2

Second Edition

Microsoft

WINDOWS® XP
PROFESSIONAL
RESOURCE KIT

The Microsoft Windows Team

PUBLISHED BY
Microsoft Press
A Division of Microsoft Corporation
One Microsoft Way
Redmond, Washington 98052-6399

Library of Congress Cataloging-in-Publication Data
Microsoft Windows XP Professional Resource Kit / Microsoft Windows Team.--2nd ed.
   p. cm.
   Includes index.
  ISBN 0-7356-1974-3
   1. Microsoft Windows (Computer File)   2. Operating systems (Computers).   I. Microsoft
Windows Team.

  QA76.76.O63M524132253   2003
  005.4'469--dc21   2003050987

Printed and bound in the United States of America.

1 2 3 4 5 6 7 8 9   QWT   8 7 6 5 4 3

Distributed in Canada by H.B. Fenn and Company Ltd.

A CIP catalogue record for this book is available from the British Library.

Microsoft Press books are available through booksellers and distributors worldwide. For further information about international e
contact your local Microsoft Corporation office or contact Microsoft Press International directly at fax (425) 936-7329.
Visit our Web site at www.microsoft.com/mspress. Send comments to *rkinput@microsoft.com*.

Acquisitions Editor: Martin DelRe
Project Editor: Julie Miller

Body Part No. X09-71501

MY 30 '06

Contents at a Glance

Contents

9   Managing Devices   357

13   File Systems   547

Part IV Networking

Thank you to those who contributed to this book:

Microsoft Windows XP Professional Resource Kit, Second Edition

Book Writing Lead: Paulette McKay
Resource Kit Tools Program Managers: Majdi Badarin and Clark Gilder
Resource Kit Tools Software Development and Test Team: Sameer Garde, Sunil Gummalla,
Venu Somineni, Kendra Yourtee, Scott Smith, and John Turner
Technical Writing Leads: Cheryl Jenkins, Randy McLaughlin, and Andrea Weiss
Writers: Ben Aguiluz, Fred Ahrends, Jim Bevan, Ross Carter, Martin DelRe, Kumud Dwivedi,
Suzanne Girardot, Douglas Goodwin, Clifton Hall, Merrilee McDonald, Chris McKitterick,
Jerry Santos, Ben Smith, Mark Wilkinson, Roland Winkler, Roger Yap, Larry Yurdin, and Jill Zoeller

Book Editing Leads: Julie Miller, Scott Turnbull, and Paula Younkin
Editing Leads: Sandra Faucett, Anika Nelson, and Scott Somohano
Editors: Sandra Faucett, Laura Graham, Justin Hall, Joan Kleps, Rebecca McKay, Sandi Resnick,
Susan F. Sarrafan, Fredrika Sprengle, Dee Teodoro, and Thelma Warren
Glossary Coordinator: Scott Somohano

Production Leads: Dave Eggleston, Patty Gardner, and Jason Hershey
Production Specialists: Barbara Arend, Heather Klauber, Elizabeth Hansford, Tess McMillan,
Barbara Norfleet, and William Teel
Documentation Tools Software Developers: Jason Hershey and Cornel Moiceanu

Indexing Leads: David Pearlstein and Krista Wall
Indexers: Lee Ross and Tony Ross

Lead Graphic Designer: Gabriel Varela
Designers: Chris Blanton and Rochelle Parry
Art Production: Jon Billow, Joel Panchot, Amy Shear, and Gabriel Varela

Test Managers: Eric Camplin and Jonathan Fricke
Test Lead: Richard Min
Testers: Keith Horton, Michael Howe, Tim Kim, Gino Sega, and Matt Winberry

Windows Lab Administrators: Dave Meyer and Robert Thingwold
Lab Partners: Cisco Systems, Inc. and Compaq, Inc.

Department Managers: Martin DelRe and Ken Western
Documentation Manager: Pilar Ackerman
Editing Manager: Kate O'Leary
Release Managers: Daretha Hodges, Neil Orint, and Karla van der Hoeven

A special recognition to the following technical experts for their exceptional contributions:
Ben Christenbury, Bob Fruth, Jeff Nemecek, and George Vordenbaum

A special thanks to the following technical experts who contributed to and supported this effort: Randy Abrams, Maximillian Aigner, Brian Andrew, Gabriel Aul, Brian Aust, Kai Axford, Arun Ayyagari, Ed Baisa, David Bakin, Smaranda Balasiu, Dan Baldo, David Baldridge, Terry Barcroft, Karl Barrus, Brad Benefield, Fred Bhesania, Susan Boher, Richard Bond, Trudy Brassell, John Brezak, Ryan Burkhardt, Franc Camara, Robert Cameron, Greg Campbell, Craig Carlston, Karen Carncross, Mira Chahine, Daniel Chan, Frank Chidsey, Jason Clark, Curtis Clay III, Jason Cobb, Shy Cohen, Joseph Conway, David Cross, Brennan Crowe, Nat Crum, Bill Curtis, Joseph Dadzie, Paul Darcy, Joseph Davies, Scott Deans, Craig Delthony, Pasquale DeMaio, Clint Denham, Michael Dennis, Dominique Domet-DeMont, Tony Donno, Bo Downey, Simon Earnshaw, Tarak Elabbady, Lisa Epstein, Levon Esibov, Brian Esposito, Glenn Evans, David Everett, Gregory Finch, Eric Fitzgerald, Zeb Fitzsimmons, Dennis Flanagan, Bob Fruth, Jason Fulenchek, Lee Fuquay, Mark Galioto, Randall Galloway, Praerit Garg, Vincent Geglia, Clark Gilder, Sunni Goeller, David Golds, Darrell Gorter, Timothy Green, Robert Griswold, Jim Groves, Bill Gruber, Robert Gu, Brian Guarraci, Keith Hageman, Jeff Hamblin, Mu Han, Bobbie Harder, Dennis Harding, William Harding, Matthew Hendel, Scott Hetzel, Emily Hill, Mike Hillberg, Mary Hillman, Greg Hinkel, Anne Hopkins, Vic Horne, Terence Hosken, Jin Huang, Ben Hutz, LaDeana Huyler, Robert Ingman, Shaun Ivory, Michael Jacquet, Raj Jhanwar, Tom Jolly, Deborah Jones, Nate Keyes, Carsten Kinder, Kristin King, Richard Knowles, Igor Kostic, Vishwa Kumbalimutt, Norbert Kusters, Justin Kwak, Michael Lai, John Lamb, John Lambert, David Lee, Thomas Lee, Benjamin Leis, Raymond Leury, Bjorn Levidow, Matt Lichtenberg, Steve Light, Yung-Shin Lin, Huisheng Liu, Daniel Lovinger, Don Lundman, Pankaj Lunia, Erik Lustig, Craig Marl, Allen Marshall, Craig Marshall, Aaron Massey, Michael Maston, Mark Maszak, Marcus Matthias, Phillippe Maurent, Greg McConel, Michael McConnell, Everett McKay, Charleta McKoy, Lonny McMichael, Joy Miller, Wes Miller, Daniel Millet, Joseph Minckler, Derek Moore, David Morehouse, Alan Morris, Jennifer Moser, Gary Moulton, David Mowers, Elliot Munger, Anand Namasivayam, Debbie Newman, Thomas Nielsen, Steve Olsson, Robert Osborne, Darwin Ou-Yang, Emanuel Paleologu, Bharti Pardasani, Cooper Partin, Annie Pearson, Daryl Pecelj, Nathan Pettigrew, Worapon Pitayaphongpat, Glenn Pittaway, Steven Poling, Jason Popp, Houman Pournasseh, Steve Powers, Jose Luis Montero Real, Cyra Richardson, Andrew Ritz, Cynda Rochester, Carmen Myriam Rodero-Scardelis, Russell Dee Rolfe, Robert Ross, Vic Rozumny, Vlad Sadovsky, Mohammed Samji, Clark Satter, John Schwartz, Joseph Seifert, Heide Shriver-Thatcher, Andy Simonds, Scott Sipe, Guy Smith, Jonathan V. Smith, Robert Smith, Bob Snead, Kirk Soluk, Sundar Srinivasan, David Stern, Christina Storm, Hakon Strande, Guhan Suriyanarayanan, Heather Swayne, Scott Tembreull, Cristian Teodorescu, Vishal Thakkar, Jim Thatcher, Mandy Tidwell, Albert Ting, Eric Torgeson, Mike Tricker, Jim Travis, Jim Truher, Mike Truitt, Gabriel Usmani, Eugene Valley, Cliff Van Dyke, Catharine van Ingen, Tonu Vanatalu, Don Velliquette, Son Voba, Stephen Walli, Charles West, BJ Whalen, Ethan Wilansky, Robert Wilhelm, Roy Williams, Jon Wojan, A-Zu Wu, Wei Wu, Edward Ye, Shuling Yu, Jason Zions, and Ethan Zoller.

Introduction

Welcome to *Microsoft® Windows® XP Professional Resource Kit, Second Edition*.

Microsoft Windows XP Professional Resource Kit, Second Edition, is a comprehensive technical resource for installing, configuring, and supporting Microsoft® Windows® XP Professional in networks that use Microsoft® Windows Server™ operating systems and other server systems. This guide also provides information to help support Microsoft® Windows® XP 64-Bit Edition in an enterprise, and information discussing feature and functionality differences among Windows XP Professional, Windows XP 64-Bit Edition, and Microsoft® Windows® XP Home Edition.

This guide provides task-based information for automating installations as well as for customizing and configuring Windows XP Professional to suit your organization's needs. This guide provides in-depth information about security and networking in Windows XP Professional, including information for wireless networks. To help you resolve problems, this guide contains extensive troubleshooting information, including a comprehensive list of the most useful troubleshooting tools and troubleshooting information focused on specific technologies.

This update to *Microsoft Windows XP Professional Resource Kit Documentation* includes more than 120 powerful tools for administering Windows clients and servers, new security chapters from the Microsoft Security Team, and a complete bonus eBook, *Automating and Customizing Installations* from the *Microsoft Windows Server 2003 Deployment Kit*, on the companion CD. The CD also includes a fully searchable electronic version (eBook) of *Microsoft Windows XP Professional Resource Kit, Second Edition*.

Document Conventions

The following sections describe text typographic style used in this book.

Reader Alert Conventions The following table describes how reader alerts are used throughout this guide.

Reader Alert	Meaning
Tip	Alerts you to supplementary information that is not essential to the completion of the task at hand.
Note	Alerts you to supplementary information.

Reader Alert	Meaning
Caution	Alerts you to possible data loss, breaches of security, or other more serious problems.
Warning	Alerts you to supplementary information that is essential to the completion of a task or alerts you that failure to take or avoid a specific action might result in physical harm to you or to the hardware.

Command-line Examples The following style conventions are used in documenting command-line tasks throughout this guide.

Element	Meaning
bold font	Characters that you type exactly as shown, including commands and parameters. User interface elements are also bold.
Italic font	Variables for which you supply a specific value. For example, *Filename.ext* can refer to any valid file name.
`Monospace font`	Code samples.
`%SystemRoot%`	Environment variable

Resource Kit Companion CD

The companion CD includes more than 120 powerful tools for administering Windows clients and servers.

Here are some of the tools that are included on the companion CD:

- **Group Policy Verification** Checks Group Policy object stability and consistency and monitors policy replication.

- **Policy Spy** Allows users to view and refresh Group Policy settings applied to the current user account and local computer.

- **Sonar.exe** Monitors key statistics and status about members a file replication service replica set, including traffic levels, backlogs, and free space.

- **Uddiconfig.exe** Enables you to adjust the configuration settings exposed by the UDDI Services MMC snap-in.

You can find additional documentation about the tools on the companion CD in the Windows Resource Kit Tools Help and Windows Resource Kit Tools Release Notes (Readme.htm). The CD also includes two complete eBooks: *Automating and Customizing Installations* from the *Microsoft Windows Server 2003 Deployment Kit*, and a fully searchable electronic version of the *Microsoft Windows XP Professional Resource Kit, Second Edition*.

Resource Kit Support Policy

Microsoft does not support the tools supplied on the *Microsoft Windows XP Professional Resource Kit, Second Edition* CD. Microsoft does not guarantee the performance of the tools, or any bug fixes for these tools. However, Microsoft Press provides a way for customers who purchase *Microsoft Windows XP Professional Resource Kit, Second Edition*, to report any problems with the software and receive feedback for such issues. To report any issues or problems, send an e-mail message to rkinput@microsoft.com. This e-mail address is only for issues related to *Microsoft Windows XP Professional Resource Kit, Second Edition*. Microsoft Press also provides corrections for books and companion CDs through the World Wide Web at http://www.microsoft.com/mspress/support/. To connect directly to the Microsoft Press Knowledge Base and enter a query regarding a question or issue you may have, go to http://www.microsoft.com/mspress/support/search.asp. For issues related to the Microsoft® Windows® XP operating system, please refer to the support information included with your product.

Part I

Deployment

Before you can begin using Microsoft® Windows® XP Professional in your organization, you need to determine how to customize it to best meet your needs, and then determine the most effective way of rolling it out to your users. The chapters in this part help you plan, implement, and troubleshoot your deployment of Windows XP Professional.

Chapter 1

Planning Deployments

Microsoft® Windows® XP Professional is designed to meet your organization's business needs. This chapter helps you determine the best way to deploy the operating system in your organization. Deploying Windows XP Professional requires careful planning. Before you install Windows XP Professional on your desktop computers, you must determine whether you need to upgrade your hardware and applications. Then you must decide which features to install, how much centralized control to maintain over users' computers, and which installation methods to use.

Related Information

- For more information about installing Windows XP Professional, see "Automating and Customizing Installations" and "Supporting Installations" in this book.

Overview of the Deployment Process

The first step in the deployment process is to assess your business needs so that you can define the project scope and objectives. Next, decide how best to use Windows XP Professional to meet those needs. Then, assess your current network and desktop configurations, determine whether you need to upgrade your hardware or software, and choose the tools for your deployment.

Having made these decisions, you are ready to plan your deployment. An effective plan typically includes the following:

- All the details for customizing Windows XP Professional.

- A schedule for the deployment.

- An assessment of your current configuration (including information about your users, organizational structure, network infrastructure, and hardware and software needs).

- Test and pilot plans.

- A rollout plan.

Create a test environment in which you can deploy Windows XP Professional by using the features and options in your plan. Have your test environment mirror, as closely as possible, your users' network, including hardware, network architecture, and business applications.

When you are satisfied with the results in your test environment, roll out your deployment to a specific group of users to test the results in a controlled production environment (a *pilot*).

Finally, roll out Windows XP Professional to your entire organization.

Creating the deployment plan is a cyclic process. As you move through each phase, modify the plan based on your experiences.

Defining Project Scope and Objectives

The scope is the baseline for creating a functional specification for your deployment project. The scope of your deployment project is defined largely by your answers to the following questions:

- What business needs do you want to address with Windows XP Professional?

- What are the long-term IT goals for the deployment project?

- How will your Windows XP Professional client computers interact with your IT infrastructure?

Assessing Your Current Environment

Document your computing environment, looking at your organizational structure and how it supports your users. Use this assessment to determine your readiness for desktop deployment of Windows XP Professional. The three major areas of your computing environment to assess include your hardware, software, and network.

Hardware   Do your desktop and mobile computers meet the minimum hardware requirements for Windows XP Professional? In addition to meeting these requirements, all hardware devices must be compatible with Windows XP Professional.

Software   Are your applications compatible with Windows XP Professional? Make sure that all your applications, including custom-designed software, work with computers running Windows XP Professional.

Network   Document your network architecture, including topology, size, and traffic patterns. Also, determine which users need access to various applications and data, and describe how they obtain access.

Where appropriate, create diagrams to include in your project plan.

Testing and Piloting the Deployment Plan

Before rolling out your deployment project, you need to test it for functionality in a controlled environment. Before you begin testing your deployment project, create a test plan that describes the tests you will run, the expected results, a schedule for performing tests, and who will run each test. The test plan must specify the criteria and priority for each test. Prioritizing your tests can help you avoid slowing down your deployment because of minor failures that can be easily corrected later; it can also help you identify larger problems that might require redesigning your deployment plan.

The testing phase is essential because a single error condition can be duplicated to all computers in your environment if it is not corrected before you deploy the image. It is recommended that you roll out the deployment to a small group of users after you test the project. *Piloting* the installation allows you to assess the success of the deployment project in a production environment before rolling it out to all users.

Create a test lab that is not connected to your network but mirrors, as closely as possible, your organization's network and hardware configurations. Set up your hardware, software, and network services as they are in your users' environment.

Perform comprehensive testing on each hardware platform, testing both application installation and operation. This can greatly increase the confidence of the project teams and the business-decision makers, resulting in a higher quality deployment.

To pilot the project, roll out the deployment to a small group of users. The primary purpose of pilot projects is not to test Windows XP Professional. Instead, the aim of your early pilots is to get user feedback for the project team. This feedback is used to further determine the features that you need to enable or disable in Windows XP Professional. This is particularly relevant if you upgrade from Microsoft® Windows® 98 or Microsoft® Windows® Millennium Edition (Me), which do not include features such as domain-based computer accounts, local security, and file system security. For pilots, you might choose a user population that represents a cross-section of your business in terms of job function and computer proficiency. Install pilot systems by using the same method that you plan to use for the final rollout.

The pilot process provides a small-scale test of the eventual full-scale rollout, so you can use the results of the pilot, including any problems encountered, to finalize your rollout plan. Compile the pilot results and use the data to estimate upgrade times, the number of concurrent upgrades you can sustain, and peak loads on the user support functions.

Rolling Out Your Deployment

After you thoroughly test your deployment plan and pilot the deployment to smaller groups of users, and you are satisfied with the results, begin rolling out Windows XP Professional to the rest of your organization.

To finalize the rollout plan, you need to determine the following:

- The number of computers to be included in each phase of the rollout.

- The time needed to upgrade or perform a clean installation for each computer to be included.

- The personnel and other resources needed to complete the rollout.

- The time frame during which you plan to roll out the installations to different groups.

- Training needed for users throughout the organization.

Throughout the rollout, gather feedback from users and modify the deployment plan as appropriate.

For more information about performing upgrades or clean installations, see "Automating and Customizing Installations" in this book.

Mapping Windows XP Professional to Your Business Needs

Some features are available only if you deploy Windows XP Professional in a domain that uses Active Directory™. Other features are available to any computer running Windows XP Professional, using any server. After you identify your business needs, you can map desktop management, security, and networking features in Windows XP Professional to those needs.

Security Features

Windows XP Professional includes features (see Table 1-1) to help you secure your network and computers by controlling user authentication and access to resources and by encrypting data stored on computers. Also included are preconfigured Security Templates for various security scenarios.

Table 1-1   Security Features in Windows XP Professional

Feature	Description	Benefit
Security Templates	Four preconfigured combinations of security policy settings that represent different organizational security needs: basic, secure, highly secure, and compatible.	Allow you to implement the appropriate templates without modifications or use them as the base for customized security configurations.
Security groups	User groupings, used to administer security, that are defined by their scope, their purpose, their rights, or their role.	Allow you to control users' rights on the system. By adding or removing users or resources from the appropriate groups as your organization changes, you can change ACLs less frequently.
Access control lists (ACLs)	Ordered lists of access control entries (ACEs) that collectively define the protections that apply to an object and its properties.	In combination with security groups, configuring ACLs on resources makes user permissions easier to control and audit.
Kerberos	The authentication protocol for computers running Microsoft® Windows® 2000 and Windows XP Professional in Active Directory domains.	Provides more efficient and secure authentication than NTLM.
NTLM	The default authentication protocol in Microsoft® Windows NT® version 4.0 and Windows XP Professional.	Allows Windows XP Professional computers to establish connections to Windows NT–based networks.

Table 1-1   Security Features in Windows XP Professional

Feature	Description	Benefit
Windows stored user names and passwords	A technology that can supply users with different credentials for different resources.	Can increase security on a per-resource basis by allowing users to store and manage credentials.
Smart card support	An integrated circuit card (ICC) that can store certificates and private keys, and perform public key cryptography operations such as authentication, digital signing, and key exchange.	Provides tamper-resistant storage for private keys and other forms of personal identification. Isolates critical security computations involving authentication, digital signatures, and key exchange. Enables credentials and other private information to be moved among computers.
Encrypting File System	A feature of NTFS that uses symmetric key encryption and public-key technology to protect files.	Allows administrators and users to encrypt data to keep it secure. This is particularly beneficial to mobile users.

Networking and Communications Features

Computers that run Windows XP Professional can be configured to participate in a variety of network environments, including Microsoft® Windows® –based, Novell NetWare–based, UNIX-based, and IBM Host Systems–based networks. Windows XP Professional can also be configured to connect directly to the Internet without being part of a network environment. Windows XP Professional includes several features, such as Zero Configuration, that simplify the process of connecting to a network and that allow mobile users to access network resources without physically reconnecting cables each time they move to a new location. Table 1-2 describes several features in Windows XP Professional that provide remote and local access to resources and support for communication solutions.

Table 1-2   Networking Features in Windows XP Professional

Feature	Description	Benefit
TCP/IP	The standard transport protocol in Windows XP Professional.	Provides communication across networks that use diverse hardware architectures and various operating systems, including computers running Windows XP Professional, devices using other Microsoft networking products, and non-Microsoft operating systems such as UNIX.

Table 1-2   Networking Features in Windows XP Professional

Feature	Description	Benefit
Dynamic Host Configuration Protocol (DHCP)	A protocol that allows computers and devices on a network to be dynamically assigned IP addresses and other network configuration information.	Eliminates the need to manually configure IP addresses and other IP settings, reducing potential conflicts and administrative overhead caused by static configurations.
Telephony and Conferencing	A service that abstracts the details of the underlying telecommunications network, allowing applications and devices to use a single command set.	Allows data, voice, and video communications to travel over the same IP-based network infrastructure.
Remote access	A connection between the local network and a remote or home office, established by dial-up modem, virtual private network (VPN), X.25, Integrated Services Digital Network (ISDN), or Point to Point Protocol (PPP).	Allows users to access the network from home or remote offices or in transit.
Client Service for NetWare	A feature that allows Windows XP Professional clients to transmit Network Core Protocol (NCP) packets to NetWare servers.	Allows Windows XP Professional client computers to connect to NetWare file and print servers.
Secure home networking	Includes Internet Connection Sharing, bridging, personal firewall, and Universal Plug and Play.	Provides easy connectivity for various devices within the home and from the home to the corporate network, along with safe access to the Internet and multiple-user accessibility over a single Internet connection.
Wireless connectivity	Protocols that are supported by Windows XP Professional to provide LAN and WAN connectivity, including security mechanisms that can make the wireless connection as secure as a cabled connection.	Provides ease of mobility by allowing users to access network resources and the Internet without using connection cables.
Zero configuration	A mechanism in which a client computer goes through a list of possible network configurations and chooses the one that applies to the current situation.	Allows the administrator to set up the initial configuration options so that users do not need to know which connection configuration to use.

Desktop Management Features

Desktop management features allow you to reduce the total cost of ownership (TCO) in your organization by making it easier to install, configure, and manage clients. These features are also designed as tools to make computers easier to use. Table 1-3 describes desktop management features in Windows XP Professional that increase user productivity.

Table 1-3 Desktop Management Features in Windows XP Professional

Feature	Description	Benefit
Group Policy Administrative Templates	Files that you can use to configure Group Policy settings to govern the behavior of services, applications, and operating system components.	Allows you to configure registry-based policy settings for domains, computers, and users.
Software Installation and Maintenance	An IntelliMirror feature that you can use to assign or publish software to users according to their job needs.	Allows you to centrally manage software installation and to repair installations by using Windows Installer.
Roaming User Profiles	A feature that ensures that the data and settings in a user's profile are copied to a network server when the user logs off and are available to the user anywhere on the network.	Provides a transparent way to back up the user's profile to a network server, protecting this information in case the user's computer fails. This is also useful for users who roam throughout the network.
Folder Redirection	An IntelliMirror feature that you can use to redirect certain folders, such as My Documents, from the user's desktop to a server.	Provides improved protection for user data by ensuring that local data is also redirected or copied to a network share, providing a central location for administrator-managed backups. Speeds up the logon process when using Roaming User Profiles by preventing large data transfers over the network.
Offline Files and Folders	A feature that you can use to make files that reside on a network share available to a local computer when it is disconnected from the server.	Allows users without constant network access, such as remote and mobile users, to continue working on their files even when they are not connected to the network. Users can also have their file synchronized with the network copy when they reconnect.

Table 1-3   Desktop Management Features in Windows XP Professional

Feature	Description	Benefit
Multilingual Options	Multilanguage support in Windows XP Professional lets users edit and print documents in almost any language.	Lets administrators customize desktop computers in their organization with the language and regional support that best meets their users' needs.

Assessing Your Current Configuration

Your deployment plan must include an assessment of your current infrastructure. The answers to the following questions can help you determine what you must do to prepare the computers in your organization for Windows XP Professional:

- Are the computers and other devices in your network compatible with Windows XP Professional?

- What applications does your organization use? Are they compatible with Windows XP Professional, or do you need to upgrade to newer versions of the software before upgrading users' computers?

- Are all of your users connecting locally, or do some of them use remote access to connect to your network?

To determine if your computers and peripheral devices are compatible with Windows XP Professional, see the Hardware Compatibility List link on the Web Resources page at http://www.microsoft.com/windows/reskits/webresources. For more information about application compatibility, see the Application Compatibility List link on the Web Resources page.

Before you can upgrade your users to Windows XP Professional, you must upgrade other software and your hardware as needed. Be sure to upgrade devices, remote access services, and your organization's applications first.

Hardware Requirements and Compatibility

Make sure that your hardware is compatible with Windows XP Professional, and that all the computers on which you plan to install the operating system are capable of supporting the installation. Table 1-4 shows the minimum and recommended hardware requirements for installing Windows XP Professional.

Table 1-4   Windows XP Professional Hardware Requirements

Minimum Requirements	Recommended Requirements
Intel Pentium (or compatible) 233-megahertz (MHz) or higher processor.	Intel Pentium II (or compatible) 300-MHz or higher processor.

Table 1-4   Windows XP Professional Hardware Requirements

Minimum Requirements	Recommended Requirements
64 megabytes (MB) of RAM.	128 MB (4 GB maximum) of RAM.
2-gigabyte (GB) hard disk with 650 MB of free disk space (additional disk space required if installing over a network).	2 GB of free disk space.
Video graphics adapter (VGA) or higher display adapter.	Super VGA (SVGA) display adapter and Plug and Play monitor.
Keyboard, mouse, or other pointing device.	Keyboard, mouse, or other pointing device.
Compact disc read-only memory (CD-ROM) or digital video disc read-only memory (DVD-ROM) drive (required for CD installations).	CD-ROM or DVD-ROM drive (12x or faster).
Network adapter (required for network installation).	Network adapter (required for network installation).

For more information about the hardware requirements for installing Windows XP Professional, see the Hardware Compatibility List link on the Web Resources page at http://www.microsoft.com/windows/reskits/webresources.

Note   Windows XP Professional supports single and dual central processing unit (CPU) systems.

Checking the BIOS

Before upgrading to Windows XP Professional, check that the computer's BIOS is the latest available version and that it is compatible with Windows XP Professional. You can obtain an updated BIOS from the manufacturer.

If the computer does not have Advanced Configuration and Power Interface (ACPI) functionality, you might need to update the BIOS. To get ACPI functionality after Windows XP Professional is installed, you are required to do an in-place upgrade of your current installation.

Warning   Microsoft does not provide technical support for BIOS upgrades. Contact the manufacturer for BIOS upgrade instructions. For more information about BIOS issues, see the Hardware Update link on the Web Resources page at http://www.microsoft.com/windows/reskits/webresources.

Hardware Compatibility List

The Windows XP Professional Hardware Compatibility List (HCL) is a list of hardware devices that have successfully passed the Hardware Compatibility Tests. All hardware on the HCL works with Windows XP Professional. Hardware not included on the HCL is not guaranteed to work successfully with Windows XP Professional.

Installing Windows XP Professional on a computer that has hardware that is not on the HCL might cause the installation to fail, or it might cause problems after installation. For more information about hardware compatibility, see the Hardware Compatibility List link on the Web Resources page at http://www.microsoft.com/windows/reskits/webresources.

Warning   A device that is not on the HCL might function, but not be supported by Windows XP Professional. For devices that do not function when the computer is running Windows XP Professional, contact the device manufacturer for a Windows XP Professional–compatible driver. If you have a program that uses 16-bit drivers, you need to install 32-bit Windows XP Professional–compatible drivers from the device manufacturer to ensure functionality with Windows XP Professional.

Hardware Compatibility with Windows Me, Windows 98, Windows 95, and Windows 3.*x*

Many updated drivers ship with the Microsoft® Windows® XP Professional operating system CD. However, when critical device drivers, such as hard-drive controllers, are not compatible with Windows XP Professional or cannot be found, Setup might halt the upgrade until updated drivers are obtained.

Note   You cannot upgrade from Microsoft® Windows® 95 or Microsoft® Windows 3.*x* to Windows XP Professional. If you are migrating from either of these operating systems you must do a clean installation of the operating system, and then install device drivers that are compatible with Windows XP Professional.

The 16-bit device drivers for Windows Me, Windows 98, Windows 95, and Windows 3.*x* were based on the virtual device driver (V*x*D) model. The V*x*D model is not supported in Windows XP Professional.

An upgrade does not migrate drivers from Windows Me or Windows 98 to Windows XP Professional. If the driver for a particular device does not exist in

Windows XP Professional, you might need to download an updated driver from the device manufacturer.

Hardware Compatibility with Windows NT Workstation 4.0

Some hardware devices that that are supported by Microsoft® Windows NT® Workstation version 4.0 also work on Windows XP Professional; however, it is best to run Setup in Check Upgrade Only mode to check for driver compatibility issues before upgrading the operating system. Windows XP Professional does not support drivers, including third-party drivers, that worked on Windows NT Workstation 4.0. You need to obtain an updated driver for Windows XP Professional from the device manufacturer.

Typically, you can address issues concerning deployment or upgrade of Windows NT Workstation 4.0 during the test phase of deployment.

Note   To access an NTFS volume that has been upgraded for Microsoft® Windows® XP, you need to be running Windows NT 4.0 Service Pack 4 or later.

Application Compatibility

Because there are new technologies in Microsoft® Windows® 2000 Professional and Windows XP Professional, you need to test your business applications for compatibility with the new operating system. Even if you currently use Windows NT 4.0, you need to test applications to make sure that they work as well on Windows XP Professional as they do in your existing environment. Also, enhancements included in Windows XP Professional, such as improved security features, might not be supported by some applications.

Identify all applications that your organization currently uses, including custom software. As you identify applications, prioritize them and note which ones are required for each business unit in your organization. Remember to include operational and administrative tools, including antivirus, compression, backup, and remote-control programs.

Applications that comply with the Windows XP Application Specification are compatible with Windows XP Professional and take advantage of the new technologies it provides. The desktop application specification applies to any software that runs on Windows XP Professional, whether it runs as a stand-alone program or as the client portion of a distributed application.

Commercial applications that comply with the Windows XP Application Specification can be certified by an independent testing organization if they meet certain requirements, such as using Windows Installer. Applications can also comply with the specification even if they are not certified. For more information about the

Windows XP Application Specification, see the Application Specification Download link on the Web Resources page at http://www.microsoft.com/windows/reskits/webresources.

Application Compatibility — Migrating from Windows Me or Windows 98

System tools in Windows 98, such as ScanDisk and DriveSpace, cannot be upgraded to Windows XP Professional. Also, client software for other networks cannot be upgraded to Windows XP Professional, so you must acquire new versions of these clients to complete the upgrade.

> **Note**   Novell has included an upgrade for their Client32 on the Windows XP Professional operating system CD. The upgrade detects and automatically upgrades a previous version of Client32 during the upgrade to Windows XP Professional. For the latest Client32 upgrade, see the Novell link on the Web Resources page at http://www.microsoft.com/windows/reskits/webresources.

Some applications written for Windows 98 or Windows Me might not run properly on Windows XP Professional without modification. For example, applications might do any of the following:

■ Maintain registry data in different locations. Windows 95, Windows 98 and Windows Me store this data in different locations than Windows XP Professional or Windows NT 4.0 and earlier.

■ Make calls to Windows 95–, Windows 98–, or Windows Me–specific application programming interfaces.

■ Install different files when installed on Windows XP Professional than when installed on Windows 98 or Windows Me.

There are four ways to address problems with applications that do not run properly on Windows XP Professional:

■ Reinstall the applications after the upgrade if the applications are compatible with Windows XP Professional.

■ Create a new Windows XP Professional–based standard configuration with compatible versions of the applications.

■ Use migration dynamic-link libraries (DLLs) for each application that is not migrated during the upgrade.

■ Run the application in Compatibility Mode by right-clicking the application, selecting **Properties**, and then clicking the **Compatibility** tab.

For more information about the Compatibility Mode tool, see "Authorization and Access Control" in this book.

Software vendors and corporate developers can use migration DLLs that move registry subkeys and entries, install new versions of files, or move files within the file system. These migration DLLs are used by Windows XP Professional Setup to resolve incompatibilities. Setup calls these DLLs to update the application installation. For more information about migration DLLs, see the Software Development Kit (SDK) information in the MSDN library link on the Web Resources page at: http://www.microsoft.com/windows/reskits/webresources.

Application Compatibility — Migrating from Windows NT Workstation 4.0 or Windows NT Workstation 3.51

Because Windows NT Workstation 4.0 and Microsoft® Windows NT® Workstation version 3.51 share common attributes with Windows XP Professional, almost all applications that run on Windows NT Workstation versions 4.0 and 3.51 run without modification on Windows XP Professional. However, a few applications are affected by the differences between Windows NT Workstation 4.0 and Windows XP Professional.

One example is antivirus software. Due to changes between the version of NTFS included with Windows NT 4.0 and the version of NTFS included with Windows XP Professional, file system filters used by antivirus software no longer function between the two file systems. Another example is third-party networking software (such as TCP/IP or IPX/SPX protocol stacks) written for Windows NT Workstation 4.0. The following features and applications cannot be properly upgraded to Windows XP Professional:

- Applications that depend on file-system filters. For example antivirus software, disk tools, and disk quota software.

- Custom power-management solutions and tools. Windows XP Professional support for Advanced Configuration and Power Interface (ACPI) and Advanced Power Management (APM) replaces these. Remove all such custom solutions and tools before upgrading.

- Custom Plug and Play solutions. These are no longer necessary, because Windows XP Professional provides full Plug and Play support. Remove all custom Plug and Play solutions before upgrading.

- Fault-tolerant options such as disk mirrors.

- Third-party network clients and services.

- Virus scanners.

- Uninterruptible power supplies.

> **Warning**   You must remove virus scanners, third-party network services, and third-party client software before starting the Windows XP Professional Setup program.

Testing Commercial Applications

You can run Windows XP Professional Setup in Check Upgrade Only mode to test commercial applications for compatibility. As Setup runs, it checks installed software against a list of applications that are known to be incompatible with Windows XP Professional and logs any that it finds.

> **Note**   Running Setup in check-upgrade-only mode can alert you to known incompatibility problems with applications installed on the computer that you are checking. However, the fact that an application does not generate a log entry does not mean that the application is compatible.

For more information about check-upgrade-only mode, see "Using Check Upgrade Only Mode" later in this chapter.

Test application installation and removal, as well as functionality. Use the features, configurations, and application suites normally used by your business to access, edit, and print data files. The following are some useful tests you might do:

- Terminate application installation before it is complete.
- Try all of the installation options used in your business.
- Test the installation by logging on as an Administrator and as a Power User.
- Log on as a User and as several members of the Users group to test the features most important to your end users.
- Apply Group Policy to users and computers.
- Test combinations of applications, such as standard desktop configurations.
- Run several applications for several days or weeks without quitting them.
- Test automated tasks that use Microsoft® Visual Basic® for Applications.
- Test to verify that long file names are consistently supported.
- Manipulate large graphics files.
- Perform rapid development sequences of edit, compile, edit, compile.
- Test object linking and embedding (OLE) custom controls.

- Test with hardware, such as scanners and other Plug and Play devices.

- Test the applications on a Terminal Services server. Test with multiple users running the same and different applications and with user-specific settings.

- Test concurrent use of a database, including simultaneous access and update of a record, and perform complex queries.

Testing Custom Applications

For custom applications, you need a more extensive testing strategy than for pre-tested commercial applications.

The Windows XP Application Compatibility Toolkit can help you develop a test plan, even for applications that were not developed internally. The test plan offers ideas about functional areas to test. To download the specification and test plan required for application certification from the MSDN Web site, see the Windows XP Application Specification link on the Web Resources page at http://www.microsoft.com/windows/reskits/webresources.

The MSDN Web site also contains information about testing, such as white papers about exploratory testing and the methods that independent testing organizations use to test applications that vendors submit for certification.

Using Check Upgrade Only Mode

Windows XP Professional Setup includes a Check Upgrade Only mode, which can be used to test the upgrade process before you do an actual upgrade. Check-upgrade-only mode produces a report that flags potential problems that might be encountered during the actual upgrade, such as hardware compatibility issues or software that might not be migrated during the upgrade. To run Setup in check-upgrade-only mode, select **Check system compatibility** from the menu displayed when you insert the installation CD.

You can also run Setup in check-upgrade-only mode by running Winnt32.exe, from the i386 folder, with the command-line parameter `-checkupgradeonly`.

The Upgrade Report is a summary of potential hardware and software upgrade issues. The following entries are in the report.

MS-DOS configuration   This includes entries in Autoexec.bat and Config.sys that are incompatible with Windows XP Professional. These entries might be associated with older hardware and software that is incompatible with Windows XP Professional. It also suggests that more technical information is provided in the Setupact.log file located in the Windows folder.

Unsupported hardware   This includes hardware that might not be supported by Windows XP Professional without additional files.

Software that must be permanently removed   This includes upgrade packs that are required for some programs because they do not support Windows XP Professional, or because they can introduce problems with Windows XP Professional Control Panel. Before upgrading to Windows XP Professional, gain disk space by using Add or Remove Programs in Control Panel to remove programs not being used.

Software that must be temporarily removed   This includes anti-virus software and upgrade packs that are recommended for programs because they use different files and settings in Windows XP Professional. If an upgrade cannot be obtained, remove the program before upgrading by using Add or Remove Programs in Control Panel. After upgrading to Windows XP Professional, reinstall or upgrade the program.

Installation requirements   This includes how much additional disk space or memory is required to install Windows XP Professional, and whether the computer contains operating systems that cannot be upgraded to Windows XP Professional.

The Upgrade Report also displays links to Microsoft Windows XP Professional Web sites, including the Hardware Compatibility List, as well as to Add or Remove Programs in Control Panel where appropriate.

If you have applications that have been identified while running in Check Upgrade Only mode as incompatible, you must remove the conflicting applications before installing Windows XP Professional.

When upgrading from Microsoft® Windows NT® Workstation, most applications can migrate. Certain proprietary applications, such as applications that were custom-made for your business, might not migrate. For more information on testing for compatibility of such programs, see "Application Compatibility" in this chapter.

Blocking Issues

If an incompatibility prevents the upgrade from continuing, a wizard appears to inform the user. You can view details about the incompatibility, if available. Unless you can fix the problem by supplying a missing file (by clicking the **Have Disk** button), you must quit Setup and fix the problem before rerunning Winnt32.exe.

Warnings

If the incompatibility does not prevent a successful upgrade to Windows XP Professional, you are warned that this application might not function correctly with Windows XP Professional. At this point, you can choose to quit, or to continue the upgrade. The **Have Disk** button is also supported in this case.

Helpful Information

The Upgrade Report also lists issues discovered by Check Upgrade Only Mode that do not prevent a successful upgrade, but might be useful for the user to know. This might include information about incompatible hardware accessories or applications that might need to be updated or are replaced by Windows XP functionality, as well as program notes. A General Information section lists information you need to be aware of before upgrading, such as files found on the computer (these might include backup files that need to be saved to a different location so they are not removed by Setup), excluded or inaccessible drives, configurations that might be lost during the upgrade process, and other reference information.

Network Infrastructure

Assess your network infrastructure by identifying existing network protocols, network bandwidth, and the network hardware. Table 1-5 describes how these issues affect your deployment plan.

Table 1-5   Basic Attributes for Assessing Your Network Infrastructure

Attribute	Effect on Project Plan
Network protocols	Network protocols determine how you customize several of the networking sections of answer files, such as [NetAdapter], [NetProtocols], and [NetServices]. For more information about creating and customizing answer files, see "Automating and Customizing Installations" in this book.
Network bandwidth	Network bandwidth affects which method of installation to use. For example, in low-bandwidth networks or on computers that are not part of a network, you might need to use a local installation method. For high-bandwidth network connections, you might choose to install Windows XP Professional by using a remote-boot CD ROM or a network-based disk image.
Network servers	The servers you have in your network affect the installation tools available to you. If you have an existing Microsoft, Windows, 2000 Server infrastructure in place, you can use a wider range of tools to automate and customize client installations, including Remote Installation Services (RIS).

Next, collect information about both the hardware and software in your work infrastructure. This should include the logical organization of your name- and address-resolution methods, naming conventions, and net in use. Documenting the location of network sites and the between them can help you decide which installation me

Document the structure of your network, includ file and print servers, directory services, domain and cols, and file structure. You should also include informa istration procedures, including backup and recovery strate and data storage and access policies. If you use multiple se note how you manage security and users' access to resources.

Network security measures should also be included in your assessment of the network. Include information about how you manage client authentication, user and group access to resources, and Internet security. Document firewall and proxy configurations.

Create physical and logical diagrams of your network to organize the information you gather. The physical network diagram should include the following information:

- Physical communication links, including cables, and the paths of analog and digital lines.

- Server names, IP addresses, and domain membership.

- Location of printers, hubs, switches, routers, bridges, proxy servers, and other network devices.

- Wide area network (WAN) communication links, their speed, and available bandwidth between sites. If you have slow or heavily used connections, it is important to note them.

The logical network diagram can include the following information:

- Domain architecture.

- Server roles, including primary and backup domain controllers, and WINS and DNS servers.

- Trust relationships and any policy restrictions that might affect your deployment.

Planning Your Preferred Client Configuration

After you identify your business needs and decide which features of Windows XP Professional to use, determine how to implement these features to simplify the management of users and computers in your organization. An important means to simplification is standardization. Standardizing desktop configurations makes it easier to

by ensuring that user settings, applications, drivers, and preferences are the same as before the problem occurred.

Determining Desktop Management Strategies

By running Windows XP Professional in a Windows 2000 Server domain, you can specify the level of control exercised over users of these computers. For example, by using Active Directory and Group Policy, you can manage desktops as follows:

- Prevent users from installing applications that are not required for their jobs.

- Make new or updated software available to users without visiting their workstations.

- Customize desktop features or prevent users from making changes to their desktop settings.

- Refresh policy settings from the server without requiring the user to log off or restart the computer.

Table 1-6 describes how you can use the desktop management features to manage computer and user settings.

Table 1-6   Desktop Management Tasks and Features

Task	Feature
Configure registry-based policy settings for computers and users.	Group Policy Administrative Templates
Manage local, domain, and network security.	Security Settings
Manage, install, upgrade, repair, or remove software.	Software Installation and Maintenance
Manage Internet Explorer configuration settings.	Internet Explorer Maintenance, MMC, Group Policy settings
Apply scripts during user logon/logoff and computer startup/shutdown.	Group Policy-based scripts
Manage users' folders and files on the network.	Folder Redirection
Manage user profiles.	Roaming User Profiles
Make shared files and folders available offline.	Offline Files and Folders (in conjunction with Folder Redirection)

If you deploy Windows XP Professional desktops in a domain that does not include Active Directory, you can still take advantage of some management features. For example, you can manage Windows XP Professional desktops locally by implementing the following IntelliMirror features:

- Roaming User Profiles
- Logon Scripts
- Folder Redirection

- Internet Explorer Maintenance

- Administrative Templates (registry-based policy)

Choosing Desktop Computer Configurations

For desktop computers that are used for specific functions, such as running certain line-of-business applications, you can use a management structure that prevents users from installing any application or device or from modifying the desktop or changing settings. To improve security and manage data storage, you can use Folder Redirection to save all data to a server location instead of on the local computer.

You can also use Group Policy settings to manage configurations, restrict user access to certain features, and limit the customizations users can make to their computer environment. To configure a computer for a single application and no other tasks, you can remove desktop features such as the Start menu and set that application to start when the user logs on.

If users need to exercise a great deal of control over their desktops, and tightly managing them is not acceptable, you can use desktop management strategies to reduce support costs and user downtime. You can allow users to install approved applications and to change many settings that affect them while preventing them from making harmful system changes. For example, you might allow users to install or update printer drivers, but not to install unapproved hardware devices. To ensure that the user's profile and data are saved to a secure location where it can be backed up regularly and restored in the event of a computer failure, use Roaming User Profiles and Folder Redirection.

For more information about implementing the preceding desktop management strategies, see "Managing Desktops" in this book. For more information about implementing and using Folder Redirection and Offline Files and Folders for desktop management, see "Managing Files and Folders" in this book. For more information about implementing Group Policy to manage desktop computers, including creating organizational unit (OU) structures and determining Group Policy strategies, see the Change and Configuration Management Deployment Guide link on the Web Resources page at http reliable fast connection to it, make sure that all necessary components are also installed. You can use scripts to make sure that all files associated with the installed applications are installed locally. A sample Visual Basic script can be found in the Implementing Common Desktop Management Scenarios white paper, available on the Web Resources page at http://www.microsoft.com/windows/reskits/webresources. To allow portable computer users to install software, make them members of the Power Users Security group. For more information about security groups, see "Determining Security Strategies" later in this chapter.

Users who connect to your network remotely might need to configure virtual private network (VPN) connections. To allow them to make necessary configuration changes, enable the following settings:

- Delete remote access connections belonging to the user.

- Rename connections belonging to the current user.

- Display and enable the New Connection Wizard.

- Display the **Dial-up Preferences** item on the **Advanced** menu.

- Allow status statistics for an active connection.

- Allow access to the following:

  - Current user's remote access connection properties.

  - Properties of the components of a local area network (LAN) connection.

  - Properties of the components of a remote access connection.

If mobile users rarely connect to your network, you might not want to use features such as Roaming User Profiles and Folder Redirection. However, these features help maintain a seamless work environment from any computer for users who frequently connect to the network or roam between portable and desktop computers.

For details about setting up portable computers and selecting features that best support mobile users, see "Supporting Mobile Users" in this book.

For more information about determining a desktop management strategy, see "Managing Desktops" in this book.

Determining a Client Connectivity Strategy

Determining how to connect clients to your network depends largely on where they are located and the type of network you are running. Those located within the corporate infrastructure can use a variety of network media, such as asynchronous transfer mode (ATM), Ethernet, or Token Ring; those outside of the corporate infrastructure need to use Routing and Remote Access or virtual private networking.

Windows XP Professional uses TCP/IP as its standard network protocol. For a Windows XP Professional–based computer to connect to a NetWare or Macintosh server, you must use a protocol that is compatible with the server. NWLink is the

Microsoft implementation of the Novell IPX/SPX protocol, which allows you to connect to NetWare file and print servers. However, the IPX/SPX protocol is not available on Windows XP 64-Bit Edition.

In the **Properties** dialog box for your network adapter, you can specify which protocols to install and enable. Windows XP Professional attempts to connect to remote servers by using the network protocols in the order specified in this dialog box.

> **Note**   Install only the necessary protocols. For example, installing and enabling Internetwork Packet Exchange (IPX) when you need only TCP/IP generates unnecessary IPX and Service Advertising Protocol (SAP) network traffic.

TCP/IP Networks

Client computers running on TCP/IP networks can be assigned an IP address statically by the network administrator or dynamically by a Dynamic Host Configuration Protocol (DHCP) server.

Windows XP Professional uses DNS as the namespace provider whether you use static IP addresses or DHCP. Networks that include Microsoft® Windows NT® Server version 4.0 or earlier or client computers running versions of Windows earlier than Windows 2000 might require a combination of DHCP and WINS.

DNS is required for integration with Active Directory, and it provides the following advantages:

- Interoperability with other DNS servers, including Novell NDS and UNIX Bind.

- Integration with networking services, by using Windows Internet Name Service (WINS) and DHCP.

- Dynamic registration of DNS names and IP addresses

The advantages of using DHCP follow:

■ Conflicts caused by assigning duplicate IP addresses are eliminated.

■ DNS or WINS settings do not need to be manually configured if the DHCP server is configured to those settings.

■ Clients are assigned IP addresses regardless of the subnet to which they connect, so IP settings need not be manually changed for roaming users.

If you assign IP addresses statically, you need to have the following information for each client:

■ The IP address and subnet mask for each network adapter installed on each client computer.

■ The IP address for the default gateway.

■ Whether the client is using DNS or WINS.

■ The name of the client computer's DNS domain and the IP addresses for the DNS or WINS servers.

■ The IP address for the proxy server.

> **Note**   It is recommended that you assign static IP addresses to servers and dynamic ones to client computers. However, there are exceptions that might require you to assign static addresses to computers running Windows XP Professional. For example, a computer that runs an application that has the IP addresses hard-coded into it requires a static address.

For more information about TCP/IP, DHCP, and DNS, see "Configuring TCP/IP" in this book. For more information about IP addressing, see "Configuring IP Addressing and Name Resolution" in this book.

IPX Protocol

Internetwork Packet Exchange (IPX) is the network protocol used by NetWare computers to control addressing and routing of packets within and among LANs. Windows XP Professional computers can connect to NetWare servers using Client Service for Netware. Windows XP Professional includes NWLink and Client Service for NetWare to transmit NetWare Core Protocol (NCP) packets to and from NetWare servers.

> **Note**   Although TCP/IP is used on some Novell NetWare-based networks, Client Service for NetWare does not support it.

NWLink and Client Service for NetWare provide access to file and print resources on NetWare networks and servers that are running either Novell Directory Services (NDS) or bindery security. Client Service supports some NetWare tools applications. It does not support IP, including NetWare/IP.

You can install Client Service or the current network client by using Novell Client. However, you cannot use Novell Client to connect a computer running Windows XP Professional to a Windows 2000 Server–based computer.

> **Caution**   Do not install both Client Service and Novell Client for Windows NT/2000 on the same computer running Windows XP Professional. Doing so can cause errors on the system.

When upgrading to Windows XP Professional from Windows Me, Windows 98, or Windows NT 4.0 Workstation, Windows XP Professional upgrades Novell Client version 4.7 or earlier to the latest version of Novell Client, allowing for a seamless upgrade. All other versions of Novell Client should be removed before upgrading the operating system, then reinstall and reconfigure Novell Client.

You can also use Microsoft Services for NetWare on a Windows 2000–based server. Services for Netware uses Client Service to connect to a NetWare network or server.

Determining Security Strategies

The Windows XP Professional

Encrypting File System (EFS) and public key technology to protect confidential data

resources, so that a user can log on to a client computer by using a single password or smart card and gain access to other computers in the domain without re-entering credential information. The Windows XP Professional authentication model protects your network against malicious attacks, such as:

- Masquerade attacks. Because a user must prove identity, it is difficult to pose as another user.

- Replay attacks. It is difficult to reuse stolen authentication information because Windows XP Professional authentication protocols use timestamps.

- Identity interception. Intercepted identities cannot be used to access the network because all exchanges are encrypted.

Kerberos V5 is the primary security protocol within Windows 2000 domains. Windows XP Professional–based clients use NTLM to authenticate to servers running Windows NT 4.0 and to access resources within a Windows NT domain.

Computers running Windows XP Professional that are not joined to a domain also use NTLM for authentication.

If you use Windows XP Professional on a network that includes Active Directory, you can use Group Policy settings to manage logon security, such as restricting access to computers and logging users off after a specified time. For more information about logon security, see "Logon and Authentication" in this book.

Authorization

Authorization controls user access to resources. Using access control lists (ACLs), security groups, and NTFS file permissions, you can make sure that users have access only to needed resources, such as files, drives, network shares, printers, and applications.

Security Groups Security groups, user rights, and permissions can be used to manage security for numerous resources while maintaining fine-grained control of files and folders and user rights. The four main security groups include:

- Domain local groups
- Global groups
- Universal groups
- Computer local groups

Using security groups can streamline the process of managing access to resources. You can assign users to security groups, and then grant permissions to those groups. You can add and remove users in security groups according to their need for access to new resources. To create local users and place them within local security groups, use the Computer Management snap-in of MMC or the **User Accounts** option in Control Panel.

Within the domain local and computer local security groups there are preconfigured security groups to which you can assign users.

Administrators   Members of this group have total control of the local computer and have permissions to complete all tasks. A built-in account called Administrator is created and assigned to this group when Windows XP Professional is installed. When a computer is joined to a domain, the Domain Administrators group is added to the local Administrators group by default.

Power Users   Members of this group have read/write permissions to other parts of the system in addition to their own profile folders, can install applications, and can perform many administrative tasks. Members of this group have the same level of permissions as Users and Power Users in Windows NT 4.0.

Users   Members of this group are authenticated users with read-only permissions for most parts of the system. They have read/write access only within their own profile folders. Users cannot read other users' data (unless it is in a shared folder), install applications that require modifying system directories or the registry, or perform administrative tasks. Users permissions under Windows XP Professional are more limited than under Windows NT 4.0.

Guests   Members of this group can log on using the built-in Guest account to perform limited tasks, including shutting down the computer. Users who do not have an account on the computer or whose account has been disabled (but not deleted) can log on using the Guest account. You can set rights and permissions for this account, which is a member of the built-in Guests group by default. The Guest account is enabled by default.

You can configure access control lists (ACLs) for resource groups or security groups and add or remove users or resources from these groups as needed. The ability to add and remove users makes user permissions easier to control and audit. It also reduces the need to change ACLs.

You can grant users permissions to access files and folders, and specify what tasks users can perform on them. You can also allow permissions to be inherited, so that permissions for a folder apply to all its subfolders and the files in them.

Group Policy

uons on resources.

For more information about managing access to resources and applications, see "Authorization and Access Control" in this book. For more information about creating disk images for installation, see "Automating and Customizing Installations" in this book.

You can use preconfigured security templates that meet the security requirements for a given workstation or network. Security templates are files with preset security settings that can be applied to a local computer or to client computers in a domain by using Active Directory.

Security templates can be used without modification or customized for specific needs. For more information about using security templates, see "Authorization and Access Control" in this book.

Encryption

You can use Encrypting File System (EFS) to encrypt data on your hard disk. For example, because portable computers are high-risk items for theft, you can use EFS to enhance security by encrypting data on the hard disks of your company's portable computers. This precaution protects data and authentication information against unauthorized access.

Before implementing EFS, it is important to understand the proper backup structure for EFS keys and to know how to restore them.

For more information about EFS, see "Encrypting File System" in this book.

Determining Client Administration and Configuration Strategies

The following sections can help you make decisions about configuring Windows XP Professional computers to make them easier to administer. Depending on the needs of your organization, you can include support for multiple language versions of the operating system and applications, specify what devices users can access, choose the file system that best suits your security and compatibility needs, and create logical disks that are more efficient to manage. Depending on the installation method you use, you can install applications along with the operating system to decrease the time it takes users to start their computers. You can enable accessibility options for users with disabilities and have those options available wherever users log on to the network.

Multilingual Options

Windows XP Professional supports companies that need to equip their users to work with various languages or in multiple locale settings. This includes organizations that:

- Operate internationally and must support various regional and language options, such as time zones, currencies, or date formats.

- Have employees or customers who speak different languages, or require language-dependent keyboards or input devices.

- Develop an internal line of business applications to run internationally or in more than one language.

If you have roaming users who need to log on anywhere and edit a document in several languages, you need the appropriate language files installed or installable on demand, on a server or workstation. You can also use Terminal Services to allow users to initiate individual Terminal Services sessions in different languages.

For more information about multilingual feature support in Windows XP Professional, see "Multilingual Solutions for Global Businesses" in this book.

You can use Setup scripts to install regional and language options on your users' computers. For more information about creating Setup scripts, see "Automating and Customizing Installations" in this book.

Hardware Devices

Windows XP Professional includes support for a range of hardware devices, including USB- and IEEE 1394–compliant devices. Device drivers for most devices are included with the operating system. Drivers can be configured to be dynamically updated by connecting to the Microsoft® Windows Update Web site and downloading the most recent versions.

If you can connect to the Internet, the Dynamic Update feature can connect to Windows Update during setup to install device drivers that were not included on the Windows XP Professional operating system CD. For more information about Dynamic Update, see "Planning for Dynamic Update" later in this chapter.

You can add devices, such as mass storage and Plug and Play devices, to your installation. For more information about adding hardware devices to your installation, see "Automating and Customizing Installations" in this book. For more information about the types of hardware devices Windows XP Professional supports, and about configuring these devices, see "Managing Devices" in this book.

File Systems

Windows XP Professional supports the FAT16, FAT32, and NTFS file systems. Because NTFS has all the basic capabilities of FAT16 and FAT32, with the added

■ Better scalability allows you to use large volumes. The maximum volume size for NTFS is much greater than it is for FAT. Additionally, NTFS performance does not degrade as volume size increases, as it does in FAT systems.

■ Recovery logging of disk activities helps restore information quickly in the event of power failure or other system problems.

When you perform a clean installation of Windows XP Professional, it is recommended that you use NTFS. If you upgrade computers that use NTFS as the only file system, continue to use NTFS with Windows XP Professional.

Converting vs. Reformatting Existing Disk Partitions Before you run Setup, you must decide whether to keep, convert, or reformat an existing partition. The default option for an existing partition is to keep the existing file system intact, thus preserving all files on that partition.

Windows XP Professional provides support for Windows 95, Windows 98, or Windows Me file systems, including FAT16 and FAT32 file systems. If you upgrade computers that use FAT or FAT32 as their file system, consider converting the partitions to NTFS.

Warning You cannot upgrade compressed Windows 98 volumes; you must uncompress them before you upgrade them to Windows XP Professional.

Use the conversion option if you want to take advantage of NTFS features, such as security or disk compression, and you are not dual-booting with another operating system that needs access to the existing partition. You cannot convert an NTFS volume to FAT or FAT32. You must reformat the NTFS volume as FAT. However, when you convert a volume from FAT to NTFS, you cannot use the uninstall feature to roll back to a previous operating system installation.

Warning Once you convert to NTFS, you cannot revert to FAT or FAT32.

You can reformat a partition during a clean installation only. If you decide to convert or reformat, select an appropriate file system (NTFS, FAT16, or FAT32). For more information about converting volumes to NTFS, see "File Systems" in this book.

> **Caution**   You can reformat a partition as either FAT or NTFS; however, refor-
> matting a partition erases all files on that partition. Make sure to back up
> all files on the partition before you reformat it.

Multiple-Booting and File System Compatibility   NTFS is the recommended file
system for Windows XP Professional. However, you might need a different file system to multiple-boot Windows XP Professional with an operating system that cannot
access NTFS volumes. If you use NTFS to format a partition, only Windows XP,
Windows 2000, and Windows NT 4.0 (with Service Pack 4) can access the volume.

If you plan to install Windows XP Professional and another operating system
on the same computer, you must use a file system that all operating systems installed
on the computer can access. For example, if the computer has Windows 95 and
Windows XP Professional, you must use FAT on any partition that Windows 95 must
access. However, if the computer has Windows NT 4.0 and Windows XP Professional, you can use FAT or NTFS because both operating systems can access all
those file systems. However, certain features in the version of NTFS included with
Windows XP Professional are not available when the computer runs
Windows NT 4.0. For more information about file system compatibility and multiple
booting, see "Determining How Many Operating Systems to Install" in this chapter.

> **Warning**   You can access NTFS volumes only when running Windows NT,
> Windows 2000, or Windows XP.

Table 1-7 describes the size and domain limitations of each file system.

Table 1-7   Comparison of NTFS and FAT File Systems

ing systems allow no access.

Table 1-7   Comparison of NTFS and FAT File Systems

Subject of Comparison	NTFS	FAT16	FAT32
Volume size	Recommended minimum volume size is approximately 10 MB. Recommended practical maximum for volumes is 2 terabytes. Much larger sizes are possible. Cannot be used on floppy disks.	Volumes up to 4 GB. Cannot be used on floppy disks.	Volumes from 512 MB to 2 terabytes. In Windows XP Professional, you can format a FAT32 volume only up to 32 GB. Cannot be used on floppy disks.
File size	Maximum file size 16 terabytes minus 64 KB (2^{44} minus 64 KB)	Maximum file size 4 GB	Maximum file size 4 GB
Files per volume	4,294,967,295 (2^{32} minus 1 files)	65,536 (2^{16} files)	Approximately 4,177,920

If you also want to use MS-DOS on your system, you must use FAT to format another partition, which is the MS-DOS operating system's native file system. MS-DOS does not recognize data on NTFS or FAT32 partitions.

For more information about FAT, NTFS, and other file systems supported in Windows XP Professional, see "File Systems" in this book.

> **Warning**   To format the active system partition you must use a file system that all the operating systems running on your computer recognize. You can have up to four primary partitions, but only the active one starts all the operating systems.

Disk Partitions

Disk partitioning is a way of dividing hard disks into sections that function as separate units. Partitions can be set up to organize data or to install additional operating systems for multiple boot configurations. Partitioning involves dividing a disk into one or more areas, each formatted for use by a particular file system.

Configuring Partitions   Depending on your existing hard disk configuration, you have the following options during setup:

- If the hard disk is unpartitioned, you can create and size the Windows XP Professional partition.

- If an existing partition is large enough, you can install Windows XP Professional on that partition.

- If the existing partition is too small but you have adequate unpartitioned space, you can create a new Windows XP Professional partition in that space.

- If the hard disk has an existing partition, you can delete it to create more unpartitioned disk space for the Windows XP Professional partition. Keep in mind that deleting an existing partition also erases any data on that partition.

Caution   Before you change file systems on a partition or delete a partition, back up the information on that partition, because reformatting or deleting a partition deletes all existing data on that partition.

If you install Windows XP Professional as part of a multiple-boot configuration, it is important to install Windows XP Professional on its own partition. Installing Windows XP Professional on the same partition as another operating system might overwrite files installed by the other operating system and overwrites the system directory unless you specify a different directory in which to install Windows XP Professional.

Warning   If you install Windows XP Professional as part of a multiple-boot configuration, make sure that you install it after you install all other operating systems. If you install another operating system after Windows XP Professional, you might not be able to start Windows XP Professional. For more information about problems with starting your computer, see "Troubleshooting Startup" in this book.

For more information about Disk Management, see "Disk Management" in this book.

> **Warning**   Windows 2000, Windows XP Professional, and Windows XP 64-Bit Edition are the only operating systems that can access a dynamic disk.
>
> If you convert the disk that contains the system volume to dynamic, you cannot start the other operating systems. For more information about basic and dynamic disks, see "Disk Management" in this book.

Applications to Install

During setup, you can choose to install standard productivity applications such as Microsoft® Office, as well as custom applications. If certain core applications need to be available to users at all times, you can install them along with the operating system. If you are automating installations by using RIS or Sysprep, you can install the applications on the disk image that you create; if you are doing unattended installations by using answer files, you can include applications and make them available from your distribution folder. For more information about adding applications to your installations, see "Automating and Customizing Installations" in this book.

If you use Active Directory, you can use the Software Installation and Maintenance feature of IntelliMirror to make applications available to users. You can assign critical applications to users and publish applications users might need to access.

Publishing an application   When you publish applications, users can install the application by using **Add or Remove Programs** in Control Panel. For more information about using Software Installation and Maintenance to make applications available to your users, see the *Distributed Systems Guide* of the *Microsoft® Windows® 2000 Server Resource Kit*.

Assigning an application to a user   When you assign an application to a user, it appears to the user that the application is already installed, and a shortcut appears in the user's **Start** menu. When the user clicks the shortcut, the application is installed from a server share.

Automating deployment and upgrades   You can also use Systems Management Server (SMS) to automate the deployment and upgrade applications during and after installing the operating system. SMS is a good option for large-scale software-deployment projects because SMS can be set to run when it will cause minimal interruption to your business, such as at night or on weekends. For more information about SMS, see the documentation included with SMS.

Accessibility Options

Windows XP Professional includes multiple features and options that improve accessibility for people with disabilities. You can use the Accessibility wizard or individual Control Panel properties to set options to meet the needs of users with vision, mobility, hearing, and learning disabilities.

For users with vision impairments or learning disabilities, you can set size and color options for the display of text and screen elements, such as icons and windows. You can also adjust the size, color, speed, and motion of the mouse cursor to aid visibility on the screen. Options such as StickyKeys, BounceKeys, ToggleKeys, and MouseKeys benefit some users with mobility impairments. SoundSentry and ShowSounds can assist users with hearing impairments.

Accessibility tools such as Magnifier, Narrator, and On-Screen Keyboard allow users with disabilities to configure and use computers without additional hardware or software. These tools also allow some users with disabilities to roam multiple computers in their organization.

Note   Accessibility features such as Narrator, Magnifier, and On-Screen Keyboard provide a minimum level of functionality for users with special needs. Most people with disabilities require tools with higher functionality.

You can use Group Policy and set user profiles to make sure that accessibility features are available to users wherever they log on in your network. You can also enable some accessibility features when you run Setup by specifying them in your answer file.

For more information about accessibility features included with Windows XP Professional, see "Accessibility for People with Disabilities" in this book. For more information about customizing answer files for unattended Setup, see "Automating and Customizing Installations" in this book.

Planning Installations

After you decide how to use Windows XP Professional in your organization and how best to manage your users and computers, you need to prepare your installations. The following questions can help you make important decisions affecting the installation

... ...sional to gain enhancements unavailable in current Windows 2000 Professional installations, upgrading might be the preferred strategy.

However, if your desktop computers run Windows 95, you must do a clean installation of Windows XP Professional. If you have an Active Directory environment in place, you can use RIS to standardize the installations across your desktops, customize and control the installation process, and determine the media on which to distribute the installation.

For more information about installing Windows XP Professional, see "Supporting Installations" and "Automating and Customizing Installations" in this book. For more detailed information about client and sever installations, see the *Microsoft*® *Windows*® *2000 Server Resource Kit Deployment Planning Guide*.

Upgrading vs. Clean Installation

Windows XP Professional provides upgrade paths from Windows 2000 Professional, Windows NT 4.0, Windows 98, and Windows Me. If you are using Windows 95, Windows 3.*x*, or another operating system you need to choose a clean install.

During an upgrade, existing user settings are retained, as well as installed applications. If you perform a clean installation, the operating system files are installed in a new folder, and you must reinstall all of your applications and reset user preferences, such as desktop and application settings.

You need to choose a clean installation of Windows XP Professional in the following cases:

- No operating system is installed on the computer.

- The installed operating system does not support an upgrade to Windows XP Professional.

- The computer has more than one partition and needs to support a multiple-boot configuration that uses Windows XP Professional and the current operating system.

- A clean installation is preferred.

The most basic advantage of a clean installation is that all of your systems can begin with the same configuration. All applications, files, and settings are reset. You can use a single disk image or answer file to make sure that all of the desktops in your organization are standardized. In this way, you can avoid many of the support problems that are caused by irregular configurations.

Note Installing multiple operating systems on the same partition is not supported and can prevent one or both operating systems from working properly. For more information about installing multiple operating systems on a single computer, see "Supporting Installations" in this book.

Upgrading from Windows 98 or Windows Me

Upgrading from Windows 98 or Windows Me to Windows XP Professional might require some additional planning because of differences in the registry structure and the setup process. For more information about software compatibility issues, see "Application Compatibility" in this chapter. If problems arise, you can choose to uninstall Windows XP Professional and revert to the previous installation. For more information about uninstalling Windows XP Professional, see "Supporting Installations" in this book.

Upgrading from Windows 2000 or Windows NT Workstation 4.0

Windows 2000 and Windows NT Workstation 4.0 provide the easiest upgrade path to Windows XP Professional because they share a common operating system structure and core features, such as support file systems, security concepts, device driver requirements, and registry structure.

If you upgrade or install Windows XP Professional on a Windows NT Workstation 4.0–based computer that uses NTFS, the installation process automatically upgrades the file system to Windows XP Professional NTFS. If you install or upgrade to Windows XP Professional and the current file system is FAT, you are asked if you want to upgrade to the NTFS file system.

> **Note**   You cannot upgrade computers that run Windows NT Workstation 3.51 to Windows XP Professional. You must do a clean installation of Windows XP Professional.

Using the User State Migration Tool

The User Sate Migration Tool allows you to save and restore users' settings and files to minimize the time required to configure users' computers after installing Windows XP Professional. You can use USMT when performing clean installations, migrating from computers running Windows 95, Windows 98, Windows Me, Windows NT 4.0, Windows 2000, or ~~Windows XP V~~

~~the tool uses to save only the settings you want to migrate to~~ Windows XP Professional.

Choosing an Installation Method

You can install Windows XP Professional on client computers in various ways. The installation method you choose is based on several factors, including:

- Whether you upgrade from an existing operating system or perform clean installations.
- How many computers will be in the deployment.
- Whether you want to allow users to install the operating system themselves, or if you want to perform unattended installations.
- How much customization is required for your installations.
- What hardware is available and how the various types differ.
- Whether you are using Active Directory.

Table 1-8 describes the installation methods available for Windows XP Professional and some of the considerations for each method.

Table 1-8   Methods and Requirements for Installing Windows XP Professional

Method and Requirements	From CD-ROM	Unattended Setup	SysPrep	Remote Operating System Installation	SMS
Upgrade or clean install	Upgrade or clean install	Upgrade or clean install	Clean install only	Clean install only	Upgrade only
Required hardware	CD-ROM drive on each computer	A network boot disk if using a remote distribution share, or a CD-ROM drive and a floppy disk drive	All desktop computers need similar hardware configurations	PXE-enabled desktop computers	A fast connection to the SMS site
Server requirements	Does not require a server	Does not require a server	Does not require a server	Requires Windows 2000 Server with Active Directory	Requires a Windows server with SMS running an SMS site
Considerations for modifying project	No changes can be made	Requires updating Unattend.txt	Requires updating and reimaging the master installation	Requires modifying the answer file	Requires creating an advertising package

For information about running Setup, see "Supporting Installations" in this book.

For more information about the relative advantages and when to use each of the installation methods, see "Automating and Customizing Installations" in this book.

Determining How Many Operating Systems to Install

You can install multiple operating systems on a computer so that the user can choose the operating system to use each time the user starts the computer. You can also specify an operating system as the default that starts when the user makes no selection.

Warning   If you install Windows XP Professional and any other operating system on a computer, you must install Windows XP Professional on a separate partition. Installing Windows XP Professional on a separate partition ensures that it will not overwrite files used by the other operating system.

Installing multiple operating systems on a computer has some drawbacks, however. Each operating system uses disk space, and compatibility issues (especially between file systems) can be complex. Also, you cannot use dynamic disks with certain operating systems. Only Windows 2000 and Windows XP Professional can access a dynamic disk.

Converting a basic disk to a dynamic disk that contains multiple installations of Windows XP Professional or Windows 2000 can cause startup problems. For more information about dynamic disks, see "Disk Management" in this book.

Note   To ensure that you can always start the computer, despite driver or disk problems, consider the disaster-recovery features available in Windows XP Professional. Safe Mode allows Windows XP Professional to restart with default settings and the minimum number of drivers. The computer will start even if a new

When you per

upgrade), by default the installation is put on a partition on which no other operating system is located. You can specify a different partition when you run Setup.

Before setting up a computer that has more than one operating system, review the following restrictions.

For computers on which you want to install MS-DOS and Windows XP Professional:

- Install MS-DOS first. Otherwise important files needed to start Windows XP Professional can be overwritten.

- Install each operating system on its own partition, and then install the applications used with each operating system on the same partition. If you intend to run an application on both operating systems, install it on both partitions.

- Format the system partition as FAT.

For computers on which you want to install Windows 95 and Windows XP Professional:

- Install Windows 95 first. Otherwise important files needed to start Windows XP Professional can be overwritten.

- Install each operating system on its own partition, and then install the applications used with each operating system on the same partition. If you intend to run an application on both operating systems, install it on both partitions.

- Format the system partition as FAT. (For Windows 95 OSR2, the primary partition must be formatted as FAT or FAT32.)

- Compressed DriveSpace or DoubleSpace volumes are not available while you run Windows XP Professional. It is not necessary to uncompress DriveSpace or DoubleSpace volumes that you access only from Windows 95.

For computers on which you want to install Windows 98 or Windows Me and Windows XP Professional:

- Install each operating system on its own partition, and then install the applications used with each operating system on the same partition. If you intend to run an application on both operating systems, install it on both partitions.

- Format the system partition as FAT or FAT32.

- Compressed DriveSpace or DoubleSpace volumes are not available while you run Windows XP Professional. It is not necessary to uncompress DriveSpace or DoubleSpace volumes that you access only from Windows 98.

For computers on which you want to install Windows NT 4.0 and Windows XP Professional:

- Make sure that Windows NT 4.0 has been updated with the latest service pack.

- Install each operating system on its own partition, and then install the applications used with each operating system on the same partition. If you intend to run an on both operating systems, install it on both partitions.

- Using NTFS as the only file system on a computer that contains both Windows XP Professional and Windows NT is *not* recommended.

- Do not install Windows XP Professional on a compressed volume unless the volume was compressed by using the NTFS compression feature.

- If the computer is part of a domain, use a unique computer name for each installation.

For computers on which you want to install Windows 2000 and Windows XP Professional, or multiple Windows XP Professional partitions:

- Install each operating system on its own partition, and then install the applications used with each operating system on the same partition. If you intend to run an application on both operating systems, install it on both partitions.

- On a computer on which you install multiple Windows XP Professional partitions, you can install any product in the Windows XP product family. For example, you can install Windows XP Professional on one partition and Microsoft® Windows® XP Home Edition on another.

> **Note**   Because Windows XP Home Edition does not support dynamic disks, you must use basic disks on computers that multiple-boot Windows XP Professional and Windows XP Home Edition.

- If the computer participates in a domain, use a different computer name for each installation. Because a unique security identifier (SID) is used for each installation of Windows XP Professional on a domain, the computer name for each installation must be unique, even for multiple installations on the same computer.

- If you use Encrypting File System (EFS), ensure that encrypted files are available from each of the installations.

Multiple Operating Systems and File System Compatibility

For Windows-based computers, the available file systems are NTFS, FAT, and FAT32. For more information, see "File Systems" in this chapter and "File Systems" in this book.

The version of NTFS included in Windows 2000 and Windows XP Professional has new features that are not available for Windows NT. You might have full access to files that use new features only when the computer is started by using Windows 2000 or Windows XP Professional. For example, a file that uses the new encryption feature is not readable when the computer is started with Windows NT 4.0, which was released before the encryption feature existed.

To set up a computer that has an NTFS partition, to run Windows NT and Windows XP Professional you must use Windows NT 4.0 with the latest released Service Pack. Using the latest Service Pack maximizes compatibility between Windows NT 4.0 and the NTFS enhancements in Windows XP Professional. Specifically, Service Pack 4 and later Service Packs provide this compatibility in file systems. Even the most recent service pack, however, does not provide access to files using later features in NTFS.

Using NTFS as the only file system on a computer that contains both Windows XP Professional and Windows NT is *not* recommended. On these computers, a FAT partition ensures that the computer has access to needed files when it is started with Windows NT 4.0.

If you set up a computer with Windows NT Workstation 3.51 or earlier on a FAT partition, and Windows XP Professional on an NTFS partition, the NTFS partition is not visible while you run Windows NT Workstation 3.51.

Multiple Operating Systems and EFS

If you configure a computer so that it contains Windows 2000 and Windows XP Professional, or contains multiple Windows XP Professional partitions, you must take certain steps to use EFS so that encrypted files are readable between the different installations. Use either of the following approaches:

- Ensure that all the installations are in the same domain and that the user has a roaming profile.

- Export the user's file encryption certificate and associated private key from one installation and import it into the other installations.

For more information about using EFS, see "Encrypting File System" in this book.

Planning for Dynamic Update

Dynamic Update is a feature in Windows XP Professional Setup that works with Windows Update to download critical fixes and drivers needed for the setup process. This feature updates the required Setup files to improve the process of getting started with Windows XP Professional. Dynamic Update also downloads device drivers from the Windows Update site that are not included on the Windows XP Professional operating system CD, which ensures that devices attached to the computer work. Updates to existing drivers are not downloaded during Dynamic Update, but you can obtain them by connecting to Windows Update after setup is complete.

Dynamic Update downloads the following types of files.

Critical fixes   Dynamic Update replaces files from the Windows XP Professional operating system CD that require critical fixes or updates. Files that are replaced also include DLLs that Setup requires. No new files are downloaded — only replacements for existing files.

Device drivers   Dynamic Update downloads new drivers for devices that are connected to the computer and are required to run Setup. Only drivers that are not included on the operating system CD are downloaded.

Using Dynamic Update

For Dynamic Update to run during Setup, the computer needs an Internet connection (or access to a network share containing updates downloaded from the corporate catalog on the Windows Update Web site) and Internet Explorer 4.01 or later. If either of these requirements is not met, Dynamic Update does not connect to Windows Update or download the required files.

The user is asked if Setup should look for updates. If the user selects **Yes**, Dynamic Update connects to the Windows Update and searches for new drivers and critical fixes. In unattended installations, Dynamic Update is enabled by default but can be disabled by setting the following key in the answer file:

```
DUDisable = yes
```

Winnt32.exe checks for required disk space, memory, and other Setup requirements. If these requirements are not met, neither the setup process nor the Dynamic Update step proceeds. If the computer meets the setup requirements, Winnt32 checks the size of the Dynamic Update download to determine if there is enough space to download the file.

The estimated size of the download is based on the size of the cabinet (.cab) files, and the total amount of disk space required for the downloaded files cannot be determined. Winnt32.exe checks the size of the files again after they are extracted from the downloaded CAB files.

For more information about creating and customizing answer files, see "Automating and Customizing Installations" in this book, and Microsoft Windows Pre-installation Reference (Ref.chm) on the Windows XP Professional operating system CD.

Using the Windows Update Corporate Site for Dynamic Update

If you plan to roll out Windows XP Professional to a large number of computers, you might not want multiple users connecting to the Microsoft® Windows® Update Web site to download critical fixes and device drivers. Using Dynamic Update, you can download the needed files from the Windows Update Corporate site and place them on a share within your network where client computers can connect during setup. This saves bandwidth and gives you more control over what files are copied to each computer. This process also lets you choose device drivers to include during the Dynamic Update phase of setup.

> **Note**   Dynamic Update might download different sets of files at different times, depending on the currently available fixes.

To download the Dynamic Update package, see the Windows Update link on the Web Resources Page at http://windows.microsoft.com/windows/reskit/webresources. The download is an executable file. Run this file to expand the Dynamic Update CAB files into the shared network folder. Prepare the shared folder by running Winnt32 with the **/DUPrepare:[*pathtonetworkshare*]** parameter.

You can point to the network share containing the Dynamic Update files by running Winnt32.exe together with the **/DUShare** parameter or by specifying the location of the share in your answer file. For more information about downloading the Dynamic Update package, preparing the downloaded files for Dynamic Update, and installing the downloaded update files during unattended setup, see "Automating and Customizing Installations" in this book.

Planning for Windows Product Activation

Windows Product Activation (WPA) deters piracy by requiring your Windows XP Professional installation to be activated. Product Activation is based on requiring each unique installation to have a unique product key.

WPA ties your Product Key and Product ID to your computer by creating an installation ID. The installation ID is made up of your Product Identification (PID) and a PC identifier, called a hardware ID, or HWID. The installation ID is sent to a Microsoft license clearinghouse, which verifies whether Microsoft manufactured that PID and that the PID has not been used to install the operating system on more hardware than is defined by the product's End-User License Agreement (EULA). For Windows XP Professional, the EULA states that you can install on one computer. If this check fails, activation of Windows XP Professional fails. If this check passes, your computer receives a confirmation ID that activates your computer. After Windows is activated, you never need to perform Product Activation again, unless you significantly overhaul the hardware in your computer. You must activate your installation within 30 days after installing Windows XP Professional.

If the Product Key is used to install Windows on a second computer, the activation fails. Additionally, if WPA detects that the current installation of Windows is running on a different computer than it was originally activated on, you must activate it again. In this way, WPA prevents casual copying of Windows.

> **Note**   WPA is not required under volume-licensing agreements.

For unattended installations that are not performed using volume-licensing media, a separate answer file, including a unique Product Key, must be created for each computer on which Windows XP Professional is installed.

> **Warning**   Because Product Keys cannot be determined from within the system, it is recommended that you create a database that lists each computer and the Product Key that corresponds to its installation.

Additional Resources

These resources contain additional information related to this chapter.

Related Information

- The *Planning, Testing, and Piloting Deployment Projects* book in the *Microsoft® Windows Server 2003 Deployment Kit* for information about planning a Windows Server 2003 environment.

- The *Deployment Planning Guide* of the *Microsoft® Windows® 2000 Server Resource Kit* for more information about designing a server environment, including planning your network and directory service infrastructure, for your organization.

Chapter 2

Automating and Customizing Installations

For organizations with many computers, automating the installation of Microsoft®
Windows® XP Professional is more efficient and cost effective than using the interactive Setup program. You can use Windows XP Professional tools to add specific
files and applications and to distribute customized installations with little or no user
interaction.

Related Information

- For more information about installing Windows XP Professional by using the
  interactive Setup program, see "Supporting Installations" in this book.

- For more information about planning Windows XP Professional deployments,
  see "Planning Deployments" in this book.

- For more detailed information about automating and customizing installations,
  see the *Automating and Customizing Installations* eBook on the companion
  CD included with this Resource Kit.

Overview of Automated and Customized Installations

Windows XP Professional includes several tools that enable you to design and deploy automated and customized installations. These tools provide different types of functionality for a variety of deployment scenarios. Each tool has specific strengths and limitations that you can evaluate to determine which tool is most appropriate for your environment. For more information about the baseline requirements for each of the tools, see "Choosing an Automated Installation and Customization Tool" later in this chapter.

Windows XP Professional includes the following automated and customized installation tools:

- **Unattended Installation (unattended Setup).** The two unattended installation tools, Winnt32.exe and Winnt.exe, are in the \i386 folder on the Microsoft® Windows® XP Professional operating system CD.

- **System Preparation Tool (Sysprep).** Sysprep is in the Deploy.cab file in the \Support\Tools folder on the Windows XP Professional operating system CD.

- **Remote Installation Services (RIS).** RIS is included in Microsoft® Windows® 2000 Server.

You can also use Systems Management Server (SMS) to deploy Windows XP Professional. For information about Systems Management Server (SMS), see the Microsoft Systems Management Server link on the Web Resources page at http://www.microsoft.com/windows/reskits/webresources.

An automated installation runs with minimal or no user interaction. During an automated installation, the Setup program uses configuration information provided by an answer file. Answer files are text files containing settings that would otherwise be manually provided by end-users. Answer files provide answers to questions that the Setup program asks during installation. In addition, answer files can contain instructions for running programs and applications.

A custom installation is a modification of a standard Windows XP Professional installation that supports specific hardware and software configurations and meets specific user needs. You can customize an installation by modifying the answer file to provide the Setup program with specific answers and instructions. You can also design a custom installation to add custom files, applications, and programs to the distribution folder.

You can automate and customize a Windows XP Professional installation to include applications, additional language support, service packs, and device drivers.

Design an Automated and Customized Installation

Windows XP Professional provides several tools for automating and customizing installations for a variety of software and hardware configurations. Before you choose a tool, assess your current configuration and evaluate your needs. With this information, you can choose the deployment tool that is most appropriate for your organization. The tool you choose also affects the customization options that you use and the procedures you must follow to implement your deployment scenario.

You can automate and customize how you install Windows XP Professional by following this process:

- **Assess your current configuration and plan your deployment.** Before you choose a tool, collect information about the types of users in your company and their needs, about the desktop environments of your users, and about your network. For information about planning Windows XP Professional deployments, see "Planning Deployments" in this book.

- **Choose an automated installation and customization tool.** The automated installation and customization tools support a variety of installation scenarios. Each of the tools is designed to take advantage of specific environments. Evaluate the tools to determine which tool or combination of tools best fits your organization. For more information about evaluating the tools, see "Choosing an Automated Installation and Customization Tool" later in this chapter.

- **Prepare for the installations.** Verify that you have the software and hardware you need, create a distribution folder, and use Setup Manager to create an answer file. For more information about software and hardware preparation, see "Preparing for the Installations" later in this chapter.

- **Customize the installations.** Design the Windows XP Professional desktop by adding hardware devices, device drivers, support information, passwords, custom language options, and applications. For more information about customizing answer files and installing applications, see "Customizing the Installations" later in this chapter.

- **Install the operating system.** Test the customized installation of Windows XP Professional. After successful testing, conduct the full-scale deployment. For more information about operating system installation, see "Installing the Operating System" later in this chapter. For more information about testing your installation before actually deploying it, see "Planning Deployments" in this book.

Windows Product Activation

To help prevent software piracy, you must use Windows Product Activation for each installation of Windows XP Professional that is not covered by a volume license or that is not preactivated by an original equipment manufacturer (OEM). You can set Windows Product Activation by using a unique product key for each computer in a bulk deployment. Create a separate answer file for each computer and then assign a unique value to ProductKey in the [UserData] section of each individual answer

file. (ProductKey is a new name for the ProductID key that was used in Microsoft®
Windows® 2000.)

For an automated installation, you can add Autoactivate = Yes to the [Unat-
tended] section of the answer file to make product activation occur automatically. If
your computer is connected to the Internet through a firewall on a network that
does not support Web Proxy Autodiscovery Protocol, you can also add AutoactivateProxy = Proxy to the [Unattended] section of the answer file. The AutoactivateProxy key enables you to configure the proxy setting so that activation by using
the HTTPS protocol can traverse a firewall.

If you add AutoactivateProxy = Proxy to the [Unattended] section of the answer
file, you can also add an optional [Proxy] section to the answer file. The [Proxy] section can contain keys and values as shown in the following example:

```
[Proxy]
Proxy_Enable = 1
Use_Same_Proxy = 1
HTTP_Proxy_Server = myproxyserver:80
Proxy_Override = <local>
```

If you specify a proxy setting in the answer file, you must also specify a brand-
ing value, as shown in the following example:

```
[Branding]
BrandIEUsingUnattended = Yes
```

You can also use a Uniqueness Database File (UDF) to provide information
that is specific to a single client computer, such as the value specified in the Product-
Key key. The .udf file provides information that overrides and replaces a section of
the answer file or appends additional sections to an existing answer file.

To support disk imaging as a deployment option, Windows Product Activation
also adds activation rollback to the standard System Preparation tool (Sysprep) and
the standard Remote Installation Preparation tool (Riprep). However, activation rollback is not supported for evaluation media or for MSDN media.

For more information about Windows Product Activation, see "Planning
Deployments" in this book. For more information about activation rollback, see
"How Sysprep Works with Windows Product Activation" and "Using the Remote
Installation Preparation Tool" later in this chapter. You can also perform automated
activation after you install Windows XP Professional by using the Windows Manage-
ment Instrumentation (WMI) provider in Windows Product Activation.

Dynamic Update

Microsoft regularly provides reliability and compatibility improvements, and also
provides emergency fixes for security issues. Some of these updates might not be
available on the Windows XP Professional operating system CD.

Updates are assembled into Dynamic Update packages, which are available on the Windows Update Web service. You can access Dynamic Update packages by selecting **Yes, download the updated setup files** on the **Get Updated Setup Files** screen of the Windows Setup wizard. Setup then downloads and installs the updated files instead of using the equivalent files on the Windows XP operating system CD.

For more information about downloading Dynamic Update packages, see the Dynamic Update link on the Web Resources page at http://www.microsoft.com/windows/reskits/webresources.

If a Dynamic Update package is available and you downloaded the package during setup, expand the downloaded package to display the .cab files. The package can contain one of the four .cab files shown in Figure 2-1. Figure 2-1 shows the structure of the network share folder and the relative location of each subfolder.

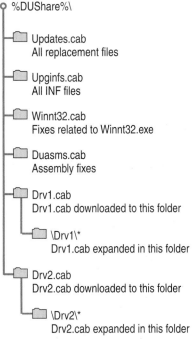

Figure 2-1   Network share folder structure

Processing Dynamic Update .cab files and driver .cab files on the network share   To process the Dynamic Update .cab files and all the driver .cab files that you downloaded from Windows Update, run Winnt32.exe with the **/DUPrepare** parameter pointing to the location of the downloaded .cab files, as shown in the following example:

```
Winnt32 /DUPrepare: path to CAB files
```

Installing the dynamic update package   To install Windows XP Professional and use the processed Dynamic Update .cab files, you can run Winnt32.exe with the

DUShare parameter, or you can specify in your answer file where Setup can find the processed .cab files. When you run Winnt32.exe with the **/DUShare** parameter, the Dynamic Update wizard is not displayed to the user and no attempt is made to connect to Windows Update.

The update files are copied from the share into the appropriate folders under %windir%\Setupupd. Setup searches the installation media for device drivers. If a device driver is not found, Setup searches the driver folder in the Dynamic Update share. Setup finds and installs a device driver.

To run Setup and connect to the Dynamic Update Share

■   At the command line, type:

```
Winnt32 /DUShare:path to dynamic update share
```

When you run Setup in unattended mode and specify a dynamic update share to connect to, dynamic update is disabled by default; the Dynamic Update wizard is not displayed to the user, and no attempt is made to connect to Windows Update.

To specify a Dynamic Update share in Unattend.txt

■   In the [Unattend] section of the Unattend.txt answer file, include the following key and value:

```
[Unattend]
DUShare = "Path to dynamic update share"
```

Choosing an Automated Installation and Customization Tool

The following questions and guidelines help you determine which of the automated installation and customization tools is most appropriate for your environment. The guidelines describe baseline requirements for each of the tools.

Do the client computers have the same Hardware Abstraction Layer (HAL) as the reference computer?   Before you can determine which tool to use, you have to find out if the client computers have Hardware Abstraction Layers (HAL) that are compatible with the reference computer. If the client and reference computers do not have compatible HALs, you cannot use Sysprep or the Remote Installation Preparation tool (Riprep.exe), which is a component of RIS. For example, if the reference computer has a Standard PC HAL, the destination computer must have the same Standard PC HAL. If the reference computer has an Advanced Configuration and Power Interface (ACPI) PC HAL, the destination computer must have the same ACPI PC HAL.

> **Note**   Standard PC and ACPI PC are the names of HALs that are detected during the initial phase of a Windows XP Professional installation, before Sysprep.exe or Riprep.exe are run.

Do the client computers have a fast and reliable network connection?   If the client and reference computers have compatible HALs, you have to determine if the network connections are fast and reliable enough to enable you to use RIS. If the client computers are not connected to a network, you cannot use RIS. If the network connections are not fast and reliable, RIS is not the appropriate tool to use.

Determine whether there is a Windows 2000 Server–based network infrastructure in place. Identify existing network protocols. Determine the speed of network links.

Table 2-1 lists key issues related to assessing your network infrastructure and describes how these issues can help you determine which tool to use.

Table 2-1   Some Important Issues for Assessing the Network Infrastructure

Issue	Effect on Your Plan
Network infrastructure	Network protocols determine how you customize the networking sections of the answer file, including [NetAdapters], [NetProtocols], and [NetServices].
Network bandwidth	Network bandwidth might affect your choice of installation tool and method. For example, locations that do not have a high-bandwidth connection to a network server might use a CD-ROM or other local installation method instead of RIS for clean installations.
Windows 2000 Server network infrastructure	Remote Installation Services (RIS) is a good option if you have an existing Windows 2000 Server infrastructure that is combined with the following: ■ High-bandwidth network connections. ■ Client computers that have remote boot-compliant network adapters that support Pre-Boot eXecution Environment (PXE) technology. You can use a Windows 2000 Server that is configured as a RIS server to copy and automatically distribute customized images of a Windows XP Professional installation to client computers over a network connection.

Do you want to upgrade an existing installation of the operating system?   If you are planning to perform a clean operating system installation on the client computers, you can use any of the installation tools. However, if you are planning to perform an operating system upgrade to the client computers, you cannot use RIS or Sysprep. Client computers running Microsoft® Windows® 3.x and Microsoft®

Windows 95 cannot be upgraded to Windows XP Professional. You must perform clean installations on these client computers. Windows XP Professional supports upgrades from the following operating systems:

- Microsoft®

- Windows NT® Workstation, version 4.0

- Microsoft®

- Windows® 2000 Professional

- Microsoft®

- Windows® 98

- Microsoft®

- Windows® Millennium Edition (Windows Me)

Choosing to perform a clean installation is a good course of action if you plan to standardize the desktop computers across your organization. If you decide to perform a clean installation, you cannot migrate customized settings from the currently installed operating system.

Depending on the status of your deployment, you might have to upgrade many of your computers in addition to installing Windows XP Professional on new computers. If you plan to use currently installed applications on existing hardware, you must perform an upgrade.

Table 2-2 provides a brief overview of tool support for upgrades and clean installations.

Table 2-2   Tool Support for Upgrades and Clean Installations

Tool	Upgrade	Clean Installation
Unattended Installation	X	X
System Preparation Tool (Sysprep.exe)		X
Remote Installation Services (RIS)		X
Systems Management Server (SMS)	X	

Do you plan to deploy and maintain a large number of client computers?   The number of client computers in a deployment can help you determine which installation tool to use. For example, if you have a large number of computers, Remote Installation Services (RIS), Systems Management Server, or third-party disk-imaging utilities in conjunction with Sysprep are good choices. For a small number of computers, using the Winnt.exe or Winnt32.exe Setup tool in unattended mode might be sufficient.

Unattended Installation

Unattended installations use setup scripts to answer installation questions and to automate the Setup process. This simplifies the installation of the operating system. Use Setup Manager to create or customize answer files that contain setup scripts.

Winnt32.exe   You can use Winnt32.exe on computers that are running Windows 98, Windows Me, Windows NT Workstation 4.0, Windows 2000, or Windows XP Professional. Use Winnt32.exe to automate the upgrade process for numerous computers without user intervention.

Winnt.exe   Winnt.exe is a less versatile tool than Winnt32.exe. You cannot use Winnt.exe to perform an operating system upgrade, and you can only use Winnt.exe from within the MS-DOS preinstallation environment. To use Winnt.exe from a network boot floppy disk, run **winnt /u:unattend.txt** /s:*source path*.

When to Use Unattended Installation

Use the Winnt32.exe unattended installation tool to upgrade a large number of client computers that have different hardware and software configurations. Unattended installation uses an answer file called Unattend.txt. You can rename Unattend.txt to reflect different installation configurations.

Advantages of Unattended Installation   Unattended installations save time and money because users do not have to attend to each computer and answer questions during installation. Unattended installations can also be configured to enable users to provide input during the installation process. You can perform unattended installations to upgrade many computers at once or to automate clean installations of the operating system.

Disadvantages of Unattended Installation   You cannot use the unattended installation tools (Winnt32.exe and Winnt.exe) to create reference configurations that include applications and that replicate the configurations across your client computers.

Unattended installation must be initiated by someone who has direct access to each client computer.

Using a Windows XP Professional Operating System CD
to Perform Unattended Installations

Use a Windows XP Professional operating system CD to initiate the installation of Windows XP Professional on client computers that are not connected to a network or on computers in low-bandwidth environments.

When to use a Windows XP Professional operating system CD to perform unattended installations   You can use a Windows XP Professional CD to install the operating system, fully configured for a network, on client computers that are not connected to a network.

Advantages of using a Windows XP Professional operating system CD to perform unattended installations   Using a Windows XP Professional Operating System CD is fast. It can save the time that is required for downloading system files from a network. Using a Windows XP Professional CD simplifies deployment of the operating system on computers that do not have high-speed connectivity.

Disadvantages of using a Windows XP Professional operating system CD to perform unattended installations   To use a Windows XP Professional operating system CD to initiate the installation of Windows XP Professional on client computers, you must be able to implement the following configuration requirements:

- The client computers must support the El Torito No Emulation CD boot specification.

- Installation must be initiated by someone who has direct access to each client computer.

- You must name the answer file Winnt.sif and place the Winnt.sif file in the root directory of a floppy disk. You must insert the floppy disk in the floppy disk drive of the client computer as soon as the computer starts from the CD.

System Preparation Tool

Disk imaging, which is also referred to as cloning, is a timesaving way to deploy Windows XP Professional. To clone a system, first configure a reference computer with the operating system, standard desktop settings, and applications that users need; then make an image of the reference computer's hard disk. Next, transfer the image to other computers, installing the operating system, settings, and applications quickly and without the need to configure each computer.

The System Preparation tool (Sysprep.exe) prepares the reference computer for cloning. Sysprep creates a unique security identifier (SID) for each cloned client computer, which makes this process secure. Sysprep detects Plug and Play devices and adjusts for systems with different devices.

You can run Setup Manager to select the screens you want displayed during Windows Welcome (Msoobe.exe) or during MiniSetup (if you use the **-mini** parameter).

These screens can be used to solicit user-specific information, such as user name or time zone selection. You can also provide these answers by using an answer file to deploy fully automated installations.

> **Warning**   Sysprep performs the preparation of the system image; however, a cloning utility from a third party is required to create the image.

When to Use Sysprep

Use Sysprep to deploy clean installations in large organizations where hundreds of computers need the same applications and desktop configurations. Use Sysprep if the computers in your organization have only a few standard hardware configurations, rather than many custom configurations.

Sysprep enables you to duplicate a custom image from a reference computer to destination computers. The reference computer and the destination computers must have the same Hardware Abstraction Layer (HAL).

Advantages of Sysprep

Sysprep greatly reduces deployment time because nearly every component, including the operating system, applications, and desktop settings, can be configured without user interaction. The reference image can be copied to a CD and physically distributed to client computers, saving the time and network capacity required to load files across a network. Using Sysprep to deploy Windows XP Professional on numerous desktops in a large organization enables you to implement standardized desktops, administrative policies, and restrictions. Additionally, by default, Sysprep does not perform full hardware Plug and Play redetection, reducing this part of the installation process to just a few minutes (instead of 20 to 30 minutes for each computer).

> **Note**   Sysprep detects any new Plug and Play hardware during the Mini-Setup Wizard; however, Sysprep does not detect hardware that is not Plug and Play.

Disadvantages of Sysprep

If you use a third-party disk-imaging utility with Sysprep to copy a reference image onto physical media, you must be able to distribute the physical media to remote client computers. The size of the reference image is limited by the capacity of the CD (approximately 650 MB). Sysprep cannot be used to upgrade earlier versions of the operating system. To preserve existing content, you must arrange to back up data and user settings prior to the installation, and then restore the data and user settings after the installation.

Remote Installation Services

Remote Installation Services (RIS) enables you to perform a clean installation of Windows XP Professional, or a clean installation of any version of Windows 2000 except Microsoft® Windows® 2000 Datacenter Server, on supported computers throughout your organization. You can simultaneously deploy the operating system on multiple clients from one or more remote locations.

> **Warning**   To deploy Windows XP images from Windows 2000 RIS Servers, you must install the Windows 2000 Remote Installation Services update. For more information about the Windows 2000 Remote Installation Services update, see the Microsoft Knowledge Base link on the Web Resources page at http://www.microsoft.com/windows/reskits/webresources. Search the Microsoft Knowledge Base using the keywords *Risetup.exe*, *RIS Servers*, and *Windows XP Images*.

System administrators can use RIS to create and store one or more images of a supported operating system on a RIS Server. A RIS image can then be downloaded over a network connection by a client computer that supports the Pre-Boot eXecution Environment (PXE). You can completely automate the installation of the downloaded RIS image or you can require users to provide input by typing a computer name or an administrator password, for example.

To use Remote Installation Services, Windows 2000 Server must be deployed with Active Directory™ configured. Then, you can deploy Windows XP Professional by using the Pre-Boot eXecution Environment (PXE) technology that enables computers to boot from their network adapters. Administrators working with a RIS server can make a preconfigured image of Windows XP Professional available for installation on a client computer.

For computers that do not support Pre-Boot eXecution Environment (PXE) technology, Remote Installation Services includes a tool called the Remote Boot Floppy Generator (RBFG.exe) that you can use to create a remote boot disk to use with RIS. You can use the RIS remote boot disk with supported network adapters that comply with the Peripheral Component Interconnect (PCI) specification.

When to Use Remote Installation Services

Use Remote Installation Services (RIS) on desktop computers that are newly added to a network or on which you want to perform a clean installation of the operating system. Use RIS when you want to standardize a Windows XP Professional configuration on new desktop computers or on computers with an existing operating system that you want to replace with Windows XP Professional.

Advantages of Remote Installation Services

Remote Installation Services offers a simple way to replace the operating system on a computer. RIS uses the Single Instance Store (SIS) method to eliminate duplicate files and to reduce the overall storage that is required on the server for system files. You can also use the Riprep option to install and configure a client computer to comply with specific corporate desktop standards.

The following list describes some of the important advantages of using RIS:

■ You can standardize your Windows XP Professional installation.

■ You can customize and control the end-user installation. You can configure the end-user Setup Wizard with specific choices that can be controlled by using Group Policy. For more information about Group Policy, see "Connecting Clients to Windows Networks" in this book.

■ You do not need to distribute physical media, and image size is not constrained by the capacity of distributed physical media.

Disadvantages of Remote Installation Services

You can use Remote Installation Services only on client computers that are connected to a network that is running Windows 2000 Server with Active Directory. RIS is restricted to working on computers that are equipped with PCI-compliant network adapters that are enabled for PXE technology, or with the Remote Boot Floppy Generator (Rbfg.exe) that is used to create a remote boot disk that can be used with supported PCI-compliant network adapters. RIS only works with images that have been created from drive C, and RIS cannot use images of other partitions on a hard disk. You cannot use RIS to upgrade an operating system; you can only use RIS for clean installations.

Systems Management Server

Systems Management Server (SMS) includes an integrated set of tools for managing Windows-based networks consisting of thousands of computers. Systems Management Server includes desktop management and software distribution tools to automate operating system upgrades.

When to Use Systems Management Server

In organizations that already use Systems Management Server to manage computers from a central location, SMS provides a convenient means for administrators to upgrade computers to Windows XP Professional.

You can only use Systems Management Server for upgrades of Windows-based client computers; you cannot use SMS for clean installations. For information about how administrators can plan for and implement a Windows XP Professional deployment by using Systems Management Server, see the Microsoft Systems Management Server link on the Web Resources page at http://www.microsoft.com/windows/reskits/webresources.

Advantages of Systems Management Server

You can upgrade computers in a locked-down or low-rights environment, and even upgrade computers after hours, without the user being logged on. Systems Management Server enables you to set deployment policies for specific client computers. Automatic load balancing between distribution points accommodates many concurrent upgrades.

As a primary advantage, Systems Management Server offers centralized control of the upgrade. For example, you can control when upgrades take place, which computers to upgrade, and how to apply network constraints.

Disadvantages of Systems Management Server

Systems Management Server is an efficient deployment tool for Windows XP Professional only if SMS is already being used within your network.

Where to Find the Tools and Related Information

Table 2-3 provides the locations of the tools and related information.

Table 2-3   Where to Find the Windows XP Professional Installation Tools and Documentation

Tool or Documentation	Go To
Winnt32.exe	\i386 on the Windows XP Professional operating system CD.
System Preparation tool (Sysprep.exe)	Deploy.cab in the\Support\Tools folder on the Windows XP Professional operating system CD. You can use Windows Explorer or you can run Extract.exe to extract Setupmgr.exe.
Remote Installation Services	Included in Windows 2000 Server.
Systems Management Server	Systems Management Server product CD.
Setup Manager (Setupmgr.exe)	Deploy.cab in the \Support\Tools folder on the Windows XP Professional operating system CD. You can use Windows Explorer or you can run Extract.exe to extract Setupmgr.exe.
Microsoft Windows XP Preinstallation Reference (Ref.chm)	Deploy.cab in the \Support\Tools folder on the Windows XP Professional operating system CD. You can use Windows Explorer or you can run the Extract.exe command to extract and view the Ref.chm file.
Microsoft Windows Corporate Deployment Tools User's Guide (Deploy.chm)	Deploy.cab in the \Support\Tools folder on the Windows XP Professional operating system CD. You can use Windows Explorer or you can run Extract.exe to extract and view the Deploy.chm file.

Preparing for the Installations

To prepare for an automated installation and customized deployment, compare the requirements of your design to the availability of the necessary software and hardware. In addition, learn how to create a distribution folder that can accommodate a variety of client computer configurations.

- **Verify hardware and software requirements.** There are distinct environmental baseline requirements for deployments that are built around each of the automated installation and customization tools. Make sure that you have evaluated the baseline requirements for the tool that you plan to use. Verify that your hardware and software configurations are capable of supporting these baseline requirements.

- **Create a distribution folder.** A distribution folder is a key component in designing a robust and versatile automated installation and customized deployment. You can create a single distribution folder for all your client computers, and you can design a distribution folder that all your answer files can reference.

Verify Hardware and Software Requirements

To determine whether the hardware components in your organization are compatible with Windows XP Professional, see the Hardware Compatibility List link on the Web Resources page at http://www.microsoft.com/windows/reskits/webresources.

Use the following guidelines to verify that your deployment scenario meets all of the hardware and software requirements.

Sysprep requirements   If you want to use Sysprep, your configuration must comply with the following guidelines:

- The reference and destination computers must have compatible HALs.

- You must have third-party disk-imaging software that can create binary images of a hard disk.

  For more information, see "Requirements to Run Sysprep" later in this chapter.

RIS requirements   To use RIS, you must have a configuration that complies with the following guidelines:

- To use the Remote Installation Preparation (Riprep) component of RIS, the reference and destination computers must have compatible HALs.

- You must have a configuration that includes a Windows 2000 Server, the Dynamic Host Configuration Protocol (DHCP) service, Domain Name System

(DNS), Active Directory, and RIS. The RIS server does not have to be the sole DNS/DHCP server or a domain controller for the domain, but it must be a member of the same domain as the client computers.

- The RIS server must contain a second partition separate from the boot partition. The second partition is required to install the Remote Installation Services. To accommodate the operating system installation images, you might want to dedicate an entire hard disk specifically to the RIS directory tree.

For more information, see "Remote Installation Services" later in this chapter.

Systems Management Server   You must have a current version of Windows 2000 Server installed and configured with Systems Management Server.

For more information about using Systems Management Server to upgrade the operating system, see the Microsoft Systems Management Server link on the Web Resources page at http://www.microsoft.com/windows/reskits/webresources.

Create a Distribution Folder

A distribution folder is structured hierarchically and contains the Windows XP Professional installation files, as well as any device drivers and other files that are required to customize the installation. Distribution folders typically reside on a server to which the destination computers can connect. Use Setup Manager to create distribution folders.

A distribution folder provides a consistent environment for installing Windows XP Professional on multiple computers. You can use the same distribution folder for all the client computers. For example, if you install Windows XP Professional on various models of similarly configured computers, all your answer files can reference the same distribution folder. In this scenario, the distribution folder must contain all the necessary device drivers for the different client computers. Then, if a hardware component changes, you can simply copy a device driver for the new hardware component to the appropriate location within the distribution folder. You do not need to change the answer file.

You can create distribution folders on multiple servers to help load balance the servers during unattended installations of Windows XP Professional. Creating distribution folders on multiple servers also improves the performance of the file copy phase of unattended installation. This enables you to run Winnt32.exe with up to eight source file locations.

Distribution Folder Structure

Figure 2-2 shows the distribution folder structure and the relative location of each subfolder.

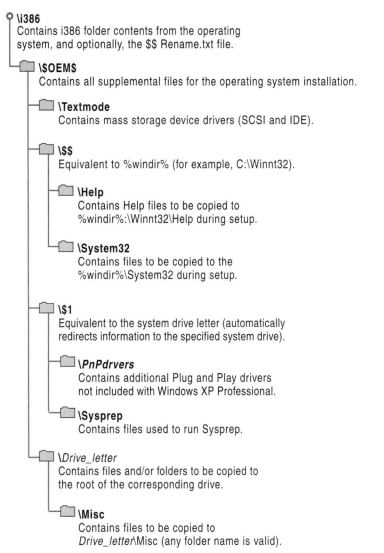

\i386
Contains i386 folder contents from the operating
system, and optionally, the $$ Rename.txt file.

\OEM
Contains all supplemental files for the operating system installation.

\Textmode
Contains mass storage device drivers (SCSI and IDE).

\$$
Equivalent to %windir% (for example, C:\Winnt32).

\Help
Contains Help files to be copied to
%windir%:\Winnt32\Help during setup.

\System32
Contains files to be copied to the
%windir%\System32 during setup.

\$1
Equivalent to the system drive letter (automatically
redirects information to the specified system drive).

\PnPdrvers
Contains additional Plug and Play drivers
not included with Windows XP Professional.

\Sysprep
Contains files used to run Sysprep.

\Drive_letter
Contains files and/or folders to be copied to
the root of the corresponding drive.

\Misc
Contains files to be copied to
Drive_letter\Misc (any folder name is valid).

Figure 2-2   Distribution folder structure

Note   The structure of a RIS distribution folder varies slightly from the
folder structure depicted in Figure 2-2. In a RIS distribution folder, the
OEM folder must be created at the same level as the i386 folder.

\i386 folder   The distribution folder that includes the i386 folder contents from the operating system and the following files and folders.

\$$Rename.txt file   An optional file that Setup uses during installations started in MS-DOS to convert specified file names from short to long. Each subfolder in the distribution folder that contains file names that you want to convert from short to long must have its own $$Rename.txt file.

\$OEM$ A folder that contains all the additional files required to complete the installation. If you use the OemFilesPath key in the [Unattended] section of the answer file, you can create the \$OEM$ folder outside the distribution folder.

> **Warning**   The OemPreinstall = Yes statement must appear in the [Unattended] section of the answer file if you are using the \OEM folder to add any more files to the system, or if you are using Cmdlines.txt.

You can instruct Setup to automatically copy directories, standard 8.3 format files, and any tools required for your automated installation to the \OEM folder.

One of the additional files that you can add to the \OEM folder is Cmdlines.txt. This file contains a list of commands that Setup carries out during its GUI mode. These commands can, for example, run an .inf file, an application installation command, or another executable file. For more information about the Cmdlines.txt file, see "Adding Applications" later in this chapter.

> **Note**   The graphical user interface (GUI) phase of Setup is referred to as "GUI mode," and the text phase of Setup is referred to as "text mode."

If the \OEM folder is in the root of the distribution folder, Setup copies all the files to the temporary directory that is created during the text phase of Setup.

\OEM\Textmode   A folder that contains the hardware-dependent files that Setup Loader and text-mode Setup install on the destination computer during text-mode setup. These files can include original equipment manufacturer HALs, mass storage device drivers, and the Txtsetup.oem file, which directs the loading and installing of these components. These files must also be listed in the [OEMBootFiles] section of Unattend.txt.

\$OEM\$\\$\$ A folder that is equivalent to the %systemroot% or %windir% environment variables. You can use OEM\\$$ to store additional files that you want copied to the folders in the Windows XP Professional system directories. For example, if you want to copy a file to the \Windows\System32 folder, place the file in OEM\\$$\System32.

You can also use OEM\\$$ to place files in a new directory (under %windir%) that is not part of the default Windows XP Professional directory structure. For example, if you want to copy OEM Plug and Play device drivers to a directory called \Windows\PnPDrvrs, place the device drivers in OEM\\$$\PnPDrvrs.

\$OEM\$\\$\$\Help   A folder that contains the OEM Help files to be copied to C:\Windows\Help during setup.

\$OEM\$\\$\$\System32   A folder that contains files to be copied to the C:\Windows\System32 folder during setup.

\$OEM\$\\$1   A folder that is equivalent to the SystemDrive environment variable. For example, if the operating system is installed on drive C, \$OEM$\\$1 refers back to drive C. The use of a variable enables rearranging drive letters without creating errors in applications that point to a hard-coded drive letter.

\$OEM\$\\$1\PnPdrvrs   A folder that contains additional Plug and Play drivers that are not included with Windows XP Professional. You can replace the name of the folder (\PnPdrvrs) with any made up of eight or fewer characters. Make sure the name of this folder matches the name used in the OemPnPDriversPath entry in Unattend.txt.

> **Note**   Microsoft® Windows® NT Workstation 4.0 used Display and Net folders to perform the \$OEM$\\$1\PnPdrvrs folder function.

\$OEM\$\\$1\Sysprep   An optional folder that contains the files required to run Sysprep. Most users do not have to run Sysprep at the end of an unattended installation. For more information about Sysprep, see "System Preparation Tool" later in this chapter.

\$OEM\$\\Drive_letter   Each \$OEM$\\Drive_letter folder contains a folder structure that is copied to the root of the corresponding drive in the destination computer during text-mode Setup. For example, files you put in an \$OEM$\C folder are copied to the root of drive C. You can also create subfolders in these folders. For example, \$OEM$\D\Misc creates a \Misc folder on drive D.

Using Setup Manager to Create a Distribution Folder

The easiest way to create a distribution folder for a Sysprep, RIS, or unattended installation is to use Setup Manager, which is available on the Windows XP Professional operating system CD in the Deploy.cab file of the \Support\Tools folder. Use the **Create a Distribution Folder** option to create a distribution folder including required Windows XP Professional source files on the network shared drive. You can also use Setup Manager to add files that you want to copy or to supply additional device drivers for use with Windows.

For more information about using Setup Manager, see "Customizing Unattended Installations" later in this chapter.

Copying a Folder to the System Drive of the Computer   You can copy an additional folder to the system drive during the customization process. For example, you might want to copy a folder containing additional device drivers.

To copy a folder to the system drive

1. In the \$OEM$ folder of the distribution share, create a folder called \$1. This folder maps to SystemDrive, which is the destination drive for the Windows XP Professional installation.

2. In the \$1 folder, copy the folder containing the files.

3. Verify that the following statement is in the [Unattended] section of the Unattend.txt answer file:

```
[Unattended]
OemPreinstall = Yes
```

Customizing the Installations

After you create a distribution folder, customize the installation by creating answer file(s) and adding devices, device drivers, applications, Help files, support information, and other components. Depending on what you want to customize, use Setup Manager to perform either or both of the following tasks:

- Add entries in the answer file to provide specific instructions to be carried out by Setup during installation.

- Populate the distribution folder by adding files, programs, and applications.

The tools you can use to customize Windows XP Professional depend on your choice of methods to install the operating system.

Table 2-4 shows the customization tools that are covered in the "Using Windows XP Professional Customization Tools" section.

Table 2-4   Customization Tools

Tool	Installation Method	Description
Unattended Installation (Winnt32.exe)	Unattend.txt	Supplies an answer file that you can either modify or use as is.
	Setup Manager	Use to create and modify answer files and distribution folders.
System Preparation (Sysprep.exe) tool	Sysprep.inf	Supplies an answer file that you can either modify or use as is.
	Sysprep Factory Mode	Use to customize the Setup for the destination computer.
	MiniSetup Wizard	Displays a configurable collection of Setup screens to gather information that has not been preconfigured in the answer file. Use Setup Manager (setupmgr.exe) to preconfigure the MiniSetup Wizard screens or Windows Welcome (Msoobe.exe). Oobe is an acronym for out-of-box experience.
		MiniSetup starts the first time a computer starts from a disk that has been duplicated using Sysprep.
	Setup Manager	Use to create and modify answer files, distribution folders, and the MiniSetup Wizard.
Remote Installation Services (RIS)	RIS template answer file (Ristndrd.sif)	Supplies an answer file that you can either modify or use as is.
	RIS Client Installation Wizard	Provides basic functionality for installing client computers.
	Setup Manager	Use to create and modify answer files and distribution folders.
Manually create an answer file	Notepad or other text editor	Use to create a new answer file or to modify an existing one.

You can customize features and components in Windows XP Professional. The examples provided at the end of this section demonstrate the following:

■ Adding hardware devices, including storage devices, Plug and Play devices, and hardware abstraction layers (HALs). When adding hardware devices to the distribution folder and specifying the devices in the answer file, consider mass storage devices such as Small Computer Systems Interface (SCSI) hard drives. Windows XP Professional Setup detects and installs most hardware devices automatically. However, to install a SCSI device that is not supported by

Windows XP Professional, you must add the device drivers for that SCSI device and its Txtsetup.oem file to the distribution folder (in the OEM\Textmode folder). To access that SCSI controller during text mode, the [MassStorageDrivers] section of the answer file must be modified with the appropriate device driver entries.

> **Note**   Ensure that hardware on the destination computer meets the minimum requirements listed in "Planning Deployments" in this book. Also to ensure that the individual components are compatible with Windows XP Professional, see the Hardware Compatibility List link on the Web Resources page at http://www.microsoft.com/windows/reskits/webresources.

- Setting passwords for local user accounts. You can also force all users or certain users to change their passwords when they log on after an upgrade from Windows 98, or Windows Me.

- Setting options for language and multilingual support, and setting key descriptions for other regional and language options, such as language-specific keyboard layouts.

- Setting time zones.

- Specifying display settings to ensure that Setup automatically detects a computer's display resolution.

- Specifying file system settings to automatically convert FAT16 and FAT 32 file systems to NTFS during installation.

- Using the $$Rename.txt file to automatically convert short file names to long file names.

- Adding applications during the GUI-mode phase of Setup using Cmdlines.txt.

- Adding applications when the user logs on for the first time using [GuiRunOnce].

- Using batch files and packaging applications to be used with the Windows Installer service.

You can customize many Windows XP Professional features after installation, such as wallpaper, screen saver settings, Active Desktop, custom toolbars and taskbars, and new Start and Programs menu options. For more information about post-installation customization, see "Managing Desktops" in this book.

Using Windows XP Professional Customization Tools

Use Setup Manager (setupmgr.exe) to create answer files or use a simple text editor (such as Notepad) to manually create them.

You can use a network connection to a RIS server to download one or more operating system images (including Windows XP Professional). If you use a RIS server to download an operating system image, RIS provides answer file templates and a Client Installation Wizard (CIW).

You can use Sysprep to distribute operating system images using removable media. Sysprep provides an answer file (Sysprep.inf) that you can customize.

Customizing Unattended Installations

An answer file or setup script is a text file that follows a specific format and syntax and contains all of the information Setup must have to automate and customize an installation. The Setup program uses this customized script to provide values for all of the settings that are required during installation.

Typically, the answer file for Winnt32.exe is named Unattend.txt; however, you can use any valid file name (for example, Sales.txt, Test.txt, and Support.txt). You must use the **/Unattend** parameter and the correct file name when you run Setup from the command line (for example, **/Unattend**:*filename.txt*). By using descriptive names to differentiate different versions of an answer file, you can build and maintain a variety of unique answer files for the workgroups within your organization.

The answer file provides Setup with the necessary information to enable interaction with the distribution folders and files that you have created.

Creating an Answer File by Using Setup Manager   You can use Setup Manager to create an answer file for an unattended installation, an automated installation using Sysprep, or an automated installation using RIS. Setup Manager is available on the Windows XP Professional operating system CD in the Deploy.cab file of the \Support\Tools folder. Setup Manager helps you create and modify an answer file by providing prompts for the information that is required and then creating the answer file. Setup Manager can create a new answer file, import an existing answer file for modification, or create a new answer file based on the configuration of the computer on which it is running.

Table 2-5 lists the parameters that you can configure with Setup Manager. The parameters are listed in the order in which they are presented. After you configure the parameters, Setup Manager generates the results as answer file keys.

Table 2-5   Setup Manager Parameters

Parameter	Description
Set user interaction	Sets the level of user interaction that is appropriate during the setup process. For example, you can select **Provide defaults** to display the configurable values supplied in the answer file, or **Fully automated** to create a setup process that does not prompt the user to review or supply configuration values.
Set default user information	Specifies an organization or user name.
Define computer names	When you enter multiple names during the setup process, Setup Manager automatically generates the Uniqueness Database File (UDF) that is required to add those unique names to each computer during setup. If the administrator imports names from a text file, Setup Manager converts each name to a Uniqueness Database File. The administrator can also set an option to generate unique computer names.
Set an administrator password	Setup Manager can encrypt the administrator password in the Unattend.txt answer file. This prevents the password from being readable if the answer file is viewed in a text editor. Setup Manager can also be set to prompt the user for the administrator password during setup. If the **Administrator Password** box is left blank, you can use the AutoLogon feature to log on to the client computer as an administrator. To disable AutoLogon, type a value in the **Administrator Password** box when you run Setup Manager.
Display settings	You can automatically set the display color depth, screen area, and refresh frequency display settings.
Configure network settings	Any custom network-setting option that can be configured from the desktop can be configured remotely using Setup Manager. The interface for setting network settings in Setup Manager is the same interface that the user sees on their desktop. Using Setup Manager, you can also add computers to a domain or workgroup, or automatically create accounts in the domain.
Set time zone and regional options	Sets the correct time zone using the same property sheet that a user would access to change the time zone locally. Specifies regional and language options such as date, time, numbers, character sets, and keyboard layout.
Set Internet Explorer settings	Performs the basic setup for Internet connections, such as connecting to proxy servers. If your organization wants to customize the browser, the administrator can use Setup Manager to access the customization tool that is part of the Internet Explorer Administration Kit (IEAK), available from www.microsoft.com.
Set telephony settings	Sets telephony properties, such as area codes and dialing rules.

Table 2-5   Setup Manager Parameters

Parameter	Description
Add Cmdlines.txt files	Files used to install additional components, such as applications. For example, the administrator can add the command line to run Microsoft® Office setup by including the command line for Office setup in the Cmdlines.txt file.
Create an installation folder	Uses the default installation folder, \\Windows, to generate a unique folder during setup or to set a custom folder.
Install printers	Sets up multiple printers as part of the installation process.
Add commands to the Run Once section	Sets up commands that run automatically the first time a user logs on. These might include running an application setup program or changing security settings.
Run commands at the end of setup	Specifies commands that run at the end of the setup process and before users log onto the system, such as starting an application setup file.
Copy additional files	Specifies additional files to be copied to the user's desktop, such as device driver libraries, and their location.
Create a distribution folder	Creates a distribution folder on the network that includes the required Windows XP Professional source files. You can also add files that you want to copy or supply additional device drivers for use with Windows XP Professional.

Setup Manager cannot perform the following functions:

- Specify system components, such as Internet Information Services.
- Create Txtsetup.oem files.
- Create subfolders in the distribution folder.

To copy Setup Manager from the Windows XP Professional CD

1. In the \Support\Tools folder, double-click the **Deploy.cab** file.
2. Copy Setupmgr.exe to a folder on the hard disk.

To run Setup Manager

- Double-click **Setupmgr.exe**. The Setup Manager Wizard helps you create an answer file and a distribution folder.

Example of an Unattend.txt Answer File   Listing 2-1 displays a typical Unattend.txt answer file. This file automates the installation or upgrade of Windows, enabling the Setup program to run without requiring user input. Comments within the answer file describe most sections, keys, and values.

Listing 2-1   Example of an Unattend.txt Answer File

```
[Unattended]
UnattendMode = FullUnattended
TargetPath = Windows
FileSystem = LeaveAlone
OemPreinstall = Yes
OemSkipEula = Yes

[GuiUnattended]
; Set the TimeZone. For example, to set the TimeZone for the
; Pacific Northwest, use a value of "004." Be sure to use the
; numeric value that represents your own time zone. To look up
; a numeric value, see the Deploy.chm file on the Windows XP Professional CD.
; The Deploy.cab file is in the \Support\Tools folder.
TimeZone = "YourTimeZone"
OemSkipWelcome = 1
; The OemSkipRegional key allows Unattended Installation to skip
; RegionalSettings when the final location of the computer is unknown.
OemSkipRegional = 1

[UserData]
; Tip: Avoid using spaces in the ComputerName value.
ComputerName = "YourComputerName"
; To ensure a fully unattended installation, you must provide a value
; for the ProductKey key.
ProductKey = "Your product key"

[LicenseFilePrintData]
; This section is used for server installs.
AutoMode = "PerServer"
AutoUsers = "50"

[Display]
BitsPerPel = 16
XResolution = 800
YResolution = 600
VRefresh = 60

[Components]
; This section contains keys for installing the components of
; Windows XP Professional. A value of On installs the component, and a
; value of Off prevents the component from being installed.
iis_common = On
iis_inetmgr = Off
iis_www = Off
iis_ftp = Off
iis_doc = Off
iis_smtp = On
; The Fp_extensions key installs Front Page Server Extensions.
Fp_extensions = On
; If you set the TSEnabled key to On, Terminal Services is installed on
; a current version of Windows Server.
```

```
TSEnabled = On
; If you set the TSClients key to On, the files required to create
; Terminal Services client disks are installed. If you set this key
; to On, you must also set the TSEnabled key to On.
TSClients = On
Indexsrv_system = On
Accessopt = On
Calc = On
Charmap = On
Chat = Off
Clipbook = On
Deskpaper = On
Dialer = On
Freecell = Off
Hypertrm = On
Media_clips = On
Media_utopia = On
Minesweeper = Off
Mousepoint = Off
Mplay = On
Mswordpad = On
Paint = On
Pinball = Off
Rec = On
Solitaire = Off
Templates = On
Vol = On

[TapiLocation]
CountryCode = "1"
Dialing = Pulse
; Indicates the area code for your telephone. This value must
; be a 3-digit number.
AreaCode = "Your telephone area code"
LongDistanceAccess = 9

[Networking]

[Identification]
JoinDomain = YourCorpNet
DomainAdmin = YourCorpAdmin
DomainAdminPassword = YourAdminPassword

[NetOptionalComponents]
; Section contains a list of optional network components to install.
Snmp = Off
Lpdsvc = Off
Simptcp = Off

[Branding]
; This section brands Microsoft® Internet Explorer with custom
; properties from the Unattended answer file.
BrandIEUsingUnattended = Yes
```

```
[URL]
; This section contains custom URL settings for Microsoft
; Internet Explorer. If these settings are not present, the
; default settings are used. Specifies the URL for the
; browser's default home page. For example, you might use the
; following: Home_Page = www.microsoft.com.
Home_Page = YourHomePageURL
; Specifies the URL for the default search page. For example, you might
; use the following: Search Page = www.msn.com
Search_Page = YourSearchPageURL
; Specifies a shortcut name in the link folder of Favorites.
; For example, you might use the following: Quick_Link_1_Name =
; "Microsoft Product Support Services"
Quick_Link_1_Name = "Your Quick Link Name"
; Specifies a shortcut URL in the link folder of Favorites. For example,
; you might use this: Quick_Link_1 = http://support.microsoft.com/.
Quick_Link_1 = YourQuickLinkURL

[Proxy]
; This section contains custom proxy settings for Microsoft
; Internet Explorer. If these settings are not present, the default
; settings are used. If proxysrv:80 is not accurate for your
; configuration, be sure to replace the proxy server and port number
; with your own values.
HTTP_Proxy_Server = proxysrv:80
Use_Same_Proxy = 1
```

Customizing Sysprep Installations

This section provides information about the components of Sysprep 2.0, including:

- The Sysprep.inf File

- The MiniSetup Wizard

- Factory Mode

- Audit Boot Mode

- Reseal Mode

- The **-msoobe** parameter (Windows Welcome)

Using Sysprep.inf   Listing 2-2 displays an example of a Sysprep.inf answer file. If you are running Sysprep with the **-mini** parameter, you can use the Sysprep.inf answer file to automate the MiniSetup process. It uses the same .inf file syntax and key names (for supported keys) as Unattend.txt. Place the Sysprep.inf file in the %SystemDrive%\Sysprep folder or on a floppy disk. If you use a floppy disk, insert it into the floppy disk drive after the Windows startup screen appears. Note that if you do not include Sysprep.inf when running Sysprep, the MiniSetup Wizard requires user input at each customization screen.

If you provided a Sysprep.inf file on the reference computer and want to individually change Sysprep.inf on each destination computer, use the floppy disk method.

Listing 2-2   Sample Sysprep.inf Answer File

```
[Unattended]
; Prompt the user to accept the EULA.
OemSkipEula = No
;Use Sysprep's default and regenerate the page file for the system
;to accommodate potential differences in available RAM.
KeepPageFile = 0
;Provide the location for additional language support files that
;might be required in a global organization.
InstallFilesPath = c:\Sysprep\i386

[GuiUnattended]
;Set the time zone.
TimesZone = 20
;Skip the Welcome screen when the system starts.
OemSkipWelcome = 1
;Do not skip the Regional and Language Options dialog box so that users can
;indicate which options apply to them.
OemSkipRegional = 0

[UserData]
ComputerName = XYZ_Computer1

[Display]
BitsPerPel = 16
XResolution = 800
YResolution = 600
VRefresh = 60

[GuiRunOnce]
"%systemdrive%\sysprep\file name.bat" = "path-1\Command-1.exe"
"path-n\Command-n.exe"
"%systemdrive%\sysprep\sysprep.exe -quiet"

[Identification]
;Join the computer to the domain ITDOMAIN.
JoinDomain = ITDOMAIN

[Networking]
```

For more information about answer file keys and values, see the Deploy.chm in the Deploy.cab file on the Windows XP Professional operating system CD. The Deploy.cab file is in the \Support\Tools folder.

Using MiniSetup   If you are running Sysprep with the **-mini** parameter, the Mini-Setup Wizard appears the first time a computer starts from a disk that was duplicated by using Sysprep. The MiniSetup Wizard gathers information that is required to customize the destination computer. If you do not use Sysprep.inf or if you leave some sections of the file blank, the MiniSetup Wizard displays screens to collect the required information that has not already been provided. The displayed screens can include:

- Welcome to Windows XP Professional Setup Wizard.

- End-User License Agreement (EULA).

- Regional and Language Options.

- User name and company.

- Product key. This screen is always displayed unless you prepopulate the system preparation procedure with product key information.

- Computer name and administrator password.

- Telephony application programming interface (TAPI) settings screen. This screen is only displayed if a modem or a new modem device exists on the computer.

- Date and time settings.

- Networking settings.

- Workgroup or computer domain.

For more information about bypassing these screens, see Table 2-6.

Note   Because Setup detects optimal settings for display devices, you no longer see the Display Settings screen when Setup or the MiniSetup Wizard is running. You can specify the settings in the [Display] section either in the answer file that is used for your reference computer or in the Sysprep.inf file used for your destination computer. If settings in the [Display] section are in the answer file that is used for your reference computer, Sysprep retains those settings unless Sysprep.inf contains different settings or unless a video adapter or monitor is detected that requires settings different from those of the reference computer.

Table 2-6   Parameters in Sysprep.inf for Bypassing the MiniSetup Wizard

Parameter	Section, Key, and Value
Set regional options	[RegionalSettings]
	LanguageGroup = 15,7,1
	SystemLocale = 00000409
	UserLocale = 00000409
	InputLocale = 0409:00000409
	[GuiUnattended]
	OemSkipRegional = 1
Define user name and company	[UserData]
	FullName = "User Name"
	OrgName = "Organization Name"
Define computer name and administrator password	[UserData]
	ComputerName = W2B32054
	[GuiUnattended]
	AdminPassword = ""
Set TAPI settings	[TapiLocation]
	AreaCode = 425
Set network settings	[Networking]
Set server licensing (Windows server only)	[LicenseFilePrintData]
	AutoMode = PerServer
	AutoUsers = 5
Define time zone selection	[GuiUnattended]
	TimeZone = "*Index*"

If you use the [RegionalSettings] section to add additional language support, make sure the language files are available. Also, make sure the C:\Sysprep\i386\Lang folder contains the files in the \i386\Lang folder on the Windows XP Professional CD. In addition, make sure the following entries appear in the Sysprep.inf file:

```
[Unattended]
InstallFilesPath = "C:\Sysprep\i386"
```

Using Sysprep Factory Mode   You can use Sysprep Factory Mode, **sysprep -factory**, to preconfigure installation options and reduce the number of displayed MiniSetup or Windows Welcome (Msoobe.exe) screens. Factory Mode enables you to prepopulate information in the [Factory] section header of the Sysprep answer file, WinBom.ini. You can prepopulate information, such as address, time zone, existing ISP, and locale. You can also use Factory Mode to update other .ini or answer files, such as Sysprep.inf, OOBEinfo.ini, or .isp and .ins files.

Factory Mode enables you to add additional device drivers and applications to the image after the computer restarts when you are running Sysprep.exe. You typically run Sysprep.exe as the final step in the preinstallation process to prepare the computer for delivery. When restarted, the computer displays the MiniSetup or Windows Welcome screens. By clicking the **Factory** button on the **OEM Reset Reminder** dialog box, or by running **Sysprep -factory** from the command line (using the **-factory** parameter), the computer restarts in a network-enabled state without starting MiniSetup or Windows Welcome. In this state, Factory.exe processes WinBom.ini and performs the following tasks:

1. Copies device drivers from a network source to the computer.

2. Starts Plug and Play enumeration.

3. Copies applications from a network source to the computer.

4. Adds customer data.

In this state, the computer can be audited. When complete, run Sysprep with the **-reseal** parameter to prepare it for delivery.

When you use Factory Mode with disk-imaging (or cloning) software, you can reduce the number of required images. You can create a reference computer image with a minimal set of device drivers, and then copy the image to the destination computers. For any destination computer that requires additional device drivers, you can run Factory Mode to update the installed image with the required drivers.

Table 2-7 lists the sections in a WinBom.ini file.

Table 2-7   WinBom.ini Sections

Section	Description
[ComputerSettings]	Configures end-user settings on the destination computer.
[Factory]	Includes entries for performing a factory installation of Windows XP Professional.
[NetCards]	Includes entries for configuring the network adapter on the destination computer if a network connection is required.
[OEMLink]	Adds a graphic and text to the Start menu to provide end users with easy access to an OEM's .htm file.

Table 2-7   WinBom.ini Sections

Section	Description
[OEMRun]	Runs external applications and command shell scripts while the Sysprep **-factory** command is running. Commands are processed asynchronously. Each application runs in the order listed in this section, but the application does not wait for a previous application to finish before it runs. These executable files or command shell scripts are the last processing performed by the Sysprep **-factory** command.
[OEMRunOnce]	Includes entries for controlling the running of external applications and command shell scripts during the running of the Sysprep **-factory** command.
[Section_name]	Preinstalls an application as specified in the [OEMRunOnce] section.
[PnPDriverUpdate]	Includes entries for updating device drivers on the installed image prior to installing the drivers with Plug and Play.
[PnPDrivers]	Lists the updated device drivers to be copied on to the computer.
[Shell]	Customizes the appearance of the Windows desktop and Start menu.
[SetupHomenet]	Sets up a firewall on a computer that uses a preconfigured Internet connection.
[StartMenuMFUlist]	Prepopulates the Most Frequently Used programs list on the Start menu with shortcuts to preinstalled applications.
[UpdateSystem]	Updates any of the computer's files or registry entries.
[UserAccounts]	Includes entries for controlling the creation of user identities on the destination computer.
[UserDefined]	Creates a user-defined section that can contain branding information or any other data for other processes.

Using Sysprep Audit Boot Mode   To test and verify installations, you can use Audit Boot Mode to quickly restart the computer before you are ready to use Reseal Mode. You can invoke Audit Boot Mode by clicking the **Audit Boot** button in the **OEM Reset Reminder** dialog box.

Using Sysprep Reseal Mode   When you have made modifications in Factory Mode, you can use Reseal Mode to prepare the computer for delivery. When the computer restarts from Factory Mode, you can invoke Reseal Mode by clicking the **Reseal** button on the **OEM Reset Reminder** dialog box, or by running **Sysprep -reseal** from the command line (using the **-reseal** parameter). To display the Windows Welcome screens on the first restart after you reseal the image, use the **-msoobe** parameter.

Customizing RIS Installations

Remote Installation Services (RIS) is a tool that enables you to perform a clean installation of a pre-configured image of a supported operating system on a client computer. You can use RIS to install the operating system over a network connection on a computer that supports the Pre-Boot eXecution Environment (PXE). You can also use RIS with the Remote Boot Floppy Generator (Rbfg.exe) to create a remote boot disk that can be used with a variety of supported PCI-based network adapters.

Using RIS Answer Files   The Remote Installation Services answer file guides the installation of the operating system. When you install RIS on a computer running a current version of Windows 2000 Server and then run Risetup.exe, a standard answer file is created and named Ristndrd.sif. You can modify this RIS answer file to perform an installation with minimal or no user intervention and place the computer account object in the domain in which the RIS server resides. Ristndrd.sif also contains the description that is displayed during the CIW when the user at the client computer selects an operating system image to install.

Listing 2-3 displays an example of a RIS answer file, Ristndrd.sif.

Listing 2-3   Sample Ristndrd.sif Answer File

```
[Data]
Floppyless = "1"
MsDosInitiated = "1"
OriSrc = "\\%SERVERNAME%\RemInst\%INSTALLPATH%\%MACHINETYPE%"
OriTyp = "4"
LocalSourceOnCD = 1

[SetupData]
OsLoadOptions = "/noguiboot /fastdetect"
SetupSourceDevice = "\Device\LanmanRedirector\%SERVERNAME%\RemInst\%INSTALLPATH%"

[Unattended]
OemPreinstall = No
FileSystem = LeaveAlone
ExtendOEMPartition = 0
TargetPath = \WINDOWS
OemSkipEula = Yes
InstallFilesPath = "\\%SERVERNAME%\RemInst\%INSTALLPATH%\%MACHINETYPE%"
LegacyNIC = 1

[UserData]
FullName = "%USERFIRSTNAME% %USERLASTNAME%"
OrgName = "%ORGNAME%"
ComputerName = %MACHINENAME%

[GuiUnattended]
OemSkipWelcome = 1
OemSkipRegional = 1
TimeZone = %TIMEZONE%
AdminPassword = "*"
```

```
[Display]
BitsPerPel = 16
XResolution = 800
YResolution = 600
VRefresh = 60

[Networking]

[NetServices]
MS_Server = params.MS_PSched

[Identification]
JoinDomain = %MACHINEDOMAIN%
DoOldStyleDomainJoin = Yes

[RemoteInstall]
Repartition = Yes
UseWholeDisk = Yes

[OSChooser]
Description = "Microsoft Windows XP Professional"
Help =
"Automatically installs Windows Professional without prompting the user for input
."
LaunchFile = "%INSTALLPATH%\%MACHINETYPE%\templates\startrom.com"
ImageType = Flat
Version = "5.1"
```

Customizing the RIS Client Installation Wizard   After you install RIS on a computer that is running a current version of Windows 2000 Server, you have access to a default set of Client Installation Wizard (CIW) screens, which provide basic functionality for installing clients. You can modify the CIW screens to meet the needs of your organization. The files are simple text files (with an .osc extension) that are in the OSCML format. CIW screens are also referred to as Operating System Chooser (OSC) screens. They have the .osc file name extension and are modeled on the HTML 2.0 format.

> **Note**   The CIW screens are modeled on HTML 2.0; they are not a subset of the HTML 2.0 specification.
>   OSCML does not support Microsoft® Visual Basic® Scripting Edition, Microsoft® JScript®, or Java.

Table 2-8 describes the screens that are displayed when a user logs on to the client computer during a RIS installation of the operating system.

After the summary screen appears, the user exits the Client Installation Wizard and proceeds to the automated installation process. The automated installation process is similar to installing the operating system from a CD, but instead of accessing the installation media locally, the client computer accesses operating system files that are stored remotely on a RIS server. Depending on the speed of your network and the load on the RIS server, this process can be much faster than an installation from a CD-ROM drive.

Table 2-8   Client Installation Wizard Screens

Screen	Description
Logon screen (Login.osc)	Requires a user to log on. The user logs on to the network by using an existing user account, password, and domain. After the user successfully logs on, RIS uses these credentials to determine which installation options to display on the Setup Options screen. If the process is not successful and the logon account, password, or domain is not recognized, the user is prompted to log on again.
Setup Options screen (Choice.osc)	Displays installation options to the user, including:
	Automatic provides the easiest operating system installation path. If there is already a computer account object in Active Directory with a Globally Unique Identifier (GUID) that matches the client computer's GUID, the existing computer account is reused. If a matching GUID is not found in Active Directory, the client computer is named based on the automatic naming format configured in the properties of the RIS server, and a new computer account is created in the location specified by the RIS server.
	Custom allows users to override the automatic computer naming process, as well as the default location within Active Directory where client computer account objects are created. The Custom Setup option is similar to the automatic option, but you can use it to set up a client computer for a subsequent user (for example, to install an operating system on a client computer within the enterprise) before delivery to a user. If either the computer name or computer location is left blank on the Custom Setup screen, the automatic name or location is used.
	Restart a Previous Setup Attempt restarts the operating system installation process by using the information entered during the previous attempt. If the installation process fails or network connectivity is disrupted during the initial text-mode phase of setup (before completing the file copy phase), a **Restart Setup** command is available for optional display to the user the next time the computer is started.
	Maintenance and Troubleshooting provides access to maintenance and troubleshooting tools, such as system flash BIOS updates and computer diagnostic tools that can be used prior to operating system installation.
	The degree to which this screen and its options are displayed is controlled by means of RIS Group Policy settings.

Table 2-8   Client Installation Wizard Screens

Screen	Description
Duplicate GUID detection screen (Osauto.osc)	This screen is not displayed to users. Osauto.osc determines if a computer account object already exists in Active Directory with the same GUID as the computer running the Client Installation Wizard. If a duplicate GUID is found, DupAuto.osc is displayed. If no duplicate GUID is found, OSChoice.osc is displayed.
Error screen (Dupauto.osc)	Displayed if a duplicate GUID is found in Active Directory. Instructs the user to contact the network administrator.
Operating system choice screen (Oschoice.osc)	Displays the list of operating system images on the RIS server that are available to a user who is logged-on. If only one image is available for the user to install, that image is automatically selected and the user does not see this screen.
aution screen (Warning.osc)	Displays a warning message that the hard disk will be formatted. The user is cautioned that an operating system will be installed on the computer, a process that requires the hard disk to be repartitioned and formatted, erasing all data currently on the disk.
Summary screen (Install.osc)	Displays information about the computer including computer name, computer GUID, and the RIS server to be used for downloading the image. Pressing any key begins the installation process.
	At this point, the RIS server has created a computer account object in Active Directory for the computer and can look up the computer and its computer name and other settings if the computer is reinstalled.
	If you were running the Client Installation Wizard to prestage the computer for another user, you can now shut down the computer and return it to the end user. The end user must have reset password permissions on the newly created computer account object in Active Directory.
Custom Setup screen (Custom.osc)	Prompts the user for a computer name and the Organizational Unit (OU) in which to create the computer account.

Using the Client Installation Wizard   Typically, when a remote boot-enabled client computer using RIS to install an operating system is turned on for the first time, the client computer contacts the boot server, and the user is prompted to press the F12 key on the keyboard of the client computer to initiate the download of the Client Installation Wizard (CIW). After the CIW is downloaded to the client computer, the Welcome screen appears and the user is prompted to log on to the network with an existing user account, password, and logon domain. After the logon process is established, RIS checks to see what installation options the user has access to based on the Group Policy settings that are applied to the user. The CIW displays a menu with the appropriate installation options tailored to the specific user. RIS has been configured so that a user is not presented with installation options by default. The Automatic setup option is automatically chosen.

Startrom.com and Startrom.n12 are two of the RIS boot files in the \RemoteInstall\OSChooser\i386 folder of the RIS hard disk partition on a RIS server.

Startrom.com   The default RIS boot file that can be sent in response to a client computer request to initiate the operating system installation procedure. If you use the default RIS boot file, the client computer prompts the user to press the F12 key to download the Client Installation Wizard (CIW).

Startrom.n12   The alternate RIS boot file that you can rename and use to streamline the process of initiating the installation of the operating system. If the client computer has a new, clean hard disk and if it is configured to boot from the network, use this alternate RIS boot file. The RIS server automatically starts downloading the CIW to the client computer. The client computer does not prompt the user to press the F12 key.

The \RemoteInstall\OSChooser\i386 folder is created and populated when you run Risetup.exe on a computer that is running Windows 2000 Server. The default Startrom.com file is the boot file that can be sent, in response to a client computer request, from a RIS server to a client computer. This default Startrom.com file prompts the user to press the F12 key to initiate the download of the CIW screens and to start the process of installing the operating system.

If you are installing Windows XP Professional on a new client computer that has a clean hard disk, you can use the Startrom.n12 file instead of the default Startrom.com file on the RIS server to eliminate the need to press the F12 key from the client computer. To do this, perform the following tasks from the RIS server:

1. In the \RemoteInstall\OSChooser\i386 folder of the hard disk partition that is used for RIS installations, change the name of the Startrom.n12 file to Startrom.com.

2. Change the boot order of the client computer so that it starts from the hard disk first and from PXE second.

The first time the client computer attempts to start from the hard disk, the boot process fails because the operating system is not yet installed on the hard disk. The client computer then starts from PXE without requiring a user to press the F12 key. After you successfully complete the operating system installation, subsequent restarts are performed by using the operating system that is now installed on the hard disk. It is necessary to perform step two in the preceding task because the client computer initiates a RIS installation on every restart if PXE is first in the boot order.

Creating an Answer File Manually

You can use a text editor, such as Notepad, to manually create an answer file. An answer file consists of section headers, keys, and values for those keys. Note that you do not have to specify all possible keys in the answer file if the installation does not require them. Invalid key values cause errors or faulty performance after Setup. Listing 2-4 displays an example of a manually created answer file.

Listing 2-4   Example of a Manually Created Answer File

```
[Section1]
; Sections contain keys and corresponding values for the keys.
; Keys and values are separated by equal signs.
; Values with spaces usually require double quotes.
; Text (like this) following semi-colons are comments.
Key = Value

[Section2]
Key = "Value with spaces"
```

Winnt.sif is the answer file that is used for performing an unattended clean installation from a CD. Listing 2-5 displays an example of a fully unattended Winnt.sif answer file.

Note   When you use Winnt.exe to perform a clean installation from a bootable CD on a computer with multiple hard disks or partitions, specify the exact location of the destination hard disk or partition to which you are installing. Add AutoPartition = 1 to the [Data] section of the Winnt.sif file to specify the location.

Listing 2-5   Sample Winnt.sif Answer File

```
[Data]
AutoPartition = 1
MsDosInitiated = 0
UnattendedInstall = Yes

[Unattended]
UnattendMode = FullUnattended
OemSkipEula = Yes
OemPreinstall = No
```

```
[GuiUnattended]
AdminPassword = *
OEMSkipRegional = 1
TimeZone = 85
OemSkipWelcome = 1

[UserData]
FullName = USERNAME
OrgName = MS
ComputerName = COMPUTERNAME

[Identification]
JoinWorkgroup = WORKGROUP

[Networking]
InstallDefaultComponents = Yes
```

Customizing Components and Features

This section describes the tools you can use and the procedures you can perform to manually customize the components and features of a Windows XP Professional installation. You also have the option of using Setup Manager Wizard to customize components and features for a Windows XP Professional installation.

Adding Hardware Device Support

The following topics describe how to add hardware device support to your installation:

- Mass Storage Devices
- Hardware Abstraction Layers
- Driver Signatures
- Plug and Play Devices

Mass Storage Devices   In Windows XP Professional, Plug and Play installs most hardware devices that can be loaded later in the setup process. However, mass storage devices, such as hard disk controllers, must be properly installed for full Plug and Play support to be available during the GUI mode of Setup. For this reason, the installation of mass storage devices is handled differently from the installation of other hardware devices.

To add small computer system interface (SCSI) devices during text-mode Setup (before full Plug and Play support is available), you must provide a Txtsetup.oem file that describes how Setup needs to install the particular SCSI device. For more information about Txtsetup.oem, see the Microsoft® Windows XP Professional Device Driver Kit.

To install a mass storage device

1.   In the distribution folder, create the Textmode folder in the \OEM folder.

2. Copy the following files into the Textmode folder. These files are available from the device vendor. In the list below, replace *Driver* with the appropriate driver name:

- *Driver*.sys

- *Driver*.dll

- *Driver*.inf

- *Driver*.cat

- Txtsetup.oem

Some drivers, such as SCSI miniport drivers, might not include a DLL file.

Note   A catalog file, for example *Driver*.cat, might not be required. Most SCSI drivers do not ship with dynamic-link library files (DLLs). Catalog files (.cat) are not used during text-mode setup.

The required files are specified in the Txtsetup.oem file. Make sure that all the files listed in Txtsetup.oem appear in the textmode directory and that the files are specified in the [OEMBootFiles] section of the Unattend.txt file.

You must also copy the driver files to the *PnPdrvrs* location that you specified for the OemPnPDriversPath key in the answer file. For example:

```
\$OEM$\$1\PnPdrvrs\Storage
```

You must include a catalog file, for example, *Driver*.cat, with the mass storage device drivers if the catalog file is listed in Txtsetup.oem. For more information about catalog files, see the Hardware Development link on the Web Resources page at http://www.microsoft.com/windows/reskits/webresources.

3. In the answer file, create a [MassStorageDrivers] section, and include the driver entries that you want to include. If you are using two mass storage devices, one to control the hard disk, and the other to control the CD-ROM drive, a possible entry in the [MassStorageDrivers] section is shown in the following example:

```
"Adaptec 2940…" = "OEM"
"Adaptec 2940…" = "retail"
```

Information for this section can be obtained from the Txtsetup.oem file, which is provided by the hardware manufacturer.

4. In the answer file, create an [OEMBootFiles] section, and include a list of the files in the OEM\Textmode folder. A possible entry to the [OEMBootFiles] section is shown in the following example:

```
[OEMBootFiles]
Driver.sys
Driver.dll
Driver.inf
Txtsetup.oem
```

   Replace the word "Driver" with the appropriate driver name.

Warning   Only add driver entries to the [MassStorageDrivers] and [OEM-BootFiles] sections for bootable mass storage devices. Do not include references to secondary mass storage devices. For secondary mass storage devices, add the drivers to the *PnPdrvrs* folder specified in the OEMPnPDriversPath key of the answer file.

If your mass storage device is a Plug and Play device, verify that a Hardware Identification Section and a reference to the catalog file for the driver (*Driver*.cat) exist in the Txtsetup.oem file. For more information, see the Driver Development Kits link on the Web Resources page at http://www.microsoft.com/windows/reskits/webresources.

5. In the Txtsetup.oem file, verify that a section named [HardwareIds.Scsi.yyyyy] exists. If not, create it by using the following format:

```
[HardwareIds.scsi. yyyyy]
id = "xxxxx" , "yyyyy"
```

   In the preceding example, xxxxx is the device identifier and yyyyy is the device service name. For the Symc810 driver, which has a device ID of PCI\VEN_1000&DEV_0001, you can create the section shown in the following example:

```
[HardwareIds.scsi.symc810]
id = "PCI\VEN_1000&DEV_0001" , "symc810"
```

Hardware Abstraction Layers   To specify Hardware Abstraction Layers (HALs) for installation, you must have a Txtsetup.oem file and the HAL files that are provided by the vendor. Use the same Txtsetup.oem file if you are installing mass storage device drivers. Only one Txtsetup.oem file can be used; therefore, if you have to install HALs and mass storage device drivers, combine the entries into one file.

To use third-party drivers, you must make appropriate changes to the answer file. For more information about answer file syntax, see the Deploy.chm in the Deploy.cab file on the Windows XP Professional operating system CD. The Deploy.cab file is in the \Support\Tools folder.

To install a HAL

1. If you have not already done so, create a Textmode folder in the \OEM folder.

2. Copy the files that you receive from the device vendor to the Textmode folder.

3. In the answer file, edit the [Unattended] section for the HAL, and add any drivers that you want to install. A possible entry for the ComputerType key is shown in the following example:

```
[Unattended]
ComputerType = "HALDescription", OEM
```

You can obtain information about the *HALDescription* from the [Computer] section of the Txtsetup.oem file, which is provided by the hardware manufacturer.

4. In the answer file, create an [OEMBootFiles] section, and enter the names of the files in the \OEM\Textmode folder.

Driver Signatures   Before using updated drivers, verify that they are signed correctly. If drivers are not correctly signed, they might not be installed. To verify that drivers are correctly signed, contact the vendor.

In the answer file, the DriverSigningPolicy key in the [Unattended] section specifies how nonsigned drivers are processed during installation.

> **Warning**   Microsoft strongly advises against using DriverSigningPolicy = Ignore unless you have fully tested the device driver in your environment and are sure that it works correctly. Using unsigned drivers increases the risk of device driver problems that can affect the performance or stability of your computer.
>
> If you are using DriverSigningPolicy = Ignore and you attempt to install a newer, unsigned copy of a driver that is protected by Windows XP Professional, the policy level is automatically updated to Warn.

For more information about driver signing policy, see the Deploy.chm in the Deploy.cab file on the Windows XP Professional operating system CD. The Deploy.cab file is in the \Support\Tools folder.

Plug and Play Devices   Windows XP Professional automatically installs most Plug and Play device drivers; however, you need to can easily add Plug and Play device drivers if necessary. When you are creating your reference installation image, check the Windows XP Professional product CD to determine if the drivers for the Plug and Play devices you are installing are listed. You can add Plug and Play device drivers that are not included on the Windows XP Professional operating system CD by performing the procedures in this section. This method works for all Plug and Play device drivers. You can also use this method to update existing Plug and Play device drivers.

The following procedures illustrate how you can add Plug and Play to these installation methods:

- Unattended Installation
- Sysprep images
- Risetup images

To add Plug and Play device drivers to an Unattended Installation

1. In the \OEM folder of the distribution folder, create subfolders for any special Plug and Play drivers and their .inf files, as shown in the following example:

```
$OEM$\$1\PnPDrvrs
```

2. Copy the driver files for the devices into the folders created in the previous step.

3. In the answer file, edit the [Unattended] key for Plug and Play and add the path to the list of Plug and Play search drives, as shown in the following example:

```
[Unattended]
OEMPnPDriversPath = "PnPDrvrs"
```

The folders must contain all of the files that are required to install the specific devices: drivers, catalog, and .inf files. You can store multiple devices.

Directories are not traversed; therefore, if you have files in both \Pnpdrivers \Video and in \Pnpdrivers\Audio, they both need to be explicitly named in the OemPnPDriversPath key.

When Setup searches .inf files for Plug and Play IDs during GUI-mode Setup, Setup alsolooks in the paths noted in the OemPnPDriversPath along with the standard default path of %windir%\Inf. The %windir%\Inf path is listed first in the search order, but if you have a device that is supported by more than one .inf file (Windows XP Professional might include a driverthat offers generic functionality), Setup continues to search all paths specified in the OemPnPDriversPath entry. Even though it might find multiple matches, Plug and Play uses the .inf file that has the best match and then installs the associated device driver to support the device.

To maintain the folders to accommodate future device drivers, create subfolders for potential device drivers. By dividing the folders into subfolders, you can store device driver files by device type rather than storing all device driver files in a single folder. Suggested subfolders include Audio, Modem, Net, Print, Storage, Video, and Other. Creating an Other folder gives you the flexibility to store new hardware devices that are not currently known.

For example, if the PnPDrvs folder contains the Audio, Modem, and Net folders, the answer file must contain the statement shown in the following example:

```
OEMPnPDriversPath = "PnPDrvs\Audio;PnPDrvs\Modem;PnPDrvs\Net"
```

Adding Plug and Play devices before performing disk duplication with Sysprep   When a client computer that has been duplicated with Sysprep starts for the first time, the installer detects all non–Industry Standard Architecture ISA hardware. If a hardware device is found for which there are no device drivers in the default Drivers.cab, the installer checks the location specified in OemPnPDriversPath. If the device drivers are not in this location, then the user is prompted for the location of the device drivers.

To improve the user experience and reduce computer startup time during the first boot, you can install additional Plug and Play device drivers before running Sysprep. If you determine that you want these OEM-supplied device drivers to be available for Windows XP Professional reinstallation, copy the OEM-supplied device driver files directly onto the hard disk before you perform the installation procedure. During MiniSetup, the installer ignores the OemPnPDriversPath information, and attempts to install these device drivers directly from their original locations on the hard disk.

To add Plug and Play devices to a Sysprep Image

1. Create a folder called Sysprep on the %SystemDrive% folder.

2. On the root of the same volume, create a folder structure to hold the drivers, as shown in the following example:

```
\Drivers
      \NIC
      \VIDEO
\Sysprep
\Windows
```

3. Copy the driver files for the devices into the folders created in the previous step. The folders must contain all of the files that are required to install the specific devices: driver, catalog, and .inf files.

4. In the Sysprep.inf answer file, edit the [Unattended] key for Plug and Play, adding the path to the list of Plug and Play search drives. You can list multiple paths in this key by separating them with a semicolon, as shown in the following example:

```
[Unattended]
OEMPnPDriversPath = Drivers\NIC;Drivers\Video
```

5. Save the Sysprep.inf file to the Sysprep folder.

If you do not want the OEM-supplied device drivers to remain on the volume after MiniSetup is complete, place the folder structure (that you created in the Sysprep folder) in the root volume. Adjust the OemPnPDriversPath key in the Sysprep.inf answer file to reflect this change. The Sysprep folder is automatically removed after Setup is complete. This automatic removal process also removes all of the subfolders that are subordinate to the Sysprep folder. To ensure that OEM-supplied device drivers are available if Windows XP Professional reinstallation is required, do not remove any of the OEM-supplied device drivers from the root volume.

When you run Sysprep.exe, any Plug and Play devices (including those found using the driver .inf files) are automatically installed during MiniSetup on the destination computers. You do not need to specify the **-PnP** command-line parameter unless there are existing (ISA) devices on the destination computers.

To add Plug and Play devices to a Risetup image

> **Warning**   To deploy Windows XP images from Windows 2000 RIS Servers, you must install the Windows 2000 Remote Installation Services update. For more information about the Windows 2000 Remote Installation Services update, see the Microsoft Knowledge Base link on the Web Resources page at http://www.microsoft.com/windows/reskits/webresources. Search the Microsoft Knowledge Base using the keywords *Risetup.exe*, *RIS Servers*, and *Windows XP Images*.

1. Create a folder structure similar to the structure shown in the following example:

    Make sure that the \oem folder is at the same level as the \i386 folder.

```
\RemoteInstall\Setup\%language%\Images\%risetup_image_name%\i386
\RemoteInstall\Setup\%language%\Images\%risetup_image_name%\$oem$\$1\Drivers
                                                            \NIC
                                                            \VIDEO
                                                            \Modem
```

2. Copy the device driver files for the devices into their respective folders. Use the folder structure that you created in the previous step.

3. In the Ristndrd.sif answer file, change the value of the OemPreinstall key in the [Unattended] section from No to Yes, and add the paths to the list of Plug and Play search drivers. You can list multiple paths by using semicolons to separate the path names, as shown in the following example:

```
[Unattended]
OemPreinstall = Yes
OEMPnPDriversPath = Drivers\NIC;Drivers\Video;drivers\modem
```

4. Save the Ristndrd.sif file in the \RemoteInstall\Setup\%language%\Images\ %risetup_image_name%\i386\Templates folder.

> **Note**   If one of the OEM-supplied drivers is for a network adapter, the RIS server must have this driver available when booting into text-mode Setup.

5. Copy the network adapter driver and the associated .inf file to the \RemoteInstall\Setup\%language%\Images\%flat_image_name%\i386 directory.

6. If the device driver that you are adding is an updated version of a driver that is already in this directory, you must delete the associated .pnf file from the \RemoteInstall\Setup\%language%\Images\%flat_image_name%\i386 directory.

7. Stop and restart the Boot Information Negotiation Layer (BINL) service on all RIS servers on which you copied the drivers. This step is required for these changes to take effect.

Customizing Regional and Language Options

You can customize the [RegionalSettings] section of your answer file to specify the regional and language options listed in Table 2-9

To use this section of your answer file, you must add, as a minimum, the **/copysource:lang** parameter to Winnt32.exe or the **/rx:lang** parameter to Winnt.exe. This enables you to copy the appropriate language files to the hard disk. For example, to copy Korean settings while installing a U.S. version of Windows XP Professional, you can specify /copysource:lang\kor if starting from Winnt32.exe.

Table 2-9 describes the keys in the [RegionalSettings] section of the answer file. To ensure that Setup completes without prompting for regional option information, do not provide keys or values for the [RegionalSettings] section when specifying

OemPreinstall = Yes. Set OEMSkipRegional = 1 in the [GuiUnattended] section of the answer file.

Table 2-9 Keys in the [RegionalSettings] Section

Key	Description
InputLocale	Specifies the input locale and keyboard layout combinations to be installed on the computer. The first keyboard layout specified is the default layout for the installation. The specified combinations must be supported by one of the language groups defined by using either the LanguageGroup key or the default language group for the language version of Windows XP Professional being installed. If an available language group does not support the combination specified, the default combination is used for the installation. This key is ignored if the Language key is specified.
Language	Specifies the language and locale to be installed on the computer. This language must be supported by one of the language groups specified by using the LanguageGroup key. If an available language group does not support the locale, the default language for the Windows XP Professional version being installed is used.
	If this value is specified, the SystemLocale, UserLocale, and InputLocale keys are ignored.
LanguageGroup	Specifies the supported language group to be installed on the computer. If this key is specified, it provides default settings for SystemLocale, InputLocale, and UserLocale keys.
	For a list of the supported language group IDs, see the Deploy.chm in the Deploy.cab file on the Windows XP Professional operating system CD. The Deploy.cab file is in the \Support\Tools folder.
SystemLocale	Enables localized applications to run and displays menus and dialog boxes in the local language.
UserLocale	Controls the settings for numbers, time, currency, and dates.

A list of valid locales and their language groups is available at the Global Software Development Web site at http://www.microsoft.com.

Note The LANG folder is automatically copied into Windows XP Professional images on a RIS server; however, the LANG folder must be manually copied into Windows 2000 images. The LANG folder must exist within images to enable locale changes.

To use [RegionalSettings] for multilingual support during MiniSetup

1. Create a folder named \i386 under \$OEM$\$1\Sysprep\ in the distribution folder.

2. To copy files from the \i386 folder of the Windows XP Professional operating system CD to the \i386 folder in the Sysprep folder, type the following at the command prompt:

```
*.nl?
kbd*.dl?
*.fo?
agt*.dl?
agt*.hl?
conime.ex?
wbcache.*
noise.*
wbdbase.*
infosoft.dl?
f3ahvoas.dl?
sylfaen.tt_
c_is*.dl_
\Lang\...
```

You can also use Setup Manager to add the necessary files and folders to the \i386 folder. However, any settings specified here are not kept if Sysprep is run on the computer.

3. In Sysprep.inf, add the InstallFilesPath key to the [Unattended] section, as shown in the following example:

```
InstallFilesPath = %systemdrive%\Sysprep\i386
```

For more information about the InstallFilesPath key, see the Deploy.chm in the Deploy.cab file, which is on the Windows XP Professional operating system CD. The Deploy.cab file is in the \Support\Tools folder.

If you specify a regional setting in the image, you must also specify the same setting in the Sysprep.inf file. In addition, you must copy the correct file to the \Sysprep\i386 folder.

The \i386 folder and its contents are only required if the end user needs language support from one of the language groups provided in that folder. The \i386 folder is deleted after MiniSetup runs on the end user's computer. If you perform an audit or if a reseller further customizes the computer, you must recreate \Sysprep\i386 and then rerun Sysprep.exe before the image is installed to allow the end user to specify the necessary regional and language options.

Presetting Time Zones

You can specify the time zone of the computers in your organization by using the TimeZone key in the [GuiUnattended] section of your answer file or the Sysprep.inf file. If the TimeZone key is not present, the user is prompted for a time zone specification during setup.

To preset time zones

- In the [GuiUnattended] section of your answer file, add the statement shown in the following example:

```
[GuiUnattended]
TimeZone = "Index"
```

In the preceding example, *Index* specifies the time zone of the reference computer. Unless the TimeZone key is specifically set in the RIS answer file, client computers that are installed with RIS use the same time zone setting as the RIS server.

For a list of valid TimeZone indexes, see the Deploy.chm in the Deploy.cab file on the Windows XP Professional operating system CD. The Deploy.cab file is in the \Support\Tools folder.

Detecting Video Mode for Computer Displays

You can customize the [Display] section of the answer file to ensure that Setup automatically detects a computer's display resolution. Specify the optimal settings (you must know the valid settings) for the keys listed in Table 2-10. If the settings that you specify are not valid, Setup finds the closest match to the selected settings, which might not be optimal.

Table 2-10   Keys in the [Display] Section

Keys	Description
BitsPerPel	Specifies the valid bits per pixel for the graphics device being installed. For example, a value of 8 implies 256 colors; a value of 16 implies 65,536 colors.
Vrefresh	Specifies a valid refresh rate for the graphics device being installed.
Xresolution	Specifies a valid x resolution for the graphics device being installed.
Yresolution	Specifies a valid y resolution for the graphics device being installed.

To ensure the video mode is properly detected by Setup

1. Check that the computer BIOS supports the set of Video ACPI extensions.

2. Check that the drivers for the video cards and displays are included in the \$1\PnPdrvrs path.

3. In the [Unattended] section of the answer file, set the OemPnPDriversPath key to the \$1\PnPdrvrs path.

4. In the [Display] section of the answer file, set the optimal settings for your computer.

To determine whether the hardware components in your organization are compatible with Windows XP Professional, see the Hardware Compatibility List link on the Web Resources page at http://www.microsoft.com/windows/reskits/webresources.

Automatically Converting FAT32 to NTFS

When upgrading, you can customize the [Unattended] section of your answer file to convert FAT32 file systems automatically to NTFS.

To automatically convert FAT32 partitions to NTFS

- In the [Unattended] section of your answer file, add the statement shown in the following example:

```
[Unattended]
FileSystem = ConvertNTFS
```

When the FileSystem key is specified, Setup automatically converts your drive just before the GUI mode of Setup starts. You must add the FileSystem = Convert-NTFS entry to the [Unattended] section if the ExtendOEMPartition entry appears in the [Unattended] section of the answer file.

For more information about the differences between the NTFS, FAT16, and FAT32 file systems, see "File Systems" in this book.

Converting Short File Names to Long File Names ($$rename.txt)

If you are starting Setup from MS-DOS, you can convert short file names to long names by creating a file called $$Rename.txt and putting that file in the folder of the distribution folder that also contains the files that you want to convert. If you are starting Setup from any other operating system, they are converted automatically.

Setup uses the list of files that you specify in $$Rename.txt to convert short names to long names during the installation process. Each folder that contains a file, or files, that you want to convert must also contain a $$Rename.txt file.

The $$Rename.txt file changes short file names to long file names during Setup. $$Rename.txt lists all of the files in a particular folder that must be renamed. Each folder that contains short file names to be renamed must contain its own version of $$Rename.txt.

To convert short file names to long file names

■ Create a $$rename.txt file by using the sections, keys, and values shown in the following example:

```
[Section_name_1]

Short_name_1 = "long_name_1"
Short_name_2 = "long_name_2"
Short_name_x = "long_name_x"

[Section_name_x]
Short_name_1 = "Long_name_1"
Short_name_2 = "Long_name_2"
Short_name_x = "Long_name_x"
```

Table 2-11 describes the variables in the preceding example.

Table 2-11   Converting Short File Names to Long File Names

Section or Key	Description
[Section_name_x]	This section name indicates the path to the folder that contains the files. A section does not have to be named, or it can have a backslash (\) as a name, which indicates that the section contains the names of the files or folders that are in the root directory of the drive.
Short_name_x	This key is the short name of the file or folder within the folder indicated by the section name. The short name must not be enclosed in quotation marks.
Long_name_x	This key Is the long name of the file or folder. This name must be enclosed in quotation marks if it contains spaces or commas.

Tip   If you are using MS-DOS to start the installation, and your MS-DOS-based tools cannot copy folders with path names longer than 64 characters, use short file names for the folders and then use $$Rename.txt to rename them later.

Adding Applications

Use any of the following methods to add applications to your installation:

■ Cmdlines.txt to add applications during the GUI mode of Setup.

■ Customized answer files. For example, customize the [GuiRunOnce] section of the answer file to install applications when the user logs on for the first time.

- Application installation programs.

- Batch files.

- Windows Installer.

Using Cmdlines.txt

The Cmdlines.txt file contains the commands that GUI mode runs when installing optional components, such as applications that must be installed immediately after Windows XP Professional installation. If you plan to use Cmdlines.txt, place it in the OEM folder of the distribution folder. If you are using Sysprep, place Cmdlines.txt in the OEM\\$1\\Sysprep\\$oem$ folder.

Use Cmdlines.txt under the following circumstances:

- You are installing from the \\OEM folder of the distribution folder.

- The application that you are installing:

  - Does not configure itself for multiple users (for example, Microsoft® Office 95).

  - Is designed to be installed by one user and to replicate user-specific information.

The section and keys for Cmdlines.txt is shown in the following example:

```
[Commands]
"Command_1"
"Command_2"
.
.
"Command_x"
```

Keys are defined as follows:

- "*Command_1*," "*Command_2*," and "*Command_x*" refer to the commands that you want to run (and the order in which you want to run them) when GUI mode calls Cmdlines.txt. Note that all commands must be within quotation marks.

When you use Cmdlines.txt, be aware of the following:

- When the commands in Cmdlines.txt are carried out during setup, there is no logged-on user and there is no guaranteed network connectivity. Therefore, user-specific information is written to the default user registry, and all users receive that information.

- Cmdlines.txt requires that you place the files that you must have to run an application or tool in directories that you can access during the setup process. This means that the files must be on the hard disk.

> **Warning** Applications that can be installed by using Windows Installer cannot be added by using Cmdlines.txt.

To specify a Cmdlines.txt file during the MiniSetup portion of Sysprep

1. Create a Sysprep.inf file to be used by Sysprep. This is a requirement and cannot by bypassed. The Sysprep.inf file must be named Sysprep.inf and must be located in the Sysprep folder on the root of the volume that contains the folder %systemroot%.

2. Place the following statement in the [Unattended] section of the Sysprep.inf file:

   ```
   InstallFilesPath = drive:\path
   ```

   In the preceding example, *path* is any folder you want to use. It is recommended that you use *drive* as the volume containing the %systemroot% folder.

3. Create the folder *drive*:*path*. You can use any folder name, but it must match the location that you specified in Sysprep.inf.

4. In the *drive*:*path* folder, create a folder named oem, and then place the Cmdlines.txt file in this folder. This file is processed at the end of MiniSetup, before saving any settings.

Using the [GuiRunOnce] Section of the Answer File The [GuiRunOnce] section of the answer file contains a list of commands that run the first time a user logs on to the computer after Setup has run. To configure the application installation program so that it starts automatically, you can add the statement shown in the following example to the [GuiRunOnce] section of the answer file:

```
[GuiRunOnce]
"%systemdrive%\appfolder\appinstall -quiet"
```

If you plan to use the [GuiRunOnce] section to initiate an installation, consider the following additional factors:

If an application forces a restart, determine how to suppress the restart. This is important because any time the system restarts, all previous entries in the [GuiRunOnce] section are lost. If the system restarts before completing entries previously listed in the [GuiRunOnce] section, the remaining items are not run. If there is no way within the application to suppress a restart, you can try to repackage the application into a Windows Installer package. Third-party products are available to provide this functionality.

Windows XP Professional contains Iexpress.exe. You can use Iexpress.exe to package .inf files into executable files. These executable files can then be included in either Cmdlines.txt or [GUIRunOnce].

> **Warning**   If you are adding an application to multiple localized language versions of Windows XP Professional, it is recommended that you test the repackaged application on the localized versions to ensure that the files are copied to the correct locations and the required registry entries are written appropriately.

If an application requires a Windows Explorer shell to install, the [GuiRunOnce] section does not work because the shell is not loaded when the Run and RunOnce commands are carried out.   Check with the application vendor to determine if there is an update that you can download that enables the application to install. If not, repackage the application as a Windows Installer package or use another means of distribution.

Applications that use the same type of installation mechanism might not run correctly if you do not use a-wait parameter.   This can happen when an application installation is running and starts another process. When Setup is still running, initiating another process and closing an active process might cause the next routine listed in the RunOnce registry entries to start. Because more than one instance of the installation mechanism is running, the second application usually fails.

Using Application Installation Programs   The preferred method for adding an application is to use the installation routine supplied with the application. You can do this if the application that you are adding can run in quiet mode (without user intervention) by using a **-q** or **-s** parameter. These parameters vary depending on how the application is written. For a list of parameters supported by the installation mechanism, see the application documentation.

To initiate the unattended installation of an application by using the application's installation program, you can add text to the [GuiRunOnce] section of the answer file that is similar to the statement shown in the following example:

```
path to setup\Setup.exe /q
```

Setup parameters vary depending on how the application is written. For example, the **-l** parameter included in some applications is useful when you want to create a log file to monitor the installation. Some applications have commands that can prevent them from automatically restarting. These commands are useful in helping to control application installations with a minimal number of restarts.

Make sure that you check with the application vendor for information, instructions, tools, and best practices information before you install any application.

> **Warning**   You must meet the licensing requirements for any application that you install, regardless of how you install it.

Using a Batch File to Control How Multiple Applications Are Installed   To control how multiple applications are installed, create a batch file that contains the individual installation commands and uses the **Start** command with the /wait parameter. This method ensures that your applications install sequentially and that each application is fully installed before the next application begins its installation routine. The batch file is then run from the [GuiRunOnce] section.

The following procedure explains how to create the batch file, install the application, and remove all references to the batch file after the installation is complete.

To install applications by using a batch file

1. Create a batch file that uses the following syntax:

   ```
   start /wait AppSetupProgram [AppSetupProgramParameters] [...]
   ```

   Table 2-12 describes the syntax that is used in the preceding example.

   Table 2-12   Batch File Parameters

File or Parameter	Description
AppSetupProgram	Specifies the path and file name for the application setup program, for example, D:\Setup.exe.
AppSetupProgramParameters	Specifies any available quiet-mode parameters for the setup program that you have specified.

2. Copy the batch file to the distribution folders or another location to which you have access during setup.

3. Using *File name*.bat as the name of the batch file, include an entry in the [GuiRunOnce] section of the answer file to run the batch file as shown in the following example. This example is based on the assumption that the batch file

was copied to the Sysprep folder on the local hard disk. However, the batch file can be in any location that is accessible to Setup during an installation.

```
[GuiRunOnce]

"path-n\Command-n.exe"
"%systemdrive%\sysprep\sysprep.exe -quiet"
```

In the preceding example, "*path-n\Command-n.exe*" and "%system-drive%\sysprep\sysprep.exe -quiet" are fully qualified paths to additional applications, tool installations, or configuration tools. They can also be paths to batch files. These paths must be available during setup.

Using Windows Installer Service   Windows Installer Service is a Windows XP Professional component that standardizes the way applications are installed on multiple computers.

When you install applications without using Windows Installer Service, every application must have its own setup executable file or script. Each application has to ensure that the proper installation rules (for example, rules for creating file versions) are followed. This is because the application setup was not an integral part of the operating system development; therefore, no central reference for installation rules exists.

Windows Installer Service implements all the Setup rules for the operating system. To follow these rules, applications must be described in a standard format known as a Windows Installer package. The data file containing the format information is known as the Windows Installer package file and has an .msi file name extension. Windows Installer Service uses the Windows Installer package file to install the application.

The package file is a database format that is optimized for installation performance. Generally, this file describes the relationships among features, components, and resources for a specific product.

The Windows Installer package file is typically located in the root folder of the Windows XP Professional operating system CD or network image, alongside the product files. The product files can exist as compressed files known as cabinet (.cab) files. Each product has its own package file. During installation, Windows Installer Service opens the package file for the product and uses the information inside the Windows Installer package to determine which installation operations must be performed for that product.

Setting Passwords

When upgrading from Windows 98 or Windows Me, you can customize your answer files to set passwords for all local user accounts and force all users or specific users to change their passwords when they first log on. You can also set passwords for the local Administrator account.

Table 2-13 describes the types of passwords that you can set in an answer file.

Table 2-13   Types of Passwords That You Can Set in an Answer File

Section	Key	Description
[GuiUnattended]	AdminPassword	Automatically sets the password for the local Administrator account. If the AdminPassword key is used in a Sysprep.inf file, the original password on the computer must be set to null. Otherwise, any AdminPassword value in the answer file is ignored.
[Win9xUpg]	DefaultPassword	Automatically sets a password for all local accounts created when you are upgrading from Windows 98 or Windows Me.
[Win9xUpg]	ForcePassword-Change	Forces users for all local accounts to change their passwords when they log on for the first time after upgrading from Windows 98 or Windows Me.
[Win9xUpg]	UserPassword	Forces specific users to change their passwords on their local accounts when they log on for the first time after upgrading from Windows 98 or Windows Me to Windows XP Professional.
		Sets user passwords for local accounts after an upgrade from Windows 98 or Windows Me to Windows XP Professional.
		If the answer file does not contain a UserPassword key and a DefaultPassword key, a password is generated for each migrated local user account. When users log on for the first time, they are required to change their password.

Prompting the User for the Administrator Password   The administrator password is set to null by default. You can customize your answer file to prompt the user for an administrator password during installation.

Locate the following entry in the [Unattended] section of the answer file:

```
[Unattended]
UnattendMode = FullUnattended
```

If the UnattendMode key is set to FullUnattended, as shown in the preceding example, do not edit the answer file as described in the following procedure. This combination of answer file settings generates an error.

To prompt for an administrator password

1. Locate the following entry in the [GuiUnattended] section of your answer file:

```
[GuiUnattended]
AdminPassword = "*"
```

2. Edit the entry to read:

```
[GuiUnattended]
AdminPassword = ""
```

> This enables the user to type the local administrator password in GUI-mode Setup.

3. To optionally put Setup in read-only mode and prevent users from changing fields (other than the Administrator password) during Setup, add the following line to the [Unattended] section of the answer file:

```
[Unattended]
UnattendMode = "ReadOnly"
```

> This enables the user to type only the local administrator password in GUI-mode Setup.

An alternative to the preceding procedure is to use Setup Manager to create the answer file and supply an administrator password. When you use Setup Manager, you can encrypt the password in the answer file so that users cannot read it.

For more information about using the RIS Client Installation Wizard to prompt users for the administrator password, see "Customizing RIS Installations" earlier in this chapter.

Setting Passwords on Local Accounts   For upgrades, you can customize your answer file to set all local account passwords to a default value.

To set passwords on all local accounts

- In your answer file, add the following entry in the [Win9xUpg] section:

```
[Win9xUpg]
DefaultPassword = "password"
```

> In the preceding example, *password* is the default password that you want to set for all local users.

> **Note** If a local account must be created for a user without a UserPassword entry and no DefaultPassword is specified, Setup creates a random password. After the first restart, the user is prompted to change the password.

For Windows 98 upgrades, you can customize your answer file to create passwords for specific local accounts. Because Windows 98 and Windows Me passwords cannot be migrated during the upgrade, Setup must create passwords for local accounts during the upgrade process. By using the DefaultPassword key, the administrator can predetermine those passwords for specific users. If a local account needs to be created for a user without a preset value for the UserPassword entry and no value is specified for DefaultPassword, Setup generates a random password.

To create passwords for specific local accounts when you are upgrading from Windows 98 or Windows Me

■ In the answer file, add the following entry in the [Win9xUpg] section:

```
[Win9xUpg]
UserPassword = user,password [,user_1,password_1]
```

Forcing All Users to Change Local Account Passwords When Upgrading from Windows 98 or Windows Me You can customize your answer file to require all users to change their passwords on their local accounts when they log on for the first time. When a user logs on for the first time, he or she is notified that his or her current password has expired and that a new password must be supplied.

To force users to change their password after upgrading from Windows 98 or Windows Me

■ In the answer file, add the following entry in the [Win9xUpg] section:

```
[Win9xUpg]
ForcePasswordChange = Yes
```

Installing the Operating System

After you have chosen the method to install the operating system and have customized your answer file and the distribution folder with the appropriate files, you are ready to install the operating system.

The following installation methods are covered in this section:

- Unattended Installations
- Image-based Installations with Sysprep
- Installations with RIS

Unattended Installations

Winnt32.exe and Winnt.exe are unattended installation tools that provide a convenient and flexible method for installing the operating system. In addition, Winnt32.exe does not require additional tools. This section explains how to use Winnt32.exe.

> **Caution**   Before upgrading to the Windows XP Professional operating system, restart the computer if you have recently upgraded any applications.

> **Note**   When you run Winnt32.exe on a computer with multiple hard disks or partitions, specify the exact location of the destination hard drive or partition to which you are installing. Use the Winnt32 **/tempdrive** parameter to specify the destination.

Use Winnt32.exe to run Setup on computers running Windows 98, Windows Me, Windows 2000, Windows NT Workstation 4.0, or Windows XP Professional operating systems.

> **Note**   Winnt32.exe is also referred to as Setup.

To run Setup in unattended mode

- At the command prompt type: **winnt32 /unattend**: *answer_file*.

  When you run the Setup program, it installs Windows XP Professional in three phases: File Copy, Text mode, and GUI mode.

File Copy

Setup copies the Windows XP Professional program files and any additional files that you specify from the distribution folder to the computer's hard disk.

Text Mode

Setup identifies the basic hardware in the computer (such as the microprocessor and motherboard type, hard disk controllers, file systems, and memory), installs the base operating system required to continue with Setup, and creates any folders that you specify.

GUI Mode

Setup configures the computer's hardware (audio, video, and so on), configures network settings, prompts you to provide an Administrator password, and allows you to personalize the installation. If you use Sysprep, the Setup program goes through a different phase called MiniSetup.

Winnt32.exe Parameters

```
Winnt32
[/checkupgradeonly]
[/cmd:command_line]
[/cmdcons]
[/copydir:folder_name]
[/copysource:folder_name]
[/debuglevel:file_name]
[/dudisable]
[/duprepare:pathname]
[/dushare:pathname]
[/m:folder_name]
[/makelocalsource]
[/noreboot]
[/s:sourcepath]
[/syspart:drive_letter]
[/tempdrive:drive_letter]
[/udf:ID,UDF_file]
[/unattend]
[/unattend:seconds][:answer_file]
```

Parameter Descriptions

To determine which parameters you want to use, refer to the following Winnt32.exe parameter descriptions:

/checkupgradeonly   Checks the current operating system for upgrade compatibility with Windows XP Professional. This is simply a verification and does not install Windows XP Professional.

/cmd:*command_line*   Specifies a command to be carried out after the GUI mode of Setup finishes. The command occurs before Setup is complete and after Setup has restarted your computer and collected the necessary configuration information. For example, this parameter can run Cmdlines.txt, which specifies the applications to be installed immediately after Setup completes.

/cmdcons   Adds a Recovery Console option for repairing a failed installation.

/copydir:*folder_name*   Creates a subfolder within the folder that contains the Windows XP Professional files. For example, if the source folder contains a Private_drivers folder that has modifications just for your site, you can type **/copydir:private_drivers** to copy that folder to your Windows XP Professional folder. You can use the **/copydir** parameter multiple times.

/copysource:*folder_name*   Temporarily creates a subfolder within the folder that contains the Windows XP Professional files. For example, if the source folder contains a Private_drivers folder that has modifications just for your site, type **/copysource:private_drivers** to have Setup copy that folder to your Windows XP Professional folder and use its files during Setup. Unlike the **/copydir** parameter, folders created by using **/copysource** are deleted when Setup finishes.

/debug[*level*][:*file_name*]   Creates a debug log at the specified level. When you use the default setting, the program creates a log file (%windir%\Winnt32.log) that has a warning level of 2. The warning levels for the log file are as follows: 0 = severe errors, 1 = errors, 2 = warnings, 3 = information, and 4 = detailed information for debugging. Each level also includes the levels below it.

/dudisable   Prevents dynamic update from running. Without dynamic update, Setup runs only with the original Setup files. This option disables dynamic update even if you set DisableDynamicUpdates = No in the [Unattended] section of the Unattend.txt file. **/dudisable** in Winnt32.exe overrides the DisableDynamicUpdates = No setting in Unattend.txt.

/duprepare:*pathname*   Prepares an installation share to be used with Dynamic Update files downloaded from the Windows Update Web site. The installation share can then be used for installing Windows on multiple client computers.

/dupshare:*pathname*   Specifies a share on which you previously downloaded Dynamic Update files (updated files for use with Setup) from the Windows Update Web site, and on which you previously ran **/duprepare:***pathname*. When run on a client computer, **/duprepare:***pathname* specifies that the client installation uses the updated files on the share that is specified in *pathname*.

/m:*folder_name*   Instructs Setup to copy replacement files from an alternate location. It directs Setup to look at the alternate location first and to copy the files from that location (if they files are present) instead of from the default location.

/makelocalsource   Instructs Setup to copy all installation source files to your local hard disk. Use /makelocalsource to obtain installation files if you begin installation from a CD and the CD becomes unavailable during the installation.

/noreboot   Instructs Setup to not restart the computer after the file copy phase of Winnt32 is complete so you can execute another command.

/s:*sourcepath* Specifies the source location of the Windows XP Professional files. The default is the current folder. To copy files simultaneously from multiple servers, you can specify up to eight sources. For example:

```
winnt32 /s:server1 … /s:server8
```

If you type the option multiple times, the first server specified must be available, or Setup fails.

This functionality speeds up the file copy phase of Setup to the destination computer and provides additional load balancing capability to the distribution servers from which you run Setup.

/syspart:*drive_letter* Specifies that you can copy Setup startup files to a hard disk, mark the disk as active, and install the disk in another computer. When you start that computer, Setup automatically starts at the next phase. Remember the following points when you use this parameter:

- You must always use the /syspart option with the /tempdrive option.

- Both /syspart and /tempdrive must point to the same partition of a secondary hard disk.

- You must install Windows XP Professional on the primary partition of the secondary hard disk.

- You can use the */syspart* parameter only from a computer that is running Windows NT 3.51, Windows NT 4.0, Windows 2000 Professional, or Windows XP Professional. You cannot use this parameter from a computer that is running Windows 98 or Windows Me.

/tempdrive:*drive_letter* Directs Setup to place temporary files on the specified partition and to install Windows XP Professional on that partition. Remember the following points as you use this parameter:

- You must always use the /tempdrive option with the /syspart option.

- Both /tempdrive and /syspart must point to the same partition of a secondary hard disk.

- You must install Windows XP Professional on the primary partition of the secondary hard disk.

/udf:*ID*[,*UDF_file*] Indicates an identifier that Setup uses to specify how a Uniqueness Database File (UDF) modifies an answer file. The UDF file overrides values in the answer file, and the identifier determines which values in the UDF file are used. For example, /udf:Roaming_user,Our_company.udf overrides settings specified for the identifier Roaming_user in the Our_company.udf file. If you do not specify a UDF file, Setup prompts you to insert a disk that contains the file $Unique$.udf.

/unattend   Upgrades a previous version of Windows by using unattended installation mode. Setup downloads the Dynamic Update files from Windows Update and includes these files in the installation. All user settings are taken from the previous installation. No user intervention is required during Setup.

User passwords cannot be migrated from a Windows 98 or Windows Me installation during an upgrade to Windows XP Professional; however, if you are upgrading from Windows NT Workstation 4.0 or Windows 2000, any user accounts that were defined in the local database are available after upgrading to Windows XP Professional.

> **Warning**   By adding the OemSkipEula key to the [Unattended] section of the answer file, you can automate Setup to affirm that you have read and accepted the End User License Agreement (EULA) for Windows XP Professional. Before using this entry to install Windows XP Professional on behalf of an organization other than your own, you must confirm that the end user (whether an individual or a single entity) has received, read, and accepted the terms of the Windows XP Professional EULA. OEMs cannot specify this key for computers being sold to end users.

/unattend[*num*][:*answer_file*]   The specified *num* value indicates the number of seconds between the time that Setup finishes copying the files and when Setup restarts. You can use *num* on any computer running Windows 98, Windows Me, Windows NT Workstation 4.0, Windows 2000, or Windows XP.

The specified *answer_file* provides Setup with your custom specifications.

Sysprep

The System Preparation tool, Sysprep.exe, is a disk-image-based deployment tool that you can use to install identical configurations on multiple computers. You can also use Sysprep to customize and automate MiniSetup and to audit computers. You can run Sysprep as many times as you want; however, if you are using a non-volume licensed version, you can only run Sysprep.exe and the MiniSetup Wizard three times on the same operating system installation. You cannot run Sysprep a fourth time. This also applies to Riprep.

On a reference computer, install the operating system and any applications that you want installed on your destination computers, and then run Sysprep. Sysprep prepares the hard disk on the reference computer for duplication to other computers. You can then run a third-party disk-imaging application. The major advantage of Sysprep installation is speed. The image can be packaged and compressed; only the files required for the specific configuration are created as part of the image. The shortened GUI-mode Setup can take five or six minutes instead of 45 to 60 minutes and prompts the user only for required and user-specified information.

Because the reference and destination computers are required to have identical HALs and ACPI support, you might be required to maintain multiple images for your environment.

> **Warning**   Before performing disk duplication, check with your software vendor to make sure that you are not violating the licensing agreement for installation of the software that you want to duplicate.

Overview of the Sysprep Process

The following steps describe the process of preparing a reference computer to use for disk duplication.

Table 2-14 describes the steps you must perform during the process of preparing a reference computer for disk duplication.

Table 2-14   Preparing a Reference Computer for Disk Duplication

Step	Description
Step 1	Install the operating system on a computer that has hardware similar to the destination computers. While preparing the computer, do not join it to a domain, and keep the local administrative password blank.
Step 2	Configure the computer. Log on as the administrator, and then install and customize Windows XP Professional and associated applications. These might include adding plug and play device drivers or productivity applications, such as Microsoft® Office, business-specific applications, and other applications or settings that you want included in a common configuration for all client computers.
Step 3	Validate the image. Run an audit, based on your criteria, to verify that the image configuration is correct. Remove residual information, including anything left behind from audit and event logs.
Step 4	Prepare the image for duplication. When the computer is configured exactly as you want it, prepare the system for duplication. If you are running Sysprep with the **-mini** parameter, you can prepare the system by running Sysprep with the optional Sysprep.inf file, which is described earlier in this chapter. After Sysprep runs, the computer shuts down automatically or indicates that it is safe to shut down.
Step 5	Duplicate. The computer hard disk is triggered to run Plug and Play detection, create new security identifiers (SIDs), and run the MiniSetup Wizard the next time the system is started. You can duplicate or create an image of the system by using hardware or software. The next time Windows XP Professional is started from this reference computer or from any destination computer created from this image, the system detects and reenumerates the Plug and Play devices to complete the installation and configuration on the destination computer.

> **Warning**   Components that depend on the Active Directory™ directory service cannot be duplicated.

Requirements for Running Sysprep

Before you can use Sysprep, your computer hardware and related devices must meet the following requirements:

- The reference and destination computers must have compatible HALs. For example, Advanced Programmable Interrupt Controller (APIC)–based MPS (multiprocessor systems) must use the same APIC HAL. A standard HAL Programmable Interrupt Controller (PIC)–based system is not compatible with either the APIC HAL or the MPS HAL.

- The reference and destination computers must have identical Advanced Configuration and Power Interface (ACPI) support.

- The Plug and Play devices on the reference and destination computers, such as modems, sound cards, network adapters, and video cards, do not have to be from the same manufacturer. However, the drivers for these devices must be available.

- Third-party disk-imaging software or disk-duplicating hardware devices are required. These products create binary images of a computer's hard disk and either duplicate the image to another hard disk or store the image in a file on a separate disk.

- The size of the hard disk on the destination computer must be at least the same size as the hard disk on the reference computer. If the destination computer has a larger hard disk, the difference is not included in the primary partition. However, you can use the ExtendOemPartition key in the Sysprep.inf file to extend the primary partition if it was formatted as NTFS.

How Sysprep Works with Windows Product Activation

In Windows XP Professional, Sysprep can reset Windows Product Activation a maximum of three times. When a computer running a disk image that was prepared with Sysprep is restarted, the activation timer is reset and the installation of Windows XP Professional is enabled with the full grace period for Windows Product Activation. After three resets, the activation timer is no longer reset. To prevent resets of the activation timer, run Sysprep from the command line, and include the **-activated** parameter and the **-reseal** parameter, as shown in the following example:

```
sysprep -activated -reseal
```

For more information about Windows Product Activation, see "Planning Deployments" in this book.

Sysprep Components

Run Sysprep.exe manually or configure Setup to run Sysprep.exe automatically by using the [GuiRunOnce] section of the answer file. Sysprep.exe and Setupcl.exe must be located in a Sysprep folder at the root of the system drive (%System-Drive%\Sysprep\). To place the files in the correct location during an automated Setup, add these files to your distribution folders under the OEM\$1\Sysprep folder. For more information about this folder, see "Create a Distribution Folder" earlier in this chapter.

Sysprep.exe and Setupcl.exe prepare the operating system for duplication and start MiniSetup. If you are running Sysprep with the **-mini** parameter, you can also include the optional answer file, Sysprep.inf, in the Sysprep folder. Sysprep.inf contains default keys that you can use to provide consistent responses where they are appropriate. This limits the requirement for user input and reduces potential user errors.

In addition, you can customize the destination computer by placing the Sysprep.inf file on a floppy disk and inserting it after the Windows startup screen appears. The floppy disk is read when the "Please Wait…" MiniSetup Wizard screen appears. When the MiniSetup Wizard successfully completes its tasks, the system restarts a final time, the Sysprep folder and all of its contents are deleted, and the system is ready for the user to log on.

The Sysprep files are defined in the following sections.

Sysprep.exe   Table 2-15 describes the optional parameters for Sysprep.exe.

Table 2-15   Sysprep.exe Optional Parameters

Parameter	Description
quiet	Runs Sysprep without displaying the Sysprep onscreen messages.
nosidgen	Runs Sysprep without regenerating SIDs that are already on the system. This is useful if you do not intend to duplicate the computer on which you are running Sysprep.
pnp	Forces full hardware detection when the computer is restarted. Setup actively seeks new devices on the system, whether or not they are Plug and Play. Because this mode increases the time required for MiniSetup, it is only useful if the computer on which the image is being loaded contains non–Plug and Play hardware that cannot be dynamically detected.
reboot	Automatically restarts the computer after Sysprep shuts it down. This eliminates the need to manually turn on the computer again.
activated	Prevents Windows Product Activation resets. If this parameter is not set, Sysprep can reset Windows Product Activation a maximum of three times.
factory	When you are running Sysprep.exe, enables you to add additional drivers and applications to the image after the computer restarts.
reseal	Enables you to reseal the image and prepare the computer for delivery after you have made modifications to the image in Factory Mode.

Table 2-15   Sysprep.exe Optional Parameters

Parameter	Description
msoobe	Displays the Windows Welcome screen (Msoobe.exe) on the next restart of the computer.
forceshutdown	Prepares the operating system as specified by Reseal Mode, and then immediately shuts down the computer without user intervention.
mini	Runs MiniSetup on the next restart of the computer.

> **Note**   For more information about optional parameters for Sysprep.exe, see Microsoft Windows Presinstallation Reference (Ref.chm) in the Deploy.cab file in the \Support\Tools folder on the Windows XP Professional operating system CD. You can use Windows Explorer or you can run Extract.exe to extract and view the Ref.chm file.

Sysprep.inf   Sysprep.inf is an answer file that is used to automate the MiniSetup process. It uses the same INI file syntax and key names (for supported keys) as Unattend.txt. Place the Sysprep.inf file in the %systemdrive%\Sysprep folder or on a floppy disk. If you use a floppy disk, insert it into the floppy disk drive after the Windows startup screen appears. Note that if you do not include Sysprep.inf when running Sysprep, the MiniSetup Wizard requires user input at each customization screen

For more information about Sysprep.inf, see "Customizing Sysprep Installations" earlier in this chapter. For details about answer file parameters and syntax, see the Deploy.chm in the Deploy.cab on the Windows XP Professional operating system CD. The Deploy.cab file is in the \Support\Tools folder.

Setupcl.exe   Setupcl.exe regenerates new security identifiers (SIDs) for the computer.

Sysprep User Interface   To run Sysprep from the user interface, double-click Sysprep.exe. The System Preparation Tool dialog box appears. The System Preparation Tool dialog box enables you to perform the following functions:

Factory mode   Run Factory Mode to add additional drivers and applications to the Sysprep image.

Audit Boot mode   Run Audit Boot mode to restart the computer before you are ready to use Reseal mode.

Reseal mode   When you have made modifications in Factory Mode, run Reseal mode to prepare the computer for delivery.

PnP flag   Select the PnP flag to force full hardware detection when the computer is restarted.

NoSIDGen flag   Select the NoSIDGen flag to run Sysprep without regenerating SIDs that are already on the computer.

MiniSetup flag   Select the MiniSetup flag to run MiniSetup the first time a computer starts from a hard disk that has been duplicated by using Sysprep.

Pre-activated flag   Select the Pre-activated flag to prevent resets of Windows Product Activation.

For more information about Factory Mode and about MiniSetup flag, see "Customizing Sysprep Installations" earlier in this chapter.

Running Sysprep

After you install the operating system, you can use Sysprep to prepare for the transfer of the operating system to other similarly configured computers.

To run Sysprep manually, first install the operating system, configure the computer, and install any applications you want to include, then run Sysprep without using the **-reboot** command-line parameter. After the system shuts down, duplicate the image of the hard disk to the similarly configured computers.

If you are running Sysprep with the **-mini** parameter, the MiniSetup Wizard runs when users start their duplicated computers for the first time. You can preassign all or some of the Sysprep configuration parameters by using Sysprep.inf. The Sysprep folder (which contains Sysprep.exe and Setupcl.exe) is automatically deleted after MiniSetup is completed.

To prepare a Windows XP Professional installation for duplication

1. From the **Start** menu, click **Run**, and then type:

   cmd

2. At the command prompt, change to the root folder of drive C, and then type:

   md sysprep

3. Insert the Windows XP Professional operating system CD into the appropriate CD-ROM drive. Open the Deploy.cab file in the \Support\Tools folder.

4. Copy **Sysprep.exe** and **Setupcl.exe** to the Sysprep folder.

   If you are using Sysprep.inf, copy this file to the Sysprep folder. For Sysprep to function correctly, Sysprep.exe, Setupcl.exe, and Sysprep.inf must all be in the same folder.

5. At the command prompt, change to the Sysprep folder by typing:

   cd sysprep

6. At the command prompt, type:

```
sysprep /optional_parameter
```

If you don't use **-reboot** as one of your optional parameters, click **Shut Down** from the **Start** menu when a message appears requesting that you shut down the computer. You are now ready to use a third-party disk-imaging tool to create an image of the installation.

> **Note**   You can add a Cmdlines.txt file to the Sysprep\i386\oem folder to be processed by Setup. This file is used to run post-setup commands, including commands for application installation. For more information about Using Cmdlines.txt, see "Adding Applications" earlier in this chapter.

Selecting Disk-imaging Tools   Use a third-party disk-imaging tool to create a Windows XP Professional image. To ensure the best outcome when you are using a third-party disk-imaging tool with Windows XP Professional, make sure the tool meets all the requirements for your environment and make sure the tool can do the following:

- Access NTFS partitions.
    Make sure your disk-imaging tool is compatible with Windows XP. Disk-imaging tools that are designed for use with the version of NTFS supported by Windows 2000, might not be compatible with the version of NTFS supported by Windows XP.

- Handle long file names.

- Create packages with short file names (for server environments that cannot read long file names).

- Open packages to add/remove files (such as new/updated drivers) without having to recreate the entire package.

Reducing the Number of Reference Images   With Sysprep, you can minimize the number of images that you need to use for preinstalling Windows XP Professional from multiprocessor (MP) to uniprocessor (UP) computers or from uniprocessor to multiprocessor computers. However, this only works for APIC or ACPI APIC computers.

> **Note**   More interrupts are available with APIC systems than with program-mable interrupt controller (PIC) uniprocessor systems. As a result, comput-ers with APIC HALs have faster response times, and they can support more hardware devices than computers with PIC HALs.

You can use one of several methods to create images for installations on mul-tiprocessor systems and deploy the images on uniprocessor systems, or to create images for installations on uniprocessor systems and deploy the images on multipro-cessor systems. Each method has advantages and disadvantages, as outlined in the following sections. Choose the method that works best for you and your preinstal-lation environment.

Table 2-16 illustrates the compatibility of computers based on their HAL type. One image is required for each compatibility group. In this table, multiprocessor is abbreviated MP and uniprocessor is abbreviated UP.

Table 2-16   HAL Compatibility

Compatibility	ACPI PIC	ACPI–APIC UP	ACPI–APIC MP	Non–ACPI UP PIC	Non–ACPI APIC UP	Non–ACPI APIC MP
ACPI PIC	X					
ACPI APIC UP		X	X			
ACPI APIC MP		X	X			
Non-ACPI UP PIC				X		X
Non–ACPI APIC UP				X	X	X
Non–ACPI APIC MP					X	X

Multiprocessor to uniprocessor   For this process, the image is created on a mul-tiprocessor reference computer. This image can be used on other multiprocessor computers or on uniprocessor computers.

The advantage of multiprocessor to uniprocessor is that you can create a single entry in the Sysprep.inf file that then prompts Windows XP Professional to deter-mine, after MiniSetup is complete, if a single processor or multiple processors are running. The correct kernel files are then used.

The disadvantage of multiprocessor to uniprocessor is that this process requires that, when you create the reference image, you include each of the Mp2up.inf files and other related Mp2up files in the distribution folders.

> **Warning**   This image can only be used in one of the following configurations depending on the HAL type you are using:
>
> ■ From an ACPI APIC MP–based reference computer for use on other ACPI APIC MP or ACPI APIC UP–based computers.
>
> ■ From a non–ACPI APIC MP–based reference computer for use on other non–ACPI APIC MP or non–ACPI APIC UP–based computers.

To create a multiprocessor to uniprocessor image

1. Copy the Mp2up.inf and associated Mp2up files to the location you are using for your Plug and Play device drivers in your distribution folders, for example, \\$OEM\$\\$1\Sysprep\Hal.

2. In Sysprep.inf, add:

   ```
   [Unattended]
   UpdateUPHAL = "hwid,%SystemDrive%\Sysprep\Hal.inf"
   ```

   In the preceding example, *hwid* is either MPS_UP or ACPI APIC_UP.

3. Install the operating system from the distribution folders to a multiprocessor computer.

4. Run Sysprep with the Sysprep.inf created in step 2.

5. Image the computer.

6. Place the image on comparable destination computers.

Uniprocessor to multiprocessor   For this process, the image is created on a uniprocessor reference computer with an APIC HAL. This image can then be used on computers with compatible hardware and compatible HALs (either APIC UP HALs or APIC MP HALs).

The advantage of uniprocessor to multiprocessor is that you do not have to install the Mp2up files on the computer.

The disadvantage of uniprocessor to multiprocessor is that before the computers can be shipped, the Sysprep.inf file must be replaced depending on the type of computer being shipped: uniprocessor or multiprocessor.

Warning This image can only be used in one of the following configurations, depending on the HAL type you are using:

■ From an ACPI APIC uniprocessor–based reference computer for use on other ACPI APIC uniprocessor or ACPI APIC multiprocessor–based computers.

■ From a non–ACPI APIC uniprocessor–based reference computer for use on other non–ACPI APIC uniprocessor or non–ACPI APIC multiprocessor–based computers.

To create the uniprocessor to multiprocessor image

1. Install the operating system on a uniprocessor computer.

2. Run Sysprep.

3. Create the image of the computer.

4. In Sysprep.inf, add:

```
[Unattended]
UpdateHAL = "hwid,%windir%\inf\hal.inf"
```

In the preceding example, hwid is either MPS_MP or ACPI APIC_MP.

5. Place the image on comparable destination computers.

6. On multiprocessor computers, use the Sysprep.inf file created in step 4 to replace all previous Sysprep.inf files.

You can use any tools you normally use to manipulate files on the hard disk when creating new computers from an image.

Using Sysprep to Extend Disk Partitions When installing Windows XP Professional, you might find it necessary to extend the partition of the destination computer. You can use Sysprep with the appropriate entries in the answer file to extend an NTFS partition. You might want to extend an NTFS partition for the following reasons:

■ To create images that can be extended into larger disk partitions and take advantage of hard disks that might have greater capacity than the original hard disk on the reference computer.

■ To create images on smaller hard disks.

Review the following steps and choose the method that works best for you, based on the third-party tools that you are using to create an image of the operating system.

> **Caution**   Make sure that you do not accidentally delete the Setupapi.log and Hyberfil.sys files (if applicable) when modifying the image. These files are recreated when the MiniSetup Wizard runs on the destination computer. Deleting these files on an active system can cause the system to function improperly.

When used in an answer file, the ExtendOemPartition key causes Setup to extend the destination partition into any available unpartitioned space that physically follows it on the hard disk.

The values for ExtendOemPartition are 0, 1, and *extra size in MB* where:

- 0 Setup does not extend the partition.
- 1 Setup extends the partition to fill out the hard disk.
- *extra size in MB* Setup increases the current partition size by this amount.

ExtendOemPartition automatically leaves the last cylinder on the hard disk free to allow dynamic disk support. ExtendOemPartition can be set to a number other than 1 to indicate a specific disk size for extending the hard disk. This is useful if more than one partition is requested on a computer.

> **Warning**   Only NTFS partitions can be extended. If the destination partition you plan to extend is FAT or FAT32, run *convert.exe /fs:ntfs* from the command line before running Sysprep. The file system is converted when the image is applied to the destination computer before the MiniSetup Wizard starts. Setup does not extend FAT16 and FAT32 partitions.
>
> ExtendOemPartition can be used with both the Unattend.txt and Sysprep.inf Setup files.
>
> When used in Sysprep.inf for imaged computers, the destination computer's hard disk must be the same size or larger than the reference computer's hard disk.
>
> To enable the extension, the partition to be extended must have contiguous unpartitioned space available.

To extend a hard disk partition when using a third-party disk-imaging product or a hardware-imaging device that supports the version of NTFS that is used by Windows XP Professional

1. Create a partition on the reference computer hard disk that is just large enough to install Windows XP Professional with all the components and applications that you intend to add. This helps keep the size of the reference image file to a minimum.

2. If the destination partition you plan to extend is FAT or FAT32, run *convert.exe /fs:ntfs* from the command line before running Sysprep. The file system is converted when the image is applied to the destination computer before the MiniSetup Wizard starts.

> **Note**   ConvertNTFS does not work in Sysprep.inf because this is a text mode-only function and Sysprep does not go through text mode.

3. In the [Unattended] section of Sysprep.inf, include the statement:

    ```
    ExtendOemPartition = 1
    ```

    You can also set the additional size in megabytes to extend the partition.

4. Install Windows XP Professional on the reference computer. Sysprep shuts down the system automatically.

5. Generate the image.

6. Place the image on the destination computer where the destination computer has the same size system partition as the reference computer.

7. Restart the destination computer.
    When you place the reference image on a destination computer, drive C is converted to NTFS when the computer starts. The computer then restarts and starts MiniSetup. During MiniSetup, Windows extends drive C to the rest of the unpartitioned space on the hard disk. The destination computer then restarts, and the end user can log on and begin using Windows XP Professional.
    The MiniSetup Wizard starts and the partition is extended.

To extend a hard disk partition when using a disk-imaging product that does not support NTFS used by Windows XP Professional

1. In the [Unattended] section of Sysprep.inf, include the statement:

    ```
    ExtendOemPartition = 1
    ```

Or additional size in megabytes to extend the partition.

2. Use Cmdlines.txt to convert short file names.

3. Run Sysprep.

The following actions occur when you restart the destination computer:

- The computer initially starts in conversion mode to convert the system partition on the destination computer to NTFS.

- The computer automatically restarts.

- The MiniSetup Wizard starts, and the partition is extended almost instantaneously.

Installing Windows XP Professional on Nonnetworked Computers   Even if you don't have a network, you can still install Windows XP Professional and various applications on client computers, one computer at a time.

To install Windows XP Professional on nonnetworked computers

1. Choose a setup method, and then start Setup.

2. Add custom information and additional files.

3. Install applications. If you have no applications to install, skip this step.

> **Warning**   Each client computer must have a CD-ROM drive.

Choose a setup method and then start Setup   Setup can typically be started from an MS-DOS bootable floppy disk, from a set of Windows XP Professional Setup floppy disks that you can create from the Web, or from the Windows XP Professional operating system CD. Starting from a CD is available only on computers that support the El Torito No Emulation CD boot specification. Choose from the setup methods provided later in this section.

> **Note**   Windows XP Professional Setup floppy disks are not provided with Windows XP Professional. To create a set of bootable floppy disks, access the Microsoft Windows Update Web site and download an application that enables you to create a set of bootable floppy disks. For more information about creating a set of bootable floppy disks, see http://www.microsoft.com.

To install from the Setup floppy disks

1. Start the computer by using the Windows XP Professional Setup floppy disks.

2. When Setup is complete, you can add applications and run Sysprep.

For more information about how to install applications, see "Customizing the Installations" earlier in this chapter.

To install from Windows 98, Windows Me, Windows NT Workstation 4.0, or Windows 2000

1. Start the computer.

2. From the **Start** menu, click **Run**, and then type:
   ***path to distribution folder* winnt32 /unattend:Unattend.txt**
   In the preceding path, *Unattend.txt* is the answer file that contains answers to installation questions that you want to automate.

3. When Setup is complete, you can add applications and run Sysprep to prepare for creating an image.

For instructions about how to install applications, see "Adding Applications" earlier in this chapter.

To install by using CD Boot

Start the computer from the Windows XP Professional operating system CD. Setup begins automatically.

1. When Setup displays the message that it is examining the hardware configuration, insert the floppy disk containing the Winnt.sif file.

2. When the floppy drive light goes off, remove the floppy disk. Setup begins copying files to the hard disk.
   For more information about how to install applications, see "Adding Applications" earlier in this chapter.

Note   The **/udf** parameter cannot be used with the CD Boot method.

Add customized information and components   During this step, you can add customized information (such as your company's name) and components (such as custom Help files and other documentation).

To add customized information and components

- Create a file called Oeminfo.ini and copy it to the %systemroot%\System32 folder. The systemroot folder is usually C:\Windows.

RIS

You can use Remote Installation Services (RIS) to install Windows XP Professional throughout an organization from remote locations. Using RIS, you can direct client computers to a RIS server and install automated, customized versions of Windows XP Professional.

RIS uses PXE/DHCP-based remote boot technology to remotely install the operating system on the client computer. The RIS server contains the operating system that can be installed on the client computer using either a Risetup or a Riprep-based image. You can contact the servers by designating the network adapter as the first in the boot order of the client computer's BIOS, or by using a remote boot disk for pre-PC98 computers. When a network boot is requested, the client computer performs the following tasks:

- The client computer requests an IP address from the DHCP server.

- The client computer requests the IP address of a boot server using PXE (if the boot server is not the DHCP server).

- The client computer contacts the boot server and downloads the Client Installation Wizard (CIW).

RIS Process

When a client computer starts, it sends out a DHCP Discover packet requesting an IP address and the location of a RIS server. In this packet, the client computer also sends out its Globally Unique Identifier (GUID). If the DHCP and RIS servers are on the same computer, all of this requested information is provided in the initial reply. If DHCP and RIS are on separate computers, the client computer sends out another broadcast DHCP Discover packet to contact a RIS server after it has successfully obtained an IP address from the DHCP server.

A RIS server running on Windows 2000 Server uses the Boot Information Negotiation Layer (BINL) service to contact the Active Directory™ service to determine if the client computer is a known client. Known clients are computers that are pre-staged to Active Directory.

The RIS server checks the Active Directory™ directory service to determine which RIS server can respond to this client request. The RIS server then provides the name of the server and the file that the client computer must download to start the installation process.

After the boot process begins, the Client Installation Wizard (CIW) screens are downloaded to the client computer and the installation begins.

When the CIW runs, the user at the client computer must log on to the domain. At this point, the user can select an image to install.

Before You Use RIS

To deploy Windows XP images from Windows 2000 RIS Servers, you must install the Windows 2000 Remote Installation Services update. For more information about the Windows 2000 Remote Installation Services update, see the Microsoft Knowledge Base link on the Web Resources page at http://www.microsoft.com/windows/reskits /webresources. Search the Microsoft Knowledge Base using the keywords *Risetup.exe*, *RIS Servers*, and *Windows XP Images*.

In addition, consider the following before you design a RIS deployment:

- **RIS server.** A RIS server is a computer running Windows 2000 Server, containing a hard disk with at least two partitions, that has been configured with the Remote Installation Services Setup Wizard (Risetup.exe) to install and run the following services:

    - Boot Information Negotiation Layer (BINL) service in Windows 2000 Server

    - Trivial File Transfer Protocol Daemon (TFTPD)

    - Single Instance Storage Groveler
      The Single Instance Storage (SIS) filter driver is also installed.

- **Remote Installation client.** The remote installation client computer can be a new personal computer that has a PXE-enabled network adapter, or an older personal computer (for example, computers built prior to the PC98/99 design specification) that can install Windows XP Professional using a remote boot disk to emulate PXE for the network adapter.

- **Active Directory.** Active Directory is a requirement for RIS. RIS setup sends a query to make sure Active Directory is running. If Active Directory is not detected on the network, RIS Setup does not continue.

- **Networking considerations.** Consider the following factors when you are designing your RIS deployment:

    - The RIS server does not have to be the domain controller for the domain.

    - You must have DNS and DHCP servers available to service the RIS client computers on the network.

    - The servers that are running DNS and DHCP do not have to be members of the same domain as the RIS server.

    - You do not have to use Microsoft DNS and DHCP services.

Table 2-17 describes the major RIS components and the users who work with each component.

Table 2-17   RIS Components, Descriptions, and Intended Users

Component	Description	User
Remote Installation Services Setup (Risetup.exe)	Sets up the RIS server. This component is not available in Windows XP Professional.	System administrator
Remote Installation Services Administrator	Configures Group Policy settings relating to RIS. This component is not available in Windows XP Professional.	System administrator
Remote Installation Preparation tool (Riprep.exe)	Creates operating system images and installs them on the RIS server. You can also use Riprep.exe to create application images to install applications with the operating system. Client computers using PXE boot ROMs or a Remote Boot Floppy Generator (RBFG) floppy disk can then download the image. Because the client computer initiates the download, starting from the text-mode portion of Setup, Riprep allows for differences in hardware among client computers (such as the boot device).	Desktop administrator
Remote Boot Floppy Generator (Rbfg.exe)	Creates the Remote Installation Services bootable floppy disk that is required to install RIS-based operating systems on client computers that do not have a PXE-enabled boot ROM.	End user
Client Installation Wizard (Oschooser.exe)	Selects the RIS image that the user must install. This wizard is used on the client computer.	End user with rights to create computer objects in the domain

Warning   To deploy Windows XP Professional Riprep-based images from Windows 2000 RIS Servers, you must install the Remote Installation Preparation tool update. For more information about the Remote Installation Preparation tool update, see the Microsoft Knowledge Base link on the Web Resources page at http://www.microsoft.com/windows/reskits/webresources. Search the Microsoft Knowledge Base using the keywords *Riprep.exe, Setupcl.exe, Imirror.dll,* and *Windows XP Images.*

The following sections discuss planning for RIS from a client perspective and explain how to use the Remote Installation Preparation tool and the Remote Installation Services boot disk.

RIS enables the administrator to configure Windows XP Professional and any applications for a single group of users, and then to apply this configuration when installing the operating system on client computers. For users, the result is a simplified and timely installation and configuration of their computer and a more rapid return to productivity if a hardware failure occurs.

Administrators have two options when using RIS:

■ **The Risetup option.** Similar to setting up a workstation directly from the Windows XP operating system CD; however, the source files reside across a network on RIS servers. Risetup images are created by using Risetup.exe, which is a server-only application.

■ **The Riprep imaging option.** Enables a network administrator to clone a standard desktop configuration, including operating system configurations and desktop customizations. After installing and configuring Windows XP Professional, its services, and any standard applications on a workstation, the network administrator runs a wizard that prepares the installation image and replicates it to available RIS servers. Remote boot–enabled client computers can then request a local installation of the image from the RIS servers over the network.

When a network service boot is requested, DHCP provides an IP address for the client computer, and the client computer can then download the Client Installation Wizard. At this point, the wizard prompts the user to log on, and, depending on the user's credentials or security group membership, displays a menu that offers appropriate customized unattended operating system installation options. The network administrator uses Group Policy settings to determine which installation options are available to a specific user, based on the policy that has been defined for that user at the client computer that initiated the network service boot request.

If you have a Windows 2000 Server operating system infrastructure with RIS installed and a client computer with the appropriate hardware, you can install Windows XP and any applications on that client computer remotely and automatically.

Preparing for Client Configuration

To ensure that a remote installation can proceed successfully, prepare the client computer for installation from a RIS server by completing the following tasks:

■ Verify the hardware compatibility of the client computer.

■ Set user rights.

■ Set permissions.

■ Specify the installation options.

■ Configure the network adapter.

■ Select and restrict client computer installation options.

- Use Riprep to prepare the client image.

- Deploy RIS.

Table 2-18 lists the tasks that the server administrator performs on a RIS server versus those that the desktop administrator performs on the client computer.

Table 2-18   Tasks for Preparing a Client Computer for a Remote Installation

Task	Description	User
Verify that the client hardware meets all requirements.	The client computer must meet the requirements for Windows XP installation and have a bootable network adapter or be enabled for remote startup. All computers that meet the PC98 0.6 and later design specification include a PXE remote–boot ROM for RIS. For client computers that do not contain a PXE ROM, use the Remote Installation boot disk to create a floppy disk that initiates the RIS process.	Desktop administrator
Set required permissions on the RIS server.	If users are allowed to use RIS to install an operating system on client computers, those users need correct permissions for creating computer accounts within the domain, specifically the Organizational Unit container specified in the Advanced Settings on the RIS Server. Use Active Directory Users and Computers to set permissions on a container that allows users to use RIS to install an operating system on their own computers.	Server administrator
Specify installation options on the RIS server.	On the RIS server, you can use Group Policy settings to restrict the installation options available to users during remote installation. To restrict images, set access control permissions on the folders containing the installation images.	Server administrator
Configure the network adapter on the client computer.	You must configure the network adapter of the client computer as the primary startup device within the system BIOS. This allows the client computer to request a network service startup from the RIS server on the network. Many computers with built-in PXE compliant network adapters have three settings for the network adapter in the BIOS: off, on, and on with PXE. After the network adapter is set to on with PXE, on with PXE is typically available as an option in the boot order section of the BIOS.	Desktop administrator

Using the Remote Installation Preparation Tool

The Remote Installation Preparation tool (Riprep.exe) provides the ability to prepare a Windows XP Professional installation for disk imaging and to replicate the image to an available RIS server on the network. The image can include locally installed applications and specific configuration settings. The wizard feature supports replication of a single partition (drive C only) installation. This means that the operating system and the applications included with the standard installation must reside on drive C before the wizard is run.

> **Warning**   To deploy Windows XP Professional Riprep-based images from Windows 2000 RIS Servers, you must install the Remote Installation Preparation tool update. For more information about the Remote Installation Preparation tool update, see the Microsoft Knowledge Base link on the Web Resources page at http://www.microsoft.com/windows/reskits/webresources. Search the Microsoft Knowledge Base using the keywords *Riprep.exe*, *Setupcl.exe*, *Imirror.dll*, and *Windows XP Images*.

It is recommended that you use RIS to install the operating system on a client computer. After the operating system is installed, you can install any applications, including line-of-business applications. You can then configure the installation to comply with company policies. For example, you might define specific screen colors, set the background bitmap to a company logo, and configure intranet proxy server settings within Internet Explorer. After the workstation has been configured and tested, you can run Riprep from the RIS server.

The destination computer (the computer that installs the image) does not need to have hardware that is identical to the computer that was used to create the image. However, the Hardware Abstraction Layer (HAL) drivers must be the same. For example, both HALs must be ACPI-based or non-ACPI-based (see Table 2.16, earlier in this chapter). In many cases, workstation class computers do not require unique HAL drivers, as server-class computers do. During image installation, the wizard uses Plug and Play to detect differences between hardware on the source and destination computers.

Riprep-based images are usually larger than Risetup-based images because Riprep-based images are a complex copy of the client computer's hard disk that is stored on the server. Riprep-based images contain the operating system in addition to preinstalled programs and tools. To store a Riprep-based image on a RIS server, your configuration must meet the following requirements:

- You must have at least one Risetup image stored on the same RIS server as the Riprep-based image.

- The Risetup image must use the same language and it must be based on the same version of the operating system as the reference computer.

The template (.sif) file refers the client computer to the RIS server to detect and load files for the client computer's network adapter. The template (.sif) file also uses the Risetup image to provide drivers to start text-mode Setup. Setup then copies the image to the installing client computer's hard disk.

When you image a client computer by using Riprep.exe, the following requirements must be met:

- At least one Risetup image must exist on the server so the user can access system files later. The Risetup image must use the same language and be based on the same version of the operating system as the reference computer.

- Only one partition is supported.

- Client computers must use the same HAL (for example, ACPI or non-ACPI).

- Destination computers must have a local hard disk that is at least equal to the size of the partition on the imaged computer.

- When you are creating the image, the client computer must not contain any encrypted files.

To run the Remote Installation Preparation tool (Riprep)

1. Install the standard operating system on the reference computer. It is recommended that you use RIS to perform this task.

2. Install applications locally on the client computer. Configure the client computer with specific corporate standard desktop settings. Make sure the client installation is correct. After the image is replicated to the RIS server, you cannot modify the configuration.

3. Copy the profile of the user used to configure the computer to the Default User profile. You should also delete any unwanted profiles at this point.

4. Connect to a RIS server from the computer on which you want to replicate this image and run Riprep.exe. The Remote Installation Preparation Wizard starts.

5. Enter the name of the RIS server where you want to replicate the contents of the client hard disk. By default, the RIS server from which the wizard is being run is filled in automatically.

6. Type the name of the folder on the RIS server where this image is to be copied.

7. When prompted, provide a description and Help text for this image. These are displayed to users during operating system image selection. Provide enough information to allow a user to distinguish between images.

8. After you complete the Remote Installation Preparation Wizard, review your selections on the summary screen that appears, and then click **Next**.

The image preparation and replication process begins. The system is prepared and files are copied to the RIS server. When the replication of the image is complete, you can use any client computer that meets the restrictions described in the next section, "Riprep Rules and Restrictions," and is enabled for PXE/DHCP-based remote boot technology to select and install the image from the Client Installation Wizard. You can also use any client computers that use the Remote Installation Services startup disk.

Riprep and Windows Product Activation   In Windows XP Professional, Riprep can reset Windows Product Activation a maximum of three times for any images that derive from an initial image and start with the installation of the initial image. When a disk image that was prepared with Riprep is rebooted, the activation timer is reset and the installation of Windows XP Professional is enabled with the full Windows Product Activation grace period. After three resets, the activation timer is no longer reset.

For more information about Windows Product Activation, see "Planning Deployments" in this book.

Riprep Rules and Restrictions   Riprep.exe is more flexible than Sysprep.exe because it starts over the network in text-mode Setup. This allows for a greater variation of hardware platforms, such as differing mass storage disk controllers. The only item that must be the same on all client computers when you use Riprep.exe is the HAL.

By default, Riprep-based images do not perform Plug and Play enumeration. If you want Plug and Play enumeration to occur, you must use the **-PnP** command-line parameter when you create your image. For example, at the command prompt, type **riprep -pnp**. After you run this command, Plug and Play enumeration always occurs. If you want to turn off Plug and Play enumeration, you must recreate the image.

To take advantage of Riprep's added functionality, be sure to follow these guidelines:

- The hard disk of the computer you want to image can have only one partition. If the hard disk of the client computer contains more than one partition, a message appears and only the system partition (containing the Windows folder) is copied. If your boot partition and system partition are different, the image is not useable.

- A Risetup image must reside on the RIS server.

- The hard disk on the destination computer must be at least the same size as, or larger than, the reference computer.

- The destination computer must also have the same HAL as the reference computer.

Using a Remote Installation Services Boot Disk

You can use the Remote Installation Services (RIS) boot disk with client computers that do not contain a remote boot-enabled ROM. The startup disk simulates the PXE startup process for computers that lack a remote boot-enabled ROM. The boot disk is analogous to a boot-enabled ROM, which uses the floppy disk drive to install the operating system from the RIS server.

This disk enables you to use RIS to install programs on a laptop computer. Because Personal Computer Memory Card International Association (PCMCIA) network adapters do not currently support PXE, you cannot use a PCMCIA network adapter with RIS. However, you can place the laptop computer in a docking station that contains a PCI-compliant network adapter and use a boot disk that you created by running Rbfg.exe.

> **Note**   Currently, Remote Boot Floppy Generator (RBFG) floppy disks only support PCI-compliant adapters. RBFG floppy disks do not support PCMCIA and ISA network adapters.

You cannot add additional network adapters to the RIS boot disk. Microsoft adds additional network adapters over time and makes the updates in the Rbfg.exe tool that is available through distribution channels, such as the Web, Windows Update, and future service packs.

Understanding GUIDs

When a client computer with a PXE-enabled network adapter connects to a RIS server, the Globally Unique Identifier (GUID) of the network adapter is among the items that are exchanged before a logon screen is displayed. The GUID is a unique 32-digit number that is stored with the computer account object that is created in Active Directory. Client computers with network adapters that are not PXE-enabled cannot supply this GUID. Instead, client computers that start from the RIS boot floppy with non-PXE-enabled network adapters send the network adapter's 12 character Media Access Control (MAC) address, prepended by 20 zeroes.

To generate a GUID in Windows 2000 Server, the Boot Information Negotiation Layer (BINL) service uses the 12 character MAC address and prepends 20 zeroes. This process creates a 32-digit number that is used as the GUID. The computer account object is associated with the network adapter, not with the computer. Even if you move the network adapter to a different computer, the GUID is still associated with the network adapter and not with the computer.

Because the computer account object is associated with the network adapter, if you move the network adapter to another computer, RIS assigns the attributes of the old computer to the new computer. Therefore, the administrator must delete the GUID from the computer account object for the old computer. If a user tries to install the new computer by using a different computer name, a message appears during the CIW that displays the names of the computers on the network that already have the same GUID. GUIDs and computer account objects must have a one-to-one relationship.

The RIS boot disk can be used with a variety of supported PCI-compliant network adapters. To determine whether the hardware components in your organization are compatible with Windows XP Professional, see the Hardware Compatibility List link on the Web Resources page at http://www.microsoft.com/windows/reskits/webresources.

One disk is used for all network adapters. The supported network adapters are listed in the Remote Boot Floppy Generator dialog box. You can display this dialog box by running Rbfg.exe. You can use this utility to create the boot disk. When RIS installation is complete, you can find Rbfg.exe on the RIS server partition, in the \RemoteInstall\admin\i386 folder.

Additional Resources

These resources contain additional information and tools related to this chapter.

Related Information

- The Hardware Compatibility List link on the Web Resources page at http://www.microsoft.com/windows/reskits/webresources.

Related Tools

- For more information about answer file sections, keys, and values, see the Deploy.chm in the Deploy.cab file on the Windows XP Professional operating system CD. The Deploy.cab file is in the \Support\Tools folder. You can use Windows Explorer or run the Extract.exe command to extract and view the Deploy.chm file.

Chapter 3

Multilingual Solutions for Global Business

A large number of corporations do business internationally, have employees or customers that communicate using more than one language, or have a need to create a single global corporate desktop image or a single code base to develop and test applications. To meet the needs of today's global business environment, Microsoft® Windows® XP Professional includes desktop configurations and application support designed to ensure multilingual compatibility.

Related Information

- For more information about supporting mobile users, see "Supporting Mobile Users" in this book.

- For more information about configuring remote desktops, see "Configuring Remote Desktop" in this book.

Overview of Multilingual Solutions for Global Business

Windows XP Professional supports companies that need to allow users (employees or customers) to work in more than one language. Typically, these companies:

- Operate internationally and must support different regional options, such as time zones, currencies, or date formats.

- Have employees or customers who speak different languages, or require language-dependent keyboards or input devices.

- Develop internal line-of-business applications that must run internationally or in more than one language.

Table 3-1 presents an overview of the most common problems that multilingual and international organizations face and outlines the possible solutions that you can apply to your Windows XP Professional deployment.

Table 3-1   Problems and Solutions for Global Business

Problem	Solution
Users need to edit documents that contain multiple languages.	All versions of Windows XP Professional contain support for editing documents in multiple languages. Some versions might require the installation of additional language collections. For advanced multilingual support, such as localized language user interface elements, dictionaries, and proofing tools, deploy Microsoft® Windows® XP Professional Multilingual User Interface Pack (MUI Pack) together with the Microsoft® Office XP Multilingual User Interface Pack.
Regional offices need automatic operating system deployments with the correct language and regional options, such as the default input language, date, time, and currency formats.	Determine each office's language and regional needs to help reduce the number of unique setup scripts. For each unique setup script, specify the appropriate [RegionalSettings] values in the answer file; use new keywords to set the default standards and formats and input language/keyboard layout combination for the default user account for new users.
Roaming users need to log on anywhere in their native languages.	Consider using Windows XP Professional MUI Pack for desktops if roaming users must log on in a native language user interface. Use Active Directory™ directory service and Group Policy to publish MUI Pack language packages to users so that they can install the correct user interface language wherever they log on.

Table 3-1   Problems and Solutions for Global Business

Problem	Solution
Multiple users need to log on to the same computer in different languages.	Consider using Windows XP Professional MUI Pack for desktops if users must log on in a native language user interface. Use Terminal Services Client to support different language sessions for different users sharing computers connected to a Microsoft® Windows® 2000 Server MultiLanguage Version–based computer running Terminal Services.
Users need language-specific keyboards, Input Method Editors, or alternative input devices.	Windows XP Professional contains built-in support for a variety of keyboard layouts and input methods and devices. Install additional language collections and input languages as needed. Place the On-Screen Keyboard on desktops where the physical keyboard might not match the operating system language version in use.
Existing line-of-business applications must accommodate language and regional differences.	Ensure proper code page support for applications developed under older operating systems; test applications by changing the language for non-Unicode programs and default input languages.
Application developers want to create single code-based applications that run in the correct local language.	Deploy Windows XP Professional MUI Pack internationally as the desktop standard; develop applications in Unicode that support the multilingual user interface. Write applications that check for the default user interface language and follow world-ready software development guidelines.
Sites on the corporate intranet must account for language and regional differences.	Use the Location setting to configure desktop browsers to receive appropriate local content, such as local weather or news.
IT wants to do simultaneous worldwide rollouts of hotfixes, patches, and Service Packs.	Deploy Windows XP Professional MUI Pack as the global desktop standard.
Users need to share folders or files containing text in other languages.	Ensure that only Unicode characters are used for Active Directory and other folder and file names; install the Complex Script and Right-to-Left or East Asian Language Collections as needed.

New Multilingual Features in Windows XP Professional

Windows XP Professional includes technologies that enhance your company's ability to do business in multiple languages and/or across multiple countries/regions.

Support for 135 locales   Versions of Microsoft® Windows® earlier than Windows XP Professional support up to 126 locales. Windows XP Professional adds support for nine additional locales: Galician, Gujarati, Kannada, Kyrgyz, Mongolian (Cyrillic), Punjabi, Divehi, Syriac, and Telugu.

Built-in language support   Each language version of Windows XP Professional provides built-in support for editing documents in hundreds of languages, grouped into three language collections. The Basic Language Collection, which is always installed, supports most Western languages. The Complex Script and Right-to-Left Language Collection can be installed to support languages such as Arabic, Hebrew, Indic, or Thai, and the East Asian Language Collection can be installed to support Simplified or Traditional Chinese, Japanese, or Korean.

Users can change input languages, keyboard layouts, and other regional options (except for the language for non-Unicode programs) without restarting the computer in order for the changes to take effect. Administrators can customize the desktop with new tools, such as the Language Toolbar, to simplify switching languages, keyboard layouts, and other regional options.

Redesigned Regional and Language Options Control Panel   The   Control Panel for regional and language options has been redesigned to make it easier to add and change input languages and keyboard layouts; change standards and formats for displaying dates, amounts, and currencies; set the default location for Web content; and change the language for non-Unicode programs. The most frequently used options are now easier to find and use.

New, simplified terminology   The terminology used in versions of Windows earlier than Windows XP Professional has been updated to simpler, more descriptive terms:

- *Standards and Formats*, which determines the formats used to display dates, times, currency, numbers, and the sorting order of text, was previously called the *User Locale*.

- *Input Language*, which specifies the combination of the language and keyboard layout used to enter text, was previously called the *Input Locale*.

- *Language for Non-Unicode Programs*, which specifies the default code pages and fonts for running non-Unicode programs, was previously called the *System Locale*.

Additional answer file and unattended mode Setup options   Windows XP Professional includes four new language keys that you can use in the [RegionalSettings] section of answer files. These keys make it easier for administrators to customize language settings, such as the default input language for new user accounts. Other features provide more options for customizing unattended mode setups and silent configurations after setup.

Updated multilingual troubleshooter   The Multilingual Document Consultant in Windows XP Professional Help and Support Center can assist you in diagnosing and resolving problems with displaying or entering different languages.

Improved Windows XP Professional Multilingual User Interface Pack   The Windows XP Professional Multilingual User Interface Pack (MUI Pack) ensures that most of the operating system user interface — including the Start and Programs menus, alerts and dialog boxes, and the Windows XP Professional Help and Support Center — appears in the localized language that has been selected as the default. (In Microsoft® Windows® 2000 Professional MultiLanguage Version, for example, a user who switches the user interface language to German might still find some user interface elements displayed in English.)

Although it is based on the code of the Microsoft® Windows® XP Professional International English language version, the MUI Pack also includes more localized components that make it easier to develop multilingual applications. New Windows Installer MUI language packages reduce storage space requirements on network servers or CD images, and make it easier for administrators to set up, and users to install, additional user interface languages.

The MUI Pack also includes improved local drivers, makes roaming easier, and simplifies remote administration over a corporate network.

Multilingual Features in Windows XP Professional

This section introduces some of the key features, concepts, and terms you need to understand as you work with a multilingual or international deployment of Windows XP Professional. Included are discussions of basic concepts, such as language collections, the use of alternative keyboard layouts, Input Method Editors, and Unicode, as well as descriptions of new terms introduced with Windows XP Professional.

Built-In Language Support

Each language version of Windows XP Professional supports hundreds of languages through 17 *language groups*, which are organized into three separately installable *language collections*, as shown in Table 3-2.

> **Note**   In Windows XP Professional — unlike Microsoft® Windows® 2000 Professional — you cannot install individual language groups. You must install the appropriate language collection as described in Table 3-2, which includes support for all of the language groups in that language collection.

Table 3-2 Language Support in Windows XP Professional

Language Collection	Installation Status	Language Group ID and Name
Basic	Always installed on every language version.	1 Western Europe and United States 2 Central Europe 3 Baltic 4 Greek 5 Cyrillic 6 Turkic
Complex Script and Right-to-Left	Always installed on the Arabic language version and the Hebrew language version; optionally installed on all other language versions.	11 Thai 12 Hebrew 13 Arabic 14 Vietnamese 15 Indic 16 Georgian 17 Armenian
East Asian	Always installed on the Simplified Chinese, Traditional Chinese, Japanese, and Korean language versions; optionally installed on all other language versions.	7 Japanese 8 Korean 9 Traditional Chinese 10 Simplified Chinese

Locales

A *locale* is a collection of Windows XP Professional operating system settings that reflects a specific country's/region's language and cultural conventions. For example, the English (Canadian), English (United Kingdom), and English (United States) locales reflect different countries/regions that share a common language but use different dialects, currencies, and so on. Windows XP Professional supports a total of 135 locales.

Standards and Formats (User Locales)

The Standards and Formats section of the Regional and Language Options Control Panel in Windows XP Professional, formerly called the *user locale*, determines the formats used to display dates, times, currency, numbers, and the sorting order of text. On a given computer, each user account can have its own unique Standards and Formats setting. The Standards and Formats setting does not affect any language settings, other than the language used to display the names of days and months, and time and date formats.

For example, an English-speaking salesperson from the Boston office logs on to a desktop in the Milan office. The Milan desktop uses the International English language version of Windows XP Professional. The salesperson selects a Standards and Formats setting of Italian (Italy), which immediately changes the currency to Lira and the date format to dd/MM/yyyy — without restarting the computer.

Input Method Editors, Input Languages, and Keyboard Layouts

For a computer to support a given language, the computer must be able to display the language on screen using the correct alphabet, characters, and fonts. The computer must be able to accept input typed on a specific language keyboard or specialized input device. The appropriate language collection must be installed, and the default input language and keyboard layout determine how characters entered on the keyboard will be displayed on the screen.

Languages such as Japanese use an *Input Method Editor (IME)*, so that a user can enter Asian text in programs by converting the keystrokes into Asian characters. The IME interprets the keystrokes as characters, and then gives the user the opportunity to insert the correct interpretation into the program being worked in. Windows XP Professional contains IMEs for Simplified and Traditional Chinese, Japanese, and Korean.

The Input Language setting of the Regional and Language Options Control Panel, formerly called an *input locale*, specifies the combination of the language being entered and the keyboard layout, IME, speech-to-text converter, or other device being used to enter it. Input languages are added to a computer user by user; each user can add multiple input languages, enabling multiple-language document editing, viewing, and printing. When you change input languages, some programs (such asMicrosoft® Office XP) offer additional features, such as fonts or spelling checkers designed for different input languages.

For example, a user in the Tokyo office who wants to write an e-mail message in both Japanese and Russian would need to install Russian as an input language to enter and display the Russian language, using a Japanese keyboard. The user can then change between the Japanese and Russian languages while composing the message.

Keyboard Layouts

Each input language that Windows XP Professional supports has a default keyboard layout associated with it. Some languages also have alternative keyboard layouts.

For example, a standard U.S. English language keyboard has 101 keys, while a typical keyboard for the Japanese localized language version of Windows XP Professional has 106 keys.

In these situations — where the physical keyboard might not match the language being entered, or a difference in the number of characters and keys makes it difficult to type — administrators or users can add layouts for additional keyboards. Also, by using the On-Screen Keyboard, users can enter text by selecting characters on the appropriate language version On-Screen Keyboard, as shown in Figure 3-1.

Figure 3-1   On-Screen Keyboard for French

Tip   Administrators can make it easier for users to change input languages and keyboard layouts by placing the Language Toolbar on the desktop or in the Taskbar, or by enabling keyboard sequences, or "hot keys." For more information, see "Simplifying Multiple Language Access on Desktops" later in this chapter.

Unicode and Code Pages

Unicode is an international standard for representing the characters in common use in the most widely used languages. Unicode provides a universal character set that can accommodate most known scripts, meaning that the text used in documents, files, and applications created in one operating system language (such as Japanese) display correctly in a different operating system language (such as English). Windows XP Professional supports Unicode as its base character encoding.

Windows XP Professional supports code pages to ensure backward compatibility and comprehensive language support for legacy documents and applications. A *code page* is an ordered set of characters in which a numeric index (code point) is associated with each character of a particular writing system. There are separate code pages for different writing systems, such as Western European and Cyrillic. In a code page–based environment, each set of characters from a specific language has its own table of characters.

Because a code page is a much smaller ordered set of characters than Unicode, code pages have limited abilities to display the characters of another code page's language. Documents based on the code page of one operating system rarely transfer successfully to an operating system that uses another code page, resulting in unintelligible text or characters. For example, if someone in Boston using the International English language version of Microsoft® Windows® 98 with the Latin code page opens a file created in the Japanese language version of Windows 98, the code points of the Japanese code page are mapped to unexpected or nonexistent characters in the Latin script.

To ensure that new applications being written for Windows XP Professional can function in any language, use Unicode as the base character encoding. Do not use code pages.

For a complete list of code pages and their associated code points, see the Microsoft OEM Code Reference link on the Web Resources page at http://www.microsoft.com/windows/reskits/webresources. For a complete listing of Unicode control characters, see "Unicode Control Characters" in Windows XP Professional Help and Support Center.

Language for Non-Unicode Programs (System Locale)

The Language for non-Unicode Programs, previously called the *system locale*, specifies the default code pages and associated bitmap font files for a given computer, and affects all of that computer's users. The default code pages and fonts enable non-Unicode applications to run as they do on a system localized to the language of the Language for non-Unicode Programs. If an application displays question marks (???) instead of the expected alphanumeric characters, the Language for non-Unicode Programs probably needs to be switched to the language in which the application was developed. Switching the Language for non-Unicode Programs to match an older application's language affects other operating system settings that will improve overall application and system compatibility.

For example, assume that a data entry clerk in the Tokyo office is using the International English language version of Windows XP Professional. If the clerk wants to run a non-Unicode accounting application designed for the Japanese localized language version of Windows 98, the clerk needs to change the Language for non-Unicode Programs of the computer to Japanese and restart the computer. Otherwise, Kanji characters would be displayed as question marks.

Note   Changing the Language for non-Unicode Programs alone does not change the language of the Windows XP Professional user interface elements, such as the system menus and dialog box display languages. Only the Windows XP Professional MUI Pack allows a user to change the language of the user interface.

User Interface Language Options (MUI Pack Only)

Using the Windows XP Professional MUI Pack, users can change the language of the user interface — such as the names of menu options, choices in dialog boxes, and Help system — to any of the localized language versions of Windows XP Professional. Administrators can specify the default user interface language by using setup scripts or silent configurations, and also can restrict users' abilities to change the user interface language by using Group Policy settings.

Windows XP Professional Language Versions

Windows XP Professional includes three different language versions: International English, individual localized language versions, and the MUI Pack. Understanding the differences between the language versions that are available will help you to choose the language version that best meets your company's specific language and international needs.

Table 3-3 shows the user needs that each language version supports.

Table 3-3   Differences Between Windows XP Professional Language Versions

User Needs	International English Version of Windows XP Professional	Localized Language Versions of Windows XP Professional	Windows XP Professional MUI Pack
Ability to read and write documents in multiple languages	X	X	X
Language and regional support for over 135 locales	X	X	X
Language and regional support for supported localized language versions			X
Localized language user interface		X	X
Ability to transact business primarily in one or more languages besides English		X	X
Ability to transact business mostly in English, but have access to additional languages	X	X	X
Extensive support for localized language applications compatibility		X	X [*]
Extensive support for localized language drivers	X	X	X [*]
Legacy DOS and BIOS support		X	
Single code base for application development	X	X	X
Single code base for application testing in different user interface languages			X
Ability to log on anywhere in any language			X
Single, simultaneous worldwide rollouts for hotfixes, patches, and Service Packs			X

[*]   Support for local drivers and applications is usually not as extensive as for localized language versions.

Windows XP Professional International English Version

The International English version of Windows XP Professional is designed for companies that do business mostly in English, but have some users with additional language needs. This version provides complete language and regional support for over 135 locales, allowing users to read and write documents in almost any language.

The Windows XP Professional user interface, however, is in English. If you require the user interface to appear in a language other than English, a localized language version or the MUI Pack is a more appropriate choice.

Windows XP Professional Localized Language Versions

Each localized language version of Windows XP Professional contains the same language and regional support that is included in the International English version, meaning that users can read and write documents in almost any language. However, the operating system user interface appears only in the localized language instead of English.

A localized language version contains more extensive application compatibility than the International English version of Windows XP Professional, as well as extra local drivers, and legacy DOS and BIOS support. If your company, or a particular office or division of your company, operates primarily in a language other than English, or requires that the operating system user interface is in a language other than English, a localized language version of Windows XP Professional is an appropriate choice. For a complete list of the localized language versions of Windows XP Professional, see the Localized Language Versions link on the Web Resources page at http://www.microsoft.com/windows/reskits/webresources.

Windows XP Professional MUI Pack

The Windows XP Professional MUI Pack allows users to change the language of the operating system user interface to any of the supported localized language versions (including English). This version is well suited for companies that:

- Want to deploy and maintain a single operating system standard or desktop image worldwide.

- Want to maintain a single code base for international application development.

- Want to do single, simultaneous worldwide rollouts for hotfixes, patches, and Service Packs.

- Have multilingual offices where different language speakers must share computers.

- Have users who need to be able to log on anywhere in any language.

The Multilingual User Interface Pack is based on the International English version of Windows XP Professional. Although the user interface can be switched to any of the supported languages, compared to a localized language version of Windows XP Professional, some parts of the operating system are not localized in the MUI Pack. These include:

- 16-bit code
- Bitmaps
- Some registry keys and values
- INF files
- Some system components, including:
    - Narrator
    - MSN® Explorer
    - NetMeeting®
    - Internet Connection Wizard

For more information about the Windows XP Professional MUI Pack, see the Locales and Language link on the Web Resources page at http://www.microsoft.com/windows/reskits/webresources.

Planning a Multilingual Deployment

To deploy the appropriate language versions of Windows XP Professional and configure regional support based on your organization's current geographic and IT infrastructure, you need to determine your language and regional requirements, as well as your hardware requirements and limitations. You also need to take into account the needs of roaming users in your organization, and whether you are upgrading an earlier localized language version of Windows. Also, consider whether your organization requires a single global image, and whether you will require specific regional builds for different offices in your organization.

Determining Language and Regional Requirements

If you do business in multiple languages or have multilingual office environments, you need to know which languages or dialects your organization must support, and whether these languages require IMEs or alternative keyboards or input devices.

If you do business internationally, you need to know which countries/regions your organization must support, and which languages or dialects are used in each. You must determine whether currency, time zone, or calendar formats vary between the different countries and regions. Additionally, you must determine which line-of-business applications you have that must accommodate such regional differences.

A four-column planning table can help you determine your language and regional needs. You can organize the table as follows:

- In column one, list your offices or divisions.

- In column two, list the languages or dialects used in those offices or divisions.

- In column three, note the corresponding Windows XP Professional language collections and locales that support those languages or dialects. For tables listing Windows XP Professional language collections and locales, see the Global Software Development List of Locale IDs and Language Groups link on the Web Resources page at http://www.microsoft.com/windows/reskits/webresources.

- In column four, note any special standards and formats settings, input language support, or default languages for non-Unicode programs required for your offices or divisions.

> **Tip**   You can use the resulting worksheet to plan your physical deployment and complete the [RegionalSettings] section of your answer files. For more information about completing your answer file, see "Using Unattended Installations and Silent Configurations" later in this chapter.

Assessing Hardware Requirements for Multilingual Support

Supporting multiple languages can impact your hardware requirements in two areas:

- **Hard disk space.** Some languages require more hard-disk storage space than others. The more languages installed on a computer, the more hard-disk space consumed. In addition, the Windows XP Professional MUI Pack requires more disk space for each user interface language installed or supported.

- **Specialized hardware devices.** Some languages or users require special keyboards, IMEs, or alternative input devices.

> **Note**   Installing a language collection enables you to view text in those languages in a document, on a Web page, and so on. However, to input text in a given language, you must also add that language as an input language. For more information about adding input languages, see "Configuring Desktops" later in this chapter.

Disk Space Requirements

If a workstation needs to support users who speak multiple languages, that workstation must have enough space on the hard disk for the appropriate language resources. The amount of disk space that you need depends, in part, on the Windows XP Professional language version that you deploy.

Language Support Requirements   Every language version of Windows XP Professional comes with support for all of the languages in the Basic Language Collection, which is installed by default. Table 3-4 lists the estimated hard drive space that you need to install additional language support.

Table 3-4   Disk Space Requirements for Language Support

Language Collection	Installation Status	Space Required in Megabytes (MB)
Basic	Always installed on every language version.	N/A
Complex Script and Right-to-Left	Always installed on the Arabic language version and the Hebrew language version; optionally installed on all other language versions.	10
East Asian	Always installed on the Simplified Chinese, Traditional Chinese, Japanese, and Korean language versions; optionally installed on all other language versions.	230

User Interface Language Requirements (MUI Pack Only)   The Windows XP Professional MUI Pack contains Windows Installer packages that allow users to install the user interface languages on demand. Because they are compressed, Windows Installer packages require less storage space on a network server or CD image.

> **Tip**   If your organization uses regional or customized builds or a CD-based deployment, include the appropriate Windows Installer packages on the custom image or CD to ensure that support for those user interface languages is available. This ensures that the specific user interface languages that each office needs are available either for unattended installations during deployment, or for on-demand installations by users post-deployment.

Providing on-demand installation also saves storage space on desktops, because users can install only the user interface languages that they need, when they need them. For a list of the storage space required on a client computer for each user interface language that is installed, see the Locales and Language link on the Web Resources page at http://www.microsoft.com/windows/reskits/webre-sources.

For more detailed information about using Windows Installer packages with the Windows XP Professional MUI Pack, see "Using Windows Installer Packages for On-Demand Installations (MUI Pack Only)" later in this chapter.

Specialized Hardware Needs

If your language requirements require you to use special keyboards, IMEs, or alternative input devices your hardware must meet minimum hardware compatibility requirements. You can find the minimum hardware compatibility requirements on the Hardware Compatibility List link on the Web Resources page at http://www.microsoft.com/windows/reskits/webresources.

Determining Roaming User Needs

If you have many roaming users who need to log on from different locations and edit documents in several languages, you must ensure that the appropriate language files are either installed or installable on demand on those users' workstations. You can also install Terminal Services so that users can sign on to unique Terminal Services sessions in different languages.

If your roaming users need to log on from different locations in their native language user interface version of the operating system, you must install the Windows XP Professional MUI Pack as appropriate.

> **Tip**   If you have deployed a Windows® 2000 Server MultiLanguage Version, you can extend the lifecycles of old desktops and functionality of thin clients for use as multilingual workstations. By installing Terminal Services on clients connected to a computer running Windows 2000 Server MultiLanguage Version, you effectively permit the client to function as a Windows XP Professional MUI Pack–based workstation that allows users to change user interface languages easily.

Upgrading from Earlier Versions of Windows

A localized language version of a Windows–based client cannot be upgraded to a different language version of Windows XP Professional, or to the Windows XP Professional MUI Pack. For example, you cannot upgrade a Japanese localized language version of Windows 2000 Professional to either the International English language version or MUI Pack of Windows XP Professional.

> **Warning**   To replace any other language versions of Windows with the Windows XP Professional MUI Pack, you must remove the previous Windows version and perform a clean installation of the Windows XP Professional MUI Pack.

You can only upgrade to the Windows XP Professional MUI Pack from an International English language version of Windows, or from the Microsoft® Windows® 2000 Professional MultiLanguage Version. Table 3-5 shows which of these earlier versions of Windows clients can be upgraded to the Windows XP Professional MUI Pack.

Table 3-5   Upgrade Matrix for Windows XP Professional MUI Pack

International English or MultiLanguage Version of Windows	Windows XP Professional MUI Pack
Microsoft® Windows NT® Workstation version 3.51	
Microsoft® Windows NT® Workstation version 4.0	X
Windows 98	X
Microsoft® Windows® Millennium Edition (Me)	X
Windows 2000 Professional	X
Windows 2000 Professional MultiLanguage Version	X
Microsoft® Windows® XP Home Edition	

Deploying a Single Global Image

The Windows XP Professional MUI Pack enables a global organization's IT department to deploy and maintain a single global desktop image. In this way, your company can create a single build that includes user interface language support for all of the languages in which you do business. The build can also include world-ready applications such as Office XP.

For example, if your company supports user interfaces in English, French, Italian, Spanish, Japanese, Simplified Chinese, and Traditional Chinese, you can create a single global image that includes user interface support for those seven languages. You can also make support for those languages available for on-demand installation after deployment by using Windows Installer packages.

> **Tip**   Deploying and maintaining a single global image can significantly improve IT efficiency and help lower many costs. It enables single-code-base application development and testing, simplifies releasing hotfixes and service patches, and reduces end-user support calls.

Creating Regional Builds

You can further customize Windows XP Professional deployments by creating specific regional builds tailored to each office's multilingual and international needs. For each office or site, you can create a regional build that specifies the appropriate language version of the operating system, the default input language, and the standards and formats appropriate to that region. You can also include the appropriate localized language versions of third-party applications, such as virus checking utilities, as well as other specialized drivers and applications required by that office.

For example, you might create the following four unique regional builds for North America:

- Two Canadian builds for the Vancouver, B.C., and Montreal offices to deploy the International English version of Windows XP Professional, with English and French (Canada) set as the default input languages, and Canada set as the default for standards and formats. English is the default input language in Vancouver, and French is the default input language in Montreal.

- A U.S. English build so that users in Seattle and other U.S. locations can install the International English version of Windows XP Professional, with English (U.S.) set as the default input language, and optional support for the East Asian Language Collection, which includes the font files, font linking, and registry settings needed for Simplified and Traditional Chinese, Japanese, and Korean language support.

- A Boston regional build that installs the U.S. English build along with optional support for the East Asian Language Collection.

The regional build for the Tokyo office, by contrast, might install the Japanese localized language version of Windows XP Professional, as well as the Japanese localized language versions of virus checking and accounting applications.

Using the Windows XP Professional MUI Pack, global organizations can also take a hybrid approach combining a single global core image, which contains the baseline operating system and applications, with additional regional core images that include localized language applications, settings, and so on. The global IT department develops and maintains the global core; individual countries/regions are responsible for building and maintaining their own regional cores. Local offices can also add a third-tier customization core image for custom stationery or templates, printer drivers, and so on.

Configuring Desktops

Using Windows XP Professional, you can customize desktops to support your company's specific language and regional needs. You can configure desktops with specific Regional and Language Options, such as a default input language or keyboard layout. You can also configure the browser to receive localized, regional content, and you can add toolbars and keyboard shortcuts to simplify switching between input languages.

Windows XP Professional enables administrators to specify the appropriate input language/keyboard layout combination and standards and formats settings for the default user account on a computer. All subsequent new user accounts created on that computer inherit the specified defaults; existing user accounts are not affected.

Administrators can specify these default settings through the user interface, or by using answer files. For more information about specifying the default settings through the user interface, see "Configuring Regional and Language Options" later in this chapter. For more information about specifying the default settings through the answer files, see "Creating Unattended Installations" and "Using Silent Configurations" later in this chapter.

Configuring Regional and Language Options

You can use the Regional and Language Options settings in Control Panel to configure input languages for user accounts, and for the MUI Pack, to specify or change the default user interface language, or install or remove user interface language packs.

To install the Complex Script and Right-to-Left Collection or East Asian Language Collection

1. In **Control Panel**, click **Regional and Language Options**.

2. Click the **Languages** tab, and then under **Supplemental language support**, select the check boxes of the language collections that you want to install.

To change the language for non-Unicode programs

1. Log on as an Administrator.

2. In **Control Panel**, click **Regional and Language Options**.

3. Click the **Advanced** tab, and then under **Language for non-Unicode programs**, select the language for which the application was developed.

For more information about language collections and languages for non-Unicode programs, see "New Multilingual Features in Windows XP Professional" earlier in this chapter.

Configuring Regional and Language Support for User Accounts

Some language versions of Windows XP Professional might require installing the Complex Script and Right-to-Left Language Collection or the East Asian Language Collection, as well as the appropriate input languages, to properly input and display all characters.

Administrators can specify which input languages are available for user selection at the Windows logon screen, and which are applied to new user accounts, by adding the appropriate input languages to the default user account.

To add an input language for the current user

1. In **Control Panel**, click **Regional and Language Options**.

2. Click the **Languages** tab, and then under **Text services and input languages**, click Details.

3. Under **Installed services**, click **Add**.

4. In the **Input Language** box, click the input language that you want to add to enable users to input text in that language.

    This installs the input language with the default keyboard layout/IME listed in the **Keyboard layout/IME** box.

To add an alternative keyboard layout/IME for an input language

1. In **Control Panel**, click **Regional and Language Options**.

2. Click the **Languages** tab, and then under **Text services and input languages**, click Details.

3. Under **Installed services**, click **Add**.

4. In the **Keyboard layout/IME** box, click the alternative keyboard layout or IME that you want to add to enable users to input text in the specified input language.

To specify the default input language for the current user

1. In **Control Panel**, click **Regional and Language Options**.

2. Click the **Languages** tab, and then under **Text services and input languages**, click **Details**.

3. Under **Default input language**, select the appropriate input language.

To add an input language for the default user account

1. Log on as an Administrator.

2. In **Control Panel**, click **Regional and Language Options**.

3. Click the **Languages** tab, and then under **Text services and input languages**, click **Details**.

4. Under **Installed services**, click **Add**.

5. In the **Input Language** box, click the input language that you want to add to enable users to input text in that language, and then click **OK**.

    If you want to add more than one input language, repeat this step for each language that you want to add.

6. Click **OK** or **Apply** to close the Text Services and **Input Languages dialog box**.

7. Click the **Advanced** tab, and then select the **Apply all settings to the current user account and to the default user profile** check box.

Configuring the User Interface Language (MUI Pack Only)

The Windows XP MUI Pack allows users to change user interface languages, as long as support for additional user interface languages has been installed, and Administrators have not locked down the desktop by using Group Policy settings.

To change the current user interface language

1. In **Control Panel**, click **Regional and Language Options**.

2. Click the **Languages** tab, and then under **Language used in menus and dialogs**, select the language that you want to use.

To specify the user interface language for the default user account

1. In **Control Panel**, click **Regional and Language Options**.

2. Click the **Languages** tab, and then under **Language used in menus and dialogs**, select the language that you want to use.

3. Click the **Advanced** tab, and then select the **Apply all settings to the current user account and to the default user profile** check box.

Configuring Localized Content

You can configure the default location to ensure that a user or group of users receives the appropriate local content, such as news and weather, from Internet or intranet content providers. You can change the default location without impacting other multilingual settings, such as the default standards and formats used for currency, sorting, dates, and so on.

The Location setting of the Regional and Language Options Control Panel enables Web content providers to redirect users to more appropriate regional sites when they visit a generic site. For example, users in the Milan office would want the default location set to Italy to ensure that they connect to the appropriate servers, content providers, and so on.

To configure localized browser content

1. In **Control Panel**, click **Regional and Language Options**.

2. Click the **Regional Options** tab, and then under **Location**, click the region or location for which you want customized content.

Simplifying Multiple Language Access on Desktops

Administrators can configure desktops to simplify working in multiple languages. For example, you can add a language toolbar to the desktop, or a language icon to the taskbar, making it easier for users to change between different input languages when they need to compose documents in multiple languages. You can also enable specific key sequences that let users quickly change between installed input languages and alternative keyboard layouts/IMEs.

To add the Language bar to the desktop or taskbar

1. In **Control Panel**, click **Regional and Language Options**.

2. Click the **Languages** tab, and then under **Text services and input languages**, click **Details**.

3. In the **Text Services and Input Languages** dialog box, under **Preferences**, click **Language Bar**.

4. In the **Language Bar Settings** dialog box, select the check boxes that correspond to the language bar and taskbar options you want to enable.

To enable or change key sequences for switching input languages or keyboard layouts/IMEs

1. In **Control Panel**, click **Regional and Language Options**.

2. Click the **Languages** tab, and then under **Text services and input languages**, click **Details**.

3. In the **Text Services and Input Languages** dialog box, under **Preferences**, click **Key Settings**.

4. In the **Advanced Key Settings** dialog box, select the options that correspond to the key sequences and actions you want to use to enable a user to change between installed input languages or keyboard layouts/IMEs.

If you want to use the On-Screen Keyboard to input text in a different language, change to the appropriate input language before enabling the On-Screen Keyboard.

To display the On-Screen Keyboard

- From the **Start** menu, point to **All Programs**, point to **Accessories**, and then point to **Accessibility**.

- Click **On-Screen Keyboard**.

Entering Special Characters or Code Points

Users can input characters that are not on the keyboard by pressing and holding the **ALT** key, and then typing the appropriate decimal code value for that character on the numeric keypad.

- If the first digit typed is 0, the value is recognized as a code point in the current input language. For example, pressing and holding the **ALT** key while typing **0163** produces £, the pound sign (U+00A3 in the format for Unicode encoding), if the default input language is English (U.S.).

- If the first digit typed is any number between 1 and 9, the value is represented as a code point in the operating system's OEM code page. For example, pressing and holding the **ALT** key while typing **163** produces ú, (U+00FA), if the code page is 437 (MS-DOS Latin US).

For a complete list of OEM code pages and their associated code points for numeric keypad input, see the Microsoft OEM Code Reference link on the Web Resources page at http://www.microsoft.com/windows/reskits/webresources.

Controlling Desktops by Using Group Policy Settings

Windows XP Professional enables administrators to automate different users' Regional and Language Options, such as the default input language or standards and formats, by using a Group Policy logon script. When a given user logs on to a computer, the Group Policy logon script silently calls the Regional and Language Options Control Panel to specify the correct settings for that user. For more information about using a Group Policy logon script to silently configure desktop settings, see "Using Silent Configurations" later in this chapter.

The Windows XP Professional MUI Pack allows administrators to use Group Policy settings to control users' abilities to change the user interface language. For more information about Group Policy settings, see "Connecting Clients to Windows Networks" in this book

Using Unattended Installations and Silent Configurations

Windows XP Professional contains keywords and options that simplify creating unattended installations of new computers and silent configuration of existing computers. In addition, when installing and configuring the Windows XP Professional MUI Pack, special considerations must be taken into account.

Creating Unattended Installations

For unattended installations of any language version of Windows XP Professional, you may need to specify additional options for running Winnt32.exe or Winnt.exe. Also, you must specify certain keywords and values in your Unattend.txt or Sysprep.inf answer file.

There are also special considerations for performing unattended installations of the Windows XP MUI Pack.

Options for Running Winnt32.exe or Winnt.exe

If your organization requires the installation of East Asian language and locale support, you must specify /`copysource:lang` or /`rx:lang` to copy the necessary language files. If you do not, and the [RegionalSettings] section of your answer file contains East Asian values, Setup will ignore everything in the [RegionalSettings] section.

> **Note** If you install one of the East Asian localized language versions of Windows XP Professional, you do not need to specify the /**copysource** or /**rx** parameters, because East Asian language and locale support are installed by default.

For Winnt32.exe, the appropriate syntax is:

```
winnt32.exe /unattend:"path to answer file" /copysource:lang /s:"path to install
source"
```

To run Winnt.exe from a 16-bit, MS-DOS network startup disk, the appropriate syntax is:

```
winnt.exe /u:"path to answer file" /rx:lang /s:"path to install source"
```

> **Note** For the MUI Pack, you must specify certain options to run Winnt32.exe. You cannot run Winnt.exe. For more information about specifying options for the MUI Pack, see "Special Considerations for Installing the Windows XP Professional MUI Pack" later in this chapter.

Defining Language and Regional Settings in the Answer File

For unattended installations of Windows XP Professional, you can customize the following sections of the answer file to address specific language and other regional needs:

- [RegionalSettings] Options

- [GuiUnattended] Options

- [TapiLocation] Options

> **Warning**   If you are creating an answer file for a localized language version of Windows XP Professional other than International English, create the answer file using that localized language version. Otherwise, change the language for non-Unicode programs to that of the localized language version, and save the answer file as ANSI text using the appropriate text encoding method for the language version that you are installing.
>
> For example, if you are creating an answer file to install the Russian localized language version on a desktop, use the Russian localized language version of Windows XP Professional to create the answer file. Otherwise, change the language for non-Unicode programs to Russian and use the Cyrillic OEM code page to author the answer file.

Specifying [RegionalSettings] Options   The [RegionalSettings] section of the answer file specifies multilingual and international settings such as the language collections installed, the input languages installed, and the language for non-Unicode programs. All of the [RegionalSettings] values can be specified in either Unattend.txt or Sysprep.inf.

> **Warning**   Any [RegionalSettings] values specified in Sysprep.inf will override any values set in Unattend.txt. In addition, if you use Sysprep, all of the appropriate additional language files specified must already be installed on the computer.

The following shows the correct syntax for the [RegionalSettings] section:

```
[RegionalSettings]
Language="locale ID"
LanguageGroup="language group ID","language group ID"…
SystemLocale="locale ID"
```

```
UserLocale="locale ID"
InputLocale="locale ID:keyboard layout ID", "locale ID:keyboard layout ID", …
UserLocale_DefaultUser="locale ID"
InputLocale_DefaultUser="locale ID:keyboard layout ID", …
```

> **Note**   The Windows XP Professional MUI Pack requires additional consider-
> ations to ensure consistency among language settings for unattended
> installations. For more information about creating unattended installations
> of the MUI Pack, see "Special Considerations for Installing the Windows XP
> Professional MUI Pack" later in this chapter.

Table 3-6 describes the [RegionalSettings] keys and identifies the corresponding settings in the **Regional and Language Options** Control Panel. For a complete
listing of valid values for these keys, see the Locales and Language link on the Web
Resources page at http://www.microsoft.com/windows/reskits/webresources.

Table 3-6   [RegionalSettings] Keys

Key	Usage	Regional and Language Options Control Panel Settings
Language	Specifies the language installed. If this key is specified, the **System-Locale**, **UserLocale**, and **Input Locale** keys are ignored.	■ Standards and Formats. ■ Input Language. ■ Language for Non-Unicode Programs.
LanguageGroup	Specifies the language groups installed on the computer. Installing one language group also installs support for all of the other language groups in the same language collection. For example, if you install the Korean language group (8), Windows XP Professional installs support for all of the other language groups in the East Asian Language Collection (i.e., Japanese (7), Traditional Chinese (9), and Simplified Chinese (10)). For a list of the language groups installed under each language collection, see "Built-In Language Support" earlier in this chapter.	Same effect as: ■ Installing support for Complex Script and Right-to-Left languages. ■ Installing support for East Asian languages.

Table 3-6 [RegionalSettings] Keys

Key	Usage	Regional and Language Options Control Panel Settings
SystemLocale	Enables non-Unicode applications to run and display menus and dialog boxes in the localized language.	Language for Non-Unicode Programs.
UserLocale	Controls settings for sorting numbers, time, currency, and dates.	Standards and Formats.
InputLocale	Specifies input language and keyboard layout combinations. The first keyboard layout specified becomes the system default. Specified combinations must be supported by one of the languages defined by using either the **LanguageGroup** key or the default language for the language version of Windows XP Professional being installed. If an available language does not support the specified combination, the default combination is used. This key is ignored if the **Language** key is specified.	Input Language(s).
UserLocale_DefaultUser*	Controls the formats for numbers, time, currency, and dates for the default user. The specified setting must be supported by one of the languages specified using the **LanguageGroup** key, or the default language for the language version of Windows XP Professional being installed.	Same effect as: ■ Setting **Standards and Formats**. ■ Selecting **Apply all settings to the current user account and to the default user profile** check box on the **Advanced** tab.
InputLocale_DefaultUser*	Sets the input language and keyboard layout combinations for the default user.	Same effect as: ■ Specifying **Input Languages**. ■ Selecting **Apply all settings to the current user account and to the default user profile** check box on the **Advanced** tab.

* Denotes new keys added in Windows XP Professional

> **Note**   If you specify a **Language** key, the value associated with it overrides all of the values specified in the **InputLocale**, **SystemLocale**, and **UserLocale** keys. Typically, using the Language key is the preferred method for specifying input languages because it prevents the occurrence of incompatible values in the **InputLocale**, **SystemLocale**, and **UserLocale** keys and installs locales appropriate for the specified language and locale combinations.

Specifying [GuiUnattended] Options   You must specify the time zone of the computer by using the **TimeZone** key in the [GuiUnattended] section of your answer file. If the **TimeZone** key is not present in Unattend.txt, the user is prompted for a time zone during setup.

To preset time zones

- In your answer file, add the following entry in the [GuiUnattended] section:

```
[GuiUnattended]
TimeZone="index"
```

  Index specifies the time zone of the computer. For a list of valid Time Zone indices, see Unattend.doc in Support\Tools\Deploy.cab on the Microsoft® Windows® XP Professional operating system CD.

> **Note**   If you specify **OemPreinstall=Yes** in the [Unattended] section of your answer file, you may want to add **OemSkipRegional=1** to the [GuiUnattended] section to ensure that setup does not prompt the user for regional information during GUI-mode setup.

Specifying [TapiLocation] Options   You can specify dialing rules specific to your country/region by using the [TapiLocation] section of your answer file. These dialing rules specify the default country code and area code that a modem uses when dialing the phone. The [TapiLocation] keys described here are supported in both Unattend.txt and Sysprep.inf, and are valid only for computers with modems.

To preset telephone dialing rules

- In your answer file, specify the appropriate values in the [TapiLocation] section:

```
[TapiLocation]
CountryCode="CountryCode"
AreaCode="AreaCode"
```

For a complete list of country codes to use for telephony, search on the Internet for "ISO 3166," or see the International Telecommunication Union link on the Web Resources page at http://www.microsoft.com/windows/reskits/webresources.

Example Answer File   In the following example, an International English language version of Windows XP Professional is configured with additional support for the East Asian Language Collection installed. English (U.S.) is the default for both the language for non-Unicode programs (the **SystemLocale**) and the standards and formats (the **UserLocale**). Additional input languages and keyboard layouts are also installed for Japanese, Chinese (Taiwan), Chinese (People's Republic of China), Korean, and German. The telephone country code is set to U.S. and the area code is 425. The time zone is Redmond (U.S.) Pacific Standard Time.

```
[GuiUnattended]
TimeZone="020"

[RegionalSettings]
LanguageGroup="1","7","8","9","10"
SystemLocale="0409"
UserLocale="0409"
InputLo-
cale="0409:00000409","0411:e0010411","0404:00000404","0804:00000804","0412:E00104
12","0407:00000407"

[TapiLocation]
CountryCode="US"
AreaCode="425"
```

Special Considerations for Installing the Windows XP Professional MUI Pack

Unattended setup of the Windows XP Professional MUI Pack is slightly different from that of the Windows XP Professional International English or localized language versions for the following reasons:

- Because the Windows XP Professional MUI Pack requires the use of files from several CD-ROMs, you should carefully review how this affects different deployment methods, including network installation, creating custom images on multiple CD-ROMs using SysPrep, or a combination of CD-ROM and network installation.

- You must specify `OemPreinstall=Yes` and `OemFilesPath="path to install source"` in the [Unattended] section of your answer file to point to the location of the user interface language files. If you are installing the MUI Pack from the default location of \i386\OEM, you do not need to specify an `OemFilesPath` value.

- The [Commands] section of Cmdlines.txt must be used to specify the execution of Muisetup.exe, the program that installs the user interface languages.

Ensuring Consistency Within [RegionalSettings]   The MUI Pack requires special attention to ensure consistency within the [RegionalSettings] section of the answer file. You must specify the language groups and locales to install to support the appropriate user interface languages and applications.

The other settings that you specify in the [RegionalSettings] section depend on your workstation configurations:

- **For single user systems.** Set locales to the same value as the default user interface language (specified when running Muisetup.exe). For example, if German is set as the default user interface language, specify one of the German locales in the answer file.

- **For shared workstations and in Terminal Services environments.** Set the default user interface language and the language for non-Unicode programs to English, the administrative language of the MUI Pack. You can set the input language according to individual preferences or requirements. Or, if specified by using the **Language** key, restrict the input language to be the same as the language for non-Unicode programs.

Warning   Install the appropriate language groups to ensure support for both the locales and the user interface languages specified. For example, if you install the Japanese (Japan) user interface language, you must also install the East Asian Language Collection to ensure Japanese language and locale support.

The following [RegionalSettings] example installs support for the East Asian Language Collection. English (U.S.) is the default for both the language for non-Unicode programs (the **SystemLocale**) and standards and formats (the **UserLocale**). Additional input language and keyboard layouts are also installed for Japanese, Chinese (Taiwan), Chinese (People's Republic of China), Korean, and German.

```
[RegionalSettings]
LanguageGroup="1","7","8","9","10"
SystemLocale="0409"
UserLocale="0409"
InputLo-
cale="0409:00000409","0411:e0010411","0404:00000404","0804:00000804","0412:E00104
12","0407:00000407"
```

Specifying [Unattended] Options   In addition to the [RegionalSettings] options, you must specify the following settings in the [Unattended] section when installing the MUI Pack:

```
[Unattended]
OemPreinstall="Yes"
OemFilesPath="path to install source"
```

The **OemFilesPath** key points to the installation share that you create to contain the MUI user interface language files. If you are installing the MUI Pack from the default location of \i386\OEM, you do not need to specify an OemFilesPath value.

Specifying [GuiUnattended] Options   The [GuiUnattended] section of the answer file lets you disable the OEM Regional prompt that would otherwise be displayed during setup. Because you specified OemPreinstall=Yes in the [Unattended] section of your answer file, you may want to add OemSkipRegional=1 to the [GuiUnattended] section to ensure that setup does not prompt the user for regional information during GUI-mode setup.

```
[GuiUnattended]
OemSkipRegional="0 | 1"
```

Set the value to 1 to bypass the user prompt.

Creating the Installation Share   For unattended installations of the Windows XP Professional MUI Pack, you must copy all of the MUI files from CD2 into a temporary directory below the top-level directory on a network share or CD. In the following example, the computer name is \\MUICORE, the share name is OEM, and the temporary directory is MUIINST.

```
\\MUICORE
    \$OEM$
        \MUIINST
            <...all MUI Pack files>
```

Tip   For CD-based deployments, if the MUI Pack files are located on the CD (and not on a network share), the user may need to change CDs to complete the installation. This would require user intervention to change CDs, effectively "breaking" the unattended nature of the installation.

Installing by Using a Cmdlines.txt File   For the Windows XP Professional MUI Pack, you must create a Cmdlines.txt file in the top level of your temporary directory. Cmdlines.txt must contain a [Commands] section that executes the Muisetup program using the appropriate parameters and values, using the following syntax:

```
[Commands]
".\temporary directory name\MUISETUP.exe [/i LangID LangID...] [/d LangID] /r /s"
```

You must use quotation marks around the command, and the path to Muisetup.exe must specify the temporary directory you created in the installation source. Table 3-7 describes the Muisetup parameters.

Table 3-7   Muisetup Parameters

Key	Description
/i	Specifies the user interface language(s) to be installed. Typically, languages are entered in four-digit hexadecimal LangID values.
/d	Specifies the default user interface language (applied to all new user accounts and used in places such as the Winlogon screen).
/r	Specifies that the restart message not be displayed.
/s	Specifies that the installation complete message not be displayed.

The following Cmdlines.txt answer file is created in the temporary directory specified by the **OemFilesPath** key in yourUnattend.txt answer file (in the example specified earlier, the location is \\MUICORE\$OEM$). If Unattend.txt does not specify a custom location for OemFilesPath, Cmdlines.txt uses the default location of \i386\$OEM$.

The following specifies that Muisetup install the Japanese (Japan) and German (Germany) user interface languages, and sets Japanese (Japan) as the default user interface language used for the Winlogon screen and applied to all new user accounts.

```
[Commands]
".\MUIINST\MUISETUP.exe /i 0411 0407 /d 0411 /r /s"
```

Installing Windows Installer User Interface Language Packages   You can use Windows Installer (.msi) packages to install additional MUI user interface language support. To do this, you must copy the .msi files for those user interface languages to the installation share, and then invoke Windows Installer in your Cmdlines.txt file to install the user interface languages on the computer. To install multiple user interface languages, repeat the msiexec invocation, specifying the appropriate .msi file for each additional user interface language that you want to install.

In the following example, the German (Germany) user interface language is silently installed from the German .msi package and the Japanese (Japan) user interface language is silently installed from the Japanese .msi package.

```
[Commands]
"msiexec.exe /i 0407.msi /q"
"msiexec.exe /i 0411.msi /q"
```

For more information about Windows Installer packages and parameters for using the **msiexec.exe** command, see the Software Development Kit (SDK) information in the MSDN Library link on the Web Resources page at http://www.microsoft.com/windows/reskits/webresources.

Additional Parameters for Installing Windows Installer Packages   When installing Windows Installer packages, you can choose whether to set a particular user interface language for the current user, the default user, or both. You can also specify whether a usere language can be uninstalled by any user. Table 3-8 describes these parameters and how to use them.

Table 3-8   Windows Installer Package Parameters

Parameter=value	Description
currentuser=1	Sets the user interface language being installed as the user interface language for the current user. If this is not specified, the user interface language will be installed without changing the current user's user interface language.
defaultuser=1	Sets the user interface language being installed as the user interface language for the default user account, which affects the logon screen and all new user accounts. If this is not specified, the user interface language will be installed without changing the default user account's user interface language.
allusers=1	Specifies that the user interface language can be uninstalled by any user of that computer.

In the following example, the German (Germany) and Japanese (Japan) user interface languages are silently installed, and the current user and default user accounts are set to Japanese. In addition, the German .msi package is to be installed per computer, allowing all users of the computer to remove it.

```
[Commands]
"msiexec.exe /i 0407.msi allusers=1 /q"
"msiexec.exe /i 0411.msi defaultuser=1 currentuser=1 /q"
```

> **Caution**   Use the `allusers=1` parameter carefully, because it allows any user to remove a user interface language from a computer — even though that user interface language might be required by another user of the same computer. If you install a given user interface language by using the `current-user=1` and/or `defaultuser=1` parameters, do not specify the `allusers=1` parameter for the same user interface language.

Using Silent Configurations

You might want to change a computer's Regional and Language Options silently after the initial installation. For example, if your organization locks down the desktop to prevent a group of users from accessing the Control Panel, you can update that group's Regional and Language Options by using a Group Policy–applied logon script.

In these situations, you can use Rundll32.exe to call the Regional and Language Options Control Panel with an answer file that specifies the appropriate settings. The syntax for calling Rundll32.exe from the command line is as follows:

```
Rundll32 shell32,Control_RunDLL intl.cpl,,/f:"c:\unattend.txt"
```

The answer file specified in c:\unattend.txt must contain a [RegionalSettings] section that specifies the appropriate regional and language settings.

Changing Language and Regional Options

The format of the answer file specified in a silent configuration is exactly the same as that used during setup. This means that all of the [RegionalSettings] options can be changed silently after the initial installation. The following is an example of a silent configuration that:

■ Adds the "German - German" input language for the current user.

■ Adds the "German - Swiss German" input language to the list of input languages for the default user.

■ Configures the language for non-Unicode programs to German.

```
[RegionalSettings]
InputLocale="0407:00000407"
InputLocale_DefaultUser="0407:00000807"
SystemLocale="0407"
```

If you specify multiple input languages for the **InputLocale** and **InputLocale_DefaultUser** keys, the first value specified will be set as the default for that particular user. In the following example, the **InputLocale** will set "German - German" as the default input language for the current user while also making "German - Swiss German" available as an input language.

```
[RegionalSettings]
InputLocale="0407:00000407", "0407:00000807"
```

Changing MUI Pack Defaults

The Windows XP Professional MUI Pack contains two new keywords that you can use after running setup to perform silent configurations. These keywords are intended for silent configuration after setup, when the specified user interface language has already been installed on the computer. Table 3.9 describes these additional [RegionalSettings] keys. For a complete listing of valid values for these keys, see the Locales and Language link on the Web Resources page at http://www.microsoft.com/windows/reskits/webresources.

Table 3-9   [RegionalSettings] Keys for Silently Configuring MUI Pack Defaults

Key	Usage
MUILanguage	Sets the user interface language for the current user.
MUILanguage_DefaultUser	Sets the user interface language for the default user account, including the logon screen and the user interface language applied to all new user accounts.

Using Windows Installer Packages for On-Demand Installations (MUI Pack Only)

The Windows XP Professional MUI Pack includes Windows Installer packages that allow users to install user interface languages on demand. For companies that support one global image, on-demand installation enables smaller and faster setups and images. If you do regional builds or CD-based deployments, include on a CD or network share the Windows Installer package for each specific user interface language your company needs to support.

To enable on-demand installations, you can publish a Windows Installer (.msi) package for each user interface language that your company supports on the appropriate Active Directory servers. The Windows Installer packages are then listed as additional user interface languages in the appropriate users' Add or Remove Programs Control Panel. If you publish the .msi packages with the **Maximum UI** option, users can choose whether to install and set a specific user interface language for the current user, the default user, or both. Alternatively, to set the user account settings automatically, you can publish the .msi packages with the **Basic UI** option and then apply transforms to the packages.

For example, assume that your company supports 12 different languages worldwide. Your IT department publishes those 12 Windows Installer user interface language packages in the global Active Directory. A clerk in the Boston office, using Windows XP Professional MUI Pack with English (U.S.) as the default user interface language, can then install Italian and Japanese user interface language support when it is needed. All that the user needs to do is open the Add or Remove Programs Control Panel and select the Italian and Japanese user interface language support packages.

For more information about Windows Installer packages and parameters for using the **msiexec.exe** command, see the Software Development Kit (SDK) information in the MSDN Library link on the Web Resources page at http://www.microsoft.com/windows/reskits/webresources.

Supporting Multilingual Applications

In a multilingual environment, it is important to ensure that your existing line-of-business applications run properly under any language version of Windows XP Professional. Multilingual and international considerations can impact legacy application support, as well as the development of new applications and the authoring of Web sites for international companies.

When you deploy Windows XP Professional in a global environment, it is important to ensure that all of your current and future applications and Web technologies are compatible with the language versions that you support.

Supporting World-Ready Applications

All versions of Windows XP Professional are built from a single world-ready source code. This simplifies supporting multilingual applications, because an application developed on any language version of Windows XP Professional following world-ready guidelines runs correctly on any other language version of Windows XP Professional. For example, a clerk in the Boston office using the International English language version of Windows XP Professional can run an application developed in the Tokyo office on a Japanese localized language version of Windows XP Professional, as long as the Boston client computer has installed the East Asian Language Collection (for Simplified and Traditional Chinese, Japanese, and Korean language support).

Supporting Non-Unicode Applications

In many organizations, legacy line-of-business applications were not developed according to world-ready guidelines. Older applications might not be Unicode-enabled, relying instead on the use of a particular code page for character encoding. These non-Unicode applications might not run correctly if the language of the application does not match the language version of the operating system (for example, running a non-Unicode Japanese order-tracking system on the International English language version of Windows XP Professional). In these situations, one of two problems commonly occurs:

- The application fails to load.

- The application loads, but text strings do not display correctly in the application's user interface.

In most cases, setting the language for non-Unicode programs of the Windows XP Professional–based computer to match the language in which the application was developed solves the problem. In the previous example, if the Boston clerk sets the Windows XP Professional–based computer's language for non-Unicode programs to Japanese, the strings in the legacy, non-Unicode Japanese order-tracking system's user interface will be correctly displayed in Kanji.

> **Note** The language for non-Unicode programs can only be set to one language at a time. If you need to run non-Unicode applications in a variety of languages, you might want to consider porting the applications to Unicode through MSLU.

The Microsoft Layer for Unicode

Another solution for porting a non-Unicode application to Unicode involves using the Microsoft® Layer for Unicode™ (MSLU) on computers running Windows 95, Windows 98, and Windows Me. MSLU is easy to integrate into applications. It requires little more than recompiling the application as a Unicode component and including the MSLU library along with the other libraries used by the program. MSLU is available and fully documented in the Windows XP Professional Platform SDK.

Determining the Compatibility of Your Current Applications

Before deploying Windows XP Professional, you need to test your internally developed line-of-business applications, and any third-party applications (such as antivirus tools), under each language version of Windows XP Professional that your organization supports in order to determine potential problems with multilingual or international compatibility. For example, if you intend to deploy the Japanese localized language version of Windows XP Professional as well as the Simplified Chinese localized language version and the MUI Pack, be sure to test your existing applications under all three configurations.

It is also important to test applications developed for one language version to see how they function while emulating the native language under a different language version of the operating system. For example, test any applications developed using the Japanese localized language version of Windows XP Professional (or earlier versions of Microsoft® Windows®) on computers running the International English language version of Windows XP Professional, after making sure that those computers have the East Asian Language Collection installed.

Basic differences in application support and backward compatibility exist between the localized language versions of Windows XP Professional and the Windows XP Professional MUI Pack. Some 16-bit applications developed on localized language versions run better on those localized language versions of Windows XP Professional than on the Windows XP Professional MUI Pack. For example, the Japanese language version of Windows 2000 supports DOS/V applications, and the Korean language version of Windows NT supports HBIOS applications, whereas the Windows XP Professional MUI Pack does not.

To determine whether a specific third-party application (such as an antivirus tool) is certified as compatible with Windows XP Professional, see the Hardware Compatibility List link on the Web Resources page at http://www.microsoft.com/windows/reskits/webresources.

Developing Multilingual Applications

The Microsoft Global Software Development Web site provides extensive information to help application developers create products that take full advantage of the multilingual and international compatibility features of Windows XP Professional. For information about how and what it means to globalize an application, see the Globalization: Step-by-Step link on the Web Resources page at http://www.microsoft.com/windows/reskits/webresources.

For more information about creating world-ready software, see the Microsoft Global Software Development link on the Web Resources page at http://www.microsoft.com/windows/reskits/webresources.

Developing Multilingual Web Sites

Developers authoring Web sites in global organizations typically require a first-time site visitor to select a preferred language, which is then stored in a client-side cookie on the visitor's computer or as a property in the visitor's profile. Thereafter, site content always appears in the user's specified language.

An alternative approach involves using a script that detects the client computer's default browser language, and then serves the appropriate language version of the Web site to the client.

The key to developing a single Web site that can serve multiple language visitors is to properly structure the following two common language-dependent strings:

- Product information or other data, such as the product name, description, and price.

- Site information, such as content in navigation bars, banner ads, and search results.

Ensuring Multilingual Compatibility

Multilingual compatibility issues can arise when you use Windows XP Professional with Active Directory objects, Terminal Services, or in mixed operating system environments. Also, special considerations arise when you use the multilingual versions of Office XP and Windows XP Professional together. You will need to be aware of these and other global compatibility issues as you prepare to deploy Windows XP Professional in a multilingual environment.

Multilingual Compatibility with Active Directory Objects, Clients, and Domain Controllers

Because Active Directory supports Unicode, there are few multilingual compatibility problems with Active Directory in any language version of Windows XP Professional. Typically, if Active Directory objects are named using Unicode characters, and both the Complex Script and Right-to-Left Language Collection and the East Asian Language Collection are installed, no problems occur in displaying Active Directory object names that combine different languages and fonts.

If you use Active Directory in a mixed operating system environment, consider the following limitations when implementing multilingual features:

- Active Directory supports a single sort order, which might not be the sort order specified by the default language version or settings of the server. If you store objects that have localized names, the returned sort order might not be what you expect.

- If your Active Directory domain controller uses a different language from that of a client computer that is a member of the same domain, you can use only the character sets common to both code pages in Active Directory naming conventions. Otherwise, the two computers might not be able to initialize a trust relationship.

- If an Active Directory client computer does not have the correct language support and fonts installed to interpret localized names in a different language used for objects stored in the directory, the client might not be able to render the names.

For example, if an Active Directory client computer in Boston does not have the East Asian Language Collection installed, it might not be able to display the Kanji characters in the Japanese name of an object stored in an Active Directory server in Tokyo.

- Localized language domain and computer names might not be supported by Windows 95, Windows 98, Windows NT 3.51, and previous DNS servers because those systems do not support UTF-8.

For more information about Active Directory, see "Connecting Clients to Windows Networks" in this book. For more information about authentication, see "Logon and Authentication" in this book.

Using Office XP and Windows XP Professional Together

Like Windows XP Professional, the English (U.S.) version of Office XP is built on an international core, meaning that it combines support for different language versions into a single product that you can run worldwide. Also like Windows XP Professional, Office XP is available in the International English and other localized language versions, and with the Multilingual User Interface Pack.

When you install Office XP on a computer running an International English or localized language version of Windows XP Professional, Office XP detects and uses the same default input language that the Windows XP Professional operating system uses. Office XP also enables support for scripts created on the Windows XP Professional operating system configuration.

Localized Versions of Office XP

Licensing localized versions of Microsoft® Office, such as Microsoft® Office XP Spanish Edition, is the best option if you need completely localized functionality and the additional content, such as templates and wizards in Word, that comes with some fully localized versions. Each localized version includes at least two sets of appropriate proofreading tools for the languages you are likely to use most (for example, the Norwegian version includes Norwegian, German, and English proofreading tools). To expand that support to more than 30 languages, you can install the Microsoft® Office XP Proofing Tools CD together with any localized version.

Organizations that work in very few languages, or that have completely decentralized IT departments that work with only the local languages, might choose to use the localized versions of Office XP.

Office XP Multilingual User Interface Pack

The Microsoft® Office XP Multilingual User Interface Pack adds key multilingual capabilities to those already built into Office by providing localized text for the user interface, online Help, wizards, and templates for Office programs.

If your company uses many languages, deploys Office XP worldwide from a central IT group, or needs to support workstations shared by many different language speakers, use the Office XP Multilingual User Interface Pack. Windows 2000 Professional and Windows XP Professional are the only operating systems that support all of the Office XP Multilingual User Interface Pack features.

When you install the Office XP Multilingual User Interface Pack on a computer running the Windows XP Professional MUI Pack, Office XP detects the default user interface language of the Windows XP Professional MUI Pack and sets that as the default for all Office programs. For example, if you install the Office XP Multilingual User Interface Pack on a computer running the Windows XP Professional MUI Pack, and the default user interface language of that computer is set to Spanish, Office XP will also use Spanish as the default user interface language for Office XP applications.

Troubleshooting Multilingual Issues

Organizations that support multilingual desktops face unique support issues. Typical problems include characters or fonts that do not display properly, applications that use the wrong currencies or sorting orders, and compatibility problems with line-of-business and third party applications and drivers. This section summarizes how to solve the most common problems that your Help desk might encounter following a multilingual deployment of Windows XP Professional.

Tools for Troubleshooting Multilingual Issues

The updated Multilingual Document Consultant in Windows XP Professional Help and Support Center is your first resource for diagnosing and resolving most common problems involving inputting or viewing documents written in multiple languages.

To start the Multilingual Document Consultant

1. In **Help and Support Center**, in the **Search** box, type **Multilingual Document Consultant**.

2. In the **Search Results** list, click **Multilingual Document Consultant**.

Problems Inputting or Displaying Multiple Languages

The following are possible solutions for some of the most common problems that users might encounter when inputting or viewing characters from multiple languages.

Characters in Complex Script, Right-to-Left, or East Asian Languages Do Not Display Correctly

If you know that the languages displayed incorrectly are part of the Complex Script and Right-to-Left Collection or the East Asian Language Collection, support for those languages probably has not been installed. Only a user logged on as an Administrator can install this support. Users might require the Microsoft® Windows® XP Professional operating system CD or access to a network resource to complete this procedure.

To install the Complex Script and Right-to-Left Collection or East Asian Language Collection

1. In **Control Panel**, click **Regional and Language Options**.

2. Click the Languages tab, and then under **Supplemental language support,** select the check boxes for the language collections that you want to install.

If you install both the Complex Script and Right-to-Left Language Collection and the East Asian Language Collection, but the document still does not display those characters correctly, verify that the font being displayed supports multiple character sets. If it does not, change the font to Tahoma or Microsoft Sans Serif.

Characters From Another Language Appear as Question Marks, Black Boxes, or Lines

Some applications might not support multiple languages, or the application might have been developed using a different language version of Windows XP Professional. Try entering characters using another program, such as WordPad, that you know contains multilingual support.

If you know that the application was developed under another language version operating system, or if you are using a 16-bit DOS character-based program, close the application, change the default input language as appropriate, and then restart the application.

To change the default input language

1. In **Control Panel**, click **Regional and Language Options**.

2. Click the **Languages** tab, and then under **Text services and input languages**, click **Details**.

3. Under **Default input language**, click the input language that you want to use.

If you suspect that the application was not developed using Unicode, you might need to change the language for non-Unicode programs.

To change the language for non-Unicode programs

1. In **Control Panel**, click **Regional and Language Options**.

2. Click the **Advanced** tab, and then under **Language for non-Unicode programs**, select the language for which the application was developed.

Finally, if none of the above solutions solve the problem, verify that the font being displayed supports multiple character sets. If it does not, change the font to Tahoma or Microsoft Sans Serif.

Characters Typed at the Command Prompt Are Not Correct

The default input language on the computer might require that you use a TrueType font, such as Tahoma, when typing at the command prompt. If you change to a TrueType font and continue to experience problems, check the mapping of your keyboard layout. Some keyboard layouts have MS-DOS keyboard mapping that differs from the normal mapping of characters.

To select a TrueType font to use at the command prompt

1. Open a command prompt window, and then on the **System Menu**, click **Properties**.

2. Click the **Font** tab, and then in the **Font** box, click a TrueType font, such as Lucida Console.

3. In the **Apply Properties to Shortcut** dialog box, do one of the following:

   ■ To use the TrueType font for this session only, click **Apply properties to current window only**.

   ■ To use the TrueType font as the default for all command prompt windows, click **Modify shortcut that started this window**.

Numbers, Currencies, Dates, or Sorting Orders Are Incorrect

Verify that you are using the correct standards and formats settings for your locale, or customize the settings to your preferences.

To change number, currency, time, date, and sort-order settings

1. In **Control Panel**, click **Regional and Language Options**.

2. Click the **Regional Options** tab, and then under **Standards and Formats**, click the country/region whose standards and formats you want to use. If you want to customize individual settings, such as how dates are displayed or numbers are sorted, click **Customize**, and then click the appropriate tabs and options.

Verifying Application Compatibility

If you have a language or regional problem with an application, the language emulation capabilities of Windows XP Professional make it easy for your IT department to verify and test an application's multilingual compatibility issues. You can test an application developed on any other language version of Windows by setting the test computer's language for non-Unicode programs to that of the application.

When testing for application compatibility, be sure to do the following:

- Anywhere that an application accepts user input, verify that any mixture of scripts works and that automated test cases are passing in randomly generated Unicode strings, not just as characters from the ANSI character set.

- For the Windows XP Professional MUI Pack, change the user interface language for one user and run an application. Check to see whether the user interface language of the application changes to match the new setting.

Some common problems you might encounter with applications include:

- **Square boxes or dots displayed instead of characters.** This indicates that the default font does not contain glyphs for the characters being displayed. The solution is to change the font to the appropriate language.

- **Question marks displayed instead of characters.** This indicates that a conversion from Unicode to ANSI was for a Unicode character that does not exist in the ANSI code page. The question mark is the default character returned instead. The solution is to change the language for non-Unicode programs to the native language.

- **Formats and sorting orders are incorrect for the locale.** This indicates that the default standards and formats settings for currency and date formats and for sorting orders might not be set to the correct language.
  For more information about resolving these problems, see "Problems Inputting or Displaying Multiple Languages" earlier in this chapter.

Additional Resources

These resources contain additional information related to this chapter.

Related Information

- "Supporting Mobile Users" in this book for more information about supporting mobile users.

- "Configuring Remote Desktop" in this book for more information about configuring remote desktops.

- "Accessibility for People with Disabilities" in this book for more information about alternative input devices and accessibility options.

- The Locales and Language link on the Web Resources page at http://www.microsoft.com/windows/reskits/webresources for a list of locale IDs for use in unattended installations.

- The Configuring and Using International Support of the MultiLanguage Version of Windows Operating Systems link on the Web Resources page at http://www.microsoft.com/windows/reskits/webresources.

- The Ask Dr. International link on the Web Resources page at http://www.microsoft.com/windows/reskits/webresources for more information about developing applications for multilingual or international use.

- The Hardware Compatibility List link on the Web Resources page at http://www.microsoft.com/windows/reskits/webresources for more information about third-party software applications that are certified as compatible with Windows XP Professional.

- The Microsoft OEM Code Reference link on the Web Resources page at http://www.microsoft.com/windows/reskist/webresources for a complete list of code pages and their associated code points

- The Locales and Language link on the Web Resources page at http://www.microsoft.com/windows/reskits/webresources for a complete list of the localized language versions of Windows XP Professional.

- The Global Software Development List of Locale IDs and Language Groups link on the Web Resources page at http://www.microsoft.com/windows/reskits/webresources for tables listing Windows XP Professional language collections and locales.

- The International Telecommunication Union link on the Web Resources page at http://www.microsoft.com/windows/reskits/webresources for a complete list of country and region codes to use for telephony.

- The Software Development Kit (SDK) information in the MSDN Library link on the Web Resources page at http://www.microsoft.com/windows/reskits/webresources for more information about Windows Installer packages and parameters for using the **msiexec.exe** command.

- The Globalization: Step-by-Step link on the Web Resources page at http://www.microsoft.com/windows/reskits/webresources for information about how and what it means to globalize an application.

- The Microsoft Global Software Development link on the Web Resources page at http://www.microsoft.com/windows/reskits/webresources for more information about creating world-ready software.

- "Unicode Control Characters" in Windows XP Professional Help and Support Center.

Chapter 4

Supporting Installations

In addition to running Setup, you might need additional tools to aid your Microsoft® Windows® XP Professional deployment. The following discussion describes the setup process, optional Windows Support Tools, service pack and hotfix deployment, and troubleshooting tips for issues that you might encounter during setup.

Related Information

- For more information about troubleshooting Windows XP Professional, see "Troubleshooting Concepts and Strategies" in this book.

- For more information about automating and customizing Windows XP Professional installations, see "Automating and Customizing Installations" in this book.

- For more information about Plug and Play and ACPI, see "Managing Devices" in this book.

The Setup Process

Windows XP Professional includes Dynamic Update and Uninstall, two new Setup features. The following discussion describes these features and what occurs during a new installation before and after each restart. During a non-scripted installation, Setup restarts your computer three times.

New Setup Features

Windows XP Professional includes new features that enhance the setup process.

Dynamic Update

Using Dynamic Update, a process that occurs during setup, the computer connects to the Microsoft® Windows Update Web site and searches for the following:

- Updated Windows XP Professional installation files
- Device driver files not included or updated on the Windows XP Professional operating system CD

Dynamic Update downloads the installation and device driver files to your computer and incorporates them into the setup process. To initiate Dynamic Update, your computer must have the following:

- Internet connection capability
- Microsoft® Internet Explorer 4.0 or later installed

For more information about Dynamic Update, see "Automating and Customizing Installations" in this book.

Note If you install Windows XP Professional by using the CD-ROM boot method, Dynamic Update does not start.

Uninstall

If your hardware or software does not function as expected after installing Windows XP Professional, you can use Uninstall to restore your computer to its previous operating system with little interruption. Uninstall removes all setup files from your computer and restores your previous operating system. Uninstall is available if you upgrade to Windows XP Professional from any of the following operating systems:

- Microsoft® Windows® 98
- Microsoft® Windows® 98, Second Edition (SE)
- Microsoft® Windows® Millennium Edition (Me)

The following are factors to consider when using the Uninstall feature:

■ Setup requires about 300 megabytes (MB) of additional space, in order to save the information it needs to be able to uninstall. Setup notifies you if your disk space is insufficient for saving the backup information.

■ Thirty days after you complete Setup, the Disk Cleanup Wizard asks whether you want to remove the Uninstall file from your computer.

■ Before removing Windows XP Professional from your computer, back up all of your important data. For information about using Backup (NTBackup.exe), see "Backup and Restore" in this book.

■ If you install an application on your computer after you have upgraded to Windows XP Professional and then decide to remove Windows XP Professional from your computer, you must reinstall the application after restoring the previous operating system.

Warning   If you convert a volume to NTFS or to dynamic disk, or if you create or delete any volume, you can no longer use the uninstall feature.

Running Setup

During Windows XP Professional setup, the following processes occur before and after each of three restarts.

Before the first restart   As it begins the installation, Setup does the following:

■ Collects information about your computer, such as whether you want to accept your license agreement or enter your product key. You can also specify installation options, including whether you want to perform an upgrade or a clean installation.

■ Runs Dynamic Update.

■ Checks disk space and builds a list of backup files to support Uninstall.

To cancel Setup at this point, click **Cancel** when prompted or close the **Setup** dialog box. Your computer's previous operating system and settings return immediately.

After the first restart   Setup runs in text mode, and does the following:

■ Provides an option to repair your existing installation.

■ Provides an option to specify a partition in which to install Windows XP Professional. Setup can also format partitions.

■ Copies files to the installation folder on your hard disk.

To cancel Setup and uninstall Windows XP Professional at this point, restart your computer, and then choose **Cancel Windows XP Professional Setup** instead of **Microsoft® Windows XP Professional Setup** on the menu that appears after your computer restarts.

Your computer's previous operating system and settings are restored.

After the second restart   Setup runs in graphical user interface (GUI) mode, and does the following:

- Installs devices.

- Sets system locale and customizes your keyboard.

- Prompts you to specify your name, organization, computer name, and administrator password.

- Installs networking components, including Client for Microsoft Networks, File and Print Sharing for Microsoft Networks, and the TCP/IP protocol with automatic addressing. Setup also determines whether your computer uses automatic IP addressing or a DHCP server to connect to the Internet, and then installs the appropriate components.

- Prompts you to join a workgroup or domain.

- Performs the basic operating system configuration.

- Installs Start menu items.

- Updates the backup file list and prepares the restore environment to support Uninstall.

- Registers components, and then saves and backs up the registry.

- Removes temporary files used during setup.

To cancel Setup and uninstall Windows XP Professional at this point, choose **Cancel Windows XP Professional Setup** instead of **Microsoft Windows XP Professional Setup** on the menu that appears after your computer restarts.

Your computer's previous operating system and settings are restored.

After the third restart   Setup has completed the installation process, and you can log on and start using Windows XP Professional. To remove Windows XP Professional after the setup process is complete, in **Control Panel**, double-click **Add or Remove Programs**, and then select **Uninstall Windows XP Professional**. Your computer's previous operating system and settings are restored.

> **Warning**   If you convert a volume to NTFS or to a dynamic disk or if you create or delete any volume, you can no longer use the uninstall feature.

Support Tools

Windows Support Tools help you deploy Windows XP Professional, manage your network, and troubleshoot problems. You can find Windows Support Tools in the \Support\Tools folder on your operating system CD. The folder also includes two cabinet files, Deploy.cab and Support.cab, which contain numerous tools in compressed form. For information about installing Support Tools, including how to extract tools within Deploy.cab and Support. cab, see Readme.htm in the \Support\Tools folder.

Table 4-1 lists some of the key deployment tools that are in the \Support\Tools folder.

Table 4-1   Support Tools That Aid in Deployment

Name	File Name	Description
Application Compatibility Program	Apcompat.exe	The Application Compatibility Program is designed to overcome the most common causes of application incompatibility with Windows XP Professional. The Application Compatibility Program does the following: ■ Fixes conflicts between operating system versions and applications ■ Finds memory management conflicts. ■ Checks for Temp folder path incompatibility. ■ Detects whether disk space is adequate. ■ Stores application compatibility settings.
Setup Manager	Setupmgr.exe	A wizard-based tool that helps you create unattended answer files. Setup Manager also creates a network distribution share, required for unattended and Sysprep deployments.
System Preparation Tool (Sysprep) 2.0	Sysprep.exe	A utility that prepares a system on a hard disk for duplication (cloning) and customization. It does not actually perform the duplication of the reference image onto destination computers (third-party utilities are required for this purpose), but ensures that the security identifiers (SIDs) are unique for each installation. In addition, Sysprep can help you customize duplicated images by adding computer-specific information such as user name, computer name, time zone, and domain membership.

Table 4-1   Support Tools That Aid in Deployment

Name	File Name	Description
Deploy.chm	Deploy.chm	A Help file that contains information about using Setup Manager, as well as a complete reference to section headers and keys that can be used in an answer file. An answer file answers the questions asked during setup. Deploy.chm replaces Unattend.doc, the answer file reference for previous Microsoft® Windows® NT–based operating systems. For more information about using answer files and automated installations, see "Automating and Customizing Installations" in this book.

Installing Service Packs and Hotfixes

A *service pack* is a collection of updates pertaining to an operating system. These updates might address operating system reliability, application compatibility, setup, and security issues.

A *hotfix* is a collection of one or more files that can be applied to the operating system to correct a problem.

Typically, Microsoft packages service packs and hotfixes with a setup program that installs updates to your computer. The service pack or hotfix setup program copies files and updates settings automatically if your operating system configuration meets requirements specific to the service pack or hotfix. Typically, you restart your computer after installing a service pack or hotfix before the updates to your computer take effect.

> **Warning**   Apply a hotfix only if directed to do so by a Microsoft Knowlege Base article that describes your problem exactly or under the direction of your support representative. For information about the Microsoft Knowledge base, see the Microsoft Knowledge Base link on the Web Resources page at http://www.microsoft.com/windows/reskits/webresources.

Service Pack and Hotfix Setup Programs

Check the documentation that comes with your service pack or hotfix for the specific name of the setup program. You can usually run service pack or hotfix setup programs from the command prompt. In addition, you can customize your installation by using parameters.

Service Pack Setup Program Naming Convention

In this chapter, *ServicePack.exe* refers to generic service pack setup programs. Table 4.2 lists parameters used for customizing Microsoft® Windows® 2000 Service Pack 1 and Windows 2000 Service Pack 2 installations. Before using these parameters, check your service pack documentation for changes.

Table 4-2   Command-Line Parameters for Service Pack Setup Programs

Command-Line Parameter	Description
`-u`	Run an unattended installation of the service pack.
`-f`	Force other applications to close at shutdown. After installing the service pack files and before restarting the computer, this parameter closes all applications.
`-n`	Do not back up files for Uninstall. In a typical service pack installation, files necessary for uninstalling the service pack are saved to your hard drive. If you use this parameter, you cannot uninstall the service pack.
`-o`	Overwrite OEM files without prompting.
`-z`	Do not restart the computer when the installation completes.
`-q`	Quiet mode—no user interaction required.
`-s:[x \distribution folder name]`	Integrated installation mode—maps to a distribution server location, where x is the letter assigned to the hard drive where your distribution share resides.

If you use the **-q** or **-u** parameter to run *ServicePack.exe* in quiet or unattended mode and want to update OEM-supplied files, you must also use the **-o** parameter. If you do not use the **-o** parameter, files such as the hardware abstraction layer (HAL) and disk miniport drivers are not updated.

Windows Hotfix Setup Program Naming Convention

For the remainder of this chapter, *Hotfix.exe* generically refers to the hotfix setup program, and Q######_XXX_YYY_ZZZ_LL.exe (described below) is used for specific examples. If you plan to install a hotfix, check its documentation for any changes to this naming convention. Typically, Windows hotfix setup programs follow this naming convention:

Q######_XXX_YYY_ZZZ_LL.exe

In the preceding naming convention, the variables have the following meanings:

- Q###### is the Microsoft® Knowledge Base article number (for example, Q123456)

- *XXX* is the platform or operating system

- *YYY* is the service pack level

- *ZZZ* is the hardware platform
- *LL* is the language

To find an article in the Microsoft Knowledge Base, click the Microsoft Knowledge Base link on the Web Resources page at http://www.microsoft.com/windows /reskits/webresources.

Table 4.3 lists parameters that you can use with *Hotfix.exe* to customize your hotfix installation. Before using these parameters, check your hotfix documentation for changes.

Table 4-3   Command-Line Parameters for Hotfix Setup Programs

Command-Line Parameter	Description
-y	Uninstall the hotfix (can be used with -m or -q).
-f	Force other applications to close at shutdown. After installing the hotfix files and before restarting the computer, this parameter closes all applications.
-n	Do not back up files for Uninstall. In a typical hotfix installation, files necessary for uninstalling the hotfix are saved to your hard drive. If you use this parameter, you cannot uninstall the hotfix.
-z	Do not restart the computer when the installation completes
-q	Quiet mode—no user interaction required
-m	Unattended mode. Use this parameter to run an unattended installation of the hotfix.
-l	List installed hotfixes. This is useful to check for compatibility against the requirements of your hotfix.

If your service pack version is newer than the hotfixes, the installation stops and silently exits if you included the **-m** or **-q** parameters. If you did not use these parameters, an error message appears, stating that the version is incorrect. In addition, if the language version of the hotfixes does not match the operating system's language, Setup is always interrupted. If no version conflict exists, Setup installs the hotfixes without user intervention.

Planning the Deployment

To successfully deploy your service pack, prepare for the deployment. Assess the updates and enhancements contained in your service pack and determine how they will affect your organization. Also, you might wish to perform other steps when planning the deployment, including these important tasks:

- Choose an installation method.
- Choose deployment tools and files.

- Check space requirements.

- Test the deployment in your environment.

Choosing an Installation Method   Depending on a number of factors, including the homogeneity of operating systems your computers are running and your company's security policies, you can choose one of the following methods to install your service pack:

- The *update installation* is the standard method used to install Windows NT–based service packs. Using this method, you install your service pack on your existing operating system.

- The *integrated installation* was introduced with Windows 2000 Service Pack 1. Using this method, you simultaneously install the operating system and your service pack.

- The *combination installation* was also introduced in Windows 2000 Service Pack 1. Using this method, you install your service pack with a variety of other components or third party applications by using a combination of update and integrated installation processes.

For more information about applying these installations and scenarios that might relate to your deployment, see "Update Installation," " Integrated Installation," and " Combination Installation" later in this chapter.

Choosing Deployment Tools and Files   After you select your installation method and one of the associated scenarios for your installation, review the scenario to determine whether you might need one or more of the following deployment tools and files:

Systems Management Server   Microsoft® Systems Management Server (SMS provides a variety of tools to help you deploy service packs. Using the SMS version 2.0 software distribution feature, you can simultaneously upgrade all of the SMS client computers in your site with your service pack. You can allow your users to run the service pack installation whenever they like, or you can schedule the service pack installation to run at a specific time. You can also schedule it to run on SMS client computers at a time when no users are logged on to the network.

> **Note**   SMS provides tools for upgrading your current computers, but not for the installation of new computers that do not have an operating system already installed.

Setup Manager   Setup Manager (Setupmgr.exe) is a wizard-based tool that can help you create or update the Unattend.txt answer file, the Cmdlines.txt file, and the network distribution share (a requirement if you want to include drivers or files from the network in your service pack installation). Setup Manager is available in the Deploy.cab file in the \Support\Tools folder on your Windows XP Professional operating system CD. For more information about Setup Manager, see "Support Tools" earlier in this chapter.

The Unattend.txt answer file identifies how Windows XP Professional Setup interacts with the distribution folders and files you create and it supplies information about your pre-installation requirements. The answer file also supplies Setup with all of the information that the end user is prompted to provide during a typical Windows XP Professional installation. For example, Unattend.txt contains a "FullName" entry in the [UserData] section, which prompts the user to provide a full name. You can create or modify the Unattend.txt answer file by using a text editor or Setup Manager. For a complete list of section headers and keys that you can use in your answer file, see Deploy.chm in the \Support\Tools folder on your Windows XP Professional operating system CD.

The Cmdlines.txt file contains a list of the commands that run during Windows XP Professional GUI–mode setup. For example, these commands can run an application setup command or another executable file. You can create the Cmdlines.txt file by using a text editor or Setup Manager.

Additional Windows XP Professional deployment and pre-installation tools   For more information about tools that to use when deploying a service pack or hotfix, see "Support Tools" earlier in this chapter.

Checking Space Requirements   A service pack requires a certain amount of space on your computer's hard drive for installation, storage, and to uninstall. Check your service pack documentation for space requirements, and then remember to reserve space for the Uninstall file if you wish to remove the service pack later.

Testing the Deployment in Your Environment   Testing a service pack in your environment can include the following steps:

1. Use a cross-section of the types of computers deployed in your environment that will receive the service pack. Test computers that have a typical sample of software and hardware devices used in your organization.

2. Install your service pack on each of these computers in the same way that you expect to install it in your environment:

   ■ Update existing Windows XP Professional–based computers to the service pack.

- Upgrade existing computers that are running Windows 98, Windows 98 Second Edition (SE), Windows Millennium Edition (Me), Microsoft® Windows® NT® Workstation 4.0, and Microsoft® Windows® 2000 Professional—to Windows XP Professional integrated with the service pack.

- Install Windows XP Professional integrated with the service pack on computers with no existing operating system (that is, a clean installation).

3. Verify that the applications and hardware continue to work as expected for the various scenarios.

Update Installation

During an update installation, a service pack is applied to a computer that is already running Windows XP Professional. The *ServicePack.exe* program automatically installs the updated system files and makes the necessary registry changes. After the computer restarts, the installation is completed and the operating system is running with an updated file set.

A number of methods for creating the update installation are supported since the release of Windows 2000 Service Pack 1. These include manually running the *ServicePack.exe* program or running a script that starts the *ServicePack.exe* program. You can use a combination of installation parameters whether you run *ServicePack.exe* manually or by using a script. Or you can use SMS to install a service pack. Also supported are a variety of distribution media, including CD-ROM, network distribution share, Web download, and Microsoft® Windows Installer. Table 4-4 lists the advantages and disadvantages of using *ServicePack.exe* versus using SMS.

Table 4-4 Comparison of Methods for Creating an Update Installation

Method	Advantages	Disadvantages
ServicePack.exe	Parameters are available to customize your installation.	You cannot set the installation to start and end at a specific time.
	Can be scripted to automate the installation.	
	You do not need to purchase additional software to install the service pack on your computers.	
SMS	Installation is automated.	You must purchase SMS separately.
	Can be scheduled to start and stop the installation automatically (for example, at night when employees do not need their computers).	

For more information about using Systems Management Server, see your SMS product documentation.

Creating an Update Installation

The update installation scenarios described in this section include procedures you can use to meet your installation requirements. These scenarios focus on the network distribution share, the distribution media most commonly used by IT professionals. For the procedures in the following scenarios, drive E is a mapped network share or a local hard disk and drive D is the CD-ROM drive.

- Scenario 1: Installing a service pack manually or by using a script

- Scenario 2: Installing a service pack by using SMS

- Scenario 3: Installing a hotfix

Scenario 1: Installing a Service Pack Manually or by Using a Script   You can use a script or manually install a service pack on Windows XP Professional–based computers from a network distribution share.

To install a service pack manually

1. Connect to the network or computer on which you want to create the distribution folder.

2. On the network distribution share, create a distribution folder for the service pack. For example, to create a distribution folder named SP, type **mkdir E:\SP**.

3. Copy the contents of your service pack onto the network distribution share.
   – or–
   To install the service pack from the network distribution share, run *ServicePack.exe*.
   For example, to install the service pack from a distribution folder named SP, type **E:\SP\ServicePack.exe**.

> **Note**   When running *ServicePack.exe* by using a script or batch file, include the following in your script: ***ServicePack.exe* -u -q**. This installs the service pack in unattended mode, with no user interaction. For more information about the parameters you can use with *ServicePack.exe,* see Table 4-2 earlier in this chapter.

Scenario 2: Installing the Service Pack by Using SMS   You can install a service pack on Windows XP Professional–based SMS client computers from a network distribution share by using SMS.

> **Warning**   SMS 2.0 Service Pack 2 is required to support Windows XP Professional service pack installations.

To use SMS to install a service pack

1. Create the SMS package by importing the package definition file for your service pack. In the package, provide the path to the service pack source files.

2. Distribute the SMS package to the distribution points.

3. Create the advertisement to notify SMS clients about the service pack.

To use SMS for an update installation, you must have an understanding of SMS as well as a working knowledge of software distribution. Also, your SMS infrastructure must be in place before you deploy the service pack. For more information about SMS, see your SMS product documentation.

Creating the SMS package   When using SMS to distribute software, first create the SMS package, which contains the files and instructions that direct the software distribution process. When you create the SMS package, you specify the location of the package source files (where SMS obtains the files) and the package definition file (.pdf) for distributing the service pack.

A package definition file is a specially formatted file that contains all of the information necessary to create the SMS package. If you import this file, SMS immediately creates the package. After you use a package definition file to create a package, you can modify it the way you would any other SMS package.

Each predefined SMS package also contains SMS programs, which are command-line executables that run on each targeted computer to control the execution of the package. Each program is a different combination of options that you create for installing the package. For example, the package definition for the service pack includes programs that install the service pack with or without user input. These SMS programs must be compatible with the installation files for the package.

To create an SMS package

1. Connect to the network or computer on which you want to place the source files.

2. On the network or computer, create a source files directory for the service pack. For example, to create a source files directory named SP, type **mkdir E:\SP**.

3. Copy the service pack executable files to the source files directory that you created in step 2. For example, to copy the service pack executable files from a service pack CD in the CD-ROM drive (D) to the source files directory named SP, type **xcopy D:\ E:\SP /e**.

4. In the **SMS Administrator** console, select **Packages**.

5. On the **Action** menu, point to **New**, and then click **Package from Definition**.

6. On the **Welcome** page, click **Next**.

7. Click **Browse** from the package definition list, and then navigate to the folder where the package definition file for the service pack was created. When you find the package definition file, click it to import the service pack package definition file, and then click **Next**.

8. On the **Source Files** page, click **Always obtain files from a source directory**, and then click **Next**.

9. In the **Source directory** box, enter the path to the package source files (see step 3).

10. Click **Next**, and then click **Finish**.

11. Select **Programs**.

12. In the details pane, double-click the service pack program.

13. In the **Program Properties** property sheet, on the **General** tab, verify that the predefined **Command line** is the correct setup command for your needs.

14. Click the **Requirements**, **Environment**, and **Advanced** tabs to check and modify the options that control the execution of your program. For more information about the options on these tabs, see your SMS product documentation.

15. Click **OK**.

> **Warning**   If you download your service pack from the Microsoft Windows Service Pack Web site, you must extract the compressed program file before you can copy it to the source files directory. Check the documentation included with your service pack for information about extracting the compressed program files.

Distributing the SMS Package to the Distribution Points   After you create the SMS package for the service pack, you can distribute the package to your distribution points. Distribution points are shares on site systems where SMS copies the package source files for access by the client computers.

To distribute an SMS package to distribution points

1. In the **SMS Administrator** console, select **Packages**, select the SMS package that you created for the service pack, and then select **Distribution Points**.

2. On the **Action** menu, point to **New**, and then click **Distribution Points**.

3. In the **New Distribution Points** wizard, click **Next**, and then select the distribution points you want to use.

   All the distribution points for all sites are listed, so you can select all the distribution points now.

4. Click Finish.

   The package is immediately distributed to the selected distribution points.

> **Note**   Your distribution points must have sufficient disk space for the SMS package. For instructions about how to check the disk space for distribution points from the SMS Administrator console, see your SMS product documentation.

Creating the SMS advertisement   After you distribute the SMS package to the distribution points, you can create the advertisement that offers the package to the SMS clients.

To create an advertisement

1. Create a collection of SMS clients to receive the installation program. You can base the collection on a query or direct membership rules. For more information about creating a collection, see your SMS product documentation.

2. Right-click the collection that will receive the program, and then click **All Tasks/Distribute Software**.

3. In the Distribute Software Wizard, click **Next**.

4. Click **Distribute an existing package**, click the SMS package for the service pack, and then click **Next**.

5. In the Distribution Points dialog box, make sure the desired distribution points are selected, and then click **Next**.

6. In the **Advertise a Program** dialog box, click **Yes. Advertise a program**, click the program you want to advertise, and then click **Next**.

7. In the **Advertisement Target** dialog box, confirm that the collection of clients selected in step 2 is listed, and then click **Next**. If this collection is not listed, click **Browse** to find the collection you want.

8. In the **Advertisement Name** dialog box, fill in the advertisement name if appropriate, and then click **Next**.

9. Specify any subgroups that should also receive this advertisement, and then click **Next**.

10. Confirm or change the time the advertisement is offered and specify whether the advertisement should expire and when.

11. On the **Assign Program** page, click **Yes** to assign the program.

12. Click **Next**, and then click **Finish**.

SMS clients refresh the list of advertised programs on a configurable polling interval, set to 60 minutes by default. After the service pack advertisement is received on a client, it is either displayed for selection by users in the Advertised Program Wizard in Control Panel, or, if assigned (mandatory), runs according to the specified schedule.

Scenario 3: Installing a Hotfix   You can install a hotfix on Windows 2000–based and Windows XP Professional–based computers from a network distribution share.

Running a Hotfix setup program   The following procedure describes how to install a hotfix by running the Q######_XXX_YYY_ZZZ_LL.exe program.

To install a hotfix

1. Connect to the network or computer on which you want to create the distribution folder.

2. On the network distribution share, create a distribution folder for the hotfix files. For example, to create a distribution folder named Hotfix, type:

   `mkdir E:\Hotfix`

3. Copy the hotfix executable file to the distribution folder that you created in step 2. For example, to copy the hotfix executable file to the distribution folder named Hotfix, type:

   `xcopy C:\Q######_XXX_YYY_ZZZ_LL.exe E:\Hotfix`

4. To install the hotfix from the network distribution share, run the Q######_XXX_YYY_ZZ.exe program. For example, to install the hotfix from the distribution folder named Hotfix, type:

   `E:\Hotfix\Q######_XXX_YYY_ZZZ_LL.exe`

Integrated Installation

You can create an integrated installation of the Windows XP Professional operating system and your service pack on a network distribution share. When you run the

ServicePack.exe program in integrated mode, it applies the service pack directly to the Windows XP Professional installation files. Therefore, you do not need to perform separate installations of the operating system and your service pack.

> **Warning**   You cannot uninstall a service pack that you install in integrated mode.

After the *ServicePack.exe* program creates the integrated installation, you can run Windows XP Professional Setup (Winnt32.exe) to install the operating system integrated with the service pack.

Creating an Integrated Installation

The following integrated installation scenarios focus on the network distribution share, the distribution media most commonly used by IT professionals. Depending on your installation requirements, choose from two integrated installation scenarios, which are detailed in the following sections. For the procedures in the following scenarios, drive E is a mapped network share or a local hard disk and drive D is the CD-ROM drive.

- Scenario 1: Installing Windows XP Professional Integrated with the service pack from a network distribution share.

- Scenario 2: Installing Windows XP Professional Integrated with the service pack by using Remote Installation Services (RIS).

Scenario 1: Installing Windows XP Professional Integrated with a Service Pack

You can create an integrated installation of the Windows XP Professional operating system and a service pack on a network distribution share. During an integrated installation, the service pack and Windows XP Professional Setup are installed at the same time.

To create an integrated installation of Windows XP Professional and your service pack

1. Connect to the network or computer on which you want to create the distribution folder.

2. On the network distribution share, create a distribution folder for the Windows XP Professional installation files. For example, to create a distribution folder named WinXP\i386 to mirror the location of the installation files on the operating system CD, type:

```
mkdir E:\WinXP\i386
```

3. Insert your Windows XP Professional operating system CD into the CD-ROM drive, and then copy the contents of the \i386 folder on the CD to the distribution folder that you created in step 2. For example, to copy the \i386 folder from the Windows XP Professional operating system CD to the distribution folder named WinXP, type:

```
xcopy D:\i386 E:\WinXP\i386 /e
```

4. From your service pack CD, run the *ServicePack.exe* program in integrated mode by using *ServicePack.exe* **-s**. For example, to apply the service pack located in the CD-ROM drive to the Windows XP Professional installation files located in the distribution folder named WinXP\i386, type:

```
D:\i386\ServicePack.exe -s:E:\WinXP\i386
```

5. Customize Windows XP Professional Setup, as needed.

After *ServicePack.exe* creates the integrated installation, you can deploy Windows XP Professional to your users' computers from the network distribution share in attended or unattended mode. During the integrated installation process, Windows XP Professional Setup (Winnt32.exe) installs the integrated operating system with the service pack already applied.

When you run the *ServicePack.exe* program in integrated mode (*ServicePack.exe* **-s**:), a .log file is created in the *systemroot* folder on the computer that is running the *ServicePack.exe* program. If you plan to update more than one version of Windows XP Professional on this computer, you should rename the Svcpack.log file after you update each version. This ensures that you do not overwrite the current log file when you update additional versions of Windows XP Professional.

Scenario 2: Using RIS to Install Windows XP Professional Integrated with a Service Pack   This scenario describes your options using Remote Installation Services (RIS) to install Windows XP Professional integrated with your service pack.

Creating a RIS image   RIS supports two types of operating system images:

■ Remote Installation Setup (RISetup) images

■ Remote Installation Preparation (RIPrep) images

Installing Windows XP Professional from a RISetup image is similar to installing directly from the Windows XP Professional operating system CD, but in this case, the source files reside on the RIS server. You use RISetup.exe to create and install from the image.

A RIPrep image is an installation of Windows XP Professional that contains specific configuration settings made by the administrator. Typically, it also contains locally installed applications. In this scenario, you install your service pack to integrate it into the Windows XP Professional installation. You use RIPrep.exe to replicate the local (RIPrep) image to a RIS server, and then restore that image to a new computer on the network. RIPrep.exe can replicate single disk partitions only, and requires that your image reside on drive C.

For more information about RIS, including creating and installing RISetup and RIPrep images, see "Automating and Customizing Installations" in this book.

Combination Installation

The combination installation uses both update and integrated installation processes to install your service pack with a variety of other components, such as the operating system, hotfixes, or additional Microsoft and third-party software that your installation might include.

Creating a Combination Installation

You can install Windows XP Professional and hotfixes, as well as additional applications, in unattended mode.

Scenario: Installing Windows XP Professional and Hotfixes in Unattended Mode   Follow these steps to create a combination installation of the Windows XP Professional operating system and hotfixes on a network distribution share. You do not need to perform separate installations of the Windows XP Professional operating system or hotfixes. This process can only be accomplished in unattended mode.

Step 1: Prepare for the installation   Before you run Setup to install the Windows XP Professional operating system and hotfixes, you must change the Hotfix file names (from Q######_XXX_YYY_ZZZ_LL to Q######), because Windows XP Professional Setup requires the 8.3 naming convention for all files and folders in the distribution folder.

Step 2: Create a distribution folder   Follow these steps to create the distribution folder:

1. Connect to the network or computer on which you want to create the distribution folder.

2. On the network distribution share, create an \i386 distribution folder. For example, to create an \i386 distribution folder, type:

    ```
    mkdir E:\i386
    ```

3. Within the \i386 folder created in step 2, create an \$OEM$ subfolder to contain any additional files, drivers, and folders you need for your installation. For example, to create an \$OEM$ subfolder within the \i386 folder, type:

    ```
    mkdir E:\i386\$OEM$
    ```

4. To install additional files (for example, device driver, application, or component files) on users' computers, within the \OEM subfolder created in step 3,

create a \$1 subfolder. For example, to create an \$1 subfolder within the \$OEM$ subfolder, type:

```
mkdir E:\i386\$OEM$\$1
```

The \$1 subfolder maps to the Windows XP Professional installation drive; for example drive C.

> **Note** The OEM and distribution folders are deleted from users' computers after Windows XP Professional Setup is completed.

Step 3: Create and customize the Unattend.txt answer file Using Setup Manager or Notepad.exe, create an Unattend.txt file that contains the following section header, key, and value:

```
[Unattended]
OemPreinstall = Yes
```

For information about using Setup Manager to customize an Unattend.txt answer file, see "Automating and Customizing Installations" in this book.

For a complete reference to answer file sections headers and keys, see Deploy.chm, which is in the Deploy.cab file in the \Support\Tools folder on your operating system CD.

Step 4: Customize the Cmdlines.txt file To run Windows XP Professional hot-fixes during Windows XP Professional setup, add the following section header and line to the Cmdlines.txt file for each hotfix:

```
[Commands]
"Q###### -n -q -z"
```

Q###### is the Microsoft Knowledge Base article number (for example, Q123456). For example, to install the Q123456.exe hotfix, add the following line to the [Commands] section header in the Cmdlines.txt file:

```
[Commands]
"Q123456 -n -q -z"
```

For information about creating and using a Cmdlines.txt file, see "Automating and Customizing Installations" in this book.

Step 5: Copy the files necessary for the installation to the distribution folder You must copy all of the files needed for the installation to your distribution folder. The distribution folder contains the installation and executable files for the Windows XP Professional operating system and the Windows XP Professional hotfixes, as well as any device driver and other files that you want to install.

To copy the files necessary for the installation

1. Copy the contents of \i386 and all its subdirectories on the Windows XP Professional operating system CD to the \i386 distribution folder on your network distribution share.

2. Copy the following files to the \i386\OEM subfolder on your network distribution share:

   ■ Hotfix executable file

   ■ Unattend.txt and Cmdlines.txt files
     For information about files contained in the \i386\OEM subfolder, see "Automating and Customizing Installations" in this book.

3. Copy any folders that contain additional device driver, application, or component files that you want to install on the system drive to the \i386\$OEM$\$1 subfolder on your network distribution share.

Step 6: Deploy the combination installation   You can deploy the installation of the Windows XP Professional operating system and the Windows XP Professional hotfixes to your users' computers from the network distribution share. During the installation process, Windows XP Professional Setup (Winnt32.exe in unattended mode) installs the operating system and applies the hotfixes.

To deploy the installation

1. Verify that the installation and executable files for the Windows XP Professional operating system and the Windows XP Professional hotfixes exist in your distribution folder.

2. Customize Windows XP Professional Setup as required.

3. Run Windows XP Professional Setup (Winnt32.exe) in unattended mode to install the Windows XP Professional operating system and the hotfixes from the network distribution share.

Note   You can also use Winnt.exe for unattended installations of the operating system, but Winnt.exe is a less versatile tool than Winnt32.exe You cannot use Winnt.exe to perform an operation system upgrade, and you can only use Winnt.exe from within the MS-DOS preinstallation environment.

For more information about running Winnt32.exe in unattended mode, see "Automating and Customizing Installations" in this book.

Uninstalling a Service Pack or Hotfix

Windows XP Professional service packs and hotfixes contain Uninstall, which is a feature that you can use to restore your computer to its previous state. When you run the *ServicePack.exe* program to install the service pack, a subfolder named $ntservicepackuninstall$ is created in your *systemroot* folder.

Uninstalling a Service Pack

You can uninstall the service pack by using Add or Remove Programs in Control Panel or by running the Uninstall program from the command prompt. Be aware of the following considerations when uninstalling a service pack:

- You cannot uninstall a service pack that you installed in integrated mode.

- If you used the **-n** parameter when running *ServicePack.exe*, you cannot uninstall the service pack.

- If you install any programs or services that require or have fixes contained in the service pack, uninstalling the service pack can adversely affect those programs.

- You should not uninstall the service pack if you have installed any applications since the service pack was installed.

- You should not uninstall the service pack if it contains system updates—such as file format, database format, and registry format changes—that Setup cannot uninstall.

To uninstall a service pack by using Add or Remove Programs

1. In Control Panel, double-click **Add or Remove Programs**, click *Service-Pack.exe*, and then click **Change/Remove**.

2. Follow the instructions that appear.

To uninstall a service pack from the command prompt

1. In the **Run** dialog box, type **cmd**, and then click **OK**.

2. Change the folder to C:\$NtServicePackUninstall$\spuninst\, where C: is the root of your hard drive.

3. Type **Spuninst.exe**, and then press **Enter**.

4. To close the command prompt window, type **Exit**.

Uninstalling a Hotfix

You can uninstall a hotfix by using Add or Remove Programs in Control Panel.

To uninstall a hotfix

1. In Control Panel, double-click **Add or Remove Programs**, click **Q######**, and then click **Change/Remove**.

2. Follow the instructions that appear.

> **Note**   If multiple hotfixes replace the same file and you want to success-
> fully return your system to its original state, you must remove the most
> recently installed hotfix first, and then all of the others in the reverse order
> of installation.

Troubleshooting Windows XP Professional Setup

Windows XP Professional includes Recovery Console, which you can use to resolve problems that might occur during setup. This section also includes a discussion about common setup problems.

Recovery Console

Recovery Console is a command-line tool that you can start from Setup. Using Recovery Console, you can start and stop services, format drives, read and write data on a local drive (including drives formatted to use NTFS), and perform many other administrative tasks. The Recovery Console is particularly useful if you need to repair your computer by copying a system file from a floppy disk or CD-ROM to your hard drive, or if you need to reconfigure a service that is preventing your computer from starting properly. Because Recovery Console is quite powerful, only advanced users who have a thorough knowledge of Windows XP Professional should use it. In addition, you must log on using the local Administrator account to use Recovery Console.

Recovery Console allows the local system administrator to access an NTFS volume without starting Windows XP Professional. When you are running Recovery Console, type **help** at the command prompt to get help for the available commands. For more information about installing and using Recovery Console, and other Start-up issues, see "Troubleshooting Startup" and "Tools for Troubleshooting" in this book.

Common Setup Errors

The following troubleshooting tips can help you resolve problems that might occur during setup.

Disk space errors   If you receive the error message "Not enough disk space for installation," use the Setup program to create a partition by using the existing free space on the hard disk. If you do not have enough space, you might have to delete files on the original partition to make space for the installation. You can delete and create partitions as needed to obtain a partition that has enough disk space to install Windows XP Professional.

If Windows XP Professional does not start, verify that all the installed hardware is detected. Check that all hardware is listed on the Hardware Compatibility List link on the Web Resources page at http://www.microsoft.com/windows/reskits/webresources. Only devices that are listed on the HCL have passed testing for compatibility with Windows XP Professional.

Stop messages   If you are installing Windows XP Professional and you encounter a Stop message, see the troubleshooting information for the Stop message in "Common Stop Messages for Troubleshooting" in this book. Also, check the HCL to determine whether the computer and its components are supported by Windows XP Professional. Reduce the number of hardware components by removing nonessential devices.

Setup stops during text mode   If possible, avoid legacy boot devices on ACPI systems because these settings cannot be reliably determined by the ACPI system. This can make the building of the device tree inaccurate, causing problems that are hard to track. For non-ACPI systems, verify that the **Plug and Play operating system** option is disabled in the BIOS. If it is not disabled, your operating system might read and write to the hardware registers.

Setup stops during GUI mode   If the computer stops responding during the GUI-mode phase of Setup, restart the computer and Setup will attempt to resume from where it stopped responding. You can usually isolate these failures to one of the following locations:

- **Device detection.** At the beginning of the GUI-mode phase of Setup, Plug and Play detects all the devices on the system. This involves external code called class installers. These class installers check the hardware settings on the computer to determine which devices are present.

- **OC Manager.** The Optional Component Manager (OCM or OC Manager) is a Setup component that allows the integration of external components into the setup process, such as Internet Information Service (IIS) and COM+, which have their own setup routines.

- **Computer configuration.** This is one of the last phases of Setup and involves the registration of object linking and embedding (OLE) control dynamic-link libraries (DLLs).

Disk input/output and file copy errors   If you receive disk input/output (I/O) errors or file copy errors during setup, your hard disk might be defective or contain defective sectors. For more information about troubleshooting and repairing your hard disk and defective sectors, see "Troubleshooting Disks and File Systems" and "Disk Management" in this book.

File copy errors   If you receive file copy errors during setup, you might need to replace RAM, or you might have defective media. For more information about troubleshooting RAM and bad media, see "Common Stop Messages for Troubleshooting" in this book.

More troubleshooting tips   For more information about troubleshooting Windows XP Professional, see "Troubleshooting Concepts and Strategies," "Tools for Troubleshooting," "Troubleshooting Disks and File Systems," and "Troubleshooting Startup" in this book.

Additional Resources

These resources contain additional information and tools related to this chapter.

Related Information

- "Automating and Customizing Installations" in this book for more information about automating your installation of Windows XP Professional, including detailed information about methods and tools available.

- "Troubleshooting Disks and File Systems" in this book for more information about troubleshooting.

- "Managing Devices" in this book for more information about Plug and Play and ACPI.

- Readme.htm in the \Support\Tools folder on your Windows XP Professional operating system CD for more information about installing and using Support Tools described in this chapter.

Part II

Desktop Management

When you configure the client computers in your organization for ease of management, you also reduce support costs. This part provides in-depth information about how to configure and manage client computers in a variety of environments to help you get the most out of Microsoft® Windows® XP Professional.

Chapter 5

Managing Desktops

Deploying standard desktop configurations and managing users' computers and settings reduces the time required to support computer users in an organization. Microsoft® Windows® XP Professional includes desktop management technologies —collectively known as Microsoft® IntelliMirror®—that allow you to centrally manage the privileges, permissions, and capabilities of users and client computers and ensure that users' data, software, and settings are available to them when they move from one computer to another. Most IntelliMirror features rely on Group Policy, which requires the Microsoft® Active Directory™ directory service, which is included with Microsoft® Windows® 2000 Server. Several of these desktop management tools and features can also be used to manage desktop computers in non–Active Directory environments.

Related Information

- For more information about deploying Group Policy and security policies, see the *Designing a Managed Environment* book in the *Microsoft Windows Server 2003 Deployment Kit*.

- For more information about implementing security for Windows-based client computers and servers, see the *Microsoft Windows Security Resource Kit*.

- For information about IntelliMirror and Group Policy, especially implementation and troubleshooting, see "Desktop Configuration Management" in the *Distributed Systems Guide* of the *Microsoft® Windows® 2000 Server Resource Kit*.

- For information about deploying Group Policy and Active Directory, see the Deployment Planning Guide of the *Microsoft Windows 2000 Server Resource Kit*.

- For information about IntelliMirror and Group Policy, especially deployment information, see the Change and Configuration Management Deployment Guide link on the Web Resources page at *http://www.microsoft.com/windows /reskits/webresources*.

Managing Desktops in Various Network Environments

Desktop Management tools and features available for managing Windows XP Professional–based clients differ depending upon whether the Windows XP Professional desktop operates exclusively in an Active Directory environment or in other network environments. IntelliMirror management technologies rely on Group Policy and most also require Active Directory; both are available in Windows 2000 Server environments. Group Policy requires Active Directory.

In an environment without Active Directory, you can use a variety of tools, such as Systems Management Server (SMS) for managing software distribution, the Internet Explorer Administration Kit for managing Internet Explorer settings, and System Policy for managing registry-based settings. In addition, each local computer has its own local Group Policy object (LGPO), regardless of whether it participates in a domain. While it is possible to set a variety of settings by using the LGPO, note that System Policy scales more easily to a large number of clients. The LGPO can be useful if you only need to apply certain settings to a small number of Windows XP Professional–based clients in a Windows NT 4.0 or other domain.

"Group Policy" refers to policy that relies on a hierarchical targeting mechanism based on Active Directory. Group Policy does not include the Local Group Policy object (LGPO), which is specific to each individual computer rather than to objects in Active Directory. Because LGPOs cannot be managed through Active Directory, they must instead be managed on each computer.

For Windows XP Professional desktops operating in other environments, such as Microsoft® Windows NT® version 4.0, Unix, or Novell, or in a mixed environment, many desktop management capabilities and tools differ. Table 5-1 summarizes the differences in desktop management tools and functionality between Active Directory and non–Active Directory environments.

Table 5-1   Desktop Management Tools and Features in Active Directory and Non–Active Directory Environments

Management Task	Active Directory	Non–Active Directory
Configure registry-based settings for computers and users.	Administrative Templates deployed using Group Policy. Administrative templates deployed using local Group Policy object (LGPO).	System Policy LGPO
Manage local, domain, and network security.	Security Settings deployed using Group Policy. Security Settings deployed using the LGPO.	LGPO
Centrally install, update, and remove software.	Systems Management Server (SMS). Group Policy–based software distribution.	SMS
Manage Internet Explorer configuration settings after deployment.	Internet Explorer Maintenance in the Group Policy MMC snap-in. Internet Explorer Maintenance deployed using the LGPO. Internet Explorer Administration Kit (IEAK).	LGPO IEAK
Apply scripts during user logon/logoff and computer startup/shutdown.	Logon/logoff and startup/shutdown scripts can be centrally configured using Group Policy or independently through the LGPO.	LGPO
Centrally manage users' folders and files on the network.	Folder Redirection in conjunction with Offline Files and Folders.	System Policy Manipulation of registry settings
Centrally manage user settings on the network.	Roaming User Profiles.	Roaming User Profiles (for Windows domains)

You can also manage Windows XP Professional desktops on Unix and Novell networks by using standards-based protocols such as TCP/IP, Simple Network Management Protocol (SNMP), Telnet, and Internetwork Packet Exchange (IPX). To enable policy-based administration on Unix and Novell networks, use a local Group Policy object or System Policy.

Managing Desktops in an Active Directory Environment

When you use Windows XP Professional or Windows 2000 Professional on Windows 2000 Server networks with Active Directory installed, you can take full advantage of IntelliMirror and Group Policy management features. If you are managing Windows XP Professional or Windows 2000 Professional desktops on networks and Active Directory is not installed, see "Managing Desktops Without Active Directory" later in this chapter.

IntelliMirror allows you to centrally manage workstations, saving you significant time while improving manageability. IntelliMirror ensures that users' data, software, and personal settings are available when they move from one computer to another, whether or not their computers are connected to the network.

IntelliMirror consists of four components: **user data management, user settings management, computer settings management, and Group Policy–based software installation and maintenance.** The IntelliMirror **components** can help you to:

- Centrally create and manage the configuration of each user's desktop.

- Enable users to access files from any location at any time by using Roaming User Profiles and Folder Redirection in combination with Offline Files.

- Manage how software is deployed and installed on computers to ensure that users have the software they need to perform their jobs. Large organizations that need advanced software distribution and inventory capabilities should consider using Microsoft® Systems Management Server (SMS) 2.0.

- Manage and enforce centralized data storage, which helps administrators keep important corporate data backed up.

- Save time when replacing computers by using Remote Installation Services(RIS) and **Group Policy–based software** installation and maintenance to easily replace applications, Roaming User Profiles to recover user profiles, and Folder Redirection to centrally manage files.

For more information about implementing IntelliMirror features, see the *Distributed Systems Guide* of the *Microsoft Windows 2000 Server Resource Kit*. For more information about deploying IntelliMirror in a Windows 2000 Server environment, see the Change and Configuration Management Deployment Guide link on the Web Resources page at http://www.microsoft.com/windows/reskits/webresources.

Implementing IntelliMirror

Active Directory and Group Policy provide the foundation for implementing IntelliMirror. Without Active Directory, you cannot take full advantage of IntelliMirror for managing clients. Table 5-2 shows the streamlined management tasks you can perform in an Active Directory environment.

Table 5-2   Management Tasks That Use IntelliMirror

Management Task	IntelliMirror Feature
Configure registry-based Group Policy settings for computers and users.	Administrative Templates
Manage local, domain, and network security.	Security Settings
Centrally install, update, and remove software.	Group Policy–based software distribution
Manage Internet Explorer configuration settings after deployment.	Internet Explorer Maintenance
Apply scripts during user logon/logoff and computer startup/shutdown.	Scripts
Centrally manage users' folders and files on the network, and make shared files and folders available offline.	Folder Redirection Offline Files and Folders
Centrally manage user profiles.	Roaming User Profiles

You can also use Group Policy to manage Remote Installation Services (RIS) by centrally setting client configuration options. For more information about using RIS, see "Automating and Customizing Installations," in this book.

Active Directory stores information about all physical and logical objects on the network. This information is automatically replicated across the network to simplify finding and managing data, no matter where the data is located in the organization. The Active Directory structure you create determines how you apply Group Policy settings. In an Active Directory environment, Group Policy allows you to define and control the state of computers and users in an organization. Group Policy allows you to control more than 600 customizable settings that you can use to centrally configure and manage users and computers.

Depending on the size of your organization, managing desktops, users, and their permissions can be a very complex task, especially because changes constantly happen. For example, users join and leave organizations, get promoted and transferred, and regularly change offices. Similarly, printers, computers, and network file shares are frequently added, removed, and relocated. When implemented in a Windows 2000 Active Directory infrastructure, Group Policy-based IntelliMirror features greatly simplify managing these ongoing changes. Once set, Group Policy automatically maintains the state you design without requiring further intervention.

You can associate or link a particular Group Policy object (GPO) to one or more sites, domains, or organizational units (OUs)in an Active Directory structure. When multiple GPOs are linked to a particular site, domain, or OU, you can prioritize the order in which the GPOs are applied by determining when in the processing order particular settings are processed.

By linking GPOs to sites, domains, and OUs, you can implement Group Policy settings as broadly or as narrowly in the organization as necessary. Consider the following when linking GPOs:

■ A GPO linked to a site applies to all users and computers in the site.

■ A GPO linked to a domain applies directly to all users and computers in the domain and by inheritance to all users and computers in all the OUs that are linked to that domain. Note that Group Policy is *not* inherited across domains.

■ A GPO linked to an OU applies directly to all users and computers in the OU and by inheritance to all users and computers in child OUs.

■ GPOs are stored in Active Directory by domain. You can, however, link a site, domain, or OU to a GPO in another trusted domain, but this is generally not recommended for performance reasons.

For detailed procedures for linking a GPO to a site, domain, or OU, see Windows 2000 Server Help. For complete technical information about Active Directory and Group Policy, see the Distributed Systems Guide of the *Microsoft Windows 2000 Server Resource Kit*. For information about planning and deploying an Active Directory structure, see "Designing the Active Directory Structure" in the *Deployment Planning Guide*. For examples of Active Directory deployment scenarios, see the Windows 2000 Server Deployment Lab Scenarios link on the Web Resources page at http://www.microsoft.com/windows/reskits/webresources.

Using IntelliMirror to Manage Desktops

Windows XP Professional, Windows 2000 Professional, and Windows 2000 Server include IntelliMirror management technologies, which are primarily enabled by Group Policy. IntelliMirror and Group Policy greatly streamline managing user data, managing user settings, managing computer settings, and installing and maintaining software.

User Data Management

Files that a user creates and uses are *user data*. Examples are word processing documents, spreadsheets, or graphics files. User data belongs to the user and is located on the user's computer or on a network share to which the user has rights.

Less obvious forms of user data include Microsoft® Internet Explorer cookies and Favorites and customized templates. User data is usually hard to recreate—for example, a template that has undergone extensive design work and customization. With IntelliMirror, users can transparently access their data from any Windows XP Professional– or Windows 2000 Professional–based computer on the network, regardless of whether or not that computer is their primary computer.

IntelliMirror technologies that support user data management include:

- Folder Redirection

- Offline Files and Synchronization Manager

- Roaming User Profiles

You can ensure that users' data is always available to them in the following ways.

Protecting user data by using Folder Redirection   You can redirect user data to a network share, where it can be backed up as part of routine system maintenance. This can be done so that the process is transparent to the user. It is recommended that users be trained to store all user data in My Documents (in the built-in subfolders My Pictures, My Music, and My Videos, and in any subfolders they create to organize their data). The My Documents folder is then redirected to a network share. This capability helps to enforce corporate directives such as storing business-critical data on servers that are centrally managed by the IT staff. If users are in the habit of storing files on their desktops, you should also consider redirecting the desktop.

Although the Application Data folder can be redirected using Folder Redirection, this is generally only recommended in the following cases:

- To reduce the size of the profile—thereby decreasing logon time—on multi-user computers where you have enabled a Group Policy setting to delete cached profiles. This gives users access to their application data, but without the need to download possibly large files every time they log on.

- To reduce the size of the profile in situations where keeping initial logon time short is a top priority, such as on terminals.

- For Terminal Services clients.

Providing users access to their data even when they are disconnected from the network   By using Offline Files and Synchronization Manager, administrators can ensure that the most up-to-date versions of a user's data reside on both the local computer and on the server. You can use Offline Files in conjunction with Folder Redirection to make available offline those folders that have been redirected to a server. Users can manually configure which files and folders are available offline, or administrators can configure them through Group Policy. The file is stored on a server, and the file on the local computer is synchronized with the network copy. Changes made while offline are synchronized with the server when the user reconnects to the network. Offline Files now supports Distributed File System (DFS) and Encrypting File System (EFS).

Enabling roaming user profiles   Although profiles are commonly used as a method of managing user settings (such as a user's shortcuts and other customizations of their environment), the profile also contains user data, including Favorites and Cookies. When roaming user profiles are enabled, users can access this data when they log on to any computer on the network. Windows XP Professional Group Policy settings allow the profile to roam correctly and free up system memory.

User Settings Management

With the user settings management tools in Windows XP Professional, you can centrally define computing environments for groups of users, and grant or deny users the ability to further customize their environments.

By managing user settings, you can:

- Reduce support calls by providing a preconfigured desktop environment appropriate for the user's job.

- Save time and costs when replacing computers by automatically restoring the user's settings.

- Help users be more efficient by automatically providing their desktop environment, no matter where they work.

The primary IntelliMirror technologies that support user settings management is Roaming User Profiles and Administrative Templates. The settings in Administrative Templates can control the desktop with pre-defined configurations; for more information, see the "Administrative Templates" section, later in this chapter.

A user profile contains:

- The portion of the registry that stores settings such as Windows Explorer settings, persistent network connections, taskbar settings, network printer connections, user-defined settings made from Control Panel, Accessories, and application settings.

- A set of profile folders that store information such as shortcut links, desktop icons, and startup applications.

User profiles are located by default on the local computer; one profile is created for each user who has logged on to that computer. By configuring user profiles to roam, you can ensure that the settings in a user's profile are copied to a network server when the user logs off from the computer and are available to the user no matter where he or she next logs on to the network.

While useful for roaming users, roaming user profiles are also beneficial for users who always use the same computer. For these users, roaming user profiles provide a transparent way to back up their profile to a network server, protecting the information from individual system failure. If a user's primary workstation needs to be replaced, the new computer receives the user's profile from the server as soon as the user logs on.

Some folders in a user profile cannot be configured to roam; these are found in the Local Settings folder, and include the subfolders Application Data (not to be confused with the "other" Application Data folder that is a peer of Local settings, which *does* roam), History, Temp, and Temporary Internet Files. These folders contain application data that is not required to roam with the user, such as temporary files, non-critical settings, and data too large to roam effectively. This data is not copied to and from the server when a user logs on or logs off.

As an illustration of using roaming and non-roaming folders, you might configure Internet Explorer to store a user's Favorites in the roaming portion of the user profile and store the temporary Internet files in the local, non-roaming portion of the user profile. By default, the History, Local Settings, Temp, and Temporary Internet Files folders are excluded from the roaming user profile. You can configure additional folders to not roam by specifying them in the Group Policy snap-in, at **User Configuration\Administrative Templates\System\User Profiles\Exclude directories in roaming profile**.

Computer Settings Management

Group Policy settings also allow you to define how desktop computers are customized and restricted on your network. For optimal control of workstations, use Group Policy objects in an Active Directory network to centralize computer management. However, if Active Directory is not deployed, you can control security on a computer-by-computer basis by using the local Group Policy object. Each computer has one LGPO that can be used to manage the computer outside of an Active Directory environment. If you configure desktop security this way, make sure to set workstation security to match corporate security standards.

The Computer Configuration tree in the Group Policy Microsoft Management Console (MMC) snap-in includes the local computer-related Group Policy settings that specify operating system behavior, desktop behavior, application settings, security settings, computer-assigned application options, and computer startup and shutdown scripts. Computer-related Group Policy settings are applied when the operating system starts up and during periodic refresh cycles. See "Using Group Policy to Manage Desktops," later in this chapter for more information.

You can also customize computer configuration settings by using the Group Policy MMC snap-in, thus simplifying individual computer setup.

Group Policy–based Software Distribution

While the advanced software deployment and management features of Systems Management Server 2.0 (SMS) offer distinct advantages in enterprise-sized organizations—such as inventory, diagnosis, and monitoring—Group Policy provides some ability to deploy software to workstations and servers running Windows 2000 or later. With Group Policy–based software deployment, you can target groups of users and computers based on their location in the Active Directory. Group Policy–based software deployment uses Windows Installer as the installation engine on the local computer.

This Software Installation and Maintenance component allows you to efficiently deploy, patch, upgrade, and remove software applications without visiting each desktop. This gives users reliable access to the applications that they need to perform their jobs, no matter which computer they are using.

Group Policy–based software distribution enables you to:

- Centrally deploy new software, upgrade applications, deploy patches and operating system upgrades, and remove previously deployed applications that are no longer required.

- Ensure that users have the software they need to be productive without an Information Technology (IT) administrator or technical support person having to visit each computer.

- Create a standard desktop operating environment that results in uninterrupted user productivity and straightforward administration.

- Maintain version control of software for all desktop computers in the organization.

- Identify and diagnose Group Policy setting failures by using Resultant Set of Policy (RSoP) in logging mode.

- Deploy, in combination with Windows Installer, 64-bit applications as well as 32-bit applications.

Using the Software Installation extension of the Group Policy MMC snap-in, you can centrally manage the installation of software on a client computer, either by assigning applications to users or computers or by publishing applications for users. You can:

- **Assign software to users**. As an administrator, you can install applications assigned to users the first time they log on after deployment, or you can have the application and its components install on demand as the user invokes that functionality.

- **Assign software to computers**. When you assign an application to a computer, the installation occurs the next time the computer starts up, and the application is available for all the users on that computer.

- **Publish software for users**. You can publish applications for users only. Those users can choose to install the software from a list of published applications located in **Add or Remove Programs** in Control Panel. **Add or Remove Programs** includes an active Web link that is associated with each application that provides users with the support information they need to install certain applications. For example, the default support link for Microsoft® Office is http://www.microsoft.com/office. Administrators can overwrite this default by using the Software Installation extension of the Group Policy snap-in.

Table 5-3 Approaches to Assigning and Publishing Software

Situation or Condition	Publish	Assign to User (Install on Demand)	Assign to User (Full Install)	Assign to Computer
Once the administrator deploys the software, it is available for installation:	The next time the user, to whom this application's Group Policy setting applies, logs on. It is also immediately visible in **Add or Remove Programs**.	The next time the user, to whom this application's Group Policy setting applies, logs on. It is also immediately visible in **Add or Remove Programs**.	The next time the user logs on. It is also immediately visible in **Add or Remove Programs**.	The next time the computer is started.
The software is installed:	By the user from **Add or Remove Programs** or, optionally, by opening an associated document (for applications deployed to auto-install).	By the user from the **Start** menu or a desktop shortcut or by opening an associated document.	Automatically when the user logs on.	Automatically when the computer is started.
The software is not installed and the user opens a file associated with the software:	The software installs only if Auto-Install is selected.	The software installs.	Does not apply. The software is already installed.	Does not apply. The software is already installed.
The user wants to remove the software by using **Add or Remove Programs**:	The user can uninstall the software, and subsequently choose to install it again by using **Add or Remove Programs**.	The user can uninstall the software, but it is re-assigned the next time the user logs on. It is available for installation again from the typical software distribution points.	The user can uninstall the software, but it is re-assigned the next time the user logs on. It is available for installation again from the typical installation points.	Only the local administrator and the network administrator can remove the software.

Using Group Policy to Manage Desktops

Group Policy is the primary tool for defining and controlling how programs, network resources, and Windows XP Professional and Windows 2000 Professional behave for users and computers in an organization. Similar to the way in which information is stored in Microsoft® Word .doc files, Group Policy settings are contained in Group Policy objects (GPOs) created by using the Group Policy MMC snap-in.

Using Group Policy in an Active Directory environment, you can specify a user or computer configuration once, and then rely on the Windows XP Professional or Windows 2000 operating system to enforce that configuration on all affected client computers until you change it. After you apply Group Policy, the system maintains the state without further intervention.

You can define configurations by implementing Group Policy settings from a central location for hundreds or even thousands of users or computers at one time. For example, you might use Group Policy to implement the following rules:

- Install Microsoft® Office 2000 on all computers used by members of the Sales Department.

- Prevent temporary personnel from accessing Control Panel.

- Manage access to adding or removing hardware.

Note   Do not confuse Group Policy settings with preferences. Group Policy settings are created by an administrator and enforced automatically. Preferences are system settings and configuration options, such as a screen saver or the view in My Documents that users set and alter without an administrator's intervention. Group Policy settings take precedence over preferences.

Group Policy Objects

Each combination of Group Policy settings that you configure is called a *Group Policy object (GPO)*. You can link GPOs to computers and users based on their location in an Active Directory structure. That is, you can link a GPO to a site, domain, or organizational unit (OU). Each GPO is applied as part of the startup process or when a user logs on to a workstation. The settings within the GPOs are evaluated by the affected clients, using the hierarchical nature of Active Directory, as described in "GPO Processing Order," later in this section.

Note   Every computer receives one LGPO, which is stored on the local computer itself. Because LGPOs must be set and modified individually on every client computer, it is recommended that you use LGPOs to manage clients only if Active Directory is not deployed in your environment, and only if you are not using the Windows XP Professional or Windows 2000 Group Policy Administrative Templates with Windows NT 4.0 System Policy.

To create, edit, and manage a GPO, use the Group Policy MMC snap-in, either as a stand-alone tool or as an extension to an Active Directory snap-in (such as the Active Directory Users and Computers snap-in or the Active Directory Sites and Services snap-in). When working in an Active Directory environment, the preferred method is to use the Group Policy snap-in as an extension to an Active Directory snap-in. This allows you to browse Active Directory for the correct Active Directory container, and then define Group Policy based on the selected scope. To access Group Policy from either the Active Directory Users and Computers snap-in or in the Active Directory Sites and Services snap-in, select the **Group Policy** tab from the **Properties** page of a site, domain, or organizational unit.

When you create a GPO, start with a template that contains all of the Group Policy settings available for you to configure. Because Group Policy settings apply to either computers or users, GPOs contain trees for each:

- **Computer Configuration**. All computer-related Group Policy settings that specify operating system behavior, desktop behavior, security settings, computer startup and shutdown scripts, computer-assigned applications, and any settings provided by applications.

- **User Configuration**. All user-related Group Policy settings that specify operating system behavior, desktop settings, security settings, user-assigned and user-published application options, folder redirection options, user logon and logoff scripts, and any Group Policy settings provided by applications.

Warning   If an Active Directory domain contains both Windows 2000– and Windows XP Professional–based clients, any new Group Policy settings specific to Windows XP Professional that you configure do not apply to the Windows 2000–based clients. See Group Policy Help or the Extended view in the Group Policy snap-in for the desktop operating system required for each setting to apply.

GPO Processing Order

Local computer Group Policy is applied during the startup process and periodic refresh cycles. User Group Policy is applied when the user logs on to the computer and during the periodic refresh cycle. When a computer starts, computer policy is applied during the boot process. Then, when a user logs on, user policy is applied in the following order: local GPO, GPOs linked to sites, GPOs linked to domains, and GPOs linked to organizational units (OUs). In the case of nested OUs, GPOs associated with parent OUs are processed prior to GPOs associated with child OUs. Keep this processing order in mind when configuring multiple GPOs to centrally manage desktops in your network environment.

> **Note** If a setting in a later-applied GPO is not configured, it does not over-write settings configured in earlier-applied GPOs.

This order of application is the default behavior. You can modify the default processing order by using the **No Override**, **Block Policy Inheritance**, or **Loop-back** Group Policy settings. These allow you to modify the rules of inheritance, either by forcing GPOs to affect groups of users or computers, or by preventing higher-level GPOs from affecting groups of users or computers.

Resultant Set of Policy

The biggest change in Group Policy for Windows XP Professional is the introduction of the Resultant Set of Policy (RSoP) MMC snap-in. RSoP gives administrators a pow-erful and flexible tool for and troubleshooting Group Policy. RSoP allows you to see the aggregate effect of Group Policy on a target user or computer, including which settings take precedence over others.

RSoP is enabled by Windows Management Instrumentation (WMI) by leverag-ing the capability of WMI to extract data from the registry, drivers, the file system, Active Directory, Simple Network Management Protocol (SNMP), Windows Installer, Microsoft® SQL Server™, various networking features, and Microsoft® Exchange Server.

Use Logging mode to determine which GPO settings are actually applied to a target user or computer. You can also use logging mode on a stand-alone computer.

For example, a help desk worker can connect to any Windows XP Profes-sional-based computer on the network and run Logging mode if they have local administrator access on the target computer.

Managing Users and Desktops by Using Group Policy Extensions

Group Policy provides several extensions you can use to configure GPOs that enable IntelliMirror features and manage users. These extensions include:

- Administrative Templates.
- Security Settings.
- Software Installation and Maintenance.
- Scripts (computer startup and shutdown scripts and user logon and logoff scripts).
- Folder Redirection.
- Internet Explorer Maintenance.
- Remote Installation Services.

> **Note**   Folder Redirection, Software Installation and Maintenance, and RIS require Active Directory; they are not present on the local Group Policy object and cannot be managed by using the local Group Policy object. If Active Directory is not deployed on your network, use System Policy instead.

You can use any of these extensions to apply Group Policy to users or computers, although settings are different for users and computers. Use the Group Policy snap-in to access the extensions. By default, all the available extensions are loaded when you start the Group Policy snap-in. Different extensions are available depending on whether you are viewing the local Group Policy object or Active Directory domain-based Group Policy.

Administrative Templates   Administrative templates (.adm files) are *Unicode* files that you can use to configure the registry-based settings that govern the behavior of many services, applications, and operating system components such as the **Start** menu. By default, the Group Policy snap-in contains four .adm files that cumulatively contain more than 600 settings. You can also access three additional .adm files that can be used with the Windows NT 4.0 System Policy Editor. The .adm files are described in Table 5-4.

Table 5-4   Administrative Template Files

.adm File	Use With	Description
System.adm	Windows XP Professional	Contains many settings that you can use to customize the user's operating environment.
Inetres.adm	Windows XP Professional	Contains settings for Internet Explorer.
Conf.adm	Windows XP Professional	Contains settings you can use to configure Microsoft® NetMeeting®.
Winnt.adm	Windows NT 4.0 System Policy Editor, Poledit.exe	Contains policy for Windows NT 4.0–based clients.
Wmplayer.adm	Windows XP Professional	Contains settings you can use to configure Windows Media Player.
Common.adm	Windows NT 4.0 System Policy Editor, Poledit.exe	Contains policy for client computers running Windows NT 4.0, Microsoft® Windows® 95, and Microsoft® Windows® 98.
Windows.adm	Windows NT 4.0 System Policy Editor, Poledit.exe	Contains policy for Windows 95– and Windows 98–based clients.

An .adm file specifies a hierarchy of categories and subcategories that together define how the Group Policy snap-in displays the options. The file also indicates the registry locations where the settings are stored if a particular selection is made, specifies any options or restrictions in values that are associated with the selection, and might specify a default value if a selection is activated.

In Windows 2000 and Windows XP Professional, all Group Policy settings set registry entries in either the \Software\Policies tree (the preferred location for all new policies) or the \Software\Microsoft\Windows\CurrentVersion\Policies tree, in either the HKEY_CURRENT_USER subtree or the HKEY_LOCAL_MACHINE subtree.

Policy settings that are stored in these registry subkeys are known as *true policy settings*. Storing settings here has the following advantages:

■ These subkeys are secure and cannot be modified by a non-administrator.

■ When Group Policy changes for any reason, these subkeys are cleaned, and then the new Group Policy–related registry entries are rewritten.

This prevents Windows NT 4.0 behavior, where System Policy settings result in persistent settings in the registry. A policy remains in effect until the value of its corresponding registry entry is reversed, either by a counteracting policy or by editing the registry. These settings are stored outside the approved registry locations above and are known as *preferences*.

By default, only true policy settings are displayed in the Group Policy snap-in. Because they use registry entries in the Policies subkeys of the registry, they will *not* cause persistent settings in the registry when the GPO that applies them is no longer in effect. The following .adm files are displayed by default:

■ System.adm, which contains operating system settings.

■ Inetres.adm, which contains Internet Explorer restrictions.

■ Conf.adm, which contains NetMeeting settings.

■ WMPlayer.adm, which contains Windows Media Player settings.

Administrators can add additional .adm files to the Group Policy snap-in that set registry values outside of the Group Policy subkeys. These settings are referred to as *preferences* because the user, application, or other parts of the system can also change the settings. By creating non–Group Policy .adm files, the administrator ensures that certain registry entries are set to specified values.

One useful feature of the Windows XP Professional Group Policy snap-in is view filtering. For example, you can hide settings that aren't configured or view only settings supported on a particular operating-system platform.

To filter the view of the Group Policy snap-in

1. Click **View**, and then click **Filtering**.

2. Select the **Filter by requirements information** check box, and then in the list box select the check boxes for the categories that you want to make visible.

3. If you want to hide settings that are not configured, select the **Only show configured policy settings** check box. If you do this, only enabled or disabled settings will be visible.

4. If you want to hide Windows NT 4.0–style system policy settings, make sure that the **Only show policy settings that can be fully managed** check box is selected. This option is recommended, and it is enabled by default.

You can also prevent administrators from viewing or using non-policy settings by enabling the **Enforce Show Policies Only** Group Policy setting in **User Configuration\Administrative Templates\System\Group Policy**.

The icon for non-policy or preference settings is red. True policy settings have a blue icon.

Use of non–Group Policy settings within the Group Policy infrastructure is strongly discouraged because of the persistent nature of these registry-based settings. To set registry-based policy settings on client computers running Windows NT 4.0, Windows 95, and Windows 98, use the Windows NT 4.0 System Policy Editor tool, Poledit.exe.

Extended View for the Group Policy snap-in now provides Explain text for the selected Group Policy setting without having to open a separate Help window. It also clearly shows which operating system client platform is required for the selected setting to apply. You can now more easily determine which settings will function depending on the existing desktop operating systems on your network.

A Group Policy settings spreadsheet is available on the Web for easy tracking of your configured Group Policy settings. See the Group Policy Object Settings spreadsheet link on the Web Resources page at http://www.microsoft.com/windows/reskits/webresources.

Security Settings   Use the Security Settings extension to set the security options for computers and users within the scope of a GPO. For information about defining security settings for the domain and network, see the Distributed Systems Guide of the *Microsoft Windows 2000 Server Resource Kit*.

The Security Settings extension of the Group Policy snap-in complements existing system security management features such as Local Security Policy snap-in. You can continue to change specific settings as needed.

You can configure security for computers to include:

■ **Account policies**, such as computer security settings for password policy, lockout policy, and Kerberos authentication protocol policy in Active Directory domains.

> **Warning**   Security settings are applied only at the domain level. If configured at the OU level, they are neither processed nor applied.

■ **Local policies**, including security settings for auditing, assigning user rights (such as who has network access to the computer), and security options (such as determining who can connect to a computer anonymously).

■ **Event logging**, which controls settings such as the size and retention method for the Application, Security, and System event logs.

■ **Restricted groups**, which allows administrators to control individual and group membership in security sensitive groups. You can enforce a membership policy regarding sensitive groups, such as Enterprise Administrators or Payroll. For more information about using security, see "Security Settings" later in this chapter.

■ **System services**, including services that control startup mode and access permissions for system services, such as who is allowed to stop and start the fax service.

■ **Registry security**, which allows you to configure security settings for registry containers, including access control, audit, and ownership.

■ **File system**, which configures security settings for file-system objects, including access control, audit, and ownership.

■ **Public Key policies**, which control and manage certificate settings.

■ **IP Security policies**, which propagates Internet Protocol security (IPSec) policy to any computer accounts affected by the GPO. For users, you can define IPSec security. This propagates IPSec policy to any user accounts affected by the GPO.

Default security templates   The following security templates are installed when Windows XP Professional is installed on an NTFS file system partition:

■ **Basicwk.inf** applies default settings for Windows XP Professional–based computers for all areas except User Rights and Group memberships.

- **Basicsv.inf** applies default settings for Windows 2000 Server–based computers for all areas except User Rights and Group memberships.

- **Basicdc.inf** applies default settings for domain controllers for all areas except User Rights and Group memberships.

User Rights and Group memberships are not modified by the basic templates because these templates are most often used for undoing file system or registry access control list (ACL) changes, or to apply the default Windows XP Professional ACLs to computers that have been upgraded from Windows NT 4.0. In these cases, administrators typically want to maintain existing User Rights and Group memberships.

Typically, you do not need to define the default security templates because they are installed by default on an NTFS partition. However, they can be useful if you have converted a drive from file allocation table (FAT) to NTFS, or if you have made customizations and want to restore the system to the default ACLs.

Do not deploy these templates by using Group Policy, because it can take a long time to reapply these basic templates. They are applied during setup. Incremental templates, on the other hand, are useful to deploy using Group Policy.

Incremental security templates   Windows XP Professional includes several incremental security templates. By default, these templates are stored in *systemroot*\Security\Templates. You can customize these predefined templates by using the Security Templates MMC snap-in or by importing them into the Security Settings extension of the Group Policy snap-in. These templates include:

- **Compatible**. The Compatible template (Compatws.inf) relaxes the default permissions for the Users group so that older applications written to less stringent security standards are more likely to run.

- **Secure**. Two templates, Securews.inf and Securedc.inf, work on workstations, servers, and domain controllers. These provide increased security compared to the access control permissions set by default when Windows XP Professional is installed. The Secure configuration includes increased security settings for Account Policy, Auditing, and some common security-related registry subkeys and entries.

- **High Secure**. The High Secure templates are Hisecws.inf and Hisecdc.inf. These provide increased **security** over the secure configuration and work on workstations, servers, and domain controllers. This configuration requires that all network communications be digitally signed and encrypted.

For more information about these templates, see "Authorization and Access Control" in this book.

Software Installation   Use the Software Installation extension of the Group Policy snap-in to centrally manage software in your organization. You can assign (make mandatory) or publish (make optionally available) software to users, and assign (but not publish) software to computers. For more information about using the Software Installation extension, see "Using IntelliMirror to Manage Desktops" earlier in this chapter.

Scripts   You can use Group Policy–based scripts to automate computer startup and shutdown, and user logon and logoff sessions. You can use any language supported by Windows Script Host (WSH), a language-independent scripting host for 32-bit Windows platforms. Your options include Microsoft® Visual Basic® Scripting Edition (VBScript), JavaScript, Perl, and batch files (with .bat and .cmd extensions) such as in Microsoft® MS-DOS®.

WSH is included in Windows XP Professional. With WSH, you can run scripts directly in Windows XP Professional by double-clicking a script file, or by typing the name of a script file at the command prompt.

You can use any WSH scripting tool including the VBScript programming system and Microsoft® JScript® development software to create scripts. Independent software vendors provide WSH support for other popular scripting languages. You can use Windows Script Host to run .vbs and .js scripts directly on the Windows desktop or command console, without having to embed the scripts in an HTML document. MS-DOS-type batch files (with .bat and .cmd extensions) also use WSH.

Windows XP Professional supports the following five scripts:

- Group Policy logon scripts

- Group Policy logoff scripts

- Group Policy startup scripts

- Group Policy shutdown scripts

- Logon scripts set on user objects

Note   Although Group Policy–based scripts are similar to logon scripts set on the user object, they often require multi-branching logic to target a specific group of users. Using Group Policy, you can target the scripts by using OUs and security group filtering. For this reason, the Windows XP Professional scripting options are a more efficient choice.

Using the **Scripts** folder located under **Computer Configuration\Administrative Templates\System** and **User Configuration\Configuration\Administrative Templates\System** in the Group Policy snap-in, you can specify when and how startup and shutdown scripts are run. See Table 5-6 later in this chapter for a partial list of script-related settings.

Folder Redirection   Use Folder Redirection to redirect Windows XP Professional certain folders from their default location in the user profile to an alternate location on an Active Directory network where you can centrally manage them and keep them secure. The Windows XP Professional that can be redirected include My Documents (and its subfolders My Pictures, My Music, and My Videos), Application Data, Desktop, and the Start menu.

Internet Explorer Maintenance   Using Internet Explorer Maintenance, you can administer and customize Internet Explorer on Windows XP Professional–based client computers by using Group Policy instead of using the Internet Explorer Administration Kit (IEAK). You can also export these settings to clients running earlier versions of Windows. For more information about managing Internet Explorer, see the Microsoft Internet Explorer Resource Kit link on the Web Resources page at http://www.microsoft.com/windows/reskits/webresources. For information about individual Internet Explorer Group Policy settings, see Group Policy Help or the Extended view in the Group Policy snap-in.

Refreshing Group Policy from the Command Line

A new command-line tool, GPUdate.exe, replaces the Secedit.exe tool to give administrators better control and flexibility in refreshing policy. Normally, Group Policy refreshes every 90 minutes for the computer and user. However, after you revise a GPO, you can use GPUpdate to refresh the GPO so that it takes effect immediately. GPUpdate replaces the Windows 2000 tool Secedit.exe and provides increased control and flexibility. The command-line parameters for this tool are described in Table 5-5.

Table 5-5   Command-Line Parameters for GPUdate.exe

Command-Line Parameter	Behavior
/target:{computer|user}	Specifies that only Computer or User policy settings are refreshed. By default, both Computer and User policy settings are refreshed.
/force	Reapplies all policy settings. By default, only policy settings that have changed are applied.
/wait:value	Sets the number of seconds to wait for policy processing to finish. The default is 600 seconds. The value "0" means not to wait. The value "-1" means to wait indefinitely. When the time limit is exceeded, the command prompt returns, but policy processing continues.

Table 5-5   Command-Line Parameters for GPUdate.exe

Command-Line Parameter	Behavior
/logoff	Causes a logoff after the Group Policy settings have been refreshed. This is required for those Group Policy client-side extensions that do not process policy on a background refresh cycle but that do process policy when the user logs on. Examples include user-targeted Software Installation and Folder Redirection. This option has no effect if there are no extensions called that require the user to log off.
/boot	Causes a reboot after the Group Policy settings are refreshed. This is required for those Group Policy client-side extensions that do not process policy on a background refresh cycle but that do process policy when the computer starts up, such as computer-targeted Software Installation. This option has no effect if there are no extensions called that require a reboot.
/sync	Causes the next foreground policy application to be processed synchronously. Foreground policy applications occur at computer boot and user logon. You can specify this for the user, computer, or both using the /target parameter. The /force and /wait parameters are ignored if specified.

Managing Desktops Without Active Directory

On a network not running the Active Directory directory service, you can implement the following IntelliMirror and Group Policy features to manage Windows XP Professional and Windows 2000 desktops:

- Roaming User Profiles and logon scripts (Microsoft® Windows NT® version 4.0 domains).

- Folder Redirection.

- Internet Explorer Maintenance.

- System Policy.

- Local Group Policy object.

Roaming User Profiles and Logon Scripts

In a Windows NT 4.0 domain, both roaming user profiles and logon scripts are configured on the user object.

My Documents Redirection

On a Windows NT 4.0 Server network you can redirect My Documents and its sub-folders, Application Data, Desktop, and the Start menu to a local or network location by using the following methods:

- You can use System Policy to redirect these folders. This will provide only limited functionality compared with true Folder Redirection, because you cannot actually move folder contents or set ACLs.

- Users can manually redirect the My Documents folder by changing the target folder location in the **My Documents** Properties page.

- Manipulation of registry settings.

  Note that you cannot configure Folder Redirection by using an LGPO.

Internet Explorer Maintenance

Instead of using Group Policy to control Internet Explorer settings, you can use the Internet Explorer Administration Kit (IEAK) to apply settings to Internet Explorer clients by using auto-configuration packages. To download the IEAK, see the Microsoft Internet Explorer Administration Kit (IEAK) link on the Web Resources page at http://www.microsoft.com/windows/reskits/webresources.

System Policy

Like Active Directory-based Group Policy objects, System Policy can define a specific user's settings or the settings for a group of users. The resulting policy file contains the registry information for all users, groups, and computers that will use the policy file. Separate policy files for each user, group, or computer are not necessary.

Group Policy includes the functionality from Windows NT 4.0 System Policy. It also provides additional policy settings for scripts, Software Installation and Maintenance, security settings, Internet Explorer maintenance, and folder redirection. Table 5-6 provides an overall comparison of Group Policy and Windows NT 4.0 System Policy.

Table 5-6   Comparison of Group Policy and System Policy

Comparison	Group Policy	Windows NT 4.0 System Policy
Tool used:	Microsoft Management Console (MMC) Group Policy snap-in.	System Policy Editor (Poledit.exe).
Number of settings:	More than 150 security-related settings and more than 620 registry-based settings.	72 settings.

Table 5-6 Comparison of Group Policy and System Policy

Comparison	Group Policy	Windows NT 4.0 System Policy
Applied to:	Users or computers in a specified Active Directory container (site, domain, or OU) or local computers and users.	Domains or local computers and users.
Security:	Secure.	Not secure.
Extensible by:	Using Microsoft Management Console (MMC) or .adm files.	Using .adm files.
Persistence:	Does not leave settings in the users' profiles when the effective policy is changed.	Persistent in users' profiles until the specified policy is reversed or until you edit the registry.
Defined by:	User or computer membership in security groups.	User membership in security groups.
Primary uses:	Implementing registry-based settings to control the desktop and user. Configuring many types of security settings. Applying logon, logoff, startup, and shutdown scripts. Implementing IntelliMirror Software Installation and Maintenance. Implementing IntelliMirror data and settings management. Optimizing and maintaining Internet Explorer.	Implementing registry-based settings that govern the behavior of applications and operating system components such as the Start Menu.

Warning System Policy settings applied to computers that have been upgraded to Windows XP Professional are persistent in ("tattoo") the registry. Applying Group Policy to a computer with persistent registry-based System Policy settings might have unpredictable results. It is recommended that you remove these settings from computers before applying GPOs.

Windows XP Professional–based clients in an Active Directory domain can process Group Policy but cannot process Windows NT 4.0 System Policy. Windows NT 4.0 policies are persistent in user profiles. This means that after a registry-based setting is applied using Windows NT 4.0 System Policy, the setting persists until the specified policy is reversed or you edit the registry to remove the corresponding entry. The effect of persistent registry-based settings can cause conflicts when a user's group membership changes. If the Windows XP Professional computer account object or user account object that you manage exists in a Windows NT 4.0 domain, you can still use certain System Policy tools to manage them.

> **Note**   You can use System Policy to deliver any of the registry-based policy settings (Administrative Templates) that are available in Windows XP Professional. The procedures described in the following subsections also work for providing System Policy from any Server Message Block (SMB)–enabled share or even from a local share.

To create a policy that is automatically downloaded from validating domain controllers, you must create a .pol file by using the System Policy Editor:

- For Windows NT 4.0 and later, the .pol file is named Ntconfig.pol and is created using the System Policy Editor for the specific operating system.

- For Windows 95, Windows 98, and Microsoft® Windows® Millennium Edition (Windows Me), the .pol file is named Config.pol and must be created by using the System Policy Editor for that operating system.

As system administrator, you can choose an alternate name for the .pol file and can direct the computer to update the policy from a path other than the Netlogon share. You can do this by using System Policy. The update path can even be a local path, so that each computer has its own policy file. However, you must make this change manually on each desktop. For more information about specifying a path to the policy file, see "Specifying a Path to the Policy File" later in this chapter.

Administrative Templates   The System Policy Editor tool uses files called *administrative templates* (.adm files) to determine which registry settings you can modify and which settings display in the System Policy Editor.

In Windows XP Professional and Windows 2000, the Administrative Templates item in the Group Policy snap-in uses administrative templates (.adm files) to specify the registry settings that can be modified through the Group Policy snap-in. This includes Group Policy for the Windows XP Professional operating system and its components as well as for applications.

Policy settings are written to the following locations in the registry:

- HKEY_CURRENT_USER\Software\Policies (preferred location)
- HKEY_LOCAL_MACHINE\Software\Policies (preferred location)

- HKEY_CURRENT_USER\Software\Microsoft\Windows\CurrentVersion\Policies

- HKEY_LOCAL_MACHINE\Software\Microsoft\Windows\CurrentVersion\Policies

Caution Do not edit the registry unless you have no alternative. The registry editor bypasses standard safeguards, allowing settings that can damage your system, or even require you to reinstall Windows. If you must edit the registry, back it up first and see the Registry Reference in the Microsoft Windows 2000 Server Resource Kit at http://www.microsoft.com/reskit.

To configure or customize Group Policy, use the Group Policy snap-in whenever possible.

A client running Windows XP Professional or Windows 2000 processes System Policy if the user or computer account, or both, are in a Windows NT 4.0 domain. The client looks for the Ntconfig.pol file used by Windows NT 4.0–style System Policy. By default, it looks for this file in the Netlogon share of the authenticating Windows NT 4.0 domain controller.

Warning It is possible for a computer account object to exist in a Windows NT 4.0 domain and a user account object for a user of that computer to exist in an Active Directory domain, or vice versa. However, operating in such a mixed environment makes the users and computers difficult to manage and might cause unpredictable behavior. For optimal central management, it is recommended that you move from a mixed environment to a pure Active Directory environment.

Setting registry-based policy in a Windows NT 4.0 domain A Windows XP Professional–based client processes System Policy if either the user or computer account exists in a Windows NT 4.0 domain. When a user logs on to a Windows XP Professional–based client in a Windows NT 4.0 domain and the client is running in the default Automatic mode, it checks the Netlogon share on the validating domain controller for the Ntconfig.pol file. If the client finds the file, it downloads it, parses it for user, group, and computer policy data, and then applies the appropriate settings. If the client does not locate the policy file on its validating domain controller, it does not check elsewhere. It is therefore critically important that the Ntconfig.pol file is replicated among the domain controllers performing authentication.

Setting registry-based policy in a workgroup environment   In the absence of a Windows NT 4.0 domain, you can configure the client to look for the Ntconfig.pol file in a specific location on the local computer or on any SMB share location. For more information about specifying a path to the policy file, see "Specifying a Path to the Policy File" later in this chapter.

Creating Ntconfig.pol files based on Windows XP Professional .adm files

You can create Ntconfig.pol files based on the Windows XP Professional .adm files and apply these settings to Windows XP Professional–based clients. To do this, you need the Windows NT 4.0 System Policy Editor tool, Poledit.exe, which is installed with Windows 2000 Server and Advanced Server. You can install Poledit.exe on Windows XP Professional–based computers by installing the Administrative Tools package that is included on the Windows 2000 Server and Microsoft® Windows® 2000 Advanced Server operating system CDs.

To install Administrative Tools on a Windows XP Professional–based computer, open the **i386** folder on the applicable Windows 2000 Server disc, and then double-click the **Adminpak.msi** file. Follow the instructions that appear in the Administrative Tools setup wizard.

When you install the Administrative Tools package, Poledit.exe and its supporting .adm files (Winnt.adm, Windows.adm, and Common.adm) are installed into the root \System directory and the \Inf directory, as in Windows NT 4.0. Poledit.exe is not added to the Start menu, but it is accessible from the command line.

Use the following procedure to create an Ntconfig.pol file.

> **Note**   The System Policy Editor from Windows NT 4.0 or earlier cannot read the Unicode-formatted .adm files shipped in Windows 2000 or later. You must use the version of System Policy Editor that ships in Windows 2000 or later, which supports Unicode. Alternatively, if you resave the .adm files as .txt files without Unicode encoding, you can use an older version of Poledit.exe.

To create an Ntconfig.pol file

1. Using a text editor such as Notepad, remove all **#if version** and **#endif** statements from the following .adm files: System.adm, Inetres.adm, and Conf.adm, and then save the files. This prevents inadvertent loading of these files by Poledit.exe.

    For example, in the Inetres.adm file, remove these lines:

    ```
    #if version <= 2
    #endif
    ```

2. Open Poledit.exe.

3. In the **System Policy Editor** window, on the **Options** menu, click **Policy Template**.

4. In the **Policy Template Options** dialog box, click **Add**, select one of the .adm files that you modified in step 1 above, and then click **OK**.

5. Specify the appropriate policy settings, as documented in System Policy Editor Help.

6. Save the file as Ntconfig.pol to the NETLOGON share of the Windows NT 4.0 domain controller.

Specifying a path to the policy file   You can change the default behavior so that a Windows XP Professional–based client looks for the policy file in a different location than the Netlogon share. The **UpdateMode** registry entry forces the computer to retrieve the policy file from a specific location (expressed as a UNC path), regardless of which user logs on.

You can set **UpdateMode** by using the System Policy Editor and the System.adm file.

To retrieve the policy file from a specific location

1. Open Poledit.exe.

2. Click **Options**, click **Policy Template**, and then in the **Policy Template Options** dialog box, make sure that System.adm is listed in the Current Policy Template(s) list box. If it is not listed, click **Add** to add this file.

3. To open the Default Computer policy, on the **File** menu, click **New Policy**, and then double-click **Default Computer** from the **Policies for** list.
   – or –
   To open the Local Computer policy, on the **File** menu, click **Open Registry**, and then double-click **Local Computer**.

4. In the **Properties** dialog box, expand **Network**, and then expand **System policies update** to display the Remote update option.

5. Select the **Remote update** box.

6. In the **Update mode** drop-down menu, select Manual **(use specific path)**.

7. In the **Path for manual update** text box, type the UNC path and file name for the policy file, then click **OK** to save your changes.

The first time the Windows XP Professional–based client is modified locally by using the System Policy Editor or receives a default System Policy file from the NETLOGON share of a domain controller, this location is written to the registry. Thereafter, the Windows XP Professional–based client does *not* look at a domain controller again to find a policy file, and all policy updates use the location you specified manually. Note that this change is permanent until you edit the policy file to reset the option to **Automatic**.

Local Group Policy Object

In addition to setting System Policy, you can set settings in the local Group Policy object (LGPO) for any computer, whether or not it participates in an Active Directory domain. Although System Policy scales more easily to a large number of clients, the LGPO can be useful if you only need to apply certain settings to a small number of Windows XP Professional–based clients in a Windows NT 4.0 or other domain.

The LGPO is located at *systemroot*\System32\GroupPolicy. Not all Group Policy extensions are available for the local GPO. Each Group Policy extension snap-in queries the Group Policy engine to get the GPO type, and then determines whether the GPO is to be displayed. To set the LGPO, use the Group Policy snap-in focused on the local computer.

Table 5-7 shows which Group Policy snap-in extensions open when the Group Policy snap-in is focused on an LGPO.

Table 5-7   Local Group Policy Object Extensions

Group Policy Snap-in Extension	Available in LGPO
Software Installation	No
Scripts	Yes
Security Settings	Yes
Administrative Templates	Yes
Folder Redirection	No
Internet Explorer Maintenance	Yes
RIS	No

You can access the Group Policy snap-in by using the following procedure.

To start the Group Policy snap-in on a Windows XP Professional–based client

1. In the MMC window, on the **File** menu, click **Add/Remove Snap-in**.

2. On the **Standalone** tab, click **Add**.

3. In the **Add Standalone Snap-in** dialog box, click **Group Policy**, and then click **Add**. The **Group Policy Wizard** appears.

4. Select **Local Computer** to edit the local GPO, or click **Browse** to select another computer.

5. Click **Finish**.

6. In the **Add Standalone Snap-in** dialog box, click **Close.**

7. In the **Add/Remove Snap-in** dialog box, click **OK**.

   The Group Policy snap-in opens with focus on the specified GPO. If you select **Local Computer**, you see Local Computer Policy. Expand the tree to see **Computer Configuration** and **User Configuration**.

   To quickly access the local Group Policy object, type **gpedit.msc** in the **Run** dialog box.

> **Note**   The Security Settings extension of the Group Policy snap-in does not support remote management for the local Group Policy object in Windows XP Professional.

Managing Desktops in UNIX and Novell Environments

You can use LGPOs and System Policy to manage Windows XP Professional Desktops in Novell and UNIX environments. For example, NTConfig.pol can exist on any network server. You can perform typical desktop-management tasks that are based on industry-standard protocols, such as Telnet and Simple Network Management Protocol (SNMP), a standards-based TCP/IP network management protocol that is implemented in many environments. For more information about using LGPOs and System Policy, see "Managing Desktops Without Active Directory," earlier in this chapter.

Standards-based Management

Windows XP Professional provides full support for SNMP, allowing you to easily manage systems that run Windows XP Professional by using a UNIX-based SNMP management suite available from independent software vendors.

Telnet Client and Server

You can use Telnet to remotely log on to and execute commands on a Windows XP Professional–based or UNIX-based system. The Telnet client included with Windows XP Professional is character- and console-based and is enhanced for advanced remote management capabilities.

   The Windows XP Professional–based Telnet client also provides NTLM authentication support. With this feature, a Windows XP Professional Telnet client can log on to a Windows XP Professional Telnet server that uses NTLM authentication.

Novell NetWare IPX Network

Internetwork Packet Exchange (IPX) is the native NetWare protocol used on many earlier Novell networks. You can integrate Network Connections clients into a Net-Ware IPX network, with the exception of clients running Microsoft® Windows® XP 64-Bit Edition.

The client must run a NetWare redirector to see a Novell NetWare network. This redirector is called Client Service for NetWare (CSNW).

A remote access server is also an IPX router and Service Advertising Protocol (SAP) agent. Once configured, remote access servers enable file and print services and the use of Windows Sockets programs over IPX on the NetWare network for Network Connections clients. Remote access servers and their Network Connections clients use the Point-to-Point (PPP) IPX Control Protocol (IPXCP), as defined in RFC 1552, "The PPP Internetwork Packet Exchange Control Protocol (IPXCP)," to configure the remote access line for IPX.

Network Connections clients are always provided an IPX address by the remote access server. The IPX network number is either generated automatically by the remote access server, or a static pool of network numbers is given to the remote access server for assignment to Network Connections.

For automatically generated IPX network numbers, the remote access server uses the NetWare Router Information Protocol (RIP) to determine an IPX network number that is not in use in the IPX network. The remote access server assigns that number to the connection.

Configure a connection by selecting **NWLink IPX/SPX/NetBIOS Compatible Transport Protocol** on the **General** tab of **Local Area Connection Properties**.

Novell ZENworks

To use Novell ZENworks, you must register Windows XP Professional with ZEN-works. A workstation record can then be imported into the Novell Directory Services (NDS) database of a Novell NetWare network. The workstation is registered by running Wsreg32.exe either from the command line or from a logon script. The following is an example of the logon script code that detects Windows XP Professional and runs the correct registry program:

```
IF " %PLATFORM" =" WINDOWS_NT" THEN BEGIN
#F:\PUBLIC\WSREG32.EXE
END
```

After the workstation is registered, you can import it into NDS by using Nnwadmn32.exe.

You can administer Windows XP Professional–based clients by using the standard ZENworks tools.

Creating and Managing Standard Desktop Configurations

IntelliMirror and Group Policy allow you to manage desktops with great efficiency. To take full advantage of these benefits, it is recommended that you define and set up default user configurations.

A standard configuration must be carefully adapted to the target users' applications, tasks, and locations. It can also increase productivity by preventing users from making system changes that could cause downtime. Because standard configurations are easier to troubleshoot or replace, they can also reduce support costs.

IntelliMirror and Group Policy are designed for use in environments where administrators need to centralize tasks such as the following:

- Managing mobile users

- Managing new users

- Creating managed desktops

- Managing multi-user desktops

- Replacing computers

Creating Managed Desktops

The managed desktop contains settings that can lower the total cost of ownership (TCO) of a desktop for any level of user. This configuration can reduce help desk costs and user downtime by providing users with just the applications and tools they need to perform their jobs. The user is permitted to install approved applications and make extensive customizations of applications and the desktop environment. At the same time, the managed desktop configuration can keep users from making potentially harmful changes to configuration settings, such as adding or disabling hardware devices, or changing system or user environment settings, such as the location of the **My Documents** folder, and can restrict access to such features as the MMC administration snap-ins and some hardware-configuration items in **Control Panel**. The user for this configuration does not usually require access to **Network Connections**.

Table 5-8 shows the desktop management features used to create a typical managed desktop configuration.

Table 5-8   Features of a Managed Desktop Configuration

Feature	Specifics	Explanation
Multiple Users	Per-user logon accounts	Users might share this computer during different shifts. Each user has a unique logon account.

Table 5-8   Features of a Managed Desktop Configuration

Feature	Specifics	Explanation
Roaming User Profiles	Yes	Makes user settings available from any computer and enables administrators to easily replace computers without losing user configuration.
Folder Redirection	**My Documents** folder	User data is saved on server shares and Group Policy prevents users from storing data locally.
Ability for User to Customize	Most	Allows users to personalize their work environment while preventing changes to critical system settings.
Assigned Applications	Multiple	Core applications are automatically installed before the user logs on.
Published Applications	Multiple	All required applications are available for users to install locally.
Group Policy Settings	Yes	Group Policy settings are used to create the managed environment.

Managing Mobile Users

Many organizations have mobile users—traveling employees who often use a portable computer. Mobile users have unique needs because, although these users usually log on to the same computer, they sometimes connect through a high-speed line and sometimes through a low-speed (or dial-up) line, and some mobile users never have a fast connection. Such users fall into two main categories:

- Users who spend the majority of time away from the office or have no fixed office. Typically, these users connect by using slow links, although they might have occasional LAN access to their logon server, data servers, and application-delivery servers.

- Users who spend most of their time in an office but occasionally work at home or in another location. The majority of their network access is at LAN-speed, but they occasionally use the Routing and Remote Access service or remote network links.

Despite the apparent differences between these two types of users, you can generally accommodate them with a single configuration. However, you might want to consider creating a slightly different GPO for users who spend the majority of their time out of the office.

Mobile users are often expected to provide much of their own computer support because on-site support is not available. For this reason, you might want to grant them more privileges than equivalent users on a desktop computer (for example, so they can install printers).

You might, however, decide to restrict mobile users from making system changes that might damage or disable their systems. For example, you might restrict mobile users from altering certain Internet Explorer settings or adding unapproved hardware devices. Although these users might need access to some of the MMC administration snap-ins, you can make available only a restricted set.

Mobile users expect transparent access to the most critical parts of their data and settings, regardless of whether the portable computer is connected to the network. They roam to desktop computers while their portable computer is in use, for example, to read mail while they are in a remote office. Finally, mobile users frequently disconnect their portable computer from the network without logging off and shutting down. This is more likely to happen with the hibernate and standby features of Windows XP Professional.

IntelliMirror provides several tools that greatly simplify managing mobile users. User data and settings management tools allow users to work on files offline and automatically update network versions of those files when they later reconnect to the network. The Offline Files feature allows users to work on network files when they are not actually connected to the network. Synchronization Manager coordinates synchronization of any changes between the offline version of a file and the network version.

Note If users are likely to disconnect from the network without logging off, it is recommended that you set Offline Files to periodically synchronize in the background. If Offline Files is set to synchronize only when users log off, users' files might not be up-to-date. You might also want to educate users to manually synchronize their data before disconnecting from the network to ensure all files are up-to-date.

Synchronization Manager also helps manage multi-user network files. If multiple users modify the same network file, Synchronization Manager notifies the users about the conflict and offers several resolution methods. The users can save the network version, their local version, or both versions. If both are to be kept, the user is asked for a new file name to store one of the versions so that uniqueness is maintained.

Software installation for the mobile user requires some additional planning. You can make sure that all important software components, defined by you or the user, are completely installed initially. This allows the user access to necessary software even when he or she is not connected to the network. That means that prior to these users leaving the office, you must ensure that all relevant features within the application are installed locally and are not just advertised. For example, make sure the spelling checker for Microsoft Office is locally installed so that the user does not trigger on-demand installation of this feature while offline.

It is not recommended that you publish software for mobile users who connect over slow links. Additionally, when mobile users connect over a slow link, user-assigned software effectively behaves the same as if you published it for these users. If you set the Group Policy slow-link detection setting to the default in the user interface, the software will not install on demand. However, you can define the connection speed that is considered to be a slow link in the Group Policy setting for slow-link detection.

> **Note**   It is recommended you treat any link that is slower than local area network (LAN) speed as a slow link.

If you determine that it is appropriate for mobile users to download software from a remote location and they experience difficulty staying connected when downloading the software, you can verify that the connection speed and Group Policy settings are set appropriately in the **Group Policy slow link detection** setting in **Computer Configuration/Administrative Templates/System/Group Policy** or **User Configuration/Administrative Templates/System/Group Policy**.

Typically, a mobile user has a single portable computer and does not roam between portable computers (unless the computer is replaced). However, roaming user profiles are useful to give some measure of protection against mobile computer failure or loss and to allow roaming to desktop computers when the mobile user is often connected to a fast network. When the mobile user is *not* often connected to a fast network, it is best not to use roaming user profiles.

Data accessed by the mobile user often falls into one or more of the following categories:

- Data that resides on a network server and which users want to access while not connected to the network. Users typically own this data (for example, their home directory), but shared data can also be stored on the local computer.

- Data that resides only on the network server (either not needed offline or volatile shared data that is inappropriate for storing offline).

- Data that resides only on the portable computer local disk. Examples are policy manuals or other read-only items or large document sets that are needed offline by the user but the performance overhead of synchronizing precludes storing them on a file server. (In this case, a suitable backup mechanism is definitely needed.) Other examples might be large database files or other data items that have their own synchronization mechanism, such as the offline storage feature in Microsoft® Outlook®.

Table 5-9 summarizes desktop management features you can use to create a mobile user configuration.

Table 5-9 Features of a Mobile User Configuration

Feature	Specifics	Explanation
Number of Users	One	Each user has a local logon account.
Roaming User Profiles	Yes, depending on connection type and frequency	Provides centralized storage of user state to help administrators replace computers without losing user configuration. Also facilitates roaming.
Folder Redirection	**My Documents** folder	Allows users to access centrally stored data and documents from anywhere. Redirected folders are automatically made available offline, to provide access when users are not connected to the network.
Ability for User to Customize	Within certain guidelines	Allows users to personalize their work environment while preventing changes to critical system settings.
Assigned Applications	Multiple	Core applications are installed on all laptops.
Published Applications	Multiple	Optional applications are available for users to install locally.
Group Policy Settings	Yes	Policy settings are used to create the managed environment.

For more information about configuring portable computers, see "Supporting Mobile Users" in this book.

Managing New Users

IntelliMirror, Group Policy, Windows Installer, and RIS greatly streamline adding new users and their computers to your network. You might use these technologies as follows to add a new managed user.

A new user logs on to a new computer and finds shortcuts to documents on the desktop. These shortcuts link to common files, data, and URLs such as the employee handbook, the company intranet, and appropriate departmental guidelines and procedures. Desktop options, application configurations, Internet settings, and so on are configured to the corporate standard. As the user customizes his or her environment (within boundaries defined by the administrator), these changes are added to the initial environment. For example, the user might change the screen resolution for better visibility, and might add shortcuts to the desktop.

In this situation, a default domain profile and Group Policy are used to configure the new user's environment based on job requirements. The advantage of using a default domain profile is that all new users start from a common, administrator-defined configuration in an existing domain structure. You create a customized domain profile that applies to all new domain users the first time they log on, and they receive the customized settings from this profile. Then, as the user personalizes desktop settings and items, these settings are saved in the user's profile that is stored locally, or in the case of a roaming user profile, in a predetermined location on the network. By implementing a default domain profile in conjunction with Roaming User Profiles, the administrator provides users with the necessary business information as a starting point, and also allows them to access their settings whenever and wherever needed. Finally, the administrator uses Folder Redirection to redirect the user's My Documents folder to a network location, so that the user's documents are safely stored on a network server and can be backed up regularly.

The administrator uses the Software Installation and Maintenance extension of Group Policy to assign Microsoft Word to a user or a specific group of users. The new user logs on for the first time and sees that the software, required to do his job, is listed in the **Start** menu. When the user selects Microsoft Word from the **Start** menu, or double-clicks on a Word document, Windows Installer checks to see whether the application is installed on the local computer. If it is not, Windows Installer downloads and installs the necessary files for Word to run and sets up the necessary local user and computer settings for an on-demand installation.

Managing Multi-User Desktops

A multi-user desktop is managed, but allows users to configure parts of their own desktops. The multi-user desktop is ideal for public shared access computers, such as those in a library, university laboratory, or public computing center. The multi-user desktop experiences high traffic and must be reliable and unbreakable while being flexible enough to allow some customization.

Users can change their desktop wallpaper and color scheme. Because many different people use the computers and security must be maintained, they cannot control or configure hardware or connection settings. The computers often require certain tools, such as word processing software, spreadsheet software, or a development studio. Students might need access to customized applications for instructional purposes and need to be able to install applications that the network administrator has published.

With the multi-user desktop configuration, users can:

- Modify Internet Explorer and the desktop.

- Run assigned or published applications.

- Configure some Control Panel options.

  However, users cannot:

- Use the Run command in the **Start** menu or at a command prompt.

- Add, remove, or modify hardware devices.

In the multi-user environment, turnover is high and a user is unlikely to return to the same computer. Therefore, local copies of roaming user profiles that are cached on the computer are removed after the user logs off, if the roaming user profile settings were successfully synchronized back to the server. Roaming user profiles use the My Documents and Application Data folders that are redirected to a network folder. However, users can log on even if their network profile is not available. In this case, the user receives a new profile based on the default profile.

The multi-user computer is assigned a set of core applications that is available to all users who log on to that particular computer. In addition, a wide variety of applications are available by publishing for user or assigning to users. Due to security risks, users cannot install from a disk, CD-ROM, or Internet location. To conserve disk space on the workstation, most applications must be configured to run from a network server. **Start** menu shortcuts and registry-based settings are configured when the user selects an application to install, but most of the application's files remain on the server. The shares that store the applications can be configured for automatic caching for programs so that application files are cached at the workstation on first use.

Table 5-10 shows the desktop management features used to create a multi-user computing environment.

Table 5-10   Features of a Multi-User Desktop Configuration

Feature	Specifics	Explanation
Multiple Users	Per-user logon accounts	Users share this computer during different shifts. Each user has a unique logon account.
Roaming User Profiles	Yes	Makes user settings available from any computer and enables administrators to easily replace computers without losing their configuration. When the user logs off, the local cached version of the profile is removed to preserve disk space.
Folder Redirection	My Documents and Application Data	User data is saved on server shares and Group Policy prevents users from storing data locally.
Ability for User to Customize	Some	Most of the system is locked down, but some personal settings are available.
Assigned Applications	Multiple	Core applications that are common to all users are assigned to the computer. Other applications are available for on-demand install by means of user assignment.
Published Applications	Multiple	Applications are available for users to install from **Add or Remove Programs** in Control Panel.
Group Policy Settings	Yes	Group Policy settings are used to create the managed environment.

Replacing Computers

When a user receives a new or different computer, it can cause a time-consuming interruption in productivity. It is extremely important that such users regain productivity in the shortest possible time and with a minimum of support. This can be accomplished by storing user data and settings independently of any specific computer. By using the Group Policy features Roaming User Profiles and Folder Redirection, you can assure that the user's data, settings, and applications are available wherever the user logs on to the network.

To further simplify setting up a new managed computer on your network, use Remote Installation Services (RIS) to create standardized operating-system configurations. RIS allows you to create a customized image of a Windows XP Professional or Windows 2000 Professional desktop from a source computer. Then you can save that desktop image to the RIS server. The image can include the operating system alone or a preconfigured desktop image, including the operating system and a standard, locally installed desktop application. You can use that preconfigured image to set up multiple desktops, saving valuable time. Create as many standard desktop images as you need to meet the needs of all types of users in your organization. For more information about using RIS, see "Automating and Customizing Installations," in this book.

These technologies might work together as follows:

A user's computer suddenly undergoes a complete hardware failure. The user calls the internal support line. Shortly, a new computer, loaded only with the Windows XP Professional operating system, arrives. Without waiting for technical assistance, the user plugs in the new computer, connects it to the network, starts it, and can immediately log on.

Because roaming user profiles are enabled, the user finds that the desktop takes on the same configuration as the computer it replaced: the same color scheme, screensaver, and all the application icons, shortcuts, and favorites are present. Because folder redirection and software installation are enabled, the user can seamlessly access data files on the server using the necessary productivity applications once they automatically install.

For more information about implementing these and other standard desktop configurations, see the Desktop Management Scenarios link on the Web Resources page at http://www.microsoft.com/windows/reskits/webresources.

Additional Resources

These resources contain additional information related to this chapter.

Related Information

- The *Designing a Managed Environment* book in the *Microsoft Windows Server 2003 Deployment Kit* for information about deploying Group Policy and security policies.

- The *Microsoft Windows Security Resource Kit* for information about implementing security for Windows-based client computers and servers.

- The *Deployment Planning Guide* of the *Windows 2000 Server Resource Kit* for information about deploying Group Policy and Active Directory.

- The Distributed Systems Guide of the *Microsoft Windows 2000 Server Resource Kit* for more information about implementing and troubleshooting IntelliMirror technologies.

- "Automating and Customizing Installations" in this book for more information about using Remote Installation Services (RIS).

- The Change and Configuration Management Guide link on the Web Resources page at http://www.microsoft.com/windows/reskits/webresources for information about deploying IntelliMirror.

- The Microsoft Internet Explorer Administration Kit (IEAK) link on the Web Resources page at http://www.microsoft.com/windows/reskits/webresources for detailed information about managing Internet Explorer.

- Group Policy Object Settings spreadsheet link on the Web Resources page at http://www.microsoft.com/windows/reskits/webresources for a complete list of Group Policy settings available for managing Windows XP Professional in .xls format for easy tracking of your configured settings.

Related Help Topics

- "Tools for Troubleshooting" in Windows XP Professional Help and Support Center for information about troubleshooting tools use and syntax.

- Group Policy Help for information about Group Policy.

- "IntelliMirror" in Windows XP Professional Help and Support Center for information about user data management, software installation and maintenance, user settings management, and Remote Installation Services (RIS).

Chapter 6

Managing Files and Folders

The Microsoft® Windows® XP Professional operating system helps you, as an administrator, to better control how files and folders are used, and makes it easier for users to work with files and folders. By using Group Policy, Folder Redirection, and Offline Files, you can centrally manage the use of files and folders. You can regulate the extent to which users can modify files and folders, back up user data automatically, and give users access to their files even when not connected to the network.

Related Information

- For an overview of managing desktops by using IntelliMirror® management technologies, see "Managing Desktops" in this book.

- For more information about managing files for mobile users, see "Supporting Mobile Users" in this book.

Overview of Managing Files and Folders

Your ability to manage files and folders differs depending upon whether the Active Directory™ directory service is available. Organizations that use Active Directory can use Group Policy settings, Folder Redirection, and Offline Files to help centrally manage files and folders. In network environments that do not use Active Directory, you can achieve some of the same functionality by using other options such as local Group Policy, System Policy, and Windows XP Professional features on client computers.

If you are managing Windows XP Professional client computers in a Microsoft® Windows® 2000 Server Active Directory environment, you can use Group Policy to implement IntelliMirror™ management using Folder Redirection and Offline Files.

Group Policy

Group Policy is the administrator's primary tool for defining and controlling programs, network resources, and the operating system. Using Group Policy, you define a configuration that is subsequently applied on all specified client computers. Group Policy lets you create as many different client configurations as needed for different kinds of users in your organization. For more information about using Group Policy, see "Managing Desktops" in this book.

Folder Redirection

By using Folder Redirection, you can redirect folders such as My Documents to network servers. Users can then access their files from any network location, and the files can be automatically backed up during routine server backups.

Offline Files and Synchronization Manager

Using Offline Files, you can make redirected user folders available offline, so users can continue working even when they are not connected to the network. Offline Files can also be used to make other files and folders that reside on the network available offline. When users reconnect, updated local copies of files can be synchronized with copies on file servers by using Synchronization Manager.

IntelliMirror

Realizing the full benefit of IntelliMirror components in an Active Directory environment takes careful planning. If your organization has implemented or is planning to implement Active Directory and you want to deploy IntelliMirror, there are many resources available to help with planning and implementation. For more information about implementing data management technologies on a Windows 2000 Server network see the *Deployment Planning Guide* of the *Microsoft® Windows® 2000 Server Resource Kit* and the Change and Configuration Management Deployment Guide link on the Web Resources page at http://www.microsoft.com/windows/reskits/webresources.

Managing Documents with Folder Redirection

Folder redirection is a component of IntelliMirror that allows administrators to redirect the path of the following folders to a new location: My Documents (and its subfolders My Pictures, My Music, and My Videos), Application Data, Desktop, and Start Menu. These folders are located by default in each user's profile on the local computer. The most commonly redirected folders are those that contain large amounts of user data—My Documents and its subfolders. Although it is not a recommended practice to store large amounts of data on the Desktop, users in some organizations do, and the Desktop folder can be redirected as well.

The new location can be a folder on the local computer or a directory on a network share. Users work with documents on a server as though the documents were stored on the local drive.

There are benefits to redirecting any folder, but redirecting the My Documents folder can be particularly advantageous:

- No matter which computer on the network the user logs on to, the user's documents are always available.

- You can use Group Policy to set disk quotas and limit the amount of space taken up by users' folders.

- You can back up data stored on a shared network server as part of routine system administration. This is safer and requires no action on the part of the user.

- User data can be redirected to a hard disk on the user's local computer other than the disk where the operating system files are located. This protects the user's data if the operating system must be reinstalled.

Combining Folder Redirection with Roaming User Profiles   You can also combine Folder Redirection and roaming user profiles to decrease logon and logoff times for roaming and mobile users. A common scenario is to redirect the **My Documents** and **My Pictures** folders, and allow the **Application Data, Desktop**, and **Start Menu** folders to roam with the profile. In addition to improved availability and backup benefits from having the data on the network, users also realize performance gains when using low-speed network connections and in subsequent logon sessions. Not all of the data in the user profile is transferred to the desktop each time the user logs on—only the data that user accesses during a session. Because only some of their documents are copied, performance is improved when the users' profiles are copied from the server.

When you combine the use of Folder Redirection and roaming user profiles, you can also provide fast computer replacement. If a user's computer needs to be replaced, the user's data can quickly be copied from the server locations to a replacement computer.

Previously, administrators who wanted to redirect folders to the network had to edit the registry or use System Policy. These methods can still be used if you are not in an Active Directory environment. For more information about registry entries that affect folder redirection, see "Folder Redirection Registry Keys" later in this chapter.

Selecting Folders for Redirection

The following folders are located by default in the user's profile, and roam by default with a roaming user profile, but you can use Folder Redirection to redirect them to another location instead.

My Documents   My Documents is the folder where users normally save their documents. Common dialog boxes in Windows XP Professional point to the **My Documents** folder by default, so there is a greater tendency for a user to save files there. It is a good practice to train users to save all their documents to this folder, and you can also enable a Group Policy setting to prevent them from saving files in other locations. Because My Documents is often too large to roam without creating excessive network traffic, it should generally be redirected.

My Pictures   A subfolder of My Documents, this is the default location for pictures and images in Windows XP Professional. If My Documents is redirected, My Pictures is also redirected by default. It is recommended that you accept the default setting, and allow **My Pictures** to follow the **My Documents** folder.

My Music   A subfolder of My Documents, this is the default location for music files. If My Documents is redirected, My Music is also redirected by default.

My Videos   A subfolder of My Documents, this is the default location for video files. If My Documents is redirected, My Videos is also redirected by default.

Application Data   This folder stores application state data, such as toolbar settings, custom dictionaries, and other non-registry-based settings. Application vendors decide what each application stores here. Because many applications incorrectly determine that the application data is local, redirecting it can cause inconsistent results. For this reason, it is recommended that you allow Application Data to roam with the profile. However, there *are three situations in which redirecting Application Data might be advantageous:*

- To reduce the size of the profile, thereby decreasing logon time, on multiuser computers where you have enabled a Group Policy setting to delete cached profiles. This gives users access to their Application Data as needed, but without having to download several possibly large files every time they log on.

- To reduce the size of the profile, thereby decreasing initial logon time, in situations where keeping initial logon time short is a priority.

- For Terminal Services clients where you have enabled a Group Policy setting to delete cached profiles.

Desktop   The Desktop folder contains items such as shortcuts and folders that are placed there for quick access. Although the Desktop is usually allowed to roam with the profile, there are two situations in which it might be advantageous to redirect the Desktop folder instead:

- To reduce the size of the profile in organizations where users store large numbers of files, rather than shortcuts, on their desktops. Because any folder that is redirected is also automatically available offline, users can still access data in their redirected folders even if they lose their connection to the server.

- To mandate a common Desktop for a group of users. Some organizations want to configure computers to use a common look and feel. By redirecting a group of users to a read-only copy of the desktop, you can ensure that all users share the same desktop, with the same desktop items. However, Group Policy and Domain Default Profiles provide better ways to accomplish this goal.

Start Menu   The Start Menu folder contains program groups and shortcuts to programs. Start menu redirection is treated differently from other redirected folders. The contents of the user's local Start menu are not copied to the redirected location. Instead, users are directed to a standard Start menu the administrator has previously created and stored on a server. It is not generally recommended to use Folder Redirection to redirect the Start menu folder; use Group Policy to control what appears on the Start menu. Redirecting the Start menu can be advantageous in the following situations:

- Mixed operating system environments. For example, for Microsoft® Windows NT® version 4.0–based client computers, you can define a path for a redirected Start menu by using System Policy. You can then use Folder Redirection to define a path for Windows XP Professional–based clients to the same location.

- Kiosk-type environments, to redirect to a read-only version of the Start menu. Redirect it only in environments where software deployment features are not being used.

Tools for Configuring Folder Redirection

Folder Redirection configuration options vary, depending on whether you have an Active Directory environment. In an Active Directory environment, you can use Group Policy to apply different configurations to different user groups; for example, you can redirect Marketing users' folders to a server in the Marketing department, and redirect Engineering users' My Documents folder to their existing home directories. In non-Active Directory environments, you have other options, such as using System Policy, as described later in this chapter; you cannot, however, configure folder redirection by using a local Group Policy object (GPO).

Windows 2000 Server Environments with Active Directory

In a Windows 2000 Server environment with Active Directory, you configure Folder Redirection by using the Group Policy Microsoft Management Console (MMC) snap-in. For details about implementing this component, see "Applying Change and Configuration Management" in the *Deployment Planning Guide.*

Other Server Environments

In Windows 2000 Server environments without Active Directory and in other server environments you can redirect folders to a local or network location by using the following methods:

- In Windows NT 4.0 environments, you can use System Policy.

- Administrators or users can also redirect the My Documents folder by changing the Target folder location on the My Documents Properties page.

Using Offline Files

Offline Files provides access to network files and folders from a local disk when the network is unavailable. This feature is particularly useful when access to information is critical, when network connections are unstable, or when using mobile computers.

Offline Files gives mobile users access to their files when they are not connected to the network and ensures that they are always working with the most current version of the files. These benefits are also useful to onsite workers who might temporarily lose network connectivity due to server maintenance or technical problems. For more information about issues relating to offline files on mobile computers, such as synchronizing with a slow link and preventing synchronization when running on battery power, see "Supporting Mobile Users" in this book.

Offline Files can be paired with Folder Redirection for higher data reliability. For example, if a folder is redirected, the contents of that folder are stored on a server drive. In Windows XP Professional, by default any redirected folders are automatically made available offline. This default behavior can be changed by enabling the Group Policy setting, **Do not automatically make redirected folders available offline**. The folder is then accessible on the user's computer in case of network inaccessibility and from any computer to which the user logs on.

In an Active Directory environment, Group Policy settings control the Offline Files feature. For details about Group Policy settings that manage Offline Files, see "Group Policy Settings that Affect Offline Files" later in this chapter, and Group Policy Help.

Implementing Offline Files

An Active Directory environment is not necessary to use Offline Files. You can make files available from any computer that supports server message block (SMB)–based File and Printer Sharing, including computers running Microsoft® Windows® 95, Microsoft® Windows® 98, Windows NT 4.0, and Windows 2000. Offline Files is not available on Novell NetWare networks or when Windows 2000 is running Terminal Services (except in single-user mode.)

Files specified for offline use are cached in a database on the hard disk of the local computer. If the network resource becomes unavailable, a message appears in the notification area. Changes made to the file while offline are saved locally, and then synchronized when the network resource becomes available again.

Before you can make files or folders on a computer available offline, you need to set up the computer to use Offline Files.

To set up a computer to use Offline Files

1. Open **My Computer**.

2. On the **Tools** menu, click **Folder Options**.

3. On the **Offline Files** tab, select the **Enable Offline Files** check box if it is not already selected.

4. Select **Synchronize all offline files before logging off** to enable a full synchronization. Leave this option unselected for a quick synchronization.

On the **Offline Files** tab, you can also set the reminder balloon options, designate the amount of disk space to use for offline files, place a shortcut to the Offline Files folder on the desktop, and encrypt the offline files local cache. Note that if an option is controlled by a Group Policy setting, it cannot be changed on the **Offline Files** tab of the local computer.

Offline Files Database

Offline files and related information are stored in a database in the system folder (*systemroot*\CSC) on the local computer.

> **Note**   Another term for Offline Files is client-side caching (CSC).

The CSC directory contains all offline files that are requested by any user on the computer. The database mimics the network resource while it is offline so that files are accessed as though the network resource is still available. File permissions and system permissions on the files are preserved. For example, a Microsoft® Word document created by Bob, given a password, and saved to a share on which only Bob has Full Control, cannot be opened from the CSC directory by Alice, because she has neither the share permissions to open the file nor the password required to open the file in Microsoft Word. You can also maintain the security of sensitive files by using Encrypting File System (EFS) to encrypt the Offline Files cache.

The Offline Files folder shows the files that are stored in the database. To open or view the files directly in the CSC folder, you must log on as a member of the Administrators group.

> **Note**   On a file allocation table (FAT) file system or a FAT file system converted to NTFS, users might be able to read information that is cached in the *systemroot*\CSC directory. This includes offline files that are requested by another user on the same computer.

It is very important not to delete files directly from the CSC directory. For information about how to delete files see "Deleting Files and Folders" later in this chapter.

Making Files Available Offline

Files are cached either automatically or manually to the computer that requests them. Automatic caching occurs when a specific file in a folder is opened, but only if the server indicates that the contents of the share must be automatically cached. Automatically cached files are marked as **Temporarily Available Offline** in the Offline Files folder because they can be removed from the cache as the cache fills up. There is no guarantee that an automatically cached file will be available when offline.

Files are manually cached when a computer specifically requests, or pins, a particular file or folder on the network to be made available offline. You pin a file or folder by selecting the file or folder, and on the **File** menu selecting **Make Available Offline**. Manually cached files are marked as **Always available offline** in the Offline Files folder.

In Windows 2000 and Windows XP Professional, the **Manual Caching for Documents** setting is enabled by default when a folder is shared. To change the setting so that documents in the shared folder are automatically cached, right-click the folder, click **Properties**, click the **Sharing** tab, and then click **Caching**. In the **Settings** box, select **Automatic Caching of Documents**. You can also disable caching.

> **Note**   You can manually pin files and folders that are configured for auto-matic caching.

By default, the following file types cannot be cached:
*.slm; *.mdb; *.ldb; *.mdw; *.mde; *.pst; *.db?

You can override the default settings by using the **Files not cached** Group Policy setting. Any file types that you specify in the Group Policy setting override the default settings. For example, if you specify that only .txt files cannot be cached, all other file types are available for caching.

The default cache size for automatically cached offline files is 10 percent of the total disk space of the hard disk. You can change the default by specifying a value between 0 and 100 percent on the **Offline Files** tab of the **Folder Options** dialog box. This setting does not affect the cache for files that are manually cached by the user, or for files pinned by the administrator using the Group Policy setting **Computer Configuration** or **User Configuration\Administrative Templates\Network\Offline Files\Administratively assigned offline files**. You can store up to 2 gigabytes (GB) of automatically cached files per computer if that much space is available; for manually cached files, you are limited only by the amount of available disk space on the drive containing the cache.

> **Note**   If the network resource is online, renaming files in the Offline Files folder takes effect immediately on the network resource.

Encrypting Offline Files

Windows XP Professional provides Encrypting File System (EFS) support for Offline Files. The local cache of Offline Files can be encrypted if the cache directory resides on an NTFS volume. When the cache is encrypted, the local copy of a cached file is automatically encrypted.

> **Tip**   This capability is particularly useful for securing data on mobile computers.

To select this option, in the **Folder Options** dialog box, click the **Offline Files** tab, and then select the **Encrypt Offline files to secure data** check box. You must be a member of the Administrators group to perform this function.

You can also use Group Policy to apply this option to groups of users. In the Group Policy snap-in, enable the **Encrypt the Offline Files cache** setting. If the setting is configured by using Group Policy, it cannot be overridden on the **Offline Files** tab on the local computer.

Reconnecting to the Network Resource

A network share automatically becomes available after being offline when three conditions are all met:

- No offline files from that network share are open on the user's computer.

- No offline files from that network share contain changes that must be synchronized.

- The network connection is not a slow link.

If these conditions are met, a user can open a file and automatically begin working on that file on the network share. The changes the user makes are saved both to the file on the network share and to the file that is cached in the Offline Files folder.

If any of these conditions is not met and a user opens a file on the network share, the user continues working offline even though the network share is available. Any changes that the user makes are saved only to the local version of the file, which must then be synchronized with the network share.

Synchronizing Files

When using Offline Files, users can synchronize some or all network resources by using Synchronization Manager. For example, users can set certain shares to be synchronized every time they log on or log off the network. Synchronization Manager quickly scans the system, and if it detects changes, the resources are automatically updated. Only the resources that have changed are updated, which speeds up the synchronization process.

Administrators can use Group Policy to specify that all offline files on a particular computer are automatically synchronized when users log off, when users log on, or when a computer enters a suspend state.

How Synchronization Works

Offline files can be synchronized with the server copies of the files:

- When the user manually forces synchronization.

- During the logon or logoff process, as specified in Synchronization Manager.

- At intervals when the computer is idle, as specified in Synchronization Manager.

- At scheduled times, as specified in Synchronization Manager.

When synchronizing offline files, you can select quick synchronization or full synchronization. The full synchronization option synchronizes every file in the local cache with the network share. The quick synchronization option only verifies that all files in the cache are complete; it does not verify that they are up-to-date.

For example if you have an autocached share containing a 10-MB file named Example.doc, when the client opens Example.doc for the first time, a directory structure is created for the file in the client database, and the file is marked as incomplete. At this point, a directory entry with the file properties exists on the client, and Example.doc is a 0-byte length file. Example.doc is then read from the server in increments. If the application is closed before the entire file is read, the file is saved in an incomplete manner in the local cache. Incomplete files are not available offline. Quick synchronization completes such files.

By default, full synchronization is performed when the user logs off. If the Group Policy setting **Synchronize all offline files before logging off** is disabled, then the system automatically performs a quick synchronization.

In order for synchronization to work, the network resources must be online or available for reconnection. How synchronization is run affects how offline changes are sent to the network resource and how new versions of cached files are downloaded. Table 6-1 describes what kind of synchronization occurs when each method is used.

Table 6-1   Synchronization Options and File Caching Behavior

Synchronization Settings and Functions	Send offline changes to the network resource?	Receive cached files from the network resource?
Automatically synchronize the selected items when I log on to my computer is enabled	Yes	No
Synchronize all offline files before logging off is enabled	Yes	Fully
Synchronize all offline files before logging off is disabled	No	Partially
Synchronize the selected items while my computer is idle	Yes	Partially
Scheduled by using Synchronization Manager	Yes	Fully
Clicking **Synchronize** from the **Start** menu or on the **Tools** menu	Yes	Fully
Clicking **Synchronize** on the **File** menu	Yes	Fully
Clicking **Make Available Offline** on the **File** menu	No	Partially
Clicking the Offline Files icon in the notification area of the task bar	Yes	No

If the network resource version of a file and the locally cached version of the file are different, you can view each file and the date and time that the files were saved, and then select one of the following options in the **Resolve file conflicts** dialog box:

- **Keep both versions**. Saves the version that resides on the local computer to the network as *filename*(*username* v*X*).doc, where *filename* is the name of the file, *username* is the user name, and *X* is the version number.

- **Keep only the version on my computer**. Replaces the network version.

- **Keep only the network version**. Replaces the version on my computer.

Configuring Synchronization

Use the following procedure to set up synchronization.

To set up synchronization

1. Open **Synchronize**.

2. Click **Setup**.

3. Use the **Logon/Logoff**, **On Idle**, and **Scheduled** tabs to configure options.

You can also initiate synchronization from the My Documents folder. After you have set up files for synchronization, **Synchronize** appears on the Start menu.

> **Note**   Synchronization works only for the user who is currently logged on.

Deleting Files and Folders

There are two methods you can use to safely remove offline files from the cache without affecting network files or folders. You can delete selected files from the Offline Files folder, or you can delete all files associated with a particular network share by using the "Delete Files" feature from the Offline Files property page. Do not directly delete or move any files from the *systemroot*\CSC folder.

Deleting Files from the Offline Files Folder

You can open the Offline Files Folder and delete files directly from the list of offline files. Deleting a file this way removes it from the cache regardless of whether it was manually or automatically cached.

Note   Deleting files and folders from the cache does not delete the network copy of the file or folder.

If an offline folder is manually cached and you delete any or all offline files in the folder, the folder remains pinned. All files in the folder are cached the next time a full synchronization occurs.

To delete files from the cache using the Offline Files Folder

1.   Click a folder, and then on the **Tools** menu, click **Folder Options**.

2.   On the **Offline Files** tab, click **View Files**.

3.   Click the files you want to delete, and then on the **File** menu, click **Delete**.

In this view of the Offline Files folder, you can see which files are automatically cached (temporarily available offline) and which are manually cached (always available offline). If you delete manually cached folders this way, the folders and files in them are no longer pinned. You need to pin the files or folders to make them available offline again.

To delete files from the cache on a network share

1.   Click a shared network folder, and then on the **Tools** menu, click **Folder Options**.

2.   On the **Offline Files** tab, click **Delete Files**.

3.   In the **Confirm File Delete** dialog box, select the shared folders containing the offline files you want to delete.

4.   Click **Delete only the temporary offline versions** if you want to delete files that were automatically cached. Click **Delete both the temporary offline versions and the versions that are always available offline** if you want to delete files that were automatically cached and files that were manually cached (pinned).

Files are also deleted from the cache whenever an offline file is deleted by using a normal user path, such as Windows Explorer, My Computer, the Run dialog box, or the command prompt. When users verify that they want to delete a file, the file is removed from the cache. This is not an effective way to clean up the cache because it also deletes files in the shared network folder. However, the files are deleted immediately only if the associated network share is online. If the share is offline, the local copy is deleted and the Synchronization Conflict notification is displayed during the next interactive synchronization.

Reinitializing the Cache

During normal operation, you delete cached files by using the procedure shown in "Deleting Files from the Offline Files Folder" earlier in this chapter. However, if normal methods of deleting files are unsuccessful, you might need to reinitialize. Reinitializing deletes all offline files in the folder and resets the Offline Files database. If any files in the cache are changed and not synchronized with the network versions, the changes are lost when the cache is reinitialized. You must restart the computer to complete the reinitialization.

To reinitialize the Offline Files cache

1. Click a folder, and then on the **Tools** menu, click **Folder Options**.

2. Click the **Offline Files** tab.

3. Press CTRL+SHIFT, and then click **Delete Files**.

4. Restart the computer.

Caution   You cannot undo the effects of reinitialization. After the cache is reinitialized all offline files are permanently removed from the computer.

Group Policy Settings That Affect Offline Files

You can use Group Policy settings to control the functioning of Offline Files. In an Active Directory environment, you can apply these settings to groups of users by applying a GPO to a site, domain, or organizational unit. In a non-Active Directory environment, you can configure these settings in the local GPO, which is found on each client computer.

Note that many of the following settings can also be configured by the user by using the My Computer interface, as described in "Implementing Offline Files" earlier in this chapter. Generally, if you apply a GPO, but leave a setting as **Not Configured**, the user can configure it by using Offline Files in Folder Options. If you either enable or disable the setting, the user cannot change it.

For more information about using Group Policy with Windows 2000 Server, see "Group Policy" and "Introduction to Desktop Management" in the *Distributed Systems Guide* of the *Microsoft Windows 2000 Server Resource Kit*.

The Group Policy settings for Offline Files are found in two locations in the Group Policy snap-in: **Computer Configuration\Administrative Templates\Network\Offline Files** for computer-based settings, and **User Configuration\Administrative Templates\Network\Offline Files** for user-based settings. Some settings are available for Computer Configuration only, while some are available for both User Configuration and Computer Configuration. If the same setting is configured for both Computer Configuration and User Configuration, the Computer Configuration setting takes precedence.

For more information about a setting, click the **Explain** tab associated with each Group Policy setting. Table 6-2 shows Group Policy settings for Offline Files.

Table 6-2   Group Policy Settings for Offline Files

Group Policy Setting	Description
Enabled	Determines whether Offline Files is enabled. Offline Files is enabled by default on Windows XP Professional–based client computers and is disabled by default on servers.
Default cache size	Limits percentage of a computer's disk space that can be used to store automatically cached offline files.
	Does not affect disk space available for manually cached offline files.
Files not cached	Allows you to exclude certain types of files from automatic and manual caching for offline use.
At logoff, delete local copy of user's offline files	Deletes local copies of the user's offline files when the user logs off.
	Caution: Files are not synchronized before they are deleted. Any changes to local files since the last synchronization are lost.
Encrypt the Offline Files cache	Determines whether offline files are encrypted in the cache on the local computer. Encrypting the offline cache enhances security on the local computer.
Disable user configuration of Offline Files	Prevents users from enabling, disabling, or changing the configuration of Offline Files. Administrators can configure other settings as they require, then enable this setting to prevent users from making any changes, thus locking in a standard configuration.
Synchronize all offline files before logging off	Determines whether offline files are fully synchronized when users log off.
Synchronize all offline files when logging on	Determines whether offline files are fully synchronized when users log on.
Synchronize all offline files before a suspend	Determines whether offline files are fully synchronized before a computer (such as a portable computer) enters suspend mode.
Action on server disconnect	Determines whether network files remain available if the computer is suddenly disconnected from the server hosting the files.
Non-default server disconnect actions	Determines how computers respond when they are disconnected from particular Offline Files servers. Administrators can enter the name of each server, and specify whether users can work offline when disconnected from that server.

Table 6-2   Group Policy Settings for Offline Files

Group Policy Setting	Description
Disable "Make Available Offline" tab	Prevents users from making network files and folders available offline.
	Removes the **Make Available Offline** option from the File menu and from all shortcut menus in Windows Explorer. Does not prevent the system from saving local copies of files that reside on network shares designated for automatic caching.
Prevent use of Offline Files folder	Disables the **View Files** button on the Offline Files tab. As a result, users cannot use the Offline Files folder to view or open copies of network files stored on their computer. Does not prevent users from working offline or from saving local copies of files available offline. Does not prevent them from using other programs, such as Windows Explorer, to view their offline files.
Administratively assigned offline files	Allows the administrator to specify files and folders available offline to users of the computer. To assign a file or folder, click Show and then click Add. In the "Type the name of the item to be added" box, type the fully qualified UNC path.
Do not automatically make redirected folders available offline	By default, local folders that are redirected are automatically made available offline. This setting allows the administrator to override the default behavior.
Prohibit "Make Available Offline" for these files and folders	Allows the administrator to specify files or folders that you do not want available offline. To assign a file or folder, click Show and then click Add. In the Type the name of the item to be added box, type the fully qualified UNC path.
Subfolders always available offline	Makes subfolders available offline whenever their parent folder is made available offline.
Disable reminder balloons	Reminder balloons appear above the Offline Files icon in the notification area to notify users when they have lost the connection to a networked file and are working on a local copy of the file. This setting hides or displays reminder balloons.
Reminder balloon frequency	Determines how often reminder balloon updates appear (in minutes).
Initial reminder balloon lifetime	Determines how long the first reminder balloon for a network status change is displayed (in seconds).
Reminder balloon lifetime	Determines how long updated reminder balloons are displayed.
Event logging level	Determines which events the Offline Files feature records in the Event Log.
Configure Slow link speed	Configures the threshold value at which the Offline Files component considers a network connection to be slow, to prevent excessive synchronization traffic.

Sharing Files and Folders

In Windows XP Professional, members of the Administrators, Power Users, and Server Operators groups can share folders. Other users who have been granted the Create Permanent Shared Objects user right can also share folders. If a folder resides on an NTFS volume, you must have at least Read permission to share the folder. When you share a folder, keep the following in mind:

- You can only share folders, not files.

- Shared folders are only relevant to users who need to access data over the network. Sharing a folder and assigning shared folder permissions has no effect on users who are locally logged on to a computer.

- When you copy a shared folder, the original shared folder is still shared, but the copy is not shared.

- When you move a shared folder, the folder is no longer shared.

- If you have a mixed environment, use 8.3 format share names so older client operating systems can recognize them.

To share a folder

1. Right-click the folder you want to share, and then click **Properties**.

2. In the folder properties dialog box, click the **Sharing** tab.

3. Click **Share this folder**, and then in **Share name**, type the name you want users to see when they browse for this folder on the network. If you append the name with the $ symbol, the folder is shared, but the folder does not appear when users browse for it across the network.

4. In **Comment**, type a description for the shared folder. This description is visible to users who browse across the network.

5. In **User limit**, make any changes you want. The default setting is **Maximum allowed**, which corresponds to the number of client access licenses you have purchased. You can also designate a user limit by clicking **Allow**, typing the number of users next to **Users**, and then clicking **OK**.

Warning By default, shared folder permissions are set so that the Full Control permission is assigned to the Everyone group. You can change the default shared folder permissions by clicking **Permissions** in the folder properties dialog box.

You can also share a folder from the command line by using the **net share** command. For more information about sharing a folder, including information about using the **net share** command, see Windows 2000 Server Help.

Configuring Shared Folder Permissions

Shared folder permissions determine who can gain access to resources on remote computers. When a folder is shared, users can connect to the folder over the network and gain access to its contents. Shared folder permissions allow you to control which users or groups can gain access to the contents of a shared folder.

Shared folders and NTFS permissions   Shared folder permissions are different from NTFS permissions. NTFS permissions use access control lists (ACLs) to limit access to resources, and can only be assigned to resources on an NTFS volume. In addition, NTFS permissions can be assigned to both files and folders. Shared folder permissions do not use access control lists, and can therefore be used on a volume that is formatted with any file system. In addition, shared folder permissions can only be assigned to folders. For more information about NTFS permissions, see "File Systems" in this book.

Administrative shares   In addition to folders you designate as shared, Windows XP Professional also creates several shared folders by default when you start a computer or when you stop and then start the Server service. These shared folders, called the *administrative shares*, are shared for administrative purposes and allow users to access administrative resources remotely. Some of the administrative shares cannot be configured, and access is restricted to users who have administrative rights. The administrative shares include folders such as the systemroot folder (ADMIN$), the root folder of every drive (C$, D$, and so on), and the printer driver folder (PRINT$).

Setting shared folder permissions   Shared folder permissions can only be set by members of the Administrators, Power Users, or Server Operators groups. Users who have been granted the Create Permanent Shared Objects user right can also assign shared folder permissions. If a folder resides on an NTFS volume, you must have at least Read permission to assign shared folder permissions.

There are three types of shared folder permissions: Read (the most restrictive), Change, and Full Control (the least restrictive). Table 6-3 describes each of these permissions.

Table 6-3   Shared Folder Permissions

Permission	Description
Read	Users can display folder and file names, display file data and attributes, run program files and scripts, and change folders within the shared folder.
Change	Users can create folders, add files to folders, change data in files, append data to files, change file attributes, delete folders and files, and perform all tasks permitted by the Read permission.
Full Control	Users can change file permissions, take ownership of files, and perform all tasks permitted by the Change permission.

You can allow or deny shared folder permissions to individual users or groups. From an administrative standpoint, it is usually most efficient to assign permissions to a group rather than to individual users. Also, deny permissions only when it is necessary to override permissions that are otherwise applied. Denied permissions take precedence over any permissions that you otherwise allow for user accounts and groups. For example, it might be necessary to deny permissions to a specific user who belongs to a group that has been granted permissions.

When you assign shared folder permissions, keep the following in mind:

■ Shared folder permissions do not restrict access to users who are locally logged on to a computer where the shared folder is located. Shared folder permissions only apply to users who connect to the folder across the network.

■ To restrict access to a folder, use shared folder permissions or NTFS permissions, but not both. The best practice is to share a folder so that the Everyone group has Full Control, and then restrict access to the folder using NTFS permissions.

■ If shared folder permissions are configured for a folder, and NTFS permissions are configured for the folder and its contents, the most restrictive permissions apply.

■ When you assign a shared folder permission to a user, and that user is a member of a group to which you assigned a different permission, the user's effective permissions are the combination of the user and group permissions. For example, if a user has Read permission and is a member of a group with Change permission, the user's effective permission is Change, which includes Read.

To configure shared folder permissions

1. Right-click the folder for which you want to configure shared folder permissions, and then click **Properties**.

2. In the folder properties dialog box, click the **Sharing** tab, and then click **Permissions**.

3. In the **Permissions for** dialog box, click **Add**.

4. In the **Select Users, Computers, or Groups** dialog box, click **Object Types**, click the **Users** check box, and then click **OK**.

5. Under **Enter the object names to select**, type the name of the group or user for which you want to set shared folder permissions, and then click **OK**.

6. In the **Permissions for** dialog box, in the **Group or user names** box, click the group or user for which you want to set shared folder permissions.

7. In the **Permissions for** dialog box, allow or deny permissions, and then click **OK**.

Simple Sharing and ForceGuest

When a Windows XP Professional–based computer is not joined to a domain, the simple sharing model is fundamentally different than the model used in previous versions of Windows. By default, all users logging on to such computers over the network are forced to use the Guest account; this is called *ForceGuest*.

How ForceGuest Works

On computers running Windows 95 and Windows 98 you can specify read-only and full-control share passwords: any user connecting to a share can enter the appropriate password and get the specified level of access. However, this share-level password model is insecure, because share passwords are passed in plaintext and can be intercepted by someone with physical access to the network.

On computers running Windows 2000 and not joined to a domain, identical user accounts with matching passwords must be created on two computers (to enable transparent sharing) or the user must type a user name and password when connecting. Windows 2000 also requires that you grant permissions to the user account on the computer hosting a share to the share and to the files and directories being shared or that you enable the Guest account. However, using the Guest account can cause broader than intended access to the share, because the Everyone group (which allows Guest access) is widely used in the default system permissions.

By default, on computers running Windows XP Professional and not joined to a domain, all incoming network connections are forced to use the Guest account. This means that an incoming connection, even if a user name and password is provided, has only Guest-level access to the share. Because of this, either the Guest user account or the Everyone group (the only group to which the Guest account belongs) must have permissions on the share and on the directories and files that are shared. It also means that, in contrast to Windows 2000, you do not need to configure matching user accounts on computers to share files. Because Windows XP

Professional supports Anonymous connections, and because it severely limits the use of the Everyone group in file system permissions, granting the Everyone group access to shared folders does not present the security problem that it does on Windows 2000–based computers.

ForceGuest is enabled by default, but can be disabled on Windows XP Professional by disabling the local security policy **Network Access: Force Network Logons using Local Accounts to Authenticate as Guest**. By contrast, on Windows XP Professional–based computers joined to a domain, the default sharing and security settings are the same as in Windows 2000. Likewise, if the ForceGuest policy setting on a Windows XP Professional–based computer not joined to a domain is disabled, then the computer behaves as in Windows 2000.

Sharing Files and Folders Using the Simple Sharing User Interface

To simplify configuring sharing and to reduce the possibility of misconfiguration, Windows XP Professional uses the Simple Sharing User Interface (UI). The simple sharing UI appears if ForceGuest is turned on; the traditional sharing and security tabs are shown if ForceGuest is turned off.

On computers running Windows XP Professional that are not joined to a domain, ForceGuest is turned on by default. To access the traditional sharing and security tabs and manage permissions manually on these computers, go to Windows Explorer or My Computer, click the **Tools** menu, click **Folder Options**, click the **View** tab, and then clear the **Use simple file sharing (Recommended)** check box. Note that changes made manually cannot be undone by using the simple sharing UI, and although you might make what appears to be a reasonable change to permissions, the resultant permissions might not work as expected if ForceGuest is subsequently turned on.

By using the simple sharing UI you can create or remove a share and set permissions on the share. When simple sharing is in effect, appropriate permissions are automatically set on shared files and folders. The following permissions are added when you use the simple sharing UI:

- Share permissions
- File permissions
- Allow others to change my files
- Don't allow others to change my files

When the Guest-only security model is used, the **Sharing** tab has only three options:

- **Share this folder on the network**. Grants the Everyone group Read permissions on the folder and its contents.
- **Share name**. The name of the share on the network.

- **Allow other users to change my files**. Grants the Everyone group Full Control permissions on folders and Change permissions on files.

Sharing the Root Directory of a Drive

You can create a share at the root of the system drive, but simple sharing does not adjust the file permissions on such shares. On a share created at the root, the simple sharing UI is displayed in the property sheet, and **Sharing** is added to the shortcut menu on the system drive icon in Windows Explorer. There are two important reasons why it is recommended that you not share the root directory of the system drive:

- By default the Everyone group is granted only Read permissions on the root of the system drive, so sharing the root of the system drive is not sufficient for most remote administration tasks.

- Sharing the root of the system drive is not secure—it essentially grants anyone who can connect to the computer access to system configuration information. For maximum security, it is recommended that you only share folders within your user profile, and only share information that you specifically want others to access.

Shared Documents Folder

The Shared Documents folder in My Documents is new in Windows XP Professional. This folder appears when two or more user accounts are created on the local computer. Files can be shared among multiple users of the same computer. In a network environment, files can be copied or moved to a folder on another computer.

By default, the Shared Documents folder is automatically shared and made accessible to all other computers on the network.

Searching for Files, Folders, and Network Resources

Searching for files, folders, and network resources is easier in Windows XP Professional than in Windows 2000. You can perform a search from the Start menu, My Computer, My Documents, or My Network Places. As in Windows 2000, from My Network Places you can connect to shared folders, a Web folder, or an FTP site.

In Windows XP Professional, using Windows Explorer is similar to using a Web browser. Forward and Back buttons, a History folder, an Address bar, custom views, and the Search Assistant are available in Windows Explorer windows and in all windows accessed by using My Computer, My Network Places, My Documents, and the **Search** command on the **Start** menu.

When you use Windows XP Professional in a Windows 2000 Server Active Directory domain, you can search the Active Directory directory service by specifying attributes for the resource you want. For example, you can search for printers capable of printing double-sided pages. For more information about searching in an

Active Directory domain, see "Searching for Network Resources In an Active Directory Environment" later in this chapter.

Finding Files and Folders

Windows XP Professional offers a number of ways to find files or folders. Each method provides access to the History folder, Search Assistant, and Indexing Service on the local computer.

Users can search for files and folders in the following ways:

■ On the **Start** menu, point to **Search**, and then click **For Files or Folders**, **On the Internet**, **For People**, or in an Active Directory domain, **For Printers**.

■ Open **Windows Explorer**.

■ Open **My Documents**, **My Computer**, or **My Network Places**.

Using the History Folder and History View

The Windows XP Professional History folder integrates Web links and network shares, so users have access to their navigation history no matter where they view the History folder. Users can sort the History folder by the following categories: **By Date**, **By Site**, **By Most Visited**, or **By Order Visited Today**.

You can also select the History view from the toolbar in Windows Explorer, which tracks the history of all Web sites and documents opened. In this view you can sort by location or by date used, or search the history list, using option buttons.

Connecting to Network Shares

Windows XP Professional allows you to map drives directly to shared subfolders on the network. In previous versions of Windows, you mapped drives to *servername**sharename*. In Windows XP Professional, you can map drives to *servername**sharename**subsharenname*.

You can use the Add Network Place wizard to connect to frequently accessed network resources. Mapped network drives do not appear in My Network Places; to view mapped drives, use My Computer or the Windows Explorer Address bar.

Using Indexing Service

Indexing Service extracts information from documents on the local hard disk drive and shared drives and organizes it in a way that makes it quick and easy to access that information by using the Search Assistant, the Indexing Service query form, or a Web browser. The information can include text contained in a document (its *contents*), and information about the document (its *properties*), such as the author's name. Indexing Service automatically stores all the index information either in the system catalog or in the Web catalog.

After the index is created, users can search, or *query*, the index for documents that contain specified words or properties. For example, a user might run a query for all documents containing the word *product* or run a query for all Microsoft® Office documents written by a specific author. Indexing Service returns a list of all documents that meet the search criteria.

To enable Indexing Service on a local computer

1. Click **Start**, point to **Search**, and then click **For Files or Folders**.

2. In the **Search Results** dialog box, under **What do you want to search for?**, click **Change preferences**, and then click **With Indexing Service (for faster local searches)**.

3. Click **Yes, enable Indexing Service**.

Indexing Service is designed to run continuously and requires little maintenance. After it is set up, all operations are automatic, including index creation, index updating, and crash recovery in the event of a power failure.

Searching for Network Resources in an Active Directory Environment

When Windows XP Professional–based computer is connected to a Windows 2000 Server domain that uses Active Directory, users can search the directory for resources such as computers, people, and shared folders, providing that the resource is *published* in Active Directory.

Active Directory contains objects, and each object is assigned specific attributes. For example, if a printer can print double-sided pages, the Active Directory administrator might specify that attribute for the printer object in Active Directory. If a user searches for printers that can print double-sided pages, the search returns all printers with that attribute. If the administrator chooses not to assign that attribute to the printer, even if it is capable of that function, the printer cannot be found by searching only for that attribute.

To help users locate resources quickly, create custom Active Directory searches and save them as query directory search (.qds) files. You can then distribute the .qds files to the workgroups or organizational units that need them.

Warning   To search using Active Directory, your computer must be part of a Windows 2000 Server Active Directory domain.

For more information about Active Directory, see the *Distributed Systems Guide* of the *Microsoft® Windows® 2000 Server Resource Kit*.

Searching for Computers

In Windows XP Professional, as in earlier versions of Windows, users can search for computers by using NetBIOS. In an Active Directory environment, users can also search for computers using Active Directory. It is important to understand the difference between the two methods.

In a NetBIOS search, if the computer the user is searching for is logged on to the network, the user can connect to it and view its shared folders.

To search for computers using NetBIOS

1. Click **Start**, point to **Search**, and then click **For Files or Folders**.

2. Click the **Computers** link.

In an Active Directory network search, computers in the directory are represented by objects. Users can locate an object even when it is disconnected from the network. When a user double-clicks the icon representing a computer found using an Active Directory search, only the properties for that computer are displayed. Users cannot locate the actual computer and its available shares by using an Active Directory search. To access shares in an Active Directory domain, the shares must be published, and the user must know the name of the share.

To search for computers using Active Directory

1. In **My Network Places**, double-click **Entire Network**.

2. Do one of the following:

   - If Web View is enabled, click the **entire contents** link, and then double-click **Directory**.

   - If Web View is not enabled, double-click **Directory**.

3. Right-click the object representing an Active Directory domain, and then click **Find**.

4. In the **Find** box, click **Computers**.

Note   You might need to specify an object in the **In** box.

Searching for Shared Files and Folders

For users to access files and folders in an Active Directory domain, the Active Directory administrator must first publish them. Folders that are shared but not published do not appear in the Search Results window. If a user searches for a computer by using an Active Directory search, no shared folders that might reside on that computer are accessible or visible. To view and access shared files and folders, the user must run a NetBIOS search.

While users can use the Search Assistant in Active Directory to locate shared folders, they must specify the exact folder name. Users cannot browse a list of shared folders. To find a shared folder in Active Directory, open the Search Assistant, and in the **Find** box, click **Shared Folders**. Then, in the **Named** box on the **Shared Folders** tab, type the shared folder name.

Troubleshooting Files and Folders Management

This section presents some common situations that might arise when managing files and folders and the most likely causes for these problems.

Folder Redirection Registry Keys

To help troubleshoot problems with Folder Redirection, you can view the registry settings to determine whether folders are redirected and see the path to the redirected location.

> **Caution**   Do not edit the registry unless you have no alternative. The registry editor bypasses standard safeguards, allowing settings that can damage your system, or even require you to reinstall Windows. If you must edit the registry, back it up first and see the Registry Reference in the Microsoft Windows 2000 Server Resource Kit at http://www.microsoft.com/reskit.

To view redirected folder information in the registry

1. In the **Run** dialog box, type **regedit.exe**, and then click **OK**.

2. Navigate to the registry subkey: HKEY_CURRENT_USER\Software \Microsoft\Windows\CurrentVersion\Explorer\User Shell Folders

If a folder has not been redirected, the Data value will be the default location in the user profile, as shown in Table 6.4.

Table 6-4   Registry Keys for Redirected Folders

Registry Key Name	Type	Data
AppData	REG_EXPAND_SZ	%USERPROFILE%\Application Data
Desktop	REG_EXPAND_SZ	%USERPROFILE%\Desktop
Personal	REG_EXPAND_SZ	%USERPROFILE%\My Documents
My Pictures	REG_EXPAND_SZ	%USERPROFILE%\My Documents\My Pictures
Start Menu	REG_EXPAND_SZ	%USERPROFILE%\Start Menu

If a folder has been redirected, the Data value will be the redirected path.

Folders Are Not Redirected

Using Group Policy, you configure a user managed by a Group Policy object to have the user's My Documents folder redirected to the server share *ServerName*\ MyDocs*Username*. When the user logs on to the network, the My Documents folder is not redirected to this server.

Possible causes

- The client computer is running Windows NT 4.0, Windows 95, or Windows 98.

- Group Policy is not applied.

- The network share is unavailable and Offline Files is not enabled.

- The user does not have sufficient access rights to the share on which you have redirected the folder.

- There is a disk quota that has been exceeded on the target folder.

- You use a mapped drive for the target path rather than a UNC path.

Diagnostic tests   To help determine the cause of the problem use the following tests.

- **Operating System**. Confirm that the client computer is running Windows XP Professional or Windows 2000 Professional. Group Policy does not work on earlier versions of the Windows operating system.

- **Group Policy**. Run Gpresult.exe in verbose mode to check whether the correct GPOs containing Folder Redirection configuration information are applied and that the expected folders are redirected.

  At the command line, type:

```
gpresult /v
```

  This displays Group Policy setting applied to the current computer for the currently logged-on user. The following output illustrates the results of this command. If similar results are not present, no Group Policy is applied for Folder Redirection.

```
The user received "Folder Redirection" settings from these Group Policy object
s:
    EU-RedirectedDesktop-Marketing
        Revision Number:    16
        Unique Name:    {C19SADC-A8E8-11D2-9BEB-00A024070A22}
        Domain Name:    ntdev.reskit.com
        Source:         Domain

    EU-FolderRedirection-Building26
        Revision Number:    11
        Unique Name:    {FBEE2508-BCAA-11D2-B3EE-00C04FA3787A}
        Domain Name:    ntdev.reskit.com
        Source:         Domain
    Desktop is redirected to \\policy1\desktop\%username%
    My Documents is redirected to \\policy1\mydocs1\%username%
    My Pictures is redirected to \\policy1\mydocs1\%username%\My Pictures
```

- **Network Connectivity**. Ping the server by its IP address to test base-level IP connectivity; ping the server by name to test Domain Name System (DNS) name resolution.

    If the server that contains redirected folders is offline, and Offline Files is disabled, users cannot access their data. For more information about how to enable Offline Files, see "Implementing Offline Files" earlier in this chapter.

    If the server that contains the redirected folders is offline, and Offline Files is enabled, users should have access to their data if those files were accessed when the users were previously online. If these files and folders are not available, see "Files Available When Online Are Not Available When Offline" later in this chapter.

- **Insufficient Access Rights**. Verify that the user has enough file security to access folders to which his or her data is redirected. You should assign a user Full Control security access on the access control lists (ACLs) of the root of the share where he or she redirects data.

- **Disk Quota**. Check whether there is a disk quota enabled on the volume that contains the redirected folder. If there is a quota enabled, make sure that this quota is not exceeded. If it is exceeded, increase the quota or have the user delete files.

- **Mapped Drive**. Check the folder redirection target in the applicable GPO. If it is a mapped drive, change it to the UNC path for the share location. Folder redirection is processed before drive mappings, so mapped drives are not recognized by the folder redirection component.

Folder Redirection Is Successful but Files and Folders Are Unavailable

Using Group Policy, you configure a user managed by a Group Policy object to have his or her My Documents folder redirected to the server share *ServerName*\ MyDocs*Username*. When the user logs on, the folders are successfully redirected, but are not available to the user on this redirected share.

Possible causes

- The network share is unavailable, and Offline Files is not enabled or the items are not available in the local cache.

- The user does not have sufficient access rights to the share on which you have redirected the folder.

- When using applications, open and save operations have hard-coded locations and do not use the redirected path.

Diagnostic tests   To help determine the cause of the problem use the following tests.

- **Network Connectivity**. Ping the server by its IP address to test base-level IP connectivity; ping the server by name to test DNS name resolution.

  If the server that contains redirected folders is offline, and Offline Files is disabled, users cannot access their data. For more information about how to enable Offline Files, see "Implementing Offline Files" earlier in this chapter.

  If the server that contains the redirected folders is offline, and Offline Files is enabled, users should have access to their data if those files were accessed when the users were previously online. If these files and folders are not available, see "Files Available When Online Are Not Available When Offline" later in this chapter.

- **Insufficient Access Rights**. Verify that the user has enough file security to access folders to which his or her data is redirected. You should assign a user Full Control security access on the access control lists (ACLs) of the root of the share where he or she will redirect data. At a minimum, the user should have Read and Write access if he or she is saving and retrieving documents.

- **Applications Using Hard-Coded Paths**. Check the applications that the user is using. Older applications might not be able to recognize the redirected folders.

  Check the applications that the user is using. Older applications might not be able to recognize the redirected folders.

Offline Files Do Not Synchronize

A user cannot synchronize certain files or folders.

Possible causes

- Files with the file name extensions .mdb, .ldb, .mdw, .mde, and .db are not synchronized by default.

- You have configured a Group Policy setting to specify additional file name extensions that cannot be synchronized.

- Network connection problems prevent accessing the files they want synchronized.

- Insufficient disk space exists on the client computer to synchronize files.

- The user does not have Read or Write permissions on files they want synchronized.

Diagnostic tests To help determine the cause of the problem use the following tests.

- **Extensions Not Synchronized**. Check the file name extensions of the files that were not synchronized to confirm that they are not on the list of files to exclude.

  Check whether you have applied any Group Policy settings that restrict other extensions from being synchronized.

  Check the following Group Policy setting:

  Computer Configuration\Administrative Templates\Network\Offline Files\Files not cached

  Using this Group Policy setting, you can designate additional file name extensions that cannot be synchronized. You can check this on your client by running the Gpresult.exe tool and looking for the following in the output:

  ```
  KeyName:    Software\Policies\Microsoft\Windows\NetCache
  ValueName:  ExcludeExtensions
  ValueType:  REG_SZ
  Value:      *.xls
  ```

  Any file name extensions listed in the **Value** line are not synchronized. In this example, any files with the extension .xls are not synchronized. The user cannot override this Group Policy setting.

- **Network Connectivity**. Ping the server by its IP address to test base-level IP connectivity; ping the server by name to test DNS name resolution.

  Use the **net view *servername*** command to view the server and its shared resources. You should be able to see the share name that stores the files. This also confirms that the user has rights to access the share.

- **Insufficient Disk Space**. Check the amount of free disk space on the client to make sure there is sufficient disk space to synchronize the missing files.

- **Insufficient Access Rights**. Check user permissions on the unsynchronized files.

User Cannot Make Files and Folders Available Offline

The user right-clicks a file or folder to make it available for offline use, but **Make Available Offline** does not appear.

Possible causes

- The file or folder selected is actually a local file or folder and not on a network file share.

- The user is trying to make his or her redirected My Documents folder available offline but does not have access to the file share.

- Offline Files is not enabled, or a Group Policy setting was applied to disable Offline Files.

- User is in a multi-concurrent user environment, such as Terminal Services or Fast User Switching. These environments are not compatible with Offline Files.

Diagnostic tests   To help determine the cause of the problem use the following tests.

- **Local File or Folder**. Validate that the file or folder is on a network file share and not a local share.

- **Insufficient Access to My Documents File Share**. If the **Make Available Offline** option appears when you right-click a file or folder, but not when you right-click a redirected **My Documents** folder, then you should check that the My Documents folder is actually redirected successfully and is not local. Then verify that the user has appropriate file security to read and write to the location where the **My Documents** folder is redirected.

- **Offline Files Not Enabled**. Check whether Offline Files is enabled.

To verify that Offline Files is enabled

1. Click **My Computer**.
2. Click **Tools**, and then select **Folder Options**.
3. Click the **Offline Files** tab.
4. Select the **Enable Offline Files** check box.

   If this procedure does not enable Offline Files, there might be a Group Policy setting that prevents Offline Files from being enabled. The Group Policy setting that controls this is:

   Computer Configuration\Administrative Templates\Network\Offline Files\Enable

   To see if this Group Policy setting is applied, run Gpresult.exe in verbose mode on the client computer. Compare the output of this tool to the following sample:

   ```
   KeyName: Software\Policies\Microsoft\Windows\NetCache
   ValueName: Enabled
   ValueType: REG_SZ
   Value:
   ```

   If the output of Gpresult.exe on your client looks like the example, this Group Policy setting is applied and Offline Files is disabled. You must change this Group Policy setting to enable Offline Files.

Note   When the Group Policy setting **Enable Offline Files** is configured with a setting of **Disable**, the Offline Files feature is disabled.

Files Available When Online Are Not Available When Offline

Documents and programs that are accessible when connected to the network are not synchronized with the local cache for offline use.

Possible causes

- The files reside on a computer that is not running Windows XP Professional or Windows 2000 Professional. Computers running previous versions of Windows do not support automatic caching of files and folders.

- Offline files are not enabled on the local computer.

- **Allow caching of files in this shared folder** is not enabled on the file share where the documents are being accessed or **Allow caching of files in this shared folder** is enabled but is not set to Automatic Caching.

Diagnostic tests To help determine the cause of the problem use the following tests.

- **Windows Version**. Check whether the server containing the file share is running Windows 2000 Server. Check that the client is running Windows XP Professional or Windows 2000 Professional.

- **Offline Files Not Enabled**. Navigate to a network file share, right-click a file or folder, and then check whether there is a **Make Available Offline** shortcut menu.

- **Caching Not Enabled or Not Automatic**. Use the following procedure to check caching settings on the file share.

To check the configuration of the file share

1. On the file server containing the file share, click **My Computer**.

2. Navigate to the folder that is shared, right-click the folder, and then select **Properties**.

3. Click the **Sharing** tab, and then click **Caching**.

4. Make sure the **Allow caching of files in this shared folder** check box is selected.

5. In the box, select one of the following:

   - **Automatic Caching for Documents** if this share contains documents.

   - **Automatic Caching for Programs** if this share contains application files.

Additional Resources

These resources contain additional information related to this chapter.

Related Information

- The *Designing a Managed Environment* book in the *Microsoft Windows Server 2003 Deployment Kit* for information about deploying Group Policy.

- The *Deployment Guide* of the *Microsoft Windows 2000 Server Resource Kit* for information about deploying Group Policy and Active Directory.

- The *Distributed Systems Guide* of the *Microsoft Windows 2000 Server Resource Kit* for more information about implementing and troubleshooting IntelliMirror technologies.

- The *Change and Configuration Management Guide* link on the Web Resources page at http://www.microsoft.com/windows/reskits/webresourcesfor information about deploying IntelliMirror.

- The Group Policy Settings link on the Web Resources page at http://www.microsoft.com/windows/reskits/webresources for a spreadsheet of Windows XP Professional Group Policy settings that facilitate tracking of configured settings.

- Group Policy Help for information about Group Policy.

- "IntelliMirror" in Windows XP Professional Help and Support Center for information about user data management, software installation and maintenance, user settings management, and Remote Installation Services (RIS).

Chapter 7

Supporting Mobile Users

For organizations that support mobile users, important considerations are hardware, power management, and security on portable computers. In addition, some administrative concerns are relevant to roaming users in organizations that use roaming user profiles or Folder Redirection. Microsoft® Windows® XP Professional can be configured and administered to provide support for mobile users, and includes features and tools that are designed specifically for portable computer users.

Related Information

- For more information about remote networking, see "Connecting Remote Offices" in this book.

- For more information about IntelliMirror® management technologies such as Offline Files, Folder Redirection, and roaming user profiles, see "Managing Files and Folders" in this book.

- For more information about implementing security for mobile users, see "Securing Mobile Computers" in the *Microsoft® Windows® Security Resource Kit* and in this book.

Overview of Windows XP Professional Support for Mobile Users

Windows XP Professional offers several new features for mobile users. In addition, several Microsoft® Windows NT® version 4.0 and Microsoft® Windows® 2000 features, as well as processes such as starting, hibernating, standby, and resuming, are enhanced in Windows XP Professional in order to increase functionality for mobile users.

Fast system startup   Windows XP Professional provides improved system boot and resume performance, resulting in fast system startup. The standby feature reduces power consumption by turning off the display, hard disk, and other system components while preserving the contents of memory. Standby also allows you to return to work quickly after waking the system. The hibernate feature saves the entire system state to the hard disk and turns off the computer. When the system restarts from hibernation, the desktop and all applications are restored to their previous state.

Folder Redirection   Folder Redirection allows the administrator to direct the contents of special shell folders, such as My Documents, to an alternate location on a server or a network share. When Folder Redirection is applied to these special folders, the redirection is transparent to the user; he or she can continue to work with documents on the server as if the documents are on the local drive. Folder Redirection is best used in conjunction with Offline Files.

Offline Files   The Offline Files feature allows users to disconnect from the network and work as if they are still connected. When the computer is offline, files and folders appear in the same directory that they appear in online. By using Offline Files, users can continue to work with copies of files that are available on a network when they are not connected to the network. Offline Files stores the data in the computer's cache to make network files available offline. When users reconnect to the network, Offline Files synchronizes the files stored on the local drive with the files on the network.

Hibernation   The hibernation feature allows the Microsoft® Windows® desktop to be restored quickly after a computer is shut down. When a computer is put into hibernation, the current system state is saved to the hard disk before the computer is turned off. Then, when a user restarts the computer, Windows restarts any programs that were running when the computer entered hibernation, and restores all previous network connections. ACPI and APM support Windows XP Professional supports the Advanced Configuration and Power Interface (ACPI) specification for robust power management and system configuration. Windows XP Professional also provides some power management features for portable computers with a legacy Advanced Power Management (APM) version 1.2–based BIOS.

Enhanced battery life Windows XP Professional provides several new features to enhance battery life. Windows XP Professional automatically dims a laptop's display when it is switched to battery power, and turns off the display panel when the laptop's lid is closed. In addition, Windows XP Professional features intelligent processor throttling to reduce CPU power consumption. Windows XP Professional also provides more accurate estimates of remaining battery life.

Processor performance control Windows XP Professional provides native support for processor performance control technologies such as Intel® SpeedStep® Technology, AMD® PowerNow!™, and Transmeta® LongRun™. Windows XP Professional also features an adaptive processor performance control algorithm that dynamically balances system performance and power consumption, based on the current CPU workload and remaining battery life.

Battery and processor metrics Windows XP Professional displays information about processor performance and battery activity in System Monitor. The processor performance data available includes the current processor frequency and power consumption. Battery information provided includes the charge and discharge rates, voltage, and remaining capacity.

Wake-on-critical battery Windows XP Professional supports wake-on-critical battery for portable computers that implement this feature. This allows a computer to awaken from standby when battery power becomes critically low and switch to hibernation to prevent data loss.

Dynamic configuration of hot added devices When you insert and remove devices such as CardBus cards or Universal Serial Bus (USB) devices, Windows XP Professional detects and configures them without requiring you to restart the computer.

Hot and cold docking or undocking With your portable computer fully powered, you can dock to a docking station and undock from a docking station without shutting down the computer.

Table 7-1 lists the new or enhanced features in Windows XP Professional that support mobile users, and indicates which of these features are available in Microsoft® Windows® 95, Microsoft® Windows® 98, Microsoft® Windows NT® Workstation 4.0, and Microsoft® Windows® 2000 Professional.

Table 7-1 Mobile User Profile Computing Features in Windows XP Professional

Windows XP Professional Feature	Windows 95	Windows 98	Windows NT 4.0	Windows 2000 Professional	Windows XP Professional
Offline Files				X	X
Folder Redirection				X	X
Roaming User Profiles			X	X	X
Briefcase	X	X	X	X	X

Table 7-1 Mobile User Profile Computing Features in Windows XP Professional

Windows XP Professional Feature	Windows 95	Windows 98	Windows NT 4.0	Windows 2000 Professional	Windows XP Professional
Hibernate				X	X
Power management	X	X		X	X
ACPI support		X		X	X
APM support	X	X		X	X
Standby (APM and ACPI only)	X	X		X	X
Battery management (APM and ACPI only)		X		X	X
Dynamic configuration of PC Cards	X	X		X	X
Hot and cold docking or undocking	X	X		X	X
Hot insertion and removal of devices in hot swappable module bays		X		X	X

Setting Up a Portable Computer

Before you can make use of mobile computing in your organization, you need to identify the critical operating system components, properties, and features that you will need to configure on your portable computers. You must also ensure that you address critical configuration issues that are specific to portable computers.

Check BIOS Compatibility

Windows XP Professional supports the Advanced Configuration and Power Interface (ACPI) specification, which enables reliable system configuration and power management features. If a portable computer has an ACPI-compliant BIOS, use the Hardware Compatibility List (HCL) to verify that it is compatible with Windows XP Professional. If it is not, upgrade the BIOS to the latest available version. If you upgrade to an ACPI-based BIOS on your portable computer after you install Windows XP Professional, and your old BIOS was either not ACPI-compliant or not compatible with Windows XP Professional, you must reinstall Windows XP Professional in order to enable ACPI and the power management features that it supports. For more information about hardware compatibility, see the Hardware Compatibility List link on the Web Resources page at http://www.microsoft.com/windows/reskits/webresources. For more information about upgrading the BIOS in a portable computer, see the Hardware Update link on the Web Resources page at http://www.microsoft.com/windows/reskits/webresources.

If a portable computer has an APM-based BIOS, run the Apmstat.exe support tool to determine whether the BIOS has any known problems. If the APM BIOS is known to be compatible with Windows XP Professional, APM power management is enabled by default. You can install Apmstat by running Setup.exe, which is located in the \Support\Tools folder on the Windows XP Professional operating system CD.

Grant Installation and Configuration Rights

If you configure a portable computer for a user who travels frequently, add this user to the Power Users group. The user can then install, uninstall, and configure software. If a hardware device fails or needs to be reinstalled while not connected to the network, a member of the Power Users Group can reinstall the device, but only if the driver package meets the following conditions:

- Is present on the system (that is, it does not need to be installed from media, such as a CD provided by a vendor).

- Is digitally signed. For more information about driver signing, see "Managing Devices" in this book.

- Can be installed without any user interface.

If a user must be able to add hardware even if the driver package does not meet these conditions, add this user to the Administrators group.

All other types of users should be members of the Users group, which does not allow them to install, uninstall, or configure software and hardware, except when the above three conditions are true. In general, no Users should be members of the Administrators group unless they need to install, uninstall, and configure non-Plug and Play hardware and drivers. For more information about driver signing or configuring hardware and drivers see "Managing Devices" in this book.

Verify Hardware Configuration

After you install new hardware on a portable computer, you need to verify that all devices function when the computer is both docked and undocked. Log on in turn as a member of the Power Users and the Users groups to test the devices, as well as the docking and undocking functionality. This testing is necessary because some hardware can be fully installed only by a member of the Administrators group. When members of the Power Users or Users group add the devices, the driver packages might not be installed.

Windows XP Professional uses one hardware profile to load drivers when the portable computer is docked (the Docked Profile) and another when the computer is undocked (the Undocked Profile). Verify that the properties are set correctly for both the Docked Profile and the Undocked Profile. For more information about docked and undocked profiles, see "Managing Hardware on Portable Computers" later in this chapter.

Configure Power Management Options

Windows power management is based on the concept of *power schemes*. A power scheme is a group of preset power options that are passed to the operating system to control a computer's power management behavior. Power schemes are presented to the user in the Power Management Control Panel option.

The power policy used when the computer is powered by AC (utility) power can be different than the policy that is used when the computer is powered by a battery.

Verify that the power schemes that are available are appropriate for the target user environments. The most useful power schemes for portable computers are Portable/Laptop, Presentation, and Max Battery. Using the default power scheme settings might not always be the best configuration. You might need to explore the best configuration for the user's needs.

Install Applications

All software and software components must be installed locally and run locally on portable computers. You must therefore make sure that you do not have any partially installed programs or distributed programs installed on a portable computer that is frequently used offline. Only Administrators can install software for personal digital assistants (PDA) because some PDA software cannot be installed by members of the Power Users group. Also, only members of the Administrators group can use the Internet Connection wizard to configure an Internet connection.

Configure Offline File Storing

If you have files and folders that you want to make available offline for mobile users, enable and configure file-storing settings on the server or network share. This is particularly important for folders such as My Documents that have been redirected to a network share or a server. Also, make sure that you have configured all offline files settings, including synchronization settings, on the portable computer.

If a user uses an e-mail program or a Web browser, be sure to configure the e-mail program and the Web browser for offline content.

Configure Security

Because portable computers are vulnerable to theft, you must ensure that they are configured securely. Format all hard disks as NTFS and apply the appropriate permissions to files and folders that contain sensitive data. Also, encrypt files and folders that contain sensitive data, and require users to use strong passwords for logging on both locally and on the network. You might also want to encrypt the Offline Files cache, so that any network files made available offline are also encrypted. For more information about encrypting files and folders, see "Encrypting File System" in this book.

Configure Roaming User Profiles and Folder Redirection

If you are supporting roaming desktop users or portable computer users who are connected directly to a network most of the time, configuring roaming user profiles and Folder Redirection can provide a number of advantages, such as fast computer replacement and the storage of backup copies of data on the network. If portable computers in your organization are rarely connected to the network or are connected remotely most of the time, however, do not use roaming user profiles or Folder Redirection. For more information about roaming user profiles and Folder Redirection, see "Configuring Roaming User Profiles and Folder Redirection" later in this chapter.

Managing Hardware on Portable Computers

The Plug and Play support in Windows XP Professional allows devices to be configured on the system without the computer having to be restarted. You can therefore add or remove a device from the computer while it is running, and Windows XP Professional will automatically allocate resources, install or uninstall the appropriate device drivers, and enable or disable the device. Full Plug and Play support is useful for portable computers because the device configuration on portable computers changes frequently to accommodate the user's environment (docked or undocked) and the user's needs (such as working remotely online, or working offline). For portable computers that are ACPI-enabled, Plug and Play makes the following functionality possible:

- Dynamic configuration of devices, such as PC Cards and CardBus.

- Hot swapping of Integrated Drive Electronics (IDE) devices in device bays, such as hard disks, floppy drives, and CD-ROM drives.

- Hot docking and undocking.

For more information about installing, configuring, and troubleshooting devices, see "Managing Devices" in this book.

Warning   Full Plug and Play support is possible only if both the device and the device drivers support Plug and Play, and the computer is ACPI-based.

Hardware Profile Creation

Windows XP Professional uses hardware profiles to determine which drivers to load when the system hardware changes. Hardware profiles are an important feature for portable computers that use a docking station. Windows XP Professional uses one hardware profile to load drivers when the portable computer is docked (the Docked Profile) and another (the Undocked Profile) when the computer is undocked. Windows XP Professional creates these two hardware profiles for portable computers when the computer is docked and undocked.

The hardware profiles are created when Windows XP Professional queries the BIOS for a dock serial ID and then assigns names for the docked and undocked configurations. You do not need to reconfigure the Docked Profile or the Undocked Profile if your system is Plug and Play-compliant. If a portable computer is fully Plug and Play–compliant, you need only these hardware profiles, and you do not need to designate which profile to use when the computer starts. The computer detects the docked or undocked state and uses the appropriate profile.

If a portable computer is not fully Plug and Play–compliant, you might need to create a new hardware profile. You can then configure the profile by enabling and disabling devices. For more information about configuring hardware profiles see Windows XP Professional Help and Support Center.

Dynamic Device Configuration

With dynamic device configuration, portable computer users can add or remove PC Cards, CardBus cards, USB and IEEE 1394 devices, and so forth without restarting the computer. The device and the device drivers must support Plug and Play in order for users to take advantage of dynamic configuration.

> **Warning**   Some ACPI-enabled computers might not be fully ACPI-compliant or support hot addition and removal of devices in hot swappable module bays. Removing such devices on these computers without first shutting down the system can physically damage the device.

Docking and Undocking

Docking and undocking of portable computers can be done either hot or cold. In a *cold dock or undock,* the computer is shut down before it is inserted into or removed from the docking station. In a *hot dock or undock*, the computer is running, with or without programs and documents open, when it is inserted into or removed from the docking station. Computer manufacturers can design the docking stations and BIOS of their mobile computers in different ways resulting in different docking and undocking behaviors. For specific information about the docking and undocking behavior of your portable computers, see the manufacturer's documentation.

Hot Docking and Undocking

Hot docking and hot undocking can only be performed on computers that are ACPI-enabled. To hot dock a system, insert the fully powered system into the docking station. To hot undock a system, click **Eject PC** on the **Start** menu before removing the system from the docking station. The **Eject PC** command appears only if a computer is ACPI-enabled. Some portable computer manufacturers support other methods of hot undocking. See manufacturer documentation for details about a given system.

Removing a portable computer without using the **Eject PC** command is not recommended. Use the **Eject PC** command to perform a hot undock. Note that undocking a portable computer while it is in standby or hibernation is not recommended. If a system is in standby or hibernation, first resume the system, and then follow the hot undock procedure.

Caution   Data loss or system instability can occur if a user does not use the Eject PC command before undocking in a fully powered state or from standby or hibernation.

You can use Group Policy to disable hot undocking, in which case the Eject PC command does not appear on ACPI-enabled computers. For more information about using Group Policy to control undocking privileges, see "Securely Undocking Portable Computers" later in this chapter.

Cold Docking and Undocking

Cold docking takes place when the computer is completely shut down before it is docked or undocked. It is recommended that you use cold docking and undocking if you have an APM-based system or other non-ACPI–based computer. To perform a cold dock, insert the computer into the docking station while the computer is shut down. To perform a cold undock, shut down the computer, and then remove or eject it from the docking station. When you shut down the computer before a cold dock or undock, you must use the **shut down** command. Do not use the **hibernate** or **stand by** commands.

Configuring Power Management

Configuring power management allows you to control how a computer consumes energy. Windows XP Professional supports the Advanced Configuration and Power Interface (ACPI) specification. The ACPI architecture is designed to provide for Operating System-Directed Power Management (OSPM). Windows XP Professional also supports the legacy Advanced Power Management (APM) version 1.2 BIOS architecture; however, APM provides only limited power management support.

If you do not have an APM-based or ACPI-based computer, it is still possible to manage some aspects of power consumption. For example, depending on the capabilities of your hardware, you can reduce the power consumed by the computer by setting timers to turn the display or disk drives off.

ACPI Power Management

Using features supported by ACPI, Windows XP Professional allows the operating system to direct and manage power usage on a system-wide basis. The operating system's *power policy* determines what devices to turn off, and when to put the computer into a low-power state. Power policy is based on a combination of application requirements, the user's preferences, and the computer's hardware capabilities. To conserve energy and prolong battery life, when the computer is idle the operating system can turn off devices such as the display panel or hard disk drive, or put the computer into a low-power sleep state such as standby or hibernation.

Each device class on the computer has a power policy owner. The policy owner for a particular device class is the component that is best aware of how the device is used. Typically this is the device class driver. Each policy owner must manage power appropriately for its class and work consistently with the operating system's policy for putting the computer into a low-power state. For example, a network adapter might sense that no network cable is plugged in, and therefore request that the operating system put the adapter in a low-power state because it is not being used.

In order to use the ACPI power management features in Windows XP Professional, your computer must have an ACPI-compliant BIOS that is compatible with Windows XP Professional.

During setup, Windows XP Professional determines which hardware abstraction layer (HAL) to install on the computer. If the computer has an ACPI-compliant BIOS, an ACPI HAL is installed and you are able to use ACPI power management features. If the computer does not have an ACPI-compliant BIOS, a non-ACPI HAL is installed and ACPI power management features are not available.

Note   The HAL directs information from the operating system and device drivers to specific devices.

In order to determine which HAL to install, Windows XP Professional performs the following process during setup:

1. Windows XP Professional checks the ACPI BIOS tables during startup. These tables list the devices that are installed on the computer and their power management capabilities.

   If this information is missing, or if the information is in the wrong form, a non-ACPI HAL is installed.

2. If the tables are correct, Setup determines whether the computer's BIOS is known to be incompatible with the ACPI standard.

   If the BIOS is on the incompatible list, a non-ACPI HAL is installed.

3. If the BIOS is not on the incompatible BIOS list, Setup checks the BIOS date.

   If the BIOS is not on the incompatible BIOS list, and the BIOS date is later than 1/1/99, an ACPI HAL is installed.

4. If the BIOS is not on the incompatible BIOS list, and the BIOS date is earlier than 1/1/99, Setup determines if the BIOS is known to be compatible with Windows XP Professional.

   If the BIOS is compatible, an ACPI HAL is installed.

   If the BIOS is not compatible, an earlier HAL is installed.

For more information about BIOS compatibility, see the Hardware Compatibility List link on the Web Resources page at http://www.microsoft.com/windows/reskits/webresources.

You can use Device Manager to determine whether your computer is operating in ACPI mode.

To determine whether Windows XP Professional is running in ACPI mode

1. In **Control Panel**, click **Performance and Maintenance**, and then click **System**.

2. In the **System Properties** dialog box, click the **Hardware** tab, and then click **Device Manager**.

3. In the details pane, click **Computer.**

   If **Advanced Configuration and Power Interface (ACPI) PC** is listed under **Computer**, the computer is operating in ACPI mode.

If you have an ACPI BIOS, but Windows XP Professional is not installed in the ACPI mode, your ACPI BIOS might be noncompliant. Check with your computer manufacturer to see if a more recent, ACPI-compatible BIOS is available. If Windows XP Professional is installed in non-ACPI mode on your computer, and you upgrade to a new BIOS version, you must reinstall Windows XP Professional to enable ACPI mode. For more information about upgrading the BIOS on a portable computer, see the Hardware Update link on the Web Resources page at http://www.microsoft.com/windows/reskits/webresources.

You must be a member of the Administrators group to view the Hal.dll file to determine which hardware abstraction layer is installed.

APM Power Management

Windows XP Professional support of APM power management is intended to provide compatibility with legacy notebook computers. The APM power management system is not designed to run on desktop computers, as power management support for the APM system is limited to battery status, suspend, resume, and auto-hibernate functions.

APM does not work with every APM-compatible system running Windows XP Professional. Microsoft has tested APM-capable systems to determine how well each system and BIOS combination supports APM.

Mobile systems can support APM if they meet the following criteria:

- Hardware must meet basic Windows XP Professional requirements.

- An ACPI-compliant BIOS is not available for end-user system upgrade.

- The APM 1.2-compliant BIOS is not on the "Disable APM List" for a particular BIOS version number and date.

- All user-defined CMOS power control features are disabled or minimized, time-outs are set to Off or to the longest possible time allowed, and the APM BIOS is enabled.

Determining APM BIOS Compatibility

In order for you to use APM-based power management features with Windows XP Professional, the APM-based BIOS on your computer must be compatible with Windows XP Professional.

Windows XP Professional supports APM version 1.2 on portable computers. The portable computer, however, must have an APM-compatible BIOS in order for APM features to work properly. Windows XP Professional determines whether a BIOS is APM-compatible during setup, and on the basis of this determination, does one of the following:

- Installs APM support (Ntapm.sys and Apmbatt.sys) and enables APM if the computer's BIOS is found on the auto-enable APM list.

- Does not install or enable APM support if the computer's BIOS is found on the disable APM list. APM on these systems does not work reliably, and if used, data loss might occur.

- Installs APM support but does not enable APM support if the computer's BIOS is not on the auto-enable APM list or the disable APM list. APM might work properly, but you must enable APM in the Windows XP Professional graphical user interface (GUI). For more information about enabling APM, see "Configuring APM BIOS" later in this chapter.

> **Warning**   APM must be enabled in the BIOS before Windows XP Professional is installed. If APM is disabled in the BIOS before installation, Windows XP Professional does not install power management support even if the APM BIOS is on the auto-enable APM list.

If APM is not enabled after you install Windows XP Professional, either the computer's BIOS is on the disable APM list, or it is not on the auto-enable APM list. You can determine whether either of these is the case by using the Apmstat.exe tool, which is included with the Windows XP Professional Support Tools on the Microsoft® Windows® XP Professional operating system CD.

To determine APM BIOS compatibility by using Apmstat.exe

- At the command prompt, type:

    apmstat

> **Caution**   If Apmstat.exe reports that an APM BIOS is known to be incompatible or that an APM BIOS is known to have problems, do not attempt to circumvent Windows XP Professional Setup by forcing it to install APM support. This might cause a computer to behave erratically and even lose data. Also, if an APM BIOS is known to be incompatible, make sure that APM is disabled in the BIOS.

If Apmstat.exe reports that an APM BIOS is not known to be compatible and it is not known to be incompatible, you might still be able to use APM, but you must enable and configure APM so that it works properly on your computer.

To verify that APM support is installed on a computer

1. In **Control Panel,** click **Performance and Maintenance**, and then click **System**.

2. Click the **Hardware** tab, and then click **Device Manager**.

3. On the **View** menu, click **Show hidden devices**.

    If **NT Apm/Legacy Support** is listed in the details pane, APM support is installed.

To enable APM

1. In **Control Panel**, click **Performance Maintenance,** and then click **Power Options**.

2. Click the **APM** tab.

3. Under **Advanced Power Management**, select the **Enable Advanced Power Management support** check box.

Note   The APM tab is present only if an APM BIOS is detected that is either APM 1.2–compliant or that might work with APM even if it is not APM 1.2–compliant. It is not recommended that you enable APM support on a computer that has a BIOS that is not APM-compliant. If problems occur after you enable APM support, disable APM and contact the computer manufacturer for an updated BIOS. The APM tab is not present if a computer has multiple processors because Windows XP Professional does not install APM support on multiprocessor computers.

Configuring APM BIOS

In order to utilize APM power management on your system, you must configure an APM-based BIOS so that power management works properly with Windows XP Professional. This might involve configuring the APM BIOS in the following way:

1.   Set BIOS time-outs to the maximum time or disable them. This allows the operating system (instead of the BIOS) to control time-outs. Because some APM BIOSs turn off or refuse to function if all time-outs are disabled, you might want to set time-outs to the maximum allowed time instead of disabling them.

2.   Make sure that screen blanking is turned off in the BIOS. Typically, you can turn off screen blanking in the BIOS by disabling the time-out for the display or by setting the time-out to the maximum value. Screen blanking reduces power to the display, which causes the computer to appear to be shut down.

Activating a pointing device typically wakes the system and restores power to the display. However, USB and other external pointing devices do not wake the system or restore power to the display.

Do not use a supplemental video card with a portable computer if you use APM. Use only the video card included with the portable computer. The APM BIOS might not detect a video card that is added to the system or a video card that is in a docking station. If the adapter is not discovered by the APM BIOS, the suspend feature does not work.

Power Management Schemes and Options

Whether you have an ACPI-based or an APM-based computer, several power management options are available for you to configure. These include choosing and configuring a power scheme, enabling the battery status indicator, configuring the power and sleep buttons, and setting low-battery alarms.

Configuring Power Schemes

Using power schemes, you can configure how and when a computer turns off devices, enters a suspend state, or changes processor performance levels on mobile systems that support this function. You can configure these settings according to the power source in use—whether the computer is plugged into a wall outlet or powered by battery. Depending on the hardware capability, you might be able to configure some of these settings even if the computer is not ACPI- or APM-enabled.

The following default power schemes are available in Windows XP Professional: Home/Office Desk, Portable/Laptop, Presentation, Always On, Minimal Power Management, and Max Battery. You can customize any scheme, or add or delete new schemes to fit a specific situation.

For more information about configuring the standby feature and the hibernate feature, see "Configuring Hibernation and Standby" later in this chapter.

The default power scheme on portable computers is Portable/Laptop; the Home/Office Desk scheme does not optimize battery power. You might need to change the power scheme based on how the computer is used. For example, you might choose the Presentation scheme to prevent the computer from turning off the display during a presentation.

To configure a power scheme

1. In **Control Panel**, click **Performance and Maintenance,** and then click **Power Options**.

2. Click the **Power Schemes** tab.

3. Select a power scheme. You can then change the settings in the power scheme to best meet your needs.

Configuring Hibernation and Standby

When a computer enters hibernation, the current state of the computer is saved to disk, and the power to the computer is turned off. When a computer wakes from hibernation, it reads the current state data from the disk and restores the system to the state that it was in before it entered hibernation. All programs that were running are restarted, and network connections are restored.

Hibernation is enabled by default. All ACPI-compatible and most APM-compatible computers can be set to enter hibernation.

Because the contents of the computer's memory are written to disk when the computer enters hibernation, you must have at least as much available disk space as you have memory.

To disable hibernation

1. In **Control Panel**, click **Performance and Maintenance,** and then click **Power Options**.

2. Click the **Hibernate** tab.

3. Clear the **Enable hibernate support** check box.

> **Note**   You must have the proper hardware to use hibernation. If the Hibernate tab is not available, the computer does not support hibernation.

When a computer enters standby, the computer's state is saved to memory and most circuitry and devices are turned off. When a computer resumes from standby, the state is restored from memory and power is restored to all devices. If power is interrupted when the computer is in standby, data might be lost. All installed devices and device driver software must properly support power management in order for standby to be available.

To provide security, you can have the computer prompt the user for a user name and password after it resumes from hibernate or standby. Password protection is enabled by default.

To disable password protection when a computer resumes from standby

1. In **Control Panel,** click **Performance and Maintenance,** and then click **Power Options**.

2. Click the **Advanced** tab.

3. Clear the **Prompt for password when computer goes off standby** check box.

> **Note**   When you must turn off your portable computer to comply with airline regulations, you must shut down the computer, rather than allowing it to remain in standby. While in standby, the operating system can reactivate itself to run preprogrammed tasks or to conserve battery power. For more information about shutting down a computer, see Windows XP Professional Help and Support Center.

Configuring the Group Policy Refresh Interval for Hibernation or Standby

You can configure the refresh interval by using Group Policy, which controls how often policies are applied on the computer. By default, the refresh interval is 90 minutes, but it can be set to any value between 0 and 64,800 minutes. You can also set an interval offset, which is a random period of time that is applied to the refresh interval. Randomizing the refresh interval prevents clients with the same refresh interval from overloading the server by simultaneously requesting policy updates. By default, the interval offset is 30 minutes, meaning that a random time between 0 and 30 minutes is applied to the refresh interval.

In some cases, Group Policy refresh settings can prevent a computer from entering hibernation or standby. This is because a policy update resets the hibernation or standby timer (as moving the mouse or pressing a key does). For example, if a computer is set to enter hibernation or standby after being idle for 45 minutes, but the Group Policy refresh interval is set at 30 minutes, the hibernation or standby timer never reaches 45 minutes. To ensure that the standby timer reaches 45 minutes (or whatever time you set), set the Group Policy refresh interval so that it is greater than the hibernation setting or standby setting in Power Options. You can also configure Group Policy so that it does not apply settings while the computer is being used.

To change the Group Policy refresh interval and the interval offset for User Configuration settings

1. In the **Run** dialog box, type **gpedit.msc**.

2. In the details pane of Group Policy, under **User Configuration**, open the **Administrative Templates** folder, and then open the **System** folder.

3. Click **Group Policy**.

4. In the details pane, double-click **Group Policy refresh interval for users**.

5. Click **Enabled**.

6. Change the settings for the refresh interval and the interval offset.

To change the Group Policy refresh interval and interval offset for Computer Configuration settings

1. In the details pane of Group Policy, under **Computer Configuration**, open the **Administrative Templates** folder, and then open the **System** folder.

2. Click **Group Policy**.

3. In the details pane, double-click **Group Policy refresh interval for computers**.

4. Click **Enabled**.

5. Change the settings for the refresh interval and the interval offset.

To disable policy updates while a computer is running

1. In the **Run** dialog box, type **gpedit.msc**.

2. In the details pane of Group Policy, under **Computer Configuration**, open the **Administrative Templates** folder, and then open the **System** folder.

3. Click **Group Policy**.

4. In the details pane, double-click **Disable background refresh of Group Policy**.

5. Click **Enabled**.

Configuring Battery Monitoring and Management

Windows XP Professional allows you to monitor and manage a portable computer's battery by using Power Meter. Windows XP Professional can also monitor multiple batteries. Battery monitoring and management are only available on ACPI-enabled and APM-enabled computers.

By default, the battery status icon will appear on the taskbar whenever the computer is operating on battery power. You must enable the battery status icon to make it appear on the taskbar at all times. This icon gives users direct access to the power meter feature, allows selection of the current power scheme, and offers direct access to power properties by means of the **Power Options** Control Panel option.

To add the battery status icon to the taskbar

1. In **Control Panel**, click **Performance and Maintenance**, and then click **Power Options.**

2. Click the **Advanced** tab.

3. Select the **Always show icon on the taskbar** check box.

> **Note** The display icon changes from a battery to a plug depending on the computer's power source—battery power or wall outlet. The display also changes to indicate that the battery is charging or fully charged and shows the remaining battery capacity when the computer is operating on battery power.

If your portable computer uses multiple batteries, you can also configure the battery meter to display the status of multiple batteries.

To configure the battery meter for multiple-battery computers

1. In **Control Panel,** click **Performance and Maintenance,** and then click **Power Options**.

2. Click the **Power Meter** tab.

3. Click **Show details for each battery**.

You can set alarms to indicate low-battery and critical-battery levels. You can select visual and audible alarm notifications, specify an action to take such as making a change in power state (standby, hibernation, shutdown), and specify the execution of a program to be run.

To configure alarms to indicate low-battery and critical-battery levels

1. In **Control Panel**, click **Performance and Maintenance,** and then click **Power Options**.

2. Click the **Alarms** tab.

3. Set the battery activation levels that you want.

4. Click **Alarm Action** to configure the behaviors of an activated alarm.

Configuring Power Button, Sleep Button, and Lid Switch Behavior

ACPI-enabled mobile computers can have up to three buttons for controlling system power: a Power button, a Sleep button, and a Lid Switch. Windows XP Professional allows you to configure the action of each button as follows:

- Do nothing
- Ask me what to do
- Sleep
- Hibernate
- Shut down

To configure power system button functionality

1. In **Control Panel**, click **Performance and Maintenance**, and then click **Power Options**.

2. Click the **Advanced** tab.

3. Under **When I close the lid of my portable computer**, select a lid-switch action.

4. Under **When I press the power button on my computer**, select a power-button action.

   Under **When I press the sleep button on my computer**, select a sleep-button action.

Enabling Devices to Wake the Computer

On ACPI-compatible systems, Windows XP Professional can enable some devices to wake the system from the hibernation or standby. Windows XP Professional supports wake events such as modem wake-on-ring, wake-on-LAN, and wake-on-critical battery. Windows XP Professional also supports wake-on-LAN for CardBus network adapters. Note that in order for the wake features to function, they must be supported by the appropriate computer hardware.

To enable a device to wake the computer

1. In **Control Panel**, click **Performance and Maintenance,** and then click **System**.

2. Click the **Hardware** tab, and then click **Device Manager**.

3. Select the device that you want to wake the system, and then double-click to open the **Properties** dialog box.

4. On the **Power Management** tab, click **Allow this device to bring the computer out of standby**.

If no **Power Management** tab appears, the device does not support system wake.

Hiding Power Options

You can prevent users from configuring power options by specifying Control Panel settings in Group Policy. You can disable Control Panel entirely, hide specific Control Panel tools, and show specific Control Panel options. Hiding Power Options can be beneficial if you have configured the power options, and you do not want users to change those options. However, if you hide Power Options, users have no means to reconfigure power management settings if they need to be changed while they are away from the office. For example, portable computer users frequently use the Portable/Laptop power scheme. When they use the portable computer for a presentation, however, it is recommended that they switch to the Presentation scheme to prevent the portable computer from turning off the display or entering standby or hibernation during the presentation. Users cannot change power schemes, or any other power option, if Power Options is not available.

To hide Power Options by using Group Policy settings

1. In the **Run** dialog box, type **gpedit.msc**.

2. In the **Group Policy** console tree, under **User Configuration**, open **Administrative Templates**.

3. Click the **Control Panel** folder.

4. In the details pane, double-click **Hide specified control panel applets**.

5. In the **Hide specified Control Panel applets Properties** dialog box, click **Enabled**, and then click **Show**.

6. Click **Add**.

7. Type **power options**.
   Typically, **Power Options** appears in the **Show Contents** dialog box, under **List of disallowed control panel applets**.

To disable Control Panel by using Group Policy settings

1. In the **Run** dialog box, type **gpedit.msc**.

2. In the **Group Policy** console tree, under **User Configuration**, open the **Administrative Templates** folder.

3. Click the **Control Panel** folder.

4. In the details pane, double-click **Disable Control Panel**.

5. Click **Enabled**.

> **Warning**   Disabling Control Panel in Group Policy prevents Control.exe from starting. This removes Control Panel from the Start menu and removes the Control Panel folder from My Computer.

Configuring Roaming User Profiles and Folder Redirection

A user profile is a group of settings and files that defines the environment that the system loads when a user logs on.

A user profile contains:

- A portion of the registry that stores registry settings such as Windows Explorer settings, persistent network connections, taskbar settings, network printer connections, user-defined Control Panel and Accessories settings, and application settings.

- A set of profile folders that store information such as shortcut links, desktop icons, and startup applications.

User profiles are located by default on the local computer; one profile is created for each user who has logged on to that computer. When administrators configure profiles to roam, the data and settings in a user's profile are copied to a network server when the user logs off of the computer. The data and settings are then available to the user no matter where he or she next logs on to the network.

While useful for mobile users, roaming user profiles are also beneficial for users who always use the same computer. Roaming user profiles provide a transparent way for such users to back up their profiles to a network server, thus protecting the information from individual system failure. If a user's primary workstation needs to be replaced, the new computer receives the user's profile from the server as soon as the user logs on.

You can use roaming user profiles together with Remote OS Installation and Software Installation and Maintenance when you replace a computer. If a computer system fails and loses its data, you can use Remote OS Installation to install Windows XP Professional, use Software Installation and Maintenance to restore applications, and use roaming user profiles to restore critical information. Because a network copy of the data exists, you can easily reestablish links to critical information.

Roaming user profiles are configured by means of the user object contained in the Active Directory™ directory service or the domain controller. For more information about configuring roaming user profiles on Microsoft® Windows® 2000 Server see the *Distributed Systems Guide* of the *Microsoft® Windows® 2000 Server Resource Kit.*

Roaming user profile considerations for mobile users   The following guidelines can be used when planning profile configurations for users of mobile computers:

- If the user regularly connects to the network via fast link, consider using a roaming user profile.

- If the user rarely connects via fast link, use a local profile. By default, roaming user profiles do not roam over slow links. For example, if a user in the field generally connects via a dial-up connection, but comes into the office twice a year and connects via the LAN, a roaming profile offers little advantage, as the server copy would only be up-to-date on those two occasions.

- If the user roams to LAN-connected computers in the domain and also has a laptop computer, use a roaming user profile for the user. For the laptop computer, enable the Group Policy setting **Only allow local user profiles**. Note that a Computer Configuration Group Policy setting takes precedence over a User Configuration setting, so the user will receive his or her User setting on desktop computers, but will receive the Computer setting on the laptop computer.

Roaming User Profiles in Windows XP Professional

Windows XP Professional includes new Group Policy settings, support for Windows XP Professional fast network logon, and more robust roaming. These features increase the usability, resilience, and performance of roaming user profiles.

New Group Policy Settings

The Group Policy settings that you use to manage user profiles have been moved to their own folders in the Group Policy snap-in, under Computer Configuration\ Administrative Templates\System\User Profiles and User Configuration\Administrative Templates\System\User Profiles. In addition, three new Computer Configuration settings are available with Windows XP Professional.

Prevent roaming-profile changes from propagating to the server   Determines whether changes users make to their roaming profiles are merged with the server copy of the profile. If this policy is set, users receive their roaming profiles when they log on, but any changes they make to their profiles will not be merged to their roaming profiles when they log off.

Add the Administrators security group to roaming user profiles In   Windows XP Professional, the default file permissions for newly generated roaming profiles are full control for the user, and no file access for the Administrators group. By default, an administrator must take ownership of a user's profile folder in order to gain access to it. Because taking ownership is an audited event, this increases the security of the profile folder. This policy allows the Administrators group to have full control of the user's profile directories, as in Windows NT 4.0.

Only allow local user profiles Determines whether roaming user profiles are available on a particular computer. By default, when a roaming profile user logs on, his or her roaming profile is copied from the server to the local computer. If the user has already logged on to this computer in the past, the roaming profile is merged with the local profile. Similarly, when the user logs off this computer, the local copy of his or her profile, including any changes that have been made, is merged with the server copy.

Using the Group Policy setting, you can prevent users configured to use roaming profiles from receiving their profile on a specific computer.

Support for Windows XP Professional Fast Network Logon

To speed the startup and logon process, Windows XP Professional does not require that the network be fully initialized before a client computer can start up or before a user can log on. If a user has previously logged on to a particular client computer, he or she is subsequently logged on using credentials cached on that computer.

When a user switches from using a local profile to using a roaming profile, Windows XP Professional copies relevant portions of the user's registry from the server instead of from the local computer, to prevent an older local copy from overwriting the server copy. Thereafter, whenever the roaming user logs on, the computer always waits for the network, so the profile can be downloaded from the server.

When fast network logon is enabled (as it is by default in Windows XP Professional), if administrators remove the profile path from a user's object, it is recommended that they also either rename or delete the corresponding profile folder. If they do not, and an administrator later reenters the same path, the user will receive the older copy of the registry from the server.

More Robust Roaming

In Windows 2000, certain applications and services keep registry keys open after the user logs off, preventing Windows from unloading the user's registry. When this occurs, profiles become locked and changes that users have made to their profiles are not saved to the server. This situation creates three problems for users:

- The user experience is impacted, as users might wonder why changes have not been saved when they log on to another computer.

- Because locked profiles are never unloaded, they use excessive memory on computers on which many users must log on (such as terminal servers).

- Profiles that are marked for deletion when users log off (to clean up the computer or for temporary profiles) are not deleted.

Windows XP Professional provides the following solutions to these problems:

- Sixty seconds after a user logs off, Windows XP Professional saves the user's registry and roams the profile correctly. In Windows 2000, if the profile is locked when a user logs off, Windows polls the profile for 60 seconds, and then quits.

- When the application or service closes the registry key that unlocks the profile, Windows XP Professional unloads the user's registry, freeing the memory used by the profile.

- If a profile is marked for deletion when the user logs off, it is deleted when the reference count drops to zero. If the application does not release the registry key, Windows XP Professional deletes all profiles marked for deletion the next time the computer starts.

Combining Folder Redirection with Roaming User Profiles

The Folder Redirection feature of IntelliMirror allows an administrator to redirect the location of certain folders in the user profile to a network location. Combining Folder Redirection with roaming user profiles allows you to decrease logon and logoff times for roaming and mobile users. A common practice is to redirect **My Documents** and **My Pictures**, and allow **Application Data**, **Desktop**, and **Start Menu** to roam with the profile. In addition to the benefits of improved availability and secure backup that having the data on the network provides, users also realize performance gains over low-speed network connections and in subsequent logon sessions. Because only some of their documents are copied, performance is improved when users' profiles are copied from the server. Not all of the data in the user profile is transferred to the desktop each time the user logs on—only the data that user accesses during a session.

When you combine the use of Folder Redirection and roaming user profiles, you can also provide fast computer replacement. If a user's computer needs to be replaced, the user's data can quickly be reestablished from the server location(s) to a replacement computer.

> **Note**   When implementing roaming user profiles or Folder Redirection for users of laptop computers, keep in mind that the user must log on at least once over a fast link in order for these features to apply. If an administrator configures the laptop in the office, he or she should make sure the user of the laptop logs on to it while still connected via fast link before taking it into the field. An alternative is to use Group Policy to change the slow link speed temporarily.

Note that Folder Redirection can be used with all types of user profiles: local, roaming, or mandatory. Using Folder Redirection with local profiles can provide some of the benefits of roaming profiles (such as having a user's data available at any computer, and maintaining data on the server) without the need to implement roaming profiles. Using Folder Redirection with a local profile, however, means that only the user's documents and files are available from all computers. To allow settings and configurations move with the user, you need to use roaming profiles.

For more information about using Group Policy to configure Folder Redirectionon a Windows 2000 Active Directory network, see the Step-by-Step Guide to User Data and User Settings link on the Web Resources page at http://www.microsoft.com/windows/reskits/webresources. For more information about alternate means of configuring Folder Redirection for non-Active Directory environments, see "Managing Files and Folders" in this book.

Table 7-2 lists the folders in a user profile, provides the default behavior for each folder, and indicates whether the folder can be redirected using Folder Redirection. For more information about selecting which folders to redirect and which to leave in the profile, see "Managing Files and Folders" in this book.

Table 7-2   Default Behavior of Profile Folders

Folder Name	Description	Roams with Profile by Default	Can Be Redirected Using Folder Redirection
Application Data[*]	Stores application state data, such as toolbar settings and other non-registry-based settings. Application vendors decide what to store here.	Yes	Yes
Cookies	Contains user's Microsoft® Internet Explorer cookies.	Yes	No
Desktop	Contains user-specific contents of the desktop.	Yes	Yes

Table 7-2 Default Behavior of Profile Folders

Folder Name	Description	Roams with Profile by Default	Can Be Redirected Using Folder Redirection
Favorites	Contains user's Internet Explorer favorites.	Yes	No
*Local Settings	Contains temporary files and per-user non-roaming application data. It is a container for application settings and data that do not roam with the profile, and cannot be redirected. This information is usually computer-specific, or too large to roam effectively. Application vendors can also opt to store temporary data here, in addition to or instead of in the Application Data folder.	No	No
History*	Contains the Internet Explorer history. This is a subfolder under Local Settings.	No	No
Temp*	Contains temporary files. A subfolder under Local Settings.	No	No
Temporary Internet Files*	Contains the Internet Explorer offline cache. A subfolder under Local Settings.	No	No
My Documents (and its subfolders My Pictures, My Music, My Videos)	The default location for documents that the user creates. Applications need to be written to save files here by default.	Yes	Yes
NetHood*	Contains shortcuts to My Network Places items.	Yes	No
PrintHood*	Contains shortcuts to printer folder items.	Yes	No
Recent*	Contains shortcuts to the most recently used documents, such as Most Recently Used (MRU) lists in applications.	Yes	No
Send To*	Contains shortcuts to document storage locations and applications.	Yes	No
Start Menu	Contains shortcuts to program items.	Yes	Yes
Templates*	Contains shortcuts to per-user customized template items, such as templates that a user creates in Microsoft Word or Microsoft Excel.	Yes	No

* These folders are hidden by default.

To view hidden folders

1. In **My Computer**, on the tools menu, select **Tools**, then click **Folder Options**.

2. Select the **View** tab, and click **Show Hidden Files and Folders**.

Configuring Offline Files for Portable Computers

By using Offline Files, users can disconnect from the network and work as if still connected. When the computer is offline, the files and folders appear in the same directory that they appear in online—as if they are still in the same location on the network. This allows the user working offline to edit files. The next time the user connects to the network, the offline changes are synchronized with the network share. Any changes that were made while the user was working offline are updated to the network.

Offline Files is especially useful for mobile users with portable computers because they can use it to access their files when they are not connected to the network. Thus users can always open, update, and work with current versions of network files when they are not connected to the network.

Offline Files stores the data in the computer's cache to make network files available offline. The cache is a portion of disk space that a computer accesses when it is not connected to the network. The view of shared network items that you make available offline is the same as the view online, even if users lose a connection to the network or remove a portable computer from the docking station. Users have the same access permissions to those files and folders that they have when they are connected to the network.

If two users on the network make changes to the same file, they can save their own version of the file to the network, keep the other user's version, or save both.

You can make shared files or folders available for offline use from any computer that shares files by using server message block (SMB)–based file and printer sharing, which includes any computer running Windows 2000, Windows 95, Windows 98, or Windows NT 4.0. The Offline Files feature is not available on Novell NetWare networks. When configuring a shared folder, you have the option to choose whether all the files in the folder are automatically available offline, or whether a user must explicitly mark a file to be available offline.

Offline Files is a stand-alone technology, which means that you do not need to pair it with Folder Redirection and set up and configure network shares. However, pairing the two technologies works well. By default, any folder that is redirected is available offline as well.

In Windows XP Professional all the files in a redirected folder, including subfolders, are automatically made available offline. You can disable automatic caching of redirected folders by using the Group Policy setting **Do not automatically make redirected folders available offline**, under User Configuration\Administrative Templates\Network\Offline Files.

> **Note** In Windows 2000, redirected folders are not automatically made available offline. To make folders available offline, administrators use the policy setting **Administratively assigned offline files**, or the users manually make all files available offline.

Configuring Files on a Network Share for Offline Use

Before you can have offline access to the files on a shared network folder, you must specify how the files in the folder are stored in a cache on the client computer—in this case, the user's portable computer. For non-executable files, such as word processing documents, spreadsheets, and bitmaps, there are two options for storing files: automatic caching, and manual caching.

Automatic Caching

Automatic caching makes a file available offline by creating a locally stored copy of the file when a user opens the file on a portable computer. Automatically stored files might not always be available in the cache because Offline Files might remove, or purge, them when the cache becomes full. Offline Files will purge files based on frequency of use. Automatic caching is most useful when you have an unreliable or unpredictable network connection. For example, if a user is working on an automatically stored file, and the portable computer is disconnected from the network, the user can continue working on the file without interruption. To make a file available offline at all times, you can use My Computer to mark the file as **Always available offline**. For more information about making files available offline, see "Managing Files and Folders" in this book.

Manual Caching

Manual caching makes a file or a folder available offline, but only when it is *pinned*, that is, manually marked on the user's computer. A manually stored file or folder that is not pinned on the user's computer is not available offline. Manual caching is useful for users who need access to a file or folder all of the time or for users who need access to entire folders, especially folders that contain documents created by or modified by other users. For example, manual caching works well for users who frequently use a portable computer away from the office without a network connection but still need access to many files on the network. In this case, you can manually pin folders on the user's portable computer to make those folders available to the user when away from the office. Automatic caching is not ideal in this case because the files in the network folder are not locally stored unless the portable computer user opens each file while the portable computer is connected to the network share.

To configure automatic or manual caching on a shared network folder

1. Right-click the shared folder that you want to configure, click **Properties**, and then click the **Sharing** tab.

2. In the **Properties** dialog box, click **Caching**.

3. In the **Setting** box, select a type of storing.

On the **Setting** box menu, you can also choose **Automatic caching of programs and documents**, which is useful if a user runs programs from the network. This option stores a copy of a network program on the user's hard disk so that the user can run the program offline. However, users of portable computers must be careful when using this feature because only the program files that are executed are stored on the local computer. For example, if you run Microsoft Word from a network share, but you do not use the spelling checker, the spelling checker is not stored. If you then run Word offline and try to run the spelling checker, the tool is not available. To avoid this problem, you can load all programs and associated tools locally on a portable computer and not use the **Automatic caching of programs and documents** option.

Configuring Synchronization for Offline Files

Synchronization ensures that any changes made to offline files and folders are propagated back to the network and that any changes that have occurred on the network are propagated to the user's computer. Some synchronization features and options relate specifically to portable computers. For more information about all synchronization options, see "Managing Files and Folders" in this book.

In order for synchronization to occur, the hard disk on a user's portable computer must be turned on so that files can be copied from the network to the local cache, and files in the local cache can be copied to the network. Synchronization might not be an optimum use of power for a portable computer running on battery power. However, certain options allow you to set synchronization to occur when a computer runs on battery power. You can also use Group Policy to synchronize all offline files before logging off.

Synchronizing Offline Files by Using Group Policy

To ensure that all offline files are fully synchronized, you must enable the Local Computer Policy setting, **Synchronize all offline files before logging off**, in the Administrative Templates\Network\Offline Files folder. When this Group Policy setting is enabled, all files in the user's redirected folder are available when the user is working offline. If this setting is not enabled, the system only performs a quick synchronization, and as a result only files that were used recently are cached. This setting appears in the Computer Configuration and User Configuration folders. If both settings are configured, the setting in Computer Configuration takes precedence over the setting in User Configuration.

Enabling Synchronization During an Idle State

By default, offline files are not synchronized when a computer is in an idle state and using battery power. This is because portable computers rely on a low-power idle state to conserve battery power, and you might not want to use battery power to synchronize files. You can change the default so that synchronization occurs when the computer is on idle and running on battery power.

To enable synchronization when a computer running on battery power is idle

1. In **All Programs,** point to **Accessories,** click **Synchronize,** and then click **Setup**.

2. In the **Synchronization Settings** dialog box, click the **On Idle** tab, and then click **Advanced**.

3. In the **Idle Settings** dialog box, clear the **Prevent synchronization when my computer is running on battery power** check box.

Preventing Scheduled Synchronization

You can schedule synchronization to occur on specific days and at specific times. Because a scheduled synchronization is often a low-priority task that consumes power, Windows XP Professional allows you to prevent scheduled synchronization from occurring when a computer is running on battery power.

To prevent scheduled synchronization from occurring when a computer is running on battery power

1. In **All Programs,** point to **Accessories,** click **Synchronize,** and then click **Setup**.

2. In the **Synchronization Settings** dialog box, click the **Scheduled** tab.

3. Click a scheduled task, and then click **Edit**.

4. On the **Settings** tab, under **Power Management,** select the **Don't start the task if the computer is running on batteries** check box.

If a scheduled synchronization is in progress, and a portable computer is switched from alternating current to battery power, you can have Windows XP Professional cancel synchronization. This might occur if scheduled synchronization starts on a docked portable computer that is using a wireless network connection, and the user performs a hot undock.

To stop scheduled synchronization when the computer is running on battery power

1. In **All Programs,** point to **Accessories,** and then click **Synchronize**.

2. In the **Items to Synchronize** dialog box, click **Setup**.

3. Click the **Scheduled** tab.

4. Click a scheduled task, and then click **Edit**.

5. On the **Settings** tab, under **Power Management**, select the **Stop the task if battery mode begins** check box.

Enabling Automatic Connection During Scheduled Synchronization

If a computer is not connected to a network when a synchronization is scheduled to start, you can configure Windows XP Professional to connect so that synchronization can occur. In this case, Windows attempts to connect to the designated network, detects that the computer is not connected to the network, and then informs the user that the network is not available. By default, Windows does not connect if there is no network connection at the time of synchronization. Although you might use this option for portable computer users who are normally connected to the network, you might not want to enable it for users who frequently use the portable computer while it is disconnected from the network.

To enable automatic connection for scheduled synchronization

1. In **All Programs,** point to **Accessories**, click **Synchronize**, and then click **Setup.**

2. On the **Scheduled** tab, under **Current synchronization tasks**, click a scheduled task, and then click **Edit**.

3. On the **Synchronization Items** tab, select **If my computer is not connected when this scheduled synchronization begins, automatically connect for me**.

Synchronizing Over a Slow Link

Windows does not provide a system-wide definition or threshold for a slow link. Instead, it allows every system component to define a slow link according to its own capabilities and requirements. For example, one component might define a slow link as 28.8 kilobits per second (Kbps) while another might define it as 56 Kbps. For Offline Files and synchronization in a Windows 2000 Active Directory environment, you can use Group Policy settings to define file synchronization behavior over a slow link. The default slow link threshold value is 64 Kbps.

A slow-link connection affects synchronization by preventing the following:

- Automatic transition of shared network folders from an offline to an online state.

- The copying of newly added files from the network share to the user's computer.

Defining the Slow Link Threshold   In Windows XP Professional and Windows 2000 Server you can use the **Configure slow link** Group Policy setting located in Computer Configuration\Administrative Templates\Network\ Offline Files to define the threshold value at which Offline Files considers a network connection to be slow.

For more information about the Group Policy settings associated with Offline Files, see "Managing Files and Folders" in this book.

Transitioning from an Offline State to an Online State   After a network share has been offline to a user—for example, if a server goes offline and is then brought back online, or a user undocks a portable computer and then docks it—the share becomes available online for the user if the following three conditions are true:

- No offline files from that network share are open on the user's computer.

- None of the offline files from that network share have changes that need to be synchronized.

- The network connection is not considered a slow link.

When these conditions are true, and a user opens a file on the network share, the user is working online on that network share. Any changes that the user makes are saved to both the file on the network share and the file stored in the Offline Files folder. If any one of the conditions is not true, and a user opens a file on the network share, the user is still working offline even though the network share is available. Any changes that the user makes are saved only to the offline version of the file.

When a user first connects to a network over a slow-link connection, the user is only working offline on any shared network folders even though the online folders are available. To start working online with a shared network folder, the user must synchronize the shared network folder. Synchronization shifts the folder to an online state and pushes any offline files that have changed to the shared network folder. To pull files from the shared network folder to the Offline Files folder, the user must perform a second synchronization, which pulls files that have changed from the network share to the Offline Files folder.

Note   When you use a slow-link connection, a second synchronization does not pull newly created files from the network share to the Offline Files folder. To make new files on the network share available offline during a slow-link connection, you must pin the files.

Making Network Shares Available Without Synchronization   Slow-link connections can prevent a network share from coming online even though the network share is available. Although you can bring the network share online by synchronizing it, this method might not be ideal. For example, when a user's portable computer is disconnected from the network, and the user requires access to a file on a shared network folder that has been made available offline, a file to which the user has made several changes offline might not be ready to synchronize with the network share. Or, the user might be in a hurry and does not want to take the time to synchronize files. The user wants only to connect to the network, get the new file from the network share, and then log off. Windows XP Professional provides a way for the user to make a folder available online without synchronizing offline files.

To make a folder available online without synchronizing offline files

1. In the notification area, click the **Offline Files** icon to open the **Offline Files Status** dialog box.

2. Select **Work online without synchronizing changes**.

> **Note**   The Offline Files icon appears in the notification area when users are working offline.

Securing Offline Files

Windows XP Professional provides several methods of protection for offline files. The Offline Files folder, including the Offline Files database and the stored offline files, is secured against unauthorized access by administrator permissions. Additionally, the same user rights that protect their network counterparts protect offline files and folders. Windows XP Professional also supports encryption of offline files.

Offline Files Folder Security

Offline files are stored (cached) in the Offline Files folder. Each computer has only one Offline Files folder, even if the computer is shared by multiple users, and all offline files are stored in this folder. By default, this folder is protected by administrator permissions so that unauthorized users cannot view the contents. However, these permissions are only applied to the folder if the folder is located on a drive that is formatted to use NTFS. Windows XP Professional notifies you of this limitation when you first cache an offline file on a FAT or FAT32 drive. For more information about file system security, see "File Systems" in this book.

Offline File and Folder Permissions

In addition to the protection afforded by the permissions on the actual Offline Files folder, offline files and folders retain the permissions set for them on the network share. This type of security is important if multiple users share a single computer. For example, if a user creates a file on a network share, changes its permissions so that only that user has access to the file, and then makes the file available offline, another user who tries to open the offline version of the file on the user's computer is denied access, just as if the second user tried to open the file directly on the network share.

This type of security is applied to offline files regardless of the formatting of the user's hard disk. Thus, if you set permissions on a file on a network share that is formatted to use NTFS, and you make that file available offline on a computer that has a FAT or FAT32 drive, the permissions carry over to the offline version of the file, even though the drive is formatted to use FAT or FAT32.

Encrypting Offline Files

You can secure data on portable computers by encrypting the offline files. Windows XP Professional provides Encrypting File System (EFS) support for Offline Files. The local cache of Offline Files can be encrypted if the cache directory resides on an NTFS volume. When the cache is encrypted, the local copy of a cached file is automatically encrypted.

To encrypt offline files

1. In **Folder Options,** click the **Offline Files** tab.

2. Select the **Encrypt Offline files to secure data** check box.

You can also use Group Policy to apply this option to groups of users. In the Group Policy snap-in, go to Computer Configuration\Administrative Templates\Network\Offline Files.

Offline files stored on local hard disks are secured by EFS, however, the files are encrypted in the system context and the encryption applies to all users of the local computer. If both the local computer and the remote computer where the files are stored are encrypted, files are encrypted at all times. If the local computer is encrypted, but the remote location of the files is not, the files are encrypted while they are stored locally.

If the remote location is encrypted and the local computer is not, however, you are warned when you try to make a file available offline that it will not be encrypted on the local computer. You can override the default and make the files available; when you attempt to synchronize the files, the local copy will be deleted.

Managing the Offline Files Folder

Portable computer users who frequently work offline might accumulate hundreds of files in the Offline Files folder on their hard disk. Because many of these files might be out-of-date, rarely used, or no longer needed offline, you might want to delete them from the Offline Files folder (the cache) to maximize the available disk space. Users might also want to delete files in the Offline Files folder if a network share has been deleted or is no longer available. In addition to deleting individual files, you can reinitialize the Offline Files cache, which deletes the entire contents of the Offline Files folder and resets the Offline Files database. Reinitializing the Offline Files cache is useful when you transfer a computer to a new user or when a user has been working offline with sensitive or proprietary documents and you want to ensure that they are no longer available offline or that they are not in the cache.

You can safely remove offline files from the cache without affecting network files or folders by deleting files from the Offline Files folder or by reinitializing the cache. Do not delete or move any files directly from the *systemroot*\CSC folder. For more information about deleting offline files from cache without affecting network files or folders, see "Managing Files and Folders" in this book.

Securing Portable Computers

Because portable computers are vulnerable to theft, it is important that you provide security for portable computers and the data that is stored on them. You can do this by formatting hard disks to use NTFS so that permissions can be set and encryption can be enabled on files and folders by means of Encrypting File System. You can also add portable computer users to the Power Users group so that they have maximum control of the portable computer without having full control of the system. Ensuring that users use strong passwords to log on to their portable computers and that administrators use strong passwords for the local administrator account is another important security measure. Also, Group Policy settings can be used to restrict access to the computer and any data that is stored on it. For more information about these security features, see "Logon and Authentication," "Managing Files and Folders," and "Encrypting File System" in this book.

Securely Undocking Portable Computers

Portable computers can be undocked in two ways, depending on the type of docking station, the type of portable computer, and the permissions and Group Policy settings that have been implemented on the computer. A portable computer can be undocked in the following circumstances:

- While the portable computer is shut down and the power is off, a user physically ejects it or removes it from the docking station (a cold undock).

- While the portable computer is running, a user uses the **Eject PC** command in Windows XP Professional to eject the computer from the docking station, before physically removing the computer (a hot undock).

To prevent an unauthorized user from undocking a portable computer from a docking station, the portable computer or docking station must include some type of physical lock. Portable computers might simply use a keyed lock that must be manually unlocked to prevent undocking by unauthorized users. Docking stations can include a lock as well, some of which can be programmatically controlled.

For example, some docking stations allow administrators to require that an authorized user log on and select **Eject PC** before freeing the lock and allowing physical removal of the portable computer from the docking station.

You can choose a local Group Policy setting that controls who has undocking privileges on a portable computer. If a user has undocking privileges, he or she is able to use the **Eject PC** command. If the user does not have undocking privileges, the **Eject PC** command is not available. However, any program can call the application programming interface (API) that controls the **Eject PC** command, which means that any program can have its own button or menu item that tries to eject a portable computer. If a user tries to use such a button or menu item and does not have undocking privileges, the command fails.

By default, undocking permissions are granted to a user during a clean installation of Windows XP Professional and during an upgrade from Windows 95, Windows 98, or Windows NT 4.0. To prevent a user from undocking, you must use Group Policy to set undocking privileges.

To set undocking privileges by using Group Policy

1. In the **Run** dialog box, type **gpedit.msc**.

2. In the details pane of Group Policy, under **Computer Configuration**, open **Windows Settings**, **Security Settings**, and the **Local Policies, and open the User Rights Assignment** folder.

3. In the details pane, right-click **Remove computer from docking station**, and then click **Properties**.

4. In the **Properties** dialog box, click **Add** to add users and groups to the list.
   – or –
   Click **Remove** to remove users and groups from the list.

> **Warning** Restricting undock privileges offers no security benefits if the docking station in question does not provide a programmatically controlled locking mechanism.

Windows XP Professional BIOS Security

Some computers allow you to implement system security or device security at the BIOS level. Typically, equipment manufacturers implement this type of security by requiring a password at startup while the BIOS is loading. If the user enters an incorrect password, the BIOS does not finish loading, and the computer does not start; or the BIOS might finish loading, but it does not transfer control of the computer to Windows XP Professional. Although this type of security is designed to control access to the computer at startup, it might also control access when the computer resumes from a low-power state such as standby or hibernation. In these cases, users might have to enter the BIOS password when the system resumes from either standby or hibernation.

To implement BIOS security on a portable computer, contact the portable computer manufacturer to verify that it operates properly with the standby and hibernate features of Windows XP Professional. Also be aware that BIOS security can super-cede Windows XP Professional security by preventing Windows XP Professional from taking control of the computer or other devices.

Using Infrared Hardware and Video Devices with Portable Computers

You can use infrared hardware and video devices with portable computers. Some devices and device types, however, have known compatibility problems with Windows XP Professional or have conflicts and limitations when they are used with Windows XP Professional.

Using Infrared Devices with Portable Computers

Windows XP Professional supports the IrTran-P image exchange protocol, which allows a computer to receive images and files from a digital camera or other digital image capture device. However, Microsoft® ActiveSync® version 3.0, the desktop synchronization technology for Microsoft® Windows® CE–based handheld comput-ers, disables the IrTran-P service. If you must use ActiveSync 3.0 and the IrTran-P service, you need to toggle between the two services to use them. You can toggle between these services either by using **Wireless Link** in Control Panel or by using ActiveSync 3.0.

> **Note**   By default, the IrTran-P protocol is turned on in Windows, meaning that you can download images and files from a digital camera to a computer.

To turn IrTran-P protocol on and off

1. In **Control Panel**, click **Printers and Other Hardware**, and then click **Wire-less Link**.

2. On the **Image Transfer** tab, select **Use Wireless Link to transfer images from a digital camera to your computer** to turn on the IrTran-P protocol.
   – or –
   Clear **Use Wireless Link to transfer images from a digital camera to your computer** to turn off the IrTran-P protocol.

To turn ActiveSync 3.0 on and off

1. Open **ActiveSync 3.0**.

2. On the **Tools** menu, click **Options**.

3. On the **Rules** tab, select **Open ActiveSync when my mobile device connects** to turn on ActiveSync.

– or –

Clear **Open ActiveSync when my mobile device connects** to turn off ActiveSync.

Windows XP Professional also supports the IrDial protocol, which gives infrared devices access to the Internet and other networks by using the Point-to-Point Protocol (PPP). Cellular telephones that use IrDial do not require special installation and configuration because IrDial network connections are managed entirely by using the Network Connections folder.

To configure a connection for IrDial

1. Double-click the connection that you want to configure.

2. Click **Properties**.

3. Under **Connect Using**, select **Infrared Modem Port**, and then click **OK**.

4. Enter your user name and your password, and then click **Dial**.

For more information about infrared device configuration and Wireless Link in Control Panel, see Windows XP Professional Help and Support Center, or see "Managing Devices" and "Connecting Remote Offices" in this book.

Using Video Devices with Portable Computers

You can use the Windows XP Professional multiple monitor feature with a docked portable computer, but only if the docking station allows you to install Peripheral Component Interconnect (PCI) or Accelerated Graphics Port (AGP) video adapters. Also, the on-board video adapter (the one that is a part of the portable computer's motherboard) must be designated as the VGA display device. Typically, this is not a problem, although the BIOS on some computers allows you to choose the video adapter that you want to use as the VGA device. In this case, you must designate the on-board video adapter.

Windows XP Professional does not support hot undocking of portable computers while they are using multiple monitors. To perform a hot undock on a computer using multiple monitors, you must first stop using all but one monitor. You can do this by detaching the secondary display before performing the hot undock.

To detach a secondary monitor

1. In **Control Panel**, click **Appearance and Themes**, and then click the **Display** icon.

2. Click the **Settings** tab, double-click the secondary monitor, and then click **Attach**.

3. Click **Apply** to detach the monitor.

Typically, the secondary monitor turns off, leaving the primary monitor running.

After you detach the secondary monitor, you can perform a hot undock.

Wireless Networking

With the rapid growth of wireless networking, users can access data from anywhere in the world, using a wide range of devices. Wireless networks offer additional benefits, by reducing or eliminating the high cost of laying expensive fiber and cabling and by providing backup functionality for wired networks. Microsoft® Windows® XP Professional provides extensive support for wireless networking technology so that businesses can extend the capabilities of their enterprise networks to wireless devices.

Wireless networking for Windows XP Professional can be categorized by the size of the area over which data can be transmitted. Wireless Personal Area Networking (WPAN) operates over a small coverage area (approximately 10 meters). Wireless Local Area Networking (WLAN) operates to a larger coverage area (approximately 100 meters). This chapter provides an overview of WPANs and WLANs and describes how you can use the wireless networking support in Windows XP Professional to exchange data over WPANs and WLANS. It does not discuss wireless wide area networks (WWANs) or wireless metropolitan area networks (WMANs).

WPAN

A Wireless Personal Area Network (WPAN) includes data communication technology that allows devices that are in very close proximity to each other to access resources and exchange data, without the use of cables. These devices can automatically create an *ad hoc network,* an informal network of devices, often by using wireless connectivity. Due to their small size and limited processing power, WPAN devices lend themselves well to ad hoc networking. In an ad hoc network scenario, the wireless devices connect to each other directly rather than through wireless access points, which are used in infrastructure networks. In infrastructure networks, wireless stations (devices with radio network cards, such as portable computers) connect to wireless access points, rather than directly to each other. These access points function as bridges between the devices and the existing network backbone.

The key WPAN technology supported in Windows XP Professional is Infrared Data Association (IrDA). IrDA is a WPAN technology that allows users with infrared-enabled devices to transfer files and images and to establish dial-up network connections and LAN access network connections.

Infrared Data Association

IrDA specifies a networking protocol that allows computers, printers, mobile phones, personal digital assistants, digital cameras, and other devices to exchange information over short distances by using infrared light. Infrared light is electromagnetic radiation covering a spectrum of wavelengths between 850 and

900 nanometers. These wavelengths are somewhat longer than visible light and are invisible to the human eye.

Due to propagation properties of light, a clear line of sight is required between the devices communication by infrared light. The clear line of sight requirement has some advantages (for example, when making a purchase with a mobile device, the required proximity between the devices ensures that you are communicating with the correct payment device), and some drawbacks (for example, you cannot connect a phone in your pocket to a portable computer on a desk) there are numerous clear advantages to using infrared light for communication:

- Infrared light offers large bandwidth.

- The exchange of data by means of infrared light is not regulated by the FCC or any other governmental agency.

- Infrared light does not interfere with radio frequency (RF) wireless networks.

- All infrared radiation is confined to a room, preventing easy eavesdropping.

IrDA is a short-range, half duplex, asynchronous serial transmission technology. Furthermore, IrDA specifies three distinct modes of transmission for different data transmission rates: Serial Ir (SIR), Fast Ir (FIR), and Very Fast Ir (VFIR). The SIR specification defines a maximum data rate of 115.2 kilobits per second (Kbps). FIR specifies a data rate of 4 megabits per second (Mbps), and VFIR specifies a data rate of 16 Mbps. A number of intermediate speeds are also available. For more information about the intermediate speeds that are available over infrared, see the Windows XP Professional Driver Development Kit (DDK) link on the Web Resources page at http://www.microsoft.com/windows/reskits/webresources.

IrDA User Profiles

The IrDA implementation in Windows XP Professional supports the following five user profiles:

- **File transfer (IrOBEX)** enables easy file transfer between IrDA devices.

- **Printing (IrLPT)** enables printing directly from IrDA devices to IrDA printers.

- **Image transfer (IrTran-P)** enables point-and-shoot one-step image transfer between digital cameras and Windows devices.

- **Dial-up networking (IrCOMM)** enables dial-up Internet access through IR-enabled cellular phones.

- **LAN access and peer-to-peer networking (IrNET)** enables network access through IR access points or through a direct network connection between two Windows devices.

These supported profiles provide the following advantages:

- **IrDA does not require use of cable.** It is impossible to mismatch connectors and wiring with IrDA. The speed and configuration parameters are negotiated transparently at connect time and a common set is used for connection. IrDA at 16 Mbps is compatible with IrDA at 9.6 Kbps. Also, the IrDA connector is completely sealed, inexpensive, and available from multiple vendors.

- **IrDA and WinSock provide a common user-space API.** The combination of IrDA and Windows Sockets (WinSock) presents the application programmer with a powerful yet simple Win32® user-space API that exposes multiple, fully error-corrected data streams. Serial and parallel ports are the only other point-to-point technologies that have a commonly available user-space API. IrDA defines rich functionality that does not exist with serial and parallel cables, and it borrows from the very successful client/server connection and programming model defined by the TCP/IP family of protocols and the WinSock APIs.

- **The open protocols of IrDA support other devices.** WinSock exposes the IrDA TinyTP protocol to the application writer. A device that implements the TinyTP protocol can easily exchange data with Windows applications.

- **IrDA is uniquely suited for ad hoc point-to-point networking.** The core IrDA services are similar to those exposed by the popular TCP protocol. Applications running on two different computers can easily open multiple reliable connections to send and receive data. As with TCP, client applications connect to a server application by specifying a device address (TCP *host*) and an application address (TCP *port*). Thus, the combination of IrDA and WinSock supports easy-to-use, zero configuration, ad hoc point-to-point networking.

For more information about installing, configuring, and using IrDA for wireless networking in Windows XP Professional, see "Wireless Networking" in Windows XP Professional Help and Support Center.

WLAN

The primary wireless Local Area Network (WLAN) solution is IEEE 802.11, which is the WLAN standard developed by the Institute of Electrical and Electronics Engineers (IEEE). The IEEE 802.11b specification, recently created and adopted, adds to the groundwork laid by IEEE 802.11. IEEE 802.11a, currently in development, will make further improvements to 802.11b. The IEEE 802.11-defined media access control is also used for the 802.11 extensions, 802.11b and 802.11a. To achieve higher data rates, 802.11b and 802.11a define different physical layer specifications.

802.11

IEEE 802.11 is a shared WLAN standard using the carrier sense multiple access media access control protocol with collision avoidance. The standard allows for both direct sequence and frequency-hopping spread spectrum transmissions at the physical layer. The original 802.11 specification defines data rates of 1 Mbps and 2 Mbps and uses a radio frequency of 2.45 GHz.

802.11b

The major enhancement to IEEE 802.11 by IEEE 802.11b is the standardization of the physical layer to support higher bandwidth. IEEE 802.11b supports two additional speeds, 5.5 Mbps and 11 Mbps, using the same frequency of 2.45 GHz. A different modulation scheme is used in order to provide the higher data rates of 5 Mbps and 11 Mbps. Direct sequence spread spectrum (DSSS) is the physical layer defined in the 802.11b standard.

802.11a

The latest standard, IEEE 802.11a, is currently being developed. This wireless standard operates at a data transmission rate as high as 54 Mbps and uses a radio frequency of 5.8 gigahertz (GHz). Instead of DSSS, which 802.11b uses, 802.11a uses Orthogonal Frequency Division Multiplexing (OFDM). ODFM allows data to be transmitted by subfrequencies in parallel. This provides greater resistance to interference and provides greater throughput. This higher speed technology allows wireless networking to perform better for video and conferencing applications. Because they are not on the same frequencies as Bluetooth or microwave ovens, OFDM and IEEE 802.11a will provide both a higher data rate and a cleaner signal.

802.11 Architecture

The 802.11 architecture contains several main components: station (STA), access point (AP), independent basic service set (IBSS), basic service set (BSS), distribution system (DS), and extended service set (ESS). The wireless STA contains an adapter card, PC Card, or an embedded device to provide wireless connectivity. The AP functions as a bridge between the wireless STAs and the existing network backbone for network access.

An IBSS is a wireless network, consisting of at least two STAs, used where no access to a DS is available. An IBSS is also sometimes referred to as an ad hoc wireless network.

A BSS includes connectivity to the existing network backbone through an AP. A BSS is also sometimes referred to as an infrastructure wireless network. All STAs in a BSS communicate through the AP. The AP provides connectivity to the wired LAN and provides bridging functionality when one STA initiates communication to another STA.

An ESS is where the APs of multiple BSSs are interconnected. This allows for mobility, because STAs can move from one BSS to another BSS. APs can be interconnected with or without wires; however, most of the time they are connected with wires. The DS is the logical component used to interconnect BSSs. The DS provides distribution services to allow for the roaming of STAs between BSSs.

Figure 7-1 shows the 802.11 architecture.

The IEEE 802 standards committee defines two separate layers, the Logical Link Control (LLC) and media access control, for the Data-Link layer of the OSI model. The IEEE 802.11 wireless standard defines the specifications for the physical layer and the media access control (MAC) layer and communicates up to the LLC layer.

All of the components in the 802.11 architecture fall into either the media access control layer or the physical layer.

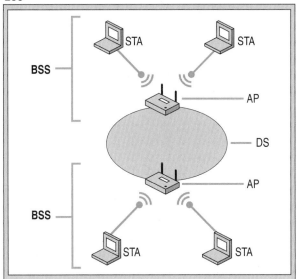
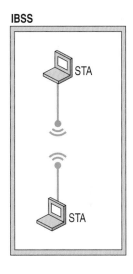

Figure 7-1   802.11 architecture

Wireless stations, when entering the range of an access point, choose a wireless access point to associate with. This selection is made automatically by using signal strength and packet error rate information. Next, the wireless station selects the assigned frequency of the access point that it is to begin communicating with. Periodically, the wireless station listens to other access points to determine whether they would provide a stronger signal or a better error rate. If a different access point provides a better signal, the workstation switches to the frequency of that access point. This process is called *reassociation*.

Reassociation can occur for many different reasons. The signal can weaken because the wireless station moves away from the access point or the access point becomes congested with too much other traffic or interference. The wireless station, by switching to another wireless station, can distribute the load over adjacent access points, increasing the performance of other wireless stations. By using a pattern of overlapping channels, coverage over large areas can be achieved. As a wireless station moves about, it can associate and reassociate from one access point to another, maintaining a continuous connection during transit.

The 802.11 media access control frame, as shown in Figure 7-2, consists of a media access control header, the frame body, and a frame check sequence (FCS). The numbers in Figure 7-2 represent the number of bytes for each field.

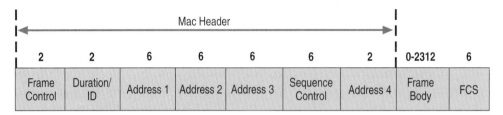

Figure 7-2 802.11 Media access control frame format

802.11 Security

The 802.11 standard provides both authentication and encryption specifications. The standard includes open system and shared key authentication types. Open system authentication is the default authentication algorithm. It involves a two-step process, consisting of an identity assertion and a request for authentication, followed by the authentication result. Shared key supports authentication of an STA either as a member of those stations that know a shared secret key, or as a member of stations that do not. The standard currently assumes that the shared key is delivered to the participating STAs by means of a secure channel that is independent of the IEEE 802.11.

Wired Equivalent Privacy (WEP) is the encryption specification that is defined by the IEEE 802.11 standard. The intention of WEP security is to provide the same security to a wireless network that is provided on a wired network. In wireless networks, because the data is broadcast using an antenna, the signals can be intercepted, and, if not encrypted, viewed by an intruder to the system.

Although the 802.11 specification does provide both authentication and encryption, it does not define or provide a WEP key management protocol. This is a limitation to IEEE 802.11 security services—especially in a wireless infrastructure network mode with a large number of STAs. The 802.1*x* draft standard addresses the security limitations of 802.11.

802.11 Authentication

All 802.11 authentication frames have the management frame type and the authentication subtype. The authentication type is determined by the authentication algorithm number field, located in the frame body of the 802.11 media access control frame. An authentication algorithm number value of 0 indicates open system authentication, and a value of 1 indicates shared key authentication. The authentication transaction sequence number field, also located in the frame body of the 802.11 media access control frame, indicates the current status of the authentication process.

Open System Authentication   Open system authentication involves a two-step communication process using plaintext. The authentication-initiating STA sends a frame consisting of an identity assertion and a request for authentication. This has the authentication transaction sequence number field of 1 and the authentication algorithm number value of 0. The authenticating STA then replies to the authentication-initiating STA with the authentication result, which has the authentication transaction sequence number field of 2.

Open system authentication allows all devices that have the authentication algorithm number for open system to authenticate.

Shared Key Authentication   Shared key authentication involves a four-step process using secure or encrypted text by means of WEP. The authentication-initiating STA sends a frame consisting of an identity assertion and a request for authentication. This has the authentication transaction sequence number field of 1. The authenticating STA then responds to the authentication-initiating STA with a frame with the challenge text created by the WEP algorithm and the transaction sequence number field of 2. The authentication-initiating STA then replies to the authenticating STA with the encrypted challenge text created by the WEP algorithm and the transaction sequence number field of 3. The authenticating STA concludes the shared key authentication process by sending the authentication result, which has the transaction sequence number field of 4.

The authentication result is positive if the authenticating STA is able to conclude that the decrypted challenge text matches the challenge text originally sent in the second frame.

802.11 Encryption

Wired networks normally require a physical connection in order to be compromised. In wireless networks, because the data is broadcast using an antenna, the signals can be intercepted, and, if not encrypted, viewed by an intruder to the system. Wireless Equivalent Privacy (WEP) security is intended to provide security that is equivalent to the security of a wired network.

WEP is the encryption standard that is specified by the IEEE 802.11 standard. *Privacy* is the encryption of data that is transmitted across the wireless network. IEEE 802.11 does not require that the same WEP keys be used by all portable devices. It also allows portable devices to maintain two sets of shared keys: a unicast session key and a multicast/global key. Current IEEE 802.11 implementations primarily support shared multicast/global keys.

WEP provides encryption services to protect authorized users of a wireless LAN from eavesdroppers. WEP functions by encrypting a data frame and its contents. The encrypted information then replaces the formerly unencrypted information. The WEP bit is set in the frame control field portion of the media access control header. This informs the receiving node that the transmission is encrypted. The receiving node unencrypts the encrypted portion of the data frame by using the same encryption scheme. It then places the unencrypted information back into the data frame, recreating the original data frame.

The IEEE 802.11 standard specifies 40-bit secret key encryption with a 24-bit initialization vector (IV). Different vendors utilize other encryption bit lengths, such as 104-bit secret key encryption with a 24-bit IV. The encryption mechanism is a symmetrical cipher that uses the same key for encryption and decryption. The secret key remains constant for a prolonged period. The initialization values are changed periodically, however, based on the degree of privacy required of the WEP algorithm.

The current IEEE 802.11 security option for access control does not scale appropriately in large infrastructure network mode (for example, corporate campuses and public places), or in an ad hoc network mode. A principal limitation to this security mechanism is that the standard does not define a key management protocol for distribution of the keys. This assumes that the secret, shared keys are delivered to the IEEE 802.11 wireless station by means of a secure channel independent of IEEE 802.11. This becomes even more challenging when a large number of stations are involved, such as on a corporate campus.

To provide a better mechanism for access control and security, a key management protocol must be included in the specification. The 802.1x draft standard addresses the key management and security limitations of the 802.11 standard.

802.1x

The 802.1x draft standard defines port-based, network access control used to provide authenticated network access for Ethernet networks. This port-based network access control uses the physical characteristics of the switched LAN infrastructure to authenticate devices attached to a LAN port. Access to the port can be denied if the authentication process fails. While this standard is designed for wired Ethernet networks, it can be applied to 802.11 wireless LANs.

The following terms are specific to the 802.1x draft standard:

- **Supplicant.** The entity that requests to be authenticated.

- **Authenticator.** The entity that allows access to resources and services on the network.

- **Authentication server.** The entity that provides the authentication service for the authenticator. The authentication server checks the credentials of the supplicant on behalf of the authenticator, and indicates in a response to the authenticator whether the supplicant is authorized to access the authenticator's services. The authentication server might be a separate entity, or its functions might be co-located with the authenticator.

The 802.1x draft standard defines two port access control methods for the authenticator: controlled and uncontrolled. Access by means of the controlled port is only allowed to those entities that have been successfully authenticated. Before authentication takes place, all communication goes through the uncontrolled port. The 802.1x authentication process is illustrated in Figure 7-3.

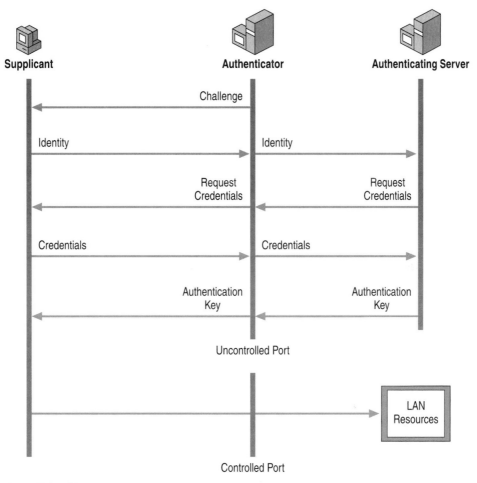

Figure 7-3   802.1x authentication

When authentication successfully takes place, the supplicant is able to access the LAN resources and services through the controlled port.

PPP Extensible Authentication Protocol   The Point-to-Point Protocol (PPP), as defined in RFC 1661, does not require authentication, but it does provide an optional authentication phase. RFC 2284, *PPP Extensible Authentication Protocol (EAP)*, defines the authentication process for PPP. The 802.1*x* draft standard lists EAP as the authentication protocol to use for the authentication process between the supplicant and the authentication server. Different EAP types are defined in RFC 2284, such as Message Digest 5 (MD5)–Challenge. Additional EAP types, such as Transport Layer Security (TLS), are also available through follow-up RFCs.

EAP-TLS   EAP-TLS, as defined in RFC 2716, is an EAP type that is used in certificate-based security environments. EAP-TLS is a Secure Channel (SChannel) authentication and encryption protocol, which provides for mutual authentication, integrity-protected cipher-suite negotiation, and key exchange between the two endpoints by means of public-key cryptography.

EAP-MD5   EAP-MD5 uses the same challenge-handshake protocol that is used by the PPP-based Challenge Handshake Authentication Protocol (CHAP), but the challenges and responses are sent as EAP messages. EAP MD5 is intended for prototyping and testing.

RADIUS and 802.1x with 802.11   While providing convenience, wireless networking technologies and wireless APs present the following security risks:

- Anyone who has a compatible wireless network adapter can gain access to the network.

- Wireless networking signals use radio waves to send and receive information. Anyone within an appropriate distance to a wireless AP can detect and receive all data sent to and from the wireless AP.

To counter the first security risk, wireless APs must require authentication and authorization of the wireless node before data can be sent to and received from the network attached to the wireless AP. To provide their own authentication and authorization, each WAP would need a user account database with each user's authentication credentials and a set of rules by which authorization is granted. Because this is administratively difficult to manage, modern WAPs are Remote Authentication Dial-In User Service (RADIUS) clients and use the industry standard RADIUS protocol to send a connection request and accounting messages to a central RADIUS server. The RADIUS server has access to a user account database and a set of rules for granting authorization. The RADIUS server processes the wireless AP's connection request and either grants the connection request or rejects it.

To counter the second security risk, the data sent between the wireless nodes and the wireless APs must be encrypted. Therefore, the authentication method used by the wireless node must allow for the determination of encryption keys that are used to encrypt data.

In addition to the security provided by authentication and encryption, using the combination of a RADIUS server and 802.1x in a WLAN also provides key management capabilities.

When using a RADIUS server and 802.1x in a WLAN, it is best if EAP-TLS is used for authentication. This is because the global key used for EAP authentication must be encrypted so that only the STA and AP can read the authentication key. The EAP authentication method used in a WLAN must be capable of generating an encryption key as part of the authentication process, which is possible with EAP-TLS.

If RADIUS is selected and configured as the authentication provider on the remote access server, then user credentials and parameters of the connection request are sent as a series of RADIUS request messages to a RADIUS server such as a computer running Windows 2000 Server and the Internet Authentication Service (IAS).

The RADIUS server receives a user-connection request from the remote access server and authenticates the client against its authentication database. A RADIUS server can also maintain a central storage database of other relevant user properties. In addition to the simple yes or no response to an authentication request, RADIUS can provide other applicable connection parameters for this user—such as maximum session time, static IP address assignment, and so on.

When a RADIUS server is used for authentication in a WLAN, the AP acts as a RADIUS client to the RADIUS server (authenticating server), and acts as the authenticator to the supplicant STA.

The AP and STA must support a multicast/global authentication key, and might also support a per-STA unicast session key. The AP has a process that listens for IEEE 802.1*x* traffic—both with and without authentication keys.

Windows XP Professional Wireless Support

Windows XP Professional has improved and built upon the wireless support provided in Windows 2000. Windows XP Professional includes support for automatic switching between different APs when roaming, auto detection of a wireless network, and automatic wireless configuration—allowing for zero client configuration. Additional security is also provided by the inclusion of an 802.1*x* client implementation in Windows XP Professional and the inclusion of wireless device authentication support in the Windows RADIUS server, Internet Authentication Service (IAS).

Roaming

Windows 2000 includes technologies that allow wireless devices to detect the availability of a network and act appropriately. Windows XP Professional enhances this technology to accommodate the transitional nature of a wireless network.

The media sense feature of Windows 2000 is enhanced in Windows XP Professional to allow for detection of a move to a new access point, thus forcing reauthentication in order to ensure appropriate network access. Media sense also allows detection of changes in the IP subnet, so that an appropriate address can be used in order to ensure optimum resource access.

Multiple IP address configurations (DHCP assigned or static) can be made available on a Windows XP Professional system and the appropriate configuration automatically chosen. When an IP address change occurs, Windows XP Professional allows for additional reconfiguration to occur, if necessary. For example, IE proxy settings can be redetected. By means of Windows Sockets extensions, applications that can be configured to be network aware (such as firewalls or browsers) can be notified of changes in network connectivity and can update their behavior based on these changes. The auto-sensing and reconfiguration effectively negates the need for a mobile IP to act as a mediator and solves most of the problems users face when roaming between networks.

When a station is roaming from access point to access point, information about the state of the station, as well as other information, must be moved along with it. This includes station location information for message delivery and other attributes of the association. Rather than recreate this information upon each transition, one access point can pass the information to the new access point. The protocols to transfer this information are not defined in the standard, but several wireless LAN vendors have jointly developed an Inter-Access Point Protocol (IAPP) for this purpose, further enhancing multivendor interoperability.

Zero Client Configuration

Automatic wireless network configuration and 802.1x authentication are selected by default. When automatic wireless configuration is enabled on your computer, you can roam between different WLANs without having to reconfigure the network connection settings on your computer for each location. These Windows XP Professional technologies allow for zero client configuration.

Zero configuration is a client-based user identification method. Zero configuration allows wireless devices to work in different modes without the need for configuration changes after the initial configuration. The zero configuration initiative automatically provides the IP address, the network prefix, the gateway router location, the DNS server address, the address of a RADIUS or IAS server, and all other necessary settings for the wireless device. It also provides security features for the client.

Zero configuration allows a wireless device to function in different environments, such as work, the airport, and home, without any user intervention. Zero configuration uses the Windows XP Professional user interface when attempting to connect wireless devices. The order of preference for zero configuration IEEE 802.11 connection using IEEE 802.1x authentication is infrastructure before ad hoc mode, and computer authentication before user authentication. You can change the default settings to allow, for example, guest access, which is not enabled by default.

WEP authentication attempts to perform an IEEE 802.11 shared key authentication if the network adapter has been preconfigured with a WEP shared key. In the event that authentication fails or the network adapter is not preconfigured with a WEP shared key, the network adapter reverts to the open system authentication.

The IEEE 802.1x security enhancements are available in Windows XP Professional. Wireless network adapters and access points must also be compatible with IEEE 802.1x for an IEEE 802.1x deployment.

Network Adapter Support   Microsoft partnered with 802.11 network adapter vendors to improve the roaming experience by automating the process of configuring the network adapter to associate with an available network.

The wireless network adapter and its Network Driver Interface Specification (NDIS) driver need to do very little beyond supporting some new NDIS Object Identifiers (OIDs) used for the querying and setting of device and driver behavior. The network adapter scans for available networks and passes those to Windows XP Professional. The Windows XP Professional Wireless Zero Configuration service then takes care of configuring the network adapter with an available network. If there are two networks covering the same area, the user can configure a preferred network order and the computer will try each network in the order defined until it finds one that is active. It is even possible to limit association to only the configured, preferred networks.

If an 802.11 network is not found nearby, Windows XP Professional configures the network adapter to use ad hoc networking mode. It is possible for the user to configure the wireless network adapter either to disable or be forced into ad hoc mode.

These network adapter enhancements are integrated with security features so that if authentication fails another network will be located to attempt association with.

Automatic Wireless Configuration   Automatic wireless configuration supports the IEEE 802.11 standard for wireless LANs (WLANs) and minimizes the configuration required to access WLANS. When automatic wireless configuration is enabled on your computer, you can roam between different WLANs without having to reconfigure the network connection settings on your computer for each location. Whenever you move from one location to another, automatic wireless configuration scans for an available WLAN in the new location, configures your network adapter card to match the settings of that WLAN, and attempts to access that WLAN. When several WLANs are available in the same location, you can create a list of preferred WLANs and define the order in which access to each is attempted. You can also specify that if an access attempt to a preferred WLAN fails, an attempt will be made to access any visible (available) WLAN of the same type.

To set up automatic wireless configuration

1. Open **Network Connections**.

2. Right-click the connection for which you want to set up automatic wireless network configuration, and then click **Properties**.

3. On the **Wireless Networks** tab, do one of the following:

    ■ To enable automatic wireless network configuration for this connection, select the **Use Windows to configure my wireless network settings** check box. This check box is selected by default.

    ■ To disable automatic wireless network configuration for this connection, clear the **Use Windows to configure my wireless network settings** check box.

4. The list of available wireless networks detected by automatic wireless network configuration appears under **Available networks**. To make changes to the **Preferred networks** list, do the following:

   ■ To add an available wireless network to the **Preferred networks** list for this connection, under **Available networks**, click the network that you want to add, and then click **Configure**.

   ■ To add a new wireless network to the **Preferred networks** list for this connection, under **Preferred networks**, click **Add**, and in **Wireless Network Properties**, specify the network name (Service Set Identifier), wireless network key (Wired Equivalent Privacy) settings, and whether the network is a computer-to-computer (ad hoc) network.

   ■ To change the order in which connection attempts to preferred networks are made for this connection, under **Preferred networks**, click the wireless network that you want to move to a new position on the list, and then click **Move up** or **Move down**.

   ■ To remove a wireless network from the list of preferred networks for this connection, under **Preferred networks**, click the wireless network that you want to remove, and then click **Remove**.

5. To refine the type of wireless network to access, click **Advanced**, and then click the network type that you want. For example, if you want to make a computer-to-computer (ad hoc) connection, and if both computer-to-computer and access point (infrastructure) networks are within range of your computer, click **Computer-to-computer (AdHoc) networks only**.

To set up 802.1x authentication

1. Open **Network Connections**.

2. Right-click the connection for which you want to enable or disable IEEE 802.1x authentication, and then click **Properties**.

3. On the **Authentication** tab, do one of the following:

   ■ To enable IEEE 802.1xx authentication for this connection, select the **Network access control using IEEE 802.1X** check box. This check box is selected by default.

   ■ To disable IEEE 802.1xx authentication for this connection, clear the **Network access control using IEEE 802.1X** check box.

4. In **EAP type**, click the Extensible Authentication Protocol type to be used with this connection.

5. If you select **Smart Card or other Certificate** in **EAP type**, you can configure additional properties if you click **Properties** and, in **Smart Card or other**

Certificate Properties, do the following:

- To use the certificate located on your smart card for authentication, click **Use my smart card**.

- To use the certificate located in the certificate store on your computer for authentication, click **Use a certificate on this computer**.

- To verify that the server certificate presented to your computer is still valid, select the **Validate server certificate** check box, specify whether to connect only if the server is located within a particular domain, and then specify the trusted root certification authority.

- To use a different user name when the user name in the smart card or certificate is not the same as the user name in the domain to which you are logging on, select the **Use a different user name for the connection** check box.

6. To specify whether the computer attempts authentication to the network if a user is not logged on and/or if the computer or user information is not available, do the following:

- To specify that the computer attempt authentication to the network if a user is not logged on, select the **Authenticate as computer when computer information is available** check box.

- To specify that the computer attempt authentication to the network if user information or computer information is not available, select the **Authenticate as guest when user or computer information is unavailable** check box.

To connect to an available wireless network

1. Right-click the network connection icon in the notification area and then click **View Available Wireless Networks**.

2. In **Connect to Wireless Network**, under **Available Networks**, click the wireless network that you want to connect to.

3. If a network key is required for Wired Equivalent Privacy (WEP), do one of the following:

- If the network key is automatically provided (for example, the key is stored on the wireless network adapter given to you by your administrator), leave **Network Key** blank.

- If the network key is not automatically provided for you, in **Network key**, type the key.

4. Click **Connect**.

5. To configure additional wireless network connection settings, or if you are having difficulty making a connection to the wireless network that you selected, click **Advanced**, and then configure the settings in the **Wireless Networks** tab.

For more information about zero client configuration for wireless network clients in Windows XP Professional, see "Wireless Networking" in Windows XP Professional Help and Support Center.

Additional Resources

These resources contain additional information related to this chapter.

Related Information

■ "Connecting Remote Offices" in this book.

■ "Managing Files and Folders" in this book.

■ "Managing Devices" in this book.

■ "Desktop Configuration Management" in the *Distributed Systems Guide* of the *Microsoft Windows 2000 Server Resource Kit*.

■ "Wireless Networking" in Windows XP Professional Help and Support Center.

■ "Securing Mobile Computers" in the *Microsoft Windows Security Resource Kit* and in this book.

Chapter 8

Configuring Remote Desktop

Remote Desktop provides access from a remote location to a computer running the Microsoft® Windows® XP Professional operating system, giving you the flexibility to work on your Windows XP Professional–based computer from anywhere, anytime. Remote Desktop in Windows XP Professional is an extension of the Microsoft® Windows® 2000 operating system Terminal Services functionality formerly available only in the Microsoft® Windows® 2000 Server family of operating systems. This chapter will help you to install, configure, and use Remote Desktop software.

Related Information

- For more information about Remote Assistance, see "Tools for Troubleshooting" in this book.

Remote Desktop Overview

Remote Desktop in Windows XP Professional provides remote access to the desktop of your computer running Windows XP Professional, from a computer at another location. Using Remote Desktop you can, for example, connect to your office computer from home and access all your applications, files, and network resources as though you were in front of your computer at the office. This ability allows more people in an organization take advantage of the flexibility provided by a distributed computing environment.

Remote Desktop is based on Terminal Services technology. Using Remote Desktop, you can run applications on a remote computer running Windows XP Professional from any other client running a Microsoft® Windows® operating system. The applications run on the Windows XP Professional–based computer and only the keyboard input, mouse input, and display output data are transmitted over the network to the remote location, as shown in Figure 8.1.

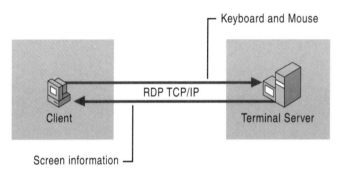

Figure 8-1   How Remote Desktop works

Terminal Services technology is also used for Remote Assistance, which allows you to invite a technical expert to connect to your computer and view your desktop.

In addition, the technical expert can take control of your computer (with your permission). For more information about using Terminal Services technology for Remote Assistance, see "Tools for Troubleshooting" in this book.

Remote Desktop Components

Remote Desktop consists of the following components:

- Remote Desktop Protocol
- Client software
  - Remote Desktop Connection
  - Remote Desktop Web Connection

These components are discussed in detail in the following sections.

Remote Desktop Protocol

The Remote Desktop Protocol (RDP) is a presentation protocol that allows a Windows-based terminal (WBT) or other Windows-based client to communicate with a Windows XP Professional–based computer. RDP works across any TCP/IP connection, such as a local area network (LAN), wide area network (WAN), dial-up, Integrated Services Digital Network (ISDN), digital subscriber line (DSL), or virtual private network (VPN) connection. RDP delivers to the client computer the display and input capabilities for applications running on a Windows XP Professional–based computer.

When using Remote Desktop Protocol from a Windows XP Professional–based client or other RDP 5.1–enabled client, many of the client resources are available within the session, including:

- **File System**. The client file system is accessible to the Remote Desktop session, as if it were a network shared drive or drives. No network connectivity software (other than Remote Desktop itself) is required for this file-system redirection feature.

- **Audio**. The audio streams, such as .wav and .mp3 files, play through the client computer's sound system.

- **Port**. The applications running within the session can have access to the serial and parallel ports on the client computer, which allows them to access and manipulate bar code readers, scanners, and other peripheral devices.

- **Printer**. The default local or network printer for the client computer becomes the default printing device for the Remote Desktop session.

- **Clipboard**. The Remote Desktop session and the client computer share a clipboard, which allows data to be interchanged between applications running on the remote computer and applications running on the client computer within a Remote Desktop session.

Client Software

Windows XP Professional includes Remote Desktop Connection client software, which you can also install on computers that are not running Windows XP Professional. You can connect using various types of client software based on the client computer's operating system and your organizational needs. Client software is available for a wide variety of hardware devices, including personal computers and Windows-based terminals. The Remote Desktop Connection software can be installed from a Windows XP Professional CD.

Windows XP Professional also includes Web-based client software, known as *Remote Desktop Web Connection* (RDWC).

Remote Desktop Connection   Remote Desktop Connection is a tool that connects your computer (the client computer) to another computer running Windows XP Professional (the remote computer). These computers could be located anywhere—

across the hall, across town, or across an ocean from each other—provided that you have network access from the client to the remote computer, and the appropriate permissions at the remote computer. The Remote Desktop Connection tool is installed by default when you install Windows XP Professional or Microsoft® Windows® XP Home Edition. You can also install this tool manually on a computer running a Microsoft® Windows® 95, Microsoft® Windows® 98, Microsoft® Windows NT® operating system, or Microsoft® Windows® 2000 Professional operating system.

Remote Desktop Web Connection   Remote Desktop Web Connection provides virtually the same functionality as Remote Desktop Connection, but delivers this functionality over the Web. When embedded in a Web page, Remote Desktop Web Connection can establish a Remote Desktop session with a remote computer running Windows XP Professional, even if Remote Desktop Connection is not installed on the client computer. Remote Desktop Web Connection must be installed on a Web server with Internet Information Services (IIS) and Active Server Pages (ASP) enabled.

Remote Desktop Web Connection offers the following advantages:

- **Efficient deployment of Remote Desktop**. With Remote Desktop Web Connection, deploying a connection can be as easy as sending a URL.

- **Support for roaming users**. Users who are away from their computers can use Remote Desktop Web Connection to gain secure access to their primary workstation from any computer running Microsoft® Windows® and Microsoft® Internet Explorer, provided you can reach the target computer on a network.

- **A lowest-common-denominator, cross-platform system**. Remote Desktop Web Connection can meet the needs of organizations that have multiple Windows operating systems and want identical client software on all their Windows-based computers.

- **Delivery of extranet applications**. Corporations that want to deploy Remote Desktop functionality to vendors, suppliers, or customers can use Remote Desktop Web Connection to distribute this functionality easily, inexpensively, and efficiently over the Internet.

Remote Desktop Features

Remote Desktop features include console security, enhanced color support, and resource redirection.

Console Security

Remote Desktop allows the user to connect to a remote console from a client location. *Console* is defined as the keyboard, mouse, and video monitor of the computer running Windows XP Professional with Remote Desktop enabled. When you enable a Remote Desktop session, the remote console "locks down" (disables display of the session on the remote computer's monitor and disables input via the remote computer's keyboard and mouse).

Enhanced, Flexible Color Support

Remote Desktop supports as many colors as the client computer will support, up to 24-bit color. It automatically detects the color depth of the remote and local computer and adapts as required. Users can modify color settings in the Display Properties sheet.

Resource Redirection

You can use resource redirection features to enhance your Remote Desktop session.

File System Redirection   Remote Desktop provides client drive redirection, making the local file system available to the Remote Desktop session. Client drives appear in Microsoft® Windows® Explorer with the designation "*driveletter* on *client-machinename*".

When you enable Remote Desktop, client-drive mapping is enabled by default. To disable it, you can use Terminal Services Group Policies. You can also disable it on an individual client computer by using Remote Desktop Connection. From the **Start** menu, point to **All Programs**, **Accessories**, **Communications** and then select **Remote Desktop Connection**. On the **Local Resources** tab, in the **Local devices** list, clear the **Disk drives** check box.

Audio Redirection   The *audio redirection* feature enables a client computer to play sounds from any application that attempts to play a .wav file on the Remote Desktop. With this feature, a user running an audio-enabled application at the remote desktop can hear the audio output from the locally attached speakers, as if the application were running on the client computer.

Advantages of the audio redirection feature include:

- Audio mixing. If two or more applications are playing sound, the resulting stream is an audio mix of the different streams.

- Minimized performance impact of the audio stream input/output (I/O) on the RDP session. If the network bandwidth between the client and remote computers changes, Remote Desktop renegotiates the sound stream quality according to the available bandwidth during transmission, and uses the best sound quality for the existing bandwidth. No user interaction required for choosing sound-stream quality.

Printer Redirection   Remote Desktop provides *printer redirection*, which routes print jobs from the Remote Desktop session to a printer attached to the client computer. When the user logs on to the remote computer, the client's local printer is detected and the appropriate printer driver is installed on the remote computer. If multiple printers are connected to the client computer, Remote Desktop will default to routing all print jobs to the client printer's default printer. Only printers whose drivers are available on the Windows XP Professional computer will appear in a Remote Desktop; you might need to manually install a driver that does not ship with Windows XP Professional.

Remote Desktop also provides network printer redirection. Network printers on a client device are redirected in addition to local printers.

The printer redirection feature is enabled by default in Windows XP Professional when you enable Remote Desktop. To disable it, you can use Terminal Services Group Policies. You can also disable the printer redirection feature on an individual computer, by using Remote Desktop Connection. On the **Local Resources** tab, clear the **Printers** check box.

Port Redirection Using the *port redirection* feature, applications running within the session have access to the serial and parallel ports on the client, which allows them to access and manipulate devices like bar code readers or scanners.

The port redirection feature is enabled by default in Windows XP Professional when you enable Remote Desktop. To disable it, you can use Terminal Services Group Policies. Or you can disable the port redirection feature on an individual computer, by using Remote Desktop Connection. On the **Local Resources** tab, clear the **Serial ports** check box.

Deploying Remote Desktop

To deploy Remote Desktop, you must:

- Enable Remote Desktop in Windows XP Professional.
- Enable users to connect to the remote computer running Windows XP Professional.
- Set up your client computer.
- Install Remote Desktop Connection software on your client computer.
- Install Remote Desktop Web Connection (if your Windows-based client is not running Windows XP Professional).

Enabling Remote Desktop in Windows XP Professional

When you install Windows XP Professional, Remote Desktop is disabled by default. You need to enable Remote Desktop before you can use it to connect to the computer remotely.

To enable Remote Desktop

1. Log on to your Windows XP Professional–based computer as an Administrator.
2. Click **Start**, right-click **My Computer**, and then click **Properties**.

3. In the **System Properties** sheet, click the **Remote** tab.

4. Select the **Allow users to connect remotely to this computer** check box.

> **Note**   You must be logged on as an Administrator (or be a member of an Administrators group) to enable Remote Desktop.

Enabling Users to Connect to the Computer Running Windows XP Professional

To remotely access your Windows XP Professional–based computer by means of Remote Desktop, you need to be a member of the Administrators group or of the Remote Desktop Users group. At your Windows XP Professional–based computer, you can add users to the Remote Desktop Users group.

To add users to the Remote Desktop Users group

1. Log on to your Windows XP Professional–based computer as an Administrator.

2. Click **Start**, right-click **My Computer**, and then click **Properties**.

3. In the **System Properties** sheet, click the **Remote** tab.

4. Click **Select Remote Users**.

5. In the **Remote Desktop Users** dialog box, click **Add**.

6. In the **Select Users** dialog box (shown in Figure 8-2), type the user name(s) you want to add, or click **Advanced** to search for objects.

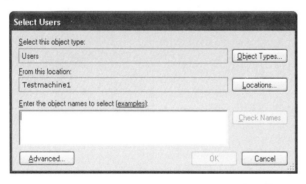

Figure 8-2   Adding users to the Remote Desktop Users group

7. Click **OK**.

    The names of the selected users appear in the **Remote Desktop Users** dialog box.

Installing Client Software

To set up your computer as a Remote Desktop client, you need to install Remote Desktop Connection (or Terminal Services Client). A web-based version of the client software, Remote Desktop Web Connection, may also be installed on the client computer. Also, your computer must be able to connect to the remote computer by means of a local area network (LAN), wide area network (WAN), dial-up, or Internet connection.

> **Note**   Terminal Services clients use TCP port 3389 to communicate with the remote computer.

Table 8-1 lists Windows operating systems and the corresponding client software that is required for deploying Remote Desktop.

Table 8-1   Client Software Versions for Various Operating Systems

Operating System	Client Software	How to Access
Windows XP (all versions)	Remote Desktop Connection (installed by default)	Start/Programs/Accessories/Communications/Remote Desktop Connection
Windows 2000 Professional	Remote Desktop Connection (installed by the user)	Install from the Windows XP Professional operating system CD.
Microsoft® Windows® 2000 Server	Terminal Services Client (installed by default if Terminal Services is installed.)	Start/Programs/Terminal Services Client Recommended: Install the latest version of Remote Desktop Connection from the Windows XP Professional operating system CD.
Windows 95 and Windows 98	Remote Desktop Connection (installed by the user)	Install from the Windows XP Professional operating system CD.
Windows NT 4.0	Remote Desktop Connection (installed by the user)	Install from the Windows XP Professional operating system CD.

Installing Remote Desktop Connection

For a client computer that is running Windows 95, Windows 98, Windows NT 4.0, or Windows 2000 Professional, you need to install Remote Desktop Connection from your Windows XP Professional operating system CD.

To install Remote Desktop Connection on computers running Windows 95, Windows 98, Windows NT 4.0, Windows 2000 Server or Windows 2000 Professional

1. Insert the Windows XP Professional operating system CD into your CD-ROM drive.

2. From the **Start** page, click **Perform Additional Tasks**, and then click **Set up Remote Desktop Connection**.

3. In the **Remote Desktop Connection-InstallShield Wizard**, follow instructions until installation is complete.

Installing Remote Desktop Web Connection

Remote Desktop Web Connection is a Web application that consists of an ActiveX® control, sample ASP pages, and HTML pages. When Remote Desktop Web Connection is deployed on a Web server, it allows users to connect to a Windows XP Professional–based computer by using Internet Explorer, even if Remote Desktop Connection or Terminal Services Client software is not installed on the computer from which the user is connecting.

Remote Desktop Web Connection is an optional World Wide Web service component of Internet Information Services (IIS), which is included in Windows XP Professional. Remote Desktop Web Connection must be installed by using **Add or Remove Programs**. For more information about installing Remote Desktop Web Connection on a Web server, see "Remote Desktop" in Windows XP Professional Help and Support Center.

When you install Remote Desktop Web Connection, the files are copied by default to the **%systemroot%\Web\Tsweb** directory of your Web server. You can use the included sample (Default.htm and Connect.asp) pages, or modify them to meet the needs of your application.

Remote Desktop Web Connection requires that the client computer have a TCP/IP connection to the Internet or a network, and run Microsoft® Internet Explorer version 4.0 or later.

> **Note**   Terminal Services clients use TCP port 3389 to communicate with the remote computer.

When a user accesses a Web page on the IIS server that contains the embedded Remote Desktop Web Connection ActiveX Client control, this control is downloaded to the client computer, and is stored in the default location for downloaded controls in Internet Explorer. The default connection page appears on the client computer, asking the user for server (name or IP address of the remote computer) and user information. The Remote Desktop session opens in the Web page. Depending on the parameters passed and the settings of the remote computer, the Windows logon screen might appear.

Figure 8-3 illustrates the processes for downloading and using the Remote Desktop Web Connection client.

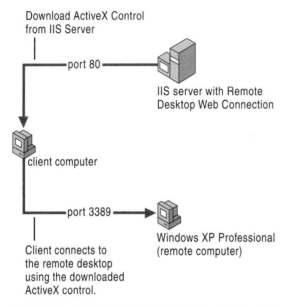

Figure 8-3   Downloading and using Remote Desktop Web Connection client

Note   Although the IIS server must download the ActiveX control to the client computer, the IIS server does not connect to the Windows XP Professional-based remote computer at any time when you use Remote Desktop Web Connection. The client computer must connect to the remote computer over a TCP/IP connection.

Establishing a Remote Desktop Session

After installing the appropriate client software on the client computer, you can connect to the remote computer. The following discussion includes tips for using Remote Desktop components, keyboard shortcuts you can use during a Remote Desktop session, information about security enhancement using encryption levels, and configuring of Remote Desktop using group policies.

You can establish a session with the Windows XP Professional–based computer by using one of the following:

- Remote Desktop Connection
- Remote Desktop Web Connection

Using Remote Desktop Connection

To create a new connection by using Remote Desktop Connection

1. Click **Start**, point to **Programs**, point to **Accessories**, and then point to **Communications**.

2. Click **Remote Desktop Connection**.

3. In the **Remote Desktop Connection** dialog box, in the **Computer** box, type the name or IP address of a computer running Windows XP Professional for which you have Remote Desktop permissions.

4. Click **Connect**.

5. In the **Log On to Windows** dialog box, type your user name, password, and domain (if required), and then click **OK**.

In Remote Desktop Connection, you can pre-configure your Remote Desktop sessions.

- If you want all of your Remote Desktop sessions to respond exactly the same each time you establish a session, click the **Options** button, pre-configure the desired settings and click **Save As** under **Connection Settings** as seen in Figure 8.4. Enter *filename* and click **Save**. Each time you want to open that session, click **Open**, and then double-click *filename*.

- If your video adapter does not support higher resolutions, you can set the display size of the Remote Desktop session to fit your display configuration. On the **Display** tab, move the **Remote desktop size** slider. Select the resolution that best fits your needs, and then click **Connect**.

- If you need to print information or check disk status from your Remote Desktop session, you can have the remote computer automatically connect to your computer's disk drives or printers. On the **Local Resources** tab, in **Local devices**, click **Disk drives** or **Printers**, and then click and **Connect**.

Figure 8-4 illustrates the client logon interface and Table 8-2 lists the features for the interface.

Figure 8-4   Remote Desktop Connection interface

Note   Configurations on the client logon interface are local policy settings; they can be overridden by Group Policy settings.

Table 8-2   Features Available on the Remote Desktop Connection Logon Interface

Tab	Settings to Configure	Notes
General	Enter or change logon and connection settings	Enter remote computer name, network user name, and network domain.
		Selecting **I'll provide my password at connection time** allows you to enter the password at connection time and stores it on the local computer. You must also enter your network password to access the session.
		Saving connection settings allows you to use a configuration throughout an enterprise.
Display	Change Remote desktop size (resolution) and colors	Selectable session resolution and color depth allow you to adjust for specific needs.

Table 8-2   Features Available on the Remote Desktop Connection Logon Interface

Tab	Settings to Configure	Notes
Local Resources	Control sound, keyboard, and local devices	Enabling sounds at the client computer enhances the session.
		Applying Windows key combinations within the Remote Desktop session enhances the session.
		Allowing the session to control local devices automatically boosts productivity.
Programs	Start a program and change an icon	Setting the session to start a specific program upon connection can improve efficiency (available only for terminal server sessions).
Experience	Set bitmap caching and compression	Allowing certain features in this tab will provide a richer visual experience at higher bandwidths.

Using Remote Desktop Web Connection

In order to use Remote Desktop Web Connection, you need to ensure that it is installed and running on the Web server. Your client computer must also have an active network connection and Internet Explorer version 4.0 or later installed.

To connect to a remote computer by using Remote Desktop Web Connection

1. On your client computer, open Internet Explorer.

2. In the **Address** box, type the Uniform Resource Locator (URL) for the home directory of the Web server hosting Remote Desktop Web Connection. The URL is "http://" followed by the Windows Networking name of your server, followed by the path of the directory containing the Remote Desktop Web Connection files (default = /Tsweb/. Note the forward slash marks). For example, if your Web site is registered with the DNS server as "Admin1", in the **Address** box you type: **http://admin1/tsweb/**, and then press ENTER.

3. From the **Remote Desktop Web Connection** page, in the **Server** box, type the name of the remote computer to which you want to connect.

   You can specify the screen size and logon information for your connection.

4. Click **Connect**.

Keyboard Shortcuts in a Remote Desktop Session

You can apply Windows key combinations to your Remote Desktop sessions, or you can use the following Remote Desktop keyboard shortcuts (shown in Table 8.3) to perform many of the same functions.

Table 8-3   Keyboard Shortcuts in a Remote Desktop Session

Windows Key Combinations for Client Computer	Equivalent Keys for Remote Desktop Session	Description
ALT+TAB	ALT+PAGE UP	Switches between programs from left to right.
ALT+SHIFT+TAB	ALT+PAGE DOWN	Switches between programs from right to left.
ALT+ESC	ALT+INSERT	Cycles through the programs in the order they were started.
	CTRL+ESC	Switches the client between a window and full screen.
CTRL+ESC	ALT+HOME	Displays the Start menu.
	ALT+DELETE	Displays the Windows menu.
PRINT SCREEN	CTRL+ALT+MINUS (–) symbol on the numeric keypad	Places a snapshot of the active window in the Remote Desktop session on the clipboard.
CTRL+ALT+DEL	CTRL+ALT+END	Displays the Task Manager or Windows Security dialog box. (Only use CTRL+ALT+END to issue this command. CTRL+ALT+DEL is always interpreted by the client computer.)
ALT+PRINT SCREEN	CTRL+ALT+PLUS (+) symbol on the numeric keypad	Places a snapshot of the entire Remote Desktop session window on the clipboard.

Security and Encryption in Remote Desktop

You can enhance the security of a Remote Desktop session by using any or all of these methods:

- Setting encryption levels to secure data communications between client and remote computer host.

- Enabling password authentication of users at logon time.

- Disabling clipboard sharing for Web-based clients.

- Disabling printer redirection for Web-based clients.

- Disabling file redirection for Web-based clients.

These five security-enhancing methods, discussed in the following sections, use Group Policy settings. For more information about using Group Policy with Remote Desktop, see "Using Group Policy with Remote Desktop" later in this chapter.

Setting Encryption Levels

Data encryption can protect your data by encrypting it on the communications link between the client and the Windows XP Professional–based computer. Encryption protects against the risk of unauthorized interception of transmitted data. By default, Remote Desktop sessions are encrypted at the highest level of security available (128-bit). However, some older versions of Terminal Services client software do not support this high level of encryption. If your network contains such "legacy" clients, you can set the encryption level of the connection to send and receive data at the highest encryption level supported by the client.

There are two levels of encryption available.

High. The **High** level encrypts data sent from client to remote computer and from remote computer to client, by using strong 128-bit encryption. Use this level only if you are sure that your client computer supports 128-bit encryption (for example, if it is running Windows XP Professional). Clients that do not support this level of encryption will not be able to connect.

Client Compatible. The **Client Compatible** level encrypts data sent between the client and the remote computer at the maximum key strength supported by the client. Use this level if your client computer does not support 128-bit encryption.

You can set the encryption level of the connection between the client and the remote computer by enabling the **Set client connection encryption level Properties** Terminal Services Group Policy setting.

Enabling Password Authentication at Logon Time

In order to enhance security of a Remote Desktop session over the Internet, you might want to prevent automatic password passing. To do this, you **can enable the Always prompt client for password** Terminal Services Group Policy setting. When this setting is enabled, you must supply your password in the Windows Logon dialog box whenever you start a Remote Desktop session.

Disabling Clipboard Redirection

For enhanced security, you might choose to disable Remote Desktop clipboard redirection for clients that connect via the Remote Desktop Web Client. You can disable clipboard redirection by using the **Do not allow clipboard redirection** Terminal Services Group Policy.

Disabling Printer Redirection

For enhanced security, you might choose to disable the printer redirection feature for clients that connect via the Remote Desktop Web Connection Client Control. You can disable printer redirection by using the **Do not allow printer redirection** Terminal Services Group Policy.

Disabling File Redirection

For enhanced security, you might choose to disable the file redirection feature for clients that connect via the Remote Desktop Web Connection Client Control. You can disable file redirection using the **Do not allow drive redirection** Terminal Services Group Policy.

Using Group Policy with Remote Desktop

In Windows XP Professional, you can use Group Policy to configure Remote Desktop connection settings, set user policy, and manage Remote Desktop sessions. You can enable Group Policy for users of a computer, for individual computers, or for groups of computers belonging to an organizational unit of a domain. To set policy for users of a particular computer, you must be an Administrator for that computer or have equivalent rights. To set policies for an organizational unit in a domain, you must be an Administrator for that domain or have equivalent rights.

Enabling Group Policy on an Individual Computer

To set Terminal Services policies settings for a particular computer or for users of that computer, open the Group Policy snap-in to edit the Local Group Policy snap-in.

The Terminal Services group policies are not configured by default. You can configure each Group Policy to be either **disabled** or **enabled**.

To access Terminal Services Group Policy

1. From the **Start** menu, click **Run**, type **mmc**, and then click **OK**.

2. On the **File** menu, click **Add/Remove Snap-in**.

3. In the **Add/Remove Snap-in** dialog box, click **Add**.

4. In the **Add Standalone Snap-in** dialog box, click **Group Policy**, click **Add**, and then click **Finish**.

5. In the **Add Standalone Snap-in** dialog box, click **Close**.

6. In the **Add/Remove Snap-in dialog box**, click **OK**.

7. In the **console pane**, double-click **Computer Configuration**, click **Administrative Templates**, click Windows Components and then click **Terminal Services**.

Terminal Services Group Policies are organized individually and in folders. Table 8-4 lists Terminal Services folders, group policies, and functions.

Table 8-4   Group Policy Settings That Affect Remote Desktop

Folder	Group Policy	Function
Terminal Services	Allow Screen Saver	Allows display of a screen saver in a Remote Desktop session.
	Set maximum color depth	Sets a limit on the color depth of any connection to a terminal server or Remote Desktop.
Client/Server data redirection	Do not allow clipboard redirection	Disables sharing of clipboard contents.
	Do not allow audio redirection	Prevents users from playing the remote computer audio at the local computer during a Remote Desktop session.
	Do not allow drive redirection	Disables mapping of client drives in Remote Desktop sessions.
	Do not allow COM port redirection	Disables redirection of data from the remote computer to client COM ports during the Remote Desktop session.
	Do not allow client printer redirection	Disables mapping of client printers in Remote Desktop sessions.
	Do not allow LPT port redirection	Disables redirection of data from the remote computer to client LPT ports during the Remote Desktop session.
	Map client printers	Directs Terminal Services to map client printers and display them in the user's printer list during Remote Desktop sessions.
	Set default client printer to be default printer in a session	Directs Terminal Services to automatically specify the client printer as the default printer in the Remote Desktop session.
Encryption and Security	Always prompt client for password upon connection	Directs Terminal Services to always prompt users for passwords at logon.
	Set client connection encryption level	Directs Terminal Services to enforce the specified encryption level for all data sent between the client and the remote computer during Terminal Services connections.

Troubleshooting Remote Desktop

This section contains troubleshooting information for Windows XP Professional Remote Desktop.

You Get a Server-Name Not Found Error Message

If the remote computer cannot be found, the following message appears:

"The specified remote computer could not be found. Verify that you have typed the correct computer name or IP address, and then try connecting again."

The problem may be in the computer name or IP address that you are using to connect. To solve this problem, verify that you have the correct computer name for the remote computer and that you have typed it in correctly. The correct computer name can be obtained from the Terminal Services administrator. If you have the correct computer name and are still unable to connect, try to connect using the actual IP address of the computer. This information can be obtained from the Terminal Services administrator.

You Cannot Open a Specified Program

If you are having problems opening a specified program on the host computer (on the Programs tab of the Remote Desktop Connection), then you may be connecting to a computer running Windows XP Professional. Specified programs will open only when connecting to a terminal server, not when starting a Remote Desktop session. Remote Desktop provides access to the actual console session of the remote computer. You cannot specify programs that open in a Remote Desktop session.

You Cannot Log On to the Remote Computer

If you do not have the correct permissions to access a remote computer running Windows XP Professional, the following message appears:

"The local policy of this system does not permit you to log on interactively."

You must add yourself to the Remote Desktop Users Group (or to a group with administrative rights) so that you can use Remote Desktop.

Your Session Ends with a Data-Encryption Error Message

If the data encryption error prevents your client computer from communicating properly with the remote computer, the following message appears:

"Because of error in data encryption, this session will end. Please try connecting to the remote computer again."

Try again to connect to the remote computer.

> **Note**   You cannot use the version of the Administrators Tools Pack (ATP) included with Windows 2000 on a computer running Windows XP Professional. Remove this version of ATP before upgrading to Windows XP Professional. To remotely manage Windows 2000 servers from a Windows XP Professional–based computer, use Terminal Services to connect to a Windows 2000–based computer running the Administrators Tools Pack. Check the Microsoft Web site for updates to ATP that are compatible with Windows XP Professional.

Additional Resources

These resources contain additional information and tools related to this chapter.

Related Information

- The Remote Desktop Protocol Features and Performance link on the Web Resources page at http://www.microsoft.com/windows/reskits/webresources.

- "Remote Desktop" in Windows XP Professional Help and Support Center.

Chapter 9

Managing Devices

The Microsoft® Windows® XP Professional operating system provides features that simplify installing, configuring, and managing computer hardware. Plug and Play is a feature that automatically configures devices, loads device drivers, and works with other Plug and Play devices to allocate resources, all without user intervention. Windows XP Professional supports devices that use the USB and IEEE 1394 buses, as well as devices that connect over other buses. Understanding hardware management features and support in Windows XP Professional helps you install, configure, and troubleshoot hardware devices.

Related Information

- For information about Universal Plug and Play, see "Connecting Remote Offices" in this book.

- For more information about using printers, see "Enabling Printing and Faxing" in this book.

- For more information about power management on portable computers, see "Supporting Mobile Users" in this book.

- For more information about troubleshooting hardware problems that prevent your system from starting, see "Troubleshooting Startup" in this book.

Plug and Play Overview

Plug and Play in Windows XP Professional allows a user to simply connect a hardware device and leave the job of configuring and starting the hardware to the operating system. However, computer hardware, device drivers, and the system BIOS must all be designed properly in order to install new devices without user intervention. For example, although Windows XP Professional provides Plug and Play functionality, if no Plug and Play–capable driver is available for a given device, the operating system cannot automatically configure and start the device.

> **Note**   In 64-bit computers, BIOS is known as Extensible Firmware Interface (EFI).

When a hardware device is connected, as when a user plugs a USB camera into a USB port, Plug and Play Manager goes through the following steps to successfully install the device:

- After receiving an insertion notification, Plug and Play Manager checks what hardware resources the device needs (such as interrupts, memory ranges, I/O ranges, and DMA channels) and to assign those resources.

- Plug and Play Manager checks the hardware identification number of the device. It then checks the hard drive, floppy drives, CD-ROM drive, and Windows Update for a driver that matches the hardware identification number of the device.

- If multiple drivers are found, Plug and Play Manager chooses the optimal driver by looking for the closest hardware ID or compatible ID match, driver signatures, and other driver features, and then installs the driver and starts the device.

Device drivers included with or installed under Windows XP Professional must meet the standards of the Windows Logo program. Device drivers that have passed the Windows Hardware Quality Lab (WHQL) compatibility tests are electronically signed and Windows XP Professional detects the digital signature. For system stability, it is recommended that you use only signed device drivers with Windows XP Professional. A message notifies the user if an unsigned driver is being installed.

When multiple drivers are available for a given device, Windows XP Professional uses driver-ranking schemes to determine the optimal driver to load. Driver rank is established based on whether the driver is signed and how closely the driver's Plug and Play ID matches the device's Plug and Play ID.

For more information about Driver Signing, see "Windows Update" and "Driver Signing" later in this chapter. For more information about driver-ranking schemes, see "Driver Ranking" later in this chapter.

The extent of Plug and Play support depends on both the hardware device and the device driver. For example, an older device that is not Plug and Play—such as a manually configured Industry Standard Architecture (ISA) sound card or an Extended Industry Standard Architecture (EISA) network adapter—can gain functionality from a Plug and Play driver.

If a driver does not support Plug and Play, its devices behave as non–Plug and Play devices. This might result in the loss of some operating system functionality. For example, power management features such as hibernation might not work.

Note   For monitors, Windows XP Professional supports Plug and Play installation only when the monitor, the display adapter, and the display driver are Plug and Play; otherwise, the monitor is detected as "Default Monitor."

If you connect the monitor by using a switch box, Plug and Play attributes of the monitor might be lost.

In Windows XP Professional, Plug and Play support is optimized for computers that include an Advanced Configuration and Power Interface (ACPI) BIOS. The ACPI BIOS is responsible for tasks such as describing hardware that is not visible to Plug and Play because the hardware is connected to a bus that does not support Plug and Play. For example, the ACPI BIOS describes and helps in configuring devices such as system timers and programmable interrupt controllers on the motherboard, which is not on a bus that supports Plug and Play.

For *all* Plug and Play features to work on a given system, it must include an ACPI BIOS and hardware devices and drivers that are Plug and Play compliant. An Advanced Power Management (APM) BIOS or a Plug and Play BIOS does not enable all Plug and Play features and is not as robust as ACPI.

When you troubleshoot or manually change resource settings, it is helpful to know whether Plug and Play functionality is provided by the operating system or by the BIOS. If Plug and Play is handled by the BIOS and you manually change resources that are allocated to hardware devices (such as interrupts or memory ranges) these changes become fixed, and the operating system cannot reallocate those resources. When any hardware resource is fixed, Windows XP Professional loses some of its ability to optimally allocate resources among all devices in the system. When Windows XP Professional cannot optimally allocate all resources, the likelihood is increased that one or more devices might not function properly due to resource allocation problems.

For more information about ACPI, see the ACPI link on the Web Resources page at http://www.microsoft.com/windows/reskits/webresources and "Power Management" later in this chapter.

On x86-based computers, the way that the system BIOS code interacts with Plug and Play devices depends on whether the system BIOS or the operating system configures hardware. If your computer has this option, the setting for the **Enable Plug and Play operating system** switch can affect this interaction.

For more information about setting Plug and Play BIOS settings, see "Setting Plug and Play BIOS Settings" later in this chapter.

> **Note** A motherboard with Itanium-based architecture relies on ACPI and the operating system to configure resources. The option to enable or disable ACPI functionality is not available on Itanium-based computers.

Some Plug and Play devices can be installed or removed while the system is running. For example, USB, IEEE 1394 and PC Card devices can be added to and removed from a fully powered system. When such hardware is added or removed, the operating system automatically detects insertion or removal of the device and manages system and/or hardware configuration as required. If the device is not designed to be removed while the system is running, it is recommended that you notify the operating system in advance to avoid problems. The Safely Remove Hardware application notifies the operating system that a device will be removed.

Table 9-1 shows the different types of Plug and Play devices, and whether or not they can be removed while the system is turned on.

Table 9-1 Plug and Play Device Connections and Installation Guidelines

Devices on these buses or connectors	Can be added to or removed from a running system	System must be turned off before device is added/ removed from system
USB, IEEE 1394, PC Card devices, CardBus devices	Yes Remove hardware by using the Safely Remove Hardware application if it appears in the notification area.	No
PCI, ISA, EISA	No	Yes
Docking station	Varies among computer manufacturers; most support docking and undocking while the computer is running.	Varies among computer manufacturers; most support docking and undocking while the computer is running.

For more information about the Safely Remove Hardware application, see "Safe Removal of Plug and Play Devices" later in this chapter. For information about the Hot Undocking feature for portable computers, see "Supporting Mobile Users" in this book.

Device Manager

Device Manager displays all devices installed in the system as shown in Figure 9.1. The devices shown in Device Manager represent the computer's hardware configuration information. The Device Manager display is recreated each time the computer is started, or whenever a dynamic change to the computer configuration occurs, such as addition of a new device while the system is running. You can use Device Manager to enable or disable devices, troubleshoot devices, update drivers, use driver rollback, and change resources such as interrupt requests (IRQs) assigned to devices.

You can open Device Manager as follows:

- On the **Start** menu, right-click **My Computer**, select **Manage**, and then select **Device Manager** under **System Tools**.

    – or –

- In **Control Panel**, click **Performance and Maintenance**, and then click **System**. On the **Hardware** tab, click **Device Manager**.

To view the property sheet for a device in Device Manager, double-click the device type. Right click the individual device and select **Properties**. The following types of information are shown for the device type:

- Driver name, vendor, date, version, and digital signature information.

- System resources allocated to the device, such as interrupt request (IRQ) lines, memory ranges, and I/O address ranges.

- Options to update the driver, roll back the driver, and uninstall the driver.

Figure 9-1 shows a Device Manager listing of system devices.

Figure 9-1 System devices in Device Manager

From the **View** menu in Device Manager you can select one of four views of system devices.

Devices by type This is the default device tree view for Device Manager. Device types include hardware such as disk drives, keyboards, Human Interface Devices (HIDs), or system devices. Double-clicking on a device type displays a list of the devices of that type on the system.

Devices by connection This view shows how devices are connected to each other. This might be useful, for example, when you connect devices to a USB hub, and then connect other devices to the devices on the hub. You can see where each device fits into the chain of connection.

Resources by type This view shows the four default resource types (and any others that are configured on your system). The four default system resource types are direct memory access (DMA), input/output (IO), interrupt request (IRQ), and reserved memory. Double-clicking on a resource type displays a list of the devices that are using a resource of that type.

Resources by connection This view shows the four default resource types (and any others that are configured on your system). Double-clicking on the system resource type shows the device types that are using a resource of that type, and how they are connected. This view might be particularly useful when you need to see whether a child device requires more memory resources than are available to a parent device.

Specific icons in Device Manager indicate device types and indicate any device problems, such as resource conflicts, or whether a device is disabled. The icons that denote device problems or disabled status are:

- A yellow exclamation point, which means that the device has a problem.

- A red "X," which means that the device is disabled.

- A blue "i" for "information," which means that the device has forced resource configurations. This icon is seen only in the two resource views.

Error codes that describe the type of problem a device might be experiencing are also displayed on the Properties pages of the device. For a list of these error codes, see "Device Manager Error Codes," an appendix in this book.

To update the driver for the device, disable or uninstall the device, scan for hardware changes, or view the device properties, right-click the device, and then make your selection on a menu.

Administrators can use Group Policy settings to prevent user access to Device Manager. For more information about Group Policy, see "Managing Desktops" in this book.

For information about using Device Manager to configure devices, see "Configuring Device Settings" later in this chapter.

Viewing Hidden Devices

Two types of devices are hidden by default in Device Manager. Non–Plug and Play drivers, printers, and other classes of devices that are not typically useful in configuring or troubleshooting hardware issues are hidden. Also hidden are devices that were previously attached but are not connected to the computer at the present time, also known as *non-present* devices. Typically you will not need to view hidden devices unless you need to configure or troubleshoot hardware. Each category of hidden device requires a different procedure for Device Manager to display the devices in that category.

To view currently attached non–Plug and Play drivers, printers, and other devices

- In **Device Manager**, on the **View** menu, select **Show hidden devices**.

The following procedure shows non-present devices for this instance of Device Manager only.

To view a list of previously attached (non-present) devices

1. At the command prompt, type:

    `Devmgmt.msc set DEVMGR_SHOW_NONPRESENT_DEVICES=1`

2. In **Device Manager**, on the **View** menu, select **Show hidden devices**.

The following procedure sets the option in Device Manager to show non-present devices whenever Device Manager is run.

To set Device Manager to always show previously attached (non-present) devices

To view the list of non-present devices Device Manager, you must select **Show hidden devices** in Device Manager, as described earlier.

1. In **Control Panel**, click **Performance and Maintenance**, and then click **System**.

2. Click the **Advanced** tab.

3. Click **Environment Variables**.

   The Environment Variables dialog box contains two sections, **User variables** and **System variables**. The changes made by adding a variable in the **User variables** section apply only to a specific user. If another user logs on to this computer, this variable will not be set for them. If you want this variable to apply to all users that log on to this computer, add it to **System variables** instead.

4. In the **User variables** or **System variables** dialog box, click **New**.

5. In the **New User Variable** or **New System Variable** dialog box, in **Variable Name,** type the following (including the underscores):

   `DEVMGR_SHOW_NONPRESENT_DEVICES`

6. In **Variable Value**, enter **1**.

7. Click **OK**, and then in the **Environment Variables** dialog box, click **OK** to apply this change.

For more information about environment variables, see "Troubleshooting Startup" in this book. For more information about using Device Manager, see Windows XP Professional Help and Support Center.

Plug and Play Device Detection

Plug and Play in Windows XP Professional provides the following services:

- Detects a Plug and Play device and determines its hardware resource requirements and device identification number.

- Allocates hardware resources.

- Dynamically loads, initializes, and unloads drivers.

- Notifies other drivers and applications when a new device is available.

- Works with power management to install and remove devices.

- Supports a range of device types.

After Windows XP Professional detects a Plug and Play device, the device driver is configured and loaded dynamically, typically without requiring user input. Some buses, such as Peripheral Component Interconnect (PCI) and USB, take full advantage of Plug and Play. Older buses, such as ISA, do not take full advantage of Plug and Play, and require more user interaction to ensure devices are correctly installed.

Plug and Play Detection on ACPI Systems

ACPI is a hardware and software interface specification that combines and enhances the Plug and Play and Advanced Power Management (APM) standards. ACPI also shifts many power management tasks to the operating system.

When a new device is plugged in, the following steps occur:

1. The function driver for the bus detects a new device on the bus.

2. The bus driver notifies Windows Plug and Play that its set of devices has changed.

3. Windows Plug and Play queries the driver for the current list of devices on the bus.

4. When Windows Plug and Play obtains the current list of devices, it determines whether any devices have been added or removed.

5. Windows Plug and Play gathers information about the new device and begins configuring it.

6. Windows Plug and Play checks the registry to determine whether the device has been installed on this computer before and if not, it stores information about the device in the registry.

7. Windows Plug and Play attempts to find and load the function and filter drivers for the device if any exist.

8. Windows Plug and Play assigns resources to the device if needed and issues an I/O request packet (IRP) to start the device.

For more information about device detection, see the Driver Development Kit (DDK) or the Driver Development Kits link on the Web Resources page at http://www.microsoft.com/windows/reskits/webresources.

Plug and Play Detection on Non-ACPI x86-based Systems

On non-ACPI x86-based computers, the system BIOS configures Plug and Play and performs the following steps:

1. Isolates any Plug and Play ISA devices for configuration.

2. Builds a map of the resources allocated to non–Plug and Play devices.

3. Maintains a list of previous resource configurations in non-volatile storage or memory.

4. Selects and enables input and output devices required during the startup process.

5. Initializes the device ROM if the device is a boot device.

6. Allocates conflict-free resources to devices that have not yet been configured.

7. Activates appropriate devices.

8. Initializes any option ROMs that are detected.

9. Starts the bootstrap loader.

Allocating System Resources

Each installed device must be allocated a set of operating system resources to operate properly. Some of these resources can be shared, while others cannot, depending upon the capabilities of the hardware and drivers. System resources allow hardware components to gain access to CPU and memory resources without conflicting with each other.

System resources include:

- Interrupt request (IRQ) lines

- Direct memory access (DMA)

- Input/output (I/O) port addresses

- Memory resources

Windows Plug and Play determines the system resources required by each device and assigns them appropriately. Windows Plug and Play can reconfigure resource assignments as necessary, such as when a new device is added that requires resources that are already in use. It can also detect ISA devices and configure non–Plug and Play hardware.

Interrupt Request Lines

IRQ lines are used by hardware devices to communicate with the CPU. The traditional architecture for x86-based computers uses sixteen IRQs (numbered from 0 to 15), some of which are reserved for devices such as the system clock, keyboard, and math co-processor. As new expansion cards are added to the computer, the remaining free IRQs are allocated to these new devices as needed. However, not all devices require IRQs to operate. Certain ISA and PCI multimedia peripherals, for example, do not require use of IRQs. Also, traditional secondary bus types (such as SCSI) and more recent types (such as USB and IEEE 1394) require only a single IRQ regardless of the number of devices connected to the host adapter.

ISA devices that use IRQs require sole access to interrupt lines to function properly, so one interrupt cannot be shared by multiple ISA devices. Because of this restriction, any system that includes ISA devices has a higher likelihood of running out of IRQs. And, once all IRQs are allocated, if a new device is added, it cannot start because no IRQ is available for it to operate. One of the major benefits of PCI over ISA is that PCI allows x86-based systems to share IRQs. Although some problems with IRQ sharing exist, most are related to high-bandwidth devices. Windows XP Professional manages IRQs using a first in, first out (FIFO) stack. The more devices that share a single IRQ, the longer it takes to traverse this stack, which can have a system wide performance impact. Performance problems might be reduced if high-bandwidth devices such as high-speed network adapters and high-end Small Computer Standard Interface (SCSI) controllers, for example, use different IRQs. More flexible interrupt handling models are available on newer x86-based ACPI systems that support the Advanced Programmable Interrupt Controller standard. Systems that incorporate the Advanced Programmable Interrupt Controller have access to more interrupts, which avoids the need to share interrupts.

Most x86-based systems do not support manual configuration of IRQ settings. However, a few do offer this capability as a troubleshooting feature. If you are experiencing problems with system lockups or stability, you have two alternatives:

1. If your system firmware supports manual configuration of IRQ settings, as a troubleshooting method, try manually assigning IRQs to specific PCI slots by using the configuration options in the BIOS. If you need to manually assign IRQ addresses for an ACPI-compliant computer and the BIOS option to disable ACPI is available, disable ACPI before installing Windows XP Professional. However, remember that it is best not to change the BIOS default or automatic settings unless you have a specific reason to do so.

2. If your system does not support manual configuration of IRQ settings, try moving high-performance peripherals to another slot.

For more information about PCI devices and IRQ sharing, see article Q252420, "General Description of IRQ Sharing in Windows 2000," in the Microsoft Knowledge Base. To find this article, see the Microsoft Knowledge Base link on the Web Resources page at http://www.microsoft.com/windows/reskits/webresources.

Caution   Changing default settings such as IRQs can cause conflicts that might make one or more devices unavailable on the system.

IRQ assignments can be reviewed using Device Manager. For more information about Device Manager, see "Device Manager" earlier in this chapter.

Direct Memory Access Channels

Direct memory access (DMA) channels allow devices to write and read directly to and from physical memory without placing a load on the CPU. This enhances system performance for devices such as network cards, because the CPU does not need to move blocks of data from memory to a device and back again. For x86-based systems, there are eight DMA channels, with several reserved for certain devices such as the DMA controller and floppy disk drive. Typically, x86-based systems have five or six available DMA channels.

I/O Port Address and Reserved Memory

Data passed between the CPU or RAM and a device must be moved through a dedicated block of memory. I/O port address ranges and memory address ranges denote a reserved area of memory that is dedicated to a specific device. Typically, these memory ranges are determined by the operating system. Manual changes are necessary only in specific cases (when using non–Plug and Play ISA hardware, for example).

Safe Removal of Plug and Play Devices

Some buses allow devices to be *hot-plugged*—added or removed while a system is running. Examples of such buses include USB, IEEE 1394, PC Card and CardBus. For devices on other buses, such as ISA and PCI, the computer must be turned off before devices are added or removed.

When removing a device from a bus that supports hot plugging, if the Safely Remove Hardware icon appears in the notification area, use the Safely Remove Hardware application as explained below to ensure a safe removal of hardware from the system. The Safely Remove Hardware application informs Windows that the user intends to remove a device. This gives Windows an opportunity to prepare for the removal by taking steps such as halting data transfers to the device and unloading device drivers.

When hardware is removed from a running system without using the Safely Remove Hardware application, it is often referred to as *surprise removal*, because the operating system is not notified in advance of the removal. Surprise removal is particularly a concern for storage devices for which write caching is enabled, because when such devices are surprise removed, data loss or corruption might occur. To reduce the likelihood of data loss or corruption due to surprise removal of consumer oriented storage devices, Windows XP Professional disables write caching by default for these devices (such as cameras that include IEEE 1394 or USB storage, small form factor storage devices such as compact flash, and so on). While write caching policy addresses this particular issue, it is recommended that users continue to use the Safely Remove Hardware application when it appears in the notification area. Also, disabling write caching might slow the performance of consumer oriented storage devices.

Write caching is enabled by default for high-performance external storage devices such as IEEE 1394 hard drives and SCSI hard drives, in addition to for storage devices inside the computer that cannot be surprise removed.

Caching policy defaults can be changed in Device Manager for high-performance external storage devices. In Device Manager, on the property sheet for the removable storage device click the **Policies** tab to view the default write caching settings for the device. If the Policies tab does not display, this option is not provided for the device. If the write caching settings are enabled, you can change the settings based on your performance and safe removal needs as follows:

- Click **Optimize for quick removal** to disable write caching on the storage device and in Windows. This allows you to remove the device without using the Safely Remove Hardware application, but can have an impact on the performance of the device.

- Click **Optimize for performance** to enable write caching in Windows, which can improve the performance of the storage device. However, you must use the Safely Remove Hardware application to disconnect the device from the computer.

If these write caching options are not enabled, your storage device is not removable without turning off the computer, and a different option displays in the dialog box. This option allows you to disable write caching for your storage device, which can affect the performance of the device.

Users should also inform the operating system before removing a portable computer from a docking station. For more information about docking and undocking procedures, see "Supporting Mobile Users" in this book.

Safely Remove Hardware Application

Before you remove a device from a bus that supports hot plugging, check to see if the Safely Remove Hardware icon appears in the notification area. If it does, it is recommended that you use the Safely Remove Hardware application to notify the operating system that the device is about to be unplugged.

To notify the operating system about removing a Plug and Play device

1. Click the **Safely Remove Hardware** icon in the notification area. The icon displays a notification bubble with a list of devices currently attached to the system.

2. Click the device you want to remove. The device is stopped and can then be unplugged.

Device Drivers

Windows XP Professional includes many features that help ensure that the device drivers installed on your computer are reliable and up to date. Drivers are signed by Microsoft after they pass a series of tests for reliability. Windows XP Professional checks for a digital signature whenever a driver is installed, and issues a message if the driver is not signed. In addition, drivers that are known cause problems in Windows are blocked from loading or installing, because Windows XP Professional checks a database of known problem drivers when the computer is started or when a device driver is loaded. If the driver is located in the database of known problem drivers, it cannot be installed or used on your computer. Another feature is Windows Update, a Web site where updated versions of signed drivers are available for download. These and other Windows XP Professional features for device drivers contribute to a stable computing environment and are discussed here in more detail.

Device Manager provides details about device drivers on the device's **Properties** page. Click the **Driver** tab, and select **Driver Details** to list all of the drivers the device is using. Driver details displayed include whether the driver is signed, its version, and whether it has been blocked from loading. For more information about Device Manager, see "Device Manager" earlier in this chapter.

Driver Signing

Microsoft uses a multi-stage process to test device drivers. Drivers are subjected to compatibility tests administered by the Windows Hardware Quality Lab (WHQL), and drivers that successfully complete the process are digitally signed. Because of this testing, signed drivers are typically more robust and reliable. Once a driver is digitally signed, Windows XP Professional recognizes it when it is loaded. Windows XP Professional notifies the user if a driver is not signed or if a driver file has been changed since its inclusion on the *Microsoft® Hardware Compatibility List (HCL)*, which is an up-to-date list of hardware that is supported by Microsoft.

The digital signature is associated with individual driver versions, and certifies to users that the driver provided with the device is identical to the driver that was tested.

The following three driver-signing policy settings in the operating system enforce signature verification and determine what the operating system does with an unsigned driver:

- **Warn**. Checks the signature on the driver before installation and displays a warning if the signature verification fails. The driver can still be installed, although installation is not recommended.

- **Block**. Checks the signature on the driver before installation and blocks installation of the driver if the signature verification fails.

- **Ignore**. Silently checks the signature on the driver, logs any unsigned driver files to a log file, and allows the installation of the driver.

> **Note**   The computer displays the **Warn** dialog box if you try to replace a signed driver with an unsigned driver, even if the policy is set to Ignore.

"Warn" is the default setting. You can change the driver-signing policy for a user without administrator permissions, but must have administrator permissions to change the driver-signing policy setting for a computer. Group Policy settings can be used to change the driver-signing policy from the defaults. For more information about using Group Policy, see "Managing Desktops" in this book.

To set signature verification options

1. In **Control Panel**, open **Performance and Maintenance**, and then open **System**.

2. Click the **Hardware** tab, and then click **Driver Signing**.

3. Under **What action do you want Windows to take?**, click the option for the level of signature verification that you want to set.

For more information about file signature verification and signature checking, see "Tools for Troubleshooting" in this book.

> **Note**   If you are logged on as a member of the Administrators group, you can apply the selected driver-signing setting as the default for all users who log on to a computer by clicking **Make this action the system default**.

Windows Update

Windows Update is an online extension of Windows XP Professional, and provides a central location for product enhancements, such as Service Packs, device drivers, and system security updates. Windows XP Professional users can install or update drivers from the Windows Update Web site. When a user accesses the Windows Update Web site, Windows Update compares the drivers installed on the user's system with the latest updates available. If newer drivers are found, Windows Update offers the list of applicable drivers to the user. The user can then choose whether to download and install the newer drivers.

Because installing drivers not included on the Windows XP Professional installation CD-ROM requires administrative rights, you must be logged on as an administrator to update a driver from Windows Update. In addition, administrators can use Group Policy to restrict users' access to Windows Update. For more information about restricting access to or configuring Windows Update, see "Tools for Troubleshooting" in this book.

Drivers are included on Windows Update only if they are digitally signed, have passed the testing requirements for the Windows Logo Program, and the vendor has given Microsoft redistribution rights for those drivers. This ensures that the drivers offered to users from Windows Update are of high quality and reliable.

Using a feature known as Automatic Updates, an administrator can configure a computer to notify a user about new updates, so the user can then download and install them, if desired, when they become available. This feature takes advantage of Windows Update to check the availability of critical updates that apply to your computer. Drivers are offered through Automatic Updates only if the driver is marked critical and no other driver is installed for a device.

You can access Windows Update by using any of the following methods:

- Open **Internet Explorer**, and on the **Tools** menu, select **Windows Update**.
- Open **Help and Support Center** and select **Windows Update**.
- Open **Programs** and select **Windows Update**.
- Use **Update Driver** in Device Manager.
- Run the **Add Printer** wizard for printer drivers.

Devices have a hardware ID that uniquely identifies the device. The *Plug and Play IDs* of devices include hardware IDs and compatible IDs. The list of hardware IDs and compatible IDs supported by an individual driver is listed in its inf file. If the hardware ID of the device exactly matches one of the hardware IDs supported by the driver, there is a *hardware match*. If some other match occurs (for example, device hardware ID to driver compatible ID) there is a *compatible match*. Drivers that have a hardware or compatible match with the device are candidates for download and installation. If a hardware or compatible match exists, Windows Update determines whether the driver on Windows Update is newer than the installed one. If it is newer, the driver is presented to the user. Also, if the hardware ID for the driver on Windows Update is a better match than the installed one, Windows Update offers that driver to the user. If the user chooses to install the offered driver, the file is downloaded, and the Windows Update ActiveX control points the Device Manager to the .inf file for installation. For more information about hardware IDs and compatible IDs, see "Driver Ranking" later in this chapter.

For more information about Windows Update, see the Windows Update link on the Web Resources page at http://www.microsoft.com/windows/reskits/webresources.

Enterprise-Wide Driver Update Using Windows Update

IT administrators can standardize the updates made to device drivers and other software by using the Microsoft® Windows Update Catalog site, which is accessible from the main Windows Update site. This site provides a comprehensive catalog of updates that can be downloaded for distribution to other computers or over a corporate network. To ensure that updates are synchronized enterprise-wide, you can download updates, and then test and approve the new software before distributing it. After the updated drivers are downloaded, tested, and approved, they can be prepared for enterprise-wide installation using standard software deployment tools and techniques.

Place the drivers to be installed on the network at a server location specified for the updated drivers. Then, each local computer can be configured to get the updated driver for a particular device from the network location instead of from the user's hard drive. You can configure users' computers in one of two ways:

- Change the registry setting for the location of that particular device driver on each local computer by using Unattend.txt. For more information about customizing the Unattend.txt file, see "Automating and Customizing Installations" in this book.

- Write a program that runs on the users' computers, which points to the new location. For more information about writing software for customizing the location of a device driver, see the Software Development Kit (SDK) information in the MSDN Library link on the Web Resources page at http://www.microsoft.com/windows/reskits/webresources.

Driver Ranking

Windows XP Professional uses driver-ranking schemes to determine which driver to load when multiple drivers are available for a device. Drivers are ranked by whether they are signed and how closely their Plug and Play ID matches the device's Plug and Play ID. The Plug and Play ID of a driver or device consists of hardware IDs and compatible IDs. If the hardware ID of the driver exactly matches one of the hardware IDs of the device, there is a *hardware match*. If some other match occurs (for example, device hardware ID to driver compatible ID) there is a *compatible match*. Driver rank also depends upon whether the device information file (.inf file) for the device includes information specifically for installations in a Microsoft® Windows NT® environment. If multiple drivers for a device exist, the lowest ranking driver is installed. The following list summarizes the driver-ranking scheme for Windows XP Professional from lowest (best match) to highest rank:

1. Signed driver with a hardware match to the device.
2. Signed driver with a compatible match to the device.

3. Unsigned driver with a hardware match to the device (with Windows NT–targeted INF section).

4. Unsigned driver with a compatible match to the device (with Windows NT–targeted INF section).

5. Unsigned driver with a hardware match to the device (without Windows NT–targeted INF section).

6. Unsigned driver with a compatible match to the device (without Windows NT–targeted INF section).

Windows Driver Protection

Windows Driver Protection features in Windows XP Professional prevent users from installing, loading, or running drivers on their system that are known to cause problems in Windows.

Microsoft maintains a database of known problem drivers that is used to determine which drivers Windows Driver Protection prevents from being installed or loaded. A driver is included in the database if there is a high probability that it will cause the system to hang or crash. The driver is identified in the database by file name, driver version, and link date. Updates to the database are downloaded to your computer from Windows Update.

If you try to install a driver that is listed in the known problem driver database, you will get a message notifying you that this is a driver that will cause system problems and the driver is not installed. The message also contains a link to a Web page that gives you more information and might offer updates to the drivers.

> **Note**   If you install drivers by using a custom executable, the problem driver database might not be checked during installation and notices about problem drivers might not be displayed. However, drivers that are missed by installation detection will be detected at load time and blocked successfully regardless of installation method.

The known problem driver database is also checked each time the computer is started and each time a driver is loaded to catch any problem drivers that might be loaded at startup. If a problem driver is installed after the computer is started, the next time you start the computer the loading process prevents the problem driver from being loaded.

When you log on to a computer where a driver has been blocked, an icon and a Help balloon display in the notification area. Clicking the icon accesses the My Computer Information-Health page in the Tools Center of Windows XP Professional

Help and Support Center, where details are provided for the list of drivers blocked since the last time the computer was started. For each driver in the list, a link is provided that opens an appropriate help file that describes in more detail the problem with the driver and contact information for the device manufacturer.

Each time a known problem driver is blocked, an entry is made in the computer's event log.

Driver Search Policy

When a new device is installed, Windows XP Professional searches four different locations for device drivers in this order: the hard drive, the floppy drive, the CD-ROM drive, and Windows Update. The default is to search all four locations in order for a device driver until the correct one is found, but you can configure the driver search locations to remove any or all of these locations. For example, you might want to prevent users from going to Windows Update to search for an updated driver.

To change driver search locations

1. In the **Group Policy** snap-in, select **Local Computer Policy**.

2. Select **User Configuration**, select **Administrative Templates**, and then expand the **System** item.

3. In the list of configuration options, double-click **Configure driver search locations**.

4. On the **Setting** tab, make sure that **Enabled** is selected.

5. Select the check boxes for the options you want to disable. Click **Apply**, and then click **OK**.

For information about installing the Local Computer Policy snap-in, see Windows XP Professional Help and Support Center.

Device Drivers in the Driver.cab File

The Windows XP Professional device drivers included on the Setup CD are stored in a single cabinet file named Driver.cab. This file is used by Setup and other system components as a driver file source. You can view the contents of the Driver.cab file by double-clicking it in Windows Explorer.

Information files (.inf files) are searched when Windows XP Professional starts or new hardware is detected. These text files provide the names and locations (typically Driver.cab) of driver related files and the initial settings required for new devices to work. During setup, Driver.cab is copied from the installation CD to the local hard disk in the *%windir%*\Driver Cache*platform* directory. (The variable *platform* describes the architecture of the system, for example, x86.) The folder where the file can be found is specified in the registry entry **DriverCachePath** in the subkey HKEY_LOCAL_MACHINE\SOFTWARE\Microsoft\Windows\CurrentVersion\Setup.

Copying a large Driver.cab file to the local hard disk instead of leaving it on the CD or network has the following advantages:

■ With the driver set on the local hard disk, users do not need the Setup CD to install new devices, which especially benefits mobile users. Exceptions are products with Windows drivers that are not included on the Setup CD.

■ Users do not need local administrator rights to install new hardware because all device drivers stored in Driver.cab are on the hard disk and are digitally signed.

■ For network-based setups, copying the Driver.cab file to the local hard disk reduces bandwidth requirements in these ways:

   1 During setup, less system and network overhead is required to copy the single large Driver.cab file than many small files.

   2 During subsequent hardware installations, driver files already reside on the local hard disk, and do not need to be copied over the network.

A new device requires corresponding driver files in order to work. Setup reads the Drvindex.inf file to find entries for the device. If an entry exists, Setup searches the following paths:

■ *systemroot*\Driver Cache*Platform*\Driver.cab

■ *systemroot*\Driver Cache*Platform*

■ The original Windows XP Professional installation source, such as a network share or a local CD-ROM drive. The Windows XP Professional source location is stored in the registry entry **SourcePath** in the subkey HKEY_LOCAL_MACHINE\Software\Microsoft\Windows\CurrentVersion\Setup.

If the required files do not exist in any of the preceding locations, or if references are not located in the Drvindex.inf file, Setup prompts the user to supply the required files.

Supported Hardware

Windows XP Professional supports a broad range of hardware, including system buses such as Universal Serial Bus (USB) and Institute of Electrical and Electronics Engineers (IEEE) 1394. Other system buses are also supported, in addition to devices such as network adapters and other internal adapters, modems, digital audio devices, DVD, Human Interface Devices (HID), still-image devices, smart cards, and video-capture devices.

Universal Serial Bus

Universal Serial Bus (USB) is a standards-based, external serial bus for the computer. USB is universal in that many types of peripheral devices can be connected to a computer by plugging them into USB ports, using standard USB cables, connectors, and sockets. USB fully supports Plug and Play, which means peripheral devices can be plugged in and unplugged while the computer is running. The operating system immediately detects a device that is plugged in and tries to load device drivers for the device.

USB hubs can be used to connect several devices to one computer. A hub provides multiple USB ports for Plug and Play devices. The hub is then plugged into the computer, directly or through another hub, using a single USB cable.

Windows XP Professional has built-in support for many USB devices (see "USB Devices" later in this chapter). When a user plugs in a USB device for which Windows XP Professional does not have built-in support, a dialog box is displayed that allows the user to manually point the Plug and Play subsystem to the location of the device drivers for that device (typically independent hardware vendor (IHV)-provided drivers on a floppy disk or CD-ROM).

USB has the following advantages:

- All USB devices connect to the computer using either the standard USB port or an A connector.

- A USB controller supports up to 127 devices. Hubs are used to obtain ports in addition to those supported by the root hub.

- USB supports *hot plugging*—plugging in or unplugging a USB device while the computer is running.

- USB supports the *selective suspend* feature, which allows USB device drivers to selectively shut down their devices when they detect that the devices are idle. When the device is put back in use, such as a user moving a USB mouse, the driver turns the device back on. This is particularly important for power management of mobile computers.

USB Topology

As illustrated in Figure 9-2, USB uses a tiered topology, so you can simultaneously attach up to 127 devices to the bus. USB supports up to seven tiers, including the root tier and five non-root hubs. The lowest tier supports only a single non-hub device. Under the USB specification, each device can be located up to 5 meters from the hub or port it is connected to.

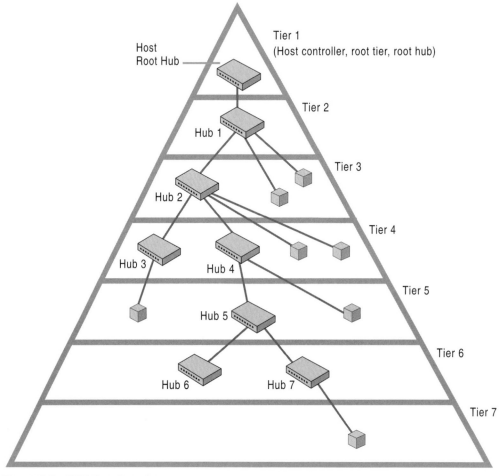

Figure 9-2 USB tiered topology

There are three types of USB components:

- *Host controller.* Also known as the *root*, the *root tier*, or the *root hub*, the host controller can be built into the motherboard of the computer or installed as an add-in CardBus or PCI card in the computer to gain additional ports and bandwidth. The host controller controls all traffic on the bus and also functions as a hub.

- *Hub.* Provides multiple ports, for attaching devices to the USB bus. Hubs are also responsible for detecting devices that are plugged in or unplugged, and for providing power for attached devices. Hubs are either *bus-powered*, drawing power directly from the USB bus, or *self-powered*, drawing power from an external AC adapter. Bus-powered hubs are capable of providing 100 milliamperes (mA) of power per port for attached devices, and can provide a maximum of four ports for devices to be plugged into. Self-powered hubs, on the other hand, typically provide 500 mA of power per port, and can provide more than four ports. Hubs can be stand-alone devices, or they can be integrated into other devices such as keyboards and monitors.

- *Device.* A USB device, which is attached to the bus through a port. A USB device can be any kind of peripheral device, such as a keyboard, mouse, game controller, printer, and so forth. Certain USB input devices such as keyboards and mice require only 100 mA of power to function. Thus, they can be plugged into both bus-powered and self-powered hubs, in addition to being plugged directly into a root port. Other devices such as printers, scanners, storage devices, and video-conferencing cameras might require 500 mA of power to function. These kinds of devices can only be plugged into root ports or self-powered hubs. If the device requires more than 500 mA of power, it includes a wall plug provided by the vendor for power.

USB Devices

A USB device typically implements a single function, for example, as a keyboard or mouse does. However, a USB device can also implement multiple functions, such as scanning, printing, and faxing. When such a multi-function device, or USB *composite device*, is plugged in, the operating system enumerates all the functions in the device, and loads device drivers for each function.

A USB device might also include a built-in hub, to enable additional devices to be plugged into it. Such a device is known as a USB *compound device*.

Each USB device contains configuration information that describes its capabilities and resource requirements. This information is read from the device by the operating system during the enumeration process.

USB devices are recognized, initialized, and ready for use when plugged in. No additional installation or configuration steps are necessary.

Windows XP Professional features built-in support for USB device types such as:

- Hubs

- Uninterruptible power supply (UPS) devices

- Input devices, such as keyboards, mice, and other pointing devices

- Game controllers, such as joysticks and game pads

- Printers

- Storage devices such as hard disk drives, CD-ROM drives, high-density disk drives, and compact flash readers

- Speakers and microphones

- Scanners

- Still image cameras

- Video-conferencing cameras (also known as "webcam" cameras)

- Modems

- USB-to-Ethernet network adapters

Windows XP Professional supports only devices that are compliant with applicable USB device class specifications as developed and published by the USB Implementers' Forum. For more information about USB specifications, see the USB link on the Web Resources page at http://www.microsoft.com/windows/reskits/webresources.

The only exception to this rule is USB-to-Ethernet adapters, which must be compliant with the Microsoft Remote Network Driver Interface Specification (NDIS) in order to benefit from built-in support in Windows XP Professional. For more information about Remote NDIS, see the Remote NDIS link on the Web Resources page at http://www.microsoft.com/windows/reskits/webresources.

Data Transfer Types and Rates Supported by USB

USB supports two different data transfer modes: *isochronous* and *asynchronous* modes. Asynchronous mode uses three asynchronous data transfer types: interrupt, control, and bulk. Isochronous mode uses the isochronous transfer type.

The USB host controller determines the data transfer rate and the priority assigned to a data stream. USB supports the following maximum data transfer rates, depending on the amount of bus bandwidth a device requires:

- 1.5 megabits per second (Mbps) for low-speed devices that do not require a large amount of bandwidth, such as mice and keyboards.

- 12 Mbps for full-speed, higher-performing devices, such as storage devices, speakers, scanners, and video cameras.

Asynchronous transfer mode   An asynchronous transfer employs a handshake system and allows data streams to be broken at random intervals. The three asynchronous data transfer types are described below.

Interrupt   Interrupt transfers reserve bandwidth and are guaranteed access to transfer data at the established rate. They are used when a device transfers unsolicited data to a host.

Control   Control transfers are used to service devices and to handle specific requests. They are typically used during device configuration.

Bulk   Bulk transfers are used to transfer large blocks of data that have no periodic or transfer rate requirement. Printers and storage devices typically deploy bulk transfers.

Isochronous transfer mode   An isochronous transfer requires a constant bandwidth within certain time constraints. Constant bandwidth is required to support the demands of streaming multimedia devices such as speakers or video cameras. Unlike asynchronous transfers, no handshaking occurs and data delivery is not guaranteed.

USB Support for Plug and Play

Windows XP Professional supports Plug and Play configuration of USB devices by using the following USB features:

Hot plug-in capability   You can plug a USB device into the system at any time. The USB driver stack enumerates the device and notifies the system that the device is present.

Persistent addressing   USB devices use descriptors to identify the device, its capabilities, and the protocols it uses. A device descriptor contains a Vendor ID (VID), a Product ID (PID), and a version number that tell the computer exactly which drivers to load. An optional serial number differentiates one device from another of the same type.

Power options   USB supports three power modes: On, Suspend, and Off.

User Interfaces for USB Device Properties

Windows XP Professional provides user interfaces to display relevant information about the status of USB devices. The information provided by the USB user interface in Device Manager provides the advanced user with property sheets for hubs and controllers that give specific USB power and bandwidth information.

In addition, an event-driven interface allows error detection and correction by notifying the user about a problem on the bus. The interface provides details about the error and suggests solutions. For information about the USB troubleshooting user interface, see "Troubleshooting a Universal Serial Bus Device" later in this chapter.

For more information about using Device Manager to display device properties, see "Device Manager" earlier in this chapter.

USB Root Hub Power Properties   The **Power Management** tab in the **USB Root Hub Properties** dialog box displays information about power usage on that hub. The **Hub information** box indicates the hub type and the amount of power available from each port (determined by hub type).

The **Attached devices** box lists devices attached to the hub's ports and the power each device requires to function. If a device requires more power to function properly than the hub's ports supply, a message notifies the user. The user can view the Device Manager property dialog box for the hub by double-clicking the device. Clicking **Refresh** updates the information in the dialog box, which shows devices that are attached or removed.

USB Host Controller Advanced Properties   The **USB Host Controller** dialog box displays information about bandwidth usage on the USB host controller and gives the user the option of turning off USB error detection. The **Advanced** tab in the **USB Universal Host Controller Properties** dialog box shows the bandwidth allocation page. The Bandwidth section of the dialog box describes USB bandwidth and how it pertains to what the user sees displayed on the property page. The list box displays all devices attached to the controller that consume isochronous bandwidth (typically, USB video cameras and USB speakers), along with the bandwidth each takes. To maintain bandwidth for control transfers, the amount of bandwidth reserved by the "System Reserved" device listing will change, depending on what devices are installed or removed. For every device that consumes one percent or more of the controller's bandwidth, there is a corresponding section in the Bandwidth Used column, which displays cumulative bandwidth usage. However, HID-compliant devices do not display here, although they do cause an increase in the System Reserved percentage.

Checking the **Don't tell me about USB errors** check box and clicking **OK** disables the display of the USB error detection and correction messages. For more information, see "USB User Interface Error Detection" later in this chapter. The default state for this button is unchecked.

IEEE 1394

Windows XP Professional supports the *Institute of Electrical and Electronics Engineers (IEEE) 1394* bus, which is designed for high-bandwidth devices, such as digital camcorders, digital cameras, digital VCRs, and various storage devices. The IEEE 1394 bus is a digital, peer-to-peer interface that supports data transport speeds from 100 to 400 Mbps. It provides a high-speed Plug and Play-capable bus that reduces the amount of power that peripheral devices require and provides support for isochronous data transfer.

IEEE 1394 can connect up to 63 devices to one IEEE 1394 bus and link up to 1023 buses to form a network of more than 64,000 devices. Each device can have up to 256 terabytes of memory available over the bus. A built-in mechanism ensures that all devices have equal access to the bus.

Windows XP Professional supports three protocol standards for data transport over the IEEE 1394 bus:

- **SBP-2 Protocol**. Used for block transfer–type devices, such as storage devices, scanners, and printers.

- **61883 Protocol**. Used with streaming data–type technologies such as networking, digital camcorders, DVD, and audio. Windows XP Professional supports the 61883-1 through 61883-4 protocols.

- **IP over 1394 Protocol**. Provides high-speed TCP/IP connectivity between PCs and is a good solution for home networking. Windows XP Professional supports the IPv4 specification for IP over 1394.

Note Microsoft® Windows® XP 64-Bit Edition only supports the SBP-2 protocol. It does not support the 61883 or IP over 1394 protocols.

Windows XP Professional supports IEEE 1394 by allowing IEEE 1394 device drivers to communicate with the IEEE 1394 bus class driver. In compliance with the Open Host Controller Interface (OHCI) 1.0 standard, Windows XP Professional includes the IEEE 1394 bus class driver with hardware-specific minidriver extensions for add-on and motherboard-based host controllers.

IEEE 1394 Bus Connector and Cable

The IEEE 1394 specification defines a standard connector and socket, which includes three interfaces: a 6-pin connector and cable, a 4-pin connector and cable, and a 6-pin-to-4-pin connector and cable. The 6-pin cables can supply power to a device over the bus, while a 4-pin cable can only carry data. An IEEE 1394 bus cable contains two pairs of twisted-pair cabling to accommodate the serial bus.

Data Transfer Rates Supported by IEEE 1394

IEEE 1394 supports both isochronous and asynchronous data transfer protocols. The IEEE 1394 specification currently supports the following bus transfer rates:

- S100 (98.304 Mbps)

- S200 (196.608 Mbps)

- S400 (393.216 Mbps)

You can link devices with different data rates; communication takes place at the highest rate supported by the lowest-rate device.

Support for Plug and Play and Other Devices

Windows XP Professional provides additional support for the IEEE 1394 bus in use with the following specifications and devices.

Plug and Play   Windows XP Professional supports hot plugging of devices that use the IEEE 1394 bus. All IEEE 1394 devices can be plugged in while the computer is on, and the device is detected and configured. For more information about Plug and Play, see "Plug and Play Overview" earlier in this chapter.

A/V Devices   Windows XP Professional supports streaming digital video and transfer of MPEG-2 data to and from IEEE 1394 devices. An application of this is video editing, where the data is retrieved from a digital camera, edited, and then written back to the camera, to a digital VCR, or to a storage device.

Storage and Other Devices   Support for IEEE 1394 storage devices, printers, and scanners is implemented by using the SBP-2 protocol. For example, SCSI class drivers can use SBP-2 to connect and use IEEE 1394 devices. Devices that use the SBP-2 protocol must be OHCI compliant.

Other Bus Support

Most buses supported by previous versions of Windows function under Windows XP Professional. The buses that are supported include PCI, AGP, PC Card, CardBus, SCSI, ISA and EISA buses.

> **Note**   Windows XP Professional does not support the Micro Channel bus. Micro Channel architecture is found mainly in older IBM PS/2 computers.

PCI Bus

The Peripheral Component Interconnect (PCI) bus, included in all computers, is used for transferring data between the CPU and hardware devices, adapters, or non-PCI bus-circuit boards. PCI is a local bus system that allows up to 10 PCI-compliant expansion cards to be installed in the computer. The PCI bus system requires the presence of a PCI controller card, which can exchange data with the system's CPU either 32 bits or 64 bits at a time, depending on the implementation, and controls data transfers between main memory and all the other devices on the PCI bus. Because of its high bandwidth, the PCI bus is capable of high-speed data transfers.

The PCI specification allows for multiplexing, a technique that permits more than one electrical signal to be present on the bus at one time. The PCI controller also allows intelligent, PCI-compliant adapters to perform tasks concurrently with the CPU using a technique called *bus mastering*. This improves performance in tasks, because it frees the CPU for other work by enabling devices to take temporary control of the PCI bus for data transfer.

AGP Bus

The Accelerated Graphics Port (AGP) bus is a dedicated video bus that provides fast, high-speed data transfers from system memory to the display adapter. For more information about AGP, see "Managing Digital Media" in this book.

PC Card and CardBus

Windows XP Professional supports the features of products designed for the PC Card standard. The 16-bit version of the PC Card is also known as PCMCIA. These products include multifunction cards, 3.3-V cards, and 32-bit PC Cards. Major advantages of PC Cards are small size, low power consumption, and Plug and Play support.

Windows XP Professional supports CardBus (also called PC Card 32), which is a combination of PC Card 16 and PCI. CardBus brings the advantages of 32-bit performance and the PCI bus to the PC Card architecture.

CardBus allows portable computers to perform high-bandwidth functions such as capturing video. For more information about PC Cards and CardBus in portable computers, see "Supporting Mobile Users" in this book.

SCSI Bus

The Small Computer Standard Interface (SCSI) standard defines a high-speed parallel bus that carries data and control signals from SCSI devices to a SCSI controller. It is an intelligent bus most often used for high-performance hard disks on multi-user systems. It is also flexible and can be used with lower throughput device such as CD-ROMs, tape drives, or scanners.

ISA Bus

The Industry Standard Architecture (ISA) bus is based on a design specification introduced for the IBM PC/AT. The specification allows components to be added as cards plugged into standard expansion slots, and has a 16-bit data path. Plug and Play ISA devices can be used on existing computers, because Plug and Play does not require any change to ISA buses. Windows XP Professional does not support non–Plug and Play ISA devices, although they work if manually configured.

EISA Bus

The Enhanced Industry Standard Architecture (EISA) bus is based on a design specification for x86-based computers introduced by an industry consortium. EISA maintains compatibility with ISA, but provides additional features. These include a 32-bit data path, and the use of connectors that can accept cards made for both EISA and ISA buses.

Other Hardware Support

In addition to USB and IEEE 1394 bus devices, Windows XP Professional supports standards for a number of other hardware devices ranging from network adapters to digital media devices.

Network and Other Internal Adapters

An adapter is a printed circuit board that allows a computer to use a peripheral device for which it does not already have connections or circuit boards. For example, a network adapter provides the physical interface (connector) and the hardware (circuitry) to connect a node or host to a local area network. A network adapter is also called an adapter card, a card, or a network adapter.

For information about troubleshooting network and other internal adapters, see "Troubleshooting Network and Other Internal Adapters" later in this chapter.

For more information about networks, see "Connecting Clients to Windows Networks" in this book.

Modems

A modem is a communications device that enables a computer to transmit information over a standard telephone line. Modems convert a digital signal from a computer to an analog signal on the telephone line, and vice versa.

Modems fall into two distinct categories, standard and controller-less modems. Although both types offer similar functions and features, the back-end hardware and the drivers used in their implementation differ significantly.

- **Standard modems**. Internal and external standard modems incorporate processing devices or chips in the modem itself and are independent of the operating system. These modems do not rely on the CPU for their internal processing. External models connect to an existing serial port and therefore do not use additional system resources. Many external models have separate on/off switches, so their power source can be cycled independently of the computer's power.

- **Controller-less modems**. Controller-less modems have only generic onboard processing devices. They rely on operating-system-specific code executed by the CPU to function.

Human Interface Devices

Windows XP Professional supports devices that are compliant with the Human Interface Device (HID) firmware specification. HID devices are those devices used by humans to control the operation of computer systems. Examples of HID devices include keyboards and pointing devices such as mouse devices and touch screens; panel controls such as knobs, switches, and buttons; consumer appliance devices such as audio/video appliances and remote controls; and devices that might not require human interaction but provide data in a similar format, such as bar code readers or voltmeters.

The HID specification was developed by the USB Implementers Forum and is mainly implemented in devices connected by USB. However, Windows XP Professional includes HID support for devices connected by using other ports or buses. For example, HID devices connected by IEEE 1394 can be developed and supplied by vendors but are not common.

An HID device is Plug and Play compliant if its underlying bus is Plug and Play compliant, and it indicates its class and HID information when plugged into the host system. Plug and Play HID devices do not require installation of additional software drivers, but non–Plug and Play HID devices might. The use of Windows Driver Model (WDM)–compliant drivers provides operating system support. Windows XP Professional supplies the HID class driver, the HID minidriver for the HID USB miniport, and the HID parser. Support for Plug and Play and power management for USB/HID devices takes place within the USB driver stack that is part of the WDM-based architecture.

From the perspective of a computer program, any HID device can be accessed either through HID application programming interfaces (APIs), or through DirectInput® Component Object Model (COM) methods. DirectInput, which is part of DirectX® digital media architecture, provides an input device API to support HID devices.

For more information about the USB Implementers Forum and HID usage, see the USB link on the Web Resources page at http://www.microsoft.com/windows/reskits/webresources.

For more information about Input and HID Devices, see the Input and HID Devices link at http://www.microsoft.com/windows/reskits/webresources.

For more information about developing minidrivers and filter drivers, see the Driver Development Kits link on the Web Resources page at http://www.microsoft.com/windows/reskits/webresources.

DVD

DVD (digital video disc) is an optical disc storage technology that can hold video, high-quality CD audio, and computer data in a single digital format. DVD devices can read multiple, digitally stored data streams concurrently for playback of digital media applications and full-length motion pictures. Two major compression technologies, MPEG-2 and AC-3 (also called Dolby Digital), are used to store from 4.7 gigabytes (GB) to 17 GB of data on a single DVD disc.

DVDs also offers copy and distribution protection. This is accomplished by encrypting the content on a disc, and by restricting playback of discs to specified geographical regions. For more information about copy and distribution protection offered by DVD, see "Managing Digital Media" in this book.

Windows XP Professional supports DVD in the following ways.

DVD video and audio playback   If the proper decoding hardware or software is present, Windows XP Professional supports playback of DVD video. This support is important for entertainment computers and any digital media platform intended to play movies. Windows XP Professional support includes the same interactivity and high-quality playback found on a standard DVD video player. DVD devices can also play most audio CDs.

DVD as a storage device   You can use DVD as a storage device on most computers that support DVD. DVD-ROM discs and devices provide cost-effective storage for large data files. The UDF file format is used to store data on most DVDs.

In Windows XP Professional, different types of DVD drives have differing capabilities, as follows:

- DVD-ROM devices can read CDs or DVD-ROM discs in both UDF and FAT32 formats.

- DVD-R/RW devices can read CD or DVD content in both UDF and FAT32 formats, but do not support DVD writing.

- DVD-RAM devices can read any CD or DVD disc, can write content in FAT32 format, and can read UDF and FAT32 formats. These discs cannot be read in most DVD-ROM devices.

For more information about DVD, see "Managing Digital Media" in this book.

For more information about the UDF and FAT32 file formats, see "File Systems" in this book.

Digital Audio Devices

Windows XP Professional uses the Windows Driver Model (WDM) audio architecture to support digital audio devices. The operating system can manage multiple audio streams, and two or more applications can play sounds simultaneously. For example, if you are listening to music on your computer, you can also hear the notification that a message has arrived. The WDM audio architecture performs audio processing in kernel mode, which significantly reduces *latency*, the time required for a signal to travel from one point to another.

Windows XP Professional also supports the Audio Codec '97 (AC '97) specification for digital audio, which defines a widely adopted audio architecture. The AC '97 controller that is typically integrated into the chipset handles the digital aspects of audio, while the AC '97 codec handles the analog aspects of audio. The AC '97 specification describes the architecture of the codec and the digital interface between the controller and the codec. Windows XP Professional includes AC '97 audio drivers to support the integrated AC '97 controllers from four major computer chipset manufacturers. As a general rule, these AC '97 audio drivers support any manufacturer's AC '97 controller when paired with any codec that is AC '97 compliant.

Because digital audio is processed by the operating system, a separate sound card is not required to process digital audio. Digital audio is supported on several bus types, including PCI, ISA, and PCMCIA, and on external digital audio devices connected with USB and IEEE 1394.

Windows XP Professional supports the following digital audio features and devices:

- Audio chipsets and sound cards implemented on the PCI, ISA and PCMCIA buses.

- USB audio devices, such as USB microphones, speakers, and MIDI devices.

- Multichannel audio output and playback of various audio formats. Volume can be set for each speaker in a multichannel configuration.

- Acoustic echo cancellation (AEC).

- Global Effects Feature (GFX), which enhances USB audio support by allowing filter drivers to support devices such as USB array microphones.

- IEEE 1394 audio devices.

- Copying of the audio capture stream so that multiple applications can have access to the stream.

- Support for Digital Rights Management (DRM) in the WDM audio architecture to allow audio drivers to be authenticated as trusted. Some DRM content can be rendered only on trusted audio devices.

- Digital Signal Processors (DSPs).

Windows XP Professional also supports DRM technology that allows content providers such as artists and record companies to protect proprietary music or other data by encrypting digital content and attaching usage rules to it. These rules determine restrictions such as the number of times content plays and the types of devices that play it. Using Windows XP Professional, you can ensure that a device or driver is trusted not to violate usage rules or allow a user to circumvent security. Trusted drivers are only relevant to DRM content that requires this security.

Driver modules that handle audio content must include a DRM signature before they can render protected content that requires a trusted audio device. Windows XP Professional uses a DRM signature in the driver's catalog files to identify a trusted device. This is not the same as the signature required for Windows drivers. To play DRM-encrypted content requiring a trusted audio device, WDM audio drivers and any associated filter components must be DRM compliant.

Still Image Devices

Windows XP Professional supports still-image devices through Windows Image Acquisition (WIA), which uses the WDM architecture. WIA provides robust communication between applications and image-capture devices, allowing you to capture images efficiently and transfer them to your computer for editing and use.

WIA supports SCSI, IEEE 1394, USB, and serial digital still image devices. Support for infrared, parallel, and serial still image devices, which are connected to standard COM ports, is provided by standard infrared, parallel, and serial interfaces. Image scanners and digital cameras are examples of WIA devices. WIA also supports Microsoft DirectShow®-based webcams and digital video (DV) camcorders to capture frames from video.

WIA supports a camera class driver that is based on Picture Transfer Protocol (PTP), a standard that enables digital cameras to communicate with each other, with printers and with computers. WIA automatically recognizes all PTP digital still cameras that support the PTP class ID and provides all of the basic still image functionality as with any other WIA device. PTP cameras that do not support the PTP class ID can also be recognized by means of a third-party .inf file that maps the device Plug and Play identifier to the WIA PTP class driver.

WIA provides a driver model for manufacturers to write drivers for cameras with proprietary protocols. When such a WIA driver is installed, all WIA features are available to this camera.

WIA also provides Mass Storage Class (MSC) device support. The storage on MSC cameras can be accessed using a drive letter that appears in My Computer If the camera uses the MSC driver provided with the operating system, the AutoPlay dialog box is displayed when it is connected to the computer, which allows the user to select the Scanner and Camera wizard.

Support for Microsoft DirectShow-based webcams and digital video camcorders is provided by a generic DirectShow filter, which identifies itself as a source of images.

WIA Architecture WIA architecture describes both an API and a device driver interface (DDI). The WIA architecture includes components provided by the software and hardware vendor, in addition to Microsoft. Figure 9-3 illustrates the WIA architecture.

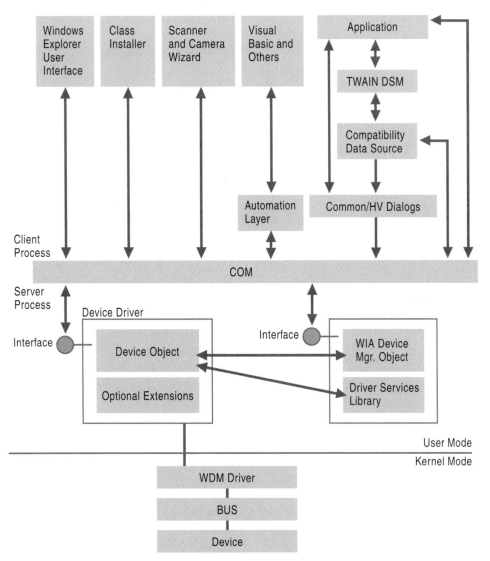

Figure 9-3   Components of WIA architecture

Windows Explorer user interface   Windows Explorer extensions such as **My Computer** and **My Pictures**, as well as **Scanners and Cameras** in Control Panel provide a user interface by which users can access WIA devices. For example, an icon for each installed WIA device appears in the **My Computer** folder. If a still image camera is installed, clicking the camera icon opens an interface that shows thumbnail pictures, controls for saving pictures, and a live preview that you can capture if the camera is a supported webcam or Digital Video (DV) camcorder.

The My Pictures folder includes thumbnails of images, a link to the WIA Scanner and Camera wizard, a built-in slide show, an enhanced preview window called the Windows Picture and Fax Viewer, and the option to print pictures from the pre-view window.

Microsoft Paint also supports WIA. When a WIA device is present, **From Scanner or Camera** is enabled on the **File** menu, and users can retrieve pictures from WIA devices.

Class Installer   The imaging class installer supports easy removal and installation of WIA devices. The installer also supports Plug and Play devices for USB, SCSI, IEEE 1394 buses, and serial-based digital still cameras.

Scanner and Camera wizard   Using the Scanner and Camera Wizard, users can retrieve images from any of the supported devices installed on the system. The Wizard provides a preview page where the user can select from several scanning options and adjust image settings. It is opened by default when WIA-enabled scanners are activated (a "scan event") and when Plug and Play still digital cameras are connected (a "connect event"). By using the AutoPlay dialog, the Wizard can also be opened when media, such as flash memory cards, that contain image files are inserted into the computer (a "media-insertion event"). Note, however, that the Wizard is not opened by default for video cameras.

Using the Wizard for a digital still camera, the user can select one or more pictures, rotate them, and view information such as picture size and resolution.

With a video camera, the user can select previously captured still images, rotate them, view picture information, and even see live video and capture still images. The user can also name the pictures, save them in the My Pictures folder, categorize pictures by using sub-folders, and publish them on the Web.

For non–Plug and Play devices, the user can start the wizard from the **Accessories** menu.

> **Note**   The WIA driver for DirectShow-supported webcams and digital video camcorders stores captured pictures in a temporary file. As a result, when you capture pictures with a webcam or DV camcorder, be sure to save the pictures you want to keep to the My Pictures folder or some other location on the PC. This ensures that the pictures are not deleted from the drive when clearing out the Temp folder, either manually or using the Disk Cleanup utility.

Visual Basic and other scripting languages   WIA includes a scripting model, which allows advanced users and IT professionals to develop WIA applications by using Microsoft Visual Basic® and other scripting languages. For more information about developing WIA applications, see the Software Development Kit (SDK) information in the MSDN Library link on the Web Resources page at http://www.microsoft.com/windows/reskits/webresources.

WIA applications   Users can start image acquisition and manipulate images by using either the WIA wizard or another application. Two primary types of WIA applications use still images:

- **Image editing applications**. Examples include Adobe PhotoShop and Microsoft® Picture It!®

- **Image display applications**. These applications are for authoring documents that include image data, but provide no or limited editing of image data. Examples include Microsoft Word and Microsoft® PowerPoint®.

TWAIN Data Source Manager   The TWAIN Data Source Manager (DSM) is an industry-standard software library used to abstract TWAIN applications from still image devices. WIA uses the TWAIN DSM implementation in Microsoft® Windows® XP together with the TWAIN compatibility driver to provide a compatibility layer for applications that support TWAIN version 1.7 or later, but don't yet support WIA.

WIA common system dialogs   All scanner and camera device drivers that ship in Windows XP Professional use the WIA common system dialogs. There are four system dialogs that are used in WIA imaging applications to access WIA-enabled scanners and cameras. The dialog that displays is tailored to the device type used. For example, when scanning an image into Paint using a WIA-enabled scanner, Paint displays a WIA dialog that allows you to preview the scanned image, crop the image, set the color, contrast and brightness, and so on. Specific dialogs for still camera and video camera display when those devices are accessed. The device selection dialog displays when more than one WIA device is active on the system.

Device object   When the WIA device driver is started, it creates a device object that allows the application to communicate with the hardware. There are four types of device objects: full WIA minidriver, WIA flatbed scanner microdriver, WIA generic PTP camera driver, and WIA video camera driver.

WIA Device Manager object   When an application first communicates with a device, the WIA Device Manager detects all the devices, creates the device objects, establishes the link between the application and the device object, and retrieves and sets device properties.

WIA Event Model   As discussed above, Still Image devices can generate various events. Some devices, such as scanners, can support multiple events, which are traditionally mapped to the buttons on the scanner itself. The most common event for scanners is Scan, which is normally mapped to the scan button.

By default, the Scanner and Camera Wizard is associated with the Scan event (for scanners) and the Connect event (for still digital cameras). Consequently, when the scan button is pressed on a WIA scanner that uses a driver supplied with Windows XP Professional, the Scanner and Camera wizard appears.

The WIA event model includes a set of pre-defined events that can be associated by means of WIA device drivers or .inf files. At the same time, these pre-defined events are available to applications so they can automatically start when the event takes place.

An application can register itself to be the default event handler by calling the WIA APIs documented on the SDK. The application has 3 handler options – global, device-specific, and device or event specific.

When an application registers as a global or device-specific event handler, a dialog appears when the event takes place. This dialog prompts the user to choose which application is to be the default event handler. The Scanner and Camera Wizard is presented as one of the options.

When an application registers as a combination device or event handler, the dialog does not appear.

When multiple applications are registered for the same event, a user can manually switch between them by using the **Events** tab on the device **Properties** page, which can be accessed by right clicking the device icon from **My Computer** and selecting **Properties**.

Image Color Management 2.0   Because colors can vary by monitor or printer, Image Color Management (ICM) version 2.0 ensures that images have accurate colors by storing standard, objective color characteristics for each output device that produces an image. As a result, a photograph taken by a digital camera looks the same on the monitor as when it was captured. In turn, the printed version of the same image accurately represents the image and colors seen through the camera and on the monitor.

Software for color management uses profiles, which are data about how each device represents color. These profiles provide the information that allows the color management software to prepare an accurate color reproduction.

ICM is based on the industry standard ICC profile, the standardized Color Management Module (CMM), and the default Standard RGB (red, green, blue) color space. Although this flexible system allows the use of any CMM, ICM uses LinoColor CMM by default. This makes Windows applications that use ICM 2.0 compatible with other platforms with respect to color management.

ICM 2.0 on Windows XP Professional is set up to run transparently for printing, which benefits users who do not need advanced color configuration options for devices. However, ICM provides full manual control with a selection of alternative color profiles—a benefit to users who need color consistency on devices and platforms that might otherwise be incompatible.

ICM supports sRGB, which complements current color management strategies by enabling a default method of handling color in the operating system and on the Internet. It efficiently provides good quality color representation and backward compatibility. *Standard RGB* (sRGB) is the default color space in Windows XP Professional for all color images that do not have another embedded profile, or are not specifically tagged with other color information. If a specific color profile is assigned to an image or a device, that color profile is used. If no color profile is assigned, then the default sRGB profile is assumed.

Video Capture

Video Capture under Windows XP Professional is based on the WDM streaming-class driver. Windows XP Professional provides minidrivers for USB and IEEE 1394 cameras, as well as PCI and videoport analog video devices. Support includes DirectShow® filters for WDM video capture interfaces and a Video for Windows (VFW)–to–WDM mapper for compatibility with previous interface versions. The mapper, also called the VFWWDM mapper, allows WDM video capture devices to take advantage of existing 32-bit VFW applications.

Capturing video with WDM has the following advantages:

- Full integration with DirectShow and streaming architecture.

- Single-class driver architecture for hardware (such as video ports and chip sets), which is shared by video capture devices and DVD or MPEG devices.

- Support for vertical blanking interval (VBI), and video port extensions.

Capture applications are available that use both DirectShow and VFW. The DirectX® version 8.1 Software Development Kit (SDK) provides four sample video capture applications. These include AMCap, PlayCap, StillCap, and DVApp. For more information about the sample video capture applications, see the Windows XP Professional Software Development Kits link on the Web Resources page at http://www.microsoft.com/windows/reskits/webresources.

Video Capture provides real-time and step-frame modes for capturing video sequences.

Real-time capture   Real-time capture of video images demands a fast computer and hard disk. A video source for real-time capture (such as a video camera or videodisc) provides an uninterrupted stream of information to the capture hardware. The capture hardware copies each frame of the video sequence and the audio portion and transfers it to the hard disk before the next frame of data enters the capture hardware. Each video frame contains one image. If the system lags during capture, frames of video data are lost.

Step-frame capture   Step-frame capture collects video frames from a video sequence in a series of steps, capturing frames one at a time, typically from a paused video device. Step-frame capture causes the video source to pause as it collects each image. If an audio source is also selected, the capture mode rewinds the media in the video source and collects audio data as the video source plays a second time. You can perform step-frame capture manually, advancing the video source by using the controls on the video device. Windows XP Professional Video

Capture also provides automatic step-frame capture for video devices that support the Media Control Interface. With this method, Video Capture issues frame-advance commands to the source device and captures the sequence frame-by-frame. When Video Capture finishes capturing the current frame, it advances the video source to the next capture point.

Step-frame capture provides an alternative for systems that cannot process a video sequence in real time due to a slow I/O subsystem. Because the system can fully process a video frame before contending with the next frame, you can use larger frame sizes and color formats, and you can compress the video sequence during capture.

Step-frame capture is also available by using WIA technology. For more information about WIA, see "Still Image Devices" earlier in this chapter.

Smart Cards

Smart Card technology is fully integrated into Windows XP Professional, and is an important component of the operating system's public-key infrastructure (PKI) security feature. A *smart card* is a small electronic device, often the size of a credit card, which contains an embedded integrated circuit. The smart card serves as a secure store for public and private keys and as a cryptographic engine for performing a digital signature or key-exchange operation. Smart card technology allows Windows XP Professional to authenticate users by using the private and public key information stored on a card.

Smart cards provide the following benefits:

■ Tamper-resistant storage for protecting private keys and other forms of personal information.

■ Isolation of security-critical computations involving authentication, digital signatures, and key exchange from other parts of the system.

■ Portability of credentials and other private information between computers at work, home, and elsewhere.

The Smart Card subsystem on Windows XP Professional supports industry standard Personal Computer/Smart Card (PC/SC)–compliant cards and readers, and provides drivers for commercially available Plug and Play smart card readers. Smart card readers attach to standard peripheral interfaces, such as RS-232, PS/2, PCMCIA, and USB. Windows XP Professional detects Plug and Play-compliant smart card readers and installs them using the Add Hardware wizard.

To install a smart card reader driver, follow the directions in the Add Hardware wizard for installing device driver software. The process requires that you use either the Windows XP Professional CD or media from the smart card reader manufacturer that contains the appropriate device driver.

> **Note**   Microsoft does not support or recommend using non–Plug and Play smart card readers. If you use a non–Plug and Play reader, you must obtain installation instructions and associated device driver software directly from the manufacturer of the smart card reader.
>
> For information about Windows XP Professional–compatiblesmart card readers see the Windows Hardware Compatibility List link on the Web Resources page at http://www.microsoft.com/windows/reskits/webresources.

Before using a smart card to log on, a user must be enrolled to do so by a user who has the privilege to enroll other users. This is required because enrollment for a smart card certificate is a controlled procedure in the same manner that employee badges are controlled for identification and physical access purposes. Enrollment provides the user with the public encryption key and certificate that is required for authentication and secure exchange of information. The user also needs a Personal Identification Number (PIN) to complete the logon process. Usually the user sets the PIN during enrollment, or is given a default PIN and is instructed to change it as soon as possible.

Using a smart card to log on to Windows XP Professional requires at least one *service provider* so that applications can access card-based services. A cryptographic service provider (CSP) makes available the cryptographic services of the smart card, such as key generation, digital signature, and key exchange. A Smart Card Service Provider (SCSP) makes the noncryptographic services of a smart card available to an application.

For more information about installing a smart card reader and smart card certificate enrollment, see Windows XP Professional Help and Support Center.

For more information about using Smart Cards for logon and authentication, see "Logon and Authentication" in this book.

Device Installation

In Windows XP Professional, how you install a device depends on whether the device and the computer are Plug and Play. When installing Plug and Play devices, Windows XP Professional detects and configures the device with little or no user intervention. Device driver installation also requires little user involvement because Windows XP Professional uses driver-ranking schemes and driver search location policies, among other features, to determine which drivers are loaded.

Installing a Device in Windows XP Professional

Windows XP Professional Setup performs an inventory of all devices on the computer and records the information about those devices in the registry. Setup gets configuration information for system devices from the .inf file associated with each device and, for Plug and Play devices, from the device itself.

When a new device is installed, Windows XP Professional uses the device's Plug and Play ID to search Windows XP Professional .inf files for an entry for that device. Windows XP Professional uses this information to create an entry for the device under the Hkey_Local_Machine subtree in the registry, and copies the drivers needed. Registry entries are then copied from the .inf file to the registry entry for the driver.

When you install a new device, rely first on Plug and Play to detect and configure it. How you install hardware depends on the type of device:

- For Plug and Play external devices, plug in the device.

- For Plug and Play internal devices, turn the computer off and install the device according to the manufacturer's documentation. You can, however, typically insert and remove PC Card, CardBus, and other Plug and Play devices without turning the computer off.

- For PCI and ISA Plug and Play cards, turn the computer off, and then install the device. When you restart the computer, Windows XP Professional detects the device and starts the Plug and Play installation procedures.

- For non–Plug and Play devices, turn the computer off, and then install the device. When you restart the computer, run the Add Hardware wizard and let Windows XP Professional detect the device. This requires administrator permissions. If Windows XP Professional cannot detect the device, you might need to manually configure it. Consult the hardware vendor's documentation if this is necessary.

Note   Whenever possible, use Plug and Play devices even in computers that do not have an ACPI BIOS in order to make available any additional Plug and Play functionality.

Installing Drivers

Many device drivers are installed with no user intervention. For example, when you plug in a USB mouse device, the drivers are automatically detected and installed. Drivers are installed without user intervention if certain conditions are met:

- Installing the driver does not require showing a user interface.

- The driver package contains all files needed to complete the installation.

- The driver package is available on the system in the Driver.cab file, or was previously installed.

- The driver package is digitally signed.

- No errors occur during installation.

If any of these conditions is not met, the device installation restarts and the user might need to respond to dialog boxes or messages. Manual installation of a driver requires administrator permissions.

Note   Drivers that support features specific to Windows XP Professional are not compatible with Microsoft® Windows® 98 or Microsoft® Windows® Millennium Edition (Me).

Windows XP Professional determines which device driver to load for a device by using these features:

- Driver-ranking schemes

- Driver search location policies

- Windows Driver Protection

- Windows Update

For more information about device drivers, including driver-ranking schemes, Windows Driver Protection, driver search location policy, and Windows Update, see "Device Drivers" earlier in this chapter.

Setting Plug and Play BIOS Settings

For x86-based systems, the way that the system BIOS code interacts with Plug and Play devices can vary, depending on whether the system BIOS or the operating system is responsible for configuring hardware. Whether the system BIOS is set to enable Plug and Play can affect this interaction if this option exists for your system. System conditions and recommended BIOS settings are listed in Table 9-2.

Table 9-2 Recommended Plug and Play BIOS Settings for x86-based Systems

Condition	Recommended BIOS Setting
Fully compliant ACPI system (ACPI BIOS present; ACPI Hardware Abstraction Layer (HAL) installed)	Windows XP Professional assigns device resources and ignores BIOS settings. This includes re-assigning IRQ, DMA, and Input Output (I/O) resources and arbitrating conflicts for all PCI devices. Because Windows XP Professional ignores the Plug and Play BIOS setting and uses ACPI, the BIOS setting can be left at either **Yes/Enabled** or **No/Disabled**. However, it is recommended that you set this option to **No/Disabled**.
Non-compliant ACPI system (ACPI BIOS present; compliance problems prevented ACPI HAL installation)	The system BIOS assigns device resources prior to the loading of the operating system, and the Plug and Play BIOS setting must be **No/Disabled.** If your devices have a static configuration, you must turn off your computer before removing or attaching most devices. For more information about whether to turn your computer off when installing a device, see "Installing a Device in Windows XP Professional" earlier in this chapter.
Non-ACPI systems	The system BIOS assigns device resources prior to the loading of the operating system, and the Plug and Play BIOS setting must be **No/Disabled.** If your devices have a static configuration, you must turn off your computer before removing or attaching most devices.
Dual boot Windows XP Professional and Microsoft® Windows® 95, Windows 98, or Windows Me operating systems	The Plug and Play BIOS setting must be **No/Disabled**. Disabling Plug and Play in the BIOS is recommended to prevent errors that might arise. For example, if the system check for Plug and Play on a Windows 98 ACPI system passes, the system check for Plug and Play might fail on a Windows XP Professional ACPI system.

For information about viewing or modifying your computer's BIOS settings, consult your computer's documentation or manufacturer's support Web site.

Note Motherboards based on Itanium-based architecture rely on ACPI and the operating system to configure resources. The option to enable or disable ACPI settings is not available on Itanium-based computers.

Configuring Device Settings

Windows XP Professional identifies devices and their hardware resource requirements. The operating system allocates the optimal resources and attempts to resolve conflicts when two or more devices request the same resource. Consequently, you must not manually change resource settings for a Plug and Play device unless it is absolutely necessary to resolve a problem with the device. Doing so fixes its settings, preventing Windows XP Professional from granting another device's request to use that resource. Changed resource settings can be returned to the original values by selecting the **Use automatic settings** check box on the **Resources** tab of the **Device Properties Page** in Device Manager. See the procedure "To change resource settings for a device by using Device Manager" later in this section.

Note   Windows XP Professional might allocate a single resource to more than one device. For example, multiple PCI devices might share the same IRQ.

During setup, Windows XP Professional detects non–Plug and Play devices that have fixed resource requirements. For example, some ISA modems require fixed I/O port settings, and cannot operate at any other I/O setting. After running Setup, you can use the Add Hardware wizard to install non–Plug and Play devices. This is the only instance in which you need to use the Add Hardware wizard to install a device.

Certain circumstances might require you to change resource settings after Windows XP Professional configures a device. For example, Windows XP Professional might not be able to configure one device without creating conflicts with another. Typically a message explains that a conflict exists and suggests a solution, such as turning off or disabling a device or assigning non-conflicting resources.

For more information about troubleshooting devices, see "Hardware Troubleshooting" later in this chapter or "Tools for Troubleshooting" in this book.

To manually change the configuration of a device, use Device Manager. Use the following strategies when using Device Manager to resolve device conflicts manually:

- Identify a free resource and assign it to the device.

- Disable or remove one of the conflicting devices to free resources.

- Remove non–Plug and Play hardware and device drivers.

- Rearrange resources used by a device or devices to free resources that the conflicting device requires.

- Use Device Manager to select non-conflicting resource values. Use device configuration software, jumpers, or DIP switches to adjust actual hardware values to match those used by Device Manager.

You can print a report about your system and device resource settings. In **Device Manager**, highlight the device that you are interested in. On the **Action** menu, select **Print**. In the **Report Type** section of the **Print** dialog box, select a system summary report, a report of the selected class or device, or a report of all devices with a system summary. Click **Print** to send the report to the printer.

The following procedure explains how to change a device's resource settings by using Device Manager.

Caution   Change resource settings only if absolutely necessary. Changing resource settings can cause conflicts and can cause you to lose Plug and Play functionality.

To change resource settings for a device by using Device Manager

Some devices do not have a Resources tab on their property sheet. You cannot manually change the resources for these devices.

1. In **Device Manager**, expand the device class to show the available devices.

2. Right-click a device, and then click **Properties**.

3. On the **Resources** tab, notice that the **Conflicting device list** shows conflicting values for resources used by other devices.

4. In the **Resource type** list, select the setting you want to change, clear the **Use automatic settings** check box, and then click **Change Setting**.

    If there is a conflict with another device, a message is displayed in **Conflict Information**.

5. If an error message says, "This resource setting cannot be modified," browse for a configuration that you can use to change resource settings without conflicting with other devices.

6. Click **OK**, and then restart Windows XP Professional.

7. Verify that the settings are correct for the device.

Note   Many legacy devices have jumpers or DIP switches that set the IRQ, DMA, and I/O addresses. If you change these settings in Device Manager, you must also change the settings on the device to match them.

Using Hardware Profiles for Alternate Configurations

Windows XP Professional uses hardware profiles to determine which drivers to load. A computer can have different profiles that describe different hardware configurations. Hardware profiles are especially important for portable computers that can be docked. Windows XP Professional uses one hardware profile to load drivers when the portable computer is docked and another when it is undocked. For example, a different profile is used at a customer site that has a monitor different from the one at the office.

Configurations are created when Windows XP Professional queries the BIOS for a dock serial ID and assigns a name for the docked and undocked configurations. Windows XP Professional then stores the hardware and software associated with these configurations. Applications access and store information for each hardware configuration used by the mobile user. Using multiple profiles enables applications to adapt to various hardware configurations.

Windows XP Professional prompts you for the name of a hardware profile only when two profiles are so similar that it cannot differentiate between them. If this happens, the operating system displays a **Hardware Profile** menu from which you can choose the correct profile.

For more information about hardware profiles for portable computers, see "Supporting Mobile Users" in this book.

Changing Hardware Acceleration Settings for Digital Audio

Windows XP Professional includes a driver that provides hardware acceleration. This driver speeds up the delivery of digital audio data, which improves Microsoft DirectSound® Audio performance. You can change the level of hardware acceleration available to DirectSound Audio applications by using the Hardware Acceleration option for Sounds and Audio Devices. You can use these settings for testing or to improve the stability of the system.

Hardware Acceleration for DirectSound Audio has four settings, which are described in Table 9-3.

Table 9-3   Hardware Acceleration for DirectSound Audio

Setting Name	Description
Emulation	Forces emulation mode, so audio applications run as though no DirectSound Audio compatible driver is on the system, and no hardware acceleration is provided. Use this setting only if other acceleration settings do not function properly.
Basic	Disables hardware acceleration, so applications run as though no hardware acceleration is present. This option is useful if you want to emulate a non-DirectSound-accelerated sound card for testing purposes.

Table 9-3 Hardware Acceleration for DirectSound Audio

Setting Name	Description
Standard	Enables hardware acceleration but disables any vendor-specific properties, so only standard acceleration features are used. This is the default setting for Windows XP Professional.
Full	Enables hardware acceleration and all vendor-specific properties, so all acceleration features are available.

To change the hardware acceleration setting for audio devices

1. In **Control Panel**, open **Sounds, Speech and Audio Devices**, and then open **Sounds and Audio Devices**.

2. Click the **Audio** tab, and under **Sound Playback**, click the **Advanced** button.

3. In the **Advanced Audio Properties** dialog box, click the **Performance** tab.

4. Under **Audio Playback**, move the **Hardware Acceleration** slider to the desired setting.

Configuring the Display

The Display option in Control Panel allows you to change the settings on your monitor and make other changes to your desktop, including the following:

- Change the display driver.

- Change screen resolution and color depth (without restarting the computer when using display drivers that support this functionality).

- Change color schemes and text styles in all screen elements, including fonts used in dialog boxes, menus, and title bars.

- View changes in colors, text, and other elements of display appearance before the changes are applied.

- Configure display settings for each hardware profile, for example, docked and undocked configurations.

- Configure multiple monitors. For information about configuring multiple monitors, see "Configuring Multiple Monitors" later in this chapter.

Windows XP Professional also includes mechanisms to ensure that incompatible display drivers cannot prevent a user from accessing the system. If a display driver fails to load or initialize when Windows XP Professional is started, Windows XP Professional automatically uses the generic VGA display driver. This ensures that you can start Windows XP Professional to fix a display-related problem.

Changing the Display Driver

You can change or upgrade a display driver by using Device Manager to view the properties for the monitor. When you select **Update Driver** from the **Driver** tab, the **Hardware Update Wizard** installs the driver automatically, or you can choose to install a different driver from a list of known drivers for the display. For more information about adding or changing a device driver, see Windows XP Professional Help and Support Center.

If you install a new Plug and Play monitor, the system detects the monitor and the **Found New Hardware** wizard guides you through the installation process. After attaching the monitor, uninstall the old monitor in Device Manager, and scan for the new hardware by clicking **Scan for hardware changes** on the **Action** menu.

Note   If a driver is not included with your monitor, check Windows Update for an updated driver for your monitor. If there is no driver in Windows Update, check the manufacturer's Web site for the most recent driver.

If the monitor is detected as **Default Monitor**, either the display adapter or the monitor is not Plug and Play. If the monitor is not detected as **Plug and Play Monitor**, the monitor is not included in the monitor .inf files. Check Windows Update or contact your hardware manufacturer for an updated Windows XP Professional .inf file.

Warning   Incorrect display settings can physically damage some monitors. Check the manual for your monitor before choosing a new setting.

Changing Hardware Acceleration Settings for Graphics Hardware

Windows XP Professional uses hardware acceleration to improve display performance. If using hardware acceleration causes a problem, such as mouse pointer problems or corrupt images, you can turn off some or all hardware acceleration features. By turning off hardware acceleration, you can manually control the level of acceleration and performance supplied by your graphics hardware, which can help you troubleshoot display problems.

Hardware acceleration for your graphics hardware has six settings. Table 9-4 shows the settings and their meanings.

Table 9-4   Hardware Acceleration for Graphics Hardware

Setting	Description
None	Disables all accelerations. Use this setting only if your computer frequently stops responding or has other severe problems.
1	Disables all but basic accelerations. User this setting to correct more severe problems.
2	Disables all DirectX® Graphics accelerations, as well as all cursor and advanced drawing accelerations. Use this setting to correct severe problems with DirectX accelerated applications.
3	Disables all cursor and advanced drawing accelerations. Use this setting to correct drawing problems.
4	Disables cursor and bitmap accelerations. Use this setting to troubleshoot mouse pointer problems or corrupt images.
Full	Enables all acceleration features. This setting is recommended if your computer has no problems.

Note   If you use multiple monitors, changing hardware acceleration settings affects all monitors.

To change hardware acceleration

1. Right-click the desktop, and then click **Properties**.

2. In the **Display Properties** dialog box, click the **Settings** tab, and then click the **Advanced** button.

3. Click the **Troubleshoot** tab, and then choose the desired level of hardware acceleration.

Windows XP Professional supports *write combining*, which improves video performance by speeding up the display of information to your screen. However, increased speed can also cause screen corruption. If display problems occur, you can disable write combining to troubleshoot this problem.

To disable write combining

1. Right-click the desktop, and then click **Properties**.

2. In the **Display Properties** dialog box, click the **Settings** tab, and then click the **Advanced** button.

3. Click the **Troubleshoot** tab, and then clear the **Enable write combining** check box.

Configuring Display Resolution and Appearance

You can configure the display resolution and colors, fonts, and backgrounds for your Windows XP Professional display. Right-click the desktop, select **Properties**, and make changes from the **Settings** tab on the **Display Properties** dialog box.

You can also adjust the refresh frequency rate for your display. A higher refresh frequency rate reduces flicker on CRT displays. On the **Settings** tab, click the **Advanced** button, and then change the refresh frequency on the **Monitor** tab.

Windows XP Professional allows you to change resolution and color depth without restarting the computer, if the installed display adapter is using a video driver provided with Windows XP Professional. You might have to restart the computer if you are not using a Plug and Play display adapter and driver.

Configuring Power Management for the Display

The **Display Properties** dialog box, accessed by right-clicking the desktop and selecting **Properties**, allows you to set the screen saver and other desktop attributes. In addition, you can use settings in Screen Saver properties to take advantage of power management support in Windows XP Professional, if your hardware supports this feature. Windows XP Professional can support screen saver power management if your computer is Energy Star Compliant. An Energy Star–compliant monitor supports the Video Electronics Standards Association (VESA) Display Power Management System (DPMS) specification. To determine whether your monitor is Energy Star compliant, look for the Energy Star logo on the **Screen Saver** tab of the Display dialog box.

The display monitor is typically one of the most "power-hungry" components of a computer. Manufacturers of newer display monitors have incorporated energy-saving features based on the DPMS specification. By using signals from the display adapter, a software control can place the monitor in standby mode or even turn it off completely, thus reducing the power the monitor uses when inactive.

You can adjust monitor power settings on the **Screen Saver** tab by clicking the **Power** button, and, on the **Power Schemes** tab, selecting the amount of time the monitor will stay on without any activity before it turns itself off.

Enabling Mode Pruning

Mode Pruning is a Windows XP Professional feature that is used to remove *display modes* that the monitor cannot support. Display modes are the combinations of screen resolution, colors, and refresh rates available for the selected video adapter. In Mode Pruning, the graphics modes of the monitor and the display adapter are compared, and only modes common to both the monitor and display adapter are available to the user.

Mode Pruning is available only if a Plug and Play monitor is detected or if a specific monitor driver is loaded in Device Manager. Mode Pruning is not available if the monitor driver is "Default Monitor." On Plug and Play monitors, Mode Pruning is enabled by default. If Mode Pruning is disabled, you can select display modes that are not supported by your monitor.

Warning Choosing a mode that is inappropriate for your monitor might cause severe display problems and might damage your hardware. You must be logged on as a member of the Administrator's group to view unsupported modes. It is not recommended that you change this setting. If you choose to view unsupported display modes, consult your hardware documentation.

To disable Mode Pruning

1. Right-click the desktop, and then click **Properties**.

2. In the **Display Properties** dialog box, click the **Settings** tab, click **Advanced**, and then click the **Monitor** tab.

3. Clear **Hide modes that this monitor cannot display**, and then click **Apply**.

Using Digital Flat Panel Monitors

Windows XP Professional supports using digital flat panel (DFP) monitors with display adapters that have the appropriate output connectors. These connectors include Digital Video Interconnect (DVI) and DFP. Most display adapters also have standard CRT connectors for more common monitors.

Using Multiple Monitors

By using the Multiple Monitors feature you can configure up to ten monitors, so that the Windows XP Professional desktop display spreads across all of the monitors. For each monitor, you can adjust position, resolution, and color depth.

In the **Display Properties** dialog box, one monitor is designated the primary display. This is the default display used for prompts and pop-up windows and has full hardware DirectX Graphics acceleration. It is also the only display that can run DirectX applications in full-screen mode.

POST vs. Primary Display Device

In Windows XP Professional, any supported VGA monitor can be used as the power-on self test (POST) device. The adapter that displays the system BIOS and system memory count when the computer is turned on is the POST device. This is the only device that can be used for MS-DOS mode operations in full screen mode. The POST device does not have to be the same as the Primary Display, which is the default display that is used for prompts and pop-up windows. The Primary Display has full hardware DirectX Graphics acceleration, and is also the only display that can run DirectX applications in full-screen mode.

Configuring Multiple Monitors

A monitor must meet the following criteria to be used as a secondary monitor. It must be a PCI or AGP device, be able to run in graphical user interface (GUI) mode without using VGA resources, and have a Windows XP Professional driver that enables it to be a secondary display. For more information about monitors that can be used as secondary monitors, see the Hardware Compatibility List link on the Web Resources page at http://www.microsoft.com/windows/reskits/webresources.

Note   To use multiple monitors a working monitor capable of VGA graphics must be connected to each installed display adapter.

In a multiple monitor environment, only one graphics device can be VGA compatible. This is a limitation of computer hardware that requires that only one device respond to any hardware address. Because the VGA hardware compatibility standard requires specific hardware addresses, only one VGA graphics device can be present in a computer, and only this device can physically respond to VGA addresses. Thus, applications that require a full-screen view will run only on the particular device that supports VGA hardware compatibility.

If you have an on-board display device, it must be used as the VGA device. Some computers cannot activate the onboard display when a VGA-capable PCI display device is present. In this case, disable the on-board hardware VGA for the secondary devices so that the onboard device runs a POST routine.

To add a second monitor to your computer

1. Verify that your primary display adapter works properly.

2. Plug in the second monitor.
   Windows XP Professional detects and installs the new monitor.

3. In the **Display Properties** dialog box, click the **Settings** tab.
   Icons for both monitors display in the dialog box.

4. Click the icon for the new monitor, labeled **2**.

5. Select **Extend my Windows desktop to this monitor**, and then click **OK**.

6. To adjust the color depth on the new monitor, use the **Color Quality** drop-down list box. To adjust the resolution, use the **Screen Resolution** slider.

7. Verify that the on-screen arrangement of the monitors matches the physical configuration of your monitors. This can be changed by dragging the icon of the monitor to the location on the screen that corresponds to the location of the monitor on your desk.

Multiple Monitors and DirectX

Only the primary monitor in a multiple monitor configuration can accelerate DirectX Graphics functions that use the full capabilities of the monitor. Additionally, only the primary monitor can run DirectX applications in full-screen mode. For this reason, you need to make sure that the monitor with the best DirectX Graphics performance and features is the primary monitor.

To set the primary monitor in a multiple monitor configuration

1. Right-click the desktop, and then click **Properties**.

2. In the **Display Properties** dialog box, click the **Settings** tab.

3. On the **Settings** tab, select **Use this monitor as the primary display**.

4. Click **OK**.

Using Multiple Monitors with Portable Computers

Dualview, another feature of Windows XP Professional, allows both portable and desktop computers to display independent output on the onboard display and an external monitor. Dualview is very similar to the multiple monitor feature, except that you cannot select the primary display. The portable computer display must be used as the VGA device.

Dualview requires that the display adapter provide dual outputs. The external VGA port on the portable computer provides the second monitor connection. Dualview can be used with docked or undocked portable computers. The display driver for the adapter must support this feature, so it is not available in all computers.

Windows XP Professional does not support hot undocking of portable computers that have an active multiple monitor configuration. To hot undock a portable computer, set up a non-multiple monitor hardware profile and log on again using that profile. You can also open **Display** in **Control Panel** to detach the secondary display before undocking.

Configuring Communications Resources

A communications resource is a physical or logical device that provides a single, asynchronous data stream. Communications ports, printer ports, and modems are examples of communications resources.

Two types of communications resources appear as ports in Device Manager:

- **Communications ports**. These ports, also called COM ports, serial ports, or RS-232 COM ports, connect RS-232- compatible serial devices, such as modems and pointing devices, to the computer. Several types of communications ports might be listed in Device Manager:

- **Serial ports**. Ports, also known as RS-232 COM ports, to which external serial devices can be attached. Typically these ports require a 9- or 25-pin plug. Serial ports designed for Windows XP Professional use the 16550A buffered UART, which has a 16-byte FIFO that gives the CPU more time to serve other processes and that can serve multiple characters in a single interrupt routine.

- **Internal modem adapters**. Internal modems are modems that are constructed on an expansion card to be installed in an expansion slot inside a computer.

- **Printer ports**. These ports, also known as LPT ports or parallel ports, connect parallel devices, such as printers, to the computer. For more information about configuring printer ports, see "Enabling Printing and Faxing" in this book.

Note   If Windows XP Professional does not detect an internal modem, the modem must be installed and configured by using the Modems option in Control Panel.

When you install a communications device, Windows XP Professional assigns COM names to communication ports, internal modem adapters, and PC Card modem cards according to their base I/O port addresses as shown in the following list:

- COM1 at address 3F8

- COM2 at address 2F8

- COM3 at address 3E8

- COM4 at address 2E8

If a device has a nonstandard base address, or if all four standard ports are assigned to devices, Windows XP Professional assigns the modem to COM5 or higher. Some 16-bit Microsoft® Windows® version 3.1–based applications might not be able to access ports higher than COM4. Thus, when using the System option in Control Panel, you must adjust the base address in Device Manager or delete other devices to free a COM port at a lower address.

Also, if some devices installed on a computer are not Plug and Play, you might need to change resource settings for their communications ports. You can change communications port settings by using Device Manager, as described in "Device Installation" earlier in this chapter.

> **Tip**   For future reference, it is recommended that you record the settings that appear on the Resources sheet for each communications port.

Configuring Scanners and Cameras

Configuration of scanners and cameras is completed during setup. Standard or default settings are applied when you run Setup, but you can change many of these settings by opening the **Scanners and Cameras Properties** dialog box in Control Panel.

Ports

For serial devices, to view the port being used by the scanner or camera, go to the **Port Settings** tab in the **Scanners and Cameras Properties** dialog box in Control Panel. On the **Port Settings** tab, you can configure the baud rate—faster to speed image transfer or slower to accommodate hardware limitations.

> **Warning**   Do not set the baud rate higher than the fastest speed supported by the hardware, or the image transfer will fail.

Image Color Management

The standard color profile is sRGB for Image Color Management (ICM 2.0) on the World Wide Web, in Microsoft® Windows®, Microsoft® Office, and similar display environments. However, you can add, remove, or select an alternate color profile for a device. In Control Panel, open the **Scanners and Cameras Properties** dialog box, and then use the **Color Management** tab.

IrTran-P

Infrared Picture Transfer (IrTran-P) is an image transfer protocol that sends images to Windows XP Professional by using infrared technology. On a camera that supports IrTran-P, when you press the Send button, the camera sends its stored images to Windows XP Professional. The IrTran-P server in Windows XP Professional then detects the connection the camera is attempting to establish, begins a session, accepts the images, and stores them in the My Pictures folder.

To use IrTran-P, you need an imaging device, typically a camera that can produce infrared transmissions, and a computer that can receive infrared transmissions. Most IrTran-P devices are Plug and Play and do not need any special configuration.

Pushbutton Scanning

Pushbutton scanning allows a scanner to associate a particular application with the push button on the scanner, and is typically configured during device installation.

However, you might need to associate an application with a scanner button, if this is not done automatically. In Control Panel, open the **Scanners and Cameras Properties** dialog box, and then use the **Events** tab to configure the button events for a scanner.

Power Management

Windows XP Professional offers enhanced power-management features for desktop and mobile computers. The operating system supports the Advanced Configuration and Power Interface (ACPI) specification, which provides reliable power management and system configuration.

On an ACPI-compliant system, Windows XP Professional manages, directs, and coordinates power so the system is instantly accessible to users when needed, but consumes the least possible power when not actively working. In earlier power management architectures such as APM, the BIOS controlled the power state of system devices without coordinating with the operating system.

By contrast, devices and applications designed in compliance with the ACPI specification work with the operating system to respond to or request a change in the system power state. For example, an active application or input from a device, such as a mouse, indicates to the operating system that the computer or device is in use. The operating system's power policy manager then allocates full power to the system. Otherwise, the operating system attempts to put the computer into a lower power or sleep state. For example, a fax modem can operate while the system is in a low-power state, consuming little energy until the phone rings, at which time the system returns to full power to receive a fax, and transitions back into a low-power state when the system is no longer needed.

For more information about power management, ACPI, and Advanced Power Management (APM), see "Supporting Mobile Users" in this book.

Power Management Features

Windows XP Professional supports power management features based on ACPI and the OnNow design initiative. The operating system also provides more limited power management support for systems based on the older APM specification. Windows XP Professional includes the following power management features:

- **Improved boot and resume performance**. Reduced startup times mean the computer is ready for use quickly when powering up from a low-power state; reduced shutdown times allow the computer to quickly enter a low-power state.

- **Wake-on support**. The computer is in a low-power state when not in use, but can still respond to wake-up events, such as a phone call or a network request.

- **Improved power efficiency**. Features that improve power efficiency, especially for portable computers, include native support for processor performance control technologies, LCD dimming when on battery power, and turning off the laptop display panel when the lid is closed.

- **Power management features in applications**. Applications designed to use power management features in Windows tell the operating system what not to put into sleep mode. For example, presentation software, which might be displaying a screen but not actively processing, can tell the operating system not to put the monitor into a sleep state.

- **Power policy ownership for individual devices**. All devices designed to use power management features in Windows can participate in power management. When they are not in use, they can request that the operating system put them into a low-power state to conserve power.

- **User interface for setting power preferences**. In Control Panel, **Power Options** provide an interface through which a user can set preferences by choosing or creating power schemes, specifying battery usage options, and setting low-power alarms. If an Uninterruptible Power Supply (UPS) is present, Power Options can also manage the UPS.

- **Decreased thermal output**. Power reduction for unused devices results in decreased thermal output, which can prolong the life of hardware components.

- **Decreased noise**. When the computer is in a low-power state, power can be reduced sufficiently to cause cooling fans to turn off, thereby decreasing noise.

> **Caution** Devices or applications that are not ACPI-compliant might prevent the operating system from putting the system into a low-power state, such as standby or hibernation. Non-compliant applications or devices might cause data loss or other failures if the computer wakes up and the application or device is not properly designed to handle a change in the system power state.

Power Policy Overview

The goal of power management is to conserve power while the computer is working and to put the computer into low-power states when it is not working. The power policy manager, in conjunction with applications and devices, implements the decisions that determine how to save energy and when to put the computer into a low-power state. Power policies are based on user preferences, the requirements of applications, and the capabilities of the system hardware. The implementation of power policy is distributed throughout the system, with system components acting as policy owners for the various devices. For example, the operating system is the policy owner responsible for determining when the computer goes into a low-power state, the level of power reduction, and how to operate the processor to reduce power consumption.

Each device in the computer has a power policy owner, which is the component that manages power for that device. Each policy owner works in conjunction with the operating system's policy for putting the computer into low-power states.

Device drivers carry out power policy –controlling devices so that when power consumption or capabilities change for each specific device, these changes are shared among the drivers in the stack. Device-specific drivers save and restore device settings across transitions to and from low-power states. When a device power policy owner detects conditions that permit or require a change in the power state of a device, it sends a request to the power policy manager in the operating system to put the device into the desired state. For example, if a network cable is unplugged, the network device driver can notify the operating system that the network adapter does not need full power and can be put into a lower power state until the network cable is plugged back in.

Another instance of the use of power management is Wake on LAN. As a network administrator, you can send information over the network to run an application or configure a system remotely. A remote system in a low-power state powers up when it receives the LAN request, accepts the information, and then returns to a low-power state when the task is complete.

Using the Power Management Interface

In Windows XP Professional, you can use **Power Options** in Control Panel to configure and monitor power management features and set power management options called power schemes. You can configure optional features, such as support for hibernation, and you can monitor the status of power components, such as the remaining power in your laptop battery. If your system has an Uninterruptible Power Supply (UPS), you can configure and view details of the UPS.

For more information about configuring power schemes for your desktop computer or power management for portable computers, see "Supporting Mobile Users" in this book. For procedural information about using the **Power Options Properties** dialog box to configure power options, see "Power Options" in Windows XP Professional Help and Support Center.

For ways to troubleshoot power management see "Tools for Troubleshooting" in this book.

Hardware Troubleshooting

Any device installed in your system can cause startup and stability problems. Thus it is important to become familiar with common issues, so that you can diagnose and troubleshoot hardware. This compilation of troubleshooting examples can help you resolve common hardware problems by using Windows XP Professional features such as Device Manager. Checklists of troubleshooting suggestions included in this section might also provide solutions to hardware problems.

Troubleshooting Hardware by Using Device Manager

The list of devices shown in Device Manager can provide valuable information about hardware problems you might encounter. For example, devices that have resource conflicts or other problems are marked with a yellow exclamation point. You can fix problems with device drivers by updating or uninstalling the driver from Device Manager. You can view a device's properties and system resources to establish where a conflict originates. You can disable a device by using Device Manager to see which device might be causing a problem.

When there is a problem with a device, Device Manager provides an error code on the device's properties page. For a list of Device Manager error codes and suggested solutions, see "Device Manager Error Codes," an appendix in this book.

For more information about Device Manager, see "Device Manager" earlier in this chapter.

Troubleshooting Network and Other Internal Adapters

Typically, installation of new internal devices in Windows XP Professional proceeds smoothly. If a problem occurs, Table 9-5 can help you identify the cause and find a solution.

Table 9-5   Suggestions for Troubleshooting Network and Other Internal Adapters

Suggestion	Course of Action
Check the HCL.	Verify that the device is listed on the Hardware Compatibility List (HCL) and then check Windows Update for newer Windows XP Professional drivers. For non-HCL devices, consult the manufacturer's Web site for Windows XP Professional updates.
Update device drivers.	Check Windows Update to determine whether updated drivers are available. If your device driver is not listed on Windows Update, check the manufacturer's Web site. If you cannot restart the computer after installing new drivers, see "Troubleshooting Startup" in this book.
Upgrade the adapter's firmware.	Upgrade the computer's firmware to the latest revision. Certain types of network cards, such as combination modem and network cards for portable computers and Preboot Execution Environment (PXE) adapters used for Remote Installation Services (RIS) might require BIOS updates to take full advantage of advanced features.
	Note: To start from a PXE device into a Windows 2000 or Windows XP Professional RIS enabled network, the system firmware **boot order** option must be set so that the network adapter is the first device on the list. Typically, the floppy disk or CD-ROM is the first device, with the network adapter set as one of the last options.
	Upgrade the adapter's firmware to the newest version. This could improve the adapter's stability and compatibility.

Table 9-5   Suggestions for Troubleshooting Network and Other Internal Adapters

Suggestion	Course of Action
Upgrade the computer's firmware.	For a discussion about keeping motherboard firmware revisions current, see "Troubleshooting Concepts and Strategies" in this book.
Verify that ISA devices operate in Plug and Play mode.	For ISA devices, verify that they are operating in Plug and Play mode. For non–Plug and Play devices, choose resource settings that do not conflict with existing settings for other devices.
Replace or move the adapter.	Replace the adapter with an identical adapter type. If problems disappear, this indicates a hardware problem with the first device.
	You can also try physically moving the adapter to another slot. Some motherboards assign resources based on slot position, and relocating a device from one slot to another might resolve hardware conflicts. Manuals for some PCI network adapters strongly advise that you use a "master" slot whenever possible to avoid problems on x86-based systems. Refer to your computer's documentation for the location of these master PCI slots. If you are experienced with hardware, some x86-based motherboards have a firmware option that allows you to assign IRQ resources manually.
Restart or shut down the computer.	Restart the computer to make sure that device drivers are activated. This is sometimes required for ISA devices that must restart to fully initialize. For multiple boot x86-based systems with Windows 95 or Windows 98 installed, each operating system might assign different resources to the same device, resulting in initialization problems. If you suspect a problem, you can use Device Manager to verify that the device is still functioning. A yellow exclamation point or a red "X" indicates malfunctioning or improperly installed hardware. Restarting the computer might work, or a full shutdown might be required before you can switch operating systems.
Verify that the network driver is properly installed.	Verify that the **Local Area Connection** icon is present in **Network Connections** in Control Panel. If an installation problem exists, no icon appears. Try refreshing the screen to display the icon.

Table 9-5 Suggestions for Troubleshooting Network and Other Internal Adapters

Suggestion	Course of Action
Verify network driver settings.	Many adapters use drivers that attempt to auto-detect network settings such as media type, media connector, and duplex. Occasionally, automatic settings are incorrectly detected, and you might need to make manual changes so that the device works (a common example is the duplex setting). If default driver settings do not work, try manually changing each parameter one at a time and observe the result.
	Note: For TCP/IP networks, Windows XP Professional uses Media Sensing, a feature that attempts to re-establish broken connections without restarting the computer. This can cause problems when two computers are connected directly to each other by a crossover network cable. For best results, avoid using crossover cables and use network hubs instead. For more information about disabling media sensing, see article Q239924, "How to Disable Media Sense for TCP/IP in Windows 2000," in the Microsoft Knowledge Base. To find this article, see the Microsoft Knowledge Base link on the Web Resources page at http://www.microsoft.com/windows/reskits/webresources.
Verify compatibility of network tools.	Bonus tools are often included with products installed by using OEM drivers. These tools might be incompatible with Windows XP Professional. Uninstall extra tools (leaving the base drivers in place) to determine whether this resolves problems. If bonus tools cause the problem, search for updated versions on the manufacturer's Web site.

Troubleshooting Modems

Typically, modem troubleshooting involves setup and installation problems. Understanding the differences between the two types of modems, standard and controllerless, can help to resolve problems. See "Modems" earlier in this chapter.

If problems arise during setup or installation of modems, use the following steps for troubleshooting:

Standard (external) modems Verify that the computer uses the serial port to communicate with the modem. If the system requests area code and dialing options information, open **Phone and Modem Options** in **Control Panel**. On the **Modems** tab, click **Properties** to verify that the information screen is not blank.

If you have difficulty, repeat the verification step mentioned above, and then check to see whether Device Manager lists your modem. If not, a specific driver for your modem was not found. Windows XP Professional might substitute a **Standard Modem** driver that provides basic functionality, but it might not support all the advanced features of the modem. You can use the Standard Modem driver temporarily until you obtain an update from the modem manufacturer.

- Shut down and restart the computer, and then repeat the above steps.
- If you are still having problems with the modem, try moving the external modem to another free serial port if one is available.
- For internal modems, see "All Modems" below.

Controller-less modems   Troubleshooting options for controller-less modems are limited to updating driver software. Controller-less modems rely on operating-system-specific code to function, so you must use the most current Windows XP Professional drivers.

All modems   Use the following suggestions to troubleshoot standard external modems, internal modems, and controller-less modems:

- If lack of system resources is an issue (especially for x86-based systems), disable unused COM ports in both the BIOS and in Device Manager. Communication ports consume resources whether they are actively used or not. Disabling unused ports might reduce the potential for hardware conflicts.

- If applicable, upgrade modem firmware to the newest version.

- Replace the modem with an identical model to verify that the current hardware is not malfunctioning.

- Refer to the troubleshooting options listed in Table 9-5, earlier in this chapter.

> **Note**   Some modems use USB interfaces. For information about troubleshooting USB devices, see "Troubleshooting a Universal Serial Bus Device" later in this chapter.

Troubleshooting Video Adapters

Video problems can stem from two common causes:

- The wrong video driver is installed.

- The settings made by using **Display** in Control Panel are incorrect, such as setting the wrong monitor type. This mismatch can result in distorted images if the monitor cannot synchronize with the video card's resolution or refresh rate.

If video distortion occurs immediately after manipulating the **Display** settings, press ESC to undo the changes. If you succeed in restoring the previous settings, select the correct monitor from the list of available models. If you cannot locate an exact match, use the **Default Monitor** or obtain a suitable driver from the manufacturer.

If you use the wrong video driver or settings, the system might stop responding and display a Stop message, or the screen might go blank soon after Windows XP Professional starts. To restore previous video settings, restart the computer, and then press **F8** to view the following choices on the Windows XP Professional **Advanced Options** menu:

- **Last Known Good Configuration**. Select **Last Known Good Configuration** to restore the registry and driver configurations to their state the last time the computer was successfully started.

- **Safe mode**. Start in safe mode and manually update, remove, or roll back the video driver.

- **Enable VGA mode**. Select the **Enable VGA mode** option to enable standard VGA 640 x 480 resolution and 16-color capability. You can then use **Display** in Control Panel to select the correct driver for your video adapter.

If the preceding suggestions do not resolve the problem, try the troubleshooting suggestions in "Troubleshooting Network and Other Internal Adapters" earlier in this chapter.

Under certain circumstances, aggressive video driver settings can cause problems with the monitor. If problems persist, try reducing graphics hardware acceleration. The appropriate setting is often determined by trial and error. For more information about changing hardware acceleration settings, see "Changing Hardware Acceleration Settings for Graphics Hardware" in this chapter.

Troubleshooting Multiple Monitors

- When using multiple monitors, you can avoid problems during Windows XP Professional startup by taking the following precautions:

    - **Keep all monitors turned on during startup**. This precaution lets you keep track of the image on your screen, which can move from one monitor to another during startup. You can then set your primary and secondary monitor preferences: in Control Panel, open **Display** and click the **Settings** tab. For more information about adjusting multiple monitor settings, see Windows XP Professional Help and Support Center.

    - **Verify the BIOS video card initialization sequence**. Some system firmware gives you the option of initializing either the PCI or Advanced Graphics Port (AGP) first. You might be able to avoid the video shift from one monitor to another by setting the BIOS values to match your primary and secondary monitor preferences in Windows XP Professional. Consult your hardware documentation before you make any changes to the BIOS.

Troubleshooting a Universal Serial Bus Device

USB devices are typically reliable and easy to install. However, problems can arise when a new USB device is installed, or when other changes are made to the system that affect a USB device. Windows XP Professional provides error messages when certain USB error conditions are encountered. Refer to the error messages, a description of the error conditions, and recommended solutions in this section to help troubleshoot these problems. Begin with the following USB troubleshooting checklist, which provides suggestions for solutions to common problems with USB devices.

For a step-by-step approach to troubleshooting USB problems, see the USB Troubleshooter in Windows XP Professional Help and Support.

USB Troubleshooting Checklist

Adding a USB device might cause your system to stop responding. If resetting the computer does not solve the problem, turn off the computer, and try restarting it. If startup or stability problems persist, try any of the following troubleshooting suggestions:

- To troubleshoot problems with the USB controller, refer to Table 9.5, earlier in this chapter. USB controllers are either built into the computer or are available as add-on PCI adapters.

- Follow the manufacturer's installation instructions for the USB device. Some installations require that you run a setup program before plugging the device into your computer.

- Plug the device into another computer to make sure that the problem is not due to your computer configuration. If you can reproduce the problem, the USB device might be malfunctioning.

- If the device is attached to a USB hub, unplug it from the hub and reconnect it. Turn the hub off and on or connect the device directly to a free USB port on the computer.

- Check the Event Log for USB-related error messages. The message can provide clues or other valuable information about the problem.

- Check Device Manager to make sure that all devices on the **Universal Serial bus controllers** tree are functioning properly. Setting Device Manager to show USB devices by connection is usually the easiest way to spot a faulty device. Check that the device is not disabled. If a yellow exclamation point precedes a device, check Windows Update or contact your hardware vendor to obtain the most recent, compatible driver.

Note   Some x86-based motherboards with built-in USB controllers feature a BIOS option labeled **Assign IRQ to USB**. This option must be set to **on** or **yes** for USB devices to function.

- Verify that you are not exceeding USB power limits. If a USB device attempts to draw more than 500 milliamps (mA) of electrical current, the device must be accompanied by a wall adapter to draw the additional power. If you are unsure about total USB power consumption for your system, use the power supply if one is furnished with your device to guarantee adequate power.

- The USB specification allows up to five external hubs to be connected in a chain.

- Always use the cables included with the device and replace damaged or worn cables with an identical type. USB cables come in many kinds and lengths, depending on the capability of the device. Using incorrect cables can degrade performance or cause the device to stop functioning.

To view information about USB power consumption

1. Open Device Manager, and then expand Universal Serial Bus controllers.

2. Double-click USB Root Hub.

3. Click the Power Management tab to view information about power consumption.

Installing Unsupported USB Devices

When you install a USB device and an appropriate driver exists in the Driver.cab file, the device is configured without the operating system requesting a device driver. However, some USB devices might not be supported with Windows XP Professional drivers.

When you attempt to install an unsupported device, Windows XP Professional prompts you for the appropriate driver. When prompted, select the location on removable media that contains the drivers supplied by the device manufacturer drivers. You can optionally specify a network location.

> **Note** The fact that a USB device functions properly in Microsoft® Windows® 98 or Microsoft® Windows® 2000 does not guarantee problem-free installation in Windows XP Professional. Some USB devices might stop functioning if you upgrade to Windows XP Professional without updating drivers. Be sure to verify that USB peripherals are on the Windows XP Professional HCL, or that the driver supplied by the manufacturer is compatible with Windows XP Professional.

USB User Interface Error Detection

The USB error detection and correction scheme uses WMI event-driven architecture to resolve errors. The interface notifies the user when a problem occurs on the bus, gives information about the error, and suggests solutions.

When the user clicks on an error message, a dialog box appears that shows the following:

■ A description of the error condition.

■ The tree-view, which is a topological view of the bus. The tree is expanded so that the device in question is displayed, selected, and in bold.

■ A recommended user action, which depends on the current topology of devices on the bus.

The following six error conditions reported for USB devices result in messages that give error descriptions, and some also give troubleshooting advice:

■ **Electrical surge on hub port**. Either a device attached to the port, or the port itself, has drawn more current than allowed, and the hub turned off the port. The port will not function correctly until you reset it. If the device is the cause, it must be detached before resetting the port. To reset the port, disconnect the device, and then click **Reset** in the dialog box. If the port is the cause, close the dialog box, and do the following to re-enable the port:

    1. Disconnect the hub.

    2. Re-attach the hub.

    3. If it is the root hub, unplug all attached USB devices from the computer, and (if they have power supplies) unplug them from the electric supply. After a few moments, reconnect the devices. The computer can be restarted at any time.

■ **USB hub port power exceeded**. A device that requires more than 100 mA has been plugged into a bus-powered hub that can supply only 100 mA to each of its ports. The device will not work until it is plugged into a self-powered hub, or into a root hub, that supplies 500 mA to each port. Disconnect the problem device and reconnect it to an unused port that meets its power requirements. (The error dialog box lists the appropriate port in bold.)

■ **USB host controller bandwidth exceeded**. A device request for allocation of bandwidth has failed because the USB host controller is in full use and has no spare bandwidth. Typically, devices support several settings at various levels of bandwidth. A device tries to allocate the highest bandwidth, progressively metering itself back after each bandwidth allocation fails. Repeated requests trigger an error condition.

It is recommended that you close some applications that are using USB devices that use bandwidth. In Device Manager you can view the property page for the host controller to see bandwidth status. Pressing **Refresh** in the dialog box after making any changes updates bandwidth data to show whether bandwidth is freed.

- **Maximum number of hubs surpassed**. Six or more USB hubs are linked in a chain, and the USB specification allows a maximum of five. It is recommended that you remove the most recently connected hub and connect it to a port that is highlighted on the tree view list in green (signifying that it is free and recommended).

- **Device enumeration failure**. A device is plugged into a USB port, but the operating system does not recognize the device. The failure can have various causes. For example, the device might not initialize properly when it is plugged in, or the device driver might be faulty. If the cause is not a permanent malfunction in the physical device, unplugging and plugging the device in again might allow it to enumerate properly.

- **Identical serial numbers**. The serial number in a device, if it exists, must be unique for each device that shares the same USB Vendor ID and Product ID. Occasionally hardware vendors mistakenly program devices with identical serial numbers. When two or more USB devices with identical serial numbers are plugged into the same system, only the first one plugged in functions. For further assistance, contact the hardware vendor.

For more information about the USB standard, see the USB link on the Web Resources page at http://www.microsoft.com/windows/reskits/webresources.

For more information about troubleshooting USB, see the Microsoft Knowledge Base link on the Web Resources page at www.microsoft.com/windows/reskits/webresources. Search the Knowledge Base using the keywords *USB* and *USB troubleshooting*.

Troubleshooting IEEE 1394 Bus Devices

Although IEEE 1394 devices are generally reliable, problems do arise with these devices, often when changes are made to the system. The following suggestions for troubleshooting IEEE 1394 devices can help to solve hardware problems:

- When installing PCI IEEE 1394 adapters, refer to the troubleshooting options listed in Table 9.5, earlier in this chapter. Some manufacturers provide IEEE 1394 controllers that are integrated into the motherboard, while others offer them as optional components.

- Follow the manufacturer's installation instructions. Some IEEE 1394 hardware installations require that you run a setup program before plugging the device into your computer.

- Install the IEEE 1394 adapter and peripherals in another computer to make sure that the problem is not due to your computer configuration. If you can reproduce the problem, the IEEE 1394 adapter or the connected device might be malfunctioning.

- Be sure to use the correct cables and follow the manufacturer's recommendations for length and type. For example, four-pin IEEE 1394 connectors do not provide power to connected devices, so you must use a separate power adapter. Six-pin connectors do provide power if IEEE 1394 bus power specifications are not exceeded and electrical current is supplied while your computer is on. If problems occur, use the power supply packaged with your device.

- For security reasons, you cannot simultaneously connect IEEE 1394 storage devices to multiple Windows XP Professional computers. By design, Windows XP Professional does not mount an IEEE 1394 storage device that is being used by another computer. You must disconnect an IEEE 1394 hard disk from one computer before another computer can use it.

- "Bus-resets" might cause a data flow interruption immediately after a device is attached or removed. Avoid connecting or detaching an IEEE 1394 device during a time-critical operation such as capturing video or burning a CD-ROM. Add or remove devices only during idle periods.

For more information about the IEEE 1394 standard, see the IEEE 1394 link on the Web Resources page at http://www.microsoft.com/windows/reskits/webresources.

Additional Resources

These resources contain additional information related to this chapter.

Related Information

- "Supporting Installations" in this book for information about device detection during system startup.

- "Connecting Remote Offices" in this book for information about Universal Plug and Play.

- "Enabling Printing and Faxing" in this book for information about using printers.

- "Supporting Mobile Users" in this book for information about power management on portable computers.

- "Tools for Troubleshooting" in this book for information about troubleshooting hardware.

- The Windows Update link on the Web Resources page at http://www.microsoft.com/windows/reskits/webresources.

- The Driver Development Kits link on the Web Resources page at http:// www.microsoft.com/windows/reskits/webresources.

- The Microsoft Knowledge Base link on the Web Resources page at http:// www.microsoft.com/windows/reskits/webresources for information about troubleshooting devices.

- The Hardware Development link on the Web Resources page at http:// www.microsoft.com/windows/reskits/webresources.

- The OnNow link on the Web Resources page at http://www.microsoft.com/ windows/reskits/webresources for information about the OnNow power management initiative.

- The ACPI link on the Web Resources page at http://www.microsoft.com/windows/reskits/webresources.

- The Plug and Play link on the Web Resources page at http:// www.microsoft.com/windows/reskits/webresources.

Chapter 10

Managing Digital Media

Microsoft® Windows® XP Professional provides applications and tools that corporate managers and network administrators can use to create, use, and manage digital media content. You can configure workstations to take advantage of digital media functionality. Audio, video, and other digital media content can be combined into live and streaming presentations that can be broadcast over your corporate intranet and on the Web.

Related Information

- For more information about telephony, videophones, and digital media conferences, see "Configuring Telephony and Teleconferencing" in this book.

- For more information about digital video cameras, see "Managing Devices" in this book.

- For more information about deploying custom configurations using Group Policy and local policy, see "Managing Desktops" in this book.

Digital Media Components Overview

Windows XP Professional includes components and applications designed to provide a rich digital-media experience, including DirectX®, DVD technologies, and Windows Media™ Technologies. Each of these is described in detail in the following sections.

DirectX 8.1

The DirectX® version 8.1 application programming interface (API) includes a group of technologies that make Microsoft® Windows®-based computers ideal for running applications that are rich in full-color video, three-dimensional (3-D) graphics, interactive music, and multi-channel sound. DirectX gives software quick and transparent access to a broad range of peripherals such as graphics cards, audio devices, and input devices.

DirectX provides a hardware abstraction layer (HAL) between digital media software and computer hardware, which makes it easier to develop device-independent applications. Digital media applications created with DirectX can run on any Windows-based computer, regardless of hardware, enabling these applications to take full advantage of high-performance hardware capabilities.

DirectX tools simplify the creation and playback of digital media content, and make it easier to integrate a wide range of digital media elements such as video and audio.

Table 10-1 describes the DirectX 8.1 technologies.

Table 10-1   DirectX 8.1 Technologies

DirectX 8.1 Technology	Description
DirectX Graphics	Combines DirectDraw® and Direct3D® APIs into one component. It manipulates display modes, displays directly from memory, provides hardware overlay support and flipping surface support, and enables a drawing interface for 3-D video display hardware.
DirectX Audio	Combines DirectSound® and DirectMusic® APIs into one component. It captures, mixes, and plays multiple audio signals; manages hardware voices; enables 3-D audio in applications; and creates interactive, variable music soundtracks. DirectSound is not a feature of Microsoft® Windows® XP 64-Bit Edition.
DirectPlay®	A media-independent networking API that connects multi-user applications over the Internet, a modem link, or an intranet.

Table 10-1   DirectX 8.1 Technologies

DirectX 8.1 Technology	Description
DirectShow®	A media-streaming API that enables digital media streams to be captured and played back by Microsoft® Windows Media™ Player. The streams can contain compressed video and audio data in a wide variety of formats.
	As part of DirectShow, Microsoft TV Technologies includes support for the Broadcast Driver Architecture, which defines a framework that supports various devices for receiving digital and analog television. Microsoft TV Technologies is not a feature of Windows XP 64-Bit Edition.
	Also a part of DirectShow, DirectX Video Acceleration is an API and a corresponding device driver interface that allows hardware acceleration of digital video decoding.
DirectInput®	Enables support for input devices, such as joysticks, and for input/output devices, such as force-feedback controllers.

The following features and tools provide additional graphics capabilities, diagnostics, and information about using DirectX.

Open Graphics Library 1.1

Windows XP Professional supports the Open Graphics Library (OpenGL) 1.1 specification. OpenGL is an API that provides high-performance 3-D graphics capabilities for applications and allows them to be independent of any operating system. The Microsoft implementation of OpenGL in Windows XP Professional provides software with which programmers can create high-quality still and animated three-dimensional color images and it supports applications running on Windows XP Professional that are developed using OpenGL, such as some computer-aided design/computer-aided manufacturing (CAD/CAM) graphics applications.

DirectX Diagnostic Tool

Windows XP Professional includes the DirectX Diagnostic Tool for diagnosing problems with DirectX drivers and digital media hardware. You can use this tool to obtain detailed information, such as the configuration of any device or driver using DirectX, as well as to test these devices specifically. For more information about using the DirectX Diagnostic Tool, see "Common Problems with Playing Digital Media" later in this chapter.

DirectX Software Development Kit

The Microsoft® DirectX® Software Development Kit (SDK) includes code samples, diagnostic tools, and sample applications. You can order the SDK on CD-ROM or download it. For more information, see the DirectX link on the Web Resources page at http://www.microsoft.com/windows/reskits/webresources.

DVD Formats and Devices

DVD (digital video disc) is an optical disc storage medium that can hold high quantities of video, high-quality audio, and application data in a single format. DVD devices can read multiple digital data streams concurrently for playback of digital media, including full-length motion pictures.

Full-motion video is stored on DVD in the Moving Pictures Experts Group (MPEG)-2 format. Most DVD implementations include a software decoder with MPEG hardware acceleration provided by the video adapter.

To be DVD-ready, a computer system must include a video card with a minimum of 4 megabytes (MB) video RAM (VRAM) (16 MB recommended) capable of displaying at least 800 x 600 pixels at 16 bits per pixel (BPP).

DVDs provide the following benefits:

- DVD discs and devices provide cost-effective storage for large data files.

- Devices that read and write DVDs provide a wide range of recording options.

- DVD discs played on a computer running Windows XP Professional yield even better video quality than discs played on standard DVD video players connected to a television because computer monitors can achieve greater image quality.

DVD Formats

DVD uses both physical and application formats. Physical formats for DVD media are the following:

- **DVD-ROM**. DVD read-only-memory.

- **DVD-R**. DVD-recordable. Supports one-time recording

- **DVD-RAM**. Supports many-time recording.

- **DVD-RW and DVD+RW**. Rewritable disc formats that are not compatible with DVD-RAM

Application formats for DVD include **DVD-Video**, which defines how video programs are stored on disc and how they are played; and **DVD-Audio**, which provides a separate DVD-Audio zone for audio content on the disc.

DVD Architecture

DVD architecture includes hardware and software components. The components of each system vary depending on whether DVD decoding is accomplished with a hardware decoder or with a software decoder. Software decoders are often bundled with multimedia PCs and vendors often include software decoders with DVD drives and video cards. Windows XP Professional supports both software and hardware decoders.

In addition, DVD architecture includes hardware and software components that operate at three different levels. The application level provides components that interact with and are produced by applications and other software. The kernel level provides drivers and file system formats such as the Windows Driver Model (WDM) streaming-class driver and the Universal Disk Format (UDF) file system. The hardware level includes DVD drives, sound cards, and video cards.

Figure 10-1 illustrates Windows XP Professional software DVD decoding architecture.

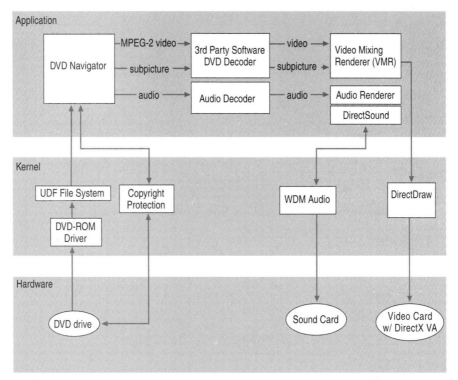

Figure 10-1   Windows XP Professional software DVD decoding architecture

Figure 10-2 illustrates the Windows XP Professional hardware DVD decoding architecture.

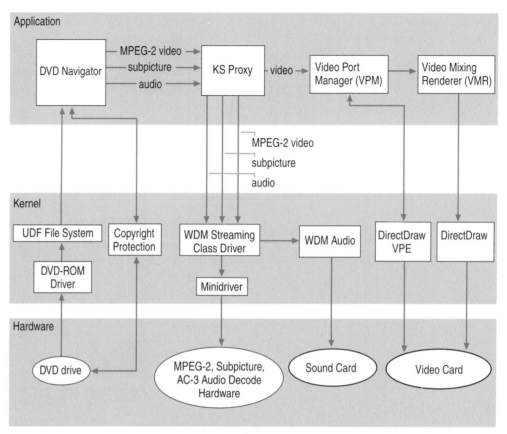

Figure 10-2 Windows XP Professional hardware DVD decoding architecture

Application Level A DVD decoder is third-party software or a third-party device that is required to decode DVD video, audio, and subpicture data. The other application-level components read the DVD data and pass it along to the decoder. The application level for DVD video display includes the components listed in Table 10-2 and discussed in detail in the following sections.

Table 10-2 Application-Level DVD Decoder Components

Component	Software	Hardware
DVD Navigator	X	X
MPEG-2	X	X
AC-3 audio	X	X
Subpicture	X	X

Table 10-2   Application-Level DVD Decoder Components

Component	Software	Hardware
Third-party software DVD decoder	X	
Audio decoder	X	
Video mixing renderer (VMR)	X	X
Audio renderer	X	
KS proxy		X
Video Port Manager (VPM)		X

DVD Navigator   DVD Navigator reads the disc and produces audio and video streams that are sent to a decoder. The decoder output is then sent to audio and video renderers. DirectShow provides support for DVD Navigator, WDM proxy filters for hardware decoders, video mixer/renderers, and audio renderers.

The data streams necessary to play a full-length DVD movie include not only the MPEG video portion (possibly with closed captioning), but also digital audio, which can have Dolby surround sound. For the same video segment, a DVD can provide multiple languages, soundtracks, subtitle tracks, camera angles, and rating levels. DVD Navigator uses DirectShow to track these various data streams and pass them to the proper codec (coder/decoder hardware that can convert audio or video signals between analog and digital forms). For more information about DirectShow, see "DirectX 8.1" in this chapter.

> **Note**   The term *codec* can stand for **coder/decoder**, which is hardware that converts audio or video signals between analog and digital forms and it can stand for **compressor/decompressor**, which is hardware or software that compresses and uncompresses audio or video data. The specific definition of the term is provided when it is used in context throughout this chapter.

MPEG-2   Moving Pictures Experts Group (MPEG)-2 is a standard for video compression that saves space by removing redundant information (such as areas of the picture that do not change) and by removing information that is not readily perceptible to the human eye.

AC-3 audio   AC-3 is a type of audio stream developed by Dolby Labs. It allows up to six separate audio channels: left and right front, left and right rear, center, and a subwoofer channel.

Subpicture   DVDs contain a data stream called a *subpicture*. The subpicture stream delivers the subtitles and any other add-on data, such as system help, director's comments, and menus, which can be displayed while playing digital media.

Third-party software DVD decoder The software decoder processes the video and subpicture data, and passes it along to the Video Mixing Renderer (VMR).

Audio decoder The audio decoder processes audio data into a form usable by an audio renderer.

Video Mixing Renderer A video mixing renderer (VMR) is the default renderer (display mechanism) for Windows XP Professional. It supports blending video input streams with transparency information. It allows third-party implementation of custom video effects.

Audio renderer The audio renderer has a DirectShow component that sends audio data to an audio driver.

KS proxy The Kernel Stream (KS) proxy is a DirectShow filter that sends data to the kernel mode drivers. It sends video data to a Video Port Manager (VPM), and sends MPEG-2, AC-3 and subpicture data to a WDM streaming-class driver.

Video Port Manager (VPM) A Video Port Manager (VPM) is a DirectShow filter that enables the VMR to work seamlessly on systems where video data is transferred directly from a video capture device or hardware decoder to the graphics chip without going over the system bus. The direct hardware connection is called a video port.

Kernel Level The kernel level for DVD video display includes the components listed in Table 10.3 and discussed in detail in the following sections.

Table 10-3   Kernel-Level DVD Decoder Components

Component	Software	Hardware
DVD-ROM driver	X	X
UDF file system	X	X
Copyright protection	X	X
WDM audio	X	X
DirectDraw	X	X
WDM streaming-class driver		X
DirectX Graphics HAL with VPE		X

DVD-ROM driver Windows XP Professional provides a DVD-ROM driver, which supports the DVD-ROM industry-defined command set known as the MMC-3 specification.

UDF file system The file system on many DVDs is UDF, which is a standard defined by the Optical Storage Technology Association (OSTA). UDF is compliant with the International Standards Organization (ISO) 13346 specification and is intended to succeed the CD-ROM File System (CDFS).

Windows XP Professional supports writing to DVD-RAM discs by using the FAT32 and FAT16 file formats. Windows XP Professional does not support writing in UDF file format, but it does support reading UDF version 2.0 files, as well as all previous versions of UDF. For more information about UDF, see "File Systems" in this book.

Copyright protection   DVDs are both copy protected and distribution protected. Encrypting the content on the disc provides copyright protection. Distribution protection is achieved by restricting playback of discs to specified geographical regions. The DVD publisher determines the region in which a disc can be played; Windows XP Professional responds to the region encoding.

The DVD Forum has set up eight worldwide regions and assigned them a region code, as shown in Table 10-4.

Table 10-4   DVD Region Codes

Code	Country/Region
1	Canada, USA, United States Territories
2	Japan, Europe, South Africa, Middle East (including Egypt)
3	Southeast Asia, East Asia (including Hong Kong SAR)
4	Australia, New Zealand, Pacific Islands, Central America, Mexico, South America, Caribbean
5	Former Soviet Union, Indian Subcontinent, North Korea, Mongolia, Africa
6	China
7	(Reserved, currently unused)
8	Special international venues (including in-flight airlines, cruise ships, and so on)

In Device Manager, on the DVD drive Properties page, the user can set the DVD region code a limited number of times. For more information, see Windows XP Professional Help and Support Center.

WDM audio   Windows Driver Model (WDM) audio receives audio data from the audio renderer. It also routes and mixes an unlimited number of audio streams, and handles software wavetable synthesis and software emulation of older hardware.

DirectDraw   DirectDraw is a DirectX Graphics component that provides a drawing interface for video display hardware.

WDM streaming-class driver   The WDM driver supports streaming data types, and supports MPEG-2 and AC-3 hardware decoders. It optimizes interconnection of devices that encode data (such as video capture devices) and devices that decode data (such as DVD hardware decoders that decode MPEG-2 streams for playing DVD movies). It also handles common operating-system tasks such as direct memory access (DMA) and Plug and Play.

DirectX Graphics HAL with VPE   The DirectX Graphics hardware abstraction layer (HAL) with Video Port Extensions (VPE) helps with data transfer. Decoded video files can become large enough to cause problems with data transfer. An encoded MPEG-2 stream travels at a rate of 5 to 10 megabits per second (Mbps). After the stream is decoded, it can easily exceed 100 Mbps. Processing this amount of information in a continuous stream can overwhelm the PCI bus. To avoid this, most of the decoding can be handled at the hardware level by using dedicated MPEG-decoder cards.

Support for these decoder cards is built into DirectX, by means of DirectX Graphics support for VPEs. The VPEs allow the MPEG stream to be written directly to the memory of the video card from the MPEG decoder card by means of a dedicated cable. DirectX Graphics tracks the display and synchronization of the data while allowing the data stream to move directly through the hardware layer. For more information about DirectX Graphics, see "DirectX 8.1" in this chapter.

Hardware Level   The hardware level for DVD video display includes the components listed in Table 10-5 and discussed in detail in the following sections.

Table 10-5   Hardware-Level DVD Decoder Components

Component	Software	Hardware
DVD decoders	X	X
Sound card	X	X
Video card		X
Video card with DirectX VA	X	
MPEG-2, subpicture, AC-3 audio decoding hardware		X

DVD decoders   DVD-Video requires a DVD drive and a decoder. A software decoder for DVD is third party software that must be purchased and installed before the DVD player can play MPEG-2 encoded video. If your system does not come with a decoder already installed by the manufacturer, you must obtain a decoder to play a DVD movie.

> **Note**   If you have installed a DVD decoder, and then you upgrade your computer from Microsoft® Windows® 98 or Microsoft® Windows® Millennium Edition to Windows XP Professional, your decoder will no longer function. You might be able to upgrade your current decoder, otherwise you will need to install a new DVD decoder. If Windows XP Professional does not automatically guide you through upgrading your decoder, then check with your decoder manufacturer for an updated decoder.

Sound card   The sound card produces the sound that is played through the speakers or headphones.

MPEG-2, subpicture, and AC-3 Audio decoding hardware   You can purchase this hardware decoder from a third-party vendor.

Video card   The video card produces the video on the display.

Video card with DirectX VA   The video card produces the video on the display. Direct X Video Acceleration (VA) is an API and corresponding Device Driver Interface (DDI) for hardware acceleration of the processing of digital video decoding.

For more information about DVD drives and decoders supported by Windows XP Professional, see "If you do not have a DVD decoder" in Windows XP Professional Help and Support Center.

Windows Media Technologies

The following are Windows Media Technologies:

- **Microsoft® Windows Media™ Player for Microsoft® Windows® XP**. A client for media playback.

- **Windows Movie Maker**. A feature that enables users to transfer video to their computers.

- **Windows Media™ Tools**. A set of content-development tools.

- **Windows Media Services**   A server for distributing digital content.

- **SDKs**   For both the client and server, enabling third parties to create commercial products that are compatible with Windows Media.

Media content is stored in Windows Media™ file formats, and is compressed and decompressed by built-in Windows Media–based codecs. You can encrypt Windows Media files by using Windows Media Digital Rights Management (DRM) to secure them against unauthorized distribution.

Windows Media Player for Windows XP

Using Windows Media Player for Windows XP, you can play both downloaded and streaming digital media content in various file formats, including:

- Advanced streaming format (.asf)

- Windows Media audio file (.wma)

- Windows Media video file (.wmv)

- MP3

- Audio-video interleaved (.avi)

- Waveform-audio (.wav)

Windows Media Player includes a number of features in a single application: CD player, DVD player, audio and video player, media jukebox, media guide, Internet radio, portable-device music-file transfer, and an audio CD recorder.

Note   Windows Media Player cannot play a DVD unless you have a decoder installed on your computer.

Windows Media Player can run the streaming and nonstreaming file types shown in Table 10-6.

Table 10-6   File Formats Supported by Windows Media Player

File Type	File Name Extensions
Windows Media audio and video formats	.asf, .asx, .wma, .wmv, .wax, .wmd, .wmp, .wvx, .wmx, .wm
Windows Media Player skins	.wmz, .wms
MPEG	.mpg, .mpeg, .m1v, .mp2,.mpa, .mpe, mp2v, .mpv2[*]
CD Audio	.cda
Intel Indeo video technology	.ivf
MIDI	.mid, .midi, .rmi
Apple QuickTime 1 & 2, Macintosh AIFF Resource	.qt, .aif, .aifc, .aiff, .mov
UNIX formats	.au, .snd
MP3	.mp3, .m3u
DVD video	.vob
Windows audio and video files	.avi, .wav
Other formats	.avi, .wav

* To play.mp2v files you must have a software or hardware DVD decoder installed on your computer.

Windows Media Player works with the server to negotiate the most efficient allocation of bandwidth and deliver high-quality streaming media. The higher the bandwidth of your Internet connection, the better the quality of the streaming digital media. The best results are achieved by using a high-speed connection such as a T1 connection, a cable modem, or a digital subscriber line (DSL).

> **Note**   Windows XP 64-Bit Edition does not support Windows Media Player.

Windows Movie Maker

Windows Movie Maker is a standard feature of Windows XP Professional. Using Windows Movie Maker, you can transfer a video into Windows Media™ Format on your PC by using base-level video or audio capture features. You can also create simple arrangements, do simple editing of video and audio, and then distribute the results by using e-mail—or over the Internet for downloaded or streaming play.

A primary feature of Windows Movie Maker is automatic shot-boundary detection. When you record or import video into Windows Movie Maker, the application detects when a shot changes, and produces a thumbnail image of the shot. This defines your video as a collection of *clips*, which provides a random-access visual index to the video and allows the video to be easily edited.

Windows Movie Maker is designed for the home user, but business users can use this technology to create videos for training and sales presentations. In addition, corporate customers can enhance their presentations by using the stand-alone application Microsoft® Producer, which is described in the following section.

For more information about Windows Movie Maker, see the Windows Media Technologies link on the Web Resources page at http://www.microsoft.com/windows/reskits/webresources.

> **Note**   Windows XP 64-Bit Edition does not support Windows Movie Maker.

Microsoft Producer

Microsoft® Producer is a stand-alone application that uses Windows Media Technologies. It allows business professionals to create, lay out, edit, and publish rich-media presentations that synchronize audio and video with slides, and translate into HTML, and other data types. You can record a new Windows Media file by using a Direct-Show supported capture device, or by importing existing audio/video files. You can create and synchronize presentation elements by using different wizards or by working directly on the timeline, which allows you to see the order and timing of the various media used throughout the presentation. Once you have completed the presentation, you can use the Publishing wizard to make the final presentation available from a corporate intranet site, the Web, a shared network location, or a CD.

For more information about Microsoft Producer, see the Windows Media Technologies link on the Web Resources page at http://www.microsoft.com/windows/reskits/webresources.

Windows Media Tools and Features

Windows Media Tools and features help you to create and publish content in Windows Media™ Format. Windows Media Tools include the following:

- **Windows Media™ Software Development Kit (SDK)**. A family of components that enable product vendors, content developers, and systems administrators to make their applications and Internet sites secure and compatible with Windows Media. You can download the Windows Media SDK from the Windows Media Technologies Web site link on the Web Resources page at http://www.microsoft.com/windows/reskits/webresources.

- **Windows Media Format**. A high-quality, secure format for film, television, computer, and CD-sourced digital media content. You can download Windows Media Format from the Windows Media Technologies Web site link on the Web Resources page at http://www.microsoft.com/windows/reskits/webresources.

- **Windows Media Rights Manager**. An end-to-end digital rights management system that offers content providers and retailers a flexible platform for secure distribution of digital media content. Windows Media Rights Manager version 7 can be installed and run on Microsoft® Windows® 2000–based servers. You can download Windows Media Rights Manager from the Windows Media Technologies Web site link on the Web Resources page at http://www.microsoft.com/windows/reskits/webresources.

- **Windows Media Encoder**. A production tool for converting both live and prerecorded audio, video, and computer screen images to Windows Media Format. Windows Media Encoder can be used to encode a stored or live stream of data by converting the data to Windows Media Format, using a file or a capture card as the source. You can also add scripts manually to the converted data while encoding from a live source. You can download Windows Media Encoder from the Windows Media Technologies Web site link on the Web Resources page at http://www.microsoft.com/windows/reskits/webresources.

- **Windows Media™ Services**. A set of services that facilitates the distribution of audio, video, and other media to client computers by providing file-access permissions. Windows Media™ Services version 4.1 is the current version, which runs on a Microsoft® Windows® 2000–based server. Windows Media Services can be installed as an optional component in Windows 2000 Server, and can be downloaded from the Windows Media Technologies Web site link on the Web Resources page at http://www.microsoft.com/windows/reskits/webresources.

Note Windows XP 64-Bit Edition does not support Windows Media Services.

For more information about Windows Media Tools, see the Windows Media Technologies link on the Web Resources page at http://www.microsoft.com/windows/reskits/webresources.

Accelerated Graphics Port

An Accelerated Graphics Port (AGP) is a dedicated high-speed port that delivers video and graphics data over PCI buses. AGP technology allows large blocks of 3-D graphic data to be moved between the computer's graphics controller and its system memory by providing higher bandwidth, reduced device contention, and the ability to render graphics directly from system memory.

AGP has the following advantages over PCI video adapters:

- AGP peak bandwidth is up to four times higher than PCI bandwidth.

- AGP has higher sustained rates due to sideband addressing and split transactions.

- AGP is a dedicated bus, which reduces conflicts with other devices.

- AGP allows the CPU to write directly to shared system memory, which is much faster than writing to local video memory.

- AGP can read 3-D graphic data from shared system memory while reading and writing other data from local video memory, thereby enabling faster rendering of high-resolution 3-D scenes.

To use an AGP video adapter, a computer must have an AGP graphics controller and a Pentium II LX–compatible or higher processor.

Optimizing Workstations for Digital Media

In Windows XP Professional, both users and network administrators can configure workstations to optimize for digital media and customize personal preferences such as audio playback levels. Network administrators can use Group Policy and local policies to configure custom desktop settings and profiles across the network. For example, your company or group can configure individualized custom sound configurations for employees and customers with special needs or alternate language requirements.

For information about setting custom desktop settings and profiles by using Group Policy, see "Managing Desktops" in this book.

The following sections discuss specific aspects of configuring for digital media.

Configuring Sounds and Video

You can assign sounds to system and program events, such as Windows XP Professional startup or when a user logs off. You can save different combinations of event and sound pairings as custom sound schemes. You can also specify default devices to use for playing and recording sound.

Configuring Sound Events and Sound Schemes

To assign a particular sound to a specific system or program event, you must configure the event and sound pairing and save it as a custom sound scheme. You can configure sound events and sound schemes in **Control Panel**. Click **Sounds, Speech, and Audio Devices**, and then click **Sounds and Audio Devices**.

For information about recording sounds to use for sound events or in your custom sound schemes, see "Using Digital Media" later in this chapter.

For more information about configuring digital-media hardware devices and options, see "Configuring Digital Media Devices" later in this chapter.

Configuring Preferred Playback and Recording Devices

If a workstation has multiple audio playback and recording devices, you can specify the preferred devices to use when playing or recording sound. You can also specify the default playback or recording volume for that device. Preferred playback and recording devices are specified using **Sounds and Audio Devices** in Control Panel or from the **Tools** menu in Windows Media Player.

To configure analog or digital audio CD playback

1. In Windows Media Player, click **Tools**, and then click **Options**.

2. On the **Devices** tab, double-click the CD device you want to use for audio CD playback and recording.

3. Under **Playback** and **Copy**, select **Digital** or **Analog**.

You can specify a default playback or recording level by setting volume controls for a device that you want to use for playing MIDI music.

To configure a preferred MIDI music playback device

1. In **Control Panel**, click **Sounds, Speech, and Audio Devices**, and then click **Sounds and Audio Devices**.

2. On the **Audio** tab, under **MIDI Music Playback**, click the preferred device for playing MIDI music.

3. To specify the default playback or recording level for the selected device, click **Volume**, and then set the volume controls.

4. To display information about the selected device, click **About**.

For more information about using MIDI devices, see "Playing Digital Media" later in this chapter.

Configuring Audio Performance Options

Windows XP Professional lets you optimize audio playback and recording performance by specifying the default hardware acceleration and sample-rate conversion quality. The default hardware acceleration setting for Windows XP Professional is "Full," which enables all acceleration features. The default sampling-rate conversion quality is "Good," which provides reasonable quality with fast performance.

You can configure audio performance options in Control Panel. Click **Sounds, Speech, and Audio Devices**, and then click **Sounds and Audio Devices**.

Configuring CD and DVD Playback Options

In Windows XP Professional, you can select a default application for playing CDs and DVDs. You can use a third-party DVD player application provided with your DVD device or you can select Windows Media Player as your default CD or DVD player application.

To select Windows Media Player as your default CD or DVD player application

1. In Windows Media Player, click **Tools**, and then click **Options**.

2. On the **File Types** tab select the file types for which Windows Media Player should be the default player.

> **Note**   If you install a third party CD or DVD player after you set Windows Media Player as your default application, the third-party player might register itself as the default. If this happens, you must set the default player to Windows Media Player again, if you want it to be your default CD or DVD player.

You can also select actions to for Windows to perform when inserting a CD or DVD that contains different media file types, such as automatically playing a file or opening the folder to view the available music files, or, for pictures, viewing a slide-show of the images or printing the pictures. You can also choose to have Windows XP Professional automatically perform the action, display a prompt to choose an action, or to take no action at all when that file type is encountered. The action is taken whenever the specific file type is encountered in the data from the CD or DVD drive. These AutoPlay settings are available for pictures, music files, video, and mixed content.

To select AutoPlay actions for different content types

1. In **Windows Explorer**, right-click the CD or DVD drive, and then click **Properties**.

2. On the **AutoPlay** tab, in the drop-down list box, select the content type you want to configure.

3. In the **Actions** area, select the **Select an action to perform** button, and then select an action from the list.

4. Click **Apply**.

5. Repeat steps 2 through 4 for each content type and click **OK** to close the dialog box.

Configuring Animations, Sounds, and Videos in Internet Explorer

By default, Microsoft Internet Explorer plays animations, sounds, and videos from intranet and Internet sites. However, you can disable any of these to ensure that pages load faster or to create a quiet work environment.

To configure animations, sounds, and videos in Internet Explorer

1. On the **Start** menu, right click the **Internet Explorer** icon and then click **Internet Properties**.

2. On the **Advanced** tab, in the **Settings** dialog box, under **Multimedia**, select or clear the **Play animations in web pages**, **Play sounds in web pages**, or **Play videos in web pages** check boxes.

Configuring Digital Media Devices

In Windows XP Professional you can configure digital media devices—such as the Accelerated Graphics Port (AGP), DVD devices, and digital video cameras—like any other supported device. Windows XP Professional also supports a wide range of Human Interface Devices (HIDs) and other peripherals connected through the Universal Serial Bus (USB) or an IEEE 1394 port. For more information about installing and configuring such devices, see "Managing Devices" in this book.

Configuring a drive to record CDs   When you are writing files to CD, it is recommended that you optimize your computer's disk space for optimal recording speed. To do this, configure your workstation to use another local drive or partition for the temporary storage area that Windows uses to preprocess files before they are written to a CD. You need to have another local drive available, or to have created a partition on your hard drive. For more information about creating partitions on your hard drive, see "Disk Management" in this book.

To select a different drive or partition on which to store temporary files for CD recording

1. In **My Computer**, right-click the CD recording drive, and then click **Properties**.

2. On the **Recording** tab, in the drop-down box, select a drive with at least 700 MB of free disk space to store temporary files.

3. Click **Apply**, and then click **OK**.

Managing digital media devices   You can view a list of installed digital media devices, determine driver versions, perform diagnostics, see what codecs are installed, and more, in Control Panel, under **Sounds and Audio Devices,** on the **Hardware** tab. The **Devices** list shows the audio, video, and digital media devices installed on the workstation. When you click a device in the **Devices** list, information about that device (such as the manufacturer and operational status) is displayed under **Device Properties**. You can also use the System Information component of Windows XP Professional Help and Support Center to view information about the digital media devices and codecs installed on your system.

To view information about installed digital media devices in Help and Support Center

1. In Help and Support Center, click **Use Tools to view your computer information and diagnose problems**, and then click **Advanced System Information**.

2. Click **View detailed system information**.

    A System Summary list of hardware resources, components, software and applications displays.

Using Digital Media

Windows XP Professional offers many possibilities for playing, creating, and distributing digital media content and for using it more effectively.

For more information about configuring audio, video, and digital media devices, and workstation defaults (such as audio playback level), see "Optimizing Workstations for Digital Media" earlier in this chapter.

Playing Digital Media

Windows XP Professional supports a wide range of playback devices and digital media sources, technologies, and file types. For example, you can play audio from a CD, a MIDI device, or a radio station that is broadcasting over the Web. You can play video or other digital media on DVD, or watch a streaming broadcast over the Web by using Windows Media Player.

For more information about specifying preferred devices for playing audio and video, see "Configuring Sounds and Video" earlier in this chapter.

Playing CDs

You can play audio CDs on a CD drive or a DVD drive, but a standard CD drive cannot read DVD discs. When you insert an audio CD into a CD drive, Windows XP Professional starts Windows Media Player.

For more information about using Windows Media Player and playing audio CDs, see "Windows Media Player for Windows XP" earlier in this chapter, or see Windows Media Player Help.

To provide the best possible performance from CD drives, Windows XP Professional includes the 32-bit CD File System (CDFS), which quickly and efficiently reads files on CD. Windows XP Professional supports the UDF file system on DVD. It also reads and writes FAT32 files on DVD, but the UDF file system is more widely used. For more information about file systems on DVD, see "DVD Formats and Devices" earlier in this chapter.

When you are playing audio CDs in Microsoft® Windows® XP, it is important to be aware of the two options for CD playback—digital and analog. With digital playback enabled, the CD drive transmits audio data digitally over the bus and requires a compatible drive. Analog playback uses a cable connected between the CD drive and a sound card in the computer. Digital playback often provides better sound quality than analog, but it results in additional performance overhead.

For more information about configuring analog or digital audio CD playback, see "Configuring Sounds and Video" earlier in this chapter.

Playing Audio from MIDI Devices

Musical Instrument Digital Interface (MIDI) is a serial interface standard that allows for the interconnection of music synthesizers, musical instruments, and computers. Windows XP Professional follows the General MIDI Specification to determine which instruments and sounds to use. This specification is an industry standard that defines a common orchestra, or set of instruments that musicians and developers can use and expect consistent results.

Musicians use MIDI as a music development tool. Virtually all sophisticated electronic music equipment supports MIDI, and MIDI offers a convenient way to precisely control the sounds produced by the equipment. You can also use MIDI for listening to music files created using the MIDI standard. You can download standard MIDI files from the Web and play them using Windows Media Player.

Unlike CDs and digital audio files, MIDI files do not capture and store actual sounds. Instead, a MIDI file is a list of events that describe the specific steps that a sound card or other playback device must take to generate certain sounds. *Events* are described in terms of the value, volume, and duration of a note, the instrument used to play the note, and so on. This allows MIDI files to be much smaller than digital audio files. You can also edit the events, edit and rearrange the music, and compose interactively.

When you play a MIDI file, there are three different locations that create and produce the sound in different ways. When you select your preferred MIDI music playback device, you are also selecting the location of the sound production. Following is a short description of each option.

MIDI devices supported by Windows XP Professional include those discussed in the following sections.

Software synthesizer   Microsoft® GS Wavetable SW Synth, a MIDI software synthesizer, is provided as a feature of Windows XP Professional but can be replaced by a third-party software synthesizer. The software synthesizer displays in the list of MIDI music playback devices as "SW Synth" or "Software Synth." The software synthesizer reproduces instrument sounds by using your computer's memory, instead of the sound card's synthesizer. MIDI software synthesis might produce a higher quality sound with a wider range of instruments than a sound card can process. It also provides a larger variety of sets of sounds, such as downloadable sounds. The MIDI data is converted to audio, which is played on speakers or headphones plugged into the sound card. Because your computer's memory is doing all of the processing and sending music, rather than MIDI instructions, to the sound card, your computer's performance might be slower than when you are using a MIDI device.

Internal sound card   If you select the computer's sound card as your default MIDI playback device, the sound card's hardware synthesizer creates and plays the music. The device listing is usually "FM Synth," "FM Synthesizer," or "Wave Table Synth." The quality of the audio depends on the quality of the sound card and the library of sounds provided with it. The sound quality might not be as good as with a software synthesizer, but the computer's performance is not significantly impacted by using the hardware synthesizer because the sound card is recreating the instrument sounds. The music is then played on speakers or headphones plugged into the sound card.

External MIDI devices   If you want to play a MIDI file on an external MIDI device such as a keyboard, you must select the correct external device from the list of MIDI music playback devices. The device listing is either MPU-401, External MIDI, or MIDI OUT, which are types of MIDI ports on the computer to which the external MIDI device is attached. The MIDI data is sent to the external device, which processes it and plays the audio through speakers or headphones connected to that device. For more information about configuring a MIDI playback device, see "Configuring Sounds and Video" earlier in this chapter.

For more information about MIDI devices and the MIDI standard, see the MIDI Manufacturers Association link on the Web Resources page at http://www.microsoft.com/windows/reskits/webresources.

For more information about playing digital media files using Windows Media Player, see Windows Media Player Help, or see the Windows Media Technologies link on the Web Resources page at http://www.microsoft.com/windows/reskits/webresources.

Creating Digital Media

You can use a wide range of input devices, such as digital video cameras, for creating audio, video, and digital media, and you can design content for a wide range of output formats (CD, DVD, and Web).

Different authoring and editing tools make it much easier to design and create digital media content. Some of the options for common authoring and editing tasks are discussed in the following sections.

Recording, Mixing, and Editing Audio

By using Windows Sound Recorder in Windows XP Professional, you can record audio from a variety of input devices, and then save audio files in a variety of different formats. To use Sound Recorder you must have an audio input device, such as a microphone or a CD-ROM player, attached to the computer.

Once you have recorded an audio file, in Sound Recorder on the **Effects** menu you can add effects (such as echo), increase or decrease the speed and volume, and insert or mix other audio files. You can save audio files in standard CD quality, radio quality, or telephone quality formats. You can also choose a custom format to maximize file compression and use a specific audio format that uses available audio codecs to change the sound quality. For more information about using Sound Recorder to record, mix, and edit audio, see Windows Sound Recorder Help.

To select an audio format

1. On the **Accessories** menu, point to **Entertainment,** and then click **Sound Recorder**.

2. On the **File** menu, click **Properties**.

3. In the **Choose from** box, click **Recording formats**, and then click the **Convert Now** button.

4. In the **Format** box, select a format, and then in the **Attributes** box, select an attribute (such as the sampling frequency or number of channels) that is available for the selected format.

Recording CDs

If you have a CD recording drive installed in your computer, you can record, or write, to a CD by using Windows Explorer in Windows XP Professional. You can write both data and audio files to a CD-R or CD-RW disc.

To create a data CD, use Windows Explorer to copy files and folders to the CD recording drive. Windows XP Professional writes the files to a temporary staging area, where they are held before they are copied to the CD. After you have copied all the files you want to put on the CD, you can record the files to the CD. In Windows Explorer, highlight the CD recording drive. On the **File** menu, click **Write these files to CD**. The CD Writing Wizard appears, and takes you through the steps to finalize writing your files to the CD.

Note   When you write to a CD, you need 1.3 gigabytes (GB) of disk space for writing a full 650 MB of data, less if you are not recording a full CD. This amount of space is necessary for the temporary staging area.

You can also write to an audio CD by using Windows Media Player. When you use Windows Media Player to write an audio CD, the file type is changed to .cda, and the audio CD can be played in any CD player. For more information about creating your own CDs in Windows Media Player, see Windows Media Player Help.

If you are using a CD-RW disc, you can delete files on the disc and append new files to a disc that already contains files.

You cannot duplicate a CD in Windows XP Professional without additional software.

Note   Windows XP 64-Bit Edition does not support writing to CDs.

For more information about writing to CDs, see Windows XP Professional Help and Support Center.

Creating Streaming Content for the Internet

Windows Media Technologies in Windows XP Professional provides a straightforward way to combine audio, video, graphics, animation, and other elements into multimedia presentations that you can broadcast live or on demand over a network.

Using Windows Media Technologies you can create, deliver, and play streaming media files in the advanced streaming format, which includes files with .asf, .wma, and .wmv file extensions. This format solves the problem of long download times by starting playback while the data is still being sent. Windows Media files send the first part of the audio or video data first and collect it in a buffer. While that data is being played, the rest of the data continues to flow in time to be played. This ensures that playback is not interrupted by network congestion. The buffer can be manually increased for best performance by clicking the **Tools** menu in Windows Media Player, clicking **Options,** selecting the **Performance** tab, and changing the buffer size under **Network buffering**.

You can stream both live and on-demand (stored) content. You can stream on-demand content from a Windows 2000-based server with Windows Media Services installed, which provides both standard *unicast streaming* (delivering individual streams of live or on-demand content to multiple clients) and bandwidth-conserving *multicast streaming* (sending a single stream of real-time content to an unlimited number of users).

Creating Digital Media Content Using Intelligent Streaming and Windows Media Encoder Intelligent Streaming is a set of features in Windows Media Technologies. It automatically detects network conditions and adjusts the properties of a video stream to maximize quality. This is important for low-bandwidth modem connections where the connection speed can vary widely depending on network congestion. *Intelligent Streaming* allows users to receive digital media content tailored to their connection speed to maintain a continuous presentation. To accomplish this, the Windows Media stream is encoded at multiple bit rates. In other words, up to 10 discrete video streams are encoded, from the same content, into a single Windows Media stream, each at a different transmission bit rate. The server and the client then automatically determine the current available bandwidth, and the server selects and serves the video stream at the appropriate bit rate.

Windows Media Encoder can encode stored content for on-demand playback. In addition, it lets you encode live audio and video feeds and then add them to dynamic mixtures of other media. Media Encoder synchronizes and compresses these media components into a single file, augments the file with error-correction information, and delivers it to the server running Windows Media Services, which then transmits it over the network.

Windows Media Technologies Codecs Windows Media Technologies codecs play an important role in transferring data over limited-bandwidth connections. Because codecs compress large volumes of raw data, data is transmitted using less bandwidth and is then decompressed when it reaches its destination.

Content providers who want to send audio or video face a problem with file size. Uncompressed broadcast-quality video requires 160 Mbps of network bandwidth. Uncompressed CD-quality audio requires approximately 2.8 Mbps. Many Internet users connect at speeds of only 28.8 kilobits per second (Kbps), a speed that is at least 1,000 times slower than audio and video require.

A codec (compressor/decompressor) is a software module that compresses and decompresses audio and video files so that smaller files can be transmitted. Codecs are typically optimized for compressing either audio or video, and there are many different compression algorithms available for each type of media. When an audio or video file is compressed, it loses some of the original data that is not apparent to the viewer or listener, and the smaller file can be transmitted more quickly. Content providers struggle to balance the trade-off between delivering high-quality content without data compression, which results in slower data transmission; and achieving high data-compression rates, which lowers the content quality.

Unlike many other codecs, Windows Media Technologies codecs are optimized to deliver both high-quality content and high data-compression rates. This means that the user hears crisp, CD-quality sound and sees clear, smooth video—even over slow Internet connections.

Content developers use codecs to compress or encode audio and video for real-time or local playback over the Internet and corporate intranets. Users do not need to know anything about codecs to play digital media content using Windows Media Player; they just click a link to the content, and it plays. Windows Media Player has an **Automatic Updates** feature that checks for updates to licensed codecs on a schedule determined by the user. The **Automatic Updates** feature can be customized in Windows Media Player on the **Tools** menu, clicking **Options**, selecting the **Player** tab, and changing the options under **Automatic Updates**.

Creating Dynamic Web Pages

You do not need special digital-media authoring software to create digital media presentations for broadcast over a network. You can use Dynamic HTML (DHTML) and HTML+TIME to add interactive digital media to your Web pages. For example, you can create slide-show-style or digital media presentations with synchronized text, images, audio, video, and streaming media. These presentations can be timed, interactive, or a both. HTML+TIME version 2.0 provides features such as animation and enhanced timing and synchronization functionality over the previous versions, and is available with Microsoft Internet Explorer version 5.5 and later.

Using HTML+TIME   You can incrementally enhance your Web pages by adding HTML+TIME elements or by adding HTML+TIME attributes to existing HTML elements. Using HTML+TIME elements, you can add media playback, animation, visual transitions and effects, and conditional rendering of content based on characteristics such as language, captioning, and connection speed to your Web page. Among other things, HTML+TIME attributes let you specify when an element appears on a page, how long it remains displayed, how many times it repeats, whether or not it is synchronized with other media or HTML elements on the page, and how the surrounding elements are affected.

The implementation of HTML+TIME builds on DirectX and Windows Media Technologies features. HTML+TIME changes properties of HTML elements or media over time. For every HTML element associated with a timeline, HTML+TIME provides scriptable properties and Document Object Model (DOM) methods.

For more information about using HTML+TIME to create dynamic Web pages that incorporate digital media, see the HTML+TIME link on the Web Resources page at http://www.microsoft.com/windows/reskits/webresources.

Note   Although some HTML+TIME features are available with Microsoft Internet Explorer version 5.0, due to the new and significantly enhanced features in HTML+TIME 2.0, use of Internet Explorer 5.5 or later is strongly encouraged.

Broadcasting Digital Media Presentations Over Your Intranet

With Windows Media Tools, you can create digital media presentations and place them on your server running Windows Media Services for broadcast over a network. You can also broadcast live events or digital media in the same way. Windows Media Tools also allow you to configure and allocate resources on your server to optimize the use of bandwidth.

You can use Windows Media Encoder to encode digitized audio and video data in Windows Media Format. After the encoded data is created, you can either save it as a file or stream it. The Windows Media file is then either hosted on a server running Windows Media Services (for streaming over your network), or hosted on a Web server (for downloading). In either case, the user plays the broadcast on a computer running Windows Media Player.

To host a Windows Media stream file for streamed delivery, place the file on a server running Windows Media Services and create a link to the file.

Optimizing Digital Media Broadcasts   Intelligent Streaming detects available bandwidth and makes full use of it to optimize multimedia playback, ensuring that users will receive the highest quality multimedia possible by adjusting for connection speed or network problems. Windows Media Services, running on the server, and Windows Media Player, running on the client, communicate with each other before and during file transmission to establish the optimum network throughput and automatically adjust the stream to changes in bandwidth while maximizing quality.

For more information about Intelligent Streaming, see "Creating Streaming Content for the Internet" earlier in this chapter.

Windows Media Player and Windows Media Services work together to maintain the quality of data transmissions through multi-datarate encoding, intelligent transmission processing, and a video playback enhancement filter.

Multi-datarate encoding   Multi-datarate encoding ensures that, when a user clicks a link, Windows Media Player and Windows Media Services automatically determine the optimum data rate and quality based on the speed of the connection.

Intelligent transmission   Windows Media Player and Windows Media Services respond to network congestion by intelligently degrading quality to preserve continuous playback. First, the server decreases the video frame rate to maintain audio quality and keep buffering to a minimum. If conditions worsen, the server stops sending video frames completely, but maintains audio quality.

Video playback enhancement filter   Windows Media Player improves overall video quality, especially at low bandwidths, by using intelligent filtering to smooth pixelation and remove *ghosting*, the dim secondary images that appear due to signal problems in transmission.

Managing Digital Media Data Transmission   Windows Media Services provides a set of services that work together to optimize digital media data transmission from the server to the client computer. The server is configured using Windows Media Administrator and network bandwidth can be controlled using Internet Information Services (IIS).

Configuring servers for broadcasting digital media presentations   Windows Media Services components, which run on Windows 2000–based servers, are a set of services that can unicast and multicast audio, video, and other media to client computers. Windows Media Encoder compresses the audio and video feed in real time and passes it to the server running Windows Media Services for delivery to client computers, where it is played as live content. On-demand digital media files must be stored on a server and passed to the network by the server running Windows Media Services.

Server-side software includes the Windows Media Administrator, which is a set of administrative tools for managing, configuring, and monitoring Windows Media Services, and Windows Media Rights Manager, an optional component that is a digital-rights tool for reducing content piracy.

Windows Media Services can deliver live broadcasts or streaming stored multimedia content at rates as low as 3 Kbps (audio only) or as high as 6 Mbps (audio and video) and can scale to meet the heaviest demands. A single server can scale to support thousands of simultaneous user connections, letting you host large Internet broadcasts.

Windows Media Services, provides high bandwidth availability, which allows delivery of full-motion, full-screen MPEG video with guaranteed performance across high-bandwidth networks.

Controlling bandwidth use and enabling process throttling   You can control the network bandwidth used by Internet Information Services (IIS) on a particular server either at the computer level or at the Web site level. With IIS, you can enable *process throttling,* which is a method for limiting the processing time used by *out-of-process applications* so that no one application can dominate processing time on a server. Process throttling is useful if you host multiple sites on one server and you are concerned that out-of-process applications on one site will use all of the CPU capacity, thereby preventing other sites from using the CPU. To enable process throttling, use IIS to set the percentage of CPU time that a site or application is limited to, and to enforce the action that is taken when a limit is exceeded. Actions include logging the error, idling the application, or halting the application. For more information about using IIS, see the *Microsoft Internet Information Services 5.0 Resource Guide* of the *Microsoft® Windows® 2000 Server Resource Kit.*

> **Note**   Before you decide to use process throttling, use System Monitor to examine the **%-Processor Time** counter in the Processor object and the specific instance counters for **Maximum CGI Requests** and **Total CGI Requests** in the Web Service object. It is also recommended that you enable process accounting and examine the DLLHOST object counters to determine the number of out-of-process Web Application Manager (WAM) and Internet Server Application Programming Interface (ISAPI) requests.

Troubleshooting Digital Media

Windows XP Professional Help and Support Center includes intuitive, step-by-step troubleshooters to help you diagnose problems with audio, video, or digital media. To find these troubleshooting tools, open Windows XP Professional Help and Support Center, click **Fixing a problem**, and then click **Games, sound and video problems**. The troubleshooters include:

- Games and Multimedia Troubleshooter
- Troubleshooting DirectX
- Microsoft Display Troubleshooter
- DVD Troubleshooter
- Sound Troubleshooter

A Hardware Troubleshooter is available in Windows XP Professional Help and Support Center under **Hardware and system device problems**.

In Windows XP Professional, you can troubleshoot digital media devices by using the following procedure.

To troubleshoot specific digital media devices

1. In **Control Panel**, click **Sounds, Speech, and Audio Devices**, and then click **Sounds and Audio Devices**.

2. On the **Hardware** tab, under **Devices**, select the device that you want to troubleshoot.

3. Click **Properties** to determine the properties of the device, such as the driver version in use.

    – or –

    Click **Troubleshoot** to troubleshoot the device.

Common Problems with Playing Digital Media

Several common problems can occur in playing media files. One common symptom is a low volume (or no sound at all) when you play media files. An improperly installed sound card or improperly connected speakers can be the cause of this problem.

You can check to see whether the volume in **Volume Control** is muted or set too low.

To check volume

1. In the Windows XP Professional notification area, right-click the **Volume Control** icon.

2. Click **Open Volume Controls** to verify whether the **Mute all** check box is clear.

    – or –

    Use the slider for **Volume Control** to adjust the volume.

> **Note**   If the **Volume Control** icon is not in the notification area, in **Programs**, point to **Accessories**, point to **Entertainment**, and then click **Volume Control**.

You can check to see whether your sound card is properly configured and whether the sound card settings conflict with settings for other hardware.

To check sound card configuration

1. On the **Start** menu, right-click **My Computer,** and select **Manage**.

2. Under **System Tools**, select **Device Manager**.

3. In the list of devices, locate your sound card. Right-click the device name, select **Properties**, and then click the **General** tab.

    The **Device status** dialog box shows whether there is a problem with the device. If there is a problem with the device, the icon for the device displays with either a yellow exclamation mark or a red "X" over it.

> **Note**   If you can play WAV files, the sound card is probably properly installed.

If headphones connect directly to a sound card, verify that the headphones are plugged into the "line out" or "audio out" jacks and not to the "line in" or "mic in" jacks.

If the headphones are connected correctly, and you still cannot hear audio, verify that the sound card is correctly installed by reviewing its properties.

> **Note** If you have **Digital CD Playback** enabled for a CD- drive, audio output from the headphone jack on the CD drive is disabled.

To check speaker connection

1. On the computer's sound card, look at the jacks that connect the speakers or headphones. Make sure the speakers or headphones are plugged into the "line out" or "speaker out" jacks.

2. Check to see that the speakers are properly connected to a power source and turned on, and that the speaker volume knob is turned up, if there is one.

Windows Media Player Help also contains a number of troubleshooting scenarios that can assist you in diagnosing and solving problems with playing digital media.

Windows XP Professional includes the DirectX Diagnostic Tool, to diagnose problems with DirectX drivers and digital media hardware. You can use the tool to obtain detailed system and driver information, such as the system configuration of anything using DirectX, as well as to test specific devices. The **More Help** tab provides access to troubleshooters for DirectX and Sound, and to the Microsoft System Information Tool. You can report result to Microsoft Product Support Services to speed up diagnosing and resolving problems. You can also use the DirectX Diagnostic Tool to change system configuration. To open the DirectX Diagnostic Tool, in the Run dialog box, type **dxdiag**.

For more information about using the DirectX Diagnostic Tool, see the DirectX Diagnostic Tool Help.

Troubleshooting Playback of WAV Files

If a digital media application is unable to play waveform-audio (.wav) files, start by reviewing the troubleshooting guidelines in "Common Problems with Playing Digital Media" earlier in this chapter.

If you are running Sound Recorder, but waveform-audio files do not play, make sure that the waveform-audio driver or audio codec is installed.

To see if a waveform-audio driver or audio codec is installed

1. In Control Panel, click **Sounds, Speech, and Audio Devices**, and then click **Sounds and Audio Devices**.

2. On the **Hardware** tab, and then examine the **Devices** list to make sure an audio driver or audio codec is in the list of devices and drivers.

3. If you have a driver installed that is not working, or you want to upgrade your driver, go to the Windows Update site to find out if there are newer drivers available. For more information about Windows Update, see "Managing Devices" in this book.

4. Check with the manufacturer of the sound card to ensure you have the proper drivers.

5. If you cannot find the correct audio codec or driver for the sound card in the list or on Windows Update, download an updated driver from the manufacturer's Web site.

Troubleshooting MIDI Files

If a digital media application cannot play MIDI files, start by reviewing the troubleshooting guidelines in "Common Problems with Playing Digital Media" earlier in this chapter.

If MIDI files do not play, the cause of the problem might be that a MIDI driver is not installed.

To see if a MIDI driver is installed

1. In Control Panel, click **Sounds, Speech, and Audio Devices**, and then click **Sounds and Audio Devices**.

2. On the **Hardware** tab, in the list of devices, select your MIDI device, and then click **Properties**.

3. Click the **Driver** tab to view details about the driver or to update, roll back, or uninstall the driver.

4. If no driver is installed, read the manufacturer's instructions to install a driver for the device.

A MIDI file plays on the default MIDI output device unless you select a different one. For information about configuring and selecting a preferred MIDI output device, see "Configuring Sounds and Video" earlier in this chapter.

If the MIDI file is still inaudible, MIDI music playback might be configured to use the wrong device. You can check whether the correct MIDI output device is selected and correctly connected.

To see if the MIDI output device is correctly connected

1. Check to see that the correct MIDI output device is selected, by checking the **Default Device** in the **MIDI Music Playback** dialog box, as described in "Configuring Sounds and Video".

2. If you have selected the sound card or the software synthesizer as your output device, make sure the headphones or speakers are connected to the sound card.

3. If you have selected an external MIDI device as your output device, check the following:

   ■ Make sure that the external MIDI device is connected to your computer using the port labeled External MIDI, MIDI OUT, or MPU-401.

   ■ Make sure there are speakers or headphones connected to the external MIDI device.

   ■ Check to see that those speakers or headphones are turned on and that the volume is turned up.

Troubleshooting DVD

Because DVD technology uses several hardware components, the first step in troubleshooting DVD is to determine which component is not functioning correctly.

■ Make sure that Device Manager shows the DVD drive as functioning correctly.

■ Make sure that Windows XP Professional can read the data on the DVD by using Windows Explorer to see the contents of the DVD. For a video DVD, there should be at least the following two folders: Video_TS and Audio_TS.

■ If you are using a hardware decoder with your DVD drive, use Device Manager to verify that the decoder is working properly. To verify that Windows XP Professional supports your hardware decoder, check the Hardware Compatibility List link on the Web Resources page at http://www.microsoft.com/windows/reskits/webresources.

■ If you are using a software decoder with your DVD drive, try reinstalling the software.

For additional help with troubleshooting problems playing DVDs, in Windows XP Professional Help and Support Center, click **Fixing a problem**, click **Games, sound and video problems**, and then click the **DVD troubleshooter**.

Troubleshooting an Audio CD

If you cannot play an audio CD, start by reviewing the troubleshooting guidelines in "Common Problems with Playing Digital Media" earlier in this chapter.

If an audio CD does not play, the cause of the problem might be that the CD drive is not properly installed.

To verify whether a CD drive is properly installed

1. Place a data CD in the CD drive.

2. Make that sure you can view the files in Windows Explorer or list the files at the command prompt. If you can view the files, the CD drive is properly installed.

3. If you cannot view the files, use Device Manager to verify that your disk drivers are properly installed.

4. Check to see whether the disk is dirty.

5. Check whether any new software has been installed that might be causing a conflict.

Windows XP Professional can use digital playback of a CD audio for digital devices, such as USB speakers. This feature works with CD devices that support Digital Audio Extraction (DAE), but compatibility problems might exist with older drives. When this option is enabled, you do not need to connect your CD drive to your sound card by using the analog audio cable. If you enable digital CD audio and encounter playback problems, such as audio skipping, or cutting in or out, your CD drive might not be compatible with DAE.

To verify whether digital CD audio is enabled

1. In **Control Panel**, click **Sounds, Speech, and Audio Devices**, and then click **Sounds and Audio Devices**.

2. On the **Hardware** tab, under **Devices**, select the CD device, and then click **Properties**.

3. On the **Properties** tab, under **Digital CD Playback**, verify whether the **Enable digital CD audio for this CD-ROM device** check box is selected.

Note   Selecting the **Enable digital CD audio for this CD-ROM device** check box disables audio output from the headphone jack on the CD drive.

If the CD is playing and there is no sound coming from the speakers, check to see whether the CD drive is connected to the sound card. If the **Enable digital CD audio for this CD-ROM device** check box is *not* selected, you must connect the CD drive to the sound card, and you can hear sound from speakers or headphones plugged into the headphone jack on the face of the CD drive.

To see if the CD drive is connected to the sound card

1. Plug the speakers or headphones into the audio jack on the face of the CD drive.

2. If you can hear sound, check the internal or external audio connection between the CD drive and the sound card.

Troubleshooting CD Recording

One of the first things to do in troubleshooting a problem with CD recording is to check how your CD-R or CD-RW drive is configured. The Properties page for the CD drive contains information about troubleshooting and fixing problems. To view the Properties page for your CD drive, right-click the CD drive in Windows Explorer and select **Properties**. The settings on the **Recording** tab show you how your CD writer is configured. On this tab you can change settings to fix problems and optimize CD writing. If the Recording tab is not present, then the drive is not capable of recording CDs. You can use the following settings on the Recording tab to help you troubleshoot problems with CD recording:

- You can see the drive where temporary files are stored when you record a CD, and you can change the location of the temporary image file used to write the CD if you have additional drives available. The location of the temporary image file defaults to the root of the drive, but you can change it by using the drive Properties. This can be helpful when there is not enough room on the default drive to hold both the temporary files (which cannot be moved) and the temporary image file.

- You can see the recording speed and change it, if necessary, for troubleshooting or for higher quality recordings, in some instances. The default setting is "Fastest".

- You can select the option to automatically eject media after recording, which is the default. If you don't want the CD to be automatically ejected after the CD writing process, clear the **Automatically eject the CD after writing** check box.

If you have trouble recording a CD, you might be able to pinpoint the problem by checking whether any of the following suggestions apply to your situation. These are some general things to look at that might affect the CD-write process:

- Make sure that your CD drive is a recording CD drive (CD-R or CD-RW).

- Check whether the drive that will be used for the temporary staging area (typically your hard drive) has sufficient free space. It is recommended that you have 1.3 GB of free space to successfully write to CD.

If you are trying to write to CD, but the Write these files to CD option does not appear on the CD Writing Tasks list in Windows Explorer, try one of the following methods to verify that the correct media is placed in the CD drive.

- Make sure that the CD is a CD-R or CD-RW disc.

- Make sure that the CD recording speed is equal to or less than the drive recording speed. Many CD drives are designed to copy files to CD at 4X speed, but some are designed to copy files at up to 10X speed. Higher speed CD drives can write at lower speeds to lower speed discs. The higher speed CD discs cannot be used in a lower speed CD drive. For more information about setting the recording speed, see the information above about setting recording speeds on the **Recording** tab.

In Windows Explorer, on the **CD Writing Tasks** list, if the only option is **Erase files on CD-RW**, you cannot write to the CD-RW you are using. This is typically either because the disc has been preformatted or it has been previously written to in UDF file format. Windows XP Professional does not support writing to UDF file format on CD. These are your options:

- If there are files currently on the CD and you want to keep these files, remove the CD-RW from the drive and use a different CD-RW for writing your files.

- If the CD does not contain any files, it was preformatted in a format not supported by Windows XP Professional. Select **Erase files on CD-RW** to erase and format the CD so you can write your files.

If you close all other programs before beginning the CD writing process, you can maintain a constant flow of data to the CD recorder. This includes disabling any screen savers that might appear during the recording process.

If you are able to copy files to the temporary staging area and to begin the write process, but the CD Writing Wizard stops before you get to the Write CD process, the following suggestions might help:

- Check that there is enough free space on the drive where the temporary staging resides.

- Consult the vendor of the CD drive to see if an upgrade is available for the firmware of the drive.

If the CD Writing Wizard stops sooner than expected, and the CD is not readable, try the following suggestions:

- Find the drive that holds the temporary staging area by looking on the **Recording** tab on the CD recorder's properties page. Run Disk Defragmenter on this drive.

- Lower the recording speed on the **Recording** tab. The recording speed should not exceed the highest speed possible for your CD drive.

Additional Resources

These resources contain additional information and tools related to this chapter.

Related Information

- "Configuring Telephony and Conferencing" in this book for more information about telephony, videophones, and digital media conferences.

- "Managing Devices" in this book for more information about digital video cameras.

- "Managing Desktops" in this book for more information about deploying custom configurations by using Group Policy and local policy.

- The MIDI Manufacturers Association link on the Web Resources page at http://www.microsoft.com/windows/reskits/webresources for more information about MIDI devices and the MIDI standard.

- The Windows Media Technologies link on the Web Resources page at http://www.microsoft.com/windows/reskits/webresources for more information about playing digital media files by using Windows Media Player.

- The HTML+TIME link on the Web Resources page at http://www.microsoft.com/windows/reskits/webresources for more information about using HTML+TIME and Dynamic HTML (DHTML) to create dynamic Web pages that incorporate digital media.

- The DirectX link on the Web Resources page at http://www.microsoft.com/windows/reskits/webresources for more information about DirectX, or to download or order the DirectX SDK.

Chapter 11

Enabling Printing and Faxing

Microsoft® Windows® XP Professional offers several new ways to install, configure, and manage printers. Many improvements that enhance performance, compatibility, and use of wizards in the Windows XP Professional printing system are transparent to users. The installation process is intuitive and efficient. After installation you can send print jobs over the Internet by using new port monitors.

Related Information

- For information about finding a printer by an attribute, such as location, see "Active Directory" in the *Distributed Systems Guide* of the *Microsoft® Windows® 2000 Server Resource Kit*.

- For information about setting permissions, see "Authorization and Access Control" in this book.

- For information about printer location, see "Configuring TCP/IP" in this book.

- For information about Plug and Play technology, see "Managing Devices" in this book.

New to Enabling Printing and Faxing

The Printers and Faxes folder (formerly Printers folder) changes appearance when you select Show Common Tasks in folders.

To change the Printers and Faxes folder view

1. In **Control Panel**, double-click **Folder Options.**

2. On the **General tab,** click **Show Common Tasks in folders**.

An unobtrusive balloon in the notification area, instead of a dialog box on the main screen, tells you the status of a print job. The balloon remains active for ten seconds or until the user clicks the icon.

The preferred port monitor in Windows XP Professional is the Standard TCP/IP Port Monitor, known as the *standard port monitor*, which uses TCP/IP as the transport protocol. When Simple Network Management Protocol (SNMP) is supported and turned on, Windows XP Professional uses it to configure and monitor the logical printer ports. Internet printing also adds a Hypertext Transfer Protocol (HTTP) port monitor.

> **Warning** Windows XP Professional no longer supports the Data Link Control (DLC) printing protocol. DLC is the default protocol for using HPMON from Hewlett Packard. Some earlier Hewlett Packard Jet Direct printers use HPMON. You can upgrade to the current Hewlett Packard Jet Direct network interface card that supports IP and use the standard port monitor.

Using Active Directory to Find Printers

A networked printer serves many users and offers better resource management and greater flexibility than stand-alone printers. However, a networked printer can be more difficult for your computer to locate because it is not directly connected to the user's computer.

The Add Printer wizard supports searching and installing printers using the Active Directory™ directory service.

Using Active Directory, users can search a range of printer attributes to find a printer. If you use subnets to define the sites within your organization, the Active Directory™ directory service can find printers near you. Locating the closest printer has formerly been difficult for both administrators and users.

For example, if you are in Los Angeles and want to find all the Los Angeles printers in your deployment, in the **Location** dialog box, type **US/LAX**. If US/LAX matches the printer location syntax in Active Directory, your search might return the following results:

- US/LAX/1/101

- US/LAX/2/103

These results indicate that two printers are available in Los Angeles. The printers are located in buildings 1 and 2 and in rooms 101 and 103.

> **Note**   A printer in Active Directory must be serviced by a print server. If you print directly to a network printer, you cannot use Active Directory. When printing over a Microsoft® Windows® 2000–based network, you can choose between printers on your local area network (LAN) and printers available on the Internet.

To search for nearby printers

1. In **Search**, click **Printers, computers, or people**, and then click **A Printer on the network**.

2. In the **Location** box, type the complete printer location string, or a partial string followed by an asterisk (*).

3. Click **Find Now**.

> **Note**   The printer location string must match the syntax specified by the administrator that describes the location in Active Directory.

Searching Active Directory Fields

When you search for printers in large environments, you might need to use a specific format to find a printer in the location you want. You can create specific formats by using a standardized format for the Location attribute of each printer. The Location field allows approximately 250 characters and permits you to describe printer locations in various ways. For example, the following formats describe a printer located in New York City in building 3 on floor 5:

- New York/Building 3/Floor 5
- NYC/Bldg III/Fifth floor
- NY/B3/F5

When you understand how a printer location is formatted in Active Directory, you can create more effective searches.

To search for a printer that has specific characteristics

1. In Search, click **Printers, computers, or people**, and then click **A Printer on the network**.
2. Click the **Features** tab.
   Use Features to create searches for printers using a predefined set of commonly sought features.
   – or –
   Click the **Advanced** tab. (Use the **Advanced** tab to search Active Directory by using Boolean operators. You can construct complex searches based on any available criteria.)
3. Enter your search criteria, and then click **Find Now**.

Active Directory returns a list of all printers that match your query. Note that if a printer query has characteristics different from the ones listed in Active Directory, you might receive misleading search results and be unable to find the appropriate printer.

Searching Active Directory Locations

You can make your search of Active Directory locations more effective by using the following:

- Location tracking, which can be enabled.
- A standardized location naming convention that is assigned to each site, subnet, or computer object.
- Sites based on one or more subnets.

If these methods are available, you can find printers in your location quickly.

To search for printers by using Active Directory location tracking

1. In **Search, click Printers**, **computers**, **or people**, and then click **A Printer on the network**.

   Your current location appears in the **Location** box if your deployment uses location tracking.

2. If your current location does not appear, click **Browse** to find printers in other locations.

3. Enter any other search criteria, and then click **Find Now**.

For more information about searching, see "Searching Active Directory Fields" earlier in this chapter.

For your users to search for nearby printers by using subnets, your deployment must have the following:

- A directory service with more than one subnet.

- A network IP addressing scheme that roughly matches the physical layout of your enterprise.

- One or more subnet objects for each site.

  You can create subnet objects, and then manage sites by using Active Directory Sites and Services, which is included with Microsoft® Windows® 2000 Server.

Your deployment can use an extended schema, although in most cases you need to use location tracking instead of extending the schema. All objects in Active Directory have a base set of attributes. You can extend this base set to accommodate the particular needs of your environment. When you use an extended schema, you must construct Boolean searches on the **Advanced** tab in the **Search** dialog box. When a limited set of available Boolean operators and choices exists, the **Advanced** tab provides the set.

Although using location tracking is typically an effective solution, if it fails, administrators might extend the schema to include attributes such as printer city, printer building, or printer floor. Entering complete and accurate descriptions of printer locations in Active Directory can save time later.

For more information about Active Directory and extending the schema, see "Active Directory Schema" in the *Distributed Systems Guide*.

For more information about setting up location tracking sites on a Windows 2000–based server, see Windows 2000 Server Help.

Warning   You can connect to another network printer by entering its printer name, using the Universal Naming Convention (UNC) or Uniform Resource Locator (URL). Using URLs to access printers requires an Internet connection. You must know the UNC or URL of the printer to which you want to connect.

Installing Printers

Windows XP Professional installs and configures printers in a several ways.

Using Plug and Play support, you can install printers that are attached directly to your computer. After you attach a Plug and Play printer to the computer, Windows XP Professional installs the necessary device drivers. When you install printers over a network, Active Directory helps you locate printers based on criteria such as the printer location, or color and resolution capabilities.

Using Point and Print to install a network printer connection, you can download all required printer drivers. After a print server is configured to support printers and provide drivers to clients, users do not need to know which driver is required for the printer or how to install the required drivers. Windows XP Professional installs the required drivers for them.

If your printer and printer monitor support bidirectional communication, the print device can actively report errors. If the printer is jammed or out of paper, Windows XP Professional lets you know.

Installing Network and Internet Printers

In Windows XP Professional you can install network printers by using the following features:

- Point and Print
- Add Printer Wizard
- Run dialog box
- Internet Printers

Users can choose the method they find most convenient.

Note   Windows XP Professional has removed the NetBEUI networking protocol from the operating system. It is recommended that you use TCP/IP, IPX/SPX, or the software provided by the Printer manufacturer in place of the NetBEUI protocol on your network.

Point and Print

When you use Point and Print to install a printer over a network, the server sends Windows XP Professional information about your printer, such as:

- Printer driver files.

- The name of the server on which printer driver files are stored.

- Printer model information that specifies which printer driver to retrieve, either from the Windows directory on a local computer or over the network.

To install a printer by using Point and Print

1. Open a network print server, and then open the **Printers and Faxes** folder.

2. Right-click a printer icon, and then click **Connect**.

Add Printer Wizard

The Add Printer wizard walks you through the steps of installing a non-Plug and Play printer.

Run Dialog Box

If you know the universal naming convention (UNC) name or the URL of the printer you want to install, you can use the following procedure to complete a fast, direct installation.

To install a printer by using the Run dialog box

- In the **Run** dialog box, type the UNC or URL.

Internet Printers

In Internet Explorer, you can find all the printers that are available on a Microsoft Internet print server. To view these printers, enter the URL of the print server in the address bar of Internet Explorer.

For more information about a printer on a Microsoft Internet print server, click the printer name. A Web page displays information such as:

- Printer model

- Location

- Comment

- Network name

- Documents in the queue

- Maximum speed

- Availability of color support

- Availability of duplexing

- Maximum resolution

To install an Internet printer by using the URL

1. In **Internet Explorer**, in the **Address** text box, type the URL of the print server (for example, http://*servername*/*printers*), and then click **Go**.

2. Click a printer icon, and then click **Connect**.

Installing Local Printers

There are several ways to install local printers. Use the one that is most convenient for you.

> **Warning**   To install local printer drivers, you must be a member of the Power User or Administrator group and have permission to Load and unload device drivers.

To grant permissions to load and unload device drivers

1. In **Programs**, point to **Administrative Tools**, and then click **Local Security Policy**.

2. In the console tree, double-click **Local Policies**, and then double-click **User Rights Assignment**.

3. In the details pane, right-click the **Load and unload device drivers** policy, and then click **Properties**.

4. Click **Add User or Group**, enter the appropriate user name, and if you are done adding users, click **OK**.

   To avoid having to grant permissions on a per user basis, you can click **Load and unload device drivers** to grant permissions to add local printers to the Power Users group.

5. Click **Add User or Group**, click **Object Types**, select the **Groups checkbox**, and then click **OK**.

6. Click **Locations**, select the local computer at the top of the network tree, and then click **OK**.

7. In the name box, type **Power Users**, and then click **OK**.

8. Click **OK**.

Plug and Play Printers

Plug and Play is a set of specifications that a computer uses to detect and configure a print device and install the appropriate drivers. This installation technique is available only for printers that are connected directly to your computer. Plug and Play is not available for networked printers.

To start Plug and Play printer installation, plug your printer into your computer. In most cases, Windows XP Professional automatically configures the printer and activates it. During this process, Plug and Play installs the appropriate drivers; and you do not need to restart your computer. If the installation fails, you can use manual detection for Plug and Play printers by using the Add Printer wizard or Device Manager.

To install a local printer by using the Add Printer wizard

1. In Control Panel, double-click **Printers and Faxes**.

2. Double-click **Add Printer**, and then follow the instructions.

Although Windows XP Professional includes drivers for many popular printers, you need to provide the driver if your printer uses a driver that is not included with Windows XP Professional. If Plug and Play detects that your computer does not have a driver for your printer, you are prompted to provide it.

You can have the Add Printer wizard search for drivers on the CD, local drive, network path, or Windows Update.

Automatic Detection and Installation

Windows XP Professional detects supported printers and completes the entire printer installation process by installing the proper drivers, updating the system, and allocating resources. You do not need to restart the computer, and the printer is immediately available for use.

All printers that Plug and Play automatically detects use Universal Serial Bus (USB) connections, Institute of Electrical and Electronics Engineers (IEEE) 1394 cables, parallel connections, or Infrared Data Association (IrDA) transmission.

Manual Detection and Installation

Manual Plug and Play detection is similar to automatic Plug and Play detection in that Windows XP Professional completes printer installation. However, you must restart your computer to prompt the automatic installation, or use the Add Hardware wizard to prompt your computer to detect the printer. When you restart the computer or use the Add Hardware wizard, Windows XP Professional updates your computer, allocates resources, and installs drivers. If drivers for the printer are not available, you are prompted to provide them.

Typically, manually detectable Plug and Play printers use parallel cables. In Windows XP Professional, for a printer using a parallel connection, you can click the **Automatically Detect** box in the Add Printer wizard to verify that the printer is installed. For more information about Plug and Play, see "Managing Devices" in this book.

Note Most Plug and Play printers use USB or parallel connections.

Printer Installation Considerations

Typically, Plug and Play automatically detects printers that use USB ports. Plug and Play also detects printers that use parallel ports, but if the print device does not have an in-box driver, you must install these print devices by using the Add Printer wizard. Windows XP Professional requires that you have Power User or greater permissions and have the **Load and unload device drivers** permissions assigned to you to install printers.

Some printers require drivers that are not included with Windows XP Professional. Using the Add Printer wizard, you can install a printer driver from a floppy disk, a network share, a CD-ROM, Windows Update, or the printer manufacturer's Web site.

Note Windows Update makes it possible for you to download updated device drivers as they become available.

If Microsoft does not supply a driver for your printer, request a printer driver from the printer's manufacturer. To ensure quality, use drivers that are Windows Hardware Quality Labs (WHQL) certified. Microsoft Product Support Services does not support systems that use drivers that are not on the WHQL list.

You can send e-mail to mswish@microsoft.com to request Microsoft support for a driver or feature. Please include the following information in your request:

- Name
- Business name
- Phone number or e-mail address
- Printer manufacturer
- Printer model
- Driver or feature name

Note Microsoft reserves the right to decide whether or not to honor your request for support of additional drivers or features.

Driver.cab File

When you install a Plug and Play device, Windows XP Professional installs a driver from the Driver.cab file.

Windows XP Professional installs the cabinet file as part of the operating system installation process. The Driver.cab file contains thousands of commonly used files, including drivers, application extensions, and color profiles. These files enable Windows XP Professional to work with a broad range of hardware devices and applications.

Windows Update

If the device drivers you need are not available in the version of Windows XP Professional you have installed, they might be available from Windows Update, which updates your system by adding new Windows XP Professional features, including device drivers and system updates.

You can gain access to Windows Update by selecting **Windows Update** from the **Start** menu.

Printing from Other Operating Systems

A network printer installed on a computer running Windows XP Professional might use a print server that is not running Windows 2000. In that case, you must install additional components so that the client computer, server computers, and printer can communicate and transfer print jobs.

NetWare Print Servers

To use a printer connected to a NetWare server, you must install a client such as Microsoft Client Service for NetWare or Novell Client 32 on your computer. These clients let your computer send print jobs to the NetWare server, which the server relays to the printer.

UNIX Print Servers

Before you can print to a remote UNIX printer configured using Line Printer Daemon (LPD), you must configure Windows XP Professional to print by using Line Printer Remote (LPR). You must first install Print Services for UNIX, and then install and configure a printer using LPR as the printer port.

To install Print Services for UNIX

1. In **Control Panel**, double-click **Network Connections**.

2. On the **Advanced** menu, click **Optional Networking Components**.

3. Select **Other Network File and Print Services**, and then click **Details**.

4. Select **Print Services for UNIX**, and then click **OK**.

To add an LPR port

1. In **Control Panel**, double-click **Printers and Faxes**.

2. Double-click **Add Printer**, and then click **Next**.

3. Click **Local printer**, clear the **Automatically detect my printer** check box, and then click **Next**.

4. Click **Create a new port**, and then click **LPR Port**.

5. Click **Next**, and then enter the following information:

   - In **Name or address of server providing LPD**, type the Domain Name System (DNS) name or IP address of the host for the printer you are adding.

   - In the **Name of printer or print queue on that server** text box, type the name of the printer as it is identified by the host, which is either the direct-connect printer itself or the UNIX computer.

6. Follow the instructions to finish installing the printer.

Note   The standard port monitor supports the RAW protocol, TCP/IP printing, and the LPR protocol.

IBM Host Printers

IBM host printers are a component of Systems Network Architecture (SNA), a computer networking architecture developed by IBM. SNA provides a network structure for IBM mainframe, midrange, and personal computer systems. SNA defines a set of proprietary communication protocols and message formats for the exchange and management of data on IBM host networks.

To send print jobs to printers that are part of an SNA environment, you can use the Add Printer wizard to connect to the LPT port or print queue that corresponds to the printer you want. An administrator must configure SNA hosts and printers to accept these connections before users can connect to them. For more information about configuring printers in an SNA environment, see the documentation provided with your printer.

Printing Preferences

You can configure printing options in the **Printing Preferences** dialog box. For some printers, advanced options are available. Refer to the documentation provided with your printer for a list of these additional features.

To access Printing Preferences

■   In the **Print** dialog box, click the **Preferences** button of the program you used to create the document.

Printing Preferences settings are maintained across different documents, so you can establish a standard output for all documents. Printing Preferences determine default print job settings, but you can override these defaults in the **Print** dialog box.

Using the **Printing Preferences** dialog box, each user can set different preferences for a printer. Because printing preferences are preserved for each user, preferences do not need to be reset each time the printer is used.

Using the **Printing Preferences** dialog box, you can print in reverse order, print multiple pages on a single page, or specify the number of copies to be printed. Windows XP Professional supports printing up to 9,999 copies of a document in one print job.

For more information about Printing Preferences, see Windows XP Professional Help and Support Center.

Print Queue Security Options

The level of access to a print job queue depends on a user's security permissions as shown in Table 11-1.

Users working with print queues include two groups:

■   **Administrative users** have Manage Printers and Manage Documents permissions. They have wide control over how the printer operates regardless of where the print job originates.

■   **General users** have Print permissions to view general printer information and to manage the documents that they send to the printer. They cannot control other users' print jobs.

Table 11-1   Default Permissions for Printer Users

Task	Administrative User	General User
See all jobs.	Yes	Yes
Pause or resume printer operation.	Yes	No
Pause, cancel, reschedule, or redirect any job.	Yes	No
Pause, cancel, reschedule, or redirect own job.	Yes	Yes
Restart a job from the beginning.	Yes	Yes
View and change job settings such as priority or user notified on completion.	Yes	Yes
View form, paper source, page orientation, and number of copies.	Yes	Yes

> **Note**   Not all applications support the new common dialog box.

Scheduling Printing

Users with administrative permissions can establish print scheduling on the Advanced tab of the printer properties dialog box as shown in Figure 11-1.

Figure 11-1   Advanced tab in a printer properties dialog box

Users with administrative permissions can schedule printer availability, printer priority, and print job priority. Printer priority affects how print jobs reach print queues. Print job priority affects jobs already in a print queue. It does not affect how jobs arrive in a print queue.

> **Note**   Windows XP Professional gives you quick access to basic information about printers. Let the mouse pointer pause on a printer to display the printer name, status, and location, and the number of documents in its queue.

Printer Availability

Printer availability determines whether a printer is available always or only during selected hours.

Printer Priority

Printer priority determines the order in which a printer is chosen relative to other available printers. Printer priority must be set for logical printers that correspond to the same physical printer. Setting printer priorities for virtual printers that correspond to different physical printers has no effect.

> **Note**   A physical printer is the printer hardware that prints a document; a logical printer is a representation of that physical print device.

Important points to remember about printer priority:

- Higher numbers correspond to higher priorities, so priority 1 printers have lowest priority.

- Printer priority determines the order in which the printer completes multiple print jobs. A printer does not stop processing a job already in process, even when the spooler receives a higher priority job that is directed to a higher priority printer on the same port.

To set printer priority

1. Open **Printers and Faxes**, right-click a printer icon, and then click **Properties**.

2. In the **Properties** dialog box, on the **Advanced** tab, enter a number in the **Priority** box.

> **Note**   To set printer priority, you must have Manage Printer permissions for the printer.

To set printer priorities for multiple virtual printers

1. Add a virtual printer to a specific port.

2. Add more virtual printers, by using different names for the physical printer you are emulating, until you have the number of virtual printers you need.

3. Right-click a printer icon, click **Properties**, and in the **Priority** box, type or select a value.

4. Repeat step 3 for other virtual printers that correspond to the same physical printer.

5. Using **Computer Management**, establish distinct groups to which you intend to add users, and then assign each group to a printer.

6. On each virtual printer's **Security** tab, add groups, and then set permissions and restrict access as needed.

For more information about setting printer priorities, see Windows XP Professional Help and Support Center.

> **Caution** If a user is a member of two groups, and one group is denied access to the printer, the **Deny** setting overrides the **Allow** setting. It is recommended that you remove the Everyone group from the printer, instead of denying access to the Everyone group.

Users can install printers based on their group membership, which ensures that the users have the correct level of priority access to printers.

Print Job Priority

A user with administrative permissions can set the print job priority for a document. However, users who submit print jobs have administrative permissions for those jobs and can change the jobs priority in a print queue.

In a print queue, multiple jobs sent to the same virtual printer are affected by job priority. The printer prints the job with highest print job priority first, and then prints jobs in the order of submission. You can set job priority in a printer's property sheet, by using the Priority field on the Advanced tab.

Consider the set of jobs in the print queue shown in Table 11-2.

Table 11-2   Sample Jobs in a Print Queue

Job	Status	Priority
1	Printing	1
2	Spooled	10
3	Spooled	1
4	Spooled	10
5	Spooled	99

Assuming that no other jobs are submitted, and no administrator changes a job priority, the printer prints these jobs in the order shown in Table 11-3.

Table 11-3   Printing Priority for Jobs in Table 11-2

Order	Explanation
Job 1	Printing
Job 5	Highest priority
Job 2	First in queue of priority-10 jobs
Job 4	Highest priority of jobs remaining
Job 3	Only job remaining; lowest priority

To set job priority on an existing print job

1. Open the print queue.

2. Double-click to select a print job.

3. On the **General** tab, move the **Priority** slider to set the print job priority.

Spooler Settings

Users with administrative permissions can configure print spooling by using the **Advanced** tab on the **Printer Properties** page. A print job can be sent to the spooler or directly to the printer. Jobs sent to the spooler can be configured to start printing as soon as possible, or after the final page in the job is sent to the spooler.

When you send a print job to a spooler, your computer does not have to render the print job, so the resources of your computer remain available. However, if the print server with the spooler is unavailable, sending the print job to the spooler fails. You might have to wait for other jobs to finish spooling before your job is processed.

If the spooler is configured to print each page as it is rendered, printing delays might occur between pages. If each spooler has many users, it is faster to have the entire job spooled before printing. If each spooler has few users, it is faster to print each page as it spools.

> **Note**   Spooling occurs on the print server for print jobs sent over the network and on the local computer when the printer is directly connected.

Creating and Sending Print Jobs

Windows XP Professional supports the following ways to create and send a print job to the printer:

- Drag a file to a printer icon in the Printer folder. The file then prints on that printer.

- Create a shortcut to a printer, and then add it to the **Send To** menu. Right-click a file, point to **Send To**, and click the name of the printer you want to use.

- Open a file in the program you used to create the file. Click **File**, and then click **Print**.

- Right-click a file, and then click **Print**. The default printer prints the file, and then closes the application.

Modifications to the Print Dialog Box

The Windows XP Professional Print dialog box includes several modifications to previous versions of Windows.

The Print dialog box includes improvements that allow you to:

- Use the **Find Printer** button to browse for printers that are not installed on your computer, but are available on the network. After you find a printer, you can use Point and Print to establish a connection with the printer and install the required drivers.

- Use the **Preferences** button to change the **Layout** or **Paper/Quality** settings.

> **Note**   The changes to the Print dialog box are not supported by all applications.

Printer Drivers

A printer driver is a software program that converts application-drawing commands to printer-ready-data. Printer drivers translate the information a user sends from the computer into commands that the printer understands.

The Microsoft Universal and PostScript drivers are enhanced printer drivers, which improve printing in the following ways.

Universal Driver

The Universal driver has been optimized for improved quality and faster printing, and Image Color Management (ICM) 2.0 ensures accurate color. The Generic Print Description (GPD) supports minidrivers, which extract the details of each printer's features and allow some unsupported printers to work with Windows XP Professional.

For more information about ICM, see "Image Color Management 2.0" later in this chapter.

The Universal driver enhances font performance and capabilities. Printer font substitution results in better output. Two-byte fonts are supported, allowing the printing of extended punctuation marks, ideographs, and character sets, such as Basic Latin, Greek, Cyrillic, Indic, Thai, Kana, and Hangul characters.

The Universal driver supports customization, allowing greater flexibility for print devices that can be used with Windows XP Professional.

PostScript 5.0 Driver

The PostScript 5.0 driver provides improved performance through enhanced virtual memory management. Color printing with the PostScript driver uses ICM 2.0, which ensures that color images are faithfully reproduced.

Microsoft has extended the PostScript driver to support more font formats and provide the structure for further customization.

PostScript continues to support the following:

- PostScript levels 1, 2, and 3.

- ICM 2.0.

- Control over output data format, allowing for CTRL+D handling, Binary Communications Protocol (BCP), Tagged Binary Communications Protocol (TBCP), and pure binary (8-bit) channels such as AppleTalk.

- PPD version 4.2 and .wpd files.

- Simplified Printer Description (.spd) files.

- Tracking of virtual memory available to the printer.

Image Color Management 2.0

Image Color Management (ICM) 2.0 ensures that printed colors are accurately reproduced. To use ICM 2.0, your printer must support it. In some cases you can use a third-party calibration tool to create or update a color profile for your printer. This compensates for color variations between different printers of the same type or the variations that occur as a printer ages.

Methods of Sending Print Jobs

By using new port monitors and newly supported connection methods, Windows XP Professional sends print jobs faster than previous versions of Windows. For sending print jobs you can use:

- **Standard port monitor**. The preferred port monitor for printers on a TCP/IP network.

- **Internet printing**. A method of sending print jobs to a printer using the URL of the printer.

- **USB**. For installing a printer quickly and easily.

- **IrDA**. For submitting print jobs by using infrared transmissions.

- **IEEE 1284. 4 protocol**. For setting up your multifunction peripheral (MFP) device in a one-step process.

Standard Port Monitor

The standard port monitor connects clients to network printers that use the TCP/IP protocol. It replaces the LPR port monitor (Lprmon) as the preferred port monitor for TCP/IP printers that are connected directly to the network through a network adapter. The new standard port simplifies the installation of most TCP/IP printers by detecting the network settings. Printers connected to a UNIX or Virtual Address eXtension (VAX) host might still require Lprmon.

The standard port monitor is the preferred port monitor in Windows XP Professional. The standard port monitor can use Simple Network Management Protocol (SNMP) to configure and monitor the printer status. In addition to the standard port monitor, Internet printing adds an HTTP print provider.

The standard port monitor communicates with network-ready printers, network adapters like Hewlett-Packard's JetDirect and external network print servers like Intel's NetPort. The standard port monitor can support many printers on a single server and is faster and easier to configure than Lprmon.

The standard port monitor sends documents to a printer by using either the RAW or LPR printing protocol. Together, these protocols support most current TCP/IP printers. Do not confuse these print protocols with transport protocols such as TCP/IP or Data Link Control (DLC).

The RAW protocol is the default print protocol for most print devices. To send a job formatted with RAW, the print server opens a TCP stream to the printer's port 9100 or another port number and selects the connections to multiport external devices. For example, on certain print devices port 9101 goes to the first parallel port, 9102 goes to the second parallel port, and so on.

The standard port monitor uses the LPR protocol when you specify LPR protocol during port installation or reconfiguration, or when the RAW protocol cannot be established.

The standard port monitor deviates from the LPR standard in the following ways:

- The standard port monitor does not conform to the RFC 1179 requirement that the source TCP port must lie between port 721 and port 731. The standard port monitor uses ports from the general, unreserved pool of ports (1024 and above).

- The standard port monitor sends a print job to the spooler without determining the actual job size and designates a default job size, regardless of the actual size of the job. The LPR standard states that print jobs must include information about the size of the job the port monitor sends. Sending a print job that contains job size information requires that the port monitor spool the job twice—once to determine size, and once to send the job to the spooler. Spooling the job once, by using the standard port monitor, improves printing performance.

The standard port monitor can send print jobs to the LPD service running on a print server. For more information about LPD, see "Port Monitor" later in this chapter.

Improved Status Information   The standard port monitor is compatible with RFC 1759, the standard printer management information bases (MIB). As a result, on devices that support SNMP and RFC 1759, the standard port monitor can provide detailed status.

For more information about printing to devices located on other platforms, see "Printing from Other Operating Systems" earlier in this chapter.

To configure a standard TCP/IP port by using the standard port monitor

1. Select an installed printer, click **File**, and then click **Properties**.

2. Click the **Ports** tab, and then click **Add Port**.

3. Click **Standard TCP/IP Port**, and then click **New Port**.

4. In the **Printer Name** or **IP Address** text box, type a name or the IP address of a print device.

5. In the **Port Name** text box, type a host-resolvable port name, which can be any character string, or use the default name that the wizard supplies, and then click **Next**.

6. If prompted by the **Additional Port Information Required** dialog box, click **Standard**, and then select one of the devices listed.
   – or –
   Click **Custom**, and then configure the port by using the **Configure Standard TCP/IP Port Monitor** dialog box. (If you do not know details about the port, use **Generic Network Card**.)

7. When prompted for the protoco483
   l, select either **RAW** (preferred) or **LPR**.

8. If the wizard detects that the device supports multiple ports, as indicated in the Tcpmon.ini file, it prompts you to select a port.

> **Warning**   The system sends an SNMP get command to the device. An SNMP get command asks for the status of a device. In this case, the system uses the SNMP get command to request a status check from that printer. By using the SNMP values returned from the get command, the system determines device details and the appropriate device options are displayed for further selection. For example, you can select the correct printer port.

9. Select a port from the list and finish the wizard.
   The new port is listed on the **Ports** tab of the **Properties** dialog box.

Reconfiguring the Standard Port Monitor   The standard port monitor port can be reconfigured in the printer **Properties** dialog box. On the **Ports** tab, click **Configure Port**. The standard port monitor has its own **Configure** dialog box.

> **Caution**   The Configure Standard TCP/IP Port Monitor dialog box does not verify that the options you select are correct. If they are incorrect, the port does not work. Check with the printer manufacturer to see if the device supports SNMP.

Status Reporting   Printers return print status over SNMP. Because the standard port monitor is compatible with SNMP, it allows detailed status reporting when the printer provides it. Printers that do not comply with the SNMP standard do not return status information, and when an error occurs during printing, the spooler either displays a general printing error or fails to detect an error.

Internet Printing

Windows XP Professional supports Internet printing. This makes it possible to use printers located anywhere in the world by sending print jobs using Hypertext Transfer Protocol (HTTP). Using Microsoft Internet Information Services (IIS) or a Web peer server, Windows XP Professional creates a Web page that provides information about printers and provides the transport for printing over the Internet. Using the Internet, printers can be used to replace fax machines or postal mail.

Use an Internet printer as you would any other Windows XP Professional installed printer.

For more information about installing an Internet printer on your computer, see "Installing Network and Internet Printers" earlier in this chapter.

For more information about managing print jobs sent by using Internet Printing Protocol (IPP) version 1.0, see "Printing Over the Internet" later in this chapter.

USB

Windows XP Professional supports printing to Universal Serial Bus (USB) printers. USB is composed of an external bus architecture for connecting USB-capable peripheral devices to a host computer, and a communication protocol that supports serial data transfers between a host system and USB-capable peripherals.

IrDA

Infrared Data Association (IrDA) is a system of exchanging information between computers by using infrared transmissions without a cable connection. IrDA can be used between any two devices that support IrDA, such as computers and printers. Windows XP Professional supports printing by using an IrDA device.

IrDA is a point-to-point protocol based on TCP/IP and Winsock APIs. IrDA can be used to exchange data between devices other than Windows that use the IrDA protocol. IrDA exchanges data at rates approaching the rates that are provided by LAN connections.

IEEE 1284.4 Protocol

Windows XP Professional supports IEEE 1284.4, a protocol that allows Windows 2000 print servers to send data to multiple parts of a single multifunction peripheral (MFP) device. IEEE 1284.4 is a driver that multiplexes data so that the operating system can communicate with multiple functions of an MFP over a single connection.

IEEE 1284.4 is installed when an IEEE 1284.4-enabled device is detected. No manual installation or configuration is required.

Monitoring and Managing Internet Print Jobs

A range of permissions affects how users manage printers and receive information about printer status.

Windows XP Professional gives you quick access to basic information about printers. In Microsoft Internet Explorer, you can make the mouse pointer pause on a printer to display the printer name, status, location, and number of documents in its queue.

Printers that are hosted by Windows XP Professional or Windows 2000 servers that have Internet Information Services (IIS) or a Peer Web Server can receive jobs sent by users who use the Internet Printing Protocol. Windows 2000 Internet print servers provide information to clients about the status of print jobs and the availability of printers.

You can view and manage the print jobs on a server by using the Internet print server's Web pages. These pages provide information about jobs in the print queue, including the job name, status, owner, number of pages, page size, and time of submission.

You can view the printer device status for more information about a particular printer. This page provides current printer information, such as:

- The text in the printer's local display.

- Paper-tray capabilities and status, such as the approximate number of pages available in each tray.

- Console lights illuminated, such as Online, Data, or Attention, depending on the printer and whether it supports the standard printer MIB.

Printing Concepts

When users print, the computer completes several steps that involve a set of components including executable files, drivers, device interfaces, and dynamic-link libraries, which work together to create the printed output. Understanding how this process works helps you understand what happens when you print a document and how to solve printing problems. Printing has two parts: printing process and the print components. The two parts make the printing process possible. When printing to an Internet print server, the print server adds to the standard print process by creating an interface for users.

Printer Pooling

A printer pool associates two or more identical printers with one set of printer software. To set up a printer pool, add a printer by using the Add Printer wizard, and then assign an output port to all printers that are identical to the original printer. Windows 2000 does not limit the number of printers in a pool. When a document is sent to the printer pool, the first available printer prints it. This configuration maximizes printer use and minimizes the wait for completed print jobs.

Efficient printer pools have the following characteristics:

- All printers in the pool are the same model.

- Printer ports can be of the same type or mixed, such as parallel, serial, and network.

- It is recommended that all printers be in one physical location because it is impossible to predict which printer receives the document, making it hard for users to find their print job.

Note   When print jobs are sent through a standard TCP/IP port to devices that are RFC 1759 compliant, and the printer in a pool stops printing after a set time, the current document is rescheduled on another port. Succeeding documents print to other printers in the pool until the nonfunctioning printer is fixed.

Printing Processes

The printing process is divided into three phases:

■ Client processes

■ Spooler processes

■ Printer processes

These groups of steps include the following specific actions, shown in Figure 11-2.

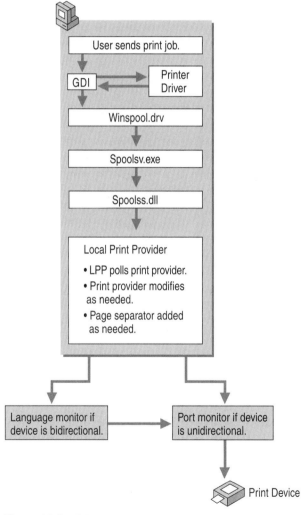

Figure 11-2   Printing process

The steps depicted in Figure 11-2 include the following:

Client Processes

The client processes include:

- A user sends a print job from an application. The application calls the Graphics Device Interface (GDI).

- The GDI calls the printer driver for information, which the GDI uses to create a job in printer language.

- The GDI delivers the job to the spooler.

Spooler Processes

The spooler processes include:

- The client side of the spooler (Winspool.drv) makes a remote procedure call (RPC) call to the server side spooler (Spoolsv.exe).

- Spoolsv.exe calls the print router (Spoolss.dll).

- The router (Localspl.dll) sends the print job to the local print provider (LPP) or the remote print server if the job is being sent to a network printer.

- The LPP polls print processors to find one that can handle the data type of the job.

- The LPP sends the job to the print processor, which modifies the job as required to make it print properly.

- The print processor sends the job to the page separator. A separator page is added if required.

- The job is sent to the appropriate port print monitor. If print is bidirectional, the job is first sent to a language monitor, such as the Printer Job Language (PJL) monitor, and then sent on to the port monitor. If the job is unidirectional, the job is sent directly to the port monitor.

Printer Processes

The printer processes include:

- The printer receives the print job from the print spooler.

- The printer translates the print language into a bitmap, which it then prints.

Printer Components

Many components work together to make the printing process possible. Different components are used at different times, depending on the type of print job being produced and the types of hardware being used.

Graphics Device Interface

The application calls the Graphics Device Interface (GDI) to begin the process of creating a print job. The GDI reads the driver information for the printer to get information about how to format the job. Using the document information from the application and the print device information from the printer driver, the GDI renders the print job in a language that the printer reads.

Printer Drivers

Printer drivers contain information that is specific to the printer that is used. Printer drivers reside on users' computers and are used by the GDI to render print jobs.

Windows XP Professional includes the most common printer drivers, but you might need to provide third-party printer drivers for some printers. When a Windows XP Professional user connects to a printer or installs a Plug and Play printer, the necessary printer drivers are loaded onto the user's computer, if they are available in Windows XP Professional.

Print Spooler

The print spooler consists of a group of components that include the print router, the local and remote print provider, the print processor, and the language and port monitors. These components can reside on both the computer sending a job and the network print server receiving print jobs. The print spooler's components take the print job that the GDI creates, and then modify it so that it has all the required information and formatting to print correctly. If part of the spooler is on a server, the server provides the processing resources for the print job, freeing the user's computer and improving performance.

Different print servers have different spooler components. In Windows 2000 Server, the print spooler is made up of a router, remote print provider, local print provider, print processor, separator page processor, and language and port monitors.

Print Router   The print router receives a print job and locates an available print provider that can handle the print job's protocol. For example, the router might look for a print provider designed to handle RPC print jobs or jobs that were transferred by using HTTP. When an acceptable print provider is found, the router relays the print job from the remote print provider to the chosen local print provider, where the job is modified as needed before printing.

Remote Print Provider   The remote print provider is part of the client side of the print process. The router gives control of the print job to the first remote print provider the router finds that recognizes the destination printer. A remote print provider sends the print job to the server router only.

Examples of remote print providers include the Windows Network Print Provider and the Novell NetWare Remote Print Provider. When a user sends a print job to a printer on a print server, the remote print provider is on the user's computer and the local print provider is on the server.

Local Print Provider   The local print provider receives the print job, writes it to a spool file, and keeps track of information about the job. Spooling a file to disk ensures that the job is saved and printed even if printers are unavailable or a power failure occurs.

The local print provider has two components that are required by the printer type and settings:

- The *print processor* makes necessary modifications to the print job, and then calls the GDI to render the job. This is important when third-party printers have special requirements. Often, modifications are not required.

- The *separator page* processor adds separator pages as required. You can specify separator pages based on your needs. Most separator pages include information such as the user and computer that created the job, or the date and time the job was created. You can configure the separator page on the **Advanced** tab of the **Printer Properties** page.

    The escape codes used in creating a separator page are listed in Table 11-4.

Table 11-4   Escape Codes and Functions for a Separator Page

Escape Code	Function
\	The first line of the separator file must contain only this character. The separator file interpreter reads the separator file command as a delimiter.
\N	Prints the user name of the person who submitted the job.
\I	Prints the job number.
\D	Prints the date the job was printed. The time is displayed in the format specified under Regional and Language Options in Control Panel.
\L*xxx*	Prints the string of text that appears after the \L escape code. If you enter \LTest, the text "Test" appears in the separator page.
\F*pathname*	Prints the contents of the file specified by the pathname, starting on an empty line. The contents of this file are copied directly to the printer without processing.
\H*nn*	Sets a printer-specific control sequence, where *nn* is a hexadecimal ASCII code sent directly to the printer. See your printer manual to determine the specific numbers.
\W*nn*	Sets the width of the separator page. The default width is 80 characters, and the maximum width is 256 characters. Characters beyond this width are deleted.
\B\S	Prints text in single-width block characters until \U is encountered.
\E	Ejects a page from the printer. Use this code to start a new separator page or to end the separator page file. If you get an extra blank separator page when you print, remove this code from your separator page file.

Table 11-4   Escape Codes and Functions for a Separator Page

Escape Code	Function
\n	Skips the number of lines specified by n (from 0 through 9). Skipping 0 lines moves printing to the next line.
\B\M	Prints text in double-width block characters until \U is encountered.
\U	Turns off block character printing.

After the local print provider passes a job through the print processor and separator page processor, it sends the job from the spooler to the appropriate port print monitor.

Print Monitors   Windows XP Professional supports two kinds of print monitors:

- Language monitors
- Port monitors

Port monitors are subdivided into:

- Local port monitors
- Remote port monitors

Windows XP Professional provides three types of print monitors: language, local port, and remote.

Language monitor   The language monitor provides the language that the client and printer use to communicate. If the printer is bidirectional, the language monitor allows you to monitor printer status. You can request configuration and status from the printer, and the printer sends unsolicited status (such as "Paper tray empty") to the client.

Local port monitor   The local port monitor (Localspl.dll) controls parallel and serial input/output (I/O) ports where a printer might be attached. It sends print jobs to local devices, including those on familiar ports such as LPT1 and COM1.

Remote port monitor   The remote port monitor includes all other port monitors supplied with Windows XP Professional, and it enables printing to remote printers. An example is Lanman Print Services Port.

Port Monitor

The local print provider (Localspl.dll) that comes with Windows XP Professional includes the local port monitor and the Winprint print processor. The local port monitor controls the parallel and serial ports to which printers are connected. The standard port monitor is used for most network print jobs. Port monitors such as the NetWare Port Monitor or AppleTalk Port Monitor control other ports, such as TCP/IP or Ethernet.

Windows XP Professional includes port monitors that enable printing to different types of printers in different network environments. Some of the port monitors included with Windows XP Professional are described in further detail below:

■ The preferred network port monitor in Windows XP Professional is the standard port monitor. SNMP is used to configure and monitor the printer ports. In addition to the standard port monitor, Internet printing adds an HTTP print provider. For more information, see "Methods of Sending Print Jobs" earlier in this chapter.

■ The local port monitor is the standard monitor for printers connected directly to your computer. If you add a printer to your computer by using a serial or parallel port (such as COM1 or LPT1), this monitor is used.

■ The USB port monitor is the monitor used for USB printers connected directly to your computer. If you plug your USB printer into your computer, this monitor is used.

■ LPR Port monitor is used to send jobs over TCP/IP to a print server or printer running an LPD service. LPR Port monitor can be used as an alternative to the standard port monitor to Unix print servers. Use LPR Port if your LPD target server requires an RFC 1179-compliant Line Printer Remote protocol.

Note   The standard port monitor is the preferred port monitor for Windows XP Professional. The standard port monitor supports the RAW protocol, TCP/IP printing, and the non-RFC LPR protocol.

■ PJL Monitor (Pjlmon.dll) communicates in printer job language (PJL). Any bidirectional print device that uses a bidirectional port monitor that uses PJL can use the PJL language monitor.

Printing Over the Internet

A user on a computer that runs Windows XP Professional can access information about available printers and send jobs to those printers on a Windows 2000 print server, or send to any print server that supports IPP v1.0. For finding an Internet printer and sending a print job to that printer, the following must occur:

1. A user connects to a Windows 2000 print server over the Internet by typing the URL for the print device.

2. The print server requires the client to provide authentication information. This ensures that only authorized users print documents on your printer, rather than making it available to everyone with an Internet connection.

3. After a user has authorized access to the print server, the server presents status information to the user by using Active Server Pages (ASP), which contain information about currently available printers.

4. Windows XP Professional users can connect to any of the available printers by using ASP and can get information about each printer's capabilities.

5. After users connect to an Internet printer, they can send documents to the print server by using IPP v1.0. IPP sends the job to the designated Internet printer.

Note   Only computers that run Microsoft® Windows® 95, Microsoft® Windows® 98, Microsoft® Windows® Millennium Edition (Me), or Microsoft Windows 2000 and that use the Internet Printing Client, can connect to available printers. Microsoft® Windows NT® and Microsoft® Windows® 3.1 cannot connect.

Figure 11-3 shows the steps that the Internet printing process might include.

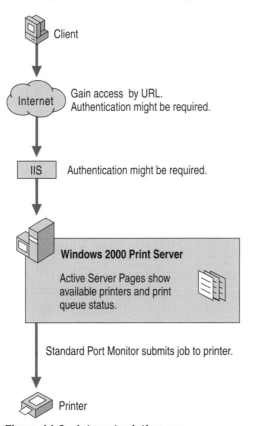

Figure 11-3   Internet printing process

Print Job Formats

Print jobs are sent in a variety of formats, each suited to different computing environments.

EMF   Enhanced Metafile (EMF) is the standard format for print jobs created on Windows XP Professional. EMF files are highly portable because the instructions for the print job are assembled on the user's computer, and the spooler completes the processing of the print job.

EMF data is created by the GDI. After an EMF job is sent to the spooler, control is returned to the user, and the spooler finishes processing the job. This limits how long the user's computer is busy.

RAW   RAW is a common data type for clients other than Windows. The spooler does not modify RAW data. It is sent directly to the printer.

RAW [FF Appended]   RAW [FF Appended] is exactly like the RAW data type, except that a form-feed character is appended to the end of each print job. The last page of a RAW document does not print on a Printer Control Language (PCL) printer, so appending a form feed is necessary.

RAW [FF Auto]   RAW [FF Auto] is exactly like the RAW data type, except the spooler checks the document for a form-feed character at the end of the job. If there is no form feed, the spooler adds one.

Text   Text tells the spooler that the data is ANSI text and modifies it if necessary. The print processor takes the text and calls GDI for playback. The text is printed using the printer's default font.

Text data is composed of values from 0 through 255. Each value represents a different character. This data type is based on the ANSI standard, and if an application that has another character set creates text data it does not print. This often presents a problem in the extended character range, represented by values above 127.

Troubleshooting Printing Problems

This troubleshooting section provides several approaches to solving printing problems. The first section describes common printing problems and solutions. The second section describes the parts of the printing process. You can learn how printing works, determine where a printing problem occurs, and fix that part of the process.

Common Printing Problems

This section describes some of the most common printing problems and their solutions. You can use the following examples to solve similar problems.

Cannot Administer Printers After an Upgrade

Power users are now required to have the **Load and unload device drivers** permission to administer printers. For more information about this new requirement, see Installing Local Printers earlier in this chapter.

Cannot Install a Plug and Play Printer

Windows XP Professional includes more printer drivers than previous versions of Windows, but if the printer driver you need is not included with Windows XP Professional, your computer does not automatically install your printer, even if it is Plug and Play. You can install the printer by using the Add Printer wizard. Click **Have Disk** to provide the required drivers.

If required drivers are available, you might want to restart your computer. If a Plug and Play printer requires manual detection, you must restart the computer before installing the printer. Manually detected Plug and Play printers typically use parallel port connections.

Cannot Find a Printer by Location

Searching for a printer by location requires that you use Windows XP Professional or another client enabled in Active Directory.

Make sure your searches match the printer location format used in your environment. For more information about printer location formats, see "Using Active Directory to Find Printers" earlier in this chapter.

Bidirectional Printer Problem

If you encounter a problem with bidirectional printing, disable bidirectional printing and resend your print job.

To disable bidirectional printing

1. In **Control Panel**, click **Printers**.

2. Right-click the bidirectional printer, and then click **Properties**.

3. Click the **Ports** tab, clear **Enable bidirectional support**, and then click **OK**.

Do Not Have Permissions

If a printer requires security permissions, you must have the appropriate permissions from your user account or your user group.

Use a printer that does not require permissions or a printer for which you have permissions. Or, ask your administrator to grant you permissions for the printer.

Bad Printer Port or Improperly Formatted Data

Incorrectly configured ports can cause printing failures. LPR ports typically include an IP address, or a fully qualified domain name (FQDN), followed by a queue name and DNS resolves the address. In that case, an FQDN resolution error can occur. A user might also enter the Windows 2000 Server queue name instead of the LPD queue name.

To find out if an incorrect FQDN name is being used, review the event log for your computer for event ID 2004. Event ID 2004 indicates that the target LPD did not respond as expected, which can occur with an incorrect FQDN.

A bad printer port or improperly formatted data error can occur if a user configures a computer to print directly to the printer or to use bidirectional communication when the hardware does not support those functions.

To troubleshoot the TCP/IP port you use for the printer, try configuring the standard TCP/IP port monitor for your printer.

For more information about configuring the Standard TCP/IP Port Monitor, see "Methods of Sending Print Jobs" earlier in this chapter.

Make the following changes to troubleshoot the TCP/IP port:

■ In the **Configure Standard TCP/IP Port Monitor** dialog box, verify the **Port Name** and the **Printer Name or IP Address**. Correct them if necessary.

■ Toggle from one protocol to another. Some printers require that you use one or the other.

■ Select **LPR Byte Counting Enabled**. Some printers require that jobs accurately represent their size.

For more information about byte counting, see "Methods of Sending Print Jobs" earlier in this chapter.

Print Jobs Go to the Queue but Do Not Print

If you use a multifunction peripheral (MFP), IEEE 1284.4 might not properly detect your print device. Shut down your computer and printer, turn on your printer, and then turn on your computer. Typically, IEEE 1284.4 recognizes all features of your MFP.

Graphic Images Not Printing as Expected

Disable enhanced metafile spooling (EMF).

To disable enhanced metafile spooling

1. In the **Printers and Faxes** folder, right-click the print server, and then click **Properties**.

2. Click the **Advanced tab**, and then clear the **Enable advanced printing features** check box.

3. Click **OK**.

Pages That Are Only Partially Printed

■ Check that sufficient memory is available to print the document.

■ Pages print only partially when the page size of the document you want to print is bigger than the page size available to the printer.

- If text is missing, verify that the font used for the missing text is installed and valid.

- The printer might need toner. Try replacing the printer's toner cartridge.

Slow printing

- If the print server is taking an unusually long time to render the job, try defragmenting the server's disk. Check that there is adequate space for temporary files on the hard disk.

- If you use printer pooling to handle a large number of jobs, and print jobs take a long time to get to the top of queue, consider adding more printers to the pool to handle the volume of print jobs.

PostScript printer returns "Out of Memory" message   To print the current document, you must allocate more memory for the printer or send smaller print jobs.

To configure PostScript memory, in the **Printer Properties** dialog box, on the **Device Settings** tab, modify **Available PostScript Memory**. You must have Manage printer rights to change **Available PostScript Memory**.

Break large print jobs into smaller parts to reduce the amount of printer memory required. For example, a ten-page print job can be divided into two five-page jobs.

Computer stalls during printing   For local printers:

- Check that the appropriate printer driver is installed. Reinstall if necessary.

- Check for adequate space on the hard disk.

  For network printers:

- Check that the server has enough free hard-disk space.

- Try to disable EMF spooling and send the job in RAW format.

Troubleshooting the Printing Process

A series of actions occurs in the process of completing a print job. Understanding significance of each part of the process can help you solve printing problems.

Administrator creates print share on print server   A print share makes the printer available to the network. The necessary drivers are stored on the server for distribution to clients, and the print server waits to receive the jobs that the printer produces.

If this step is not properly completed, users might be unable to connect to the printer on the server even if the printer is correctly installed.

Client system connects to the share   Using any Windows XP Professional features, such as Point and Print, the Add Printer wizard, or the list of printers in My Network Places, you can connect the client to the printer. If necessary, appropriate drivers are downloaded to the client computer and information about the printer is recorded.

If client system connection is not completed properly, the user might not be able to locate the printer in the list of available printers.

Client system creates print job   Users initiate this process by choosing to print a document. If the printer drivers for a user's computer are not available, the GDI cannot properly create the print job.

Client system sends print job to print share   A network connection between client and print server must be available.

Print server receives, spools, and modifies print job   The print server must have enough space to accommodate print jobs.

Print server sends print job to printer   The proper port or language monitor must be available for the printer type. The network connection between print server and printer must be working.

Printer interprets print job and prints it   The printer must be turned on, online, connected to the network, and functioning properly.

Troubleshooting Printing from an Operating System Other Than Windows

If you have problems printing from Windows XP Professional to a non-Windows print server, the following sections might be helpful.

UNIX

If printing to a UNIX server fails, make sure that the Lprmon is installed. If it is not installed, you might not be able to produce print information that the server can interpret. For more information about installing the LPR port monitor, see "Methods of Sending Print Jobs" earlier in this chapter. For more information about working with UNIX, see "Printing from Other Operating Systems" earlier in this chapter.

NetWare

If printing to a NetWare server fails, make sure that you have a client installed on your computer, such as Microsoft Client Service for NetWare or Novell Client 32. These clients let your computer send print jobs to the NetWare server, which the server then relays to the printer. If this type of client is not installed, you might not be able to produce usable information for the print server. For more information, see "Printing from Other Operating Systems" earlier in this chapter.

IBM

If printing from an IBM server fails, make sure that you have connected to the LPT port that corresponds to the printer where you send the job. For more information about the standard port monitor, see "Methods of Sending Print Jobs" earlier in this chapter. If your clients need to communicate with a mainframe computer, make sure that 3270 host emulation software is installed. If your clients need to communicate with an AS/400 system, make sure that 5250 host emulation software is installed.

Troubleshooting Font-Related Printing Problems

Typically, problems with fonts occur only when you try to print a document. If printing is taking a very long time, or if the result is not as expected, the cause might be your fonts. To solve a font problem, try reinstalling the font that does not print as expected or try printing from another computer.

Font does not print correctly   Sometimes fonts become corrupted. Reinstalling the font might solve the problem even if the font does not appear to be corrupted.

Printed font is distorted or unreadable   Try a different font size or a different font to see if the problem is specific to the particular font and font size you use.

Paste the text into another document and try to print. If the problem persists, the problem might be specific to the font. Reinstall the font.

Print page is clipped   Pages only partially print when the page size of the document you are trying to print is bigger than the page size available in the printer. Check to confirm that you are not sending documents that cover a larger size of paper than the printer can accommodate.

The printer might not have enough memory to print large documents. If this is the case, increase the available virtual memory, add more RAM to the printer, or print smaller sections of the document.

Slow performance   If you are working with an unusually large number of fonts, system performance degrades. Keeping fewer than 1,000 fonts installed on your computer helps maintain performance.

New fonts are added the first time you restart your computer after installing them. This slows the startup process. When the computer is restarted later, the process finishes more quickly due to font caching, but startup might still be slower than before. Enumeration of fonts can also slow your system. Font enumeration can occur when an application starts up or when all the available fonts must be listed, such as when you select a font or open the Fonts folder.

Faxing in Windows XP Professional

If you have a fax modem attached to your computer, you can send or receive fax documents directly from your computer.

Windows XP Professional detects fax modems, but it is recommended that you refer to the documentation for your fax modem for other steps that you must take to install your modem. To use the fax service that Windows XP Professional provides, you must manually install the service.

To add fax service

1. In **Add or Remove Programs**, click **Add/Remove Windows Components**.

2. Select **Fax Service**, click **Next**, and then click **Finish**.

Configuring Fax Service

You can configure Fax Service to archive and print received faxes, to archive sent faxes, to retry sending faxes that could not be sent, and to automatically cleanup unsent faxes after a certain period.

Configuring Fax Service Options

You might want to configure several attributes of your fax service first, such as security settings and how fax jobs are stored and sent.

To configure fax service options

1. In **All Programs**, point to **Accessories, point to Communications**, point to **Fax, and then click Fax Console.**

2. In the **Fax Console**, click **Tools**, and then click **Fax Printer Configuration**.

3. Set your preferences:

   ■ To set archiving preferences for sent and received faxes, click the **Archive** tab.

   ■ To set notification preferences, click the **Tracking** tab.

   ■ To set retry preferences on sent faxes and an automatic cleanup for unsent faxes, click the **Devices** tab, and then click **Properties**.

   The **Fax (Local) Properties** dialog box is shown in Figure 11-4.

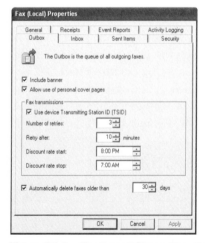

Figure 11-4   Fax (Local) Properties dialog box

Entering User Information for Faxing

This is the default information for the fax cover sheet. The **User Information** tab is shown in Figure 11-5.

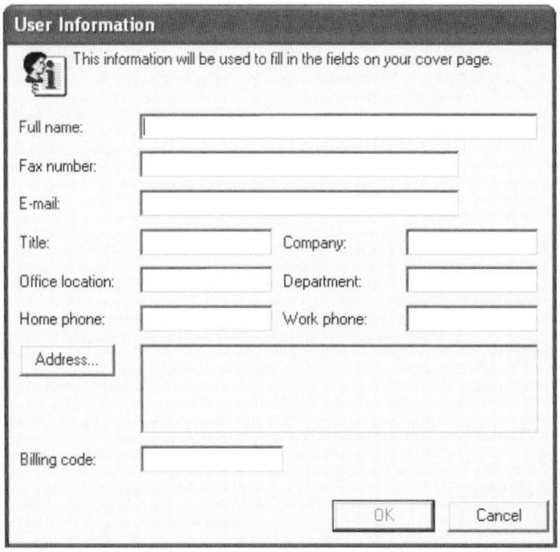

Figure 11-5   User Information in the Fax Properties dialog box

To configure fax user information by using the fax configuration wizard

1. In **All Programs**, point to **Accessories, point to Communications**, point to **Fax**, and then click **Fax Console**.

2. On the **Fax Configuration Wizard** properties page, click **Next**, and then enter your information.

The information you enter on this page creates the default information in the Send Fax wizard, which appears when you send a fax. You can change this information each time you send a fax.

Setting Printing Preferences for Faxes

You can configure the default options for sending fax jobs to a particular fax printer. By configuring fax options, you can control the resolution, orientation, and paper size.

To configure fax job defaults

1. In **Control Panel**, double-click the **Printers and Faxes** icon.

2. Right-click the **Fax** icon, and then click **Printing Preferences**.

3. Make your choices on the **Fax Printing Preferences** properties page.

Sending Faxes

When you prepare a fax to be sent, use the Send Fax wizard to provide the information needed to send your fax. The fax wizard includes a number of optional pages that you can use to configure fax job attributes.

Recipient information   Use this page to enter the phone number or numbers to which you want to send the fax, including fax numbers in your Microsoft® Windows or Microsoft® Outlook address book. Specify special dialing rules, such as first dialing 9 for an outside line.

Preparing the cover page   Use this page if you would like to add a cover page and a note for the recipient.

Schedule   Use this page to determine when to send the fax. By scheduling transmissions, you can take advantage of lower rates during specific times.

Summary page   Use this page to confirm the configuration you have chosen before sending the fax.

Preview Fax button   Use this button to preview your fax before sending.

After you use the Send Fax wizard, Windows XP Professional uses the modem to send your job to the fax numbers you have indicated unless you specified that the job be sent at a later time. If the transmission fails, Windows XP Professional tries to resend the job at regular intervals depending on your preferences.

To configure the number and frequency of retries

1. In **Control Panel,** double-click **Printers and Faxes**.

2. Right-click **Fax**, click **Properties**, click the **Devices** tab, and then select a device.

3. Click the **Properties** button.

4. On the **Send** tab, set your Retries preferences.

Additional Resources

These resources contain additional information related to this chapter.

Related Information

- "Active Directory" in the *Distributed Systems Guide* for information about finding a printer by an attribute, such as location.

- "Authorization and Access Control" in this book for more information about setting permissions.

- "Configuring TCP/IP" in this book for information about printer location.

- "Managing Devices" in this book for information about Plug and Play technology.

Chapter 12

Disk Management

Administrators can use the Disk Management snap-in or the new DiskPart command-line tool to manage disks and volumes in Microsoft® Windows® XP Professional. Both tools support dynamic disks and volumes, which were introduced in Microsoft® Windows® 2000. Microsoft® Windows® XP 64-Bit Edition also introduces a new partition style, giving administrators additional choices for configuring disk storage.

Related Information

- For more information about the NTFS file system and the file allocation table file systems FAT and FAT32, see "File Systems" in this book.

- For more information about troubleshooting problems related to disks and using Chkdsk and Disk Defragmenter, see "Troubleshooting Disks and File Systems" in this book.

- For more information about the startup process and Boot.ini, see "Troubleshooting Startup" in this book.

New in Disk Management

The Windows XP Professional operating system provides improved disk management. Table 12-1 summarizes the enhancements made from Microsoft® Windows® 2000 Professional to Windows XP Professional.

Table 12-1   Enhancements and Changes Since Windows 2000

New Feature	Feature Description
Manage disks at the command line by using DiskPart.	Use the new command-line tool DiskPart to perform disk-related tasks at the command line as an alternative to using the Disk Management snap-in. When you use DiskPart, you can create scripts to automate tasks, such as creating volumes or converting disks to dynamic.
Extend simple and spanned volumes that were converted from basic to dynamic.	You can now extend most simple and spanned volumes after converting them from basic to dynamic. For more information, see "Converting Basic Disks to Dynamic Disks" later in this chapter.
Extend basic volumes by using DiskPart.	Use DiskPart to extend primary partitions and logical drives on basic disks that use the MBR partition style.
Use a new partition style for disks in Itanium-based computers.	Windows XP 64-Bit Edition supports a new partition style called GUID partition table (GPT). The GPT partition style offers benefits such as support for volumes up to 18 exabytes and 128 partitions per disk.
Use NTFS when you format dynamic volumes and GPT disks by using Disk Management.	When you use the Disk Management snap-in, NTFS is the only file system available for dynamic volumes and for disks that use the GPT partition style. If you want to format dynamic volumes and GPT disks by using the file allocation table (FAT) file systems, you must use the **format** command at the command line.
Use dynamic disks to create volumes that span multiple disks.	Dynamic disks are the mandatory storage type for volumes that span multiple disks. Therefore, before you upgrade from Windows 2000 Professional to Windows XP Professional, you must convert basic disks to dynamic if they contain volume sets or stripe sets created by using Microsoft® Windows NT® Workstation 4.0.

If you are migrating from Microsoft® Windows NT® version 4.0, the enhancements in Table 12-2 apply in addition to those outlined in Table 12-1.

Table 12-2   Enhancements and Changes Since Windows NT 4.0

New Feature	Feature Description
Basic and dynamic disk storage	Windows XP Professional offers two types of disk storage: basic and dynamic. Basic disks use the same disk structures as those used in Windows NT 4.0.
	Dynamic disks, which offer features not available in basic disks, were introduced in Windows 2000 and are supported and enhanced by Windows XP Professional.
Online disk management	You can perform most disk-related tasks without shutting down the computer or interrupting users, and most configuration changes take effect immediately. For example, you can create or extend a volume without restarting the computer. You can also add disks without restarting. For information about changes that do require restarting the computer, see "Converting Basic Disks to Dynamic Disks" later in this chapter.
Disk Management snap-in	The Disk Management snap-in replaces the Disk Administrator program used in Windows NT 4.0.
Local and remote disk management	By using the Disk Management snap-in, you can manage any remote computer running Windows 2000, Windows XP Professional, or Windows XP 64-Bit Edition on which you are a member of the Administrators group.
Limited support for multidisk volumes created by using Windows NT 4.0	Because Windows XP Professional offers limited support for multidisk volumes created by Windows NT 4.0, you must perform certain steps before you upgrade to Windows XP Professional. For more information, see "Preparing Multidisk Volumes for Windows XP Professional" later in this chapter.

Disk Management Overview

Use the Disk Management snap-in in Windows XP Professional to perform disk-related tasks, such as creating basic and dynamic volumes, formatting them, and assigning drive letters.

You must be a member of the Administrators group to use Disk Management.

To open Disk Management

1. From the **Start** menu, click **Run**.

2. In the **Open** box, type **diskmgmt.msc**, and then click **OK**.

Note If you upgrade from Microsoft® Windows® 98, Microsoft® Windows® 98, Second Edition (SE), or Microsoft® Windows® Millennium Edition to Windows XP Professional, a message appears when you open Disk Management during the first 30 days after installation. The message indicates that making any changes to your disk configuration, such as creating or deleting partitions or converting them to dynamic, prevents you from uninstalling Windows XP Professional. For more information, see "Supporting Installations" in this book.

After you install a new disk, you must choose a partition style and storage type to use on the disk. Your choices vary according to which operating system you are running and whether the computer is an x86–based computer or an Itanium–based computer. Table 12-3 describes the storage types and partition styles that are available for each edition of Microsoft® Windows XP and Windows 2000.

Table 12-3 Storage Types and Partition Styles Available in Windows XP and Windows 2000

| Operating System | Storage Types | | | Partition Styles | |
	Basic Volumes	Dynamic Simple, Spanned, and Striped Volumes	Dynamic Mirrored and RAID-5 Volumes	MBR Disks	GPT Disks
Microsoft® Windows® XP Home Edition	X			X	
Windows XP Professional	X	X		X	
Windows XP 64-Bit Edition	X	X		X	X
Windows 2000 Professional	X	X		X	
Windows 2000 Server family	X	X	X	X	

Windows XP Professional offers two *storage types*: basic disk and dynamic disk. Basic disks use the same disk structures as those used in Windows Me or earlier, Microsoft® Windows NT® 4.0, and Microsoft Windows 2000. When using basic disks, you are limited to creating four primary partitions per disk, or three primary partitions and one extended partition with unlimited logical drives. Primary partitions and logical drives on basic disks are known as basic volumes.

Dynamic disks were introduced in Windows 2000 and are supported and enhanced by Windows XP Professional. Dynamic disks provide features that basic disks do not, such as the ability to create volumes that span multiple disks. All volumes on dynamic disks are known as dynamic volumes.

The term *partition style* refers to the method that Windows XP Professional uses to organize partitions on the disk. All x86-based computers use the partition style known as the master boot record (MBR). The MBR contains a partition table that describes where the partitions are located on the disk. Because MBR is the only partition style available on x86-based computers, you do not need to choose this style; it is used automatically.

Itanium-based computers running the Windows XP 64-Bit Edition use a new partition style called the globally unique identifier (GUID) partition table (GPT). The GPT partition style supports partitions up to 18 exabytes and 128 partitions per disk.

The introduction of GPT makes understanding the partition styles a bit more challenging, but most disk-related tasks are unchanged. You can still use basic disks and dynamic disks as you did in Windows 2000, and these storage types are available on disks that use either partition style.

Disk Management differentiates between partition styles by referring to disks that use the master boot record as MBR disks and disks that use the GUID partition table as GPT disks. Figure 12-1 shows how Disk Management displays GPT and MBR disks in an Itanium-based computer.

Note   You can use Windows XP 64-Bit Edition to manage MBR disks and GPT disks. However, you cannot start Windows XP 64-Bit Edition from an MBR disk.

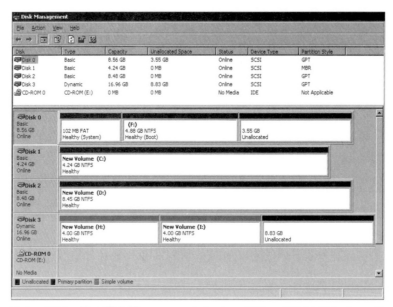

Figure 12-1   How Disk Management displays GPT and MBR disks in an Itanium-based computer

For more information about GPT disks, see "Managing GPT Disks in Itanium-based Computers" later in this chapter. For sector-level details about MBR and GPT disks, see "Troubleshooting Disks and File Systems" in this book.

Basic and Dynamic Disks and Volumes

You can use both basic and dynamic disks on the same computer system and with any combination of file systems. However, all volumes on a physical disk must be either basic or dynamic, and each disk must use either the MBR or GPT partition style. For more information about the file systems available in Windows XP Professional, see "File Systems" in this book.

Basic Disks

The term *basic disk* refers to a physical disk that contains basic volumes, such as primary partitions and logical drives. In x86-based computers, basic disks use the same partition style (the MBR partition style) as the disks used by Microsoft' MS–DOS', Windows Me or earlier, Windows NT 4.0 or earlier, and Windows 2000. Therefore, use basic disks if you want to use these operating systems to access data in an x86-based computer that also runs Windows XP Professional.

Itanium-based computers also support basic disks, but you can choose either partition style (MBR or GPT) for each basic disk. The partition style determines the number of basic volumes you can create on the disk as well as the operating systems that can access the disk. For more information about GPT disks, see "Managing GPT Disks in Itanium-based Computers" later in this chapter.

You must convert a basic disk to dynamic before you can create simple volumes, spanned volumes, and striped volumes. For more information, see "Converting Basic Disks to Dynamic Disks" later in this chapter.

Basic Volumes

The term *basic volume* refers to a partition on a basic disk. Windows XP Professional supports the following basic volumes:

- Primary partitions (MBR and GPT disks).

- Logical drives within extended partitions (MBR disks only).

The number of basic volumes you can create on a basic disk depends on the partition style of the disk:

- On MBR disks, you can create up to four primary partitions, or you can create up to three primary partitions and one extended partition. Within the extended partition, you can create unlimited logical drives.

- On GPT disks, you can create up to 128 partitions. Because GPT disks do not limit you to four partitions, extended partitions and logical drives are not available on GPT disks. For more information about GPT disks, see "Managing GPT Disks in Itanium-based Computers" later in this chapter.

If you want to add more space to existing primary partitions and logical drives, use the **extend** command in DiskPart. The requirements for extending a basic volume are as follows:

- You must use NTFS to format the basic volume. If the volume is formatted by using FAT, you must convert it to NTFS before you can extend it. For more information about converting FAT volumes to NTFS, see "File Systems" in this book.

- You can extend a basic volume on the same disk only, and the basic volume must be followed by contiguous unallocated space.

- You can extend a logical drive within contiguous free space in the extended partition that contains it. If you extend a logical drive beyond the free space available in the extended partition, the extended partition grows to contain the logical drive as long as the extended partition is followed by contiguous unallocated space.

For more information about using DiskPart, see Windows XP Professional Help.

Dynamic Disks

A *dynamic disk* is a physical disk that contains dynamic volumes. Dynamic disks provide features that basic disks do not. For example, use dynamic disks if you need to:

- Increase the size of a volume by extending the volume onto the same disk by using unallocated space that is not contiguous. You can also extend a volume onto other dynamic disks.

- Improve disk input/output (I/O) performance by using striped volumes.

Dynamic disks offer greater flexibility for volume management because they use a hidden database to track information about dynamic volumes on the disk and about other dynamic disks in the computer. Because each dynamic disk in a computer stores a replica of the dynamic disk database, Windows XP Professional can repair a corrupted database on one dynamic disk by using the database on another dynamic disk.

The location of the database is determined by the partition style of the disk.

- On MBR disks, the database is contained in the last 1 megabyte (MB) of the disk.

- On GPT disks, the database is contained in a 1-MB reserved (hidden) partition known as the Logical Disk Manager (LDM) Metadata partition.

When you move dynamic disks to a computer that has existing dynamic disks, you must import the dynamic disks to merge the databases on the moved disks with the databases on the existing dynamic disks. For more information about importing dynamic disks, see "Importing Foreign Disks" later in this chapter.

All dynamic disks in a computer must be members of the same disk group, which is a collection of dynamic disks. Each disk in a disk group stores a replica of the same dynamic disk database. A disk group uses a name consisting of the computer name plus a suffix of Dg0. The disk group name is stored in the registry.

The disk group name on a computer never changes as long as the disk group contains dynamic disks. If you remove the last disk in the disk group or convert all dynamic disks to basic, the registry entry remains. However, if you then create a dynamic disk again on that computer, a new disk group name is generated. The computer name in the disk group remains the same, but the suffix is Dg1 instead of Dg0.

When you move a dynamic disk to a computer that has no dynamic disks, the dynamic disk retains its disk group name and ID from the original computer and uses them on the local computer.

For more information about disk groups, see article Q222189, "Description of Disk Groups in Windows 2000 Disk Management," in the Microsoft Knowledge Base. To find this article, see the Microsoft Knowledge Base link on the Web Resources page at http://www.microsoft.com/windows/reskits/webresources.

For more information about converting basic disks to dynamic, including the limitations of dynamic disks, see "Converting Basic Disks to Dynamic Disks" later in this chapter.

Dynamic Volumes

A *dynamic volume* is a volume that is created on a dynamic disk. Dynamic volume types include simple, spanned, and striped volumes. Windows 2000 Server also supports mirrored and RAID-5 volumes, which are fault tolerant. Dynamic disks and volumes are not available on computers running Windows XP Home Edition.

Regardless of the partition style used (MBR or GPT), you can create about 2,000 dynamic volumes per disk group, although the recommended number of dynamic volumes is 32 or fewer per disk group.

To help you understand dynamic volumes, the following descriptions are provided.

Simple Volumes

Simple volumes are the dynamic-disk equivalent of the primary partitions and logical drives that you used in Windows NT 4.0 and earlier versions. When creating simple volumes, keep these points in mind:

- If you have only one dynamic disk, you can create only simple volumes.

- You can increase the size of a simple volume to include unallocated space on the same disk or on a different disk. The volume must be unformatted or formatted by using NTFS. You can increase the size of a simple volume in two ways:

  - By extending the simple volume on the same disk. The volume remains a simple volume.

  - By extending a simple volume to include unallocated space on other disks on the same computer. This creates a spanned volume.

> **Note** If the simple volume is the system volume or the boot volume, you cannot extend it. For more information about determining which volumes are the system and boot volumes, see "Converting Basic Disks to Dynamic Disks" later in this chapter.

Spanned Volumes

Spanned volumes combine areas of unallocated space from multiple disks into one logical volume. The areas of unallocated space can be different sizes. Spanned volumes require two disks, and you can use up to 32 disks. When creating spanned volumes, keep these points in mind:

- You can extend only NTFS volumes or unformatted volumes.

- After you create or extend a spanned volume, you cannot delete any portion of it without deleting the entire spanned volume.

- You cannot stripe spanned volumes.

- Spanned volumes do not provide fault tolerance. If one of the disks containing a spanned volume fails, the entire volume fails, and all data on the spanned volume becomes inaccessible.

Striped Volumes

Striped volumes improve disk I/O performance by distributing I/O requests across disks. Striped volumes are composed of stripes of data of equal size written across each disk in the volume. They are created from equally sized, unallocated areas on two or more physical disks. In Windows XP Professional, the size of each stripe is 64 kilobytes (KB).

Striped volumes cannot be extended and do not offer fault tolerance. If one of the disks containing a striped volume fails, the entire volume fails, and all data on the striped volume becomes inaccessible.

Mirrored Volumes

A mirrored volume is a fault-tolerant volume that provides a copy of a volume on another physical disk. Mirrored volumes provide data redundancy by duplicating the information contained on the volume. The two volumes that make up a mirrored volume are known as mirrors. Each mirror is always located on a different disk. If one of the physical disks fails, the data on the failed disk becomes unavailable, but the system continues to operate by using the unaffected disk.

Mirrored volumes are available only on computers running the Windows 2000 Server family of operating systems. Mirrored volumes are not available on computers running Windows XP.

RAID-5 Volumes

A RAID–5 volume is a fault-tolerant volume that stripes data and parity across three or more physical disks. Parity is a calculated value that is used to reconstruct data if one physical disk fails. When a disk fails, Windows 2000 Server continues to operate by recreating the data that was on the failed disk from the remaining data and parity.

RAID–5 volumes are available only on computers running the Windows 2000 Server family of operating systems. RAID–5 volumes are not available on computers running Windows XP.

Converting Basic Disks to Dynamic Disks

You can convert a basic disk to dynamic by using Disk Management or by using Disk-Part, a command-line tool that provides the same functions as Disk Management. When you convert a disk to dynamic, the following occurs:

- All existing primary partitions and logical drives become simple volumes.

- The disk joins the local disk group and receives a copy of the dynamic disk database.

Before you convert a disk to dynamic, read the section "Before Converting Disks to Dynamic" later in this chapter to review the scenarios that are affected by dynamic disks. For example, converting disks to dynamic in a multiple-boot computer can cause startup problems if you do not configure your disks properly. If you decide to perform the conversion, see "How to Convert a Basic Disk to Dynamic" later in this chapter.

> **Note**   For certain disks, the menu command to convert the disk to dynamic is unavailable in Disk Management. For more information, see "Disks That You Cannot Convert to Dynamic" later in this chapter.

You can convert basic disks to dynamic at any time. In most cases, you do not need to restart your computer to complete the conversion. However, you must restart the computer if the disks you are converting contain any of the following volumes:

- **System volume (x86-based computers only)**. The system volume contains hardware-specific files such as Ntldr, Boot.ini, and Ntdetect.com. These files are needed to load Windows XP Professional in x86-based computers.

- **Boot volume**. The boot volume contains the Windows XP Professional operating system and its support files. In x86-based computers, the boot volume can be, but does not have to be, the same volume as the system volume. In Itanium-based computers, the boot volume is never the same volume as the EFI System partition. For more information about the EFI System partition, see "Managing GPT Disks in Itanium-based Computers" later in this chapter.

- **Volumes that contain the paging file**. The paging file is a hidden file on the hard disk that Windows XP Professional uses to hold parts of programs and data files that do not fit in memory.

> **Warning** When you convert MBR disks that contain the system, boot, or paging file volumes to dynamic, you are prompted to restart the computer two times. You must restart the computer twice to complete the conversion.

As shown in Figure 12-2, the Disk Management snap-in identifies these volumes in the graphical and disk list views. If you have a combined system and boot volume that also contains the paging file (the most common scenario), then only **System** is shown.

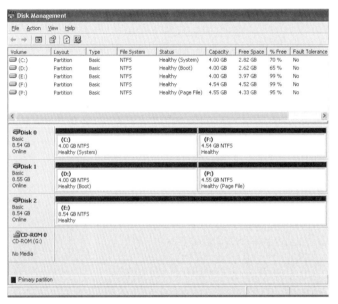

Figure 12-2 How Disk Management identifies separate system, boot, and paging file volumes for an x86-based computer

The **list volume** command in DiskPart also shows the system, boot, and paging file volumes as follows:

Volume ###	Ltr	Label	Fs	Type	Size	Status	Info
Volume 0	G			Unknown	0 B		
Volume 1	C		NTFS	Partition	4096 MB	Healthy	System
Volume 2	F		NTFS	Partition	4651 MB	Healthy	
Volume 3	D		NTFS	Partition	4096 MB	Healthy	Boot
Volume 4	P		NTFS	Partition	4664 MB	Healthy	Pagefile
Volume 5	E		NTFS	Partition	9 GB	Healthy	

For more information about using DiskPart, see "Managing Disks from the Command Line by Using DiskPart" later in this chapter.

Even after you convert a disk to dynamic, some types of primary partitions do not become dynamic volumes. These partitions retain their partition entries in the partition table and are shown as primary partitions in Disk Management. These partitions are:

- Known OEM partitions (usually displayed in Disk Management as EISA Configuration partitions).

- EFI System partitions.

Before Converting Disks to Dynamic

Converting a disk to dynamic changes the partition layout on the disk and creates the dynamic disk database. The result of these changes is increased flexibility for volume management in Windows 2000 and Windows XP Professional. However, these changes are not easily reversed, and the structure of dynamic disks is not compatible with some operating systems. Therefore, you must consider the following issues before you convert disks to dynamic.

If you want to uninstall Windows XP Professional   Do not convert a disk to dynamic if you upgraded from Windows 98 or Windows Me, and you later want to uninstall Windows XP Professional and revert to your previous operating system. Making any changes to disk configuration, including converting a disk to dynamic, prevents you from uninstalling Windows XP Professional. For more information, see "Supporting Installations" in this book.

If a disk contains multiple copies of Windows XP Professional or Windows 2000   Do not convert a disk to dynamic if it contains multiple copies of Windows XP Professional or Windows 2000. Even though these operating systems support dynamic disks, they require certain registry entries that allow them to start from dynamic disks. If the operating systems are installed on the same disk and you use one of the operating systems to convert the disk to dynamic, the registry of the other operating system becomes out-of-date because the drivers required to start the operating system from a dynamic disk are not loaded. Therefore, you can no longer start the other operating system.

One way that you can use dynamic disks with Windows XP Professional and Windows 2000 in a multiple-boot configuration is to install each operating system to a different disk. For example, install Windows 2000 on disk 1 and Windows XP Professional on disk 2. Use Windows 2000 to convert disk 1 to dynamic, and then use Windows XP Professional to convert disk 2 to dynamic. By using this method, you ensure that the registries are updated for each operating system.

If you want to access the disk by using Windows Me or earlier, or Windows NT 4.0   You can access dynamic disks only from computers that are running Windows 2000, Windows XP Professional, or Windows XP 64-Bit Edition. You cannot access dynamic disks from computers running MS-DOS, Windows 95, Windows 98, Windows Me, Windows NT 4.0 or earlier, or Windows XP Home Edition.

This restriction also means that you cannot start any of these operating systems if you convert the disk containing the system volume to dynamic.

To avoid this restriction, use two hard disks: install the other operating system on the first disk, which contains the system volume, and then install Windows XP Professional on the second disk. Using this method, you can convert the disk that is running Windows XP Professional to dynamic and still start the other operating system on the basic disk. However, this method prevents the other operating system from accessing the dynamic disk or any of its volumes and data. Therefore, in computers that start multiple operating systems, you must use caution when you convert disks to dynamic.

Access to dynamic disks is further restricted by the partition style used on the dynamic disk:

- **Dynamic MBR disks**. Only computers running Windows 2000, Windows XP Professional, or Windows XP 64-Bit Edition can access dynamic MBR disks.

- **Dynamic GPT disks**. Only Itanium-based computers running Windows XP 64-Bit Edition can access dynamic GPT disks.

> **Note**   Volumes on dynamic MBR and GPT disks are available across a network to computers running MS-DOS, Windows 95, Windows 98, Windows Me, Windows NT 4.0 or earlier, or Windows XP.

If the disk contains partitions displayed as Healthy (Unknown) in Disk Management   Do not convert a disk to dynamic if it contains unknown partitions created by other operating systems. Windows XP Professional converts unknown partitions to dynamic, making them unreadable to other operating systems. For more information about unknown partitions, see "Troubleshooting Disks and File Systems" in this book.

If the disk contains an OEM partition that is not at the beginning of the disk   Do not convert a disk to dynamic if it contains an OEM partition that is not at the beginning of the disk. (In Disk Management, an OEM partition usually appears as an EISA Configuration partition.) When you convert a disk to dynamic, Windows XP Professional preserves the OEM partition only if it is the first partition on the disk. Otherwise the partition is deleted during the conversion to dynamic.

If you want to extend a dynamic volume   You can extend dynamic volumes that do not retain their partition entries in the partition table. The following volumes retain their entries in the partition table and cannot be extended:

- The system volume and boot volume of the operating system that you used to convert the disk to dynamic.

- Any basic volume that was present on the disk when you converted the disk from basic to dynamic by using the version of Disk Management included with Windows 2000.

- Simple volumes on which you run the DiskPart command **retain**. The **retain** command adds a partition entry to the partition table. However, after you use this command, you can no longer extend the volume.

> **Note**   The **retain** command adds an entry to the partition table of an MBR disk only for simple volumes that are contiguous, start at cylinder-aligned offsets, and are an integral number of cylinders in size. If a volume does not meet these requirements, the **retain** command fails. The following examples describe volumes on which the **retain** command will succeed:
>
> - The simple volume is contiguous and starts at the beginning of the disk
> - The simple volume was present on the disk when the disk was converted to dynamic.

The only way to add more space to the system or boot volume on a dynamic disk is to back up all data on the disk, repartition and reformat the disk, reinstall Windows XP Professional, convert the disks to dynamic, and then restore the data from backup.

The following volumes do not have partition entries and can be extended:

- Simple volumes and spanned volumes created from unallocated space on a dynamic disk.

- A basic volume that is not the system or boot volume and that is on a disk that was converted from basic disk to dynamic disk by using Windows XP Professional.

In addition, you cannot extend striped volumes. Although striped volumes do not have entries in the partition table, Windows XP Professional does not support extending them. You can add more space to a striped volume by backing up the data, deleting the volume, recreating the volume by using Windows XP Professional, and then restoring the data.

If you want to install Windows XP Professional on a dynamic volume   You can install Windows XP Professional only on dynamic volumes that retain their partition entries in the partition table. The only dynamic volumes listed in the partition table are the following:

- The system volume and boot volume of the operating system (Windows XP Professional or Windows 2000) that you used to convert the disk to dynamic. The system volume and boot volume must be simple volumes.

- Any basic volume that was present on the disk when you used Windows 2000 to convert the disk from basic to dynamic.

- Simple volumes on which you run the DiskPart command **retain**. The **retain** command adds a partition entry to the partition table so that you can install Windows XP Professional on the simple volume.

Because these dynamic volumes retain their partition entries, you can install Windows XP Professional on them. However, you cannot extend any of these volumes because you can only extend volumes that do not have entries in the partition table.

If you want to format a dynamic volume by using FAT   Disk Management does not offer FAT as a formatting option for dynamic volumes because NTFS is the preferred file system for dynamic volumes. If you want to format a dynamic volume by using FAT, you must use My Computer, Windows Explorer, or the **format** command. For more information about FAT and NTFS, see "File Systems" in this book.

How to Convert a Basic Disk to Dynamic

After you review the section titled "Before You Convert Disks to Dynamic" earlier in this chapter, you can use this procedure to convert a basic disk to dynamic.

To convert a basic disk to dynamic by using Disk Management

1. From the **Start** menu, click **Run**.

2. In the **Open** box, type **diskmgmt.msc**, and then click **OK**.

3. Right-click the disk you want to convert to dynamic, and then click **Convert to Dynamic Disk**.

    Make sure that you right-click the disk, not a volume on the disk. If the **Convert to Dynamic Disk** command is unavailable or if the conversion fails, you cannot convert the disk to dynamic. For more information, see "Disks That You Cannot Convert to Dynamic" later in this chapter.

Although you can convert a basic disk to dynamic without losing data, you cannot convert a dynamic disk to basic if the disk contains volumes. You must delete all volumes on a dynamic disk before you can convert it to basic. If you want to keep your data, you must back it up or move it to another disk before you delete the volumes. After you convert the disk to basic, you can create a new partition that uses the same drive letter or drive path that you used with the dynamic volume and then restore the data. For more information about drive paths and mounted drives, see Windows XP Professional Help.

To convert an unpartitioned dynamic disk to basic

- In Disk Management, right-click the dynamic disk, and then click **Convert to Basic Disk**.

Disks That You Cannot Convert to Dynamic

Windows XP Professional Setup and Disk Management ensure that disks initialized by Windows XP Professional can be converted to dynamic. However, on some disks the conversion fails or the **Convert to Dynamic Disk** command is not available when you right-click a basic disk. The following conditions prevent you from converting a basic disk to dynamic.

The computer is running Windows XP Home Edition   Dynamic disks are not available on computers running Windows XP Home Edition.

The disk is in a portable computer   Windows XP Professional does not support dynamic disks in portable computers. However, on some older portable computers that are not Advanced Configuration and Power Interface (ACPI) compliant, you might be able to convert the disk to dynamic, but it is neither recommended nor supported.

The disk is a removable disk   You cannot use dynamic disks on the following:

■ Removable media, such as Iomega Zip or Jaz disks.

■ Detachable disks that use universal serial bus (USB) or IEEE 1394 (also called FireWire) interfaces.

The sector size is larger than 512 bytes   A sector is a unit of storage on a hard disk. The majority of hard disks use 512-byte sectors. Windows XP Professional supports converting basic disks to dynamic only if the sector size of the basic disk is 512 bytes.

Partitions on a GPT disk are not contiguous   If an unknown partition lies between two known partitions on a GPT disk, you cannot convert the disk to dynamic. Unknown partitions are created by operating systems or utilities that use partition type GUIDs that Windows XP 64-Bit Edition does not recognize. For more information about partition type GUIDs supported by Windows XP 64-Bit Edition, see "Troubleshooting Disks and File Systems" in this book.

An MBR disk does not have space for the dynamic disk database   An MBR disk requires 1 MB of disk space at the end of the disk to be used for the dynamic disk database. Windows XP Professional and Windows 2000 automatically reserve 1 MB or one cylinder, whichever is greater, when creating partitions on a disk, but in rare cases, disks with partitions created by other operating systems might not have this space available. If this space is not available, you cannot convert the disk to dynamic.

To convert the disk to dynamic, you must back up or move the data, delete the partitions, recreate the partitions, restore the data, and then convert the disk to dynamic. By using Windows XP Professional to create the partitions, you ensure that the necessary space is available for the dynamic disk database.

This limitation does not affect GPT disks because the database is created in its own partition with space borrowed from the Microsoft Reserved partition. For more information about the Microsoft Reserved partition, see "Required Partitions on GPT Disks" later in this chapter.

Managing Volumes During Windows XP Professional Setup

Before you begin Windows XP Professional Setup on an x86-based computer, either as a new installation or as an upgrade, review your current disk configuration and determine whether you need to create additional volumes during Setup. Because your options for creating and formatting volumes are limited during Setup, you might want to create only the system and boot volumes during Setup, and then wait until Setup completes before you create and format additional volumes.

If your computer uses multidisk volumes created by using Windows NT 4.0, you must follow the guidelines provided in the next section.

Warning   If you upgrade from Windows 98 or Windows Me to Windows XP Professional, do not make any changes to your disk configuration after Setup completes if you want to uninstall Windows XP Professional and revert to the previous operating system. For example, converting a volume to NTFS, converting a disk to dynamic, or deleting volumes can prevent you from uninstalling Windows XP Professional. For more information, see "Supporting Installations" in this book.

To ensure that you can successfully install Windows XP Professional, you must verify that the computer's mass storage controllers, such as Advanced Technology Attachment (ATA), IDE, SCSI, RAID, or Fibre Channel adapters, are listed in the Hardware Compatibility List (HCL). You might also need to obtain from the device manufacturer a separate device driver for use with Windows XP Professional. After you obtain the device driver, copy it to a floppy disk before you begin Setup. During the early part of Setup, a line of text at the bottom of the screen prompts you to press F6. Additional prompts help you install the device driver so that Setup can gain access to the mass storage controller.

If you are unsure whether Windows XP Professional supports your mass storage controller, you can try running Setup. If the controller is not supported, you receive the Stop message 0x7B INACCESSIBLE_BOOT_DEVICE.

For more information about the HCL, see the Microsoft Windows Hardware Compatibility List link on the Web Resources page at http://www.microsoft.com /windows/reskits/webresources. For information about managing volumes in Itanium-based computers during Setup, see "Creating Partitions During Setup of Windows XP 64-Bit Edition" later in this chapter.

Preparing Multidisk Volumes for Windows XP Professional

Ftdisk.sys was the fault-tolerant driver that was used to manage volume sets and stripe sets in Windows NT Workstation 4.0 and earlier. To encourage administrators to begin using dynamic volumes, Windows 2000 offers limited support for Ftdisk volumes. Completing this transition, Windows XP Professional does not support volume sets or stripe sets. Therefore, before you install Windows XP Professional on an x86-based computer, you must do one of the following:

- If you are upgrading from Windows NT Workstation 4.0 to Windows XP Professional, you need to back up and then delete all multidisk volumes before you upgrade because Windows XP Professional cannot access these volumes. Be sure to verify that your backup was successful before deleting the volumes. After you finish upgrading to Windows XP Professional, create new dynamic volumes and then restore the data.

    If you do not back up the volumes before you upgrade to Windows XP Professional, Disk Management shows the volumes as Failed. You must use Ftonline.exe to restore the volumes to Healthy so that you can access data on them. Access is only valid for the current session so that you can back up the data before you delete the volumes. If you reboot, you must run Ftonline again. For more information about using Ftonline.exe, click **Tools** in Help and Support Center, and then click **Windows Support Tools**.

> **Note**   Before you can upgrade a computer that is running Windows NT 4.0 to Windows XP Professional, you must first install Service Pack 6 or later.

- If you are upgrading from Windows NT Workstation 4.0 to Windows XP Professional and the paging file resides on a volume set or stripe set, you must use **System** in Control Panel to move the paging file to a primary partition or logical drive before beginning Setup.

- If you are upgrading from Windows 2000 Professional to Windows XP Professional, you must use Disk Management to convert all basic disks that contain multidisk volumes to dynamic disks before beginning Setup or Setup does not continue.

Creating Volumes During Windows XP Professional Setup

During Windows XP Professional Setup, you can create basic volumes by using unallocated space from the basic disks that are installed in the computer. For example, on a single unformatted hard disk, you can create a system volume and separate boot volume, or you can create a single combined system and boot volume that uses all unallocated space on the disk. You can also create additional basic volumes on the same disk and on other disks in the computer if unallocated space is available. However, you cannot create additional volumes on dynamic disks during Setup.

Although you can specify the size of each basic volume, you cannot specify whether to create a primary partition, extended partition, or logical drive. Setup determines the type of volume as follows:

- If no partitions exist on the disk, Setup creates a primary partition of the size you specified.

- If a single primary partition exists, Setup creates an extended partition by using the remaining contiguous, unallocated space on the disk. Setup then creates a logical drive (within the extended partition) of the size you specified.

- If a primary partition and an extended partition exist on the disk and no free space exists within the extended partition, Setup creates an additional primary partition of the size you specified.

Note   When you create basic volumes during Setup, Setup reserves 1 MB or one cylinder, whichever is greater, at the end of the disk. Setup reserves the space for the dynamic disk database so that you can convert the disk to dynamic if you want to.

After you create each volume, Setup assigns it a drive letter. The drive letter that Setup chooses depends on whether other basic volumes, dynamic volumes, and removable disks have drive letters already assigned. For all volumes and removable disks without drive letters, Setup assigns drive letters by using the following method:

1. Scans all fixed hard disks as they are enumerated. Assigns drive letters starting with any active primary partition (if one exists); otherwise, scans the first primary partition on each disk. Assigns the next available letter starting with C.

2. Scans all fixed hard disks and removable disks, and assigns drive letters to all logical drives in an extended partition or the removable disk(s) as enumerated. Assigns the next available letter starting with C.

3. Scans all fixed hard disks and assigns drive letters to all remaining primary partitions. Assigns the next available letter starting with C.

4. Scans floppy drives and assigns the next available drive letter starting with A.

5. Scans CD-ROM drives and assigns the next available letter starting with D.

Windows XP Professional and Windows 2000 assign drive letters differently from how Windows 98, Windows Me, and Windows NT 4.0 assign drive letters. Therefore, if the computer starts multiple operating systems, the drive letters might vary depending on which operating system is running. For more information about how Windows XP Professional and Windows 2000 assign drive letters, see the Microsoft Knowledge Base link on the Web Resources page at http://www.microsoft.com /windows/reskits/webresources. Search the Knowledge Base by using the keywords "LDM" and "cmdcons."

If an existing removable disk is not turned on during Setup, Windows XP Professional might give its drive letter to a new volume. For example, if a removable disk had drive letter G in Windows 2000 but was turned off during Windows XP Professional Setup, a newly created volume might be given drive letter G. To ensure that drive letter assignments remain constant, you must keep removable disk devices turned on when you create new volumes.

After Setup is complete, you can change drive letters for most volumes and removable disks by using Disk Management or the DiskPart command-line tool.

To change a drive letter by using Disk Management

1. From the **Start** menu, click **Run**.

2. In the **Open** box, type **diskmgmt.msc**, and then click **OK**.

3. Right-click the volume whose drive letter you want to change, and then click **Change Drive Letter and Paths**.

4. Click **Change**, and then select the drive letter you want to use.

> **Note**   You can assign drive letters A and B to removable disks, such as Iomega Zip drives, and also to floppy drives. You cannot assign these drive letters to fixed hard disks.

For information about using DiskPart to change drive letters, see Windows XP Professional Help.

> **Note**   The DiskPart **retain** command adds an entry to the partition table of an MBR disk only for simple volumes that are contiguous, start at cylinder-aligned offsets, and are an integral number of cylinders in size. If a volume does not meet these requirements, the **retain** command fails. The following examples describe volumes on which the **retain** command will succeed:
>
> ■ The simple volume is contiguous and starts at the beginning of the disk
>
> ■ The simple volume was present on the disk when the disk was converted to dynamic.

You cannot use Disk Management to change the drive letter of the system or boot volumes. Instead, you must change the drive letter by making certain changes in the registry. This procedure is not recommended unless you are changing the drive letter back to the original letter.

For more information about changing the drive letter of the system or boot volume, see the Microsoft Knowledge Base link on the Web Resources page at http://www.microsoft.com/windows/reskits/webresources. Search the Knowledge Base by using the keywords "mounted," "devices," and "partition."

For more information about formatting volumes during Setup, see "File Systems" in this book.

Installing Windows XP Professional on Dynamic Disks

You can install Windows XP Professional on the following dynamic volumes:

- Any basic volume that was present on the disk when you converted the disk to dynamic by using Windows 2000.

- Simple volumes on which you run the DiskPart command **retain**. This command adds a partition entry to the partition table so that you can install Windows XP Professional on the simple volume.

> **Note**   The DiskPart **retain** command adds an entry to the partition table of an MBR disk only for simple volumes that are contiguous, start at cylinder-aligned offsets, and are an integral number of cylinders in size. If a volume does not meet these requirements, the **retain** command fails. The following examples describe volumes on which the **retain** command will succeed:
>
> - The simple volume is contiguous and starts at the beginning of the disk
> - The simple volume was present on the disk when the disk was converted to dynamic.

- An existing simple volume that is the boot or system volume.

> **Caution**   Do not install Windows XP Professional on a mirrored system or boot volume. Although the installation completes successfully, Windows XP Professional cannot start because it does not support mirrored volumes.

During a new installation of Windows XP Professional, Setup displays a list of all disks and volumes installed in the computer. However, Setup does not differentiate between basic and dynamic disks, nor does Setup differentiate between installable and non-installable dynamic volumes. Therefore, before you begin Setup, decide which volume you plan to install Windows XP Professional on, and then ensure that the volume is installable.

If you choose a dynamic volume that is not installable, Setup displays a message that the partition is unrecognized and that you cannot install Windows XP Professional on it.

Caution   Use caution when deleting volumes during Setup, especially if the computer contains dynamic disks. Deleting a single dynamic volume during Setup deletes all volumes on the disk and converts the disk to basic. As a result, all data on the disk is lost.

If you want to delete a dynamic volume without causing all other dynamic volumes on the disk to become inaccessible, wait for Setup to complete, and then use the Disk Management snap-in to delete the volume.

If you try to delete a dynamic volume during Setup, you are warned about this issue before any data is destroyed. You can then choose to continue with the deletion, which deletes all volumes and their data, or cancel the deletion.

For more information about installing Windows XP Professional on dynamic volumes, see "Converting Basic Disks to Dynamic Disks" earlier in this chapter.

Adding, Moving, and Importing Disks

As you administer disk storage, you might need to add new hard disks or move hard disks from one computer to another. If a hard disk fails, you need to remove it and replace it with a new hard disk. After you connect the hard disk to the computer, you must perform certain steps before you can access or create volumes on the disk.

This section discusses the following:

- Adding new disks to a computer.

- Moving and removing disks.

- Importing foreign disks.

Adding New Disks to a Computer

When you first start Disk Management after installing a new hard disk, a wizard appears that provides a list of the new disks detected by Windows XP Professional. Follow the instructions in the wizard to initialize the disk by creating the partition structures, such as the MBR or the GUID partition table, necessary for data storage.

Next, the wizard offers to convert the disks to dynamic. Click to select the check box next to each disk that you want to convert to dynamic, and then follow the instructions to complete the wizard.

> **Note**   If you cancel the wizard before the partition structures are written, the disk status remains **Not Initialized** until you right-click the disk, and then click **Initialize Disk**.

After you complete the wizard that installs the disk, the Plug and Play Manager assigns a number to the disk, which appears in Disk Management. The disk numbers are not necessarily assigned in a certain order, and disk numbers might change after you restart the computer.

For more information about Plug and Play Manager, see "Managing Devices" in this book.

Moving Disks

You can move basic and dynamic disks from one computer to another. For example, if a computer becomes inoperable but you know the hard disk still works, you can move the disk to a computer that is running Windows XP Professional and access the data on the disk.

Before You Move Disks

Before you move disks and install them in a computer that is running Windows XP Professional, you must review these guidelines.

If you are moving dynamic disks   Do not move dynamic disks to computers running Windows 95, Windows 98, Windows Me, Windows NT 4.0 or earlier, or Windows XP Home Edition because these operating systems cannot read dynamic disks. If you want to make the disk readable by an operating system that cannot read dynamic disks, you must use Windows XP Professional or Windows 2000 to back up or move the data to another disk, delete all volumes, and then right-click the dynamic disk and click **Convert to Basic Disk**.

If you are moving disks that contain multidisk volumes   Move all disks that contain multidisk volumes, such as spanned and striped volumes, at the same time.

If you move only one disk and leave the other disk in the original computer, the data in the striped or spanned volumes becomes inaccessible on both disks. You must move the disks at the same time to ensure the data is accessible on the target computer. For more information about moving multidisk volumes, see "Importing Foreign Disks" later in this chapter.

If you are moving GPT disks   Move GPT disks only to other Itanium-based computers because x86-based computers cannot read the partition structures on the disk. If you move a GPT disk to an x86-based computer running Windows 2000 with Service Pack 1 or greater or Windows XP Professional, the Disk Management snap-in shows that the GPT disk contains one volume with the status GPT Protective Partition. However, you cannot access any data on the GPT disk nor can you delete the volume. As a result, the disk is unusable in any x86-based computer unless you convert the disk to an MBR disk.

In Windows XP Professional, you can convert a GPT disk to MBR by using the **clean** command in DiskPart, which removes all data and partition structures from the disk. You cannot use the Disk Management snap-in in Windows XP Professional to perform the conversion. However, you can use Disk Management in Windows XP 64–Bit Edition to convert a GPT disk to an MBR disk and vice versa, but the disk must be empty. For more information about changing the partition style of a disk, see "Managing GPT Disks in Itanium-based Computers" later in this chapter.

If the disk contains volume sets or stripe sets   Windows XP Professional cannot access volume sets or stripe sets that were created by using Windows NT 4.0. If you must move disks that contain volume sets or stripe sets to Windows XP Professional, you have three choices:

- You can back up and then delete these volumes before you move the disks, and then create new dynamic volumes and restore the data.

- If the volume sets or stripe sets are in a computer running Windows 2000, you can convert the disks that contain them to dynamic before you move the disks to a computer running Windows XP Professional. If you use this method, it is recommended that you back up the data as a precaution before converting the disks to dynamic. After you move the disks, Windows XP Professional can access them normally.

- If the volume sets or stripe sets are in a computer running Windows NT 4.0, you can use the command-line tool Ftonline.exe after you move the disks to access the volumes in Windows XP Professional. Access is only valid for the current session so that you can back up the data before you delete the volumes. If you reboot, you must run Ftonline again. For more information about using Ftonline.exe, click **Tools** in Help and Support Center, and then click **Windows Support Tools**.

Do not move disks that contain mirror sets or stripe sets with parity to a computer running Windows XP Professional. You can, however, move disks from computers running Windows NT 4.0 to computers running Windows XP Professional if the disks contain primary partitions, extended partitions, and logical drives.

If the dynamic disk contains the system or boot volume   Do not move a dynamic disk that contains the system or boot volume to another computer unless you have no other way to recover data. Startup problems can occur if you move the disk back to the original computer and attempt to start Windows XP Professional from the disk.

You can, however, move a basic disk that contains a system or boot volume to another computer, access data on the disk, and then move the disk back to the original computer and successfully start Windows XP Professional.

If the target computer has no dynamic disks   If you move a dynamic disk that does not contain a system or boot volume to a computer that has never contained dynamic disks, the target computer uses the disk group identity from the original computer. This is not a problem unless you try to move the disk back to the original computer, and the original computer contains other dynamic disks. In this case, the original computer cannot import the foreign disk. To resolve this problem, move the disk to a different computer that has an existing disk group (that is, the computer has existing dynamic disks), import the disk, and then take the disk back to the original computer and import it.

How to Move Disks

To move a hard disk from one computer to another, follow this procedure:

1. Review the preceding limitations to ensure that you can access the data on the disks after you move them.

2. As a precaution, back up the data on the disk.

3. Remove the disk from the original computer.

   Although you do not need to turn off the computer to remove an external disk or hot-swappable disk, if the Safely Remove Hardware icon appears in the taskbar notification area, you must use the Safely Remove Hardware application to alert Windows XP that you are removing the disk. If the Safely Remove Hardware icon is not in the notification area, you must use Device Manager to uninstall the disk before you unplug it. However, to move an internal disk, you must turn off and unplug the original computer before you remove the disk. Then turn off and unplug the target computer before you add the disk. For more information about removing external disks, see "Managing Devices" in this book.

4. Install the disk in a computer that is running Windows XP Professional.

5. Log on to Windows XP Professional as a member of the Administrators group, and then open Disk Management.

6. On the **Action** menu, click **Rescan Disks**. If the disk does not appear in Disk Management, open Device Manager, and then from the **Action** menu click **Scan for hardware changes**.

All newly attached disks appear in the Disk Management snap-in, but only basic disks are immediately accessible. If the disks you moved were dynamic disks, they appear as Foreign disks and you must import them before you can access data on them. For more information, see "Importing Foreign Disks" later in this chapter.

Basic volumes are assigned the next available drive letter, which might differ from the drive letter used by the previous operating system. For more information about how Windows XP Professional assigns drive letters, see the Microsoft Knowledge Base link on the Web Resources page at http://www.microsoft.com/windows /reskits/webresources. Search the Knowledge Base by using the keywords "LDM" and "cmdcons."

Removing Disks from the Dynamic Disk Database

After you remove a dynamic disk from a computer, the remaining online dynamic disks retain information about the removed disk and its volumes in the dynamic disk database. As a result, Disk Management still displays the removed hard disk but shows it as **Offline** and assigns it the status of **Missing**.

You can delete all references to the removed disk by updating the dynamic disk database. To do this, use Disk Management to remove all volumes on the missing disk. After you remove all the volumes, right-click the missing disk, and then click **Remove Disk**. The missing disk is no longer displayed in Disk Management.

You need at least one online dynamic disk to retain information about missing disks and their volumes. When you remove the last dynamic disk, you lose the information, and the missing disks are no longer displayed in Disk Management.

For more information about disk and volume error conditions, see "Troubleshooting Disks and File Systems" in this book.

Importing Foreign Disks

If you move one or more dynamic disks from a disk group to another computer that has its own disk group, the dynamic disks you moved are marked as Foreign until you import the disks into the existing disk group. You must import the disks before you can access volumes on the disk.

In computers that are running any combination of Windows 2000 and Windows XP Professional, you do not need to import existing dynamic disks because the disks are imported automatically each time you start either operating system.

You cannot import dynamic disks into computers running Windows XP Home Edition because it cannot read dynamic disks.

How to Import Disks

1. In Disk Management, right-click any disk that is marked as Foreign, and then click **Import Foreign Disks**.

2. Select the disk group that you want to import.

   Even if multiple disk groups are present, you must import one group at a time. If you want to view the disks that are part of a disk group, select the disk group, and then click the **Disks** button.

3. Carefully review the information in the **Foreign Disk Volumes** dialog box to ensure that you can access the volumes after you import the disks.

As Figure 12-3 shows, the **Foreign Disk Volumes** dialog box describes what will happen to each volume after you import the disks. If a volume condition shows as **OK**, you can access the volume after you import the disks. However, if a volume condition shows as **Data incomplete**, you must import the remaining disks that contain the multidisk volume before you can access the volume.

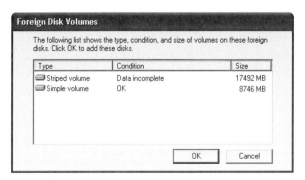

Figure 12-3   Foreign Disk Volumes dialog box

Because spanned and striped volumes span multiple disks, the status of a multidisk volume can become complicated if you do not move all of the disks at the same time. Another complication can arise when you move a disk and then later move additional disks. Although you can move volumes incrementally, the procedure can be complicated and is therefore not recommended. For this reason, when you move volumes that span multiple disks, you need to move them all at the same time.

The following describes the volume states that occur when you move the specified volume types:

Importing Spanned or Striped Volumes

You can import spanned or striped volumes into computers running Windows XP Professional, Windows XP 64–Bit Edition, or any edition of Windows 2000.

Whenever possible, move all disks that contain spanned or striped volumes at the same time. Moving the disks at the same time ensures that the volumes have the Healthy status after import. If you move only some disks from one system to another, the volume becomes disabled during import and also becomes disabled on the original system. As long as you do not delete the volume on either the original or the target system, you can move the remaining disks later. When you move all disks over to the other system, the volume returns its original state.

Importing Mirrored or RAID-5 Volumes

Do not import mirrored or RAID–5 volumes into computers running Windows XP Professional or Windows 2000 Professional. Because these operating systems do not support mirrored or RAID–5 volumes, you cannot access data on these volumes after the import. You must move the volume back to a computer running Windows 2000 Server to access the volume.

Drive Letter Assignments for Imported Dynamic Volumes

Because dynamic disks store drive letter information in the dynamic disk database, imported volumes use their existing drive letters unless those drive letters are already used. If the previous drive letter is unavailable, then Disk Management assigns the next available drive letter to the imported volume.

For more information about how Windows XP Professional assigns drive letters, see the Microsoft Knowledge Base link on the Web Resources page at http://www.microsoft.com/windows/reskits/webresources. Search the Knowledge Base by using the keywords "LDM" and "cmdcons."

For more information about disk groups and importing disks, see article Q222189, "Description of Disk Groups in Windows 2000 Disk Management," in the Microsoft Knowledge Base. To find this article, see the Microsoft Knowledge Base link on the Web Resources page at http://www.microsoft.com/windows/reskits/webresources.

Managing GPT Disks in Itanium-based Computers

Instead of using a BIOS, computers with an Intel Itanium processor use the Extensible Firmware Interface (EFI) between the computer's hardware and the operating system. EFI defines a new partition style called GUID partition table (GPT) that offers advantages over master boot record (MBR) partition tables. Table 12-4 compares MBR and GPT disks.

Table 12-4 Comparison of MBR and GPT Disks

Characteristic	MBR Disk (x86-based computer)	GPT Disk (Itanium-based computer)
Number of partitions on basic disks	Supports up to either: ■ Four primary partitions per disk, or ■ Three primary partitions and an extended partition with unlimited logical drives.	Supports up to 128 partitions.
Compatible operating systems	Can be read by: ■ Microsoft MS-DOS ■ Microsoft Windows 95 ■ Microsoft Windows 98 ■ Microsoft Windows Me ■ Windows NT, all versions ■ Windows 2000, all versions ■ Windows XP	Can be read by Windows XP 64-Bit Edition.
Maximum size of basic volumes	Supports basic volumes up to 2 terabytes.	Supports basic volumes up to 18 exabytes.
Maximum size of dynamic volumes	Supports the maximum volume size of the file system used to format the volume.	Supports the maximum volume size of the file system used to format the volume.
Partition tables (copies)	Contains one copy of the partition table.	Contains primary and backup partition tables for redundancy and checksum fields for improved partition structure integrity.
Locations for data storage	Stores data in partitions and in unpartitioned space. Although most data is stored within partitions, some data might be stored in hidden or unpartitioned sectors created by OEMs or other operating systems.	Stores user and program data in partitions that are visible to the user. Stores data that is critical to platform operation in partitions that Windows XP 64-Bit Edition recognizes but does not make visible to the user. Does not store data in unpartitioned space.
Troubleshooting methods	Uses the same methods and tools that you use in Windows 2000.	Uses tools designed for GPT disks. (Do not use MBR troubleshooting tools on GPT disks.)

By default, Windows XP 64–Bit Edition initializes new disks on Itanium-based computers as GPT disks. You can have both GPT and MBR disks on an Itanium-based computer, but you must have at least one GPT disk that contains the EFI System partition and a primary partition or simple volume that contains Windows XP 64–Bit Edition. For more information about the required GPT partitions, see "Required Partitions on GPT Disks" in this chapter.

You can convert a disk from GPT to MBR or vice versa as long as the disk is empty.

To change the partition style of an empty disk

■ Right-click the disk, and then click **Convert to GPT Disk** or **Convert to MBR Disk**.

You can configure GPT disks and MBR disks as basic or dynamic. You can perform the same tasks on GPT disks that you perform on MBR disks with the following exceptions:

■ You can use the Disk Management snap-in to format partitions on GPT disks by using NTFS. If you want to format GPT disks by using FAT or FAT32, you must use the **format** command at the command prompt.

■ You cannot use GPT on the following:

  ■ Removable media.

  ■ Detachable disks that use universal serial bus (USB) or IEEE 1394 (also called FireWire) interfaces.

  ■ Cluster disks that connect to shared SCSI or Fibre channel buses used by Cluster service.

Required Partitions on GPT Disks

Windows XP 64-Bit Edition creates special partitions on GPT disks to store private system data, such as the dynamic disk database. On MBR disks, this system data is often stored in unused regions of the disk. However, GPT disks do not support the storing of data in unused space, so Windows XP 64-Bit Edition creates the partitions required to store private system data when you initialize a GPT disk.

The partitions on a GPT disk vary depending on whether the disk is basic or dynamic. Table 12-5 describes the required partitions on basic and dynamic GPT disks.

Table 12-5   Required Partitions on Basic and Dynamic GPT Disks

Partition Type	Basic GPT Disks	Dynamic GPT Disks
EFI System partition	X	X
Microsoft Reserved (MSR) partition	X	X
Primary partition	X	

Table 12-5 Required Partitions on Basic and Dynamic GPT Disks

Partition Type	Basic GPT Disks	Dynamic GPT Disks
Logical Disk Manager (LDM) Metadata partition		X
LDM Data partition		X

The partitions described in Table 12-5 are not required in these situations:

■ The EFI System partition is not required on all GPT disks. In a computer with one GPT disk, the EFI System partition is typically the first partition on the disk. Additional GPT disks in an Itanium-based computer do not require an EFI System partition.

■ A basic GPT disk might not contain primary partitions. For example, when you install a new disk and configure it as a GPT disk, Windows XP 64-Bit Edition automatically creates the Microsoft Reserved partition but does not create primary partitions. You must create one or more primary partitions before you can store data on a basic GPT disk.

Figure 12-4 illustrates the partition layout of a basic GPT disk with three primary partitions and a dynamic GPT disk with three simple volumes.

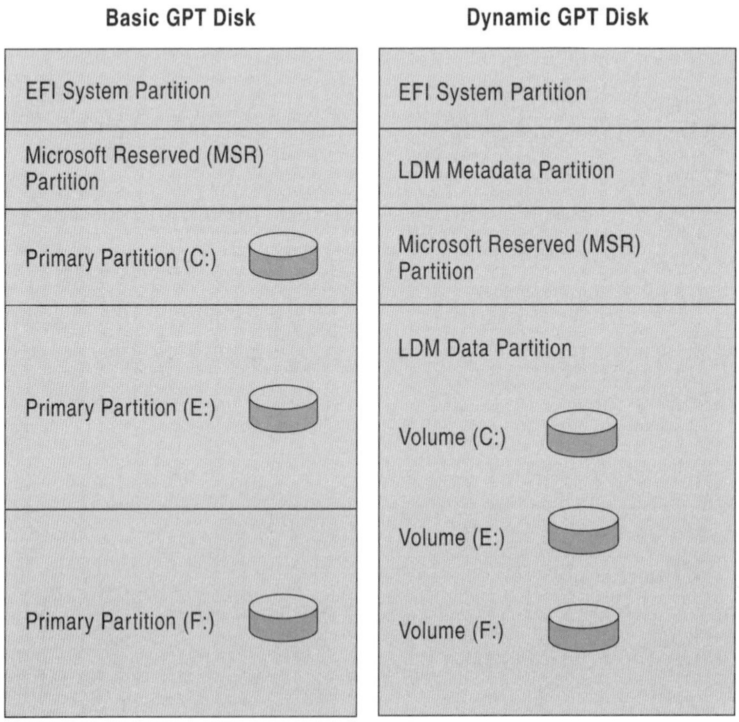

Figure 12-4 Partition layout on basic and dynamic GPT disks

EFI System Partition

An Itanium-based computer must have one GPT disk that contains an EFI System partition, which is analogous to the system volume on an x86-based computer because it contains the files that are required to start Windows XP 64-Bit Edition. Windows XP 64-Bit Edition creates the EFI System partition during Setup and formats it by using FAT. The size of the EFI System partition is 1% of the disk, with a minimum size of 100 MB and a maximum size of 1,000 MB.

Windows XP 64-Bit Edition creates the following subdirectories in the EFI System partition:

- \EFI\Microsoft\WINNT50, which contains Ia64ldr.efi and other files that are necessary to start Windows XP 64-Bit Edition.

- \Msutil, which contains utilities such as Nvrboot.efi.

Other subdirectories created by operating system vendors, original equipment manufacturers (OEMs), BIOS vendors, and other tools vendors might also be present.

The EFI System partition is shown in Disk Management, but all commands associated with it are disabled. You cannot store data on it, assign a drive letter to it, or delete it by using Disk Management or DiskPart. Instead, you must use the EFI firmware's Boot Manager or the Windows XP 64-Bit Edition **mountvol** command to access the EFI System partition. For more information about using the **mountvol** command, see Windows XP 64-Bit Edition Help.

> **Caution**   Do not copy files to, delete files from, or change existing files in the EFI System partition unless you know exactly what you are doing. Incorrect changes to the files in this partition might prevent an Itanium-based computer from starting.

Microsoft Reserved Partition

The Microsoft Reserved (MSR) partition is required on every GPT disk. Windows XP 64-Bit Edition reserves the space in the MSR so that system components are guaranteed space to allocate new partitions for their own use. For example, when you convert a basic GPT disk to dynamic, the system removes 1 MB of the MSR partition and uses that space to create the LDM Metadata partition.

If the GPT disk contains an EFI System partition as the first partition on the disk, the MSR partition is usually the second partition on the disk. If the GPT disk does not contain an EFI System partition, then the MSR partition is typically the first partition on the GPT disk. In rare cases, the MSR partition is the last partition on the disk.

The size of the MSR partition varies. For GPT disks that are smaller than 16 gigabytes (GB), it is 32 MB. For disks larger than 16 GB, the MSR partition is 128 MB.

Windows XP 64-Bit Edition creates an MSR partition in the following situations:

- Setup creates an MSR partition on the disk on which you install Windows XP 64-Bit Edition.

- OEMs create the MSR partition on computers running Windows XP 64-Bit Edition before they are shipped.

- The Disk Management snap-in and DiskPart create an MSR partition on any disk that is converted from MBR to GPT.

- The Disk Management snap-in and DiskPart create an MSR partition on any GPT disk that does not contain an MSR partition. Windows XP 64-Bit Edition usually places the MSR partition at the beginning of the disk. However, if primary partitions exist at the beginning of the disk, then the MSR is placed at the end of the disk.

Note   The MSR partition is not shown in Disk Management and does not receive a drive letter.

Primary Partition

You create primary partitions on basic disks to store data. Every primary partition you create appears in the GUID partition entry array (similar to the partition table in MBR disks). The GUID partition entry array supports up to 128 partitions, including primary partitions and other required partitions. For example, if a GPT contains an EFI System partition and a Microsoft Reserved partition, you can create an additional 126 primary partitions. For more information about the GUID partition entry array, see "Troubleshooting Disks and File Systems" in this book.

If you convert a basic disk that contains primary partitions to dynamic, the primary partitions become simple volumes, and information about them is stored in the dynamic disk database, not in the GUID partition entry array.

LDM Data Partition

Windows XP 64-Bit Edition creates LDM Data partitions during the conversion to dynamic disk. LDM Data partitions act as containers for dynamic volumes, allocating the disk for use by the dynamic disk database. A GPT disk can have multiple LDM Data partitions as follows:

- If the boot volume spans the entire disk that is converted to dynamic, then only one LDM Data partition is present after the conversion to dynamic disk.

- If the disk contains a boot volume and one or more primary partitions, then two LDM Data partitions are present after the conversion: one for the boot volume, and one that allocates the remaining space on the disk.

- If the disk contains a boot volume that is surrounded by partitions or unallocated space on either side, then three LDM Data partitions are present after the conversion.

If you use the DiskPart **retain** command on a simple volume and the other volumes on the disk meet any of the above conditions, more than three LDM Data partitions might be present.

OEM or Unknown Partition

Original equipment manufacturers (OEMs) and operating systems that support the GPT partition style can create additional partitions on GPT disks. Windows XP 64-Bit Edition displays these partitions in Disk Management as Healthy (Unknown Partition), but you cannot assign drive letters to these partitions, delete them, or view or store data in them by using Windows XP 64-Bit Edition. In addition, if an unknown partition lies between two known partitions on a GPT disk, you cannot convert that disk to dynamic. For more information about problems converting GPT disks to dynamic, see "Disks That You Cannot Convert to Dynamic" earlier in this chapter.

Creating Partitions During Setup of Windows XP 64-Bit Edition

If you install Windows XP 64-Bit Edition on a blank disk, Setup initializes the disk as a GPT disk. Setup offers to create the EFI System partition and then automatically creates the Microsoft Reserved partition. Next, Setup formats the EFI System partition by using FAT. You can then create additional primary partitions, including the boot volume.

For all partitions and removable disks without drive letters, Setup assigns drive letters by using the following method:

1. Scans all fixed hard disks as they are enumerated. If the disk is an MBR disk, Setup assigns a drive letter to the first primary partition starting with C. If the disk is a GPT disk, then Setup assigns drive letters to all primary partitions on the GPT disk starting with C.

2. Scans all fixed hard disks and removable disks, and assigns drive letters to all logical drives in an extended partition on MBR disks or the removable disk(s) as enumerated. Assigns the next available letter starting with C.

3. Scans all fixed hard disks and assigns drive letters to all remaining primary partitions on MBR disks. Assigns the next available letter starting with C.

4. Scans floppy drives and assigns the next available drive letter starting with A.

5. Scans CD-ROM drives and assigns the next available letter starting with D.

After you choose the partition in which to install Windows XP 64-Bit Edition, Setup formats the boot volume by using the file system you selected. If you create other partitions during Setup, you must wait for Setup to complete; then use Disk Management or the **format** command to format the partitions.

Remote Disk and Command-Line Disk Management

You can manage remote computers that are running Windows XP Professional, Windows XP 64-Bit Edition, or Windows 2000 by using the Disk Management snap-in. After you select the remote computer you want to manage, you can remotely perform the same tasks that you normally perform while sitting at the remote computer.

By using the DiskPart command-line tool, you can create scripts to automate disk-related tasks, such as creating volumes or converting disks to dynamic. Scripting these tasks is useful if you are deploying Windows XP Professional by using Unattended Installation or the System Preparation (Sysprep) tool, which does not support creating volumes other than the boot volume.

Note   Sysprep.exe is part of Deploy.cab, which is located in the \Support \Tools folder on the Windows XP Professional operating system CD.

Managing Disks on Remote Computers

You can use Disk Management to manage disks on remote computers that run Windows XP Professional, Windows XP 64-Bit Edition, or Windows 2000. You must be a member of the Administrators group on both the local and remote computers, and the computers must be within the same domain or within trusted domains.

When managing disks and volumes on remote computers, you can:

- Use a computer that is running Windows XP Professional or Windows XP 64-Bit Edition to manage disks on a remote computer that is running Windows 2000 and vice versa.

- Use an x86-based computer to manage an Itanium-based computer and vice versa.

The types of volumes and disks you can create depend on the operating system that you are running on the remote computer, not the local computer. For example, only the Windows 2000 Server family supports mirrored volumes and RAID-5 volumes. Therefore, you can use a computer running Windows XP Professional to create mirrored or RAID-5 volumes on a remote computer running Windows 2000 Server. See Table 12-3 earlier in this chapter for more information about the types of volumes and disks available on each edition of Windows XP Professional and Windows 2000 Server.

To manage disks on a remote computer

1. Click **Start**, and then click **Run**.

2. In the **Open** box, type **compmgmt.msc**, and then click **OK**.

3. In the Computer Management snap-in, right-click **Computer Management (Local)**, and then click **Connect to another computer**.

4. In **Another Computer**, type the name of the computer that you want to connect to remotely.

    When you manage disks in a remote computer, the following limitations apply:

■ If you use a computer that is running Windows 2000 to manage a remote Itanium-based computer that is running Windows XP 64-Bit Edition, you cannot manage dynamic disks in the remote computer if one of the disks in the disk group is a GPT disk.

■ If you use a computer that is running Windows XP Professional to manage a remote computer that is running Windows 2000, the property page for IEEE 1394 and USB detachable disks does not show all information.

Managing Disks from the Command Line by Using DiskPart

DiskPart.exe is a text-mode command interpreter that is separate from the Windows XP Professional command prompt. DiskPart allows you to manage fixed (non-removable) disks and volumes by using scripts or direct input.

To run DiskPart, at the command prompt, type:

```
diskpart
```

To view a list of DiskPart commands, at the DiskPart command prompt, type:

```
commands
```

For more information about using the DiskPart commands, see Windows XP Professional Help.

Creating DiskPart Scripts

You can create DiskPart scripts in text files by using any extension. To run a DiskPart script from the command line, type:

```
diskpart /s testscript.txt
```

To create a log file of the DiskPart session, type:

```
diskpart /s testscript.txt > logfile.txt
```

DiskPart does not have a **format** command. You must run the **format** command from the command prompt either manually or by using a batch file. The following example shows a batch file called Formatpart.bat and a DiskPart script called Createpart.txt. The batch file executes the DiskPart script and then runs the **format** command.

In Formatpart.bat:
```
diskpart /s createpart.txt
format g: /fs:ntfs
```

In Createpart.txt:
```
select disk 1
create volume simple size 4096
assign letter g
```

When to Use DiskPart Scripting

A common scenario for using DiskPart scripts is when you deploy Windows XP Professional by using Unattended Installation or Sysprep.

■ **Unattended Installation**. A hands-free method of installing Windows XP Professional that is convenient for system administrators, original equipment manufacturers (OEMs), value-added resellers (VARs), and other users who install Windows XP Professional on many computers or who frequently install Windows XP Professional on the same computer.

■ **System Preparation (Sysprep) Tool**. A simple utility that you can use together with third-party disk imaging utilities to prepare a system that you want to duplicate. Sysprep uses an answer file to automate Mini-Setup, which shortens the graphical user interface (GUI) setup mode. In GUI setup mode, the end user is prompted only for required and user-specific information, such as accepting the Microsoft End-User License Agreement (EULA), entering the Product Key, and adding user and company names.

You can create additional volumes or perform other disk-related tasks when you use Unattended Installation or Sysprep by using answer files to run DiskPart scripts. An answer file contains answers to questions that Windows XP Professional Setup asks during installation; the answer file automates the responses so that Setup runs without user intervention. It consists of section headers, parameters, and the values for each parameter. The answer file for Unattended Installation is called Unattend.txt, and the answer file for Sysprep is called Sysprep.inf.

For more information about using Unattended Installation and Sysprep, see "Automating and Customizing Installations" in this book.

Creating partitions by using DiskPart scripts in the [GuiRunOnce] section of Unattend.txt or Sysprep.inf   Table 12-6 describes a scenario in which you create and format two primary partitions by using a batch file called Formatpart.bat. The batch file executes a DiskPart script called Createpart.txt to create the partitions, and then the batch file formats the partitions by using the **format** command.

Table 12-6   DiskPart Scenario Using [GuiRunOnce]

Scenario	Sample Script
Disk 0: 20 GB basic disk	**In Createpart.txt:**[*]
C: 4 GB NTFS system volume (already created)	
| D: 16 GB NTFS data volume (uses the remaining unallocated space on the disk) | ```
select disk 0
create partition primary
assign letter d
select disk 1
create partition primary
assign letter r
``` |
| **Disk 1: 60 GB basic disk** | |
| R: 60 GB NTFS data volume (uses all unallocated space on the disk) | **In Formatpart.bat:** |
| | ```
diskpart/s createpart.txt
echo y | format d: /fs:ntfs
echo y | format r: /fs:ntfs
``` |

[*]   You do not need to specify the DiskPart size= parameter in this example because the partitions use all the unallocated space on their respective disks.

You can use Windows Setup Manager to specify Formatpart.bat by following the example shown in Figure 12-5. Programs that you enter in the **Command to run** box appear in the [GuiRunOnce] section of Unattend.txt or Sysprep.inf.

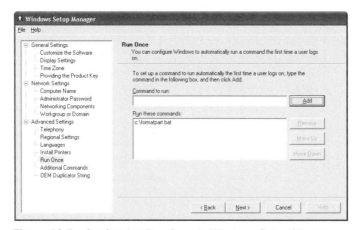

Figure 12-5   Configuring Run Once in Windows Setup Manager

[GuiRunOnce] contains a list of commands that Windows XP Professional executes the first time a user logs on to the computer after GUI-mode Setup has completed. Each line specifies a command to be executed by the GuiRunOnce registry entry. For example:

```
[GuiRunOnce]
Command0 = c:\formatpart.bat
```

Note   For each command line that contains spaces, be sure to place the command in quotation marks when you add the command to the answer file. If you use Windows Setup Manager to specify a command, Windows Setup Manager automatically adds the quotation marks to the answer file.

Commands run by using the GuiRunOnce key run in the security context of the user who is currently logged on. If the user does not have the permissions necessary to run the command completely, the command fails.

Converting disks to dynamic by using DiskPart scripts in the [GuiRunOnce] section of Unattend.txt or Sysprep.inf   Table 12-7 describes a scenario in which you execute a DiskPart script called Convertdyn.txt in the [GuiRunOnce] section of Sysprep.inf. The Convertdyn.txt script converts Disk 0 to dynamic.

Table 12-7   DiskPart Scenario Using Cmdlines.txt

Scenario	Sample Script

Disk 0: 24 GB basic disk to be converted to dynamic
 	
C: 4 GB NTFS system volume (already created)
 	
D: 20 GB NTFS data volume (already created)
	In Convertdyn.txt:
	
	`select disk 0`
	`convert dynamic`

After the conversion, both basic volumes become dynamic simple volumes. If you need to increase the size of volume D, you can extend the volume to another disk to create a spanned volume.

Most third-party imaging tools are not compatible with dynamic disks. Therefore, you must convert the disk to dynamic after you create the images, and then deploy the images to target computers. Perform the following steps to complete this scenario:

1. Use Windows Setup Manager to create the Sysprep.inf file or modify an existing file.

2. Prepare the system for imaging by using Sysprep. Both basic volumes can be present when you create the image, but the disk must be a basic disk.

3. Clone the image by using a third-party imaging tool.

4. Download the image to the target systems.

5. Use Sysprep.inf to execute the DiskPart script that converts Disk 0 to dynamic. You are prompted to restart the computer twice to complete the conversion because the disk contains the system volume. For more information about converting the system volume to dynamic, see "Converting Basic Disks to Dynamic Disks" earlier in this chapter.

Managing Disks from the Command Line by Using Fsutil

You can use the Fsutil.exe command-line tool from the command prompt to perform many disk and volume-related tasks on NTFS volumes. Table 12-8 summarizes many of the Fsutil commands related to disks and volumes. For more information about using Fsutil, including the commands not listed here, see Windows XP Professional Help.

Table 12-8   Fsutil Commands Related to Disks and Volumes

Command	Description
fsutil fsinfo drives	Lists the drive letters for all volumes on the computer.
fsutil fsinfo drivetype	Displays the drive type for the specified drive. For example, this command can return Fixed Drive, CD-ROM Drive, and Removable Drive.
fsutil fsinfo volumeinfo	For a specified NTFS volume, displays information about the file system, such as volume name, serial number, and whether the volume supports NTFS-related features, such as disk quotas, encryption, and compression.
fsutil fsinfo statistics	Displays statistics about the specified NTFS volume.
fsutil fsinfo ntfsinfo	Displays information about the specified NTFS volume, such as the total clusters, free clusters, bytes per sector, bytes per cluster, and information about the master file table (MFT).
fsutil volume dismount	Dismounts the specified volume.
fsutil volume diskfree	Displays the total number of bytes in the volume, the number of free bytes, and the number of bytes available for data storage.

Guidelines for Maintaining Disks and Volumes

Table 12-9 describes the guidelines for maintaining disks and volumes as well as the frequency and benefits of performing each task. By following these guidelines as part of a regular maintenance program, you can minimize the chances of excessive downtime or data loss due to disk or file system errors.

Table 12-9   Disk and File System Maintenance Guidelines

Guideline	Frequency	Result
Run Disk Defragmenter.	Weekly (during idle times) or as needed	Defragmenting volumes increases file system performance.
		For more information about using Disk Defragmenter, see "Troubleshooting Disks and File Systems" in this book.
Back up data.	Daily	Backing up data prevents data loss caused by hard disk failures, power outages, virus infection, and many other possible computer problems.
		For more information about backing up files, see "Backup and Restore" in this book.
Perform a trial restoration to ensure the integrity of your backups.	Monthly	A trial restoration confirms that your files are properly backed up and can uncover hardware problems that do not show up with software verifications.
Review Event Viewer logs.	Daily	Careful monitoring of logs in Event Viewer can help you predict and identify the sources of system problems. For example, if log warnings show that a disk driver can only read or write to a sector after several retries, the sector is likely to go bad.
		For more information about using Event Viewer, see Windows XP Professional Help.
Use the Chkntfs command to determine whether volumes are flagged as dirty.	Daily	Running Chkntfs can help you identify volumes that have file system errors. If a volume is flagged as dirty, Windows XP Professional runs Chkdsk when the computer is restarted. You can, however, run Chkdsk immediately or postpone Chkdsk by using the Chkntfs command, although it is recommended that you run Chkdsk as soon as possible. To assess the damage without repairing the volume, you can run Chkdsk in read-only mode.
		For more information about using Chkdsk and Chkntfs, see "Troubleshooting Disks and File Systems" in this book.

Additional Resources

These resources contain additional information and tools related to this chapter.

Related Information

- "File Systems" in this book.

- "Troubleshooting Disks and File Systems" in this book for more information about troubleshooting problems related to disks, and about using Chkdsk and Disk Defragmenter.

- "Troubleshooting Startup" in this book for more information about the startup process and about Boot.ini.

- "Managing Devices" in this book for more information about the Device Manager snap-in and about disconnecting Plug and Play storage devices.

- *Inside Windows 2000 Server* by William Boswell, 2000, Indianapolis: New Riders Publishing.

- *Inside Microsoft Windows 2000, Third Edition* by David A. Solomon and Mark E. Russinovich, 2000, Redmond: Microsoft Press.

- The Extensible Firmware Interface link on the Web Resources page at http://www.microsoft.com/windows/reskits/webresources.

Chapter 13

File Systems

On readable/writable disks, Microsoft® Windows® XP Professional supports the NTFS file system and three file allocation table (FAT) file systems: FAT12, FAT16 and FAT32. On CD-ROM and DVD media, Windows XP Professional supports two file systems: Compact Disc File System (CDFS) and Universal Disk Format (UDF).

When choosing a file system for readable/writable disks, you must consider the features associated with each file system. You must also consider limitations, such as maximum volume size, cluster size, file size, and compatibility with other operating systems.

Related Information

- For more information about boot sectors, defragmenting volumes, and using Chkdsk.exe, see "Troubleshooting Disks and File Systems" in this book.

- For more information about disks and volumes, see "Disk Management" in this book.

- For more information about system recovery, see "Tools for Troubleshooting" in this book.

- For more information about sharing folders and shared folder permissions, see "Managing Files and Folders" in this book.

New in File Systems

Windows XP Professional provides improved file system performance and features. Table 13-1 summarizes the enhancements made from Microsoft® Windows® 2000 to Windows XP Professional.

Table 13-1 Enhancements Since Windows 2000

Enhancement	Description
NTFS performance is improved.	Some data structures on newly formatted NTFS volumes have been moved to a different location on the physical disk. This new location improves performance from 5 to 8 percent, making NTFS performance similar to FAT.
A quick-format option is available during Windows XP Professional Setup.	If the volume is already formatted and you are sure the disk is not damaged, you can use this option during Setup to decrease the time necessary to format the volume.
Variable cluster sizes are now available on volumes converted to NTFS.	The **format** command in Windows XP Professional now aligns FAT data clusters at the cluster size boundary. This alignment improves the conversion of FAT volumes to NTFS because the **convert** command can now use a variable cluster size, up to a maximum of 4 kilobytes (KB), for converted volumes, instead of a fixed 512-byte cluster size as used in Windows 2000.
Default permissions are applied to volumes converted to NTFS.	Convert.exe now applies default permissions on volumes converted to NTFS. This change ensures that converted NTFS volumes receive the same access control lists (ACLs) as natively formatted NTFS volumes.
A new parameter prevents the master file table (MFT) from becoming fragmented during the conversion to NTFS.	To prevent the MFT from becoming fragmented during the conversion to NTFS, the **/cvtarea** parameter in Convert.exe allows you to specify a contiguous placeholder file at the root folder to be used for the MFT. Using this parameter improves NTFS performance after the conversion by ensuring that the MFT occupies a contiguous space on the hard disk.
More options are available for defragmenting volumes.	Windows XP Professional offers two choices for defragmenting volumes: the Disk Defragmenter snap-in and a new command-line tool called Defrag.exe. Both tools can defragment NTFS volumes that use any cluster size and files smaller than 16 clusters. Both tools can also defragment the MFT on NTFS volumes.
Portable Operating System Interface (POSIX) support is provided by Windows Interix 2.2.	The POSIX subsystem included with Microsoft® Windows NT® and Windows 2000 is not included with Windows XP Professional. The broad functionality found on most UNIX systems beyond the POSIX.1 standard is included as part of Microsoft® Windows® Interix 2.2.

Table 13-1   Enhancements Since Windows 2000

Enhancement	Description
Format DVD-RAM discs.	Windows XP Professional supports formatting DVD-RAM discs as FAT32 volumes.
Perform file system tasks at the command line by using Fsutil.exe.	Use Fsutil.exe to perform file system tasks such as disabling long file names, checking whether a volume is flagged as dirty, viewing NTFS-related information about a volume, creating hard links, and managing quotas and sparse files.
Create a Microsoft MS-DOS startup floppy disk.	When you format a floppy disk by using My Computer, you can select the **Create an MS-DOS startup disk** option. An MS-DOS startup disk is useful when you need to update a computer's BIOS.

If you are migrating from Microsoft Windows NT version 4.0, the enhancements in Table 13-2 apply in addition to those outlined in Table 13-1.

Table 13-2   Enhancements Since Windows NT 4.0

New Feature	Feature Description
An updated version of NTFS provides new features exclusive to NTFS volumes.	NTFS — the recommended native file system for Windows XP Professional — is more functional, robust, and secure than the FAT file systems. The version of NTFS included with Windows 2000 introduced features such as encryption, disk quotas, mounted drives, distributed link tracking, sparse files, and so on. These improvements are also available in Windows XP Professional.
FAT32 support allows greater flexibility for computers that start other versions of Windows.	FAT32 was a new option in Windows 2000 and continues to be supported by Windows XP Professional. FAT32 formats much larger volumes than FAT16 and stores files on large volumes more efficiently than FAT16.

File Systems Overview

A *file system* is the structure in which files are named, stored, and organized. File systems supported by Windows XP Professional include FAT16, FAT32, and NTFS. You can use any combination of these file systems on a hard disk, but each volume on a hard disk can be formatted by using only one file system. When choosing the appropriate file system to use, you need to determine the following:

How the computer is used (dedicated to Windows XP Professional or multiple-boot) On computers that contain multiple operating systems, file system compatibility becomes more complex because different versions of Windows support different combinations of file systems.

The number and size of locally installed hard disks   Each file system has a different maximum volume size. As volume sizes increase, your choice of file systems becomes limited. For example, to create volumes larger than 32 gigabytes (GB) in Windows XP Professional, you must use NTFS.

Security considerations   NTFS offers security features, such as encryption and file and folder permissions. These features are not available on FAT volumes.

Interest in using advanced file system features   NTFS offers features such as disk quotas, distributed link tracking, compression, and mounted drives. These features are not available on FAT volumes.

Advantages of Using NTFS

NTFS provides performance, reliability, and advanced features not found in any version of FAT. Use NTFS wherever possible to gain the maximum benefits from Windows XP Professional, including the following:

Robust, reliable performance
- NTFS guarantees the consistency of the volume by using standard transaction logging and recovery techniques. In the event of a system failure, NTFS uses its log file and checkpoint information to restore the consistency of the file system when the computer is restarted.

- In the event of a bad-sector error, NTFS dynamically remaps the cluster containing the bad sector and allocates a new cluster for the data. NTFS also marks the cluster as bad and no longer uses it.

Built-in security features
- When you set permissions on a file or folder, you specify the groups and users whose access you want to restrict or allow, and then select the type of access. For example, you can let one group read the contents of a file, let another group make changes to the file, and prevent all other groups from accessing the file.

- The Encrypting File System (EFS) is the technology used to store encrypted files on NTFS volumes. After you encrypt a file or folder, you work with the encrypted file or folder just as you do with any other files and folders. However, an intruder who tries to access your encrypted files or folders is prevented from doing so, even if the intruder has physical access to the computer.

Supports large volumes

- Using the default cluster size (4 KB) for large volumes, you can create an NTFS volume up to 16 terabytes. You can create NTFS volumes up to 256 terabytes using the maximum cluster size of 64 KB. NTFS also supports larger files and more files per volume than FAT.

- NTFS manages disk space more efficiently than FAT by using smaller cluster sizes. For example, a 30-GB NTFS volume uses 4-KB clusters. The same volume formatted by using FAT32 uses 16-KB clusters. Using smaller clusters reduces wasted space on hard disks.

Designed for storage growth

- By enabling disk quotas, you can track and control disk space usage for NTFS volumes. You can configure whether users are allowed to exceed their limit, and you can also configure Windows XP Professional to log an event when a user exceeds a specified warning level or quota limit.

- To create extra disk space, you can compress files on NTFS volumes. Compressed files can be read and written by any Windows-based application without first being decompressed by another program.

- If you run out of drive letters or need to create additional space that is accessible from an existing folder, you can mount a volume at any empty folder on a local NTFS volume to create a mounted drive. Mounted drives make data more accessible and give you the flexibility to manage data storage based on your work environment and system usage.

- You can increase the size of most NTFS volumes by adding unallocated space from the same disk or from another disk. For more information about increasing the size of NTFS volumes, see "Disk Management" in this book.

Other advanced features found only on NTFS volumes

- Distributed link tracking maintains the integrity of shortcuts and OLE links. You can rename source files, move them to NTFS volumes on different computers within a Windows 2000 domain, change the computer name or folder name that stores the target — all without breaking the shortcut or OLE links.

- Sparse files consist of large, consecutive areas of zeroes. NTFS manages sparse files by tracking the starting and ending point of the sparse file, as well as its useful (non-zero) data. The unused space in a sparse file is made available as free space.

- The NTFS change journal provides a persistent log of changes made to files on a volume. NTFS maintains the change journal by tracking information about added, deleted, and modified files for each volume. Programs such as Indexing Service can take advantage of the change journal to boost search performance.

- Hard links are NTFS-based links to a file on an NTFS volume. By creating hard links, you can have a single file in multiple folders without duplicating the file. You can also create multiple hard links for a file in a folder if you use different file names for the hard links. Because all of the hard links reference the same file, applications can open any of the hard links and modify the file.

When to Use FAT

If your computer runs only Windows XP Professional and you do not plan to install other operating systems, use NTFS. However, if you have other operating systems installed and want to access the volumes, you must use FAT16 or FAT32, depending on which operating systems are on your computer. For example, to start a Windows XP Professional-based computer in Microsoft MS-DOS, Microsoft, Windows® 3.*x*, or Microsoft, Windows 95, you must use FAT16. For a multiple-boot configuration that has Microsoft, Windows, 95 OEM Service Release 2 (OSR2), Microsoft, Windows 98, or Microsoft, Windows Millennium Edition (Me), use FAT32. Table 13-3 shows the file system formats supported by various operating systems.

Table 13-3   Operating System and File System Compatibility

Operating System	FAT16	FAT32	NTFS
Windows XP	X	X	X
Windows 2000	X	X	X
Windows NT 4.0[*]	X		X
Windows 95 OSR2, Windows 98, and Windows Me	X	X	
Windows 95 (prior to OSR2)	X		
MS-DOS	X		

[*]   Computers running Windows NT 4.0 require Service Pack 4 or later to access NTFS volumes previously mounted by Windows 2000 or Windows XP Professional.

In multiple-boot configurations, you can use NTFS for the Windows NT 4.0 with Service Pack 4 or later boot volume, Windows 2000 boot volume, or Windows XP boot volume if you do not want to access these volumes from other operating systems. However, you must format the system volume according to Table 13-3 if you want to start other operating systems. For more information about NTFS compatibility in computers running Windows NT 4.0 and Windows XP Professional, see "NTFS Compatibility with Windows NT 4.0" later in this chapter. For more information about the system and boot volumes, see "Disk Management" in this book.

Although NTFS is the preferred file system for hard disks, Windows XP Professional uses FAT12 when you format floppy disks and FAT32 when you format DVD-RAM discs. For removable media that can be ejected unexpectedly, you must use FAT16 or FAT32. NTFS is disabled for some removable media because NTFS does not flush data to the disk immediately, and removing NTFS-formatted media without using the Safe Removal application can result in data loss.

If you do not plan on removing the media and want to use NTFS, you can change the Safe Removal policy.

To enable NTFS on removable media

1. In Device Manager, right-click the device, and then click **Properties**.

2. On the **Policies** tab, click **Optimize for performance**.

For more information about removing disks and the Safe Removal policies, see "Managing Devices" in this book.

You no longer need to use FAT for the system and boot volumes because Windows XP Professional offers two troubleshooting tools designed to access NTFS volumes:

■ Safe Mode starts Windows XP Professional by using only the basic set of device drivers and system services loaded.

■ Recovery Console is a special command-line environment that enables you to copy system files from the operating system CD, fix disk errors, and otherwise troubleshoot system problems without installing a second copy of the operating system.

For more information about Safe Mode and the Recovery Console, see "Tools for Troubleshooting" in this book.

Cluster Size

A *cluster* (or *allocation unit*) is the smallest amount of disk space that can be allocated to hold a file. All file systems used by Windows XP Professional organize hard disks based on cluster size, which is determined by the number of sectors that the cluster contains. For example, on a disk that uses 512-byte sectors, a 512-byte cluster contains one sector, whereas a 4-KB cluster contains eight sectors.

FAT16, FAT32, and NTFS each use different cluster sizes depending on the size of the volume, and each file system has a maximum number of clusters it can support. The smaller the cluster size, the more efficiently a disk stores information because unused space within a cluster cannot be used by other files. And the more clusters supported, the larger the volumes you can create and format by using a particular file system.

Table 13-4 provides a comparison of FAT16, FAT32, and NTFS volume and default cluster sizes.

Table 13-4   Default Cluster Sizes for Volumes with Windows XP Professional File Systems

Volume Size	FAT16 Cluster Size	FAT32 Cluster Size	NTFS Cluster Size
7 MB–16 MB	2 KB	Not supported	512 bytes
17 MB–32 MB	512 bytes	Not supported	512 bytes
33 MB–64 MB	1 KB	512 bytes	512 bytes
65 MB–128 MB	2 KB	1 KB	512 bytes
129 MB–256 MB	4 KB	2 KB	512 bytes
257 MB–512 MB	8 KB	4 KB	512 bytes
513 MB–1,024 MB	16 KB	4 KB	1 KB
1,025 MB–2 GB	32 KB	4 KB	2 KB
2 GB–4 GB	64 KB	4 KB	4 KB
4 GB–8 GB	Not supported	4 KB	4 KB
8 GB–16 GB	Not supported	8 KB	4 KB
16 GB–32 GB	Not supported	16 KB	4 KB
32 GB–2 terabytes	Not supported	Not supported[*]	4 KB

*   Windows XP Professional formats FAT32 volumes up to 32 GB regardless of cluster size. To format volumes larger than 32 GB, you must use NTFS. However, Windows XP Professional can mount FAT32 volumes larger than 32 GB that were created by other operating systems.

In the Disk Management snap-in, you can specify a cluster size of up to 64 KB when you format a volume. If you use the **format** command to format a volume, but do not specify a cluster size by using the **/a:**size parameter, the default values in Table 13-4 are used. If you want to change the cluster size after the volume is formatted, you must reformat the volume.

Before you choose a cluster size other than the default, note the following important limitations:

■   For Microsoft® Windows® NT, Windows 2000, and Windows XP Professional, the cluster size of FAT16 volumes from 2 GB through 4 GB is 64 KB, which can create compatibility issues with some applications. For example, setup programs do not compute free space properly on a volume with 64-KB clusters and cannot run because of a perceived lack of free space. For this reason, you must use either NTFS or FAT32 to format volumes larger than 2 GB. The **format** command in Windows XP Professional displays a warning and asks for a confirmation before formatting a volume that has 64-KB clusters using FAT16.

- Windows XP Professional, like Windows NT 4.0 and Windows 2000, supports file compression. Because file compression is not supported on cluster sizes above 4 KB, the default NTFS cluster size for Windows XP Professional never exceeds 4 KB. For more information about NTFS compression, see "File Compression" later in this chapter.

To check the cluster size of an existing volume, use the **chkdsk** command or the **fsutil fsinfo ntfsinfo** command. For more information about using Chkdsk, see "Troubleshooting Disks and File Systems" in this book. For more information about using Fsutil, see Windows XP Professional Help.

Size Limitations in NTFS and FAT File Systems

Each file system supports a maximum volume size, file size, and number of files per volume. Because FAT16 and FAT32 volumes are limited to 4 GB and 32 GB respectively, you must use NTFS to create volumes larger than 32 GB. If you use FAT16 or FAT32 in computers that start multiple operating systems, you must note the following size limitations:

- FAT volumes smaller than 16 MB are formatted as FAT12.

- FAT16 volumes larger than 2 GB are not accessible from computers running MS-DOS, Windows 95, Windows 98, Windows Me, and many other operating systems. This limitation occurs because these operating systems do not support cluster sizes larger than 32 KB, which results in the 2 GB limit.

- In theory, FAT32 volumes can be about 8 terabytes; however, the maximum FAT32 volume size that Windows XP Professional can format is 32 GB. Therefore, you must use NTFS to format volumes larger than 32 GB. However, Windows XP Professional can read and write to larger FAT32 volumes formatted by other operating systems.

- If you create multidisk volumes such as spanned or striped volumes, the amount of space used on each disk is applied to the total size of the volume. Therefore, to create a multidisk volume that is larger than 32 GB, you must use NTFS.

For more information about FAT16 and FAT32, see "FAT File System" later in this chapter.

Maximum Sizes on NTFS Volumes

In theory, the maximum NTFS volume size is 264 clusters minus 1 cluster. However, the maximum NTFS volume size as implemented in Windows XP Professional is 232 clusters minus 1 cluster. For example, using 64-KB clusters, the maximum NTFS volume size is 256 terabytes minus 64 KB. Using the default cluster size of 4 KB, the maximum NTFS volume size is 16 terabytes minus 4 KB.

Because partition tables on master boot record (MBR) disks only support partition sizes up to 2 terabytes, you must use dynamic volumes to create NTFS volumes over 2 terabytes. Windows XP Professional manages dynamic volumes in a special database instead of in the partition table, so dynamic volumes are not subject to the 2-terabyte physical limit imposed by the partition table. Therefore, dynamic NTFS volumes can be as large as the maximum volume size supported by NTFS.

Itanium-based computers that use GUID partition table (GPT) disks also support NTFS volumes larger than 2 terabytes.

> **Note** If you use large numbers of files in an NTFS folder (300,000 or more), disable short-file name generation, especially if the first six characters of the long file names are similar. For more information, see "Optimizing NTFS Performance" later in this chapter.

Table 13-5 lists NTFS size limits.

Table 13-5   NTFS Size Limits

Description	Limit
Maximum file size	Theory: 16 exabytes minus 1 KB (2^{64} bytes minus 1 KB)
	Implementation: 16 terabytes minus 64 KB (2^{44} bytes minus 64 KB)
Maximum volume size	Theory: 2^{64} clusters minus 1 cluster
	Implementation: 256 terabytes minus 64 KB (2^{32} clusters minus 1 cluster)
Files per volume	4,294,967,295 (2^{32} minus 1 file)

Maximum Sizes on FAT32 Volumes

A FAT32 volume must have a minimum of 65,527 clusters. Windows XP Professional can format FAT32 volumes up to 32 GB, but it can mount larger FAT32 volumes created by other operating systems. Table 13-6 lists FAT32 size limits.

Table 13-6   FAT32 Size Limits

Description	Limit
Maximum file size	4 GB minus 1 byte (2^{32} bytes minus 1 byte)
Maximum volume size	32 GB (implementation)
Files per volume	4,177,920
Maximum number of files and subfolders within a single folder	65,534 (The use of long file names can significantly reduce the number of available files and subfolders within a folder.)

Maximum Sizes on FAT16 Volumes

FAT16 supports a maximum of 65,524 clusters per volume. Table 13-7 lists FAT16 size limits.

Table 13-7   FAT16 Size Limits

Description	Limit
Maximum file size	4 GB minus 1 byte (232 bytes minus 1 byte)
Maximum volume size	4 GB
Files per volume	Approximately 65,536 (216 files)
Maximum number of files and folders within the root folder	512 (Long file names can reduce the number of available files and folders in the root folder.)

Formatting a Volume

You choose a file system when you format a volume. During the format, Windows XP Professional places key file system structures on the volume. These structures include the boot sector, the file allocation table (for FAT volumes), and the master file table (for NTFS volumes). Depending on the program you use to format a volume, you can also choose one or more of the following formatting options.

Volume label   Specifies the name of the volume using up to 11 characters for FAT volumes and 32 characters for NTFS volumes. Volume labels make it easy to identify volumes when you view them in Microsoft® Windows® Explorer, My Computer, and Disk Management.

Quick format   Creates the file system structure on the volume without verifying the integrity of every sector in the volume, which increases the formatting speed. If the volume is already formatted and you are sure the disk is not damaged, you can use this option. If quick format fails, perform the format again without using quick format. A full format identifies and tracks bad sectors so that they are not used for storing data.

> **Note**   You must use the quick format option if you format a volume created on a third-party hardware-based RAID array that supports pre-allocating space for future use even though the physical disks do not have this space available. In this case, if you do not choose the quick format option, the format does not complete because Windows XP Professional cannot read every sector on the disk.

Enable compression   Compresses all files in the NTFS volume. For more information about compression, see "File Compression" later in this chapter.

Allocation unit (cluster) size   Specifies the cluster size to be used when the volume is formatted. Use the default size unless you want to choose a different cluster size for performance reasons. For more information about the impact of cluster sizes on performance, see "Optimizing NTFS Performance" later in this chapter.

The available formatting options vary according to the program you use to format the volume. Table 13-8 describes the programs that you can use to format a volume as well as the available options for each program.

Table 13-8   Options Available When You Format a Volume

Format Option	Where the Option Is Available			
	Setup	**My Computer or Windows Explorer**	**Disk Management**	**Format Command**
Volume label	No option to create a volume label.	Available for all volumes.	Available for all volumes.	Use the **/v:**_label_ parameter to specify the volume label.
Quick format	Available for all volumes.	Available for all volumes.	Available for all volumes.	Use the **/q** parameter to specify the quick format option.
Enable compression	No option to compress the volume.	Available for NTFS volumes.	Available for NTFS volumes.	Use the **/c** parameter to enable compression for NTFS volumes.
Allocation unit (cluster) size	Uses the default cluster size only.	Offers default cluster sizes for FAT volumes and clusters sizes up to 4 KB for NTFS volumes.	Offers all available cluster sizes.	Use the **/a:**_size_ parameter to specify the cluster size.

When you format a volume during Windows XP Professional Setup, you can choose between NTFS and FAT. The version of FAT that Setup uses depends on the size of the volume. For volumes smaller than 2 GB (2048 MB), Setup uses FAT16. For volumes 2 GB or larger, Setup uses FAT32. For volumes 32 GB or larger, Setup uses NTFS and does not offer FAT.

Disk Management requires you to format volumes on dynamic disks and GPT disks as NTFS. Use the **format** command to format these volumes as FAT or FAT32. For more information about dynamic disks and GPT disks, see "Disk Management" in this book.

Note   The **format** command is also available in Recovery Console. For more information about using Recovery Console, see "Tools for Troubleshooting" in this book.

You cannot format a volume that contains the paging file. Disk Management disables the Format menu command for paging file volumes. My Computer, Windows Explorer, and the **format** command display an error message when you try to format a paging file volume. You must move or delete the paging file before you can format the volume. For more information about identifying the volume that contains the paging file, see "Disk Management" in this book.

NTFS File System

NTFS is the preferred file system for all computers running Windows XP Professional. By formatting new volumes as NTFS — or converting existing FAT volumes to NTFS — you can take advantage of features unique to NTFS such as mounted drives, encryption, disk quotas, and file and folder permissions. This section describes many of the features available on NTFS volumes as well as issues including recoverability, performance, and compatibility.

Features Available on NTFS Volumes

This section describes the following NTFS features that are exclusive to NTFS volumes:

- File and Folder Permissions
- Encryption
- Disk Quotas
- File Compression
- Mounted Drives
- Distributed Link Tracking
- Sparse Files
- Multiple Data Streams
- POSIX Compliance
- NTFS Change Journal
- Indexing Service

File and Folder Permissions

On NTFS volumes you can set permissions on files and folders that specify which groups and users have access, and what level of access is permitted. NTFS file and folder permissions apply to users on the local computer and to users accessing the file or folder over the network. File and folder permissions are maintained in discretionary access control lists.

> **Note**   You can also set shared folder permissions, which operate on shared folders in combination with NTFS file and folder permissions. File attributes (read-only, hidden, and system) also limit file access. For more information about shared folder permissions, see "Managing Files and Folders" in this book.

File and folder permissions on NTFS volumes are inheritable by default. This feature reduces the time required to change the permissions of many files and sub-folders. For example, you might want to change the permissions on a tree of folders containing several thousand files. If the files and subfolders inherit permissions, you need to set permissions for only the top-level folder. In addition, you can prevent files or folders from inheriting permissions from the parent folder, allowing you to give a file or subfolder permissions different from its parent folder.

When you view the Advanced Security Settings dialog box, you can see the individual permission entries assigned to the object. Permissions acquired through inheritance are called inherited permissions. Permissions that are not inherited, but are instead defined directly on an object, are called explicit permissions. Both types of permissions are shown in the Advanced Security Settings dialog box as shown in Figure 13-1.

To open the Advanced Security Settings dialog box

1. Right-click a file or folder on an NTFS volume.

2. Click **Properties**, click the **Security** tab, and then click **Advanced**.

Figure 13-1   Advanced Security Settings dialog box

If the Security tab does not appear, the computer is not part of a domain, and simple file sharing is enabled. To view the Security tab, you must disable simple file sharing.

To disable simple file sharing

1. In My Computer, click the **Tools** menu, and then click **Folder Options**.

2. On the **View** tab, in **Advanced settings**, clear the **Use simple file sharing (Recommended)** check box.

> **Warning**   You can back up and restore data on FAT and NTFS volumes. However, if you back up data from an NTFS volume and then restore it to a FAT volume, you lose security settings and other file information specific to NTFS.

Windows XP Professional offers an easy way to view which permissions are effectively granted to any specified user or group for the current object. You can view this information in the Effective Permissions dialog box.

Effective permissions reflect the work of combining permissions, both allowed and denied, from all matching entries, whether explicit or inherited. Matching entries name either the user or group directly, or a group in which the specified user or group is a member. The effective permissions are indicated by a checkmark next to each permission that is granted to the user or group. Figure 13-2 shows the permissions assigned to the Art folder for user2.

Figure 13-2   Effective Permissions tab

Although NTFS provides access control to individual files and folders, users can perform certain actions even if permissions are set on a file or folder to prevent access. For example, you have a folder (MyFolder) containing a file (File1), and you grant Full Control to a user for the folder MyFolder. If you deny Full Control for File1, the user can still delete File1 because the Full Control permission for MyFolder consists of a set of special permissions that include Delete Subfolders and Files. This special permission allows the user to delete files within the folder, even if the special permission Delete has been denied (or not granted) to the user for File1. You can view the special permissions assigned to a file or folder by clicking the Edit button in the Advanced Security Settings dialog box.

To prevent File1 from being deleted, you must ensure that the user is not granted the Delete Subfolders and Files special permission on the parent folder (MyFolder), explicitly or through group membership. To do this, use the Effective Permissions tab to view the folder's special permissions that are granted to the user. If Delete Subfolders and Files is selected, the user can delete all files within the folder.

To give the user access to the folder and its files without the ability to delete them, clear the Full Control check box and ensure that the user is not also granted Full Control via membership in another group. Although explicit permissions override inherited permissions, you cannot deny Full Control without also denying Modify, Read & Execute, List Folder Contents, Read, and Write. To prevent a user who is granted Full Control, by way of inherited group permissions, from deleting MyFolder and its files, you can do one of the following:

- Explicitly deny the Delete Subfolders and Files special permission for either the group or for the individual user.

- Remove inheritance from the folder and then reset the permissions for the group.

Note Anyone who has List Folder Contents permission for a folder can view file properties on any file in the folder, even if file permissions prevent them from seeing the contents of the file.

For more information about file and folder permissions, see "Authorization and Access Control" in this book.

Encryption

The Encrypting File System (EFS) uses symmetric key encryption in conjunction with public key technology to protect files and folders. Encryption ensures that only the authorized users and designated recovery agents of that file or folder can access it.

Users of EFS are issued a digital certificate with a public key and a private key pair. EFS uses the key set for the user who is logged on to the local computer where the private key is stored.

Users work with encrypted files and folders just as they do with any other files and folders. Encryption is transparent to any authorized users; the system decrypts the file or folder when the user opens it. When the file is saved, encryption is reapplied. However, intruders who try to access the encrypted files or folders receive an "Access denied" message if they try to open, copy, move, or rename the encrypted file or folder.

To encrypt or decrypt a folder or file, set the encryption attribute for NTFS folders and files just as you set attributes such as read-only or compressed. If you encrypt a folder, all files and subfolders created in the encrypted folder are automatically encrypted.

> **Warning** It is recommended that you encrypt at the folder level to ensure that new files are automatically encrypted and that temporary files created during the editing process remain encrypted.

EFS is not available in Microsoft® Windows® XP Home Edition. For more information about EFS, see "Encrypting File System" in this book.

You can also encrypt or decrypt a file or folder by using the command-line tool Cipher. For more information about Cipher, see Windows XP Professional Help.

Disk Quotas

Disk quotas track and control disk space usage for NTFS volumes. By using disk quotas, you can configure Windows XP Professional to:

- Log an event when a user exceeds a specified disk space warning level. The warning level specifies the point at which a user is nearing the quota limit.

- Prevent further use of disk space or log an event when a user exceeds a specified disk space limit.

Disk quotas are tracked on a per-user, per-volume basis; users are charged *only* for the files they own. Quotas are tracked per volume, even if the hard disk contains multiple volumes. If you have multiple shared folders on the *same* volume, the quotas apply to all shared folders equally, and a user's use of all shared folders cannot exceed the assigned quota on that volume.

The disk space used by each file is charged to the user who owns the file. The file owner is identified by the security identifier (SID) in the security information for the file. The total disk space charged to a user is the sum of the length of all data streams; property set streams and resident user data streams affect the user's quota. Small files contained entirely within the file's master file table (MFT) record also affect the user's quota.

Because disk quotas are based on file ownership, they are independent of the location of the files on the volume. Moving files from one folder to another on the same volume does not change volume space usage. However, copying the files to a different folder on the same volume results in duplicate files in both locations. Thus, the available volume space usage against the user's quota decreases by the number of bytes copied.

Disk quotas are transparent to the user. When a user views the available disk space for the volume, the system reports only the user's available quota allowance. If the user exceeds this allowance, the system indicates that the disk is full. To obtain more disk space after exceeding the quota allowance, the user must do one of the following:

- Delete files.

- Reduce the size of existing files.

- Have another user claim ownership of some files.

- Have the administrator increase the quota allowance.

Disk quotas are based on uncompressed file sizes. Users cannot increase the amount of free space by using NTFS compression to compress the files.

For sparse files, disk quotas are based on the nominal size of the sparse file, not the actual allocated amount of disk space. For example, creating a 50-MB file with all zero bytes consumes 50 MB of that user's quota. This means the user can write data to the sparse file without exceeding the quota limit because the user has already been charged for the space. For more information about sparse files, see "Sparse Files" later in this chapter.

To enable quotas

1. Right-click a volume in Windows Explorer or My Computer.

2. Click **Properties**, and then click the **Quota** tab (see Figure 13-3).

3. Do the following:

   - Enable or disable disk quotas.

   - Deny disk space to users who have exceeded their quota limit.

   - Set the default warning level and quota limit assigned to new volume users.

   - Specify whether to log an event in the system log when a user reaches the quota or warning level.

Figure 13-3   Quota tab

If the volume is not formatted by using NTFS, or if you are not a member of the Administrators group on the computer, the Quota tab is not displayed on the volume's Properties dialog box.

Note   You can also use the command-line tool Fsutil.exe to manage quotas. For more information about Fsutil.exe, see Windows XP Professional Help.

Disk Quota States

As the administrator, you can turn quota enforcement on and off. There are three quota states, as shown in Table 13-9.

Table 13-9   Disk Quota States

State	Description
Quota disabled	Quota usage changes are not tracked, and the quota limits are not removed. In this state, performance is not affected by disk quotas. This is the default state.
Quota tracked	Quota usage changes are tracked, but quota limits are not enforced. In this state, no quota violation events are generated and no file operations fail because of disk quota violations.
Quota enforced	Quota usage changes are tracked, and quota limits are enforced.

Warning Levels and Disk Quota Limits

When you enable disk quotas, you can set both the warning level and the quota limit.

Warning level   Specifies when a user is nearing the limit. When the disk space charged to the user exceeds the warning level, the system can generate an event in the system log on the computer hosting the volume. The user is not notified when this level is surpassed.

Quota limit   Specifies the amount of disk space allocated to a user. When the disk space charged to the user exceeds the quota limit, the system generates an event in the system log or denies additional disk space to the user. When you set quota limits on a computer that many users share, make sure to set the limit to at least 2 MB, which is greater than the default 1 KB, to ensure that Windows XP Professional can create a user profile when a user logs on to the computer.

For example, you can set a user's disk quota limit to 500 MB, and the disk quota warning level to 450 MB. The user can store no more than 500 MB of data on the volume. If more than 450 MB are stored on the volume, the disk quota system can log an event in the system log.

Increasing Quotas for Individual Users

Figure 13-4 shows the Quota Entries window, which you open by clicking the **Quota Entries** button. In the Quota Entries window, you can view each user's quota limit, warning level, and quota usage. You can also change the quota limit and warning level for individual users who need more disk space than the default quota.

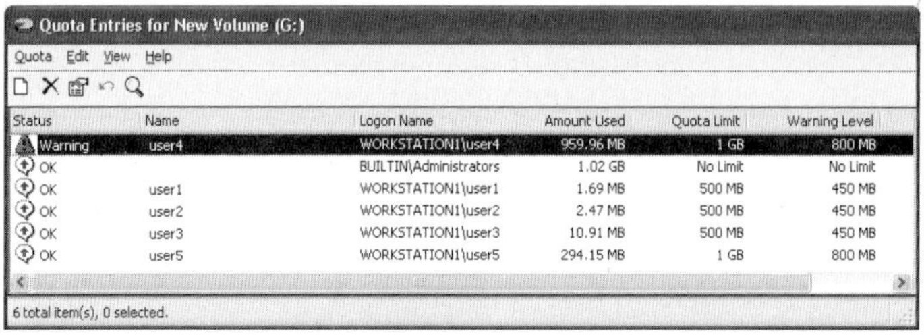

Figure 13-4   Quota Entries window

For example, on a volume that contains a shared folder named \\Workstation1\Public, you can set a quota of 500 MB per user while giving two users each a 1-GB limit because they work with large files. If both users have files stored on \\Workstation1\Public, their current usage is displayed in the Quota Entries window.

To change the quota for an individual user

1. Open the **Properties** dialog box for the appropriate volume.

2. Click the **Quota** tab, and then click **Quota Entries**.

3. Select the appropriate user, right-click, and then click **Properties** to set the quota.

   -or-

   For a new user who does not have files stored on the volume, on the **Quota** menu, click **New Quota Entry,** and then set the quota higher than the default.

> **Note**   Disk quotas do not prevent you from allocating more space than is available on the disk. For example, on a 40-GB volume used by 50 users, each user might be allocated 1 GB.

Disk Quotas and Administrators

A new Group Policy setting allows you to specify the default owner of objects (such as files) created by members of the Administrators group. You can access the Group Policy setting **System objects: Default owner for objects created by members of the administrators group** in Local Computer Policy\Computer Configuration \Windows Settings\Security Settings\Local Policies\Security Options\. In Windows XP Professional, the default owner is the object creator. To change the default owner to the Administrators group, use the Group Policy snap-in. For more information about using the Group Policy snap-in, see "Managing Desktops" in this book.

Although members of the Administrators group do not have quotas enabled by default, you can set quotas for all members of the Administrators group except the built-in Administrator account. In Windows 2000, you cannot set quotas for any member of the Administrators group.

Exceeding Disk Quota Limits

When you select **Deny disk space to users exceeding quota limit** on the Quota tab of the Properties dialog box, users who exceed their limit receive an "Insufficient disk space" error message and cannot write additional data to the volume without deleting or moving files. Individual programs determine their own error handling for this condition. The program treats the volume as full.

By leaving the **Deny disk space to users exceeding quota limit** check box cleared, you can let users exceed their quota. This is useful when you want to track use of disk space without denying users access to a volume. You can also specify whether to log an event to the volume host computer's system log when users exceed either their quota or warning level.

Event Viewer keeps a chronological record of users who exceed their quota or warning level. However, it does not provide information about which users are currently over their quota warning level.

> **Note** You can use the **fsutil behavior set quotanotify** command to set the interval between quota-related events that NTFS records in the system log. For more information about this command, see Windows XP Professional Help.

Deleting Quota Entries

To delete the quota entry for a user, you must do any of the following:

- Permanently delete the files.
- Take ownership of the files and folders.
- Move the files to a different volume.

You cannot delete quota entries if a user owns files or folders on the volume. If you try to delete a quota entry for a user who still owns files or folders on the volume, a dialog box appears as shown in Figure 13-5.

Figure 13-5 The Disk Quota dialog box

If the user owns files on the volume, you can use the Disk Quota dialog box to delete the files, take ownership of them, or move them to another volume. However, if the user owns folders on the volume, you can only use the Disk Quota dialog box to take ownership of the folders, not delete or move them. To make it easier to take ownership of folders, you can click the **Show folders only** check box.

Local and Remote Implementations of Disk Quotas

You can enable disk quotas on local computers and remote computers. On local computers, use quotas to do the following:

- Prevent users from using excessive disk space on a shared folder on your computer.

- Limit the amount of space available to users who log on to the local computer.

    On remote computers, quotas can ensure the following:

- Disk space on public servers is not monopolized by one or a few users.

- Information technology (IT) budget for mass storage is managed efficiently by making users account for the use of shared disk space by using public disk space only for necessary files.

You can manage NTFS volumes on remote computers running Windows XP Professional and Windows 2000. The volumes must be formatted by using NTFS and be shared from the root folder of the volume. You can set quotas on the remote volume by mapping to it using Windows Explorer or My Computer.

To set quotas on a mapped remote volume

1. Right-click the mapped remote volume.

2. Click **Properties**, and then click the **Quota** tab.

> **Note**   You must be a member of the Administrators group on the remote computer to enable, disable, or manage quotas.

Auditing Disk Space Use

Enabling quotas causes a slight decrease in file system performance. By periodically enabling and disabling quotas, you can take advantage of the auditing capabilities provided by Windows XP Professional disk quotas without permanently affecting performance.

    To create a record of the audit, save a copy of the system log data from Event Viewer to a comma-delimited file that can be read by programs such as Microsoft Excel. These files can be useful for analyzing the data captured.

> **Note**   When you disable quotas, the tracking information displayed in the **Quota Entries** window is no longer updated. To refresh this information (including the current disk space used by each user), enable disk quotas again.

Disk Quotas in Multiple-Boot Configurations

Disk quotas are not enforced and can be exceeded in multiple-boot configurations when an NTFS volume is mounted by using Windows NT 4.0. However, when that computer resumes running Windows XP Professional, users who exceeded their quotas must delete or move files to a different volume — that is, until they are under their limit — before they can store new files to the quota volume. Disk quotas are enforced on computers configured as a multiple-boot system with Windows XP Professional and Windows 2000.

Using WMI to Script Disk Quotas

Microsoft® Windows® Management Instrumentation (WMI) is the application programming interface (API) that allows all system components to be monitored and controlled, either locally or remotely. By using the WMI classes Win32_DiskQuota, Win32_QuotaSettings, and Win32_VolumeQuotaSetting, you can create scripts that help you to do the following:

View and modify the quota settings for users for all disks on a computer by:

- Viewing the status of the quota.

- Reporting or setting the warning level.

- Reporting or setting the quota limit.

- Reporting how much space is being used for a specified user.

View and modify the quota settings and defaults for each disk on a computer by:

- Reporting or setting the operational state of quotas on a disk (disabled, tracked, or enforced).

- Reporting or setting the default warning level.

- Reporting or setting the default quota limit.

- Enabling or disabling the logging of warning levels being exceeded.

- Enabling or disabling the logging of quota limits being exceeded.

By using these classes, you can take advantage of other standard WMI features such as WMI Query Language (WQL) query support and event generation based on changes in the data in these classes. For example, a program can request that it be notified when a user is within 2 MB of the quota limit. When this criterion is met, WMI sends an event notification to the program, allowing an action such as increasing the quota or sending an e-mail message to the user.

Note   WQL is a subset of Structured Query Language (SQL).

For more information about WMI, see the Microsoft Windows Management Instrumentation (WMI) SDK link on the Web Resources page at http://www.microsoft.com/windows/reskits/webresources.

File Compression

NTFS supports compression on individual files, all files within a folder, and all files within NTFS volumes. Because compression is implemented within NTFS, any Windows-based program can read and write compressed files without determining the compression state of the file. When a program opens a compressed file, NTFS decompresses only the portion of the file being read and then copies that data to memory. By leaving data in memory uncompressed, NTFS performance is not impacted when it reads or modifies data in memory. NTFS compresses the modified or new data in the file when the data is later written to disk.

The compression algorithms in NTFS support cluster sizes of up to 4 KB. When the cluster size is greater than 4 KB on an NTFS volume, none of the NTFS compression features are available.

Using Windows Explorer or My Computer to Compress Files   Using Windows Explorer or My Computer, you can set the compression state of a file on an NTFS volume. You can also set the compression state of a folder or volume without changing the compression state of existing files in that folder.

If you have Modify permission for a file or folder, you can change its compression state locally or across a network.

To set the compression state of a volume

1. In **My Computer** or **Windows Explorer**, right-click the volume that you want to compress or uncompress.

2. Click **Properties** to display the **Properties** dialog box.

3. On the **General** tab, select or clear the **Compress drive to save disk space** check box, and then click **OK**.

4. In the **Confirm Attribute Changes** dialog box, select whether to make the compression apply to the entire volume or only to the root folder.

Any change to the compression attribute is applied to the files you specified. If you compress all files in the volume, the process might take a few minutes to finish, depending on the size of the volume, the number of files to compress, and the speed of the computer. The delay occurs because Windows XP Professional must change the compression state of every folder on the volume and compress or uncompress every file on the volume. Changing the compression state of folders is relatively fast because for each folder Windows XP Professional changes only the compression attribute. However, compressing or uncompressing every file on the volume takes longer because NTFS must read data in its current form (compressed or uncompressed) from the disk, convert the data to its new form in memory, and then write the data back to disk.

To set the compression state of a folder or file

1. In My Computer or Windows Explorer, right-click the file or folder that you want to compress or decompress.

2. Click **Properties** to display the **Properties** dialog box.

3. On the **General** tab, click **Advanced**.

4. In the **Advanced Attributes** dialog box, select or clear the **Compress contents to save disk space** check box, and then click **OK**.

5. In the **Properties** dialog box, click **OK**.

6. If the compression state was altered for a folder, in the **Confirm Attribute Changes** dialog box, select whether to make the compression apply only to the selected folder, or to the selected folder and all its files and subfolders. Click **OK** when done.

> **Note**   Windows XP Professional can compress closed paging files. However, when you restart Windows XP Professional, the paging files revert to an uncompressed state. For information about paging files, see the topics on virtual memory in Windows XP Professional Help.

You can set Windows Explorer to display alternate colors for compressed files and folders by using the following procedure:

To display alternate colors for compressed files and folders

1. In My Computer or Windows Explorer, click the **Tools** menu, and then click **Folder Options**.

2. On the **View** tab, select the **Show encrypted or compressed NTFS files in color** check box.

3. Click **OK** to return to Windows Explorer or My Computer.

Using Compact to Compress a Volume   Compact.exe is the command-line version of the compression feature in Windows Explorer and My Computer. Compact displays and alters the compression of folders and files on NTFS volumes. It also displays the compression state of folders.

Three reasons that you might want to use Compact instead of Windows Explorer or My Computer follow:

- You can use Compact in a batch script.

- If the system fails during compression or decompression, the operation might not have finished. You can use the **/f** parameter to force the operation to finish in the background.

- You can compress or uncompress files that match certain criteria. For example, to compress all .txt files in the current folder, type:

  ```
  compact /c *.txt
  ```

  The following list provides examples of Compact syntax.

- To compress a volume, from the root folder of the volume, type:

  ```
  compact /c /i /s:\
  ```

  The preceding example sets the compression state of the root folder and all folders on the volume and compresses every file on the volume. Using the **/i** parameter ensures that error messages do not interrupt the compression process.

- To set the compression state of the current folder and its subfolders and existing files, from the current folder, type:

  ```
  compact /c /s
  ```

- To set the compression state of files in the current folder, subfolders in the current folder, and files within all subfolders — without altering the compression state of the current folder — from the current folder, type:

  ```
  compact /c /s *.*
  ```

For more information about Compact, see Windows XP Professional Help.

Effects of Compression on Moving and Copying Files   Moving and copying files and folders can change their compression state. The resulting compression state depends on whether you move or copy the files and whether you move files between NTFS volumes or to FAT volumes.

> **Note** The default behavior for dragging and dropping files and folders in Windows Explorer and My Computer depends on the relationship between the source and the target location. If the selected item is dragged to a folder on the same volume, the item is moved. If the selected item is dragged to a folder on a different volume, the item is copied. To force a copy, press CTRL as you drag and drop the item to its new location. To move the item, press SHIFT as you drag and drop it to the new location. If you right-click and drag the selected item, a shortcut menu appears so that you can choose to copy, move, create a shortcut to the item, or cancel the task.

Moving Files or Folders within an NTFS Volume   When you move an uncompressed file or folder to another folder on the same NTFS volume, the file remains uncompressed, regardless of the compression state of the folder to which it was moved. For example, if you move an uncompressed file to a compressed folder, the file remains uncompressed after the move, as shown in Figure 13-6.

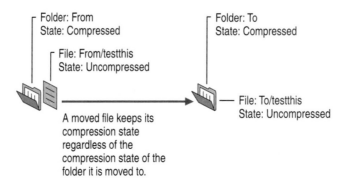

Figure 13-6   Moving an uncompressed file to a compressed folder

When you move a compressed file or folder to another folder, the file remains compressed after the move, regardless of the compression state of the folder, as shown in Figure 13-7.

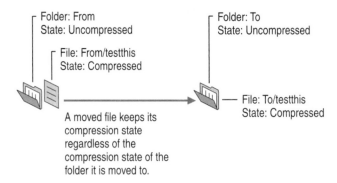

Figure 13-7   Moving a compressed file to an uncompressed folder

Copying Files or Folders on NTFS Volumes   When you copy a file to a folder, the file takes on the compression attribute of the target folder. For example, if you copy a compressed file to an uncompressed folder, the file is uncompressed when it is copied to the folder, as shown in Figure 13-8.

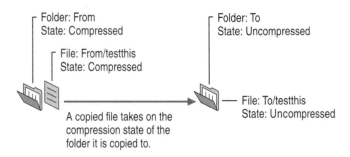

Figure 13-8   Copying a compressed file to an uncompressed folder

When you copy a file to a folder that already contains a file of the same name, the copied file takes on the compression attribute of the target file, regardless of the compression state of the folder, as shown in Figure 13-9.

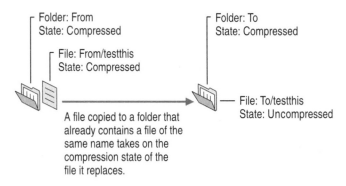

Figure 13-9   Copying a file to a folder that contains a file of the same name

Copying Files Between FAT and NTFS Volumes Like files copied between NTFS folders, files copied from a FAT folder to an NTFS folder take on the compression attribute of the target folder. Because Windows XP Professional supports compression only on NTFS volumes, compressed NTFS files copied to a FAT volume are uncompressed. Similarly, compressed NTFS files copied to a floppy disk are uncompressed.

> **Caution** If you copy a file from an NTFS volume to a FAT volume, any NTFS-specific properties associated with that file, such as permissions and data streams, are permanently lost.

Adding Files to an Almost Full NTFS Volume As a best practice for using compression, ensure that you have at least 15 percent free space on the volume. If you copy files to a compressed NTFS folder that does not have room for the files in an uncompressed state, an error message indicates the disk lacks adequate space. A message might also appear if you attempt to read a compressed file on a volume that is almost full. These messages appear because NTFS must support the possibility that any file that is read into memory might be modified, and the modified data must eventually be written to disk. Therefore, NTFS must reserve enough space on the disk for the file based on the worse possible compression scenario: that the file must be saved, uncompressed, to disk. After the files are flushed to disk, NTFS releases any remaining reserved space.

You can regain space that NTFS has reserved for open files by dismounting and then remounting the volume or by restarting the computer. You can temporarily dismount a volume by using the **fsutil volume dismount** command. The volume is remounted the next time you access it.

NTFS Compression Performance Workstations are good candidates for compression because compression and decompression are performed locally. Heavily loaded servers that have substantial input/output (I/O) traffic are poor candidates for data compression. Because the server must decompress files before sending them across the network, the decompression workload can cause performance degradation on the server. However, read-only servers, read-mostly servers, or servers that store infrequently accessed files might not get performance degradation. For example, if 50% of the files on a server are frequently accessed and are close to 100% of the server's I/O workload, do not compress those files. If the other 50% are accessed once every few days, and account for less than 1% of the server workload, you might want to compress them.

If your workload involves asynchronous I/O, do not use compression. Compression converts all I/O to synchronous.

If you have programs that use transaction logging and constantly write to a database or log, have the programs store their files on an uncompressed volume. If a program modifies data by using mapped sections in a compressed file, it can produce dirty pages faster than the mapped writer can write them. (A dirty page is a page that has been modified in the cache, but is not yet written to disk.) For example, programs such as Microsoft® Message Queue cannot function on compressed NTFS volumes.

It is recommended that you avoid placing user home folders and roaming profiles on compressed NTFS volumes because of the large number of read and write operations performed in these folders.

For information about the effect of compression on NTFS performance, see "Optimizing NTFS Performance" later in this chapter.

Other Compression Methods   In addition to using NTFS compression, you can use the Compressed (zipped) Folders feature in Windows XP Professional and other compression tools.

Using the Compressed (zipped) Folders Feature   You can use the Compressed (zipped) Folders feature in Windows XP Professional to create, add files to, and extract files from zipped files. In Windows Explorer and My Computer, a zipper on the folder icon identifies Compressed (zipped) Folders. Unlike in NTFS compression, you can create Compressed (zipped) Folders on any FAT or NTFS volume. In addition, Compressed (zipped) Folders are compatible with other programs that create zipped files, so you can share them with users who use other compression programs that support zipped files.

To create a Compressed (zipped) Folder

- In Windows Explorer or My Computer, click the **File** menu, point to **New**, and then click **Compressed (zipped) Folder**.

After you create a Compressed (zipped) Folder, you can compress files, programs, or other folders by dragging them to it. You can open files directly from Compressed (zipped) Folders, or you can extract files before opening them.

For more information about using the Compressed (zipped) Folders feature, see Windows XP Professional Help.

Other Compression Tools   Other compression tools are available to compress files on computers running Windows XP Professional. These tools differ from NTFS compression in the following ways:

- They typically run from either the command line or as a stand-alone application.

- They can be used to compress files on FAT volumes as well as NTFS volumes.

■ Files cannot be opened when they are in a compressed state; the file must first be decompressed. When you close the file, it is saved in an uncompressed state, and you must use a program to compress it.

NTFS compression differs from DoubleSpace, DriveSpace, and DriveSpace 3 compression in several ways. For example, NTFS provides faster compression and decompression with minimal loss of compression for a typical text file. Another difference is that these programs compress the entire volume, including the metadata associated with each file and folder. By using NTFS compression, you can compress individual files or folders instead of the entire volume, and you can compress only files you use infrequently.

> **Note**   You can use the Disk Cleanup tool to compress files that have not been accessed for a specified number of days. For more information about Disk Cleanup, see Windows XP Professional Help.

Mounted Drives

Mounted drives, also known as volume mount points or drive paths, are volumes attached to an empty folder on an NTFS volume. Mounted drives function the same way as any other volume, but are assigned a label or name instead of a drive letter. Mounted drives are robust against system changes that occur when devices are added or removed from a computer. They are not subject to the 26-volume limit imposed by drive letters, so you can use them for access to more than 26 volumes on your computer.

The version of NTFS included with Windows XP Professional and Windows 2000 must be used on the host volume. However, the volume to be mounted can be formatted in any file system supported by Windows XP Professional, including NTFS, FAT16, FAT32, CDFS, or UDF.

One volume can host multiple mounted drives, providing a way for you to easily extend the storage capacity of any particular volume on a Windows XP Professional system. Users on the local system or users who connect to it over a network can continue to use the same drive letter for access to the volume, but multiple volumes can be in use simultaneously from that drive letter.

> **Note**   To identify and manage mounted drives from the command line, use the Mountvol.exe tool. For more information about Mountvol.exe, see Windows XP Professional Help.

The following scenario is an example of mounted drives. A user recently installed Windows XP Professional on volume C, an NTFS volume. She is concerned about storage space on this volume because she uses her computer extensively to create and edit digital photos, graphic art, and desktop publishing (DTP) files. The user knows that the default document folder, My Documents, is on volume C, but she wants to use the E volume on her second hard disk to store her work. She creates a mounted drive on volume C under the My Documents folder labeled Art. Any sub-folder of the Art folder actually resides on volume E, thus saving space on volume C.

To create a mounted drive, you must be a member of the Administrators group on the local computer.

To create a mounted drive under C:\My Documents

1. Log on to the computer using an account that is a member of the Administrators group.

2. Click **Start**, click **Run**, type **diskmgmt.msc**, and then click **OK**.

3. Right-click volume E, and then click **Change Drive Letter and Paths**.

4. In the **Change Drive Letter and Paths** dialog box, click **Add**, click **Mount in the following empty NTFS folder**, and then click **Browse**.

5. In the **Browse for Drive Path** dialog box, expand drive C, go to the C:\Documents and Settings*username*\My Documents folder, and then click **New Folder**.

6. In the folder name placeholder in the Explorer tree, type the name **Art** over the default name **New Folder**, and then close the dialog boxes.

7. In My Computer or Windows Explorer, go to volume E and create new folders such as Photos, LineArt, and DTP for the graphic arts documents.

As shown in Figure 13-10, all files stored in the My Documents\Art folder are stored in the root folder of volume E, the mounted drive. Any other folder created within Windows Explorer or My Computer under the My Documents folder still resides on volume C.

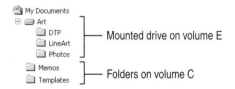

Figure 13-10   A mounted drive in My Documents

Hard Links

You can use the **fsutil hardlink create** command to create hard links. A hard link is an NTFS-based link to a given file. When you create a hard link to a file on an NTFS volume, NTFS adds a directory entry for the hard link without duplicating the original file. By creating hard links, you can:

- Create hard links that use the same file name as the original file but appear in different folders.

- Create hard links that use different file names from the original file but appear in the same folder.

- Create hard links that use different file names from the original file and appear in different folders.

Because a hard link is a directory entry for a file, an application can modify a file by using any of its hard links. Applications that use any other hard link can detect the changes. However, directory entries for hard links are updated only when a user accesses a file by using the hard link. For example, if a user opens and modifies a file by using its hard link, and the size of the original file changes, the hard link that is used to access the file also shows the new size.

> **Warning**   NTFS updates the properties of a hard link only when a user accesses the original file by using the hard link, not every time a user makes a change to the original file.

Hard links do not have security descriptors; instead, the security descriptor belongs to the original file to which the hard link points. Thus, if you change the security descriptor of any hard link, you actually change the underlying file's security descriptor. All hard links that point to the file allow the newly specified access. You cannot give a file different security descriptors on a per-hard-link basis.

When creating hard links, consider the following:

- You can create hard links only on NTFS volumes; not on FAT volumes.

- You cannot create a hard link on one volume that refers to a file on another volume.

To delete a file that has multiple hard links, you must delete the file and all its associated hard links.

For more information about using the **fsutil hardlink create** command, see Windows XP Professional Help.

Distributed Link Tracking

Distributed link tracking ensures that shell shortcuts and OLE links continue to work after the target file is renamed or moved. When you create a shortcut to a file on an NTFS volume, distributed link tracking stamps a unique object identifier (ID) into the target file, known as the link source. Information about the object ID is also stored within the referring file, known as the link client. Distributed link tracking uses this object ID to locate the link source in any combination of the following events that occur on NTFS volumes within a Windows 2000-based domain:

- The link source is renamed.

- The link source is moved to another folder on the same volume or to a different volume on the same computer.

- The link source is moved from one shared network folder to another shared network folder on other computers within the same domain.

- The computer containing the link source is renamed.

- The name of the shared network folder containing the link source has changed.

- The volume containing the link source is moved to another computer within the same domain.

Note   Distributed link tracking works only on NTFS volumes in computers running Windows 2000 or Windows XP. The NTFS volumes cannot be on removable media.

Distributed link tracking attempts to maintain links even when they do not occur within a domain, such as cross-domain, within a workgroup, or on a single computer that is not connected to a network. Links can always be maintained in these events when a link source is moved within a computer, or when the network shared folder on the link source computer is changed. Typically, links can be maintained when the link source is moved to another computer; however, this form of tracking is less reliable over time.

Distributed link tracking uses different services for client and server:

- The Distributed Link Tracking Client service runs on all Windows 2000 and Windows XP Professional computers. In computers that are not part of a network, the Client service performs all activities related to link tracking.

■ The Distributed Link Tracking Server service runs on Windows 2000 domain controllers. The Server service maintains information relating to the movement of link sources. Because of this service and the information it maintains, links within a domain are more reliable than those outside a domain. For computers that run in a domain, the Distributed Link Tracking Client service takes advantage of this information by communicating with the Distributed Link Tracking Server service.

The Distributed Link Tracking Client service monitors activity on NTFS volumes and stores maintenance information in a file called Tracking.log, which is located at the root of each volume in a hidden folder called System Volume Information. This folder is protected by permissions that allow only the system to have access to it. The System Volume Information folder is also used by other Windows XP Professional services such as Indexing Service.

Sparse Files

Sparse files provide a method of saving disk space for files that contain meaningful data as well as large sections of data composed of zeros. If an NTFS file is marked as sparse, then NTFS allocates disk clusters only for the data explicitly specified by the application. Non-specified ranges of the file are represented by non-allocated space on the disk. When a sparse file is read from allocated ranges, the data is returned as it was stored. Data read from non-allocated ranges is returned as zeros. An example of a program that uses sparse files is Indexing Service, which stores its catalogs as sparse files on NTFS volumes.

File system application programming interfaces (APIs) allow for the file to be copied or backed as actual bits and sparse stream ranges. File system APIs also allow for querying allocated ranges. Programs that implement these APIs then need only to read allocated ranges to recover all data in the file. The result is efficient file system storage and access. Figure 13-11 shows how data is stored with and without the sparse file attribute set.

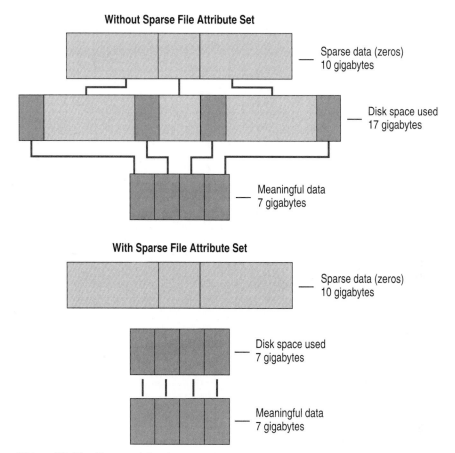

Figure 13-11   Sparse data storage

Figure 13-12 shows the properties of a 1-GB sparse file. Although the file is 1 GB, it occupies only 64 KB of disk space.

Figure 13-12   Properties of a sparse file

Warning   Only NTFS volumes mounted by Windows 2000 or Windows XP support sparse files. If you copy or move a sparse file to a FAT volume or an NTFS volume mounted by an operating system other than Windows XP or Windows 2000, the file is built to its originally specified size. If the required space is not available, the operation fails.

Multiple Data Streams

A data stream is a sequence of bytes. An application populates the stream by writing data at specific offsets within the stream. The application can then read the data by reading the same offsets in the read path. Every file has a main, unnamed stream associated with it, regardless of the file system used. However, NTFS supports additional named data streams in which each data stream is an alternate sequence of bytes as illustrated in Figure 13-13. Applications can create additional named streams and access the streams by referring to their names. This feature permits related data to be managed as a single unit. For example, a graphics program can store a thumbnail image of bitmap in a named data stream within the NTFS file containing the image.

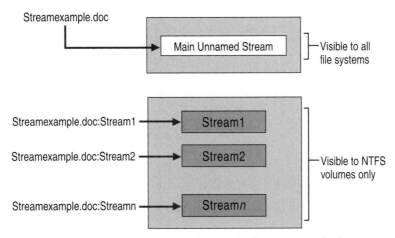

Figure 13-13   Unnamed and named streams for Streamexample.doc

To see how data streams work, you can create a file that contains multiple data streams by adding summary information to a file on an NTFS volume.

To create a data stream for a file on an NTFS volume

1. Right-click a text file or Wordpad document, and then click **Properties**.

2. On the **Summary** tab, add information about the file, such as the title, subject, and author.

The file information is stored in separate named streams. Figure 13-14 shows the Summary tab of the file Streamexample.doc.

Figure 13-14   Creating alternate data streams by using the Summary tab

FAT volumes support only the main, unnamed stream, so if you try to copy or move Streamexample.doc to a FAT volume or floppy disk, you receive an error message as shown in Figure 13-15. If you copy the file, all named data streams and other attributes not supported by FAT are lost.

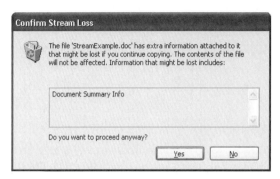

Figure 13-15   Message that confirms loss of named data streams

POSIX Compliance

NTFS provides a several features to support the Portable Operating System Interface (POSIX) standard, which is defined by the Institute of Electrical and Electronic Engineers (IEEE) standard 1003.1-1990 (also known as ISO/IEC 9945-1:1990).

NTFS includes the following POSIX-compliant features.

Case-sensitive naming   For example, POSIX interprets README.TXT, Readme.txt, and readme.txt as separate files.

Hard links   A file can have more than one name. This allows two different file names, which can be in different folders on the same volume, to point to the same data.

Additional time stamps   These show when the file was last accessed or modified.

The POSIX subsystem included with Windows NT and Windows 2000 is not included with Windows XP Professional. A new subsystem supporting the broad functionality found on most UNIX systems beyond the POSIX.1 standard is shipped as part of Interix 2.2. The Interix subsystem can be certified to the NIST FIPS 151-2 POSIX Conformance Test Suite.

For more information about Interix 2.2, see the Microsoft Interix 2.2 link on the Web Resources page http://www.microsoft.com/windows/reskits/webresources.

Caution   You must use Interix-based programs to manage file names that differ only in case. You cannot use standard Windows XP Professional command-line tools (such as **copy**, **del**, and **move**, or their equivalents in Windows Explorer or My Computer) to manage file names that differ only in case.

NTFS Change Journal

The change journal provides a persistent log of changes made to files on a volume. NTFS uses the change journal to track information about added, deleted, and modified files for each volume. The change journal describes the nature of any changes to files on the volume. When any file or folder is created, modified, or deleted, NTFS adds a record to the change journal for that volume.

The total size of all the records currently in the journal varies, but there is a configurable maximum size. The change journal can exceed the maximum size until the size reaches an outer threshold, at which point a portion of the oldest records are deleted until the change journal is restored to its maximum size. The maximum size of the change journal is configurable but cannot be reduced, only increased.

The change journal conveys significant scalability benefits to applications that might otherwise need to scan an entire volume for changes. File system indexing, replication managers, virus scanners, and incremental backup applications can benefit from using the change journal.

The change journal is much more efficient than time stamps or file notifications for determining changes in a particular namespace. Applications that must rescan an entire volume to determine changes can now scan once and subsequently refer to the change journal. The I/O cost depends on how many files have changed, not on how many files exist on the volume.

The APIs are fully documented and can be leveraged by independent software vendors (ISVs). Microsoft uses the change journal in Windows XP Professional components such as the Indexing Service and File Replication Service. ISVs can use this feature to enhance the scalability and robustness of a range of products including backup, antivirus, and auditing tools.

For more information about the change journal, see the Platform SoftwareDevelopment Kit (SDK) link on the Web Resources page at http://www.microsoft.com/windows/reskits/webresources.

Indexing Service

Indexing Service extracts information from a set of documents and organizes it for easy access through the Windows XP Professional Search function, the Indexing Service query form, or a Web browser. After the index is created, users can query the index for documents that contain key words, phrases, or properties. For example, a user can query all documents containing the word "product," or query for all Microsoft® Office documents written by a specific author. Indexing Service returns a list of all documents that meet the search criteria.

Although you can run Indexing Service on volumes formatted using any supported file system, Indexing Service works best on NTFS volumes because it uses several NTFS advanced features.

Change journal   After you enable Indexing Service and it completes the first scan of the NTFS volume, additional time-intensive disk scans are not required because Indexing Service uses the change journal to detect file additions, deletions, and modifications. On NTFS volumes, the disk I/O required to update the index is proportional to the number of files that have actually changed. On FAT volumes, Indexing Service must periodically scan all files to locate changes, making the disk I/O proportional to the number of files on the computer that are marked for indexing. Without using Indexing Service, Windows XP Professional must open, read, and close every file in the search, resulting in thousands of disk I/Os per search.

Sparse files   Indexing Service stores the index as a sparse file on NTFS volumes, reducing the size of the index by half when compared to the index size on FAT volumes.

Permissions   Indexing Service does not compromise information security. On NTFS volumes, if a user does not have Read permission for a file, Indexing Service does not return that file in the results list to the user. Similarly, Indexing Service does not indicate that a match was found if the file cannot be accessed.

Encryption   Indexing Service never indexes encrypted documents. If a document is encrypted after it is indexed, it is removed from the catalog.

Indexing Service is disabled by default. For more information about enabling Indexing Service, see Windows XP Professional Help.

Converting Volumes to NTFS

Windows XP Professional can convert FAT16, FAT32, and previous versions of NTFS to the new version of NTFS used in Windows XP.

Converting NTFS Volumes Formatted By Using Windows 2000

When Windows XP Professional first mounts an NTFS volume that was formatted in Windows 2000, Windows XP Professional converts the NTFS volume to NTFS 3.1. The conversion consists of changing the NTFS version from 3.0 to 3.1. No other changes are made to existing metadata or files on the volume. However, Windows XP Professional uses a different header style for new files created on NTFS 3.1 volumes. As a result of this change, some third-party imaging programs cannot create images of NTFS 3.1 volumes. Contact the manufacturer of your imaging program to find out if a version is available that supports NTFS 3.1 volumes in Windows XP Professional.

Computers running Windows NT 4.0 with Service Pack 4 or later or Windows 2000 can access NTFS 3.1 volumes without any conversion or additional service packs.

Converting NTFS Volumes Formatted by Using Windows NT 4.0 and Earlier

When you upgrade from Windows NT 4.0 to Windows XP Professional, all local volumes formatted by using the version of NTFS used in Windows NT 4.0 and earlier are upgraded to NTFS 3.1. The upgrade occurs when Windows XP Professional mounts the volume for the first time after Windows XP Professional Setup is completed. (The upgrade does not take place during Setup.) Any NTFS volumes that are removed or turned off during Setup, or added after Setup, are converted when Windows XP Professional mounts the volumes.

The Ntfs.sys driver performs the conversion by determining which version of NTFS is used on the volume and converting the volume if necessary. The conversion takes only a few seconds on any size volume and consists of the following new records in the master file table:

- $Secure, which contains unique security descriptors for all files within a volume.

- $Extend, which is used for extensions such as quotas, reparse point data, and object identifiers. The conversion process also adds three new files the to $Extend directory:

    - $Quota, used for disk quotas.

    - $Reparse, used for reparse points.

    - $ObjID, used for distributed link tracking.

Both $Secure and $Extend take the place of previously unused master file table (MFT) records, so sufficient space always exists in the volume for these two records. However, $Quota, $Reparse, and $ObjID are new additions to the MFT, and you must have enough free space in the volume to contain these files, or the conversion fails.

If the conversion fails, the volume is still available, but you can only perform NTFS-related tasks that were available in Windows NT 4.0 or earlier. To convert the volume to the version of NTFS used in Windows XP Professional, you must free disk space by deleting or moving files and then dismount the volume by using the **fsutil volume dismount** command. When Windows XP Professional mounts the volume and enough space exists, the conversion is completed. (You can also restart the computer to dismount the volume and complete the conversion.)

> **Note**   Removable media that is formatted by using the previous version of NTFS is upgraded after the installation or upgrade process, or when you insert the media and Windows XP Professional mounts it.

NTFS Conversion Issues for FAT Volumes

Before you convert a FAT or FAT32 volume to NTFS, you must consider the following issues:

- You cannot uninstall Windows XP Professional if you convert any volume to NTFS. For more information, see "Supporting Installations" in this book.

- Despite a minimal chance of corruption or data loss during the conversion from FAT to NTFS, it is recommended that you perform a full backup of the data on the volume to be converted before you execute the **convert** command. It is also recommended that you verify the integrity of the backup before proceeding.

- The conversion is a one-way process. After you convert a volume to NTFS, you cannot reconvert the volume to FAT without backing up your data, reformatting the volume as FAT, and then restoring your data.

- The first step of the conversion process is running the Chkdsk tool. Because Chkdsk can increase the time required to complete the conversion, you must take this factor into account when you plan the conversion. Until the conversion is completed, the FAT volume and its data are unavailable. For more information about determining how long Chkdsk will run, see "Troubleshooting Disks and File Systems" in this book.

- To convert the file system, the Convert tool requires a certain amount of free space on the volume and sufficient memory to update the cache. For a detailed description of the amount of free space required for a conversion, see article Q156560, "Free Space Required to Convert FAT to NTFS," in the Microsoft Knowledge Base. To find this article, see the Microsoft Knowledge Base link on the Web Resources page at http://www.microsoft.com/windows/reskits/webresources.

- In multiple-boot configurations, NTFS volumes are accessible only by using Windows NT 4.0 with Service Pack 4 or later, Windows 2000, or Windows XP. For more information about using NTFS in multiple-boot configurations, see "NTFS Compatibility with Windows NT 4.0" later in this chapter.

- When you install Recovery Console onto a volume that is formatted for either the FAT16 or FAT32 file systems, and then use Convert.exe to convert the volume to NTFS, the Recovery Console no longer runs. This problem occurs because the file-system-specific boot files (in the cmdcons folder of the system volume) that are used to run Recovery Console are not valid for a volume that has been converted to NTFS. To resolve this problem, re-install Recovery Console from the Windows XP Professional operating system CD after the conversion. You can also use the Windows XP Professional operating system CD to start Recovery Console.

■ Because the **format** command in Windows XP Professional aligns FAT data clusters at the cluster size boundary, Convert.exe can preserve the cluster size for the size of the volume (up to 4 KB) instead of using the 512-byte cluster size used in Windows 2000 for converted volumes. Table 13-10 lists the cluster sizes used for volumes converted to NTFS.

Table 13-10   Cluster Sizes for Volumes Converted to NTFS

Original FAT Cluster Size	Converted NTFS Cluster Size
512 bytes	512 bytes
1 KB	1 KB
2 KB	2 KB
4 KB and larger	4 KB

Note   If the FAT volume was formatted using an operating system other than Windows XP, the cluster size of the converted volume is usually 512 bytes. However, if the FAT clusters happen to be aligned at the cluster size boundary, Windows XP Professional can use the variable cluster size for the converted volume.

Using Convert.exe to Convert FAT Volumes to NTFS

To convert FAT16 and FAT32 volumes to NTFS, use Convert.exe from the command line. The syntax of Convert follows:

```
convert volume: /fs:ntfs [/v] [/x] [/cvtarea:filename] [/nosecurity] [/?]
```

Table 13-11 describes the parameters available with Convert.

Table 13-11   Convert Parameters

Parameter	Description
volume	Specifies drive letter (followed by a colon), mounted drive, or volume name that you want to convert.
/fs:ntfs	Specifies that you want to convert the volume to NTFS.

Table 13-11 Convert Parameters

Parameter	Description
/v	Specifies verbose mode. All messages are displayed during conversion.
/x	Causes the volume to dismount, if necessary, before it is formatted. Any open handles to the volume become invalid.
/cvtarea:*filename*	Specifies that the MFT and other NTFS metadata files are written to an existing, contiguous placeholder file. This file must be in the root folder of the volume to be converted.
/nosecurity	Specifies that you do not want to apply default NTFS permissions to the volume. Using the **convert** command together with the **/nosecurity** parameter mimics the behavior of the **convert** command in Windows 2000.
/?	Displays user help.

Converting Volumes in Use

When you use the **convert** command, you might see the following messages:

```
Convert cannot run because the volume is in use by another process. Convert may run
if this volume is dismounted first. ALL OPEN HANDLES TO THIS VOLUME WOULD THEN BE
INVALID. Would you like to force a dismount on this volume (Y/N)?
```

-or-

```
Convert cannot gain exclusive access to the [driveletter] drive, so it cannot convert
it now. Would you like to schedule it to be converted the next time the system
restarts (Y/N)?
```

> **Caution** Forcefully dismounting a volume can cause data loss if files are open when the volume is dismounted. Therefore, the safest way to convert a volume that cannot be locked is to schedule the conversion to take place when the computer restarts.

These messages appear if any of the following three conditions exist.

The current folder (where you run the Convert command) is on the volume to be converted For example, you cannot immediately convert the F volume if you type **convert f: /fs:ntfs** at the F:\> prompt. If you have multiple volumes, you can solve this problem by changing to a folder on another volume (by typing **c:** for example) and retyping the command to start the conversion. If you have only one volume, you must schedule the conversion to occur the next time you start Windows XP Professional.

A program has a file open on the volume to be converted To solve this problem, close all programs that might be accessing the volume and ensure that remote users are not accessing files on the volume from across the network. If this does not work, run the command again and type **Y** to dismount the volume. If you do not want to dismount the volume, type **N**. Convert then prompts you to schedule the conversion to occur the next time you restart the computer.

Windows XP Professional is installed on the volume to be converted, or the volume contains the paging file You cannot convert the Windows XP Professional boot volume while Windows XP Professional is running, nor can you force a dismount of the volume that contains the paging file. In these situations, you must schedule the conversion to occur the next time you start Windows XP Professional.

If you must restart the computer to complete the conversion, Windows XP Professional provides a 10-second delay before the conversion begins.

If necessary, you can cancel the conversion before the computer restarts by editing the registry.

> **Caution** Do not edit the registry unless you have no alternative. The registry editor bypasses standard safeguards, allowing settings that can damage your system, or even require you to reinstall Windows. If you must edit the registry, back it up first and see the Registry Reference in the Microsoft Windows 2000 Server Resource Kit at http://www.microsoft.com/reskit.

To edit the registry and cancel an NTFS conversion before the computer restarts

1. Click **Start**, click **Run**, and then type:
    regedit.exe

2. Click **OK**.

3. In the registry editor, navigate to HKEY_LOCAL_MACHINE\SYSTEM\ CurrentControlSet\Control\Session Manager.

4. Delete the following value from the **BootExecute** entry, where **x** is the volume that is to be converted:
    autocheck autoconv \??\x: /FS:NTFS

5. Close the registry editor.

Using the /CVTAREA Parameter

For optimal performance after the conversion, you can use the **/cvtarea** parameter to prevent the MFT from becoming fragmented during the conversion. Before you use the **/cvtarea** parameter, you must first use the **fsutil file createnew** command to create a large file (typically 1/8th of the total volume size) in the root folder. This file is overwritten by the MFT during the conversion. If the file is larger than the space required for the MFT, the unused space becomes available space. If the file does not reside in contiguous clusters, an error message appears and the conversion fails. Defragment the volume, and then try running the conversion again. For more information about the **fsutil file createnew** command, see Windows XP Professional Help.

If you do not use the **/cvtarea** parameter, volumes that are converted from FAT to NTFS (instead of being initially formatted by using NTFS) lack some performance benefits because the MFT becomes fragmented after the conversion. You can defragment the MFT after the conversion by using Disk Defragmenter. For more information, see "Defragmenting NTFS Volumes" later in this chapter.

How Convert.exe Safeguards Data During the Conversion

To guard against the possibility of corruption caused by failure during conversion, Convert.exe must build the NTFS metadata files by using only the space designated as free space by the FAT file system. Then, if the conversion does not finish, the FAT representation of the user files remains valid. A complication is that one sector of NTFS data must occupy a specific location on the disk, and a small number of other structures must occupy contiguous sectors.

During the conversion process, Convert.exe performs the following steps:

1. Runs Chkdsk or Autochk to verify the integrity of the file system. Chkdsk runs when the conversion takes place while Windows XP Professional is running. If Chkdsk encounters an error, the conversion stops. You must use the **chkdsk /f** command to fix any file system errors, and then run Convert again. Autochk runs when you schedule the conversion to take place when the computer restarts. If Autochk encounters an error, Autochk attempts to repair the error, and the conversion continues. For more information about Chkdsk and Autochk, see "Troubleshooting Disks and File Systems" in this book.

2. Relocates FAT clusters for the fixed-location NTFS structure and other contiguous data (if necessary) and saves the new file allocation table. If the necessary sectors cannot be made available because they are unreadable, for example, the conversion process fails, and the FAT volume remains in the same state it was in before the attempted conversion.

3. Creates NTFS elementary data structures in FAT free space. These are the fixed-size tables and structures common to any NTFS volume. The size of these tables varies depending on the size of the volume, but does not depend on the number of files on the volume.

4. Creates the NTFS master file table and directory listings in the FAT free space. The space required for this step is variable and depends on the total number of files and folders on the FAT volume.

5. Marks as free, in the NTFS bitmap, those NTFS clusters being used by FAT-specific structures. After the conversion is complete, the FAT metadata overhead can be reclaimed as free space to NTFS.

6. Writes the NTFS boot sector. This is the final action that causes the volume to be recognized as NTFS instead of FAT. If the conversion fails at any step prior to this, the volume is still a valid FAT volume and is recognized as such.

Almost all writes are to FAT free space, so a failure preserves the FAT intact. The following situations are the only times when a failure might cause problems.

At the end of Step 2, when Convert.exe overwrites the FAT   The algorithm for relocating clusters guarantees that if a failure occurs during this stage, Chkdsk can fix the disk without any loss of data.

In Step 6, when Convert.exe writes the boot sector   If a failure occurs during this step, and the volume being converted is the system volume (the active, primary partition used to start the system), there is a chance that the system could be left in a state where it would not start. In the unlikely event that this takes place, you can start the system by using a Windows XP Professional startup floppy disk. For more information about creating a Windows XP Professional startup floppy disk, see article Q119467, "How to Create a Bootable Disk for an NTFS or FAT Partition." To find this article, see the Microsoft Knowledge Base link on the Web Resources page at http://www.microsoft.com/windows/reskits/webresources.

Defragmenting NTFS Volumes

Windows XP Professional provides two methods of defragmenting NTFS volumes: the Disk Defragmenter snap-in and the new **defrag** command-line tool. You can use either tool as part of a frequent and regular maintenance program to maintain the optimum performance of NTFS volumes.

Disk defragmentation is improved in Windows XP Professional. Both tools in Windows XP Professional can now defragment the following:

NTFS volumes that use any cluster size   In Windows 2000, you can defragment only NTFS volumes that have cluster sizes smaller than or equal to 4 KB. Using Disk Defragmenter in Windows XP Professional, you can defragment volumes that use any cluster size.

Files smaller than 16 clusters   Disk Defragmenter in Windows 2000 cannot move files smaller than 16 clusters, so free space smaller than 16 clusters is ignored. In Windows XP Professional, Disk Defragmenter can defragment files of any cluster size.

The MFT   The master file table (MFT) is defragmented along with other files on the volume. Because the first fragment of the MFT cannot be moved, the MFT is typically contained within two fragments when sufficient space is available on the volume. In this case, the MFT is considered defragmented. If the MFT is contained within three or more fragments, Disk Defragmenter looks for free space where the MFT might fit. If sufficient free space exists, the MFT is moved as a whole (minus the first fragment). If space is not available, the MFT is not defragmented.

> **Note**   Windows XP Professional reserves a portion of the volume for the MFT known as the MFT zone. Neither Disk Defragmenter nor the **defrag** command moves files into this area. For more information about the MFT Zone, see "The MFT Zone" later in this chapter.

For more information about using Disk Defragmenter on FAT and NTFS volumes, see "Troubleshooting Disks and File Systems" in this book.

Optimizing NTFS Performance

NTFS performance is affected by many factors, such as cluster size, fragmentation level, and the use of programs such as antivirus software. In addition, NTFS features such as compression and Indexing Service can also affect performance. You can optimize the performance of NTFS volumes by using the following guidelines.

Cluster Size

Before you format an NTFS volume, evaluate the types of files to be stored on the volume so that you can determine whether to use the default cluster size. Some important questions to answer include:

- Are the files typically the same size?

- Are the files smaller than the default cluster size?

- Do the files remain the same size or grow larger?

If the files are typically smaller than the default cluster size (for example, 4 KB) and do not increase, use the default cluster size to reduce wasted disk space. However, smaller clusters can increase fragmentation, especially when files grow to fill more than one cluster. Therefore, adjust the cluster size accordingly when you format the volume. If the files you store tend to be large or increase in size, use 16- or 32-KB clusters instead of the default 4-KB cluster size.

> **Note**   Compression is supported only on volumes that use 4 KB or smaller clusters.

Cluster size is also an issue for volumes that were converted from FAT to NTFS in Windows 2000 or earlier because the default cluster size for converted volumes is 512 bytes, and the MFT was most likely fragmented during the conversion. For optimum performance, back up the data on the volume, reformat the volume, specify the appropriate cluster size, and then restore the data.

For more information about choosing a cluster size, see "Cluster Size" earlier in this chapter.

Short File Names

Every time you create a file with a long file name, NTFS creates a second file entry that has a similar 8.3 short file name. A file with an 8.3 short file name has a file name containing 1 to 8 characters and a file name extension containing 1 to 3 characters. The file name and file name extension are separated by a period.

If you have a large number of files (300,000 or more) in a folder, and the files have long file names with the same initial characters, the time required to create the files increases. The increase occurs because NTFS bases the short file name on the first six characters of the long file name. In folders with more than 300,000 files, the short file names start to conflict after NTFS uses all of the 8.3 names that are similar to the long file names. Repeated conflicts between a generated short file name and existing short file names cause NTFS to regenerate the short file name from 6 to 8 times.

To reduce the time required to create files, you can use the **fsutil behavior set disable8dot3** command to disable the creation of 8.3 short file names. (You must restart your computer for this setting to take effect.) For more information about disabling 8.3 short file names, see "MS-DOS-Readable File Names on NTFS Volumes" later in this chapter.

If you want NTFS to generate 8.3 names, you can improve performance by using a naming scheme in which long file names differ at the beginning instead of at the end of the name.

For more information about short file names, see "File Names in Windows XP Professional" later in this chapter.

Folder Structure

NTFS supports volumes with large numbers of files and folders, so create a folder structure that works best for your organization. Some guidelines to consider when designing a folder structure include:

- Avoid putting a large number of files into a folder if you use programs that create, delete, open, or close files quickly or frequently. The better solution is to logically separate the files into folders so that you can distribute the workload on multiple folders at a time.

■ If there is no way to logically separate the files into folders, put all the files into one folder, and then disable 8.3 file name generation. If you must use 8.3 names, use a file naming scheme that ensures that the first six characters are unique.

Warning   The time required to run Chkdsk.exe increases with larger folders. For more information about determining how long Chkdsk takes to complete, see "Troubleshooting Disks and File Systems" in this book.

Fragmentation

Heavily fragmented volumes do not perform as well as volumes that are defragmented regularly. You can reduce fragmentation by running the Disk Defragmenter snap-in or the command-line tool Defrag.exe weekly during idle times. For more information about defragmenting NTFS volumes, see "Defragmenting NTFS Volumes" earlier in this chapter.

Antivirus Programs

Antivirus programs add overhead to the system to scan for viruses, thus impacting file system performance. However, the impact varies among antivirus programs. When you evaluate antivirus programs, measure baseline performance to determine which programs cause the least impact in your environment. Many antivirus software vendors offer tuning guides that you can use to customize the software for your organization while minimizing performance impact.

Compression

Compression adds overhead to the system because a compressed NTFS file is decompressed, copied, and then recompressed as a new file even when the file is copied in the same computer. If your server is CPU-bound, avoid using compression. For more information about compression, see "File Compression" earlier in this chapter.

Indexing Service

If users frequently search for files on NTFS volumes in computers running Windows 2000 or Windows XP Professional, you can reduce search times dramatically by enabling Indexing Service. Indexing Service also works well when users search for content inside documents.

After you enable Indexing Service, it uses system resources to build and maintain its index, and NTFS begins tracking all file changes in the NTFS change journal. Both of these actions result in a slight performance decrease. However, for volumes that contain frequently searched files, the benefits gained from increased search speed outweigh the performance impact caused by enabling Indexing Service.

For more information about Indexing Service, see "Indexing Service" earlier in this chapter.

Last Access Time

Each file and folder on an NTFS volume contains an attribute called Last Access Time. This attribute shows when the file or folder was last accessed, such as when a user performs a folder listing, adds files to a folder, reads a file, or makes changes to a file. The most up-to-date Last Access Time is always stored in memory and is eventually written to disk within two places:

- The file's attribute, which is part of its MFT record.

- A directory entry for the file. The directory entry is stored in the folder that contains the file. Files with multiple hard links have multiple directory entries.

The Last Access Time on disk is not always current because NTFS looks for a one-hour interval before forcing the Last Access Time updates to disk. NTFS also delays writing the Last Access Time to disk when users or programs perform read-only operations on a file or folder, such as listing the folder's contents or reading (but not changing) a file in the folder. If the Last Access Time is kept current on disk for read operations, all read operations become write operations, which impacts NTFS performance.

> **Note** File-based queries of Last Access Time are accurate even if all on-disk values are not current. NTFS returns the correct value on queries because the accurate value is stored in memory.

NTFS eventually writes the in-memory Last Access Time to disk as follows.

Within the file's attribute NTFS typically updates a file's attribute on disk if the current Last Access Time in memory differs by more than an hour from the Last Access Time stored on disk, or when all in-memory references to that file are gone, whichever is more recent. For example, if a file's current Last Access Time is 1:00 P.M., and you read the file at 1:30 P.M., NTFS does not update the Last Access Time. If you read the file again at 2:00 P.M., NTFS updates the Last Access Time in the file's attribute to reflect 2:00 P.M. because the file's attribute shows 1:00 P.M. and the in-memory Last Access Time shows 2:00 P.M.

Within a directory entry for a file NTFS updates the directory entry for a file during the following events:

- When NTFS updates the file's Last Access Time and detects that the Last Access Time for the file differs by more than an hour from the Last Access Time stored in the file's directory entry. This update typically occurs after a program closes the handle used to access a file within the directory. If the program holds the handle open for an extended time, a lag occurs before the change appears in the directory entry.

- When NTFS updates other file attributes such as Last Modify Time, and a Last Access Time update is pending. In this case, NTFS updates the Last Access Time along with the other updates without additional performance impact.

Note   NTFS does not update a file's directory entry when all in-memory references to that file are gone.

If you have an NTFS volume with a high number of folders or files, and a program is running that briefly accesses each of these in turn, the I/O bandwidth used to generate the Last Access Time updates can be a significant percentage of the overall I/O bandwidth. To increase the speed of access to a folder or file, you can use the **fsutil behavior set disablelastaccess** command to disable updating the Last Access Time. After you use this command and restart the computer, the Last Access Time is no longer updated. If you create a new file, the Last Access Time remains the same as the File Creation Time. For more information about using the **fsutil behavior set disablelastaccess** command, see Windows XP Professional Help.

NTFS Compatibility with Windows NT 4.0

Your ability to access your NTFS volumes when you use a multiple-boot configuration to start Windows NT and Windows XP Professional depends on which version of Windows NT you are using. If you are running Windows NT 4.0 Service Pack 4 or later, you can read basic volumes formatted by using the new version of NTFS. Computers running Windows 2000 and Windows XP Professional can read the new version of NTFS on both basic and dynamic volumes.

Note   Computers accessing NTFS volumes across the network are not affected.

When a Windows XP Professional volume is mounted in a computer running Windows NT 4.0 Service Pack 4 or later, most of the new NTFS features are not available. However, most read and write operations are permitted if they do not make use of any new NTFS features. The following features are affected by this configuration.

Reparse points   Windows NT cannot perform any operations that make use of reparse points.

Disk quotas   When you run Windows NT on a multiple-boot configuration that also runs Windows XP Professional, Windows NT ignores disk quotas implemented by Windows XP Professional, allowing you to use more disk space than your quota allows.

Encryption   Windows NT cannot perform any operations on files encrypted by Windows XP Professional.

Sparse files   Windows NT cannot perform any operations on sparse files.

Change journal   Windows NT ignores the change journal. No entries are logged when a user accesses files.

> **Warning**   Because NTFS data structures are not the same for Windows NT 4.0 and Windows XP Professional, Windows NT 4.0 disk tools such as Chkdsk and Autochk do not work on NTFS volumes formatted or upgraded by Windows XP Professional. These tools check the version stamp of NTFS. After installing Windows XP Professional, you must run the updated version of these disk tools on their NTFS volumes.

Cleanup Operations on Windows NT Volumes

Because files on volumes formatted by using the version of NTFS included with Windows XP Professional can be read and written to by Windows NT 4.0 Service Pack 4 or later, Windows XP Professional might need to perform cleanup operations to ensure the consistency of the data structures of a volume after it is mounted on a computer running Windows NT.

Windows XP Professional does not perform cleanup operations on volumes previously mounted by using Windows 2000.

Cleanup operations affect the following features.

Reparse points   Computers running Windows NT 4.0 or earlier cannot access files that have reparse points, so no cleanup operations are necessary.

Disk quotas   If disk quotas are turned off, Windows XP Professional performs no cleanup operations. If disk quotas are turned on, Windows XP Professional cleans up the quota information by rebuilding the index. If a user exceeds the disk quota while the NTFS volume is mounted by a Windows NT 4.0 Service Pack 4 or later system, and disk quotas are strictly enforced, all further disk allocations of data by that user using Windows XP Professional fail. The user can still read and write data to any existing file but cannot increase the size of a file. However, the user can delete and shrink files. When usage falls below the assigned disk quota, disk allocations of data can resume.

Encryption   Encrypted files cannot be accessed by computers that are running Windows NT 4.0 or earlier, so no cleanup operations are necessary.

Sparse files   Computers running Windows NT 4.0 or earlier cannot access sparse files, so no cleanup operations are necessary.

Change journal   Computers that are running Windows NT 4.0 or earlier do not log file changes in the change journal. When Windows XP Professional starts, the change journals on volumes accessed by Windows NT are reset to indicate that the journal history is incomplete. Applications that use the change journal must be able to accept incomplete journals.

Object identifiers   Windows XP Professional maintains two references to the object identifier: one on the file and one in the volume-wide object identifier index. If you delete a file that has an object identifier, Windows XP Professional must scan and clean up the entry in the index.

NTFS Recoverability

NTFS is a recoverable file system that guarantees the consistency of the volume by using standard transaction logging and recovery techniques. In the event of a system failure, NTFS runs a recovery procedure that accesses information stored in a transaction log file. The NTFS recovery procedure guarantees that the volume is restored to a consistent state. Transaction logging requires very little overhead.

NTFS ensures the integrity of all NTFS volumes by performing disk recovery operations whenever a volume is mounted after the computer is restarted or after the volume is dismounted.

NTFS also uses a technique called cluster remapping to minimize the effects of a bad sector on an NTFS volume.

> **Warning**   If either the MBR or boot sector is corrupted, you might not be able to access data on the volume. For more information about recovering from MBR or boot sector errors, see "Troubleshooting Disks and File Systems" in this book.

Recovering Data with NTFS

NTFS views each operation that modifies a file on a volume as a transaction and manages each one as an integral unit. NTFS might also break a single complex operation into multiple transactions. After a transaction is started, it is either completed, or it is rolled back if an event occurs that causes the operation to fail, and the NTFS volume returns to its state before the transaction began. Events that can cause an operation to fail include bad sectors, transient low-memory conditions, and disconnected devices.

To ensure that a transaction can either be completed or rolled back, NTFS performs the following steps for each transaction:

1. Records the metadata operations of a transaction in a log file cached in memory.

2. Records the actual metadata operations in memory.

3. Marks the transaction in the cached log file as committed.

4. Flushes the log file to disk.

5. Flushes the actual metadata operations to disk.

The preceding steps 4 and 5 occur in a *lazy* fashion after the transaction is completed, meaning that the flush operations are not tied to the transaction itself. Instead, NTFS modifies the log and metadata quickly in memory, and then flushes later at a convenient time to boost performance.

NTFS guarantees that the log records containing the metadata operations of the transaction are written to disk before the metadata that is modified in the transaction is written to disk. After NTFS updates the cache, NTFS commits the transaction by recording in the cached log file that the transaction is complete. After the cached log file is flushed to disk, all committed transactions are guaranteed to be completed, even if the system crashes before the changes are written to disk.

Note Applications can specify the FILE_FLAG_WRITE_THROUGH Win32 flag to instruct the system to write through any intermediate cache and go directly to disk. The system can still cache write operations, but cannot lazily flush them.

If a system failure occurs, NTFS has enough information in the log to complete or abort any partial NTFS transaction. During recovery operations, NTFS redoes each committed transaction found in the log file. Then NTFS locates in the log file the transactions that were not committed at the time of the system failure and undoes each metadata operation recorded in the log file. Because NTFS flushes the log to disk before any metadata changes are written to disk, NTFS has complete information available about any metadata changes that need to be rolled back during recovery.

Caution   NTFS uses transaction logging and recovery to guarantee that the volume structure is not corrupted. For this reason, all file system data is accessible after a system failure. NTFS guarantees user data only if the program used to create the data uses the FILE_FLAG_WRITE_THROUGH Win32 flag. If the program does not use this flag, user data can be lost due to a system failure. If a system failure does occur, NTFS shows either the previous data, the new data, or zeros. Users do not see random data on the volume as the result of a crash.

Caching and Data Recovery

The cache is the area of RAM that contains the most recently used data. When you write data to disk, the lazy-write technique in Windows XP Professional indicates that the data is written when it is still in the cache. Cache memory can also be on the disk controller, such as cache memory available on SCSI controllers, or on the disk unit, such as cache memory available on Advanced Technology Attachment (ATA) disks. The following information can help you decide whether to enable the disk or the controller cache:

- Write caching improves disk performance, particularly if large amounts of data are being written to the disk.

- Control of the write-back cache is a firmware function provided by the disk manufacturer. See the documentation supplied with the disk or disk controller. You cannot configure the write-back cache from Windows XP Professional.

- Write caching does not impact the reliability of the file system's own metadata. NTFS instructs the disk device driver to ensure that metadata is written whether or not write caching is enabled. Non-metadata is typically written to disk and can be cached.

- Read caching in the disk does not affect the reliability of a file system.

Cluster Remapping

When NTFS detects a bad sector, NTFS dynamically remaps the cluster containing the bad sector — a recovery technique called *cluster remapping* — and allocates a new cluster for the data. If the error occurred during a read, NTFS returns a read error to the calling program, and the data is lost. If the error occurs during a write, NTFS writes the data to the new cluster, and no data is lost.

NTFS puts the address of the cluster containing the bad sector in the bad cluster file, $BadClus, in the MFT so that the bad sector is not reused.

> **Warning** Cluster remapping is *not* a backup alternative. After errors are detected, the disk must be monitored closely and replaced if the detect list grows. This type of error is displayed in the system log of Event Viewer.

FAT uses a form of cluster remapping, but only when the volume is initially formatted. If a bad sector occurs on a FAT volume after it is formatted, data stored within the associated cluster can be permanently lost. NTFS handles cluster remapping dynamically and continuously, ensuring the integrity of your data.

NTFS Data Structures

This section is useful for administrators who need information about the on-disk structures of NTFS volumes. These structures give NTFS basic advantages over other file systems used in Windows XP Professional.

Master File Table and Metadata Files

When you format a volume using NTFS, Windows XP Professional creates a master file table (MFT) and metadata files. The MFT is a relational database that consists of rows of file records and columns of file attributes. It contains at least one entry for every file on an NTFS volume, including the MFT itself.

Because the MFT stores information about itself, NTFS reserves the first 16 records of the MFT for metadata files (approximately 16 KB), which are used to describe the MFT. Metadata files that begin with a dollar sign ($) are described in Table 13-12. The remaining records of the MFT contain the file and folder records for each file and folder on the volume.

Table 13-12   Metadata Files Stored in the Master File Table

System File	File Name	MFT Record	Purpose of the File
Master file table	$Mft	0	Contains one base file record for each file and folder on an NTFS volume. If the allocation information for a file or folder is too large to fit within a single record, other file records are allocated as well.
Master file table mirror	$MftMirr	1	Guarantees access to the MFT in case of a single-sector failure. It is a duplicate image of the first four records of the MFT.

Table 13-12   Metadata Files Stored in the Master File Table

System File	File Name	MFT Record	Purpose of the File
Log file	$LogFile	2	Contains a list of transaction steps used for NTFS recoverability. The log file is used by Windows XP Professional to restore consistency to NTFS after a system failure. The size of the log file depends on the size of the volume, but you can increase the size of the log file by using the Chkdsk command. For more information about the log file, see "NTFS Recoverability" earlier in this chapter. For more information about Chkdsk, see "Troubleshooting Disks and File Systems" in this book.
Volume	$Volume	3	Contains information about the volume, such as the volume label and the volume version.
Attribute definitions	$AttrDef	4	Lists attribute names, numbers, and descriptions.
Root file name index	.	5	The root folder.
Cluster bitmap	$Bitmap	6	Represents the volume by showing free and unused clusters.
Boot sector	$Boot	7	Includes the BPB used to mount the volume and additional bootstrap loader code used if the volume is bootable.
Bad cluster file	$BadClus	8	Contains bad clusters for a volume.
Security file	$Secure	9	Contains unique security descriptors for all files within a volume.
Upcase table	$Upcase	10	Converts lowercase characters to matching Unicode uppercase characters.
NTFS extension file	$Extend	11	Used for various optional extensions such as quotas, reparse point data, and object identifiers.
		12–15	Reserved for future use.

The data segment locations for both the MFT and the backup MFT, $Mft and $MftMirr respectively, are recorded in the boot sector. The $MftMirr is a duplicate image of either the first four records of the $Mft or the first cluster of the $Mft, whichever is larger. If any MFT records in the mirrored range are corrupted or unreadable, NTFS reads the boot sector to find the location of the $MftMirr. NTFS then reads the $MftMirr and uses the information in $MftMirr instead of the information in the MFT. If possible, the correct data from the $MftMirr is written back to the corresponding location in the $Mft. For more information about the NTFS boot sector, see "Troubleshooting Disks and File Systems" in this book.

Note   To improve NTFS performance, the $LogFile and $Bitmap metadata files on newly formatted NTFS volumes are located in a different position on the disk than they were in Windows 2000. (The MFT record numbers do not change.) This new location improves performance by 5 to 8 percent, making NTFS performance similar to FAT.

NTFS creates a file record for each file and a folder record for each folder created on an NTFS volume. The MFT includes a separate file record for the MFT itself. These file and folder records are 1 KB each and are stored in the MFT. The attributes of the file are written to the allocated space in the MFT. Besides file attributes, each file record contains information about the position of the file record in the MFT. Figure 13-16 shows the contents of an MFT record for a small file or folder. Small files and folders (typically, 900 bytes or smaller) are entirely contained within the file's MFT record.

Standard Information	File or Directory Name	Data or Index	Unused Space

Figure 13-16   MFT record for a small file or folder

Typically, each file uses one file record. However, if a file has a large number of attributes or becomes highly fragmented, it might need more than one file record. If this is the case, the first record for the file, the base file record, stores the location of the other file records required by the file.

Folder records contain index information. Small folder records reside entirely within the MFT structure, while large folders are organized into B-tree structures and have records with pointers to external clusters that contain folder entries that cannot be contained within the MFT structure.

The benefit of using B-tree structures is evident when NTFS enumerates files in a large folder. The B-tree structure allows NTFS to group, or index, similar file names and then search only the group that contains the file, minimizing the number of disk accesses needed to find a particular file, especially for large folders. Because of the B-tree structure, NTFS outperforms FAT for large folders because FAT must scan all file names in a large folder before listing all of the files.

MFT Zone

To prevent the MFT from becoming fragmented, NTFS reserves 12.5 percent of volume by default for exclusive use of the MFT. This space, known as the MFT zone, is not used to store data unless the remainder of the volume becomes full.

Depending on the average file size and other variables, as the disk fills to capacity, either the MFT zone or the unreserved space on the disk becomes full first.

■ Volumes that have a small number of large files exhaust the unreserved space first.

■ Volumes with a large number of small files exhaust the MFT zone space first.

In either case, fragmentation of the MFT occurs when one region or the other becomes full. You can change the size of the MFT zone for newly created volumes by using the **fsutil behavior set mftzone** command. This command uses four settings, 1–4, which correspond to a percentage of the disk to be used as the MFT zone. The MFT zone sizes follow:

■ Setting 1, the default, reserves approximately 12.5 percent of the disk.

■ Setting 2 reserves approximately 25 percent.

■ Setting 3 reserves approximately 37.5 percent.

■ Setting 4 reserves approximately 50 percent.

In most computers, the default setting of 1 is adequate. The default setting accommodates volumes with an average file size of 8 KB. If you want to store a large number of smaller files (between 2 KB and 7 KB), you can use the **fsutil behavior set mftzone** command to increase the size of the MFT zone for new volumes. You must restart the computer before the new MFT zone size takes effect.

After you increase the size of the MFT zone, NTFS does not immediately allocate space to accommodate the size of the new MFT zone. Instead, NTFS exhausts the original reserved space before increasing the size of the MFT zone. When the original space is exhausted, NTFS looks for the next contiguous space large enough to hold the additional MFT zone, which can cause the MFT to become fragmented. Therefore, the **fsutil behavior set mftzone** command works best when you use the command to set the zone size, reboot, and then create the volume.

To determine the current size of the MFT zone on a Windows XP Professional-based computer, use the **fsutil behavior query mftzone** command. If you have not modified the size of the MFT zone, a message appears that indicates the MFT zone is not currently set, which means that the default setting of 1 is used. Otherwise, the command returns the current value, either 1, 2, 3, or 4. The current setting applies to all NTFS volumes in the computer.

NTFS File Attributes

Every allocated sector on an NTFS volume belongs to a file. Even the file system metadata is part of a file. NTFS views each file (or folder) as a set of file attributes. File elements such as its name, its security information, and even its data are file attributes. Each attribute is identified by an attribute type code and an optional attribute name.

When a file's attributes can fit within the MFT file record for that file, they are called resident attributes. Attributes such as file name and time stamp are always resident. When the amount of information for a file does not fit in its MFT file record, some file attributes become nonresident. Nonresident attributes are allocated one or more clusters of disk space. A portion of the nonresident attribute remains in the MFT and points to the external clusters. NTFS creates the Attribute List attribute to describe the location of all attribute records. Table 13-13 lists the file attributes currently defined by NTFS.

Table 13-13   NTFS File Attribute Types

Attribute Type	Description
Standard Information	Information such as timestamp and link count.
Attribute List	Locations of all attribute records that do not fit in the MFT record.
File Name	A repeatable attribute for both long and short file names. The long name of the file can be up to 255 Unicode characters. The short name is the 8.3, case-insensitive name for the file. Additional names, or hard links, required by POSIX can be included as additional file name attributes.
Data	File data. NTFS supports multiple data attributes per file. Each file typically has one unnamed data attribute. A file can also have one or more named data attributes, each using a particular syntax.
Object ID	A volume-unique file identifier. Used by the distributed link tracking service. Not all files have object identifiers.
Logged Tool Stream	Similar to a data stream, but operations are logged to the NTFS log file just like NTFS metadata changes. This attribute is used by EFS.
Reparse Point	Used for mounted drives. This is also used by Installable File System (IFS) filter drivers to mark certain files as special to that driver.
Index Root	Used to implement folders and other indexes.
Index Allocation	Used to implement the B-tree structure for large folders and other large indexes.
Bitmap	Used to implement the B-tree structure for large folders and other large indexes.
Volume Information	Used only in the $Volume system file. Contains the volume version.
Volume Name	Used only in the $Volume system file. Contains the volume label.

MS–DOS-Readable File Names on NTFS Volumes

By default, Windows XP Professional generates MS-DOS-readable file names on all NTFS volumes for use by 16-bit programs that run under Windows XP Professional. To improve performance on volumes with many long, similar names, you can use the **fsutil behavior set** command to disable 8.3 name creation. For more information about using this command, see Windows XP Professional Help.

> **Warning**   Although disabling 8.3 name creation increases NTFS performance under Windows XP Professional, some 16-bit applications might not be able to access files and folders that have long file names. Also, some third-party programs cannot be installed on NTFS volumes if 8.3 names are disabled. In this case, use the **fsutil behavior set** command to enable short file names, restart the computer, and then try installing the program again.

Windows XP Professional does not generate short (8.3) file names for files created by POSIX-based applications on an NTFS volume — whether short file names are disabled or not. This means that MS-DOS-based and 16-bit Windows-based applications cannot view these file names if they are not valid 8.3 file names. Therefore, you must use standard MS-DOS 8.3 naming conventions if you want to use MS-DOS-based or 16-bit Windows-based applications to work with files that are created by POSIX applications.

FAT File System

The FAT file system locates the file allocation table near the beginning of the volume. FAT16 works best on small disks with simple folder structures. FAT32 works well on large disks with complex folder structures. Both FAT file systems store two copies of the file allocation table on the volume. If one copy of the file allocation table is corrupted, the other is used. The location of the file allocation table is specified in the FAT boot sector's BIOS Parameter Block (BPB). For more information about the FAT boot sectors, see "Troubleshooting Disks and File Systems" in this book.

> **Note**   Windows XP Professional uses the Fastfat driver to mount and fully support FAT volumes.

Comparing FAT File Systems

The numerals in the names FAT12, FAT16, and FAT32 refer to the number of bits required for a file allocation table entry as follows:

- FAT12 uses a 12-bit file allocation table entry (212 clusters).

- FAT16 uses a 16-bit file allocation table entry (216 clusters).

- FAT32 uses a 32-bit file allocation table entry. However, FAT32 reserves the first 4 bits of a FAT32 file allocation table entry, which means FAT32 has a theoretical maximum of 228 clusters.

> **Note**   In Windows XP Professional, FAT12 is used only on floppy disks and on volumes smaller than 16 megabytes.

There are additional advantages and disadvantages between FAT16 and FAT32.

Advantages of FAT16

Advantages of FAT16 include:

- MS-DOS, Windows 95, Windows 98, Windows Me, Windows NT, Windows 2000, Windows XP, and some UNIX operating systems can use FAT16.

- Many software tools can address problems and recover data on FAT16 volumes.

- If you have a startup failure, you can start the computer by using an MS-DOS bootable floppy disk to troubleshoot the problem.

- FAT16 is efficient, in speed and storage, on volumes smaller than 256 MB.

Disadvantages of FAT16

Disadvantages of FAT16 include:

- The root folder can manage a maximum of 512 entries. The use of long file names can significantly reduce the number of available entries.

- FAT16 is limited to 65,536 clusters, but because certain clusters are reserved, it has a practical limit of 65,524. Therefore, the largest FAT16 volume on Windows XP Professional is limited to just under 4 GB and uses a cluster size of 64 KB. To maintain compatibility with MS-DOS, Windows 95, Windows 98, and Windows Me, a FAT16 volume cannot be larger than 2 GB.

- FAT16 is inefficient on larger volume sizes because the cluster size is much larger when compared to NTFS and FAT32 cluster sizes. For example, a 10-KB file stored on a 1.2-GB FAT16 volume, which uses a 32-KB cluster, wastes 22 KB of disk space. FAT32 and NTFS use 4-KB and 2-KB clusters, respectively, for a 1.2-GB volume.

- The boot sector, a critical disk structure for starting your computer, is not backed up.

- FAT16 has no built-in file system security or compression scheme.

Advantages of FAT32

FAT32 has the following enhancements:

- The root folder on a FAT32 volume is an ordinary cluster chain and can be located anywhere on the volume. For this reason, FAT32 does not restrict the number of entries in the root folder.

- FAT32 uses smaller clusters (4 KB for volumes up to 8 GB), so it allocates disk space more efficiently than FAT16. Depending on the size of your files, FAT32 creates the potential for tens and even hundreds of megabytes of additional free disk space on larger volumes compared to FAT16.

- The boot sector is backed up at a specified location on the volume, so FAT32 volumes are less susceptible to single points of failure than FAT16 volumes.

Disadvantages of FAT32

Disadvantages of FAT32 include:

- Windows XP Professional is designed to format FAT32 volumes up to 32 GB. To format volumes larger than 32 GB in Windows XP Professional, you must use NTFS.

- MS-DOS, Windows 95 (prior to OSR2), and Windows NT 4.0 and earlier cannot access FAT32 volumes.

- If you have a startup failure, you cannot start the computer by using an MS-DOS or Windows 95 bootable floppy disk because these operating systems cannot read FAT32 volumes. You must use a floppy disk created by using Windows 95 OSR2, Windows 98, or Windows Millennium Edition.

- FAT32 has no built-in file system security or compression scheme.

FAT16 File System

FAT16 is included in Windows XP Professional for the following reasons:

- It provides backward compatibility in the form of an upgrade path for earlier versions of Windows-compatible products.

- It is compatible with most other operating systems.

When relatively small files are placed on a FAT16 volume, FAT16 manages disk space inefficiently. Therefore, FAT16 is not recommended for volumes larger than 511 MB, and you cannot use FAT16 on volumes larger than 4 gigabytes (GB).

Using FAT12 in Windows XP Professional

On volumes with fewer than 32,680 sectors, the cluster sizes can be up to 8 sectors per cluster. In this circumstance, the format program creates a 12-bit FAT. Typically, volumes less than 16 MB are formatted for a 12-bit FAT, but the exact size depends on the disk geometry. The disk geometry also determines when a larger cluster size is needed because the number of clusters on the volume must fit into the number of bits used by the file system managing the volume. Therefore, you might have a 33-MB volume that has only 1 sector (512 bytes) per cluster.

FAT12 is the original implementation of FAT and is intended for very small media. The file allocation table for FAT12 is smaller than the file allocation table for FAT16 and FAT32, because it uses less space for each entry, leaving more space for data. All 1.44-MB 3.5-inch floppy disks are formatted by using FAT12.

Figure 13-17 illustrates how FAT16 maps clusters on a volume. The file allocation tables (labeled FAT1 and FAT2) identify each cluster in the volume as one of the following:

- Unused

- Cluster in use by a file

- Bad cluster

- Last cluster in a file

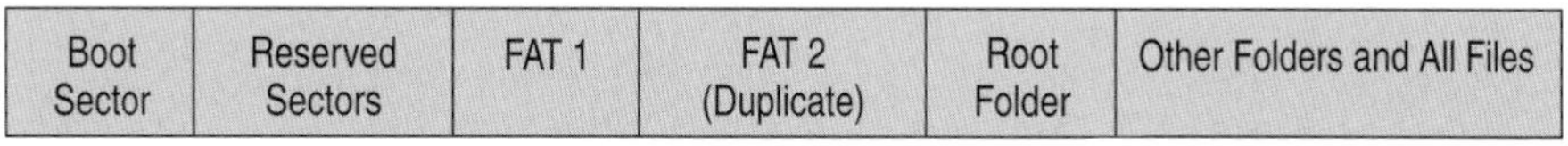

Boot Sector	Reserved Sectors	FAT 1	FAT 2 (Duplicate)	Root Folder	Other Folders and All Files

Figure 13-17   Organization of a FAT16 volume

The root folder has the maximum number of available entries fixed at 512. The maximum number of entries on a floppy disk depends on the size of the disk.

Note   Each folder and 8.3 file name in the root folder counts as an entry. For example, because the maximum number of entries is fixed at 512, if you have 100 folders in the root folder, you can create only 412 more files or folders in the root folder. If those folders or files use names longer than the 8.3 format, fewer files and folders can be created.

Folders contain a 32-byte entry for each file and folder they contain. The entry includes the following information:

- Name in 8.3 format (11 bytes)
- Attribute (1 byte, described later in this section)
- Create time (3 bytes)
- Create date (2 bytes)
- Last access date (2 bytes)
- Last modified time (2 bytes)
- Last modified date (2 bytes)
- Starting cluster number in the file allocation table (2 bytes)
- File size (4 bytes)

Note Three bytes in each 32-byte folder entry are held in reserve.

In the file allocation table of a FAT16 volume, files are given the first available location on the volume. The starting cluster number is the address of the first cluster used by the file. Each cluster contains a pointer to the next cluster in the file, or an end-of-file indicator at (0xFFFF), which indicates that this cluster is the end of the file. These pointers and end-of-file indicators are shown in Figure 13-18.

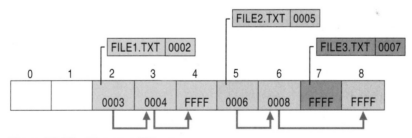

Figure 13-18 Files on a FAT volume

Figure 13-18 shows three files in a folder. File1.txt uses three clusters. File2.txt is a fragmented file that requires three clusters. File3.txt fits in one cluster. In each case, the file allocation table entry points to the first cluster of the file.

The information in the folder is used by all operating systems that support FAT. Windows XP Professional can store additional timestamps in a FAT folder entry. These timestamps show when the file was created or last accessed.

The attribute byte for each entry in a folder describes what kind of entry it is. For example, one bit indicates that the entry is for a subfolder, and another bit marks the entry as a volume. Typically, the operating system controls the settings of these bits.

The attribute byte includes four bits that can be turned on or off by the user— archive, system, hidden, and read-only.

FAT32 File System

The FAT32 on-disk format and features on Windows XP Professional are similar to those on Windows 95 OSR2, Windows 98, and Windows Me.

The size of a FAT32 cluster is determined by the system and can range in size from 1 sector (512 bytes) to 128 sectors (64 KB), incremented in powers of 2.

Note   Using 64-KB clusters in FAT32 can lead to compatibility problems with certain programs. The maximum cluster size recommended for a FAT32 volume is 32 KB.

Because FAT32 requires 4 bytes to store cluster values, many internal and on-disk data structures have been revised or expanded. Most programs are unaffected by these changes; however, disk tools that read the on-disk format must be updated to support FAT32.

The most significant difference between FAT16 and FAT32 is the maximum number of clusters supported, which in turn affects a volume's maximum size and storage efficiency. FAT32 breaks the 4-GB volume limitation of FAT16 by extending the maximum number of clusters.

Due to the greater number of available clusters within FAT32, each cluster can be made smaller for a particular volume, increasing the efficiency of data storage. For example, FAT16 volumes between 2 and 4 GB use a 64-KB cluster, whereas FAT32 volumes between 16 GB and 32 GB use a 16-KB cluster.

> **Note**   The 127.5-GB limit on FAT32 volumes imposed in Windows 98 no
> longer applies to Windows Me. In Windows Me, using a cluster size of
> 32 KB, a FAT32 volume can theoretically be about 8 terabytes. However, the
> 32-bit fields in the partition table (and in the FAT32 boot sector) limit the size
> of an individual volume (regardless of file system) on a basic MBR disk using
> a sector size of 512 bytes to approximately 2 terabytes.
>
> Although Windows 2000 and Windows XP Professional can mount
> FAT32 volumes of any size, Windows 2000 and Windows XP Professional
> can format FAT32 volumes up to 32 GB only. Use NTFS to format larger vol-
> umes. For more information about the benefits of formatting Windows XP
> Professional volumes by using NTFS, see "Advantages of Using NTFS" ear-
> lier in this chapter.

The largest possible file for a FAT32 volume is 4 GB minus 1 byte. FAT32 contains 4 bytes per cluster in the file allocation table; FAT16 contains 2 bytes per cluster; and FAT12 contains 1.5 bytes per cluster. A FAT32 volume must have at least
65,527 clusters. For more information about clusters, see "Cluster Size" earlier in this
chapter.

File Names on FAT Volumes

Files created or renamed on FAT volumes use attribute bits to support long file names
in a way that does not interfere with how MS-DOS gains access to the volume.

When you create a file that has a long file name, Windows XP Professional creates a conventional 8.3 name for the file and one or more secondary folder entries
for the file, one for each set of 13 characters in the long file name. Each secondary
folder entry stores a corresponding part of the long file name in Unicode. MS-DOS
accesses the file by using the conventional 8.3 file name contained in the folder
entry for the file.

Windows XP Professional marks the secondary folder entries as part of a long
file name by setting the volume ID, read-only, system, and hidden attribute bits.
MS-DOS typically ignores folder entries with all these attribute bits set.

Figure 13-19 shows all of the folder entries for the file Thequi~1.fox, which has
a long name of The quick brown.fox. The long name is in Unicode, so each character in the name uses 2 bytes in the folder entry. The attribute field for the long-name
entries has the value 0x0F. The attribute field for the short name has the value 0x20.

2nd Long Entry
(And Last)

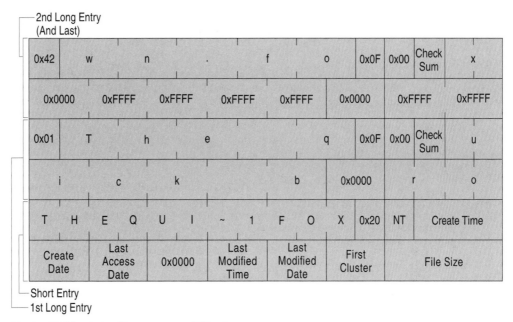

Short Entry
1st Long Entry

Figure 13-19   Long file name on a FAT volume

Note   Windows NT and Windows XP Professional do not use the same algorithm to create long and short file names as Windows 95, Windows 98, and Windows Me. However, on computers that use a multiple-boot configuration to start these operating systems, files that you create while running one operating system can be accessed while running another.

For more information about how Windows XP Professional creates short file names, see "File Names in Windows XP Professional" later in this chapter.

By default, Windows XP Professional supports long file names on FAT volumes. You can disable long file names on FAT volumes if you use MS-DOS–based disk tools regularly on the computer. These tools might either eliminate the long file names created by Windows XP Professional or delete the files that have long file names.

To prevent a FAT file system from creating long file names, set the value of the **Win31FileSystem** registry entry (in the subkey HKEY_LOCAL_MACHINE\SYSTEM\CurrentControlSet\Control\FileSystem) to 1. This value prevents Windows XP Professional from creating new long file names on all FAT volumes. However, existing long file names remain intact but are not displayed in My Computer, Windows Explorer, or at the command prompt.

Caution   Do not edit the registry unless you have no alternative. The registry editor bypasses standard safeguards, allowing settings that can damage your system, or even require you to reinstall Windows. If you must edit the registry, back it up first and see the Registry Reference in the Microsoft Windows 2000 Server Resource Kit at http://www.microsoft.com/reskit.

Compact Disc File System

The Windows XP Professional Compact Disc File System (CDFS) can read compact discs (CDs) formatted according to the ISO 9660 file system standard. The ISO 9660 specification defines three methods, or interchange levels, for recording and naming files on a CD. Windows XP Professional supports up to interchange level 3.

Windows XP Professional also supports Joliet, an extension to ISO 9660, which supports CDs that are recorded using file names containing Unicode characters. Joliet supports file and folder names on CDs as follows:

■ File and folder names can contain up to 64 Unicode characters.

■ Folder names can contain file name extensions.

■ Folder hierarchy can be recorded deeper than 8 levels.

Note   CDFS does not support the Rock Ridge Interchange Protocol extensions to ISO 9660 and reads only the ISO 9660 structures on such discs.

If the computer uses a compatible CD-ROM drive, Windows XP Professional can also read CDs recorded by using the following standards:

■ Red Book (CD-Audio), including Enhanced CD

■ Yellow Book (CD-ROM)

■ CD-XA

■ White Book (Video CD)

■ Photo CD

■ Orange Book Part II (CD-recordable, including multisession) and Part III (CD-Rewritable)

■ Blue Book (CD Extra)

> **Note**   You might need a special program or player to interpret the information on CD-XA, White Book, and Photo CDs. Also, Windows XP Professional cannot read CD-R or CD-RW discs that have not been closed by the writing software.

Windows XP Professional provides integrated support for writing data to CD-R and CD-RW. When writing data to CD, Windows XP Professional automatically uses the Joliet and ISO 9660 formats. When writing audio files to CD, Windows XP Professional uses the Red Book format. For more information about burning CDs, see Windows XP Professional Help.

Universal Disk Format

Universal Disk Format (UDF) is a file system defined by the Optical Storage Technology Association. UDF is based on the ISO 13346 (ECMA-167) standard and is the successor to the ISO 9660 (CDFS) format.

UDF is used for removable media like DVD, CD, compact disc–recordable (CD-R), compact disc–rewritable (CD-RW), write once, read many (WORM), and magneto-optical (MO) discs. Because UDF is based on open standards, it is intended to facilitate data interchange between operating systems and between consumer devices. The standard supports a number of advanced features, including:

- Long and Unicode file names
- Deep directory trees
- Sparse files
- Large (64-bit) file sizes
- Access control lists (ACLs)
- Named streams

Windows XP Professional reads UDF versions 1.02, 1.50, 2.0, and 2.01 on CD, CD-R, CD-RW, DVD, DVD-RAM, and magneto-optical discs. Support is implemented in the Udfs.sys driver. If you have a DVD-RAM drive, you can use Windows XP Professional to format DVD-RAM discs by using FAT32. Windows XP Professional does not include built-in support for formatting DVD-RAM discs by using NTFS, although some third-party tools might enable this capability.

Windows XP Professional does not support writing to UDF volumes. In addition, Windows XP Professional does not implement the following UDF features:

- Named streams
- Access control lists
- Extended attributes

Note   Windows XP Professional reads the File Create Time from an embedded FileTimes extended attribute recorded in a basic file entry.

File System Tools

The tools described in this chapter are installed along with Windows XP Professional in the *systemroot*\System32 folder. Table 13-14 describes these tools. For more information about tools found in s*ystemroot*\System32, see Windows XP Professional Help.

Table 13-14   Location of File System Tools

Tool	Description
Cacls.exe	Displays and modifies ACLs of files or folders.
Chkntfs.exe	Displays or specifies whether automatic system checking is scheduled to be run on a FAT, FAT32, or NTFS volume when the computer is started.
Cipher.exe	Displays or alters the encryption of folders and files on NTFS volumes.
Compact.exe	Displays and alters the compression of files or directories on NTFS volumes.
Convert.exe	Converts a FAT16 or FAT32 volume to NTFS.
Defrag.exe	Locates and consolidates fragmented boot files, data files, and folders on local or remote volumes.
Expand.exe	Extracts a file from a compressed file. Use this command to extract a file from a cabinet (.cab) or compressed file.
Fsutil.exe	Performs many tasks related to file systems — such as managing reparse points, sparse files, and file system behavior — and more.
Mountvol.exe	Creates, deletes, or lists a mounted drive.

File Names in Windows XP Professional

File names in Windows XP Professional can be up to 255 characters and can contain spaces, multiple periods, and special characters that are not allowed in MS-DOS file names. Windows XP Professional makes it possible for other operating systems to access files that have long names by generating an MS-DOS-readable (8.3) name for each file. These MS-DOS-readable names also enable MS-DOS-based and Windows 3.*x*–based applications to recognize and load files that have long file names. When a program saves a file on a computer running Windows XP Professional, both the 8.3 file name and long file name are retained.

> **Note**   The 8.3 format means that files can have between 1 and 8 characters in the file name. The name must start with a letter or a number and can contain any characters except the following:
>
> . " / \ [ ] : ; | = , * ? (space)
>
> An 8.3 file name typically has a file name extension that is from one to three characters long and has the same character restrictions. A period separates the file name from the file name extension.
>
> Several special file names are reserved by the system and cannot be used for files or folders:
>
> CON, AUX, COM1, COM2, COM3, COM4, LPT1, LPT2, LPT3, PRN, NUL

To see both the long and short file names for each file in the folder, at the command line, type:

```
dir /x
```

Long File Names at the Command Prompt

At the command prompt, if you type the long name of a file or folder that contains spaces, you must enclose the name in quotation marks. For example, if you have a program called Dump Disk Files that you want to run from the command prompt and you enter the name without quotation marks, it generates the error message "Cannot find the program Dump or one of its components."

You must also use quotation marks around each referenced set of long file names when a path typed at the command line includes spaces, as in the following example:

```
move "c:\This month's reports\*.*" "c:\Last month's reports"
```

Caution   Use wildcard characters such as the asterisk (*****) and question mark (**?**) carefully in conjunction with the **del** and **copy** commands. Windows XP Professional searches both long and short file names for matches to the wildcard character combination you specify, which can cause additional files to be deleted or copied. It is always a good idea to run the **dir** command first on the specified files to make sure you are affecting only the files you intend to use.

Generating Short File Names

In Windows XP Professional, both FAT and NTFS use the Unicode character set, which contains several prohibited characters that MS-DOS cannot read, for their names. To generate a short MS-DOS-readable file name, Windows XP Professional deletes all of these characters from the long file name and removes any spaces. Because an MS-DOS-readable file name can have only one period, Windows XP Professional also removes extra periods from the file name. If necessary, Windows XP Professional truncates the file name to six characters and appends a tilde (**~**) and a number. For example, each non-duplicate file name is appended with **~1**. Duplicate file names end with **~2**, then **~3**, and so on. After the file names are truncated, the file name extensions are truncated to three or fewer characters. Finally, when displaying file names at the command line, Windows XP Professional translates all characters in the file name and extension to uppercase.

Note   You can permit extended characters by using the **fsutil behavior set** command. You must restart the computer before this setting takes effect. For more information about using the **fsutil behavior set** command, see Windows XP Professional Help.

When five or more files exist that can result in duplicate short file names, Windows XP Professional uses a slightly different method for creating short file names. For the fifth and subsequent files, Windows XP Professional:

■ Uses only the first two letters of the long file name.

■ Generates the next four letters of the short file name by mathematically manipulating the remaining letters of the long file name.

■ Appends **~1** (or another number, if necessary, to avoid a duplicate file name) to the result.

This method substantially improves performance when Windows XP Professional must create short file names for a large number of files with similar long file names. Windows XP Professional uses this method to create short names for files on both FAT and NTFS volumes.

Table 13-15 shows the short file names for files created by six tests.

Table 13-15 Short File Names Created by Windows XP Professional — Example One

Long File Name	Short File Name
This is test 1.txt	THISIS~1.TXT
This is test 2.txt	THISIS~2.TXT
This is test 3.txt	THISIS~3.TXT
This is test 4.txt	THISIS~4.TXT
This is test 5.txt	THA1CA~1.TXT
This is test 6.txt	THA1CE~1.TXT

If the long file names in Table 13-5 are created in a different order, their short file names are different, as shown in Table 13-16.

Table 13-16 Short File Names Created by Windows XP Professional — Example Two

Long File Name	Short File Name
This is test 2.txt	THISIS~1.TXT
This is test 3.txt	THISIS~2.TXT
This is test 1.txt	THISIS~3.TXT
This is test 4.txt	THISIS~4.TXT
This is test 5.txt	THA1CA~1.TXT
This is test 6.txt	THA1CE~1.TXT

When you delete a file, its short file name is also deleted. When you create new files in the same folder, Windows XP Professional might re-use short file names that have been deleted. For instance, in Example 1, if you delete the file "This is test 1.txt," and then create a new file called "This is test 7.txt," its short file name becomes THISIS~1.TXT.

Additional Resources

- "Troubleshooting Disks and File Systems" in this book for more information about boot sectors, defragmenting volumes, and using Chkdsk.exe.

- "Managing Files and Folders" in this book for more information about shared folders and shared folder permissions.

- "Disk Management" in this book.

- "Tools for Troubleshooting" in this book.

- *Inside Windows 2000 Server* by William Boswell, 2000, Indianapolis: New Riders Publishing.

- *Inside Microsoft Windows 2000, Third Edition* by David A. Solomon and Mark E. Russinovich, 2000, Redmond: Microsoft Press.

Chapter 14

Backup and Restore

Backup is a tool in Microsoft® Windows® XP Professional that allows users to back up and restore data. The ability to restore data from backup media in the event of an emergency is critical to the success of an organization.

Backup uses the Removable Storage feature to manage the storage devices attached to your system. Because backing up the data on your system is one of the most important aspects of data management, Windows XP Professional integrates Backup with Removable Storage to help you protect your data.

Related Information

- For more information about the NTFS file system and the file allocation table (FAT) file system, see "File Systems" in this book.

- For more information about disaster recovery, see "Troubleshooting Concepts and Strategies" in this book.

- For more information about System Restore, see "Tools for Troubleshooting" in this book.

Technology Features

Volume shadow copies Windows XP Professional introduces volume shadow copies, a technology that provides a copy of the original volume at the instant a shadow copy is made. Volume shadow copies allow users or applications to continue working while a backup occurs on a shadow copy of the original volume. The uninterrupted backup allows the files to appear unchanged while changes are made during the backup, which might take hours to be completed. Additionally, the backup application can back up files that are held open exclusively by their respective applications. In previous versions of Backup, files open at the time of the backup were skipped. For more information about volume shadow copies, see "Volume Shadow Copy Technology" later in this chapter.

Automated System Recovery Windows XP Professional introduces the Automated System Recovery (ASR) tool, an advanced option of the Backup Tool (NTBackup.exe). ASR replaces the Emergency Repair Disk found in Microsoft® Windows® 2000 and Microsoft® Windows® NT 4.0.

ASR in Backup is a last-resort feature to use before reformatting your disk and re-installing Windows XP Professional. ASR enables you to restore the system state and critical files on the system and boot partitions. Use ASR only when Windows XP Professional cannot start in normal, safe, or Recovery Console mode. For more information about ASR, see "Automated System Recovery" later in this chapter.

> **Tip** You can also do a full backup with the ability to restore your system by using the Backup and Restore wizard. In the wizard choose **All information on this computer** and have a blank floppy disk available to use when prompted.

Backup Overview

Regular backup of local hard disks prevents data loss from a disk or drive failure, disk controller errors, power outages, viruses, and other serious problems. Careful planning of backup operations and reliable equipment can make file recovery easier and faster.

Using Backup, you can back up data to tape, optical disc, or a compressed file. You can also store your backup files on a network share.

Backup Types

Deciding which type of backup to use depends on your organization's needs. The two major considerations are the value of the data and the amount of data that has changed since the last normal or incremental backup.

You can perform any of the following types of backup:

Normal   A normal backup copies all selected files and marks each as having been backed up. Normal backups are the easiest to use for restoring files because you need only the most recent backup file or tape to restore all of the backed up files. Normal backups take the most time because every file that is selected is backed up, regardless of whether it has changed since the last backup.

Incremental   An incremental backup reduces the time required to complete the backup process by saving only files that have been created or changed since the last normal or incremental backups. It marks files so that you will know if a specific file has been backed up. You need to create a complete normal backup of your system before you can run incremental backups. If you use a combination of normal and incremental backups to restore your data, you must have the last normal backup set of media as well as every incremental backup in chronological order since the last normal backup.

Differential   A differential backup can reduce the time required to complete the backup process by copying files that have been created or changed since the last normal or incremental backup. It does not mark files as backed up. You need to create a complete normal backup of your system before you run differential backups. If you use a combination of normal and differential backups, you must have the last normal backup media set and the last differential backup sets to restore your data.

Copy   A copy backup copies all selected files, but it does not mark each copied file as backed up. Copying is a useful temporary method to back up files between normal and incremental backups; it does not affect other backup operations.

Daily   A daily backup copies all selected files that have been modified on the day that the daily backup is performed. The backed up files are not marked as backed up.

Some backup types use a backup marker, also known as an "archive attribute," to track when a file has been backed up. When the file changes, Windows XP Professional marks the file to be backed up again. Files or directories that have been moved to new locations are not marked for backup. Backup allows you to back up only files with this marker set and to choose whether or not to mark files when they are backed up.

Caution Backup protects against data loss caused by a virus. Because some viruses take weeks to appear, keep normal backup tapes for at least a month to make sure that you can restore a system to its uninfected status.

Storage and Media

Windows XP Professional can back up files to a variety of storage devices. Data can be backed up to tape drives, disk volumes, removable disks, and network shares, or to a library of discs or tapes in a media pool controlled by a robotic changer. If you do not have a separate storage device, you can back up to a local hard disk or to floppy disks.

Storage Devices

Storage technology changes rapidly, so it is important to research the merits of various media before you make a purchase. When you select a storage device, consider storage device and media costs, as well as reliability and capacity. Ideally, a storage device has more than enough capacity to back up the combined data of all local hard disks and can detect and correct errors during backup-and-restore operations. For information about specific storage devices, see the Hardware Compatibility List (HCL) link on the Web Resources page at http://www.microsoft.com/windows/res-kits/webresources.

Tip To make sure that your storage devices and media work correctly, verify your backups by performing test restores.

Media Types

The most common medium is magnetic tape. Commonly used tape drives for backup include a quarter-inch cartridge, digital data storage (DDS), 8mm cassette, and digital linear tape (DLT). High-capacity, high-performance tape drives typically use small computer system interface (SCSI) controllers. Other types of media include magnetic discs, optical discs, and CD-ROMs — recordable CD-ROM (CD-R) and rewritable CD-ROM (CD-RW).

Note Backup does not support backing up directly to CD-R or CD-RW devices. You can back up to a file, and then copy that backup file to a CD-R or CD-RW. The restore process can be accomplished directly from the CD-R.

Security Considerations

Several steps are required to enhance the security and operation of your backup-and-restore operations. You need to take steps to secure your backup media.

When you develop a backup plan, consider the following methods:

■ Secure both the storage device and the backup media. Data can be retrieved from stolen media and restored to another computer.

■ Back up an entire volume by using the normal backup procedure. In case of a disk failure, it is more efficient to restore the entire volume in one operation.

■ Always back up the System State data to prevent the loss of local user accounts and security information.

■ Keep at least three current copies of backup media. Store one copy at an off-site location in a properly controlled, secure environment.

Backup and Restore Rights

In many cases, the local administrator performs backup and restore operations on Windows XP Professional systems. However, when Windows XP Professional is used as a file server in a peer-to-peer, local area network (LAN), backup and restore rights can be given to a user without granting full administrative privileges.

If you are the system administrator of a networked computer with shared volumes or of a publicly used computer, you need to extend backup and restore rights only to those users who are responsible for backing up the computer. You can do this by adding users to the Backup Operators local group. In a high-security environment, only you need the ability to restore files, although it is a good idea to train personnel to perform all restore tasks in the event that you are unavailable.

To add a user to the Backup Operators group

1. In **Control Panel**, double-click **Administrative Tools**.

2. Double-click the **Computer Management** icon.

3. In the console tree, click **Local Users and Groups**, and then double-click **Groups** in the details pane.

4. Double-click the **Backup Operators** group, and then click **Add**.

5. Enter the user's name, and then click **OK**.

Caution   A person who does not have permission to write to a file might have permission to restore the file. During a restore operation, such permission conflicts are ignored and the existing file can be overwritten.

File Permissions

In Windows XP Professional, access to NTFS files is limited by NTFS file and folder permissions, share permissions, and file attributes. You cannot back up or restore NTFS files to which you do not have access rights unless you are a member of either the Administrators or Backup Operators local group.

> **Note**   Neither of the file allocation table (FAT) file systems (FAT16 and FAT32) provides file permissions.

Backup Media Storage

Store some data off-site for long-term storage or to have available in the event of a disaster; however, other data needs to be readily available.

> **Caution**   Tape cartridges last longer in cool, humidity-controlled locations. Your storage area must also be free of magnetic fields, such as those near the backs of computer terminals and telephone equipment.

Daily backups — full and incremental   Store media in a fireproof safe or cabinet to protect against natural disaster, theft, and sabotage.

Copies of cartridges   If more than one copy of a software program is purchased, store one off-site if possible. If you have only one copy, back it up to a cartridge, label it as a backup, and store the original off-site. If you have to reinstall software, you can restore it from the backup cartridge to a computer that is running Windows XP Professional.

For highly confidential data that must be stored off-site, consider assistance from a company that specializes in secure data storage. If the cost or logistics of such protection is too great, use an alternative solution, such as a safe-deposit box or an off-site fireproof safe that is designed to protect magnetic media.

For maximum security, store the following items off-site:

- A full, normal backup of the entire system, performed weekly.

- Original software that is installed on computers. (Keep only copies on-site.)

- Documents that are required for processing an insurance claim, such as purchase orders or receipts.

- Information that is required to get network hardware reinstalled or reconfigured.

- Information that is required to reconfigure your storage subsystem.

Tip   Make sure that your off-site storage location is bonded.

Establishing a Backup Plan

When you develop your backup plan:

- Keep spare hardware and media on hand in case of a failure. To avoid a problem, compare the spare hardware with the original hardware in advance to make sure that the firmware revision is the same as the original equipment. For more information about firmware revisions, check the documentation provided by the manufacturer.

- Test backed-up data regularly to verify the reliability of your backup procedures and equipment.

- Include stress testing of backup hardware (storage drives, optical drives, and controllers) and software (backup program and device drivers).

Several different system configurations can affect your backup strategies. At one end of the range is a simple, stand-alone computer with one user. At the other is a workgroup network with a computer that is hosting a network public file share.

Caution   Backup does not back up files on computers running Microsoft® MS-DOS®, unless you create a share that Backup can access over the network. Consider reserving space on a network share so that users of MS-DOS and Microsoft Windows version 3.1 can copy important files. Files on the network share can be backed up during regular file server backups.

You can work out a backup solution by doing these four tasks:

1. Research and select a storage device. When considering new backup hardware, be sure to consider its reliability, speed, capacity, cost, and compatibility with Windows XP Professional. The media must provide more than enough space to back up all of your data.

2. If necessary, install a controller card in the computer. If you choose to use a SCSI-based tape drive, put the tape drive on its own controller.

3. Connect your new storage device to the computer so that you can back up the System State data. If you are using an external SCSI drive, start the drive before you start the computer so that the driver can be loaded properly.

4. Establish a backup media rotation schedule. You need to continue making backups as long as data is created or changed.

Over a period of time, you need to use several separate discs or tapes when you run your backup regimen. By using multiple discs or tapes instead of repeatedly using the same disc or tape, you gain additional benefits with your backup program:

■   It preserves access to multiple versions of data files in case a user needs to restore an older copy of a data file.

■   If the last backup is unsuccessful as a result of a bad cartridge, you have a backup from the previous process.

■   You extend the useful life span of each cartridge.

Tip   Have several extra, new, blank, formatted media available in case of media failure. Regularly scan the Backup log for errors that might indicate that a backup cartridge is beginning to fail.

Make sure to clean a tape drive's recording heads regularly. Failure to do so can lead to unusable backups and the premature failure of the tape drive. See the tape drive manufacturer's recommendations for the proper method and frequency of cleaning.

Stand-Alone Computer

You need to choose a backup medium to use. If the quantity of data that you need to back up is small, a removable hard disk or rewritable DVD disc (DVD RAM) might be all that you need. However, for more flexibility and capacity for growth, a tape cartridge is still the backup medium of choice.

To back up to a CD-R or CD-RW, you must back up to a file first, and then copy that file to the CD-R or CD-RW. You can then restore the file directly from the CD-R or CD-RW. Because space on CD-R or CD-RW is limited from 650 to 700 MBs, you might have to divide your backups into smaller jobs.

After your storage device is installed, decide on a backup schedule and the type of backup. If the data that is created on a daily basis is irreplaceable, daily backups are recommended. If the data is less valuable, the frequency of backups can be less often. Recognize, however, that the longer the period between backups, the greater the potential for loss. Just as it is unwise to work on a document all day without saving the file, it is unwise to work on a document all week without backing it up. The value of the data helps you determine the appropriate frequency of backups.

The type of backup you make determines how easy or difficult it is to restore the data in an emergency. The compromise is between security and convenience. If you choose to run full, normal backups every day, you can restore lost data easily, but the backups can take a substantial amount of time (depending upon the quantity of data to be backed up and the data transfer speed of the storage device). If you choose to make incremental backups for a month after making a full backup, you save substantial time in the backup process. However, fully restoring a corrupted hard disk might require you to restore the normal backup, and then each incremental backup in succession. Substituting a differential backup for the incremental backup shortens the restore process, but as the backup process takes more time each day, the total accumulation of changed files continues to grow, so the time you gain by using a differential backup might be minimal. You must also use a separate cartridge for each differential backup to prevent losing the ability to retrieve earlier versions of files.

Stand-Alone Method One

Computers that contain frequently changing data that is hard to replace or reproduce, or computers that provide a public network share need to be backed up daily. Run a full, normal backup every Friday. Every Monday through Thursday run a differential backup to a different tape or disc. After the second Friday, when a second full backup has been successfully made, store the first full backup as a temporary archive. Then after every following Friday's full backup, alternate the full backups as temporary archives. On every eighth Friday, save the full backup as a permanent archive, which needs to be stored in a secure, off-site location. Over the course of a year, this method uses at least 14 tapes or discs.

> **Note**   If a computer is used seven days a week, add a Saturday and Sunday differential backup to the schedule.
> Use new tapes if you choose to make permanent archives on tape.

Stand-Alone Method Two

If the computer is used less often or if the data is not as valuable, consider making one incremental backup each week for three weeks and one full, normal backup every fourth week. Alternating the full backups between two cartridges ensures that at least one always exists. This reduces the amount of time spent creating backups, but it also reduces protection against data corruption or erasure. Over the course of a year this method uses at least fives tapes or discs.

LAN Workgroups

The following scenario illustrates a possible approach for backing up a small network that consists of a computer that is running Windows XP Professional and that is hosting a public file share for 20 other client computers.

Connect a storage device to the share host computer. From the share host computer, you can back up user files on remote computers that are running the following operating systems: Microsoft® Windows® for Workgroups, Microsoft® Windows® 95, Microsoft® Windows® 98, Microsoft® Windows NT 4.0®, Microsoft® Windows® 2000, and Windows XP Professional. (See the two suggested methods for doing this that follow.) Establish a media rotation schedule. If conserving media is a requirement, back up clients less frequently than you back up the share host and encourage users to copy critical files to the network share at the end of the day.

Volume shadow copies cannot be used on remote shares. The success of your backup is more reliable if it is run on an individual Windows XP Professional–based computer and saved to the server that you are backing up. Using this method provides a shadow copy of the data volumes, and you can then schedule periodic system state backups. However, this backup method must be managed and scheduled for each computer individually, which is not practical if you manage many computers.

In the descriptions of the following methods for backing up remote computers, the computer that contains the data to be backed up is called "Data." The computer that runs the backup process is called "Target."

Workgroup Method One

Back up Data locally to disk. Use Backup over the network or the **xcopy** command to move the resulting backup file to Target. Make sure you run a backup verification pass that compares the data on Data and the data on Target on a regular basis. Typical transfer speeds for Ethernet or Token Ring are approximately 1 megabyte (MB) per second if the network is not busy. You can use this transfer rate and the total amount of data being transferred to estimate the transfer time. If the transfer time is too long, you might need to use a faster network connection or a different backup method.

For more information about using the **xcopy** command, type the following at the command prompt:

```
xcopy /?
```

Workgroup Method Two

Copy the data that you want to back up to another disk or disks on Data. Bring Data online, and copy the data by using the data storage device that is connected to Data. You can also back up Data over the network to Target. Whether to perform the backup from Data or from Target depends on the following factors:

- Availability of a target computer
- Policies requiring backups on designated computers

- Time and cost of performing backup from Data
- Time and cost of transferring files to Target

LAN Backup Schedule

After you have determined the best method for giving Target access to the data it needs to back up, you can begin your backup schedule plan. On Target, run a full, normal backup every Friday. Every Monday through Thursday, run a differential backup to a different tape. Run this program for four weeks before you reuse tapes in the backup program. On every fourth Friday, save the full backup as a permanent archive stored in a secure, off-site location. Over the course of a year, this method uses at least 31 tapes.

> **Note**   To allow users access to even more old versions of document files, you can lengthen the backup schedule to six weeks before tapes are reused. This increases the number of tapes used in a year to at least 41.
>
> If a computer is used seven days a week, add a Saturday and Sunday differential backup to the schedule.

Documenting Backup-and-Restore Procedures

Keeping accurate backup records is essential for locating backed up data quickly, particularly if you have accumulated a large number of backup cartridges. Thorough records include cartridges labels, catalogs, and online log files and log books.

Cartridge labels   Labels for write-once cartridges need to contain the backup date, the type of backup (normal, incremental, or differential), and a list of contents. If you are restoring from differential or incremental backups, you need to be able to locate the last normal backup and either the last differential backup or all incremental backups that have been created since the last normal backup. Label reusable media, such as tapes or removable discs, sequentially and keep a log book in which you note the content of cartridges, the backup date, the type of backup, and the date the medium was placed in service. If you have to replace a defective cartridge, label the new cartridge with the next unused sequential ID, and record it in the log book.

Catalogs   Most backup software includes a mechanism for cataloging backup files. Backup stores catalogs on a backup cartridge and temporarily loads them into memory. Catalogs are created for each backup set or for each collection of backed up files from one drive.

Log files   Log files include the names of all backed up and restored files and folders. A log file is useful when you are restoring data because you can print or read this file from any text editor. Keeping printed logs in a notebook makes it easier to locate specific files. For example, if the tape that contains the catalog of the backup set is corrupted, you can use the printed logs to locate a file. It is recommended that you carefully review log files following each backup session to ensure that the session completes successfully.

Verify Operations

A verify operation compares the files on disk to the files on the backup media. It occurs after all files are backed up or restored, and it takes about as long as the backup procedure. Recommended times for performing verify operations follow:

- After every backup, especially if you back up to a set of cartridges for long-term storage.
- After a file restore operation.

Choosing a verify operation while backing up system files might cause the verify operation to falsely report files that are in use by the operating system and continuously changing.

If a verify operation is unsuccessful for a particular file, check the date that the file was last modified. If the file changes between a backup operation and a verify operation, the verify operation is unsuccessful. A change in the size of a file, or corruption of data on the backup disc or cartridge also might make a verify operation unsuccessful.

Backing Up System State Data

System State data includes the following:

- Boot files, including the system files
- Files protected by Windows File Protection (WFP)
- The registry
- Performance counter configuration information
- The Component Services class registration database

The System State data does not represent the entire system. To restore a system to an operational condition, the boot files, system volumes, and System State must all be restored together.

Restoration of the System State replaces boot files first and commits the system hive of the registry as a final step in the process.

System State backup and restore operations include all System State data. You cannot choose to back up or restore individual components because of dependencies among the System State components. However, you can restore System State data to an alternate location in which only the registry files and system boot files are restored. The Component Services class registration database is not restored to the alternate location.

Although you cannot change which components of the System State are backed up, you can back up all system-protected files at the same time as the System State data by setting advanced backup options.

The system-protected files only change if you install a service pack or application, or upgrade your operating system. Typically, the system-protected files represent a very large portion of System State data— the default, including the protected files, is about 180 MB. Include these system-protected files only if new programs have been installed. Otherwise a restore causes the new application to fail.

To back up System State data

1. From the **Start** menu, point to **All Programs**, click **Accessories**, click **System Tools**, and then click **Backup**.

2. Click **Advanced Mode**.

3. Click the **Backup** tab, and then select the **System State** check box.

4. Click **Start Backup**.

This backs up the System State data along with any other data that you have selected for the current backup operation. Keep the following in mind when you are backing up System State data:

- You must be an administrator or a backup operator to back up files and folders.

- You can back up the System State data only on a local computer.

- You must also back up the Boot and System volumes to ensure that the system starts properly.

- You can use the Backup wizard to back up System State data.

- You cannot use an incremental backup while backing up System State data.

Boot and System Files

Backup depends on the functionality of WFP when backing up and restoring boot and system files. System files are backed up and restored as a single entity. In Microsoft Windows NT version 4.0 and earlier, backup programs can selectively back up and restore operating system files as they do data files, allowing for incremental backup and restore operations of most operating system files. Windows XP Professional, however, does not allow incremental restoration of operating system files.

The advanced backup options give you additional backup choices. Descriptions of the options and information about setting them follows.

To set advanced backup options

1. Open Backup, and then click **Advanced Mode**.

2. In the **Backup Utility** dialog box, click the **Backup** tab, and then select the files and folders that you want to back up.

3. Click **Start Backup**.

4. In the Backup Job Information dialog box, click **Advanced**.

5. Set the advanced backup options that you want, and then click **OK**.

   The advanced backup options are described in Table 14-1.

Table 14-1   Advanced Backup Options

Option	Description
Back up migrated Remote Storage data.	Backs up data that has been designated for Remote Storage. You can restore Remote Storage data only to an NTFS volume that is used with Windows 2000 and Windows XP Professional.
	Note that Remote Storage is available only on Windows 2000–based computers.
Verify data after backup.	Verifies that the backed up data is exactly the same as the original data. This can substantially increase the time it takes to perform a backup.
Use hardware compression, if available.	Compresses the data that you are backing up so you can save more data on a tape. If this option is disabled, you do not have a tape drive on your computer or your tape drive cannot compress data.
Automatically back up system-protected files along with the System State.	Backs up all system files in your systemroot directory in addition to the boot files included with the System State data.
Disable volume shadow copy.	Allows you to disable volume shadow copy technology.

Using the Backup Tool

Backup is a graphical tool that is used with a variety of storage media to back up and restore files on volumes using any file system supported by Windows XP Professional. Backup also simplifies archiving and allows you to schedule jobs to automate backups.

Removable Storage does tasks such as mounting and dismounting a tape or disc. It tracks and controls backup cartridges, which are typically organized into pools, on storage devices, and allows applications such as Backup to share robotic changers and cartridge libraries. After Removable Storage is started, it is transparent, so you only need access to it when you change cartridges, not when you perform a backup or restore operation.

> **Note**   Removable Storage does not manage backing up to files on a random access medium, such as a hard disk or removable disk.

Because of Removable Storage technology in Windows XP Professional, target media of Backup are not drive-oriented as in the past. In versions of Backup included in Windows NT 4.0, backup data was written to drives (for example, tape or disc drives).

In Windows XP Professional, Backup uses cartridges in media pools to store backed-up data. Backup still writes backup data to tapes or files on discs; but Removable Storage, which references media instead of drives, manages the media. Backup determines whether each cartridge to which it gains access is a member of an existing media pool or unallocated media. The significance of this change can be seen when a user sets up a regular backup schedule.

In the past, users scheduled Backup to run on specified days, and they could use any cartridge for that day's job. Removable Storage tracks the use of all cartridges, so it does not allow indiscriminate use of unrecognized cartridges by the applications that use Removable Storage to manage the media associated with their respective applications.

Each cartridge that Backup uses is added to Backup's application media pool, and you must identify a cartridge for each job you schedule. If you choose to back up your data to a different cartridge each night over the course of a week, you have to create seven scheduled jobs, or one job for each tape. This is because the job scheduler you can use with Backup requires that you specify a cartridge name in the scheduled job. (Each cartridge has a unique name recorded in the header of the data area.) If you place the Tuesday cartridge in the recording drive on Friday, the scheduled job is unsuccessful because the criteria required for completing the job are not met.

You can enhance the likelihood of success in the following way: Run the backup manually the first time the cartridge is used and assign the cartridge a unique name (such as "Monday"). After you give each a cartridge a unique name, you can create a set of scheduled backup jobs.

This feature is very important to pay attention to using a scheduled backup to a single drive (a drive that does not include a changer). In this case Removable Storage cannot load the proper media into the drive. If the media left in the drive is not the expected media, the job will fail. Backup running in scheduled mode has no way of reporting failures to the user on an interactive basis, therefore, the backup log is the only way to determine if failures of this type have occurred. If you do not review the backup logs, failures could prevent any backup from occurring during that session.

A new feature Windows XP Professional offers is the ability to view the media pools directly from Backup. In Windows 2000, you must view media pools by opening the Removable Storage snap-in in Microsoft Management Console (MMC).

For more information about Removable Storage, see "Removable Storage" later in this chapter.

> **Note**   If you use a multi-cartridge library device (such as a tape drive that contains a magazine of tapes) and set Backup to always draw cartridges from the free media pool, you only need to schedule one job. However, data on each previously used cartridge must be deleted, which places the cartridge back into the free media pool so to be used again.

Files Skipped During Backup

Using volume shadow copy technology in Windows XP Professional, you can reduce the number and type of files skipped during backup. If the volume shadow copy fails, Backup defaults to non-shadow copy techniques used in previous editions of Windows.

If non-shadow copy technology is used, Backup skips the following files:

- Files that are open in other applications
- Files that Backup skips by default

Files Skipped by Default

Files that Backup skips by default include temporary files, such as Pagefile.sys, Hiberfil.sys, Win386.swp, 386spart.par, Backup.log, and Restore.log. These files are neither backed up nor restored by Backup.

Backup also skips files on remote computers that are on a network share if the files are in use at the time of the backup.

Volume Shadow Copy Technology

Volume shadow copy technology provides an instant copy of the original volume. A shadow copy of the volume is made at the time a backup is initiated. Data is then backed up from the shadow copy instead of from the original volume. The original volume continues to change as the process continues, but the shadow copy of the volume remains constant. This is helpful if users need access to files while a backup is taking place.

Other important advantages of this technology include the following:

- A computer can be backed up while applications and services are running.
- Files are not skipped during the backup process.

- Files open at the time of the shadow copy appear closed on the shadow copy volume.

- The need for scheduling a *backup window* is eliminated. A backup window requires that applications be shut down to ensure a successful volume backup.

Using volume shadow copy technology, Windows XP Professional works with running applications to determine when a volume shadow copy occurs. The Volume Shadow Copy service then allows a backup application to access the volume and back it up. Applications continue running uninterrupted on the actual volumes. After the backup is completed and the data is saved on the backup media, the shadow copy is deleted.

By default, Windows XP Professional uses free disk space on any NTFS volume to store a record of the differences between the original volume and the shadow copy volume. The data on the shadow copy volume exists only while the shadow copy is being taken. The amount of disk space temporarily consumed depends on how much file data on the volume has changed during backup.

If sufficient temporary disk space is not available, Windows XP Professional cannot complete a volume shadow copy and Backup skips open files. Thus you must provide sufficient disk space to create a shadow copy of open files. Applications that can use Backup can register writer interfaces, which help coordinate the backup activity with the backup application.

Windows XP Professional uses volume shadow copy technology by default. If you only want to back up a few files or directories, you might want to disable shadow copies to avoid delays.

For more information about volume shadow copy technology, see Windows XP Professional Help and Support Center.

Note   Volume shadow copies require that you use NTFS for your file system.

Automated System Recovery

The Automated System Recovery (ASR) tool, an advanced option of the Backup Tool (NTBackup.exe), is new in Windows XP Professional. The ASR feature replaces the Emergency Repair Disk found in Windows 2000 and Windows NT 4.0. Use ASR to restore your system only if other disaster recovery tools are unavailable.

ASR allows you to restore the operating system to a previous state so that you can start Windows XP Professional when other recovery methods do not work. For example, disk damage might prevent you from starting Windows XP Professional in normal or safe mode, or prevent using Recovery Console and Last Known Good Configuration. ASR gives you another way to start your system.

ASR consists of two parts that automate the process of saving and restoring system state information: ASR backup and ASR restore. To learn more about disaster recovery tools, see "Tools for Troubleshooting" in this book.

ASR Backup

The ASR wizard guides you through the process of saving ASR backups to removable media. When using the wizard to create an ASR backup, you need to decide where to store the ASR backup data and have a blank floppy disk available.

To locate the ASR wizard

1. In **All Programs**, point to **Accessories, System Tools**, and then click **Backup**.

2. Click **Advanced Mode**, and then click **Automated System Recovery Wizard**.

On the floppy disk, the wizard saves only hard-disk configuration information (not user data), such as disk signatures, the partition table, and volume data. If you run the ASR restore operation later, ASR Restore configures disks by using the saved data on the ASR floppy disk. The ASR backup operation scans your system and lists files to save for an ASR Restore.

ASR Restore

The ASR restore text-mode process relies on Windows XP Professional Setup along with the information stored on an ASR floppy disk. Before you begin, gather the following items:

- The most recent ASR floppy disk.
- The Windows XP Professional operating system CD.
- The most recent ASR backup media set, typically removable media such as data tape cartridges.

To restore your system by using ASR

1. Insert the Windows XP Professional operating system CD, and then restart your computer.

2. At the **Press any key to boot CD** prompt, press any key.

3. At the **ASR** prompt, press **F2**.

4. At the prompt, insert an ASR floppy disk.

5. At the prompt, insert ASR backup media (typically one or more pieces of removable media such as data tape cartridges).

6. At the prompt, provide a destination folder, such as C:\Windows or C:\Winnt.

ASR checks the backup media. To avoid application configuration issues, it is recommended that you give the destination folder the same directory name that you used when you created the ASR backup.

Restoring from network shares is not an ASR option. Therefore, you must use locally attached devices such as the following devices attached to ATA or SCSI adapters:

- Tape backup drives

- Removable disks, including CDs

- Other hard disks

ASR Considerations   ASR is not a replacement for regular backups in which files stored on one or more volumes are saved to backup media. Because ASR saves only the files necessary to restore system state, data loss might occur. Therefore, always consider other recovery options before using ASR.

For more information about Recovery Console, see "Tools for Troubleshooting," in this book.

Before using ASR, consider the following points:

- ASR formats the *systemdrive* partition as part of the restore process. When you have dedicated space for user data files on the system partition (*systemdrive*), personal data or application files are not restored, and data loss is possible.

- ASR restores only operating system files that it determines need repair. However, ASR might initialize operating system volumes that also contain users' personal files. Therefore, there is a risk to user files stored on these volumes.

- ASR is different from the System Restore feature. ASR is a recovery tool that backs up all files on the system partition and is used to bring a system back online if startup fails. System Restore saves only incremental changes, or shadow copies, and lets you start Windows XP Professional in normal or safe mode. Always try System Restore before resorting to ASR.

- ASR supports FAT16 volumes up to 2.1 GB only. ASR does not support 4 GB FAT16 partitions that use a cluster size of 64 kilobytes (KB). If your system contains 4-GB FAT16 partitions, convert them from FAT16 to NTFS before using ASR. For more information about volumes and clusters, see "File Systems" in this book.

For more information about Automated System Recovery, see Windows XP Professional Help and Support Center.

Removable Storage

Removable Storage provides services to applications and system administrators that facilitate the use, sharing, and management of removable media devices, such as tape drives and robotic storage libraries. The availability of Removable Storage technology eliminates the need for independent software vendors (ISVs) to develop customized solutions and support for these devices on a per-device basis. More importantly, Removable Storage enables multiple storage applications to share expensive removable media storage devices. Thus the focus of storage applications can be directed to customer features rather than hardware issues.

As shown in Figure 14-1, Removable Storage provides a single set of application programming interfaces (APIs) that allow applications to catalog all removable media (except floppy disks and similar small-capacity media), such as disc, tape, and optical media, which are either stored on shelves (offline) or in libraries (online). Also, by disguising the complexities of underlying robotic library systems, Removable Storage lowers the costs of developing and operating storage applications and provides consistency for customers who purchase these applications.

Before Removable Storage

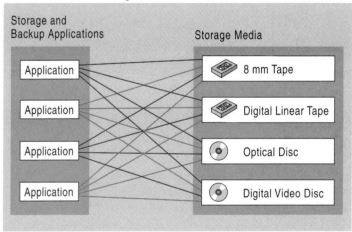

After Removable Storage

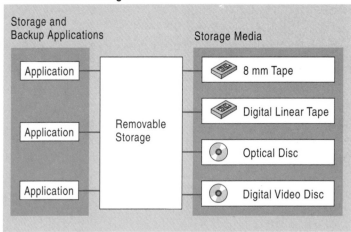

Figure 14-1 Removable media with and without Removable Storage

Removable Storage uses media pools to organize media. Media pools control access to media, group media into media types according to use, allow media to be shared across applications, and allow Removable Storage to track application sharing.

Basic Concepts

Removable Storage can be described in terms of five basic concepts: media units, media libraries, media pools, work queue items, and operator requests. The first item in this list, *media*, is fundamental and affects all others. The remaining four items in the list are the top-level nodes in the Removable Storage snap-in.

Media Units

Media are classified into media units (also known as cartridges or discs) of a certain type, such as 8mm tape, magnetic disc, optical disc, or CD-ROM.

While both sides of double-sided media must be contained in the same library, the state of each side can be different. For example, one side can be allocated, and the other side can be available.

Media Libraries

Removable Storage manages two classes of libraries: online libraries and offline media physical locations. Libraries include both cartridges and the means to read and write them. The offline media physical location is a special holder for cartridges that are cataloged by Removable Storage but do not reside in a library.

Online Libraries   In its simplest form, a *library* consists of the following components:

- A data storage cartridge
- A means of reading and writing to the cartridge

For example, a CD-ROM drive is a simple library with one drive, no slots, an insert/eject port, and no transport.

In comparison, a robotic-based tape library can hold up to several thousand tapes, have one or more tape drives, and have a mechanical means of moving tapes into and out of the drives.

Robotic library   A robotic library can contain any of the following components: Cartridges, slots to hold the cartridges, one or more drives, a transport, and either a door or an insert/eject port. No user intervention is required to place a cartridge in a library in one of its drives.

Stand-alone drive library   In a stand-alone drive library (also known as a stand-alone drive), the user or a transport must place a cartridge in a drive. The CD-ROM drive on most desktop computers is a stand-alone drive library. Removable Storage treats any drive that has an insert/eject port as a stand-alone library.

Offline media physical location In an online library, the location of a cartridge is the library in which it resides. Cartridges that are not in an online library, such as archived backup tapes on a shelf, are offline media that reside in an offline media physical location. When a user or administrator moves an offline medium into an online library, Removable Storage tracks its location to the library into which it is placed. When a cartridge is taken out of an online library, Removable Storage designates its location as the offline media physical location.

Media Pools

A media pool is a logical collection of cartridges that share some common attributes. A media pool contains media of only one type, but a media pool can contain more than one library. Both sides of a two-sided cartridge are always in the same pool.

Each media pool can control access to the media that belong to it. Although a media pool does not control access to the data that is contained on the cartridges, it does control how the cartridges are manipulated, including an application's ability to move a cartridge from the pool or to allocate a cartridge for its own use.

Media pools can be used hierarchically to hold other media pools or to hold cartridges. An application that needs to group media of several types into one collection can create one application media pool for the whole collection and additional media pools within the original pool—one for each media type. A *free pool* contains a media pool for each media type. Media pools are categorized into two classes: system media pools and application media pools. The system and application media pools are defined as follows:

- System pools, which are created by Removable Storage for its own use, include free pools, import pools, and unrecognized pools.

- Application pools, which are created by applications to group media, allow several applications to share the libraries attached to a system.

System pools The following three kinds of system pools hold cartridges when they are not in use:

- **Free pool**. Holds unused cartridges that are available to applications.

- **Import pool**. Temporarily holds cartridges newly placed in a library.

- **Unrecognized pool**. Temporarily holds unidentifiable cartridges newly placed in a library.

Free pool Free pools support sharing cartridges among applications. The pools contain blank or recycled cartridges that are available to any application. An application can draw cartridges from the free pools, and it can return cartridges to the free pools when the cartridges are no longer needed.

Import pool   When a cartridge is placed in a library, if Removable Storage can identify the format or the application that is associated with it, but has not seen it before, Removable Storage places the cartridge in the import pool. For example, if an administrator places a tape written by Backup on one computer into a library that is attached to a second computer, Removable Storage on the second system recognizes that the tape was written using Microsoft Tape Format (MTF) and places it in the import pool for its media type.

Unrecognized pool   When a cartridge is placed in a library, if Removable Storage cannot identify the format or the application that is associated with it and has not seen the cartridge before, Removable Storage places the cartridge in the unrecognized pool for its media type. Blank cartridges are treated this way. Cartridges in unrecognized pools might have data on them, but Removable Storage cannot read data on these cartridges and cannot catalog them. Cartridges in the unrecognized pool are not available for backup media. Instead, they must be moved to the free pool to be used by Backup. When Backup first starts, it checks the unrecognized pool for media. If media is found there, Backup offers the user the option to move the media to the free pool.

> **Caution**   Moving media to the free pool deletes all data contained on the media.

Application pools   Each application that uses cartridges managed by Removable Storage uses one or more application pools. Applications can create these pools, or you can create them by using Removable Storage. You can set permissions for application pools that allow applications to share pools or that assign each application its own set of pools.

Work Queue Items

When applications make a library request, Removable Storage places the request in a queue and processes it as resources become available. For example, a request to mount a tape in a library results in a mount work queue item, which might wait until a drive or slot is available.

Operator Requests

Sometimes, even with robotic libraries, manual assistance is required to complete a request or perform maintenance. If an application requests that a cartridge in an offline location be mounted, the cartridge must be manually entered into the online library. This generates a request to the administrator or an operator to enter the cartridge.

Available Backup Media

Backup displays a list of all available storage devices in the **Backup destination** list on the **Backup** tab. If Backup does not detect any external storage devices, you can back up data to a file on the hard disk. If you want to back up to a medium that Removable Storage does not manage, make sure that you load the medium in the appropriate storage device.

When you back up data to cartridges that are managed by Removable Storage, make sure that Removable Storage is running (you can confirm this in the Services console of the MMC). To back up to new cartridges, first make the cartridges available in the media pool. In an existing media pool, cartridges must be loaded in a library.

Locked Files

In Windows XP Professional, you can back up local files that the operating system locks, such as event logs and registry files. However, Backup skips event logs and registry files if they are open in other applications, and you do not use the shadow copy method to back up files.

To minimize the number of files that are not backed up, it is recommended that you use the default method of backing up files, which uses volume shadow copy technology. If you choose to use another method of backing up files, avoid running applications while Backup is running.

Encrypted Files

Encrypted files remain encrypted when they are backed up. Therefore, it is important to ensure that user keys, particularly the recovery agent keys, are also stored safely on backup cartridges. The Certificates console provides methods for exporting keys to floppy disks or to other removable media so that they can be secured.

For information about Encrypting File System (EFS), see "File Systems" in this book.

Backing Up Files on Your Local Computer

Using Backup, you can back up any file on your local hard disk.

Because most changes on a server occur as users add, modify, or delete files from their computers, it is recommended that you back up changes to users' folders daily.

Some users keep most of the files that they want backed up on network shares. Other users require that data on local computers be backed up. Your backup procedures need to take both situations into account.

Network users primarily use applications such as Microsoft® Word. You can reinstall the executable files from the original distribution medium, but the time and productivity that is lost doing this make the approach less than ideal. In addition, if you have customized the applications to suit the needs of your organization, reproducing those settings can be more difficult than reloading the programs themselves.

Because the applications rarely change, backing them up as part of your backup procedure uses minimal offline storage space and ensures that the latest version is always available.

Backing Up Files on Remote Computers

You can use Backup on any computer to which you can connect remotely. This allows a single-medium drive to be shared across an entire network and one backup policy to be in effect for the entire network.

You cannot back up System State data directly from a remote computer by using Backup. You can back up files and folders on a remote computer only by using a shared folder.

To back up the System State data of a remote computer

1. Run Backup locally on the remote computer to save the System State data to a file on a shared volume.

2. Back up the System State data file remotely to the shared volume.

To restore the System State data of a remote computer

1. Restore the System State data file remotely to the shared volume.

2. Restore the System State data file locally on the local computer.

Restoring Data

If files or directory services are not accessible, you must restore them. Restore operations are only possible if you have used Backup or another program to back up the files. Using Backup, you can restore the entire backup medium, one or more backup sets, or individual files. After the restore operation starts, you can restore the System State data as well.

Typically, all catalog information is maintained on the corresponding medium for that backup set.

When you insert a backup medium to restore data, only information about the first backup set is displayed. To restore the entire medium, first load the catalog by right-clicking the media and selecting **Catalog**. Otherwise, when you select a medium, you select only the displayed sets.

Restoring System State Data

When you restore the System State data, all System State data that is relevant to your computer is restored. However, due to dependencies among the system state components, you cannot back up or restore individual components of the System State data.

To restore System State data

1. Log on to the computer as the administrator.

2. Start **Backup**.

3. Click the **Restore** tab, and then select the check box for any drive, folder, or file that you want to restore.

4. Select the **System State** check box to restore the System State data and any other data you selected for the current restore operation.

> **Caution**   If you restore the System State data, and you do not designate an alternate location for the restored data, Backup replaces the System State data on your computer with the System State data you are restoring.

Files from Third-Party Backup Programs

You can use Backup to restore data from a tape that was backed up by using a program other than Backup if the tape is in Microsoft Tape Format (MTF). Although the tape might not have the full on-tape catalog information that Backup produces, it must have equivalent information. Also, some older tape backup devices might not support creating full on-tape catalogs by using Backup. Contact the vendor if you suspect that your tape backup device does not support creating a full on-tape catalog.

File Security Settings

Backup preserves permissions, ownership, and audit flags on files restored to NTFS volumes, but not on files restored to FAT volumes. It is not possible to secure that type of information on FAT volumes.

When you restore files to a new computer or hard disk, you do not have to restore security information. The files inherit the permissions of the NTFS directory in which they are placed. If the directory has no permissions, the file retains its previous permissions, including ownership.

Additional Resources

These resources contain additional information and tools related to this chapter.

- "File Systems" in this book.
- "Troubleshooting Concepts and Strategies" in this book.
- "Tools for Troubleshooting" in this book.

Part III

Security

Managing users' access to the network and the resources on it are vital to protecting your organization's sensitive information. This part discusses strategies for authenticating users and controlling their access to network resources, as well as strategies for securing computers and files on your network.

Chapter 15

Logon and Authentication

When a user logs on to a computer, a series of steps begins that makes up the authentication process. Authentication validates user identity and defines resources that a user can access. Windows operating systems use NTLM or the Kerberos V5 authentication protocol. Authentication is mostly automatic, but understanding the protocols, policies, and other elements involved can help you configure and manage authentication—and strengthen security.

Related Information

- For more information about authorization, see "Authorization and Access Control" in this book.

- For more information about authentication by using remote access services, see "Connecting Remote Offices" in this book.

- For more information about Kerberos V5 authentication, see "Authentication" in the *Distributed Systems Guide* of the *Microsoft® Windows® 2000 Server Resource Kit*.

- For more information about implementing security for Windows-based client computers and servers, see the *Microsoft® Windows® Security Resource Kit*.

Authentication Overview

Microsoft® Windows® XP Professional assures security by using the following processes:

- *Authentication*, which verifies the identity of something or someone.

- *Authorization*, which allows you to control access to all network resources, such as files and printers.

Authentication takes place all around us. For example, you are required to authenticate your identity and purpose when crossing international borders or completing business transactions. Similarly, in Windows, the identity of a user or computer must be authenticated before the user or computer has access to files, folders, and applications.

The following discussion provides detailed information about the configuration, management, and maintenance of authentication functions for Windows XP Professional–based clients, whether they are stand-alone clients or members of an Active Directory™ or other network environment.

New in Windows XP Professional

If you are already familiar with the security model in Microsoft® Windows NT® version 4.0 and Microsoft® Windows® 2000, you will recognize many of the features in Windows XP Professional. At the same time, you will also find a number of familiar features that have changed significantly, and new features that will improve your ability to manage system security.

The following are among the changed security-related features in Windows XP Professional:

- **Everyone membership.** The built-in Everyone group includes Authenticated Users and Guests, but no longer includes members of the Anonymous group.

- **Simple sharing.** By default, on Windows XP Professional systems that are not connected to a domain, all attempts to log on from across the network will be forced to use the Guest account. In addition, on computers that are using the simple sharing security model, the **Security Properties** dialog box is replaced by a simplified **Shared Documents Properties** dialog box.

- **Administrative ownership.** In Windows NT 4.0 and Windows 2000, all resources such as files and folders that are created by a member of the Administrators group belong to the group as a whole. In Windows XP Professional, these resources by default belong to the individual who creates them.

- **Encrypting File System (EFS) recovery agent.** In a Windows 2000 environment, if you attempt to configure an EFS recovery policy with no recovery agent certificates, EFS is automatically disabled. In a Windows XP Professional environment, the same action enables users to encrypt files without a Data Recovery Agent (DRA). In an environment with computers running both Microsoft® Windows® XP and Windows 2000, an empty EFS recovery policy turns off EFS on Windows 2000–based computers, but eliminates the requirement for a DRA only on Windows XP Professional–based computers.

- **Permissions for installing printers.** In order to install a local printer in Windows XP Professional, you must belong to the Power Users or Administrators group and have the Load/Unload Device Driver privilege. Administrators have this privilege by default, but it must be granted to Power Users.

- **Blank password restriction.** To protect users who do not password-protect their accounts, Windows XP Professional accounts without passwords can only be used to log on at the physical computer console.

The following are among the new security related features in Windows XP Professional:

- **Restricted software policy.** New security policy options allow you to prevent certain software applications from running based on a file path, Internet zone, certificate, or hashed file path.

- **Fast user switching.** On computers running Windows XP Professional that are not connected to a domain, users can switch from one user account to another without logging off or closing their applications.

- **Stored user names and passwords.** This utility provides secure storage for user names and credentials needed to access network or Internet resources.

- **New service accounts.** Windows XP Professional includes two new service accounts, LocalService and NetworkService, to enable graduated levels of permissions on services. Services can run as LocalService on the local computer, as NetworkService on the network, or as part of the Local System. Any service not running as one of the three built-in service accounts must have its own account.

- **Password Reset Wizard.** This wizard makes it possible for users to create a secure reset disk, which they can use at a later date in case they forget the password for their local account.

For more information about these features and changes, see the applicable discussions in this chapter, and see "Authorization and Access Control" and "Encrypting File System" in this book.

Credentials and Validation

The authentication process has two fundamental parts—credentials and validation.

Credentials   Credentials assert the identity of the applicant. A validating agent either confirms or denies the validity of the credentials, determining the level of trust granted the applicant. At an international border, for example, a passport issued by a recognized national government would be a traveler's credentials, and a crossing guard representing the government of the country/region one attempts to enter would be the validating agent. Typically, a passport is considered a strong guarantee of a bearer's identity. On the other hand, a business card is another kind of a credential—or proof of identity—that is validated with much less rigor.

In Windows 2000 and Windows XP Professional, a user's credentials can be supplied by a password, a Kerberos ticket, or a smart card if the computer is equipped to handle a smart card. For more information about smart cards, see "Smart Cards" later in this chapter.

Validation   Validation in Windows is performed by a protected subsystem called the *Local Security Authority* (LSA), which maintains information about all aspects of local operating system security. In addition to providing interactive user authentication services, the LSA does the following:

- Manages local security policy.

- Manages audit policy and settings.

- Generates tokens that contain user and group information as well as information about the security permissions for the user.

The LSA validates your identity based on which entity issued your account. If it was issued by:

- **LSA.** The LSA can validate your information by checking its own Security Accounts Manager (SAM) database. Any workstation or member server can store local user accounts and information about local groups. However, these accounts can only be used for accessing that workstation or computer.

- **Security authority for the local domain or for a trusted domain.** The LSA contacts the entity that issued your account and asks it to verify that the account is valid and that you are the account holder.

Security Principals

In Windows XP Professional, any user, group, or computer that can initiate action is *a security principal*. Security principals have accounts, which can be local to a computer or they can be domain-based. A local Security Accounts Manager (SAM) database manages local accounts on the computer. A domain-based SAM manages accounts in a Windows NT 4.0 domain. Active Directory manages domain accounts in Active Directory domains.

For example, Windows XP Professional computers participate in a network domain by communicating with a domain controller even when no human user is logged on. To initiate communications, the computer must have an active account in the domain. Before accepting communications from the computer, the LSA on the domain controller authenticates the computer's identity and then defines the computer's security context just as it would for a human security principal. This security context defines the identity and capabilities of a user or service on a particular computer or a user, service, or computer on a network. For example, it defines the resources (such as a file share or printer) that can be accessed and the actions (such as Read, Write, or Modify) that can be performed by a user, computer, or service on that resource.

The security context of a user or computer can vary from one computer to another, such as when a user logs on to a server or a workstation other than the user's own primary workstation. It can also vary from one session to another, such as when an administrator modifies the user's rights and permissions. In addition, the security context is usually different when a user or computer is operating on a standalone basis, in a mixed network domain, or as part of an Active Directory domain. For more information about security principals and how the security context is created, see "Authorization and Access Control" in this book.

About Services

Even though most Windows applications run in the security context of the user who starts them, this is not true of services. Many Windows services, such as network and printing services, are launched by the service controller when you start your computer. Services continue to run after the last human user logs off. Services have to log on to accounts to access domain resources just as human users and Windows XP Professional–based computers do.

> **Note** Services normally run in security contexts known as Local System, Network Service, or Local Service.

Before starting a service, the service controller logs on to the account designated for the service and presents the service's credentials for authentication by the LSA. For example, when a Windows XP Professional computer joins a domain, the messenger service on the computer connects to a domain controller and opens a secure channel to it. To obtain an authenticated connection, messenger must have credentials that the remote computer's LSA trusts. LSA uses the credentials for the local computer's domain account, as do all other services running in the security context of the Local System.

Security Identifiers

The rights and permissions for a user, computer, or group are determined by access control lists (ACLs), contain security identifiers (SIDs) for a user, computer, or group. A security identifier (SID) is a unique value that identifies a user, group, or computer account within an enterprise. Every account is issued a SID when it is created. Access control mechanisms in Windows XP Professional identify security principals by SID instead of by name. Thus, even if the name of a security principal changes, the SID remains the same.

In addition to your own unique SID, you are identified by the SIDs of the groups to which you belong. This information is stored in an access token, which encapsulates all data that relates to your identity and security context during a given session.

Access Tokens   An access token is recreated every time a security principal logs on, and contains the following information:

- The SID for the user's account.

- A list of SIDs for security groups that include the user and the privileges held on the local computer by the user and the user's security groups. This list includes SIDs both for domain-based security groups, if the user is a member of a domain, and for local security groups.

- The SID of the user or security group that becomes the default owner of any object that the user creates or takes ownership of.

- The SID for the user's primary group.

- The default DACLs that the operating system applies to objects created by the user if no other access control information is available.

- The source, such as the Session Manager or LAN Manager, that caused the access token to be created.

- A value indicating whether the access token is a *primary token* (which represents the security context of a process) or *impersonation token*, which is an access token that a thread within a service process can use to temporarily adopt a different security context, such as the security context for a client of the service.

- A value that indicates to what extent a service can adopt the security context of a client represented by this access token.

- Statistics about the access token that are used internally by the operating system.

- An optional list of SIDs added to an access token by a process to restrict use of the token.

- A session ID that indicates whether the token is associated with a Terminal Services client session. (The session ID also makes fast user switching possible.)

A copy of the access token is attached to every thread and process that the user runs. The security reference monitor (SRM) then compares the security IDs in the token with the security IDs for every file, folder, printer, or application that the user attempts to access. In this way, the access token provides a security context for the security principal's actions on the computer.

For more information about ACLs and SIDs, see "Authorization and Access Control" in this book.

Security Groups

Organizing users and other objects into groups simplifies access administration. Security groups can be described according to their scope (such as Global or Universal) or according to their purpose, rights, and role (such as the Everyone, Administrators, Power Users, or Users groups).

Using Microsoft® Windows® 2000 Server and Windows XP Professional security groups, you can assign the same security permissions to many users. This ensures consistent security permissions across all members of a group. Using security groups to assign permissions means that access control of resources remains constant and easy to manage and audit. By adding and removing users who require access from the appropriate security groups as needed, you can minimize the frequency of changes to ACLs.

Types of Logon

There are four types of logon processes in Windows 2000 Server and Windows XP Professional:

- **Interactive.** Logs on to a local computer to which you have direct physical access. Terminal Services and Remote Desktop logon processes are interactive even though they take place remotely.

- **Network.** Accesses a system that is running Windows NT 4.0, Windows 2000, or Windows XP Professional across the network from the computer where you logged on. In this case, the LSA on your workstation will attempt to establish your identity with the LSA on a remote computer by using the credentials that were used during your initial interactive network logon process.

- **Service.** When a Win32®-based service starts up, it logs on to the local computer using the credentials of a local or domain user account or the LocalSystem account. A service running in the security context of the LocalSystem account on a Microsoft® Windows® 2000 domain controller would have unrestricted access to Active Directory™. On the other hand, a service running in the security context of a local user account would have no access to network resources.

- **Batch.** A batch logon is rarely used in the Windows operating system because it is usually reserved for applications that run as batch jobs, such as bank account reconciliation and big print spools. The account that is logging on must have the logon as a batch job privilege. If it does not, the account will fail to log on.

An interactive logon process confirms the user's identification to either a domain account or a local computer. This process differs, depending on whether the user account is local to the computer or resides in Active Directory:

- **Domain account.** A user logs on to the network with a password or smart card, using credentials stored in Active Directory. By using a domain account to log on, an authorized user can access resources in the domain and any trusting domains.

- **Local user account.** A user logs on to a local computer by using credentials stored in the SAM database. Any workstation or member server can store local user accounts, but those accounts can only be used to access that local computer.

Windows XP Professional can use a user principal name (UPN) to identify users in an interactive logon process.

If you want to log on to a Windows 2000 domain, and **Logon domain** does not appear in the dialog box, click the **Options** button to open an expanded dialog box. Or, type your user name and the Windows 2000 domain name as follows:

- Your user principal name prefix (your user name) and your user principal name suffix (your Windows 2000 domain name), joined by the "@" character. For example, user@sales.westcoast.microsoft.

Tip The suffix in the preceding example is a fully qualified DNS domain name. An administrator might create an alternative suffix to simplify the logon process. For example, by creating a user principal name suffix of "microsoft," the same user can log on by using the simpler address, user@microsoft.com.

Components Used in Interactive Logon

The interactive logon process in Windows XP Professional involves a number of components and a sequence of events that are not visible to the user. The logon process involves the following components, whose relationship to each other is illustrated in Figure 15-1.

- **Winlogon.** A secure process, responsible for managing the security-related user interactions that coordinate the logon and logoff processes and start the user's shell.

- **Microsoft Graphical Identification and Authentication (MSGINA).** A DLL that is called by Winlogon to obtain a user's account name and password and pass it back to Winlogon. MSGINA displays the standard logon dialog box.

> **Note**   Some organizations create their own GINAs or use third-party GINAs.

- **Local Security Authority (LSA).** The entity that receives the user name and password from Winlogon and determines whether the logon process is to be authenticated on the local computer or across the network.

- **Security Account Manager (SAM).** The protected subsystem that manages user and group account information. If the logon process is to be authenticated locally, the SAM database on the local computer is used to verify the user's credentials. If the logon process is to be authenticated on a Windows NT 4.0 domain controller, the SAM database on the domain controller is used.

- **Net Logon service.** The service used, together with the NTLM protocol, to query the SAM on a domain controller to validate the user's credentials.

- **Kerberos Key Distribution Center (KDC) service.** The service used, together with the Kerberos authentication protocol, to authenticate logon requests to Active Directory.

- **Active Directory.** The directory service in Windows 2000 and later. If the logon process is to be authenticated on a Windows 2000 domain controller, the KDC service queries Active Directory to verify the user's credentials.

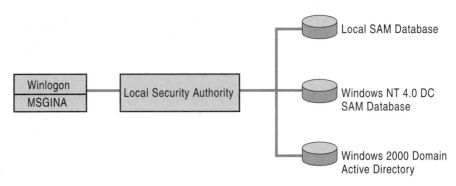

Figure 15-1   Components involved in interactive logon

Using RunAs to Start a Program

Administrators require a greater range of permissions than other users to perform their tasks, such as accessing files, installing and running applications, or modifying systems. However, running Windows XP Professional all the time as an administrator or a member of an administrative group makes the network more vulnerable to viruses, such as the Trojan horse, and other security risks. To reduce risk, it is recommended that you perform non-administrative tasks by using accounts that have only Users or Power Users rights and use your Administrator account only when you perform administrative tasks.

You can use administrative rights and privileges even while logged on as a member of the Users or Power Users group. The **RunAs** program and the **RunAs Service** let you log on by using one security context and then, within the initial logon session, authenticate and use a second account. Figure 15-2 illustrates the **RunAs** dialog box.

Figure 15-2   RunAs dialog box

The **RunAs Service** logs on an account with expanded permissions. For example, when you log on as a member of the Users group, you can perform routine tasks such as running programs and visiting Internet sites without exposing your computer to unnecessary risk. As a member of the Power Users group, you can perform routine tasks and install programs, add printers, and use most Control Panel items. Then, when you use the **RunAs** program to log on as an administrator, you can start a program in the Administrators group security context. You can use the **RunAs** program to start any program, program shortcut, saved MMC console, or Control Panel item if the following conditions exist:

■ You provide the appropriate user account and password information.

■ The user account can log on to the computer.

■ The program, MMC snap-in, or Control Panel item is available on the system and to the user account.

> **Note**   Some applications are started indirectly by Windows XP Professional and therefore cannot be started by the **RunAs** program.

To use RunAs to start a program as an administrator

1. In Windows Explorer, click the program you want to open, such as an MMC console or Control Panel.

2. Press SHIFT, right-click the program, tool, or item, and then click **Run As**.

3. In the **Run As** dialog box, click **The following user**.

4. In the **User name** and **Password** boxes, type the user name and password for the administrator account you want to use.

5. In the **Domain** box, do one of the following:

   ■ If you want to use the local administrator account on your computer, type the name of your computer.
   – or –

   ■ If you want to use the domain administrator account from the domain your computer is a member of or any trusted domain on your computer, type the name of the domain.

You can perform a secondary logon from a command prompt by using the following syntax:

```
runas /user: domain_name\administrator_account program name
```

If the Administrator account in the microsoft.com domain is named Administrator, you can use the following command to start MMC as Administrator:

```
runas /user:microsoft\administrator mmc
```

If you attempt to start a program, an MMC console, or a Control Panel item from a network location by using the **RunAs** dialog box or command, it might fail if the credentials used to connect to the network share are different from the credentials used to start the program.

> **Note**   If the **RunAs** program fails, the **RunAs Service** might not be running. You can set the **RunAs Service** to start when the system starts by using the Services MMC snap-in.

Authentication Protocols

Windows 2000 Server and Windows XP Professional support several protocols for verifying the identity of users who claim to have accounts on the system. These include protocols for authenticating dial-up connections and protocols for authenticating external users who try to connect to the network over the Internet. However, the following authentication protocols are the primary choices for network authentication between Windows NT 4.0, Windows 2000, and Windows 2000 Server domains, and Windows XP Professional–based clients:

- **Kerberos V5 protocol.** The default authentication protocol for Windows 2000 and Windows XP Professional.

- **NTLM protocol.** The default authentication protocol in Windows NT 4.0.

Even though the Kerberos V5 authentication protocol is the default for Windows 2000 Server and Windows XP Professional, both the network domain controllers and the client computers must be running Windows 2000 or Windows XP Professional for Kerberos authentication to be used. The alternative NTLM protocol is used for authentication if the following conditions exist:

- Computers running Microsoft® Windows® 3.11, Microsoft® Windows® 95, Microsoft® Windows® 98, or Windows NT 4.0 use the NTLM protocol for network authentication in Windows 2000 domains.

- Computers running Windows 2000 Professional or later or Microsoft® Windows® 2000 Server or later use the NTLM protocol to authenticate to servers running Windows NT 4.0.

- Computers running Windows 2000 Professional or later and Windows 2000 Server or later use the NTLM protocol to authenticate when they are not participating in a domain. That is, when they operate as stand-alone computers or as part of a workgroup.

Protocol Selection

The following processes determine whether the Kerberos or NTLM protocol is used to complete the network authentication process:

1. After the user name and password are entered, the LSA passes this information to the *Security Support Provider Interface* (*SSPI*), an interface that communicates with both the Kerberos and NTLM services.

> **Tip**   SSPI also allows developers to write "security-aware" applications whether the Kerberos or NTLM protocol is used.

2. SSPI passes the user name and password to the Kerberos Security Support Provider (SSP), which exchanges messages directly with the domain's Kerberos Key Distribution Center (KDC). The Kerberos SSP determines whether the target computer name is the local computer or the domain name.

3. If the domain name is referenced, and the KDC recognizes the user name, the Kerberos authentication process proceeds.

4. If the user name is not recognized, the KDC passes an internal error message to the SSPI. If a KDC cannot be found, the following message (transparent to the user) is passed back to the LSA:
   "No logon server available."

5. The internal error message triggers the process to start over again. MSGINA passes the information to LSA again, and then LSA passes the information back to SSPI.

6. SSPI then passes the user name and password to the NTLM driver, MSV1_0 SSP. MSV1_0 then uses the Net Logon service to complete the NTLM authentication process.

If both the Kerberos and NTLM protocols fail to authenticate the user account, the following error message appears, and the user can try to log on again:

```
"The system could not log you on. Make sure your User name and domain are correct,
then type you password again. Letters in passwords must be typed using the correct
case. Make sure that Caps Lock is not accidentally on."
```

> **Note** The same error message appears whether the password is typed incorrectly or the user name is not in the local SAM database. This is done to make it more difficult for an intruder to determine the reason that the logon attempt failed.

NTLM

The NTLM protocol authenticates users and computers based on a challenge/response mechanism. When the NTLM protocol is used, a resource server must contact a domain authentication service on the domain controller for the computer or user's account domain to verify its identity whenever a new access token is needed.

> **Note** In the absence of a domain, the NTLM protocol can also be used for peer-to-peer authentication.

NTLM authentication in Windows 2000 and Windows XP Professional supports the following three methods of challenge/response authentication:

- **LAN Manager (LM).** The least secure form of challenge/response authentication that is supported by Windows XP Professional, (but more secure than cleartext). LM is available so that computers running Windows XP Professional can connect to file shares on computers running Microsoft® Windows® for Workgroups, Windows 95, or Windows 98.

- **NTLM version 1.** A more secure form of challenge/response authentication than LM. It is available so that computers running Windows XP Professional can connect to servers in a Windows NT domain that has at least one domain controller running Windows NT 4.0 Service Pack 3 or earlier.

- **NTLM version 2.** The most secure form of challenge/response authentication that is supported by Windows XP Professional. It is used when computers running Windows XP Professional connect to servers in a Windows NT domain where all domain controllers are upgraded to Windows NT 4.0 Service Pack 4 or later. It is also used when computers running Windows 2000 or

Windows XP Professional connect to servers running Windows NT in a Windows 2000 domain. In addition, computers running Windows 95 or Windows 98 can use this form of challenge/response authentication if the Directory Service Client Pack has been installed.

By default, all three challenge/response mechanisms are enabled so that clients running Microsoft® Windows® for Workgroups, Windows 95, or Windows 98 can access network resources. You can disable authentication that uses weaker variants by setting the LAN Manager authentication level security option in Local Security Policy\Computer Configuration\Windows Settings\Local Policies\Security Options or in the appropriate security template. If you do so, however, computers that rely on the weaker variants for authentication might not be able to access network resources.

For more information about configuring the LAN Manager authentication level, see "Account Policies" later in this chapter.

Interactive Logon with NTLM

The following process, shown in Figure 15-3, is essentially the same on any version of NTLM you use:

1. The user presses CTRL+ALT+DEL, which is the *Secure Attention Sequence* (*SAS*) on computers that have a standard Windows XP Professional configuration. Winlogon calls a replaceable *Graphical Identification and Authentication* (*GINA*) dynamic-link library (DLL) to display a logon user interface.

2. After the user enters a user name and password, Winlogon sends the information to the LSA.

3. If the user's account is local to the computer, the LSA uses the MSV1_0 authentication package to compare the user's logon information with data in the computer's SAM database. If the user is not local to the computer, the LSA validates the user's credentials by using the MSV1_0 authentication package and Net Logon service to query the SAM on a Windows NT domain controller.

4. If the user's logon name and password are valid, the SAM communicates this information back to the LSA, along with the user's security identifier (SID) and the SIDs that apply to any groups that the user belongs to. The LSA uses this information to create an access token that includes the user's SIDs.

5. Winlogon starts the user's shell with the token attached.

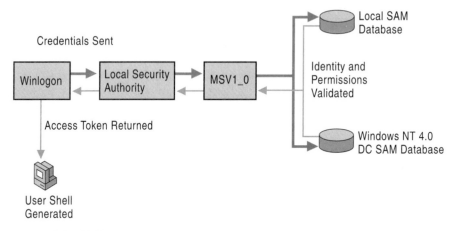

Figure 15-3   NTLM logon process

Kerberos V5 Authentication Protocol

The Kerberos V5 protocol provides a means for mutual authentication between a client, such as a user, computer, or service, and a server. This is a more efficient means for servers to authenticate clients, even in the largest and most complex network environments. The Kerberos protocol is based on the assumption that initial transactions between clients and servers take place on an open network—an environment in which an unauthorized user can pose as either a client or a server and intercept or tamper with communication between authorized clients and servers. Kerberos V5 authentication also provides secure and efficient authentication for complex networks of clients and resources.

The Kerberos V5 protocol uses secret key encryption to protect logon credentials that travel across the network. The same key can then be used to decrypt these credentials on the receiving end. This decryption and the subsequent steps are performed by the Kerberos Key Distribution Center (KDC), which runs on every domain controller as part of Active Directory.

An *authenticator*—a piece of information such as a time stamp that is different each time it is generated—is included with the encrypted login credentials to verify that previous authentication credentials are not being reused. A new authenticator is generated and incorporated with the KDC's encrypted response to the client to confirm that the original message was received and accepted. If the initial logon credentials and the authenticator are accepted, the KDC issues a ticket-granting ticket (TGT) that is used by the LSA to get service tickets. These service tickets can then be used to access network resources without having to re-authenticate the client as long as the service ticket remains valid. These tickets contain encrypted data that confirms the user's identity to the requested service. Except for entering an initial password or smart-card credentials, the authentication process is transparent to the user.

Interactive Logons Using Kerberos Authentication

The Kerberos authentication process was designed to be more secure and scalable across large, diverse networks than NTLM authentication. The Kerberos authentication process includes the following actions:

1. The user presses CTRL+ALT+DEL, the SAS on computers that have a standard Windows XP Professional configuration. Winlogon calls a replaceable Graphical Identification and Authentication (GINA) dynamic-link library (DLL) to display a logon user interface.

2. After the user enters a user name and password, Winlogon sends the information to the LSA.

3. When the logon request reaches the LSA, it passes the request to the Kerberos authentication package. The client sends an initial authentication request (AS_REQ), which includes the user's credentials and an encrypted timestamp to the KDC. This is a request for authentication and a TGT.

Note   The logon request uses the principal name of krbtgt@ *domain_name*, where *domain_name* is the name of the domain in which the user account is located. The first domain controller in the domain generates the krbtgt@ *domain_name* account.

4. The KDC uses the secret key to decrypt the timestamp and issues a TGT to the client. This TGT (AS_REP) contains a session key, the name of the user to whom the session key was issued, the maximum lifetime of the ticket, and any additional data fields or settings that might be required. The AS_REP is encrypted in the user's key and returned to the user. The ticket is encrypted in the KDC's key and enclosed in the AS_REP. The authorization data portion of the TGT contains the SID for the user account and SIDs for any global and universal groups to which the user belongs.

Note   The SIDs are returned to the LSA for inclusion in the user's access token. The maximum lifetime of a ticket is defined by the domain policy. If a ticket expires during an active session, the client requests a new ticket.

5. When the user attempts to access a resource, the client system uses the TGT to request a service ticket (TGS_REQ) from the Kerberos ticket-granting service on the domain controller (see Figure 15-4). The TGS then issues a service

ticket (TGS_REP) to the client. This service ticket is encrypted using the server's secret key. The SIDs are copied by the Kerberos service from the TGT into all subsequent service tickets obtained from the Kerberos service.

> **Note** This TGS session uses a separate session key than the earlier TGT transaction.

6. The client presents this service ticket directly to the requested network service. The service ticket proves both the user's identity and permissions to the service, and the service's identity to the user.

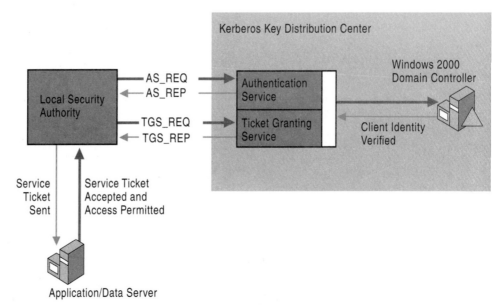

Figure 15-4 Logon process using the Kerberos V5 authentication protocol

For more information about Kerberos V5 authentication, see "Logon and Authentication" in the *Distributed Systems Guide*. For more information about configuring the Kerberos V5 authentication service, see "Account Policies" later in this chapter.

Kerberos Ticket Cache

Windows stores tickets and keys obtained from the KDC in a *credentials cache*, an area of memory protected by the LSA. Only processes running in the LSA's security context have access to the cache. Its memory is never paged to disk. All tickets and keys are stored per user logon session, which means that they are destroyed when a security principal logs off or the system is turned off.

The credentials cache is managed by the Kerberos SSP, which runs in the LSA's security context. Whenever tickets and keys must be obtained or renewed, the LSA calls the Kerberos SSP to accomplish the task.

The credentials cache is also used to store a copy of an interactive user's password-derived key. If the user's TGT expires during a logon session, the Kerberos SSP uses its copy of the key to obtain a new TGT without interrupting the user's logon session. The key is not stored permanently on the computer, and the local copy in the credentials cache is destroyed when the credentials cache is flushed.

Password-derived keys for services and computers are handled differently. They are stored in a secure area of the computer's registry just as they are in Windows NT. Password-derived keys for user accounts on the local system, which are used only for access to computers in stand-alone mode, are also stored in the registry. These keys are never used for network access.

Kerberos Interoperability

The Windows 2000 implementation of the Kerberos V5 protocol supports Internet Engineering Task Force (IETF) standard RFC 1510 to help ensure interoperability with other vendors' implementations of Kerberos V5 authentication. This interoperability allows single sign-on to be provided within large mixed environments.

Applications or other operating systems based on the Generic Security Service Application Program Interface (GSSAPI) can obtain service tickets from a Windows 2000 Server domain. A Windows 2000 Professional, Windows 2000 Server, or Windows XP Professional client likewise can authenticate to a third-party Kerberos KDC for authentication.

A Kerberos realm is not a Windows domain. As a result, the computer running Windows XP must be configured as a member of a workgroup and it must be configured to locate the Kerberos realm by its name. A Windows XP Professional client that uses a non-Windows Kerberos V5 realm must be configured to locate the realm, available KDC servers, and available Kerberos password servers.

> **Note**   Kerberos V5 configuration tools are available on the Windows distribution media in the Support folder.

You can use the command-line tool Ksetup to configure Windows XP Professional clients to use a third-party Kerberos V5 KDC.

To enable user logon to a non-Windows Kerberos realm

1. In the **Run** dialog box, type **cmd**, and then click **OK**.

2. At the command line, type:

```
ksetup /addkdc REALM.MYDOMAIN.COM kdc.realm.mydomain.com
ksetup /addkdc REALM.MYDOMAIN.COM kdc-master.realm.mydomain.com
```

This configures the computer to use two KDCs for the realm REALM.*MYDOMAIN*.COM.

3. If the Kerberos realm supports the Kerberos change password protocol, then the kpasswd servers can be configured. This will allow the user to change their password after they press CTRL+ALT+DEL. To configure the kpasswd server, at the command line, type:

```
ksetup /addkpasswd REALM.MYDOMAIN.COM kdc-master.realm.mydomain.com
```

Note   Windows XP can also locate the KDC and kpasswd servers based on the DNS SRV records if no KDCs or kpasswd entries exist for the configured realm.

4. The computer needs to have a local account that is authorized with the interactive logon right to the appropriate Kerberos principal. To map a local account with the username "alice," at the command line, type:

```
ksetup /mapuser alice@REALM.MYDOMAIN.COM username
```

This maps the local account "alice" to the Kerberos principal "alice@REALM.*MYDOMAIN*.COM". When the user "alice@REALM.*MYDO-MAIN*.COM" logs on to the computer, the local identity "alice" is used for access control and to locate a user profile.

Note   It is best not to trust all users to access your computer. If no mapping exists for a particular user, they cannot log on.

5. If you want to grant guest access to any users, an explicit mapping for the guest account needs to be set up and the guest account must be enabled. To map the guest account, at the command line, type:

```
ksetup /mapuser * guest
```

6. Restart the computer in order to implement your changes.

You might also want to enable Windows XP Professional users to access services by presenting the Kerberos credentials associated with their mapped identities.

To enable Kerberos authentication for services

1. In the **Run** dialog box, type **cmd,** and then click **OK.**

2. Because a Kerberos realm is not a Windows domain, the computer running Windows XP Professional must be configured as a member of a workgroup and the computer configured to locate the Kerberos realm by its name. To do this, at the command line, type:

   ```
   ksetup /addkdc REALM.MYDOMAIN.COM kdc.realm.mydomain.com
   ksetup /addkdc REALM.MYDOMAIN.COM kdc-master.realm.mydomain.com
   ```

   This configures the computer to use two KDCs for the realm REALM.*MYDOMAIN*.COM configuration.

3. Configure the computer to authenticate to the realm in which the computer's host service principal was created. To accomplish this, create a new KDC entry by typing:

   ```
   ksetup /setrealm REALM.MYDOMAIN.COM
   ```

4. Configure the computer's password so that it corresponds to the host service principal created for the computer in the Kerberos realm. At the command line, type:

   ```
   ksetup /setmachpassword the-password
   ```

5. To set up mappings for users to control explicit access, at the command line, type:

   ```
   ksetup /mapuser alice@REALM.MYDOMAIN.COM alice
   ```

   This will map the Kerberos principal "alice@REALM.*MYDOMAIN*.COM" to the local account "alice". You can use the local account "alice" on access control lists on resources or local groups on the computer to grant or deny access to specific resources.

   Note   If no mapping exists for a Kerberos principal, the user will be anonymous and will be able to access any resource for which anonymous access is allowed.

6. Restart the computer.

Managing Credentials

Authentication is an organization's first defense against malicious intruders. As a result, many organizations have implemented stringent validation criteria, including strong passwords and smart cards.

Passwords can be the weakest link in a computer security scheme. Network passwords that once took weeks to break can now be broken in hours. However, it still can take months to crack a strong password. A strong password that is hard to break has the following characteristics:

- Contains at least six characters.

- Contains characters from each of the following three groups:

    - Uppercase and lowercase letters (A, a, B, b, C, c, and so on)

    - Numerals

    - Symbols (characters that are not defined as letters or numerals, such as !, @, #, and so on)

- Contains at least one symbol character in the second through sixth positions.

- Is significantly different from prior passwords.

- Does not contain your name or user name.

- Is not a common word or name.

Windows XP Professional passwords can have up to 127 characters. However, if you use Windows XP Professional on a network that also has computers using Windows 95 or Windows 98, consider using passwords no longer than 14 characters. If your password is longer, you might not be able to log on to your network from those computers.

Warning   Require users to change passwords frequently. Although a strong password can help protect against intruders, given enough time, automated password-cracking tools can crack any password. Changing passwords can minimize the risk of an intruder determining a password. It also minimizes potential damage when a password is compromised without the user's knowledge.

Blank Password Restrictions

By default, Windows XP Professional does not require users with local accounts, including administrators, to have passwords. Users can choose to set passwords on their own accounts, or administrators can assign passwords to users on a local computer.

To protect users who do not password-protect their accounts, Windows XP Professional accounts without passwords can only be used to log on at the physical computer console. By default, accounts with blank passwords can no longer be used to log on to the computer remotely over the network, or for any other logon activity *except* at the main physical console logon screen. For example, you cannot use the secondary logon service (RunAs) to start a program as a local user with a blank password.

> **Caution**   If your computer is not in a physically secured location, it is recommended that you assign passwords to all local user accounts. Failure to do so allows anyone with physical access to the computer to log on using an account that does not have a password. This is especially important for portable computers, which should always have strong passwords on all local user accounts.

Assigning a password to a local account removes the restriction that prevents logging on over a network and permits that account to access any resources it is authorized to access, even over a network connection.

> **Note**   This restriction does not apply to domain accounts. It also does not apply to the local Guest account. If the guest account is enabled and has a blank password, it will be permitted to log on and access any resource authorized for access by the Guest account. For more information about managing network logons using the Guest account, see "Authorization and Access Control" in this book.

If you want to disable the restriction against logging on to the network without a password, you can do so through Local Security Policy. The policy setting that controls blank password restriction can be modified using the Local Security Policy or Group Policy MMC snap-ins. You can use either tool to find this policy option at **Security Settings\Local Policies\Security Options**. The name of the policy is **Accounts: Limit local account use of blank passwords to console logon only**. It is enabled by default.

> **Caution**   Disabling this policy setting might degrade the security of your Windows XP Professional computer. Before disabling this policy setting, ensure that all local accounts have strong passwords, or that the computer is in a secure and trusted environment where it will not be subject to attack.

Password Management

You can use **User Accounts** in Control Panel or the **Local Users and Groups** MMC snap-in to add and remove local user accounts, add and remove users from groups, and work with passwords. When the Windows XP Professional–based computer is connected to a Windows NT or Windows 2000 Server domain, you can use **Local Users and Groups** to add and remove domain user accounts to local groups. When the Windows XP Professional–based computer is not connected to a domain, you can use **User Accounts** to add and remove local user accounts and assign users to a local group.

To change the password for a user

1. In **Control Panel**, open **User Accounts**. In the **User Accounts** dialog box, click the user's name, and then click **Reset Password**.

2. Enter the new password twice in the **Reset Password** dialog box.

3. If desired, type in a word or phrase in the box provided for password hints.

To perform advanced password-related tasks

1. In the **Local Users and Groups** MMC snap-in, double-click the **Users** folder.

2. Select and right-click the name of the user who has a local account that you want to manage, and then select **Properties**.

3. On the user's **Properties** page, select one or more of the following options:

    ■ **User must change password at next logon**.

    ■ **User cannot change password**.

    ■ **Password never expires**.

    ■ **Account is disabled**.

    ■ **Account is locked out**.

Group Policy

You can use Group Policy to perform more advanced password management tasks, such as setting a minimum password length or the interval between password changes. When you review your password security policies, establish your Account Lockout Policy at the same time. This policy locks a user account after a certain number of incorrect passwords are tried in succession. For more information about password-related policy options, see "Account Policies" later in this chapter.

> **Note**   You must log on as an administrator or be a member of the Administrators group to add and delete user accounts, assign users to a local group, and set or change user passwords.

Stored User Names and Passwords

It is not always desirable to use one set of credentials for access to different resources. For example, when an administrator accesses a remote server, you might want him or her to use administrative rather than user credentials. Similarly, if a user will be accessing external resources such as a bank account, you might prefer that he or she use credentials that are different than their network username and password.

Stored User Names and Passwords in Control Panel simplifies the management and use of multiple sets of logon credentials, including X.509 certificates used with smart cards and Passport credentials. The credentials—part of the user's profile—are stored until needed. This can increase security on a per-resource basis by ensuring that if one password is compromised it does not compromise all security.

> **Note**   Microsoft Passport provides a single name, password, and wallet that can be used on multiple Web sites.

After a user logs on and attempts to access additional password-protected resources, such as a share on a server, and if the user's default logon credentials are not sufficient to gain access, then **Stored User Names and Passwords** is queried. If alternate credentials with the correct logon information have been saved in **Stored User Names and Passwords**, these credentials are used to gain access. Otherwise, the user is prompted to supply new credentials, which can then be saved for reuse, either later in the logon session or during a subsequent session.

Several restrictions apply:

- If **Stored User Names and Passwords** contains invalid or incorrect credentials for a specific resource, access to the resource will be denied, and the **Stored User Names and Passwords** dialog box will not appear.

■ **Stored User Names and Passwords** stores credentials only for NTLM, Kerberos, Passport, and SSL authentication. Microsoft® Internet Explorer maintains its own cache for basic authentication.

These credentials become an encrypted part of a user's local profile in the \Documents and Settings\Username\Application Data\Microsoft\Credentials directory. As a result, these credentials can roam with the user if the user's network policy supports Roaming Profiles. However, if you have copies of **Stored User Names and Passwords** on two different computers and change the credentials that are associated with the resource on one of these computers, the change will not be propagated to **Stored User Names and Passwords** on the second computer.

To store a new user name and password

1. In **Control Panel**, open **User Accounts**.

2. On computers joined to a domain, click the **Advanced** tab, click **Manage Passwords**.

    – or –

    On computers not joined to a domain, click the icon that represents your user account, and then, under **Related Tasks**, click **Manage your stored passwords**.

3. Click **Add**.

4. Type the appropriate information in the spaces provided.

> **Warning** Educate your users about the importance of using strong passwords for all credentials stored in **Stored User Names and Passwords**.

To store a Passport ID

1. In **Control Panel**, open **User Accounts**.

2. On computers not joined to a domain, click the icon that represents your user account, and then, under **What do you want to change about your account?**, click **Create a Passport**.

    – or –

    On computers joined to a domain, click the **Advanced** tab, then click **.NET Passport Wizard**.

3. Type the appropriate information in the spaces provided.

4. In the **When accessing** box, type *.passport.com.

> **Warning**   Some credentials are used infrequently. Others might be for extremely sensitive resources that the user wants to protect more carefully. When appropriate, have users store credentials for "This logon session only." Credentials for a single logon session are typically stored by selecting the appropriate check box in the **User Names and Password** dialog box.

Some administrators might not feel comfortable with allowing users to store network credentials for later use. This might be due to concern about reduced security, or a potential increase in the number of account lockouts when credentials stored in **User Names and Passwords** expire. As a result, a Group Policy setting has been introduced to allow you to limit use of **Stored User Names and Passwords**.

To limit use of Stored User Names and Passwords

1. In the **Group Policy** MMC snap-in, double-click the **Security Options** folder (Computer Configuration\Windows Settings\Security Settings\Local Policies\ Security Options).

2. Right-click **Network access: Do not allow storage of credentials or .NET Passports for network authentication.**

3. Click **Enabled**, and then click **OK**.

Backing Up and Restoring Passwords

Forgetting passwords is one of the most common problems users—including administrators—encounter on local computers. To prevent users from being locked out of their computers, a **Password Reset Wizard** has been added to Windows XP Professional. The wizard allows users to create a backup disk, which they can use later to reset their password if they forget their Windows password.

> **Note**   The ability to back up and restore passwords applies only to local user accounts. It does not apply to network-based passwords and accounts. Also, users can back up passwords only for accounts that they are logged on to. Administrators can create password backups only for their own accounts, not for other users.

The backup disk does not actually store the user's password—that would pose a security risk. Instead, the disk contains a private and public key pair that the backup process generates. A file containing the user's password encrypted with the public key is stored on the computer, but is separate from the Security Accounts Manager database.

The following procedure describes the password backup process, which can be performed when a password is set or at any time the user chooses.

To back up a password

1. In **Control Panel**, click **User Accounts**, and then select your own account.

2. In the **Related Tasks** pane, click **Create a Password Reset Disk** to launch the **Password Reset Wizard**, and then click **Next**.

> **Note** If the computer is joined to a domain, the domain-based version of User Accounts is used even when the user logs on by using a local account. To access the Password Reset Wizard in this situation, press CTRL-ALT-DEL, click **Backup**, and then click **Next**.

3. Insert removable media into the drive where the backup key will be stored, and then click **Next**.

> **Note** The backup can be stored only to removable media, not to the local computer.

4. In **Current User Account Password**, in the **Current user account password** box, type your existing password, and then click **Next**.

5. A progress indicator appears. During this phase:

   a. A file containing a 2048-bit public key is created on the local computer. This file is a self-signed certificate containing the SID of the user and the user's password encrypted by the public key.

   b. The certificate and the private key are written to removable media.

6. Click **Finish**.

The **Password Reset Wizard** allows users to backup their passwords without having to create a new backup disk for every password change. Every time a user changes a password, the new password is encrypted using the public key and a function of the previous encrypted password. The encrypted password is then added to a list of previous password changes in the file where the public key resides.

To restore a password, Windows XP Professional includes the **Password Reset Wizard**, which appears when the user enters an incorrect password. This wizard asks for the drive where the backup disk is located and prompts the user for a new account password. After the new password is entered, the user's private key is retrieved from the backup media, the user's profile is loaded, and the wizard attempts to decrypt the last encrypted password by using the private key. If the process succeeds, the password entered earlier in the process becomes the new password and the user is allowed to access the system. If the decryption fails, the user is informed that the reset disk is invalid and the wizard closes.

Note   You cannot reset the user password if the hard disk is reformatted or the file containing the chain of encrypted passwords is deleted.

Smart Cards

A *smart card* is an integrated circuit card (ICC) approximately the size of a credit card. You can use it to store certificates and private keys and to perform public key cryptography operations, such as authentication, digital signing, and key exchange.

A smart card enhances security as follows:

- Provides tamper-resistant storage for private keys and other forms of personal identification.

- Isolates critical security computations involving authentication, digital signatures, and key exchange from parts of the system that do not require this data.

- Enables moving credentials and other private information from one computer to another (for example, from a workplace computer to a home or remote computer.)

A smart card uses a personal identification number (PIN) instead of a password. The smart card is protected from misuse by the PIN, which the owner of the smart card selects. To use the smart card, the user inserts the card into a smart card reader attached to a computer, and then enters the PIN.

A PIN offers more protection than a standard network password. The strength of the password depends on its length, how well it is protected, and how difficult it is to guess. In contrast, a PIN never travels on the network. In addition, smart cards allow a limited number (typically three to five) of failed attempts to key in the correct PIN before the card locks itself. After the limit is reached, entering the correct PIN does not work. The user must contact a system administrator to unlock the card.

Windows 2000 supports industry-standard, Personal Computer/Smart Card (PC/SC)–compliant smart cards and Plug and Play smart card readers that conform to specifications developed by the PC/SC Workgroup. To function with Windows 2000 Server and Windows XP Professional, a smart card must conform physically and electronically to ISO 7816-1, 7816-2, and 7816-3 standards.

Smart card readers attach to standard personal computer peripheral interfaces such as RS-232, PC Card, and Universal Serial Bus (USB). Some RS-232 readers have an extra cable that plugs into the PS/2 port to draw power for the reader. However, the reader does not communicate through the PS/2 port. Readers are standard Windows devices, and they carry a security descriptor and a Plug and Play identifier. Smart card readers are controlled by standard Windows device drivers, and you can install and remove them by using the Hardware wizard.

Windows 2000 Server and Windows XP Professional include drivers for various commercially available Plug and Play smart-card readers that are certified to display the Windows-compatible logo. Some manufacturers might provide drivers for noncertified smart card readers that currently work with the Windows operating system. Nevertheless, to ensure continued support by Microsoft, it is recommended that you purchase only smart card readers that display the Windows-compatible logo.

Logging On by Using a Smart Card

Smart cards can only be used to log on to domain accounts, not local accounts. When you use a password to log on interactively to a domain account, Windows 2000 Server and Windows XP Professional use the Kerberos V5 protocol for authentication. If you use a smart card, the operating system uses Kerberos V5 authentication with X.509 v3 certificates unless the domain controller is not running Windows 2000 Server.

To initiate a typical logon session, a user must prove the user's identity to the KDC by providing information known only to the user and the KDC. The secret information is a cryptographic *shared key* derived from the user's password. A shared secret key is symmetric, which means that the same key is used for both encryption and decryption.

To support logging on by using a smart card, Windows 2000 Server implement a public key extension to the Kerberos protocol's initial authentication request. In contrast to shared secret key cryptography, public key cryptography is asymmetric; that is, two different keys are needed—one to encrypt, another to decrypt. Together, the keys needed to perform both operations make up a private/public key pair.

When a smart card is used in place of a password, a private/public key pair stored on the user's smart card is substituted for the shared secret key derived from the user's password. The private key is stored only on the smart card. The public key can be made available to anyone with whom the owner wishes to exchange confidential information.

In the public key extension to the Kerberos protocol, the client encrypts its part of the initial Authentication Service Exchange (AS Exchange) with the private key and passes the certificate to the KDC. The KDC encrypts the user's logon session key with the public half of the user's key pair. The client then decrypts the logon session key by using the private half of the key pair.

Initiating a smart card logon session involves the following process:

1. The user inserts a smart card into a card reader attached to the computer.

2. The insertion of the card signals the SAS just as pressing CTRL+ALT+DEL signals the SAS on computers configured for logging on using a password.

3. In response, Winlogon dispatches to MSGINA, which displays a modified logon dialog box. In this case, however, the user types only the personal identification number (PIN).

4. MSGINA sends the user's logon information to the LSA just as it does with a logon session using a password.

5. The LSA uses the PIN for access to the smart card, which contains the user's private key along with an X509 v3 certificate that contains the public half of the key pair.

6. The Kerberos SSP on the client computer sends the user's public key certificate to the KDC as pre-authentication data in its initial authentication request.

7. The KDC validates the certificate, extracts the public key, and then uses the public key to encrypt a logon session key. It returns the encrypted logon session key and a TGT to the client.

8. If the client owns the private half of the key pair, it can use the private key to decrypt the logon session key. Both the client and the KDC then use this logon session key in all future communications with one another.

> **Warning** All cryptographic operations that use these keys take place on the smart card.

The rest of the authentication process is the same as for a standard logon session.

For information about the types of smart cards and smart card readers supported by Windows 2000 Server and Windows XP Professional, see **Compatible Hardware and Software** in Windows XP Professional Help and Support Center.

Automating Logon

Using Windows XP Professional, you can automate the logon process by storing your password and other pertinent information in the registry. Using this feature, other users can start your computer and use the account you enable to log on automatically.

Caution   Although enabling autologon can make it more convenient to use Windows XP Professional, using this feature is a security risk. Setting a computer for autologon means that anyone who can physically obtain access to the computer can gain access to all of the computer's contents, potentially including any network or networks it is connected to. A second risk is that enabling autologon causes the password to be stored in the registry in plain text. The specific registry key that stores this value is remotely readable by the Authenticated Users group. As a result, this setting is appropriate only when the computer is physically secured, and unauthorized users are prevented from remotely accessing the registry.

You can enable autologon by using the following procedure to edit the registry:

Caution   Do not edit the registry unless you have no alternative. The registry editor bypasses standard safeguards, allowing settings that can damage your system or even require you to reinstall Windows. If you must edit the registry, back it up first and see the Registry Reference in the *Microsoft® Windows® 2000 Server Resource Kit* at http://www.microsoft.com/reskit.

To add logon information by editing the registry

1. In the **Run** dialog box, type **regedit.exe**, and then click **OK**.

2. Navigate to the registry subkey HKEY_LOCAL_MACHINE\SOFTWARE \Microsoft\Windows NT\CurrentVersion\Winlogon

3. Double-click the **DefaultUserName** entry.

4. In the **Value data** box, type your user name, and then click **OK**.

5. If the **DefaultPassword** entry does not exist, click **New** on the **Edit** menu, and then select **String Value**.

   a. In the **Name** box, type:
      DefaultPassword

   b. Double-click **DefaultPassword.**

   c. In the **Value Data** field, type your password.

6. Double-click **AutoAdminLogon**, and then enter **1** in the **Value data** box.

7. Close the registry editor.

8. Restart your computer.

   Starting the computer now causes the logon process to occur automatically.

Disabling the Welcome Screen

On computers running Windows XP Professional that are not members of a domain, the default is for users to see a Welcome screen that includes the names of all users with accounts on the computer. The user's password prompt is revealed when the user clicks his or her name. Because the names of all user accounts are made visible on this Welcome screen, this behavior is less secure than using the CTRL+ALT+DEL user interface.

To disable the Welcome screen and require CTRL+ALT+DEL to be used for logons

1. In **Control Panel**, click **User Accounts**.

2. Click **Change the way users log on or off**.

3. Clear the **Use the Welcome screen** check box. This also disables the **Use Fast User Switching** option.

   Users will now log on using the CTRL+ALT+DEL user interface.

Authentication Policy Options

Authentication policies and other security policies can be applied to stand-alone computers, as well as member computers and domain controllers, by using the Security Configuration Manager Tools. The Security Configuration Manager tools consist of:

■ Local Security Policy

■ Security Settings extension to Group Policy

■ Security Templates snap-in

■ Security Configuration and Analysis snap-in

■ Secedit.exe command-line tool

To set or modify individual security settings on individual computers, use Local Security Policy. To define security settings that are enforced on any number of computers, use the Security Settings extension to Group Policy. To apply several settings in batch, use Security Templates to define the settings, and then apply those settings by using Security Configuration and Analysis or Secedit.exe, or import the template that contains your settings into Local or Group Policy. Figure 15-5 shows the Group Policy snap-in with the Security Settings extensions expanded.

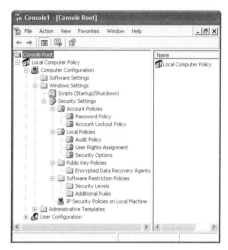

Figure 15-5   Group Policy snap-in

Note   For more information about working with Group Policy, see "Managing Desktops" in this book. For more information about security-related Group Policy, see "Authorization and Access Control" in this book.

The following security policy options are logon options and authentication options that can be configured on a computer running Windows XP Professional. This section does not include security policy options that impact other areas of desktop security management.

Account Policies

Account policies affect Windows XP Professional computers in two ways. When applied to a local computer, account policies apply to the local account database that is stored on that computer. When applied to domain controllers, the account policies affect domain accounts for users logging on from Windows XP Professional computers that are joined to that domain.

Domain-wide account policies are defined in the Default Domain Group Policy object (GPO). All domain controllers pull the domain-wide account policy from the Default Domain GPO regardless of the organizational unit in which the domain controller exists. Thus, while there might be different local account policies for member computers in different organizational units, there cannot be different account policies for the accounts in a domain.

By default, all computers that are not-domain controllers will also receive the default domain account policy for their local accounts. However different account policies might be established for local accounts on computers that are not domain controllers by setting an account policy at the organizational unit level. Account policies for stand-alone computers can be set using Local Security Policy.

Password Policy

To modify the following password policy settings, open Local Security Policy or Group Policy and go to Computer Configuration\Windows Settings\Security Settings\Account Policies\Password Policy.

- **Maximum password age.** The number of days a password can be used before the user must change it. Changing passwords regularly is one way to prevent passwords from being compromised. Typically, the default varies from 30 to 42 days.

- **Enforce password history.** The number of unique, new passwords that must be associated with a user account before an old password can be reused. When used in conjunction with Minimum password age, this setting prevents reuse of the same password over and over. Most IT departments set a value greater than 10.

- **Minimum password age.** The number of days a password must be used before the user can change it. The default value is zero, but it is recommended that this be reset to a few days. When used in conjunction with similarly short settings in Enforce password history, this restriction prevents reuse of the same password over and over.

- **Minimum password length.** The minimum number of characters a user's password can contain. The default value is zero. Seven characters is a recommended and widely used minimum.

- **Passwords must meet complexity requirements.** The default password filter (Passfilt.dll) included with Windows 2000 Server and Windows XP Professional requires that a password have the following characteristics:

- Does not contain your name or user name.

- Contains at least six characters.

- Contains characters from each of the following three groups: uppercase and lowercase letters (A, a, B, b, C, c, and so on), numerals, symbols (characters that are not defined as letters or numerals, such as !, @, #, and so on).

  This policy is disabled by default.

Tip   It is strongly recommended that you enable this policy setting.

Account Lockout Policy

Account lockout policy options disable accounts after a set number of failed logon attempts. Using these options can help you detect and block attempts to break passwords. To modify lockout policy settings, launch Local Security Policy or Group Policy and go to Computer Configuration\Windows Settings\Security Settings\Account Policies\Account Lockout Policy.

- **Account lockout threshold.** The number of failed logon attempts before a user account is locked out. A locked out account cannot be used until an administrator resets it, or until the account lockout duration expires. You can set values between 1 and 999 failed logon attempts, or you can specify that the account is never locked out by setting the value to 0.

- This setting is disabled in the Default Domain Group Policy object and in Local Security Policy for workstations and servers. You must change this to enable lockout after a specified number of attempts.

- Unsuccessful attempts to log on to workstations or member servers that have been locked using either CTRL+ALT+DEL or password-protected screen savers do not count as failed logon attempts under this policy setting. Failed attempts to log on remotely do count.

Account lockout duration. The number of minutes (from 1 to 99999) an account remains locked out before it unlocks. By setting the value to 0, you can specify that the account remains locked out until an administrator unlocks it. By default, this policy is not defined because it has meaning only when an account lockout threshold is specified.

Reset account lockout counter after. Determines how many minutes (1 to 99999) must elapse after a failed logon attempt before the counter resets to 0 bad logon attempts. This value must be less than or equal to the account lockout duration. Typically, a reset time of 30 minutes is sufficient because the purpose of an account lockout is to delay an attack on a password.

To manually reset an account that has been locked out, open the user's property sheet in Active Directory Users and Computers. On the **Account** tab, clear the **Account is Locked Out** check box. Even though it is a good practice to reset the user's password at the same time, changing the password does not unlock the account.

Kerberos Policy

Kerberos policy does not apply to local account databases because the Kerberos authentication protocol is not used to authenticate local accounts. Therefore, the Kerberos policy settings can be configured only by means of the default domain GPO, where it affects domain logons performed from Windows XP Professional computers.

For information about Kerberos policy, see "Authentication" in the *Distributed Systems Guide*.

Local Policies

In Local Security Policy and Group Policy, three categories of security policy are located under Computer Configuration\Windows Settings\Security Settings\Local Policies:

- Audit Policy
- User Rights Assignment
- Security Options

> **Note**   For information about Audit Policy see "Auditing and Troubleshooting" in this chapter.

User Rights Assignment

User rights are typically assigned on the basis of the security groups to which a user belongs, such as Administrators, Power Users or Users. The policy settings in this category are typically used to allow or deny users permission to access to their computer based on the method of access and their security group memberships.

In the Local Security Settings and Group Policy snap-ins, the following policy options that affect user rights based on their method of accessing the computer are located under the Computer Configuration\Windows Settings\Security Settings\Local Policies\User Rights Assignment extension:

> **Note**   The User Rights Assignment extension includes additional policy options that are not listed here.

- **Access this computer from the network.** Allows a user to connect to the computer over the network. By default, permissions are granted to members of the Administrators, Everyone, and Power Users groups.

- **Deny access to this computer from the network.** A user cannot connect to the computer over the network. By default, permissions are not granted to anyone who connects to the computer from the network.

- **Allow logon through Terminal Services.** Allows a user to connect to the computer by means of a terminal services session.

- **Deny logon through Terminal Services.** A user cannot connect to the computer by means of a terminal services session.

- **Log on as a batch job.** Allows a user to log on by means of a batch-queue facility. For example, when a user submits a job by using the task scheduler, the task scheduler logs that user on as a batch user instead of as an interactive user. This user right is defined in the Default Domain Controller Group Policy object and in the local security policy of workstations and servers. By default, only the *LocalSystem* account has permissions to be logged on as a batch job.

- **Deny logon as a batch job.** Certain accounts cannot log on as a batch job. This policy setting supercedes the **Log on as a batch job** policy setting if a user account is subject to both policies. This user right is defined in the Default Domain Controller Group Policy object and in the local security policy of workstations and servers. By default, no users are prevented from logging on as a batch job.

- **Log on as a service.** Certain service accounts can register a process as a service. This user right is defined in the Default Domain Controller Group Policy object and in the local security policy of workstations and servers. By default, no user or computer accounts have permissions to log on as a service. By default, only System, LocalService, and NetworkService have the right to log on as a service.

- **Deny logon as a service.** A security principal cannot log on as a service to establish a security context. The LocalSystem account always retains the right to log on as a service. Any service that runs under a separate account must be granted this right.

- **Log on locally.** Allows certain users to log on at the computer. This user right is defined in the Default Domain Controller Group Policy object and in the local security policy of workstations and servers. The default groups that have this right on Windows XP Professional are Administrators, Backup Operators, Power Users, Users, and Guest.

- **Deny logon locally.** Certain users cannot log on at the computer. This policy setting supercedes the **Log on locally** policy setting if an account is subject to both policies. This user right is defined in the Default Domain Controller Group Policy object and in the local security policy of workstations and servers. By default, no accounts are denied local logon permission.

Security Options

You might want to set the following security options in order to modify logon-related behaviors:

- Interactive logon
- Microsoft network server
- Network access
- Network security

- Recovery console
- Shutdown

The following policy options are located under Computer Configuration\Windows Settings\Security Settings\Local Policies\Security Options:

> **Note**   The Security Options extension includes additional policy options that are not listed here.

- **Do not display last user name.** Determines whether the name of the last user to log on to the computer is displayed in the Windows logon screen. If this policy is enabled, the name of the last user to successfully log on is not displayed in the **Log On to Windows** dialog box. If this policy is disabled, the name of the last user to log on is displayed. This policy is defined in Local Computer Policy, where it is disabled by default.

- **Do not require CTRL+ALT+DEL.** Determines if a user must press CTRL+ALT+DEL to log on. If this policy is enabled, a user is not required to press CTRL+ALT+DEL to log on. This policy is disabled by default on workstations and servers that are joined to a domain. It is enabled by default on stand-alone workstations.

> **Caution**   Not having to press CTRL+ALT+DEL leaves the user's password vulnerable to interception. Requiring CTRL+ALT+DEL before logging on ensures that the user is communicating by means of a trusted path when entering a password.

- **Message text for users attempting to log on.** Specifies message text that appears when a user logs on. This text is often used for legal reasons, such as to warn users against misusing company information or to tell them that their actions might be audited. For servers, this policy is enabled, but no default text is specified. This policy is defined by default, but no default text is specified.

- **Message title for users attempting to log on.** Allows the specification of a title to appear in the title bar of the window that contains the message for users attempting to log on. For servers, this policy is enabled, but no default text is specified. This policy is defined by default, but no default text is specified.

- **Number of previous logons to cache (in case a domain controller is not available).** Windows 2000 Server and Windows XP Professional store previous user's logon information locally so that a subsequent user can log on even if a domain controller is unavailable. This setting determines how many unique previous logons are cached. If a domain controller is unavailable and a user's logon information is stored, the user is prompted by the message: "A domain controller for your domain could not be contacted. You have been logged on using cached account information. Changes to your profile since you last logged on may not be available." If a domain controller is unavailable and a user's logon information is not stored, the user is prompted by this message: "The system cannot log you on now because the domain *DOMAIN_NAME* is not available." In this policy setting, a value of 0 disables logon storing. Any value above 50 stores only 50 logon attempts. For servers, this policy is defined by default in Local Computer Policy, and the default value is 10 logons.

- **Prompt user to change password before expiration.** Determines how far in advance the operating system warns users that their password is about to expire. Advanced warning gives the user time to construct a strong password. The default value is 14 days.

- **Require domain controller authentication to unlock**. If a computer is locked, a user must authenticate against a domain controller in order to unlock the computer. Otherwise cached credentials can be used.

- **Smart card removal behavior.** Allows you to configure one of three consequences if a smart card is removed in the middle of a session: Lock workstation, Force Logoff, and No action.

- **Allow anonymous SID/Name translation.** Makes it possible for anonymous users to translate SIDs into user names and user names into SIDs. This policy is disabled by default.

- **Do not allow anonymous enumeration of SAM accounts.** Prevents anonymous users from generating a list of accounts in the SAM database. This policy is enabled by default.

- **Do not allow anonymous enumeration of SAM accounts and shares**. Prevents anonymous users from generating a list of accounts and shares in the SAM database. This policy is disabled by default.

- **Do not allow Stored User Names and Passwords to save passports or credentials for domain authentication.** Prevents Stored User Names and Passwords from saving passport or domain authentication credentials after a logon session has ended. This policy is disabled by default.

- **Sharing and security model for local accounts.** Allows you to choose between the **Guest only** security model or the **Classic** security model. In the

Guest only model, all attempts to log on to the local computer from across the network will be forced to use the Guest account. In the **Classic** security model, users who attempt to log on to the local computer from across the network authenticate as themselves. This policy does not apply to computers that are joined to a domain. Otherwise, **Guest only** is enabled by default.

- **Let Everyone permissions apply to Anonymous users.** Restores Everyone permissions to users logging on anonymously. In Windows 2000, Anonymous logons received Everyone permissions by default. This default behavior was removed in Windows XP Professional.

- **Do not store LAN Manager hash value on next password change.** Clears the LAN Manager hash value the next time a password is changed. This policy is disabled by default.

- **Force logoff when logon time expires.** Determines whether to disconnect users who are connected to the local computer outside their valid logon hours. This setting affects the Server Message Block (SMB) component of a Windows 2000 server. When this policy is enabled, client sessions with the SMB server are disconnected when the client's logon hours expire. If this policy is disabled, an established client session can continue after the client's logon time expires.

- **LAN Manager Authentication Level.** Determines which challenge/response authentication protocol is used for network logons. These policy options affect the level of authentication protocol used by clients, the level of session security negotiated, and the level of authentication accepted by servers. The following options are available:

    - **Send LM & NTLM responses.** Clients use LM and NTLM authentication, and never use NTLMv2 session security; domain controllers accept LM, NTLM, and NTLMv2 authentication.

    - **Send LM & NTLM - use NTLMv2 session security if negotiated.** Clients use LM and NTLM authentication, and use NTLMv2 session security if the server supports it; domain controllers accept LM, NTLM, and NTLMv2 authentication.

    - **Send NTLM response only.** Clients use NTLM authentication only, and use NTLMv2 session security if the server supports it; domain controllers accept LM, NTLM, and NTLMv2 authentication.

    - **Send NTLMv2 response only.** Clients use NTLMv2 authentication only, and use NTLMv2 session security if the server supports it; domain controllers accept LM, NTLM, and NTLMv2 authentication.

    - **Send NTLMv2 response only\refuse LM.** Clients use NTLMv2 authentication only, and use NTLMv2 session security if the server supports it; domain controllers refuse LM and accept only NTLM and NTLMv2 authentication.

> **Caution** The more restrictive NTLM settings are, the more they can affect the ability of clients running Windows XP Professional to communicate over the network with clients running Windows NT 4.0 or earlier.

- **Minimum session security for NTLM SSP based (including secure RPC) clients.** Allows you to configure the following options for Windows XP Professional clients:

    - Require message integrity

    - Require message confidentiality

    - Require NTLMv2 session security

    - Require 128-bit encryption

- **Allow system to be shut down without having to log on.** Determines whether a computer can be turned off without logging on. When this policy is enabled, the **Shut Down** command is available on the logon screen. When this policy is disabled, the option to turn off the computer does not appear on the logon screen. In this case, users must be able to log on to the computer successfully and have the **Shut down the system** user right to turn off the system. By default, this option is enabled on workstations and disabled on servers in Local Computer Policy.

Auditing and Troubleshooting

You can monitor logon activity in Windows 2000 Server and Windows XP Professional in a very detailed way by enabling success-and-failure auditing in the system's Audit policy.

Security Options

You can also monitor logon events. The following option is under Computer Configuration\Windows Settings\Security Settings\Local Policies\Security Options.

- **Shut down system immediately if unable to log security audits.** Determines whether the system turns off when it is unable to log security events. If this policy is enabled, the system halts if a security audit cannot be logged. Typically, an event fails to be logged when the security audit log is full, and the retention method specified for the security log is either **Do Not Overwrite Events** or **Overwrite Events by Days**. By default, this policy is disabled.

Audit Policy

Monitoring logon attempts and account management activity can help you to identify when unwanted logons are taking place. The following audit policy options, which allow you to monitor these activities, can be found under Computer Configuration\Windows Settings\Security Settings\Local Policies\Audit Policy.

- **Audit account logon events**. Governs auditing of each instance when a user logs on or logs off another computer than was used to validate the account. For domain controllers, this policy is defined in the Default Domain Controllers Group Policy object. The default setting is **No auditing**.

  If you define this policy setting, you can specify whether to audit successes and failures, or not to audit the event at all. **Success auditing** generates an audit entry when an account logon process is successful. **Failure auditing** generates an audit entry when an attempted account logon process fails. You can select **No auditing** by defining the policy setting and clearing the **Success auditing** and **Failure auditing** check boxes.

  You can use this policy to track logon attempts that occur on remote computers. For example, if **Success auditing** is enabled for account logon events on a domain controller, an entry is logged for each user who is validated against that domain controller even though the user is actually logging on to a workstation joined to the domain.

- **Audit account management.** Determines whether the system audits each event of account management on a computer. Examples of account management events include:

  - A user account or group is created, changed, or deleted.

  - A user account is renamed, disabled, or enabled.

  - A password is set or changed.

    By default, this value is set to **No auditing** in the Default Domain Controller Group Policy object and in the local policies of workstations and servers. If you define this policy setting, you can specify whether to audit successes or failures, or not to audit the event type at all. **Success auditing** generates an audit entry when any account management event is successful. **Failure auditing** generates an audit entry when any account management event fails. You can select **No auditing** by defining the policy setting and clearing the **Success auditing** and **Failure auditing** check boxes.

- **Audit logon events.** Determines whether to audit each instance of a user logging on, logging off, or making a network connection to this computer. If you are auditing successful **Audit account logon events** on a domain controller, workstation logons do not generate logon audits. Only interactive and network logons to the domain controller itself generate logon events. Account logon events are generated on the local computer for local accounts and on the domain controller for network accounts. Logon events are generated where the logon occurs. By default, this value is set to **No auditing** in the Default Domain Controller Group Policy object and in the local policies of workstations and servers. If you define this policy setting, you can specify whether to audit successes or failures or not to audit the event at all. **Success auditing** generates an audit entry when a successful logon occurs. **Failure auditing** generates an audit entry when an attempted logon fails. You can select **No auditing** by defining the policy setting and clearing the **Success auditing** and **Failure auditing** check boxes.

Security Event Messages

Auditing logon attempts can generate numerous security events, depending on whether you are auditing successes or failures or both. You can view these audit events with Event Viewer, which maintains logs about program, security, and system events on your computer. The Event Log service starts automatically when you start Windows XP Professional.

To view the error messages generated by your audit events

1. On the **Start** menu, click **Control Panel**.

2. Click **Performance and Maintenance**, click **Administrative Tools**, and then click **Event Viewer**.

   – or –

   Start Event Viewer by installing it in a custom MMC console.

   Event logs consist of a header, a description of the event, and optional additional data as shown in Figure 15-6.

Figure 15-6   Typical security event message

For more information about security event messages, see the appendix "Security Event Messages" in this book.

Additional Resources

These resources contain additional information and tools related to this chapter.

Related Information

- "Logon and Authentication" in the *Distributed Systems Guide*.

- "Authorization and Access Control" in this book.

- "Connecting Remote Offices" in this book for more information about authentication by using Remote Access Service.

- "Security Event Messages" in this book.

- *Inside Microsoft Windows 2000, Third Edition*, by David A. Solomon and Mark E. Russinovich, 2000, Redmond: Microsoft Press.

- *Microsoft Windows 2000 Security Handbook* by Jeff Schmidt, Theresa Hadden, Travis Davis, Dave Bixler, and Alexander Kachur, 2000, Indianapolis: Macmillan Computer Publishing.

Related Help Topics

- "Security" in Windows XP Professional Help and Support Center.

- "Stored User Names and Passwords" in Windows XP Professional Help and Support Center.

- "Smart Cards" in Windows XP Professional Help and Support Center.

- "Logon Scripts" in Windows XP Professional Help and Support Center.

- The *Microsoft Windows Security Resource Kit,* by Ben Smith and Brian Komar with the Microsoft Security Team, 2003, Redmond, WA: Microsoft Press.

Chapter 16

Authorization and Access Control

The Microsoft® Windows® XP Professional operating system includes a number of features that you can use to protect selected files, applications, and other resources from unauthorized use. These features, which include access control lists, security groups, and Group Policy, along with the tools that allow you to configure and manage these features, provide a powerful, yet flexible access control infrastructure for your local resources and network. Understanding what these features are, why they are necessary, and how they function will help you to manage rights and permissions on network and local resources more effectively.

Related Information

- For more information about the authentication process and how security contexts are created, see "Logon and Authentication" in this book.

- For more information about implementing security for Windows-based client computers and servers, see the *Microsoft® Windows® Security Resource Kit*.

- For more information about authorization in Active Directory™ directory service environments, see "Access Control" in the *Distributed Systems Guide* of the *Microsoft® Windows® 2000 Server Resource Kit*.

Overview of Access Control

Every user and computer has a specific role and purpose in an organization. In order to accomplish their goals, each user and computer must be able to access certain resources and perform specific tasks. However, allowing users and computers unlimited access to system and network resources and functionality can compromise an organization's security and stability. The access control infrastructure of Windows XP Professional functions to balance the resource access and system security needs of an organization.

For example, Alice works in Accounting and needs to be able to view—but not create or modify—certain Personnel Department files that are off limits to other users in the organization. The Personnel department, which controls these files, uses access control to define which users can have Read-only access to Personnel files, which users can have Write and Modify access, and which users have no access to the Personnel share. Alice is given Read-only access to the Personnel files. Similarly, IT determines that prohibiting users such as Alice from making significant changes to their systems can reduce costs and improve security and supportability. IT makes Alice and other users members of the Users group, thus limiting their ability to install applications and reconfigure their operating system environments. In this way, Alice has the access to resources that she needs, the security of the organization is enforced, and the stability of the network is maintained.

Important Terms

In order to understand the basic principles of access control, it is necessary to understand how the following terms are defined in the context of the access control model for Windows XP Professional.

Security principal   In Windows XP Professional, any entity that can be authenticated. A user, group, computer, or service can be a security principal. Security principals have accounts. Local accounts are managed by the Local Security Accounts Manager (SAM) on the computer. If the account is in a Microsoft® Windows® 2000 Server domain, it is managed by Active Directory. If the account is in a Microsoft® Windows NT® version 4.0 domain, it is managed by a SAM database on the primary domain controller.

Security identifier (SID)   A value that uniquely identifies a user, group, service, or computer account within an enterprise. Every account is issued a SID when it is created. Access control mechanisms in Windows XP Professional identify security principals by SID rather than by name.

Security context   Information that describes a particular security principal's identity and capabilities on a computer. In Windows XP Professional, all users in an organization exist in a specific security context that is redefined every time they log on. All activities, such as installing or running applications, take place in this security context. The security subsystem uses the security context to determine what a process and its threads of execution can do to objects on the computer, and who will be held accountable for what they have done.

Access token   A data structure containing the SID for a security principal, SIDs for the groups that the security principal belongs to, and a list of the security principal's rights on the local computer. An access token is created for every security principal that logs on locally at the computer or remotely through a network connection. Each process has a primary access token that it inherits by default from its creating process. The access token provides a security context for the security principal's actions on the computer. It also provides a security context for any application threads that act on the security principal's behalf.

Object   Any resource that can be manipulated by a program or process. Objects include resources that you can see through the user interface, such as files, folders, printers, registry subkeys and entries, Active Directory objects, and the Microsoft® Windows® desktop. They also include resources that you cannot see, such as sessions, processes, threads, and access tokens. An object can function as a logical container for other objects.

Inheritance   A mechanism for propagating access control information down through a tree of objects. In Microsoft® Windows NT®, an object (such as a file) inherits access control information from its parent object (such as a folder) only when the object is first created. In Windows XP Professional, objects inherit access control information not only when they are created, but also when the parent object's access control list changes.

Owner   The only security principal who has an inherent right to allow or deny permission to access an object. An object's owner can give another security principal permission to take ownership. By default, the built-in Administrators group on a computer is assigned a user right that allows this group to take ownership of all objects on the computer.

Security groups   Groups that can be used to organize users and domain objects, thus simplifying administration. Security groups allow you to assign the same security permissions to a large numbers of users, such as employees in a single department or in a single location, ensuring that security permissions are consistent across all members of a group.

Security descriptor   A data structure containing the security information associated with a securable object. A security descriptor identifies an object's owner by SID. If permissions are configured for the object, its security descriptor contains a discretionary access control list (DACL) with SIDs for the users and groups that are allowed or denied access. If auditing is configured for the object, its security descriptor also contains a system access control list (SACL) that controls how the security subsystem audits attempts to access the object.

Access control list (ACL)   An ordered list of access control entries (ACEs) that define the permissions that apply to an object and its properties. Each ACE identifies a security principal and specifies a set of access rights allowed, denied, or audited for that security principal.

Security settings   Security configuration settings that can be applied to individual computers. These settings can be configured locally on the computer by using the Local Security Policy administration tool, the Microsoft Management Console (MMC) Security Configuration and Analysis snap-in, or, if the computer is a member of an Active Directory domain, through the Security Settings extension to Group Policy.

Key Concepts

The security systems in Windows XP Professional are based on technologies originally developed for Windows NT. The access control models in Windows NT, Microsoft® Windows® 2000, and Windows XP Professional share the same key concepts and characteristics, which are described in the following sections.

Discretionary access to securable objects   The user who owns an object has ultimate control over who has permission to use it and in what way. An object's owner can give permission for different kinds of access to particular users or groups of users. For example, the owner of a file object can give Read and Write permission to all members of one group while denying Write access to members of another group. In Windows XP Professional, owners can Allow or Deny other users access to individual properties of certain types of objects as well as to the entire object. The properties that can be delegated include permissions that Allow or Deny other users access to the object.

Inheritance of permissions   You can control permissions for new objects created in a container object by setting inheritable permissions on the container. The permissions that you set on a container are inherited by existing objects in the container, as well as by newly created objects. For example, the permissions that are set on an NTFS file system folder are inherited by new subfolders and files created within the folder.

Auditing of system events   You can use the auditing feature to detect attempts to circumvent protections on resources or to create an audit trail of administrative actions on the system. For example, you can audit failed attempts to open a file. You can also set security policy so that failed logon attempts are recorded in the security event log. If another administrator changes the auditing policy so that failed logon attempts are no longer audited, the log can record this event as well. In Windows 2000, you can use Group Policy to centrally control who is allowed to manage security logs on computers joined to a domain.

Rights and Permissions

Access control involves the configuration of *rights* and *permissions*, which apply to both the objects on the local computer or network and the potential users (including individuals, computers, and services) of those objects.

A right, which is also commonly referred to as a privilege, is authorization to perform an operation. From an administrator's point of view, there are two types of rights: privileges and logon rights. In Windows XP Professional, only one user right is inherent—the right to allow or deny access to resources that you own. All other user rights must be granted, which means that they can also be withdrawn.

A permission is authorization to perform an operation on a specific object, such as a file. Permissions are granted by owners. If you own an object, you can grant any user or security group permission to do whatever you are authorized to do with it.

When permission to perform an operation is not explicitly granted, it is implicitly denied. For example, if Alice allows the Marketing group, and only the Marketing group, permission to read her file, users who are not members of the Marketing group are implicitly denied access. The operating system will not allow users who are not members of the Marketing group to read the file.

Permissions can also be explicitly denied. For example, Alice might not want Bob to be able to read her file, even though he is a member of the Marketing group. She can exclude Bob by explicitly denying him permission to read the file. In fact, this is exactly how explicit denials are best used—to exclude a subset (such as Bob) from a larger group (such as Marketing) that has been given permission to do something.

Each permission that an object's owner grants to a particular user or group is stored as part of an ACE in a DACL that is part of the object's security descriptor.

User-based Authorization

Every application that a user starts runs in the security context of that user.

When a user logs on, an access token is created. The access token contains key security-related information, including the user's SID, the SIDs of the groups to which the user belongs, and other information about the user's security context. This access token is then attached to every process that the user runs during that logon session.

An application runs as a process with threads of execution. When an application performs an operation on a user's behalf, one of the threads performs the operation. For example, when Alice opens a Word document, Microsoft® Word, and not Alice, actually opens the file. More precisely, one of the threads of execution performs the operation.

In order for a thread to gain access to an object such as a file, it must identify itself to the operating system's security subsystem. Threads and applications do not have a security identity, so they must borrow one from a security principal, such as Alice. When Alice starts an application, it runs as a process within her logon session.

When one of the application's threads needs to open a file, the thread identifies itself as Alice's agent by presenting her access token. Alice is therefore ultimately responsible for anything that the thread does to the file or system on her behalf.

Before allowing the thread of execution to proceed, the operating system performs an access check to determine whether the security principal associated with the thread has the degree of access that the thread has requested. This access check involves the following steps:

1. The security subsystem checks the file object's DACL, looking for ACEs that apply to the user and group SIDs referenced in the thread's access token.

2. If a DACL does not exist, access is granted. Otherwise, the security subsystem steps through the DACL until it finds any ACEs that either allow or deny access to the user or one of the user's groups.

3. If a deny is found at the user or group level, the access is denied.

4. If the security subsystem comes to the end of the DACL and the thread's desired access is still not explicitly allowed or denied, the security subsystem denies access to the object. Therefore, if a DACL exists, but is empty, access is by definition denied.

At the conclusion of this process, access is either allowed and the file is opened, or access is denied, in which case the file remains closed and an "Access Denied" message is generated.

Figure 16-1 illustrates this process.

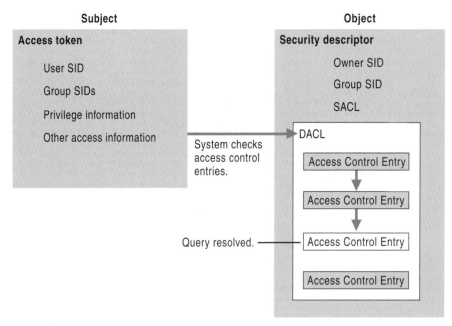

Figure 16-1   Validating a request for access

In the case of the Personnel files, Alice's administrators set a DACL on the folders and files that she needs to work with to explicitly define the extent (Read) or limits (not Create or Write) of access that she as an individual or member of a security group has to those files.

Every computer and service on the network also has a security context that governs the resources that it is permitted to access and the actions that it is permitted to take.

Security Descriptors

Access control information is first written to an object's security descriptor when the object is created. Then, when a user tries to perform an action with the object, the operating system examines the object's security descriptor to determine whether the user is allowed to do what the user wants to do.

The information that is included in a security descriptor depends on the type of object in question and how it was created. In general, security descriptors can include the following information:

- Which user owns the object

- Which users and groups are allowed or denied access to the object

- Which users' and groups' access to the object must be audited

This information can later be modified. In both cases, the information that goes into a security descriptor is supplied by one of the following:

- The subject

- The parent object

- The object manager

When a subject creates a new object, it can assign the object a security descriptor. If the subject does not assign a security descriptor, the operating system uses access control information inherited from the parent object to create one. If no information is available to inherit, the operating system uses default access control information provided by the object manager for the particular type of object that the subject wants to create.

After an object is created, the object's owner or any user who has the permission to change permissions can change information in the object's security descriptor. The owner can assign the permission to change permissions to other users. Changes can also come from the parent object when that object's owner modifies its security descriptor. This process is called inheritance. Every time the security descriptor on a container object is changed, the object manager propagates any changes marked as inheritable to all objects in the container, as long as those objects are not protected. For more information about managing inheritance, see "Modifying Inheritance of Permissions" later in this chapter.

Planning for Effective Access Control

Managing security groups, ACLs, and security settings requires careful planning. Developing an access control plan can help to prevent basic security problems, such as inadequately protected resources, users granted greater rights and permissions than they need to do their jobs, or ad hoc security configurations that are not based on a well-thought-out, manageable security plan. Ad hoc security management might provide adequate protection for small organizations, but will quickly break down as the organization grows.

Although Windows XP Professional incorporates highly advanced security features, effective access control must combine the proper use of Windows XP Professional–based technologies with good planning. Security features are only as good as the methods used to employ and manage them.

> **Tip**   To improve the security of your network, provide each user, computer, and service with the least number of privileges needed to perform their tasks and run their applications. Windows XP Professional includes improved features—including well-defined default security groups, Restricted Software settings, and the Secondary Logon Service (SLS)—to make this possible. For information about SLS, see "Logon and Authentication" in this book. For information about Restricted Software settings, see "Software Restriction Policies" later in this chapter.

Consider developing an access control plan that describes how you will use Windows XP Professional features to establish a secure, usable environment. A typical access control plan might include the following sections:

- **Security goals.** Define the resources and processes that you are protecting.

- **Security risks.** Enumerate the types of security hazards that affect your enterprise, including what poses the threats and how significant these threats are.

- **Security strategies.** Describe the general security strategies necessary to meet the threats and mitigate the risks.

- **Security group descriptions.** Define the security restrictions or permissions that might apply to different groups of users and resources, and then create security groups to help you implement these sets of permissions and restrictions.

- **Security policy.** If you add your Windows XP Professional–based clients to an Active Directory environment, you can use the Security Settings extension to Group Policy to define and enforce your security strategy on any number of computers.

- **Information security strategies.** Define how you plan to implement information security solutions, such as an encrypting file system (EFS), and access authorization using permissions. For more information about EFS, see "Encrypting File System" in this book.

- **Administrative policies.** Document policies for delegation of administrative tasks and monitoring of audit logs to detect suspicious activity.

Your access control plan can contain additional sections, but these are suggested as a starting point. If possible, test and revise all aspects of your access control plans using a test laboratory that closely resembles your organization's computing environment. Also, conduct pilot deployments to further test and refine your access control plans.

User Accounts and Security Groups

Creating and deleting user accounts and defining and using security groups are important security tasks. Defining the security restrictions or permissions that might apply to different groups of users and resources in your network will help to simplify the implementation and management of the permissions and restrictions in your organization. For example, you can create a Printer Operators group and give it precisely delineated administrative control over a finite group of printers.

In order for you to effectively manage security groups in your organization, you need to be familiar with the relationship between accounts, security groups, and built-in security principals. It is also important for you to become familiar with the techniques and tools available for managing group membership.

User Account Creation

Every user has an *account* containing unique credentials that allow the user to access resources on a local computer or domain. Accounts can be local to a computer or domain based. If the account is specific to a local computer, the user will not be able to access network based resources unless the resources have been configured to allow Anonymous access. If the account is domain based, the user will be able to access network resources from the local computer. However, his or her permissions as a user of network resources might be quite different than his or her rights on the local computer. For more information about how accounts are authenticated, see "Logon and Authentication" in this book.

Two user accounts—Administrator and Guest—are created automatically when Windows XP Professional is installed. The Administrator account can be used to initially log on and configure the computer. For example, the Administrator can install software, configure printers, join the computer to a domain, and so on. After the computer has been configured, it is necessary to log on as Administrator only to perform administrative tasks.

> **Tip**   It is best if the Administrator account has a password that meets complexity requirements. You can also rename the Administrator account to make it more difficult for potential hackers to gain access to your system.

The Guest account can be used to allow different users to log on and access local resources without having to create an account for each user. The Guest account can also be enabled to simplify file and printer sharing with other Windows-based computers that are configured in a workgroup environment. Otherwise, it is recommended that you turn off the Guest account.

Except for the Administrator and Guest accounts, local user accounts are not created automatically when Windows XP Professional is installed. Instead, local user accounts must be created by a member of the Administrators group after the installation is complete. In turn, only domain-level Administrators and Account Operators can create domain accounts.

User accounts, which include information such as the user's name, alias, password, and unique security identifier (SID), enable users to log on to the network or local computer and to access local and network resources. Any domain or local user can then manage permissions on resources on the local computer—as long as the user has change permission rights on the resource.

To create, delete, and manage user accounts, administrators can use **User Accounts** in Control Panel, the Local Users and Groups snap-in to the Microsoft Management Console (if the user account is local to a particular computer) or the Active Directory Users and Computers snap-in (if the account is to participate in a domain). For more information about creating, deleting, and managing user accounts, see "Local Users and Groups" in Windows XP Professional Help and Support Center.

Types of Security Groups

User accounts are also members of security groups. Depending on the organizational environment, groups used to administer security can be defined by their scope, their purpose, their rights, or their role. The scope of a security group can be a single computer, a single domain, or multiple domains within a forest. In general, Windows 2000 and Windows XP Professional groups fall into one of several categories.

Computer local groups   Computer local groups are security groups that are specific to a computer and are not recognized elsewhere in the domain. These groups are a primary means of managing rights and permissions to resources on a local computer.

Domain local groups   Domain local groups are local to the domain in which they are created, and thus can be given permissions and user rights only to objects on computers within the domain.

Global groups   Global groups, which are also created on domain controllers, are used for combining users who share a common access profile based on job function or business role. Global groups can contain user accounts from the same domain and other global groups from the same domain, and can be granted permissions to any computer running Windows NT 4.0, Windows 2000, or Windows XP Professional in any domain in a forest.

Universal groups   Universal groups are used in larger, multi-domain organizations where there is a need to grant access to similar groups of accounts defined in multiple domains in a forest. Universal groups are used only in multiple domain trees or forests that have a global catalog. They can contain groups from any Windows 2000 domain, and can be used to grant access on any computers running Windows 2000 or Windows XP Professional in any domain in the forest.

Built-in security principals   Built-in security principals, also called special identities, apply to any account that is using the computer in specified ways, such as for Anonymous and Remote logons. Unlike the other types of security groups, built-in security principals do not have specific memberships that you can view or modify, nor do you even see them when you administer groups. However, they are available for use when you assign rights and permissions to group members.

The scope of a group determines where in the network you are able to use the group and assign permissions, and the amount of network traffic the group creates. Using the most appropriate group for a task simplifies administration and, in a domain environment, reduces network traffic by reducing the amount of replication required. The following sections discuss the computer local and special identity groups in greater detail.

Computer Local Security Groups

Windows XP Professional includes a number of built-in computer local security groups. You can manage the membership of these groups by using the Local Users and Groups snap-in to the Microsoft Management Console (MMC) or by using User Accounts in Control Panel. However, if you are using Windows XP Professional in a stand-alone or workgroup configuration, by using User Accounts in Control Panel you can manage only three of these built-in security groups—Administrators, Users (which are also referred to as Limited users), and Guests. If you are using Windows XP Professional in a stand-alone or workgroup configuration and want to use other security groups in addition to these three, you need to manage them from the Local Users and Groups snap-in.

The following sections describe the roles and privileges associated with each computer local security group.

Administrators Members of this group have total control of the local computer. The default Windows XP Professional security settings do not restrict administrative access to any registry object or file system object. Administrators can perform any and all functions supported by the operating system. Any right that Administrators do not have by default, they can grant to themselves.

> **Warning** If a hacker or virus gains access to a computer while a member of the Administrators group is logged on, the hacker or virus can use the administrator's security context to perform any task on the local computer— or, in the case of a network administrator, on the network—that the administrator can perform. Impress upon all members of the Administrators group the importance of minimizing the amount of time that they are logged on with these privileges.

Default members of the local Administrators group include the first account created on a clean installation, existing members of the local Administrators group in an upgrade, and members of the Domain Administrators group.

Administrators can create or delete user accounts and modify permissions for users and resources. Administrative access to the system is ideally used only to:

- Install the operating system and components (including drivers for hardware, system services, and so forth).
- Install service packs and hot fixes.
- Install Windows updates.
- Upgrade the operating system.
- Repair the operating system.
- Configure critical computer-wide operating system parameters.
- Take ownership of objects.

In some cases, administrative accounts must also be used to install and run legacy Windows-based applications.

> **Tip** Limit the membership of the Administrators group. The greater the number of members in the Administrators group, the greater the number of accounts that a hacker or virus can potentially use to gain access to a computer.

Backup Operators   Members of this group can back up and restore files on the computer, regardless of the permissions that protect those files. They can also log on to the computer and shut it down, but they cannot change security settings.

Guests   By default, members of the Guests group are denied access to the application and system event logs. Otherwise, members of the Guests group have the same access rights as members of the Users group. This allows occasional or one-time users to log on to a workstation's built-in Guest account and be granted limited abilities. Members of the Guest group can also shut down the system.

> **Note**   The Guest account, which is a member of the Guests group by default, is not an authenticated user. When logged on interactively, the Guest account is a member of both the Guests group and the Users group. However, when logged on over the network, the Guest account is not a member of the Users group.

HelpServicesGroup   Members of this group can use helper applications to diagnose system problems. This group, in conjunction with the Support and HelpAssistant accounts, can be used by members of Microsoft Help and Support Center to access the computer from the network and to log on locally.

Network Configuration Operators   Members of this group have limited administrative privileges that allow them to configure networking features, such as IP address assignment.

Power Users   Power Users have less system access than Administrators but more than Users. By default, members of this group have Read/Write permissions to other parts of the system in addition to their own profile.

The default Windows 2000 and later security settings for Power Users are backward compatible with the default security settings for Users in the Windows NT 4.0 operating system. This allows Power Users to run legacy applications that are not certified for Windows 2000 and Windows XP Professional and therefore cannot be run under the more secure Users context.

Power Users can perform many system-wide operations, such as changing system time and display settings, and creating user accounts and shares. Power Users also have Modify access to:

- HKEY_LOCAL_MACHINE \Software
- Program files
- %windir%
- %windir%\System32

Although Power Users have Modify access to the %windir% and %windir%\System32 directories, they have Read-only access to the files that are installed in these directories during Windows XP Professional text-mode setup. This allows non-certified applications to write new files into the system directories but prevents Power Users from modifying the Windows XP Professional system files.

While Power Users have the permissions necessary to install most applications, not all application installations will succeed. For example, many applications check for explicit membership in the Administrators group before installing. Other applications attempt to replace operating system files, which Power Users cannot do. Finally, because Power Users cannot install services, they cannot install applications that have a service component.

To install local printer drivers, you need to be a member of the Power Users or Administrators group and have the **Load and unload device drivers** privilege assigned to you.

To add the Load and unload device drivers privilege for Power Users

1. In **Control Panel**, click **Performance and Maintenance**, click **Administrative Tools**, and then double-click **Local Security Policy**.

2. In the console tree, double-click **Local Policies**, and then double-click **User Rights Assignment**.

3. In the right pane, right-click the **Load and unload device drivers** policy, and then click **Properties**.

4. Click **Add**, enter the **Power Users** group, and then click **OK**.

Like Users, Power Users are not allowed to access data stored in other users' profiles.

Replicator　Members of this group are allowed to replicate files across a domain.

Remote Desktop Users　Members of this group have the right to log on remotely.

Users　Unlike Administrators, Users have limited access on the system. By default, members of the Users group have Read/Write permissions only to their own profile.

> **Note**   Users are referred to as Limited users in stand-alone or workgroup installations of Windows XP Professional when viewed in User Accounts in Control Panel.

User security settings are designed to prohibit members of the Users group from compromising the integrity of the operating system and installed applications. Users cannot modify computer-wide registry settings, operating system files, or program files, and they cannot install applications that can be run by other Users. As a result, the Users group is secure to the extent that members also cannot run viruses or Trojan horse applications that affect the operating system or other users of the operating system.

> **Note**   Users can install peripherals, such as printers, only if the following three conditions are met: The driver package is already present on the system or available via a trusted path, the driver package is signed, and the driver package can be installed without any user interface. For more information about installing printers with Windows XP Professional, see "Enabling Printing and Faxing" in this book. For more information about installing other peripherals, see "Managing Devices" and "Supporting Mobile Users" in this book.

Only applications that are certified for Windows 2000 or Windows XP Professional run successfully under the secure Users context. Many legacy applications were not designed with operating system security in mind, and as a result, members of the Users groups cannot run them.

The best way to increase the security and manageability of the operating system is to make all end users members of the Users group only, and deploy only applications that are certified for Windows 2000 and Windows XP Professional.

> **Warning**   To ensure that users can run all the applications they need to run, it is recommended that you test all of your applications at the privilege levels of the users who need to run them.

About the Program Compatibility Wizard

Windows XP Professional includes a Program Compatibility wizard that allows Users to run applications in a security context appropriate for legacy applications. Using the Program Compatibility wizard, users can specify that individual applications run in a security context appropriate to the following operating systems:

- Microsoft® Windows® 95
- Windows NT 4.0 (Service Pack 5)
- Microsoft® Windows® 98 or Microsoft® Windows® Millennium Edition (Me)
- Windows 2000

> **Caution**   The Program Compatibility wizard is not intended to make it possible to run operating system–specific applications such as anti virus or backup software. Doing so can damage important system files and cause serious problems.

To open the Program Compatibility wizard

- On the desktop, double-click the **Run in Compatibility Mode** icon.

For more information about using the Program Compatibility wizard, see Windows XP Professional Help and Support Center.

Domain Local Security Groups

Domain local versions of all except the Power Users and HelpServices groups—plus a number of additional server-specific built-in groups—are included on domain controllers. Users' access to the local computer and network depends primarily on the computer local and domain local security groups to which their account belongs. In other words, users' accounts identify who they are, and in some cases permissions and restrictions are set on an individual basis. However, the security groups to which the user belongs are primarily responsible for determining what permissions and restrictions govern their activities on the local computer and on the network.

For more information about the rights and permissions of computer local groups, see "Managing User Rights by Using Security Groups" later in this chapter.

Built-in Security Principals

Built-in security principals apply to any account that is using the computer in a specified way. Built-in security principals allow you to configure security based on the manner in which a resource is being accessed.

The following built-in security principals apply to any user account that is using a computer running Windows XP Professional in the ways specified:

> **Note**   Several additional built-in security principals are available on computers running Windows 2000 Server.

- **Anonymous Logon.** Network logons for which credentials are not provided. Users cannot log on anonymously and interactively at the same time.
- **Authenticated Users.** Any user, except a user of the Guest account, who is authenticated locally by a trusted domain controller. This identity provides users with the rights necessary to operate the system as an end user. (The Guest account is never treated as an Authenticated User.)
- **Creator Group.** A placeholder in an inheritable ACE. When the ACE is inherited, the system replaces this SID with the SID for the primary group of the object's current owner.
- **Creator Owner.** A placeholder in an inheritable ACE. When the ACE is inherited, the system replaces this SID with the SID of the object's current owner.
- **Dialup.** Any user who accesses the computer over a dial-up connection.
- **Everyone.** All users who access the computer, including Guests and Users from other domains. By default, Everyone includes Authenticated Users and Guests, but not Anonymous logons.
- **Interactive.** Any user who logs on locally.
- **Network.** Any user who logs on over the network.
- **Remore Interactive Logon.** All users who log on to the computer by using a Remote Desktop connection.
- **Terminal Server User.** Any user who accesses the computer by using a terminal server session.

The following security principals apply to any non-human user that is using the computer in a specified way:

- **Batch.** Any batch process that is accessing a resource on the computer.
- **Local Service.** Services that are local to the computer, have no need for extensive local privileges, and do not need authenticated network access. A service running as Local Service has significantly less authority than a service running as System, both locally and on the network. When services running as Local Service access local resources, they do so as members of the local Users group. When they access network resources, they do so as Anonymous users.
- **Network Service.** Services that have no need for extensive local privileges but do need authenticated network access. A service running as Network Service has the same network access as a service running as System, but has significantly reduced local access. When services running as Network Service access

local resources, they do so as members of the local Users group. When they access network resources, they do so using the SID assigned to the computer.

- **Service.** Any service.

- **System.** The operating system.

     Built-in security principals are used to manage the rights and restrictions that apply to users based on the type of logon session they have initiated. For example, suppose there is a file or share that you want Alice to be able to access—but only when she is logged on interactively. You can accomplish this by allowing Alice access to the resource but denying access to requests accompanied by access tokens that include the Dialup security principal.

The following security principles are available when a computer running Windows XP Professional is a member of a domain:

- **Enterprise Domain Controllers.** Includes all domain controllers in a forest of domains.

- **Restricted.** An identity used by a process that is executing in a restricted security context. When code executes at the restricted security level, the Restricted SID is added to the user's access token.

- **Self.** A placeholder in an ACE on a user, group, or computer object in Active Directory. When you grant permissions to Self, you grant these permissions to the security principal represented by the object. During an access check, the operating system replaces the SID for Self with the SID for the security principal represented by the object.

> **Warning**   It is recommended that you not remove or change the permissions that pertain to the built-in security principals themselves.

Memberships Associated with Default Groups

In Windows NT 4.0, the Everyone group is used as a catchall for file system ACLs, registry ACLs, and user rights. An administrator cannot define who does and does not belong to the Everyone group. Instead, Windows NT 4.0 automatically controls the group membership so that everyone is a member of the Everyone group. If an administrator wants more granular access control, the default ACLs have to be modified in order to remove the Everyone group and add groups that the administrator can control.

     In Windows 2000 and later, groups whose membership is automatically configured by the operating system, such as Everyone and Authenticated Users, are not used to assign permissions to file and registry objects. Only those groups whose membership can be controlled by an administrator—primarily Users, Power Users, and Administrators—are used to assign permissions. When users are members of a group, they automatically have the permissions that have been assigned to that group.

The users that constitute the default memberships in these groups are listed in Table 16-1.

Table 16-1   Default Group Memberships

Local Group	Default Workstation Members
Administrators	Administrators
Power Users	None
Users	Authenticated Users, Interactive Users

With a clean installation of Windows 2000 and Windows XP Professional, the Authenticated Users group and the Interactive group are added to the Users group. Thus, by default, any non-administrative user accessing a Windows 2000– or Windows XP Professional–based system interactively is a member of the Users group. Because the Guest account and Anonymous logons are not considered to be authenticated, these users do not receive User level access over the network.

On upgrades from Windows NT 4.0, the Interactive users group is added to the Power Users group. Because Windows 2000 and Windows XP Professional Power Users have the same file system and registry permissions that Windows NT 4.0 Users have, Interactive users on Windows 2000– and Windows XP Professional–based computers that were upgraded from Windows NT 4.0 can run any application that Windows NT 4.0 Users could run.

Deploying certified applications and then removing Interactive Users from the Power Users group secures a Windows XP Professional–based workstation that was upgraded from Windows NT 4.0. In this way, non-administrators who log on will be subject to the secure permissions granted to the Users group without having to change any file or registry ACLs.

For more information about security group permissions on systems that have been upgraded see "Managing User Rights by Using Security Groups" later in this chapter.

Well-Known SIDs   SIDs are associated with a user's account, security groups, and security principals. Most of these SIDs are unique. However, the values of some specific SIDs are constant across all systems. These are called well-known SIDs because they identify generic users or generic groups. For example, well-known SIDs identify the following users and groups:

- **Everyone (S-1-1-0).** The identifier authority value for this SID is 1 (World Authority). It has only one subauthority value, 0 (Null relative identifier (RID)).

- **Creator Owner (S-1-3-0).** The generic user Creator Owner is a placeholder in an inheritable ACE. When the ACE is inherited, the system replaces the SID for Creator Owner with the SID for the object's current owner. The identifier authority value for this SID is 3 (Creator Authority). It has only one subauthority value, 0 (Null RID).

■ **Self (S-1-5-10).** The generic user Self is a placeholder in an ACE on a User, Group, or Computer object in Active Directory. When you grant permission to Self, you grant it to the security principal represented by the object. During an access check, the operating system replaces the SID for Principal Self with the SID for the security principal represented by the object. The identifier authority for this SID is 5 (NT Authority). It has only one subauthority value, 10 (Self RID).

For information about other well-known SIDs, see the appendix "Well-Known Security Identifiers" in the *Distributed Systems Guide.*

Using Whoami   The Whoami utility, which is available in the Support/Tools directory on the Windows XP Professional operating system CD, allows you to view the rights and permissions that apply to an individual user. This command-line tool returns the domain or computer name and the user name of the user who is currently logged on to the computer on which the tool is run, as well as the complete contents of the current user's access token. It displays the user name and security identifiers (SIDs), the groups and their SIDs, the privileges and their status (for example, enabled or disabled), and the logon ID.

> **Note**   To install Whoami, double-click Setup.exe in the Support/Tools directory on the Windows XP Professional operating system CD. Then complete the steps in the Support Tools Setup Wizard to complete the installation.

To view an individual's user rights and permissions

■ At the command line, type:

`Whoami`

You can use the following command-line options to customize the results you receive from **whoami**:

■ **/ALL.** Displays all information in the current access token.

■ **/USER.** Displays the user identified in the current access token.

■ **/GROUPS.** Displays groups listed in the current access token.

■ **/PRIV.** Displays privileges associated with the current access token.

■ **/LOGONID.** Displays the logon ID used for the current session.

■ **/SID.** Displays the SIDS associated with the current session (must be used in combination with the **/USER, /GROUPS, /PRIV,** or **/LOGONID** switches).

- **/NOVERBOSE.** Displays minimal information (must be used in combination with the **/USER**, **/GROUPS**, **/PRIV**, or **/LOGONID** switches).

For example, on a clean installation of Windows XP Professional, **whoami** used with the **/GROUPS** option reveals that an Administrator user belongs to the following default groups:

```
Everyone
Builtin/Administrators
NT Authority/Users
Local
NT Authority/Interactive
NT Authority/Authenticated Users
```

A Standard or Power User who runs **whoami** would generate the following group results:

```
Everyone
Builtin/Power Users
NT Authority/Users
Local
NT Authority/Interactive
NT Authority/Authenticated Users
```

A member of the Limited or User group who runs **whoami** would generate the following group results:

```
Everyone
NT Authority/Users
Local
NT Authority/Interactive
NT Authority/Authenticated Users
```

When used with the **/USER /SID** switches, **whoami** also allows you to identify the unique security identifiers that are associated with a given logon session, as the following output illustrates:

```
[User] = "HQ-RES-PRO-01\Limited" S-1-5-21-1454471165-1645522239-1547161642-1009
```

Managing Permissions by Nesting Groups

Nesting groups, or adding groups to other groups, can reduce the number of permissions that need to be assigned to users or groups individually. As you assign members of your organization to global groups in order to apply security settings based on a user's job or business unit, you can nest the groups into the Users and Power Users groups, and in this way apply the security settings that are inherent to Users and Power Users to the members of the global groups contained within them.

For example, Alice and other employees in the Accounting department can be added to a group that is specific to that department. An administrator responsible for the Accounting department can control the membership of this group. The administrator can assign organization-wide security permissions to these users by making the Accounting department security group a member of the Users domain local group. The administrator thus only needs to configure the Accounting department security group to allow members access to the resources specific to the Accounting department.

This also facilitates the management of employees who are reassigned within an organization. It is much easier, for example, to move a user from the Accounting security group to the Marketing group than it is to reconfigure the many ACEs and ACLs required to permit the user to access the resources needed to perform the new job, and remove access to resources the user no longer needs.

Nesting Groups in Domain Environments

The process of creating groups across domains involves the following steps:

■ Administrators in each domain create global groups and add user accounts that have the same resource requirements to the global groups.

■ A domain administrator creates a domain local group for each resource that exists within a domain, such as file shares or printers, and then adds the appropriate global groups from each domain to this domain local group.

■ A domain administrator assigns the appropriate permissions for the resource to the domain local group. Users in each global group receive the required permissions because their global group is a member of the domain local group.

Effectively nesting groups in a multi-domain environment reduces network traffic between domains and simplifies administration in a domain tree. The extent to which you can use nesting in your organization depends on whether you are operating in mixed mode or in native mode. In mixed mode, only one type of nesting is available: global groups can be members of domain local groups. Universal groups do not exist in mixed mode. In native mode, multiple levels of nesting are available. The nesting rules for group memberships for Windows 2000 are listed in Table 16-2.

Table 16-2 Nesting Rules for Group Memberships

Group Scope	Can contain	Can be a member of
Domain Local Group	User accounts and universal and global groups from any trusted domain.	Domain local groups in the same domain.
	Domain local groups from the same domain.	
Global Group	User accounts and global groups from the same domain.	Universal and domain local groups in any domain.
		Global groups in the same domain.
Universal Groups	User accounts, and universal and global groups from any domain.	Domain local or universal groups in any domain.

Working with Access Control Lists

If you configure ACLs for resource groups or security groups and add or remove users or resources from the appropriate groups when your organization changes, it is easier to control and audit user rights and permissions and reduces the need to change ACLs.

There are two types of ACLs—Discretionary Access Control Lists (DACLs), which identify the users and groups that are allowed or denied access, and System Access Control Lists (SACLs), which control how access is audited. For more information about the use of SACLs, see "Auditing and Analyzing Access Control" later in this chapter.

Viewing ACLs

The access control list for an object is generally found on the Security tab of the object's property sheet. This tab lists the groups and users that have access to this object, and provides a summary of the permissions allowed to each group.

> **Note**   The Security tab for an object can be viewed only by users who have the appropriate permissions on the object. In addition, users on computers running Windows XP Professional in stand-alone or workgroup environments will not be able to view the security tab if simple sharing has been enabled. For more information about simple sharing, see "Managing Network Authentication" later in this chapter.

Figure 16-2 shows the Properties page with a number of ACEs visible.

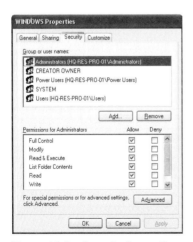

Figure 16-2   Security Properties page for a Windows folder

The **Group or user names** box lists the security principals that have permissions assigned for this resource. The **Permissions for** box lists the permissions allowed or denied for the security principal highlighted in the **Group or user names** box. The **Add** and **Remove** buttons allow you to add new security principals for this resource or to delete existing principals from the list.

> **Note** Generally, the **Group or user names** box includes the resolved network names for the security principal. If the name does not resolve—if the computer is disconnected from the network, for example—the user or group's SID might appear instead.

To view the Security tab on your system

1. Right-click an object such as a file, folder, or printer, and select **Properties**.

2. Click the **Security** tab.

Clicking the Advanced button opens the Advanced Security Settings page, which provides additional information about the permissions that apply to a user or group.

Figure 16-3 shows an example of an Advanced Security Settings page.

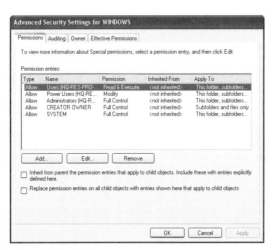

Figure 16-3 Advanced Security Settings for a Windows folder

The **Advanced Security Settings** page allows you to use more advanced features for granting permissions, such as:

- Modifying special permissions that apply to each user or group.

- Modifying access inheritance options for the object and any child objects.

- Auditing attempts to access the object.

- Modifying ownership information for the object and any child objects.

- Viewing effective permissions.

Note   As long as settings are inherited from a parent object rather than explicitly defined on the object you are assessing, you have to go back to the source ACL in order to change access control settings on the child object.

The **Permissions** tab shows permissions that have been explicitly configured on the object, permissions that have been inherited, where inherited permissions are inherited from, and what child objects they apply to. A new advanced option in the Windows XP Professional, the **Effective Permissions** tab, allows you to see all of the permissions that apply to a security principal for a given object, including the permissions derived from memberships in security groups. The **Effective Permissions** tab is illustrated in Figure 16-4.

Figure 16-4   Effective Permissions tab

To view the Effective Permissions for a user or group

1. On the **Effective Permissions** tab, click the **Select** button to open the **Select User or Group** dialog box.

2. In the **Name** box, type the name of the built-in security principal, group, or user, for which you would like to view **Effective Permissions**.

    – or –

    Click the **Object Types** button, and then select **Built-in security principals**, **Groups**, or **Users**.

3. Click **OK**.

> **Tip** If the security principal is network based, you can click **Locations** and select a target, or you can type in the domain name together with the group name, such as reskit\users.

It is important to specify the correct object types and the locations for your search. Failure to do so will result in an error message and the suggestion that you refine your search before searching again.

Access Control Entries

Access control lists contain a wide variety of ACEs that can be viewed on the Permissions and Effective Permissions tabs. All ACEs include the following access control information:

-   A SID that identifies a user or group, such as Alice, the Accounting department, or users in the Denver office.

-   A list of special permissions that specify access rights, such as List Folder/Read Data.

-   Inheritance information that determines whether new files created in a particular folder will receive access permissions from the parent folder.

-   A flag that indicates whether the ACE is an Allow or Deny ACE.

To view a specific ACE

1. Navigate to the **Advanced Security Settings** page for the file, folder, or object.

2. Double-click the entry or entries you want to view in the **Permission entries** box.

Figure 16-5 shows the ACE for the Windows folder.

Figure 16-5   ACE for the Windows folder

How Access Control Is Applied to New Objects

The operating system uses the following guidelines to set the DACL in the security descriptors for most types of new securable objects:

1. The new object's DACL is the DACL from the security descriptor specified by the creating process. The operating system merges any inheritable ACEs from the parent object into the DACL.

2. If the creating process does not specify a security descriptor, the operating system builds the object's DACL from inheritable ACEs in the parent object's DACL. For example, in the case of a new file, this might be the inheritable ACEs from the folder in which the file is being created.

3. If the parent object has no inheritable ACEs, for example if the file is being created in the root directory, the operating system asks the object manager to provide a default DACL.

4. If the object manager does not provide a default DACL, the operating system checks for a default DACL in the access token belonging to the subject (the user, for example).

5. If the subject's access token does not have a default DACL, the new object is assigned no DACL, which allows Everyone unconditional access.

> **Warning**   Failure to set DACLs or setting DACLs improperly might have undesirable consequences. For example, an empty DACL, where neither Allow nor Deny has been configured, denies access to all accounts. On the other hand, if there is no DACL then all accounts have full access.

Modifying Inheritance of Permissions

Inheritance is one of the primary tools for managing access control. By default, permissions assigned to a parent folder are inherited by the subfolders and files that are contained in the parent folder. You can block inheritance, however, so that permission changes made to parent folders will not affect child folders and files. This is useful when permissions on individual files need to be more restrictive than the permissions that apply to a parent folder, for example.

To block permission changes made to parent folders from affecting child folders and files

1. Open the **Advanced Security Settings** page for the file or folder.

2. Click the **Permissions** tab.

3. Clear the **Inherit from parent the permission entries that apply to child objects. Include these with entries explicitly defined here** check box.

4. Click **OK**.

Permissions can also be denied. By denying a user or group permission to a folder or file, you are denying a specific level of access regardless of the other permissions assigned to the user or group. Even if a user has access permissions to the file or folder as a member of one group, denying permission to the user as a member of a second group blocks any other permissions the user has.

Managing Ownership Permissions

You can take ownership of a resource if you are a member of the Administrators group. It is important for administrators to take full ownership or reassign ownership for key resources, so that if an employee creates a resource, such as a file share, and then leaves the organization, that resource remains accessible.

To view the ownership information associated with a resource

1. Right-click the file or folder and select **Properties** from the secondary menu.

2. On the **Security** tab, click the **Advanced** button to view the **Advanced Security Settings** of the resource.

3. Click the **Owner** tab.

> **Note**   You must have Read permission on the object in order to view ownership data.

Figure 16-6 shows the Owner tab.

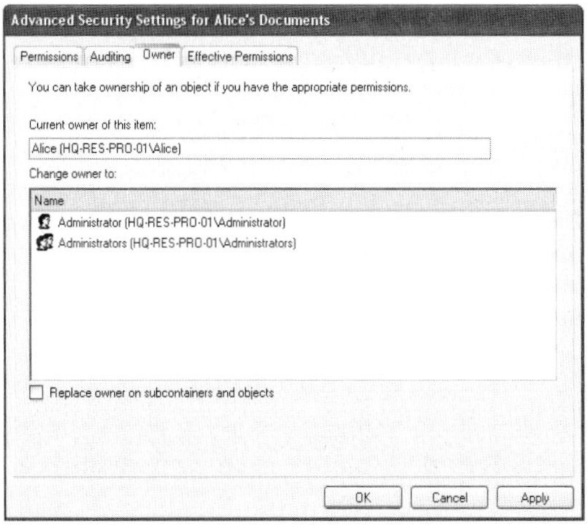

Advanced Security Settings for Alice's Documents

Permissions | Auditing | Owner | Effective Permissions

You can take ownership of an object if you have the appropriate permissions.

Current owner of this item:

Alice (HQ-RES-PRO-01\Alice)

Change owner to:

Name
- Administrator (HQ-RES-PRO-01\Administrator)
- Administrators (HQ-RES-PRO-01\Administrators)

☐ Replace owner on subcontainers and objects

OK | Cancel | Apply

Figure 16-6   Owner tab

Every object has an owner, usually the user who created the object. The owner has an implied right to Allow or Deny other users permission to use the object. This right cannot be withdrawn. Owners can give other users permission to Change Permissions (WRITE_DAC). This permission, unlike the owner's inherent right, can be withdrawn.

By default, a new object's owner is the security principal identified as the default owner in the access token attached to the creating process. When an object is created, the SID stored in the access token's Owner field is copied to the security descriptor's Owner field. The default owner is normally an individual—the user who is currently logged on.

In Windows XP Professional, you can use Group Policy to modify this rule of object ownership as it pertains to members of the Administrators group. The Group Policy option allows you to reassign ownership of objects created by members of the Administrators group to all members of the group rather than to the individual who created the object.

To make the Administrators group the owner of all objects created by its members

1. In **Control Panel**, click **Performance and Maintenance**, click **Administrative Tools**, and then double-click **Local Security Policy**.

2. Under **Security Settings**, double-click **Local Policies**, and then click **Security Options**.

3. Double-click the policy **System objects: Default owner for objects created by members of the administrators group**.

4. In the drop-down list box, select **Administrators group**, and then click **OK**.

Owners of NTFS objects can allow another user to take ownership by giving that user Take Ownership permission. In addition, certain users can take ownership without having permission if they have been assigned the **Take ownership of files or other objects** (SeTakeOwnershipPrivilege) privilege. By default, this privilege is assigned only to the Administrators group.

Determining Ownership of Objects   You can use the **dir** command to determine the owners of objects in a share or folder. At the command line, type the **dir** command using the following syntax:

```
dir /q [share or folder name]
```

Default Permissions

Windows XP Professional offers a very fine degree of security control over access to a wide variety of objects. A local file folder, for example, has 14 available permissions, beginning with Read, Write, Modify, and Delete. Both basic and special permissions are available for files and folders.

Basic File and Folder Permissions

The number and type of permissions that are available for any object depend on the security context of the object. For example, the following permissions are available for folders on NTFS partitions:

■ **Read.**   Allows a user to see the files and subfolders in a folder and view folder attributes, ownership, and permissions.

■ **Write.**   Allows a user to create new files and subfolders with the folder, change folder attributes, and view folder ownership and permissions.

■ **List Folder Contents.**   Allows a user to see the names of files and subfolders in the folder.

■ **Read & Execute.**   Gives a user the rights assigned through the Read permission and the List Folder Contents permission. It also gives the user the ability to traverse folders. Traverse folders rights allow a user to reach files and folders located in subdirectories even if the user does not have permission to access portions of the directory path.

■ **Modify.**   Gives a user the ability to delete the folder and perform the actions permitted by the Write and Read & Execute permissions.

- **Full Control.** Allows a user to change permissions, take ownership, delete subfolders and files, and perform the actions granted by all other permissions.

The following basic permissions apply to files on NTFS partitions:

- **Read.** Allows a user to read a file and view file attributes, ownership, and permissions.

- **Write.** Allows a user to overwrite a file, change file attributes, and view file ownership and permissions.

- **Read & Execute.** Gives a user the rights required to run applications and perform the actions permitted by the Read permission.

- **Modify.** Gives a user the ability to modify and delete a file and perform the actions permitted by the Write and Read & Execute permissions.

- **Full Control.** Allows a user to change permissions, take ownership, and perform the actions granted by all other permissions.

> **Note** Share permissions for NTFS volumes work in combination with file and directory permissions. By default, the permissions for a new share on an NTFS partition allow Everyone Full Control. Using Full Control permission for Everyone on all NTFS shared directories is the easiest way to manage NTFS file security. This way, you need only manage the underlying file and directory permissions.

Advanced File and Folder Permissions

A number of more detailed permissions are available when you click the **Advanced** button on the **Properties** page; select a user, group, or security principal; and then click **Edit**. These permissions include:

- **Traverse Folder/Execute File.** Allows or denies moving through folders to reach other files or folders, even if the user has no permissions to the folders being traversed (the permission applies only to folders). Traverse Folder takes effect when a group or user is not granted the Bypass Traverse Checking user right in the Group Policy snap-in. (By default, the Everyone group is given the Bypass Traverse Checking user right.) The Execute File permission allows or denies running program files (the permission applies only to files).

> **Note** Setting the Traverse Folder permission on a folder does not automatically set the Execute File permission on all files within that folder.

- **List Folder/Read Data.**   Allows or denies viewing filenames and subfolder names within the folder (the permission applies only to folders). The Read Data permission allows or denies viewing data in files (the permission applies only to files).

- **Read Attributes.**   Allows or denies viewing the attributes of a file or folder (for example, the read-only and hidden attributes). Attributes are defined by NTFS.

- **Read Extended Attributes.**   Allows or denies viewing the extended attributes of a file or folder. Extended attributes are defined by programs and can vary by program.

- **Create Files/Write Data.**   Allows or denies creating files within the folder (the permission applies only to folders). Also, the Write Data permission allows or denies making changes to the file and overwriting existing content (the permission applies only to files).

- **Create Folders/Append Data.**   Allows or denies creating folders within the folder (the permission applies only to folders). The Append Data permission allows or denies making changes to the end of the file but not changing, deleting, or overwriting existing data (the permission applies only to files).

- **Write Attributes.**   Allows or denies changing the attributes of a file or folder.

- **Write Extended Attributes.**   Allows or denies changing the extended attributes of a file or folder. Extended attributes are defined by programs and might vary by program.

- **Delete Subfolders and Files.**   Allows or denies deleting subfolders and files, even if the Delete permission has not been granted on the subfolder or file.

- **Delete.**   Allows or denies deleting the file or folder. If you don't have Delete permission on a file or folder, you can still delete it if you have been granted Delete Subfolders and Files permission on the parent folder.

- **Read Permissions.**   Allows or denies reading permissions of a file or folder, such as Full Control, Read, and Write.

- **Change Permissions.**   Allows or denies changing permissions on the file or folder, such as Full Control, Read, and Write.

- **Take Ownership.**   Allows or denies taking ownership of a file or folder. The owner of a file or folder can always change permissions on it, regardless of any existing permissions that protect the file or folder.

Many of the advanced permissions are already configured when you select certain basic permissions. As a result, in general, you do not need to manually configure advanced permissions in order to benefit from them. For example, Table 16-3 illustrates the links between basic and advanced permissions for folders.

Table 16-3   Advanced Folder Permissions

Special Permissions	Full Control	Modify	Read & Execute	List Folder Contents	Read	Write
Traverse Folder/Execute File	Yes	Yes	Yes	Yes	No	No
List Folder/Read Data	Yes	Yes	Yes	Yes	Yes	No
Read Attributes	Yes	Yes	Yes	Yes	Yes	No
Read Extended Attributes	Yes	Yes	Yes	Yes	Yes	No
Create Files/Write Data	Yes	Yes	No	No	No	Yes
Create Folders/Append Data	Yes	Yes	No	No	No	Yes
Write Attributes	Yes	Yes	No	No	No	Yes
Write Extended Attributes	Yes	Yes	No	No	No	Yes
Delete Subfolders and Files	Yes	No	No	No	No	No

Table 16-4 illustrates the links between basic and advanced permissions for files.

Table 16-4   Advanced File Permissions

Special Permissions	Full Control	Modify	Read & Execute	Read	Write
Traverse Folder/Execute File	Yes	Yes	Yes	No	No
List Folder/Read Data	Yes	Yes	Yes	Yes	No
Read Attributes	Yes	Yes	Yes	Yes	No
Read Extended Attributes	Yes	Yes	Yes	Yes	No
Create Files/Write Data	Yes	Yes	No	No	Yes
Create Folders/Append Data	Yes	Yes	No	No	Yes
Write Attributes	Yes	Yes	No	No	Yes
Write Extended Attributes	Yes	Yes	No	No	Yes
Delete	Yes	Yes	No	No	No
Read Permissions	Yes	Yes	Yes	Yes	No
Change Permissions	Yes	No	No	No	No
Take Ownership	Yes	No	No	No	No

> **Note**   File and folder security permissions are available only with the NTFS file system. File and folder permissions are not available with the FAT or FAT32 file systems.

Applying Folder and Share Permissions at Setup

Default NTFS file and folder permissions for the installation partition are applied during setup by the Security Configuration Manager using the Setup security template.

The Security Configuration Manager also secures the root directory during setup if the current root security descriptor grants Everyone Full Control. This is a change from previous releases of Windows NT and provides increased security for non-Windows directories that are created off of the root. Because of the ACL inheritance model, any non-Windows subdirectories that inherit permissions from the root directory will also be modified during setup. The new Windows XP Professional root ACL (also implemented by Format and Convert) is as follows:

- Administrators, System: Full Control (Container Inherit, Object Inherit)
- Creator Owner: Full Control (Container Inherit, Object Inherit, Inherit Only)
- Everyone: Read & Execute (No Inheritance)
- Users: Read & Execute (Container Inherit, Object Inherit)
- Users: Create Directory (Container Inherit)
- Users: Add File (Container Inherit, Inherit Only)

The Setup Security.inf template can be used to reapply default security settings. For more information about applying templates, see "Using Security Templates" later in this chapter.

Using CACLs

Although the Properties page is the basic user interface for viewing and modifying ACLs and ACEs, it is not usable for configuring security for all types of objects on a network or Windows XP Professional–based computer. In some cases you can use the tool Cacls.exe to perform security configuration tasks.

Cacls.exe can be used to display or modify access control lists (ACLs) for one or more files at time. It includes options that can be used to grant (**/g**), revoke (**/r**), replace (**/p**), or deny (**/d**) specific user access rights. For example, you can use the **cacls** command to grant an access right to a user. At the command line, type the **cacls** command using the following syntax:

```
cacls [filename] /g [username:right]
```

In this command, the user name of the user is followed by a colon and the specific user right that you want.

Managing User Rights by Using Security Groups

It is easier to manage groups than individual users. The rights granted to a user are based on the user's security group memberships. For this reason, a significant portion of Windows XP Professional operating system security is defined by the default access permissions granted to the Administrators, Power Users, and Users groups. If you already have a managed user environment, or if you want to move to a managed user environment, consider the capabilities and restrictions that apply to each of these security groups. Also, determine which of your users require higher levels of permissions, and which users need fewer permissions.

Security Group Upgrade from Windows NT 4.0

In the case of an upgrade from Windows NT 4.0 to Windows XP Professional, existing Users automatically become members of the Power Users group. This is because the permissions that apply to Users in Windows 2000 and Windows XP Professional are more restrictive than the permissions that apply to Users in Windows NT 4.0. As a result, after upgrading to Windows XP Professional, certain applications might not run for users who are members of the Users group. Placing Windows NT 4.0 Users in the Power Users group enables them to continue to run non-certified applications.

From a security standpoint, deploying certified applications and placing users only in the Users group is preferred. The default access control settings for the Users group on NTFS systems prevents users (or malicious applications run by users) from compromising the operating system or other users' data.

> **Note**   If you need to run non-certified applications but do not want to use the Power Users group, the Compatible security template can be used to open up permissions for Users in a manner that is consistent with the access control requirements of most legacy applications. For more information about the Compatible template, see "Security Templates" later in this chapter.

Security Group Creation in a Clean Installation

In a clean installation of Windows 2000 or Windows XP Professional, security group membership depends on how users are created:

- If the user is a domain user logging on to the Windows XP Professional–based computer for the first time, the user becomes a member of the Users (Restricted) group on the local computer.

- If the user is local and the account was created with the Local Users and Groups MMC snap-in, then the user becomes a member of the Users (Restricted) group on the local computer.

- If the user is local and the account was created with User Accounts in Control Panel, then the user becomes a member of the Power Users (Standard) group on the local computer.

The Administrators, System, and Creator Owner groups are given Full Control on all file system and registry objects that exist at the beginning of GUI-mode setup. The Users group is explicitly granted Write access to specific locations, and Read-only (or less) access to the rest of the system.

Table 16-5 lists the default Write access permissions for Users in Windows XP Professional.

Table 16-5   Default Write Access Permissions for Users in Windows XP Professional

Object	Permission	Comment
HKEY_Current_User	Full Control	User's portion of the registry
%UserProfile%	Full Control	User's Profile directory
All Users\Shared Documents	Write	Shared Documents location
All Users\Application Data	Write	Shared Application Data location
%Windir%\Temp	Synchronize, Traverse, Add File, Add Subdir	Per-computer temp directory. This is a concession made for service-based applications so that Profiles do not need to be loaded in order to get the per-User temp directory of an impersonated user.
\ (Root Directory)	Create Directory and Create Files under Subdirectories	Per share directory.

Table 16-6 lists the default user rights for clean-installed workstations.

Table 16-6   User Rights for Clean-installed Workstations

User Right	Default Workstation
Replace a Process-Level Token	Not assigned.
Generate Security Audits	Not assigned.
Log On as a Batch Job	Not assigned.
Backup Files and Directories	Administrators, Backup Ops

Table 16-6   User Rights for Clean-installed Workstations

User Right	Default Workstation
Bypass Traverse Checking	Administrators, Backup Ops, Power Users, Users, Everyone
Create a Pagefile	Administrators
Create Permanent Shared Objects	Not assigned.
Create a Token Object	Not assigned.
Debug Programs	Administrators
Increase Scheduling Priority	Administrators
Increase Quotas	Administrators
Log On Interactively	Administrators, Backup Ops, Power Users, Users, Guest
Load and Unload Device Drivers	Administrators
Lock Pages in Memory	Not assigned.
Add workstations to the domain	Not assigned.
Access this computer from the network	Administrators, Backup Ops, Power Users, Users, Everyone
Profile a single process	Administrators, Power Users
Force shutdown from a remote system	Administrators
Restore files and directories	Administrators, Backup Ops
Manage audit and security logs	Administrators
Log On as a service	Not assigned.
Shut down the system	Administrators, Backup Ops, Power Users, Users
Modify firmware environment variables	Administrators
Profile system performance	Administrators
Change system time	Administrators, Power Users
Take ownership of files or other objects	Administrators
Act as part of the operating system	Not assigned.
Deny Interactive Logon	Not assigned.
Deny Batch Logon	Not assigned.
Deny Service Logon	Not assigned.
Deny Network Logon	Not assigned.
Remove Computer from a Docking Station	Administrators, Power Users, Users
Synchronize directory service data	Not assigned.
Enable computer and user accounts to be trusted for delegation	Not assigned.

Managing Anonymous Logons

It is recommended that you do not grant access to Anonymous users unless you have specific reasons for doing so. To help you implement this restriction, when a Windows 2000–based system is upgraded to Windows XP Professional, resources with access control lists that grant access to the Everyone group (and not explicitly to the Anonymous Logon group) will no longer be available to Anonymous users.

In most cases, this is an appropriate restriction on Anonymous access. However, you might need to permit Anonymous access in order to support pre-existing applications that require it. In this case, you can explicitly add the Anonymous Logon security group to the access control lists for a specific resource and grant Anonymous users the right to access the computer over the network.

In some situations, however, it might be difficult or impossible to determine which resource on the computer running Windows XP Professional must grant Anonymous access, or to modify the permissions on all of the necessary resources. If this is the case, you might need to force the computer running Windows XP Professional to include the Everyone group in the Anonymous Logon security token. You can do this through the **Let Everyone permissions apply to anonymous users** local security setting. The security setting can be set to either **Enabled** or **Disabled**. The default setting is **Disabled**.

To change whether Everyone permissions apply to anonymous users

1. In **Control Panel**, click **Performance and Maintenance**, click **Administrative Tools**, and then double-click **Local Security Policy**.

2. Under **Security Settings**, double-click **Local Policies**, and then click **Security Options**.

3. Right-click **Network Access: Let Everyone permissions apply to anonymous users**, and then click **Properties**.

4. To allow Anonymous users to be members of the Everyone security group, select **Enabled**. To revoke the Everyone security group security identifier in the Anonymous user's access token (the Windows XP Professional default), select **Disabled**.

Managing Network Authentication

An increasing number of Windows XP Professional–based systems are connected directly to the Internet and participate in home or small business networks rather than in domains. In order to simplify the sharing and security model used in these non-domain environments, network logons performed against unjoined Windows XP Professional–based computers are automatically mapped to the Guest account by default. This simplifies the sharing of resources in home or small business networks by eliminating the need to synchronize user names and passwords across all computers in the network. Authenticating users logging on to the network as Guest can provide an additional measure of security for computers connected to the Internet by eliminating the ability to access the computer remotely by using administrative credentials.

Forcing network logons to authenticate as Guest does not affect the following:

- **Interactive logons.** In addition to console logons, this also includes remote access sessions using Terminal Services or Telnet, which are essentially "remote" occurrences of interactive logon sessions.

- **Computers that are joined to a domain.** This is not the default for Windows XP Professional–based computers that are joined to a domain because the domain provides single sign-on capabilities for all computers that are in the domain.

- **Outbound connections.** The authentication and access control settings of the computer that you are attempting to access govern outbound connections.

While forcing network logons to authenticate as Guest can simplify the sharing of resources, it does not expose the detailed access control permissions that Windows XP Professional is capable of and that many advanced users might want. For example, requiring all users to authenticate as Guest means that all users must be granted the same level of permissions to the same resource. You cannot grant Alice Read-only access to one share while granting Bob Modify access to the same share, because both Alice and Bob authenticate as Guest user.

> **Note**   When Guest-only network logons are being used, Read-only and Modify are the only permissions that can be granted to shared files.

This also means that the actions performed remotely by Alice and Bob cannot be individually audited.

To ensure that remote administration of domain-based computers running Windows XP Professional is possible, you must include a domain-based account in the local administrators group.

You can use the Group Policy snap-in to select between the Classic and Guest-only security models that regulate the use of the Guest account and sharing behavior for Windows XP Professional in stand-alone and workgroup environments. The Classic model allows you to have explicit control over access to resources. Using the Classic model, you can grant different users different types of access to the same resource.

To select the Classic security model

1. In **Microsoft Management Console**, open **Group Policy** and navigate to the **Security Settings** container.

   The file path is Local Computer Policy\Computer Configuration\Windows Settings\Security Settings\Local Policies\Security Options.

2. Double-click **Network access: Sharing and security model for local accounts**, and then click **Properties**.

3. Select **Classic - local users authenticate as themselves**, and then click **OK**.

The alternative policy setting, **Guest only – local users authenticate as Guest**, requires all users to be treated equally—that is, all users authenticate as Guest and thus receive the same level of access to a given resource. When the computer is not joined to a domain, this setting configures the file sharing and security tabs in Windows Explorer to correspond to the sharing and security model in use.

> **Caution**   When using the Guest-only model, any user who can access your computer over the network (including anonymous Internet users) will be able to access your shared resources. Therefore it is important to have a firewall or similar device to protect your computer from unauthorized access. Similarly, when using the Classic model, it is important that local accounts be password protected; otherwise those user accounts can be used by anyone to access shared system resources.

Sharing Files and Folders Under the Guest-Only Option

The Guest-only security model is designed to simplify many details of security management for users, including the procedures used to share files and folders. This is apparent on the **Sharing** tab of a folder's **Properties** page. When the Guest-only security model is used, the **Sharing** tab has only three options:

- **Share this folder on the network.** Allows Everyone Read permissions on the folder and its contents.

- **Share name.** The name of the share on the network.

- **Allow other users to change my files.** Allows Everyone Full Control permissions on folders and Change permissions on files.

You can create a share at the root of the system drive; however, the default sharing model does not change the file permissions on shares created there. The Everyone group only has Read permissions on the root of the system drive, so sharing the root does not provide sufficient permissions for performing the majority of tasks associated with remote administration.

For more information about using the Home Network Wizard to enable the Guest account for sharing files and folders, and ensuring that the personal firewall is properly configured, see Windows XP Professional Help and Support Center and "Connecting Remote Offices" in this book.

Using Security Policy

By using Local Security Policy you can modify numerous security-relevant settings, including file system ACLs, registry ACLs, service ACLs and group membership. These settings can be used to manage a single computer or many computers at once. For computers that are not joined to an Active Directory domain, the Security Templates and Security Configuration and Analysis MMC snap-in components of Security Configuration Manager can be used to create security templates and apply them to individual computers.

> **Note**   Security settings that are defined via domain-based Group Policy always override security settings that are configured locally.

Windows XP Professional allows you to configure security settings in the following areas:

- **Account Policies.** This includes password policies such as minimum password length and account lockout parameters.

- **Local Policies.** This includes auditing policy, assignment of user rights and privileges, and various security options that can be configured locally on a particular Windows XP Professional–based computer.

- **Event Log Settings.** This is used to configure auditing for security events such as successful and failed logon and logoff attempts.

- **Public Key Policies.** These are used to configure encrypted data recovery agents, domain roots, and trusted certificate authorities.

- **Software Restriction Policies.** This is a new Windows XP Professional policy-driven feature that allows you to prevent unwanted applications, such as viruses or other harmful software, from running.

- **IP Security Policy.** This is used to configure network Internet Protocol (IP) security.

- **Restricted Groups.** This is used to manage the members of built-in groups that have certain predefined capabilities. These groups include built-in groups such as Administrators, Power Users, Print Operators, Server Operators, and so on, as well as domain groups, such as domain Administrators. You can also add groups that you consider to be sensitive or privileged to the Restricted Groups list, along with their membership information. This allows you to track and manage these groups as part of system security configuration or policy.

- **System Services.** This is used to configure and manage security settings for areas such as network services, file and print services, telephony and fax services, and Internet/intranet services. Security policy allows you to configure the service startup mode (automatic, manual, or disabled) as well as security on the service.

- **Registry.** This is used to manage the security descriptors on registry subkeys and entries.

- **File System.** This is used to configure and manage security settings on the local file system. The configuration file contains a list of fully qualified file or directory paths and security descriptors for each.

Administrators who have implemented an Active Directory domain structure can configure and apply additional security configuration options, such as Kerberos policy, for their clients running Windows 2000 Professional and Windows XP Professional.

Note For information about the use and management of Group Policy in Active Directory environments, see "Group Policy" in the *Distributed Systems Guide*. For more information about individual policy settings, see "Security Event Messages" in this book.

Software Restriction Policies

When users run applications, they do so in the security context defined by their rights and restrictions. For example, a user might have the right to view and edit documents by using Microsoft Word, but not have the right to install or modify the application itself. These rights and restrictions do not always prevent untrusted applications from taking advantage of the security contexts of trusted applications. The increasing number of "stealth" applications distributed through e-mail and the Internet create a need for a more precise level of administrative control over the relationship between applications and the user's security context.

Software Restriction Policies are designed to assist you in regulating unknown or untrusted applications by allowing you to classify applications as trusted or untrusted. After trusted and untrusted applications have been identified, you can then apply a policy that regulates each application's ability to execute. This policy can apply to an entire computer or to individual users.

How Software Restriction Policies Work

Software Restriction Policies includes two key items:

- Security Levels, which define the default authorization level at which a user is allowed to run a piece of software.

- Additional Rules, which specify the maximum authorization level at which a piece of software is allowed to run on that computer.

When a user attempts to run a software application, the computer uses the maximum values of these two components to determine the authorization level at which the application is allowed to run.

Security Levels   There are two default Security Levels, **Unrestricted** and **Disallowed**. You can use Unrestricted settings to define just the set of programs that are allowed to run. **Disallowed** can be used to specify only the programs that are forbidden to run.

Configuring applications as Disallowed is more secure than configuring applications as Unrestricted because it allows you to isolate specific unacceptable applications based on well-defined criteria. You can define default Security Level rules for each of the following criteria associated with an application:

- **Path.** You can allow or disallow an application by creating a rule based on the application's file path.

    When a path rule specifies a folder, it matches any program contained in that folder and any programs contained in subfolders. A path rule can use environmental variables, such as %WINDIR%. This makes the rule adaptable to a particular user's environment. A path rule can also incorporate wildcards, so that specifications such as *.VBS, for example, match all Visual Basic Script files.

- **Hash.** You can allow or disallow an application based on the application's hashed file contents.

    A *hash* is a fingerprint that uniquely identifies a file even if the file is moved or renamed. If software is renamed or moved, the hash rule will still apply because it is based on a cryptographic calculation derived from the contents of the file.

- **Certificate.** You can allow or disallow an application based on the certificate associated with that application.

    A certificate rule can apply to a self-signed certificate, a certificate issued from a commercial certification authority, or a certificate issued from a Windows 2000 public key infrastructure. Because they use signed hashes contained in the file signature, certificate rules are applied to files regardless of file name or location.

- **Internet Zone.** You can allow or disallow an application based on the Internet zone from which the application is downloaded.

  Applications can be downloaded from the following zones: Internet, Intranet, Restricted Sites, Trusted Sites, and My Computer. The Internet zone rules apply only to Windows Installer packages.

Additional Rules   The following Additional Rules allow you to further refine your Software Restriction Policies:

- **Enforcement Properties.** Determines whether software library files are excluded from the software policy restrictions. Also, you can use this option to prevent software policy restrictions from applying to local administrators.

- **Designated File Types.** Allows you to add or delete file types from the list of what is considered to be executable code.

- **Trusted Publishers.** Allows you to define who (end users, local administrators, or enterprise administrators) can select trusted publishers. In addition, you can use this option to specify revocation-checking options.

Using Software Restriction Policies

How you use Software Restriction Policies depends in large part upon how well you know what software applications your users are running. If you know all of the client software that will be allowed, then you can use Software Restriction Policies to enforce the use of allowed software only. If you do not know all of the applications that your users will run, you can still use Software Restriction Policies in a more limited way by disallowing applications that you are certain you do not want.

You can use Software Restriction Policies to protect users from viruses without preventing useful programs from running. For example, a number of recent worm viruses were authored using a language called Visual Basic Script. Many system administrators also use VB Script to perform system management tasks. An administrator might want to protect his computers from all VB Script–based viruses, but still use VB Script for systems management and login scripts.

To do this, he or she can create a path rule such as *.VBS that disallows all VB Script files, and create a certificate rule identifying the certificate used by the IT department to sign administrative scripts. The IT department would sign all VB scripts using that trusted certificate. Any script not signed by that certificate would be prevented from running.

Security Templates

Windows XP Professional provides predefined security templates as a starting point for creating security policies that can be customized to meet different organizational requirements. You can customize the templates by using the Security Templates snap-in.

After the predefined security templates are customized, they can be used to configure an individual computer or thousands of computers. Individual computers can be configured by using the Security Configuration and Analysis snap-in or the Secedit.exe command-line tool, or by importing the template into the Local Security Settings snap-in. You can configure multiple computers by importing a template into Group Policy.

You can also use a security template in conjunction with the Security Configuration and Analysis snap-in as a baseline for analyzing a system for potential security holes or policy violations. To examine the proposed changes, import the template into a database and then perform an analysis against that database. Performing an analysis does not change any system settings, but will highlight the differences between the settings specified in the template and the settings as they currently exist on the system.

Note   The predefined security templates should not be applied to production systems without comprehensive testing to ensure that they meet the security and functionality requirements for your specific organization.

By default, the predefined security templates are stored in the *Systemroot* \Security\Templates folder. The predefined templates include:

- Compatible (Compatws.inf)

- Secure (Secure*.inf)

- High Secure (Hisec*.inf)

- Root Directory Permissions (Rootsec.inf)

- Setup Security (Setup Security.inf)

Compatible (Compatws.inf)

Default permissions for workstations and servers are primarily granted to three local groups: Administrators, Power Users, and Users. Administrators have the most privileges, while Users have the least. Thus, you can significantly improve the security, reliability, and total cost of system ownership by:

- Ensuring that end-users are members of the Users group.

- Deploying applications that run successfully under a User context.

Applications that comply with the Windows 2000 Application Specification can run successfully under a User context. However, applications that are not certified for Windows 2000 are not likely to run under a User context. Thus, if non-certified applications must be supported, there are two primary options:

- Allow users of such applications to be members of the Power Users group.

- Relax the default permissions granted to the Users group.

Because Power Users have inherent capabilities such as creating users, groups, printers and shares, some administrators would rather relax the default User permissions than allow users of non-certified applications to be members of the Power Users group. This is precisely what the Compatible template is for. It loosens the default file and registry permissions granted to the Users group in a manner that is consistent with the requirements of most non-certified applications. Also, because it is assumed that the administrator applying the Compatible template does not want users of non-certified applications to be Power Users, the Compatible template also removes all members of the Power Users group.

Because of the heightened security guidelines that must be applied to domain controllers, it is best if the Compatible template is not applied to domain controllers or imported into the default domain or default domain controller Group Policy objects.

Secure (Secure*.inf)

The Secure templates define enhanced security settings that are least likely to impact application compatibility. For example, the Secure templates define stronger password, lockout, and audit settings.

The Secure templates limit the use of the NTLM authentication protocol by configuring clients to send only NTLM version 2 responses and configuring servers to refuse LanManager responses.

In order to apply Securews.inf to a member computer, all of the domain controllers that contain the accounts of users that log on to the client must be running Windows NT 4.0 Service Pack 4 or higher. If a server is configured with Securews.inf, a client with a local account on that server will not be able to connect to it from a LanManager client using that local account. If a domain controller is configured with Securedc.inf, a user with an account in that domain will not be able to connect to any member server from a LanManager client by using their domain account.

Note   You can use LanManager on clients running Microsoft® Windows® for Workgroups, as well as Microsoft® Windows® 95 and Microsoft® Windows® 98, without the DS Client Pack installed. If the DS Client Pack is installed on clients running Windows 95 and Windows 98, those clients can use NTLMv2. Windows Me supports NTLMv2.

The Secure templates also provide further restrictions by preventing anonymous users (for example, users from untrusted domains) from:

- Enumerating account names and shares

- Performing SID to name or name to SID translations

Finally, the Secure templates enable server-side Server Message Block (SMB) packet signing, which is disabled by default for workstations and servers. Because client-side SMB packet signing is enabled by default, SMB packet signing will always be negotiated when workstations and servers are operating at the secure level.

High Secure (Hisec*.inf)

The High Secure templates are supersets of the secure templates and impose further restrictions on the levels of encryption and signing required for authentication and for the data that flows over Secure Channels and between SMB clients and servers. For example, while the Secure templates cause servers to refuse NTLM responses, the High Secure templates cause servers to refuse both LanManager and NTLM responses. While the Secure templates enable server-side SMB packet signing, the High Secure templates require it. Also, the High Secure templates require strong (128-bit) encryption and signing for the Secure Channel data that constitute domain-to-member and domain-to-domain trust relationships. Therefore, in order to apply Hisecws.inf to a member computer:

- All of the domain controllers that contain the accounts of all users that will log on to the client must be running Windows NT 4.0 Service Pack 4 or higher.

- All of the domain controllers for the domain that the client is joined to must be running Windows 2000 or later.

The following rules also apply to the High Secure template:

- In order to apply Hisecdc.inf to a domain controller, all of the domain controllers in all trusted or trusting domains must be running Windows 2000 or later.

- If a server is configured with Hisecws.inf, a client with a local account on that server will not be able to connect to it from a client that does not support NTLMv2.

- If a server is configured with Hisecws.inf, all clients that wish to use SMB to connect to that server must have client-side SMB packet signing enabled. Client-side SMB packet-signing is enabled by default for all Windows XP Professional–based computers.

- If a domain controller is configured with Hisecdc.inf, a user with an account in that domain will not be able to connect to any member server from a client that does not support NTLMv2.

- If a domain controller is configured with Hisecdc.inf, Lightweight Directory Access Protocol (LDAP) clients will not be able to bind with the Active Directory LDAP server unless data signing is negotiated. Thus, bind requests that use ldap_simple_bind or ldap_simple_bind_s are rejected. By default, all Microsoft LDAP clients that ship with Windows XP Professional request data signing if Transport Layer Security\Secure Sockets Layer (TLS\SSL) is not already in use. If TLS\SSL is in use, data signing is considered to be negotiated.

In addition to further restrictions on the use of downlevel LanManager protocols and the requirements for encryption and signing of secure channel and SMB traffic, the High Secure templates also limit the use of cached logon data such as those data stored by Winlogon and Stored User Names and Passwords.

Finally, the template Hisecws.inf removes all members of the Power Users group based on the assumption that only applications that are certified for Windows 2000 have been deployed. With certified applications in place, neither the insecure Compatible template nor the insecure Power Users group is needed. Instead, users can successfully run certified applications under the secure context of a normal User.

Root Directory Permissions (Rootsec.inf)

By default, the Rootsec.inf template specifies the new permissions, introduced in Windows XP Professional, for the root of the system drive. This template can be used to reapply the default root directory permissions if they are inadvertently changed. In addition, the template can be used to apply the same root permissions to other volumes.

> **Note** This template does not overwrite explicit ACEs defined on child objects. It propagates only the permissions that are inherited by child objects.

Setup Security (Setup security.inf)

Setup security is a computer-specific template that represents the default security settings applied during installation of the operating system, including the file permissions for the root of the system drive. This template, or portions thereof, can be used for disaster recovery purposes. Setup security.inf replaces the combination of Basic.inf and Ocfiles.inf that existed in versions of Windows earlier than Windows XP Professional. Setup security.inf should not be applied by using Group Policy.

No Terminal Server SID (Notssid.inf)

The default file system and registry ACLs on servers grant permissions to a Terminal Server SID. The Terminal Server SID is used only when Terminal Server is running in application compatibility mode. If Terminal Server is not in use, this template can be applied to remove the unnecessary Terminal Server SID from these file system and registry locations. Removing the ACE for the Terminal Server SID does not, however, increase the security of the system. Therefore, instead of removing the Terminal Server SID, it is recommended that you run Terminal Server in full security mode rather than application compatibility mode. When Terminal Server is running in full security mode, the Terminal Server SID is not used.

Working with Local Security Policy

To view and implement security policy on a local computer, you must have Administrator rights to the computer. Administrators can use the following Windows XP Professional tools to view and configure security policy settings:

- **Local Security Policy.**   This Group Policy snap-in can be used to configure security settings on individual computers. The Local Security Policy snap-in can be used to configure Account Policies, Audit Policies, User Rights, and numerous other security options.

- **Security Settings extension to Group Policy.**   This Group Policy snap-in can be used to establish security policies for domains or organizational units (OUs). The Group Policy snap-in can be used to configure the same settings that Local Security Policy configures, as well as Event Log settings, Restricted Groups, System Services, file ACLs and registry ACLs.

- **Security Templates snap-in.**   This is a stand-alone Microsoft Management Console snap-in that can be used to create a text-based template file that contains security settings for all security areas. The security templates snap-in can be used to configure Account Policies, Local Policies, Event Log settings, Restricted Groups, System Services, registry settings, and File System settings.

- **Security Configuration and Analysis snap-in.**   This is a stand-alone MMC snap-in that can configure or analyze Windows XP Professional operating system security. Its operation is based on the contents of a security template that was created by using the Security Templates snap-in.

- **Secedit.exe.**   This is a command-line version of the Security Configuration and Analysis snap-in. It allows security configuration and analysis to be performed without a graphical user interface (GUI).

Viewing Local Security Policy Settings

You can use the following procedure to view the security policy settings on a computer running Windows XP Professional.

To view Local Security Policy settings

■ In **Control Panel**, click **Performance and Maintenance**, click **Administrative Tools**, and then double-click **Local Security Policy**.

The Local Security Settings snap-in is illustrated in Figure 16-7. You can also view the Local Security Settings container from the command line.

Figure 16-7   Local Security Settings snap-in

To view the Local Security Settings container from the command line

■ In the **Run** dialog box, type:

  secpol.msc

Modifying Local Security Policy Settings

To modify a local security policy setting, double-click the security item and revise the policy as needed. For example, you can use the following procedure to set the local policy **Prevent users from installing printer drivers**.

To set the Prevent users from installing printer drivers local policy

1. In the **Local Security Settings** snap-in, in the left pane under **Security Settings**, click the PLUS SIGN (+) to expand **Local Policies**.

2. Click **Security Options**.

3. In the right pane, double-click **Devices: Prevent users from installing printer drivers**.

4. Click **Enabled**, and then click **OK**.

5. In the left pane, right-click **Security Settings**, and then click **Reload**.

Permissions on Group Policy Objects   To edit a Group Policy object, the user must have both Read and Write access to the Group Policy object, and must be one of the following:

■ A member of the Administrators group for the local computer, domain, or enterprise.

■ A member of the Group Policy Creator Owners group who has previously created the Group Policy object.

■ A user with delegated access to the Group Policy object. That is, an administrator or a user who has had access delegated to him or her by someone with the appropriate rights using the **Security** tab on the **Group Policy Object Properties** page.

By default, Group Policy objects allow members of the Domain Administrators, Enterprise Administrators, and Group Policy Creator Owners groups Full Control without the Apply Group Policy attribute set. This means that they can edit the Group Policy object, but the policies contained in that Group Policy object do not apply to them.

By default, Authenticated Users have Read access to the Group Policy object with the Apply Group Policy attribute set. This means that Group Policy affects them.

Domain Administrators and Enterprise Administrators are also members of Authenticated Users; therefore, members of those groups are, by default, affected by Group Policy objects unless you explicitly exclude them.

When a non-administrator creates a Group Policy object, this person becomes the Creator Owner of the Group Policy object (GPO) and can edit the GPO. When an administrator creates a Group Policy object, the Domain Administrators group becomes the Creator Owner of the GPO; therefore any member of the Domain Administrators group can edit the GPO.

Creating Group Policy MMC Consoles to Delegate Group Policy   You can delegate Group Policy by creating and saving the Group Policy snap-in consoles (.msc files), and then specifying which users and groups have access permissions to the Group Policy object or to an Active Directory container. You can define permissions for a Group Policy object by using the **Security** tab on the **Properties** page of the Group Policy object; these permissions grant or deny access by specified groups to a Group Policy object.

This type of delegation is also enhanced by the policy settings available for MMC. Several policies are available in the Administrative Templates node, which is located under Windows Components in the Microsoft Management Console. These policies enable the administrator to define which MMC snap-ins the affected user can or cannot run. The policy definitions can be inclusive, which allows only a specified set of snap-ins to run, or they can be exclusive, which does not allow a specified set of snap-ins to run.

Using Security Templates

The Security Templates snap-in allows you to create a text-based template file that can contain security settings for all of the security areas supported by local security policy. You can then use these template files to configure or analyze system security in the following ways:

- You can import a template file into the Security Settings extension to configure local, domain, or OU security policy.

- You can use the Security Configuration and Analysis snap-in to configure or analyze system security based on a text-based security template.

- You can use the Secedit.exe command-line tool directly or in conjunction with other management tools such as Microsoft® Systems Management Server or Task Scheduler to deploy a security template or trigger a security analysis.

To load the Security Templates snap-in and view security policy settings

1. In the **Run** dialog box, type:
    mmc /s

2. Click **OK**.

3. On the **File** menu, click **Add\Remove Snap-in**, and then click **Add**.

4. In **Available Standalone Snap-ins**, select **Security Templates**.

5. Click **Add**, and then click **Close**.

6. Click **OK**.

7. In the left pane, click the PLUS SIGN (+) to expand **Security Templates**.

8. Expand **C:\Windows\security\templates**.
    The Security Templates snap-in is illustrated in Figure 16-8.

Note   If you installed Windows XP Professional in a different drive or directory, that path will display instead of C:\Windows.

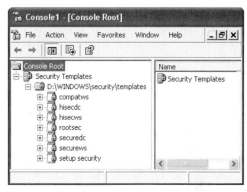

Figure 16-8   Security Templates snap-in with the default templates

Creating and Applying Security Templates   You can create your own security template, or you can select the existing template that most closely meets your needs and make any additions or changes that you want to that template.

To create a new security template

■ Double-click **Security Templates**, right-click the default templates folder, and then click **New Template**.

This creates a blank template file without any security settings. You can now completely customize the template to meet the needs of your organization.

Once you create your template or make all of the desired changes to an existing template, it is automatically saved to the templates directory. By using Save As, you can overwrite the existing template of that name or save the template under a new name.

> **Tip**   Do not overwrite the default templates in case you later realize that the template you create does not work as desired.

To save a new or modified security template

■ Right-click the template name, select **Save As** from the shortcut menu, fill in a new name, and then click **OK**.

After you create a security template for your environment, you need to apply it to your computer. When you apply a template to existing security settings, the settings in the template are merged into the computer's security settings.

To apply a security template to a computer

1. In the Group Policy snap-in, double-click **Computer Configuration\Windows Settings**.

2. Right-click **Security Settings**, and then click **Import Policy**.

3. Select the template file that you want to import into your environment.

4. Click **OK**.

You can also export the security template for your system from the Group Policy snap-in.

To export a security template

1. In the **Group Policy** snap-in, double-click **Computer Configuration\Windows Settings**.

2. Right-click **Security Settings**, and then click **Export List**.

3. Type in the name and location for the text file that you are exporting.

Alternatively, you can navigate to the \%systemroot%\Security\Templates folder and copy the appropriate template file to another network location or to a floppy disk.

Performing Security Configuration Tasks Using Security Templates You can perform the following key security-related tasks by using Windows XP Professional security templates:

- Configure permissions for a file system directory.

- Create a restricted Group Policy.

- Inherit, overwrite, and ignore policy changes.

Configuring Permissions for File System Directories You can use the following procedure to configure permissions for file system directories.

To configure permissions for file system directories

1. Open the **Security Templates** snap-in and expand **Securews.inf**.

2. Right-click **File System** in the left pane, and then click **Add File**.

3. Click the **%systemroot%\repair** folder, and then click **OK**.
   This brings up the Security Properties dialog box, which allows you to specify permissions for the %systemroot%\repair directory in the Securews.inf template.

4. Click the **Add** button, and in the drop-down box select **Administrators** group.

5. Click **Add**, and then click **OK**.

6. Select the **Full Control** check box.

7. Click the **Advanced** button. Clear the **Inherit from parent the permission entries that apply to child objects** check box.

8. Click **OK**.

9. Select the **Replace existing permission on all subfolders and files with inheritable permissions** button, and then click **OK**.

Creating a Restricted Group Policy   A restricted Group Policy allows you to define who can and cannot belong to a specific group. When a template (or policy) that defines a restricted group is applied to a system, the Security Configuration Tool Set adds members to the group and removes members from the group to ensure that the actual group membership coincides with the settings defined in the template (or policy). The following procedure describes how to create a restricted Group Policy.

To create a restricted Group Policy

1. In the left pane, in **Security Templates**, double-click a security template.

2. Right-click **Restricted Groups**, and then select **Add Group**.

3. In the **Group** dialog box, type the group name, and then click **OK**.

4. Double-click the **Restricted Groups** folder.

> **Tip**   To assist in troubleshooting, use a name that indicates that the group is affected by a restricted Group Policy.

5. In the right pane, double-click the new group name. You can now define who can be a member of the restricted group and specify other groups of which that group can be a member.

6. Click **Add** in the **Members of this group** section and then click **Browse**.

7. In the **Select Users** dialog box, locate and select user names.

8. Click **Add**, and then click **OK**.

The restricted Group Policy defines which users can be members of the specified local group when the specified template is used to configure a Windows 2000– or Windows XP Professional–based system. During configuration, the Security Configuration Tool Set removes all other users that belong to the group at the time of configuration. Similarly, if at the time of configuration the specified user does not belong to the specified group, the Security Configuration Tool Set adds the user to the group.

If no users are specified as members of a defined restricted group, the Security Configuration Tool Set removes all current members of that group when the template is used to configure a system.

If no groups are specified for a restricted group to belong to, no action is taken to adjust membership in other groups.

Inheriting, Overwriting, and Ignoring Policy Changes   After you define permissions for a file system or registry object, you can use the Security Configuration Tool Set to configure the object's children.

If you select **Propagate inheritable permissions to all subfolders and files**, normal Windows XP Professional ACL inheritance procedures are put into effect—that is, any inherited permissions on child objects are adjusted according to the new permissions defined for this parent. Any explicit access control entry (ACE) defined for a child object remains unchanged.

If you select **Replace existing permissions on all subfolders and files with inheritable permissions**, all explicit ACEs for all child objects (which are not otherwise listed in the template) are removed, and all child objects are set to inherit the inheritable permissions defined for this parent.

To prevent a child object from being overwritten by a parent, the child object can be added to the template and ignored. If a child object is added to the template and ignored, that child's inheritance mode and explicit ACEs remain untouched.

Choosing the option **Do not allow permissions on this file or folder to be replaced** makes sense only if an ancestor of that object is configured to overwrite children. If no ancestor exists in the template, ignoring an object has no impact. If an ancestor exists but is configured so that children inherit, then ignoring a child has no impact.

By saving a security template file, you can copy the file containing your desired configuration settings to multiple computers running Windows XP Professional.

You can analyze, summarize, and evaluate your security policy configuration by using Security Configuration and Analysis tools. For more information about using the Security Configuration and Analysis tools, see "Auditing and Analyzing Access Control" later in this chapter.

Auditing and Analyzing Access Control

On many computers, the state of the operating system changes frequently. If you, other administrators, or users periodically make changes to computer configurations, auditing and regular analysis will enable you to validate the security configuration on each computer and to verify that security has not been breached. For example, you might want to track who or what is attempting to perform certain tasks, or you might want to obtain information about why certain events are taking place or not taking place.

Windows XP Professional provides a number of auditing and analysis features—including audit policies, Event Viewer, and the Security Configuration and Analysis snap-in—that can aid you in effectively validating the security configurations on the computers in your organization.

Enabling Auditing Policies

You can monitor many different types of events on a Windows XP Professional–based system, including user actions such as logging on and logging off, and the success and failure of key application events. Administrators need to monitor these events to track security, system performance, and application errors.

You can set up audit policies to track authorized and unauthorized access to resources. By default, auditing is not enabled. Before you enable auditing, it will be important for you to define exactly what needs to be audited and why you want it to be audited. Auditing can slow down system performance, and it will also require effort on your part to evaluate audit logs; therefore, advanced planning is recommended to ensure that you track appropriate system events without creating excess administrative overhead.

For example, if you decide to audit account logon sessions, you need to consider what the information will be used for. Your security administrators group might be interested in logging failed logon events because this can indicate that someone is trying to log on with an account for which he or she does not have the correct password. Alternatively, you might want to log successful logon attempts to determine whether users are accessing workstations in areas of the network that they are not permitted to use.

To enable auditing, use the Microsoft Management Console with the Group Policy snap-in focused on the local computer. To see the different types of objects for which auditing can be configured, navigate to the following folder: Computer Configuration\Windows Settings\Security Settings\Local Policies\Audit Policy.

There you will find a number of configuration audit policies, which can be used to audit events that fall into the following categories:

- **Account logon events.** Logs an event each time a user attempts to log on. For example, specific events logged include: logon failures for unknown user accounts; time restriction violations; user account has expired; user does not have the right to log on locally; account password has expired; account is locked out. Successful logons also can be tracked through events.

- **Account management.** Logs an event each time an account is managed. This is a useful function if you are concerned about changes being made to user accounts in your environment.

- **Logon events.** Logs an event for logon events that are occurring over the network or generated by service startup (such as an interactive logon events or service starting events).

- **Object access.** Logs an event each time a user attempts to access a resource such as a printer or shared folder.

- **Policy changes.** Logs an event each time a policy is successfully or unsuccessfully changed in your environment.

- **Use of privileges.** Logs an event each time a user attempts, successfully or unsuccessfully, to use special privileges, such as changing system time.

- **Process tracking.** Logs an event for each program or process that a user launches while accessing a system. Administrators can use this information to track the details of a user's activities while he or she is accessing a system.

- **System events.** Logs designated system events, such as when a user restarts or shuts down a computer.

For each of these categories, determine whether you want to log Success, Failure, or both Success and Failure for the events they represent. Then configure the object that you want to monitor so that the policy and the object are linked.

For example, to audit file and folder access, first mark the activities (Success, Failure, or both) that you want to track under Object Access. Then, for each of the files and folders that you want audited, configure the SACLs that enable auditing.

To enable auditing

1. Right-click the file or folder, and then click **Properties**.

2. On the **Security** tab, click the **Advanced** button.

3. On the Advanced Security Settings for Shared Documents page, click the **Auditing** tab.

    The **Auditing** tab is shown in Figure 16-9.

Figure 16-9   Auditing tab

4. Click the **Add** button, and then select the users, or groups whose activity you want to monitor.

5. For each entry, determine whether you want to track successes or failures or both.

6. Determine whether auditing must be configured on this object only or other child objects. For example, if the object is a folder and you want to audit activity on files and subfolders, select **Apply these auditing entries to objects and/or containers within this container only**.

7. Configure settings for the Users, Computers, and Groups whose activities you want to track, complete the process by clicking **OK**.

8. In the **Group Policy** snap-in, navigate to:
   Local Computer Policy\Computer Configuration\Windows Settings \Security Settings\Local Policies\Audit Policy

9. Double-click **Audit object access**.

10. Select the appropriate check boxes for logging **Success, Failure,** or both.

11. Click **OK**.

The list of configurable entries is almost identical to the list of Access Control Entries for files and folders. For more information about ACEs for files and folders, see "Access Control Entries" earlier in this chapter.

Auditing the Use of Privileges

Windows XP Professional provides the option to audit the use of privileges. Although this setting can be either enabled or disabled, it cannot be applied selectively to individual rights.

> **Warning**   Auditing the use of user privileges generates a very large number of audits, and in most cases the value of the information this provides does not outweigh the associated management costs. Therefore, do not audit the use of user privileges unless it is strictly necessary for your environment. If you must audit the use of user privileges, it might be worthwhile to obtain or write an event-analysis tool that can gather information about only the user rights that are of interest to you.

Enabling the Use of Privileges category in the system's Audit policy does not enable the audit of all user rights. The following user rights are never audited:

- Bypass Traverse Checking (SeChangeNotifyPrivilege)
- Generate Security Audits (SeAuditPrivilege)
- Create A Token Object (SeCreateTokenPrivilege)
- Debug Programs (SeDebugPrivilege)
- Replace A Process Level Token (SeAssignPrimaryTokenPrivilege)

The following user rights are audited only if a specific registry entry is present:

- Backup Files and Directories (SeBackupPrivilege)
- Restore Files and Directories (SeRestorePrivilege)

You can enable auditing of these privileges by using the security policy user interface in Windows XP Professional.

Auditing Account Management

Account Management audit policy is very detailed in Windows 2000 and Windows XP Professional and in later service packs of Windows NT 4.0. Enabling auditing for this event category allows you to record the success or failure of the domain and local events that are listed with their event numbers in the Appendix "Security Event Messages" in this book.

Using the Event Viewer

The Event Viewer is an MMC snap-in that enables you to view three different logs that are stored by Windows XP Professional:

- **System log.**   The System log contains events logged by the Windows XP Professional system components, such as drivers or other system components that failed to load during startup. Windows XP Professional predetermines the event types logged by the system components.

- **Application log.**   The Application log contains events logged by applications or programs. For example, a database program might record a file error in the application log. The program developer decides which events to record. Many Windows XP Professional services (such as DHCP, DNS, and File Replication Services) use the application log.

- **Security log.**   The Security log, if configured to do so, records security events, such as valid and invalid logon attempts. Events that are related to resource use, such as creating, opening, or deleting files, can also be logged. An administrator can specify the events that are recorded in the security log policy.

When you select the log type in the left pane of the Event Viewer, the corresponding log data displays in the right pane.

The data in the right pane can be filtered and resorted. In addition, you can select which columns of data to display by selecting **Choose Columns** from the **View** menu.

The Event Viewer tracks five types of events:

- **Error.** A significant problem, such as loss of data or loss of functionality.

- **Warning.** An event that is not necessarily significant but might indicate a possible future problem.

- **Information.** An event that describes the successful operation of an application, driver, or service.

- **Success Audit.** An audited security event in which a user's attempt to access a resource succeeds.

- **Failed Audit.** An audited security event in which a user's attempt to access a resource fails.

In addition, the Event Viewer records the following:

- The date of the event.

- The time at which the event occurred.

- The source (such as a service or process) that reported the event to the Event Viewer.

- The category of the event. In many cases, the category relates to the subsystem that reported the event.

- The user account associated with the event.

- The computer on which the event occurred.

- The Event ID, which is a numeric code that can be used to obtain additional information regarding the event being logged.

- A description of the event.

Using the Security Configuration and Analysis Snap-in

You can use the Security Configuration and Analysis snap-in at any time to analyze current system settings against a baseline template. Performing this analysis allows you to do the following:

- Identify security holes that might exist in the current configuration.

- Identify the changes that a potential security policy will transmit to a system before actually deploying the security policy.

- Identify deviations from a policy that is currently imposed on a system.

For example, if you have created a custom security template, the Security Configuration and Analysis tools will allow you to compare your system's current settings against the settings that are defined by the security template that you created. If the custom security template defines a more secure configuration than the current settings provide, the analysis will identify the security holes that exist in the current system configuration, as well as the changes that will take place if the custom template is used to configure the system.

To load the Security Configuration and Analysis MMC snap-in

1. In the **Run** dialog box, type:
   mmc /s

2. On the **File** menu, click **Add\Remove Snap-in**, and then click **Add**.

3. In **Available Standalone Snap-ins**, select **Security Configuration and Analysis**.

4. Click **Add**, click **Close**, and then click **OK**.

Creating and Analyzing a Security Configuration Database

All configurations and analyses are database-driven. The security configuration and analysis database, which is also referred to as the local computer policy database, is a computer-specific data store that is generated when one or more configurations are imported to a particular computer. A security configuration and analysis database is the starting point for all configurations and analyses done on a system.

An initial database is created during a clean installation of Windows 2000 or Windows XP Professional. Initially, it contains the default security configurations that are provided with the system. You can export and save this database to a security configuration file immediately after the installation for use in the event that you want to restore the initial security configuration at some point.

This database defines the security policy that is in force for that system. The system runs with the configuration defined in security policy. However, security policy might not define the entire configuration. For example, security might not be defined for every file or folder path. This means that security configuration attributes that are not enforced by policy can take any value for file and folder security—either a default value or a value defined by another mechanism. Attributes that are not enforced by policy might also be configured manually using personal databases. However, any custom configurations that conflict with the policy are overridden by the definitions in the policy. Personal database configurations are useful in areas such as the registry and the file system, where multiple users on the system can secure their own registry portions and home directory subtrees.

You can use the Security Configuration and Analysis snap-in to compare the current system configuration against the stored configuration in the database. Performing this analysis provides you with information about where a particular system deviates from the stored configuration. This information is useful for troubleshooting problems, tuning the security policy, and, most importantly, detecting any security flaws that might open up in the system over time.

The database is initially created from the computer-independent configuration file described above. New configurations can be added to the database incrementally without overwriting the entire configuration.

To generate a security configuration database

1. In the left pane, right-click **Security Configuration and Analysis**.

2. Click **Open Database** (see Figure 16-10).

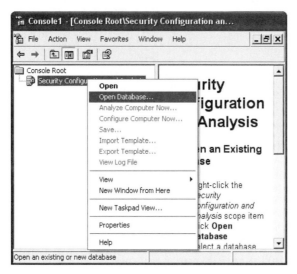

Figure 16-10   Opening a Security Configuration and Analysis database

3. In the **Name** dialog box, type a name for your new database.

4. Click **Open**.

5. Select an existing security template to import into the database.

6. Click **Open**.

    The name of the database appears in the result pane. Several more options are available when you right-click **Security Configuration and Analysis**.

To analyze the security configuration database

1. Right-click **Security Configuration and Analysis**, and then click **Analyze Computer Now**.

2. In the **Error log file path** dialog box, specify a log file for the analysis results, such as the following:

    %windir%\security\logs\Mysecurews.log

3. Click **Open**, and then click **OK**. A progress indicator displays as the analysis proceeds (see Figure 16-11).

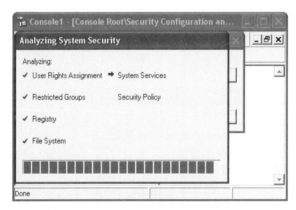

Figure 16-11 Progress dialog for Security Configuration and Analysis

Reviewing the Results of a Database Analysis After a database analysis is complete, you can view the security information under the Security Configuration and Analysis node.

To view the results of a database analysis

1. In **Security Configuration and Analysis**, click **View**, and then click **Customize**.

2. Select the **Description Bar** to expose the database you are currently working with.

3. In the left pane, click **Security Configuration and Analysis**.

    You can double-click any setting in the result pane to investigate discrepancies and modify database settings if desired.

    Configuration results are displayed for the following areas:

■ **Account policies.** This includes password, account lockout, and Kerberos authentication policies. Kerberos authentication policies are relevant only on Windows 2000 domain controllers.

- **Event log.** This includes audit policies such as object access, password changes, and logon and logoff activities.

- **Local policies.** This includes audit policy, user rights assignment, and computer security options.

- **Restricted groups.** This includes group memberships for selected groups that you consider to be sensitive.

- **Object trees.** This includes directory objects (in Windows 2000 domain controllers), registry subkeys and entries, and the local file system.

> **Note**   For each object tree, defined configuration files allow you to configure (and analyze) settings for security descriptors, including object ownership, the access control list (ACL), and auditing information.

In the right pane, both database and actual system settings are displayed for each object. Discrepancies are highlighted with a red flag. Consistencies are highlighted with a green check mark. If neither a flag nor a check mark appears, the security setting is not specified in the database (that is, the security setting was not configured in the template that was imported).

Modifying Baseline Analysis Settings   After you review the results of the analysis, you might change your mind about the relevance of the security specification that was originally defined for an object. If so, you can update the baseline database used to perform the analysis.

If you consider an object to be relevant to security, check the **Define this policy in the database** check box when viewing the detailed analysis results. If this box is clear, the object is removed from the configuration and receives its inheritance from its parent object.

If you want to base future configurations or analyses on a different security specification, you can click the **Edit Security Settings** control to modify the security definition currently stored in the database.

Configuring and Analyzing Operations by Using Secedit.exe

The configuration and analysis operations available from the Security Configuration and Analysis snap-in can also be performed by using the Secedit.exe command-line tool. Using the command-line tool allows you to perform security configuration and analysis in conjunction with using other administrative tools, such as Microsoft Systems Management Server or the Task Scheduler built into Windows XP Professional. Secedit.exe also provides some capabilities that are not available in the graphical user interface, such as performing a batch analysis.

The Secedit.exe command-line tool allows the following high-level operations:

- **Analyze.** Also available from the Security Configuration and Analysis snap-in.
- **Configure.** Also available from the Security Configuration and Analysis snap-in.
- **Export.** Also available after opening a database from the shortcut menu of the Security Configuration and Analysis snap-in. This dumps database configuration information into a template (.inf) file.
- **Validate.** This verifies the syntax of a template created by using the Security Templates snap-in.

Note For information about command-line syntax for Secedit.exe, see "Security Configuration Manager tools" in Windows XP Professional Help and Support Center.

All Secedit.exe configurations and analyses are database-driven. Therefore, Secedit.exe supports switches for specifying a database (**/db**) as well as a configuration file (**/cfg**) to be imported into the database before performing the configuration.

By default, the configuration file is appended to the database. To overwrite existing configuration information in the database, use the **/overwrite** switch. As with the Security Configuration and Analysis snap-in, you can specify a log file (**/log**).

Note While the Security Configuration and Analysis snap-in always configures all security areas, Secedit.exe allows you to specify areas (**/areas**) to be configured. Security areas not specified with the **/areas** switch are ignored even if the database contains security settings for those areas.

Additional Resources

These resources contain additional information and tools related to this chapter.

Related Information

- The *Microsoft Windows Security Resource Kit* for implementing security for Windows-based client computers and servers.

- "Logon and Authentication" in this book for more information about the authentication process and how security contexts are created.

- "Access Control" in the *Distributed Systems Guide* for more information about authorization in Active Directory environments.

- "Security Event Messages" in this book.

- "User Rights" in this book.

- "Set up your user account to use a .NET Passport" in Windows XP Professional Help and Support Center.

- "Fast User Switching" in Windows XP Professional Help and Support Center.

- "Local users and Groups overview" in Windows XP Professional Help and Support Center.

- "Permissions and user rights" in Windows XP Professional Help and Support Center.

- "Security Templates overview" in Windows XP Professional Help and Support Center.

- "Remote Desktop overview" in Windows XP Professional Help and Support Center.

Chapter 17

Encrypting File System

Microsoft® Windows® XP Encrypting File System (EFS) enables users to encrypt individual files, folders, or entire data drives. Because EFS provides strong encryption through industry standard algorithms and public key cryptography, encrypted files are confidential even if an attacker bypasses system security. EFS users can share encrypted files with other users on file shares and in Web folders. Many EFS features can be configured through Group Policy settings or command-line tools, facilitating enterprise management.

Related Information

- For more information about NTFS, see "File Systems" in this book.

- For more information about solutions for mobile users, see "Supporting Mobile Users" in this book.

Overview of EFS

Security features such as logon authentication or file permissions protect network resources from unauthorized access. However, anyone with physical access to a computer such as a stolen laptop can install a new operating system on that computer and bypass the existing operating system's security. In this way, sensitive data can be exposed. Encrypting sensitive files by means of EFS adds another layer of security. When files are encrypted, their data is protected even if an attacker has full access to the computer's data storage.

Only authorized users and designated data recovery agents can decrypt encrypted files. Other system accounts that have permissions for a file—even the Take Ownership permission—cannot open the file without authorization. Even the administrator account cannot open the file if that account is not designated as a data recovery agent. If an unauthorized user tries to open an encrypted file, access is denied.

Benefits of EFS

EFS allows users to store confidential information about a computer when people who have physical access to your computer could otherwise compromise that information, intentionally or unintentionally. EFS is especially useful for securing sensitive data on portable computers or on computers shared by several users. Both kinds of systems are susceptible to attack by techniques that circumvent the restrictions of access control lists (ACLs). In a shared system, an attacker can gain access by starting up a different operating system. An attacker can also steal a computer, remove the hard drive(s), place the drive(s) in another system, and gain access to the stored files. Files encrypted by EFS, however, appear as unintelligible characters when the attacker does not have the decryption key.

Because EFS is tightly integrated with NTFS, file encryption and decryption are transparent. When users open a file, it is decrypted by EFS as data is read from disk. When they save the file, EFS encrypts the data as it is written to disk. Authorized users might not even realize that the files are encrypted because they can work with the files as they normally do.

In its default configuration, EFS enables users to start encrypting files from My Computer with no administrative effort. From the user's point of view, encrypting a file is simply a matter of setting a file attribute. The encryption attribute can also be set for a file folder. This means that any file created in or added to the folder is automatically encrypted.

How EFS Works

1. EFS uses a public-private key pair and a per-file encryption key to encrypt and decrypt data. When a user encrypts a file, EFS generates a file encryption key (FEK) to encrypt the data. The FEK is encrypted with the user's public key, and the encrypted FEK is then stored with the file.

2. Files can be marked for encryption in a variety of ways. The user can set the encryption attribute for a file by using Advanced Properties for the file in My Computer, by storing the file in a file folder set for encryption, or by using the Cipher.exe command-line utility. EFS can also be configured so that users can encrypt or decrypt a file from the shortcut menu accessed by right- clicking the file.

3. To decrypt files, the user opens the file, removes the encryption attribute, or decrypts the file by using the cipher command. EFS decrypts the FEK by using the user's private key, and then decrypts the data by using the FEK.

New for Windows XP Professional

EFS in Windows XP Professional includes the following new features:

- Additional users can be authorized to access encrypted files.

- Offline Files can be encrypted.

- Data Recovery Agents are recommended but optional.

- The triple-DES (3DES) encryption algorithm can be used to replace DESX.

- A password reset disk can be used to safely reset a user's password.

- Encrypted files can be stored in Web folders.

Configuring EFS for Your Environment

EFS is enabled by default. Users can encrypt files if they have permission to modify the files. Because EFS relies on a public key to encrypt files, users need a public-private key pair and a public key certificate for encryption. Because EFS can use self-signed certificates, however, EFS does not require administrative effort before use.

> **Note**   The use of self-signed certificates for EFS is not recommended in a domain environment. Configuring certification authorities to deliver EFS certificates to users as part of your public key infrastructure simplifies the manageability for recovery agents.

If EFS is not appropriate in your environment, or if you have files that you do not want to be encrypted, you can disable EFS in various ways. There are also a number of ways in which you can configure EFS to meet the specific needs of your organization.

In order to use EFS, all users must have EFS certificates. If you do not currently have a public key infrastructure (PKI), you can use self-signed certificates. If you have certification authorities, however, you might want to configure them to provide EFS certificates.

You will also need to consider a disaster recovery plan if you use EFS on your system.

Components of EFS

EFS consists primarily of the following operating system components: the EFS service, the EFS driver, the EFS File System Run-Time Library (FSRTL), and an application programming interface (API). Like many other security services, EFS uses the Microsoft Cryptographic Application Programming Interface to obtain services from a cryptographic service provider such as the RSA Base Provider that is included with Windows XP Professional. Figure 17-1 shows the architecture of EFS.

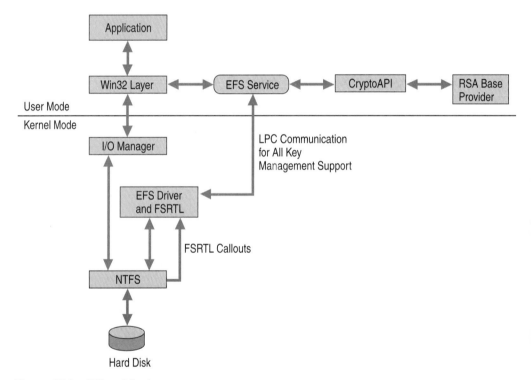

Figure 17-1   EFS architecture

EFS Service

The EFS service is part of the security subsystem. It uses the existing local procedure call (LPC) communication port between the Local Security Authority (LSA) and the kernel-mode security reference monitor to communicate with the EFS driver. In user mode, it interfaces with CryptoAPI to obtain file encryption keys and to generate data decryption fields (DDFs) and data recovery fields (DRFs). The EFS service also provides support for Win32 APIs.

The EFS service calls CryptoAPI to acquire the file encryption key (FEK) for a data file and then to encode the FEK, thus producing the DDF. The EFS service also returns the FEK, DRF, and DDF by way of the FSRTL to the EFS driver.

EFS Driver

EFS is tightly integrated with NTFS. The EFS driver is essentially a file system filter driver logically layered on top of NTFS. It communicates with the EFS service to request file encryption keys, DDFs, DRFs, and other key management services. It passes this information to the EFS FSRTL to perform various file system operations (open, read, write, and append) transparently.

CryptoAPI

CryptoAPI provides services that enable application developers to add cryptography to their Win32 applications. CryptoAPI consists of a set of functions that allow applications to encrypt or digitally sign data in a flexible manner, while providing protection for private key data. Applications can use the functions in CryptoAPI without knowing anything about the underlying implementation.

CryptoAPI provides the underlying security services for secure channels and code signing. CryptoAPI supports public key and symmetric-key operations such as key generation, key management and secure storage, key exchange, encryption, decryption, hashing, digital signatures, and verification of signatures. Developers can use certificates with these public key operations and perform the necessary encapsulations and encoding to apply certificates within their applications.

EFS uses CryptoAPI for all of its cryptographic operations.

Cryptographic Service Provider

By default, EFS uses the DESX algorithm, a variation of the U.S. government's Data Encryption Standard (DES) algorithm, for file encryption. The public-private key pairs for EFS users and recovery agent accounts are obtained from the Microsoft base cryptographic service provider (CSP), also called the RSA base provider. This CSP is included with Windows XP Professional and is approved for general export worldwide. The Microsoft enhanced CSP can also be used for EFS.

3DES Algorithm Support   Windows XP Professional can be configured to use the triple-DES (3DES) algorithm instead of DESX. 3DES, which is compliant with Federal Information Processing Standards (FIPS 140-1 Level 1), offers significantly stronger encryption using a 128-bit or 168-bit key.

3DES is enabled through a Group Policy setting.

Note   When 3DES is enabled, it is used as the encryption algorithm for IP Security as well as for EFS. For more information about configuring 3DES support, see "Enabling 3DES" later in this chapter.

When 3DES is enabled, all new encryptions are completed by using 3DES. Note that DESX and 3DES are always available for decryption, regardless of the encryption policy.

Data Protection API

The Data Protection API (DPAPI) is a set of function calls that provide data protection services to user and system processes. Applications either pass plaintext data to DPAPI and receive protected data back, or pass the protected data to DPAPI and receive plaintext data back. For example, after a CSP generates keys for certificates, it calls CryptProtectData(), one of the primary functions of DPAPI, to protect those keys. When the keys are needed, DPAPI decrypts them.

EFS FSRTL

The EFS FSRTL is a module within the EFS driver that implements NTFS callouts to handle various file system operations such as reads, writes, and opens on encrypted files and directories, and operations to encrypt, decrypt, and recover file data when it is written to or read from disk. The EFS driver and FSRTL are implemented as a single component. However, they never communicate directly. They use the NTFS file control callout mechanism to pass messages to each other. This ensures that NTFS participates in all file operations. The operations implemented by using the file control mechanisms include writing the EFS attribute data (DDF and DRF) as file attributes and communicating the FEK computed in the EFS service to FSRTL so that it can be set up in the open file context. This file context is then used for transparent encryption and decryption on writes of file data to disk and reads of file data from disk.

Win32 API

EFS provides an API set to expose its features. This API provides a programming interface for operations such as encrypting plaintext files, decrypting or recovering ciphertext files, and importing and exporting encrypted files (without decrypting them first). The API is remoted to support remote encryption, decryption, backup, and restore operations. The API is supported in a standard system DLL, Advapi32.dll.

Encrypting and Decrypting by Using EFS

Encryption and decryption are the primary tasks of EFS. Several different encryption and decryption options are available to users. Users can encrypt and decrypt files by using My Computer and by using the **cipher** command, and optionally by using the shortcut menu accessed by right-clicking a file or folder.

EFS also allows users to encrypt offline files. Additionally, EFS provides several options for users to determine the encryption status of files and folders.

What Can Be Encrypted

Individual files and file folders (or sub-folders) on NTFS volumes can be encrypted. Although it is common to refer to file folders with the encryption attribute set as "encrypted," the folder itself is not encrypted. When encryption is set for a folder, EFS automatically encrypts all new files created in the folder and all files copied or moved into the folder by using My Computer. Offline Files can also be encrypted.

Note   When offline files are encrypted, the entire offline files database is encrypted rather than individual files. Individual files do not display the encryption attribute. The database is encrypted using the system's startup key.

System files and any files in the systemroot folder or its subfolders cannot be encrypted. No files or directories in a roaming user profile can be encrypted. A file cannot be both compressed and encrypted. Being compressed does not prevent encryption, but when the file is encrypted, it is uncompressed.

How Files Are Encrypted

EFS uses a combination of public key and symmetric key encryption to ensure that files are protected from all but the most computationally infeasible methods of attack. Public key encryption algorithms use asymmetric keys for encryption and decryption, which means that different keys are used to encrypt and decrypt the same data. Public key encryption involves the use of a private key (which is held only by its owner) and a public key (which is publicly available on the network). Information that is encrypted by using the public key can be decrypted only by using the corresponding private key. The two keys together are called a key pair or a key set.

Asymmetric cryptography, however, requires a significant amount of processing time for its mathematical operations. Public key operations are often used as part of initial key exchange or key protection operations. As soon as possible, cryptographic services change from public key to symmetric operations, in which the same key is used for both encryption and decryption. Compared with public key operations, symmetric encryption is commonly 100 to 1,000 times faster.

EFS follows the industry standard cryptographic procedure of key encipherment. Data is encrypted using a symmetric file encryption key (FEK) for speed and then the FEK is secured asymmetrically for maximum security. When a user requests that a file be encrypted, EFS uses a uniquely generated FEK to encrypt a file and then encrypts the FEK by using the public key taken from the user's public key certificate. The encrypted FEK is stored in a file header. When a user requests decryption, EFS decrypts the FEK using the user's private key, and then uses the FEK to decrypt the file.

Structure of an Encrypted File

An encrypted file contains encrypted data and a header with fields to store copies of the encrypted FEK for authorized users and designated data recovery agents (DRA). For more information about DRAs, see "Data Recovery and Data Recovery Agents" later in this chapter.

The structure for an encrypted file is shown in Figure 17-2.

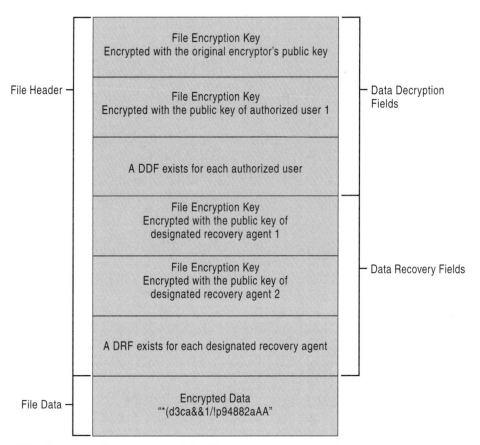

Figure 17-2   Structure of an encrypted data file

Data Decryption Field   An encrypted file contains a minimum of one stored FEK, the FEK encrypted by using the initial encryptor's public key. The storage field for this encrypted FEK is called the *data decryption field* (DDF). Additionally, if an EFS-encrypted file is shared, a copy of the FEK is encrypted by using the newly authorized user's public key, and the encrypted FEK is stored in another DDF.

For more information about sharing encrypted files, see "Authorizing Multi-User Access to Encrypted Files" later in this chapter.

Data Recovery Field   If a computer's effective security policy designates one or more data recovery agent (DRA), then copies of the FEK are encrypted for each DRA using each DRA's public key and stored in another file header field called the *data recovery field* (DRF).

The Encryption Process

When a user encrypts an existing file, the following process occurs:

1. The EFS service opens the file for exclusive access.

2. All data streams in the file are copied to a plaintext temporary file in the system's temporary directory.

3. An FEK is randomly generated and used to encrypt the file by using DESX or 3DES, depending on the effective security policy.

4. A DDF is created to contain the FEK encrypted by using the user's public key. EFS automatically obtains the user's public key from the user's X.509 version 3 file encryption certificate.

5. If a recovery agent has been designated through Group Policy, a DRF is created to contain the FEK encrypted by using RSA and the recovery agent's public key. For more information about using Group Policy to configure data recovery agents, see "Configuring Data Recovery Policy in a Stand-Alone Environment" later in this chapter.

    EFS automatically obtains the recovery agent's public key from the recovery agent's X.509 version 3 certificate for file recovery, which is stored in the EFS recovery policy. If there are multiple recovery agents, a copy of the FEK is encrypted by using each agent's public key, and a DRF is created to store each encrypted FEK.

> **Note**   The file recovery property in the certificate is an example of an enhanced key usage (EKU) field. An EKU extension and extended property specify and limit the valid uses of a certificate. File Recovery is one of the EKU fields defined by Microsoft as part of the Microsoft public key infrastructure (PKI).

6. EFS writes the encrypted data, along with the DDF and the DRF, back to the file. Because symmetric encryption does not add additional data, file size increase is minimal after encryption. The metadata, consisting primarily of encrypted FEKs, is usually less than one kilobyte. File size in bytes before and after encryption is normally reported to be the same.

7. The plaintext temporary file is deleted.

> **Note**   Data from deleted files might not be erased when the file is deleted. The **cipher /w** command can be used to remove data from available unused disk space on the entire volume. For more information about the **cipher** command, see Windows XP Professional Help and Support Center, or use the **cipher /?** command at a command prompt.

When a user saves a file to a folder that has been configured for encryption, the process is similar except that no temporary file is created.

Figure 17-3 illustrates the process of obtaining an FEK to encrypt the data and obtaining public keys to encrypt the FEK, and shows the structure of the encrypted file.

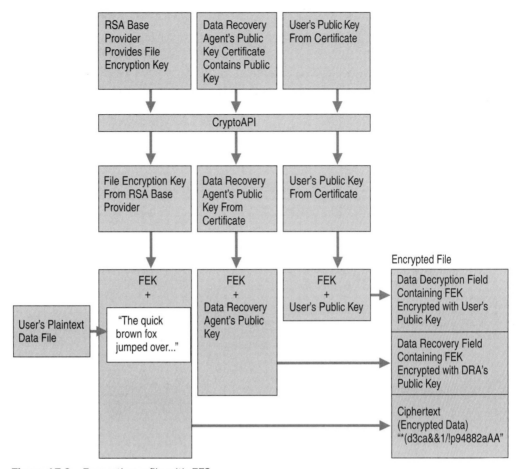

Figure 17-3   Encrypting a file with EFS

The Decryption Process

When an application accesses an encrypted file, decryption proceeds as follows:

1. NTFS recognizes that the file is encrypted and sends a request to the EFS driver.

2. The EFS driver retrieves the DDF and passes it to the EFS service.

3. The EFS service retrieves the user's private key from the user's profile and uses it to decrypt the DDF and obtain the FEK.

4. The EFS service passes the FEK back to the EFS driver.

5. The EFS driver uses the FEK to decrypt sections of the file as needed for the application.

> **Note** When an application opens a file, only those sections of the file that the application is using are decrypted because EFS uses cipher block chaining. The behavior is different if the user removes the encryption attribute from the file. In this case, the entire file is decrypted and rewritten as plaintext.

6. The EFS driver returns the decrypted data to NTFS, which then sends the data to the requesting application.

Figure 17-4 illustrates the process of obtaining the user's private key from the user's profile, using it to decrypt the FEK, and using the FEK to decrypt the data for a user.

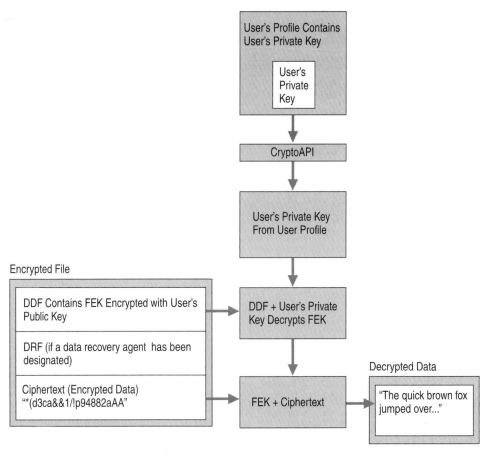

Figure 17-4 Decrypting a file for a user

Working with Encryption and Decryption

When encrypting files, it is best to turn on encryption for folders rather than to encrypt files individually. By using encrypted folders, you do not have to encrypt each file when you save it. This also ensures that any temporary or backup files that the application creates remain encrypted during and after editing, provided that the application does its editing in the same folder. When files or folders are encrypted or decrypted, the date and time stamps on the files and folders are updated to the current date and time.

> **Note**   Applications do not always use the same folder for temporary files or backup files. Microsoft, Word, for example, uses the folder where the encrypted file is located for temporary and backup files but can be configured to use alternate folders. Also, if EFS is appropriate for a specific user, it is a good practice to encrypt the user's My Documents folder because many applications use this folder as the default location to save files. Remember, though, that no files or directories in roaming profiles can be encrypted.

Encrypting and Decrypting Files and Folders by Using My Computer

Applying encryption to a folder by using My Computer is simply a matter of assigning an attribute.

To apply encryption to a folder by using My Computer

1. In **My Computer**, select the folder to encrypt.

2. Right click the folder and click **Properties**.

3. On the **General** tab, click the **Advanced** button.

4. Select the **Encrypt contents to secure data** check box, and then click **OK**.
    When you click OK, if the folder contains unencrypted files or subfolders, another dialog box appears to ask you if you want to apply the changes to just the folder or to the folder, its subfolders, and all files.

Table 17-1 shows the results of selecting the **Apply changes to this folder only** option.

Table 17-1   Results of Selecting the Apply Changes to This Folder Only Option

File Description	Encryption Status
Already stored in the folder and its subfolders.	Unchanged. Files remain either encrypted or unencrypted.
Created in or copied to the folder by you later.	File encrypted and FEK encrypted by using your public key.
Created in or copied to the folder by another user later.	File encrypted and FEK encrypted by using the other user's public key.
Created in or copied to subfolders later.	Unchanged.
Moved to the folder or subfolders later.	Unchanged.

Table 17-2 shows the results of choosing the **Apply changes to this folder, subfolders, and files** option.

Table 17-2   Results of Selecting the Apply Changes to This Folder, Subfolders, and Files Option

File Description	Encryption Status
Already in the folder and its subfolders.	If you have Write permission, file encrypted and FEK encrypted by using your public key; otherwise, files are unchanged.
Later created in or copied to the folder or subfolders by you.	File encrypted and FEK encrypted by using your public key.
Later created in or copied to the folder or subfolders by another user.	File encrypted and FEK encrypted by using the other user's public key.
Later moved to the folder or subfolders.	Moving unencrypted files into an encrypted folder will automatically encrypt those files in the new folder.

With either choice, the folder's list of files remains in plaintext and you can enumerate files as usual.

Caution   EFS lets you encrypt files you do not own, provided that you have Write Attributes, Create Files/Write Data, and List Folder/Read Data permissions for the files. If you select **Apply changes to this folder, subfolders, and files** in folders where other users also store files, no one but you will be able to decrypt the files. If this occurs, you can recover the files by reversing the process. Select the folder and clear the **Encrypt contents to secure data** check box. On a shared computer, it is better to encrypt folders like My Documents for each individual user. If users have roaming profiles, the My Documents folder cannot be encrypted because no files in a roaming profile can be encrypted. In this case, it is better to create individual data folders outside the user profile for each user.

You can turn on EFS for an individual file by using My Computer in the same way that you apply encryption to a folder. However, when you encrypt a single file, the following warning appears: "You have chosen to encrypt a file that is not in an encrypted folder. The file can become decrypted when it is modified." If you select the **Always encrypt only the file** check box, the warning no longer appears, and EFS encrypts only the file that you select.

To decrypt a file or folder by using My Computer

1. Right-click the file or folder, and then click **Properties**.

2. Click **Advanced**, and then clear the **Encrypt contents to secure data** check box.

    This causes EFS to decrypt the selected folder and mark it as unencrypted. When you apply your choice, you also have the option to decrypt all files and subfolders in the folder.

Encrypting and Decrypting Files and Folders by Using the Cipher Command

You can encrypt and decrypt folders or files by using the Cipher.exe command-line utility. Table 17-3 lists the parameters for the tasks that you can perform by using the **cipher** command.

Note   You can use wildcard characters and multiple parameters with the cipher command. A space is required between multiple parameters.

Table 17-3   Tasks and Parameters for the Cipher Command

Task	Parameter(s)
Display the encryption status of files and folders.	Use the **cipher** command with no parameters or with the name of a specific file or folder.
Set the encryption attribute for folders in the current directory.	**/e**
Encrypt files in the current directory.	**/e /a**
Remove the encryption attribute from folders in the current directory.	**/d**
Decrypt files in the current directory.	**/d /a**
Display all of the options available with cipher.	**/?**

In the following example, a folder called "project docs" is encrypted and decrypted. `Cipher "project docs"` displays the status as "U" or unencrypted. `Cipher /e "project docs"` encrypts the folder. `Cipher /d` decrypts the folder.

```
X:\>cipher "project docs"
Listing X:\
New files added to this directory will not be encrypted.
U Project docs

X:\>cipher /e "project docs"
Encrypting directories in X:\
Project docs        [OK]
1 directorie(s) within 1 directorie(s) were encrypted.

X:\>cipher "project docs"
Listing X:\
New files added to this directory will not be encrypted.
E Project docs

X:\>cipher /d "project docs"
Decrypting directories in X:\
Project docs [OK]
1 directorie(s) within 1 directorie(s) were decrypted.

X:\>cipher "project docs"
Listing X:\
New files added to this directory will not be encrypted.
U Project docs
```

Enabling EFS Options on the Shortcut Menu

Some organizations might choose to enable EFS on the shortcut menu. Encrypt and Decrypt are then available when a user right-clicks a file or folder in My Computer.

To enable EFS options on the shortcut menu by editing the registry

1. In the **Run** dialog box, type **regedit.exe**.

2. Navigate to the subkey **HKEY_LOCAL_MACHINE\SOFTWARE\Microsoft\Windows\CurrentVersion\Explorer\Advanced**.

3. On the **Edit** menu, point to **New**, and then click **DWORD Value**.

4. Enter **EncryptionContextMenu** for the value name, and **1** for the value data.

This change takes effect the next time My Computer is opened. When the user right-clicks a file or folder on an NTFS volume, the option to encrypt or decrypt appears on the shortcut menu.

> **Caution**   Do not edit the registry unless you have no alternative. The registry editor bypasses standard safeguards, allowing settings that can damage your system, or even require you to reinstall Windows. If you must edit the registry, back it up first and see the Registry Reference in the Microsoft® Windows® 2000 Server Resource Kit at http://www.microsoft.com/reskit.

Encrypting Offline Files

Microsoft® Windows® 2000 introduced client-side caching functionality, now called Offline Files, which is an IntelliMirror™ management technology that allows network users to access files on network shares even when the client computer is disconnected from the network. When disconnected from the network, mobile users can still browse, read, and edit files by using the same UNC path that is used on the network because the files have been cached on the client computer. When the user later connects to the server, the system reconciles the changes with the server. The Windows XP Professional client can use EFS to encrypt offline files and folders. This feature is especially attractive for traveling professionals who need to work offline periodically and maintain data security.

To encrypt offline files

1. In **My Computer**, on the **Tools** menu, click **Folder Options**.

2. On the **Offline Files** tab, select **Enable Offline Files** and **Encrypt offline files** to secure data, and click **OK**.

Offline files will now be encrypted when cached locally, even if they were not encrypted in the network folder.

Determining Encryption Status By Using My Computer

Because encryption is an attribute of a file or folder, it is possible to determine whether a file or folder is already encrypted by examining its attributes. You can open the Advanced Properties sheet for the file or folder and see that the **Encrypt contents to secure data** check box is selected. You can also add the **Attributes** column to the **Details** view. When you do this, any file with an **E** attribute is encrypted, and any folder with an **E** attribute has the encryption attribute set.

Both encrypted and compressed files can be displayed with alternate colors in My Computer. Encrypted files are green, and compressed files are blue. Files and folders can either be encrypted or compressed, but they cannot be both encrypted and compressed.

To display encrypted files in an alternate color

1. In **My Computer**, on the **Tools** menu, click **Folder Options**.

2. On the **View** tab, select the **Show encrypted or compressed NTFS files in color** check box, and click **OK**. All encrypted file and folder names are displayed in green.

Determining Encryption Status by Using the Cipher Command

Use the **cipher** command with no parameters or with a file or folder name to display encryption status. In the following example, the encryption status of files and folders in the **X:\Project docs** directory is displayed. **Cipher** is executed without any parameters. An "**E**" in the left column means that the file or folder is encrypted, and a "**U**" means that it is unencrypted.

```
X:\Project docs>cipher
Listing X:\Project docs\
New files added to this directory will be encrypted.
E cipher
E plan2.txt
E plan3.txt
E plan4.txt
E plan5.txt
E plan6.txt
E plan7.txt
E plan8.txt
E secretplan.txt
```

Remote EFS Operations on File Shares and Web Folders

Users can encrypt and decrypt files that are stored on network file shares or on Web Distributed Authoring and Versioning (WebDAV) Web folders. Web folders have many advantages compared to file shares, and Microsoft recommends the use of Web folders whenever possible for remote storage of encrypted files. Web folders require less administrative effort and are more secure than file shares. Web folders can also securely store and deliver encrypted files over the Internet by using standard HTTP file transfers. Using file shares for remote EFS operations requires a Windows 2000 or later domain environment because EFS must impersonate the user by using Kerberos delegation to encrypt or decrypt files for the user.

The primary difference between remote EFS operations on files stored on file shares and files stored on Web folders is where the operations occur. When files are stored on file shares, all EFS operations occur on the computer on which the files are stored. For example, if a user connects to a network file share and chooses to open a file that he or she previously encrypted, the file is decrypted on the computer on which the file is stored and then transmitted in plaintext over the network to the user's computer. When files are stored on Web folders, all EFS operations occur on the user's local computer. For example, if a user connects to a Web folder and chooses to open a file that he or she previously encrypted, the file remains encrypted during transmission to the user's computer and is decrypted by EFS on the user's computer. This difference in where EFS operations occur also explains why file shares require more administrative configuration than Web folders.

Remote EFS Operations in a File Share Environment

Remote EFS operations on files stored on network file shares are possible in Windows 2000 or later domain environments only. Domain users can remotely encrypt or decrypt files, but this capability is not enabled by default. The following are requirements for successful remote EFS operations in a file share environment:

1. The files to be encrypted must be available to the user through a network share. Normal share-level security applies.

2. The user must have Write or Modify permissions to encrypt or decrypt a file.

3. The user must have either a local profile on the computer where EFS operations will occur or a roaming profile. If the user does not have a local profile on the remote computer or a roaming profile, EFS creates a local profile for the user on the remote computer.

   If the remote computer is a server in a cluster, the user must have a roaming profile.

4. To encrypt a file, the user must have a valid EFS certificate. If EFS cannot locate a pre-existing certificate, EFS contacts a trusted enterprise certification authority for a certificate. If no trusted enterprise certification authorities are known, a self-signed certificate is created and used. The certificate and keys are stored in the user's profile on the remote computer or in the user's roaming profile if available.

Note   In order to verify a certificate's authenticity, a certification authority signs the certificates that it issues with its private key. EFS creates and uses a self-signed certificate if no file encryption certificate is available from a certification authority. A self-signed certificate indicates that the issuer and subject in the certificate are identical, and that no certification authority has signed the certificate.

5. To decrypt a file, the user's profile must contain the private key associated with the public key used to encrypt the FEK.

6. EFS must impersonate the user to obtain access to the necessary public or private key. This requires the following:

   a. The computer must be a domain member in a domain that uses Kerberos authentication because impersonation relies on Kerberos authentication and delegation.

   b. The computer must be trusted for delegation.

   c. The user must be logged on with a domain account that can be delegated.

Note   Use the Active Directory Users and Computers snap-in to configure delegation options for both users and computers. To trust a computer for delegation, open the computer's Properties sheet, and select **Trusted for delegation**. To allow a user account to be delegated, open the user's Properties sheet. On the Account tab, under Account Options, clear the **The account is sensitive and cannot be delegated** check box. Do not select **The account is trusted for delegation**. This property is not used with EFS.

Remote decryption is a potential security risk because files are decrypted prior to transmission and are transmitted unencrypted. EFS decrypts the file on the computer that stores the encrypted file, and the data is then transmitted over the network in plaintext. Organizations need to consider whether this level of risk is acceptable. You can greatly reduce or eliminate this risk by enabling IP Security to use Encapsulating Security Payload (ESP), which will encrypt transmitted data, enabling another network layer security protocol, or by using Web folders. For more information about configuring IP Security, see "Internet Protocol Security" in the *TCP/IP Core Networking Guide* of the *Microsoft® Windows® 2000 Server Resource Kit.*

Remote Encryption on File Shares

Encrypting files and then encrypting the user's FEK by using the user's public key requires access to the user's EFS certificate. If the user is encrypting a file stored on the computer at which he or she is logged on, EFS uses the existing EFS certificate, obtains a certificate from an enterprise certification authority (CA), or creates a self-signed certificate.

If the user is encrypting a file on a remote computer, EFS must first impersonate the user by using Kerberos delegation. If this impersonation is successful, EFS determines whether the user has a roaming profile and/or a local profile. If the user has a roaming profile, EFS loads it. If not, EFS loads the local profile, if one is available. If no profile can be located, EFS creates one for the user.

EFS looks for a valid EFS certificate and its associated private key in the user's profile. If no certificate exists, or if the profile contains a certificate but not the associated private key, EFS attempts to locate a trusted enterprise CA and obtain an EFS certificate for the user. As part of this attempt, EFS generates a public-private key pair. If a trusted enterprise CA can be contacted, EFS requests a certificate. If a certificate cannot be obtained from a CA, EFS self-signs a certificate.

After EFS has a user profile and a valid certificate, an FEK is created and used to encrypt the file's data. The public key is then used to encrypt the FEK, and the encrypted FEK is stored in the file header.

If EFS creates a public-private key pair, both keys are stored in the user's profile on the remote computer.

Remote Decryption on File Shares

To decrypt a file, EFS must first obtain the user's private key. More specifically, EFS needs the private key associated with the public key used to encrypt the file's FEK. EFS uses the private key to decrypt the FEK and then uses the FEK to decrypt the file. The private key is stored in the user's profile. Before decrypting the file, EFS must:

1. Locate the user's profile. The user is not currently logged on at the remote computer where the decrypting is taking place, so EFS impersonates the user. The user might have a local profile or a roaming profile.

2. Find the appropriate private key. When a profile is located, EFS checks any private keys contained in the profile for a match with the public key that encrypted the FEK.

> **Note**   Public-private key pairs share a "thumbprint" value, a unique hash value stored with each key.

3. Decrypt the FEK. If the user profile contains the correct private key, EFS uses it to decrypt the FEK.

When EFS decrypts a file on the computer at which the user is logged on, the user is already accessing his or her user profile. When the user attempts to decrypt a remote file, however, EFS needs to impersonate the user in order to get access to the user's profile, in which the user's private keys are stored. This requires the computer to be trusted for delegation.

In a remote decryption scenario, then, EFS determines if the computer has been trusted for delegation. If not, the decryption process fails.

The user account must also not be designated as a sensitive account that cannot be delegated. Domain administrator accounts, for example, are flagged as non-forwardable (identity cannot be delegated). Any account that cannot be delegated cannot use EFS remotely.

If the computer is trusted for delegation and the user account that EFS needs to impersonate can be delegated, EFS can next locate the user's profile. The process is similar to that used after a new key pair has been generated and the private key needs storage. EFS looks for a local profile and a roaming profile, and uses the roaming profile if it exists. If the user does not have a local or a roaming profile, the decryption process fails. EFS cannot create a user profile in this situation because it needs the existing private key (and thus the profile in which it is stored) to decrypt the FEK.

If a user profile is located, EFS looks for a private key to match the public key used to encrypt the FEK. If found, the private key is used to decrypt the FEK, and file decryption can begin. If the private key is not found, the decryption process fails.

When the FEK is decrypted and used to decrypt the file, the data is ready to be transmitted in plaintext across the network.

Note that an attacker can use network monitoring software to access the plaintext data as it is transmitted over the network. You can prevent this by using IP Security with ESP and encryption to secure data as it is transmitted, or by storing encrypted files on Web folders.

Local and Remote File Operations in a File Share Environment

Encrypted files and folders can be renamed, copied, or moved. Renaming an encrypted file or folder either locally or remotely does not cause decryption. However, moving or copying a file or folder can result in decryption. The effects of moving or copying encrypted files and folders vary according to whether the files or folders are moved or copied locally or remotely.

For more information about renaming, copying, or moving encrypted files and folders, see Windows XP Professional Help and Support Center.

Local File Operations and Encrypted Files   Encrypted files or folders retain their encryption after being either copied or moved, either by using My Computer or by using command-line tools, to local volumes, provided that the target volume uses the version of NTFS used in Windows 2000 or later. Otherwise, encrypted files are stored as plaintext, and encrypted folders lose the encryption attribute.

Note   Most floppy disk drives are FAT volumes, so encryption is lost when files are copied to disk unless the files are backed up by using the Backup tool before they are copied. Encrypted files that are copied or moved to servers or workstations running Microsoft® Windows NT® 4.0 also lose their encryption.

Local File Operations and Plaintext Files   When plaintext files are copied or moved in My Computer to an encrypted folder on a local NTFS volume, they are encrypted. Plaintext files are also encrypted if they are copied to an encrypted folder on a local volume by using the **copy** or **xcopy** commands.

The **move** command produces different results if the plaintext file is moved to an encrypted folder on the same volume or on a different local volume. If the **move** command is used to move a plaintext file to an encrypted folder on the same volume, the file remains in plaintext. This is because the move command simply renames the file, unless the file is moved to a different volume. If the file is moved to an encrypted folder on a different local volume, it is encrypted.

Renaming plaintext files that are in encrypted folders produces different results at the command line and in My Computer. If a plaintext file in an encrypted folder is renamed in My Computer, the resulting file is encrypted. If the file is renamed by using the **ren** command, it remains in plaintext.

Remote File Operations   When encrypted files or folders are copied or moved to or from a network file share on a remote computer, the files are decrypted locally, transmitted in plaintext, and then re-encrypted on the target volume if possible. Encrypted files transmitted to or from Web folders remain encrypted during transmission. With remote file operations, EFS must impersonate the encryptor, so the encryptor's account must be configured to enable delegation, and the remote computer must be trusted for delegation. EFS makes use of either an existing EFS certificate for the encryptor if one is available, a certificate obtained from a trusted enterprise CA, or a self-signed certificate.

Encrypted files or folders retain their encryption after being either copied or moved from a local to a remote computer, provided that the remote computer is trusted for delegation and the target volume uses the version of NTFS used in Windows 2000 or later. A moved or copied file is re-encrypted on the target volume, so it has a new FEK, and the FEK is encrypted by using the user's public key if it is available or by using a new public key EFS generates if the profile is unavailable. In the latter case, a new user profile is generated for the user on the remote computer to store the new private key.

If all of the conditions necessary for remote encryption are not met, the transfer might fail. If the computer is not trusted for delegation, EFS cannot impersonate the user. When this occurs, the user receives an "Access is denied" message. If EFS can successfully impersonate the user, but the target volume does not use the version of NTFS used in Windows 2000 or later, the transfer will succeed, but the file or folder loses its encrypted status.

File Operations to Non-EFS Capable Volumes   Encrypted files might need to be decrypted before the files can be copied or moved to volumes that are not EFS-capable. For any file operation in My Computer, if the destination volume is not capable of re-encrypting the file, the following message is displayed to the user: "The file *filename* cannot be copied or moved without losing its encryption. You can choose to ignore this error and continue, or cancel." If the user chooses to ignore the message, the file is copied or moved, but is stored in plaintext on the destination volume.

Attempts to copy encrypted files by using either the **copy** or **xcopy** commands to non-EFS capable volumes fail. In both cases an error message informs the user that the operation failed because the file could not be encrypted. If used with appropriate parameters, however, the **copy** and **xcopy** commands can be used to copy encrypted files to non-EFS capable volumes.

Note   The **copy** and **xcopy** command-line parameters that enable copying of encrypted files to non-EFS capable volumes are available in Windows XP Professional, but are not available in earlier versions of Windows.

Table 17-4 lists the parameters for the tasks that you can perform by using the copy and xcopy commands.

Table 17-4   Tasks and Parameters for the Copy and Xcopy Commands

Task	Parameter
Copy encrypted files to non-EFS capable volumes by using the copy command.	**copy /d**
Copy encrypted files to non-EFS capable volumes by using the xcopy command.	**xcopy /g**

Remote EFS Operations in a Web Folder Environment

When users open encrypted files stored on Web folders, the files remain encrypted during the file transfer, and EFS decrypts them locally. Both uploads to and downloads from Web folders are raw data transfers, so even if an attacker could access the data during the transmission of an encrypted file, the captured data would be encrypted and unusable.

EFS with Web folders eliminates the need for specialized software to securely share encrypted files between users, businesses, or organizations. Files can be stored on common intranet or Internet file servers for easy access while strong security is maintained by EFS.

The WebDAV redirector is a mini-redirector that supports the WebDAV protocol, an extension to the HTTP 1.1 standard, for remote document sharing over HTTP. The WebDAV redirector supports the use of existing applications, and it allows file sharing across the Internet (for example, using firewalls, routers) to HTTP servers. Internet Information Services (IIS) version 5.0 (Windows 2000) supports Web folders.

Users access Web folders in the same way that they access file shares. Users can map a network drive to a Web folder by using the **net use** command or by using My Computer. Upon connecting to the Web folder, the user can choose to copy, encrypt, or decrypt files exactly as they would by using files on file shares.

> **Note**   Web folders are not included in browse lists. To connect to a Web folder, the user must specify the full path (for example, \\Server-Name\WebShareName).

Creating a Web Folder

You can create a Web folder on a server that is running Internet Information Services 5.0 or later. WebDAV is an Internet standard protocol, and WebDAV implementations are possible with other third-party Internet servers.

To create a Web folder

1. Right-click a folder on the server, and then select **Properties**.

2. On the **Web Sharing** tab, click the **Share this folder** button.

3. On the **Edit Alias** screen, enter an alias (equivalent of a share name) and appropriate permissions.

   For more information about configuring WebDAV folders, see Internet Information Services 5.0 Help.

Remote Encryption of Files on Web Folders

When a user chooses to encrypt a file on a Web folder, the file is automatically copied from the Web folder to the user's computer, encrypted on the user's computer, and then returned to the Web folder. The advantage to this is that the computer hosting the Web folder does not need to be trusted for delegation and does not require roaming or remote user profiles. No other administrative tasks beyond creating the Web folder and assigning user permissions are required. The disadvantage is that the file must be transmitted from the Web folder to the local computer in order to be encrypted. Organizations need to consider whether the bandwidth requirements for Web folders outweigh the administrative effort necessary to maintain file shares for encrypted file storage. It must also be considered that Web folders are not recommended for files over 60 MB in size.

> **Note**   Bandwidth requirements are reduced if the user encrypts the file locally and then stores the file on the Web folder. The encrypted file is also transmitted in ciphertext when it is transmitted to a Web folder.

Remote Decryption of Files on Web Folders

When a user chooses to decrypt a file on a Web folder, the file is automatically copied from the Web folder to the user's computer in ciphertext. EFS then decrypts the file on the user's computer. If the user opens the encrypted file for use in an application, the file is never decrypted anywhere except on the user's computer. If the user chooses to decrypt a file on the Web folder rather than on the local computer, the file is transmitted in plaintext and stored in plaintext on the Web folder after it is decrypted on the user's computer. The computer hosting the Web folder does not require any configuration except for the creation of the Web folder and the assigning of user permissions in order for remote decryption to function.

File Copy from a Web Folder

Encrypted files are copied from Web folders in the same way that plaintext files are copied from file shares. The **copy** and **xcopy** commands do not require any special parameters. The file is transmitted in ciphertext and remains encrypted on the local computer if possible. The encryption status for files copied from Web folders is the same as that for files copied locally. For more information about encryption status for files copied locally and about the **copy** and **xcopy** commands, see "Local and Remote File Operations in a File Share Environment" earlier in this chapter.

Delivering EFS Certificates to Users

All EFS users must have valid certificates for use with EFS. All designated DRAs must have valid file recovery certificates. These certificates can be created and self-signed by EFS if no certification authorities (CA) are available. Users can request certificates from an enterprise CA.

How EFS Uses Certificates

When a user sets the encrypted attribute for a file or folder, EFS attempts to locate the user's certificate in the personal certificate store. If the user does not have a certificate that has been authorized for use with EFS, EFS requests a certificate from an available enterprise certification authority (CA). If an enterprise CA is not available, EFS automatically generates its own self-signed certificate for the user.

In either case, a public-private key pair for use with the certificate is generated by CryptoAPI. The public key is stored in the user's certificate, the certificate is stored in the user's personal certificate store, and the private key is securely stored in the user's profile.

Each time a user accesses an encrypted file or creates a new encrypted file, EFS needs to access the user's EFS certificate to obtain the public key and/or to access the user's private key. In all cases, the private key is used to decrypt FEKs, and the public key is used to encrypt FEKs.

If the EFS user certificate expires, EFS ensures that the certificate is renewed if possible or if not, that a new public-private key pair and a new public key certificate are issued for the user the next time an EFS operation is performed for that user.

> **Note**   Certificates that EFS generates are self-signed rather than signed by a CA. Therefore, the certification path is the same as for root CA certificates, which are also self-signed. EFS certificates that are self-signed are identified by Windows XP Professional as "not trusted" because the certifying authority does not have a certificate in the Trusted Root Certification Authorities store. Nevertheless, self-signed EFS certificates are valid for use by EFS.

Determining Whether an EFS Certificate Exists

If you upgraded from Windows 2000 Professional, a certificate might already exist for you. If your computer is not joined to a domain, and you have encrypted a file, EFS has generated a self-signed certificate for you. You can determine whether you have an existing certificate by using the Certificates snap-in.

To view your certificates by using the Certificates snap-in

1. Open the Certificates snap-in configured for **My user account**.

2. Expand the **Personal** folder, and then right-click **Certificates**.

Figure 17-5 shows the EFS certificate for the account **alice**.

Figure 17-5   Certificates snap-in and EFS certificate

If the issuer (**Issued By**) is the same as the subject (**Issued To**), the certificate is self-signed. If the certificate is issued by a certification authority, its name is listed in the **Issued By** column.

Obtaining an EFS Certificate in a Stand-Alone Environment

In a stand-alone environment, EFS automatically generates EFS certificates. Users obtain a certificate by encrypting a file. Each user who logs on at the computer can encrypt files, and EFS generates a unique certificate and key pair for each user. Unless a user shares the encrypted files for others to access, no user can access another user's files.

You can also request certificates by using the Advanced Certificate page Web form.

Using Enterprise Certification Authorities to Issue Certificates

Domain environments can be configured so that EFS works just as it does in a stand-alone environment, creating self-signed certificates for users. Enterprise CAs can also be configured in the domain to create certificates for users. Certificates that are issued by enterprise certification authorities (CA) are based on certificate templates. Certificate templates are stored in Active Directory and define the attributes of certificate types to be issued to users and computers. The following three version 1 certificate templates support EFS user operations by default:

- User

- Administrator

- Basic EFS

Administrator and user certificates have a number of uses in addition to EFS. A basic EFS certificate can be used for EFS operations only.

Enterprise CAs use Access Control Lists (ACLs) for certificate templates in Active Directory to determine whether to approve certificate requests. If a user has the Enroll permission for a certificate template, the CA will issue a certificate of the type defined by the template to the user.

By default, members of the Domain Admins and Domain Users security groups have Enroll permission for basic EFS certificates and user certificates. By default, members of the Domain Admins and Enterprise Admins security groups have Enroll permission for administrator certificates.

Users can obtain an EFS certificate from an Enterprise CA by using one of these methods:

- On-demand enrollment using an Enterprise CA and properly configured certificate templates

- Manual enrollment by the end-user

Using an Enterprise CA ensures that users can easily and seamlessly obtain EFS certificates. This is also the lowest-cost option for certificate deployment.

Certificates can be requested from a CA by using the Certificates snap-in.

To request a certificate from a CA

1. Open the **Certificates** snap-in, expand **Personal folder**, right-click **Certificates**, and then select **All Tasks** and **Request New Certificate**. The Request New Certificate wizard starts.

2. On the **Certificate Types** screen, select **Basic EFS**, and click **Next**.

3. Enter a **Friendly name** and a **Description**, and click **Next**.

4. Click **Finish** to close the Request New Certificate wizard.

Open the Certificates folder to see the new certificate. In Figure 17-6, the administrator has a self-signed recovery certificate that EFS generated for the default EFS recovery policy. You can tell that the File Recovery certificate is self-signed because Issued To is the same as Issued By. Below it is the EFS certificate that was just requested. The EFS certificate was issued by a certification authority named CA1.

Figure 17-6   Certificates snap-in

Renewing Certificates and Keys

EFS automatically renews certificates if possible. Self-signed certificates are valid for 100 years, so renewal is not an issue if you use these certificates. Certificates issued by certification authorities are typically valid for only a few years. You can view a certificate's expiration date in the Certificates snap-in. If EFS is unable to automatically renew an expired certificate, you are unable to encrypt more files by using the existing certificate. You can still decrypt files, however, because EFS stores existing private keys. If EFS cannot renew the certificate, it requests a new certificate from a trusted enterprise CA if one is known and available. Otherwise, EFS creates a new self-signed certificate.

If for any reason you want to generate a new self-signed certificate for a user, you can use the **cipher** command.

To generate a new certificate by using the cipher command

- At the command line, type:

```
cipher /k
```

The output is the identifier that links the new private and public keys. You can view this identifier in the EFS certificate in the Certificates snap-in.

The following is an example of output from the **cipher** command.

```
X:\>cipher /k
Your new file encryption certificate thumbnail information on the PC named WK-01 is:
   AEE8 15AD 68EE B640 9CD7 C25F 4E98 4CBC C2D9 7378
```

> **Note**   If you generate a new certificate and key by using **cipher /k**, new files are encrypted using the new public key. Existing encrypted files are decrypted by using the old private key, which continues to be stored in the user's profile.

Replacing Self-Signed Certificates with CA-issued Certificates

Self-signed certificates enable users to use EFS in the absence of a public key infrastructure or Active Directory. When a CA is deployed, however, PKI administrators need to migrate users from their existing self-signed certificates to CA-issued certificates. Otherwise, EFS continues to use the self-signed certificate, even if a CA has issued a new certificate.

Users can request new CA-issued file encryption certificates for EFS to replace their existing self-signed file encryption certificates by using the **cipher** command.

To request a CA-issued file encryption certificate

- At the command line, type:

```
cipher /k
```

   This causes Windows XP Professional to archive the existing self-signed certificate and request a new one from a trusted CA. Any files that have been encrypted by using the earlier public key can still be decrypted, and when they are subsequently saved, they can be encrypted by using the new public key.

> **Warning**   Archived certificates must not be deleted. When a certificate is deleted, the corresponding private key is also deleted. Without the private key, files previously encrypted cannot be decrypted. Users can use the **cipher /u** command to update encrypted files on local drives by using the new keys.

The **cipher** utility can be called in a logon script to automatically and invisibly migrate users. This utility only works locally. It cannot request new certificates for files that have been encrypted on remote servers.

> **Note**   If the **cipher /k** command is used to replace a self-signed certificate, but no trusted enterprise CA can be located, the existing self-signed certificate is replaced with a new self-signed certificate.

Authorizing Multi-User Access to Encrypted Files

Users can share encrypted files with other local, domain, and trusted domain users. Authorizing user access to encrypted files is a separate process from sharing files for network access by using share-level security and access control lists. Because there is no method to issue a certificate for a group, only individual user accounts can be authorized for access to an encrypted file. Groups cannot be authorized for access.

How Users Are Authorized for Access to Encrypted Files

After a file has been encrypted, additional users can be authorized to access encrypted files by using the Advanced Attributes dialog box in the file's properties. When the original encryptor or another authorized user shares the encrypted file with another user, EFS uses the following process:

1. An authorized user opens the **Advanced Attributes** dialog box for the encrypted file and clicks the **Details** button.

2. In the **Encryption Details** dialog box, the user clicks the **Add** button to open the **Select User** dialog box. EFS certificates stored in the user's profile in the **Other People** and **Trusted People** certificate stores are automatically displayed. To locate user certificates that are stored in Active Directory, the user can click the **Find User** button, and then click the **Find Now** button to locate the selected user(s). A dialog box will display any users that hold valid EFS certificates in the Active Directory based on the search criteria.

   EFS certificates can also be imported to the user's profile. If the EFS certificate is self-signed, it is added to Trusted People. If the EFS certificate was issued by a CA, it is added to Other People. Certificates added to either container appear in the **Select User** dialog box.

Note If you import someone's certificate, you have the option to manually select its location. If you import a self-signed certificate, be sure to add it to Trusted People. Certificates in Trusted People are the only certificates that are not chain validated because the certificates are already trusted. Self-signed certificates will always fail chain validation because no CA was involved in certifying them, so placing them anywhere other than in Trusted People makes them unusable.

3. Before a user can be authorized to access an encrypted file and be added to the file, EFS needs to determine whether the certificate can be trusted. When a user's certificate is selected, EFS attempts to validate the certificate chain. If the chain validation fails, CryptoAPI also checks to see if the certificate is in Trusted People store. If not, the certificate cannot be used.

   Imported self-signed certificates are automatically placed in Trusted People, and there is no certificate chain to validate, so the user can be added to the encrypted file.

   If the certificate was signed by a CA, EFS attempts to build a certification chain and validate the certificate. If the chain ends with an untrusted root CA, EFS will not use the certificate, and the user is not added to the file. If the user's EFS certificate is signed by a CA and includes information about certificate revocation list (CRL) distribution points, EFS attempts to connect with the distribution points to check for certificate revocation. If a CRL distribution point cannot be reached, the certificate will not be used, even if the root is trusted. Finally, if the EFS certificate is signed by a CA, the CA is trusted, and the CA does not use CRL distribution points, EFS accepts the certificate and adds the user.

4. For the next part of the process, assume that Alice already has access to the encrypted file. She is either the original encryptor, or she has been authorized for access. Alice is authorizing Bob to access the file.

5. EFS obtains Alice's private key from her user profile to decrypt the FEK contained in the file's data decryption field.

6. EFS obtains Bob's public key from his certificate and uses it to encrypt the FEK.

7. Bob's encrypted FEK is stored in a new data decryption field with the file.

Note At no time in this process is the file itself decrypted, so it is not at risk directly. However, the FEK is briefly decrypted. Because EFS performs this operation in nonpaged memory, the decrypted FEK is never paged and so is never exposed.

Figure 17-7 shows what happens when Alice shares an encrypted file with Bob.

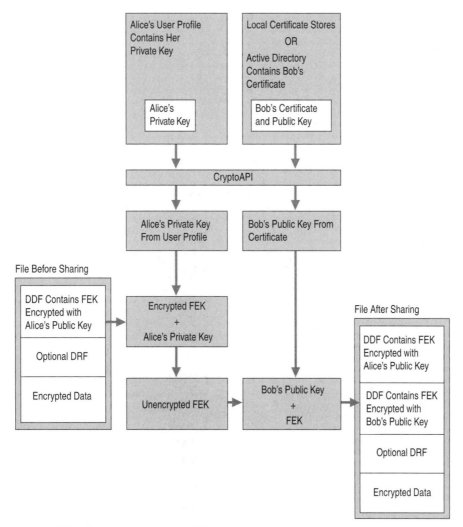

Figure 17-7   Sharing an encrypted file

Considerations for Sharing Encrypted Files

It is important that users electing to share encrypted files keep the following points in mind:

1. Shared EFS files are not file shares. If authorized users need to access shared EFS files over the network, a file share or a Web folder is required. Alternatively, users could establish remote sessions with computers that store encrypted files by using Terminal Services.

2. Any user who is authorized to decrypt a file can authorize other users to access the file. Granting access is not limited to the file owner. Caution users to share files only with trusted accounts, because those accounts can authorize other accounts. Removing the Write permission from a user or group of users can prevent this problem, but it also prevents the user or group from modifying the file.

3. EFS sharing requires that the users who will be authorized to access the encrypted file have EFS certificates. These certificates can be located in roaming profiles or in the user profiles on the computer on which the file to be shared is stored, or they can be stored in and retrieved from Active Directory.

4. EFS sharing of an encrypted file often means that the file will be accessed across the network. It is best if Web folders are used for encrypted file storage whenever possible. For more information about using Web folders to share encrypted files, see "Remote EFS Operations on File Shares and Web Folders" earlier in this chapter.

5. If a user chooses to remotely access an encrypted file stored on a file share and to authorize other users to access the file, the authorization process and requirements are the same as on the local computer. Additionally, EFS must impersonate the user in order to perform this operation, and all of the requirements for remote EFS operations on files stored on file shares apply. For more information about the requirements for EFS operations, see "Remote EFS Operations on File Shares and Web Folders" earlier in this chapter.

6. If a user chooses to remotely access an encrypted file stored on a Web folder and to authorize other users to access the file, the file is automatically transmitted to the local computer in ciphertext. The authorization process takes place on the local computer with the same requirements as for encrypted files stored locally.

Sharing Encrypted Files

You can authorize individual users to access encrypted files.

To share an encrypted file with other users

1. In **My Computer**, right-click the encrypted file, and then click **Properties**.

2. On the **General** tab, select **Advanced**.

3. In the **Advanced Attributes** dialog box, under **Compress or Encrypt Attributes**, select **Details**.

> **Note**   If you select an encrypted folder instead of an encrypted file, the **Details** button appears dimmed. You can add users to individual encrypted files but not to folders.

4. In the **Encryption Details** dialog box, click **Add**.

5. Add a user from the local computer or from Active Directory.

To add a user from the local computer

- In the **Select Users** dialog box, click the user's certificate, and then click **OK**.

To add a user from Active Directory

1. Click **Find User**. In the **Find Users, Contacts, and Groups** dialog box, click **Browse** to search for users.

2. In the **Browse for Container** dialog box, click the folder or domain in which you want to begin your search. You can perform your search in the entire directory or start searching from a folder or domain within the directory.

3. To narrow the search, click **Advanced** and then click **Field** to search for users by using conditions and values.

4. Select the user, and then click **OK**.

> **Caution**   Any authorized user of an encrypted file can authorize other users' access, so it is important to authorize access for trusted accounts only.

Taking Recovery Precautions

Encrypting a file always includes a risk that it cannot be read again. The owner of the private key, without which a file cannot be decrypted, might leave the organization without decrypting all of his or her files. Worse yet, he or she might intentionally or accidentally encrypt critical shared files so that no one else can use them. A user's profile might be damaged or deleted, meaning that the user no longer has the private key needed to decrypt the file's FEK. Because losing data is often disastrous, there are four methods of recovering when encrypted files cannot be decrypted. You can use data recovery agents, export and import of EFS recovery keys, and Backup for file backup and restoration.

Data Recovery and Data Recovery Agents

You can use Local Policy on stand-alone computers to designate one or more users, typically Administrator accounts, as data recovery agents. These DRAs are issued recovery certificates with public and private keys that are used for EFS data recovery operations.

The default design for the EFS recovery policy is different in Windows XP Professional than it was in Windows 2000 Professional. Stand-alone computers do not have a default DRA, but Microsoft strongly recommends that all environments have at least one designated DRA.

In a Windows 2000 environment, if an administrator attempts to configure an EFS recovery policy with no recovery agent certificates, EFS is automatically disabled. In a Windows XP Professional environment, the same action enables users to encrypt files without a DRA. In a mixed environment an empty EFS recovery policy turns off EFS on Windows 2000 computers, but only eliminates the requirement for a DRA on Windows XP Professional computers.

When a domain user logs on at a domain computer that is within the scope of the EFS recovery policy, all DRA certificates are cached in the computer's certificate store. This means that EFS on every domain computer can easily access and use the DRA's public key (or multiple public keys if multiple DRAs are designated). On computers where an EFS recovery policy is in effect, every encrypted file contains at least one data recovery field, in which the file's FEK is encrypted by using the DRA's public key and stored. By using the associated private key, any designated DRA can decrypt any encrypted file within the scope of the EFS recovery policy.

Warning   The private key for a DRA must be located on the computer where recovery operations are to be conducted.

Because each DRA has a distinct private key that can decrypt a file's FEK, data recovery discloses only the encrypted data, not the private keys of any user other than the DRA. A private key for recovery cannot decrypt the DDF. If there are multiple recovery agent accounts, each private key for recovery decrypts only its own DRF and no other. Thus, there is no danger that an unauthorized recovery agent account can access information from the file that enables access to other files.

Note   It is best not to encrypt files when you are logged on with a DRA account. The effectiveness of EFS recovery is compromised if a file's creator is both the user and the recovery agent.

For more information about encrypted file recovery, see Windows XP Professional Help and Support Center.

For more information about how to change EFS recovery policy for the local computer, see Windows XP Professional Help and Support Center and "Configuring Data Recovery Policy in a Stand-Alone Environment" later in this chapter.

Data Recovery Implementation Considerations

When designating DRAs for your files, it is important to keep the following considerations in mind:

1. Files are more secure, but less recoverable, if only one person can decrypt them. If you choose not to designate any DRAs, be sure that user profiles are backed up regularly. The user's private key, without which the file cannot be decrypted, is stored in the user profile. Additionally, because users can have multiple profiles on multiple computers or might have a roaming profile, be sure that all profiles are being backed up. This is especially true for notebook computers. If the user logs on with a local account and encrypts a file, the private key for that transaction is contained in the user profile for the local account, not the user's domain account profile.

   The most effective way for users to ensure access to encrypted files is to export their EFS certificates and private keys. For more information about exporting EFS certificates and keys, see "Exporting and Importing EFS and DRA Certificates and Private Keys" later in this chapter.

2. Files are less secure, but more recoverable, if more than one person can decrypt them. If you want the ability to recover encrypted files, designate one or more DRAs by using the EFS recovery policy.

3. For more flexible EFS recovery management, consider issuing EFS recovery certificates to designated recovery agent accounts, in addition to the default Administrator account. Also, legal or corporate policy might require that the recovery agent account be different from the domain Administrator account. You can also configure EFS recovery policy for portable computers to use the same recovery agent certificates, whether the computers are connected to domains or are operated as stand-alone computers.

4. EFS is normally used to encrypt user data files. Application files (for example, .exe, .dll, .ini files) are rarely encrypted. If computers are configured to use System Restore as part of recovery policy, application files are saved at restore points. These files can then be restored to return the system to a previous state. If application files that System Restore is monitoring are encrypted, it is important to note the following expected results of restoration:

   - If you decrypt a previously encrypted monitored file or folder, and then restore to a point before the file or folder was decrypted, the restored file or folder remains decrypted. If you undo the restore, the file or folder remains decrypted.

- If you encrypt a monitored file, and then restore to a point before the monitored file was encrypted, the restored file is unencrypted. If you undo the restore, the file remains unencrypted.

- If you modify a monitored file that is encrypted for multiple users, and then restore to a point before the modification occurred, the file will be accessible only to the first user who modified the file after the restore point was created. If you undo the restore, only the user who ran the restore will be able to access the file. The filter will back up the file during restore in the context of the user who is running the restore operation.

- If you delete a monitored encrypted file and then restore to a point before the deletion, the deleted file is restored with its encryption attributes intact. If you undo the restore, the file is again deleted.

- If you encrypt a directory and then restore to a point before it was encrypted, the directory remains encrypted. Monitored files created in this directory after the restore point are encrypted, but they will be deleted by a restore. Monitored files moved into this directory retain the encryption status from the directory in which they were created. After the restore, monitored files will be moved back to their original directory and retain the encryption status from that directory. If you undo the restore, the directory remains encrypted, and files are returned.

- If you modify an encrypted directory (for example, change its name) and then restore to a point before the modification, the modification is lost, but the directory remains encrypted. If you undo the restore, the modification returns and the directory remains encrypted.

- If you delete a directory that is encrypted and then restore to a point before it was deleted, the directory retains its encryption status. If you undo the restore, the directory is again deleted.

If you encrypt application files, consider these recommendations:

- The best practice is to place these files in a partition/drive that is excluded from System Restore protection. This reduces the risk of restoring files to a pre-encrypted state.

- If you choose to encrypt application files and use System Restore on the partition/drive storing the files, turn off System Restore (losing all previous restore points), complete the encryption settings, and then turn System Restore back on. This ensures that the files cannot be reverted to a pre-encrypted state.

To configure System Restore

1. On the **System Tools** menu, click **System Restore**.

2. Select **System Restore Settings**, and configure the options as appropriate for your environment.

> **Note**   You must be an administrator to configure System Restore.

Data Recovery Agent Decryption Process

The process for decrypting a file for a DRA is identical to that described earlier for a user except that the copy of the FEK encrypted by using the DRA's public key is taken from the file's DRF, decrypted, and used to decrypt the file.

Figure 17-8 illustrates the process of obtaining the DRA's private key from his or her user profile, using it to decrypt the FEK, and using the FEK to decrypt the data.

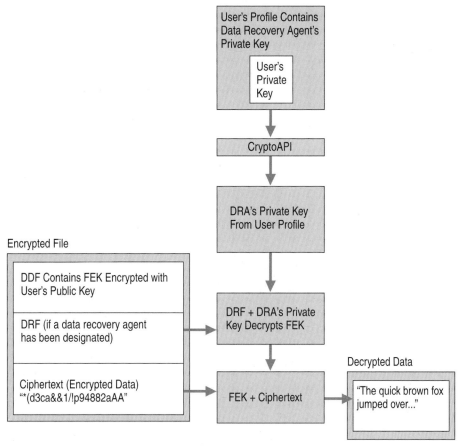

Figure 17-8   Decrypting a file for a data recovery agent

Configuring Data Recovery Policy in a Stand-Alone Environment

In a stand-alone environment, an administrator for the computer needs to generate a recovery agent certificate and designate a DRA.

Designating a Data Recovery Agent in a Stand-Alone Environment

For stand-alone computers, Windows XP Professional does not create a default recovery agent. A DRA can be added by using Group Policy on the local computer, but the intended DRA must first have a recovery certificate. Because the computer is stand-alone, EFS creates a self-signed certificate for the DRA. This requires the **cipher.exe** command-line utility.

To generate a recovery agent certificate

1. Log on as an administrator.

2. At a command prompt, type:

   ```
   cipher /r:filename
   ```

   This generates importable .pfx and .cer files with the file names you specify.

To designate a DRA

1. Log on as the intended DRA.

2. Open the Certificates snap-in, and import the .cer file containing the recovery agent certificate.

   – or –

   Import the .pfx file containing the recovery key.

> **Note**   For more information about importing certificates, see "Exporting and Importing EFS and DRA Certificates and Private Keys" later in this chapter.

The local administrator can now open the Group Policy MMC snap-in and add the DRA.

To remove a DRA

1. In **Local Computer** node of Group Policy, expand **Computer Configuration**.

2. Expand **Windows Settings, Security Settings, Public Key Policies,** and **Encrypting File System**.

3. Select the DRA to remove and delete the certificate.

Exporting and Importing EFS and DRA Certificates and Private Keys

As added protection in the event that a user's certificate or private key is damaged or lost, certificates and private keys can be exported. The certificate is stored in a file with a .cer extension, and the certificate and private key are stored in a password-protected file with a .pfx extension. These archive files can be stored on a floppy disk or other medium, and can be imported easily from these files.

Exporting these keys does not automatically remove them from the system; however, it is possible to remove the private key after it has been exported. Public keys are always available. They do not need to be removed. Circumstances might warrant removal of the private key, however.

If an EFS user wants to safeguard against loss of a private key through, for example, a damaged or deleted user profile, it can be exported and protected it with a strong password. Keys can be exported to a floppy disk, and the disk can be stored off-site or locked in a vault, depending on the level of security needed.

If one or more DRAs have been designated by Group Policy, it is important that those keys be exported. In addition, it is recommended that you:

- Protect exported private keys by using strong passwords.

- Delete exported private keys from the system after export.

- Store exported DRA keys on a floppy disk or other media in a physically secure location (for example, a vault).

In a domain environment, when DRAs are designated by Group Policy, any DRA can recover (decrypt) any domain user's encrypted files. Each encrypted file can have one or more data recovery fields, in which a copy of the file's FEK is encrypted by using a DRA's public key and stored. The DRA's private key, however, is not needed unless an EFS user is unable to decrypt a file. If a file needs to be recovered, a DRA can either import his or her private key on the computer where the encrypted file is stored, or the user can use the Backup utility included with Windows XP Professional to back up the encrypted file and make it available for the DRA to restore on a computer used for data recovery.

> **Caution**   Every DRA has a personal EFS certificate and private key. Normally, when the DRA recovers a file, the DRA's personal private key is used. However, recovery certificates and keys are not bound to a specific user. Anyone who has access to a DRA's private key can import that key and use it to decrypt any files for which the DRA is a recovery agent. Therefore, it is extremely important to protect exported private keys by using strong passwords and physically secure storage.

Exporting Certificates and Keys

You can use the Certificate Export wizard to export a certificate and private key to a removable medium. The same process is used to export any certificate.

To export a certificate

1. Open the Certificates snap-in, and then expand the **Personal** folder.

2. Double-click **Certificates**, and then right-click the certificate you want to export.

3. Select **All Tasks**, and then select **Export**.

4. Select **Yes, export the private key**.

   The export format is PCKS #12. You have the option of deleting the private key or leaving it on the computer. If you are backing up an EFS certificate and keys, you might want to leave the private key on the computer so that you can decrypt your files without importing the private key. If you are backing up a file recovery certificate and keys, it is best if you delete the private key after the export. The private key is only needed for disaster recovery, and files are more secure if the private key is removed.

5. Select an option, and then click **Next**.

6. Enter a password to protect your exported private key. It is best if you use a strong password.

7. Click **Next**.

8. Enter a file name for the exported certificate and private key.

9. Click **Next**, review the final information, and then click **Finish**.

   The export file has a .pfx extension.

Importing Certificates

The same process is used to import either an EFS certificate or a File Recovery certificate.

To import a certificate

1. Open the Certificates snap-in, and then expand the **Personal** folder.

2. Right-click the **Certificates** folder, click **All Tasks** and click **Import**.

   This starts the Certificate Import Wizard. You can also start this wizard by double-clicking a certificate file.

3. In the dialog box, enter the name of your certificate file.

4. Enter the password that protects the private key. This password was created during export. You have the option of protecting the imported private key by using the same password. If you enable this option, you will be prompted to enter this password when you attempt to open an encrypted file.

> **Note**   Enabling the option to protect the imported private key adds another layer of protection. However, if the password needed to open the file is forgotten, you will not be able to open the files. A designated data recovery agent would have to import the file recovery private key and open the file.

You also have the option of marking the key as exportable. If you are importing from a backup copy of your keys and plan to keep the backup copy, it is best not to select this option. This prevents an attacker from exporting your EFS private key.

5. Designate a location for the certificate. The default location is the personal certificate store.

Backing Up and Restoring Encrypted Files or Folders

In Windows XP Professional, encrypted files and folders remain encrypted if you back them up by using Backup in Administrative Tools. You can also use the **ntbackup** command, the backup APIs, or other backup products designed for use with Windows XP Professional. Backup files remain encrypted when transferred across the network or when copied or moved onto any storage medium, including non-NTFS volumes. If backup files are restored to volumes formatted by using the version of NTFS used in Windows 2000 or later, they remain encrypted. Along with providing excellent disaster recovery, backups can also be used to securely move files between computers, sites, and so on.

Opening restored, encrypted files is no different from decrypting and opening any encrypted files. However, if files are restored from backup onto a new computer, in a new forest, or at any location at which the user's profile (and thus the private key needed to decrypt the files) is not available, the user can import an EFS certificate and private key. After importing the certificate and private key, the user can decrypt the files.

Recovering Encrypted Files

Any data recovery agent can recover an encrypted file when a user's private key fails to decrypt the file.

To recover an encrypted file

1. Log on to a computer that has access to the user's profile; for example, a computer that has a designated recovery console or a recovery key on removable media such as a floppy disk. You might log on at the user's computer or the user might have a roaming profile.

2. Locate the encrypted file. For example, the user might have made a backup of the file by using Backup or sent the file to a WebDAV Web folder.

3. Decrypt the file by using either the **cipher** command or My Computer. This will make the file available to the user.

    For more information about decrypting files, see "Working with Encryption and Decryption" earlier in this chapter.

Strengthening Key and File Security

When an encrypted file is saved, Windows XP Professional automatically provides four levels of encryption and a fifth, the startup key, can be configured. These levels of encryption protect the encryption keys that are used to protect the file:

1. EFS provides the FEK, which encrypts the data in the file.

2. EFS uses the public key in the user's EFS certificate to encrypt the FEK. The public key and certificate are stored by default in the computer's certificate store. The corresponding private key, used to decrypt the FEK, is stored in an encrypted form in the user's profile for the corresponding user or the data recovery agent account in the RSA folder.

3. The Data Protection API generates the user's master key that is used to encrypt the user's private keys.

4. The Data Protection API generates a symmetric password encryption key, derived from a hash of the file creator's credentials, which encrypts the user's master key.

5. A startup key (also called the syskey) can be used to protect all master keys as well as a variety of other secrets that are stored on computers. At system startup, the startup key is used to encrypt all of the private keys on the computer, including private keys that are used for EFS. Startup keys are automatically generated and used for computers in a domain but must be manually configured on stand-alone computers. Startup key security can be increased by storing the key on removable media or by requiring a system startup password.

Windows XP Professional provides several configuration options that increase security. To prevent loss of access to your master keys on stand-alone computers, you can create a password reset disk (PRD). To provide stronger encryption for files, you can enable the 3DES encryption algorithm. In addition, you can implement options to prevent your computer from entering hibernation mode and to delete paging files at system shutdown so that data is not needlessly exposed.

Certificate and Public Key Storage

Windows XP Professional stores a user's public key certificates in the user's personal certificate store. Certificates are stored in plaintext because they are public information, and they are digitally signed by certification authorities to protect against tampering.

User certificates are located in the Documents and Settings*username* \\Application Data\\Microsoft\\SystemCertificates\\My\\Certificates folder for each user profile. These certificates are written to the user's personal store in the system registry each time the user logs on to the computer. For roaming profiles, users' certificates are located on the domain controller and follow users when they log on to different computers in the domain.

Private Key Storage

Private keys for the Microsoft RSA-based cryptographic service providers (CSPs), including the Base CSP and the Enhanced CSP, are located in the user profile under *RootDirectory*\\Documents and Settings*username*\\Application Data\\Microsoft \\Crypto\\RSA. In the case of a roaming user profile, private keys reside in the RSA folder on the domain controller and are downloaded to the user's computer until the user logs off or the computer is restarted.

Because private keys must be protected, all files in the RSA folder are automatically encrypted by using a random symmetric key called the user's master key. The user's master key is 64 bytes in length and is generated by a strong random number generator. 3DES keys are derived from the master key and are used to protect private keys. The master key is generated automatically and is periodically renewed. It encrypts each file in the RSA folder automatically as the file is created.

For more information about CryptoAPI, see the Software Development Kit (SDK) link on the Web Resources page at http://www.microsoft.com/windows/reskits /webresources.

For more information about Data Protection API, see the Technet link on the Web resources page at http://www.microsoft.com/windows/reskits/webresources.

Caution   The RSA folder must never be renamed or moved. This is the only place the CSPs look for private keys. If you need additional protection for this folder, the administrator can provide additional file system security for users' computers or use roaming profiles.

Master Key Storage and Security

The Data Protection API automatically encrypts the user's master key or keys. Master keys are stored in the user profile under *RootDirectory*\Documents and Settings *username*\Application Data\Microsoft\Protect. For a domain user who has a roaming profile, the master key is located in the user's profile and is downloaded to the user's profile on the local computer until the computer is restarted.

While the user is logged on, when a master key is not being used for a cryptographic operation, it is encrypted and stored on disk. Before master keys are stored, they are 3DES-encrypted using a key derived from the user's password. When a user changes his or her logon password, master keys are automatically unencrypted and re-encrypted using the new password.

Master Key Loss and Data Recovery

If a logon password is forgotten or if an administrator resets a user password, the user's master keys become inaccessible. Because the decryption key is derived from the user's password, the system is unable to decrypt the master keys. Without the master keys, EFS-encrypted files are also inaccessible to the user, and can only be recovered by a data recovery agent, if one has been configured, or through the use of a password reset disk (PRD), if one has been created.

> **Note** The password reset disk feature is available for local accounts only. Domain account passwords cannot be backed up by using a PRD.

For example, Alice uses EFS on her stand-alone computer to encrypt her private files. She forgets her password but remembers the password for the built-in administrator account. She logs on as the administrator and resets the password for her account named Alice. When she resets the password, she is able to log on as Alice, but files that she encrypted as Alice are inaccessible because the master keys are inaccessible.

Alice can recover her encrypted data in two ways. First, if a data recovery agent was configured for Alice's computer before she encrypted the files, the DRA can recover the files. Second, even without a DRA, if Alice created a PRD before she lost or reset her password, she can use the PRD to safely change her password and recover her data.

Password Reset Disk Creation

PRDs protect against loss of access to master keys and encrypted files on stand-alone computers. Users can create PRDs for their own user accounts. When a user creates a PRD, the system creates a public-private key pair and a self-signed certificate. The user's password is encrypted by using the public key and stored locally in the registry at HKEY_LOCAL_MACHINE\SECURITY\Recovery*<user SID>*.

The private key is exported to a removable media and deleted from the local computer.

To create a password reset disk for your user account

1. In **Control Panel**, click **User Accounts**.

2. Click your user account.

3. Under **Related Tasks**, select **Prevent a forgotten password**. This starts the Forgotten Password wizard.

4. On the welcome screen, click **Next**.

5. Select the removable drive on which you would like to store your password key, and then click **Next**.

6. Enter your current password, and click **Next**.

If you have created a PRD and you forget your password or enter the wrong password, you will be prompted with the following message: "Did you forget your password? You can use your password reset disk." You can then use the Password Reset wizard to reset your password. The system will do the following:

1. Use the private key stored on the PRD to decrypt the stored copy of your old password.

2. Create a decryption key based on an SHA-1 hash of your old password.

3. Decrypt your master keys by using the decryption key.

4. Prompt you for a new password.

5. Encrypt master keys by using your new password.

To use the PRD to reset your password

1. At the logon screen, click **use your password reset disk** to start the Password Reset wizard, and then click **Next**.

2. Insert the removable media that contains your password key, and then click **Next**.

3. Enter your new password in the Reset the User Account Password dialog box, and then click **Next**.

Enabling the Startup Key

The Syskey wizard enables startup key protection. If enabled, the startup key protects the following sensitive information:

- Master keys that are used to protect private keys.

- Protection keys for user account passwords stored in Active Directory.

- Protection keys for passwords stored in the registry in the local Security Accounts Manager (SAM) registry key.

- Protection keys for LSA secrets.

- The protection key for the administrator account password that is used for system recovery startup in safe mode.

You must be a member of the local Administrators group to use the **syskey** command. Using this utility, an administrator can configure the system to do one of the following:

1. Use a computer-generated random key as the startup key, and store it on the local system by using a complex obfuscation algorithm that scatters the startup key throughout the registry. This option enables computer restarts without the need to enter the startup key.

2. Use a computer-generated random key, but store it on a floppy disk. The floppy disk must be inserted into a drive during system startup for the startup sequence to complete. This option is more secure than the first, but effectively rules out restarting the computer remotely.

> **Warning** If the startup key password is forgotten or the floppy disk that contains the startup key is lost, it might not be possible to start the system. If this occurs, the only way to recover the system is to use a repair disk to restore the registry to a state prior to when startup key protection was enabled. Any changes that were made after that time would be lost. Therefore it is important to store the startup key safely. If it is on a floppy disk, make backup copies and store them in different locations.

3. Use a password chosen by the administrator to derive the startup key. The administrator is prompted for the password during the initial startup sequence.

> **Note** After startup key protection is enabled, it cannot be disabled, but it can be configured to operate at different security levels.

To enable startup key protection

1. At the command line, type:

```
syskey
```

2. Click **Encryption Enabled**, and then click **OK**.

   – or –

   Click **Update**, if encryption was previously enabled.

3. Select an option for the key.

   The default option is a system-generated password that is stored locally. If you use the password-derived startup key option, **syskey** does not enforce a minimum password length. However, passwords longer than 12 characters are recommended. The maximum length is 128 characters.

4. Click **OK** to restart the computer.

   When the system restarts, you might be prompted to enter the startup key, depending on the key option you selected. The first use of the startup key is detected and a new random password encryption key is generated. The password encryption key is protected by using the startup key, and then all account password information is strongly encrypted.

   After the startup key has been enabled, the following process occurs at system startups:

- The startup key is retrieved from the locally stored key, the password entry, or insertion of a floppy disk, depending on the option you selected.

- The startup key is used to decrypt the master protection key.

- The master protection key is used to derive the per-user account password encryption key, which is then used to decrypt the password information in Active Directory or the local SAM registry key.

   The **syskey** command can be used again later to change the startup key storage option or to change the password. Changing the startup key requires knowledge of, or possession of, the current startup key.

To change the startup key option or password

1. At the command line, type:

   `syskey`

2. In the first dialog box, click **Update**.

3. In the next dialog box, select a key option or change the password, and then click **OK**.

4. Restart the computer.

Enabling 3DES

You can strengthen security by replacing the default DESX algorithm with 3DES. In a stand-alone environment, enabling 3DES is recommended. In a domain environment, the appropriate encryption algorithm is typically determined by corporate policy.

3DES can be enabled by using the system cryptography Group Policy setting. If this setting is configured for 3DES, IP Security and EFS both use 3DES for encryption. Not all IP Security implementations are capable of encrypting by using 3DES, however. Windows 2000 without the High Encryption Pack, for example, cannot use 3DES. It is also possible to configure EFS to use 3DES without affecting encryption elsewhere. This requires modification of a registry setting.

To enable system-wide 3DES by using Group Policy

1. In **Computer Configuration**, expand **Windows Settings**, **Security Settings**, **Local Policies**, and then expand **Security Options**.

2. Double-click **System cryptography: Use FIPS compliant algorithms for encryption**.

3. Select **Enabled**, and then click **OK**.

   To enable 3DES for EFS only, a registry entry must be added.

To enable 3DES for EFS only

1. In the **Run** dialog box, type **regedit.exe**.

2. Navigate to the subkey **HKEY_LOCAL_MACHINE\SOFTWARE\Microsoft \Windows NT\CurrentVersion\EFS**.

3. On the **Edit** menu, point to **New**, and then click **DWORD Value**.

4. Enter **AlgorithmID** for the value name and **0x6603** for the value data to enable 3DES.

5. Restart the computer.

6. To disable 3DES and enable DESX, simply delete the AlgorithmID setting and restart the computer.

> **Caution** Do not edit the registry unless you have no alternative. The registry editor bypasses standard safeguards, allowing settings that can damage your system, or even require you to reinstall Windows. If you must edit the registry, back it up first and see the Registry Reference in the Microsoft Windows 2000 Server Resource Kit at http://www.microsoft.com/reskit.

7. When 3DES is enabled, files encrypted by using both the DESX and 3DES algorithms can be decrypted. However, all new files are encrypted by using the 3DES algorithm.

Caution   If a user needs to access an encrypted file from both Windows 2000 and Windows XP Professional, do not enable the 3DES algorithm. The Windows 2000 operating system does not support the 3DES algorithm by default. However, if the High Encryption Pack has been installed on Windows 2000, it can use 3DES.

Increasing Security for Open Encrypted Files

File data is decrypted before it is sent to an application. This means that the FEK is also decrypted. Although the FEK is not exposed, file data might be.

Because the EFS File System Run-Time Library (FSRTL) is located in the Windows operating system kernel and uses the nonpaged pool to store the FEK, FEKs cannot be leaked to paging files. However, because the contents of paging files are not encrypted, the plaintext contents of encrypted files might temporarily be copied to paging files when open for application use. If the plaintext contents of encrypted files are copied to a paging file, the plaintext remains in the paging file until the contents are replaced by new data. Plaintext contents can remain in paging files for a considerable amount of time even after applications close the encrypted files.

A paging file is a system file, so it cannot be encrypted. (By default, the name of the paging file is Pagefile.sys.) The file system security for paging files prevents any user from gaining access to and reading these files, and these security settings cannot be changed. However, someone other than the authorized user might start the computer under a different operating system to read a paging file.

To prevent others from reading the contents of paging files that might contain plaintext of encrypted files, you can do either of the following:

- Disable hibernation mode on your computer.

- Configure security settings to clear the paging files every time the computer shuts down.

Disabling Hibernation Mode

When a computer hibernates, the contents of system memory and any open files are written to a storage file on the hard drive, and the system is powered off. This saves energy and allows the computer to be restarted with the same applications and files that were open when the system hibernated. However, hibernation can be a security risk because files are decrypted for use in applications. If an encrypted file is opened and then the system is hibernated, the contents of the open encrypted file will be in the hibernation storage file as plaintext. An attacker could potentially access the storage file used during hibernation. For this reason, EFS users might want to disable hibernation so that encrypted files are not placed at risk. If you choose to use hibernation mode, be sure to close any open encrypted files before letting the system hibernate.

To disable hibernation

1. In **Control Panel**, double-click **Performance and Maintenance**, and then click **Power Options**.

2. On the **Hibernate** tab, clear the **Enable hibernate** check box.

3. Click **Apply**.

Clearing the Paging File at Shutdown

When a file is encrypted or decrypted, plaintext data can be paged. This can be a security problem if an attacker boots the system by using another operating system and opens the paging file. The paging file can be cleared at shutdown by means of Group Policy.

To clear the paging file at shutdown

1. In the Group Policy snap-in, select a Group Policy object to edit.

2. Expand Computer Configuration and Windows Settings, Security Settings, Local Policies, and then expand Security Options.

3. Double-click **Shutdown: Clear virtual memory pagefile**.

4. Click **Enabled**, and then click **OK**.

Disabling EFS

EFS is enabled by default but can be disabled for individual files or individual file folders, or disabled entirely for a computer or domain. Disabling EFS for a stand-alone computer requires adding an entry to the registry.

Disabling EFS for an Individual File

Although files can be made unencryptable by setting the system attribute or placing the file in the %systemroot% folder or any of its subfolders, these options are unde-sirable in many cases. For example, system files are also normally hidden from view, and a user might want a file that is unencryptable to be visible to other users.

> **Note**   Even with Write permission, users cannot encrypt files or folders in the %systemroot% folder, or files or folders that have their system attribute set. If these types of files and folders could be encrypted, it might render the system useless. This is because many of these files are needed for the system to start up, and decryption keys are not available during the startup process to decrypt them.

Denying Write permissions for a file also makes it unencryptable by the users or groups within the scope of the denial. Simply attributing the file as read-only, however, does not prevent encryption. A user who has Write permissions can encrypt read-only files.

In most cases, the best solution is to disable EFS for a folder rather than an individual file.

Disabling EFS for a File Folder

To disable encryption within a folder, create a file called Desktop.ini that contains:

```
[Encryption]
Disable=1
```

Save the file in the directory in which you want to disable EFS. If a user attempts to encrypt the folder or any files in the folder, a message tells the user that "An error occurred applying attributes to the file: *filename.* The directory has been disabled for encryption."

> **Note**   The Desktop.ini file affects only the current folder and the files in it. If you create a subfolder, both the subfolder and any files in it can be encrypted. Also, encrypted files can be copied or moved, without losing their encryption, into the directory that contains the Desktop.ini file.

Disabling EFS for a Stand-Alone Computer

A registry entry must be added to disable EFS for a stand-alone computer.

To disable EFS on a stand-alone computer by editing the registry

1. In the **Run** dialog box, type **regedit.exe**.

2. Navigate to the subkey **HKEY_LOCAL_MACHINE\SOFTWARE\Microsoft \Windows NT\CurrentVersion\EFS**.

3. On the **Edit** menu, point to **New**, and then click **DWORD Value**.

4. Enter **EfsConfiguration** for the value name and **1** for the value data to disable EFS (a value of **0** enables EFS).

5. Restart the computer.

6. If EFS is disabled and a user tries to encrypt a file or folder, a message tells the user that "An error occurred applying attributes to the file: filename. The directory has been disabled for encryption."

> **Note**   Do not edit the registry unless you have no alternative. The registry editor bypasses standard safeguards, allowing settings that can damage your system, or even require you to reinstall Windows. If you must edit the registry, back it up first and see the Registry Reference in the Microsoft Windows 2000 Server Resource Kit at http://www.microsoft.com/reskit.

Tips for Implementing EFS

Encryption is a sensitive operation. It is important that encrypted data not become decrypted inadvertently. To this end, it is recommended that users do the following:

- The most important practice is to have users export their EFS certificates and private keys to removable media, and store the media securely. It is best if users do not remove the private keys from their computers because they will not be able to decrypt any files without importing the private key. The most common EFS-related problem that users encounter is the inability to decrypt files after losing access to the EFS private key in the user profile. Users who switch between operating systems can also benefit from exporting their EFS certificates and private keys. If both operating systems can use EFS, users can import their certificates and keys. This enables them to access their encrypted files when they are logged on to either operating system.

- Export the private keys for recovery accounts, store them in a safe place on secure media, and remove the keys from computers. This prevents someone from using the recovery account on the computer to read files that are encrypted by others. This is especially important for stand-alone computers where the recovery account is the local Administrator or another local account. For example, a portable computer that contains encrypted files might be lost or stolen, but if the private key for recovery is not on the computer, no one can log on as the recovery account and use it to recover files.

- The private keys associated with recovery certificates are extremely sensitive. Export each such key into a .pfx file, protected under a strong password, to removable media, and then physically secure the media.

- Do not use the recovery agent account for any other purpose.

- Do not destroy recovery certificates and private keys when recovery agent policy changes. Keep them in archives until you are sure that all files that are protected by them have been updated with new recovery agent information.

- Encrypt the My Documents folder (*RootDirectory\UserProfile*My Documents). This ensures that personal folders where most Microsoft Office documents are saved are encrypted by default. Remember, however, that no files or directories in roaming profiles can be encrypted. Encrypt folders rather than individual files. Applications work on files in various ways; for example, some applications create temporary files in the same folder during editing. These temporary files might or might not be encrypted, and some applications substitute them for the original when the edit is saved. Encrypting at the folder level ensures that files do not get decrypted transparently in this way.

- Never rename or move the RSA folder. This is the only place EFS looks for private keys.

- In a domain, change the default recovery agent account (the Administrator of the first domain controller installed for the domain) as soon as possible, and set a password for each recovery agent account. This adds an extra layer of protection in case the Administrator account is compromised, and provides easy tracking of use of the recovery account.

- Designate two or more recovery agent accounts per organizational unit (a subgroup of computers, or even a single computer, within a domain), depending on the size of the organizational unit. Designate one computer for each designated recovery agent account, and give permission to appropriate administrators to use the recovery agent accounts.

- Implement a recovery agent archive program to ensure that EFS files can be recovered by means of obsolete recovery keys. Recovery certificates and private keys must be exported and stored in a controlled and secure manner. It is recommended that you store archives in a controlled-access vault, and that you have a master archive and a backup archive. The master archive is located onsite; the backup archive is located in a secure off-site location.

- Configure Syskey for stand-alone computers that are not members of a domain to provide startup key protection for the EFS users' private keys.

- Encourage users in stand-alone environments to create password reset disks in case they forget their passwords. This enables recovery of the master key for stand-alone computers.

- Use WebDAV folders to store encrypted files that must be transmitted across the network, especially public networks. This ensures that the data is encrypted during transmission.

Troubleshooting EFS

In some situations EFS might not operate as expected. Some EFS issues can be resolved very simply, while others require complex high-level administrative solutions. Understanding how EFS works is the basis for resolving EFS issues. This section presents some common situations that might arise with EFS and the most likely causes for these problems.

For more information about troubleshooting EFS, see Windows XP Professional Help and Support Center.

Unable to Encrypt Files

If you find that you are unable to encrypt files or folders, one of the following might be the cause:

- The file is not an NTFS volume.

- You do not have Write access to the file.

- If you are having trouble encrypting a remote file, check to see that your user profile is available for EFS to use on that computer (this typically means having a roaming user profile), make sure the remote computer is trusted for delegation, and make sure your account is configured to enable delegation. Sensitive accounts are not enabled for delegation by default, so users like Enterprise Administrator might not be able to encrypt or decrypt files remotely.

Note   Sometimes users think that a file is not encrypted because they can open it and read the file. You can verify whether a file is encrypted by checking the file's attributes.

For more information about formatting volumes as NTFS, see Windows XP Professional Help and Support Center.

For more information about the encryption process, requirements, and procedures, see "Encrypting and Decrypting By Using EFS" earlier in this chapter.

For more information about remote EFS operations, see "Remote EFS Operations in a File Share Environment" earlier in this chapter.

Unable to Decrypt Remote Files

The following are the major causes of and solutions for remote decryption failure (usually indicated by an "Access is denied" message):

- The computer on which the encrypted file is stored is not trusted for delegation. Every computer that stores encrypted files for remote access must be trusted for delegation. To check a computer's delegation status, open the computer's properties sheet in the Active Directory Users and Computers snap-in.

- The user account that EFS needs to impersonate cannot be delegated. To check a user's delegation status, open the user's Properties sheet in the Active Directory Users and Computers snap-in.

- The user's profile is not available. Using roaming user profiles is the solution for this problem.

- One of the user's profiles is available, but it does not contain the correct private key. Using roaming user profiles is the solution for this problem.

For more information about the decryption process, requirements, and procedures, see "Encrypting and Decrypting By Using EFS" earlier in this chapter.

For more information about remote EFS operations, see "Remote EFS Operations in a File Share Environment" earlier in this chapter.

Unable to Open Encrypted Files

If you are unable to open an encrypted file, you might not have the correct EFS certificate and private key for the file. If the file is old, the public key and private key set might no longer be available. Although expired certificates and private keys are archived, users can delete archived certificates and private keys, or they can be damaged. If this has occurred, you can recover the file.

This problem can also occur when a computer that previously operated in stand-alone mode is now a member of a domain. The file might have been encrypted by a local self-signed certificate issued by the computer, but the CA designated at the domain level is now the issuing authority.

To access a file that was encrypted while the computer was in stand-alone mode, log off, and then log back on to the local computer instead of the domain.

The same conditions apply for encrypting and decrypting remote files. The user's profile must be available for EFS to use, the computer must be trusted for delegation, and the user's account must be enabled for delegation.

For information about how to recover files, see "Recovering Encrypted Files" earlier in this chapter.

For more information about encryption and decryption processes, requirements, and procedures, see "Encrypting and Decrypting By Using EFS" earlier in this chapter.

For more information about remote EFS operations, see "Remote EFS Operations in a File Share Environment" earlier in this chapter.

Determining Whether the Certificate Used to Encrypt a File is Still Available for Decryption

The public key certificate is not used for decryption because it does not contain the private key. However, if a file cannot be decrypted, you can determine who is authorized to access the file and which certificate and public key were used to encrypt the file. This information is listed in the Encryption Details dialog box under a file's advanced properties. When you determine whether the user has been authorized to access the file, you can determine what certificate was used to encrypt the file. Then you can determine whether the certificate is still available. If the certificate is not available, the private key will not be available, and the user will not be able to decrypt the file. If the certificate is available, the user might have exported the private key and deleted it from the computer.

To view authorized users and certificate thumbprint information

1. Right-click the encrypted file and then click **Properties**.

2. On the General tab, in the **Attributes** section, click **Advanced**.

3. In the **Advanced Attributes** dialog box, click **Details** to open **Encryption Details**. Users who are authorized to access the file are listed under **Users Who Can Transparently Access This File**. The thumbprint for the certificate used to encrypt the file is listed with the name of the authorized user.
   Note that any data recovery agents are listed as well.

To compare the certificate thumbprint associated with the encrypted file with other certificate thumbprints

1. Open the **Certificates** snap-in and locate the user's certificates.

2. Double-click a certificate and then click the **Details** tab. The certificate thumbprint is one of the listed details.

3. Compare the certificate thumbprint associated with the encrypted file with the thumbprints of each of the user's EFS certificates.

Determining Whether the Access Problem Is Related to the Availability of the Necessary Private Key

If the user who wants to access the file is not listed in Users Who Can Transparently Access This File, the user has not been authorized to access the file or has been deleted from the authorized user list. You can then determine whether the user is supposed to be authorized to access the file.

If the user is already authorized to access the file, you can compare the certificate thumbprint listed next to the users' name with thumbprints of the user's certificates in the Certificates snap-in.

- If the thumbprint listed in Users Who Can Transparently Access This File matches the thumbprint for the user's EFS certificate, an access problem probably results from either exporting the private key and deleting it from the system or from other access rights issues. Determine whether the user has exported and saved the private key. If so, the private key can be imported and access to the file is restored.

- If the thumbprint listed in Users Who Can Transparently Access This File does not match any thumbprints for the user's certificates, it is likely that the certificate has been deleted. This means that the private key has also been deleted. Determine whether the user exported the certificate and keys before deleting the certificate. If so, the certificate and keys can be imported to restore access to the file.

If the EFS certificate used to encrypt the file is available, determine whether the user has the necessary read and write permissions for the file. If the user does have read and write permission, it is likely that the private key was exported and deleted from the computer.

If the necessary private key is not available and cannot be imported, you can use the Encryption Details dialog box to determine whether any other users or any data recovery agents are authorized to access the file. If so, you can have any of these authorized users decrypt the file.

If the necessary private key is not available and cannot be imported, and there are no other authorized users or any data recovery agents, the file cannot be recovered. Determine whether the user's profile is available for restore from backup.

Encrypted File Is Unencrypted When Copied or Moved

Encrypted files are decrypted when they are copied or moved to non-EFS capable volumes. If the user copies or moves files by using My Computer, the system provides a warning to the user if the destination volume is not EFS capable. If the user copies or moves files by using the **copy /d** command or the **xcopy /g** command, the files will be decrypted on the target volume with no warning that this has occurred.

For more information about changes to encryption status when files are copied or moved, see "Remote EFS Operations In A File Share Environment" earlier in this chapter.

Virus Check Program Cannot Check All Files

When your virus check program tries to check all the files on your hard disk, you get an "Access is denied" error message. Your virus check program can only read files that have been encrypted by you. If other users have encrypted files on your hard disk, access to these files is denied to the virus check program. To perform a virus check for files that have been encrypted by other users, the other users must log on and run the virus check program.

Common Error Messages

While performing EFS tasks, users might encounter error messages. The following are the most common messages that can occur and the possible causes for them.

Access is denied You might receive an "Access is denied" message in one of the following situations:

- You do not have basic permissions to access the file (for example, the file is read-only).

- You are trying to encrypt a system file or folder. System files and folders cannot be encrypted.

- You are trying to share an encrypted file with someone but you are not authorized.

- You are trying to decrypt a file that you did not encrypt and for which you have not been authorized.

- You are trying to decrypt a file that you encrypted or that you are authorized to access, but your private key (and probably your user profile) is not available.

The directory has been disabled for encryption This message appears if a user tries to encrypt a folder (or files in the folder) in which a Desktop.ini file has been placed with encryption disabled.

The server is not trusted for remote encryption operation This message might appear if the remote server that stores a file or folder you are attempting to encrypt or decrypt is not trusted for delegation.

The disk partition does not support file encryption EFS cannot be enabled on a non-NTFS disk partition. To use EFS, the disk partition must be NTFS.

No valid key set This message typically occurs in remote encryption or decryption operations. It means that EFS could not locate the correct keys for the operation. This is most likely to occur in remote decryption scenarios. EFS needs to locate your user profile and the private key associated with the public key used to encrypt the file's FEK. This error message might occur if the profile cannot be found, or if the profile can be found but does not contain the correct private key.

Additional Resources

These resources contain additional information and tools related to this chapter.

Related Information

- "File Systems" in this book for more information about NTFS.

- "Supporting Mobile Users" in this book for more information about solutions for mobile users.

- "Cryptography for Network and Information Security" in the *Distributed Systems Guide* of the *Microsoft® Windows® 2000 Server Resource Kit* for more information about cryptography.

- "Windows 2000 Certificate Services and Public Key Infrastructure" in the *Distributed Systems Guide* of the *Microsoft® Windows® 2000 Server Resource Kit* for information about the public key infrastructure in Windows.

- *Microsoft® Internet Information Services 5.0 Resource Guide*, 2000, Redmond, WA: Microsoft Press for more information about WebDAV.

- The Software Development Kit (SDK) link on the Web Resources page at http://www.microsoft.com/windows/reskits/webresources for more information about CryptoAPI.

- The Technet link on the Web resources page at http://www.microsoft.com/windows/reskits/webresources for more information about Data Protection API.

Chapter 18

Implementing TCP/IP Security

This chapter is from the Microsoft® Windows® Security Resource Kit *by Ben Smith and Brian Komar with the Microsoft Security Team (Microsoft Press, 2003).*

TCP/IP is an industry-standard suite of protocols designed to facilitate communication between computers on large networks. TCP/IP was developed in 1969 by the U.S. Department of Defense Advanced Research Projects Agency (DARPA), as the result of a resource-sharing experiment called ARPANET (Advanced Research Projects Agency Network). Since 1969, ARPANET has grown into a worldwide community of networks known as the Internet, and TCP/IP has become the primary protocol used on all networks. Unfortunately, TCP/IP was not designed with security in mind and thus has very few security components by default. Consequently, it is often a source of network vulnerabilities. On your Microsoft Windows 2000 and Windows XP computers, you can secure the TCP/IP protocol in several ways, which include securing the TCP/IP stack itself and using IP Security (IPSec). We will examine both techniques in this chapter.

Securing TCP/IP

You cannot successfully secure computer networks without knowing how TCP/IP works. Nearly all computers today use TCP/IP as their primary network communication protocol. Thus, without physical access to a computer, an attacker must use TCP/IP to attack it. Consequently, TCP/IP security is often your first line of defense against attackers attempting to compromise your organization's network and therefore should be part of any defense-in-depth strategy for securing networks. You can secure the TCP/IP protocol in Windows 2000 and Windows XP to protect a computer against common attacks, such as denial-of-service attacks, and to help prevent attacks on applications that use the TCP/IP protocol.

Understanding Internet Layer Protocols

TCP/IP primarily operates at two levels in the OSI model: the Internet layer and the transport layer. The Internet layer is responsible for addressing, packaging, and routing functions. The core protocols of the Internet layer include the Internet Protocol (IP), Address Resolution Protocol (ARP), and Internet Control Message Protocol (ICMP):

- **IP**   A routable protocol responsible for logical addressing, routing, and the fragmentation and reassembly of packets

- **ARP**   Resolves IP addresses to Media Access Control (MAC) addresses and vice versa

- **ICMP**   Provides diagnostic functions and reporting errors for unsuccessful delivery of IP packets

The TCP/IP protocol suite includes a series of interconnected protocols called the *core protocols*. All other applications and protocols in the TCP/IP protocol suite rely on the basic services provided by several protocols, including IP, ARP, and ICMP.

IP

IP is a connectionless, unreliable datagram protocol primarily responsible for addressing and routing packets between hosts. *Connectionless* means that a session is not established to manage the exchange data. *Unreliable* means that delivery is not guaranteed. IP always makes a best-effort attempt to deliver a packet. An IP packet might be lost, delivered out of sequence, duplicated, or delayed. IP does not attempt to recover from these types of errors. The acknowledgment of packets delivered and the recovery of lost packets is the responsibility of a higher-layer protocol, such as TCP. IP is defined in RFC 791.

An IP packet consists of an IP header and an IP payload. The IP header contains information about the IP packet itself, and the IP payload is the data being encapsulated by the IP protocol to be transmitted to the receiving host. The following list describes the key fields in the IP header:

- **Source IP Address**   The IP address of the source of the IP datagram.

- **Destination IP Address**   The IP address of the destination of the IP datagram.

- **Identification**   Used to identify a specific IP datagram and all fragments of a specific IP datagram if fragmentation occurs.

- **Protocol**   Informs IP at the destination host whether to pass the packet up to TCP, UDP, ICMP, or other protocols.

- **Checksum**   A simple mathematical computation used to verify the integrity of the IP header. If the IP header does not match the checksum, the receiving host will disregard the packet. This checksum does not include any information outside the IP header.

- **Time To Live (TTL)**   Designates the number of networks on which the datagram is allowed to travel before being discarded by a router. The TTL is set by the sending host and used to prevent packets from endlessly circulating on an IP network. When forwarding an IP packet, routers decrease the TTL by at least one.

- **Fragmentation And Reassembly**   If a router receives an IP packet that is too large for the network to which the packet is being forwarded, IP fragments the original packet into smaller packets that fit on the downstream network. When the packets arrive at their final destination, IP on the destination host reassembles the fragments into the original payload. This process is referred to as fragmentation and reassembly. Fragmentation can occur in environments that have a mix of networking technologies, such as Ethernet and Token Ring. The fragmentation and reassembly works as follows:

  1. When an IP packet is sent, the sending host places a unique value in the Identification field.

  2. The IP packet is received at the router. If the router determines that the Maximum Transmission Unit (MTU) of the network onto which the packet is to be forwarded is smaller than the size of the IP packet, the router fragments the original IP payload into multiple packets, each of which is smaller than the receiving network's MTU size. Each fragment is sent with its own IP header that contains the following:

     The original Identification field, which identifies all fragments that belong together.

The More Fragments flag, which indicates that other fragments follow. The More Fragments flag is not set on the last fragment because no other fragments follow it.

The Fragment Offset field, which indicates the position of the fragment relative to the original IP payload.

3. When the fragments are received by the destination host, they are identified by the Identification field as belonging together. The Fragment Offset field is then used to reassemble the fragments into the original IP payload.

ARP

Address Resolution Protocol performs IP address–to–MAC address resolution for outgoing packets. As each outgoing addressed IP datagram is encapsulated in a frame, source and destination MAC addresses must be added. Determining the destination MAC address for each frame is the responsibility of ARP. ARP is defined in RFC 826.

ICMP

Internet Control Message Protocol provides troubleshooting facilities and error reporting for packets that are undeliverable. For example, if IP is unable to deliver a packet to the destination host, ICMP sends a Destination Unreachable message to the source host. Table 18-1 shows the most common ICMP messages.

Table 18-1   Common ICMP Messages

Message	Description
Echo Request	Troubleshooting message used to check IP connectivity to a desired host. The Ping utility sends ICMP Echo Request messages.
Echo Reply	Response to an ICMP Echo Request.
Redirect	Sent by a router to inform a sending host of a better route to a destination IP address.
Source Quench	Sent by a router to inform a sending host that its IP datagrams are being dropped because of congestion at the router. The sending host then lowers its transmission rate.
Destination Unreachable	Sent by a router or the destination host to inform the sending host that the datagram cannot be delivered.

When the result of an ICMP request is a Destination Unreachable message, a specific message is returned to the requestor detailing why the Destination Unreachable ICMP message was sent. Table 18-2 describes the most common of these messages.

Table 18-2   Common ICMP Destination Unreachable Messages

Unreachable Message	Description
Host Unreachable	Sent by an IP router when a route to the destination IP address cannot be found
Protocol Unreachable	Sent by the destination IP node when the Protocol field in the IP header cannot be matched with an IP client protocol currently loaded
Port Unreachable	Sent by the destination IP node when the destination port in the UDP header cannot be matched with a process using that port
Fragmentation Needed and DF Set	Sent by an IP router when fragmentation must occur but is not allowed because of the source node setting the Don't Fragment (DF) flag in the IP header

ICMP does not make IP a reliable protocol. ICMP attempts to report errors and provide feedback on specific conditions. ICMP messages are carried as unacknowledged IP datagrams and are themselves unreliable. ICMP is defined in RFC 792.

Understanding Transport Layer Protocols

The transport layer is responsible for providing session and datagram communication services over the IP protocol. The two core protocols of the transport layer are the Transmission Control Protocol (TCP) and User Datagram Protocol (UDP):

- **TCP**   Provides a one-to-one, connection-oriented, reliable communications service. TCP is responsible for the establishment of a TCP connection, the sequencing and acknowledgment of packets sent, and the recovery of packets lost during transmission.

- **UDP**   Provides a one-to-one or one-to-many, connectionless, unreliable communications service. UDP is used when the amount of data to be transferred is small (such as data that fits into a single packet), when the overhead of establishing a TCP connection is not desired, or when the applications or upper layer protocols provide reliable delivery.

How TCP Communication Works

When two computers communicate using TCP, the computer that initiates the communication is known as the client, regardless of whether it is running a client or server OS, and the responding computer is known as the host. If the client and host are on the same network segment, the client computer first uses ARP to resolve the host's MAC address by sending a broadcast for the IP address of the host. Once the client has the MAC address of the host, it can commence communication to the port on the host by using the transport layer protocol specified by the application. There are 65,535 TCP and UDP ports, beginning with 0. Ports 1023 and below are regarded as well-known ports for legacy reasons, and ports above 1023 are known as high ports. Functionally, no difference exists between the well-known ports and the high ports. On the host, an application is bound to a certain port it specifies and is initialized in a listening state, where it waits for requests from a client. When the client initiates a connection to a TCP port, a defined series of packets, known as a *three-way handshake* and illustrated in Figure 18-1, constructs a session for reliable packet transmission. The steps for establishing connections follow:

1. The client sends the host a synchronization (SYN) message that contains the host's port and the client's Initial Sequence Number (ISN). TCP sequence numbers are 32 bits in length and used to ensure session reliability by facilitating out-of-order packet reconstruction.

2. The host receives the message and sends back its own SYN message and an acknowledgement (ACK) message, which includes the host's ISN and the client's ISN incremented by 1.

3. The client receives the host's response and sends an ACK, which includes the ISN from the host incremented by 1. After the host receives the packet, the TCP session is established.

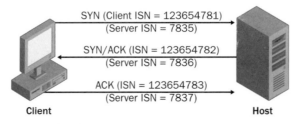

Figure 18-1 Three-way TCP handshake

When the communication between the client and host is complete, the session is closed once the following steps occur:

1. The client sends a finalization (FIN) message to the host. The session is now *half closed*. The client no longer sends data but can still receive data from the host. Upon receiving this FIN message, the host enters a passive closed state.

2. The host sends an ACK message, which includes the client's sequence number augmented by 1.

3. The server sends its own FIN message. The client receives the FIN message and returns an ACK message that includes the host's sequence number augmented by 1.

4. Upon receiving this ACK message, the host closes the connection and releases the memory the connection was using.

The Netstat.exe Command

To see port activity on your Windows 2000 or Windows XP computers, you can use the Netstat.exe command. Netstat.exe will also show the status of TCP ports. The syntax for using Netstat.exe follows, and Table 18-3 describes the options available when using this command.

NETSTAT [-a] [-e] [-n] [-o] [-s] [-p proto] [-r] [interval]

Table 18-3   Netstat.exe Options

Option	Description
-a	Displays all connections and listening ports.
-e	Displays Ethernet statistics. This can be combined with the -s option.
-n	Displays addresses and port numbers in numerical form.
-o	Displays the owning process ID (PID) associated with each connection. This option exists in Windows XP only.
-p *protocol*	Shows connections for the protocol specified by *protocol*, which can be TCP, UDP, TCPv6, or UDPv6. If used with the -s option to display per-protocol statistics, the value for protocol can be IP, ICMP, TCP, or UDP.
-r	Displays the routing table.
-s	Displays per-protocol statistics. By default, statistics are shown for IP, ICMP, TCP, and UDP.
interval	Determines the refresh interval for the data displayed by Netstat.

Tip   To find the process associated with a given active port in Windows XP, you can locate the PID associated with the port by typing **netstat –aon**. You can then find the process associated with the PID by typing **tasklist –FI "PID eq *XX*"**, where *XX* is the PID of the process.

As mentioned in Table 18-3, the -o option of Netstat.exe is not available in Windows 2000; however, you can download utilities from the Internet that have similar functionality and will run on Windows 2000.

Common Threats to TCP/IP

Several types of threats to TCP/IP can either compromise network security or lead to information disclosure. Although these attacks are more prevalent on the Internet, you should be concerned about them on internal computers as well. These common threats include:

- Port scanning
- Spoofing
- Denial of service

Port Scanning

In order to communicate with TCP/IP, applications running on host computers must listen for incoming TCP or UDP connections, and host operating systems must listen for broadcast and other network maintenance traffic. By scanning a computer to see what ports a host is listening for and what protocols it uses, an attacker might be able to locate weaknesses in the host that he can later use to attack the computer. Attackers often perform port scans to reveal this information. Several types of port scans exist:

- **Ping sweeps** An attacker might use an automated tool to send ICMP Echo Request packets to entire networks or subnets. By default, all active hosts will respond. This lets the attacker know that the host exists and is active. An attacker can also analyze the structure of the ICMP packet to determine the OS running on the host.

- **Port enumeration** At attacker might want to enumerate all the services running on a host computer. Because hosts must respond to client computers to carry out legitimate operations, attackers can exploit this behavior to obtain critical information.

> **Tip** You can download a command-line port-scanning tool from Microsoft called Portqry.exe. This tool, found at http://www.microsoft.com/downloads/release.asp?ReleaseID=37344, tests the security of hosts and performs network diagnostics. In addition, many free utilities that can perform port scans are available on the Internet.

- **Banner grabbing** Many common services respond with banners when sessions are initiated or requested. These banners contain basic information on the service or server. For example, by using Telnet to connect to port 25 of a Windows 2000 server running the default Simple Mail Transfer Protocol (SMTP) service, you can retrieve this banner:

```
220 SFOFS001.finance.woodgrovebank.com Microsoft ESMTP MAIL Service,
   Version: 5.0 .2195.5329 ready at Sat, 12 Oct 2002 16:18:44 -0800
```

From interpreting this banner, you can determine that the target server is named SFOFS001. SFOFS001 is probably a file server running Windows 2000 with Service Pack 3 installed and is physically located in the Pacific Time zone—most likely in San Francisco. The server is running a built-in instance of the SMTP service, which is installed as part of Microsoft Internet Information Services (IIS) 5.0. Knowing that IIS is installed by default in Windows 2000 and that this server does not appear to be a Web server, it is likely that the server has a default installation of Windows 2000.

> **Warning**   Changing service banners can also break applications that rely on them for information about the server they are communicating with. Furthermore, changing banners can break an application running on the computer that uses the information from service banners from other services running on the computer.

- **Half scan**   This type of port scanning does not follow the precise TCP three-way handshake protocol and leaves TCP connections half open. Because most host system logs do not log packets until the host receives the final ACK, half scans can enable an attack to gain information about a host without being detected.

Spoofing

Attackers might want to spoof, or mimic, a legitimate TCP/IP packets to attack a computer or network. Usually spoofing a packet requires that the attacker handcraft a TCP/IP packet and send it to either the host he wants to attack or a third party host that he has previously compromised in order to attack the targeted host or network. Many types of spoofing attacks exist. These following three are among the most well-known:

- **Land attack**   Takes advantage of security flaws in the many implementations of TCP/IP. To carry out a land attack, an attacker opens a legitimate TCP session by sending a SYN packet but spoofs the packet so that the source address and port and the destination address and port match the host IP address and the port the packet is being sent to.

    For example, to carry out a land attack on an e-mail server with the IP address 192.168.183.200, an attacker can create a packet with the source address of 192.168.183.200 and the source port of 25, rather than using the source address and port of his own computer. Now the source and destination addresses will be the same, as will the source and destination ports. If not patched to protect against the land attack, the e-mail will continually attempt to make a connection with itself on its own port 25, resulting in a denial-of-service situation.

- **Smurf attack**   Uses a third-party network to carry out a denial-of-service attack on a host system by spoofing an ICMP Echo Request packet. The attacker obtains the host IP address and creates a forged ICMP Echo Request packet that looks like it came from the host IP address. The attacker sends thousands of copies of the spoofed packet to the broadcast address on an improperly secured third-party network. This results in every computer in the third-party network responding to each spoofed packet by sending an ICMP Echo Reply packet to the host system. The amount of ICMP traffic that is generated by this attack will deny legitimate traffic from reaching the target host.

- **Session hijacking**   Takes advantage of flaws in many implementations of the TCP/IP protocol by anticipating TCP sequence numbers to hijack a session with a host. To hijack a TCP/IP session, the attacker creates a legitimate TCP session to the targeted host, records the TCP sequence numbers used by the host, and then computes the round-trip time (RTT). This step often takes many exchanges in sequence. Using the stored sequence numbers and the RTT, the attacker can potentially predict future TCP sequence numbers. The attacker can then send a spoofed packet to another host, using the targeted host IP address as the source address and the next sequence number. If successful, the second host system will believe the packet originated from the targeted system and accept packets from the attacker. This type of attack is particularly effective when the second host trusts the targeted host.

> **More Info**   IP spoofing by predicting TCP/IP sequence numbers was the basis for the famous Christmas 1994 attack on Tsutomu Shimomura by Kevin Mitnick. The attack is chronicled in the book *Takedown: The Pursuit and Capture of Kevin Mitnick, America's Most Wanted Computer Outlaw—By The Man Who Did It* (Hyperion, 1996).

Denial of Service

Denial-of-service attackers attempt to exploit the way the TCP/IP protocol works to prevent legitimate traffic from reaching the host system. One of the most common types of denial-of-service attacks is a SYN flood. A SYN flood attempts to create a situation in which the host system's maximum TCP connection pool is locked in a half-open state, thus denying legitimate traffic to and from the host. To carry out a SYN flood, the attacker creates a spoofed IP packet with an unreachable IP address for a source address, or she clips the receive wire on the Ethernet cable she is using. When the host receives the packet, it responds by sending a SYN/ACK response and waits for the final ACK in the TCP three-way handshake, which never comes. The session will remain in the half-open state until the predefined time-out is reached. This process is repeated until no more TCP sessions are allowed by the host system, which then cannot create any new sessions.

Configuring TCP/IP Security in Windows 2000 and Windows XP

The remainder of this section presents several ways you can secure your Windows 2000 and Windows XP computers against attacks on TCP/IP, including basic TCP/IP binding configurations, custom registry settings, and TCP/IP filtering.

Implementing Basic TCP/IP Security

Three basic settings, outlined in the following list, will increase the security of TCP/IP for each network adapter in Windows 2000 and Windows XP. You will need to ensure that each of these settings is compatible with your network and the applications that either run on the computer or must be accessible from the computer.

- **File And Printer Sharing For Microsoft Networks**   By default, File and Printer Sharing for Microsoft Networks is bound on all network interfaces. The File and Printer Sharing for Microsoft Networks component enables other computers on a network to access resources on your computer. By removing the binding to File and Printer Sharing for Microsoft Networks from a network interface, you can prevent other computers from enumerating or connecting to files and printers that have been shared through that network interface. After removing this binding from a network interface, the computer will no longer listen for direct Server Message Block (SMB) connections on TCP ports 139 or 445 of that interface. Removing this setting will not interfere with the computer's ability to connect to other shared files or printers. You can unbind File and Printer Sharing for Microsoft Networks in the Network And Dial-Up Connections Control Panel applet or on the properties of the network interface.

- **NetBIOS Over TCP/IP**   Windows 2000 and Windows XP support file and printer sharing traffic by using the SMB protocol directly hosted on TCP. This differs from earlier operating systems, in which SMB traffic requires the NetBIOS over TCP/IP (NetBT) protocol to work on a TCP/IP transport. If both the direct hosted and NetBT interfaces are enabled, both methods are tried at the same time and the first to respond is used. This allows Windows to function properly with operating systems that do not support direct hosting of SMB traffic. NetBIOS over TCP/IP traditionally uses the following ports:

NetBIOS name	137/UDP
NetBIOS name	137/TCP
NetBIOS datagram	138/UDP
NetBIOS session	139/TCP

Note   Direct hosted "NetBIOS-less" SMB traffic uses port 445 (TCP and UDP). If you disable NetBIOS Over TCP/IP (NetBT) and unbind File And Printer Sharing For Microsoft Networks, the computer will no longer respond to any NetBIOS requests. Applications and services that depend on NetBT will no longer function once NetBT is disabled. Therefore, verify that your clients and applications no longer need NetBT support before you disable it.

- **DNS Registration**   By default, Windows 2000 and Windows XP computers attempt to automatically register their host names and IP address mappings in the Domain Name System (DNS) for each adapter. If your computer is using a public DNS server or cannot reach the DNS server, as is often seen when the computer resides in a screened subnet, you should remove this behavior on each adapter.

Configuring Registry Settings

Denial-of-service attacks are network attacks aimed at making a computer or a particular service on a computer unavailable to network users. Denial-of-service attacks can be difficult to defend against. To help prevent denial-of-service attacks, you can harden the TCP/IP protocol stack on Windows 2000 and Windows XP computers. You should harden the TCP/IP stack against denial-of-service attacks, even on internal networks, to prevent denial-of-service attacks that originate from inside the network as well as on computers attached to public networks. You can harden the TCP/IP stack on a Windows 2000 or Windows XP computer by customizing these registry values, which are stored in the registry key HKLM\System\CurrentControlSet\Services\Tcpip\Parameters\:

- **EnableICMPRedirect**   When ICMP redirects are disabled (by setting the value to 0), attackers cannot carry out attacks that require a host to redirect the ICMP-based attack to a third party.

- **SynAttackProtect**   Enables SYN flood protection in Windows 2000 and Windows XP. You can set this value to 0, 1, or 2. The default setting, 0, provides no protection. Setting the value to 1 will activate SYN/ACK protection contained in the TCPMaxPortsExhausted, TCPMaxHalfOpen, and TCPMaxHalfOpenRetried values. Setting the value to 2 will protect against SYN/ACK attacks by more aggressively timing out open and half-open connections.

- **TCPMaxConnectResponseRetransmissions**   Determines how many times TCP retransmits an unanswered SYN/ACK message. TCP retransmits acknowledgments until the number of retransmissions specified by this value is reached.

- **TCPMaxHalfOpen**   Determines how many connections the server can maintain in the half-open state before TCP/IP initiates SYN flooding attack protection. This entry is used only when SYN flooding attack protection is enabled on this server—that is, when the value of the SynAttackProtect entry is 1 or 2 and the value of the TCPMaxConnectResponseRetransmissions entry is at least 2.

- **TCPMaxHalfOpenRetried**   Determines how many connections the server can maintain in the half-open state even after a connection request has been retransmitted. If the number of connections exceeds the value of this entry,

TCP/IP initiates SYN flooding attack protection. This entry is used only when SYN flooding attack protection is enabled on this server—that is, when the value of the SynAttackProtect entry is 1 and the value of the TCPMaxConnect-ResponseRetransmissions entry is at least 2.

- **TCPMaxPortsExhausted**   Determines how many connection requests the system can refuse before TCP/IP initiates SYN flooding attack protection. The system must refuse all connection requests when its reserve of open connection ports runs out. This entry is used only when SYN flooding attack protection is enabled on this server—that is, when the value of the SynAttackProtect entry is 1, and the value of the TCPMaxConnectResponseRetransmissions entry is at least 2.

- **TCPMaxDataRetransmissions**   Determines how many times TCP retransmits an unacknowledged data segment on an existing connection. TCP retransmits data segments until they are acknowledged or until the number of retransmissions specified by this value is reached.

- **EnableDeadGWDetect**   Determines whether the computer will attempt to detect dead gateways. When dead gateway detection is enabled (by setting this value to 1), TCP might ask IP to change to a backup gateway if a number of connections are experiencing difficulty. Backup gateways are defined in the TCP/IP configuration dialog box in Network Control Panel for each adapter. When you leave this setting enabled, it is possible for an attacker to redirect the server to a gateway of his choosing.

- **EnablePMTUDiscovery**   Determines whether path MTU discovery is enabled (1), in which TCP attempts to discover the largest packet size over the path to a remote host. When path MTU discovery is disabled (0), the path MTU for all TCP connections will be fixed at 576 bytes.

- **DisableIPSourceRouting**   Determines whether a computer allows clients to predetermine the route that packets take to their destination. When this value is set to 2, the computer will disable source routing for IP packets.

- **NoNameReleaseOnDemand**   Determines whether the computer will release its NetBIOS name if requested by another computer or a malicious packet attempting to hijack the computer's NetBIOS name.

- **PerformRouterDiscovery**   Determines whether the computer performs router discovery on this interface. Router discovery solicits router information from the network and adds the information retrieved to the route table. Setting this value to 0 will prevent the interface from performing router discovery.

Table 18-4 lists the registry entries that you can make to harden the TCP/IP stack on your Windows 2000 and Windows XP computers.

Table 18-4 Registry Settings to Harden TCP/IP

Value	Data (DWORD)
EnableICMPRedirect	0
SynAttackProtect	2
TCPMaxConnectResponseRetransmissions	2
TCPMaxHalfOpen	500
TCPMaxHalfOpenRetired	400
TCPMaxPortsExhausted	5
TCPMaxDataRetransmissions	3
EnableDeadGWDetect	0
EnablePMTUDiscovery	0
DisableIPSourceRouting	2
NoNameReleaseOnDemand	1
PerformRouterDiscovery	0

> **Tip** Tcpip_sec.vbs is a script that automatically configures the registry in Windows 2000 and Windows XP to use the settings for securing TCP/IP shown in Table 18-4. This script is located on the CD that is included with the *Microsoft Windows Security Resource Kit*.

Additionally, you can secure the TCP/IP stack for Windows Sockets (Winsock) applications such as FTP servers and Web servers. The driver Afd.sys is responsible for connection attempts to Winsock applications. Afd.sys has been modified in Windows 2000 and Windows XP to support large numbers of connections in the half-open state without denying access to legitimate clients. Afd.sys can use dynamic backlog, which is configurable, rather than a static backlog. You can configure four parameters for the dynamic backlog:

- **EnableDynamicBacklog** Switches between using a static backlog and a dynamic backlog. By default, this parameter is set to 0, which enables the static backlog. You should enable the dynamic backlog for better security on Winsock.

- **MinimumDynamicBacklog** Controls the minimum number of free connections allowed on a listening Winsock endpoint. If the number of free connections drops below this value, a thread is queued to create additional free connections. Making this value too large (setting it to a number greater than 100) will degrade the performance of the computer.

- **MaximumDynamicBacklog**   Controls the maximum number of half-open and free connections to Winsock endpoints. If this value is reached, no additional free connections will be made.

- **DynamicBacklogGrowthDelta**   Controls the number of Winsock endpoints in each allocation pool requested by the computer. Setting this value too high can cause system resources to be unnecessarily occupied.

Each of these values must be added to the registry key HKLM\System\Current-ControlSet\Services\AFD\Parameters. Table 18-5 lists the parameters and the recommended levels of protection.

Table 18-5   Registry Settings to Harden Winsock

Value	Data (DWORD)
DynamicBacklogGrowthDelta	10
EnableDynamicBacklog	1
MinimumDynamicBacklog	20
MaximumDynamicBacklog	20,000

Tip   Winsock_sec.vbs is a script that automatically configures the registry in Windows 2000 and Windows XP to use the settings for securing Winsock shown in Table 18-5. This script is located on the CD that is included with the *Microsoft Windows Security Resource Kit*.

Using TCP/IP Filtering

Windows 2000 and Windows XP include support for TCP/IP filtering, a feature known as TCP/IP Security in Windows NT 4.0. TCP/IP filtering allows you to specify which types of inbound local host IP traffic are processed for all interfaces. This feature prevents traffic from being processed by the computer in the absence of other TCP/IP filtering, such as that provided by Routing and Remote Access (RRAS), Internet Connection Firewall (on Windows XP), and other TCP/IP applications or services. TCP/IP filtering is disabled by default.

When configuring TCP/IP filtering, you can permit either all or only specific ports or protocols listed for TCP ports, UDP ports, or IP protocols. Packets destined for the host are accepted for processing if they meet one of the following criteria:

- The destination TCP port matches the list of TCP ports.

- The destination UDP port matches the list of UDP ports.

- The IP protocol matches the list of IP protocols.

- The packet is an ICMP packet.

Note   TCP/IP port filtering applies to all interfaces on the computer and cannot be applied on a per-adapter basis. However, you can configure allowed ports and protocols on a per-adapter basis.

In addition to being able to configure TCP/IP filtering on the Options tab of the TCP/IP advanced properties in the user interface, you can apply the settings directly to the registry. Table 18-6 lists the registry values to configure TCP/IP filtering. TCP/IP filtering is set in the key HKLM\SYSTEM\CurrentControlSet\Services\Tcpip\Parameters, while the specific settings for each interface are configured in the key HKLM\SYSTEM\CurrentControlSet\Services\Tcpip\Parameters\Interfaces*Interface_GUID*.

Table 18-6   Registry Values for TCP/IP Filtering

Setting	Type	Description
EnableSecurityFilters	DWORD	1 enables TCP/IP filtering; 0 disables TCP/IP filtering.
UdpAllowedPorts	MULTI_SZ	0 allows all UDP ports; an empty (null) value blocks all UDP ports; otherwise, the specific allowed UDP ports are listed.
TCPAllowedPorts	MULTI_SZ	0 allows all TCP ports; an empty (null) value blocks all TCP ports; otherwise, the specific allowed TCP ports are listed.
RawIpAllowedProtocols	MULTI_SZ	0 allows all IP protocols; an empty (null) value blocks all IP protocols; otherwise, the specific allowed IP protocols are listed.

Using Internet Connection Firewall in Windows XP

Windows XP includes a personal firewall called Internet Connection Firewall (ICF). ICF is a stateful firewall—it monitors all aspects of the communications between the Windows XP computer and other hosts, and it inspects the source and destination address of each message that it handles. To prevent unsolicited traffic from the public side of the connection from entering the private side, ICF keeps a table of all communications that have originated from the ICF computer. When used in conjunction with Internet Connection Sharing (ICS), ICF creates a table for tracking all traffic originated from the ICF/ICS computer and all traffic originated from private network computers. Inbound Internet traffic is allowed to reach the computers in your network only when a matching entry in the table shows that the communication exchange originated within your computer or private network. You can enable ICF on a per-interface basis on the Advanced tab of the interface.

You can configure services to allow unsolicited traffic from the Internet to be forwarded by the ICF computer to the private network. For example, if you are hosting an HTTP Web server service and have enabled the HTTP service on your ICF computer, unsolicited HTTP traffic will be forwarded by the ICF computer to the HTTP Web server. A set of operational information, known as a *service definition*, is required by ICF to allow the unsolicited Internet traffic to be forwarded to the Web server on your private network. The Services tab of ICF is shown in Figure 18-2.

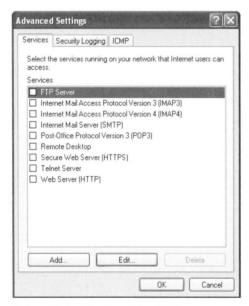

Figure 18-2   Services tab of ICF

In addition, you can add custom services to the Services tab of ICF. ICF can also perform port translation for incoming connections. When you create a custom service, you will need to specify the following:

- **Description of service**   Determines how the service is displayed on the Services tab

- **Name or IP address**   Determines the host name or IP address of the computer offering the service if the service is not hosted on the local computer

- **External port**   Defines the TCP or UDP port on the ICF computer that will listen to inbound traffic to the service

- **Internal port**   Defines the TCP or UDP port to which the ICF computer will forward the inbound traffic to the computer defined in the Name Or IP Address field

Communications that originate from a source outside the ICF computer, such as the Internet, are dropped by the firewall unless an entry in the Services tab is made to allow passage. ICF silently discards unsolicited communications, preventing common attacks, such as port scanning and NetBIOS enumeration. ICF can create a security log so you can view the activity that is tracked by the firewall. You can choose whether to log dropped, successful, or dropped and successful packets. By default, packets are logged to c:\windows\pfirewall.log. The log file has a default maximum size of 4098 KB. Table 18-7 describes the fields in the packet log file.

Table 18-7   Description of Information Logged by ICF

Field	Description
Date	Specifies date that the recorded transactions occurred in the format YY-MM-DD.
Time	Specifies time that the recorded transaction occurred in the format HH:MM:SS.
Action	Specifies which operation was observed by the firewall. The options available to the firewall are OPEN, CLOSE, DROP, and INFO-EVENTS-LOST. An INFO-EVENTS-LOST action indicates the number of events that happened but were not placed in the log.
Protocol	Specifies which IP protocol was used for the communication.
Src-ip	Specifies the source IP address of the computer attempting to establish communications.
Dst-ip	Specifies the destination IP address of the communication attempt.
Src-port	Specifies the source port number of the sending computer. Only TCP and UDP will return a valid src-port entry.
Dst-port	Specifies the port of the destination computer. Only TCP and UDP will return a valid dst-port entry.
Size	Specifies the packet size in bytes.
Tcpflags	Specifies the TCP control flags found in the TCP header of an IP packet: ■ **ACK** Acknowledgment field significant ■ **FIN** No more data from sender ■ **PSH** Push function ■ **RST** Reset the connection ■ **SYN** Synchronize sequence numbers ■ **URG** Urgent Pointer field
Tcpsyn	Specifies the TCP synchronization number in the packet.
Tcpack	Specifies the TCP acknowledgment number in the packet.
Tcpwin	Specifies the TCP window size in bytes in the packet.
Icmptype	Specifies a number that represents the Type field of the ICMP message.
Icmpcode	Specifies a number that represents the Code field of the ICMP message.
Info	Specifies an information entry that depends on the type of action that occurred. For example, an INFO-EVENTS-LOST action will create an entry of the number of events that happened but were not placed in the log since the last occurrence of this event type.

Using IPSec

By its design, TCP/IP is an open protocol created to connect heterogeneous computing environments with the least amount of overhead possible. As is often the case, interoperability and performance design goals do not generally result in security—and TCP/IP is no exception to this. TCP/IP provides no native mechanism for the confidentiality or integrity of packets. To secure TCP/IP, you can implement IP Security. IPSec implements encryption and authenticity at a lower level in the TCP/IP stack than application-layer protocols such as Secure Sockets Layer (SSL) and Transport Layer Security (TLS). Because the protection process takes place lower in the TCP/IP stack, IPSec protection is transparent to applications. IPSec is a well-defined, standards-driven technology.

The IPSec process encrypts the payload after it leaves the application at the client and then decrypts the payload before it reaches the application at the server. An application does not have to be IPSec aware because the data transferred between the client and the server is normally transmitted in plaintext.

IPSec is comprised of two protocols that operate in two modes with three different authentication methods. IPSec is policy driven and can be deployed centrally by using Group Policy. To deploy IPSec, you must determine the

- Protocol
- Mode
- Authentication methods
- Policies

Securing Data Transmission with IPSec Protocols

As mentioned, IPSec is comprised of two protocols: IPSec Authentication Header (AH) and IPSec Encapsulating Security Payload (ESP). Each protocol provides different services; AH primarily provides packet integrity services, while ESP provides packet confidentiality services. IPSec provides mutual authentication services between clients and hosts, regardless of whether AH or ESP is being used.

Using AH

IPSec AH provides authentication, integrity, and anti-replay protection for the entire packet, including the IP header and the payload. AH does not provide confidentiality. When packets are secured with AH, the IPSec driver computes an Integrity Check Value (ICV) after the packet has been constructed but before it is sent to the computer. With Windows 2000 and Windows XP, you can use either the HMAC SHA1 or HMAC MD5 algorithm to compute the ICV. Figure 18-3 shows how AH modifies an IP packet.

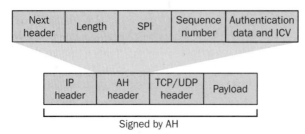

Figure 18-3 AH modifications to an IP packet

The fields in an AH packet include these:

- **Next Header** Indicates the protocol ID for the header that follows the AH header. For example, if the encrypted data is transmitted using TCP, the next header value would be 6, which is the protocol ID for TCP.

- **Length** Contains the total length of the AH.

- **Security Parameters Index (SPI)** Identifies the security association (the IPSec agreement between two computers) that was negotiated in the Internet Key Exchange (IKE) protocol exchange between the source computer and the destination computer.

- **Sequence Number** Protects the AH-protected packet from replay attacks in which an attacker attempts to resend a packet that he has previously intercepted, such as an authentication packet, to another computer. For each packet issued for a specific security association (SA), the sequence number is incremented by 1 to ensure that each packet is assigned a unique sequence number. The recipient computer verifies each packet to ensure that a sequence number has not been reused. The sequence number prevents an attacker from capturing packets, modifying them, and then retransmitting them later.

- **Authentication Data** Contains the ICV created against the signed portion of the AH packet by using either HMAC SHA1 or HMAC MD5. The recipient performs the same integrity algorithm and compares the result of the hash algorithm with the result stored within the Authentication Data field to ensure that the signed portion of the AH packet has not been altered in transit. Because the TTL, Type of Service (TOS), Flags, Fragment Offset, and Header Checksum fields are not used in the ICV, packets secured with IPSec AH can cross routers, which can change these fields.

Using ESP

ESP packets are used to provide encryption services to transmitted data. In addition, ESP provides authentication, integrity, and antireplay services. When packets are sent using ESP, the payload of the packet is encrypted and authenticated. In Windows 2000 and Windows XP, the encryption is done with either Data Encryption Standard (DES) or 3DES, and the ICV calculation is done with either HMAC SHA1 or HMAC MD5.

> **Tip**   When designing an IPSec solution, you can combine AH and ESP proto-
> cols in a single IPSec SA. Although both AH and ESP provide integrity protec-
> tion to transmitted data, AH protects the entire packet from modification,
> while ESP protects only the IP payload from modification.

ESP encrypts the TCP or UDP header and the application data included within
an IP packet. It does not include the original IP header unless IPSec tunnel mode is
used. Figure 18-4 shows how ESP modifies an IP packet.

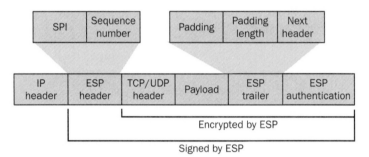

Figure 18-4   ESP modifications to an IP packet

The ESP header has two fields that are inserted between the original IP header
and the TCP or UDP header from the original packet:

- **Security Parameters Index (SPI)**   Identifies the SA that was negotiated
  between the source computer and the destination computer for IPSec communication. The combination of the SPI, the IPSec protocol (AH or ESP), and the
  source and destination IP addresses identifies the SA used for the IPSec transmission within the ESP packet.

- **Sequence Number**   Protects the SA from replay attacks. This field is incremented by 1 to ensure that packets are never received more than once. If a
  packet is received with a previous sequence number, that packet is dropped.

The ESP trailer is inserted after the application data from the original packet
and includes the following fields:

- **Padding**   A variable length from 0–255 bytes that brings the length of the
  application data and ESP trailer to a length divisible by 32 bits so that they
  match the required size for the cipher algorithm.

- **Padding Length**   Indicates the length of the Padding field. After the packet is
  decrypted, this field is used to determine the length of the Padding field.

- **Next Header**   Identifies the protocol used for the transmission of the data,
  such as TCP or UDP.

Following the ESP trailer, the ESP protocol adds an ESP authentication trailer to the end of the packet. The ESP authentication trailer contains a single field:

- **Authentication Data**   Contains the ICV, which verifies the originating host that sent the message and ensures that the packet was not modified in transit. The ICV uses the defined integrity algorithm to calculate the ICV. The integrity algorithm is applied to the ESP header, the TCP/UDP header, the application data, and the ESP trailer.

ESP provides integrity protection for the ESP header, the TCP/UDP header, the application data, and the ESP trailer. ESP also provides inspection protection by encrypting the TCP/UDP header, the application data, and the ESP trailer.

Choosing Between IPSec Modes

IPSec operates in two modes: transport mode and tunnel mode. IPSec transport mode is used for host-to-host connections, and IPSec tunnel mode is used for network-to-network or host-to-network connections.

Using IPSec Transport Mode

IPSec transport mode is fully routable, as long as the connection does not cross a network address translation (NAT) interface, which would invalidate the ICV. Used this way, IPSec must be supported on both hosts, and each host must support the same authentication protocols and have compatible IPSec filters configured and assigned. IPSec transport mode is used to secure traffic from clients to hosts for connections where sensitive data is passed.

Using IPSec Tunnel Mode

IPSec tunnel mode is used for network-to-network connections (IPSec tunnels between routers) or host-to-network connections (IPSec tunnels between a host and a router). Used this way, IPSec must be supported on both endpoints, and each endpoint must support the same authentication protocols and have compatible IPSec filters configured and assigned. IPSec tunnel mode is commonly used for site-to-site connections that cross public networks, such as the Internet.

Selecting an IPSec Authentication Method

During the initial construction of the IPSec session—also known as the Internet Key Exchange, or IKE—each host or endpoint authenticates the other host or endpoint. When configuring IPSec, you must ensure that each host or endpoint supports the same authentication methods. IPSec supports three authentication methods:

- Kerberos
- X.509 certificates
- Preshared key

Authenticating with Kerberos

In Windows 2000 and Windows XP, Kerberos is used for the IPSec mutual authentication by default. For Kerberos to be used as the authentication protocol, both hosts or endpoints must receive Kerberos tickets from the same Active Directory directory service forest. Thus, you should choose Kerberos for IPSec authentication only when both hosts or endpoints are within you own organization. Kerberos is an excellent authentication method for IPSec because it requires no additional configuration or network infrastructure.

> **Warning**   Some types of traffic are exempted by default from being secured by IPSec, even when the IPSec policy specifies that all IP traffic should be secured. The IPSec exemptions apply to Broadcast, Multicast, Resource Reservation Setup Protocol (RSVP), IKE, and Kerberos traffic. Kerberos is a security protocol itself, can be used by IPSec for IKE authentication, and was not originally designed to be secured by IPSec. Therefore, Kerberos is exempt from IPSec filtering.
>
> To remove the exemption for Kerberos and RSVP, set the value *NoDefault-Exempt* to 1 in the registry key HKEY_LOCAL_ MACHINE\SYSTEM\Current-ControlSet\Services\IPSEC. Nodefaultexempt.vbs is a script that automatically removes the exemption for Kerberos and RSVP. This script is located on the CD that is included with the *Microsoft Windows Security Resource Kit*.

Authenticating with X.509 Certificates

You can use X.509 certificates for IPSec mutual authentication of hosts or endpoints. Certificates allow you to create IPSec secured sessions with hosts or endpoints outside your Active Directory forests, such as business partners in extranet scenarios. You also must use certificates when using IPSec to secure VPN connections made by using Layer Two Tunneling Protocol (L2TP). To use certificates, the hosts must be able to validate that the other's certificate is valid.

Authenticating with Preshared Key

You can use a preshared key, which is a simple, case-sensitive text string, to authenticate hosts or endpoints. Preshared key authentication should be used only when testing or troubleshooting IPSec connectivity because the preshared key is not stored in a secure fashion by hosts or endpoints.

Creating IPSec Policies

IPSec is a policy-driven technology. In Windows 2000 and Windows XP, you can have only one IPSec policy assigned at a time. IPSec policies are dynamic, meaning that you do not have to stop and start the IPSec service or restart the computer when assigning or unassigning IPSec policies. You can also use Group Policy to deploy IPSec policies to Windows 2000 and Windows XP clients. Windows 2000 and Windows XP include three precreated IPSec policies:

- **Client (Respond Only)**   A computer configured with the Client policy will use IPSec if the host it is communicating with requests using IPSec and supports Kerberos authentication.

- **Server (Request Security)**   A computer configured with the Server policy will always attempt to negotiate IPSec but will permit unsecured communication with hosts that do not support IPSec. The Server policy permits unsecured ICMP traffic.

- **Secure Server (Require Security)**   A computer configured with the Secure Server policy will request that IPSec be used for all inbound and outbound connections. The computer will accept unencrypted packets but will always respond by using IPSec secured packets. The Secure Server policy permits unsecured ICMP traffic.

In addition to the built-in policies, you can create custom IPSec policies. When creating your own IPSec policies, you must configure rules that include the following settings:

- IP Filter List

- Tunnel Settings

- Filter Actions

- Authentication Methods

- Connection Types

IPSec rules determine what types of network traffic will initiate IPSec between the computer and the host or endpoint it is communicating with. A computer can have any number of IPSec filters. You should ensure that only one rule is created for each type of traffic. If multiple filters apply to a given type of traffic, the most specific filter will be processed first.

IP Filter List

The IP filter list defines the types of network traffic that the IPSec rule applies to. You must define the following details for each entry in the filter list:

- **Source address**   Can be a specific IP address, a specific IP subnet address, or any address.

- **Destination address**   Can be a specific IP address, a specific IP subnet address, or any address.

- **Protocol**   The protocol ID or transport protocol used by the protocol. For example, Point-to-Point Tunneling Protocol (PPTP) uses Generic Routing Encapsulation (GRE) packets. GRE packets are identified by their protocol ID, which is protocol ID 47. Telnet, on the other hand, uses TCP as its transport protocol, so an IPSec filter for Telnet would only define the protocol type as TCP.

- **Source port**   If the protocol were to use TCP or UDP, the source port could be defined for the protected connection. The source port is set to a specific port or to a random port, depending on the protocol being defined. Most protocols use a random port for the source port.

- **Destination port**   If the protocol uses TCP or UDP, the protocol uses a specific port at the server to accept transmissions. For example, Telnet configures the server to listen for connections on TCP port 23.

When configuring IP filter lists for transport mode connections, you should always choose to have the IPSec rule mirrored to secure the return communication defined in the rule. For tunnel mode connections, you must manually specify both the inbound and outbound filter list.

Tunnel Settings

The tunnel setting determines whether IPSec operates in transport or tunnel mode. If you want IPSec to operate in transport mode, select This Rule Does Not Specify A Tunnel when creating an IPSec rule using the Security Rule Wizard. If you want the filter to operate in tunnel mode, you must specify the IP address of the endpoint of the tunnel.

Filter Actions

For each filter rule, you must choose a filter action. The filter action defines how the traffic defined in the IP filter will be handled by the filter rule. The three filter actions are listed here and shown in Figure 18-5.

- **Permit**   Allows packets to be transmitted without IPSec protection. For example, Simple Network Management Protocol (SNMP) includes support for devices that might not be IPSec aware. Enabling IPSec for SNMP would cause a loss of network management capabilities for these devices. In a highly secure network, you could create an IPSec filter for SNMP and set the IPSec action to Permit to allow SNMP packets to be transmitted without IPSec protection.

- **Block**   Discards packets. If the associated IPSec filter is matched, all packets with the block action defined are discarded.

- **Negotiate Security**   Allows an administrator to define the desired encryption and integrity algorithms to secure data transmissions if an IPSec filter is matched.

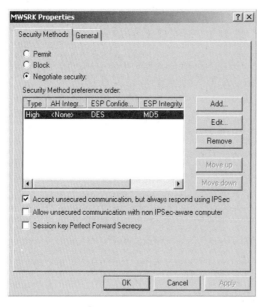

Figure 18-5   IPSec filter actions

In addition to these three basic actions, you can define settings that indicate how the Windows 2000–based computer will react if non-IPSec protected data is received and how frequently new session keys are defined to protect the IPSec data. Options include the following:

- **Accept Unsecured Communication, But Always Respond Using IPSec**   You use this option when the IPSec protection is enforced only at the servers, not at the clients. In a typical IPSec deployment, clients are configured to use IPSec if requested by the server but to never initiate an IPSec SA. This setting allows the initial packet to be received by the server, which then starts the IKE process to negotiate an SA between the client and the server. Although it is riskier to have the initial packet of a data transmission accepted by using plaintext, the response packet sent from the server will not be transmitted until an SA is established.

- **Allow Unsecured Communication—With Non-IPSec-Aware Computers**   In a mixed network, this option allows non-IPSec aware clients to connect to the server. Windows 2000 clients, if configured to do so, will connect to the server and negotiate IPSec protection. Non-IPSec-aware clients will still be allowed to connect by using unprotected data streams.

- **Session Key Perfect Forward Secrecy**   Using Perfect Forward Secrecy will ensure that an existing key is never used as the foundation of a new key. When you use Perfect Forward Secrecy, all keys will be generated without using existing keys. This reduces the risk of continual data exposure should a key be compromised because previous keys cannot be used to determine future keys.

Authentication Methods

For each filter rule, you must choose an authentication method. You can enable multiple authentication methods for each rule and determine their order of precedence by editing the filter rule after it has been created.

Connection Types

You must specify what type of interfaces each filter rule applies to. In Windows 2000 and Windows XP, you can choose to have the rule apply to the following:

- All network connections

- Local area network (LAN) connections

- Remote access connections

> **Note**   You can create IPSec policies by using Ipsecpol.exe from the command line or from batch files and scripts, in addition to using the user interface.

How IPSec Works

IPSec can be initiated by either the sending host or the receiving host. The two hosts or endpoints enter into a negotiation that will determine how the communication will be protected. The negotiation is completed in the IKE, and the resulting agreement is a set of security associations, or SAs.

IKE has two modes of operation, main mode and quick mode. We will examine each mode momentarily. IKE also serves two functions:

- Centralizes SA management, reducing connection time

- Generates and manages the authenticated keys used to secure the information

The SA is used until the two hosts or endpoints cease communication, even though the keys used might change. A computer can have many SAs. The SA for each packet is tracked using the SPI.

Main Mode

During the main mode negotiation, the two computers establish a secure, authenticated channel—the main mode SA. IKE automatically provides the necessary identity protection during this exchange. This ensures no identity information is sent without encryption between the communicating computers, thus enabling total privacy. Following are the steps in a main mode negotiation:

1. **Policy negotiation** These four mandatory parameters are negotiated as part of the main mode SA:

   - The encryption algorithm (DES or 3DES)

   - The hash algorithm (MD5 or SHA1)

   - The authentication method (certificate, preshared key, or Kerberos v5 authentication)

   - The Diffie-Hellman (DH) group to be used for the base keying material

   If certificates or preshared keys are used for authentication, the computer identity is protected. However, if Kerberos v5 authentication is used, the computer identity is unencrypted until encryption of the entire identity payload takes place during authentication.

2. **DH exchange (of public values)** At no time are actual keys exchanged; only the base information needed by DH to generate the shared, secret key is exchanged. After this exchange, the IKE service on each computer generates the master key used to protect the final step: authentication.

3. **Authentication** The computers attempt to authenticate the DH exchange. Without successful authentication, communication cannot proceed. The master key is used, in conjunction with the negotiation algorithms and methods, to authenticate identities. The entire identity payload—including the identity type, port, and protocol—is hashed and encrypted by using the keys generated from the DH exchange in the second step. The identity payload, regardless of which authentication method is used, is protected from both modification and interpretation.

   After the hosts have mutually authenticated each other, the host that initiated the negotiation presents an offer for a potential SA to the receiving host. The responder cannot modify the offer. Should the offer be modified, the initiator rejects the responder's message. The responder sends either a reply accepting the offer or a reply with alternatives. After the hosts agree on an SA, quick mode negotiation begins.

Quick Mode

In this mode, SAs are negotiated on behalf of the IPSec service. The following are the steps in quick mode negotiation:

1. **Policy negotiation**   The IPSec computers exchange their requirements for securing the data transfer:

   ■ The hash algorithm for integrity and authentication (MD5 or SHA1)

   ■ The algorithm for encryption, if requested (3DES or DES)

   ■ A description of the traffic to protect

2. **Session key material refresh or exchange**   IKE refreshes the keying material, and new, shared, or secret keys are generated for authentication and encryption (if negotiated) of the packets. If a rekey is required, a second DH exchange takes place or a refresh of the original DH exchange occurs.

3. **SA exchange**   The SAs and keys are passed to the IPSec driver, along with the SPI.

   A common agreement is reached, and two SAs are established: one for inbound communication, and one for outbound communication.

During the quick mode negotiation of shared policy and keying material, the information is protected by the SA negotiated during main mode. As mentioned in step 3, quick mode results in a pair of SAs: one for inbound communication and one for outbound communication, each having its own SPI and key. Figure 18-6 shows a summary of what is negotiated during main mode and quick mode.

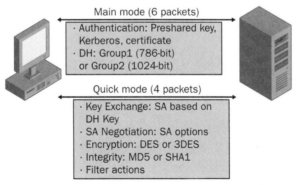

Figure 18-6   Main mode and quick mode negotiation

IPSec, Routers, and NAT

IPSec creates a new IP header for a packet that can be routed as normal IP traffic. Routers and switches in the data path between the communicating hosts simply forward the packets to their destination. However, when a firewall or gateway lies in the data path, you must enable IP forwarding at the firewall for the following IP protocols and UDP ports:

- **IP protocol ID 50**   Create inbound and outbound filters to allow ESP traffic to be forwarded.

- **IP protocol ID 51**   Create inbound and outbound filters to allow AH traffic to be forwarded.

- **UDP port 500**   Create inbound and outbound filters to allow IKE traffic to be forwarded.

Because of the nature of the NAT and port address translation (PAT) technologies, which require that packets be altered to change IP address and port information, IPSec is not compatible with NAT. IPSec does not allow manipulation of packets during transfer. The IPSec endpoint will discard packets that have been altered by NAT because the ICVs will not match. At the time of the printing of this book, research into encapsulating IPSec packets in UDP packets so that they can pass through NAT devices is under way.

Monitoring IPSec

You can monitor IPSec in Windows 2000 with IPSecmon.exe and in Windows XP the IP Security Monitor Microsoft Management Console (MMC) snap-in. In addition, you can create log files in both Windows 2000 and Windows XP to view IPSec negotiations.

Using IPSecmon in Windows 2000

In Windows 2000, you can view the status of IPSec SAs and basic information on IPSec sessions by running IPSecmon from the Run prompt. IPSecmon displays information about each SA and the overall statistics of IPSec and IKE sessions. Figure 18-7 shows IPSecmon in Windows 2000. The built-in Server IPSec policy is applied to the Windows 2000 computer named SFOFS001. The SFOFS001 computer has attempted to negotiate IPSec with three other computers: SEADC001, SFODC001, and SFOXP001. However, SFOFS001 has successfully negotiated an SA with SFOXP001 only. The IPSec session with SFPXP001 uses the IPSec protocol ESP with 3DES as the encrypting algorithm and HMAC SHA1 as the authentication algorithm.

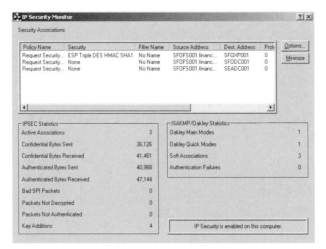

Figure 18-7   Using IPSecmon in Windows 2000

Using the IP Security Monitor MMC Snap-In

In Windows XP, IPSecmon has been replaced with an MMC snap-in that provides all the information that IPSecmon did in Windows 2000, only in much greater detail. You can use the IP Security Monitor MMC snap-in to view details of each SA, whereas in Windows 2000, you could view only the basic details of an SA. Figure 18-8 shows the IP Security Monitor MMC snap-in in Windows XP, which enables you to view the exact SA details negotiated during both main mode and quick mode.

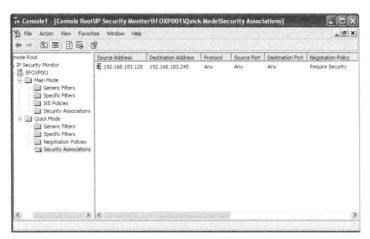

Figure 18-8   Using IP Security Monitor MMC snap-in in Windows XP

Using IPSec Logs in Windows 2000 and Windows XP

In both Windows 2000 and Windows XP, you can have IPSec log the IKE exchanges to a log file on the hard drive for troubleshooting or monitoring needs. To have your computer log IKE exchanges, you must create a registry value named *EnableLogging* in the registry key HKLM\System\CurrentControlSet\Services\PolicyAgent\Oakley. To enable logging, set the value to 1 and restart the IPSec services. The log file will be written to the file %systemroot%\debug\oakley.log.

> **Note**   Although the IPSec log file will contain more detailed information than a network capture made with Network Monitor, you can also use Network Monitor to determine how IPSec SA negotiations function in relation to the other traffic on the network. Ipseclog.vbs is a script that automatically configures the registry in Windows 2000 and Windows XP to enable IPSec logging. This script is located on the CD that is included with the *Microsoft Windows Security Resource Kit*.

Best Practices

- **Create a TCP/IP hardening policy.**   Ensure that the TCP/IP stack on your Windows 2000 and Windows XP computers is appropriately secure, based on the threats to it. This is especially true of any computer directly connected to the Internet or in screened subnets.

- **Use ICF for mobile and home computers running Windows XP.**   ICF provides an excellent degree of protection for mobile clients and home computers. Be certain to provide training to users on how to enable and disable ICF.

- **Use IPSec hardware accelerators when possible**   By using IPSec hardware accelerators on computers that will have many IPSec sessions at a time, such as servers, you can prevent the computer's CPU performance from being overly taxed.

Additional Information

- Internet Assigned Numbers Authority's (IANA) TCP and UDP port number assignment list (http://www.iana.org/assignments/port-numbers)

- IANA's IP protocol ID number list (http://www.iana.org/assignments/protocol-numbers)

- "5-Minute Security Advisor—Essential Security Tools for Home Office Users" (http://www.microsoft.com/technet/columns/security/5min/5min-105.asp)

- Internet Connection Firewall Overview—Windows XP Help File (http://www.microsoft.com/windowsxp/home/using/productdoc /en/hnw_understanding_firewall.asp)

- "IPSec Architecture" white paper (http://www.microsoft.com/technet/security/prodtech/network/ipsecarc.asp)

- "IPSec Implementation" white paper (http://www.microsoft.com/technet/security/prodtech/network/ipsecimp.asp)

- "Security Considerations for Network Attacks" white paper (http://www.microsoft.com/technet/security/prodtech/network/secdeny.asp)

- "Best Practices for Preventing DoS/Denial of Service Attacks" white paper (http://www.microsoft.com/technet/security/bestprac/dosatack.asp)

- 309798: "How to Configure TCP/IP Filtering in Windows 2000"

Note   The previous article can be accessed through the Microsoft Knowledge Base. Go to http://support.microsoft.com and enter the article number in the Search The Knowledge Base text box.

Chapter 19

Securing Mobile Computers

This chapter is from the Microsoft® Windows® Security Resource Kit *by Ben Smith and Brian Komar with the Microsoft Security Team (Microsoft Press, 2003).*

Mobile computers present a special security risk because of their portability and small size. They are at much greater risk of physical compromise and are much more difficult to manage. Often, when people hear the term *mobile computers*, they think it applies to only laptop computers. But mobile computers also include Microsoft Tablet PCs, PDAs, Microsoft Pocket PCs, and wireless phones. Each of these devices can carry secret information, such as passwords, or information that could be used to break into their respective networks.

Understanding Mobile Computers

Mobile computers face all the threats that desktop computers do, but they also face additional threats. These vulnerabilities include the following:

- Increase in the possibility of being lost or stolen
- Difficulty in applying security updates
- Exposure to untrusted networks
- Eavesdropping on wireless connectivity

Increase in the Possibility of Being Lost or Stolen

Laptops and other mobile devices have a much greater chance of being stolen because of their mobility and small size. A thief could easily hide a laptop in a briefcase or under a coat. Even organizations that have tight physical security are susceptible to this type of theft. For example, in February 2000, a laptop belonging to a U.S. State Department employee and containing top-secret information was stolen from a conference room inside the State Department. Furthermore, although some laptops will always remain within the boundaries of company facilities, most users will work on their laptops away from the office. Consequently, the network security of such laptop computers is enforced by those organizations' corporate security and IT departments. But the users themselves are responsible for the physical security of their laptops. Users take their laptops home, on business and personal trips, and to school, and they sometimes leave their laptops in their cars—unattended and in plain view—during those stops. In July 2000, a commander in the British Royal Navy had his laptop stolen from his car, which was parked outside his house. His laptop was reported to hold top-secret information.

Thieves target laptops because they are small, high-value items that can easily be sold. If a thief is sufficiently computer-savvy or sells the laptop to an attacker, he can potentially retrieve all the information from the laptop. This information includes cached passwords for network accounts; cached personal information from Microsoft Internet Explorer; personal information, such as names, addresses, and birthdates for people in address books; and the actual company data on the laptop. An attacker can use this information to attack the organization's network or steal the identity of the user or her friends and family. Furthermore, the stolen laptop might contain information that is confidential or secret. An information leak resulting from a stolen laptop could have a tremendous impact on your organization if that information falls into the wrong hands. This might sound alarmist, but several high-profile incidents of laptop theft have occurred in the past few years, including those government incidents mentioned earlier.

The corporate world has not been immune to such incidents of laptop theft. In 2000, the laptop belonging to the CEO of Qualcomm was stolen after he delivered a presentation at an industry conference. According to the media, the CEO was less than 30 feet away when his laptop was stolen from the podium from which he had been speaking. Because the CEO had been using his laptop to give the presentation, it is likely that he left it unlocked when he walked off the podium, rendering many types of data protection, such as encrypting file system (EFS), useless. Although the thieves in the cases we have mentioned so far might not have been targeting the organizations whose laptops they stole or the information on those laptops, no evidence to the contrary exists.

Some organizations face a greater threat of their having laptops stolen. For example, hardware and software companies might be targeted by attackers hoping to steal the companies' latest and greatest inventions. And law enforcement and government agencies might be targeted by attackers hoping to gain access to the secret information contained on their networks.

Mobile telephone devices also have a high incidence of theft and loss. At the very least, a thief can use a stolen phone to make long-distance and international phone calls, creating very expensive phone bills for the owner. A thief can also retrieve contact information from a phone's address book, potentially subjecting the phone owner's friends and family to identity theft. A more serious vulnerability, however, is that many mobile phones have Internet access, or even full computing power, such as the Pocket PC Phone Edition devices. Such devices can have confidential information stored on them, such as passwords and private e-mail messages. Other types of devices in this category include handheld e-mail devices such as the BlackBerry, PDA devices such as Palm Pilots, and handheld PCs such as the Compaq iPAQ. Because it is often difficult for users to input data into these devices, perhaps because they must use an onscreen keyboard or handwriting recognition software, users of these devices frequently store network credentials, such as passwords, persistently. An attacker could retrieve these credentials to later attack the network of the device user's organization. These mobile devices also have the capability to store files, which an attacker could retrieve from the device if stolen.

Laptop computers and mobile devices often have accessories and add-ons that might hold confidential information. Such accessories include conventional removable media, such as floppy disks and CDs. Another class of removable media includes high-capacity, solid-state devices, such as CompactFlash cards, Secure Digital (SD) cards, smart cards, and Subscriber Identity Module (SIM) cards for cellular and wireless phones. Smart cards and SIM cards, in particular, can contain data such as private keys and personal information that could be used to attack the network of the device user's organization, if they fall into the wrong hands.

Difficulty in Applying Security Updates

Unlike desktop computers, which have a somewhat static place in the network infrastructure, laptop computers often roam among many subnets and networks, not to mention leaving the local area network (LAN) altogether. The mobility of laptop computers makes them much more difficult to manage centrally, which greatly increases the difficulty in applying security updates, including hotfixes, service packs, and virus definition files. This mobility also increases the difficulty in assessing how current the security updates are. Traditional methods of applying security updates, including manual application and the use of network management software such as Microsoft Systems Management Server (SMS), are often ineffective with laptop computers. This is because these methods depend on computers being in a static physical location as well as a logical one on the network.

This issue is especially problematic for laptop computers that rarely or never are connected to the LAN. When these computers do connect to the network, they often do so through low-bandwidth connections, such as modems. For all intents and purposes, these computers are self-managed by their users, making these users responsible for knowing how to locate and apply security updates themselves. If security updates are not installed, the laptop computer will be vulnerable to known exploits, which is particularly alarming because these computers are often directly connected to untrusted networks.

Exposure to Untrusted Networks

Desktop computers are always connected to the LAN on which their security settings can be managed and are protected from the Internet and other untrusted networks by firewalls. On the other hand, network administrators cannot be sure which networks laptop users will connect to. When at home or in hotels, a laptop user will connect directly to the Internet without any protection—and the machine will be exposed to the legions of attackers scanning for vulnerable computers connected to the Internet. A user might also connect her laptop to the networks of her business partners and the semipublic networks at industry conventions, where confidential information can be exposed to anyone who succeeds in breaking into the laptop. Once the user connects her computer to such an untrusted network, a network administrator can do little to protect the machine from attacks that can be launched against it. For example, enabling Internet Connection Firewall (ICF) in Microsoft Windows XP will provide excellent protection against attacks attempted over the organization's network when a user is connected to untrusted networks; however, when the user is connected to the corporate network, ICF will prevent the application of Group Policy.

Eavesdropping on Wireless Connectivity

Many laptops and mobile devices are now equipped with 802.11b or Bluetooth wireless network interfaces. Many users do not realize that connecting their laptop or mobile device to a wireless network that is not secure is similar to having a sensitive conversation in a crowded restaurant or subway—anyone who wants to listen in can. Public and private wireless networks are becoming more common in public areas, such as airport terminals and cafes. Users might be temped to connect their laptop or mobile device to these networks for the convenience it affords, not realizing that the information they are sending and receiving might be traveling via an untrusted network.

Many home computer users and businesses are installing 802.11b wireless networks these days. Unfortunately, the built-in security measure of these networks—Wired Equivalent Privacy (WEP)—has an inherent security vulnerability. When exploited by an attacker, this vulnerability can enable the attacker to connect to the wireless network directly. In addition, many users and administrators are lulled into a false sense of security by the signal strength of their wireless access points. These users and administrators assume that their laptops can achieve this maximum signal strength, but in reality, attackers can build or purchase inexpensive wireless antennas to intercept wireless network transmissions from more than half a mile to a mile away.

Implementing Additional Security for Laptop Computers

Mobile computers are one of the most difficult IT assets to secure because network administrators must rely on users to be responsible for the security of their computers on a daily basis. To secure mobile computers, you not only must implement technology-based security, you must ensure that users understand the threats to their mobile computers and can make appropriate judgments about using their machines so that they do not jeopardize the security of information on their mobile computers or the network itself.

When implementing security for laptop computers beyond the baseline configuration, you should have two goals in mind: to secure the information on the laptop, and to prevent a compromise of the laptop from leading to the compromise of the network. To accomplish these goals you must address the following areas:

- Hardware protection
- Boot protection
- Data protection
- User education

Hardware Protection

The first area of additional security for laptop computers is protecting the laptop itself. To help prevent a laptop from being stolen when left unattended, you can use hardware locks. Several types of hardware locks exist, and they vary in cost and degree of protection. The most basic type of lock is a passive cable lock. Passive cable locks use a cable connected to the security slot on a laptop that wraps around an unmovable object. For example, a user storing a laptop in the trunk of a car could wrap the cable around the frame of the car. Typically, these locks use a key or combination lock and have cables that cannot be easily cut with handheld cable cutters. To circumvent a passive hardware lock, an attacker must pick the lock, cut the cable, or figure out a way to move the object the laptop is attached to. Some passive cable locks have alarms built into them. When the cable is looped around an object and reattached to the cable lock base, the lock creates a weak electric circuit that passes through the cable. If the circuit is broken because the cable is cut, the alarm sounds. These alarms are typically loud enough to be heard clearly from 100 yards or more. The alarm will continue to sound until the lock is unlocked or the internal battery runs out.

The effectiveness of a cable lock is dependent on the laptop user using the lock properly. Two common mistakes that users make with cable locks are leaving the key to the lock in an obvious location and attaching the cable to an object that is not secure. For example, users might leave the key to the lock in their laptop carrying case and place the case on the floor near the locked laptop, or they might loop the cable around the leg of a table, which could easily be picked up. Thus, if you implement hardware locks, you must train users in how to properly use them; otherwise, the locks can be ineffective. Hardware locks are by no means undefeatable, but if properly used, they can deter would-be thieves. The addition of an alarm to such a lock increases the likelihood of capturing the thief immediately after he steals the laptop.

Instead of (or in addition to) using passive cable locks, you can use active security systems. The most common types of active security systems use a hardware token that detects unusual motion of the laptop and sounds an alarm. If an unusual amount of motion is detected, the security system will activate. In the event of unusual motion—depending on the computer you are protecting—the security system might prevent the computer from being booted without the deactivation code, encrypt sensitive information (including data already encrypted by the OS, such as passwords), and sound an alarm. Some active security systems use proximity switches instead of motion detectors. These hardware protection systems prevent computers from leaving a confined area, such as an office building or a particular floor in the building. Active security systems typically cost two to three times more than passive cable locks.

In addition to using locks, alarms, and countermeasures to protect laptops that have highly confidential information, you might consider using a hardware tracking system. Such a system enables you to locate the laptop after it has been stolen and thereby catch the thief (and have her arrested). Hardware tracking systems for laptops or desktops typically rely on one of two mechanisms: an Internet tracking system, or a Global Positioning System (GPS). The client-side tracking agent is installed in protected areas on the computer's hard drive or in hardware tokens installed inside the laptop's case. The agent contacts the tracking service periodically with information about where the computer is located, on the Internet or physically. If the computer is reported stolen, the tracking service can wait for the device to contact it. When contacted by the agent running on the device, the tracking service can retrieve the information about the location of the device. You can then give this information to law enforcement officials to attempt to track the stolen computer. Obviously, not all laptops need this degree of protection. This type of protection is very expensive. You might want to consider hardware tracking services on laptops that you know could hold information that, if compromised, might result in the loss of human life. For example, such hardware tracking services might be more appropriate for laptops that are used by government agencies, law enforcement agencies, or mission-critical assets, such as offline root Certification Authorities (CAs).

One other type of hardware protection for computers that you should consider is to remove removable media drives from the laptop. One of the most common methods of breaking into a computer running Microsoft Windows NT 4.0 or later is to boot the computer by using a bootable floppy disk or CD. Although this is by no means a foolproof security measure, by removing these drives, you make compromising the laptop computer much more difficult and time-consuming. If you remove the floppy disk and CD-ROM drives from a computer, you should also disable the use of USB ports in the BIOS. Otherwise, the attacker might be able to attach a USB floppy or CD-ROM drive to the computer and use it as a boot device.

Boot Protection

One way that you can protect information contained on a laptop and protect account information stored on the laptop from being used to attack your organization's network if the computer is stolen is to prevent the OS from loading. You can do this by using BIOS passwords or the Windows System Key feature (Syskey).

Although different BIOS versions have different names for passwords, most BIOS versions on laptop computers have two types of passwords that you can install: *boot passwords* and *setup passwords*. Both password types are configured in the BIOS. A boot password prevents the BIOS from transferring control to the OS installed on the hard drive or any other type of media, including bootable floppy disks and CDs, without entering the password. A boot password does not prevent a user or attacker from entering the BIOS configuration; however, in newer BIOS versions, you must enter the existing password to change the boot password. BIOS setup passwords prevent a user or attacker from entering the BIOS configuration and changing information stored in the BIOS, such as the boot password or the order of precedence for boot devices.

There are only two ways to reset the BIOS setup password and boot password: by entering the existing password, or by clearing the CMOS. To clear the CMOS memory on a laptop, you must disassemble the laptop and remove the CMOS battery, which completely clears the BIOS settings. Although BIOS passwords will not completely prevent an attacker from booting the computer, under most conditions, these passwords will buy network administrators enough time to disable the user's user account and any other accounts that need to be disabled. The use of BIOS passwords also gives the user enough time to change any Web site account passwords that have been persistently stored on the laptop.

You can also use the Windows System Key utility to prevent the OS from being loaded by unauthorized people. To do so, set System Key to use Mode 2 or Mode 3 (explained in the following list). You can configure System Key by typing **syskey** at the command prompt. Only members of the Administrators group can initialize or change the system key level. The system key is the *master key* used to protect the password database encryption key. System keys have three modes:

- **Mode 1**   Uses a machine-generated random key as the system key and stores the key on the local system. Because the key is stored on the OS, it allows for unattended system restart. By default, System Key Mode 1 is enabled during installation on all computers running Microsoft Windows 2000 and Windows XP.

- **Mode 2**   Uses a machine-generated random key and stores the key on a floppy disk. The floppy disk with the system key is required for the system to start before the system is available for users to log on. The OS will not load unless the floppy disk is in the floppy drive. When System Key is enabled in Mode 2, the OS will never be able to be loaded if the floppy disk is damaged or lost, unless you have previously created a repair disk.

- **Mode 3**   Uses a password chosen by the administrator to derive the system key. The OS will prompt for the system key password when the system begins the initial startup sequence, before the system is available for users to log on. The system key password is not stored anywhere on the system; instead, an MD5 hash of the password is used as the master key to protect the password encryption key. If the password is forgotten, the OS will be rendered unbootable.

Setting the System Key to Mode 2 or Mode 3 will greatly increase the security of the OS and the password-based keys it contains, such as the contents of the Security Accounts Manager (SAM) database and local security authority (LSA) secrets.

Caution   Because there is no way to recover from a damaged or lost floppy disk or a forgotten System Key password, you should implement System Key Mode 2 or Mode 3 with great caution. Develop a secure method of archiving system keys if you decide to implement System Key Mode 2 or Mode 3 on your network.

Data Protection

Regardless of whether you use hardware alarms or boot protection mechanisms, you should implement protection for data that is stored on a laptop computer. On network servers, discretionary access control lists (DACLs) are the primary method of protecting files. Unfortunately, access control lists (ACLs) are of little use when a computer is in the possession of an attacker. Unlike network servers, whose physical security can be protected by network administrators, laptop computers can be easily stolen. An attacker can remove the hard drive from a laptop and install it in a computer that they are the administrator of. The attacker can take ownership of the files and folders on the laptop computer's hard drive and read the files and folders.

To lessen this risk, you can use the EFS to secure the information on a laptop. When you use EFS properly, the only way to retrieve the information contained in the files is by performing a brute force attack on the encryption algorithm. In Windows 2000 and Windows XP, EFS uses the 56-bit DESX algorithm. Although computationally feasible, this algorithm is difficult to break. Windows XP also allows you to use the 3DES algorithm, which is computationally infeasible and thereby makes performing a brute force attack virtually impossible, given current hardware constraints.

The other data protection issue to address with laptop computers is the logical security of the laptop. Unlike desktop computers, which are protected from untrusted networks by firewalls and routers, laptop computers might be connected to untrusted networks on a regular basis. For example, a user might use the high-speed connection in her hotel room to create a virtual private network (VPN) connection to the corporate network. By doing this, the user creates a relatively unprotected, authenticated route to the corporate network from the Internet, not to mention placing the data stored locally on her laptop in danger. To prevent this situation, users can use personal firewall applications, such as Internet Connection Firewall, or ICF, in Windows XP.

Note   ICF is covered in detail in Chapter 18, "Implementing TCP/IP Security," of this book.

You might have certain users in your organization who have especially high security requirements, such as those needed to safeguard information that, if disclosed, could lead to the loss of life. You should avoid storing any important information persistently on the laptops of these users. You should also require these users to create a VPN connection to the corporate network and then use Terminal Services to connect to a computer on the network to access information. Furthermore, you should disable the option of storing cached credentials by setting the number of cached credentials to 0 in Group Policy or in the local Group Policy object (GPO) if the laptop is not a member of a domain. When you prevent credentials from being cached on the laptop, the user will not be able to log on to his laptop when a domain controller cannot be located to authenticate his credentials. You also should not install any applications locally on the laptop. This means the laptop will have little functionality other than acting as a remote access point to the network, but it will not place precious data or the network in danger.

Securing Mobile Devices

Securing mobile devices, such as Pocket PCs and Pocket PC Phone Edition devices, is similar to securing laptop computers. Mobile devices should have user passwords to prevent unauthorized users and attackers from accessing them. For example, Pocket PC 2002 supports both four-digit passwords and alphanumeric passwords for protecting access to the device. Each time an incorrect password is attempted, a time delay is activated before the logon screen will reappear. The delay increases exponentially upon each successive incorrect attempt.

In addition, if the mobile device will be connecting to the Internet or untrusted networks, such as public 802.11b wireless networks, you should ensure that the computer securely transmits authentication packets and data. For example, Pocket PC 2002 supports connecting to Web sites that have Secure Sockets Layer (SSL) connections enabled and wireless networks that use WEP.

Although no viruses or Trojan horses that specifically attack the Pocket PC platform or other types of mobile devices have been reported, as with laptop computers, you must install and maintain antivirus software on mobile devices and ensure that all security updates are applied as soon as they are released.

User Education

All the security measures discussed so far are completely dependent on the user properly protecting his laptop. Consequently, you must train users in the potential threats to their laptops and the measures they must take to secure their computers. Although most of the measures users must take to protect their laptops might seem obvious to you—such as not leaving a laptop in the car while buying groceries, or at least using a hardware lock to secure the laptop inside the trunk—they might not be obvious to your users. As with any type of training, it's best to be creative in how you get your message across to users in a way that they will understand. For example, when explaining to users the level of attention they should give to protecting their laptops, you can use this analogy: tell them to secure their laptops as though they were $2000 bundles of cash. Few people would ever consider locking $2000 in a car or leaving it on a table in a restaurant while they used the restroom. Posters, wallet cards, and e-mail reminders containing laptop security tips are also particularly effective in helping train users.

Securing Wireless Networking in Windows XP

Windows XP natively supports automatic configuration for the IEEE 802.11 standard for wireless networks, which minimizes the configuration that is required to access wireless networks. Users can roam between different wireless networks without the need to reconfigure the network connection settings on their computer for each location. When a user moves from one wireless network to another, Windows XP searches for available wireless networks and connects to them or prompts the user to select a wireless network to connect to. From a usability standpoint, the automatic—and even transparent—configuration of wireless networking in Windows XP is great. From a security standpoint, it presents some serious problems. Not all wireless networks are secure, and thus, a user could unwittingly endanger his laptop computer or even the corporate network.

Using Wireless Zero Configuration in Windows XP

The Wireless Zero Configuration service in Windows XP enables automatic connection to the following:

- **Infrastructure networks**   Computers and devices connect to wireless access points. Access points function as network bridges between the wireless clients and a wired network infrastructure. When a user enters the transmission area of an infrastructure network, where the access points broadcast their service set identifier (SSID), Windows XP will automatically attempt to connect to the access point it gets the strongest signal from. For example, your organization might have more than one building equipped with a wireless network. When a user moves between buildings, Windows XP will always connect to the wireless network without intervention from the user.

> **Tip** Enable wireless access points to broadcast their SSID only if you intend the network to be public. Consider disabling the broadcasting of SSIDs for networks connected to your corporate network to prevent potential attackers from gaining valuable information about your network. This will, however, prevent the use of the Wireless Zero Configuration functionality.

■ **Ad hoc networks** Ad hoc networks are formed when computers and devices with wireless network connectivity connect directly to each other, instead of connecting to access points. Unlike infrastructure networks, which operate as network bridges to other networks, ad hoc networks only allow you to access resources on the computer or devices that you connect to.

By default, Windows XP connects to both infrastructure networks and ad hoc networks, even those that the computer has not connected to before. For security purposes, you might not want the laptop computers in your organization to connect to untrusted networks automatically. You can define how Windows XP connects to wireless networks in the advanced wireless network connection properties. To increase the security of Windows XP laptops with wireless network cards, you should select to connect to only infrastructure networks and deselect the option to automatically connect to *nonpreferred networks*, which are networks that are not stored as preferred networks in the wireless network configuration utility (shown in Figure 19-1).

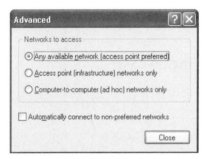

Figure 19-1 Advanced wireless network connection properties

Configuring Security for 802.11 Wireless Network Connectivity

The most basic type of security for 802.11 wireless networks is Wired Equivalent Privacy, or WEP. WEP provides for authentication and data transmission security for wireless clients to protect against unauthorized access and eavesdropping. Unlike

Windows XP, Windows 2000 does not have integrated wireless network manage-ment features. In Windows XP, you can configure the network key that is used for WEP. The key is used for authentication to the wireless network. In addition, the data encryption is enabled, which means a shared encryption key is generated to encrypt the data transmission between the computer and the wireless access point. In Windows 2000, 802.11 configuration must be done in the application provided by the wireless network interface vendor.

Configuring 802.11 Security with WEP

802.11 supports two subtypes of network authentication service: open system and shared key. When open system authentication is used, any computer or device can request authentication for the access point, and consequently, any computer or device can connect to the network. Using open system authentication does not pre-vent data transmission encryption. Unlike open system authentication, shared key authentication requires that the client computer or device have knowledge of a secret key that is shared by the wireless access point and all other wireless clients.

When using shared key authentication, the access point generates a random 64-bit or 128-bit number that is used as a challenge. The wireless client returns the challenge, which is encrypted with the WEP shared key. The encryption process involves using the RC4 stream cipher to perform an exclusive or (XOR) binary oper-ation on the plaintext payload. The RC4 keystream is generated by using a random number generator (RNG). The seed of the RNG is the result of concatenating the 40-bit or 104-bit WEP key with a 24-bit initialization vector. The encrypted payload and the initialization vector are sent to the access point. The access point concatenates the WEP key with the initialization vector to seed the keystream for RC4 to perform an XOR binary operation on the encrypted payload to reveal the plaintext payload.

Unfortunately, an attacker who captures these frames possesses the plaintext challenge, the ciphertext challenge, and the initialization vector. Because of the way that XOR operations work, the attacker will now know the keystream that was used, which is the concatenated initialization vector and the WEP key. Although the attacker still does not know the WEP key, she can attempt to authenticate to the access point and use the keystream derived from the captured packets to encrypt the challenge and retransmit the captured initialization vector.

Note   Several utilities available on the Internet automate this process of compromising shared key authentication.

How XOR Operations Work

To understand how an attacker can compromise WEP security, you must know how the binary XOR operation works. An XOR takes two binary numbers of equal length and performs a comparison of each bit, yielding a result of bits that is equal to the two numbers. The following list shows the result of XOR operations:

```
0 XOR 0 = 1
0 XOR 1 = 0
1 XOR 0 = 0
1 XOR 1 = 1
```

The XOR is frequently used by stream ciphers to encrypt data. For example, the name *BEN* can be represented in ASCII as 0x42 0x45 0x4E and converted to the binary. The RC4 algorithm might generate the keystream shown next. You then perform an XOR on the plaintext with the keystream. The result is the ciphertext.

```
Plaintext             01000010    01000101    01001110
Keystream     XOR     01101100    00010111    01101111
Ciphertext            11010001    10101101    11011110
```

If you convert the ciphertext back to ASCII characters, you get the following: Þ -Ñ. The problem with using XOR for encryption is that if you know any two of the three elements, you can determine the one you do not know. For example, if you can intercept the plaintext and the ciphertext, you can determine the keystream by performing an XOR on the plaintext with the ciphertext:

```
Plaintext             01000010    01000101    01001110
Ciphertext    XOR     11010001    10101101    11011110
Keystream             01101100    00010111    01101111
```

Although shared key authentication is not completely secure, it does provide more protection than Open System authentication. Thus, when combined with Media Access Control (MAC) address filtering, implementing shared key authentication provides a base level of security for wireless networks against novice attackers. If your organization issues laptops to users with wireless network cards, the users will likely install a home wireless network. To ensure that employees do not expose information contained on their laptops to potential attackers, you should create guidelines for installing home wireless networks, and these guidelines should include enabling shared key authentication.

WEP also provides data encrypted services by using the same process as defined for shared key authentication. Because only 2^24 (roughly 16 million) initialization vectors exist, if you assume that each packet uses a new initialization vector, the probability is that one initialization vector will be repeated after about 4500 packets have been transmitted. This is an example of a birthday attack on a cryptography algorithm. Thus, if an attacker can get the access point to send known plaintext (such as ping packets) and then capture all encrypted packets, he will be able to compute the keystream by performing an XOR on the plaintext with the ciphertext. The attacker could then place the keystream in a database organized by the initialization vector. The next time that the attacker intercepts a packet with that initialization vector, he can look up the keystream in the database and decrypt the packet.

In addition, a known vulnerability exists in the scheduling algorithm in RC4, meaning that a small subset of initialization vectors will be weak. Researchers at AT&T labs estimate that this vulnerability could be exploited by intercepting as few as 1,000,000 packets. By exploiting this vulnerability, an attacker could retrieve the static WEP key. If the attacker knows what the WEP key is, he can decrypt any packet he wants to view. Most newer, enterprise-oriented access points and wireless network cards are programmed not to use these weak initialization vectors. You can protect your wireless clients that use Windows XP by using 802.1x.

Configuring 802.11 Security with 802.1x

At the time of the printing of this book, IEEE 802.1x is a draft standard for port-based network access control, which provides authenticated network access to 802.11 wireless networks and to wired networks. Port-based network access control uses the physical characteristics of a switched LAN infrastructure to authenticate devices that are attached to a LAN port and to prevent access to that port in cases where the authentication process fails.

During a port-based network access control interaction, a LAN port adopts one of two roles: *authenticator* or *supplicant*. In the role of authenticator, a LAN port enforces authentication before it allows user access to the services that can be accessed through that port. In the role of supplicant, a LAN port requests access to the services that can be accessed through the authenticator's port. An authentication server, which either can be a separate entity or an entity colocated with the authenticator, checks the supplicant's credentials on behalf of the authenticator. The authentication server then responds to the authenticator, indicating whether the supplicant is authorized to access the authenticator's services.

The authenticator's port-based network access control defines two logical access points to the LAN, through one physical LAN port. The first logical access point, the *uncontrolled port*, allows data exchange between the authenticator and other computers on the LAN, regardless of the computer's authorization state. The second logical access point, the *controlled port*, allows data exchange between an authenticated LAN user and the authenticator.

IEEE 802.1x uses standard security protocols, such as Remote Authentication Dial-In User Service (RADIUS), to provide centralized user identification, authentication, dynamic WEP management, and accounting. In Windows XP, you can use X.509 certificates or the Protected Extensible Authentication Protocol (PEAP) with Microsoft Challenge Handshake Authentication Protocol version 2 (MS-CHAPv2) to authenticate clients on the Authentication tab on the profile of a preferred wireless network connection, as shown in Figure 19-2.

Figure 19-2   Configuring 802.1x authentication for wireless connections in Windows XP

The PEAP authentication has two phases. First, an encrypted TLS channel is established to the RADIUS server using a PEAP exchange. Second, MS-CHAPv2 is used to authenticate the wireless client to the network. After the wireless user and computer have been authenticated, encryption keys can be exchanged.

Best Practices

- **Educate your users.**   Ultimately, the security of information stored on laptop computers and mobile devices will rest with how seriously users take securing these assets and how well users follow guidelines and security polices for protecting their laptops. Although you can use technology to secure these devices to a certain extent, you must train users to do their part in securing laptop computers and mobile devices.

- **Use hardware locks for laptop computers.**   If the risk to your organization from supplying users with laptop computers is high enough, consider using hardware locking devices.

- **Use BIOS or System Key passwords.**   Passwords that prevent an attacker from booting a laptop computer, even temporarily, will increase the security of your network and the information stored on a stolen computer.

- **Install personal firewall applications for mobile users.**   For users that will be connecting to untrusted networks, install Windows XP or a personal firewall application to prevent an attacker from compromising the computer. Be sure to show the user how to use the application.

- **Implement 802.1x to secure corporate wireless networks.**   The security provided by WEP is not strong enough to prevent knowledgeable and skilled attackers from compromising data sent on wireless networks. 802.1x provides secure authentication, dynamic key exchanges, and data transmission security.

- **Create guidelines for home wireless network configuration.**   To protect information on laptops issued to employees who will install wireless networks in their homes, create guidelines on what wireless access point to install and how to implement basic security measures, such as disabling SSID broadcasting, enabling WEP with shared key authentication, and MAC address filtering.

Additional Information

- "Overview of Mobile Information Server Security" white paper (http://www.microsoft.com/technet/prodtechnol/mis/evaluate/security.asp)

- "Enterprise Deployment of IEEE 802.11 Using Windows XP and Windows 2000 Internet Authentication Service" white paper, which covers 802.1x (http://www.microsoft.com/windowsxp/pro/techinfo/deployment/wireless/default.asp)

- "RADIUS Protocol Security and Best Practices" white paper (http://www.microsoft.com/windows2000/techinfo/administration/radius.asp)

- "5-Minute Security Advisor: The Road Warrior's Guide to Laptop Protection" (http://www.microsoft.com/technet/columns/security/5min/5min-205.asp)

- 314647: "How to Increase Information Security on the Pocket PC"

- 143475: "Windows NT System Key Permits Strong Encryption of the SAM"

Note   The previous two articles can be accessed through the Microsoft Knowledge Base. Go to http://support.microsoft.com and enter the article number in the Search The Knowledge Base text box.

Part IV

Networking

Determining how best to client computers to your network and ensure that they have access to network resources, even when they are working from home or from a remote office, is vital to the success of any network environment. This part helps you to design and implement client connectivity solutions for all of your users' needs.

Chapter 20

Connecting Clients to Windows Networks

Microsoft® Windows® XP Professional can be a member of a variety of network configurations, from a small home network consisting of two computers to a large enterprise network that includes thousands of computers worldwide. This chapter describes the network environments in which Windows XP Professional can be used.

Related Information

- For more information about configuring TCP/IP in Windows XP Professional, see "Configuring TCP/IP" in this book.

- For more information about account authentication in Microsoft® Windows® 2000 domains, see "Authorization and Access Control" in this book.

- For more information about deploying Windows Server 2003 client network services, see the *Deploying Network Services* book of the *Microsoft® Windows Server™ 2003 Deployment Kit*.

Microsoft Networking Overview

The networking capabilities of Windows XP Professional include refinements of features introduced in Windows 2000. These refinements allow you to maintain a scalable networking presence in a variety of environments.

New in Microsoft Networking

The networking innovations, first appearing in Windows 2000 Professional and further refined in Windows XP Professional can be categorized into three areas: directory services, account authentication, and policy handling.

Directory Service

Windows XP Professional, Windows 2000, and Windows Server 2003 use the Active Directory™ directory service as its domain-based directory service. A *directory service* provides information about objects in a network environment, including user and computer accounts, and shared resources such as printers and other directories. It provides a consistent way to name, describe, locate, access, manage, and secure information about each of these resources. Active Directory, the directory service used in Windows 2000 and Windows Server 2003 domains, organizes information in a hierarchical, object-based fashion.

Account Authentication

In Windows 2000 and Windows Server 2003 domains, Account Authentication is performed using a protocol called *Negotiate*. Negotiate, in turn, uses the Kerberos V5 authentication protocol to authenticate any Windows XP–based computers, Windows 2000–based computers, and Windows Server 2003–based computers. The Kerberos V5 authentication protocol, as defined in RFC 1510, is an industry-supported distributed security protocol based on Internet standard security.

Negotiate uses the NTLM protocol where local authentication is needed and to authenticate any computer based on versions of Windows prior to Windows 2000. NTLM is also used as the account authentication method in Microsoft® Windows NT® domains and for authentication to Microsoft® Windows NT® version 4.0–based domain controllers.

For more information about the Kerberos V5 protocol and Windows XP Professional, see "Account Authentication" later in this chapter.

Policy Handling

Windows XP Professional supports the use of both System Policy and Group Policy to specify user and computer configurations. System Policy, introduced in Windows NT 4.0, is more limited than Group Policy, introduced in Windows 2000. In a Windows NT domain, domain administrators use System Policy to manage the user's work environment and to enforce system configuration settings. In a

Windows 2000 or Windows Server 2003 domain, Group Policy settings are your primary method for enabling centralized change and configuration management. A domain administrator can create Group Policy settings at a Windows 2000–based or Windows Server 2003–based domain controller to create a specific system configuration for a particular group of users, computers, or both. You can use Group Policy to do the following:

- Automatically install applications assigned to users or computers or both and provide location independence for roaming users.

- Permit desktop customization and lockdown.

- Configure security policies.

For more information about Group Policy, see "Group Policy and System Policy Settings" later in this chapter.

Fundamental Configuration Tasks

To allow your Windows XP Professional–based computer to take its place in a Microsoft network, you must first perform these fundamental tasks: assess the current network environment, install and configure your transport protocol, connect your computer to the appropriate network environment, verify that that you are logged on, and then troubleshoot any problem that might have occurred in the process.

Determining the Current Networking Environment

Before adding a Windows XP Professional–based computer to a network, you must determine whether you want to add the computer to a Windows 2000 or Windows Server 2003 domain, a Windows NT domain, to a workgroup of computers running Microsoft® Windows® 95 and Microsoft® Windows® 98 or to a non-Windows–based environment such as Netware. Typically, the network environment determines the authentication method you choose to access the network, the means you choose to enforce desktop and security rules (Group Policy or System Policy), and the method you use to handle logon scripts.

Installing and Configuring TCP/IP or Another Network Protocol

Before you can add a Windows XP Professional–based computer to an existing network, you must establish client connectivity with the network. Transmission Control Protocol/Internet Protocol (TCP/IP) has become the universal network protocol suite due to its scalability and its role as an Internet standard.

For all recommended tasks, it is assumed that the Windows XP Professional–based computer on the Microsoft network runs IP protocol as the default network protocol. Windows XP Professional supports NetBIOS over TCP/IP (NetBT), Windows Sockets (WinSock), and the Internetwork Packet Exchange/Sequenced Packet Exchange protocol (IPX/SPX). NetBT and WinSock are installed by default. IPX/SPX can be added if needed for connectivity to legacy Novell networks.

For more information about the Windows XP Professional implementation of TCP/IP and IP configuration, see "Configuring TCP/IP" in this book.

For more information about network protocol installation and configuration, see "TCP/IP and Other Network Protocols" later in this chapter.

Connecting to the Right Network Environment

A user who has appropriate permissions can do the following:

- Join a domain or workgroup. No rights are required for joining a workgroup.

- Create the computer account in a domain during Windows XP Professional installation. For workgroups, no permissions are required

- Use the Network Identification wizard to make the Windows XP Professional–based computer a member of a specified domain or workgroup.

- Manually add a computer to a network by specifying the appropriate domain or workgroup on the **Computer Name** tab of the **System Properties** dialog box.

For more information about joining a domain or workgroup, see "Microsoft Network Environments" later in this chapter.

Verifying a Successful Client Logon Attempt

To verify that a Windows XP Professional–based client is added to the network, attempt to log on to the domain where you added the computer; or if you added the computer to a workgroup, log on locally. If you are in a domain environment, make sure that logon scripts function as expected and that no conflicts occur between the following:

- Local Group Policy and Windows NT System Policy
    – or –

- Local Group Policy and Windows 2000 or Windows Server 2003 domain Group Policy settings

> **Note**   Domain Group Policy always overrides Local Group Policy.

For more information about confirming a Windows XP Professional–based computer's membership in a workgroup or domain, see "Confirming Domain and Workgroup Membership" later in this chapter.

Troubleshooting a Failed Logon Attempt

If a user cannot log on to a workgroup by using a local account or to a domain by using an account on a domain controller, troubleshoot the logon failure to determine its cause and solution.

For examples of logon-related problems and how to solve them, see "Troubleshooting Logon Problems" later in this chapter.

Microsoft Network Environments

There are two distinct kinds of Microsoft network environments — the peer-to-peer or workgroup (non-server-based) and the domain (server-based). Peer-to-peer networking is geared to small groups of users sharing resources on a one-to-one basis. Networks with Novell 3.x servers or standalone Windows NT-based, Windows 2000–based, or Windows Server 2003–based servers fall into the peer-to-peer group The domain model is enterprise networks built around a central directory database.

Peer-to-Peer Network Environment

A *peer-to-peer network* or *workgroup* is a single-subnet network that is used as a convenient way to connect a small number of users to share resources. Peer-to-peer clients have the identical level of authority on a network, which eliminates the need for domain controllers. User authentication is decentralized by the use of the local account database located on each client. A user must have a user account on each computer to gain access. Figure 20-1 shows an example of a peer-to-peer network.

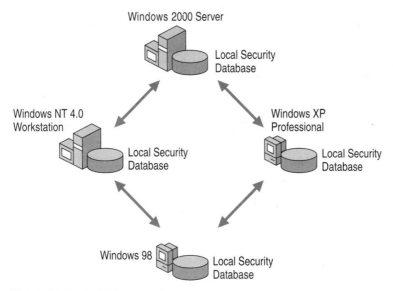

Figure 20-1   Peer-to-peer network

Peer-to-peer networks are ideal for small office/home office (SOHO) configurations that have from two to 10 computers. They can also be helpful for users who work with more than one computer and share resources (such as files, applications, or printers) with other users. For more information about small office/home office local connections, see "Connecting Remote Offices" in this book.

Windows XP Professional is compatible with all Microsoft products that use the Server Message Block (SMB) protocol. SMB functionality includes support for peer-to-peer networking with all other Microsoft networking products.

A Windows XP Professional–based computer in a peer-to-peer environment performs account authentication locally. Because the Kerberos V5 protocol is only used for domain authentication, Windows XP Professional uses NTLM to authenticate users in the local account database. For more information about account authentication, see "Account Authentication" later in this chapter.

Windows–based computers communicate with each other on peer-to-peer networks by using a common protocol. Due to dominance of the Internet, TCP/IP has become the protocol of choice for peer-to-peer networks. For more information about configuring protocols for peer-to-peer networking, see "TCP/IP and Other Network Protocols" later in this chapter.

Windows Domain Environment

A *domain* is a logical grouping of networked computers that share a central directory database that contains user account and security information for resources within the domain.

In a domain, the directory database is stored on computers that are configured as domain controllers. A domain controller manages all security-related aspects of interactions between users and domains. Security and administration are centralized. Figure 20-2 illustrates a domain configuration.

In a domain that has more than one domain controller, the domain accounts database is replicated between domain controllers within the domain for increased scalability and fault tolerance. If a domain controller becomes unavailable, directory information is still available from the other domain controllers. For more information about Windows 2000 Server domain controller placement in a Windows 2000 domain, see "Designing the Active Directory Structure" in the *Deployment Planning Guide* of the *Microsoft Windows 2000 Server Resource Kit*. For more information about Windows Server 2003 domain controller placement, see the *Microsoft Windows Server 2003 Deployment Kit*.

Windows 2000 and Windows Server 2003 domains improve on Windows NT domains. In Windows 2000 and Windows Server 2003 domains, all domain controllers can receive updates to the directory database. In Windows NT domains, the single-master model allows only one domain controller to be updated, which then replicates the changes to the other domain controllers. In Windows 2000 and Windows Server 2003 domains, the directory is distributed, and it uses a hierarchical namespace based on the Domain Name System (DNS). In Windows NT domains, the directory is centralized, and a flat namespace is used.

Windows XP Professional is fully compatible with Windows NT, Windows 2000, and Windows Server 2003 domains. For more information about whether to migrate an existing Windows NT domain to Windows 2000, see "Determining Domain Migration Strategies" in the *Deployment Planning Guide*.

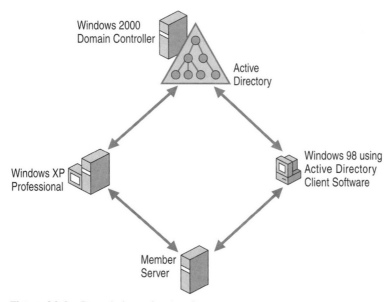

Figure 20-2   Domain-based network

Active Directory

Active Directory is the directory service included with Windows 2000 Server and Windows Server 2003. The service provides a place to store information about network-based entities (such as applications, files, printers, and users) and the means to locate and manage resources. Active Directory provides a consistent way to name, describe, locate, access, manage, and secure information about network resources.

Active Directory is available only in domains with Windows 2000–based or Windows Server 2003–based domain controllers. Active Directory presents domain information in a hierarchical, object-based format and protects network data from unauthorized access. It replicates directory data across a network so that data remains available if one domain controller fails.

Active Directory Clients   Active Directory supports clients running Windows XP Professional, Windows 2000, Windows NT, and Windows 9x. These computers can have access to shared resources within a domain to the extent allowed by the security on the resources. However, a computer that runs Windows 98, Windows 95, or Windows NT 4.0, or must have the Active Directory client software installed to search for information in Active Directory about the shared resources.

Active Directory Objects   In Active Directory, network resources such as users, groups, and computers are represented as *objects*. An object is a unique namespace within the directory with object specific attributes that represents something concrete, such as a user, a printer, or an application. An Active Directory object is defined by a set of rules, or *schema*. When you create an Active Directory object, Active Directory generates values for some of the object's attributes, and you provide other values. For example, when creating a new user account, Active Directory automatically assigns a globally unique identifier (GUID) but requires the administrator to provide values, at least for the minimally required attributes such as the user name and the logon identifier.

Organizational Units   An Active Directory domain can contain an organizational unit hierarchy. Organizational units are containers to which you can delegate administrative authority over sets of objects. Organizational units can also be used to apply policies to users and computers. An organizational unit can contain Active Directory objects, such as users, groups, computers, printers, and shared folders, as well as other organizational units. Each domain can have its own hierarchy of organizational units that implements domain-specific administration.

An Active Directory organizational unit can represent a group of users, such as the marketing department, or a collection of related objects, such as printers. You can create a tree structure by nesting organizational units, objects, and containers in the same way that a Windows file system uses folders and files. Storing objects in an organizational unit allows an administrator to use Group Policy to apply restrictions to all users or all computers within that unit. Objects can still be stored in containers other than organizational units when such container-level policies are not required.

Global Catalog   Windows 2000 Server introduced the *global catalog*, which provides forest-wide Active Directory searches. Ordinarily, a domain controller stores objects for only one domain. A global catalog server is a special domain controller that stores complete objects for one domain and partial objects (every object but only a limited set of each object's attributes) for every other domain in the forest. The global catalog is also required for user logon. There can be multiple global catalog servers in a forest.

The global catalog makes directory structures within an enterprise transparent to end users seeking information. In an enterprise that contains many domains, the global catalog allows clients to easily perform searches across all domains without having to search each domain separately.

Administration Tools   Administrators who have the required permissions can use the Windows Server 2003 Administration Tools Pack to remotely create Active Directory objects and perform other administration tasks from a Windows XP Professional client that meets the following criteria:

- The Windows Server 2003 Administration Tools Pack has been installed locally.

- The Windows XP Professional Client has been updated with Service Pack 1 or the hotfix included with Knowledge Base Article Q329357.

- The Windows XP Professional client is a 32-bit client. The tools support 32-bit and 64-bit server operating systems. However, the Windows Server 2003 Administration Tools Pack does not install on 64-bit systems.

> **Warning**   You must have administrative permissions on the local computer to install or run Windows Server 2003 Administration Tools Pack. For security reasons, Windows Server 2003 Administration Tools Pack should be *uninstalled* if the Windows XP Professional computer is to be used by a non-administrator. In addition, you should be aware of specific security requirements for each tool.

The Administration Tools Pack is available as adminpak.msi on the Windows Server 2003 family operating system CDs. For more information about installing the Administration Tools Pack, see the Windows Server 2003 Help and Support Center.

Active Directory Security   A *security identifier* (SID) is a unique number created by the security subsystem of the Windows XP Professional, Windows 2000, Windows Server 2003 or Windows NT operating system and assigned to *security principal objects* such as user, group, and computer accounts. Every account on a network is issued a unique SID when that account is first created. For example, when you join a computer to a Windows 2000 or Windows Server 2003 domain, a SID is created for that computer account. Internal processes in the Windows XP Professional, Windows 2000, Windows Server 2003, and Windows NT operating systems refer to an account by its SID instead of its user name or group name.

Each object is protected by an access control list (ACL) that contains *access control entries* (ACEs) that specify the users or groups who are permitted access to that object and what these access rights are. An ACE is created for an object by assigning permissions. Each ACE contains the SID of a user or group who is allowed (or explicitly denied) access to that object. An ACE also defines the level of access allowed. For example, a user might have read-only access to some objects, read-and-write access to other objects, and no access to the remaining objects.

If you create an account, delete it, and then create a new account that has the same user name, the new account does not have the rights or permissions previously granted to the old account because the accounts have different SIDs. For more information about planning and implementing access permissions, see "Authorization and Access Control" in this book.

DNS and Active Directory Domains   Domain Name System (DNS) is required for support of Active Directory for the following reasons:

■ Active Directory domains are named with DNS names.

■ Active Directory uses DNS as its location service, to enable clients to locate domain controllers.

Active Directory can also benefit DNS. DNS zone information can be copied to Active Directory domain controllers to enhance zone replication and provide security.

To implement Active Directory, one or more DNS servers must be available to the Windows 2000 or Windows Server 2003 domain, and the DNS client service must be configured at each member computer. This can be done automatically through DHCP.

Active Directory domains are named with DNS names. The DNS hierarchical naming structure is an inverted tree structure, or a single-root domain, under which can be parent and child domains. For example, a Windows 2000 domain name such as *seattle.noam.reskit.com* identifies a specific computer in a domain named *noam,* which is a child domain of the domain *reskit.* The *com* domain is a top-level domain on the Internet by which *reskit.com* and any of its child domains might be located.

Each computer in a DNS domain is identified by a unique, fully qualified domain name (FQDN). The FQDN of a computer located in the domain noam.reskit.com is *computername*.noam.reskit.com. Figure 20-3 illustrates a Windows 2000 domain that uses the DNS hierarchical naming structure.

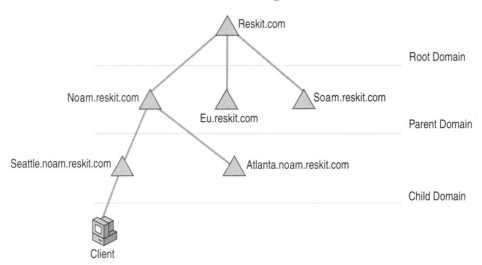

Figure 20-3   Windows 2000 domain hierarchy

Every Windows 2000 (or Windows Server 2003) domain and every Windows XP Professional–based computer has a DNS name. Thus, domains and computers are represented both as Active Directory objects and as DNS nodes (a node in the DNS hierarchy represents a domain or a computer). When you add a computer to a Windows 2000 or Windows Server 2003 domain, you need to specify the FQDN, consisting of the computer name and domain name. This information is provided when you add the computer account to the domain during or after initial Windows XP Professional Setup. For more information about adding Windows XP Professional–based clients to a Windows 2000 or Windows Server 2003 domain, see "Joining the Network Environment" later in this chapter.

Although the two namespaces can share an identical domain structure, it is important to understand that they are not the same namespace. Each stores different data and therefore manages different objects. DNS stores zones and resource records, and Active Directory stores domains and domain objects.

Note   Not every client needs to be visible to the Internet and not every company that wants to implement Active Directory needs to be on the Internet.

For more information about configuring the DNS client, see "Configuring IP Addressing and Name Resolution" in this book. For more conceptual information about DNS and the Windows 2000 DNS service, see "Introduction to DNS" and "Windows 2000 DNS" in the *Microsoft Windows 2000 Server TCP/IP Core Networking Guide.*

Windows NT 4.0 Compatibility

In addition to being able to use Active Directory domain controllers, Windows XP Professional–based computers can access domain controllers used in Windows NT 4.0 domains. Like Active Directory, the Windows NT 4.0 account database includes the following two types of accounts in its domain environment:

- **Computer accounts.** Windows NT 4.0–based, Windows 2000–based, and Windows XP Professional–based computers that can access the domain.

- **User accounts.** Users who can access the domain.

Shared resources defined within the domain are associated with accounts by using ACEs, which determine the permissions to domain resources such as shared files and printers. A Windows XP Professional–based computer can access objects stored in a Windows NT account database without modification.

Typically, a Windows XP Professional–based computer uses Kerberos V5 authentication to find a Windows 2000–based or Windows Server 2003–based domain controller. A Windows XP Professional–based computer that is authenticating against a Windows NT 4.0 domain controller uses NTLM as its security protocol. For information about Kerberos V5 authentication, see "Account Authentication" later in this chapter.

Account Authentication

Typically, a computer and its stored information must be protected from unauthorized access. Windows XP Professional secures the computer by using account authentication, which can prevent a user from accessing a computer or domain. Account authentication is the process of confirming the identity of a user by verifying a user's login name and password or smartcard information against data stored in an account database either locally or on a domain server. After authentication identifies the user, the user is granted access to a specific set of network resources based on permissions. Authorization takes place by means of the mechanism of access control, using access control lists (ACLs), which define permissions on file systems, network file and print shares, and entries in the account database. For more information about account authentication, see "Logon and Authentication" in this book.

Authentication Methods

Account authentication is performed by one of the following two methods:

- Authentication by the local account database for computers in workgroups and stand-alone computers.

- Authentication by a domain account database located on a domain controller for computers in a domain.

Windows XP Professional uses the Kerberos V5 authentication protocol as the default authentication method for domain access and NTLM for local access.

When you log on to a Windows domain, Windows XP Professional attempts to use Kerberos V5 security procedures as the primary source of user authentication, searching for the Kerberos Key Distribution Center (KDC) service on the domain controller. KDC is the account authentication service that runs on all Windows 2000–based and Windows Server 2003–based domain controllers.

In a Windows NT 4.0 environment, Windows 2000 and Windows XP Professional use NTLM to authenticate to the domain's Windows NT Security Accounts Manager (SAM) database on a Windows NT–based domain controller.

When users log on locally to a workstation or to a stand-alone or member server, authentication to the local database occurs by way of NTLM rather than by way of the Kerberos V5 protocol. The local accounts database on Windows XP Professional–based and Windows 2000–based computers is a SAM database, similar to the database used in Windows NT 4.0 and earlier.

Logon Names

A user must have a unique logon name to access a domain and its resources. In a domain environment, a user is a type of security principal. Every account, domain or local, has a user name, which is also called the SAM account name.

The logon name for a user on the local computer is the same as the user name for the account stored on the local computer.

The logon name for a user in the domain can be one of two types (every Windows 2000 or Windows Server 2003 domain user has both by default), both of which contain the user name of the domain account:

User Principal Name   The user principal name consists of the SAM account name, the *at* sign (@), and a user principal name suffix. The user principal name suffix is the DNS domain name of the forest root domain, but you can change the suffix. For example, the user John Doe, who has a user account in the reskit.com domain, might have the user principal name JDoe@reskit.com. This form of the logon name can be used to log on to Windows 2000 or Windows Server 2003 networks.

User Logon Name (Pre-Windows 2000)   The SAM account name is combined with the NetBIOS domain name, separated by a backslash (for example, reskit\ JDoe). This form of the logon name is used to log on to Windows NT networks or to log on to a Windows 2000 or Windows Server 2003 network from a client that is running an earlier version of Windows or accessing a server that is running an earlier version of Windows.

The user principal name of the user object is independent of the *distinguished name*, which is the name that identifies the object and its location within Active Directory. Theoretically two accounts that log on to the same domain can have the same SAM account name. In such a situation, it is the distinguished name that differentiates the object, not the SAM or user principal name. While this sharing of one principal name by two user objects is possible, it is never recommended as it can cause confusion. Also, you can move or rename a user object without affecting the user principal name, and you can have multiple user principal names.

TCP/IP and Other Network Protocols

Because TCP/IP is the standard network protocol suite, IP is the protocol installed by default on Windows XP Professional. For backward compatibility, Windows XP Professional also supports NetBIOS over TCP/IP (NetBT) and Internetwork Packet Exchange/Sequenced Packet Exchange (IPX/SPX).

Benefits of TCP/IP

Windows XP Professional includes a complete implementation of the standard, routable TCP/IP protocol suite. TCP/IP provides the following benefits:

- Support for Internet connectivity.

- Ability to route packets, which allows you to divide networks into subnets to optimize networking performance or to facilitate network management.

- Connectivity across interconnected networks that use different operating systems and hardware platforms, including communication with many non-Microsoft systems, such as Internet hosts, Apple Macintosh systems, IBM mainframes, UNIX systems, and Open Virtual Memory System (VMS) systems.

- Support for automatic TCP/IP configuration by using Dynamic Host Configuration Protocol (DHCP).

- Support for Automatic Private IP Addressing (APIPA), allowing computers in small networks without a DHCP server to automatically assign themselves IP addresses.

- Support for automatic mapping of IP addresses to NetBIOS names by using Windows Internet Name Service (WINS) servers.

- Support for NetBIOS over TCP/IP (NetBT).

- Performance enhancements, including a larger default TCP receive window size and selective acknowledgments.

- Hypertext Transfer Protocol (HTTP), File Transfer Protocol (FTP), and other communications protocols used for Internet access.

- Alternate IP Configuration, a new feature that allows users to have a DHCP assigned IP address as well as a static IP address mapped to the same network adapter and thus allows the user to roam between different networks seamlessly.

When you install Windows XP Professional, TCP/IP and NetBIOS over TCP/IP (NetBT) are installed by default. Either can be configured during or after installation. IPX/SPX is also included with Windows XP Professional and can be installed if needed.

For more information about features of TCP/IP in Windows XP Professional, see "Configuring TCP/IP" in this book.

Configuring the Protocol Binding Order

If multiple network protocols are installed on your Windows XP Professional–based computer, you can determine the *binding order* of each protocol for each service that uses the protocol. The binding order determines which protocol a service uses to connect to another client or service. To reduce the time needed to find required clients and services, place the most-frequently-used protocol first.

Multiple services can bind with each protocol, but the service that controls access to the network is the **Client for Microsoft Networks,** shown in Figure 20-4. The binding order appears on the **Adapters and Bindings** tab of the **Advanced Settings** property sheet of a selected network adapter.

Figure 20-4   Configure protocol binding order

To change the binding order of network protocols

1. In **Control Panel**, click **Network and Internet Connections**.

2. Click **Network Connections**.

3. Select the connection you want to modify, and then on the **Advanced** menu, click **Advanced Settings**.

4. On the **Adapters and Bindings** tab, in **Connections** select **Local Area Connection** or the specific Remote Access connection for which to change the binding order. Then, in **Bindings** for the selected connection, select the protocol to move up or down in the list, and then click the **Up** or **Down** button.

Locating Resources by Publishing Objects

Typically, users want to locate shared resources when they log on to the network. Windows XP Professional provides shared resources by publishing objects in domains and by using the *browse* function in SMB-based networks, such as Windows NT.

Publishing   *Publishing* is the act of creating objects in Active Directory that either contain the information you want to make available or that provide a reference to that information. For example, a user object contains useful information about the user, such as a telephone number and an e-mail address. Similarly, a volume object might contain a reference to a shared file system volume. Published objects are available to Windows XP Professional–based and Windows 2000–based clients, and to Windows NT 4.0–based, Windows 95–based, and Windows 98–based clients that have Active Directory client software installed. Publishing can be implemented only in an Active Directory domain where TCP/IP is the transport protocol.

Share publishing and printer publishing are two examples of file and print objects published in Active Directory.

Share publishing   Network administrators and authorized users can publish a shared folder as a shared folder object in Active Directory by using the Active Directory Users and Computers snap-in of the Microsoft Management Console (MMC). Users can then query Active Directory for a shared folder.

Printer publishing   In a Windows 2000 or Windows Server 2003 domain, Active Directory simplifies managing, locating, and connecting to printers. When you add a printer by using the Add Printer wizard, and then share the printer, Windows 2000 Server publishes it in the domain as an object in Active Directory. Publishing printers in Active Directory lets users locate the most convenient printer. Users can now query Active Directory for any of these printers by specifying printer attributes such as type (PostScript or legal-sized paper, for example) and location. When you remove a printer from the server, it is unpublished by the server.

Computer Browser and Browsing Roles

The Computer Browser service provides a method of locating shared resources within a domain or workgroup environment. The service transparently designates certain workstations or servers as browse servers, which maintain master *browse lists*, or directories of all shared resources on the network. The Computer Browser service designates other workstations and servers as browsers, which contact the nearest browse server to obtain the master browse list.

Browsing is required by network applications that use SMB, such as My Network Places, the **net view** command, and Windows Explorer.

Typically, domains that allow browsing are controlled by computers that run earlier versions of Windows operating systems, such as Windows 98 or Windows NT. For compatibility, Windows 2000 and Windows Server 2003 domains support browsing for clients that use these operating systems. However, you can enhance the functionality of browsing by publishing shared resources to Active Directory and to global catalogs.

Table 20-1 describes the browser roles and functions that computers using this service can perform.

Table 20-1   Browser Roles and Functions

Browser Role	Function
Domain master browser	A browse server that collects and maintains the master browse list of available network servers for its domain, as well as any names for other domains and workgroups used in the network. The domain master browser distributes and synchronizes the master browse list for master browsers on other subnets that have computers belonging to the same domain. It is used only in domain environments. By default, the primary domain controller for a domain has this role. A Windows XP Professional–based computer cannot become a domain master browser but it can function as a browse server.
Master browser	A browse server that collects and maintains the list of available network servers in its subnet. The master browser replicates its listed information by relying on the domain master browser to obtain a complete browse list for the network. This browser then distributes its completed list to backup browsers located on the same subnet.
Backup browser	Receives a copy of the browse list from the master browser for its subnet. Distributes the browse list to other computers on request.
Potential browser	Under normal conditions, operates similarly to a nonbrowser. It is capable of becoming a backup browser if instructed to by the master browser for the subnet. This is the default configuration for a Windows XP Professional–based computer.
Nonbrowser	Can operate as a browse client, requesting browse lists from other computers that have browser roles on the same subnet. However, it does not maintain a browse list. It is configured so it cannot become a browser.

Under certain conditions, such as failure or shutdown of a computer that is designated for a specified browser role, browsers or potential browsers might change to a different role by using a process known as *browser election*.

When a Windows XP Professional–based computer starts, it checks the registry entry **MaintainServerList** to determine if it can become a browser. This entry is found in:

HKEY_LOCAL_MACHINE\SYSTEM\CurrentControlSet\Services\Browser\ Parameters

Table 20-2 describes the values that you can assign to the **MaintainServerList** entry to specify how a computer participates in browser services.

Table 20-2   Allowable Values for the MaintainServerList Registry Entry

Value	Description
No	Prevents the computer from participating as a browser.

Table 20-2   Allowable Values for the MaintainServerList Registry Entry

Value	Description
Yes	Makes the computer a browser. At startup, the computer attempts to contact the master browser to get a current browse list. If the master browser cannot be found, the computer forces a browser election. The computer becomes either an elected master browser or a backup browser.
Auto	Makes the computer a potential browser. It might become a browser, depending on the number of currently active browsers. If necessary, the master browser instructs the computer if it must become a backup browser. The Auto value is the default for computers running Windows XP Professional, Windows 2000 Professional, and Windows NT Workstation 4.0.

> **Tip** Set the **MaintainServerList** entry to **No** on computers that are frequently turned off or removed from the network, such as portable computers. This ensures that a browse server remains available, helps to reduce browser elections, and reduces network overhead caused by a browser. Disabling browsing on client computers also reduces the network overhead that results from browser announcements.

Another entry in this registry location, **IsDomainMaster**, determines if a Windows XP Professional–based computer can become a preferred master browser. A *preferred master browser* has priority over other computers in master browser elections. Whenever a preferred master browser starts, it forces an election. The default setting for a Windows XP Professional–based computer is **False**.

> **Caution** Do not edit the registry unless you have no alternative. The registry editor bypasses standard safeguards, allowing settings that can damage your system, or even require you to reinstall Windows. If you must edit the registry, back it up first and see the Registry Reference in the Microsoft Windows 2000 Server Resource Kit at http://www.microsoft.com/reskit.

Browser Elections

After the browsing role for a Windows XP Professional–based computer is determined, the computer checks to see if a master browser is present on the domain. If a master browse server does not exist, a *browser election* determines which computer becomes a master browse server for the workgroup. A browser election occurs when the following circumstances exist:

- A computer cannot locate a master browser.

- A preferred master browser comes online.

- A Windows NT–based domain controller starts.

Note   In a Computer Browser service context, a *server* is any computer that can provide resources to the rest of the network. For example, a computer that can share files or print resources with other computers on the network is considered a server in the context of the browser system even if the computer is not actively sharing resources.

If a master browse server already exists, Windows XP Professional checks the number of computers in the workgroup and the available browse servers. If the number of computers in the workgroup exceeds the defined ratio of browse servers to computers (typically one browse server for every 32 computers), and the **MaintainServerList** registry entry is set to **Auto**, the master browser can select a Windows XP Professional–based computer to act as a backup browser.

Building the Browse List for Microsoft Networks

In Windows XP Professional, the Computer Browser service maintains an up-to-date list of domains, workgroups, and computers and provides this list to applications at the user's request. The user sees the list in the following circumstances:

- If a user requests a list of computers in a workgroup, the Computer Browser service on the local computer randomly chooses a browse server and sends the request.

- If a user selects a workgroup to which the user's computer does not belong:

  - Windows XP Professional requests a list of the computers that belong to the selected workgroup. A browse server in the selected workgroup provides the list.

  - The selected browse server sends a list of the workgroups that are on the network and a list of computers in the user's workgroup.

The browse list is displayed anywhere that Windows XP Professional presents lists of browsable resources. You can also use the **net view** command to view the browse list. The list can contain the names of domains, workgroups, and computers that run the file and printer sharing service, including the following:

- Computers running Windows 98, Windows 95, Microsoft® Windows® for Workgroups, and Windows NT Workstation.

- Windows NT domains and servers.

- Workgroups defined in Windows 98, Windows 95, Windows for Workgroups, Windows NT Server, and Windows NT Workstation.

- Workgroup Add-on for Microsoft® MS-DOS® peer servers.

- LAN Manager 2.*x* domains and servers.

Adding to and Removing from the Browse List

When a user starts or properly shuts down a computer running Windows XP Professional on the network, it announces that event to the master browse server for its workgroup. The master browse server either adds or removes that computer from the list of available computers in the workgroup. Next, the master browse server notifies backup browse servers that a change to the browse list is available. The backup browse servers then request the new information to update their local browse lists. New computers on the network do not show up in a user's request for a browse list until the backup browse server receives an updated browse list, which can take up to 15 minutes.

If a user turns off the computer without properly shutting it down, the computer does not notify the master browse server. In such cases, the computer name continues to appear in the browse list until the name entry times out, which can take up to an hour.

Logon Scripts

A logon script is a batch file (.bat or .cmd), executable file, or procedure (including VBScript, JavaScript or Windows Script Host) that you can use to configure the user environment after the System Policy or Group Policy is enabled. An administrator can use logon scripts to set up network directory and printer shares or start maintenance applications, such as an anti-virus application.

The functionality of logon scripts that are designed for a Windows NT domain is the same for Windows XP Professional–based clients. However, after migrating to a Windows 2000 or Windows Server 2003 domain, test logon scripts to verify that your applications and procedures are compatible with Windows XP Professional.

Group Policy and System Policy Settings

System Policy is based on registry settings made by using Poledit.exe, the System Policy Editor tool. Windows NT 4.0 introduced Poledit.exe, which specifies user and computer configurations stored in the Windows NT registry. By using Poledit.exe, administrators can create a System Policy to control the user work environment and to enforce system configuration settings for all computers that run either Windows NT 4.0 Workstation or Windows NT 4.0 Server.

Windows NT 4.0 includes 72 policy settings that:

- Assign the values only for registry entries based on .adm files.

- Apply only to users on Windows NT–based computers, or Windows 95–based and Windows 98–based computers within a domain.

- Apply only to controls exercised by user name and membership in security groups.

- Remain in user profiles only until the specified policy is reversed or until the user edits the registry.

- Function primarily for customizing desktop environments; they do not perform as well in other circumstances.

- Lack security.

Beginning with Windows 2000, the Group Policy snap-in replaced the System Policy Editor tool used in Windows NT 4.0. The Group Policy snap-in gives you increased control over configuration settings for groups of computers and users. In Windows XP Professional, as in Windows 2000 and Windows Server 2003, Group Policy settings are your primary means for enabling centralized change and configuration management. A domain administrator can use Group Policy at a Windows 2000–based or Windows Server 2003–based domain controller to create a specific desktop configuration for a particular group of users and computers. You can also create local Group Policy settings for individual workstations to customize environments that differ from the domain environment.

A Windows 2000 domain Group Policy has more than 100 security-related settings and more than 450 registry-based settings that provide a broad range of options for managing the user environment. Windows Server 2003 offers additional options and settings. Group Policy settings are:

- Defined either locally or in the Windows 2000 or Windows Server 2003 domain.

- Extended by using MMC or .adm files.

- Not left in user profiles.

- Applied to users or computers in a specified Active Directory container (sites, domains, and organizational units).

- Controlled further by user or computer membership in security groups.

- Configures many types of security settings.

- Applies to logon, logoff, startup, and shutdown scripts.

904   Part IV   Networking

- Used to install and maintain software (Windows 2000 and Windows Server 2003 domain policies only).

- Used to redirect folders (such as My Documents and Application Data).

- Used to perform maintenance on Microsoft® Internet Explorer (Windows 2000 and Windows Server 2003 domain policies only).

- Used to ensure security.

You can use the Group Policy snap-in to edit local Group Policy objects to make the following changes at the local computer:

- Define security settings for a local computer only, not for a domain or network.

- Use administrative templates to set more than 450 operating system behaviors.

- Use scripts to automate computer startup, shutdown, and user logon and logoff processes.

On a stand-alone computer running Windows XP Professional, local Group Policy objects are located at *systemroot*\System32\GroupPolicy.

For more information about implementing Group Policy within a Windows 2000 domain, see "Group Policy" in the *Distributed Systems Guide* of the *Microsoft Windows 2000 Server Resource Kit*. For more information about implementing Group Policy in a Windows Server 2003 domain, see the *Designing a Managed Environment* book of the *Microsoft Windows Server 2003 Resource Kit*.

System Policy and Group Policy Coexistence

You might have instances in which Windows NT System Policy must coexist with Windows 2000 and Windows Server 2003 Group Policy. Two possible scenarios follow:

- A Windows XP Professional–based computer uses local Group Policy together with Windows NT 4.0 System Policy to enable Windows 2000 security settings.

- A Windows XP Professional–based computer is in a Windows NT 4.0 domain that you are in the process of migrating to a Windows 2000 or Windows Server 2003 domain, and user and computer accounts are split between the two domains.

In an environment where Windows NT System Policy coexists with Windows 2000 or Windows Server 2003 Group Policy, the resulting computer and user configuration is determined by the following factors:

- The location of the user account (Windows NT–based or Windows 2000–based or Windows Server 2003–based domain controller).

- The location of the computer account (Windows NT–based or Windows 2000–based or Windows Server 2003 –based domain controller).

- The activity taking place, such as a computer starting up, a user logging on, or the refreshing of a user or system account.

Table 20-3 summarizes the expected behavior of computer and user accounts in an environment where Windows NT System Policy coexists with Windows 2000 or Windows Server 2003 domain Group Policy.

Table 20-3   Expected Behaviors of System Policies and Group Policy Settings

Environment	Account Object Location	Result at Windows XP Professional–based Client
Windows NT 4.0 domain	Computer: Windows NT 4.0	**At computer startup:** Computer local Group Policy (only if changed).
		Every time the user logs on: Computer System Policy.
Windows NT 4.0 domain	Computer refresh	**Before Control-Alt-Delete:** Computer local Group Policy only.
		After the user logs on: Computer local Group Policy and computer System Policy.
Windows NT 4.0 domain	User: Windows NT 4.0	**When the user logs on:** User System Policy.
		If local Group Policy changes: User local Group Policy and user System Policy.
Windows NT 4.0 domain	User refresh	User local Group Policy and user System Policy.
Mixed domain (migration)	Computer: Windows NT 4.0	**At computer startup:** Computer local Group Policy (only if changed).
		Every time the user logs on: Computer System Policy.
Mixed domain (migration)	Computer refresh	**Before Control-Alt-Delete:** Computer local Group Policy only.
		After the user logs on: Computer local Group Policy and computer System Policy.
Mixed domain (migration)	User: Windows XP Professional	Group Policy is processed by the local computer.
		Windows NT 4 does not recognize Group Policy. Thus a user logging on to an Windows NT 4 computer does not get any portion of Group Policy.
Mixed domain (migration)	User refresh	User Group Policy.

Table 20-3   Expected Behaviors of System Policies and Group Policy Settings

Environment	Account Object Location	Result at Windows XP Professional–based Client
Mixed domain (migration)	Computer: Windows 2000 Server, Windows Server 2003, or Windows XP Professional	**During system startup:** Group Policy.
Mixed domain (migration)	Computer refresh	Computer Group Policy.
Mixed domain (migration)	User: Windows NT 4.0	**When the user logs on:** User System Policy. **If local Group Policy changes:** User local Group Policy and user System Policy.
Mixed domain (migration)	User refresh	User local Group Policy and user System Policy.
Windows 2000 or Windows Server 2003 domain	Computer: Windows XP Professional	Computer Configuration part of Group Policy is processed when the computer starts and at designated intervals thereafter (period is configurable).
Windows 2000 or Windows Server 2003 domain	User: Windows XP Professional	User Configuration part of Group Policy is processed when the user logs on.
Workgroup	Local	Local Group Policy only.

In a system environment where local Group Policy on a Windows XP Professional–based computer coexists with a Windows NT 4.0 domain System Policy, make sure that the policy settings do not conflict or override each other. For example, in a Windows NT 4.0 domain that has system policies enabled, a Windows XP Professional–based computer with local Group Policy enabled enforces both policy settings whenever the computer is restarted immediately after the user logs on.

For more information about implementing Windows 2000 Group Policy on a Windows XP Professional client, see "Defining Client Administration and Configuration Standards" in the *Deployment Planning Guide* of the *Microsoft Windows 2000 Server Resource Kit*. For more information about implementing Windows Server 2003 Group Policy on a Windows XP Professional client, see the *Designing a Managed Environment* book of the *Microsoft Windows Server 2003 Deployment Kit*.

Checking Local and Domain Policy Compatibility

Check to see if existing local Group Policy and Windows NT System Policy are compatible. Does configuring Group Policy with Windows NT System Policy or Windows 2000 or Windows Server 2003 domain Group Policy produce unexpected results? For example, if you configure local Group Policy to remove entries from the

Start menu, does the domain Group Policy override the entries when the user logs on to the domain? For more information about the coexistence of local Group Policy with domain Group Policy or Windows NT System Policy, see "Troubleshooting Group Policy and System Policy" later in this chapter.

Group Policy Settings for Network Connections

You can use Group Policy settings or a combination of Group Policy and System Policy settings to control access to the Network Connections folder and the way the folder is used. For example, a Group Policy setting can be applied to make the **Advanced Settings** menu unavailable in the Network Connections folder. For more information about using Group Policy with Windows 2000 Server, see Windows 2000 Server Help. For more information about using Group Policy with Windows Server 2003, see the Windows Server 2003 Help and Support Center.

The location in the Group Policy snap-in for these settings is shown in Figure 20-5.

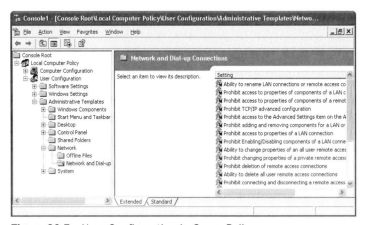

Figure 20-5   User Configuration in Group Policy

Descriptions of local Group Policy settings and all setting and registry information that you can apply in Windows XP Professional follow.

Allow configuration of connection sharing   The **Allow configuration of connection sharing** setting determines whether administrators can enable, disable, and configure the Internet Connection Sharing (ICS) feature of a dial-up connection.

> **Note**   This setting appears in the **Computer Configuration** and **User Configuration** folders. If both settings are configured, the setting in **Computer Configuration** takes precedence over the setting in **User Configuration**. Also, this setting applies only to users in the Administrators group.

If you enable this setting or do not configure it, the **Sharing** tab is displayed in the **Properties** dialog box for a dial-up connection. On Windows 2000 Server for example, it also displays the Internet Connection Sharing (ICS) page in the Network Connection Wizard. If you disable this setting, the **Sharing** tab and Internet Connection Sharing wizard page do not appear.

Warning Allowing users to enable ICS allows them to create an unauthorized DHCP server on the subnet on which the computer is located. An ICS-enabled computer allocates incorrect IP address configurations to all other DHCP clients on the same subnet and prevents them from communicating with computers on other subnets.

Prohibiting deletion of remote access connections   The **Prohibit deletion of remote access connections** setting determines whether users can delete their private dial-up network connections. By default, only administrators can delete connections available to all users. If you enable this setting, users cannot delete their private dial-up connections, and the **Delete** option is disabled on the context menu for a dial-up connection and on the **File** menu in Network Connections. If you disable this setting, users can delete any dial-up connection. For information about using Group Policy to manage user desktops, see "Managing Desktops" in this book.

Note   The **Prohibit deletion of remote access connections** setting appears in the Computer Configuration and User Configuration folders. If both settings are configured, the setting in Computer Configuration takes precedence over the setting in User Configuration. Even when the setting in User Configuration is not overridden, that setting applies only to users in the Administrators group.

Ability to change properties of an all user remote access connection   The **Ability to change properties of an all user remote access connection** setting determines whether a user can view and change the properties of dial-up connections that are available to all users of the computer. This setting also determines whether the **Dial-up Connection Properties** dialog box is available to users.

If you enable this setting, users can delete shared dial-up connections. If you do not configure this setting, only administrators can delete shared dial-up connections. If you disable this setting, no one can delete shared dial-up connections. By default, users can still delete their private connections, but you can change the default by using this setting.

Also, if you disable this setting, administrators are restricted from changing properties of all user remote access connections the same as any other user.

The **Ability to change properties of an all user remote access connection** setting overrides settings that remove or disable parts of **the Dial-up Connection Properties** dialog box, such as those that hide tabs, remove the check boxes for enabling or disabling components, or that disable the **Properties** button for components that a connection uses. If you disable this setting, it overrides these subsidiary settings.

Prohibit access to the properties of components of a remote access connection   The **Prohibit access to the properties of components of a remote access connection** setting determines whether users can connect and disconnect dial-up connections.

If you enable this setting, the **Connect** and **Disconnect** options on the **File** menu for dial-up connections are not available to users in the group.

Ability to enable/disable a LAN connection   The **Ability to enable/disable a LAN connection** setting determines whether users can enable and disable local area network connections.

If you enable this setting, users in the group can enable and disable LAN connections. If you disable it, even administrators are blocked from enabling and disabling LAN connections.

Prohibit access to properties of a LAN connection   The **Prohibit access to properties of a LAN connection** setting determines whether users can view and change the properties of a LAN connection. It also determines whether the **Local Area Connection Properties** dialog box is available to users.

If you enable this setting, users cannot open the **Local Area Connection Properties** dialog box. If you disable or do not configure this setting, the **Local Area Connection Properties** dialog box is displayed when users right-click the icon representing a local area connection, and then click **Properties**. The **Properties** option is also available on the **File** menu when users select the connection.

Prohibit changing properties of a private remote access connection   The **Prohibit changing properties of a private remote access connection** setting determines whether users can view and change the properties of their private dial-up connections.

Private connections are available to one user only. Typically, a user can create a private connection on the **Connection Availability** page in the Network Connection wizard by clicking **Only for myself**. You can use the **Prohibit changing properties of a private remote access connection** setting to make the **Dial-up Connection Properties** dialog box unavailable to users.

If you enable this setting, users cannot open the **Local Area Connection Properties** dialog box. If you disable or do not configure this setting, the **Local**

Area Connection Properties dialog box is displayed when users right-click the icon representing a local area connection, and then click **Properties.** The **Properties** option is also available on the **File** menu when users select the connection.

Ability to rename all user remote access connections   The **Ability to rename all user remote access connections** setting determines whether users can rename the dial-up and local area connections available to all users.

If you enable this setting, the **Rename** option is enabled. Users can rename connections by clicking the icon representing a connection or by using the **File** menu. If you disable this setting, the **Rename** option is disabled. This setting has no effect on administrators.

Prohibit renaming of private remote access connections   The   **Prohibit renaming of private remote access connections** setting determines whether users can rename their private dial-up connections.

Private connections are available only to one user. To create a private connection, on the **Connection Availability** page in the Network Connection wizard, click **Only for myself.**

Prohibit adding or removing components for a LAN or remote access connection   The **Prohibit adding or removing components for a LAN or remote access connection** setting determines whether administrators can add and remove network components.

If you enable this setting, the **Install** and **Uninstall** buttons for components of connections in Network Connections are disabled. Also, when this setting is enabled, administrators cannot gain access to network components in the Windows Components wizard. If you disable or do not configure this setting, the **Install** and **Uninstall** buttons for components of connections are enabled, and administrators can gain access to network components in the Windows Components wizard.

When this setting is disabled, the **Install** button opens the dialog boxes used to add network components. Clicking the **Uninstall** button removes the selected component in the components list (preceding the button). The **Install** and **Uninstall** buttons display when administrators right-click a connection, and then click **Properties**. These buttons are on the **General** tab for local area connections and on the **Networking** tab for dial-up connections.

Tip   When this setting is disabled, the Windows Components wizard permits administrators to add and remove components. To use the wizard, double-click **Add or Remove Programs** in Control Panel. To go directly to the network components in the Windows Components wizard, click the **Advanced** menu in Network Connections, and then click **Optional Networking Components**.

Prohibit enabling /disabling components of a LAN connection   The **Prohibit enabling/disabling components of a LAN connection** setting determines whether administrators can enable and disable the components used by local area connections.

If you disable or do not configure this setting, the **Properties** dialog box for a connection includes a check box for each component that the connection uses. Selecting the check box enables the component, and clearing the check box disables the component. Enabling this setting dims the check boxes for enabling and disabling components. As a result, administrators cannot enable or disable the components that a connection uses.

Prohibit access to properties of components of a LAN connection   The **Prohibit access to properties of components of a LAN connection** setting determines whether administrators can change the properties of components used by a local area connection.

This setting determines whether the **Properties** button for components of a local area connection is enabled. If you enable this setting, the **Properties** button is disabled. If you disable this setting or do not configure it, the **Properties** button is enabled.

To find the **Properties** button, right-click the connection, and then click **Properties**. You then see a list of the network components that the connection uses. To view or change the properties of a component, click the name of the component, and then click **Properties**.

Not all network components have configurable properties. For components that are not configurable, the **Properties** button is always disabled.

Prohibit access to the Network Connection wizard   The **Prohibit access to the Network Connection wizard** setting determines whether users can use the Network Connection wizard, which creates new network connections.

If you disable or do not configure this setting, **Make New Connection** appears in the Network Connections folder. Clicking **Make New Connection** starts the Network Connection wizard. If you enable this setting, **Make New Connection** does not appear. As a result, users cannot start the Network Connection wizard.

Prohibit viewing of status for an active connection   The **Prohibit viewing of status for an active connection** setting determines whether users can view the **Status** page for an active connection.

Status displays information about the connection and its activity. It also provides buttons to disconnect and to configure the properties of the connection.

If you disable or do not configure this setting, **Status** appears when users double-click an active connection. Also, an option to display **Status** appears on a menu when users right-click the icon for an active connection, and the option appears on the **File** menu when users select an active connection. If you enable this setting, **Status** is disabled, and **Status** does not appear.

Prohibit access to the Dial-up Preferences item on the Advanced menu   The **Prohibit access to the Dial-up Preferences item on the Advanced menu** setting determines whether **Dial-up Preferences** on the **Advanced** menu in Network Connections is enabled.

If you enable this setting, **Dial-up Preferences** is disabled. If you disable or do not configure this setting, it is enabled. By default, **Dial-up Preferences** is enabled.

Dial-up Preferences allows users to configure Autodial and callback features.

Prohibit access to the Advanced Settings item on the Advanced menu   The **Prohibit access to the Advanced Settings item on the Advanced menu** setting determines whether **Advanced Settings** on the **Advanced** menu in Network Connections is enabled.

If you enable this setting, **Advanced Settings** is disabled. If you disable or do not configure this setting, it is enabled. By default, **Advanced Settings** is enabled.

By enabling **Advanced Settings,** an administrator can view and change bindings and the order in which the computer accesses connections, network providers, and print providers.

Prohibit use of Internet connection sharing on your DNS domain network   The **Prohibit use of Internet connection sharing on your DNS domain network** setting determines whether administrators and can enable, disable, and configure the ICS feature of a dial-up connection.

If you enable this setting or do not configure it, the **Sharing** tab does not appear in the **Properties** dialog box for a dial-up connection. If you disable this setting, the **Sharing** tab and the **Internet Connection Sharing** wizard appear.

This setting appears in the Computer Configuration and User Configuration folders. If both settings are configured, the setting in Computer Configuration takes precedence over the setting in User Configuration.

Prohibit TCP/IP advanced configuration   The **Prohibit TCP/IP advanced configuration** setting determines whether users can use Network Connections to configure TCP/IP, DNS, and WINS settings.

If you enable this setting, the **Advanced** button on **Internet Protocol (TCP/IP) Properties** is disabled. As a result, users cannot open **Advanced TCP/IP Settings**. If you disable this setting, the **Advanced** button is enabled, and the users can open **Advanced TCP/IP Settings** and modify IP settings, such as DNS and WINS server information.

Warning   If the **Prohibit access to properties of a LAN connection** setting or the **Prohibit access to properties of components of a LAN connection** setting are enabled, users cannot gain access to the **Advanced** button. As a result, this setting is ignored.

If multiple network protocols are installed on your Windows XP Professional–based computer, you can determine the binding order of each protocol for each service that uses the protocol.

> **Note**   Windows Server 2003 Group Policy provides an updated set of configuration settings for Windows XP Professional-based computers. For more information, see the Windows Server 2003 Help and Support Center.

Joining the Network Environment

Adding a Windows XP Professional–based computer to a logical grouping of computers is called *joining* the domain or workgroup. To add a computer to the domain, you must be logged on to the computer with an account that is a member of the local Administrators group. If the account does not have administrative rights at the domain controller, another administrative account that does must be used. You can add a computer to a domain by using the Network Identification wizard.

> **Note**   In a Windows 2000 or Windows Server 2003 domain, permissions to add computers to a domain can be delegated to non-administrative user accounts. A domain administrator determines the delegation strategy used in an enterprise. For more information about delegation, see "Authorization and Access Control" in this book.

Network Identification Wizard

The Network Identification wizard provides a simple interface for joining a Windows XP Professional–based computer to a Windows NT domain, Windows 2000 or Windows Server 2003 domain, or a Windows XP Professional workgroup.

To start the Network Identification wizard

1. Right-click **My Computer**, and then click **Properties**.

2. On the **Computer Name** tab, click **Network ID**, and then click **Next**.

3. Select **This computer is part of a business network, and I use it to connect to other computers at work**, and then click **Next**.

Follow the subsequent instructions to complete the process.

Changing Windows Workgroup Membership

In the default Setup configuration, a Windows XP Professional–based computer is a member of a workgroup called WORKGROUP. You can change workgroup membership by logging on to an account that has administrative permissions. You can also enable your Windows XP Professional–based computer to manually join a Windows workgroup.

> **Warning**   If your computer was a member of a domain before you joined the workgroup, it is disjoined from the domain, and your computer account is disabled.

To join a Windows workgroup

1. In Control Panel, click **Performance and Maintenance**.
2. Click **System**.
3. In the **System Properties** dialog box, click **the Computer Name** tab.
4. Click **Change**.
5. Under **Member of**, click **Workgroup**.
6. Type the name of the workgroup that you want to join, and then click **OK**.
7. Click **OK** twice to return to the **System Properties** dialog box.
8. Click **OK**, and then click **Yes** to restart the computer.

Manually Joining a Windows Domain

As mentioned earlier, in the default Setup configuration, a Windows XP Professional–based computer is a member of a workgroup called WORKGROUP. You can move from a workgroup to a domain by logging on to an account that has administrative permissions. You can also manually configure a Windows XP Professional–based computer to join a Windows domain.

To join a Windows domain

1. In Control Panel, click **Performance and Maintenance**.
2. Click **System**.
3. In the **System Properties** dialog box, select the **Computer Name** tab.

4. Click **Change**.

5. If the computer account has been created at the domain controller, enter the user name, password, and domain, and then click **Next**.

– or –

If the computer account has not been created at the domain controller do the following:

   a. Enter the user name, password, and domain name, and then click **Next**.

   b. At the prompt, enter the user name and password of an Administrator account, and then click **OK**.

6. Click **OK** twice to return to the **System Properties** dialog box.

7. Click **OK**, and then click **Yes** to restart the computer.

Confirming Domain and Workgroup Membership

After you add the Windows XP Professional–based computer to the domain or workgroup, you should verify that the move is successful. To do so, restart the computer. After you press CTRL+ALT+DEL, the **Log On to Windows** dialog box appears. Use the arrow to the right of the **Log on to** text box to review the **Log on to** list. If you have joined a domain, the list will include the logon domain and any of its trusted domains. Reviewing the list is the first step toward confirming that you have successfully added the computer account to the logon domain.

Testing a Workgroup User Account

To test workgroup membership, log on to the local computer by using a valid user name and password. Typically, you can access all local computer resources and view other workgroup computers in **My Network Places**. A failure to access other workgroup computers might indicate problems with addressing or name resolution or a failure to connect to an intervening computer.

Testing a Domain User Account

You can test the validity of a user account by logging on to the trusted or logon domain. If you can log on by using the logon credentials at the domain controller, you've been granted access to a user account at the selected domain. If a message indicates that you've connected by using credentials stored in the cache, that means that the domain controller could not be contacted during the account authentication process. It is important to verify that the physical connection (network adapter and cables) and logical connection (transport protocol configuration) permit access to the domain controller.

You can use Nltest.exe, a command-line tool included with Windows Support Tools on the Windows XP Professional operating system CD, to test the logical connection between a Windows XP Professional–based computer and a domain controller. By using Nltest.exe, you can determine if a domain controller can authenticate a user account. Nltest.exe also establishes which domain controller performs the authentication and provides a list of trusted domains. For more information about Nltest.exe, click **Tools** in Windows XP Professional Help and Support Center, and then click **Windows Support Tools**.

Establishing a Secure Channel

The logical connection between the Windows XP Professional–based computer and the domain controller is known as a *secure channel*. A secure channel acts to authenticate computer accounts on computers running Windows XP Professional, Windows Server 2003, Windows 2000, and Windows NT. A secure channel also authenticates user accounts when a remote user connects to a network resource. The user account exists in a trusted domain. This process is called pass-through authentication. A secure channel must exist for account authentication to be performed. Nltest.exe can test secure channels and reset them at the discretion of the user.

The following examples show a Windows XP Professional computer, Client1, that is a member of the Windows NT 4.0 domain Main_dom. The account User1, in this instance, has been created within the domain.

To identify the domain controllers in the Main_dom domain, at the command prompt, type:

```
nltest /dclist:Main_dom
```

Your output shows this information:

```
List of DCs in Domain Main_dom
  \\NET1 (PDC)
The command completed successfully
```

To determine if the domain controller Net1 can authenticate the user account User1, at the command prompt, type:

```
nltest /whowill:Main_dom User1
```

Your output shows this information:

```
[20:58:55] Mail message 0 sent successfully (\MAILSLOT\NET\GETDC939)
[20:58:55] Response 0: S:\\NET1 D:Main_dom A:User1 (Act found)
The command completed successfully
```

In this example, **S:** indicates the domain controller that authenticates the account, **D:** indicates the domain of which the account is a member, and **A:** indicates the account name.

To determine if the workstation Client1 has a secure connection with a domain controller within the Main_Dom domain, enter:

```
nltest /server:Client1 /sc_query:Main_Dom
```

Your output shows this information:

```
Flags: 0
Connection Status = 0 0x0 NERR_Success
Trusted DC Name \\NET1
Trusted DC Connection Status Status = 0 0x0 NERR_Success
The command completed successfully
```

When computer and user account authentication is completed, make sure all logon scripts perform as expected. Make sure that network shares, batch files, and tools are configured as indicated by the logon script.

Troubleshooting Microsoft Networking

Tools and techniques are available that can help you identify and resolve problems that you might encounter in a networking environment.

When troubleshooting a network connection in Windows XP Professional, first establish that the following conditions exist:

- The cable connection between the network adapter and the port is secure. If it is, restart the computer in case you have temporarily lost connection.

- The network adapter is correctly installed. Use Device Manager to verify that it is functioning correctly.

- Event Viewer is correctly logging system and application events so that the problem can be fully analyzed. For more information about using Event Viewer and the event logs, see "Tools for Troubleshooting" later in this chapter.

- At least one domain controllers is available and functioning.

For more information about troubleshooting techniques and tools, see "Troubleshooting Concepts and Strategies" and "Tools for Troubleshooting" in this book and Windows XP Professional Help and Support Center.

Tools for Troubleshooting

Windows XP Professional includes tools to help you diagnose and resolve networking problems. For information about the use and syntax of the troubleshooting tools, see "Tools for Troubleshooting" in this book.

Event Viewer   Event Viewer allows you to monitor events in your system. It maintains logs about program, security, and system events on your computer. You can use Event Viewer to view and manage the event logs, gather information about hardware and software problems, and monitor Windows XP Professional security events. The Event Log service starts by default when you start Windows XP Professional. All users can view application and system logs.

An event log consists of a header, a description of the event (based on the event type), and additional data (optional). A typical log entry consists of the header and a description as shown in Figure 20-6.

Figure 20-6   Typical event log entry

To use Event Viewer to access a security log

1. Right-click **My Computer**, and then click **Manage**.

2. Click **System Tools**, click **Event Viewer**, and then click **Security**.

3. In the list of specific security events, double-click the most recent one.

4. In the **Event Properties** dialog box of the specific security event, read the information about the event and relevant data.

5. Event Viewer categorizes events by log type (for example, security or system) and displays a separate log for every event, which includes date, time, source, category, ID, user account, and computer name.

The log types that directly relate to a user logging on are the security and system logs. Table 20-4 provides a description of the log types and how they can be used in troubleshooting.

Table 20-4   Log Types

Log Type	Description
Security	The Security Log records security events, such as valid and invalid logon attempts, and events related to resource use, such as creating, opening, or deleting files or other objects. For example, the Security log records a user's inability to log on to a domain account due to an incorrect or invalid user ID/password combination.
System	The System Log records events logged by the Windows XP Professional system components. For example, if a driver or other system component fails to load during startup, it is recorded in the System Log. Also, the System Log records a duplicate computer name on the domain as an error message sent by NetBT.

For more information about Event Viewer, see Windows XP Professional Help and Support Center.

Network Connectivity Tester (Netdiag.exe)   This command-line diagnostic tool helps isolate networking and connectivity problems by performing a series of tests to determine the state of your network client and its functionality. Netdiag.exe performs LAN connectivity and domain membership tests, including network adapter status, IP configuration, domain membership, and Kerberos V5 security tests. The tests can be performed as a group or individually.

For more information about the function and syntax of Netdiag.exe, see "Tools for Troubleshooting" in this book.

Status Menu Command   If your computer is set up to accept incoming connections, an icon with an assigned user name appears in the Network Connections folder as each user connects. You can view the progress of incoming connections by right-clicking a named connection, and then clicking **Status**.

By using the **Status** menu command, you can view the following data:

- The duration of a connection.

- The speed at which you initially connected. For a single-link connection and for individual links in a multilink connection, this speed is negotiated (and fixed) at the time the connection or link is established. For multilink connections, this speed is equal to the sum of the speeds of the individual links. For multilink connections, this speed varies as links are added or deleted.

- For local area connections, the number of bytes transmitted and received during a connection. For other types of connections, the number of bytes transmitted and received during a connection, and the associated compression and error statistics.

- The diagnostic tools that you can use for a connection, if any. For example, the Windows Network Troubleshooter, TCP/IP Autoping, and TCP/IP Windows IP Configuration.

The Support tab in the Local Area Connection Status Dialog box   The **Support** tab in the **Local Area Connection Status** dialog box allows you to do the following:

- View the address type, IP address, subnet mask, and default address of a connection.

  Use the **Details** button to view a detailed summary of the network connection, which includes its physical address, the IP address of its DHCP, DNS and WINS servers, the date the DHCP lease of the address was obtained, and the date the DHCP lease is due to expire. This is in addition to the IP address, subnet mask, and default address of the connection.

- Open the **Network Diagnostics** page of Windows XP Professional Help and Support Center.

- Repair your settings by pressing the Repair button. This does the following:

  - Releases current TCP/IP settings.

  - Renews your TCP/IP settings.

  - Registers the DNS resource records for all adapters on your Windows XP Professional–based computer. All errors are reported in the Event Viewer within 15 minutes of the time registration is initiated. On the command line, you can achieve similar results by using "ipconfig /registerdns".

  - Flushes the ARP cache

  - Does a DHCP broadcast renew for the IP lease.

  - Purges and reloads the remote cache name table of NetBT. On the command line, you can achieve similar results by using "Nbtstat -R".

  - Sends Name Release packets to WINS and then starts refresh. On the command line, you can achieve similar results by using "Nbtstat -RR".

  - Purges the dns resolver cache and re-registers the DNS recodes. On the command line, you can achieve similar results by using "ipconfig /flushdns".

Troubleshooting Joining Networks

You can use the following techniques and procedures to troubleshoot problems that might occur when you join a Windows XP Professional–based computer to a Windows NT domain, Windows 2000 domain, or a workgroup consisting of other Microsoft networking clients.

Unable to join a domain   When you attempt to add a computer running Windows XP Professional to a domain, the following message appears:

```
"Unable to connect to the domain controller for this domain. Either the user name or
password entered is incorrect."
```

To join a Windows XP Professional–based computer to a domain, you must provide an account name that is a member of the Domain Admins group (Windows NT, Windows 2000 or Windows Server 2003 domains) or that is a member of a group that has permissions to add computers to a domain.

Unable to find a domain controller   When you attempt to add a computer running Windows XP Professional to a domain or workgroup or a Windows XP Professional workgroup by using the Network Identification wizard or by manually adding the computer, the following message appears:

```
"The specified domain does not exist or could not be contacted."
```

When you receive the preceding message, verify that the correct domain or workgroup names are entered in the Workgroup and Domain fields on athe Computer Name tab of the System Properties dialog box..

If TCP/IP is the transport protocol used, the problem might be caused by the configuration of TCP/IP options on the client. Log on to a local administrative account and do the following tasks to resolve the problem:

1. Attempt to ping the domain controller by using its NetBIOS name (for example, DomainController1) or a fully qualified DNSdomain name (for example, DomainController1.domain1.reskit.com). If unsuccessful, attempt to ping the domain controller by using the IP address.

2. If the attempt to ping the domain controller by name is not successful, and DNS or WINS is used for name resolution, verify the IP addresses of the name servers. Then, try again to ping the domain controller by name.

3. If the attempt to ping the domain controller by name is unsuccessful, and the Windows XP Professional–based client is in the same subnet as the domain controller, verify the client's IP address.

4. If the Windows XP Professional–based client is in a different subnet from the domain controller, verify that you have specified the correct default gateways.

5. If Internet Control Message Protocol (ICMP)-enabled routers are used within your network, you can use a method called ICMP Router Discovery to automate the discovery and configuration of default gateways. For more information about ICMP Router Discovery, see "Configuring TCP/IP" in this book.

6. If Routing Information Protocol (RIP)–enabled routers are used in the network, install RIP support.

7. If a domain controller has an Internet Protocol security (IPSec) policy set at **Secure Server**, it denies transfer of IP packets to clients that do not have IPSec enabled by local or domain-based security policies. Contact the domain administrator to revise the IPSec policy on the domain controller. For more information about IPSec, see "Configuring TCP/IP" in this book.

Unable to rename a computer   When you attempt to name or rename a computer with a name that is similar to the domain or workgroup name, the following message appears:

```
"The new computer name may not be the same as the Workgroup (Domain) name."
```

In a Windows NT workgroup or domain or a Windows 2000 or Windows Server 2003 domain where NetBIOS is not disabled on all clients and servers, the first 15 characters of the name of the Windows XP Professional–based computer must not duplicate the name of an existing client, workgroup, or domain. For example, if the domain name is *Reskit1domainSEA*, you must select a different name for a computer in that domain.

Troubleshooting Logon Problems

After joining a Windows XP Professional–based computer to a workgroup or domain, the computer running Windows XP Professional typically communicates with other clients in the network environment. You can use the following techniques and procedures to identify and resolve problems that occur when you attempt to log on to a domain or to a workgroup consisting of other Microsoft networking clients.

Unable to log on at a local workstation   After creating a computer account at the domain, you attempt to log on locally by using a non-administrative account. The following message appears:

```
"The system could not log you on. Make sure your user name and Domain are correct,
then type your password again."
```

Unable to log on to a domain   After your computer joins a Windows 2000 or Windows Server 2003 domain, and you attempt to log on to the domain, the following message appears:

```
"The system cannot log you on due to the following error: There is a time difference
between the Client and Server. Please try again or consult your system administrator."
```

The Kerberos V5 authentication protocol inspects the timestamp of the authentication request sent by the logged-on client. The timestamp is compared to the current time of the domain controller. If a significant difference exists between the times (default is five minutes), authentication fails. Log on locally to an administrative account and make sure that the Windows XP Professional–based client time is the same as that of the domain controller. It is also important that the time zone be entered correctly because the Kerberos protocol converts all times to Greenwich Mean Time and then compares them that way.

Each user account object in Active Directory contains a **User must log on using a smart card** option. If the account is configured for using a smart card, and the user selects this option, and then tries to log on without using a smart card, the following message appears:

```
"Your account has been disabled. Please see your system administrator."
```

The preceding message appears even though the account is not disabled. The user must contact the domain administrator to disable the **User must log on using a smart card** option.

Look for these common causes of logon failure:

1. Password or user name incorrectly typed.

2. Password typed with CAPS LOCK on.

3. No common protocol between a Windows XP Professional–based client and a domain controller.

For the first two causes of logon failure, you should receive an error that begins with "Make sure your User name and domain are correct..." For the third cause of failure, you should get an error stating that the domain controller could not be contacted.

Assuming that TCP/IP is the protocol that you used in the network, the client configuration might have changed since initial installation. Look for these causes:

- Incorrect static addresses or subnet masks.

- DHCP enabled in an environment where no DHCP server is available.

- Improperly configured default gateways.

- Incorrect addresses for DNS or WINS servers.

- Incorrectly configured Hosts or Lmhosts files.

Unable to log on to a domain after renaming the computer   Often your logon domain does not recognize the new name of your client computer. To troubleshoot this problem, you must rename the Windows XP Professional–based computer that belongs to a Windows NT domain.

To rename a Windows XP Professional–based computer that is a member of a Windows NT domain

1. Create a new computer account (or have one created for you) that uses the new computer name.

2. Leave the domain by temporarily joining a workgroup.

3. When prompted, restart the computer.

4. Join the domain by using the new computer name.

5. When prompted, restart the computer.

Troubleshooting Group Policy and System Policy

Configuration conflicts can occur between local Group Policy settings and Windows NT System Policy, which can impede user access to system features and functions. For example, if a Windows XP Professional–based computer that was originally a stand-alone computer or a member of a workgroup is added to a Windows NT domain that uses System Policy, both the local Group Policy and Windows NT System Policy might be processed at various points in the logon process. To anticipate the behavior of a Windows XP Professional–based computer by following local Group Policy in a Windows NT domain that uses system policies, see "System Policy and Group Policy Coexistence" earlier in this chapter.

Troubleshooting My Network Places

A common problem is that you cannot use **My Network Places** to access all local computer resources or to see other workgroup computers. A typical problem, a likely cause, and possible solutions follow.

After successfully logging on to a workgroup or domain, you attempt to view shared resources either by typing **net view** at the command prompt or by opening **My Network Places**. The resulting window does not show any computers or members of the workgroup or domain.

Likely cause   A browser election has taken place, and the browse list is being updated on the domain master browser, on master browsers in the domain or workgroup, and on backup browsers.

Possible solution one   Attempt to force an update of the browse list by refreshing the **My Network Places** window. Otherwise, it might take up to 15 minutes for all browsers to receive an updated browse list.

Possible solution two   If your computer is a member of a workgroup, make sure that you have changed the default name, WORKGROUP, to the specified workgroup name.

Additional Resources

These resources contain additional information and tools related to this chapter.

Related Information

- "Configuring TCP/IP" in this book for more information about configuring TCP/IP.

- "Authorization and Access Control" in this book for more information about account authentication.

- The *Deploying Network* Services book of the *Microsoft Windows Server 2003 Deployment Kit* for more information about Windows networks.

- "Defining Client Administration and Configuration Standards" in the *Deployment Planning Guide* of the *Microsoft Windows 2000 Server Resource Kit* for more information about implementing Group Policy.

Chapter 21

Configuring TCP/IP

Transmission Control Protocol/Internet Protocol (TCP/IP) is the high-performance, scalable suite of communications protocols now accepted as the industry standard protocol for intranets and the Internet. Microsoft has adopted TCP/IP as the strategic enterprise network transport for its platforms. This chapter introduces you to the fundamentals of TCP/IP client configuration, IP security issues, and TCP/IP troubleshooting for Microsoft® Windows® XP Professional. A more detailed explanation of IP addressing and name resolution is available in a subsequent chapter.

Related Information

- For more information about IP addressing and name resolution configuration details, see "Configuring IP Address and Name Resolution" in this book.

- For more information about configuring virtual private networks, see "Connecting Remote Offices" in this book.

- For more information about TCP/IP security, see "Implementing TCP/IP Security" in this book.

- For more information about creating Internet Protocol Security policies, see "Internet Protocol Security" in the *TCP/IP Core Networking Guide* of the *Microsoft® Windows® 2000 Server Resource Kit*.

- For information about troubleshooting IP multicast forwarding, see "IP Multicast Support" in the *Internetworking Guide* of the *Microsoft Windows 2000 Server Resource Kit*.

- For more information about TCP/IP routing, see "Unicast IP Routing" in the *Internetworking Guide* of the *Microsoft Windows 2000 Server Resource Kit*.

Overview of Windows XP Professional TCP/IP

TCP/IP provides communication across interconnected networks that use diverse hardware architectures and various operating systems. TCP/IP can communicate with computers running Windows XP Professional and other Microsoft operating systems, or non-Microsoft systems such as UNIX.

TCP/IP in Windows XP Professional builds upon the Microsoft® Windows® 2000 TCP/IP implementation, which in itself is an improvement over the TCP/IP functionality found in Microsoft® Windows NT® Workstation version 4.0. Table 21-1 shows some of the features of the TCP/IP implementation in Windows XP Professional.

Table 21-1   Features of TCP/IP in Windows XP Professional

Feature	Description
Logical and physical multihoming	Allows association of multiple IP addresses to single or multiple network adapters for internetwork connectivity.
Internal IP routing capability	Allows a Windows XP Professional–based computer to route packets between multiple network adapters.
Multiple configurable default gateways	Allows configuring multiple default gateways to improve network reliability and availability.
Virtual private networking	Permits secured transmission of data across public networks through encapsulated and encrypted packets.
Windows Sockets Version 2 (Winsock2) interface	Standard application programming interface (API) permits access to networking features.
NetBIOS interface	Allows the use of NetBIOS sessions, datagrams, and name management over TCP/IP.
My Network Places browsing support	Lists of network resources for My Network Places can span a TCP/IP internetwork.
Simple Network Management Protocol (SNMP) agent	Permits performance and resource monitoring of a TCP/IP host.
TCP/IP connectivity tools	Command-line tools such as Finger, Ftp, Rcp, Rexec, Rsh, Telnet, and Tftp allow access to heterogeneous hosts across a TCP/IP-based network.

Table 21-1   Features of TCP/IP in Windows XP Professional

Feature	Description
Simple TCP/IP tools	Chargen, Daytime, Discard, Echo, and Quote of the Day client and server tools.
TCP/IP management and diagnostic tools	Command-line tools such as Arp, Ipconfig, Nbtstat, Ping, Netsh, Route, Nslookup, Tracert, and PathPing provide maintenance and diagnostic features.
TCP/IP network printing	Permits printing on other-connected devices, such as UNIX-connected devices.

Defining TCP/IP

TCP/IP is a suite of interconnected protocols, which has evolved with the Internet as its communications standard. Because Internet connectivity is now a dominant force in networking, TCP/IP has all but eclipsed other networking protocols. All other protocols in the TCP/IP suite rely on the basic services provided by the following protocols: *Internet Protocol (IP), Address Resolution Protocol (ARP), Internet Control Message Protocol (ICMP), Internet Group Management Protocol (IGMP), Transmission Control Protocol (TCP), and User Datagram Protocol (UDP)*.

TCP/IP in Windows XP Professional offers the following advantages:

- A standard, routable enterprise networking protocol that is the most complete and accepted networking protocol suite available.

  All current network operating systems offer TCP/IP support, and most large networks rely on TCP/IP for much of their network traffic.

- A technology for connecting dissimilar systems.

  A number of protocols in the TCP/IP suite are available to access and transfer data between dissimilar systems, including File Transfer Protocol (FTP) and Telnet, a terminal emulation protocol. Several of these standard tools are included with Windows XP Professional.

- A dependable, scalable, cross-platform client/server framework.

  TCP/IP in Windows XP Professional uses the Windows Sockets interface, which is ideal for developing client/server applications that can run on Windows Sockets–compliant stacks from other vendors.

- A method of gaining access to the Internet.

  The Internet is a world-wide collaboration of networks, connecting research facilities, universities, libraries, private companies, and individuals.

TCP/IP Features in Windows XP Professional

The following features are part of the TCP/IP implementation in the Windows XP Professional operating system.

Automatic determination of interface–based metrics for default gateway assignment   Every computer that runs TCP/IP makes routing decisions. These decisions are controlled by the IP routing table. The routing table is built automatically, based on the current TCP/IP configuration of your computer. Each route occupies a single line in the displayed table. The routing table is searched by your computer for an entry that is the most specific match to the destination IP address.

Your computer uses the default route if no other host or network route matches the destination address included in an IP datagram. The default route typically forwards an IP datagram (for which there is no matching or explicit local route) to a default gateway address for a router on the local subnet.

Because the router that corresponds to the default gateway contains information about the network IDs of the other IP subnets within the larger TCP/IP internet, it forwards the datagram to other routers until the datagram is eventually delivered to an IP router that is connected to the specified destination host or subnet within the larger network.

A metric allows you to select the best path to a destination by indicating the "cost" or logical distance to a specific address. In this instance, it allows your computer to choose, as your default gateway, the router interface that is the shortest distance (or has the lowest metric cost) from your computer. In the case of the Routing Information Protocol (RIP), the metric indicates the number of hops to the destination.

If your default gateway has been automatically assigned, you can use the **Advanced TCP/IP Settings** dialog box to indicate whether you want that automatically assigned default gateway to have an automatically assigned or a static metric. If you choose a static metric, you are able to specify that metric in a text box.

If you have multiple interfaces and you configure a default gateway for each interface, TCP/IP by default automatically calculates an interface metric that is based on the speed of the interface. The interface metric becomes the metric of the default route in the routing table for the configured default gateway. The interface with the highest speed has the lowest metric for its default route. The result is that whenever multiple default gateways are configured on multiple interfaces, the fastest interface will be the one used to forward traffic to its default gateway.

In previous implementations of TCP/IP in Windows, multiple default gateways all had a default route metric set to 1, and the default gateway used depended on the order of the interfaces. This sometimes caused difficulty in determining which default gateway the TCP/IP protocol was using.

On Windows XP Professional–based computers, the automatic determination of the interface metric is enabled by default through the **Automatic metric** check box on the **IP Settings** tab on the advanced properties of the **Internet Protocol (TCP/IP)** protocol.

You can disable the automatic determination of the interface metric and type a new value for the interface metric. If multiple interfaces have the same lowest interface metric, the default gateway of the first network adapter is used. The default gateway for the second network adapter is used when the first is unavailable.

To access the Advanced TCP/IP Settings dialog box

In Control Panel (default view), click **Network and Internet Connections**.

1. Click **Network Connections**.

2. In Network Connections, right-click the local area connection you want to modify, and then click **Properties**.

3. In the **Local Area Connection Properties** dialog box, select **Internet Protocol (TCP/IP)**, then click **Properties**.

4. In the **Internet Protocol (TCP/IP) Properties** dialog box, click **Advanced**.

5. The **Advanced TCP/IP Settings** dialog box appears.

If you plan instead to assign one or more static default gateways to an interface, you can use the **Advanced TCP/IP Settings** dialog box to do so by selecting **Add** beneath **Default gateways**. When you enter the static address of a default gateway, you can also indicate if you want that static default gateway to have an automatically assigned or a static metric. If you want a static metric, you can specify that metric in a text box.

For more information about configuring default gateways and interface-based metrics, see "Configuring IP Address and Name Resolution" in this book.

Alternate Configuration   Laptops that participate on more than one network often use a static IP address at home and a dynamically assigned IP address at the office. In earlier versions of Windows, this required reconfiguration of TCP/IP settings. By configuring an alternate configuration, you can configure TCP/IP to first try Dynamic Host Configuration Protocol (DHCP), and then configure an alternate static IP address setting if a DHCP configuration is not received. For more information about alternate configuration, see "Configuring IP Address and Name Resolution" in this book.

IGMP v3   *Multicast* is communication between a single sender and multiple receivers on a network. Internet Group Management Protocol (IGMP) is used to exchange membership status data between members of multicast groups and neighboring IP routers that support multicast forwarding.

Earlier versions of Windows support only IGMP version 1 and version 2. IGMP Version 3 (IGMPv3) adds support for source filtering, which enables a multicast group member to specify that they want to receive multicast traffic from specified sources or from all but a specific set of sources.

Network Diagnostics   Network Diagnostics provides improved network and connectivity testing and validation. Network Diagnostics is a feature of the new Help and Support Center in Windows XP. To run Network Diagnostics, click **Start**, then click **Help and Support**. Under **Pick a Task**, click **Use Tools** to view your computer information and diagnose problems, and then click **Network Diagnostics**.

Determining Network Requirements for TCP/IP

Before installing and configuring a network protocol on your Windows XP Professional–based computer, it is important to understand the requirements of your network. Most networks have come to depend almost entirely upon TCP/IP. Before configuring TCP/IP on your desktop computer, it is important to understand which network protocols are being used on the network and how the protocols are implemented.

For example, if you want your Windows XP Professional–based computer to connect to both a Windows 2000 domain and NetWare servers running Internetwork Packet Exchange/Sequenced Packet Exchange (IPX/SPX), one set of configuration choices are required. If, on the other hand, you might need to connect your computer to a Windows NT 4.0 domain running NetBIOS over TCP/IP (NetBT), and using Windows Internet Name Service (WINS) servers, an entirely different set of configuration choices are necessary.

Before configuring TCP/IP on your Windows XP Professional–based computer, it is important to know whether your IP address is statically or dynamically assigned. Make sure you also know what kind of name resolution scheme is in place on your network. For more information about addressing and name resolution, see "Configuring IP Address and Name Resolution" in this book.

Installing and Configuring TCP/IP

The installation and configuration process for TCP/IP requires either the manual or default installation of TCP/IP, as well as IP address assignment, the resolution of names, and the verification that the Windows XP Professional implementation of TCP/IP is properly installed. The following sections provide some installation and configuration details.

Default and Manual Installation of TCP/IP

Windows XP Professional Setup installs TCP/IP by default. If you are upgrading to Windows XP Professional, however, Setup updates your existing network configuration, if such an update is available.

If your original Windows installation included a third-party TCP/IP protocol stack, Setup replaces the existing implementation of TCP/IP. If there are features that are required by your third-party stack, you must determine whether or not they are supported by the TCP/IP implementation in Windows XP Professional. If these required features are not supported by Windows XP Professional, you must install the third-party stack by using the installation tool provided by the stack's vendor.

Configuring IP Properties

Configuring TCP/IP on a Windows XP Professional–based computer includes choosing a method for the assignment of IP addresses and a method for name resolution. There are four methods of assigning IP addresses to TCP/IP clients:

- Dynamic Host Configuration Protocol (DHCP), which automatically assigns IP addresses in an environment with a DHCP server.

- Automatic Private IP Addressing (APIPA), which automatically assigns an IP address and subnet mask to clients on a subnet if there is no DHCP server (or if no DHCP request to the subnet is received by the DHCP server).

- Alternate Configuration, which allows the user to set the computer to first try DHCP, and then configure an alternate, manually configured TCP/IP address setting if a DHCP configuration is not received.

- Manual configuration of IP addresses.

Similarly, there are four methods supported by Windows XP Professional for resolving names to IP addresses:

- Domain Name System (DNS) for applications and services that require host name to IP address resolution, such as the Active Directory™ directory service.

- Windows Internet Name Service (WINS), for compatibility with applications and services that require NetBIOS name to IP address resolution, such as file and print sharing functions of pre–Windows 2000 versions of Windows.

- Hosts and LMHosts files, which provide host name to IP address resolution and NetBIOS name to IP address resolution, respectively, through the use of local files that are maintained manually.

- Subnet broadcasts, which can be used for NetBIOS name resolution within the local subnet.

For more information about address assignment and name resolution, see "Configuring IP Address and Name Resolution" later in this book.

Verifying IP Installation

After you have configured TCP/IP, you can use two command-line tools, IPConfig and Ping, to test the configuration and connections to other TCP/IP hosts and networks. This type of testing ensures that TCP/IP is functioning properly.

> **Note** In TCP/IP terms, a host is defined as any computer on the network, regardless of its operating system or its role as client or server, that is not forwarding packets between subnets.

Using IPConfig   Use the IPConfig tool to verify the TCP/IP configuration parameters on a host. This helps to determine whether the configuration is initialized, or whether a duplicate IP address exists. Use the **ipconfig** command with the **/all** parameter to verify configuration information.

> **Tip**   At the command prompt, type **ipconfig /all|more** to prevent the ipconfig output from scrolling off the screen; to scroll down and view additional output, press the Spacebar.

The result of the **ipconfig /all** command is as follows:

- If a configuration has initialized, the IP address and subnet mask appear, and, if assigned, the default gateway for each TCP/IP interface also appears. When appropriate, IPConfig also displays the host name, the primary DNS suffix, the DNS suffix search list, the media access control (MAC) address, the IP address of each DNS server, the IP address of each WINS server, and the IP address of the DHCP server.

- If TCP/IP is configured with a static IP address and a duplicate IP address exists, the IP address appears; however, the subnet mask is 0.0.0.0.

- If the computer is configured for automatic addressing and APIPA, and cannot obtain an IP address from a DHCP server on the network, the IPConfig tool displays the IP address as the address provided by APIPA. This is an address in the range of 169.254.0.1 to 169.254.255.254. APIPA also configures the subnet mask of 255.255.0.0.

Using Ping   After you have verified the TCP/IP configuration, use the Ping tool to test connectivity. Ping is a diagnostic tool that you can use to test TCP/IP configurations and diagnose connection failures. Use the Ping tool to determine whether a particular TCP/IP host is available and functional. To test connectivity, use the **ping** command with the following syntax:

```
ping hostname
```

As an example of the results you receive using the Ping tool, if you were to successfully ping 172.31.23.17, you might receive the following response:

```
==========================================================================
Pinging 171.31.23.17 with 32 bytes of data:

Reply from  172.31.23.17: bytes=32 time<1ms TTL=128
Reply from  172.31.23.17: bytes=32 time<1ms TTL=128
Reply from  172.31.23.17: bytes=32 time<1ms TTL=128
Reply from  172.31.23.17: bytes=32 time<1ms TTL=128

Ping Statistics for 172.31.23.17:
      Packets: Sent = 4, Received = 4, Lost = 0 (0% loss),
Approximate round trip times in milli-seconds:
   Minimum = 0ms, Maximum = 0ms, Average = 0ms
==========================================================================
```

Using IPConfig and Ping   The following steps verify a computer's network configuration and test router connections:

1. Use the **ipconfig** command to verify that the TCP/IP configuration is initialized.

2. Use the **ping** command with the IP address of the default gateway to verify that the default gateway is operational and that your computer can communicate with the local network.

3. Use the **ping** command with the IP address of a remote host to verify that the computer can communicate through a router.

The Network Diagnostics feature of Windows XP Professional provides network and connectivity testing and validation. Test results can be viewed in a command window or by using a browser. The Network Diagnostics feature can effectively replace the command-line processes used for IPConfig and Ping.

For more information about using the **ping** command, see "Testing the Network Connection with Ping and PathPing" later in this chapter.

> **Note**   Many hosts on the Internet discard the ICMP traffic of the Ping command and do not reply to ping messages. If pinging to one remote host does not work, try several different ones.

Using Netsh to Configure and Monitor Computers

The Netsh tool provides a command-line, scripting interface for configuring and monitoring computers running Windows XP Professional. By using the Netsh tool, you can issue *context commands* to the appropriate helper, and the helper then carries out the command. A *helper* is a dynamic-link library (DLL) file that extends the functionality of the Netsh tool by providing configuration, monitoring, and support for one or more services, tools, or protocols. The helper can also be used to extend other helpers.

Context commands are groupings of Netsh commands for specific networking components. A specific context is identified by a string that is appended to commands. Commands entered in a specific context are passed to an associated helper. The contexts available depend on the Windows XP Professional components installed. For example, type **routing** at the **netsh** prompt to change to the routing context.

You can use commands in the Netsh Interface IP context to configure the TCP/IP protocol (including addresses, default gateways, DNS servers, and WINS servers) and to display configuration and statistical information.

You can run these commands from the Windows XP command prompt or from the command prompt for the Netsh Interface IP context. For these commands to work at the Windows XP command prompt, you must type Netsh **interface ip** before typing commands and parameters as they appear in the syntax below. To run these Netsh commands on a remote Windows 2000 Server, you must first use Remote Desktop Connection to connect to a Windows 2000 Server that is running Terminal Server. There might be functional differences between Netsh context commands on Windows 2000 and Windows XP.

As an example of how to use Netsh to configure an interface, the following command configures the interface named **Local Area Connection** with the static IP address 10.0.5.99, the subnet mask of 255.255.255.0, and a default gateway of 10.0.5.1:

```
set address name="Local Area Connection"
source=static addr=10.0.5.99 mask=255.255.255.0 gateway=10.0.5.1
```

Netsh command-line options include the following:

- **-a** *AliasFile*

  Specifies that an alias file is used. An alias file contains a list of **netsh** commands and an aliased version so that you can use the aliased command line in place of the **netsh** command. You can use alias files to map commands that are more familiar in other platforms to the appropriate **netsh** command.

- **-c** *Context*

  Specifies the context of the command that corresponds to an installed helper DLL.

- *Command*

  Specifies the **netsh** command to carry out.

- **-f** *ScriptFile*

  Specifies that all of the **netsh** commands in the *ScriptFile* file are executed.

- **-r** *RemoteMachine*

  Specifies that the **netsh** commands are carried out on a remote computer specified by either its name or IP address.

You can abbreviate commands to the shortest unambiguous string. For example, issuing the command **sh ip int** is equivalent to issuing **show ip interface**. **Netsh** commands can be either global or context-specific. Global commands can be issued in any context and are used for general Netsh tool functions. Context-specific commands vary according to the context. You can log commands issued to a log file to create an audit trail of a **netsh** command session.

Table 21-2 lists the **netsh** global commands.

Table 21-2   Netsh commands and descriptions

Command	Description
..	Moves up one context level
? or help	Displays command-line Help
show version	Displays the current version of Windows and the Netsh tool
show netdlls	Displays the current version of installed Netsh helper DLLs
add helper	Add a Netsh help DLL
delete helper	Removes a Netsh help DLL
show helper	Displays the installed Netsh helper DLLs
cmd	Opens a command window
online	Sets the current mode to online
offline	Sets the current mode to offline
set mode	Sets the current mode to online or offline
show mode	Displays the current mode
flush	Discards any changes in offline mode
commit	Commits changes made in offline mode
set audit-logging	Turns on or turns off the logging facility
show audit-logging	Displays current audit logging settings
set loglevel	Sets level of logging information
show loglevel	Displays the level of logging information
set machine	Configures the computer on which the netsh commands are executed
show machine	Displays the computer on which the netsh commands are executed
exec	Executes a script file containing netsh commands
quit or bye or exit	Exits the Netsh tool
add alias	Adds an alias to an existing command
delete alias	Deletes an alias from an existing command
show alias	Displays all defined aliases
dump	Writes configuration to a text file

Table 21-2   Netsh commands and descriptions

Command	Description
popd	A scripting command that pops a context from the stack
pushd	A scripting command that pushes the current context on the stack

The Netsh tool has the following command modes:

- **Online.**   In online mode, commands issued at a Netsh command prompt are executed immediately.

- **Offline.**   In offline mode, commands issued at a Netsh command prompt are accumulated and carried out as a batch by issuing the **commit** global command. You can discard accumulated commands by issuing the **flush** global command.

- **Script.**   By using either the **-f** command-line option or by issuing the **exec** global command at a Netsh command prompt, all the **netsh** commands in the specified file are executed.

Advanced IP Configuration

A segment is a section of a network that is bounded by a bridge or other Layer 2 device. A network segment is a section of a network that is bounded by a router or other Layer 3 device. A network (or internetwork) is two or more TCP/IP network segments that are interconnected by routers. A router is a device that forwards IP packets from one network segment (also known as a subnet) to another. The router might be a dedicated hardware device built for that purpose or routing software running on a computer.

Understanding Internetwork Routing Strategy

Routing is the forwarding of packets based on the contents of a local routing table.

In the context of internetworking, the terms *routed protocol* and *routing protocol* are often confused. Routed protocols are protocols, such as IP, that support addressing for multiple network segments in an internetwork. Routing protocols are used by routers to communicate network segment reachability information.

Routing protocols are typically not of concern to a user of a Windows XP Professional client connected to a network. A general awareness of routing on the internetwork, however, can be helpful, as described in the following sections.

IP Packet Transmission

When IP prepares to send a packet, it inserts the source IP address and the destination IP address of the packet in the IP header. Next, it examines the destination address, compares it to a locally maintained routing table, and takes appropriate action based on what it finds. There are three possible actions:

- IP can pass the packet up to a protocol layer above IP on the local host.
- The packet can be forwarded through one of the locally attached network adapters.
- The packet can be discarded.

IP looks for a match of the destination address in the routing table from the most specific to the most general in the following order:

- The destination address (host route).
- A portion of the destination address (subnet route).
- No part of the destination address (default route).

IP always finds the route(s) that is closest to the destination address of the packet being forwarded.

If a default gateway is not specified and no other match is found, the packet is discarded.

The default gateway forwards the packet to other routers until the packet is eventually delivered to a router connected to the subnet of the destination. This example of routing is shown in Figure 21-1.

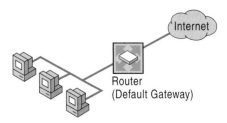

Figure 21-1   IP packet routing

For each Windows XP Professional–based computer on a TCP/IP network, you can maintain a routing table with an entry for every subnet with which the local computer communicates. For a limited number of subnets, this method can be used for network connectivity. But for most networks, this is not a practical solution due to the large number of subnets that must be listed and maintained in the routing table. Therefore, in most cases, rather than configuring the Windows XP Professional-based computer with routes for every subnet, a default gateway is configured.

Configuring the Local IP Routing Table

A Windows XP Professional–based computer uses its local IP routing table to determine how to forward an IP packet to reach a specified destination. The local routing table can be configured in the following ways:

- The routing table is manually maintained at the Windows XP Professional–based computer.

- The routing table is automatically maintained at the Windows XP Professional–based computer by the Routing Information Protocol (RIP) Listener.

- The default gateway is manually configured or specified by using the Dynamic Host Configuration Protocol (DHCP).

- The default gateway is automatically configured and maintained by using Internet Control Message Protocol (ICMP) Router Discovery.

Determining Methods for Identifying Gateways and Managing Routing Paths

In an enterprise with multiple subnets, a route to remote destinations must exist to enable communication with hosts on other networks. Windows XP Professional supports manual entry of the default gateways, as well as the use of ICMP Router Discovery to find and specify default gateways. Routing table maintenance is supported by means of manual configuration of the routing table and a Routing Information Protocol (RIP) Listener for automated maintenance of the routing table. Select the methods that reflect your network configuration.

Manually Configuring Default Gateways

If a specific route for the destination does not exist in the routing table, the packet is directed to the default gateway. Windows XP Professional allows you to specify multiple default gateways. You can list them in order, based on availability, load balancing, or other criteria.

You can also assign a value to each gateway, known as the cost metric, which determines the cost of forwarding an IP packet to the specific router. For multiple routes to the same destination, the route with the lowest cost metric is the most preferred entry in the routing table. You can either manually assign the cost metric of the gateway or have Windows XP Professional automatically determine the metric based on the speed of the networking interface.

To specify default gateways

1. In Control Panel, click **Network and Internet Connections** (default view).

2. Click **Network Connections**.

3. In Network Connections, right-click the local area connection you want to modify, and then click **Properties**.

4. Select **Internet Protocol (TCP/IP)**, click **Properties**, and then click **Advanced**.

5. Verify that the **Automatic metric** check box is selected (it is selected by default) to enable automatic determination of interface-based metrics.

6. In the **Default gateways** box, click **Add**.

7. Type the IP address and metric for the default gateway.

   This interface provides automatic determination for the default gateway. The metric is the cost of using a specified route. The gateway with the lowest metric is used first. The default metric value for each gateway is **Automatic metric**.

8. Click **Add**.

9. Click **OK** when you have specified all the default gateways for the connection.

Alternately, default gateway addresses and metrics can be provided by a DHCP server. However, gateway configuration information specified in connection properties override addresses provided through DHCP. For more information about configuring DHCP, see "Configuring IP Addressing and Name Resolution" in this book.

Configuring ICMP Router Discovery   ICMP Router Discovery automates the discovery and configuration of the default gateways for a Windows XP Professional–based client. If ICMP Router Discovery-enabled routers are used on your network, you can use this method of configuring default gateways.

ICMP Router Discovery provides an effective method of detecting and configuring default gateways. Instead of configuring a default gateway manually or by using DHCP, Windows XP Professional–based computers can dynamically discover the best default gateway to use on a subnet and can automatically switch to another default gateway if the first default gateway fails or the network administrator changes router preferences.

The ICMP Router Discovery messages are called Router Advertisements. The Router Advertisement parameter can be controlled by any router that is compliant with RFC 1256. Windows 2000 Server with the Routing and Remote Access service supports ICMP Router Discovery.

When a Windows XP Professional–based computer configured for ICMP Router Discovery initializes, it joins the all-hosts IP multicast group (224.0.0.1) and listens for ICMP Router Advertisement messages. ICMP Router Discovery-enabled routers periodically send ICMP Router Advertisements containing their IP address, a preference level, and a period of time after which they can be considered down. Each host in the IP multicast group (224.0.0.1) receives the ICMP Router Advertisements and selects the router with the highest preference level as its default gateway.

A Windows XP Professional– based computer can also send ICMP Router Solicitation messages to the all-routers IP multicast address (224.0.0.2) at initialization, or at a point when it has not received a ICMP Router Advertisement for the current default gateway within the advertised lifetime of the default gateway router. Windows XP Professional–based hosts send a maximum of three solicitations at intervals of approximately 600 milliseconds.

The use of ICMP Router Discovery is determined by the value of a registry entry. If the value of "PerformRouterDiscovery" is 1, ICMP Router Discovery is enabled.

- **PerformRouterDiscovery** in the subkey HKEY_LOCAL_MACHINE\SYSTEM \CurrentControlSet\Services\Tcpip\Parameters\Interfaces*interface*. To enable ICMP Router Discovery for a specific interface, add the entry to the registry, with a value of 1 (REG_DWORD). By default, the value is 2, which indicates that it is off by default but can be enabled through the receipt of the **Perform router discovery** DHCP option.

The value of another registry entry will allow you to send ICMP Router Discovery Solicitation messages as limited broadcasts instead of multicasts.

- **SolicitationAddressBcast** in the same subkey HKEY_LOCAL_MACHINE\ SYSTEM\CurrentControlSet\Services\Tcpip\Parameters\Interfaces*interface*. To enable SolicitationAddressBcast for a specific interface, add the entry to the registry, with a value of 1 (REG_DWORD).

Windows XP Professional does not add this entry to the registry. You can add it by editing the registry or by using a program that edits the registry. This entry is used only when router discovery is enabled, that is, when the value of Perform-RouterDiscovery is 1.

Caution Do not edit the registry unless you have no alternative. The registry editor bypasses standard safeguards, allowing settings that can damage your system, or even require you to reinstall Windows. If you must edit the registry, back it up first and see the Registry Reference in the Microsoft Windows 2000 Server Resource Kit at http://www.microsoft.com/reskit.

Manually Editing the Routing Table

There are several instances when you might need to manually edit the local routing table for your Windows XP Professional–based computer:

- The computer has multiple network adapters (that is, multihomed), and must access different routers for each adapter.

If your computer is multihomed and has connections to two separate IP network segments, such as the corporate network and the Internet, the default gateway for the Internet is used. For the computer to communicate with the corporate network, routes must be manually added to the routing table.

■ The default route is present, but you want to define customized forwarding.

You can display the current routing table to determine whether any changes are required. To see the routing table for your computer, at the command prompt type:

```
route print
```

The **route print** command produces a routing table display such as the following:

```
===========================================================================
Interface List
0x1 ......................... MS TCP Loopback interface
0x2000002 ...00 c0 4f 49 f3 b2 ...... 3Com EtherLink PCI (QoS Packet Scheduler)
===========================================================================
===========================================================================
Active Routes:
Network Destination       Netmask          Gateway      Interface     Metric
0.0.0.0                   0.0.0.0          172.16.0.1   172.16.4.120    30
127.0.0.0                 255.0.0.0        127.0.0.1    127.0.0.1        1
172.16.0.0                255.255.248.0    172.16.4.120 172.16.4.120    30
172.16.4.120              255.255.255.255  127.0.0.1    127.0.0.1       30
172.16.255.255            255.255.255.255  172.16.4.120 172.16.4.120    30
224.0.0.0                 240.0.0.0        172.16.4.120 172.16.4.120     1
255.255.255.255  255.255.255.255           127.0.0.1    127.0.0.1        1
Default Gateway:     172.16.4.1
```

The routing table shows a computer with the IP address 172.16.4.120, subnet mask of 255.255.248.0, and a default gateway of 172.16.4.1. The routing table contains the following seven entries:

1. The default route, used when forwarding packets to all locations off the local subnet.

2. The loopback route, the route a host uses when sending packets to itself.

3. A subnet route for the locally attached subnet.

4. A host route for the local host (the route for packets sent to this host computer).

5. A host route for a special type of IP broadcast address called the all-subnets directed broadcast.

6. The IP multicast route, the route used when the computer sends packets to an IP multicast group.

7. A host route for the limited broadcast address.

Network Destination   The network address in the routing table is the destination address. The network destination column can have three different types of entries, as listed here in order from most to least specific:

1. Host address (a route to a single, specific destination IP address).

2. Subnet address (a route to a subnet).

3. Default route of 0.0.0.0 (a route used when there is no other match).

If no match is found, the packets are discarded.

Netmask   The netmask defines which part of the destination must match the network address in order for that route to be considered a match with the destination address of the packet being forwarded. When the mask is written in binary, a 1 indicates a bit that must match, and a 0 indicates a bit that does not have to match.

For example, the mask of all 1s (255.255.255.255) means that the destination address of the packet to be forwarded must exactly match the entire host address for this route to be considered a match. For another example, if the network address 192.168.232.0 has a netmask of 255.255.255.0, then the first three octets must match exactly, but the last octet need not match.

Gateway Address   The gateway address in the routing table is used to determine the forwarding IP address. This will be either the host's own IP address or the address of a router on the local attached subnet. If the gateway address of the route is the host IP address, then the forwarding IP address is set to the destination IP address in the IP datagram, that is the IP address of the host you are attempting to contact whether that host is on the local subnet or on a remote subnet. If the gateway address of the route is not the host IP address, then the forwarding IP address is set to the gateway address, which is typically the address of a router on the local subnet.

Interface   The interface is the IP address of the network adapter from which the packet must be sent. 127.0.0.1 is the software loopback address.

Metric   The metric indicates the cost of the route. In the case of RIP routes, the cost is determined by the number of hops (routers to cross) to the destination. Anything on the local subnet is one hop, and each router crossed after that is an additional hop. The metric is used to decide which route to use when there are multiple closest matching routes with the destination address.

To add static routes, use the following format:

```
Route add subnet mask netmask gateway metric metric if interface
```

The following is an example route:

```
Route add 172.20.255.0 mask 255.255.255.0 172.20.234.232 metric 2 if 33554434
```

The route in this example demonstrates that to reach the subnet 172.20.255.0 with a mask of 255.255.255.0, use gateway 172.20.234.232, and that the route has a cost metric of 2 (for example, the subnet is 2 hops away), using interface 33554434.

> **Note**   The interface number used in the route print command is the decimal version. The interface number, as it appears in the route print display is the hexadecimal version. For example, 0x200002 is the hexadecimal version of 33554434 decimal.

Limitations of Manual Maintenance   The creation of static routes and the manual maintenance of routing tables has several major limitations:

- It is susceptible to human error. An error in one of the routes can prevent reachability to a location on the network.

- Each change in the status of a network segment or router might require an equivalent alteration in the routing table. For example, routers can fail, new subnets or routers might be added, or the metric of a route might change. Under manual maintenance, changes in the network might require immediate modification of the routing table by an administrator.

- The challenge of manually maintaining local routing tables is multiplied when supporting a large number of computers in a department or enterprise.

- Manually added routes might be lost when the TCP/IP stack is reinitialized. To prevent this from happening, use the **–p** (persistent) parameter with the **route add** command.

Configure RIP Listening Support

Routing Information Protocol (RIP) can be used to address the challenges of supporting routing in an enterprise environment. If one or more of the routers on your subnet uses RIP to send routing information, your Windows XP Professional–based computer can be configured to listen to RIP messages. By configuring your computer to listen in, it can learn other routes on the network and then add the appropriate routes to the IP routing table. This process is called *RIP listening* or *silent RIP*.

Network administrators can use RIP listening on multihomed hosts to solve the problem of multiple default gateways without manually adding routes to the routing table. Figure 21-2 shows an example of a multihomed host that uses RIP listening.

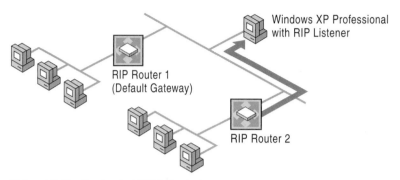

Figure 21-2   Host using RIP listening

In Figure 21-2, Both Router 1 and Router 2 are RIP routers. The Windows XP Professional–based computer is enabled as a RIP listener. It adds routes to both subnets. The Windows XP Professional–based computer is not configured with a default gateway.

Windows XP Professional supports routers using either RIP version 1 or RIP version 2 as long as the RIP messages are sent as subnet-level broadcasts. RIP version 2 messages sent as multicasts are not received by the RIP listener.

RIP listening support is installed as an optional service to Windows XP Professional.

To install RIP listening support

1. In **Control Panel**, double-click **Add or Remove Programs**.

2. Select **Add/Remove Windows Components**.

3. In the Windows Components Wizard, click **Networking Services**.

4. Click **Details**.

5. Select the **RIP Listener** check box.

6. Click **OK**, and then click **Next**.

IP Security and Filtering

Windows XP Professional supports two methods of securing and controlling the transmission of IP packets: Internet Protocol security (IPSec), an industry-defined set of standards that verifies, authenticates, and optionally encrypts data at the IP packet level; and TCP/IP filtering, which controls the ports and packet types for incoming local host data. Either or both of these methods can be implemented on the same Windows XP Professional–based client.

IPSec might be enabled for the Windows XP Professional–based computer by using local policies, or implemented by using Group Policy objects in Active Directory within an enterprise environment. If implemented locally, built-in or custom policies created by using the IP Security Policy Management snap-in can determine the rules required for secured communications with other hosts. For more information, see "Configuring IPSec Policies" later in this chapter.

You can also restrict the type of IP traffic that can be received by a Windows XP Professional–based computer as the destination. TCP/IP packet filtering can be used to limit packet reception by TCP or UDP port, or by IP protocol. For more information, see "TCP/IP Filtering" later in this chapter.

IPSec

The need for IP-based network security is almost universal in the interconnected business world of the Internet, intranets, branch offices, and remote access. Because sensitive information constantly crosses the networks, the challenge for network administrators and other information service professionals is to ensure that this traffic is:

- Safe from data modification while in transit.

- Safe from viewing.

- Safe from being impersonated by unauthenticated parties.

- Safe from being captured and replayed later to gain access to sensitive resources; typically, an encrypted password can be used in this manner.

These security services are known as data integrity, data confidentiality, data authentication, and replay protection.

IP does not have a default security mechanism and IP packets are easy to read, modify, replay, and forge. Without security, both public and private networks are susceptible to unauthorized monitoring and access. While internal attacks might be the result of minimal or nonexistent intranet security, risks from outside the private network stem from connections to both the Internet and extranets. Password-based, user access controls alone do not protect data transmitted across a network.

As a result, IPSec was designed by the Internet Engineering Task Force (IETF) to supports network-level data authentication, data integrity, data confidentiality, and replay protection. IPSec integrates with Windows 2000 and Windows XP Professional security to provide the ideal platform for safeguarding intranet and Internet communications. It uses industry-standard encryption algorithms and a comprehensive security management approach to provide security for all TCP/IP communications on both sides of an organization's firewall. The result is an end-to-end security strategy for Windows 2000 and Windows XP Professional that defends against both external and internal attacks.

IP security is deployed below the transport layer, sparing network managers the difficulty and expense of trying to deploy and coordinate security one application at a time. By deploying Windows XP Professional and Windows 2000 IPSec, network managers provide a strong layer of protection for the entire network, with applications automatically inheriting security from IPSec-enabled servers and clients.

How IPSec Prevents Network Attacks

Without security measures in place, data might be subjected to an attack. Some attacks are passive; that is, the information is simply monitored. Others are active, meaning that the information is used or altered with intent to corrupt or destroy the data or the network itself. Table 21-3 shows some common security risks found in networks and prevention methods using IPSec.

Table 21-3   Types of Network Attacks and Preventing Them Using IPSec

Attack Type	Description	IPSec Prevention Method
Eavesdropping (also known as sniffing or snooping)	Monitoring of plaintext or unencrypted packets.	Data is encrypted before transmission, preventing access to the original data even when the packet is monitored or intercepted. Only the peers have knowledge of the encryption key.
Data modification	Alteration and transmission of modified packets.	Data hashing attaches a cryptographic checksum to each packet, which is checked by the receiving computer to detect modification.
Identity spoofing	Use of constructed or captured packets to falsely assume the identity of a valid address.	The Kerberos V5 authentication protocol, public key certificates, or pre-shared keys authenticate peers before secure communication begins.
Denial-of-service	Preventing access to a network server by valid users. An example is to flood the network or server with traffic.	Ports or protocols can be blocked.
Man-in-the-middle	Diversion of IP packets to an unintended third party, to be monitored and possibly altered.	Authentication of peers.
Known-key	Used to decrypt or modify data.	In Windows XP Professional, cryptographic keys are periodically refreshed, reducing the possibility that a captured key can be used to gain access to secure information.
Application layer	Mainly directed at application servers, this attack is used to cause a fault in a network's operating system or applications, or to introduce viruses into the network.	Because IPSec is implemented at the network layer, packets that do not meet the security filters at this level are never passed to applications, protecting applications and operating systems.

IPSec prevents attacks, described in Table 21-3, by using cryptography-based mechanisms. Cryptography allows information to be transmitted securely by hashing and encrypting the information.

A combination of an algorithm and a key is used to secure information:

- The algorithm is the mathematical process by which the information is secured.

- A key is the secret code or number required to read, modify, or verify secured data.

IPSec uses a policy-based mechanism to determine the level of security required during a communications session. Policies can be distributed throughout a network by means of Windows 2000–based domain controllers, or created and stored locally within the registry of a Windows XP Professional–based computer.

Before the transmission of any data, an IPSec-enabled computer negotiates the level of security to be maintained during the communications session. During the negotiation process, the authentication method is determined, a hashing method is determined, a tunneling method is chosen (optional), and an encryption method is determined (also optional). The secret authentication keys are determined locally at each computer by using information that is exchanged at this time. No actual keys are ever transmitted. After the keys are generated, identities are authenticated, and secured data exchange can begin.

The resulting level of security can either be low or high, dependent upon the IP security policy of the sending or receiving computer. For example, a communications session between a Windows XP Professional–based computer and a non-IPSec-aware host might not require a secure transmission channel. Conversely, a communications session between a Windows 2000–based server containing sensitive information and an intranet host might require high security.

Example of IPSec

These seven steps, as shown in Figure 21-3, demonstrate a typical implementation of IPSec.

1. An application on Computer A generates outbound packets to send to Computer B across the network.

2. The IPSec driver on Computer A determines that communications with Computer B must be secured.

3. Computer A begins security negotiations with Computer B. The two computers negotiate the use of a shared, secret key, using the Internet Key Exchange (IKE) protocol. The same shared cryptographic key is determined independently at both ends without being transmitted across the network.

4. The IKE negotiation establishes two types of agreements, called *security associations* (SA), between the two computers. One type specifies how the two

computers trust each other and protects their ongoing negotiation. The other type specifies how to protect a particular type of application communication.

5. After the IKE negotiation is complete, the cryptographic key is passed by IKE to the IPSec driver. The IPSec driver on Computer A hashes the outgoing packets for integrity, and optionally, encrypts them for confidentially. It transmits the packets to Computer B.

6. Routers and servers along the network path from Computer A to Computer B do not require IPSec. They pass along the packets in the usual manner.

7. The IPSec driver on Computer B checks the packets for integrity and decrypts their content if necessary. It then transfers the packets to the receiving application.

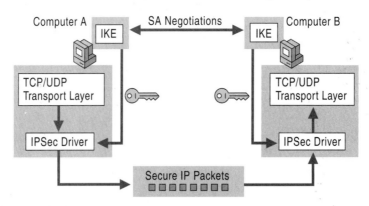

Figure 21-3   Establishing an IPSec session

Considerations for IPSec

IPSec provides encryption of outgoing IP packets, but at the cost of local computer performance. The encryption and decryption of packets is a processor-intensive task. Consequently, the encryption and decryption of a large amount of IP packets can place significant demands on the workstation.

Alternately, you can offload cryptographic processing to the network adapter. Many network adapters include onboard processors that can perform tasks otherwise performed by the computer's central processor, including packet encryption. Consult the product documentation for your network adapter to see if it supports encryption-processing offload.

Configuring IPSec Policies

IPSec policies, rather than applications, are used to configure IPSec services. The policies provide variable levels of protection for most traffic types in most existing networks.

There are two storage locations for IPSec policies:

- Active Directory
- The registry on a local computer.

A network security administrator can configure IPSec policies to meet the security requirements of a domain, site, or organizational unit for an Active Directory domain. IPSec policy can also be implemented in a non-Active Directory domain environment by using local IPSec policies.

IPSec policies are based on your organization's guidelines for secure operations. For more information about planning, creating, and implementing IPSec policies on a Windows 2000–based domain controller, see Windows 2000 Server Help.

Configuring Domain–based IPSec Policies

For an organization that chooses to implement IP security, creating and assigning IP security policies at the domain level provide the most efficient method of controlling enterprise security policy. Windows 2000 Server and Windows XP Professional offer an administrative interface, the **IP Security Policy Management** snap-in, to create and administer security policies. An IP security administrator can create security policies at varying levels of granularity from the site, domain, or organizational unit.

After an IPSec policy is created, it can be assigned to a specific container. For example, if Computer A is a member of an organizational unit (OU) that has a IPSec policy applied to it, the IPSec policy for the OU is automatically applied at startup. No user intervention is required. By using domain-based policies, you ensure that the proper security is always implemented at user's computer, overriding the local IPSec policies.

When a computer that is normally a member of a Windows 2000 domain is temporarily disconnected, the domain-based IPSec policy information is cached in the local registry.

IPSec Policy Precedence

IPSec policy precedence is identical with that of other Group Policy settings. In a domain, Group Policy is applied hierarchically from the least restrictive object, such as a site, to the most restrictive object, such as an organizational unit (OU).

For more information about Active Directory and Group Policy, see "Active Directory" and "Desktop Configuration Management" in the *Distributed Systems Guide* of the *Microsoft Windows 2000 Server Resource Kit*.

Configuring Local IPSec Policies

Local IPSec policies can be selected and stored locally on a Windows XP Professional–based computer. This can be done to implement local IP security in the following situations:

- The computer is a member of a Windows 2000 domain that does not implement IPSec policies.

- The computer is a member of a Windows NT 4.0 domain.

- The computer is part of a workgroup.

- The computer is not a member of a local domain or workgroup, but is connected to other hosts by means of an enterprise intranet or the Internet.

By implementing local IP security, the Windows XP Professional–based computer can secure IP packets based on the security policy stored in its registry. Three preconfigured local IPSec policies are provided at system installation: Client (Respond Only), Server (Request Security), and Secure Server (Require Security). Table 21-4 describes the attributes of each of these default security policies.

Table 21-4 Default Local IP Security Policies

Policy Name	Security Requirements	Attributes
Client (Respond Only)	Low	Enables a Windows XP Professional–based computer to respond to requests for secured communications. Unsecured communications can be used with non-IPSec hosts.
Server (Request Security)	Moderate	Enables a Windows XP Professional–based computer to accept unsecured communications, but attempts to establish a secure channel by requesting security from the sending host. Communications are unsecured if the requesting host is not IPSec-enabled.
Secure Server (Require Security)	High	Requires that all communications with Windows XP Professional–based computers are secure. All unsecured incoming communications are discarded, with the exception of an initial incoming communication request, and all outgoing communications are secured.

The default security policies are intended to provide an example. They are not designed for operational use without modification. A knowledgeable IPSec network administrator or advanced user should design new, custom polices for operational use. You must have administrative privileges to assign or change IPSec policies.

By default, no local IPSec policies are assigned. To assign one of the default local IPSec policies, right-click the policy in the **IP Security Policy Management** snap-in, and then click **Assign**.

IP Security Policy Management Snap-in

The IP Security Policy Management snap-in allows you to perform the following tasks:

- Create and manage local and domain-based IPSec policies.

- Manage IP filter lists and filter actions.

- Restore default IPSec policies.

- Import and export IPSec policies.

To create a console with the IP Security Policy Management snap-in, perform the following steps while logged on to an account with administrative rights.

To install the IP Security Policy Management snap-in

1. Click **Start**, and then click **Run**.

2. In the **Run** dialog box, type **mmc**, and then click **OK**.

3. On the File menu, click **Add/Remove Snap-in**.

4. Using the **Standalone** tab of the **Add/Remove Snap-In** dialog box, click **Add**.

5. In the **Available Standalone Snap-ins** box, select **IP Security Policy Management**, and then click **Add**.

6. In the **Select which computer or domain this snap-in will manage** dialog box, select the option that matches the security policy environment to be managed by your computer.

    You can manage the security policy of a computer (as stored in its registry), the IP security policy of the local domain or another domain (if appropriate permissions are granted), or manage the local security policy of another computer, as stored in the registry of that computer.

7. Click **Finish**, click **Close**, and then click **OK**.

Creating Local IPSec Policies

New IPSec policies can be created by selecting **Create IP Security Policy** from the **Actions** menu of the IP Security Policy Management snap-in, or by right-clicking the **IP Security Policies on Local Computer** in the console tree, and then selecting **Create IP Security Policy**. This action starts the IP Security Policy Wizard.

The IP Security Policy Wizard prompts you for the information needed to configure the new policy. The following information is required:

- Policy name and description

- Application of default response rule

    A security rule determines how IPSec policy secures communication. Selecting this option ensures responses to requests for secure communications. Additional rules can be created by editing the IPSec policy.

- Authentication method for default response rule

An authentication method for the two computers must be determined before secure communications can begin. Use this option to select the method of authentication for the default response rule, if chosen:

- Kerberos V5
- Certificate-based
- Preshared key

For more information about IPSec policy and rule creation, see Windows XP Professional Help and Support Center.

TCP/IP Filtering

Windows XP Professional includes support for TCP/IP filtering. TCP/IP filtering allows you to specify exactly which types of incoming IP traffic are processed as the destination for each IP interface. This feature is designed to isolate the traffic being processed by Internet and intranet clients in the absence of other TCP/IP filtering provided by IPSec, the Routing and Remote Access service, or other TCP/IP applications or services. TCP/IP filtering is disabled by default.

TCP/IP filtering is a set of input filters for non-transit TCP/IP traffic (traffic destined for the local host). Non-transit traffic is traffic that is processed by the host because the destination IP address of inbound IP datagrams is directed to an assigned interface address, appropriate subnet broadcast address, or multicast address. TCP/IP filtering does not apply to transit or routed traffic that is forwarded between interfaces.

A packet is accepted for processing if it meets one of the following criteria:

- The destination TCP port matches the list of TCP ports. By default, all TCP ports are permitted.

- The destination UDP port matches the list of UDP ports. By default, all UDP ports are permitted.

- The IP protocol matches the list of IP protocols. By default, all IP protocols are permitted.

- It is an ICMP packet.

You cannot filter ICMP traffic by using TCP/IP filtering. If you need ICMP filtering, configure IP packet filters by using Routing and Remote Access. For more information, see "Unicast IP Routing" in the *Internetworking Guide* of the *Microsoft Windows 2000 Server Resource Kit.*

Note Protocols that are members of the TCP/IP protocol suite are frequently referred to simply as "IP Protocols."

To configure TCP/IP filtering

1. In Control Panel (default view), click **Network and Internet Connections**.

2. Click **Network Connections**.

3. In Network Connections, right-click the local area connection you want to modify, and then click **Properties**.

4. On the **General** tab, click **Internet Protocol (TCP/IP)** in the list of components, and then click **Properties**.

5. Click **Advanced**.

6. Click the **Options** tab, click **TCP/IP filtering**, and then click **Properties**.

7. In the **TCP/IP Filtering** dialog box, select the **Enable TCP/IP Filtering** check box and then add the numbers of all TCP and UDP ports and all IP protocols for which you want filtering enabled.

8. Click **OK**.

TCP/IP filtering can be enabled and disabled for all adapters by selecting a single check box. This helps troubleshoot connectivity problems that might be related to filtering. Filters that are too restrictive might unnecessarily limit connectivity options. For example, if you decide to allow only specific types of UDP traffic and do not include RIP (UDP port 520), then the RIP Listener service does not function.

Configuring Multihoming

When a computer is configured with more than one IP address, it is referred to as a multihomed system. Multihoming is supported in two different ways:

- Multiple network adapters or media types per physical network.

    The network adapters can be for similar or dissimilar networks. For example, a host with one Ethernet and one Token Ring adapter installed, each linked to a separate network, requires IP addresses to be bound to both adapters. There are no restrictions other than hardware.

- Multiple IP addresses per network adapter.

    A computer can access multiple subnets that are logically separated, but bound to a single network adapter. Such a configuration might be used in an environment where a host requires access to different divisions of a corporation network that are separated by different subnets.

    Figure 21-4 shows an example of a Windows XP Professional–based computer using multihoming to connect to two subnets. These subnets can be physically separated by disparate or disconnected cabling, or logically separated through the use of multinetting.

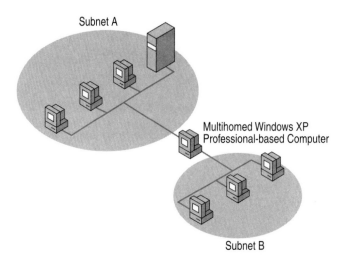

Figure 21-4   Multihomed Windows XP Professional–based computer connected to two separate subnets

Configuring Multiple Network Adapters or Media Types

Windows XP Professional places no restrictions on physically multihomed computers, so you can add as many network adapters as the computer hardware can accommodate, and assign each a separate address.

As each new network adapter is installed, Windows XP Professional Plug and Play autodetects the adapter. The device driver for each adapter is installed and any internal resources are automatically configured. The network adapter is bound to the TCP/IP protocol. If the network adapter is not Plug and Play–compliant, the adapter software must be installed and configured manually using the manufacturer's instructions.

For a multihomed computer that uses multiple network adapters for physical connections to the LAN, each adapter appears as a separate adapter in the Network Connections folder.

For a system configured to support multiple network or media types, there are no restrictions for this type of configuration other than hardware and media support. The TCP/IP implementation in Windows XP Professional supports the following:

- Ethernet (Ethernet II and IEEE 802.3 SNAP encapsulation).
- Token Ring (IEEE 802.5 encapsulation).
- Asynchronous Transfer Mode (ATM) over IP
- ATM Lane Emulation (LANE).
- Fiber Distributed Data Interface (FDDI).

- WAN, using circuit-switched media such as ISDN and dial-up, dedicated asynchronous lines, dedicated synchronous lines such as T-Carrier, and virtual-circuit wide-area media such as X.25 and Frame Relay.

By default, each new network adapter is set for automatic TCP/IP configuration.

To manually configure IP addresses on a multihomed system

1. In Control Panel (default view), click **Network and Internet Connections**.

2. Click **Network Connections**.

3. In Network Connections, right-click the local area network connection you want to modify, and then select **Properties**.

4. On the **General** tab, in the **This connection uses the following items** list, click **Internet Protocol (TCP/IP)**, and then click **Properties**.

5. Configure TCP/IP as described in "Configuring an IP Address Manually" in "Configuring IP Addressing and Name Resolution" in this book.

6. Start at step 3 and configure the second adapter for TCP/IP.

For more information about how to configure a multihomed system using a single network adapter, see "Configuring IP Addressing and Name Resolution" in this book.

Multihoming Considerations

If TCP/IP is configured for multiple network adapters, or for a single network adapter with multiple IP addresses, you must consider the following issues.

NetBIOS over TCP/IP (NetBT) binds to the first IP address for each network adapter only   When a NetBIOS name registration message is sent out, only one IP address is registered per adapter. This registration occurs for the IP address that is listed first in the properties of the TCP/IP settings for the adapter.

A unique IP address and subnet mask are defined for each adapter   For each network adapter, an instance of TCP/IP is bound to the adapter. You can choose to have IP addresses automatically assigned (by DHCP or through Automatic Private IP Addressing [APIPA] or alternate configuration if a DHCP server is not present) or defined manually as static addresses.

Domain Name System (DNS) configuration settings are global, unless otherwise noted   The default settings on the **DNS** tab in **Advanced TCP/IP Properties** dialog box are used for all adapters on the computer. It is possible to change this default setting by entering the DNS suffix for a particular connection in the appropriate text box. If this is not done, for a multihomed computer, you must carefully define options for DNS that apply to all adapters using TCP/IP.

To access the Advanced TCP/IP Settings dialog box

1. In Control Panel (default view), click **Network and Internet Connections**.

2. Click **Network Connections**.

3. In Network Connections, right-click the local area connection you want to modify, and then click **Properties**.

4. On the **General** tab, in the **This connection uses the following items** list, click **Internet Protocol (TCP/IP)**, and then click **Properties**.

5. In the **Internet Protocol Properties** dialog box, click **Advanced**.
    The **Advanced TCP/IP Settings** dialog box appears.

Windows Internet Name Service (WINS) configuration settings are defined for each adapter   The settings on the **WINS** configuration tab are used only for the adapter you are configuring. For example, NetBIOS over TCP/IP (NetBT) can be enabled or disabled for each network adapter. If you select the **Disable NetBIOS over TCP/IP** check box for a LAN adapter, this setting is disabled only for that adapter, not for other LAN adapters on the computer.

The default gateway can be different for each adapter   While it is possible to configure a default gateway IP address for each network interface, there is only a single active default route in the IP routing table. In earlier versions of Windows, if there were multiple default routes in the IP routing table (assuming a metric of 1), then the specific default route was chosen randomly when TCP/IP was initialized. This behavior often lead to confusion and loss of connectivity. Windows XP Professional now provides the network administrator (or a user who has appropriate permissions) with two options. One enables the automatic determination of a routing metric based on the speed of the interface. The metric indicates the cost of the route. The other option is the traditional one, allowing you to enter a static interface-based metric.

Although you can have a different default gateway for each adapter, Windows XP Professional uses only one default gateway at a time. This means that only certain hosts are reachable:

- Hosts on the local subnet.

- Hosts that are reachable by the default gateway.

As a result, you might lose network connectivity in some cases; for example, if your computer is first connected to the corporate TCP/IP network and you make a Point-to-Point Protocol (PPP) dial-up connection to the Internet. Your computer stops using the default gateway that connects your computer to the corporate network and instead uses the default gateway that connects your computer to the Internet. Therefore, you can reach hosts on your local subnet, but you cannot reach other hosts on your network.

For information about methods to access multiple gateways, see "Configuring the Local IP Routing Table" earlier in this chapter.

Default gateways and disjointed networks   Disjointed networks are networks that are not connected together. A good example is an intranet that uses both private addressing and the Internet. While both are IP networks, they are not designed to be connected together. You cannot configure default gateways on multiple interfaces connected to disjointed networks. You should configure a default gateway on the interface that is attached to the network that contains the most subnets (typically the Internet). Then, you either add static routes or use a dynamic routing protocol to provide connectivity to subnets reachable on the other network (typically your intranet).

TCP/IP Troubleshooting

Many network troubleshooting tools are available to assist in diagnosing TCP/IP problems for Windows XP Professional. The following sections describe the tools and configuration details necessary to resolve typical troubleshooting problems.

TCP/IP Troubleshooting Tools

Table 21-5 lists the diagnostic tools discussed in this section.

Table 21-5   TCP/IP Diagnostic Tools

Tool	Function
Hostname	Displays the host name of the computer.
IPConfig	Displays current TCP/IP network configuration values, updates or releases Dynamic Host Configuration Protocol (DHCP) allocated leases, and displays, registers, or flushes Domain Name System (DNS) names.
Nbtstat	Displays status of current NetBIOS over TCP/IP connections, updates the NetBIOS name cache, and displays the registered names and scope ID.
Pathping	Displays a path to a TCP/IP host and reports packet losses at each router along the way.
Ping	Sends ICMP Echo Request messages to verify that TCP/IP is configured correctly and that a TCP/IP host is available.
Route	Displays the IP routing table and adds or deletes IP routes.
Tracert	Displays the path to a TCP/IP host.

To view the proper syntax for each command, type **-?** after each command. Typing **/?** produces the same results except after **hostname** and **tracert** where it has no effect.

In addition to the TCP/IP-specific tools, the following Windows XP Professional tools can be used:

- **Event Viewer**. Records system errors and events.

- **Control Panel**. Allows changes to networking and other system components.

- **Registry editor**. Regedit.exe allows viewing and editing of registry settings.

Checking the Configuration with Ipconfig

When troubleshooting a TCP/IP networking problem, begin by checking the TCP/IP configuration on the computer experiencing the problem. Use the **ipconfig** command to get the host computer configuration information, including the IP address, subnet mask, and default gateway.

When Ipconfig is used with the **/all** parameter, it produces a detailed configuration report for all interfaces, including any configured remote access adapters. Ipconfig output can be redirected to a file and pasted into other documents. To do so, type `ipconfig directory\file name`. The output is placed in the directory you specified with the file name you specified.

The output of Ipconfig can be reviewed to find any problems in the computer network configuration. For example, if a computer is manually configured with an IP address that is a duplicate of an existing IP address that has already been detected, the subnet mask appears as 0.0.0.0.

If no problems appear in the TCP/IP configuration, the next step is to test the ability to connect to other host computers on the TCP/IP network.

Testing the Network Connection with Ping and PathPing

Ping is a tool that helps to verify IP-level connectivity. PathPing is a tool that detects packet loss over multiple-hop paths. The **ping** command is used to send an ICMP Echo Request message to a target host. Use Ping whenever you want to verify that a host computer can send IP packets to a destination host. You can also use the Ping tool to isolate network hardware problems and incompatible configurations.

Note If you run **ipconfig /all** and the IP configuration is displayed, there is no need to ping the loopback address and your own IP address; Ipconfig has already performed these tasks to display the configuration.

When troubleshooting, it is best to verify that a route exists between the local computer and a network host by first using Ping and the IP address of the network host to which you want to connect. The command syntax is:

`ping IP address`

Perform the following steps when using Ping:

1. Ping the loopback address to verify that TCP/IP is installed and configured correctly on the local computer.

   `ping 127.0.0.1`

   If the loopback step fails, the IP stack is not responding. This might be because the TCP drivers are corrupted, the network adapter might not be working, or another service is interfering with IP.

2. Ping the IP address of the local computer to verify that it was added to the network correctly. If the routing table is correct, this simply forwards the packet to the loopback address of 127.0.0.1.

   `ping` *IP address of local host*

3. Ping the IP address of the default gateway to verify that the default gateway is functioning and that you can communicate with a local host on the local network.

   `ping` *IP address of default gateway*

4. Ping the IP address of a remote host to verify that you can communicate through a router.

   `ping` *IP address of remote host*

5. Ping the host name of a remote host to verify that you can resolve a remote host name.

   `ping` *Host name of remote host*

6. Run a PathPing analysis to a remote host to verify that the routers on the way to the destination are operating correctly.

   `pathping` *IP address of remote host*

If your local address is returned as 169.254.*y*.*z*, with a subnet mask of 255.255.0.0, you were assigned an IP address by the Automatic Private IP Addressing (APIPA) feature of Windows XP Professional. This means that TCP/IP is configured for automatic configuration, a DHCP server was not found, and an alternate configuration is not specified.

If your local address is returned as 0.0.0.0, the DHCP Media Sensing feature override started because the network adapter detected that it is not connected to a network or because TCP/IP has detected an IP address that duplicates a manually configured IP address.

Ping uses name resolution to resolve a computer name to an IP address. Therefore, if pinging by IP address succeeds, but fails by name, then the problem lies in host name resolution and not network connectivity.

If you cannot use Ping successfully at any point, make sure that:

- The local computer's IP address is valid and appears correctly in the **General** tab of the **Internet Protocol (TCP/IP) Properties** dialog box or when using the Ipconfig tool.

- A default gateway is configured and the link between the host and the default gateway is operational. For troubleshooting purposes, make sure that only one default gateway is configured. While it is possible to configure more than one default gateway, gateways beyond the first one are only used when the IP stack determines that the original gateway is not functioning. Because the point of troubleshooting is to determine the status of the first configured gateway, delete all others to simplify your troubleshooting.

- IP Security is not currently enabled. Depending on IPSec policy, Ping packets might be blocked or require security. For more information about IPSec, see "Configuring IPSec Policies" earlier in this chapter.

Warning   If the remote system being pinged is across a high-delay link such as a satellite link, responses might take longer to be returned. The **-w** (wait) parameter can be used to specify a longer time-out period than the default time of four seconds.

Clearing the ARP Cache

If you can ping both the loopback address and your own IP address, but not any other IP addresses, you might have to clear out the Address Resolution Protocol (ARP) cache. This can be done by using the Arp tool. Use commands **arp -a** or **arp -g** to display the cache contents. Delete the entries by using **arp -d** *IP address*. Flush the ARP cache by using **netsh interface ip delete arpcache**.

Verifying the Default Gateway

The gateway address must be on the same network as the local host; if not, messages from the host computer cannot be forwarded to any location outside the local network. Next, ensure that the default gateway address is correct as entered. Finally, make sure that the default gateway is a router, not just a host, and that it is enabled to forward IP datagrams.

Pinging a Remote Host

If the default gateway responds correctly, ping a remote host to ensure that network-to-network communications are operating as expected. If this fails, use Tracert to trace the path to the destination. For IP routers that are computers running

Windows XP Professional, Windows 2000, or Windows NT, use the Route tool or the Routing and Remote Access snap-in on those computers to examine the IP routing table. For IP routers that are not computers running Windows XP Professional, Windows 2000, or Windows NT, use the vendor-designated appropriate tool or facility to examine the IP routing table.

Four error messages are commonly returned by Ping during troubleshooting, as shown in Table 21-6.

Table 21-6   Ping Error Messages

Error Message	Meaning and Action
TTL Expired in Transit	The number of required hops exceeds Time to Live (TTL). Increase TTL by using the **ping -i** parameter.
	A routing loop exists. Use the **tracert** command to check if there is a routing loop due to misconfigured routers.
Destination Host Unreachable	A local or remote route does not exist for a destination host either at the sending host or at a router. Troubleshoot the local host or router's routing table.
Request Timed Out	Echo Reply messages were not received within the designated time period (default of 4 seconds). Increase time period by using the **ping -w** parameter.
Ping request could not find host	Destination host name cannot be resolved. Verify name and availability of DNS or WINS servers.

Checking IP Security

While IPSec can increase the defenses of a network, it can also make it more difficult to change network configurations or resolve troubleshooting problems. In some cases, IPSec policies requiring secured communication on a Windows XP Professional–based computer can create difficulties in connecting to a remote host. If IPSec has been implemented locally, you can disable the IPSEC Services service in the **Services** snap-in.

If the problem disappears when IPSec services are stopped, IPSec policies are either blocking the necessary traffic or requiring security for the needed traffic. Contact the security administrator to modify the IPSec policy.

For more information about IPSec issues, see "Configuring IPSec Policies" earlier in this chapter.

Checking Packet Filtering

Any mistakes in packet filtering can cause address resolution or connectivity to fail. To determine if packet filtering is the source of a network problem, you must disable TCP/IP packet filtering.

To disable TCP/IP packet filtering

1. In Control Panel (default view), click **Network and Internet Connections**.

2. Click **Network Connections**.

3. In Network Connections, right-click the local area connection you want to modify, and then click **Properties**.

4. On the **General** tab, in the **This connection uses the following items** list, click **Internet Protocol (TCP/IP)**, and then click **Properties**.

5. Click **Advanced**, and then click the **Options** tab.

6. In the **Optional Settings** dialog box, click **TCP/IP Filtering**, and then click the **Properties** tab.

7. Clear the **Enable TCP/IP Filtering (All adapters)** check box, and then click **OK**.

Try pinging an address by using its DNS name, NetBIOS computer name, or IP address. If the attempt succeeds, the packet filtering options might be misconfigured or might be too restrictive. For example, the filtering might permit the computer to act as a Web server, but in the process disable tools, such as remote administration. You can restore a wider range of permissible filtering options by changing the permitted TCP port, UDP port, and IP protocol values.

If the attempt still fails, another form of packet filtering could still be interfering with your networking. For more information about IPSec packet filtering, see "Internet Protocol Security" earlier in this chapter. For information about Routing and Remote Access service packet filtering, see "Unicast IP Routing" in the *Internetworking Guide* of the *Microsoft Windows 2000 Server Resource Kit*.

Troubleshooting Routing

Windows XP Professional supports routing on both single-adapter and multihomed computers. The Routing and Remote Access service provided with Windows 2000 Server includes two routing protocols: Routing Information Protocol (RIP) and Open Shortest Path First (OSPF). Windows 2000 routers can use RIP or OSPF to dynamically exchange routing information.

Cannot connect to a specific server   To determine the cause of connectivity problems when trying to connect to a specific server using NetBIOS-based connections, use the **nbtstat -n** command on the server to determine what name the server registered on the network.

Nbtstat -n output lists several names that the computer has registered. A name resembling the computer's name, as configured on the **Computer Name** tab in **System** in **Control Panel**, must be present. If not, try one of the other unique names displayed by Nbtstat.

The Nbtstat tool can also display the cached entries for remote computers from either #PRE entries in the Lmhosts file or from recently resolved names. If the name the remote computers are using for the server is the same, and the other computers are on a remote subnet, be sure that they have the computer's name-to-address mapping in their Lmhosts files or WINS servers.

Connection to a remote host hangs   To determine why a TCP/IP connection to a remote computer is not working properly, use the **netstat -a** command to show the status of all activity for TCP and UDP ports on the local computer.

A good TCP connection usually shows 0 bytes in the Sent and Received queues. If data is blocked in either queue or if the state is irregular, the connection is probably faulty. If not, you are probably experiencing network or application delay.

Using the Route tool to examine the routing table   For two hosts to exchange IP datagrams, they must both have a route to each other, or use default gateways that know of a route. Normally, routers exchange information with each other by using a routing protocol, such as RIP or OSPF. For information about how to examine and configure the local routing table, see "Configuring the Local IP Routing Table" earlier in this chapter.

Examining paths with Tracert   *Tracert* is a route-tracing tool that sends ICMP Echo Request messages with incrementally higher values in the IP header TTL field to determine the path from one host to another through a network. It then analyzes the ICMP messages that are returned. Tracert allows you to track the path from router to router for up to 30 hops. If a router has failed or if the packet is routed into a loop, Tracert reveals the problem. After the problem router is found, its administrator can be contacted if it is an offsite router, or the router can be restored to fully functional status if it is under your control.

Troubleshooting Gateways

If you see the message "**Your default gateway does not belong to one of the configured interfaces...**" during configuration, find out whether the default gateway is located on the same logical network as the computer's network adapter. Compare the network ID portion of the default gateway's IP address with the network IDs of the computer's network adapters. Specifically, check that the bitwise logical AND of the IP address and the subnet mask equals the bitwise logical AND of the default gateway and the subnet mask.

For example, a computer with a single network adapter, configured with an IP address of 172.16.27.139 and a subnet mask of 255.255.0.0, requires a default gateway of the form 172.16.*y.z*. The network ID for this IP interface is 172.16.0.0.

Additional Resources

These resources contain additional information related to this chapter.

- "Implementing TCP/IP Security" in this book for more information about TCP/IP security and best practices.

- The *Deploying Network Services* book of the *Microsoft® Windows Server™ 2003 Deployment Kit* for more information about Windows TCP/IP network services.

- "Introduction to TCP/IP" in the *TCP/IP Core Networking Guide* of the *Microsoft® Windows® 2000 Server Resource Kit* for more general information about the TCP/IP protocol suite.

- "Unicast Routing Overview" in the *Internetworking Guide* of the *Microsoft® Windows® 2000 Server Resource Kit* for more information about routing principles.

- "TCP/IP Troubleshooting" in the *TCP/IP Core Networking Guide* of the *Microsoft® Windows® 2000 Server Resource Kit* for more information about IP packet filtering.

Chapter 22

Configuring IP Addressing and Name Resolution

Address assignment and name resolution are two complex and often-misunderstood areas of IP functionality. You can configure Microsoft® Windows® XP Professional TCP/IP to automatically obtain an IP address for your computer each time that one is needed, or you can manually specify an IP address. Additionally, you can use one of several methods to identify your Windows XP Professional–based computer by name, rather than IP address.

Related Information

- This chapter expands upon the discussion of TCP/IP first covered in another chapter. For information on TCP/IP configuration issues see "Configuring TCP/IP" in this book.

- For more information about installing and configuring a DHCP server, see "Dynamic Host Configuration Protocol" in the *TCP/IP Core Networking Guide* of the *Microsoft® Windows® 2000 Server Resource Kit*.

- For more information about deploying TCP/IP network services, see the *Deploying Network Services* book of the *Microsoft® Windows Server™ 2003 Deployment Kit*.

- For more information about address translation, see "Unicast IP Routing" in the *Internetworking Guide* of the *Microsoft Windows 2000 Server Resource Kit*.

- For more information about DNS, see *"DNS"* in the *TCP/IP Core Networking Guide*.

Overview of Addressing and Name Resolution

In Windows XP Professional TCP/IP, 32-bit addresses are used to identify each node in the network. This means that every interface on every device has its own address. There are two types of authorized addresses: public authorized addresses and private authorized addresses. Unauthorized addresses can also be used. Four different methods can be used to assign IP addresses. Additionally, several methods exist for resolving device names to IP addresses.

Types of IP Addresses

In order to communicate on a private network or the Internet, each computer on a TCP/IP network must be identified by a unique 32-bit IP address. *Public* IP addresses and authorized *private* IP addresses on the Internet are assigned and managed by the Internet Assigned Numbers Authority (IANA). It is also possible, although not always advisable, to assign an *unauthorized private address* (that is, an address of your own choosing.)

Public IP Addresses

In order for a computer to be visible on the Internet, it must be reachable through a public IP address. The IANA assigns ranges of *public IP addresses* to organizations that can then assign IP addresses within those ranges to individual computers. This prevents multiple computers from having the same IP address.

The public IP address for your Windows XP Professional– based computer can either be assigned through a Dynamic Host Configuration Protocol (DHCP) server available in your enterprise network, configured manually, or provided by an Internet service provider (ISP) through a dial-up connection.

Authorized Private IP Addresses

The IANA has reserved a certain number of IP addresses that are never used on the global Internet. These *private IP addresses* are used for networks that do not want to directly connect to the Internet, but nevertheless require IP connectivity. For example, a user wanting to connect multiple Windows XP Professional– based computers in a home network can use the Automatic Private IP Addressing (APIPA) feature to allow each computer to automatically assign itself a private IP address. The user does not need to configure an IP address for each computer, nor is a DHCP server needed. For more information about APIPA, see "Types of IP Address Assignment" later in this chapter.

Computers on a network using authorized private IP addressing can connect to the Internet through the use of another computer with either proxy or network address translator (NAT) capabilities. Windows XP Professional includes the Internet

Connection Sharing (ICS) feature that provides NAT services to clients in a private network. For more information about Internet Connection Sharing, see "Connecting Remote Offices" in this book.

Unauthorized Private IP Addresses

It is possible, when there is an absolute certainty that your network will never access the Internet, to assign to a node a 32-bit *unauthorized private IP address* of your choosing. Keep in mind that if any Internet connectivity is ever established with any node on your network, these unauthorized private IP addresses could generate significant problems that would require you to immediately change the IP address of every node that you had assigned in this manner.

Types of IP Address Assignment

Windows XP Professional provides four methods for assigning IP addresses to TCP/IP clients:

- **Dynamic Host Configuration Protocol (DHCP)**. Provides automatic configuration of IP addresses and other configuration options (*auto-configuration*) for clients in a network with one or more DHCP servers. This is the default addressing method in Windows XP Professional.

- **Automatic Private IP Addressing (APIPA)**. Automatically assigns a private IP address to clients in a single-subnet environment where no DHCP server is available. When communicating within their own subnet, computers using APIPA addresses can communicate only with other computers using APIPA addresses. For more information about APIPA, see "Enabling IP Address Assignment" later in this chapter.

- **Static IP Addressing**. Allows you to manually configure the IP address if DHCP and APIPA are not available or are not feasible. This method can be time-consuming and prone to error, especially on larger networks.

- **Alternate IP Configuration**. Allows a single interface to make use of more than one IP address as long as only one is used at a time. New in Windows XP Professional, Alternate IP Configuration allows the user to configure a Windows XP Professional–based computer to use one address (either a specified static address or an automatically configured one) and then if that attempt is not successful, to make another pre-configured attempt.

For more information about choosing a method for IP address assignment that best meets the needs of your environment, see "Choosing an IP Address Assignment Method" later in this chapter.

Types of TCP/IP Name Resolution

In general, users prefer to use computer names instead of IP addresses. In Windows XP Professional, TCP/IP allows a computer to communicate over a network with another computer by using a host name or a NetBIOS name in place of an IP address. The mechanisms for name resolution that Microsoft® Windows® supports include:

- **Domain Name System (DNS)**. A global, distributed database based on a hierarchical naming system. The hierarchical naming structure of DNS complements the hierarchical planning structure implemented in the Active Directory™ directory service, and is used as its naming service. DNS name resolution is used on the Internet to map friendly names to IP addresses, and vice versa. In Microsoft® Windows® 2000 and Microsoft® Windows® XP environments, DNS is the default name resolution method.

- **NetBIOS over TCP/IP (NetBT)**. Provides name resolution and connection services for clients using Microsoft® Windows® 95, Microsoft® Windows® 98, and Microsoft® Windows® Millennium Edition (Windows Me) operating systems, applications, and services. Microsoft® Windows® 2000 Server includes a NetBIOS name server known as the Windows Internet Name Service (WINS). NetBIOS over TCP/IP(NetBT) name resolution can take the form of any of four standard name-resolution node types defined in RFCs 1001 and 1002, as well as a fifth node type unique to the Windows implementation of IP name resolution. For more information about these node types, see "Configuring NetBIOS Name Resolution" later in this chapter.

When one computer attempts to communicate with another computer using one of these mechanisms for name resolution, the device name must be resolved to an IP address and ultimately to a hardware address.

Enabling IP Address Assignment

Windows XP Professional provides three methods for assignment of IP addresses to TCP/IP clients, as well as an additional technique that allows more than one IP address to be assigned per interface:

- DHCP
- APIPA
- Static IP Addressing
- Alternate IP Configuration

Choosing an IP Address Assignment Method

You can choose one of three methods for the assigning of an IP address to an interface. In addition, there is a technique that can add some flexibility to your decision making process. Each of the three addressing schemes available in Windows XP Professional is designed to meet different connectivity needs.

Choosing DHCP

DHCP dynamic addressing allows the automatic assignment of a public address for a specified period of time. A configured DHCP server provides a database of available IP addresses. The server can also be set up to provide configuration options for DHCP clients, including addresses of DNS and WINS servers, gateway addresses, and other information. DHCP provides an efficient IP configuration option for larger networks, providing simplified client configuration and reuse of IP addresses.

At startup, each DHCP client requests configuration data from the server, allowing auto-configuration of the IP address, subnet masking, and other options. The IP address is assigned to each client for an amount of time determined by the server, called a *lease*, which can be renewed periodically. Halfway through the lease duration, the DHCP client requests a lease renewal. If this attempt is not successful, the IP address is returned to the database and made available to other DHCP clients. For more information about the DHCP lease process, see "DHCP Lease Process" later in this chapter.

Choosing APIPA

Automatic Private IP Addressing (APIPA) is appropriate for simple networks that have only one subnet. With APIPA, if no DHCP server is available, the computer automatically assigns itself a private IP address. If a DHCP server later becomes available, the computer changes its IP address to one obtained from the DHCP server.

Using APIPA, a Windows XP Professional–based client assigns itself an IP address from a range reserved for authorized private class B network addresses (169.254.0.1 - 169.254.255.254), with a subnet mask of 255.255.0.0. A computer with an authorized private address cannot directly communicate with hosts outside its subnet, including Internet hosts. APIPA is most suitable for small, single-subnet networks, such as a home or small office. APIPA is enabled by default if no DHCP servers are available on the network.

Note   APIPA assigns only an IP address and subnet mask; it does not assign a default gateway, nor does it assign the IP addresses of DNS or WINS servers. Use APIPA only on a single-subnet network that contains no routers. If your small office or home office network is connected to the Internet or a private intranet, do not use APIPA.

Choosing Static IP Addressing

Static addressing involves the manual assignment of a designated fixed address. If your network does not include a DHCP server, and APIPA cannot be used, use manual IP addressing. You must configure the IP address and subnet mask to meet the client computer's connectivity requirements.

Choosing Alternate IP Configuration

With alternate IP Configuration, you can configure an interface that has more than one address. If you need to connect to more than one network (presumably from different locations), you can configure a second address (either static or APIPA) for the same interface. Alternate IP Configuration will allow your Windows XP Professional–based computer to look for the first address and, if that address is not available, to look for the second.

Configuring DHCP

In an effort to make implementing the TCP/IP protocol more manageable, Microsoft worked with other industry leaders to create an Internet standard called Dynamic Host Configuration Protocol (DHCP) for the automatic allocation of TCP/IP configuration. DHCP is not a Microsoft standard, but a public Request for Comments standard, RFC 2131, that Microsoft has implemented.

By implementing a DHCP server within an enterprise, a network administrator is able to establish a range of valid IP addresses to be used by each subnet, as well as a series of options for configuring the subnet mask, the default gateway, and addresses for DNS and WINS servers. An individual IP address from the range, and the options associated with that range, are assigned dynamically to any DHCP client requesting an address. If DHCP is available company-wide, users can move from subnet to subnet and always have a valid IP address. DHCP permits the administrator to assign a lease time that defines how long an IP address configuration remains valid. A Microsoft® Windows NT® version 3.5 or later or a Windows 2000–based server running the DHCP service, or any computer or network device running RFC 2131–compliant software, can act as a DHCP server.

For more information about installing and configuring the DHCP service in Windows 2000, see "Dynamic Host Configuration Protocol" in the *Networking Guide* of the *Microsoft Windows 2000 Server Resource Kit*.

DHCP Lease Process

The first time that a Windows XP Professional–based client (with DHCP enabled) attempts to join a network, it automatically follows an initialization process to obtain a lease from a DHCP server. Figure 22-1 shows the lease process.

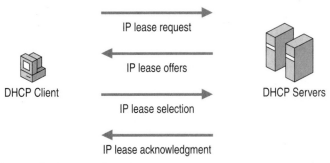

IP lease request

IP lease offers

IP lease selection

IP lease acknowledgment

DHCP Client

DHCP Servers

Figure 22-1   The DHCP lease process

The lease process involves the following steps:

1. The Windows XP Professional DHCP client requests an IP address by broadcasting a message (known as a DHCPDiscover message) to the local subnet.

2. The client is offered an address when a DHCP server responds with a DHCPOffer message containing an IP address, and associated configuration information, available for lease to the client.

3. The client selects the offered address and replies to the server with a DHCPRequest message.

4. The client is assigned the address and the DHCP server sends an acknowledgment message (DHCPAck) approving the lease. Other DHCP option information, such as default gateway and DNS server addresses, might be included in the message.

5. After the client receives acknowledgment, it configures its TCP/IP properties using any DHCP option information in the DHCPAck message, and completes the initialization of TCP/IP.

If no DHCP server responds to the client request, the Windows XP Professional–based client can proceed in one of two ways:

If APIPA is enabled, the client self-configures a unique IP address in the range 169.254.0.1 through 169.254.255.254. For more information about self-configuring IP addresses, see "Configuring APIPA" later in this chapter.

If APIPA has been disabled, the client network initialization fails. The client continues to re-send DHCPDiscover messages in the background until it receives a valid lease from a DHCP server. The client makes four attempts to obtain a lease, one every five minutes.

In rare cases, a DHCP server might return a negative acknowledgment (DHCP-Nack) to the client. This can happen if a client requests an invalid or duplicate address. If this occurs, the client must begin the entire lease process again.

Restarting a DHCP Client

When a Windows XP Professional–based client that had previously leased an IP address restarts, it broadcasts a DHCPRequest message containing a request for its previously assigned IP address. If the requested IP address is available, the DHCP server responds with an acknowledgment message, and the client joins the network.

If the client cannot use the IP address because it is in use by another client, or if the address is no longer valid because the client has been physically moved to a different subnet, the DHCP server responds with a negative acknowledgment (DHCPNack), causing the client to restart the lease process.

DHCP Lease Renewals

To ensure that addresses are not left assigned when they are no longer needed, the DHCP server places an administrator-defined time limit on the lease, known as a *lease duration*.

Halfway through the lease duration, the DHCP client requests a lease renewal, and the DHCP server extends the lease. If at any time a computer stops using its assigned IP address (for example, if a computer is moved to another network segment or is removed), the lease expires and the address becomes available for reassignment.

Configuring the Windows XP Professional DHCP Client

When TCP/IP is installed, Windows XP Professional automatically enables the option to obtain an IP address from a DHCP server. You can disable this option if you want to manually enter an IP address. For more information about disabling DHCP, see "Configuring an IP Address Manually" later in this chapter.

The IP configuration tool (Ipconfig.exe) allows users or administrators to examine the current IP address configuration assigned to the computer, the IP address lease time, and other useful data about the TCP/IP configuration.

Configuring APIPA

In Windows XP Professional, *Automatic Private IP Addressing (APIPA)* allows home users and small business users to create a functioning, single subnet TCP/IP network without the use of either static addressing or a DHCP server.

Manually configuring IP addresses can be tedious work in all but the very smallest networks and is prone to human error. Generally, autoconfiguration is a better choice. APIPA allows a Windows XP Professional client to assign itself an IP address in the following circumstances:

- The client is configured to obtain a lease DHCP, but a DHCP server cannot be found, is unavailable, or is not used (for example, in a small office/home office network).

- The client used DHCP to obtain a lease, but the client's attempts to renew the lease through a DHCP server have failed.

In these cases, the Windows XP Professional client selects an IP address from the range of IANA-designated, private class B addresses (169.254.0.1 - 169.254.255.254) with the subnet mask 255.255.0.0. The client performs duplicate-address detection to ensure that the IP address that it has chosen is not already in use. If the address is in use, the client will select another IP address up to 10 times. After the client has selected an address that is verifiably not in use, it configures the interface with that address. In the background, the client continues to check for a DHCP server every five minutes. If a DHCP server is found, the APIPA autoconfiguration information is abandoned and the configuration offered by the DHCP server is used instead.

You can use the Ipconfig.exe command-line tool to determine whether APIPA is enabled.

To determine whether Automatic Private IP Addressing is currently enabled

- At the command prompt, type:
  ipconfig /all

The resulting text identifies your IP address and other information. Check the line that reads "Autoconfiguration Enabled." If the text reads "YES" and the IP address is in the 169.254.0.1 - 169.254.255.254 range, Automatic Private IP Addressing is enabled.

You can disable automatic private IP addressing in one of two ways:

- Manually configure TCP/IP. This method also disables DHCP. For information about manually configuring TCP/IP, see "Configuring an IP Address Manually" later in this chapter.

- Disable automatic private IP addressing (but not DHCP) for a particular network interface by editing the registry.

> **Caution**   Do not edit the registry unless you have no alternative. The registry editor bypasses standard safeguards, allowing settings that can damage your system, or even require you to reinstall Windows. If you must edit the registry, back it up first and see the Registry Reference in the Microsoft Windows 2000 Server Resource Kit at http://www.microsoft.com/reskit.

To disable APIPA by editing the registry

1. You do this by adding the registry entry **IPAutoconfigurationEnabled** with a value of 0 (REG_DWORD data type) in the following subkey:
   HKEY_LOCAL_MACHINE\SYSTEM\CurrentControlSet\Services\Tcpip\ Parameters\Interfaces*interface-name*

2. Use the registry editor Regedit.exe to add the above entry, and then restart the computer.

To disable APIPA for multiple adapters by editing the registry

1. Set the value of the **IPAutoconfigurationEnabled** entry to 0x0 (REG_DWORD data type) in the following registry subkey:

    HKEY_LOCAL_MACHINE\SYSTEM\CurrentControlSet\Services\Tcpip\ Parameters

2. Use the registry editor Regedit.exe to add the above entry, and then restart the computer.

Configuring an IP Address Manually

If you cannot use DHCP or APIPA for IP address and subnet assignment, the IP address for the Windows XP Professional–based client must be manually configured. The required values include the following:

- The IP address for each network adapter installed on the computer.

- The subnet mask corresponding to each network adapter's local network.

To configure an IP address manually

1. In **Control Panel**, select **Network and Internet Connections**.

2. On the **Network and Internet Connections** sheet, select **Network Connections**.

3. In **Network Connections**, right-click the local area connection that you want to modify.

4. Select **Properties**.

5. On the **General** tab of the **Properties** sheet, select **Internet Protocol (TCP/ IP)**.

6. Click **Properties**.

7. On the **General** tab of the TCP/IP **Properties** sheet, select the **Use the following IP address** option.

8. Type the IP address, subnet mask, and default gateway for the selected adapter in the respective text boxes. The network administrator must provide these values for individual users, based on the IP addressing plan for your site.

    The value in the **IP Address** text box identifies the IP address for this network adapter. The value in the **Subnet Mask** text box is used to identify the network ID for the selected network adapter.

9. Click **OK** to save the IP addressing information.

10. Click **OK** to save the connection properties.

Configuring Multiple IP Addresses on a Network Adapter

Multihoming involves the placement of more than one network adapter in a single computer. In addition, Windows XP Professional supports *logical multihoming*, by which multiple addresses are assigned on a single network adapter. This configuration is useful in an environment in which a single physical network is logically divided into subnets. For more information about multihoming, see "Configuring TCP/IP" in this book.

To configure a multihomed system using a single network adapter

1. In **Control Panel**, **select Network and Internet Connections**.

2. In the **Network and Internet Connections** sheet, select **Network Connections**.

3. In **Network Connections**, right-click the local area connection that you want to modify, and then select **Properties**.

4. In the **Local Area Connection Properties sheet**, click the **General** tab. Select **Internet Protocol (TCP/IP)**, and then click **Properties**.

5. In the **Internet Protocol (TCP/IP)** sheet, click the **General** tab. Select **Use the following IP address**. Add TCP/IP configuration information for the first IP address, and click **Advanced**.

   Figure 22-2 shows the advanced TCP/IP Settings dialog box.

Figure 22-2   Advanced TCP/IP Settings dialog box

6. In the **Advanced TCP/IP Settings** dialog box, under **IP address**, click **Add** to assign one or more additional IP addresses to the same interface.

7. In the **TCP/IP Address** box, enter an IP address and a subnet mask to assign an additional address to the same interface. Click **Add**. Repeat the process for each additional address that you want to assign to that interface.

8. In the **Advanced TCP/IP Settings** page, under **Default Gateways**, click **Add** to assign one or more additional default gateways to the same interface.

9. In the **TCP/IP Gateway Address** box, enter an IP address for an additional default gateway for the same interface. Use the checkbox to indicate whether the gateway's metric is to be assigned automatically. If a metric is not to be assigned automatically, enter the metric. Upon completion, click **Add**. Repeat the process for each additional default gateway address that you want to assign to that interface.

Caution   As a general recommendation, do not specify multiple default gateways.

Figure 22-3 shows the TCP/IP Gateway Address dialog box.

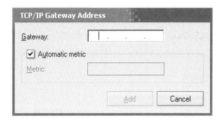

Figure 22-3   TCP/IP Gateway Address dialog box

10. Click **OK** three times, so that all changes take effect.

Note   A metric indicates the cost of the route (which, in the case of the Routing Information Protocol indicates the number of hops to the destination). The TCP/IP Gateway Address dialog box allows you to indicate whether the default gateway is to have an automatically assigned or a static metric. If it is to have a static metric, you can enter that metric in a text box. For more information about assigning a static metric, see "Configuring TCP/IP" in this book.

For more information about the automatic determination of the default gateway address and about interface-based metrics, see "Configuring TCP/IP" in this book.

Configuring an Alternate IP Address

Laptops and other mobile devices that participate on more than one network often use a static IP address at one location and a dynamically assigned IP address at another. For example, your computer might use dynamic addressing (DHCP) at the office but need to use a static IP address when at home to connect to a broadband ISP.

Windows XP Professional solves this problem by allowing the user to configure the computer to first try DHCP, and then, if the attempt fails, to try alternate static IP address setting(s).

To configure a dynamically assigned private IP alternate address

1. In **Control Panel**, select **Network and Internet Connections.**

2. In the **Network and Internet Connections** properties sheet, select **Network Connections**.

3. In Network Connections, right-click **Local Area Connections** and click **Properties.**

4. In the **Local Area Connection Properties** properties **sheet**, click the **General** tab. Select **Internet Protocol (TCP/IP)** and click **Properties**.

5. On the **Alternate Configuration tab of the Internet Protocol Properties page**, select **Automatic private IP address** to specify a dynamically assigned private address as your alternate IP address.

6. Click **OK**.

To configure a static IP alternate address

1. In **Control Panel**, select **Network and Internet Connections**.

2. In the **Network and Internet Connections** sheet, select **Network Connections**.

3. In **Network Connections**, right-click **Local Area Connections** and click **Properties**.

4. In the **Local Area Connection Properties sheet**, click the **General** tab. Select **Internet Protocol (TCP/IP)** and click **Properties**.

5. On the **Alternate Configuration** tab, select **User configured** for a static address as your alternate IP address.

6. Enter your alternate IP address, alternate subnet mask, and alternate default gateway.

7. Type the preferred and alternate DNS server address for this network.

8. Type the preferred and alternate WINS server address for this network.

9. Click **OK**.

Configuring TCP/IP Name Resolution

TCP/IP-based services use IP addresses to identify each other, but users and applications frequently require computer names for host identification. A name resolution mechanism must be available on a TCP/IP network to resolve names to IP addresses.

To resolve a name to an IP address, the Windows XP Professional resolver first submits the name query to DNS. If DNS name resolution fails, the resolver checks the length of the name. If it is longer than 15 bytes, resolution fails. If not, the resolver then checks to determine whether NetBIOS is running. If it is not running, resolution fails. If it is running, the resolver then tries NetBIOS name resolution. Figure 22-4 illustrates this process.

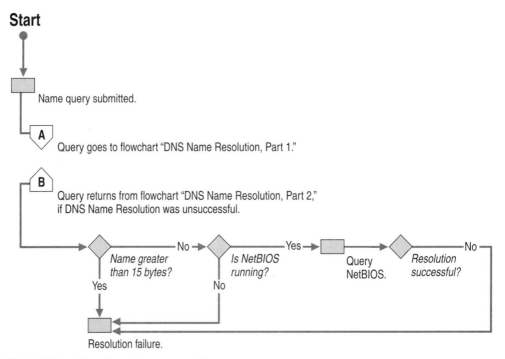

Figure 22-4   Overview of name resolution

Windows XP Professional provides several different types of name resolution, including DNS, WINS, Hosts and Lmhosts files, and broadcast. Generally, a Windows XP Professional–based computer uses a combination of name-resolution types, to be chosen by the user.

Windows XP Professional supports DNS dynamic update. *Dynamic update* is a standard, specified in RFC 2136, that provides a means of dynamically updating host data in a DNS database. Updates can come from DNS clients and/or DHCP servers. For more information about dynamic update, see "Configuring Dynamic Update" later in this chapter.

Choosing a Name Resolution Method

Windows XP Professional provides four methods for resolving names to IP addresses:

- Domain Name System (DNS), accomplished by querying DNS servers. This is for applications and services that require host-to-IP name resolution.

- NetBIOS name resolution, accomplished by querying WINS servers. This is included for compatibility reasons for applications and services that require NetBIOS-to-IP name resolution, such as the browsing function of Microsoft® Windows® NT 4.0, Windows 98, and Windows 95.

- IP Host and NetBIOS name resolution, accomplished through Hosts files and Lmhosts files respectively. These provide host name-to-IP and NetBIOS name-to-IP name resolution through manually maintained local files.

- NetBIOS name resolution, accomplished by means of b-node broadcasts. B-node broadcasts are used for name resolution within the local subnet.

For Windows XP Professional–based clients, you need to determine whether the client needs to be configured to use DNS, WINS, or a combination of the two. In general, DNS is needed under the following circumstances:

- The client is a member of an Active Directory domain. Active Directory uses DNS as its locator service and is tightly integrated with it. A locator service assists clients in finding other hosts and services, using only the domain names.

- The client accesses the Internet.

- The client is on a network that uses DNS to resolve host names.

Windows XP Professional supports NetBIOS over TCP/IP for backward compatibility with earlier versions of Windows. If a WINS server is available within your network, configure your Windows XP Professional–based computer to use WINS if the client uses applications or services that require NetBIOS name resolution.

If a WINS server is not available, configure the Windows XP Professional client to use Lmhosts for NetBIOS name resolution. If this is not possible, NetBIOS name resolution is provided by broadcasts, which cannot be used to resolve host names that are outside the local subnet.

You also need to determine whether autoconfiguration is available at the DHCP server. If you use DHCP for autoconfiguration, a DHCP server can provide client configuration details (including subnet mask, DNS and WINS servers, and other options). If you do not use DHCP, you must manually configure these parameters.

Configuring DNS Settings

DNS is the default name resolution method for Windows XP Professional clients, and is required for their integration into a Windows–based Active Directory domain. However, in order for the network to use this method of name resolution, DNS must be properly configured. Table 22-1 indicates where you can find information about the DNS settings that you need to configure.

Table 22-1   DNS Configuration Topics

To configure this DNS setting...	...refer to this section
Configure domain name Configure primary DNS suffix Configure connection-specific DNS suffix	"Configuring DNS to Resolve Host Names and Domain Names"
Specify addresses of available DNS servers	"Specifying DNS Servers"
Specify how DNS client should resolve host names	"Configuring DNS Query Settings"
Optimize local DNS cache Prevent DNS client from accepting non-queried servers	"DNS Caching, Network Prioritization and Security"
Configure dynamic update, if used	"Configuring Dynamic Update"

Configuring DNS to Resolve Host Names and Domain Names

DNS provides name-to-IP mapping by means of a distributed database. In general, each organization runs its own DNS servers and maintains the name mapping database records, or *resource records*, for its domain. When a name resolution request is made, a DNS server first checks its own records for the corresponding IP address. If it does not have the answer, it will query other DNS servers for the information.

A Windows XP Professional client configured for DNS name resolution can utilize one or more DNS servers for name-resolution services. This section describes the procedures for performing the following tasks:

- Configuring DNS host name and domain names

- Configuring DNS query settings

- Specifying DNS servers

- DNS caching, network prioritization, and security

Table 22-2 summarizes the differences between each kind of name used in TCP/IP in Windows 2000 and Windows XP Professional. By default, the host name, a period, and the primary DNS suffix are concatenated to create a fully qualified domain name (FQDN) for the computer.

Table 22-2   DNS and NetBIOS Names

Name Type	Description
NetBIOS name	A NetBIOS name is used to uniquely identify a NetBIOS service that is "listening" on the first IP address that is bound to an adapter. This unique NetBIOS name is resolved to the IP address of the server through broadcast, WINS, or the Lmhosts file. By default, it is the same as the host name and can be up to 15 characters long.
	The NetBIOS name is also known as a *NetBIOS computer name.*
	For example, a NetBIOS name might be client1.
Host name	The term *host name* can mean either the FQDN, or the first label (or part) of an FQDN. In this chapter, *host name* refers to the first label of an FQDN. For example, the first label of the FQDN client1.reskit.com is client1.
	The host name is also often referred to as the *Computer name* (as opposed to *Full computer name*, which is used to represent the full DNS computer name).
Primary DNS suffix	Every Windows XP Professional and every Windows 2000 Server–based computer can be assigned a primary DNS suffix to be used in name resolution and name registration. The primary DNS suffix is specified on the **Computer Name** tab of the **My Computer** properties sheet.
	The primary DNS suffix is also known as the *primary domain name* and the *domain name.*
	For example, the FQDN client1.reskit.com has the primary DNS suffix reskit.com.

Table 22-2 DNS and NetBIOS Names

Name Type	Description
Connection-specific DNS suffix	The connection-specific DNS suffix is a DNS suffix that is assigned to an adapter.
	The connection-specific DNS suffix is also known as an *adapter DNS suffix*.
	For example, a connection-specific DNS suffix might be reskit.com.
Fully qualified domain name (FQDN	The FQDN is a DNS name that uniquely identifies the computer on the network. By default, it is a concatenation of the host name, the primary DNS suffix, and a period.
	The fully qualified domain name is also known as the *full computer name*.
	For example, an FQDN might be client1.reskit.com.

DNS and NetBIOS Names

The DNS host name is taken from the computer name assigned to it during Windows XP Professional installation. The host name can be 63 bytes (or characters) long, and uses the character set specified in RFC 2181. The host name is used in combination with the primary domain name to form the fully qualified domain name (FQDN).

The NetBIOS computer name is used to identify the local computer for authentication by hosts and tools that use NetBIOS over TCP/IP (NetBT) for name resolution. NetBIOS names contain 15 bytes. In a new Windows XP Professional installation, the NetBIOS name is initially taken from the assigned DNS host name. If the DNS host name exceeds 15 bytes, the host name is shortened to form the NetBIOS computer name. For more information about NetBIOS names, see "Configuring NetBIOS Name Resolution" later in this chapter.

You can change the DNS host name after installation, by means of the Computer Name tab in the System dialog box. When you do this, the same change will be made to the NetBIOS computer name, to the degree that the new name is in accordance with NetBIOS naming rules.

To change the DNS host name

1. In **Control Panel**, select **Performance and Maintenance**.

2. In the **Performance and Maintenance Connections** sheet, select **System**.

3. In the **System Properties** sheet (as shown in Figure 22-5), select **the Computer Name** tab.

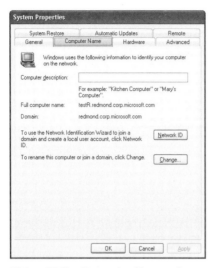

Figure 22-5   Computer Name tab

4. Click **Change**.

5. Type the new host name in the **Computer name** text box, and click **OK**.

6. When prompted, click **Yes** to restart the computer.

Note   If you enter a name that includes characters other than a-z, A-Z, 0-9 and "-", a warning message appears suggesting that you use only these characters.

In Windows 95, Windows 98, and Windows NT, NetBIOS is used to name the computer. If a Windows XP Professional–based computer has been migrated from an earlier version of Windows, its host name is taken from the preexisting NetBIOS-based computer name. In a network that contains hosts that are not running Windows XP Professional or Windows 2000, this might present problems, because some characters that are allowed in NetBIOS names are not supported as legal characters in DNS names.

Primary DNS Suffix   The primary DNS suffix is the name of the DNS domain to which the host belongs. If a Windows XP Professional–based computer is a member of an Active Directory domain, its primary DNS domain name is set by default to the DNS name of its Active Directory domain. This information is provided during Windows XP Professional installation, during migration to Windows XP Professional, or when the computer joins a Windows 2000 domain.

If a computer is a member of a workgroup, or a member of a Windows NT domain, a DNS suffix is not automatically indicated. In such a circumstance, you can manually specify the primary DNS suffix.

To set or change the primary DNS suffix

1. In **Control Panel**, select **Performance and Maintenance Connections**.

2. In the **Performance and Maintenance** sheet, select **System**.

3. In the **System Properties** sheet, select the **Computer Name** tab.

4. Click **Change**.

5. Click **More**.

6. In the **Primary DNS suffix of this computer** text box, type the primary DNS suffix, and then click **OK**.

When a Windows XP Professional–based computer changes membership in an Active Directory domain, its DNS domain membership can be changed as well. To allow Windows XP Professional to automatically change the computer's primary DNS domain name when its Active Directory domain membership changes, make sure that the checkbox for **Change DNS domain name when domain membership changes** is selected (it is selected by default).

Connection-Specific Domain Name   Windows XP Professional permits each adapter to have a unique domain name, known as the *connection-specific domain name.*

For example, suppose the computer Client1 has the primary DNS suffix reskit.com, and it is connected to both the Internet and the corporate intranet. For each connection, you can specify a connection-specific domain name. For the connection to the Internet, you specify the name isp01.com, and the FQDN is then Client1.isp01.com.

Connection-specific domain names for each adapter can be assigned dynamically by DHCP server or can be specified manually.

To set or change the connection-specific DNS suffix

1. In **Control Panel**, under **Pick a Category**, **select Network and Internet Connections**.

2. On the **Network and Internet Connections** sheet, under **pick a Control Panel icon**, select **Network Connections**.

3. In Network Connections, right-click the local area connection you want to modify, and then select **Properties**.

4. Select **Internet Protocol (TCP/IP)**, and then click **Properties**.

5. Click **Advanced**.

6. Select the **DNS** tab.

7. In the **DNS suffix for this connection** text box, type the domain name for the connection. Then click OK.

You can also specify whether a dynamic update client registers the computer's FQDN containing the connection-specific DNS suffix. For more information about this configuration, see "Configuring Dynamic Update" later in this chapter.

Fully Qualified Domain Name   By default, the primary DNS suffix combines with the host name to create a fully qualified domain name (FQDN). During DNS queries, the primary DNS suffix, connection-specific suffix(es), and devolved primary DNS suffixes could be appended to a single-label name, for example, **client1**. In that form, the name could then be submitted for DNS name resolution. In this example, when querying the DNS server for the IP address of client1, the primary DNS suffix reskit.com is appended to the shorter name **client1**, and the DNS server is actually asked to resolve the FQDN **client1.reskit.com**.

> **Note**   If an entry is specified in the **Search these DNS domains (in order)** box on the DNS tab of the Advanced TCP/IP Settings dialog box, that entry is used instead of the DNS suffixes to create an FQDN.

DNS Naming Restrictions

Different DNS implementations impose different character and length restrictions. Table 22-3 shows the restrictions for each implementation.

Table 22-3   Naming Restrictions

Restriction	Standard DNS (as included in Windows NT 4.0)	DNS in Windows XP Professional and Windows 2000 Server	NetBIOS
Characters	Supports RFC 1123, which permits A- Z, a-z, 0-9, and the hyphen (-).	Supports RFC 2181, which permits more characters than RFC 1123. It is advisable, however, to use only the characters permitted by RFC 1123.	Unicode characters, numbers, white space, and these symbols: ! @ $ % ∧ & ') (. - _ { } ~
Computer/host name length	63 octets per label and 255 bytes for FQDN.	63 octets per label and 255 bytes for FQDN.	15 octets.

According to RFC 1123, the only characters that can be used in DNS labels are A-Z, a-z, 0-9, and the hyphen (-). The period (.) character is also used in DNS names, but only between DNS labels and at the end of a FQDN. Many DNS servers, including Windows NT 4.0 DNS servers, follow RFC 1123.

Compliance with RFC 1123 can present a problem, however, on Windows XP Professional–based or Windows 2000–based computers that are upgraded from Windows NT 4.0. During the upgrade from Windows NT 4.0 to Windows 2000 or Windows XP Professional, a computer's host name (also known as Computer name) is set to the computer's Windows NT 4.0 NetBIOS name. NetBIOS names can use characters that are illegal in DNS names according to RFC 1123, and it can be time-consuming to convert all of the NetBIOS names to standard DNS names that are compliant with RFC 1123.

To simplify the migration process from Windows NT 4.0 and Windows 2000, DNS servers support a wider character set. RFC 2181, "Clarifications to the DNS Specification," extends the character set allowed in DNS names. Based on this definition, the Windows 2000 DNS servers have been adjusted to accommodate UTF-8 character encoding, a larger character set. as described in RFC 2044. UTF-8 character encoding is a superset of ASCII and a translation of UCS-2 (also known as Unicode) character encoding. The UTF-8 character set includes characters from most of the world's written languages, allowing a greater range of possible names.

Before using the extended character set, you must consider the following:

■ If a client name containing characters not in compliance with RFC 1123 is to be used, all DNS servers to which the client is to be registered must support RFC 2181. Avoid using UTF-8-compliant host names that contain characters other than those specified in RFC 1123 if your network includes any DNS servers that do not comply with this standard.

■ Some third-party resolver software supports only the characters listed in RFC 1123. Computers in your network using such software probably cannot look up clients with names that include nonstandard characters.

DNS Query Process

The DNS resolver attaches a domain name suffix to a name specified in a query, if the name meets either of the following conditions:

■ The name is a single-label unqualified (that is, non-dot-terminated) name.

■ The name is a multiple-label unqualified (that is, non-dot-terminated) name and the resolver cannot resolve it as a fully qualified domain name.

The query process is shown in Figure 22-6 (part 1) and Figure 22-7 (part 2).

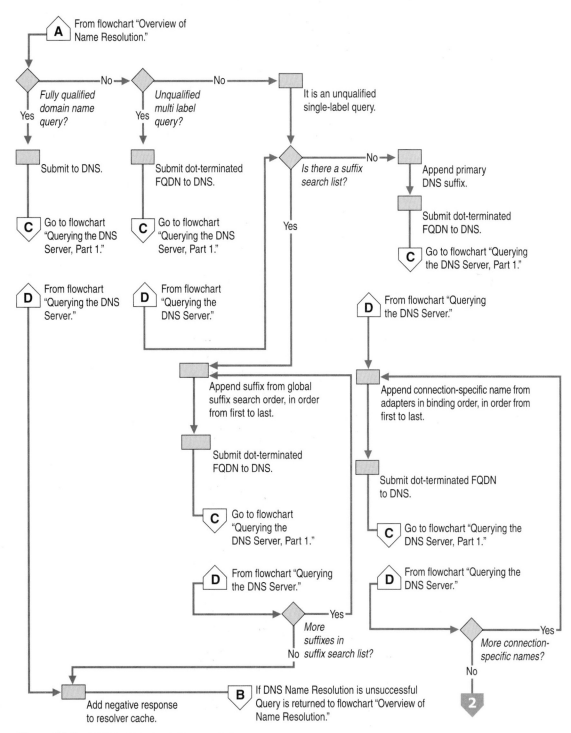

Figure 22-6   DNS name resolution, part 1

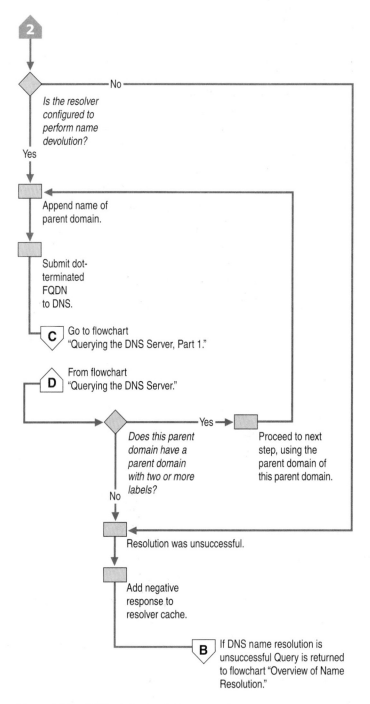

Figure 22-7 DNS name resolution, part 2

Adding Suffixes to Queries

You can use the DNS tab in the Advanced TCP/IP Settings dialog box to configure how suffixes are added to queries.

Figure 22-8 shows the DNS tab of the Advanced TCP/IP Settings dialog box.

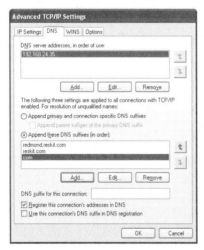

Figure 22-8   Advanced TCP/IP Settings DNS tab

The option **Append primary and connection specific DNS suffixes** is selected by default. When enabled, it causes the resolver to append the primary DNS suffix to the name submitted for DNS name resolution, as defined on the Computer Name tab of the System Properties sheet, as well as the DNS suffix as defined in the **DNS suffix for this connection** field of each network connection.

For example, if your primary DNS suffix is dom1.acquired01-int.com, and this suffix is queried for the unqualified (non-dot-terminated) single-label name client1, the resolver queries for the following FQDN: client1.dom.acquried01-int.com.

If the query in the previous step fails, and if you have specified a connection-specific DNS suffix in the **DNS suffix for this connection** box or if the suffix is assigned by a DHCP server, the resolver appends that suffix.

For example, if you entered the name acquired01-ext.com in the **DNS suffix for this connection** box and then queried for the unqualified, single-label name client1, the resolver queries for the following FQDN: client1.acquired01-ext.com.

If the query in the previous step fails, and if the **Append parent suffixes of the primary DNS suffix** option is selected (it is selected by default): the resolver performs name devolution on the primary DNS suffix; that is, it strips off the leftmost label, and attempts to devolve the resulting domain name until only two labels remain.

For example, if your primary DNS suffix is dom1.acquired01-int.com, and you selected the check box **Append parent suffixes of the primary DNS suffix** and then queried for the unqualified, single-label name client1, the resolver queries the following FQDN: client1.acquired01-int.com.

You can disable the name devolution option on the DNS tab of the Advanced TCP/IP Settings dialog box.

To disable name devolution

1. In **Control Panel, select Network and Internet Connections**.

2. In the **Network and Internet Connections** sheet, select **Network Connections**.

3. In Network Connections, right-click the local area connection that you want to change, and then select **Properties**.

4. Select **Internet Protocol (TCP/IP)**, and then click **Properties**.

5. Click **Advanced, and then** click the **DNS** tab.

6. Clear the check box **Append parent suffixes of the primary DNS suffix**.

7. Click **OK**.

The text box **Append these DNS suffixes (in order)** allows you to specify a list of domains to try, called a *domain-suffix search list*. If you enter a domain suffix search list, the resolver adds those domain name suffixes in order and does not try any other domain names. For example, if the **Append these DNS suffixes (in order)** box includes the names listed in Figure 22-8 and you enter the unqualified, single-label query "coffee," the resolver looks for fully qualified domain names in this order:

- coffee.redmond.reskit.com.
- coffee.reskit.com.
- coffee.com.

To add entries to the domain-suffix search list

1. In **Control Panel, select Network and Internet Connections**.

2. In the **Network and Internet Connections** sheet select **Network Connections**.

3. In Network Connections, right-click the local area connection that you want to change, and then select **Properties**.

4. Select **Internet Protocol (TCP/IP)**, and then click **Properties**.

5. Click **Advanced**.

6. Click the **DNS** tab.

7. Select **Append these DNS suffixes (in order)**.

8. Click **Add**.

9. To add a domain suffix to the list, type the domain suffix(es) that you want to include, and click **Add**.

    - or -

    To remove a domain suffix from the list, select the domain suffix, and then click **Remove**.

10. To change the domain suffix search order, select a suffix, and then click the up-arrow or down-arrow button to move the suffix up or down the list.

Specifying DNS Servers

When a name is submitted to the DNS resolver (client) for name resolution, the Windows XP Professional resolver first checks the local cache. If the requested data is in the cache, the data is returned to the user. If the data is not in the cache, the resolver queries the DNS servers that are listed in the TCP/IP properties for each adapter.

The resolver can query through all of the computer's network connections, including remote access connections. In Windows NT 4.0, the resolver queries all servers through all adapters. In Windows 2000 and Windows XP Professional, however, you can specify a list of DNS servers to query for each adapter.

Figures 22-9 (part 1), 22-10 (part 2), and 22-11 (part 3) illustrate the process by which the resolver queries the servers on each adapter.

Querying DNS Servers

Windows XP Professional allows multiple DNS servers to be specified. The first DNS server specified, known as the *preferred* DNS server, can be followed by an unlimited number of *alternate* DNS servers. The resolver queries the DNS servers in the following order:

1. The resolver sends the query to the first server on the preferred adapter's search list and waits one second for a response.

2. If the resolver does not receive a response from the first server within the allotted time, it sends the query to the first DNS server on the search list of each adapter still under consideration. The resolver waits two seconds for a response.

3. If the resolver does not receive a response from any server within this allotted time, the resolver sends the query to all DNS servers on all adapters still under consideration and waits another two seconds for a response.

4. If the resolver still does not receive a response from any server within this time period, it sends the query to all DNS servers on all adapters still under consideration and waits four seconds for a response.

5. If, after these four seconds, the resolver does not receive a response from any server, it sends the query to all DNS servers on all adapters still under consideration and waits eight seconds for a response.

6. If the resolver receives a positive response within that time, it stops querying for the name, adds the response to the cache, and returns the response to the client.

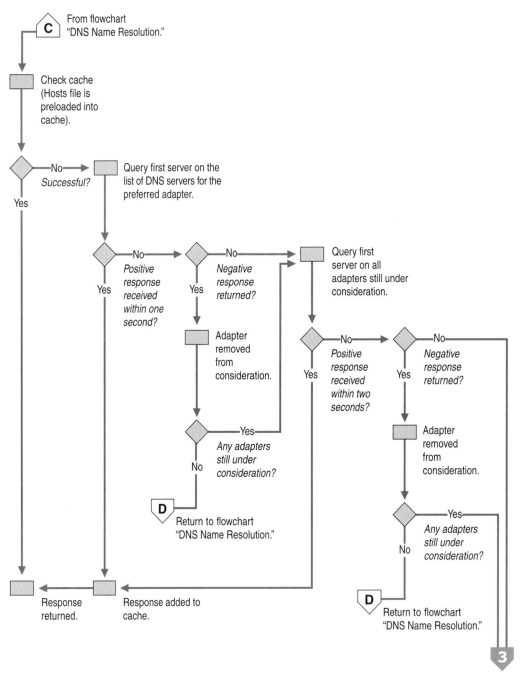

Figure 22-9 Querying the DNS server, part 1

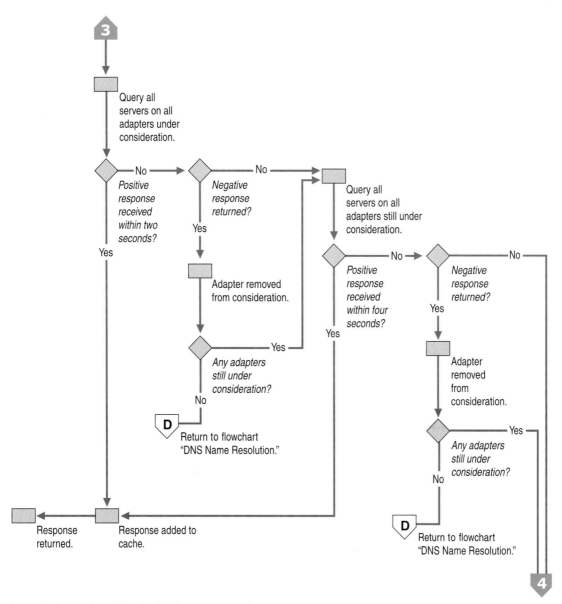

Figure 22-10   Querying the DNS server, part 2

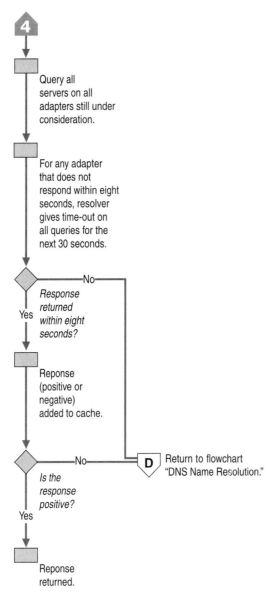

Figure 22-11   Querying the DNS server, part 3

If it has not received a response from any server within those eight seconds, the resolver responds with a time-out. Also, if it has not received a response from any server on a specified adapter's search list, then for the next 30 seconds, the resolver responds to all queries destined for servers on that adapter's search list with a time-out and does not query those servers.

If, at any point, the resolver receives a negative response from a server, it removes every server connected to that adapter from consideration during this search. For example, if in step 2, the first server on alternate adapter A gave a negative response, the resolver would not send the query to any other server on the list for alternate adapter A.

The resolver also keeps track of which servers answer queries more quickly, and might move servers up or down on the list based on how quickly they reply to queries.

If all DNS servers on an adapter are queried and none reply, either positively or negatively, all subsequent name queries to any server listed on that adapter will fail for a default period of 30 seconds. This feature decreases network traffic.

Figure 22-12 shows how the resolver queries each server on each adapter.

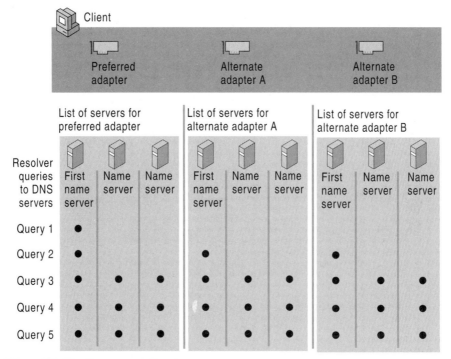

Figure 22-12   Name resolution for a multihomed client

To specify a preferred and alternate DNS server

1. In **Control Panel**, **select Network and Internet Connections**.

2. In the **Network and Internet Connections** sheet, select **Network Connections**.

3. In **Network Connections**, right-click the local area network connection that you want to change, and then click **Properties**.

4. Select **Internet Protocol (TCP/IP)**, and then click **Properties**.

5. On the **General** tab of the TCP/IP **Properties sheet**, select the method to be used to access the DNS servers for your network:

   ■ If a DHCP server is available for automatic IP addressing and is configured to provide parameters for automatic DNS server configuration, select **Obtain DNS server address automatically**.

   ■ If the IP addresses for the DNS servers are to be manually configured, select **Use the following DNS server addresses** option button. Type the IP addresses of the preferred and alternate DNS servers in the appropriate boxes.

To specify additional alternate DNS servers

1. In **Control Panel, select Network and Internet Connections**.

2. In the **Network and Internet Connections** sheet, select **Network Connections**.

3. On the **General** tab of the **Network Connections Properties** sheet, click **Advanced**.

4. Click the **DNS** tab.

5. Under **DNS server addresses, in order of use**, click **Add**.

6. Type the IP address of the DNS server that you want to add.

7. Click **Add**.

   To remove an IP address from the list, select it, and then click **Remove**.
   The order of the IP addresses, and thus the search order, can be rearranged as needed to reflect changes in name server availability or performance, or to implement load balancing.

To set the DNS server search order

1. In **Control Panel, select Network and Internet Connections**.

2. In the **Network and Internet Connections** sheet, select **Network Connections**.

3. Right-click **Local Area Connections**, and click **Properties**.

4. On the **General** tab, in the **Local Area Connection Properties** dialog box, select **Internet Protocol (TCP/IP)**, and click **Properties**.

5. On the **General** tab, in the **Internet Protocol (TCP/IP)** dialog box, click **Advanced**.

6. In the **Advanced TCP/IP Settings** dialog box, click the **DNS** tab.

7. In the **DNS server addresses, in order of use** box, select the IP address of the DNS server that you want to reposition.

8. Click the up-arrow or down-arrow button to reposition the selected IP address within the list of DNS servers, and click **OK**.

DNS Caching, Network Prioritization, and Security

The default settings of DNS might need to be changed in order to optimize the performance and security of the Windows XP Professional DNS client. You can make configuration changes in order to:

- Configure caching and negative caching.

- Configure Subnet prioritization.

- Prevent the resolver from receiving responses from nonqueried servers.

Configuring Caching and Negative Caching   When the Windows XP Professional resolver receives a positive or negative response to a query, it adds that positive or negative response to its cache, thus creating a *DNS resource record*. The resolver always checks the cache before querying any DNS server, so if a DNS resource record is in the cache, the resolver uses the record from the cache rather than querying a server. This expedites queries and decreases network traffic for DNS queries.

You can use the Ipconfig tool to view and to flush the DNS resolver cache.

To view the DNS resolver cache

- At the command prompt, type:
  ipconfig /displaydns

Ipconfig displays the contents of the DNS resolver cache, including the DNS resource records preloaded from the Hosts file as well as any recently queried names that were resolved by the system.

After a certain amount of time, specified in the Time to Live (TTL) associated with the DNS resource record, the resolver discards the record from the cache. You can also flush the cache manually. After you flush the cache, the computer must query DNS servers again for any DNS resource records previously resolved by the computer.

To flush the cache manually by using Ipconfig

■ At the command prompt, type:
ipconfig /flushdns

The local Hosts file is preloaded into the resolver's cache and reloaded into the cache whenever Hosts is updated.

The length of time for which a positive or negative response is cached depends on the values of entries in the following registry subkey:

HKEY_LOCAL_MACHINE\SYSTEM\CurrentControlSet\Services\DNSCache\ Parameters

The TTL for positive responses is the lesser of the following values:

■ the number of seconds specified in the query response the resolver received

■ the value of the registry entry **MaxCacheEntryTtlLimit**

The default TTL for positive responses is 86,400 seconds (1 day).

The TTL for negative responses is the number of seconds specified in the registry entry **NegativeCacheTime**.

The default TTL for negative responses is 300 seconds. If you do not want negative responses to be cached at all, set the value of **NegativeCacheTime** to 0.

> **Caution**   Do not edit the registry unless you have no alternative. The registry editor bypasses standard safeguards, allowing settings that can damage your system, or even require you to reinstall Windows. If you must edit the registry, back it up first and see the Registry Reference in the Microsoft Windows 2000 Server Resource Kit at http://www.microsoft.com/reskit.

Configuring Subnet Prioritization   Each DNS database consists of resource records. In general, resource records contain information related to a particular host computer, such as its IP address, owner of the host, or the type of services it provides. Table 22-4 lists some of the common types of resource records.

Table 22-4   Common Types of Resource Records

Resource Record Type	Description	Explanation
SOA	Start of Authority	This record designates the start of a zone. It contains information such as the name of the zone, the e-mail address of the zone administrator, and settings that control how secondary DNS servers update the zone data files.
A	Address	This record lists the IP address of a particular host name. This is the key record for name resolution.
PTR	Pointer	This record designates a reverse mapping of a host IP address to a host DNS domain name.
CNAME	Canonical Name	This record specifies an alias or nickname for the standard (canonical) host name.
MX	Mail Exchanger	This record lists the host computer that is responsible for receiving e-mail sent to a domain.
NS	Name Server	This record specifies the name server responsible for a given zone.

If the resolver receives multiple IP address mappings (A resource records) from a DNS server, and some of the records have IP addresses from networks to which the computer is directly connected, the resolver places those resource records first. This reduces network traffic across subnets by forcing computers to connect to network resources that are closer to them.

For example, suppose there are three Web servers that all host the Web page for www.reskit.com, and they are all located on different subnets. The DNS name server for the network contains the following resource records:

```
www.reskit.com.IN  A172.16.64.11
www.reskit.com.IN  A172.17.64.22
www.reskit.com.IN  A172.18.64.33
```

When a Windows XP Professional–based computer's DNS resolver (client) receives a response to the query for the A record of www.reskit.com, it returns A records in order starting with the IP addresses from subnets to which the computer is directly connected. For example, if a computer with the IP address 172.17.64.93 is queried for www.reskit.com, the resolver returns the resource records in the following order:

```
www.reskit.com.IN  A172.17.64.22
www.reskit.com.IN  A172.16.64.11
www.reskit.com.IN  A172.18.64.33
```

Subnet prioritization prevents the resolver from choosing the first IP address returned in the DNS query and using the DNS server's round robin feature (defined in RFC 1794.) With *round robin* enabled, the server rotates the order of resource records returned when multiple A resource records exist for a queried DNS domain name. Thus, in the example described earlier, if a user queried for www.reskit.com, the name server replies to the first client request by ordering the addresses as follows:

```
172.16.64.11
172.17.64.22
172.18.64.33
```

It replies to the second client request by ordering the addresses as follows:

```
172.17.64.22
172.18.64.33
172.16.64.11
```

It replies to the third client request by ordering the addresses as follows:

```
172.18.64.33
172.16.64.11
172.17.64.22
```

With round robin enabled, if clients are configured to use the first IP address in the list that they receive, different clients will use different IP addresses, thus balancing the load among multiple network resources with the same name. However, if the resolvers are configured for subnet prioritization, the resolvers reorder the list to favor IP addresses from networks to which they are directly connected, reducing the effectiveness of the round robin feature.

Although subnet prioritization does reduce network traffic across subnets, in some cases you might prefer to have the round robin feature work as described in RFC 1794. If so, you can disable the subnet prioritization feature on your clients by adding the registry entry **PrioritizeRecordData** with a value of 0 (REG_DWORD data type) in the following registry subkey:

HKEY_LOCAL_MACHINE\SYSTEM\CurrentControlSet\Services\DnsCache\ Parameters

Preventing the Resolver from Accepting Responses from Nonqueried Servers By default, the resolver accepts responses from servers that it did not query, as well as from those it did. This presents a possible security liability, in that unauthorized DNS servers might pass along invalid A resource records for the purpose of misdirecting subsequent DNS queries. If you want to disable this feature, add the registry entry

QueryIpMatching with a value of 1 (REG_DWORD data type) to the following registry subkey:

HKEY_LOCAL_MACHINE\SYSTEM\CurrentControlSet\Services\DnsCache\Parameters

> **Caution**   Do not edit the registry unless you have no alternative. The registry editor bypasses standard safeguards, allowing settings that can damage your system, or even require you to reinstall Windows. If you must edit the registry, back it up first and see the Registry Reference in the Microsoft Windows 2000 Server Resource Kit at http://www.microsoft.com/reskit.

Configuring Dynamic Update

Windows XP Professional–based computers can dynamically update DNS entries in a manner compliant with RFC 2136. Dynamic update allows clients and servers to register DNS domain names (PTR resource records) and IP address mappings (A resource records) to an RFC 2136–compliant DNS server. This frees administrators from the time-consuming process of manually updating DNS entries.

Using Windows XP Professional, clients can send dynamic updates through three types of network connections: DHCP configured connections, statically configured connections, and remote access connections. By default, the DNS client on Windows XP Professional does not attempt dynamic update over a Remote Access or Virtual Private Network (VPN) connection. Regardless of which connection type is used, the DHCP client service sends dynamic updates to the authoritative DNS server. The DHCP client service runs on all computers regardless of whether they are configured as DHCP clients.

Configuring Dynamic Update for DHCP Clients

By default in Windows XP Professional, the DHCP client feature is configured to request that the client register the A resource record, and that the DHCP server register the PTR resource record. By default, the name used in the DNS registration is a concatenation of the computer name and the primary DNS suffix. You can change this default by using the TCP/IP Properties sheet for your network connection.

To change the dynamic update defaults on the dynamic update client

1. In **Control Panel**, **select Network and Internet Connections**.

2. In the **Network and Internet Connections** sheet, **select Network Connections**.

3. In **Network Connections**, right-click the local area network connection that you want to change, and then click **Properties**.

4. Right-click the connection that you want to configure, and then click **Properties**.

5. Select **Internet Protocol (TCP/IP)**, click **Properties**, click **Advanced**, and then select the **DNS** tab.

6. To configure the client to make no requests for DNS registration, cancel the selection of **Register this connection's address in DNS**. Under this configuration, the client will not attempt to register any A or PTR DNS records corresponding to this connection.

   - or -

   To change the dynamic update default, select **Use this connection's DNS suffix in DNS registration**.

If you choose to select **Use this connection's DNS suffix in DNS registration**, the client requests that the server update the PTR record, using the name that is a concatenation of the computer name and the connection-specific DNS suffix. If the DHCP server is configured to register DNS records according to the client's request, the client will then register the following:

- The PTR record, using the name that is a concatenation of the computer name and the primary DNS suffix.

- The A record, using the name that is a concatenation of the computer name and the primary DNS suffix.

- The A record, using the name that is a concatenation of the computer name and the connection-specific DNS suffix.

Statically Configured and Remote Access Clients

Statically configured clients and remote access clients do not communicate with the DHCP server.

Statically configured Windows XP Professional clients dynamically update their A and PTR resource records every time they start, just in case the records become corrupted in the DNS database.

Remote access clients dynamically update their A and PTR resource records when a dial-up connection is made. They also attempt to cancel the registration of the A and PTR resource records when the user terminates the connection. However, if a remote access client fails to cancel the registration of a resource record within four seconds, it terminates the connection and the DNS database contains a stale record. If the remote access client fails to de-register a resource record, it adds a message to the event log, which you can view by using the Event Viewer. The remote access client never deletes stale records.

> **Note** By default, the DNS client on Windows XP Professional and Windows XP Home Edition do not attempt dynamic update over a Remote Access Service or Virtual Private Network connection.

Multihomed Clients

If a dynamic update client is *multihomed* (has more than one adapter and associated IP address), by default it registers DNS A record(s) containing the first IP address on each network connection. If you do not want the dynamic update client to register all of its IP addresses, you can configure it to not register A and PTR records containing the IP address(es) of one or more network connections. For more information about multihoming, see "Configuring TCP/IP" in this book.

To prevent the computer from registering A and PTR records containing the IP address on a specific network connection

1. In **Control Panel**, select **Network and Internet Connections**.

2. In the **Network and Internet Connections** sheet, select **Network Connections**.

3. In Network Connections, right-click the local area network connection that you want to change, and then click **Properties**.

4. Select **Internet Protocol (TCP/IP)**, click **Properties**, click **Advanced**, and then select the **DNS** tab.

5. Clear the **Register this connection's address in DNS** check box.

The dynamic update client does not register all IP addresses with all DNS servers. For example, Figure 22-13 shows a multihomed computer, client1.noam.reskit.com, which is connected to both the Internet and the corporate intranet. Client1 is connected to the intranet by adapter A, a DHCP adapter with the IP address 172.16.8.7. Client1 is also connected to the Internet by adapter B, a remote access adapter with the IP address 131.107.0.16. Client1 resolves intranet names by using a name server on the intranet, NoamDC1, and resolves Internet names by using a name server on the Internet, ISPNameServer.

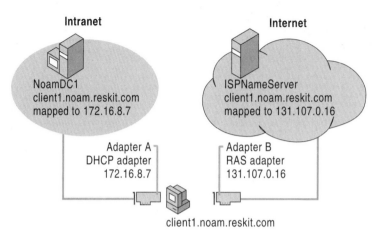

Intranet

NoamDC1
client1.noam.reskit.com
mapped to 172.16.8.7

Internet

ISPNameServer
client1.noam.reskit.com
mapped to 131.107.0.16

Adapter A
DHCP adapter
172.16.8.7

Adapter B
RAS adapter
131.107.0.16

client1.noam.reskit.com

Figure 22-13 Dynamic update for multihomed clients

Note that although Client1 is connected to both networks, the IP address 172.16.8.7 is reachable only through adapter A, and the IP address 131.107.99.1 is reachable only through adapter B. Therefore, when the dynamic update client registers the IP addresses for Client1, it does not register both IP addresses with both name servers. Instead, it registers the name-to-IP address mapping for adapter A with NoamDC1 and the name-to-IP address mapping for adapter B with ISP-NameServer.

Disabling Dynamic Update

Dynamic update is configured on Windows XP Professional clients by default. Dynamic update can be disabled for all network interfaces on the computer by adding the registry entry **DisableDynamicUpdate** with a value of 1 (REG_DWORD data type) to the following registry subkey:

HKEY_LOCAL_MACHINE\SYSTEM\CurrentControlSet\Services\Tcpip\Parameters

> **Caution** Do not edit the registry unless you have no alternative. The registry editor bypasses standard safeguards, allowing settings that can damage your system, or even require you to reinstall Windows. If you must edit the registry, back it up first and see the Registry Reference in the Microsoft Windows 2000 Server Resource Kit at http://www.microsoft.com/reskit.

To disable dynamic update for the network interface card with the device ID of *interface,* add the entry **DisableDynamicUpdate** with a value of 1 (REG_DWORD data type) to the following registry subkey:

HKEY_LOCAL_MACHINE\SYSTEM\CurrentControlSet\Services\Tcpip\Parameters\Interfaces*interface-name*

If this entry exists in both the Interfaces subkey and the specific interface-name subkey, the more global of the two subkeys takes precedence.

Editing Hosts Files

For networks without access to a DNS name server, the creation of a local host table file, called a Hosts file, can provide host name resolution for applications and services. This file can also be used in an environment where name servers are available, but not all hosts are registered. For example, a Hosts file can be used for a server that is not available for general use, but is only to be accessed by a limited number of clients. This file must be manually created, and must be updated as host names and addresses change.

TCP/IP in Windows XP Professional can be configured to search Hosts for mappings of remote host names to IP addresses. The Hosts file format is the same as the format for host tables in the 4.3 Berkeley Software Distribution (BSD) UNIX */etc/ Hosts file*. For example, the entry for a computer with an address of 192.176.73.6 and a host name of client1.reskit.com looks like this:

```
192.176.73.6      client1.reskit.com
```

The Hosts file can be created and modified with an ordinary text editor. An example of the Hosts format is provided in the file named Hosts in the Windows XP Professional *systemroot*\System32\Drivers\Etc directory That Hosts file can be edited to include remote host names and IP addresses for each computer with which you communicate.

Configuring NetBIOS Name Resolution

Microsoft TCP/IP uses NetBIOS over TCP/IP (NetBT) as specified in RFCs 1001 and 1002, which define a software interface that supports name resolution for NetBIOS client and server programs in the LAN and WAN environments. Although DNS is the default name-resolution method for Windows XP Professional, NetBT is still provided to support NetBIOS methods of name resolution for clients running versions of Windows earlier than Windows 2000, and for Windows 2000 domains and Windows XP Professional and Windows 2000 workgroups that do not implement Active Directory.

The following discussion describes the types of name-resolution methods that are available through NetBIOS over TCP/IP (including WINS) and contains procedures for configuring the different resolution methods.

NetBIOS Name-Resolution Basics

RFCs 1001 and 1002 define the following four node types:

- **B-node**. Uses broadcasts to resolve names.

- **P-node**. Uses point-to-point communications with a NetBIOS server (such as a WINS server) to resolve names.

- **M-node**. Uses broadcasts first (b-node), then uses directed name queries (p-node) if broadcasts are not successful.

- **H-node**. Uses name queries first (p-node), and then uses broadcasts (b-node) if the name server is unavailable or if the name is not registered in the WINS database.

A fifth node type is unique to the Windows implementation of IP name resolution and is defined by Microsoft:

- **Microsoft-enhanced**. Uses the local Lmhosts file plus Windows Sockets **gethostbyname( )** calls (using standard DNS and/or local Hosts files) in addition to standard node types.

Windows includes a NetBIOS name server known as the Windows Internet Name Service (WINS). If WINS is enabled on a Windows XP Professional–based computer, the system uses h-node by default. Without WINS, the system uses b-node by default. Non-WINS clients can access WINS through a WINS proxy, which is a WINS-enabled computer that listens to name query broadcasts and then queries the WINS server on behalf of the requesting client.

To see which node type is configured on a Windows XP Professional–based computer

- At the command prompt, type:
  ipconfig /all
  The node type is indicated to the right of the heading **Node type**.

Using a name server to locate resources is generally preferable to broadcasting, for two reasons:

- Broadcasts are not usually forwarded by routers. Therefore, only local subnet NetBIOS names can be resolved.

- Broadcast frames are processed by all computers on a subnet.

Figures 22-14 (part 1) and 22-15 (part 2) illustrate the NetBIOS name-resolution methods used by Windows XP Professional.

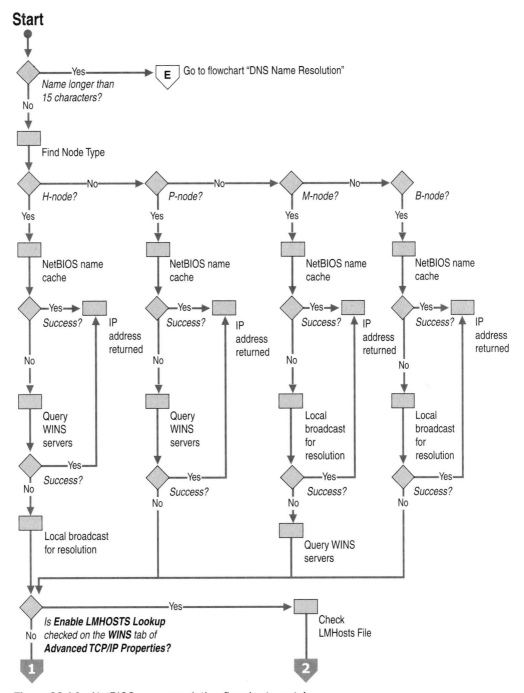

Figure 22-14   NetBIOS name-resolution flowchart, part 1

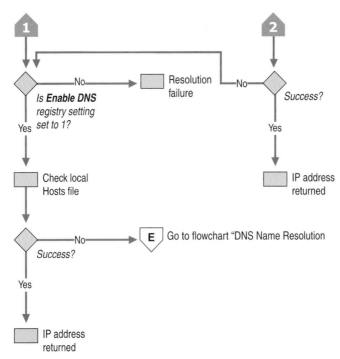

Figure 22-15   NetBIOS name-resolution flowchart, part 2

Name Resolution Using WINS

Windows Internet Name Service (WINS) is a service that runs on Windows 2000 Server to provide NetBIOS name resolution. It provides a database for registering and querying dynamic NetBIOS name-to-IP address mappings in a routed network environment. You can use WINS either alone or in conjunction with DNS.

WINS reduces the use of local broadcasts for name resolution and allows users to locate computers on remote networks. Furthermore, when dynamic addressing through DHCP results in new IP addresses for computers that move between subnets, the changes are updated automatically in the WINS database. Neither the user nor the network administrator needs to make manual accommodations for name resolution.

WINS consists of two components: the WINS server, which handles name queries and registrations, and the client software (NetBIOS over TCP/IP), which queries for computer name resolution. The IP addresses of a WINS server need to be configured on your Windows XP Professional client to provide NetBIOS name resolution. In a network where dynamic update is not available, a WINS server can provide a DNS server configured for WINS lookup with dynamic updates of host names, provided that WINS is enabled at each client.

A WINS server is a Windows Server–based (that is, Windows NT Server version 3.5 or later) computer running the WINS server service. When TCP/IP is implemented under Windows XP Professional, WINS client software is installed automatically. WINS client support is configured with Windows XP Professional to maintain compatibility with computers not running Windows 2000 or Windows XP Professional operating systems, including clients and servers running versions of Windows earlier than Windows 2000.

If there are WINS servers installed on your network, you can use WINS in combination with broadcast name queries to resolve NetBIOS computer names to IP addresses. If you do not use this option, Windows XP Professional can use name query broadcasts (b-node mode of NetBIOS over TCP/IP), and the local Lmhosts file to resolve computer names to IP addresses. However, broadcast resolution is limited to the local network.

Additionally, a WINS server can be used in conjunction with a DNS server to provide dynamic registration of hosts in an environment without DNS update. When configured to use WINS lookup, a DNS server can forward queries to a WINS server for resolution of unknown A resource records for all WINS clients.

If DHCP is used for autoconfiguration, WINS server parameters can be provided by the DHCP server. Otherwise, you must configure information about WINS servers manually. WINS configuration is local for each network adaptor on a computer. The WINS server(s) for one network adaptor on a computer does not necessarily have to be the WINS server(s) for another network adaptor on the same computer.

Configuring WINS

The following procedure describes how to configure WINS and how to enable DHCP

To configure a computer to use WINS for name resolution

1. In **Control Panel**, select **Network and Internet Connections**.

2. In the **Network and Internet Connections** sheet, select **Network Connections**.

3. In **Network Connections**, right-click the local area network connection that you want to change, and then click **Properties**.

4. Select **Internet Protocol (TCP/IP)**, and then click **Properties**.

5. If a DHCP server is available, that is configured to provide information on available WINS servers, select **Obtain an IP address automatically**.

   - or -

   If the WINS server information is not available from a DHCP server, do the following:

   a. Click **Advanced**.

    b. Select the **WINS** tab.

    c. Click **Add**.

    d. Enter the address of the WINS server, and click **Add**.

Figure 22-16 shows the WINS tab of the Advanced TCP/IP Settings dialog box.

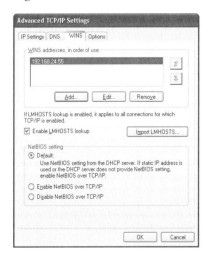

Figure 22-16   WINS tab of the Advanced TCP/IP Settings dialog box

The order of the IP addresses can be rearranged as needed to reflect changes in name server availability or performance, or to implement load balancing.

To set the WINS server search order

1. On the **WINS** tab, under the **WINS addresses, in order of use** box, select the IP address of the WINS server that you want to reposition.

2. Click the up-arrow or down-arrow button to reposition the selected IP address within the list of WINS servers.

B-Node Broadcasts and Lmhosts

By default, a Windows XP Professional–based computer that is not configured as a WINS client or WINS server is configured as a *b-node* computer. A b-node computer is one that uses IP broadcasts for NetBIOS name resolution.

IP broadcasts can provide dynamic name resolution by registering address-to-name mappings in the computer's cache. However, IP broadcasts have the following disadvantages:

- They can lead to increase network traffic.

- They are ineffective in routed networks. Resources located outside the local subnet do not receive name queries that are sent as IP broadcasts, because IP-broadcast packets are not passed to remote subnets by the router (default gateway) on the local subnet.

For networks without access to a WINS name server, Windows XP Professional enables you to manually provide NetBIOS name and IP address mappings for remote computers by using the Lmhosts file. This file can also be used in an environment where name servers are available, but not all hosts are registered; for example, a server that is not available for general use, but is only to be accessed by a limited number of clients.

Selected mappings from the Lmhosts file are maintained in a limited cache of NetBIOS computer names and IP address mappings. This memory cache is initialized when a computer is started. When the computer needs to resolve a name, the cache is examined first and, if there is no match in the cache, Windows XP Professional uses b-node IP broadcasts to try to find the NetBIOS computer. If the IP broadcast name query fails, the complete Lmhosts file is parsed to find the NetBIOS name and the corresponding IP address. This strategy enables the Lmhosts file to contain a large number of mappings, without requiring a large amount of static memory to maintain an infrequently used cache.

The Lmhosts file can be used to map computer names and IP addresses for computers outside the local subnet, an advantage over the b-node broadcast method. You can use the Lmhosts file to find remote computers for network file, print, and remote procedure services. The Lmhosts file is typically used for smaller networks that do not have name servers.

The Lmhosts file is a local text file that maps IP addresses to NetBIOS names. It contains entries for Windows-networking computers located outside of the local subnet. The Lmhosts file is read when WINS or broadcast name resolution fails; resolved entries are stored in a local cache for later access.

You can create an Lmhosts file by using a text editor. Lmhosts is a simple text file. An example of the Lmhosts format is provided in the file named Lmhosts.sam in the Windows XP Professional *systemroot*\System32\Drivers\Etc directory. This is only an example file. To activate the Lmhosts file, rename Lmhosts.sam to Lmhosts. Edit the Lmhosts file to include remote NetBIOS names and IP addresses for each computer with which you communicate.

The keywords listed in Table 22-5 can be used in the Lmhosts file in Windows XP Professional.

Table 22-5 Lmhosts Keywords

Keyword	Description
\0x*nn*	Support for nonprinting characters in NetBIOS names. Enclose the NetBIOS name in double quotation marks and use \0x*nn* notation to specify a hexadecimal value for the character. This enables custom applications that use special names to function properly in routed topologies. However, Microsoft® LAN Manager TCP/IP does not recognize the hexadecimal format.
	Note that the hexadecimal notation applies only to one character in the name. Use blanks to pad the name so that the special character is last in the string.
BEGIN_ALTERNATE	Used to group multiple INCLUDE statements. Any single successful INCLUDE statement causes the group to succeed.
END_ALTERNATE	Used to mark the end of an INCLUDE statement grouping.
DOM: *domain*	Part of the computer name-to-IP address mapping entry that indicates that the IP address is a domain controller in the domain specified by *domain*. This keyword affects how the Browser and Logon services behave in routed TCP/IP environments. To preload a DOM entry, you must first add the PRE keyword to the line. DOM groups are limited to 25 members.
INCLUDE *filename*	Forces the system to seek the specified *filename* and parse it as if it were local. Specifying a Uniform Naming Convention (UNC) *filename* allows you to use a centralized Lmhosts file on a server. If the server on which the specified *filename* exists is outside of the local broadcast subnet, you must add a preloaded entry for the server.
MH	Part of the computer name-to-IP-address-mapping entry that defines the entry as a unique name that can have more than one address. The maximum number of addresses that can be assigned to a unique name is 25. The number of entries is equal to the number of network adapters in a multihomed computer.
PRE	Part of the computer name-to-IP address mapping entry that causes that entry to be preloaded into the name cache. (By default, entries are not preloaded into the name cache but are parsed only after WINS and name query broadcasts fail to resolve a name.) The PRE keyword must be appended for entries that also appear in INCLUDE statements; otherwise, the entry in the INCLUDE statement is ignored.
SG *name*	Part of the computer name-to-IP address mapping entry that associates that entry with a user-defined special (Internet) group specified by *name*. The SG keyword defines Internet groups by using a NetBIOS name that has 0x20 in the 16th byte. A special group is limited to 25 members.

The following example shows how all of these keywords are used:

```
192.176.94.102    "appname        \0x14"            #special app server
192.176.94.123    printsrv    #PRE                  #source server
192.176.94.98     localsrv    #PRE
192.176.94.97     primary     #PRE   #DOM:mydomain  #PDC for mydomain

#BEGIN_ALTERNATE
#INCLUDE \\localsrv\public\lmhosts       #adds Lmhosts from this server
#INCLUDE \\primary\public\lmhosts        #adds Lmhosts from this server
#END_ALTERNATE
```

In the preceding example:

- The servers named printsrv, localsrv, and primary are defined, by the #PRE keyword, as entries to be preloaded into the NetBIOS cache at system startup.

- The servers named localsrv and primary are defined as preloaded and also identified in the #INCLUDE statements as the location of the centrally maintained Lmhosts file.

- Note that the server named "appname   \0x14" contains a special character after the first 15 characters in its name (including the blanks) and so its name is enclosed in double quotation marks.

- The number sign, when not used with a keyword, designates the start of a comment.

WINS Proxy

RFC 1001 cautions against using the b-node method for name resolution in a routed network — that is, relying on broadcasts for name queries. However, in practice, b-nodes are sometimes useful in routed networks, and sometimes b-nodes cannot be removed or updated. For this reason, Microsoft introduced WINS Proxies. A *WINS Proxy* is a WINS-enabled computer that helps to resolve name queries for computers that are not WINS-enabled in routed TCP/IP networks.

By default, computers that are not WINS-enabled use b-node name resolution. The WINS Proxy listens on the local subnet for b-node name-service broadcasts, and responds on behalf of those names that are not on the local network. A WINS Proxy communicates with the WINS server, by means of directed datagrams, to retrieve the information necessary to respond to these broadcasts.

Because the WINS server does not respond to broadcasts, it is best if a computer configured as a WINS Proxy is installed on subnets containing computers that are not WINS-enabled.

The WINS Proxy checks broadcast name registrations against the WINS database by sending name-query requests to ensure that the names do not conflict with other names in the database. If a name exists in the WINS database, by default the WINS Proxy will send a negative name-registration response to the computer trying to register the name. In response to a name-release request, the WINS Proxy simply deletes the name from its cache of remote names.

The WINS Proxy always differentiates name queries for names on the local subnet from queries for remote names elsewhere in the network. It compares the subnet mask of any name it has resolved against its own subnet mask; if the two match, the WINS Proxy does not respond to the name query.

When the WINS Proxy receives a name query, it checks its remote name table. If the WINS Proxy does not find the name in the remote name table, it queries the WINS server, and then enters the name into the remote name table in a "resolving" state. If the WINS Proxy receives a query for the same name before the WINS server has responded, the WINS Proxy does not query the WINS server again. When the WINS Proxy receives the response from the WINS server, the WINS Proxy updates the remote table entry with the correct address and changes the state to "resolved." The WINS Proxy only sends a reply message to the Windows XP Professional client if the WINS Proxy has the response already in its cache.

The behavior of a b-node client does not change when a WINS Proxy is added to the local subnet. If the first name-resolution query times out, the client tries again. If the WINS Proxy has the answer cached by the time it intercepts the new query, the WINS Proxy answers the Windows XP Professional client.

Disabling NetBT

Windows XP Professional file and print sharing components use NetBT to communicate with versions of Windows earlier than Windows 2000 and with non-Windows clients. However, the Windows XP Professional file and print sharing components (the redirector and server) support *direct hosting* for communicating with other computers running Windows XP Professional and Windows 2000. With direct hosting, DNS is used for name resolution. No NetBIOS name resolution (WINS or broadcast) is used and no NetBIOS sessions are established.

By default, both NetBT and direct hosting are enabled, and both are tried in parallel when a new connection is being established. The first method to succeed is used to establish the connection. You can disable NetBIOS support so that all traffic must use direct hosting.

To disable NetBT support

1. In **Control Panel**, select **Network and Internet Connections**.

2. In the **Network and Internet Connections** sheet, select **Network Connections**.

3. In **Network Connections**, right-click the local area network connection that you want to change, and then click **Properties**.

4. Select **Internet Protocol (TCP/IP)**, and then click **Properties**.

5. Click **Advanced**.

6. Select the **WINS Address** tab.

7. Select **Disable NetBIOS over TCP/IP**.

> **Warning**   If you disable NetBIOS support, applications and services that depend on NetBIOS over TCP/IP will no longer function. Therefore, it is imperative that you verify that clients and applications no longer need such support before you disable it. Disabling NetBT can prevent creation of file- and print-sharing connections with clients and servers that are not running Windows XP Professional or Windows 2000.

Troubleshooting Name Resolution and Addressing

When troubleshooting any connectivity issues, it is important to first ascertain whether the error condition was caused by a failure in host name resolution (for example, www.reskit.com) or in NetBIOS name resolution (for example, *computername*). If name resolution does not appear to be the problem, use TCP/IP troubleshooting tools such as Ping and Tracert to verify that IP addressing has been correctly configured on the Windows XP Professional–based client. For more information about TCP/IP troubleshooting tools, see "Configuring TCP/IP" in this book.

The easiest way to distinguish host name resolution problems from NetBIOS name resolution problems is to find out whether the failing application uses NetBIOS or Windows Sockets. Most Internet or intranet-based applications (such as Internet Explorer and other Web browsers, ftp clients and telnet) use Windows Sockets. If the application uses Windows Sockets, the problem lies with host name resolution. If the application uses NetBIOS, the problem is with NetBIOS name resolution (broadcast, Lmhosts or WINS). You can troubleshoot NetBIOS name-resolution problems with the various **net** commands and with the Windows NT 4.0 administrator tools.

Checking NetBIOS Name Resolution

Several methods are available for detecting and resolving the most common types of NetBIOS name-resolution problems.

Resolving NetBios Error 53

The most common symptom of a problem in NetBIOS name resolution is that the Ping tool returns an Error 53 message. The Error 53 message is generally returned when name resolution for a particular computer name fails, but Error 53 can also occur when there is a problem establishing a NetBIOS session. You can use the **net view** command to distinguish between these two cases.

To determine the cause of an Error 53 message

- At the command prompt, type:
  net view * *hostname*
  where *hostname* is a network resource that you know is active.

  If the hostname and a list of the host's shares appear on the screen, name resolution is probably not the source of the problem. It is possible, on occasion, for name resolution to be functioning properly and yet **net use** still returns Error 53 (for example, when a DNS or WINS server has a bad entry).

To confirm that name resolution is definitely not the source of your problem, try pinging the host name. If Ping also shows that name resolution fails (by returning the "Unknown host" message), check the status of your NetBIOS session.

To check the status of your NetBIOS session

- At the command prompt, type:
  net view *ip address*
  where *ip address* is the same network resource that you used to determine the cause of the Error 53 message. If this also fails, the problem is in establishing a session.

If the computer is on the local subnet, confirm that the name is spelled correctly and that the target computer is running TCP/IP as well. If the computer is not on the local subnet, be sure that its name and IP address mapping are available in the DNS database, the Hosts or Lmhosts file, or the WINS database.

If all TCP/IP elements appear to be installed properly, Ping the remote computer to be sure that it has TCP/IP enabled.

Checking the Lmhosts File

The name resolution problem might be in your Lmhosts file, which looks for addresses sequentially from the top down. If more than one address is listed for the same host name, TCP/IP returns the first value it encounters, whether or not that value is accurate.

You can find the Lmhosts file in *systemroot*\\System32\\Drivers\\Etc. Note that this file does not exist by default; a sample file named Lmhosts.sam is supplied. This file must be renamed to Lmhosts before it can be used.

> **Note**   Although *systemroot*\System32\Drivers\Etc is the default directory for the Lmhosts file, exactly which Lmhosts file is parsed depends on the value of the registry entry **databasepath** located in the subkey HKEY_LOCAL_MACHINE\SYSTEM\CurrentControlSet\Services\Tcpip\ Parameters.
>
> The database path tells the local computer where to look for the Lmhosts file.

Checking the WINS Configuration

Check to see that the WINS configuration is correct. In particular, check the address for the WINS server.

To check your WINS configuration

1. In **Control Panel, select Network and Internet Connections**.

2. In the **Network and Internet Connections** sheet, **select Network Connections**.

3. In **Network Connections**, right-click the local area connection that you want to change, and then click **Properties**.

4. In the **Local Area Connection Properties** sheet, select **Internet Protocol (TCP/IP)**, and then click **Properties**.

5. In the **Internet Protocol (TCP/IP) Properties** sheet, click **Advanced**.

6. In the **Advanced TCP/IP Settings** dialog box, click the **WINS** tab.

7. In the **WINS configuration** dialog box, add the server's IP address (if none is listed).

8. Check to see whether Lmhosts lookup is enabled.

9. Check to see whether NetBIOS settings are taken from the DHCP server, or whether NetBIOS is enabled or disabled. If you are using DHCP for this host computer, select **Use NetBIOS setting from the DHCP server**. Otherwise, select **enable NetBIOS over TCP/IP**.

Checking Hosts Files and DNS Name Resolution

If your problem is with Windows Sockets, rather than with NetBIOS, you might have either a Hosts file error or a DNS configuration error. If you are using a Hosts file for host name resolution, you need to verify that the settings in the file are correct. If you are using DNS for host name resolution, verify that the DNS configuration is correct.

Checking the Hosts File

If you are having trouble connecting to a remote system using a host name, and you use a Hosts file for name resolution, the problem might be with the contents of that file. Make sure that the name of the remote computer is spelled correctly in the Hosts file and by the application using the file.

The Hosts file or a DNS server is used to resolve host names to IP addresses whenever you use TCP/IP tools such as Ping. You can find the Hosts file in *systemroot*\System32\Drivers\Etc.

This file is not dynamic; all entries are made manually. The file format is the following:

```
172.16.48.10    testpc1.reskit.com
```

The IP address and the friendly host name are always separated by one or more space or tab characters.

The following Hosts file problems can cause networking errors:

- The Hosts file does not contain the specified host name.

- The host name is misspelled, either in the Hosts file or in the command.

- The IP address for the specified host name, as it appears in the Hosts file, is invalid or incorrect.

- The Hosts file contains multiple entries for the same host on separate lines. Because the Hosts file is parsed from the top, the first entry found is used.

Checking Your DNS Configuration

If you are using DNS, be sure that you have checked the DNS tab of the Advanced TCP/IP Settings dialog box to confirm that the IP addresses of the DNS servers are correct and in the proper order. Use Ping with the remote computer's host name, and then use its IP address to determine whether the host address is being resolved properly. If the host name ping fails and the IP address ping succeeds, the problem is with name resolution.

To check DNS configuration

1. In **Control Panel**, **select Network and Internet Connections**.

2. In the **Network and Internet Connections** sheet, select **Network Connections**.

3. In **Network Connections**, right-click the local area connection that you want to change, and then click **Properties**.

4. Click **Internet Protocol (TCP/IP)**, and then click **Properties**.

5. In the **Microsoft TCP/IP Properties** sheet, click the **Advanced** tab.

6. Click the **DNS** tab.

7. Confirm that DNS is configured properly. If you find that the IP address of a particular DNS server is missing, be sure to add it to the list of DNS server addresses.

> **Note** This procedure does not apply to network connections configured by DHCP servers, as DHCP servers configure network connections with preferred and alternate DNS servers.

You can test whether the DNS servers are running by pinging their IP addresses or by opening a Telnet session to port 53 on the DNS server. If the connection is established successfully, the DNS service is working on the DNS server. After you have verified that the DNS service is running, you can perform **Nslookup** queries to the DNS server to further verify the status of the DNS records for which you are looking. For more information about **Nslookup** and other aspects of DNS configuration, see "Windows 2000 DNS" in the *TCP/IP Core Networking Guide* of the *Microsoft Windows 2000 Server Resource Kit*.

If both pinging by IP address and pinging by name fail, the problem is with the network connection, possibly physical connectivity or routing. For more information about troubleshooting network connectivity, see "Configuring TCP/IP" in this book.

For more information about how DNS resolves host names, see "Configuring DNS to Resolve Host Names and Domain Names" earlier in this chapter.

DNS Error Messages

Errors in name resolution can occur when the entries in a DNS server or client are not configured correctly, when the DNS server is not running, or when there is a problem with network connectivity. To determine the cause of any name resolution problem, you can use the **nslookup** command-line tool.

Failed queries return a variety of messages, depending on whether the name cannot be resolved, the server does not provide a response, or the request times out. These messages generally indicate one of the following:

- The server is offline.

- The host computer does not have the DNS client service enabled.

- There is a hardware or routing problem.

Troubleshooting IP Addressing

If host name resolution is successful, the problem must be something else. The solution might simply be a matter of correcting the IP configuration.

TCP/IP troubleshooting generally follows a set pattern. First, verify that the TCP/IP configuration on the problem computer is correct. The **ipconfig** command can be used to get the host computer configuration information, including the IP address, subnet mask, and default gateway. For more information about **ipconfig**, see "Configuring TCP/IP" in this book.

Next, verify that a connection and a route exist between the computer and the destination host by using Ping and/or PathPing. Ping helps to verify IP-level connectivity; PathPing detects packet loss over multiple-hop trips. For more information about how these tools can be used to troubleshoot IP addressing problems, see "Configuring TCP/IP" in this book.

If you have successfully pinged both your own machine and the loopback address, clear out the Address Resolution Protocol (ARP) cache and restart your computer (for information about clearing out the ARP cache, see "Configuring TCP/IP" in this book). In addition, make certain that the default gateway is on the same network that your client is on, that it is a router, and that its name has been entered correctly. Then, try Pinging a remote host to ensure that network-to-network communications are operating as expected. Use Tracert to examine the path to the destination.

For more information about troubleshooting IP addressing, see "Configuring TCP/IP" in this book.

Additional Resources

These resources contain additional information related to this chapter.

- "Configuring TCP/IP" in this book for more information on the TCP/IP fundamentals on which this chapter is based.

- *The Deploying Network Services book* of the *Microsoft® Windows Server™ 2003 Deployment Kit* for more information about deploying Windows TCP/IP network services.

- "Introduction to TCP/IP" in the *TCP/IP Core Networking Guide* for more information about types of IP addresses and IP address assignment.

- "Dynamic Host Configuration Protocol" in the *TCP/IP Core Networking Guide* for more information about DHCP.

- "Introduction to DNS" in the *TCP/IP Core Networking Guide* for more information about DNS.

- "Windows Internet Name Service" and "Lmhosts File" in the *TCP/IP Core Networking Guide* for more information about NetBIOS name resolution.

- "TCP/IP Troubleshooting" and "TCP/IP Tools and Troubleshooting Utilities" in the *TCP/IP Core Networking Guide* for more information about troubleshooting name resolution and addressing.

Chapter 23

Connecting Remote Offices

You can use your Microsoft® Windows® XP Professional–based computer to configure a remote office network connecting computers and other devices in your home, in your small business, or in the branch office of a larger corporation. You can also establish and maintain a connection between your remote office and private networks, such as your organization's main office, and the Internet.

Related Information

- For more information about TCP/IP, see "Configuring TCP/IP" in this book.

- For more information about troubleshooting network and dial-up connections with diagnostic tools, see "Troubleshooting Concepts and Strategies" in this book.

- For more information about remote access server, see "Remote Access Server" in the *Internetworking Guide* of the *Microsoft® Windows® 2000 Server Resource Kit*.

- For more information about connecting remote offices, deploying remote access services, and deploying virtual private networks, see the *Deploying Network Services* book of the *Microsoft® Windows Server™ 2003 Deployment Kit*.

Remote Office Overview

For the purposes of this chapter, a *remote office* is defined as any home office, branch office, or sole office of a small business connected to either a private network or to the Internet. In this chapter, attention is paid to the local connections within a remote office as well as to the connections from that office to either a private network or to the Internet.

Local Connections in a Remote Office

You can link several computers and other devices in a remote office together to form a local area network (LAN) that functions as a workgroup (also known as a peer-to-peer network). The LAN can be based on any of the several technologies that are covered in this chapter, and allows the sharing of resources, such as printers or disks. In such an environment, a Windows XP Professional–based computer can allow several home devices to connect to school or the workplace, or it can link multiple systems at the same remote location to a central site or main office. Windows XP Professional, with its *Internet Connection Sharing* (ICS) functionality, allows the sharing of an Internet connection. By using a single telephone line, digital subscriber line (DSL) line, or cable modem, all the devices within the home or small office can connect to the Internet, thereby reducing the cost of access for the entire home or office.

There are now numerous technologies that you can use to connect Windows XP Professional–based computers and other devices within your home and small office, including traditional LAN technologies:

- Ethernet
- Token Ring
- Fiber Distributed Data Interface (FDDI)

Windows XP Professional also supports newer technologies such as:

- 802.11*x* for wireless LANs
- Home Phoneline Network Adapter (HPNA)
- Infrared Data Association (IrDA) protocols
- Direct cable connection
- IP over ATM

- Asynchronous Transfer Mode (ATM) LAN Emulation (LANE)
- Microsoft Ethernet permanent virtual connection (PVC)

Remote Connections to a Private Network

You can use a Windows XP Professional–based computer to connect to a private network so you can work at home, at a field office, or at another remote location. You can dial directly to a private network using either an analog phone line with a modem or an Integrated Services Digital Network (ISDN) phone line. You can maintain a persistent connection to the private network using either Frame Relay or a leased line such as T1. A third approach that has been gaining in popularity allows you to access a private network by means of an encrypted virtual private network (VPN) connection over the Internet.

Connecting to the Internet

Typically, you can connect to the Internet using an analog phone line with a modem or an ISDN phone line. Another option that is growing in popularity is a high-speed broadband connection using either cable modem or DSL. Whatever your choice, each system can directly connect to the Internet using its own public IP address (statically or dynamically assigned) or, as was mentioned earlier, one Windows XP Professional–based computer can function as a gateway, providing shared Internet access to all the systems on your small LAN.

What's New

Windows XP Professional builds on the Microsoft® Windows® 2000 local networking, dial-up, and other remote connection functionality and adds the following features:

- **IEEE 802.1D Transparent Bridge.** Users can add multiple LAN segments (usually made of different media types) to create a single IP subnet.

- **ICS Discovery and Control.** Private network clients can locate the ICS host, know its status, and control its Internet connection.

- **Internet Connection Firewall.** Basic packet filtering–based Internet security is provided for the computer, or when used in conjunction with ICS, for the remote office network.

Connection Types

To place the connectivity needs of the remote office in perspective, Table 23-1 includes both commonly used connection types as well as some of those less often used in the remote office environment.

Table 23-1   Connection Types

Connection Type	Communication Method	Example
Remote access	■ Dial-up modem ■ ISDN ■ X.25 ■ Point-to-Point Protocol over Ethernet (PPPoE) ■ Microsoft Ethernet PVC	Connection to an organization's network or the Internet by using dial-up access.
VPN	■ Point-to-Point Tunneling Protocol (PPTP) ■ Layer Two Tunneling Protocol (L2TP)	Secure connection to a corporate network over an existing connection to the Internet.
Local	■ Ethernet ■ Token Ring ■ FDDI ■ LAN Emulation ■ HPNA ■ 802.11x ■ IP over ATM ■ IrDA	Connection within a corporate network. (Ethernet is most suitable for Small Office/Home Office LAN.)
WAN	■ T-Carrier leased lines ■ Cable modem ■ DSL ■ Dial-up ■ Frame Relay	Persistent connections between geographically dispersed areas.
Direct cable	■ USB ■ Serial cabling ■ Direct parallel cabling ■ Infrared link ■ IEEE 1394 (Firewire)	Direct data transfer between two devices (for example, information synchronization between a handheld Microsoft® Windows® CE–based computer and a desktop computer).
Incoming	■ Dial-up ■ VPN ■ Direct connections	Connections from other computers to dial in to this computer.

Remote Access Connection Types

Remote access allows remote clients running Windows to access a network. You can use the following remote access connection types.

Dial-up Modem

Dial-up modem is the most commonly used form of remote access connection. Also called a slow link, an analog dial-up connection makes use of the PSTN rather than a dedicated circuit or some other type of private network.

ISDN

Integrated Services Digital Network (ISDN) technology makes it possible to offer telephone customers digital data and voice services using a single wire by dividing the capacity of the wire into separate channels. A basic rate ISDN line can offer speeds of up to 128 kilobits per second (Kbps) using two 64 Kbps channels. An ISDN line must be installed by the phone company at both the server site and the remote site. In most instances, ISDN is used for intermittent, dial-up connectivity rather than for a persistent or permanent connection.

X.25

X.25 is a standard that defines the connection between a terminal and a packet-switching data network. When X.25 originated in the early 1970s, the noisy, copper-based telephone infrastructure dictated devoting a great deal of overhead to ensure packet reliability. Media reliability improvements since then, including optical fiber lines, has made the costly focus on data-link reliability unnecessary. ISDN and Frame Relay have largely replaced X.25 as preferred remote connectivity solutions. X.25, however, remains the most widely accepted worldwide data communications standard. Consequently, X.25 continues to be used, often in tandem with newer technologies. X.25 is supported in Windows XP Professional.

PPPoE

Point-to-Point Protocol (PPP) is a set of framing and authentication protocols included with Windows remote access to ensure interoperability with third-party remote access software.

PPP over Ethernet (PPPoE) provides the ability to connect a network of hosts over a simple bridging access device to a remote access concentrator. With this model, each host uses its own PPP connection and the user is presented with a familiar user interface. Access control, billing, and type of service can be accomplished on a per-user, rather than a per-site, basis.

To provide a point-to-point connection over Ethernet, each PPP session must learn the Ethernet address of the remote peer, as well as establish a unique session identifier. PPPoE includes a discovery protocol that allows this to take place.

Microsoft Ethernet PVC

Microsoft Ethernet PVC provides support for Ethernet and IP data encapsulation over ATM. This enables the encapsulation and transport of IP or Ethernet packets over ATM between a client connected by means of an ATM permanent virtual connection to a supporting infrastructure. To accomplish this, Microsoft Ethernet PVC acts as a bridging Ethernet adapter for the TCP/IP protocol or a routing adapter for the TCP/IP protocol alone and uses the PVC on the ATM or internal ADSL adapter to transfer encapsulated data.

Windows XP Professional supports the two encapsulation methods defined in RFC 2684: LLC Encapsulation and VC Multiplexing. Both Ethernet and IP protocols are supported using either encapsulation method on both bridged and routed PDUs (protocol data units). For example, protocols supported by Microsoft Ethernet PVC in Windows XP Professional include PPPoE (PPP over Ethernet), L2TP (Layer 2 Tunneling Protocol), Ethernet, or Ethernet encapsulated in IP.

A typical situation in which Microsoft Ethernet PVC might provide remote connectivity for a home or small office involves using an internal ADSL modem. In Windows XP Professional you configure the ADSL modem as Microsoft Ethernet PVC. As shown in Figure 23-1, the ADSL modem connects by means of the Public Switched Telephone Network (PSTN) to a Digital Subscriber Line Access Multiplexer (DSLAM) located at the service provider, most likely the central office of the local telephony carrier. The DSLAM either bridges the encapsulated data directly to a network or connects to an external bridge, router, or ATM switch located at the service provider. A connection can then be made to the targeted network, such as a corporate office or the Internet.

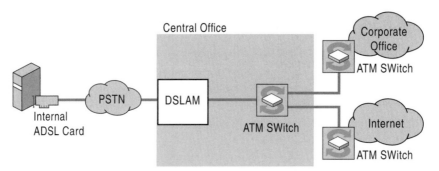

Figure 23-1   Connectivity with Ethernet PVC

For information about configuring Ethernet PVC, see Windows XP Professional Help and Support Center.

VPN Connection Types

A virtual private network (VPN) connection simulates a secure private link over a shared public infrastructure such as the Internet by encapsulating and encrypting all traffic from the remote access client to the VPN server. VPN offers affordable, secure access for home and small offices over any networking technology that transports IP packets. A Windows XP Professional remote access VPN connection makes use of one of two tunneling protocols to encapsulate all traffic.

PPTP

Point-to-Point Tunneling Protocol (PPTP), while developed by Microsoft and others, is an open industry standard that supports the tunneling of PPP frames. PPP frames can include IP and other networking protocols. Although L2TP used in conjunction with the IP security (IPSec) protocol provides greater security, PPTP is considerably easier to set up. PPTP uses Point-to-Point Protocol (PPP) authentication, compression, and encryption and can provide good security when used with Microsoft Challenge-Handshake Authentication Protocol version 2 (MS-CHAPv2) and a strong password. Companies can use PPTP to outsource their remote dial-up needs to an Internet service provider (ISP) or other carrier to reduce cost and complexity.

L2TP

Layer 2 Tunneling Protocol (L2TP) is an industry-standard Internet tunneling protocol with roughly the same functionality as PPTP. In Windows XP Professional, L2TP is designed to run natively over IP networks. Like PPTP, L2TP encapsulates PPP frames, which in turn encapsulate the frames of other protocols, thereby allowing users to run applications remotely that are dependent upon specific network protocols. Figure 23-2 demonstrates how an L2TP tunnel can connect a remote computer to a private network. That tunnel can be configured to run over the Internet or an intermediary private network.

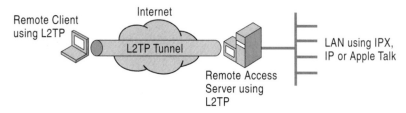

Figure 23-2   L2TP tunneling

The use of L2TP, in tandem with IPSec, provides data authentication, data integrity, and data encryption that greatly improves security when sending data over non-secure networks. For more information about IPSec, see "IPSec" later in this chapter.

> **Note**   UDP Ports 500 and 1701 need to be open when using L2TP with IPSec for encryption.

For more information about VPNs, see Windows 2000 Server Help or Windows XP Professional Help and Support Center.

Local Connection Types

Local connection types, in this context, refer to the following LAN technologies.

Ethernet

Ethernet, the 10 megabits per second (Mbps) standard for LANs, is the connection type used for most LANs. In this context, the term *Ethernet* can also include the 100 Mbps standard and the 1 gigabit per second (Gbps) standard. For 10 Mbps and 100 Mbps Ethernet, hosts connected to a shared media contend for network access using a collision detection scheme.

Token Ring

Token Ring is a shared access LAN technology that operates very differently from Ethernet. The term generally refers to the IEEE 802.5 standard, largely based on the token passing technology developed by IBM in the 1970s.

A token ring network consists of nodes wired into a physical ring. Each node (or device) passes a control message (token) to the next node. Whichever node has the token is entitled to send a message. Although Token Ring is fully supported by Windows XP Professional, it tends to be more complex and expensive than Ethernet. For this reason, it is rarely used in a home or small office.

FDDI

Fiber Distributed Data Interface (FDDI) is a 100 Mbps token-passing topology that operates in a similar fashion to Token Ring, but unlike Token Ring, FDDI is designed to be used with fiber-optic cabling. For redundancy, FDDI employs a dual-counter rotating ring. Data is generally transmitted on a primary ring. The secondary ring is used if the primary ring fails. Like Token Ring, FDDI is supported by Windows XP Professional, although it is unlikely to be used to connect nodes within a small office or home office LAN.

LAN Emulation

LAN Emulation (LANE) is a group of software components that allows Asynchronous Transfer Mode (ATM) to work with Ethernet or Token Ring networks and applications. Using LANE, you can run your traditional LAN-aware applications and protocols on an ATM network without modification.

LANE provides an intermediate step between fully using ATM and not using ATM at all. For example, LANE allows your current system and software to run on ATM, and it facilitates communication with nodes attached to legacy networks. You can increase the speed of data transmission for current applications and protocols when ATM is used over high speed media. However, LANE does not take advantage of ATM features such as Quality of Service (QoS).

IP over ATM

IP over ATM is a group of components that do not necessarily reside in one place, providing services not usually available on an ATM switch. (For the purposes of this discussion, it is assumed the IP over ATM server services reside on a Windows 2000–based server.)

IP over ATM provides several advantages over LANE. For example, it can support Quality of Service (QoS) connections, which are required by multimedia and other time-sensitive network applications. IP over ATM also provides lower overhead (because it requires no media access control (MAC) header) and a large IP packet size (9,180 bytes).

The core components required for IP over ATM are roughly the same as those required for LANE, as both approaches require the mapping of a connectionless medium to a connection-oriented medium, and vice versa. In IP over ATM, an IP ATMARP (ATM Address Resolution Protocol) server on each IP subnet maintains a database of IP and ATM addresses and provides configuration and broadcast emulation services.

Although Windows XP Professional supports both LANE and IP over ATM, it is unlikely that a small branch office or home office LAN would employ either technology.

Home Phoneline Network Adapter (HPNA)

Windows XP Professional supports HomePNA, a networking technology that uses existing telephone wiring in your home to connect devices without interrupting standard telephone service.

802.11x for wireless LANs

Windows XP Professional improves and builds upon the wireless support provided in Windows 2000. Windows XP Professional includes support for automatic switching between different access points (APs) when roaming, auto detection of wireless networks, and automatic wireless configuration — allowing for zero client configuration. Additional security is also provided by the inclusion of an 802.1*x* client implementation in Windows XP Professional and the inclusion of wireless device authentication support in the Windows Remote Authentication Dial-In User Service (RADIUS) server, Internet Authentication Service (IAS).

For more information about wireless LANs, see "Supporting Mobile Users" in this book.

IrDA

The *Infrared Data Association* (IrDA) has defined a group of short-range, high speed, bidirectional wireless infrared protocols, generically referred to as IrDA. IrDA allows a variety of wireless devices to communicate with each other. Cameras, printers, portable computers, desktop computers, and personal digital assistants (PDAs) can communicate with compatible devices using this technology.

Current IrDA standards are:

- Serial Infrared (SIR) physical layer specification, which provides for serial infrared connections running at speeds up to 115.2 Kbps. High-speed physical layer specifications have been approved by IrDA that support data speeds of 1.152 Mbps and 4 Mbps.

- IR Link Access Protocol, which provides a reliable point-to-point link, which effectively replaces a three-wire serial cable connection.

- IR Link Management Protocol, which provides for multiple sessions over a single point-to-point connection.

IrDA also specifies an Information Access Service that a device can use to determine the services offered by another device.

Infrared link, along with both serial cabling and direct parallel cabling, can be used to synchronize information between a handheld Windows CE–based computer and a desktop computer.

Direct Cable Connections

Direct Cable Connection (DCC) represents several technologies, which can each allow two devices to communicate with one another. They include the Universal Serial Bus (USB), serial (or null modem) cable, and the high-speed port-to-port transmission standard, IEEE 1394, also known as *Firewire*.

Infrared connections are sometimes also included in this category, but they are listed separately here because they also share some of the characteristics of more conventional network topologies.

When you install and configure DCC networking functionality on your Windows XP Professional–based computer, serial ports with external devices attached are listed as available for DCC connection. If you select a serial port that has an attached device, you disable the port and cannot use it for DCC networking, even though the device functions normally. If a modem is installed on the serial port, that port is removed from the list of available DCC ports. Examples of external devices include:

- Infrared devices
- Smart-card readers

USB

The *Universal Serial Bus* (USB) provides device-to-device connectivity without the need to restart your computer. It is a serial bus with a bandwidth of 1.5 Mbps designed to connect peripherals to a personal computer. USB can connect up to 127 peripherals, such as external CD-ROM drives, printers, modems, mice, and keyboards, to the system through a single, general-purpose port. This is accomplished by chaining peripherals together. USB supports hot plugging and multiple data streams. A USB port is usually located on the back of your computer near the serial port or parallel port.

Serial Cabling

A *serial (or null-modem) cable*, as the name implies, emulates modem communication. It eliminates the modem's need for asynchronous communications between two computers over short distances. When the host computer is at the same location as the target computer, or when you need to put a local host computer with remote access server capabilities between the target and a remote host, a serial cable is used to connect the serial ports of the target system to that of the local host.

Direct Parallel Cabling

A parallel cable can also be used to enable file transfers between two computers. Parallel cable connections are faster than serial cable connections because parallel cables transfer data one byte at a time. Windows XP Professional supports the following parallel cables for use with Direct Cable Connection:

- Standard or basic 4-bit cables
- Enhanced Capabilities Port (ECP) cables
- Universal Cable Module cables

IEEE 1394 (Firewire)

IEEE 1394 (or *Firewire*) is a standard for ports developed by the Institute of Electrical and Electronics Engineers (IEEE) that lets you connect high-speed digital devices, such as digital video cameras and audio/video editing equipment. Firewire provides transmission speeds of 98 Mbps to 393 Mbps. In contrast, USB provides transmission speeds of 1.5 Mbps to 12 Mbps.

Wide Area Network Connection Types

Wide area network (WAN) refers to a communications network that uses links provided by telecommunications service providers and connects geographically separated areas. In most instances, WAN refers to persistent connections as opposed to short term ones (such as Analog Dial-up and ISDN). WAN connection types include:

- T-Carrier line
- Cable modem
- DSL
- Frame Relay

T-Carrier Line

The *leased line* has traditionally been a fast, permanent alternative to dial-up remote access. In most instances, this has been in the form of a T-Carrier line, such as a T1 or fractional T1 line that transmits digital data at a maximum of 1.544 Mbps by using the telephone-switching network. E1, transmitting digital data at a maximum of 2.048 Mbps is the European counterpart of T1. Today, this legacy technology is being challenged by several other solutions that appear to be more cost effective and easier to install. T-Carrier leased lines are, nonetheless, still a corporate standard in widespread use and are supported by Windows XP Professional with the appropriate T-Carrier adapter and driver.

Cable Modem

Cable modems, with a maximum throughput of 2.8 Mbps, provide two-way, high-speed connectivity to the Internet and, by means of a VPN connection, to private networks as well. Cable modem technology employs the same coaxial lines that transmit cable television, accomplishing data transmission at speeds that makes it ideal for transferring large amounts of digital information rapidly, including complex files such as video clips, audio files, and large amounts of data.

> **Note**   Because cable modem is based upon a shared network contention topology, bandwidth is not always available on demand, and download speeds can differ.

Cable connectivity operates at higher speeds than leased lines and is more affordable and easier to install. When the cable infrastructure is in place in an area, a firm can easily connect by using the installation of a cable modem or router. Cable modems do not use the telephone system infrastructure and, consequently, there are no local-loop charges.

Perhaps the biggest obstacle preventing widespread cable adoption by businesses is availability. Eighty-five percent of all households in the United States are outfitted for cable reception and a growing number of those now support cable transmission. In contrast, few office buildings support either.

DSL

Digital subscriber line (DSL) technology provides dedicated, high-speed Internet access by using copper telephone lines. DSL partitions the telephone line and dedicates the partition so it is always available for data transmission. Thus, DSL provides high-speed Internet access without interfering with regular phone service.

A DSL circuit is much faster than an analog modem (up to 64 Kbps) or ISDN (BRI; up to 128 Kbps) connection, even though the wires coming into the subscriber's premises are the same (copper) as used for regular phone service. One form of digital subscriber line, Asymmetric Digital Subscriber Line (ADSL), for example, provides a one-way data channel to the subscriber at up to 6.4 Mbps and an upstream flow of 640 Kbps.

Like a leased line such as a T1, DSL is a dedicated connection providing continuous Internet and e-mail access, but, unlike a leased line, DSL does not require the installation of a special cable, nor does it require the costly local-loop charges of a T1. Use of a private phone line makes DSL more secure than cable, whose lines are shared by many users. In addition, unlike cable, DSL allows companies to increase their bandwidth on request.

Frame Relay

Frame Relay is a virtual circuit–based packet switching technology that permits WAN implementations of up to DS3 speeds (44.7 Mbps). It uses virtual circuits (VCs) that are either statically configured by a service provider or created dynamically when needed. Most implementations of Frame Relay use permanent virtual circuits (PVCs). Although technically not a leased line, from the point of view of the end user, a permanent virtual connection performs just like a leased line. It is always available for data transmission and there is no connection maintenance. The circuit is permanently mapped by using the service provider's network and does not change unless there is a failure in the service provider's switching network. A switched virtual circuit (SVC), less common in the world of Frame Relay, behaves more like a dial-up modem or ISDN connection although it is faster. It processes call setup, call maintenance, and call breakdown any time it is used.

Incoming Connection Types

By creating an incoming connection, a computer running Windows XP Professional can act as a remote access server. You can configure an incoming connection to accept the following connection types: dial-up (modem, ISDN, X.25), VPN (PPTP, L2TP), or direct cable connection as shown in Table 23-1. On a Windows XP Professional–based computer, an incoming connection can accept up to three incoming calls, up to one of each of these types. This can be an effective, low-cost option in a telecommuter's home office or a remote office to which the corporate network occasionally needs to send data.

For more information about setting up and configuring incoming connections, see "Managing Incoming Connections" later in this chapter.

Connection-defined Connections

All of the connections that appear in the Network Connections folder contain a set of features that you can use to create a link between your computer and another computer or network. These features establish end-to-end connectivity, define authentication negotiation, and set data encryption rules for those connections configured for remote access. For example, you might configure a dial-up connection with the following settings:

- A standard modem, capable of 56 Kbps, for dialing.

- A phone number to dial.

- Any encrypted authentication protocol. Your computer will negotiate with the remote access server to decide whether to use Challenge Handshake Authentication Protocol (CHAP), Microsoft Challenge Handshake Authentication Protocol (MS-CHAP), or Microsoft Challenge Handshake Authentication Protocol version 2 (MS-CHAPv2).

- Data encryption required (when dialing the corporate network, for example).

- TCP/IP protocol enabled, with the address obtained automatically.

When you double-click this connection, it dials the number by using the specified modem. The connection only allows the session to continue if the remote access server uses one of the specified encrypted authentication protocols, and if the remote access server encrypts data. When connected, the remote access server assigns the connection a unique IP address. This ensures a unique and non-conflicting address for the connection so you can access remote network resources, such as file shares. Properties of a dial-up connection provide all of the parameters required to dial the connection, negotiate password and data handling rules, and provide remote network connectivity.

Unlike a remote connection, you can modify a local area connection at any time, but you cannot manually create a new one. A local area connection is created for each network adapter detected by the Plug and Play service.

Setup automatically creates a local area connection for each network adapter. This connection is preconfigured with the services needed for file and print sharing and the TCP/IP protocol. All other types of connections can be created by using **Create a new connection** in the Network Connections folder.

Managing Outgoing Connections

You can configure your Windows XP Professional–based computer to initiate a remote connection. Such a connection can be any one of a number of different types, including:

- A dial-up connection to the Internet, using analog modem, ISDN, or X.25.

- A broadband connection to the Internet, using PPPoE, cable modem, DSL, or a leased line.

- A direct dial-up or broadband connection to a private network.

- A VPN connection, using the Internet to exchange data with a private network.

It is also possible to use your Windows XP Professional–based computer to establish a connection locally with another device in your office.

Local area connections can be configured at any time. The network adapter is detected; the connection is created and placed in the Network Connections folder.

Along with a display of existing connections, the Network Connections folder contains a list of network tasks including **Create a new connection**, which you can double-click to start the **New Connection Wizard**. Use the New Connection Wizard to create dynamic connections, including Internet connections, VPN connections to the workplace, direct connections to another computer, and incoming connections. Outgoing connections contact a remote access or VPN server by using a configured access method, such as a LAN, dial-up modem, or ISDN line, to establish a connection with the network.

Whether you are connected locally (by a LAN), remotely (by dial-up, ISDN, and so on), or both, you can configure a connection so that it performs any network function that you want. For example, you can print to network printers, access network drives and files, browse other networks, and access the Internet. If you are upgrading to Windows XP Professional from Microsoft® Windows® Millennium Edition (Me), Microsoft® Windows® 98 or Microsoft® Windows NT® Workstation version 4.0, Network Connections dynamically detects Dial-up Networking phone books and create a connection for each phone book entry.

> **Note**   Certain conditions, such as a malfunctioning network adapter, can keep your connection from appearing in the Network Connections folder.

Using the New Connection Wizard to Choose Connection Types

The **New Connection** icon always appears in the Network Connections folder. It starts the New Connection Wizard, which guides you through the process of creating all connection types, except for local area connections. The steps in the wizard guide you through the configuration options for each type of connection. The wizard enables you to select among three common connection types. Each connection type is then automatically configured with the most appropriate defaults for most cases. Figure 23-3 shows the three connection types: **Connect to the Internet**, **Connect to the network at my workplace**, and **Set up an advanced connection**.

Figure 23-3   New Connection Wizard

Internet Connection

Select this connection type to start the Internet Connection Wizard and connect to the Internet. File and Printer Sharing for Microsoft Networks is disabled, protecting your computer's file and print shares from computers on the Internet. The Internet Connection Wizard allows you to select a dial-up or broadband connection.

Dial-up Connection   By selecting the dial-up connection you can configure your Windows XP Professional–based computer to access the Internet for a finite period of time using a dial-up technology such as a dial-up analog modem, ISDN, or X.25. A modem or comparable piece of data circuit-terminating equipment (DCE) should be installed within or attached to your computer before such a logical configuration is attempted.

The Internet Connection Wizard automatically connects you to the Microsoft Referral Service to help you select an ISP if you select **Dial-up to the Internet** and either of the following:

- **I want to sign up for a new Internet account. (My telephone line is connected to my modem.)**

- **I want to transfer my existing Internet account to this computer. (My telephone line is connected to my modem.)**

The Microsoft Referral Service automates the process and provides the phone numbers to you.

Before you create an Internet connection, check with your Internet service provider (ISP) to verify the required connection settings. A connection to your ISP might require one or more of the following settings:

- A specific IP address

- Domain Name System (DNS) addresses and domain names

- Other optional settings

Broadband Connection   Select **Broadband Connection** to configure your Windows XP Professional–based computer for a persistent connection to the Internet using a faster broadband technology such as PPPoE, cable modem, DSL, or a leased line such as a T1. Unless you supply specific information about your broadband connection, Windows XP Professional dynamically detects and configures your broadband connection, assuming that the device necessary to establish such a connection is already in place.

Connecting to the Network at My Workplace

Select this connection type to connect to a private network from home, a field office, or another location.

Direct Connection   This option allows you to connect directly by dial-up or broadband into a corporate (or other private) network.

Internet Connection   This option allows you to access the corporate network by means of the Internet by creating a secure VPN connection. Depending upon how the VPN server has been configured, the VPN connection uses either PPTP or L2TP as its tunneling protocol.

Advanced Connection

Select the **Advanced Connection** type for two other selections.

Set Up This Computer to Accept Incoming Connections   Select this option to configure a Windows XP Professional–based computer to act as a remote access server accepting incoming connections. For more information about configuring a Windows XP Professional–based computer to act as a remote access server, see "Managing Incoming Connection" later in this chapter.

Connecting Directly to Another Computer   Select this option to connect your Windows XP Professional–based computer directly to another computer by means of a parallel, serial, or infrared port-to-port connection.

You can designate your computer to act either as the Host or the Guest computer. The Host makes data available to another computer. The Guest is the computer that accesses data on the Host computer.

To connect directly to another computer

1. In **Control Panel**, click **Network and Internet Connections**.

2. In **Network and Internet Connections**, click **Network Connections**.

3. In **Network Connections**, under **Network Tasks**, click **Create a new connection**. In the **New Connection Wizard**, click **Next**.

4. Select **Set up an advanced connection**, and then click **Next**.

5. In the **Advanced Connection Options** dialog box, select **Connect directly to another computer**, and then click **Next**.

6. Select **Host**, and then click **Next**.

7. In the **Connection Device** dialog box, select the appropriate device for this connection, and then click **Next**.

8. In the **Users allowed to connect** dialog box, select the check box next to the name of the user to whom you want to assign the right to connect this computer, and then click **Next**.

    Note that a disabled account affects the user's ability to connect. (If you wish to add a user name to the account list, click **Add**, and then type the User name, Full name, Password and Password confirmation of the user.)

9. In the **Completing the Network Connection Wizard** dialog box, type the connection name in the text box, and then click **Finish**.

What Can I Configure?

Group Policy enforces specified requirements for user environments. For example, by using Group Policy, you can enforce local and domain security options, specify logon and logoff scripts, and redirect user folder storage to a network location. Local Group Policy can be applied at the local computer or workgroup level. In the domain environment, Group Policy can be applied using Active Directory™, the directory service included with Windows 2000.

For more information about Group Policy in Windows XP Professional, see "Authorization and Access Control" in this book.

Your ability to configure connections depends on several factors, including your administrative rights, whether a connection was created by using **Only for myself** or **For all users** in the New Connection Wizard, and which Group Policy settings are applied to you.

Configuration Privileges

If you are logged on as an administrator or as a member of the Network Configuration Operators local group, the New Connection Wizard prompts you to select whether a connection that you are creating is **For all users** or **Only for myself**. If you select **For all users**, this connection is available to any user who logs on to that computer, and only an administrator who is logged on to that computer can modify the connection. If you select **Only for myself**, then only you can modify or use it.

Group Policy settings, which are designed to help manage large numbers of users in enterprise environments, can be used to control access to the Network

Connections folder, and the connections in it. Settings can be used that enable or disable the option to create connections, delete connections, or modify connection properties. For more information about these Group Policy settings, see "Connecting Clients to Windows Networks" in this book.

> **Note** If you choose **Log on using dial-up connection** when you start your Windows XP Professional session, you see only the **For all users** connections. This is because before you log on, you are not authenticated to the network. After you have logged on and your identity is authenticated, you see the **Only for myself** connections.

Configuring Remote Connections

Because all services and communication methods are configured within the connection, you do not need to use external management tools to configure dial-up, VPN, or direct connections. For example, the settings for a dial-up connection include the features to be used before, during, and after connecting. These include the modem you use for dialing, the type of password authentication and data encryption you use upon connecting, and the remote network protocols you use after connecting.

Because settings are established per connection, you can create different connections that apply to different connection scenarios and their specific needs. For example, you can configure a connection with a static TCP/IP address when you dial into your corporate office. You might also have a connection configured for an ISP. If your ISP allocates IP addresses using PPP, set the TCP/IP settings for the connection to **Obtain an IP address automatically**.

Connection status, which includes the duration and speed of a connection, is viewed from the connection itself; you do not need to use an external status tool. All connections are configured by right-clicking the connection, and then clicking **Properties**. For more information about configuring connections, see Windows XP Professional Help and Support Center.

Configuring Advanced Settings

The settings in the **Advanced** menu of the Network Connections folder allow you to choose from a range of advanced settings including operator-assisted dialing, dial-up preferences, bridge creation (Layer 2 connectivity), and network identification options. Another option allows you to install optional networking components such as the Simple Network Management Protocol (SNMP) service or the printing service. You can also modify the order in which connections are used by network services, or the order in which your computer uses network protocols and providers.

Operator-Assisted Dialing

If you choose this setting, automatic dial-up settings can be overridden where intervention is required. Typically, you can use this setting where you have to call by using a manually operated switchboard to establish your dial-up connection.

Dial-up Preferences

The settings in **Dial-up Preferences** affect connection creation privileges, Autodial options, and callback options.

You can enable or disable **Dial-up Preferences** on your users' desktops by using the **Enable the Dial-up Preferences item on the Advanced menu** Group Policy setting.

Autodial   The **Autodial** tab on the **Dial-up Preferences** page lists the available locations where you can enable Autodial. Autodial maps and maintains network addresses to connection destinations, which allows the destinations to be automatically dialed when referenced, whether from an application or from a command prompt. To enable Autodial for a location, select the check box next to the location. To disable Autodial for a connection, clear the check box next to the location.

The following is an example of how Autodial works:

1. You are not connected to your ISP, and you click an Internet address that is embedded in a word processing document.

2. You are asked to choose the connection used to reach your ISP, that connection is dialed, and then you access the Internet address.

3. The next time you are not connected to your ISP and you click the Internet address in the word processing document, the connection that you selected the first time is automatically dialed.

The Autodial feature works only when the Remote Access Auto Connection Manager service is on. Remote Access Auto Connection Manager is on by default in Windows XP Professional–based computers that are not members of a domain and in Microsoft® Windows® XP Home Edition.

To start the Remote Access Auto Connection Manager service

1. Right-click **My Computer**, and then click **Manage**.

2. In the details pane, right-click **Remote Access Auto Connection Manager**, and then click **Start**.In the console tree, double-click **Services and Applications**, and then click **Services**.

Callback   The **Callback** tab on the **Dial-up Preferences** page provides you with cost advantages. Callback instructs your dial-up server to disconnect your initiating call after authenticating your credentials and then call you back, thereby reducing your phone charges.

Callback behavior is determined by a combination of the settings that you specify in Network Connections, and by the user account settings you designate. Table 23-2 illustrates callback behavior based on these settings.

Table 23-2   Callback Behavior

Callback Setting on the Calling Computer	Callback Setting on the User Account	Behavior
No callback	**No callback**	The connection stays up.
No callback	**Set by caller**	The remote access server offers callback, the client declines, and the connection stays up.
No callback	**Always callback to**	The remote access server offers callback, the client declines, and the remote access server disconnects the connection.
Ask me during dialing when the server offers	**No callback**	The connection stays up.
Ask me during dialing when the server offers	**Set by caller**	The **Callback** dialog box appears on your computer. Type the current callback number in the dialog box, and then wait for the server to disconnect and return the call. Optionally, you can press **ESC** at this point to cancel the callback process and remain connected.
Ask me during dialing when the server offers	**Always callback to**	The remote access server disconnects, and then returns the call by using the number specified on the remote access server.
Always call me back at the number(s) below	**No callback**	The connection stays up.
Always call me back at the number(s) below	**Set by caller**	The remote access server disconnects, and then returns the call, using the number specified in Network Connections.
Always call me back at the number(s) below	**Always callback to**	The remote access server disconnects and then returns the call by using the number specified on the remote access server.

After your call reaches the remote access server, the server determines that your user name and password are correct and then acts, based upon pre-configured Network Connections and remote access server callback settings.

Callback can also provide security advantages to your network. Requiring callback to a particular number enhances network security by ensuring that only users from specific locations can gain access to the server. Dropping the call and then immediately calling back to the pre-assigned callback number makes impersonation more difficult. You cannot use this aspect of callback if you are dialing in from multiple locations.

The settings in **Callback** indicate the conditions under which you want to use the feature. For example, you can configure callback to prompt you for a phone number during the dialing process, or you can specify that callback always call you back at a specific number.

Callback options can also be configured on a per-user basis on the dial-up properties of a user account. The **Always Callback to** server setting overrides Network Connections settings. Therefore, if you have specified **Ask me during dialing when the server offers** in Network Connections, but your user account designates **Always Callback to** (with a corresponding phone number), callback does not prompt you for a number when you dial in; it always calls you back at the number specified on the server. For more information about how to configure your callback options, see Windows XP Professional Help and Support Center.

If you have specified **No callback**, but the user account is set to **Always Callback to**, you cannot connect. With this combination of settings, the remote access server requests callback, your computer refuses, and then the remote access server disconnects your connection. If your computer is configured to accept incoming connections, you can enforce callback options on that computer. For more information about configuring incoming connections, see "Managing Incoming Connections" later in this chapter.

Dynamic Multiple Device Dialing

The PPP Multilink Protocol (MP), defined in RFC 1990, combines multiple physical links into a logical bundle, called multilink lines, and the resulting aggregate link increases your connection bandwidth. Network Connections can dynamically control the use of these multilink lines through a combination of support for MP and Bandwidth Allocation Protocol (BAP). BAP is a PPP control protocol that is used on an MP connection to dynamically manage links. This procedure can be accomplished by dialing over multiple ISDN, X.25, or analog modem lines.

To dial multiple devices, both your connection and your remote access server must have MP enabled. BAP enables the dynamic use of multiple-device dialing by allocating lines only as they are required, thereby limiting communications costs to the bandwidth requirements. You can realize a significant efficiency advantage by doing this. The conditions under which extra lines are dialed, and underused lines are disconnected, are configured by using the **Options** property page of a dial-up connection. For more information, see Windows XP Professional Help and Support Center.

Network Identification

Network Identification displays your computer name, and the workgroup or domain to which the computer belongs. You can change the name of your computer, or join a domain by changing the settings on the **System Properties** sheet.

To change the name of your computer

1. In **Control Panel**, click **Performance and Maintenance**.

2. In **Performance and Maintenance**, click **System**.

3. Click the **Computer Name** tab.

4. **In the Computer description** text box, you can type a name for the computer (for example, "Mary's Computer"), and then click **Apply**.

5. The computer name appears under **Full Computer Name**. To change that name, click **Change**.

6. **In Computer Name Changes,** type the new computer name, and then click **OK**.

7. In the **Computer Name Changes** dialog box, enter the name and password of an account with permission to rename this computer in the domain. Click **OK**.

Advanced Settings

Windows XP Professional uses network providers and bindings in the order specified in the **Advanced Settings** dialog box.

To open the Advanced Settings dialog box

1. In **Control Panel**, click **Network and Internet Connections**.

2. In **Network and Internet Connections**, click **Network Connections**.

3. In **Network Connections**, select the appropriate **LAN or High Speed Internet** connection.

4. On the **Advanced drop-down menu**, click **Advanced Settings**.

By changing your provider order, and by changing the order of protocols bound to those providers, you can improve performance. For example, suppose your LAN connection is enabled to access Novell NetWare and Microsoft Windows networks, which use IPX and TCP/IP respectively, but your primary connection is to a Microsoft Windows network that uses TCP/IP. You can move **Microsoft Windows**

Network to the top of the **Network Providers** list on the **Provider Order** tab, and move **Internet Protocol (TCP/IP)** to the top of the **File and Printer Sharing for Microsoft Networks** binding on the **Adapters and Bindings** tab.

> **Note**   Microsoft® Windows® XP 64-Bit Edition does not support Client Service for NetWare.

An administrator can enable or disable the **Advanced Settings** option by using the **Enable the Advanced Settings item on the Advanced menu** setting in the Microsoft Management Console (MMC) Group Policy snap-in. For more information about Advanced Settings, see "Connecting Clients to Windows Networks" in this book.

Optional Networking Components

Optional networking components support network operations that are not automatically installed with Windows XP Professional. The components consist of the following:

- **Management and Monitoring Tools**
    - Simple Network Management Protocol (SNMP)
    - WMI SNMP Provider
- **Networking Services**
    - RIP Listener
    - Simple TCP/IP Services
    - Universal Plug and Play
- **Other Network File and Print Services**
    - Print Services for UNIX

To configure optional networking components

1. In **Control Panel**, click **Add or Remove Programs**.

2. In **Add or Remove Programs**, click **Add/Remove Windows Components**.

3. In the **Windows Components Wizard**, select the networking components you want to add, and then click **Next**.

4. When the wizard completes, click **Finish**.

Deploying Connection Manager

Connection Manager 1.3 is a client dialer, included in Windows XP Professional, whose several advanced features make it a superset of basic dial-up networking. Microsoft® Windows® 2000 Server includes a set of tools that enables a network manager to deliver pre-configured connections to network users. These tools are the Connection Manager Administration Kit (CMAK) and Connection Point Services (CPS).

Connection Manager provides support for local and remote connections to your service provider using a network of access points, such as those available worldwide by means of ISPs. If your service provider requires secure connections over the Internet, you can also use Connection Manager to establish VPN connections. Connection Manager's features are covered in greater detail in Table 23-3. Two features new to Windows XP Professional — Access Points and Improved Help — are included in Table 23-3.

Table 23-3   Connection Manager Features

Feature	Description
Branding	Enables the graphics, icons, messages, Help, and phone book support in Connection Manager to be customized to provide an identity that is unique to a service or corporation. For example, you can include custom logos, customer support, and phone book information to identify and represent a company.
Custom actions and monitored applications	Custom functionality, including original programs can be incorporated to enhance the connection experience of users. These programs can be automatically run at various points during the connection process, such as when users log on or log off. Monitored applications can be set up to automatically disconnect after the original program closes.
Multiple instances of Connection Manager 1.3	Allows remote users to run more than one Connection Manager service profile at a time. For example, users can run an Internet solution at the same time they run a corporate VPN tunnel.
Multiple user support for each service profile	Supports users who share computers. User profiles allow two or more people to use the same computer and the same service profile. Credentials are maintained, based on the logon ID of the user, so users do not have to re-enter them for each connection.
Simplified distribution	CMAK wizard can be used on a Windows 2000–based server to automatically build a service profile, the customized software required for a user to run Connection Manager on Windows XP Professional. The service profile is created as an executable file that can be distributed on compact disc or downloaded to the client.

Table 23-3   Connection Manager Features

Feature	Description
Access Points	Used to save frequently used connection settings.
Improved Help	Provides informational balloon help for Access Points and Dialing Rules.

Additional Connection Manager client features introduced in Windows XP Professional include connection logging, VPN server selection, terminal window support, automatic route addition, and improved ISDN support.

CMAK

A network administrator can use CMAK to tailor the appearance and behavior of a connection made with Connection Manager. Using CMAK, an administrator can develop client dialer and connection software that allows users to connect to the network by using only the connection features that the administrator defines for them. Connection Manager supports a variety of features that both simplify and enhance implementation of connection support for you and your users, most of which can be incorporated using the CMAK wizard.

CMAK allows you to build profiles customizing the Connection Manager installation package that you deliver to your customers, so that Connection Manager reflects the identity of your organization. It allows you to determine which functions and features you want to include and how Connection Manager appears to your customers.

For more information about CMAK and the configuration of connection manager service profiles, see "Customizing Connection Management and Settings" in the *Microsoft Internet Explorer 5 Resource Kit* of the *Microsoft® Windows® 2000 Server Resource Kit*.

CPS

Connection Point Services (CPS) work in conjunction with Connection Manager to automate the process of updating users' computers with new Points of Presence (POP) entries. Each POP entry supplies a telephone number that provides dial-up access to an Internet access point.

CPS consists of Phone Book Service, a tool for distributing phone books, and Phone Book Administrator, a tool for creating and maintaining your phone book files. The phone books provide users with complete POP information, so they can connect to different Internet access points rather than being restricted to a single POP during travel.

CPS eliminates a user's need to contact technical support to obtain changes in POP information and reconfigure their client dialer software.

Accessing Network Resources

Network Connections provides access to your network, based on the user name and, in the case of PPP connections, password credentials that you supply. This access does not imply privilege to use resources on the network. The network access control process confirms your access rights each time that you attempt to access any network resource. For more information about authentication and access control methods, see "Authentication" later in this chapter.

After you have connected to your network, access to network resources, such as files and printers, might be affected by one or more of the following administrative controls on both your own computer and on the resources you are trying to access.

File and Printer Sharing

File and Printer Sharing is established by each resource, and permissions depend on user name or group membership.

Group Policy

Group Policy enforces specified requirements for your users' environments. For example, by using Group Policy, you can enforce local and domain security options, specify logon and logoff scripts, and redirect user folder storage to a network location.

Local Group Policy

Local Group Policy can be applied at the local computer or workgroup level. In the domain environment, Local Group Policy is overridden by domain-based Group Policy.

> **Note**   If your computer is connecting to a domain-protected network, you must have a user account on that network before you can be granted access to network resources that are protected by domain-based access control lists (ACLs).

For more information about Group Policy and Local Group Policy, see "Connecting Clients to Windows Networks" in this book.

Managing Incoming Connections

By configuring a Windows XP Professional–based computer to accept incoming connections, you permit other computers to dial in to your computer. Plug and Play automatically detects and enumerates devices, such as modems and COM ports.

> **Note**   Callback options, discussed in "Callback" earlier in this chapter, can only be enforced if your computer has been configured to accept incoming connections.

To configure your computer to accept incoming connections

1. In **Control Panel**, click **Network and Internet Connections**.

2. Click **Network Connections**.

3. Under **Network Tasks**, click **Create a new connection** to start the **New Connections Wizard.**

   The first time you start the New Connections Wizard, the Location Information dialog box appears, requesting country or region, area code and, if necessary, a carrier code and an outside access number. You also need to indicate whether your phone system uses tone or pulse dialing. After typing this information in the dialog box, click **OK**.

4. In **New Connection Wizard**, click **Next**.

5. On the **Network Connection Type** dialog box, select **Set up an advanced connection**, and then click **Next**.

6. On the **Advanced Connection Options** page, select **Accept incoming connections**, and then click **Next**.

   This allows other computers to connect to your Windows XP Professional–based computer by means of the Internet, a phone line, or a direct cable connection.

7. On the Devices for **Incoming Connections** page, select the check box next to each device you want to use for incoming connections, and then click **Next**.

8. On the **Incoming Virtual Private Connection** page, select **Allow virtual private connections**, and then click **Next**.

   This enables a virtual private connection so that another computer can use the Internet or another public network to access your computer. For this to occur, your computer must have a known name or an IP address on the Internet.

9. On the **User Permissions** page, select the check box next to each existing user name you want to add, or click **Add** for each new user you wish to add. Click **Next**.

   This specifies the name of each user you permit to access your computer.

10. On the **Networking Software** page, select the check box next to each type of networking software that should be enabled for incoming connections. Click **Next**, and then click **Finish**.

This allows your computer to accept connections from other kinds of computers. The components listed by default include **TCP/IP**, **File and Print Sharing for Microsoft Networks**, **QoS Packet Scheduler**, and **Client for Microsoft Networks**.

Configuring Home Networks

Using Windows XP Professional, you can easily set up a home office network between desktops without using a server. Its Microsoft® Windows NT®–style user account management and permissions offer an environment ready-made for secure home and small office networking. You can also integrate other hardware devices such as printers, scanners, or cameras into your home network. The Network Setup Wizard guides you through the process of setting up your home network including Internet Connection Sharing (ICS), naming your workgroup, and naming your computer.

You can use Home Networking to:

- Share an Internet connection with all of the computers on your home network.

- Work on files stored on any computer on the network.

- Share printers from any computer.

- Play multiplayer games.

- Use one computer to secure your entire network and protect your Internet connection.

In addition, Windows XP Professional is compatible with previous versions of Windows. You can introduce Windows XP Professional into a peer-to-peer network configured between clients running Microsoft® Windows® 95, Microsoft® Windows® 98, or Microsoft® Windows® Millennium Edition (Me), or introduce clients running Windows 95, Windows 98, or Windows Me into a Windows XP Professional network.

You can set up one computer to communicate to the Internet using Internet Connection Sharing. ICS provides access to the public network (the Internet) for all computers in your home network to communicate with the Internet at the same time. The computers that do not have a direct Internet connection, called clients, rely on the host computer to provide access to the Internet. The ICS host computer manages network addressing. Besides providing Internet access, the ICS host computer in your network assigns itself a permanent private address and acts as a

Dynamic Host Configuration Protocol (DHCP) server for ICS clients, assigning a unique address to each ICS client and, therefore, providing a way for computers to communicate with other computers on the network.

For more information about ICS, see "Internet Connection Sharing" later in this chapter.

Successfully setting up your home network is a two-part process:

1. Install and configure the appropriate hardware on each computer.

2. Run the Windows XP Professional Network Setup Wizard on each computer in your home network.

Before you run the Network Setup Wizard, be sure you have addressed these concerns:

- The Network Setup Wizard is only supported on computers running Windows XP Professional, Microsoft® Windows® XP Home Edition, Windows Me, or Windows 98.

- Before setting up your home network, make sure that the ICS host computer has the Internet connection configured.

- Before running the Network Setup Wizard, install a network adapter in your Windows XP Professional–based computer. If you plan to enable ICS, you will need 2 network connections.

- When planning to run the Network Setup Wizard, make sure your computer is not a member of a domain. These setup options do not appear on a Windows XP–based computer that is a domain member.

Home Network Hardware Requirements

Make sure your network hardware, such as devices and cables, is installed and set up correctly before you run the Network Setup Wizard. When planning your home or small office network, pick the type of hardware to use for connecting your computers. In the business world, the standard network connection technology is Ethernet, which requires a network adapter and dedicated physical cabling. Depending on its complexity, an Ethernet network might also require other interconnecting devices to perform the negotiation the configuration requires.

There are several components that you need to create a home network:

- **Computers.** You need two or more computers for a network.

- **Network adapter.** Often called a network interface card, network adapters connect your computers to the network and allow your computers to communicate with each other.

- **Network hubs and cables.** A hub connects multiple computers at a central location. A hub is typically used when connecting two or more computers to an Ethernet network. A hub is not required if you are going to connect your computers through your phone lines using Home Phoneline Networking Alliance (HPNA) or if you use wireless adapters. Using Ethernet or HPNA, you need cables to connect to either a hub or the phone lines.

- **Modem.** This includes 28.8 or 56 Kbps analog modems, wireless modems, ISDN adapters, Digital Subscriber Line (DSL) adapters, and cable modems.

In addition, you'll want to make sure that the computers on your network meet the following minimum requirements:

- The computer sharing its Internet connection is running Windows XP Home Edition or Windows XP Professional. This is called the host computer.

- The Network Setup Wizard can only be run on computers using Windows 98, Windows Me, Windows XP Home Edition or Windows XP Professional.

After you install all of the required hardware in each of your computers, you can run the Home Networking Wizard.

Home Network Configuration Instructions

In Windows XP Professional, setup of the ICS host and client computers is greatly simplified by using the Network Setup Wizard. Run the Network Setup Wizard on the ICS host computer first. Then, run the wizard on the client computers. After you answer some basic questions, the wizard configures the computers to operate correctly on the network.

When running the Network Setup Wizard, be aware of the following:

- You must run the Network Setup Wizard on every computer in your network.

- Run the Network Setup Wizard on the host computer first. The host computer is the one that will share its Internet connection. When the Network Setup Wizard is run on subsequent computers, it automatically looks for a host computer that has shared its Internet connection.

- To run the Network Setup Wizard in Windows 98 or Windows Me, you must use a Windows XP Professional or Windows XP Home Edition CD-ROM. You can also use a Microsoft® Windows® XP–based computer with Network Setup Wizard to create Network Setup Wizard diskettes for use on other computers.

- To start the Network Setup Wizard on a Windows XP Professional–based computer, in **Control Panel**, click **Network and Internet Connections**, and then click **Network Connections**. Under **Common Tasks**, click **Network Setup Wizard**.

Note   You must be logged on as an administrator or a member of the Administrators group in order to complete this procedure.

To configure other computers on your home network

1. Insert the Windows XP Professional or Windows XP Home Edition operating system CD.

2. Under **What do you want to do?**, click **Perform additional tasks**.

3. In **Perform additional tasks**, click **Set up a home or small office network**.

4. In the dialog box welcoming you to the Network Setup Wizard, click **yes** to continue.

5. Follow the instructions on your screen.

Home and Small Office Local Connections

A local area connection is automatically created for each network adapter in your computer that is detected by Plug and Play. After a network adapter is installed, it is detected by the Plug and Play service. Network Connections enumerates the adapter and populates the Network Connections folder with a local area connection. Because local area connections are dependent upon a network card being recognized in the computer, they cannot be created by using **Create a new connection**.

For the adapter to be detected and the connection created, Plug and Play, Network Connections, and Remote Procedure Call (RPC) services must be started. All of these services start automatically; no user interaction is required.

A local area connection might not appear in the Network Connections for any of the following reasons:

■ The network adapter was removed. A local area connection only appears if an adapter is detected.

■ The installed network adapter is malfunctioning.

■ If your network adapter is a legacy adapter that is not detected by the Add Hardware Wizard or Plug and Play, then you might need to use the Add Hardware Wizard to set up the adapter manually in Device Manager before you see a local area connection in the Network Connections folder.

■ If the network adapter driver is not recognized, the adapter appears in Device Manager but you cannot see a local area connection. If your network adapter driver needs to be updated, use the **Update Driver** feature in the adapter's property sheet.

If your computer has one network adapter, but you need to connect to multiple LANs (for example, you use Dynamic Host Configuration Protocol (DHCP) at work but a static IP address configuration at home), you can configure TCP/IP with an alternate configuration. With an alternate configuration, your computer first tries to locate a DHCP server, and then if one is not found, it configures TCP/IP with the static configuration. For further information on alternate address configuration, see "Configuring IP Addressing and Name Resolution" in this book.

> **Note**   Windows XP Professional peer-to-peer networking can comfortably handle as many as 10 computers. (Microsoft added a software limitation to Windows XP Professional to prevent you from peer-to-peer networking more than 10 computers. Beyond 10 computers, you will want to configure a Windows 2000 Server–based computer as a domain controller.)

Use the network adapters that are supported by Windows XP Professional and listed in the Hardware Compatibility List link on the Web Resources page at http://www.microsoft.com/windows/reskits/webresources.

Clients, Services, and Protocols

By default, the following clients, services, and protocols are installed with a local area connection:

- **Clients.** Client for Microsoft Networks (allows you to access file and print shares of other Windows–based computers).

- **Services.** File and Print Sharing for Microsoft Networks (allows you to share your own computer resources) and QoS Packet Scheduler (enforces QoS parameters for a particular data flow).

- **Protocols.** TCP/IP, with automatic addressing enabled.

Any other clients, services, and protocols, including Internetwork Packet Exchange/Sequenced Packet Exchange (IPX/SPX), must be installed separately.

For information about configuring TCP/IP for a local area connection, see "Configuring TCP/IP" in this book.

Local Area Connection Status

Like other connections, the appearance of the local area connection icon changes according to the status of the connection. The icon appears in the Network Connections folder, or if the network cable is disconnected, an additional icon appears on the taskbar. If a network adapter is not detected by your computer, a local area connection icon does not appear in the Network Connections folder. Table 23-4 describes the different local area connection icons.

Table 23-4   Local Area Connection Icons

Icon	Description	Location
Local Area Connection	The local area connection is active.	Network Connections folder
Local Area Connection	The cable is unplugged from your computer, or from the wall or hub.	Network Connections folder
	The cable is unplugged from your computer, or from the wall or hub.	Taskbar
Local Area Connection	The driver is disabled.	Network Connections folder
None	The network adapter was not detected.	No icon appears in the Network Connections folder

To view the status of a local area connection

1. Right-click the local area connection, and then click **Status**.

   The **General** tab in the **Local Area Connection Status** dialog box, which is visible by default, provides information about the connection including its status, its duration, its speed, and the number of packets sent and received.

2. The **Support** tab on the **Local Area Connection Status** dialog box displays data including address type, IP address, subnet mask, and default gateway. Clicking the **Details** button displays a summary of advanced network data, including the network adapter's physical (or MAC) address and the IP addresses of DHCP, DNS, and WINS servers. The **Support** tab is the equivalent to the Winipcfg.exe tool provided with Windows Me, Windows 98, and Windows 95.

3. To automatically enable the Status monitor each time the connection is active, right-click the local area connection, click **Properties**, and then select the **Show icon in taskbar when connected** check box. By default, the Status monitor is disabled for local area connections, but enabled for all other types of connections.

WAN Adapters

Permanent connection WAN adapters such as T1, Frame Relay, and ATM, also appear in the Network Connections folder as local area connections. For these adapters, some settings are autodetected, and some need to be configured. For example, for a Frame Relay adapter, the appropriate management protocol, Committed Information Rates (CIR), Data Link Connection Identifiers (DLCIs), and line signaling must be configured. For these settings, contact your Frame Relay service provider. Default settings might vary according to the adapter.

The Network Bridge

The Network Bridge provides an IEEE 802.1D transparent bridge for grouping network interfaces at the media access control (MAC) sublayer of the OSI data-link layer. The bridge implements the spanning tree algorithm for prevention of bridged loops in the LAN segment topology.

A bridge in Windows XP Professional simplifies the setup and administration of a subnetted home network. The classic model of a subnetted IP network involves:

- Assigning each network segment a subnet identifier (ID).

- Correctly assigning IP addresses and subnet masks and configuring packet forwarding on the computers connecting the subnets.

- Configuring name resolution servers.

Bridging the LAN segments that comprise a home network simplifies the situation by creating a single subnet. The entire home network can then operate with a single subnet. DHCP client computers on any LAN segment in the home network automatically obtain an IP address, subnet mask, and default gateway from the host computer on which ICS is enabled.

Note   Bridging is a MAC layer activity, making use of a single subnet ID. ICS is a network layer activity, employing a single public IP address. The two are not related. However, the Network Bridge only works with TCP/IP.

Remote Network Security

You can configure your dial-up, virtual private network (VPN), and direct connections to enforce various levels of password authentication and data encryption. Authentication methods range from unencrypted to custom, such as the Extensible Authentication Protocol (EAP). EAP provides flexible support for a wide range of authentication methods, including smart cards, certificates, one-time passwords, and public keys. You can also specify the type of data encryption, depending on the type of authentication protocol (MS-CHAP, MS-CHAPv2, or Extensible Authentication Protocol-Transport Level Security (EAP-TLS)) that you choose. Finally, if you have sufficient permissions, you can configure callback options to save telephone charges and increase dial-up security.

Advanced settings, such as Autodial, callback preferences, network identification, and binding order, are configured on the **Advanced** menu in the Network Connections folder. Optional networking components, such as the SNMP service, can also be installed on the **Advanced** menu. For more information about callback options and other advanced settings, see "Managing Outgoing Connections" earlier in this chapter.

If your Windows XP Professional–based computer connects to a Windows 2000–based server, the remote access permissions granted to your computer by the server are based on the dial-up settings of your user account and *remote access policies*. Remote access policies are a set of conditions and connection settings that give network administrators more flexibility in granting remote access permissions and specifying connection requirements and restrictions. If the settings of your connection do not match at least one of the remote access policies, the connection attempt is rejected, regardless of your dial-up settings.

The network administrator can configure Windows 2000 Server user accounts and domains to provide security by forcing encrypted authentication and encrypted data for remote communications. For more information about Windows 2000 security, see Windows 2000 Server Help.

Authentication

For dial-up, virtual private network (VPN), and direct connections, Windows XP Professional authentication is implemented in two processes: interactive logon and network authorization. Successful user authentication depends on both of these processes.

Interactive Logon Process

The interactive logon process confirms a user's identity to either a domain account or a local computer. Depending on the type of user account and whether the computer is connected to a network protected by a domain controller, the process can vary as follows:

- **A domain account.** A user logs on to the network with a password or smart card, using credentials that match those stored in Active Directory. By logging on with a domain account, an authorized user can access resources in the domain and any trusting domains. If a password is used to log on to a domain account, Windows XP Professional uses the Kerberos V5 protocol for authentication. If a smart card is used instead, Windows XP Professional uses Kerberos V5 authentication with certificates.

■ **A local computer account.** A user logs on to a local computer, using credentials stored in Security Accounts Manager (SAM), which is the local security account database. Any workstation can maintain local user accounts, but those accounts can only be used for access to that local computer.

Network Access Control

The network access control process confirms the user's identity to any network service or resource that the user is attempting to access. To provide this type of access control, the Windows 2000 security system supports many different mechanisms, including the Kerberos V5 protocol, Secure Socket Layer/Transport Layer Security (SSL/TLS), and, for compatibility with Microsoft® Windows NT® version 4.0, the NTLM protocol.

> **Note** *NTLM* is a Microsoft protocol that serves as default for authentication in Windows NT version 4.0. It is retained in Windows XP Professional and Windows 2000 for compatibility with clients and servers that are running Windows NT 4.0 and earlier. It is also used to authenticate logon attempts to stand-alone computers that are running Windows XP Professional, or Windows 2000.

Users who have logged on to a domain account do not see network access control challenges during their logon session. Users who have logged on to a local computer account might have to provide credentials (such as a user name and password) every time they access a network resource.

Logging On Using Domain Credentials

The credentials that you use to initially log on to your computer are also the credentials that are presented to a domain when attempting to access a network resource. Therefore, if your local logon and network authorization credentials differ, you might be prompted to provide Windows 2000 domain credentials each time you access a network resource. You can avoid this by logging on to your computer by using your domain name, your domain user name, and your domain password before you try to connect to a network resource. If you log on without being connected to the network, Windows 2000 Server recognizes that your credentials match a previous successful logon attempt, and you receive the following message: "Windows cannot connect to a server to confirm your logon settings. You have been logged on using previously stored account information." Whenever you connect to your network, your cached credentials are sent to your domain and you can access network resources without having to provide your password again.

Authentication Protocols

You can use Network Connections with the following authentication protocols and methods.

PAP   Password Authentication Protocol (PAP) uses plaintext (unencrypted) passwords and is the least sophisticated authentication protocol. PAP is typically used when your connection and the server cannot negotiate a more secure form of validation. You might need to use this protocol when you are attempting to connect to a non-Windows-based server.

SPAP   Shiva Password Authentication Protocol (SPAP) uses a two-way encryption scheme to encrypt passwords. By using SPAP, Shiva clients can dial in to computers running Windows 2000 Server and Windows XP Professional clients can dial in to Shiva network access servers.

CHAP   The Challenge Handshake Authentication Protocol (CHAP) negotiates a secure form of encrypted authentication by using Message Digest 5 (MD5), an industry-standard hashing scheme. A *hashing scheme* is a method for transforming data (for example, a password) in such a way that the result is unique and cannot be changed back to its original form. CHAP uses challenge-response with one-way MD5 hashing on the response. In this way, you can prove to the server that you know your password without actually sending the password over the network. By supporting CHAP and MD5, Network Connections can authenticate users to almost all third-party PPP servers.

> **Note**   If your server requires you to use PAP, SPAP, or CHAP, you cannot use data encryption for dial-up or PPTP connections.
>
> If the connection is configured to require data encryption, and connects to a server that is only configured for PAP, SPAP, or CHAP authentication, the client terminates the connection.

MS-CHAP   Microsoft created *Microsoft Challenge Handshake Authentication Protocol* (MS-CHAP), an extension of CHAP, to authenticate remote Windows-based workstations. Like CHAP, MS-CHAP uses a challenge-response mechanism.

Where possible, MS-CHAP is consistent with standard CHAP. Its response packet is in a format specifically designed for networks with computers running Windows XP Professional, Windows XP Home Edition, Windows 2000, Windows NT, Windows Me, Windows 98, and Windows 95.

A version of MS-CHAP is available specifically for connecting to a Windows 95–based computer. It is available as part of the Windows Dial-up Networking 1.3 Performance and Security Upgrade for Windows 95. This is required only if your connection is being made to a Windows 95–based computer.

MS-CHAPv2   Windows XP Professional also includes Microsoft Challenge Handshake Authentication Protocol version 2 (MS-CHAPv2). This protocol provides mutual authentication, stronger initial data encryption keys, and different encryption keys for sending and receiving. To minimize the risk of password compromise during MS-CHAP exchanges, MS-CHAPv2 supports only a newer, more secure, version of the MS-CHAP password change process.

In Windows XP Professional and Windows 2000, both dial-up and VPN connections can use MS-CHAPv2. Windows NT 4.0, Windows 98, and Windows 95–based computers can only use MS-CHAPv2 authentication for VPN connections.

For VPN connections, Windows 2000 Server offers MS-CHAPv2 before offering MS-CHAP. Updated Windows-based clients accept MS-CHAPv2 when it is offered and MS-CHAP is enabled. Dial-up connections are not affected.

EAP   The *Extensible Authentication Protocol* (EAP) is an extension to the Point-to-Point Protocol (PPP). EAP was developed in response to an increasing demand for remote access user authentication that uses third-party security devices. EAP provides an infrastructure to support additional authentication methods within PPP. By using EAP, support for any number of authentication methods might be added, including token cards, one-time passwords, public key authentication using smart cards, certificates, and others. EAP is a critical technology component for secure VPN connections, because it offers stronger authentication methods (such as public key certificates) that are more secure against brute-force attacks, dictionary attacks, and password guessing than older password-based authentication methods.

Certificate Authentication   A certificate is an encrypted set of authentication credentials, including a digital signature from the certification authority that issued the certificate. In the certificate authentication process, your computer presents its user certificate to the server, and the server presents its computer certificate to your computer, enabling mutual authentication. As shown in Figures 23-4 and 23-5, if a user certificate is installed either in the certificate store on your computer or on a smart card, and EAP-TLS is enabled, you can use certificate-based authentication in a single network logon process. This provides tamper-resistant storage of authentication information.

Figure 23-4   Authentication tab on the Local Area Connection Properties sheet

Figure 23-5   Smart Card or other Certificate Properties dialog box

Certificates are validated by verifying the digital signature by means of a public key. The public key is contained in a trusted authority root certificate of the certification authority that issued the certificate. These root certificates are the basis for certificate verification and are supplied only by a system administrator.

Smart Cards   A smart card is a credit card–sized device that is inserted into a smart card reader, which is either installed internally in your computer or connected externally to your computer.

Certificates can reside either in the certificate store on your computer or on a smart card. When setting the security options of a connection, you can use a smart card or other certificate, and you can specify particular certificate requirements. For example, you can specify that the server's certificate must be validated.

When you double-click **New Connection** in the Network Connections folder, if a smart-card reader is installed, Windows XP Professional detects it and prompts you to use it as the authentication method for the connection. If you decide not to use the smart card at the time you create a connection, you can later modify the connection to use another certificate or authentication method.

How the Remote Access Authentication Process Works

Your computer dials a remote access server. Depending on the authentication methods you have chosen, one or more of the following might happen:

- If you are using PAP or SPAP:

   1. Your computer sends its password as plaintext (PAP) or using two-way encryption (SPAP) to the server.

   2. The server checks the account credentials against the user database.

- If you are using CHAP or MS-CHAP:

   1. The server sends a challenge to your computer.

   2. Your computer sends an encrypted response to the server.

   3. The server checks the response against the user database.

- If you are using MS-CHAPv2:

   1. The server sends a challenge to your computer.

   2. Your computer sends an encrypted response and a challenge to the server.

   3. The server checks the response against the user database, and sends back an encrypted challenge response.

   4. Your computer verifies the encrypted challenge response.

- If you are using certificate-based authentication:

   1. The server requests credentials from your computer and sends its own computer certificate.

   2. If you configured your connection to **Validate server certificate**, it is validated. If not, this step is skipped.

   3. Your computer presents its user certificate to the server.

   4. The server verifies that the user certificate is valid, and that it has not been revoked.

- If the account is valid and permitted through the dial-up properties of the user account and remote access policies, the server authorizes the connection.

- If the connection is authorized, the server accepts your connection.

- If callback is enabled, the remote access server calls your computer back and repeats the authentication process.

Note If you are using an L2TP-enabled VPN connection, IP Security (IPSec) performs a computer-level authentication and provides encryption before any of these steps take place. For more information about IPSec, see "Data Encryption" later in this chapter.

Data Encryption

Think of data encryption as a key you use to lock valuables in a strong box. Sensitive data is encrypted by using a key algorithm, which renders the data unreadable without the key. Data encryption keys are determined when your computer connects to the computer on the other end. Data encryption can be initiated by your computer or by the server to which you are connecting.

For dial-up, VPN and direct connections, Network Connections supports two types of encryption: Microsoft Point-to-Point Encryption (MPPE), which uses Rivest-Shamir-Adleman (RSA) RC4 encryption, and an implementation of Internet Protocol security (IPSec) that uses Data Encryption Standard (DES) encryption. Both MPPE and IPSec support multiple key strengths for encryption.

Server controls are flexible. They can be set to deny the use of encryption or require a specific encryption strength. By default, most servers are set to allow encryption and allow clients to choose their encryption strength. The system administrator can set encryption requirements on a Windows 2000 remote access or VPN server by using the encryption settings on the profile of a remote access policy.

The encryption method used by a VPN connection depends on the type of protocol used by the server to which it connects. If the VPN connection is using PPTP, MPPE is used. If the VPN connection is using L2TP, IPSec encryption methods and strengths are used. If the VPN connection is configured for an automatic server type (which is the default selection), then PPTP is attempted first, followed by L2TP.

MPPE

Microsoft Point-to-Point Encryption (MPPE) encrypts data in PPP-based dial-up connections or PPTP VPN connections. Strong (128-bit key) and standard (56-bit key or

40-bit key) MPPE encryption levels are supported. MPPE provides data security between your computer and your dial-up server (for dial-up PPP connections) and between your computer and your PPTP-based VPN server (for VPN connections).

To use MPPE-based data encryption for dial-up or VPN connections, the client and server must use the MS-CHAP, MS-CHAPv2, or EAP-TLS authentication methods. These authentication methods generate the keys used in the encryption process.

IPSec

IP security (IPSec) is a suite of cryptography-based protection services and security protocols. Because it requires no changes to applications or protocols, you can easily deploy IPSec for existing networks.

The Windows XP Professional implementation of IPSec is based on industry standards developed by the Internet Engineering Task Force (IETF) IPSec working group.

IPSec provides computer-level authentication, as well as data encryption, for L2TP-based VPN connections. IPSec provides per packet data authentication (proof that the data was sent by the authorized user), data integrity (proof that the data was not modified in transit), replay protection (prevention from resending a stream of captured packets), and data confidentiality (captured packets cannot be interpreted without the encryption key). In contrast, PPTP only provides per-packet data confidentiality. IPSec negotiates a secure connection between your computer and the VPN server before an L2TP connection is established, which secures user names, passwords, and data.

> **Note**   UDP Ports 500 and 1701 need to be open when using L2TP with IPSec for encryption.

IPSec encryption does not rely on the PPP authentication method to provide initial encryption keys. Therefore, L2TP connections use all standard PPP-based authentication protocols, such as EAP-TLS, MS-CHAPv2, MS-CHAP, EAP-MD5, CHAP, SPAP, and PAP, to authenticate the user after the secure IPSec communication is established. However, the use of EAP-TLS or MS-CHAPv2 is recommended.

Encryption is determined by the IPSec *security association (SA)*. An SA is a combination of a destination address, a security protocol, and a unique identification value, called a Security Parameters Index (SPI). The available encryptions include:

- Data Encryption Standard (DES), which uses a 56-bit key.
- Triple DES (3DES) uses three 56-bit keys. It is designed specifically for high-security environments.

Internet Connection Sharing

The Internet Connection Sharing (ICS) feature in Windows XP Professional provides a simple solution to allow all of the computers on a home or small business network to share the same connection to the Internet.

You can use the Internet Connection Sharing (ICS) feature of Network Connections to connect your remote office network to the Internet. For example, you might have a home network, with only one of the home network computers connected to the Internet by using a dial-up connection. By enabling ICS on the computer that uses the dial-up connection, you provide Internet access to all of the computers on your home network, with only one computer physically connected to the Internet.

After ICS is enabled and users verify their networking and Internet options, remote office network users can use applications, such as Microsoft® Internet Explorer and Microsoft Outlook Express, as if they were already connected to the Internet. If the ICS host computer is not already connected to the Internet, it dials the ISP and creates the connection so that the user can reach the specified Web address or resource.

Using ICS, you designate one remote office computer as the ICS host computer. Typically, this is the computer with the fastest outgoing connection, such as a DSL or cable modem. Use the ICS host computer to establish the connection to the Internet. All of the other computers on your remote office intranet — referred to from this point as "clients" to distinguish them from the ICS host computer — use the shared connection on the ICS host computer to access the Internet. In general, this is a three-step process:

1.   Configure the ICS host computer for Internet access. How you set up the ICS host computer depends on whether it uses an analog modem or ISDN connection, or a DSL or cable modem connection to the outside world.

2.   Enable Internet Connection Sharing on the ICS host computer to provide Internet access to everyone on the branch intranet.

3.   Configure your client computers for dynamic IP addressing.

To use the Internet Connection Sharing feature, users on your remote office network must configure TCP/IP on their local area connection to obtain an IP address automatically. ICS provides network address translation, IP address allocation, and DNS name resolution services for all computers on your remote office network or home network that are configured for automatic addressing.

The following protocols, services, interfaces, and routes shown in Table 23-5 are configured when you enable Internet Connection Sharing.

Table 23-5   Settings for Internet Connection Sharing

Item	Configuration
IP address 192.168.0.1	Configured with a subnet mask of 255.255.255.0 on the network adapter that is connected to the small office/home office network.
Autodial feature	Enabled.
Static default IP route	Created when the dial-up connection is established.
Internet Connection Sharing service	Started automatically.
DHCP allocator	Enabled with the default range of 192.168.0.2 to 192.168.0.254 and a subnet mask of 255.255.255.0.
DNS proxy	Enabled.

> **Note**   Throughout this chapter, *remote office* is defined as any home office, branch office or sole office of a small business connected to either a private network or to the Internet.

For a detailed scenario about setting up ICS in a branch office network, see "ICS Scenario: Connecting Your Branch Office's Intranet to the Internet" later in this chapter.

Using DHCP with ICS

The computer functioning as your ICS host maintains two connections. At least one of these is by means of a network adapter, the one which connects the ICS host computer to the other computers within the remote office. The other, whether by means of a second network adapter or a modem, connects your network to the Internet. You need to ensure that ICS is enabled on the connection that connects your remote office network to the Internet. As a result, the ICS host computer, through its local network connection appropriately allocates TCP/IP addresses to its own users, the shared connection connects the network to the Internet, and users outside your remote office network are not at risk of receiving inappropriate addresses from your local network. By enabling ICS on a connection, the ICS host computer becomes a Dynamic Host Configuration Protocol (DHCP) allocator for the remote office network. DHCP distributes IP addresses and other configuration information to users as they start up. If ICS is enabled on the wrong network adapter, users outside your local network might be granted IP addresses by the your network DHCP allocator, causing problems on their own networks.

There are groups of IP addresses that are specifically reserved for small networks. One of the groups of IP addresses is used by ICS — 192.168.0.1 to 192.168.0.254. These addresses are used with a subnet mask of 255.255.255.0.

Understanding the IP addressing scheme and using it appropriately can be difficult. The DHCP service enables the ICS host computer to assign IP addresses to its clients automatically. By default, when ICS is installed, the DHCP service begins assigning addresses to computers on the network.

Your ISP might use a DHCP service to assign your computer an dynamic IP address when you connect to the Internet. Quite possibly, each time your computer connects to the Internet, a different, but unique IP address might be assigned to it. Keep in mind that the DHCP dynamic address assignment, referred to here, does not affect the ICS private adapter which always has the same address.

If your ICS host computer has two adapters — one for the device connecting you to the Internet and another for connecting to your remote office network — an IP address of 192.168.0.1 is always assigned to the network adapter connected to your network. This is assigned permanently and is referred to as a static IP address because it does not change. Next, the DHCP client service is loaded into memory so that a dynamic IP address can be assigned to the computer's external adapter by your ISP.

Each client computer on your remote office network must request an IP address from your ICS computer. It is important that the ICS host computer remains on all the time or is started prior to starting the other computers on your network. Otherwise, the client computers will be unable to obtain an IP address.

For more information about DHCP, see "Configuring IP Addressing and Name Resolution" in this book.

Note Internet Connection Sharing does not work with some versions of AOL. For more information, contact AOL.

ICS Scenario: Connecting Your Branch Office's Intranet to the Internet

This scenario describes how to connect a branch office of a corporation to the Internet. It also explains the differences between setting up an analog modem or ISDN connection, and setting up a cable modem or DSL connection, and discusses how to configure a computer on the intranet of a branch office to use a VPN to connect to the corporate network. Figure 23-6 shows the initial configuration for a branch office.

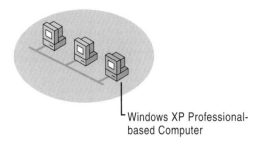

Windows XP Professional-
based Computer

Figure 23-6   Initial configuration of a branch office

The Internet Connection Sharing (ICS) feature in Windows XP Professional provides a simple solution to allow all of the computers on a local intranet to share the same outgoing connection to the Internet.

> **Note**   Never turn off the ICS computer while any of the clients are running, as the ICS computer provides IP address configuration, name resolution services, and a gateway to the Internet. If you do lose power to the ICS computer, the other remote office clients cannot access the Internet because the shared connection on the ICS computer is not available.

Configuring the ICS Computer

How you configure the ICS host computer depends on whether it connects to the Internet using an analog modem or ISDN connection, or a high-speed device such as a DSL or cable modem.

> **Note**   The ICS host computer automatically assigns IP addresses, forwards DNS names to the Internet for resolution, and assigns itself as the default gateway for connecting to the Internet. If any of the clients on the remote office's intranet are providing these functions, Internet Connection Sharing might not work.

Configuring an ICS Computer with an Analog Modem or ISDN Connection   In this configuration, the ICS computer connects to the Internet using an analog modem or ISDN connection. The ICS computer and all of the other computers in the branch office are connected to that office's intranet using network adapters. Figure 23-7 shows how an Internet connection is shared using an analog modem or an ISDN connection.

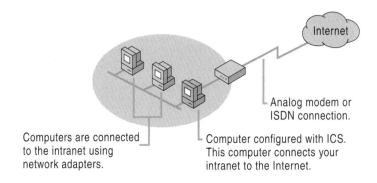

Figure 23-7   Internet Connection Sharing using an analog modem or ISDN connection

Install the analog modem (or make sure you have a modem installed) on the ICS computer you want to use to access the Internet. If you are installing an analog modem in the ICS computer for the first time, Windows XP Professional Plug and Play automatically detects and configures the analog modem.

Open the Network Connections folder, and then double-click **New Connection Wizard**. The New Connection Wizard sets up the connection to your Internet service provider (ISP). Configure the connection by using the settings provided by your ISP.

After the wizard has created the new connection to your ISP, Windows XP Professional adds a new icon for the connection in the Network Connections folder. Test the new Internet connection by connecting to your ISP and verifying that you can browse the World Wide Web.

To allow other users to connect to your computer

1. In **Control Panel**, click **Performance and Maintenance**.

2. In **Performance and Maintenance**, click **System**.

3. Click the **Remote** tab.

4. Under **Remote Desktop**, make sure the **Allow users to connect remotely to this computer** checkbox is enabled, and then click **Select Remote Users**.

5. In the **Remote Desktop Users** dialog box, click **Add**.

6. In the **Select Users** dialog box, click **Locations** to specify the search location.

7. Click **Object Types** to specify the types of objects for which you want to search.

8. In the **Enter the object names to select (examples)** box, type the names of the objects for which you want to search.

9. Click **Check Names**.

10. When the name is located, click **OK**. The name now appears in the list of users on the **Remote Desktop Users** dialog box.

> **Note** You must be logged on as an administrator or a member of the Administrators group to add a user to the Remote Users Group.

Check the configuration of the clients as described later in this section. Finally, verify the shared ICS connection by browsing the World Wide Web from one of the clients on the remote office intranet.

Configuring an ICS Computer with a DSL or Cable Modem Connection In this configuration, the ICS computer connects to the Internet using a network adapter connected to a high-speed DSL or cable modem. The ICS computer connects to the other computers in the branch office's intranet using a second network adapter. The rest of the computers in the branch office connect to the local intranet using other network adapters. Figure 23-8 shows how an Internet connection is shared by using a DSL or cable modem connection.

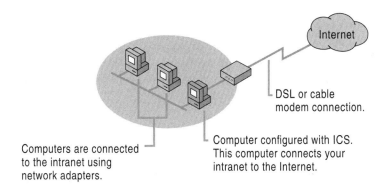

Computers are connected to the intranet using network adapters.

DSL or cable modem connection.

Computer configured with ICS. This computer connects your intranet to the Internet.

Figure 23-8 Internet Connection Sharing using a DSL or cable modem connection

Rename the local area connection on the ICS computer that you want the branch office intranet ("Office Intranet," for example) to use to access the Internet, and then install the second network adapter to connect to the DSL or cable modem connection. If you are installing the second network adapter for the first time, Plug and Play automatically detects and configures it.

Next, right-click the connection icon in the Network Connections folder to view the **Properties** of the new connection, and configure the connection by using the settings provided by your ISP. Click the **Advanced** tab, and then select the **Allow other users to connect through this computer's Internet connection** check box.

Rename the new external connection to the Internet to differentiate it from the branch office's intranet, and then test the new Internet connection by connecting to your ISP and verifying that you can browse the Web.

Finally, check the configuration of the clients (as described in the following section) and then verify the shared ICS connection by browsing the Web from one of the clients.

Configuring Remote Office Client Computers for ICS   To verify that the network settings on each client in the remote office are configured properly to use the new ICS computer to connect to the Internet, do the following:

- Verify that the local area connection to the branch office intranet uses the Client for Microsoft Networks, File and Printer Sharing, and Internet Protocol (TCP/IP) components. (These are the default settings in Windows XP Professional and Windows XP Home Edition.)

- Verify that the TCP/IP properties for the connection are configured to obtain an IP address and a DNS server address automatically. (These are the default settings in Windows XP Professional.)

- After the ICS computer has been initially configured and tested, restart all of the clients. Do not restart the ICS computer.

> **Tip**   If you have trouble accessing the Internet from a client, verify that the Internet browser for the client is configured to connect using the LAN. If this is not the problem, ping the ICS computer by typing **ping 192.168.0.1** at the command prompt. If this also fails, verify the physical connection from the client to the office intranet. Finally, you can use the **Support** tab of a Local Area Connection **Status** dialog box to view details of the IP configuration of the client. Alternatively, open a command prompt, and type **ipconfig** for IP configuration details.

The only necessary modification for client applications is to configure Internet Explorer to use the branch office LAN connection to the Internet.

Configurations to Avoid   ICS is designed to enable a computer to be a translating gateway to the Internet. Some cable modem or DSL configurations duplicate this function. To properly use ICS, do not connect a cable or DSL modem, the ICS computer, and all of the other clients on the branch office intranet directly into a network hub.

You can use this type of configuration when your ISP has assigned a static IP address to each client on your intranet. When you use a network hub, ICS is not needed for Internet access. However, in this configuration, you must disable **File and Printer Sharing** on all computers to prevent access to your computers from Internet users. Most remote offices avoid this configuration because it disables file and printer sharing between the clients on the remote office's intranet.

Some cable or DSL modems provide a built-in network hub. In this scenario, do not connect the network adapters of all the computers on your intranet directly into the cable modem.

Creating a VPN Connection to the Corporate Network   As network administrator of the branch office, you want to configure a few individual clients for access to the corporate network to send and receive e-mail, install software updates, transfer files, and otherwise access network servers and company-wide resources.

You can create a virtual private network (VPN) connection from one of the branch office's clients that tunnels through the Internet to the corporate network by using PPTP (L2TP connections cannot be made from branch office intranet client computers). It is a safe, secure way of connecting directly to the corporate network from a computer on the branch office network. Figure 23-9 shows how one client on the office intranet is connected to a corporate network by means of a PPTP-based VPN tunnel.

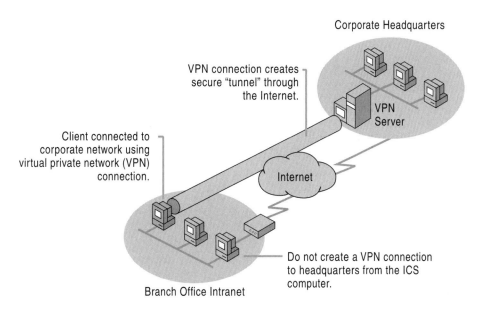

Figure 23-9   Connect a remote office client to the corporate network using a PPTP-based VPN connection

Do not create a VPN connection to the corporate network from the ICS computer. If you do, then by default all traffic from the ICS computer, including traffic from intranet clients, is forwarded over the VPN connection to the corporate network. This means that Internet resources are not reachable and that all branch office computers will send data over a logical connection by using the credentials of the ICS computer user, a questionable security practice.

The first time you start a new VPN connection, it takes a few moments to connect using PPTP, and then tries to connect usingL2TP and IPSec. Subsequent connections do not take as long because the VPN connection remembers which VPN protocol was successful for the initial connection.

After the VPN connection is made, the client on the remote office's intranet has access to the shared resources (such as file servers and printers) on the corporate network.

Likewise, while the client is connected to the corporate network using a VPN, the client is logically disconnected from the Internet unless the corporate network provides its own Web access. To access the Web through the corporate network, a client must be configured to use the rules established for Web access from the corporate network. For example, many corporations use a proxy server. In this scenario, you need to configure the browser of the client to use the corporate proxy server to access the Web. You can configure Internet Explorer to use specific proxy settings with specific Internet connections. After doing so, the client can easily shift between accessing the Internet by using the shared connection on the ICS computer or by using a VPN connection through the corporate network.

Internet Connection Firewalls

The Windows XP Professional Internet Connection Firewall (ICF) provides a solution for both novice and advanced users to protect desktop computers from passive and active Internet network threats while still providing a rich Internet experience and ease of integration for the system within a remote office network.

The ICF functions as a stateful packet. Although the ICF is a stand-alone feature, it is only necessary to run the ICF on the shared adapter to protect your home network. This functionality is included with Windows XP Home Edition and Windows XP Professional.

When enabled, this stateful filter blocks all unsolicited connections originating from the public network. To accomplish this, the ICF uses a flow table and validates any incoming flow against the entries in the flow table. Incoming data flows are only allowed if there is an existing flow table mapping that originated from the firewall system or from within the internal protected network. In other words, if the network communication did not originate within the protected network, the incoming data is dropped.

End users employing the Windows XP Professional ICF can feel comfortable that hackers should not be able to scan their systems or connect to their resources. Windows XP Professional provides a simple check box which allows users to easily and safely host Web and FTP servers.

The Windows XP Professional ICF is targeted for use by novice end users. End-user scenarios include:

- **Stand-alone computer in the home.** An end user installs the system in the home. The ICF is enabled by default for Internet connections when configured with the New Connection Wizard or the Network Setup Wizard.

- **Computer in a home or small business network.** An end user buys a more than one Windows XP Professional–based computer. When the network is setup, ICF is enabled by default on the ICS host.

Troubleshooting Remote Office Network Connections

The following sections describe common troubleshooting issues with the Network Connections feature in remote office environments as well as the relevant trouble-shooting tools provided with Windows XP Professional.

Troubleshooting Tools

There are many tools within Windows XP Professional that allow you to monitor modem or Point-to-Point Protocol (PPP) activity and diagnose network and dial-up connections, including:

- PPP logging
- Modem logging
- Modem diagnostics
- Netdiag
- Device Manager

PPP Logging

PPP logging records the series of programming functions and PPP control messages during a PPP connection. The PPP logs are a valuable source of information when you are troubleshooting the failure of a PPP connection.

Note   Routing and Remote Access service must be restarted for changes in logging settings to take effect.

To enable PPP logging on the client that is initiating the connection, use the Netsh command line tool. The syntax for the command is:

```
netsh set ras tracing * enabled
```

Conversely, if you want to stop PPP logging, the command syntax is:

```
netsh set ras tracing * disabled
```

Modem Logging

By using **Phone and Modem Options** in Control Panel, you can record a log of commands as they are sent to your modem by communication programs or the operating system. On Windows XP Professional, logging is always turned on and the log is overwritten at the beginning of every session unless you select the **Append to Log** check box.

> **Note**   Commands sent to the modem are captured in the file *system-root*\ModemLog_*Model*.txt. In this file path, *Model* is the name of the modem as it appears in the list of installed modems on the **Modems** tab of **Phone and Modem Options**.

Modem Diagnostics

When you query a modem, Windows XP Professional runs the commands and displays the results, as shown in Table 23-6. You can verify whether your modem is working properly by using the diagnostic queries that are available by means of **Phone and Modem Options** in Control Panel.

Table 23-6   Modem Query Commands and Responses

Command	Response
ATQ0V1E0	Initializes the query.
AT+GMM	Identifies the modem model (ITU V.250 recommendation is not supported by all modems).
AT+FCLASS=?	Identifies the fax classes supported by the modem, if any.
AT#CLS=?	Shows whether the modem supports the Rockwell voice command set.
ATIn	Displays manufacturer's information for n = 1 through 7. This provides information such as the port speed, the result of a checksum test, and the model information. Check the manufacturer's documentation for the expected results.

Device Manager

Device Manager provides information about how the hardware on your computer is installed and configured. It can help you determine the source of resource conflicts and the status of COM ports. You can also use Device Manager to check the status of your hardware and update device drivers, such as modem drivers, on your computer.

To open Device Manager

1. Right-click **My Computer**.

2. Click **Manage**.

3. In **Computer Management** window, select **Device Manager** in the console tree.

Troubleshooting Common Local Area Configuration Problems

The following sections describe common local area–related problems that you might encounter, and possible causes and solutions for them.

No response when using a local area network connection   There are two possible causes for the lack of response when using a LAN connection:

- There might be problems with your network adapter. Check the appearance of the local area connection icon in the Network Connections folder. Depending on the status of the local area connection, the icon appears in different ways. Use Device Manager to verify that your network adapter is working correctly.

- The LAN cable might not be plugged into the network adapter. If this is the case, a status icon is displayed in the taskbar. Check to make sure the LAN cable is inserted into the network adapter.

Troubleshooting Common Remote Access Configuration Problems

The following sections describe common remote access–related problems that you might encounter, and possible causes and solutions for them.

Modem not working
- The modem is not connected properly or is turned off. Verify that the modem is connected properly to the correct port on your computer. If the modem is external, verify that the power is on.

- The modem cabling is faulty. Do not use the 9-to-25-pin converters that are included with most mouse hardware because some of them do not carry modem signals. To be safe, use a converter made especially for this purpose.

- You dialed the wrong number, or you dialed the correct number but forgot to dial an external line-access number, such as 9. Verify that the number is correct as dialed.

- The modem is incompatible. If you have access to another computer with an Internet connection, check the list of compatible modems in the Hardware

Compatibility List link on the Web Resources page at http://www.microsoft.com/windows/reskits/webresources.

■ You do not have a valid user account, or you do not have remote access permission. Verify that your user account has been established, and that you have remote access permission.

■ The telephone line does not accommodate your modem speed. Select a lower bits-per-second (bps) rate or find a direct line.

■ The line you are trying to use is digital. Most modems work only with analog phone lines. Verify that you have analog phone lines installed or, if you have digital phone lines installed, verify that the servers and clients have digital modems.

■ Your modem cannot negotiate with the modem of the server. Try using the same type of modem as the server.

■ The remote access server is not running. Verify that the remote access service is not running. The administrator needs to carefully check the error and audit logs to see why the service stopped. After the problem is fixed, restart the service. If the service is running, the administrator needs to check whether other remote access clients can connect properly. If other clients can connect, the problem might be specific to your workstation.

When trying to connect, an error message indicates that the remote access server is not responding

■ The line you are dialing is affecting the speed. If you can connect to your remote access server by using more than one number, try another number and see if the speed improves.

■ At higher data rates, your modem is incompatible with the modem of the server. Select a lower bps rate.

■ The modem appears to have a problem connecting. If there is a lot of static on the phone line, this might be preventing the modem from connecting at a higher data rate. Select a lower bps rate.

■ The modem and telephone line are not operating correctly. This might be the result of dropped sessions caused by excessive static on the telephone line. Although the symptoms might be different than the previous problem, the cause might be the same. You can use modem diagnostics to confirm correct modem operation.

■ Your modem software needs to be updated. Check with your modem manufacturer for modem software updates.

■ There is some kind of switching equipment between the client and server that prevents the two modems from negotiating at a higher data rate. Adjust the speed of your modem to a lower data rate.

- The quality of your line is insufficient. Contact your telephone company to verify the quality of your line.

- The remote access server is not running properly. Try connecting to the same server from another workstation. If other workstations are having the same problem, there might be problems with server applications or hardware. If other clients don't have the same difficulty, the problem could be specific to your workstation.

- The remote access server is not running. This might be caused by the modem's tendency to connect at a lower data rate than specified. Verify that the server is running.

Connections to a remote access server keep getting dropped

- The remote access server disconnected you because of inactivity. Try calling again.

- Call waiting is disrupting your connection. Verify that the phone has call waiting. If so, disable call waiting, and then try calling again.

- Someone picked up the phone. Picking up the phone automatically disconnects you. Try calling again.

- Your modem cable is disconnected. Verify that the modem cable is connected properly.

- Your modem software needs to be updated. Check with your modem manufacturer for modem software updates.

- Your modem settings need to be changed because of a remote access server change. Verify the modem settings.

Connections are disconnecting abnormally

- The remote access server is not running. Verify that the server is running.

- Your modem cannot negotiate correctly with the modem of the remote access server. The serial port of the computer cannot match the speed you have selected. Try to connect at a lower initial port speed.

- Your modem software needs to be updated. Check with your modem manufacturer for modem software updates.

When trying to connect, a hardware error message is received

- The external modem is turned off. Verify that the external modem is turned on. If the external modem is turned off, turn it on and redial.

- Your modem is not functioning properly. Start modem logging to test the connection.

- Your cable is incompatible. If your modem communicates by using Hyper Terminal, but not through Network Connections, the cable that attaches your modem to the computer is probably incompatible. You need to install a compatible cable.

Connections do not appear in the Network and Dial-up Connections folder

- The folder might need to be refreshed. Press F5 to refresh the folder.

Conflicts between serial ports are causing connection problems

- The serial ports are conflicting. COM1 and COM3 share interrupt request (IRQ) 4. COM2 and COM4 share IRQ 3. To avoid such serial communications problems, do not use COM1 and COM3 simultaneously, or COM2 and COM4 simultaneously. For example, avoid using Network Connections on COM1 and Terminal on COM3.

- This rule applies if you are using a serial mouse in addition to other serial communications programs such as Network Connections. The rule does not apply if you are using an intelligent serial adapter, such as a DigiBoard serial adapter.

When trying to connect by using ISDN, a "No Answer" message is received

- The line is busy. Try calling later.

- A poor line condition (for example, too much static) interrupted your connection. Wait a few minutes, and then try dialing again.

- Your ISDN switching facility is busy. Try again later.

- Your phone number is not configured correctly. In some cases, each B channel on an ISDN line has its own number, although in other cases both B channels share a single number. Contact your telephone company to determine how many numbers your ISDN line has.

- If you are located in the United States or Canada and using ISDN, your Service Profile Identifier (SPID) is configured incorrectly. The SPID normally consists of the phone number with additional digits added to the beginning, the end, or both. The SPID helps the switch understand what type of equipment is attached to the line and routes calls to appropriate devices on the line. If an ISDN channel requires a SPID, but it is not entered correctly, then the device cannot place or accept calls. Verify that the SPID is entered correctly.

- You did not enable line-type negotiation, or a connection cannot be made with the line type you selected. Enable line-type negotiation.

- There is a problem with the hardware. Verify that the ISDN adapters are installed and configured correctly.

- Your DigiBoard adapter is too old. If you do not have the latest PCIMAC-ISA DigiBoard adapter, serial number A14308 or greater, contact DigiBoard for a replacement.

- The remote server did not answer because it is turned off or the modem is not connected. Contact that server's system administrator.

Connections made by using X.25 fail

- The dial-up packet assembler/disassembler (PAD) is configured with the wrong X.3 parameters or serial settings. If the remote access server is running and you cannot connect to it directly by using an X.25 smart card or an external PAD, modify the dial-up PAD X.3 parameters or serial settings. If they are available, obtain the correct settings.

- New Pad.inf entries are incorrect. Check other Pad.inf entries for direct connections and external PADs, and view the comments that appear with them. You might need a line analyzer or a terminal program to see the response for the PAD.

- Your modem is incompatible. If the modem that connects to a dial-up PAD connects at a lower speed than it should, replace the modem with a compatible one.

- The leased line for the remote access server is congested. This could be caused by congestion on the leased line for the remote access server. Typically, in such an instance, a connection has been established, but the network drives are disconnecting. As a result, you might be dropping sessions or getting network errors.

  - For example, four clients connecting at 9,600 bps (through dial-up PADs) require a 38,400-bps (four times 9,600) leased line on the server. If the leased line does not have adequate bandwidth, it can cause timeouts and degrade performance for connected clients. This is most likely the case if all bandwidth is dedicated to Routing and Remote Access.

  - Keeping all of this in mind, verify that the speed of the leased line can support all the COM ports at all speeds clients use to dial in.

PPTP connections fail

- TCP/IP connectivity problems are keeping you from connecting to the PPTP server. You can use the **ipconfig** and **ping** commands to verify the reachability of the server. Keep in mind that ping will typically fail to a VPN server because of packet filtering at the server.

- A legacy Winsock Proxy client, used in Proxy Server 2.0, is active. The Winsock Proxy service requires a protocol definition to identify valid network protocols when access control is enabled. The WinSock Proxy service uses the defined protocols to determine which Windows Sockets applications can be used to access the Internet. A VPN connection cannot operate with an active Winsock Proxy client. Winsock Proxy immediately redirects packets to the proxy server before they can be processed by a virtual private network connection for encapsulation. Disable the Winsock Proxy client. One alternative is to upgrade Proxy Server 2.0 to Microsoft® ISA Server 2000, allowing you to run the computer as an ISA Server Firewall client.

- You do not have the appropriate connection and domain permissions on the remote access server. Obtain appropriate permissions.

- If you are using TCP/IP, you do not have a unique public IP address. Obtain an authorized public IP address.

- Name resolution problems are keeping you from resolving names to IP addresses. Specify fully qualified domain names or IP addresses in your connection.

- You cannot connect to the PPTP-based VPN server with your DSL modem. Configure the DSL modem to pass TCP port 1723 and IP protocol 47 (most cannot by default). This must occur before a PPTP connection can be established. Some DSL modems refer to this as PPTP passthrough.

- You cannot connect to the L2TP-based VPN server with your DSL modem. Configure the DSL modem to pass UDP port 500 and IP protocol 50 (most cannot by default). This must occur before an IPSec SA can be established.

Connections made by using PPP or TCP/IP tools fail

- The server does not support Link Control Protocol (LCP) extensions. If you cannot connect to a server by using PPP, or the remote computer terminates your connection, the server might not support LCP extensions.

- IP header compression is keeping TCP/IP tools from running. If you successfully connect to a remote server by using PPP, but TCP/IP tools do not work, the problem might be IP header compression.

To disable LCP extensions

1. In **Network Connections**, click the dial-up or VPN connection you want to configure.

2. Under **Network Tasks**, click **Change settings of this connection**.

3. On the **Networking** tab, click **Settings**, and then clear the **Enable LCP extensions** check box.

To disable IP header compression

1. In **Network Connections**, click the dial-up connection you want to configure.

2. Under **Network Tasks**, click **Change settings of this connection**.

3. On the **Networking** tab, click **Internet Protocol (TCP/IP)**, and then click **Properties**.

4. Click **Advanced**, and then clear the **Use the IP Header Compression** check box.

Troubleshooting Common Internet Access Configuration Problems

The following sections describe common Internet access–related problems that you might encounter, and possible causes and solutions for them.

ICS connections fail

- The wrong network adapter is shared. An ICS host computer needs two connections. One connection, typically a network adapter, connects to the computers on the home (or small office) network and the other connection connects the home network to the Internet. Ensure that ICS is enabled on the connection that connects your home network to the Internet.

- TCP/IP is not installed on home network computers. By default, the TCP/IP protocol is installed on computers running Windows XP Professional and Windows XP Home Edition, Windows 2000, Windows Me, Windows 98, and Windows NT 4.0. If users on your home network are running operating systems other than these, verify that TCP/IP is installed on their computers.

- Users on your home network fail reach the Internet. TCP/IP is incorrectly configured on home network computers. Verify that the following TCP/IP settings are established on home network local area connections:

  - IP address. Obtain an IP address automatically (by using DHCP).

  - DNS server. Obtain DNS server address automatically.

  - Default gateways. None specified.

  For computers running Windows 95, Windows 98, or Windows NT 4.0, you can find the TCP/IP settings in **Network Control Panel**.

- Internet Connection Sharing is not started. Use the Services and Applications section of the Computer Management console tree to verify that the Internet Connection Sharing service is started. If "stopped" appears as the service status, click **Start** and **OK** to start the service.

- The Internet Connection Sharing computer is not properly configured for name resolution. If computers on the remote office network cannot resolve names to IP addresses, you might need to configure the DNS name resolution services on the ICS host computer. Check the name resolution configuration of the ICS host computer by using the **ipconfig** command.

  If your remote office accesses the Internet through an ISP, there are two ways that your ISP can configure name resolution:

  - Statically assigning name servers.
    You must manually configure the TCP/IP protocol with the IP address (or addresses) of the name servers provided by the ISP. If you have statically assigned name servers, you can run the **ipconfig** command at any time to get the IP addresses of your configured name servers.

  - Dynamically assigning name servers.

Manual configuration is not required. The IP addresses of the name servers provided by the ISP are dynamically assigned whenever you dial the ISP. If you have dynamically assigned name servers, you must run the **ipconfig** command after a connection to the ISP has been made.

- The protocol used by a game played on the Internet is not translatable. Try running the game application from the ICS computer. If the game works from the ICS computer but not from a computer on the home network, then the game might not be translatable.

- Internet users cannot see services on your home network, such as a Web server. Verify that the ICS service, including port numbers and IP addresses, is configured correctly.

- Users on your home network cannot reach the Internet sites by using friendly names. This is a DNS resolution problem. Users on your home network must use fully qualified domain names or IP addresses when accessing Internet resources.

For more information about Internet Connection Sharing, see Windows XP Professional Help and Support Center.

Applications do not run properly on a laptop connecting to an ISP   The Winsock Proxy client might be preventing your applications from running properly. If you are a mobile user and use your portable computer in your corporate environment, your applications might not be able to locate the resources or servers they need. Disable the Microsoft Winsock Proxy client (WSP Client in Control Panel) when you use the same computer to dial to an ISP or other network.

Connections to my ISP succeed, but not to the Internet   DNS options might need to be configured. Check with your ISP to see if you need to configure DNS settings for that connection. For example, you might need to specify a preferred or alternate DNS server IP address, rather than letting the DNS server IP address be assigned dynamically.

Additional Resources

These resources contain additional information and tools related to this chapter.

Related Information
- "Configuring TCP/IP" in this book for more information about TCP/IP.
- "Troubleshooting Concepts and Strategies" in this book for more information about troubleshooting network and dial-up connections with diagnostic tools.
- "Remote Access Server" in the *Internetworking Guide* of the *Microsoft® Windows® 2000 Server Resource Kit* for more information about remote access server issues.

Chapter 24

Configuring Telephony and Conferencing

Microsoft® Windows® XP Professional provides support for telecommunications in a variety of environments, including Internet Protocol (IP) telephony networks. The following discussion includes installation and configuration details for traditional and IP-based telephony and conferencing, and technical details relating to modems and communications tools.

Related Information

- For more information about installing and troubleshooting hardware devices, see "Managing Devices" in this book.

- For more information about configuration of telephony and conferencing services on a computer running Microsoft® Windows® 2000 Server, see "Telephony Integration and Conferencing" in the *Internetworking Guide* of the *Microsoft® Windows® 2000 Server Resource Kit*.

- For more information about planning and deploying Group Policy in a Windows 2000 domain, see "Group Policy" in the *Distributed Systems Guide* of the *Microsoft Windows 2000 Server Resource Kit*.

- For more information about deploying Group Policy in a Windows Server 2003 domain, see the *Designing and Managed Environment* book of the *Microsoft® Windows Server™ 2003 Deployment Kit*.

Overview of Telephony and Conferencing

IP Telephony and conferencing allow you to converge data, voice, and video—communication traditionally implemented through separate networks—over the same IP-based network infrastructure. The Windows XP Professional telephony platform allows for both IP telephony and conferencing solutions, the use of IP over an existing computer network for telephony and conferencing, and computer-telephony integration (CTI), the integration of existing circuit-switched telephony equipment with computer-based Telephony Application Programming Interface (TAPI) applications.

Telephony Environments

Windows XP Professional can provide telephony and conferencing services within a variety of communications environments, including:

- IP telephony
- Client/server telephony
- Public Switched Telephone Network (PSTN)
- Integrated Services Digital Network (ISDN)
- Private Branch Exchange (PBX)

IP Telephony

Using IP telephony and conferencing technologies, a personal computer (or other device) captures audio and video signals from the user by using, for example, a microphone attached to a sound card, and a video camera connected to a video capture device. The computer compresses and sends this information to the intended receivers over the local area network (LAN) or the Internet. For the recipient, a computer restores the signals to their original form and plays back audio by using speakers attached to a sound card and video by creating a window on the display of the computer.

IP telephony in Windows XP Professional supports:

- Session Initiation Protocol (SIP)
- H.323 protocol
- IP multicast conferencing

You can integrate IP telephony systems with the public telephone system by using an IP-PSTN gateway, allowing users to place telephone calls from an enabled computer. Users can place audio and video calls to external users by using the Internet with an H.323 proxy, allowing administrators to control host access.

Session Initiation Protocol   SIP is a text-based application-layer signaling and call control protocol. The main function of SIP is to create, modify, and terminate SIP sessions. SIP supports both unicast and multicast communication. The main components in a SIP environment are SIP servers and SIP user agents.

There are two different types of SIP user agents, as shown in Table 24-1.

Table 24-1   SIP User Agents

SIP User Agent	Function
User Agent Client	Initiates SIP requests.
User Agent Server	Receives SIP requests.

Most SIP-based applications act as both a user agent client and server. Each user agent is associated with a SIP address.

All SIP servers accept and reply to SIP requests. The function that the specific SIP server performs determines which SIP requests it processes. Table 24-2 lists the different SIP servers and their functions.

Table 24-2   SIP Servers

SIP Server	Function
Proxy server	Acts as an intermediary between a SIP user agent client and a SIP user agent server. Depending upon the direction of the communication between client and server, the proxy server performs the functions of either a SIP user agent client or SIP user agent server. The proxy server can simply forward the SIP request or modify it before sending it.
Registrar server	Receives REGISTER requests, which contain both the IP address and SIP address (Uniform Resource Locator or URL) of the user agent. This allows the Registrar server to keep track of the location of user agents, of which the Registrar server has received REGISTER requests.
Redirect server	Accepts initiation, a SIP INVITE request, of a SIP session from the calling User Agent, obtains the correct SIP address of the called User Agent and replies back to the calling User Agent with the correct SIP address. The calling User Agent then uses the correct SIP address to directly initiate a SIP session with the called User Agent.

The SIP servers can be developed as separate applications or as a single application with the functionality of all the servers. The combination of both a registrar and proxy server is sometimes referred to as a rendezvous server.

RTC Client APIs   RTC (Real Time Communication) client APIs are included with Windows XP Professional. RTC client APIs are a set of Component Object Model (COM) interfaces and methods that create computer-computer, computer-phone, phone-phone audio/video calls or text only Instant Messaging (IM) sessions over the Internet. Application Sharing and Whiteboard can also be added to computer-computer sessions.

These features can be configured so that they are also available to users in an audio/video conference. Instant Messaging, where a text message is sent to a URL or IP address, allows users the ability to communicate with other Instant Messaging users in real time. Application Sharing allows for a user to give real-time access and control of an application to another user. Whiteboard support allows for real time creation, collaboration, and viewing of sketches or diagrams.

H.323 Protocol H.323, an application-layer signaling and call control protocol, is an International Telecommunication Union-Telecommunications (ITU -T) protocol that provides voice and video services over data networks. At the most basic level, H.323 allows users to make point-to-point audio and video phone calls over an intranet. H.323 also supports voice-only calls made to conventional phones by using an IP-PSTN gateway and Internet audio/video calls made by using a proxy server.

H.323 Gateway You configure H.323 gateways as part of your enterprise's IP telephony network. Using the configuration of H.323 gateways, IP telephony integrates data networks and information with the traditional Public Switched Telephone Network (PSTN). The H.323 protocol provides client support of H.323 gateways.

Figure 24-1 shows an example of an H.323 gateway.

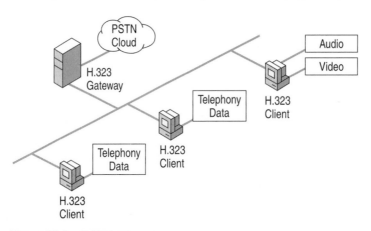

Figure 24-1 H.323 gateway

For example, a call from an IP telephony client to a conventional telephone is routed over the IP network to the H.323 gateway, which translates H.323 signaling to conventional telephone signaling, such as Signaling System 7 (SS7), and then routes the call over the conventional telephone network to its destination.

IP Multicast Conferencing The Multicast Conference Service Provider included with TAPI 3.1 provides support for IP multicast-based audio and video conferencing between multiple participants. IP multicasts support multi-user conferences using a single connection instead of multiple connections, which conserves network bandwidth.

All routers between the Windows XP Professional client and other conferencing participants must support IP multicasting. Windows 2000 Server provides a multicast-enabled Dynamic Host Configuration Protocol (DHCP) server that can allocate a unique IP address for the duration of the conference.

Client/Server Telephony

You can configure a computer running Windows 2000 Server as a telephony server, providing an interface between the PBX switch and workstations enabled to use TAPI. For example, a LAN server might have multiple telephone-line connections to a local telephone switch or PBX. An associated client starts TAPI operations and forwards them over the LAN to the server. The server uses third-party call control between the server and the PBX to implement the client's call-control requests. Figure 24-2 shows an example of a PBX system configured with a telephony server.

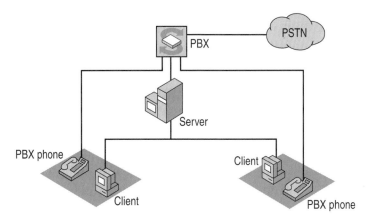

Figure 24-2   Client/server telephony using PBX

The PBX switch can connect to the server using a switch-to-host link. You can also directly connect a PBX switch to the LAN on which the server and associated clients reside. Within these distributed configurations, different subconfigurations are possible, such as:

■ **Single-line device model.** To provide personal telephony to each client, the service provider can model the PBX line associated with the client as a single-line device with one channel. Each client would have one line device available.

■ **Separate-line device model.** Each third-party station can be modeled as a separate-line device to allow applications to control calls on other stations. (A *station* is anything to which a wire leads from the PBX switch.) This subconfiguration requires that the application open each line it wants to manipulate or monitor.

Windows XP Professional workstations locate the telephony server through auto discovery of the published telephony service object in Active Directory™. After communication is established with the telephony server, users at the Windows XP

Professional computer can perform basic and advanced call control functions, such as placing, answering, and terminating calls to the PBX switch or PSTN through the computer. Installation of third-party telephony services that conform to TAPI 3.1 standards can enable advanced functions, such as computer-telephony integration (CTI) functions.

For more information about client/server telephony, see "Configuring Client/Server Telephony Support" later in this chapter.

Public Switched Telephone Network

Historically, most telephone connections in the world have been made by using the PSTN. Most PSTN calls are transmitted digitally except while in the local loop, the part of the telephone network between the telephone and the telephone company's central switching office. Within this loop, speech from a telephone is usually transmitted in analog format.

Digital data from a computer must first be converted to analog by a modem. The modem is installed in the computer, connected to the computer by the serial port, or by a Universal Serial Bus connection. The data is converted at the receiving end by another modem, which changes the data from audio to its original data form.

Windows XP Professional provides basic telephony call support for modems using PSTN lines, such as dialing and call termination. Windows XP Professional provides device drivers for a number of internal and external analog modems, which can be automatically installed by using Plug and Play, or manually installed by using the Add Hardware Wizard in Control Panel.

Integrated Services Digital Network

The need for high-speed telecommunications support within the existing telecommunications infrastructure has led to the development of new technologies, such as Integrated Services Digital Network (ISDN). ISDN is a digital phone service using existing copper telephone cabling that is provided by regional and national phone companies.

To use ISDN, you need either an ISDN modem or an ISDN adapter. You might also need an NT-1 (the equivalent of the phone jack into which you plug your device) and an ISDN line from your telephone company. Some ISDN equipment comes with the NT-1 built in.

ISDN modems are available in internal and external configurations. Internal ISDN modems are more commonly used and are installed in the same manner as a network adapter. External ISDN modems hook up to your computer by using a serial port, the same as regular modems. Thus, because a serial port cannot exceed 115 kilobits per second (Kbps) (which is lower than the total effective bandwidth of the ISDN line), some throughput is lost if you are using the maximum ISDN bandwidth. An ISDN adapter, which operates at bus speed, provides the higher rate that ISDN needs.

The same company that supports the PSTN typically supplies ISDN. However, ISDN differs from analog telephone service in several ways, including:

- Data transfer rate

- Available channels per call

- Availability of service

- Cost of service

- Quality of connection

Data transfer rate   ISDN can provide data transfer rates of up to 128 Kbps. These speeds are slower than those of LANs supported by high-speed data communications technology, but faster than those of analog telephone lines. In addition to the difference in data transfer rates, ISDN calls can be established much faster than analog phone calls. While an analog modem can take up to a minute to set up a connection, you usually can start transmitting data in about two seconds with ISDN. Because ISDN is fully digital, the lengthy process used by analog modems is not required.

Channels   PSTN provides a single channel, which can carry either voice or digital communications, but not both simultaneously. ISDN service is available in several configurations of multiple channels, each of which can support voice or digital communications. In addition to increasing data throughput, multiple channels eliminate the need for separate voice and data telephone lines.

Availability   ISDN is available throughout the United States.

Cost   The cost of ISDN hardware and service is higher than for PSTN modems and service.

Connection quality   ISDN transmits data digitally and, as a result, is less susceptible to static and noise than analog transmissions. Analog modem connections must dedicate some bandwidth to error correction and retransmission. This overhead reduces the actual throughput. In contrast, an ISDN line can dedicate all its bandwidth to data transmission.

Private Branch Exchange

A PBX is a private telephone switching system owned by a company or organization. The PBX is connected to a common group of PSTN lines from one or more of the telephone company's central switching offices to provide service to a number of individual phones, such as in a hotel, business, or government office. PBX solutions are available in a number of third-party hardware and software configurations, ranging from large dedicated switches, to server-based solutions, to internal cards that can be inserted into individual workstations. In Windows XP Professional, TAPI supports computer call control, voice mail, Caller ID, and other advanced features in conjunction with a PBX.

TAPI 3.1

The Telephony Application Programming Interface, also known as Telephony API or TAPI, is a set of Microsoft Win32 function calls and Component Object Model (COM) interfaces used by telephony applications. These function calls are processed internally by TAPI, and result in calls to service providers, which control the hardware needed by the telephony application. Windows XP Professional includes TAPI 3.1 and TAPI 2.2, which are compatible with TAPI 3.0 and TAPI 2.1 respectively.

The following are some of the enhancements TAPI 3.1 provides to TAPI 3.0:

- New audio codec, DVI4 at 16 kilohertz (KHz) sample rate, in H.323 Service Provider.

- New audio codecs, DVI4 at both 8 KHz and 16 KHz sample rates, in Multicast Conference Service Provider.

- Acoustic Echo Cancellation (AEC) support in H.323 Service Provider and Multicast Conference Service Provider.

- Data encryption for Real-Time Transport Protocol (RTP) in Multicast Conference Service Provider.

- Improved jitter management in H.323 Service Provider and Multicast Conference Service Provider.

- Supplemental Services for H.323, which has the following features enabled:

  - Call Forwarding with the following options: unconditional, on busy, and on no answer.

  - Call Diversion, which allows you to forward a call while it is ringing.

  - Blind Transfer, which allows you to transfer a caller to a third person without consulting the called person.

  - Consultative Transfer, which allows you to transfer a caller to a third person after consulting the called person.

  - Call Hold/Unhold, which allows you to stop and restart the media on a call without dropping the call.

Figure 24-3 shows the architecture of TAPI.

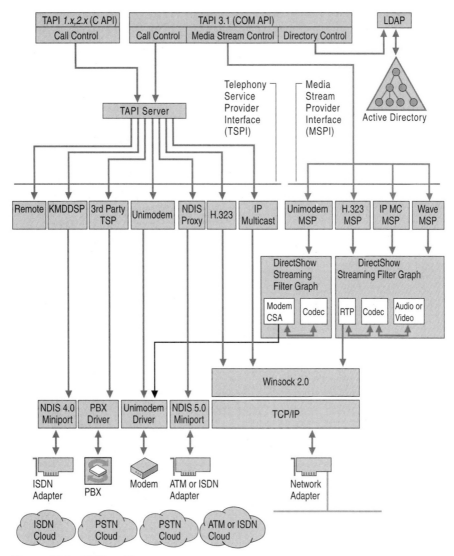

Figure 24-3   TAPI architecture

TAPI 3.1 provides a standard method for communications applications to control telephony functions for data, fax, and voice calls. TAPI manages all signaling between a computer and a telephone network, including basic functions such as dialing, answering, and ending a call. It also manages supplemental services such as hold, transfer, conference, and call park, found in PBX, ISDN, and other telephone systems. The support of supplemental services varies by service provider.

In addition to support for conventional telephony, TAPI 3.1 provides support for IP telephony; that is, telecommunications through IP-based networks. TAPI 3.1 supports user-to-user and multiparty audio and video conferencing through the H.323 and IP multicast. TAPI 3.1 interfaces with user directories to associate user and conference objects with call information, such as IP address and computer name.

Service Providers

TAPI 3.1 supports two classes of service providers: telephony and media. Telephony service providers (TSPs) provide implementation of telephony signaling and connection control features, and media service providers (MSPs) provide access to and control the media content associated with those connections, such as the audio and video streams of a videoconference.

For more information about media service providers in TAPI, see "Telephony Integration and Conferencing" in the *Internetworking Guide* of the *Microsoft Windows 2000 Server Resource Kit*.

A telephony service provider (TSP) is a dynamic-link library (DLL) that supports communications over a telephone network to one or more specific hardware devices through a set of exported service functions. The service provider responds to telephony requests sent by TAPI, and completes the basic tasks necessary to communicate over the telephone network. In this way, the service provider, in conjunction with TAPI, shields applications from the service-dependent and technology-dependent details of telephone network communication.

The installation tool for a service provider registers the application with TAPI and associates that service provider with the hardware devices it supports. Multiple service providers can share the same device: for example, the H.323 TSP and Multicast Conference TSP can both use the same network adapter. Existing applications can be associated with new telephony devices, or the function of existing devices can be extended by using the development and implementation of new service providers.

Table 24-3 lists the telephony and media service providers included with Windows XP Professional.

Table 24-3   Service Providers in Windows XP Professional

Service Provider	Function
H.323 Telephony Service Provider H.323 Media Service Provider	Provides voice and video services over data networks using the H.323 protocol. Support calling conventional phones through IP-PSTN gateways and Internet audio/video calls.
Multicast Conference TAPI Service Provider Multicast Conference Media Service Provider	Provides multiple-user conference support over intranets and the Internet.

Table 24-3   Service Providers in Windows XP Professional

Service Provider	Function
NDIS Proxy TAPI Service Provider	Permits TAPI applications to access wide area network (WAN) devices, such as ISDN modems and Asynchronous Transfer Mode (ATM) devices, using a standard Network Driver Interface Specification (NDIS) 5.0 interface.
TAPI Kernel-Mode Service Provider	Provides TAPI support for NDIS 4 WAN drivers.
Unimodem 5 Telephony Service Provider Unimodem 5 Media Service Provider	Provides device abstraction and TAPI support for a wide variety of modem devices. The Unimodem 5 MSP is used when using full-duplex voice modems.
Wave Media Service Provider	Used with any TSP that provides an audio wave driver. For example, when Unimodem 5 TSP is used with half-duplex voice modems, Wave MSP is used.

Additional service providers can be obtained from hardware vendors for use with their hardware and existing telephony applications, such as a PBX hardware solution.

Note   To install TSPs and MSPs from hardware vendors, follow the instructions provided by the vendor.

Quality of Service

Quality of Service (QoS) refers to a combination of mechanisms that cooperatively provide a specific quality level to application traffic crossing a network or multiple, disparate networks. QoS helps ensure a constant, reliable, steady data stream when using real-time communications, such as IP telephony and video conferencing, over packet-based networks.

Support for QoS in Windows XP Professional

Applications that use QoS can take advantage of the QoS infrastructure supported in Windows XP Professional.

QoS features in Windows XP Professional provide traffic shaping, smoothing bursts and peaks in traffic to an even flow. Packet marking (802.1p marking for layer 2, and Diff-serv Code Point (DSCP) marking for layer 3) helps achieve efficient traffic shaping. The QoS Packet Scheduler enforces QoS parameters for data flow. The QoS Packet Scheduler retrieves the packets from the queues and transmits them according to the QoS parameters. The marked packets then receive priority over non-marked packets when processed by network devices (switches and routers) along the data path.

QoS Components for Windows XP Professional

The components for QoS support are built into Windows XP Professional. Windows XP Professional provides an interface (QoS API) so that applications can support QoS technologies.

The QoS Packet Scheduler is not automatically installed with Windows XP Professional. After selecting and installing QoS Packet Scheduler, you might also have to configure Windows XP Professional to use 802.1p. Select the option for 802.1p support on the properties page for the network adapter. The network adapter must support 802.1p.

Configuring Telephony and Conferencing

IP telephony support is also installed during Windows XP Professional setup, including TAPI 3.1 and all telephony and media service providers. During installation, Windows XP Professional automatically detects, installs, and configures most Plug and Play modems, adapters, and other telephony devices. Use the Add Hardware Wizard to install and configure devices that are not automatically configured and require installation information, such as the driver location. Support for telephony devices added after initial Windows XP Professional installation can also be provided in this manner.

For a list of supported telecommunications devices, see the Hardware Compatibility List link on the Web Resources page at http://www.microsoft.com/windows/reskits/webresources.

If Windows XP Professional is installed over a previous version of Microsoft® Windows® that included telephony services (such as Microsoft® Windows® 95, Microsoft® Windows® 98, or Microsoft® Windows NT® version 4.0), any previous versions of the TAPI programming interface are upgraded. Previous versions of Windows with TAPI 1.4 or TAPI 2.1 are upgraded to TAPI 2.2. Previous versions of Windows with TAPI 3.0 are upgraded to TAPI 3.1. In some instances TAPI 2.2 and TAPI 3.1 will coexist on the same computer. For example, if the previous version of Windows included TAPI 1.4 or TAPI 2.1, TAPI is upgraded to TAPI 2.2. The upgraded computer would then have both the upgraded TAPI 2.2 and TAPI 3.1, which is installed with Windows XP Professional. The correct version of TAPI would be used depending upon the TAPI version for which the application was written.

Configuring Modems

A modem is a communications tool that enables a computer to transmit information over a standard telephone line. Using Windows XP Professional, you can install a modem in one of three ways:

- Plug in your Plug and Play modem or USB modem.

- In Control Panel, use Phone and Modem Options.

- In Control Panel, add a modem by using Add Hardware.

In each of these cases, the Add Hardware Wizard appears and asks if you want Windows XP Professional to automatically detect the modem or if you want to manually select a modem from the list of known manufacturers and modem models. If you choose the detection option, the wizard detects and then queries the modem to configure it. If it cannot detect the modem, it prompts you to select one.

After the modem is selected, you can, if necessary, adjust its properties, such as the volume for the modem speaker, the time to wait for the remote computer to answer the call, and the maximum data transmission speed. These adjustments are made by using Phone and Modem Options in Control Panel.

Depending on the type of modem you have, installing and configuring it might vary slightly as follows:

- If the modem supports Plug and Play, make sure it is configured to respond as a Plug and Play device, rather than manually configured for resource settings. This is normally performed by using a configuration application provided with the modem.

- If you install a modem that does not support Plug and Play, you must configure its built-in COM port by using the Add Hardware Wizard before it is installed by using Phone and Modem Options in Control Panel. In most cases, the Add Hardware Wizard does this automatically for you.

- If you are using Personal Computer Memory Card International Association (PCMCIA) drivers with Windows XP Professional, Windows XP Professional detects and configures PCMCIA modems automatically when they are first inserted.

- If you are using a USB modem, it is automatically detected when installed.

Note   This procedure is for both internal and external modems. PCMCIA and USB modems automatically install when inserted. Before you install a modem, see "Modems" in Windows XP Professional Readme.txt.

To install a modem by using Phone and Modem Options

1. In **Control Panel**, open **Phone and Modem Options**.

2. Select the **Modems** tab, as shown in Figure 24-4, then click **Add** to start the Add Hardware Wizard. The Add Hardware Wizard leads you through the steps for installing a modem.

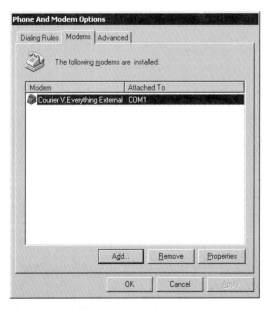

Figure 24-4   Phone and Modem Options dialog box

In most cases, let the Add Hardware Wizard detect the modem for you. If it cannot detect the exact manufacturer and model, the wizard picks a standard configuration that is usually compatible; your modem still functions at its maximum speed and according to factory default settings. A few advanced features, such as enabling and disabling compression, error control, and flow control, might be disabled.

For information about installing a modem or about finding a better match than a standard modem type, see "Troubleshooting Modems" later in this chapter.

Windows XP Professional automatically makes COM port assignments to communications ports, internal modem adapters, and PCMCIA modems according to their base input/output (I/O) port addresses. For more information, see "Managing Devices" in this book.

Defining a Location

A location is information that the modem uses to analyze telephone numbers in international format and to determine the correct sequence of numbers to be dialed. It does not need to correspond to a particular geographic location, but it usually does. For example, a user on a portable computer might require a dialing prefix of "9" to dial an external number from an office location or require a dialing prefix of "*70" to disable a call waiting feature when placing calls from home. A location would be created for each dialing prefix and selected when dialing from each environment. Table 24-4 shows the information associated with a location.

Table 24-4   Location Information

Location Property	Description
Location name	A recognizable name that identifies the location
Country/Region	The country or region for the dialing location
Area or city code	The calling prefix for the area code
Dialing rules	Specifies which prefixes, if any, need to be dialed prior to dialing the area code and number, whether call waiting needs to be enabled or disabled, and if tone or pulse dialing method needs to be used to place the call.
Area code rules	Determines how phone numbers are dialed from the area code used in the current location to other area codes, or within the area code. For example, if your current location is area code 425, and all calls to area code 206 require the 206 area code to be omitted, then you can create a rule to enforce this whenever phone numbers are passed to TAPI.
Calling card information	Specifies the calling card type, account number, and personal identification number (PIN) to be used for the location.

The first time you set up a modem, the Add Hardware Wizard prompts you for the default dialing information about the location from which you usually call (My Location), including your area code and country/region code.

To set default dialing location information

- Run the **Add Hardware Wizard**, and then type the area code and country/region code information in the **New Location** dialog box.

    – or –

    In **Control Panel**, open **Phone and Modem Options**. Select the location (for example, My Location) to modify, and then click **Edit**. The **Edit Location** dialog box appears, as shown in Figure 24-5. Type the dialing information when prompted.

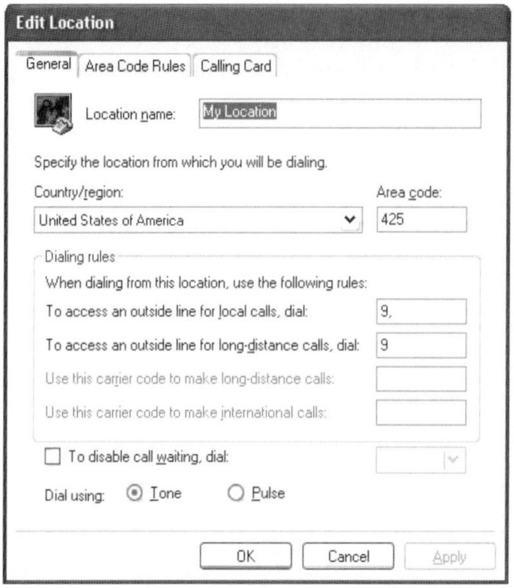

Figure 24-5   Edit Location dialog box

After you install the modem, you can enter more specific location information, such as calling card numbers or rules for dialing outside your local area code, by editing the fields in the **Edit Location** dialog box. Additional dialing rules can also be created from this location. For more information about configuring dialing properties, see Windows XP Professional Help and Support Center.

Setting Modem Properties

In Phone and Modem Options, you can globally change default modem settings for all communications applications and tools created for Windows XP Professional. For example, if you do not want to listen to the modem speaker, you can turn it off for all tools and applications that use that modem. You can also adjust these settings individually within each application.

Note   For Microsoft® Windows® 3.1–based or Microsoft® MS-DOS®-based applications, you need to configure the modem settings within each application.

To view general properties for a modem

1. In **Control Panel**, click **Phone and Modem Options**.

2. Select the **Modem** tab.

3. Select the modem or device you want, and then click **Properties**.

Modem settings are listed on the **General**, **Diagnostics**, and **Advanced** tabs. Table 24-5 describes the **General** settings.

Table 24-5   General Modem Settings

Setting	Description
Port	A port is either a COM port or an LPT port to which an external modem is attached, or a COM port name that identifies an internal or PCMCIA modem. Windows XP Professional automatically assigns a port name (COM1, COM2, COM3, or COM4) to any device it detects. Usually, the port name is adjusted only if you move an external modem from one COM port to another. For PCMCIA modems, the port cannot be changed.
Speaker volume	Sets the volume for the telephone speaker, which broadcasts the dial tone, modem connection, and voices, if applicable, on the other end. To change the volume, move the slider bar to the right or left.
Maximum speed	Sets the speed at which Windows XP Professional communicates with the modem. It is limited by the central procesing unit (CPU) speed of the computer and the speed supported by the communications port. Windows XP Professional selects a conservative default speed so that slower computers do not lose data during transfers.
	You can set the speed lower if the faster rate causes data errors. Set it higher for faster performance. For example, 57,600 might work better than the Windows XP Professional default setting of 38,400 for v.32bis (14,400 bps) modems on fast computers. If applications report data errors, set a lower speed (for example, change it from 38,400 to 19,200 for v.32bis modems).
Dial control	Clear the **Wait for dial tone before dialing** check box if you are making calls from a country or region other than where your modem was purchased and your modem fails to properly detect the dial tone.

> **Tip**   If you have a slower computer and an external modem, you can install a 16550A Universal Asynchronous Receiver/Transmitter (UART)–based COM port adapter to increase speeds. Some internal modems have an integrated 16550A UART adapter.

The **Diagnostics** tab provides hardware information that can be used in hardware configuration and problem determination. Table 24 -6 describes the **Diagnostics** settings.

Table 24-6 Diagnostics Modem Settings

Setting	Description
Modem Information	Displays manufacturer-specific information identifying the modem.
Query Modem	Click **Query Modem** to display your modem's responses to standard AT commands sent to it. This information can be used to assist in troubleshooting.
Append to Log	Windows XP Professional records commands and responses to and from the modem in the Modemlog.txt file in the Windows folder. If the box is not checked, Windows XP Professional erases the old log and records a new log at the beginning of each call. If the check box is selected, Windows XP Professional appends new call logs to this file.
View log	The modem log is a powerful tool for diagnosing problems, particularly with connection problems. However, the interpretation of the contents of the file requires modem documentation, technical support, or experience with modems. The problems diagnosed might be in the local modem, its configuration, the telephone system, the remote modem (for example, the Internet service provider [ISP]), or in some combination.

The **Advanced** tab of the Phone and Modem Options dialog box allows you to override the hardware and connection settings that were configured for the modem and serial port. The **Extra initialization commands** text box allows you to append to the standard initialization commands used to set up the modem at the start of a communications session. These can be standard AT-type commands, or commands specific to your modem or communications device. Refer to the manufacturer's documentation for a description of available commands.

The **Advanced Port Settings** button allows you to change the default configuration for the communications port used by your modem. The advanced COM port settings are available only for certain brands of modems. If you do not have one of these modems and want to change the assigned COM port, you must reinstall the modem and choose the desired COM port during the installation procedure. Table 24-7 describes the advanced port settings.

Table 24-7   Advanced Port Settings

Setting	Description
Use FIFO buffer	A serial port containing a Universal Asynchronous Receiver/Transmitter (UART) chipset allows inbound and outbound information to be stored in associated first-in, first-out (FIFO) buffers until it can be received by the computer or dispatched by the modem.
	The sizes of the inbound and outbound buffers can be enabled by checking the **Use FIFO buffers (requires 16550 compatible UART)** option. The sizes of the inbound buffer (**Receive buffer**) and outbound buffer (**Transmit buffer**) can be modified by using the slider bars.
	Increasing the buffer sizes in 16550 UART-compatible serial ports can improve performance in high-speed modems. However, if you experience data loss or overrun errors, try lowering the buffer sizes or disabling the FIFO buffers.
COM Port Number	If Windows XP Professional detected your modem automatically, it assigned it to an available serial communications (COM) port. If you want to force the COM port assignment, select the available port here. For example, if you have three serial devices that are never used simultaneously, you can change the port settings and have all three devices share the same serial port.

Click **Change Default Preferences** to modify the default settings for call handling and data connection preferences. Table 24-8 describes the available settings.

Table 24-8   Change Default Preferences

Setting	Description
Disconnect a call	Change the number of minutes listed in the **Disconnect a call if idle for more than x minutes** field if there is no activity on the line; for example, increase the number if you want to stay connected to a computer bulletin board even though there is no activity.
Cancel a call	Change the number of seconds listed in the **Cancel a call if not connected within x secs** field if it takes a long time to make a connection; for example, this might occur when you are making an international call and there are long delays before the call is connected.
Port speed	Determines the speed of the flow of data from the modem to the serial port. The speed is normally set correctly during modem installation; however, some modems can transfer data at a rate faster than the 115.2 Kbps supported by the standard serial ports for most computers. For more information, see your modem documentation.

Table 24-8   Change Default Preferences

Setting	Description
Data Protocol	Enables error correction, allowing your modem to negotiate the error correction that is to be used for a communications session with another modem. Available error correction protocols are **V.42**, **MNP4**, **MNP3**, **MNP2**, or **None**.
Compression	Select **Enable** to allow hardware-based compression. Compression boosts transmission speeds by compressing data between the modems. This feature is available on most modems. When it is enabled, modems sometimes have trouble connecting. If this occurs, select **Disable** and try again. Using modem compression can sometimes reduce performance if the data being sent is already compressed by the application.
Flow control	Select **Hardware** for all external modems to avoid loss of data. If your modem cable has RTS (Request To Send) and CTS (Clear To Send) wires connected, you can use hardware flow control; otherwise, select **None** to use software flow control.

Default hardware settings can be changed by selecting the **Advanced** tab of the **Default Preferences** dialog box.

With hardware settings, connection settings usually correspond to what the computer on the other end is using. Therefore, do not change connection settings by using Phone and Modem Options. Rather, use a specific tool or application, such as HyperTerminal, to change these settings connection by connection.

Preferences include Data bits, Parity, Stop bits, and Modulation. For information about these values, see Windows XP Professional Help and Support Center.

If you have installed an external ISDN modem, an additional **ISDN** tab appears in Phone and Modem Options dialog box. The ISDN settings must be configured before the modem can be used.

Configuring ISDN Support

Windows XP Professional provides built-in support for ISDN. Before configuring ISDN on a computer running Windows XP Professional, you need the following:

- Installed internal or external ISDN adapter.

- ISDN telephone line service at the location where you use dial-up networking to connect to the Internet.

- ISDN telephone line service at the remote location to which you want to connect, usually either your ISP or a remote access server.

If your ISDN adapter supports Plug and Play, Windows XP Professional automatically installs the required support. If the ISDN adapter is not automatically installed, use the following procedure to install the device support.

To install your ISDN device

1. In **Control Panel**, open **Add Hardware**.

2. In the **Add Hardware Wizard**, click **Next**.

3. Select **Add/Troubleshoot a device**, and then click **Next**.

4. If Windows XP Professional does not automatically detect the ISDN adapter, select **Add a new device**, and then click **Next**.

5. If you want Windows XP Professional to attempt to find the ISDN adapter, select **Yes, search for new hardware**.

   - or -

   If you want to manually select the ISDN adapter, select **No, I will select it from a list**, and then follow the instructions.

   After the device support for the ISDN adapter has been installed, you are prompted to provide the information necessary to configure ISDN support. Table 24-9 shows the information required in order to configure ISDN in Windows XP Professional.

Table 24-9   ISDN Configuration Information

Option	Description
Switch type	Most ISDN hardware adapters need to know the type of switch to which they are connected. The switch type simply refers to the brand of equipment and software revision level that the telephone company uses to provide you with ISDN service. The switch types listed are **ESS5 (AT&T)**, **National ISDN1**, and **Northern Telecom DMS 1000**.
Service Profile Identifier (SPID)	The SPID usually consists of the telephone number with some additional digits added at the beginning and end. The SPID helps the switch understand what kind of equipment is attached to the line. If multiple devices are attached, it helps route calls to the appropriate device on the line. The SPID is generally used only within the United States and Canada.
Telephone number	In some cases, each B channel on an ISDN line has its own number, while in other cases both B channels share a single telephone number. Your telephone company tells you how many numbers are in your ISDN line. Separate numbers might be useful if you plan to take incoming calls on your ISDN line.

You can change the ISDN configuration information by performing the following steps.

To configure an ISDN adapter

1. In **Control Panel**, double-click **System**, and then select the **Hardware** tab.

2. Click **Device Manager**.

3. Right-click the ISDN device whose settings you want to change, and then select **Properties**.

4. Select the **ISDN** tab.

    To change the switch type, select an item in the list. To change the telephone number and SPID information, click **Configure**.

Configuring Client/Server Telephony Support

Windows XP Professional supports access and control of telephony features on a PBX by using a telephony server. An example of the architecture of a client/server TAPI implementation is shown in Figure 24-6.

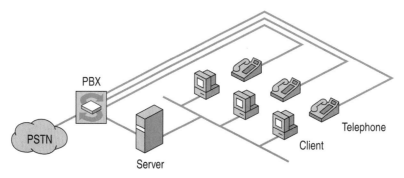

Figure 24-6   Client/server TAPI architecture

The TAPI client is installed with Windows XP Professional. To specify the Windows 2000 TAPI servers to be used by the TAPI clients, you must use the Tcmsetup tool on Windows XP Professional. The Tcmsetup tool allows you to specify the servers that provide the telephony services used by the network.

The following section describes the configuration of a Windows XP Professional client to access the telephony server.

To identify telephony servers to a TAPI client

1. Log on to the client computer with an account that is a member of the Administrators group.

2. In the **Run** dialog box, type:

    tcmsetup /c *telephonyserver1* [*telephonyserver2*]... [*telephonyserverx*]
    The variable *telephonyserver* is the name of the TAPI server.

3. Click **OK**.

The parameters for the **tcmsetup** command are described in Table 24-10.

Table 24-10   Tcmsetup Command Parameters

Parameter	Description
/q	Suppresses message boxes during setup.
/x	Specifies connection-oriented callbacks (default is connectionless).
/c *telephonyserver*	Sets the telephony server to be used by this client to *telephonyserver*. Multiple servers can be listed, each name separated by a space.
/d	Deletes the current telephony server list and disables TAPI services on this client.
/r	Disables automatic server discovery.

The telephony client must be in the same domain as the telephony server, or must be a member of a domain that is fully trusted by the domain of the telephony server.

The servers specified in the **tcmsetup** command override any previous telephony servers specified previously in the **tcmsetup** command. All servers required by the client must be specified in a single instance of the command.

The **tcmsetup** command can only be performed when logged on to the client with an account that is a member of the Administrators group. Alternately, if you logged on by using an account in the Users or Power Users group, you can use the **runas** command to perform the **tcmsetup** command as an administrator. For example:

```
runas /user:mydomain\adminacct "tcmsetup /c servername"
```

Type the password for the administrative account when prompted.

Configuring TAPI IP Telephony

This section discusses the procedures necessary for configuring a Windows XP Professional–based client to access IP telephony services by using the H.323 protocol in an environment where an H.323 proxy or gateway is present. If your Windows XP Professional–based computer connects directly to the Internet, or an H.323 gateway is not used, this configuration is not required. Microsoft Internet Security and Acceleration (ISA) Server provides an H.323 proxy and gatekeeper.

Specifying the H.323 Gateway

The H.323 protocol incorporates support for placing calls from data networks to the switched circuit PSTN network, and vice versa by using an IP-PSTN gateway. The H.323 Telephony Service Provider provides support for gateway calling by using a static configuration option, accessible through **Phone and Modem Options** in Control Panel.

To specify the address of the IP-PSTN gateway

1. In **Control Panel**, click **Phone and Modem Options**.

2. Click the **Advanced** tab, and then select **Microsoft H.323 Telephony Service Provider**.

3. Click **Configure**. Select the **Use H.323 gateway** check box, as shown in Figure 24-7, and then type the computer name or IP address of the IP-PSTN gateway in the text box.

Figure 24-7   Configure H.323 Service Provider dialog box

The telephony application running at the gateway must conform to ITU-T H.323 v1.0 standards.

For information about the installation and configuration of an IP-PSTN gateway, see "Telephony Integration and Conferencing" in the *Internetworking Guide*.

Specifying the H.323 Proxy

The Microsoft H.323 TSP incorporates support for firewall traversal. Use Phone and Modem Options to specify the inner IP address of the firewall computer. This allows calls to be made and received across the Internet.

To specify the IP address of the H.323 proxy

1. In **Control Panel**, click **Phone and Modem Options**.

2. Click the **Advanced** tab, and then select **Microsoft H.323 Telephony Service Provider**.

3. Click **Configure**. Select the **Use H.323 proxy** check box, and then type the computer name or IP address of the inner edge of the H.323 proxy or firewall computer in the text box.

Specifying the H.323 Gatekeeper

The Microsoft H.323 TSP incorporates H.323 gatekeeper support. A *gatekeeper* is a server in a network that manages client access to telephony services. A gatekeeper provides address resolution, call routing, call logging, and other services to other computers within the local communications network, or to external users. Use Phone and Modem Options to specify the name or IP address of the gatekeeper, log-on credentials (phone number or account name), and timeout and port values.

To configure the H.323 gatekeeper

1. In **Control Panel**, click **Phone and Modem Options**.

2. Click the **Advanced** tab, and then select **Microsoft H.323 Telephony Service Provider**.

3. Click **Configure**. Select the **Use H.323 gatekeeper** check box, and then type the name or IP address of the H.323 gatekeeper in the corresponding text box. If needed, you can enter nondefault values in the text boxes for both the **H.323 Call Alerting timeout** and **H.323 Call Listening Port**.

Using Windows Directory Service

A directory service can be used to facilitate the process of making H.323-based IP telephony calls. The directory service provides transparent translation from either a user name or computer name to the associated IP address. For example, if you enter a known user name or computer name when making a call through an H.323-based IP telephony application, the directory service translates the information to an IP address. You can also use the directory service to publish IP multicast conferences.

Windows XP Professional uses a combination of the Lightweight Directory Access Protocol (LDAP) directory service and Active Directory for H.323-based IP telephony calls. The Internet Locator Service (ILS) of Microsoft® Site Server is another directory service that can be used with TAPI applications on Windows 2000–based computers. This service is distinct from Active Directory in that it is less scalable, and does not provide persistent, centrally-administered data storage.

Troubleshooting Telephony and Conferencing

You can use the following techniques and procedures to determine and resolve problems within telephony applications and in telephony device configuration, and H.323 and multicast conferencing.

Troubleshooting Modems

The following sections detail troubleshooting procedures for analog and ISDN modems.

An analog or ISDN modem is not listed   If your modem is not on the Windows XP Professional Hardware Compatibility List (HCL) or is not detected by the Add Hardware Wizard, use one of the following procedures to install it:

■ Check the modem. If it is an external modem, make sure it is turned on, and all cables are tightly connected. If the modem is internal, verify that it is properly installed.

   If the modem is a Plug and Play device, open Device Manager in Control Panel and select **Scan for hardware changes** on the **Action** menu to reinstall the modem. To open Device Manager, open **Control Panel**, and then double-click **System**. Click the **Hardware** tab, and then click **Device Manager**. If the modem is not a Plug and Play device, reinstall the modem using **Add Hardware**.

■ Obtain an .inf (installation) file from the modem manufacturer specifically for Windows XP Professional. Follow the manufacturer's instructions for installing the modem in Windows XP Professional, or contact the modem manufacturer for assistance.

■ Install your modem as a standard modem by using the Add Hardware Wizard. This option provides basic dialing and connectivity support for the modem, although manufacturer-specific features might be unavailable.

Application cannot dial selected modem   If you cannot use an application to dial your modem, test the modem to verify that Windows XP Professional can connect to it. In the **Phone and Modem Options** dialog box, select the **Modems** tab, click **Properties** for the modem you want, and then select the **Diagnostics** tab. Click **Query Modem** to send a set of AT commands to the modem. If the modem response is not displayed in the **Response** area, then perform the following steps to diagnose the problem:

■ If an external modem is experiencing problems, make sure that the serial cable connection between the computer and the modem is secure and that the cable is not broken or frayed.

■ Verify that Windows XP Professional recognizes your COM ports by displaying Device Manager. Verify that the COM port is not experiencing a hardware or resource problem (identified by an exclamation point icon next to the device listing) or has been disabled (identified by the international "No" symbol). If the connected port is listed without any additional icons, the COM port is recognized and available.

If the COM port is disabled in Device Manager, a hardware or a configuration problem is likely. Use the following steps to troubleshoot the problem for an external modem:

- Verify that the port is not disabled in the BIOS (also called the CMOS) setup of the computer. Refer to the documentation for your computer to obtain information about configuring options in the BIOS setup.

- Make sure there are no other adapters or devices that are configured for the same base I/O address or interrupt request (IRQ) as the COM port to which the modem is attached.

- Verify that the serial port is not defective. If the modem and any other serial devices fail on the COM port but work on other COM ports, and you have verified the two steps above, the serial port might be defective.

If the modem experiencing problems is internal, perform the following steps to diagnose and resolve the problem:

- If the internal modem is not Plug and Play–compatible, it might use jumpers to specify the COM port. Make sure the jumpers on the modem are configured properly. There might or might not be jumpers that allow you to set the base I/O address and IRQ to be used by the modem as well. Verify that they are properly set. Some modems use a configuration application to change these settings.

- If the modem is configured for a COM port number that is assigned to a COM port on the motherboard or a serial card (physical port), you must either set the modem to use a different COM port, or use the BIOS setup to disable the COM port that has the same number as the internal modem.

- Make sure that no other adapters or devices are configured for the same base I/O address or IRQ as the internal modem.

- Verify that the internal modem is not defective. Also, check with the vendor of your modem to see if there is an upgrade available for your modem.

Troubleshooting PSTN Telephony

The following sections outline common problems and solutions for conventional (non-IP) PSTN telephony deployment.

Computer cannot find the telephony server   If the telephony server cannot be reached by means of the network, for example, a user cannot "ping" the telephony server, it is possible that:

- The telephony server is not available or has not been correctly set up. Contact the administrator of the telephony server.

- The Tcmsetup tool has not been run. Run the Tcmsetup tool with the **/c** parameter to specify the correct servers.

- The Tcmsetup tool has been run, but an incorrect telephony server was specified. Run the Tcmsetup tool with the **/c** parameter to specify the correct servers.

- The Tcmsetup tool has been run multiple times, overwriting the original telephony configuration. Run the Tcmsetup tool with the **/c** parameter, listing all telephony servers in the single command.

- The Tcmsetup tool has been run with the **/d** (delete) parameter. Run the tcmsetup tool with the **/c** parameter to enable telephony services and to specify the correct server(s).

One or more clients cannot find a line for the telephony server   If one or more client computers cannot find the lines for a telephony server, it might be because they cannot be authorized for access to lines on the telephony server. When a TAPI application first accesses lines on the telephony server, the user context associated with the application process is authenticated. This means that those lines must have been configured on the server to allow access by that client. Contact the system administrator for the server.

After the lines have been configured, the new settings are not available until TAPI restarts on the client. Stop all client TAPI applications and restart Windows XP Professional. When the client applications restart, they can find the newly assigned lines.

An application fails to start after you have canceled the Location Information dialog box   If an application fails to start after you have canceled the Location Information dialog box, the problem might be that address translation required by TAPI applications has not been specified. Use the Location Information dialog box to enter your country/region code, local area code, and pulse or tone and external line access settings.

A client cannot find a new line, even though the server administrator has assigned the line to the client   When you assign a currently running client to a line on the telephony server, the new settings are not available until TAPI restarts on the client. Stop all client TAPI applications so that TAPI shuts down. When the client applications restart, they can find the newly assigned lines.

Troubleshooting Conferencing Applications

Users of H.323 or multicast conferencing might encounter problems connecting with other users or receiving audio or video.

Audio problems in conferencing applications   If audio problems occur in H.323 or multicast video conferences, the microphones or sound cards on the clients might be incorrectly configured or malfunctioning.

To diagnose sound hardware on Windows XP Professional–based computers, start the Sound Recorder application. In **Accessories**, point to **Entertainment**, and then click **Sound Recorder**. You can also open Sound Recorder by typing **sndrec32** at the command prompt. Make a recording of your own voice using Sound Recorder, and then play it back. If there is no sound, make sure that the microphone is properly plugged in.

If the Sound Recorder test works properly but you continue to have audio problems, verify the sound settings using Volume Control.

To verify sound settings by using Volume Control

1. In **Accessories**, point to **Entertainment**, and then click **Volume Control**.

2. In the **Options** menu, click **Properties**, and then click **Playback**. Make sure that the **Wave** and **Microphone** check boxes are selected. You might have to scroll the list to see these settings.

3. Click **OK**.

4. Select the **Mute** check box in the **Microphone** column if it is not checked. This prevents speech from being echoed locally (played back on the speaker's computer).

5. If the voices of all other conference participants are too loud or too quiet, adjust the **Volume Control** or **Wave** sliders downward or upward as needed.

6. On the **Options** menu, click **Properties**, and then click **Recording**. Select all of the check boxes in the list at the bottom of the dialog box. You might have to scroll the list to see these settings.

7. Click **OK**.

8. Select the **Mute** check boxes in all of the columns except for the **Microphone** column if they are not already checked. Make sure that the **Mute** check box in the **Microphone** column is not selected. This allows your speech to be sent to the conference, but prevents other sounds, including those of other conference participants, from being transmitted from your computer.

9. If other conference participants are dissatisfied with the level of sound, adjust the **Microphone** slider downward or upward as needed.

Note   A single incorrectly configured computer can cause audio problems or echoes for all other conference participants.

If you continue to encounter audio problems after adjusting the sound settings, make sure that the affected computers have full-duplex sound cards. Full-duplex sound cards can capture and play audio simultaneously, while half-duplex sound cards can only do one at a time. Most modern sound cards are full-duplex, but many older sound cards are only half-duplex.

To check if the sound card on your computer supports full-duplex audio, start Sound Recorder and record a speech sample for approximately 30 seconds. After this is complete, open a second instance of Sound Recorder. Play the sample you recorded using the first instance of Sound Recorder, and while this is playing, attempt to record a sample using the second instance of Sound Recorder. If the second instance of Sound Recorder cannot record a sample while the first instance is playing, the sound card does not support full-duplex audio, and thus does not work with TAPI.

If sound is distorted or otherwise continues to malfunction after you attempt the above procedures, there is most likely a problem with the microphone, sound card hardware, or sound card driver. Contact the manufacturer of your sound cards to ensure that you have the most recent Windows XP Professional drivers. Also, replace the microphones and sound cards on affected computers and attempt these tests again.

Eliminating audio echo   Audio echo is a common problem with audio conferencing systems. Audio echo is often more detectable when using a microphone and speakers, as opposed to using a headset, which has an integrated microphone and speakers. For example, echo can originate in the local audio loopback that happens when a user's microphone picks up sounds from the user's speakers and transmits it back to the other participants. Normal conversation can become impossible for other participants in the conference when sensitive microphones are used, speaker level is high, or the microphone and speakers are placed in close proximity to each other.

TAPI 3.1 applications written to use the acoustic echo cancellation capabilities of either the H.323 Service Provider or Multicast Conference Service Provider allow for the elimination of acoustic echo when using a microphone and speakers.

Another way to completely eliminate audio echo is to use audio headsets. These eliminate the possibility of a user's microphone picking up sound that is being received from other conference participants.

A more expensive solution is to use special microphones with built-in echo-canceling capabilities. These microphones detect and cancel out echo. The main advantage to these is that users do not have to wear headsets. Echo-canceling microphones are also a necessity for conference rooms because using headphones is not a practical solution.

Video problems in conferencing applications   If the video image of an H.323 conference participant cannot be seen by the other party, or if the image of a multicast conference participant cannot be seen by all of the other endpoints, the computer's video capture device might not be working properly. See the camera troubleshooter in Windows XP Professional Help and Support Center.

Unable to publish multicast conference invitations   If you cannot publish multicast conference invitations, confirm with your network administrator that a Windows directory service is available at your site. The directory service provides the ability to publish IP multicast conferences.

Additional Resources

These resources contain additional information and tools related to this chapter.

- For more information about installing and troubleshooting hardware devices, see "Managing Devices" in this book.

- For more information about H.323, see the International Telecommunication Union link on the Web Resources page at http://www.microsoft.com/windows/reskits/webresources.

- For more information about SIP, see RFC 2543: *SIP: Session Initiation Protocol*.

- The Internet Engineering Task Force (IETF) link on the Web Resources page at http://www.microsoft.com/windows/reskits/webresources.

- Telephony Client Setup (Tcmsetup.exe)

    You can use the Telephony Client Setup tool to set up the telephony client. For more information about Tcmsetup, see Windows XP Professional Tools help.

Part V

System Troubleshooting

This part helps you support computers that are running Microsoft® Windows® XP Professional. In addition to an introduction to developing troubleshooting strategies, it includes in-depth information to help you troubleshoot problems with disks and file systems and those encountered during startup.

Chapter 25

Troubleshooting Concepts and Strategies

Microsoft® Windows® XP Professional provides a comprehensive set of troubleshooting tools for diagnosing and resolving hardware and software problems. Using these tools effectively requires an understanding of basic troubleshooting concepts and strategies.

Related Information

- For more information about enabling, disabling, and managing devices, see "Managing Devices" in this book.

- For more information about troubleshooting tools use and syntax, see "Tools for Troubleshooting" in this book.

- For more information about troubleshooting Stop messages, see "Common Stop Messages for Troubleshooting" in this book.

- For more information about system and performance monitoring, see "Overview of Performance Monitoring" in the *Operations Guide* of the *Microsoft® Windows® 2000 Server Resource Kit.*

Troubleshooting Overview

Whether an issue stems from a hardware or a software problem, you need a reliable troubleshooting plan. Guesswork and random solutions are unreliable and often unsuccessful. An effective troubleshooting plan starts with gathering information, observing symptoms, and doing research.

Figure 25-1 illustrates a six-step troubleshooting model used by Microsoft Product Support Services engineers, who call it the *"detect method."*

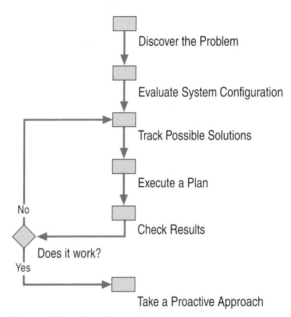

Figure 25-1   Troubleshooting Model

Based on research in problem solving, the six steps of this troubleshooting model are:

1. **Discover the problem.**   Identify and document problem symptoms, and search technical information resources to determine if the problem is a known condition. For more information, see "Identify Problem Symptoms" and "Check Technical Information Resources" later in this chapter.

2. **Evaluate system configuration.**   Review your system's history to determine what configuration changes occurred since the computer last worked correctly. Did you install new hardware or software? Did you verify that the hardware or software is fully compatible with Windows XP Professional? For more information, see "Review Your System's History", "Check Firmware Versions", and "Avoid Common Pitfalls" later in this chapter.

3. **Track possible solutions.**   Instead of using the trial-and-error approach, review Microsoft Knowledge Base articles. You can simplify troubleshooting by temporarily removing hardware and software that is not needed for starting Windows XP Professional. Consider enabling Windows XP Professional logging options to better evaluate your troubleshooting efforts. For more information, see "Troubleshooting Strategies" later in this chapter.

4. **Execute a plan.**   Test potential solutions and have a contingency plan if these solutions do not work or have a negative impact on the computer. Be sure to back up critical system or application files. For more information, see "Avoid Common Pitfalls" later in this chapter.

5. **Check results.**   Determine if your plan was successful. Have another plan in place to address unresolved issues.

6. **Take a proactive approach.**   Document changes that you make along the way while troubleshooting the problem. After resolving the problem, organize your notes and evaluate your experience. Think about ways to avoid or reduce the impact of the problem in the future. For more information, see "Document and Evaluate the Results" and "Take Proactive Measures" later in this chapter.

For more information about the preceding steps, see "Troubleshooting Concepts" and "Troubleshooting Strategies" later in this chapter.

Troubleshooting Concepts

The immediate goal of any troubleshooting session is to restore service as quickly as possible. However, the larger goal is to determine the cause of the problem. Root-cause analysis is the practice of searching for the source of problems to prevent them from recurring.

Problems represent deviations from known or expected behavior and the most effective way to solve a problem is to gather information before acting, and then isolate and eliminate variables.

Identify Problem Symptoms

Start by observing and identifying symptoms of the problem. You need to learn more about the circumstances in which problems occur and become familiar with system behavior when issues arise. Here are some questions that you can use to help identify symptoms:

- **Do error messages appear?** If so, record the error numbers, the exact message text, and a brief description of the activity. This information is useful when researching the cause of the problem or when consulting with technical support. In your description, include events that precede or follow a problem and the time and date of the error. For complex or lengthy messages, you can use a program such as Microsoft® Paint (Mspaint.exe) to record the error message as a bitmap.

To capture an on-screen error message

1. Click the window or dialog box that contains the error message.

2. To capture the contents of the entire desktop, press PRINT SCREEN (or PrtScn).
   – or –
   To capture an image of the active (foreground) desktop window only, press ALT + PRINT SCREEN (or PrtScn).

3. In the Run dialog box, in the Open box, type:
   mspaint

4. On the Edit menu, click Paste.

5. If the prompt **The image in the clipboard is larger...** appears, click Yes.

6. On the **File** menu, type a file name for the image, and then click **Save**.

Error messages might appear before Windows XP Professional starts. For example, motherboard or storage adapter firmware might display an error message if self-tests detect a hardware problem. If you are unable to record the message quickly enough, you can pause the text display by pressing PAUSE BREAK. To continue, press CTRL+PAUSE BREAK.

- **Did you check Event Viewer logs?** Entries in Event Viewer's application, security, and system logs might contain information helpful for determining the cause of the problem. Look for symptoms or signs of problems that occur at frequent or regular intervals. For more information about Event Viewer, see Windows XP Professional Help and Support Center and "Tools for Troubleshooting" in this book.

- **Did you check log files on your computer?** Error messages sometimes direct you to view a log file on your computer. The operating system or an application typically saves log files in text format. By using Notepad or an equivalent text editor, you can view the contents of a text log file to determine if it contains information useful for troubleshooting your problem.

- **Does the problem coincide with an application or activity?** If the problem occurs when an application is running or during activities such as network printing or Internet browsing, you can reproduce the error to observe details and gather information for troubleshooting purposes. Be sure to record what applications and features are being used when the problem occurs.

■ **Do previous records exist?** Check to see if there are records that describe changes, such as the software installed or hardware upgraded. If records are not available, you might query users or other support technicians. Pay special attention to recent changes such as Service Packs applied, device drivers installed, and motherboard or peripheral firmware versions. This information can help you determine if the problem is new or a condition that has worsened.

■ **Is baseline information available?** Baseline information is system configuration and performance data taken at various times to mark hardware and software changes. If possible, compare current baselines with previous ones to determine the effects of recent changes on system performance. If previous baselines are not available, you can generate a baseline to evaluate recent efforts to troubleshoot your current system configuration. For more information about generating configuration baselines of your systems' performance and hardware, see Windows XP Professional Help and Support Center and "Overview of Performance Monitoring" in the *Operations Guide* of the *Microsoft Windows 2000 Server Resource Kit*.

■ **Does the problem seem related to user profiles?** Do other users who log on to the same computer have similar problems? Are all users who do not experience problems using Administrator accounts or do they share other common attributes? For example, check if the problem occurs when using a newly created user account.

■ **Does the problem seem network related?** Determine if the same error occurs on more than one computer on a network. See if the error happens when you log on locally or use a domain account. For a network-related error that occurred during startup, try disconnecting the network cable and restart the computer. For more information about troubleshooting startup problems, see "Troubleshooting Startup" in this book.

■ **Is incompatible or untested software installed?** Are you using unsigned or beta drivers? Installing software not fully tested for compatibility with Windows XP Professional or using unsigned drivers can cause erratic behavior or instability.

■ **Do you have backups to examine?** If you can establish a time frame for the problem, try to locate earlier system backups. Examining the differences between current and previous configurations can help you identify system components or settings that have changed. In addition to examining backups, you can use the System Restore tool to save or restore system states. By comparing the current state to past states, you might be able to determine when the changes occurred and identify the components or settings affected. For more information about System Restore, see Windows XP Professional Help and Support Center and "Tools for Troubleshooting" in this book.

Check Technical Information Resources

After you gather information about key symptoms, check internal and external technical information sources for ideas, solutions, and similar or related symptoms reported by others.

Information resources such as Windows XP Professional–related newsgroups and the Microsoft Knowledge Base can save you time and effort. The ideal situation is that your problem is a known issue, complete with solutions or suggestions that point you in the right direction. See sources of information shown in Table 25-1.

Table 25-1   Help and Information Sources

Source	Description
Diagnostic Solutions Guide (DSG)	A Microsoft Web site that helps you search TechNet articles pertaining to your problem. For more information about the DSG, see the Diagnostic Solutions Guide link on the Web Resources page at http://www.microsoft.com/windows/reskits/webresources.
Help and Support Center	Provides access to troubleshooting tools, wizards, information, and links that cover a wide range of Windows XP Professional–related topics including:

- Hardware devices, such as modems and network adapters.
- Networking and the Internet.
- Multimedia applications and devices.
- E-mail, printing, and faxing.
- Working remotely.
- Remote assistance and troubleshooting.
- System information and diagnostics.
- Troubleshooting tools and diagnostic programs provided by Windows XP Professional.

To do a search using this feature, on the **Start** menu, click **Help and Support**.

Source	Description
Help Desk, Problem Management Department	Technicians who have access to a wide range of information and history, including common problems and solutions.
International Technology Information Library (ITIL) and Microsoft Operations Framework (MOF) Web sites	Sites that provide information for developing, troubleshooting, planning, organizing, and managing information technology (IT) services. The ITIL Web site provides an online glossary of commonly used industry terms used in IT-related documents. For more information, see the ITIL and MOF links on the Web Resources page at http://www.microsoft.com/windows/reskits/webresources.

Table 25-1   Help and Information Sources

Source	Description
Internet newsgroups	Technical newsgroups offer peer support for common computer problems. You can exchange messages in an appropriate forum to request or provide solutions and workarounds. Newsgroup discussions cover a wide range of topics and provide valuable information that might help you track down the source of your problem. Viewing newsgroup messages requires newsreader software, such as Outlook Express.
Manufacturers' Web sites	Web sites offered by manufacturers of computers, peripherals, and applications to provide Web support for their products.
Microsoft Knowledge Base	An extensive list of known problems and solutions that you can search. If you are unfamiliar with searching the Microsoft Knowledge Base, see article Q242450, "How to Query the Microsoft Knowledge Base Using Keywords." To find this article and for more information about the Microsoft Knowledge Base, see the Microsoft Knowledge Base link on the Web Resources page at http://www.microsoft.com/windows/reskits/webresources.
Microsoft Product Support Services	A Web site that contains technical information, useful links, downloads, and answers to frequently asked questions (FAQs). To access the support options available from Product Support Services, see the Microsoft Product Support Services link on the Web Resources page at http://www.microsoft.com/windows/reskits/webresources.
Microsoft TechNet	A subscription-based service for IT professionals that enables you to search technical content and topics about Microsoft products. For more information about TechNet, see the Microsoft TechNet link on the Web Resources page at http://www.microsoft.com/windows/reskits/webresources.
Other online information Web sites	Many Web sites maintained by individuals and organizations provide troubleshooting information for Microsoft® Windows®98, Microsoft® Windows®Me, Microsoft® Windows NT®version 4.0, Microsoft® Windows 2000, Microsoft® Windows 2000, and Windows XP Professional. Some of these Web sites specialize in hardware issues; others, in software.
Readme files	Files that contain the latest information about the software or driver installation media. Typical file names are "Readme.txt" or "Readme1st.txt."
Reference books	Reference books such as the *Microsoft Windows 2000 Server Resource Kit* provide helpful information for diagnosing problems.
Technical support	Technical support can help you solve a complex problem that might otherwise require substantial research time.
Training	Instructor-led or self-paced training can increase your troubleshooting efficiency.

Table 25-1 Help and Information Sources

Source	Description
Windows Update Web site	A site that contains downloadable content, including current information about improving system compatibility and stability. For more information about Windows Update, see the Windows Update link on the Web Resources page at http://www.microsoft.com/windows/reskits/webresources.

Before you apply a solution or workaround, or test an upgraded or updated application, use Backup to back up your system. Backups allow you to restore the computer to the previous state if you are not satisfied with the results. For information about backing up your system, see "Backup and Restore" in this book.

If your organization has test labs to use, consider testing workarounds and updates in a lab environment before applying them to multiple systems. For more information about software compatibility testing, see "Avoid Common Pitfalls" later in this chapter.

Review Your System's History

Review the history of your computer to know about recent changes, including all hardware and software installed. If baseline or change records exist, look for information about new devices, new applications, updated drivers, and change dates—as well as descriptions of the work done. If records are not available, you can learn much about your computer by querying users and internal support personnel or by using tools such as Device Manager and System Information. For more information about Device Manager and System Information, see Windows XP Professional Help and Support Center and "Tools for Troubleshooting" in this book. Also, see "Managing Devices" in this book.

Here are a few points to consider when reviewing the history of your computer:

- **Did problems occur shortly after the installation of a particular application?**

- **Was a "hotfix" applied?** Microsoft technical support might provide a hotfix for an urgent or critical issue. Hotfixes address a specific issue and might not be fully tested for compatibility. For example, a hotfix that works for one computer might cause unwanted results in another. Carefully read and follow the instructions before applying a hotfix.

- **Did the problem occur soon after new hardware was installed?**

- **Why were hardware or software updates made?** Are the motherboard and peripheral firmware current? Can you establish a relationship between the problem and the recent change?

- **Are any non-Plug and Play devices installed?** If so, you can check for proper configuration by using hardware diagnostic programs and Device Manager. Try replacing non-Plug and Play devices with hardware that is compatible with Windows XP Professional. For more information about selecting hardware, see "Avoid Common Pitfalls" later in this chapter.

- **Was a new user recently assigned to the computer?** If so, review system history to determine if the user has installed incompatible hardware or software.

- **When was the last virus check performed?** Does the virus scanning software incorporate the latest virus signature updates? For more information about virus signature versions and updates, see the documentation provided with your antivirus software.

- **If a Service Pack is installed, is it the latest version?**

To determine the version of a Service Pack

- In the **Run** dialog box, type: **winver**

Compare System Settings and Configurations

If similar computers in your organization are problem free when you are troubleshooting a problem, you can use those problem-free computers as a reference for your root-cause analysis. The properly functioning system can provide valuable baseline data. By comparing the following elements, you can speed up the process of identifying contributing causes.

Installed services and applications   Generate a list of applications and services installed on the baseline computer to compare with applications and services on the problem system. To gather a list of applications installed on your system, use **Add or Remove Programs** in Control Panel. To gather a list of services enabled on your system, use Services (Services.msc) or System Information. For more information about using Add or Remove Programs, Services, and System Information, see Windows XP Professional Help and Support Center. Also, see "Tools for Troubleshooting" and "Troubleshooting Startup" in this book.

Software revisions   Check the application and driver revisions to see if differences exist between the two systems. Update the problem system's software to match the versions used on the problem-free system. For applications, you can usually find version information by clicking **Help**, and then clicking **About** *application name*. For drivers, you can use Device Manager or System Information to find version information. For more information about determining device driver versions, see "Managing Devices" in this book.

System logs   Compare Event Viewer logs for problem indications such as signs of hardware stress. For example, unexpected system shutdowns are logged with a "1076" event identification number in the System event log. The associated descriptive text can provide essential information to diagnose the problem. Baseline and problem systems might have similar problems, but the symptoms are more noticeable on one computer because it performs a unique or very demanding role. For example, a server that provides multimedia content typically consumes more system resources than a server that stores infrequently used Microsoft Word documents. Problems with disk, audio, video, or network devices and drivers typically appear earlier on computers that are stressed. Additionally, logging options for most Windows XP Professional components exist, and these can help you with features such as authentication, security, and remote access.

Hardware revisions   A minor hardware component upgrade might not be significant enough to cause a manufacturer to change a product model number. Consider this hypothetical scenario:

A computer company uses a revision 1.0 motherboard when assembling a Model ZZXZ1234 computer. On reordering components, the company receives notice from the original equipment manufacturer (OEM) stating plans to correct certain problems by substituting updated revision 1.1 motherboards. The computer company then incorporates the updated components into all Model ZZXZ1234 computers. These minor changes might require you to exercise more care when updating drivers or firmware in your Model ZZXZ1234 computers. For example, a support Web page for Model ZZXZ1234 computers might post specific firmware versions, V3.0 for revision 1.0 motherboards and V4.0 for revision 1.1 and higher motherboards. Using firmware version V4.0 for computers that use revision 1.0 motherboards might cause problems.

Check Firmware Versions

When you turn on or cycle power to a computer, the central processing unit (CPU) begins to carry out programming instructions, or code, contained in the motherboard system firmware. Firmware, known as basic input/output system (BIOS) on x86-based computers and internal adapters, and as Extensible Firmware Interface (EFI) on Itanium-based computers, contains operating system independent code necessary for the operating system to perform low-level functions such as startup self-tests and the initialization of devices required to start Windows XP Professional. If instability or setup problems affect only a few Windows XP Professional–based computers in your organization, check the motherboard and peripheral firmware.

Motherboard firmware revisions   Compare the BIOS or EFI versions on the problem and problem-free systems. If the versions differ, check the computer manufacturer's Web site for the latest firmware revisions. For example, if your firmware revision A was stable, but upgrading to firmware revision B causes problems, you might find firmware revision C on the Web site. If no revision C exists, temporarily downgrade to revision A until an update becomes available.

> **Note**   The EFI specification defines a new model for the interface between operating systems and platform firmware. The specification abstracts the operating system from a computer's low-level hardware and firmware details and provides a standard environment for starting an operating system and running pre-boot applications (EFI tools that you can use prior to starting Windows XP Professional). For more information about EFI, see the Extensible Firmware Interface link on the Web Resources page at http://www.microsoft.com/windows/reskits/webresources.

Peripheral firmware revisions   It might be necessary to check peripheral firmware revisions and upgrade firmware for individual peripherals, such as small computer system interface (SCSI) adapters, CD and DVD-ROM drives, hard disks, video cards, and audio devices. Peripheral firmware contains device-specific instructions, but is independent from the operating system. Peripheral firmware enables a device to perform specific functions. Upgrading firmware can enhance performance, add new features, or correct compatibility problems. In most cases, you can upgrade device firmware by using software the manufacturer provides. Outdated motherboard system firmware can cause problems, especially for Advanced Configuration and Power Interface (ACPI) systems.

OEMs periodically incorporate updated firmware into existing products to address customers' issues or to add new features. Sometimes similar computers using the same hardware components have different motherboard and peripheral firmware versions. Upgrading firmware on older devices might require you to replace components (such as electronic chips) or exchange the part for a newer version. To avoid firmware problems, be sure to check the firmware (BIOS or EFI) revision your computer uses.

To check the firmware version on your computer

1. In the **Run** dialog box, in the **Open** box, type:
    msinfo32

2. In the **Item** column, locate **BIOS Version**.

Compare the firmware version listed for your system against the most recent revision available on the OEM's Web site. Figure 25-2 shows an example of this.

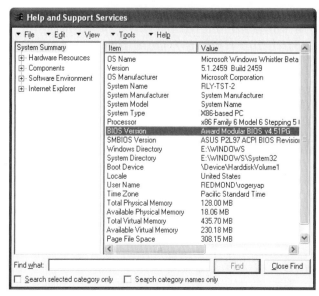

Figure 25-2   Motherboard firmware revision in System Information

Note   Windows NT 4.0 Windows Diagnostics (Winmsd.exe) is not available in Windows XP Professional. Typing **winmsd** from the command prompt now starts System Information, which contains similar information.

To check if your firmware is ACPI compliant

- In the **Run** dialog box, in the **Open** box, type:
  devmgmt.msc

Figure 25-3 shows a Device Manager display for a computer that is not using ACPI features.

Figure 25-3   Non-ACPI computer in Device Manager

As shown in Figure 25-4, if the text **ACPI** appears under **Computer**, this means that Windows XP Professional is using ACPI functionality.

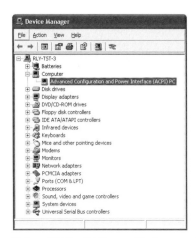

Figure 25-4   ACPI-compliant computer in Device Manager

For additional information about the ACPI specification, see the ACPI link on the Web Resources page at http://www.microsoft.com/windows/reskits/webresources.

> **Warning**   Failure to follow the manufacturer's instructions for updating firmware might cause permanent damage to your computer. If you are unfamiliar with this process, request assistance from trained personnel. Back up important data before you attempt to upgrade your firmware, in case you are unable to start your computer.

During installation, Windows XP Professional checks system firmware to determine if your computer is ACPI compliant. This prevents system instability, which can manifest in symptoms from hardware problems to data loss. If your system firmware does not pass all tests, it means that the ACPI Hardware Abstraction Layer (HAL) is not installed. If you are certain that your computer is equipped with ACPI-compliant system firmware, but Windows XP Professional does not use ACPI features (the computer is listed as a non-ACPI **Standard PC**, for example), contact the computer manufacturer for updated motherboard firmware. After upgrading from non-ACPI to ACPI firmware, you must reinstall Windows XP Professional to take advantage of ACPI features.

Caution   If you attempt to override the default ACPI settings selected by Windows XP Professional, setup problems occur. The remedy is reinstallation of the operating system. For more information about how Windows XP Professional determines ACPI compatibility, see articles Q216573, "How Windows 2000 Determines ACPI Compatibility," and Q197055, "Disabling ACPI Support in BIOS Results in Error Message," in the Microsoft Knowledge Base. To find these articles, see the Microsoft Knowledge Base link on the Web Resources page at http://www.microsoft.com/windows/reskits/webresources.

For more information about the ACPI specification, see the ACPI link on the Web Resources page at http://www.microsoft.com/windows/reskits/webresources.

For more information about System Information and Device Manager, see Windows XP Professional Help and Support Center, "Tools for Troubleshooting," and "Managing Devices" in this book.

Troubleshooting Strategies

After you observe symptoms, check technical information sources, and review your system's history, you might be ready to test a possible solution based on the information that you have gathered. If you are unable to locate information that applies to your problem or find more than one solution that applies, try to further isolate your problem by grouping observations into different categories such as software-related symptoms (due to a service or application), hardware-related symptoms (by hardware types), and error messages. Prioritize your list by frequency of occurrence and eliminate symptoms that you can attribute to user error. This enables you to methodically plan the diagnostic steps to take, or to select the next solution to try.

Isolate and Resolve Hardware Problems

When troubleshooting hardware, start with and work toward the simplest configuration possible by disabling or removing devices. Then incrementally increase or decrease complexity until you isolate the problem device. In safe mode, Windows XP Professional starts with only essential drivers and is useful for diagnosing problems. For more information about safe-mode troubleshooting, see Windows XP Professional Help and Support Center, and "Tools for Troubleshooting" in this book.

Check Your Hardware   If your diagnostic efforts point to a hardware problem, you can run diagnostic software available from the manufacturer. These programs run self-tests that confirm if a piece of hardware has malfunctioned or failed and needs replacing. You can also install the device on different computers to verify that the problem is not due to system-specific configuration issues. Replacing defective hardware and diagnosing problems on a spare or test computer minimizes impact to the user due to the system being unavailable. If diagnostic software shows that the hardware is working, consider upgrading or rolling back device drivers.

Reverse Driver Changes   If a hardware problem causes a Stop error that prevents Windows XP Professional from starting in normal mode, you can use the Last Known Good Configuration startup option. The Last Known Good Configuration enables you to recover from problems by reverting driver and registry settings to those used during the last user session. If you are able to start Windows XP Professional in normal mode after using the Last Known Good Configuration, disable the problem driver or device. Restart the computer to verify that the Stop message does not recur. If the problem persists, repeat this procedure until you isolate the hardware that is causing the problem.

Another method to recover from problems that occur after updating a device driver is by using Device Driver Roll Back in safe or normal mode. If you updated a driver since installing Windows XP Professional, you can roll back the driver to determine if the older driver restores stability. If another driver is not available, disable the device by using Device Manager until you are able to locate an updated driver.

Using Device Manager to disable devices is always preferable to physically removing a part because using Device Manager does not risk damage to internal components. If you cannot disable a device by using Device Manager, uninstall the device driver, turn off the system, remove the part, and restart the computer. If this improves system stability, the part might be causing or contributing to the problem and you need to reconfigure it.

For more information about or the Last Known Good Configuration startup option and Device Driver Roll Back, see Windows XP Professional Help and Support Center. Also, see "Troubleshooting Startup" and "Tools for Troubleshooting" in this book. For more information about disabling devices and drivers, see "Managing Devices" in this book. For more information about Stop messages, see "Common Stop Messages for Troubleshooting" in this book.

Isolate and Resolve Software Issues

If you suspect that a software problem or a recent change to system settings is preventing applications or services from functioning properly, use safe mode to help diagnose the problem. You can also use the Last Known Good startup option or System Restore to undo changes made by a recently installed application, driver, or service. You can isolate issues by using the following methods.

Closing applications and processes   Close applications one at a time, and then observe the results. A problem might occur only when a specific application is running. You can use Task Manager to end applications that have stopped responding. For more information about ending applications and processes using Task Manager, see Windows XP Professional Help and Support Center.

Temporarily disabling services   By using the Services snap-in (Services.msc) or the System Configuration Utility (Msconfig.exe), you can stop and start most system services. For some services, you might need to restart the computer for changes to take effect. For more information about disabling services by using the Services snap-in and the System Configuration Utility, see Windows XP Professional Help and Support Center and "Troubleshooting Startup" in this book.

To isolate a service-related problem, you can choose to do the following:

- **Disable services one at a time until the problem disappears.** You can then enable all other services to verify that you found the cause of the problem.

- **Disable all non–safe mode services and then re-enable them one at time until the problem appears.** Use the System Configuration Utility and boot logging to determine the services and drivers initialized in normal and safe mode. You can then disable all non–safe mode drivers and re-enable them one at a time until the problem returns.

For more information about System Restore, System Configuration Utility and boot logging, see Windows XP Professional Help and Support Services and "Tools for Troubleshooting" in this book. For more information about disabling applications and services while troubleshooting startup problems, see "Troubleshooting Startup" in this book.

Avoid Common Pitfalls

You can complicate a problem or troubleshooting process unnecessarily by acting too quickly. Avoid the following common pitfalls that can hinder your efforts:

- Not adequately identifying the problem before taking action

- Not observing the effects of diagnostic changes

- Not documenting changes while troubleshooting

- Not restoring previous settings
- Troubleshooting several problems at one time
- Using incompatible or untested hardware
- Using incompatible software

Not Identifying the Problem Adequately

If you fail to make essential observations before responding, you can miss important information in the critical moments when symptoms first appear. Here are some typical scenarios.

Failing to record information before acting   An error occurs and you start your research without recording important information such as the complete error message text and the applications running. During your research, you check technical information resources but find that you are unable to narrow the scope of your search due to insufficient information.

For more information about the types of information to record during troubleshooting, see "Identify Problem Symptoms" earlier in this chapter.

Restarting the computer too soon   In response to frequent random errors users experience with a certain application, you restart the affected computers without observing and recording the symptoms. Although users can resume work for the day, a call to technical support later that day is less effective because you cannot reproduce the problem. You must wait for the problem to recur before you can gather critical information needed to determine the root cause. For example, symptoms can be caused by power surges, faulty power supplies, excessive dust, or inadequate ventilation. Restarting the computer might be a temporary solution that does not prevent recurrence.

Failing to check for scheduled maintenance events or known service outages   A user comes to work early and finds that network resources or applications are not responding. You spend time troubleshooting the problem without success only to discover that both you and the user failed to read e-mail announcing that scheduled maintenance would cause temporary early morning outages.

Assuming that past solutions always work   Prior experience can shorten the time to solve a recurring problem because you already know the remedy. However, the same solution might not always solve a problem that looks familiar. Always verify the symptoms before acting. If your initial assumptions are incorrect, and you misdiagnose the problem, your actions might make the situation worse. Keep an open mind when troubleshooting. When in doubt, verify your information by searching technical information sources (including technical support) and obtain advice from experienced colleagues. Do not ignore new information and question past procedures that seem inappropriate.

Neglecting to check the basics   A user cannot print to a new local inkjet printer. You verify cable and power connections, check the ink cartridge, and run the printer's built-in diagnostics, but find nothing wrong. Windows XP Professional cannot detect the printer, so you manually install the most recent drivers without success. Reinstalling Windows XP Professional does not solve the problem, and you later realize that you neglected to find out if printing to any local printer from this computer has ever been successful. You find that the user has never tried this, and a firmware check reveals that the parallel port is disabled. Enabling the parallel port resolves all printing problems.

Not Observing the Effects of Diagnostic Changes

System setting changes do not always take effect immediately. For example, when troubleshooting replication issues, you must wait to observe changes. If you do not allow adequate time to pass, you might prematurely conclude that the change was not effective. To avoid this situation, familiarize yourself with the feature that you are troubleshooting and thoroughly read the information provided by technical support before judging the effectiveness of a workaround or update.

Not Documenting Changes while Troubleshooting

Documenting the steps that you take while troubleshooting allows you to review your actions after you have resolved the problem. This is useful for very complex problems that require lengthy procedures to resolve. Documenting your steps allows you to verify that you are not duplicating or skipping steps and enables others to assist you with the problem. It also allows you to identify the exact steps to take if the problem recurs and enables you to evaluate the effectiveness of your efforts.

Not Restoring Previous Settings

If disabling a feature or changing a setting does not produce the results you want, restore the feature or setting before trying something else. For example, record firmware settings before changing them to diagnose problems. Not restoring settings can make it difficult to determine which of your actions resolved the problem. When verifying solutions that require you to make extensive changes or restart the computer multiple times, perform backups before troubleshooting so that you can restore the system if your actions are ineffective or cause startup problems.

Review backup procedures   Backups are essential for all computers, from personal systems to high-availability servers. If you suspect that your troubleshooting efforts might worsen the problem or risk important data, perform a backup. This enables you to restore your system if you experience data loss, Stop errors, or other startup problems. Backups allow you to partially or completely restore the system and continue where you left off. When you evaluate or create backup procedures, consider the following:

- Use the verification option of your backup software to check that your data is correctly written to backup media.

- Routinely check the age and condition of backup media and follow the manufacturer's recommendations for using backup media.

- Follow the hardware manufacturer's recommendations for maintaining the backup device.

For more information about using Backup for troubleshooting, see "Tools for Troubleshooting" in this book. For more information about performing and planning backups, see "Backup and Restore" in this book.

Windows XP Professional also provides other ways to restore system settings such as System Restore and the Last Known Good Configuration startup option. For more information, see Windows XP Professional Help and Support Center and "Tools for Troubleshooting" in this book.

Troubleshooting Several Problems at One Time

If multiple problems affect your system, avoid troubleshooting them as a group. Instead, identify shared symptoms, and then isolate and treat each separately. For example, faulty video memory can cause Stop messages, corrupted screen images, and system instability. While diagnosing the symptoms, you might find that errors occur only with multimedia applications that use advanced three-dimensional rendering. When you attempt to rule out the possibility of failed video hardware by replacing the VGA adapter, you might find that this action also resolves the other issues.

Using Incompatible or Untested Hardware

For many organizations, standards for selecting hardware and purchasing new systems and replacement parts do not exist, are not fully defined, or are simply ignored. Standards that are well defined, refined, maintained, and followed can reduce hardware variability and optimize troubleshooting efforts.

If you need to replace hardware, record your troubleshooting actions as thoroughly as possible. Before installing a new device or replacement part, verify that it is on the Windows Hardware Compatibility List (HCL), that the firmware version for the system motherboard and devices are current, and that any replacement part is pre-tested or "burned-in" before deployment.

Checking the Windows Hardware Compatibility List   Hardware problems can occur if you use devices that are not compatible with Windows XP Professional. The HCL is a Web-based searchable database, which is continuously updated as additional hardware is tested and approved. The HCL outlines the hardware components that have been tested for use with Windows XP Professional.

If several variations of a device are available from one manufacturer, it is best to select only models listed in the HCL.

Table 25-2 explains the differences between HCL logo designations.

Table 25-2 Logo Icons and Compatible Icon in the HCL

HCL Designation	Description
Logo	Indicates that this product has met all Windows Logo requirements.
Logo	Indicates that this product has met all Windows Logo requirements and that a driver is available for download.
Logo	Indicates that this product has met all Windows Logo requirements and that a driver is available on the Windows XP Professional operating system CD.
Compatible	Indicates that this product might not meet all Windows Logo requirements, but has been deemed compatible with the operating system. A driver for the compatible device is available on the Windows XP Professional operating system CD.

When you upgrade to Windows XP Professional, device hardware resource settings are not migrated. Instead, all devices are redetected and enumerated during installation. Typically, upgrades to Windows XP Professional follow this migration path:

- An upgrade to Windows XP Professional from Windows 98, Microsoft® Windows Millennium Edition (Me), Microsoft® Windows NT 4.0 Workstation, or Windows 2000 Professional.

You might find after installation that devices that functioned before the upgrade behave differently or do not work after the upgrade. This problem might be due to the following:

- A driver for the device is not on the Windows XP Professional operating system CD and Device Manager lists it as unknown or conflicting hardware.

- Windows XP Professional Setup installed a generic driver that might be compatible with your device, but it does not fully support enhanced features. Many hardware manufacturers also provide tools that add value to their products, but they are not available in Windows XP Professional. Windows XP Professional Setup installs the basic feature set needed to enable your product to function. For additional software that enhances functionality or adds additional features, download the latest Windows XP Professional compatible drivers and tools from the manufacturer's Web site.

Do not attempt to re-install older drivers because doing so might cause system instability, startup problems, or Stop errors and other startup problems. For more information about troubleshooting Stop errors and startup problems, see "Common Stop Messages for Troubleshooting" and "Troubleshooting Startup" in this book.

For best results, always use HCL-specified devices. It is especially important to refer to the HCL before purchasing modems, tape backup units, and SCSI adapters. If you must use non-HCL hardware, check the manufacture's Web site for the latest updated device driver.

Note   If your system has non-HCL hardware installed, uninstall drivers for these devices before installing Windows XP Professional. If you cannot complete setup, remove the hardware from your system temporarily and rerun Setup.

For more information about the HCL, see the Hardware Compatibility List link on the Web Resources page at http://www.microsoft.com/windows/reskits/webresources.

Testing new and replacement parts   If you must replace or upgrade older parts with newer ones, first purchase a small number of new parts and conduct performance, compatibility, and configuration tests before doing a general deployment. The evaluation is especially important when a large number of systems are involved, and it might lead you to consider similar products from other manufacturers.

When replacing devices, use pre-tested or *burned-in* parts whenever possible. A burn-in involves installing an electronic component and observing it several days for signs of abnormal behavior. Typically, computer components fail early or not at all, and a burn-in period reveals manufacturing defects that lead to premature failure. You can choose to do additional testing by simulating worst-case conditions. For example, you might test a new hard disk by manually copying files or creating a batch file that repeatedly copies files, filling the disk to nearly full capacity.

Using Incompatible Software

Before installing software on multiple computers, test it for compatibility with existing applications in a realistic test environment. Observe how the software interacts with other programs and drivers in memory. If only the test application and the operating system are active, testing does not provide a realistic or valid indication of compatibility or performance. Testing is necessary even if a manufacturer guarantees full Windows XP Professional compatibility, because older programs might affect new software in unpredictable ways.

For large organizations, consider limited pre-deployment test rollouts to beta users who can provide real-world feedback. Select testers who have above-average computer skills to get technically accurate descriptions of problems they observe.

Setup and stability criteria are equally important in evaluating software and hardware for purchase. Testing is critical for upgrading systems from earlier versions of Windows such as Windows 98 or Windows NT 4.0. Software and drivers that were installable and stable on earlier versions of Windows might exhibit problems or not function in the Windows XP Professional environment. Video, sound, and related multimedia drivers and tools (such as audio, CD ROM mastering, and DVD playback software) are especially sensitive to operating system upgrades.

For more information about application testing guidelines, see "Planning Deployments" in this book and the Windows Application Compatibility link on the Web Resources page at http://www.microsoft.com/windows/reskits/webresources. Also see "Testing Applications for Compatibility with Windows 2000" in the *Deployment Planning Guide* of the *Microsoft Windows 2000 Server Resource Kit* and article Q244632, "How to Test Programs for Compatibility with Windows 2000," in the Microsoft Knowledge Base. To find this article, see the Microsoft Knowledge Base link on the Web Resources page at http://www.microsoft.com/windows/reskits/webresources.

Document and Evaluate the Results

You can increase the value of information collected during troubleshooting by keeping accurate and thorough records of all work done. You can use your records to reduce redundant effort and to avoid future problems by taking preventive action.

Create a configuration management database to record the history of changes, such as installed software and hardware, updated drivers, replaced hardware, and altered system settings. Periodically verify, update, and back up this data to prevent permanent loss. To maximize use of your database, note details such as:

- Changes made
- Times and dates of changes
- Reasons for the changes
- Users who made the changes
- Positive and negative effects the changes had on system stability or performance
- Information provided by technical support

When planning this database, keep in mind the need to balance scope and detail when deciding which items or attributes to track. For more information, see the Information Library (ITIL) and Microsoft Operations Framework (MOF) Web site links provided in "Check Technical Information Resources" earlier in this chapter.

Update baseline information after installing new hardware or software to compare past and current behavior or performance levels. If previous baseline information is not available, use System Information, Device Manager, the Performance tool, or industry standard benchmarks to generate data.

Baselines combined with records kept over time enable you to organize experience gained, evaluate maintenance efforts, and judge troubleshooting effectiveness. Analysis of this data can form the basis of a troubleshooting manual or lead to changes in control policy for your organization.

A post-troubleshooting review, or post-mortem, can help you pinpoint troubleshooting areas that need improvement. Some questions you might consider during this self-evaluation period include:

- What changes improved the situation?

- What changes made the problem worse?

- Was system performance restored to expected levels?

- What work was redundant or unnecessary?

- How effectively were technical support resources used?

- What other tools or information not used might have helped?

- What unresolved issues require further root-cause analysis?

Write an Action Plan

An action plan is a set of relevant troubleshooting objectives and strategies that fits within your organization's configuration and management strategies. After you identify the problem and find a potential solution or workaround that you have tested on one or more computers, you might need an action plan if the solution is to be deployed across your organization, possibly involving hundreds or thousands of computers. Coordinate your plan with supervisors and staff members in the affected areas to keep them informed well in advance and to verify that the schedule does not conflict with important activity. Include provisions for troubleshooting during non-peak work hours or dividing work into stages over a period of several days. Evaluate your plan, and as you uncover weaknesses, update it to increase its effectiveness and efficiency.

As the number of users grows, the potential loss of productivity due to disruption increases. Your plan must account for dependencies and allow last-minute changes. Factor in contingency plans for unforeseen circumstances.

For more information about creating a configuration management database, see the ITIL and MOF links listed in Table 25-1.

Take Proactive Measures

You can combine information gathered while troubleshooting major and chronic problems to create a proactive plan to prevent or minimize problems for the long term. When planning a maintenance or upgrade process for your organization, consider the following goals:

- Improving the computing environment
- Monitoring system and application logs
- Documenting hardware and software changes
- Anticipating hardware and software updates

Improve the Computing Environment

External factors can have a major impact on the operation and lifespan of a computer. Some basic precautions include labeling connecting cables, periodically testing uninterruptible power supply (UPS) batteries, and placing computers far from high-traffic areas where they might be bumped or damaged. It is important to check environmental factors such as room temperature, humidity, and air circulation to prevent failures due to excessive heat. Dust can clog cooling equipment such as computer fans and cause them to fail. Install surge suppressors, dedicated power sources, and backup power devices to protect equipment from electrical current fluctuations, surges, and spikes that can cause data loss or damage equipment. Other precautions include:

- Performing regular file and system state backups to prevent data loss. For more information about Windows Backup, see Windows XP Professional Help and Support Center and "Backup and Restore" in this book.

- Using Windows XP Professional compatible virus-scanning software and regularly download the latest virus signature updates. A virus signature data file contains information that enables virus-scanning software to identify infected files.

Monitor System and Application Logs

Monitor your system to detect problems early and avoid having software or hardware failure be your first or only warning of a problem. When using a monitoring tool such as Performance (Perfmon.msc) to evaluate changes that might affect performance, compare baseline information to current performance. The resulting data helps you isolate bottlenecks and determine if actions such as upgrading hardware, updating applications, and installing new drivers are effective. You can also use the data to justify expenditures, such as additional CPUs, more RAM, and increased storage space. Checking the Event Viewer regularly helps you to identify chronic problems and detect potential failures. This allows you to take corrective action before a problem worsens. For more information about monitoring your system, see "Overview of Performance Monitoring" in the *Operations Guide* of the *Microsoft Windows 2000 Server Resource Kit*.

Document Changes to Hardware and Software

In addition to recording computer-specific changes, do not neglect to record other factors that directly affect computer operation such as Group Policy and network infrastructure changes. For more information about developing and implementing a standard process for recording configuration changes, see "Document and Evaluate the Results" earlier in this chapter.

Plan for Hardware and Software Upgrades

Regardless of how advanced your system hardware or software is at the time of purchase, computer technologies have a limited lifespan. Your maintenance plan must account for the following factors that can make updates and upgrades necessary.

Increased demand for computing resources   When computing needs grow beyond the capability of your hardware, it makes sense to upgrade hardware components or entire systems. Performance degradation might be due to system bottlenecks caused by hardware that has reached maximum capacity. Optimizing drivers and updating applications can help in the short term, but user demand for computing resources eventually makes it necessary to upgrade to more powerful hardware.

Discontinued support for a device or software   Operating system or manufacturer support for a device or software might be discontinued, causing compatibility issues that can block upgrades to new operating systems or prevent full use of certain features in Windows XP Professional. To minimize effort when upgrading hardware and software for many computers, purchase similar computers and follow replacement standards for your organization. Failure to standardize applications and hardware can make upgrading more difficult and expensive, especially if technicians and users need retraining.

Added capabilities   Having a process for upgrading operating systems or installing application patches, hotfixes, and operating system Service Packs helps to maintain the stability, performance, and reliability of your equipment. Schedule time to stay current with new developments and product updates.

Summary and Checklist

A guaranteed "system" for troubleshooting all computer-related problems does not exist. Effective troubleshooting requires technical research and experience, careful observation, resourceful use of information, and patience. During the troubleshooting process, you can consult the checklist in Table 25-3.

Table 25-3   Troubleshooting Checklist

Task	Action
Identify problem symptoms.	Observe the symptoms:
	■ Under what conditions does the problem occur?
	■ Which aspects of the operating system control these conditions?
	■ What applications or subsystems does the problem seem related to?
	■ Record all error information for future reference, including the exact message text and error numbers.
	Do not forget to check the basics:
	■ Verify that the power cables are properly connected and are not damaged or worn.
	■ Check firmware settings to verify that devices are enabled.
Check technical information resources.	Research the problem:
	■ What actions were tried for this or similar problems in the past?
	■ Is this a known issue for which a solution or workaround exists? What were the results?
	■ What information is available from product documentation, internal support sources, or outside resources, such as a manufacturer's Web site or newsgroups?
	■ What information can you obtain from support staff, such as Help Desk, or other users who might have experienced similar problems?
Review your system's history.	Analyze the events that led up to the problem:
	■ What happened just before the problem occurred?
	■ What hardware was recently installed? Are driver and firmware revisions current?
	■ What software or system file updates were made? Are the software revisions current?
	■ Does the software and hardware configuration match the documented configuration? If not, try to determine the differences.
	■ Did you examine the event logs for clues to the problem?
	Gather baseline information or compare to a reference system:
	■ Did this application or hardware work correctly in the past? What has changed since then?
	■ Does the application or hardware work correctly on another computer? If so, what is different on that computer?
	■ Generate performance data by using the Performance tool or benchmark programs. If previous baselines exist, compare current and past performance.

Table 25-3   Troubleshooting Checklist

Task	Action
Document and evaluate the results.	Record the results:
	■ Record information using a common report format such as a database.
	■ Provide a detailed record of all of the work done to correct the problem, for future reference.
	■ Record who, what, when, and why—and identify positive and negative cause and effect.
	Evaluate the results:
	■ Was the work done efficiently?
	■ Was the solution effective? What remains unresolved?
	■ When a solution was implemented, was system performance restored to expected levels?
	■ What processes can be changed or implemented to prevent the problem from recurring?
	■ Are systems being adequately monitored? Can this problem be caught early if it happens again?
	■ What additional information, tools, or tests are needed?

Additional Resources

These resources contain additional information related to this chapter.

- ■ "Managing Devices" in this book.
- ■ "Tools for Troubleshooting" in this book.
- ■ "Common Stop Messages for Troubleshooting" in this book.
- ■ "Backup and Restore" in this book.
- ■ "File Systems" in this book.
- ■ "Troubleshooting Disks and File Systems" in this book.
- ■ "Overview of Performance Monitoring" in the *Operations Guide* of the *Microsoft Windows 2000 Server Resource Kit* for more information about monitoring performance.
- ■ The ACPI link on the Web Resources page at http://www.microsoft.com/windows/reskits/webresources.
- ■ The Extensible Firmware Interface link on the Web Resources page at http://www.microsoft.com/windows/reskits/webresources.

Chapter 26

Troubleshooting Disks and File Systems

Hard disk and file system errors can result from a variety of problems, such as hardware failures, power outages, poor system maintenance, viruses, and human error. When you are troubleshooting problems related to disks and file systems, you can refer to this chapter for information about troubleshooting tools, volume and disk error conditions, viruses, and stop messages. You can also use this chapter to obtain detailed descriptions of the master boot record (MBR), the GUID partition table (GPT), and the boot sectors.

Related Information

- For more information about the file allocation table (FAT) and NTFS file systems, see "File Systems" in this book.

- For more information about managing disks and volumes, see "Disk Management" in this book.

- For more information about the tools that Microsoft® Windows® XP Professional provides for troubleshooting, see "Tools for Troubleshooting" in this book.

- For more information about how to troubleshoot, see "Troubleshooting Concepts and Strategies" in this book.

New in Troubleshooting Disks and File Systems

Microsoft® Windows® XP Professional provides improved troubleshooting tools for disks and file systems. Table 26-1 summarizes the enhancements made from Microsoft® Windows® 2000 to Windows XP Professional.

Table 26-1   Enhancements Since Windows 2000

New Feature	Feature Description
Automated System Recovery (ASR)	Automated System Recovery (ASR) is a two-part recovery system that allows you to restore the operating system state by using files saved to tape media and hard disk configuration information saved to a floppy disk.
Disk Defragmenter has new capabilities, including a command-line option.	Windows XP Professional offers two choices for defragmenting disks: the Disk Defragmenter snap-in and a new command-line version of the tool (Defrag.exe). Both tools can defragment NTFS volumes that have cluster sizes larger than 4 KB and files smaller than 16 clusters. Both tools can also defragment the master file table (MFT) on NTFS volumes.
Troubleshoot disks and volumes at the command line by using DiskPart.	Use the new command-line tool DiskPart to troubleshoot disks and volumes at the command line as an alternative to using the Disk Management snap-in.
Create GUID partition table disks on Itanium-based computers.	Windows XP 64-Bit Edition supports a new partition style called GUID partition table (GPT). GPT disks contain redundant partition tables for improved partition structure integrity.
Use the Fsutil.exe tool to determine whether a volume is marked as dirty.	The Fsutil.exe command-line tool offers many commands that you can use to manage file system behavior. For example, you can use the **fsutil dirty** command to determine if a volume is dirty. If a volume is dirty, it has experienced file system errors, and you must run Chkdsk on the volume to repair the problem. You can also use the **fsutil dirty** command to mark a volume as dirty.

If you are migrating from Microsoft® Windows NT® version 4.0, the enhancements in Table 26-2 apply in addition to those outlined in Table 26-1.

Table 26-2   Enhancements Since Windows NT 4.0

New Feature	Feature Description
Chkntfs.exe	Chkntfs.exe is a command-line tool that you can use to disable the automatic running (at restart) of Chkdsk on dirty volumes. You can also use Chkntfs to cancel a scheduled session of Chkdsk so that it does not run when the computer restarts.
New Chkdsk parameters	Chkdsk offers two new parameters, **/c** and **/i**, to reduce the length of time required to run Chkdsk on NTFS volumes.
Recovery Console	Recovery Console is a command-line startup environment that allows you to gain access to the hard disk for basic troubleshooting and system maintenance.
Dmdiag.exe	Dmdiag.exe is a command-line tool that displays the location and layout of dynamic disks and volumes. Dynamic disks were new in Windows 2000 and do not use the traditional partition layout that was used by disks in Windows NT 4.0 and earlier.

Maintenance and Troubleshooting Tools

Windows XP Professional provides many tools that you can use to maintain and troubleshoot disks and file systems. The tools described in this section are:

- Chkdsk

- Disk Defragmenter

- Recovery Console

- Automated System Recovery

- DiskProbe

- Dmdiag

For more information about troubleshooting problems with Windows XP Professional, see "Tools for Troubleshooting" and "Troubleshooting Concepts and Strategies" in this book.

Chkdsk

Chkdsk.exe is a command-line tool that verifies the logical integrity of a file system on a Windows XP Professional volume. If file system structures become damaged, Windows XP Professional automatically schedules Chkdsk to run the next time the computer is restarted. At any time, you can manually run Chkdsk at the command prompt or from Windows Explorer or My Computer. For more information about running the graphical version of Chkdsk, see "Running Chkdsk from My Computer or Windows Explorer" later in this chapter.

Volumes that have file system errors are known as dirty volumes. To indicate that a file system problem has occurred and that the volume is dirty, Windows XP Professional displays a message similar to the following when you attempt to open, delete, or rename a file or folder by using Microsoft® Windows® Explorer or the command prompt:

```
The file or directory filename is corrupt and unreadable. Please run the Chkdsk
utility.
```

You might also see messages in the system log in the Event Viewer snap-in. Figure 26-1 illustrates a Chkdsk entry in the system log.

Figure 26-1   Chkdsk message in the system log in Event Viewer

You can also determine whether a volume is dirty by using the **fsutil dirty query** command or the **chkntfs** command.

For example, to determine whether volume C is dirty, you can type:

```
fsutil dirty query c:
```

—or—

```
chkntfs c:
```

Running Chkdsk to Repair File Systems

You can run Chkdsk in two modes:

- **Chkdsk without parameters.**   When you run Chkdsk without parameters, it runs in read-only mode. In this mode, Chkdsk examines the disk and then reports whether it found any file system errors but does not repair the errors.

- **Chkdsk with parameters.**   When you run Chkdsk with parameters, such as /**f** or /**r**, Chkdsk repairs errors related to file system structures.

Before running Chkdsk to repair a volume   Before running Chkdsk to repair a volume, you must do the following:

- Back up key data files or make sure that you have a known good backup.

- Be prepared to let the Chkdsk process complete.

If you use the **/f** or **/r** parameter on a large volume (for example, 70 GB) or on a volume with a very large number of files (in the millions), Chkdsk can take a long time to complete. The volume is not available during this time because Chkdsk does not relinquish control until it is done. If a volume is being checked during the startup process, the computer is not available until the Chkdsk process is complete.

Chkdsk does not include parameters that let you cancel the Chkdsk process; however, when you run Chkdsk you can specify parameters that shorten the process. For more information about minimizing downtime during Chkdsk, see "Reducing the Time Required to Run Chkdsk on NTFS Volumes" later in this chapter.

Running Chkdsk on the boot volume   When you use the **/f** or **/r** parameters to run Chkdsk on the boot volume, Chkdsk displays the following message:

```
Chkdsk cannot run because the volume is in use by another process. Would you like to
 schedule this volume to be checked the next time the system restarts? (Y/N)
```

Chkdsk cannot gain exclusive use of the boot volume because it contains the Windows XP operating system files. Therefore, Chkdsk must always restart the computer to check the boot volume. If you press the **Y** key, a version of Chkdsk known as Autochk runs the next time the computer restarts. After Autochk checks the boot volume, the computer automatically restarts.

Running Chkdsk on a volume other than the boot volume   When you use the **/f** or **/r** parameters on a volume other than the boot volume, Chkdsk must lock the volume for exclusive use before it can repair errors. If the volume has open files or programs, Chkdsk displays the following message:

```
Chkdsk cannot run because the volume is in use by another process. Chkdsk may run if
 this volume is dismounted first. ALL OPEN HANDLES TO THIS VOLUME WOULD THEN BE
 INVALID. Would you like to force a dismount on this volume? (Y/N)
```

If you press the **Y** key, Chkdsk attempts to close all handles and lock the volume. If Chkdsk is successful in locking the volume, the repair process begins. The duration of the repair process is determined by the number of files and folders on the volume and the level of damage, if any.

If Chkdsk cannot lock the volume, or if you press the **N** key, you can specify that you want to check the volume by running Autochk the next time the computer restarts. For more information about Autochk, see "Running Autochk When the Computer Restarts" later in this chapter.

Chkdsk Syntax   The command-line syntax for Chkdsk is as follows:

```
chkdsk [volume[[path] filename]] [/f] [/v] [/r] [/x] [/i] [/c] [/l[:size]]
```

Chkdsk Parameters   Table 26-3 lists all Chkdsk command-line parameters.

Table 26-3   Chkdsk Parameters

Parameter	Description
volume	Specifies the volume that you want Chkdsk to check. You can specify the volume by using any of the formats in the following examples: ■ To run Chkdsk on the C volume, specify: **c:** ■ To run Chkdsk on a mounted volume called **data** that is mounted on the C volume, specify: **c:\data** ■ To run Chkdsk on a volume, you can specify the symbolic link name for a volume, such as: **\\?\Volume{2d9bd2a8-5df8-11d2-bdaa-000000000000}** You can determine a symbolic link name for a volume by using the **mountvol** command. For more information about mountvol, see Windows XP Professional Help.
path	FAT/FAT32 only. Specifies the location of a file or set of files within the folder structure of the volume.
filename	FAT/FAT32 only. Specifies the file or set of files to check for fragmentation. Wildcard characters (* and ?) are allowed.
/f	Fixes errors on the disk. The volume must be locked. If Chkdsk cannot lock the volume, Chkdsk offers to check it the next time the computer restarts.
/v	On FAT/FAT32: Displays the full path and name of every file on the disk. On NTFS: Displays additional information or cleanup messages, if any.
/r	Locates bad sectors and recovers readable information (implies **/f**). If Chkdsk cannot lock the volume, it offers to check it the next time the computer starts. Because NTFS also identifies and remaps bad sectors during the course of normal operations, it is usually not necessary to use the **/r** parameter unless you suspect that a disk has bad sectors.
/x	Forces the volume to dismount first, if necessary. All opened handles to the volume are then invalid (implies **/f**). This parameter does not work on the boot volume. You must restart the computer to dismount the boot volume.
/i	NTFS only. Performs a less detailed check of index entries, reducing the amount of time needed to run Chkdsk.
/c	NTFS only. Skips the checking of cycles within the folder structure, reducing the amount of time needed to run Chkdsk.

Table 26-3   Chkdsk Parameters

Parameter	Description
/l:*size*	NTFS only. Changes the size of the log file to the specified number of kilobytes. Displays the current size if you do not enter a new size.
	If the system loses power, stops responding, or is restarted unexpectedly, NTFS runs a recovery procedure when Windows XP Professional restarts that accesses information stored in this log file. The size of the log file depends on the size of the volume. In most conditions, you do not need to change the size of the log file. However, if the number of changes to the volume is so great that NTFS fills the log before all metadata is written to disk, then NTFS must force the metadata to disk and free the log space. When this condition occurs, you might notice that Windows XP Professional stops responding for 5 or more seconds. You can eliminate the performance impact of forcing the metadata to disk by increasing the size of the log file. For more information about NTFS recoverability, see "File Systems" in this book.
/?	Displays this list of Chkdsk parameters.

For more information about the Chkdsk parameters, see Windows XP Professional Help. For more information about running the graphical version of Chkdsk, see "Running Chkdsk from My Computer or Windows Explorer" later in this chapter.

Chkdsk Examples   To run Chkdsk to repair errors on the D volume, type:

```
chkdsk d: /f
```

If you need to run Chkdsk on a large D volume and you want Chkdsk to complete as quickly as possible, type:

```
chkdsk d: /f /c /i
```

You can script Chkdsk and Autochk by using the Windows Management Instrumentation (WMI) classes Win32_LogicalDisk, Win32_AutoChkSetting, and Win32_OperatingSystemAutochkSetting. For more information about WMI, see the Microsoft Windows Management Instrumentation (WMI) SDK link on the Web Resources Page at http://www.microsoft.com/windows/reskits/webresources.

The Chkdsk Process on NTFS Volumes

When you run Chkdsk on NTFS volumes, the Chkdsk process consists of three major stages, and optional fourth and fifth stages. Chkdsk displays its progress for each stage with the following messages:

```
CHKDSK is verifying files (stage 1 of 3)...
File verification completed.
CHKDSK is verifying indexes (stage 2 of 3)...
Index verification completed.
CHKDSK is verifying security descriptors (stage 3 of 3)...
Security descriptor verification completed.
```

The following describes each of the Chkdsk stages.

Stage 1: Chkdsk verifies each file record segment in the master file table
During stage 1, Chkdsk examines each file record segment in the volume's master file table (MFT). A specific file record segment in the MFT uniquely identifies every file and directory on an NTFS volume. The percent complete that Chkdsk displays during this phase is the percent of the MFT that has been verified.

Stage 2: Chkdsk checks the directories in the volume   During stage 2, Chkdsk examines each of the indexes (directories) on the volume for internal consistency and verifies that every file and directory represented by a file record segment in the MFT is referenced by at least one directory. Chkdsk also confirms that every file or subdirectory referenced in each directory actually exists as a valid file record segment in the MFT and checks for circular directory references. Chkdsk then confirms that the time stamps and the file size information associated with files are up-to-date in the directory listings for those files.

The percent complete that Chkdsk displays during this phase is the percent of the total number of files on the volume that are checked. For volumes with many thousands of files and folders, the time required to complete this stage can be significant.

Stage 3: Chkdsk verifies the security descriptors for each volume   During stage 3, Chkdsk examines each of the security descriptors associated with each file and directory on the volume by verifying that each security descriptor structure is well formed and internally consistent. The percent complete that Chkdsk displays during this phase is the percent of the number of files and directories on the volume that are checked.

Stages 4 and 5 (optional stages): Chkdsk reads every sector on the volume to confirm stability   Chkdsk performs stages 4 and 5 if you specify the **/r** parameter when you run Chkdsk. The **/r** parameter confirms that the sectors in each cluster are usable. Specifying the **/r** parameter is usually not necessary because NTFS identifies and remaps bad sectors during the course of normal operations, but you can use the **/r** parameter if you suspect the disk has bad sectors.

During stage 4, Chkdsk verifies all clusters in use; during stage 5, Chkdsk verifies unused clusters.

The percent complete that Chkdsk displays during stage 4 is based on the percent of used clusters that are checked. The percent complete that Chkdsk displays during stage 5 is the percent of unused clusters that are checked. Used clusters typically take longer to check than unused clusters, so stage 4 lasts longer than stage 5 on a volume with equal amounts of used and unused clusters. For a volume with mostly unused clusters, stage 5 takes longer than stage 4.

During stages 1 and 3, the percent complete indicator advances relatively smoothly, although some unevenness might occur in the rate at which these phases progress. For example, file record segments that are not in use require less time to process than do those that are in use, and larger security descriptors take more time to process than do smaller ones. Overall the percent complete is a fairly accurate representation of the actual time required for that phase.

The duration of stage 2 varies because the amount of time required to process a directory is closely tied to the number of files or subdirectories listed in that directory. Because of this dependency, the percent complete indicator might not advance smoothly during stage 2, though the indicator continues to advance even for large directories. Therefore, do not use the percent complete as a reliable representation of the actual time remaining for this phase.

For more information, see "Determining How Long Chkdsk Will Run" later in this chapter.

Running Autochk When the Computer Restarts

Autochk.exe is a version of Chkdsk that runs only before Windows XP Professional starts. Autochk runs in the following situations:

- **Autochk runs if you try to run Chkdsk on the boot volume.**   Chkdsk cannot dismount the boot volume, so Chkdsk offers to run the repair process by using Autochk when the computer is restarted. If you press the **Y** key to schedule Autochk, you have 10 seconds after the computer restarts to press any key and cancel the repair process. If you cancel Autochk before the 10-second delay lapses, Autochk does not run the next time you restart the computer. If you want to run Chkdsk again, you can do so from the command line.

- **Autochk runs if Chkdsk cannot gain exclusive use of the volume.**   If Chkdsk cannot gain exclusive use of a volume when you run Chkdsk from the command line, Chkdsk offers to dismount the volume. If you press the **Y** key and Chkdsk still cannot dismount the volume, or if you press the **N** key, then Chkdsk offers to run the repair process by using Autochk when the computer is restarted. If you press the **Y** key to schedule Autochk, you have 10 seconds after the computer restarts to press any key and cancel the repair process. If you cancel Autochk before the 10-second delay lapses, Autochk does not run the next time you restart the computer. If you want to run Chkdsk again, you can do so from the command line.

- **Autochk runs if the volume is flagged as dirty.**   If the file system has flagged the volume as dirty, Autochk runs the repair process at startup. Volumes are flagged as dirty when the file system detects an error on the volume. If Autochk detects a dirty volume, it provides a 10-second delay and then begins the repair process. If you cancel Autochk when a volume is dirty, Autochk attempts to run again after a 10-second delay each time the computer is restarted.

You can use the Chkntfs.exe command-line tool to change the Autochk delay from 0 seconds to up to 3 days (259,200 seconds). However, a long delay means that the computer does not start until the time elapses or until you press a key to cancel Autochk.

If you choose to let Autochk run, you can review the Autochk report in the application log of the Event Viewer snap-in. Autochk information is logged by the Winlogon service, so look for entries with **Winlogon** listed as the source of the entry.

> **Note**   You can use the **fsutil dirty** command to query and set the volume as dirty, but you must use the **chkntfs** command to exclude a dirty volume from being repaired by Autochk. For more information about using the **fsutil dirty** command, see Windows XP Professional Help.

Using Chkntfs to Prevent Autochk from Running

For heavily used computers that cannot be offline for the length of time required to complete the repair process, you can use the Chkntfs.exe command-line tool to exclude dirty volumes from being checked by Autochk. You can also use Chkntfs to cancel previously scheduled sessions of Autochk and to check the status of a volume.

For example, by typing **chkntfs c:** at the command prompt, you can find out:

- Whether you manually scheduled Autochk to run on volume C the next time the computer is restarted.

- Whether volume C is dirty, in which case Autochk runs automatically the next time the computer is restarted unless you manually run Chkdsk on volume C, cancel Autochk during the delay at startup, or exclude volume C by using the **/x** parameter.

> **Caution**   If a volume is flagged as dirty, do not postpone running Chkdsk indefinitely. File system damage can become worse over time, so you must consider dirty volumes at risk until you run Chkdsk. Use Chkntfs only if you need to control when Chkdsk is run.

Chkntfs Syntax   The command-line syntax for Chkntfs is as follows:

```
chkntfs volume [...]
chkntfs [/d]
chkntfs [/t[:time]]
chkntfs [/x volume [...]]
chkntfs [/c volume [...]]
```

Chkntfs Parameters   Table 26-4 lists all Chkntfs command-line parameters. When using Chkntfs, you can specify only one parameter at a time.

For more information about the Chkntfs parameters, see Windows XP Professional Help. For more information about the registry changes that occur when you use Chkntfs, see article Q218461, "Enhanced Chkdsk, Autochk, and Chkntfs Tools in Windows 2000." To find this article, see the Microsoft Knowledge Base link on the Web Resources page at http://www.microsoft.com/windows/reskits/webresources.

Table 26-4   Chkntfs Parameters

Parameter	Description

`volume [...]`	Specifies the volume that you want to check. You can specify the volume by using any of the formats in the following examples:
	
	■ To run Chkntfs on the C volume, specify:
	  c:
	
	■ To run Chkdsk on a mounted volume called **data** that is mounted on the C volume, specify:
	  c:\data
	
	■ To run Chkntfs on a volume you can specify the symbolic link name for a volume, such as:
	  \\?\Volume{2d9bd2a8-5df8-11d2-bdaa-000000000000}
	
	You can determine a symbolic link name for a volume by using the **mountvol** command. For more information about mountvol, see Windows XP Professional Help.

`[/d]`	Restores all Chkntfs default settings except the countdown time for Autochk. The **/d** parameter clears the list of volumes you excluded by using the **/x** parameter and also cancels any sessions of Autochk previously scheduled to take place when the computer restarts. After you use the **/d** parameter, Autochk runs on volumes that are flagged as dirty when the computer restarts.
`[/t[:time]]`	Changes the Autochk initiation countdown time to the specified amount of time entered in seconds. The default countdown time is 10 seconds. If you use the **/t** parameter without using **:**time, the countdown time that you last used is displayed.
`[/x volume [...]]`	Excludes the specified volume from being checked when the computer starts. This parameter excludes only dirty volumes; Autochk still checks the volumes that you manually schedule.
`[/c volume [...]]`	Schedules Autochk to run on the specified volumes if they are dirty when the computer starts, overriding any volumes excluded by the **/x** parameter.

Using the /x Parameter to Exclude Volumes   Use the **/x** parameter to prevent Autochk from running at startup on dirty volumes. Although it is not recommended that you use this parameter to postpone running Autochk indefinitely, you can use this parameter to prevent Autochk from running. For example, when you know the volume is dirty, you can use the **/x** parameter to postpone running Autochk until a period of low computer activity, such as overnight or during the weekend.

The **/x** parameter is not cumulative. Each time you use the **/x** parameter, you override the previous entry. For example, typing **chkntfs e: /x**, followed by **chkntfs f: /x**, excludes only the F volume from being checked.

To exclude multiple volumes, list them all in one command. For example, you can exclude both the E and F volumes by typing:

```
chkntfs e: f: /x
```

Note   You can configure physical disk resources in cluster disks so that Chkdsk is skipped when the system mounts the disk. You can also configure the system to mount the disk even if Chkdsk encounters errors. For more information about configuring Chkdsk to run on a cluster disk, see article Q223023, "Enhanced Disk Resource Private Properties Using Cluster Server." To find this article, see the Microsoft Knowledge Base link on the Web Resource page at http://www.microsoft.com/windows/reskits/webresources.

Using the /c Parameter to Run Autochk on Excluded Volumes   If you use Chkntfs to determine that an excluded volume is marked as dirty and if you want Autochk to run on the volume when the computer starts, use the **/c** parameter. The **/c** parameter overrides the **/x** parameter so that you can run Autochk on volumes that you previously excluded. After Autochk runs on the volume, the volume remains on the excluded list.

Note   You can also use the **chkdsk /f** or **chkdsk /r** command to check volumes that you previously excluded by using the **chkntfs /x** command. The **chkntfs /c** command runs Autochk only at startup and only if the volume is marked as dirty.

The **/c** parameter is cumulative. For example, you can specify multiple volumes by typing:

```
chkntfs c: /c
chkntfs d: /c
chkntfs e: /c
```

You can specify multiple volumes at the same time by typing:

```
chkntfs c: d: e: /c
```

Reducing the Time Required to Run Chkdsk on NTFS Volumes

NTFS is a journaling file system because it guarantees the consistency of the volume by using standard transaction logging and recovery techniques. If a disk becomes corrupted, NTFS runs a recovery procedure that accesses information stored in a transaction log file. The NTFS recovery procedure guarantees that the volume is restored to a consistent state. For this reason, it is unlikely that NTFS volumes might become corrupted.

> **Caution**   NTFS does not guarantee the integrity of user data following an instance of disk corruption, even when a full Chkdsk is run immediately after corruption is detected. Chkdsk might not recover all files, and files that are recovered might be internally corrupted. Therefore, you must protect important data by performing periodic backups.

If file system errors do occur on an NTFS volume, you must run Chkdsk to repair the damage. The recommended procedure is to run **chkdsk /f** as soon as possible, but you can also run a shorter version of Chkdsk by using the **/c** and **/i** parameters. These parameters were designed for administrators who manage exceptionally large NTFS volumes and who require flexibility in managing the downtime that is incurred when Chkdsk is running.

> **Caution**   Using the **/c** and **/i** parameters can result in a volume remaining corrupted after Chkdsk completes. Therefore, you must use these parameters only in situations where you need to keep system downtime to a minimum.

Table 26-5 provides a brief overview of each parameter and the potential reduction in Chkdsk duration. The actual reduction depends on a combination of factors, such as the ratio of files to directories and the relative speed of disk input/ output (I/O) versus CPU speed, making the completion time difficult to predict.

Table 26-5   Overview of the /c and /i Chkdsk Parameters

Parameter	What It Does	Potential Reduction in Chkdsk Duration
/c	Skips the process that detects cycles in the directory structure.	1 to 2 percent
/i	Skips the process that compares directory entries to the file record segments that correspond to those entries.	50 to 70 percent

Using the /c Parameter   Use the **/c** parameter to skip the process that detects cycles in the directory structure. Cycles are a rare form of corruption in which a subdirectory has itself as a parent. Although you can speed up the Chkdsk process by using the /c parameter, using the /c parameter can also leave directory loops on an NTFS volume. Such loops might be inaccessible from the rest of the directory tree and could result in orphaned files. Files can become orphaned when file record segments remain but are not referenced by any directory entry. The file represented by the file record segment might be intact in all ways except that the file is invisible to all programs, including backup programs.

Using the /i Parameter   Use the /i parameter to skip the process that compares directory entries to the file record segments that correspond to those entries. A file record segment in the master file table (MFT) uniquely identifies every file and directory in an NTFS volume. When you use the /i parameter, the directory entries are checked to verify that they are self-consistent, but the directory entries are not necessarily consistent with the data stored in their corresponding file record segments.

When you use the /i parameter, files can become orphaned if directory entries remain, but the directory entries refer to incorrect file record segments. In this case, the files exist, but programs encounter errors when attempting to access them.

For more information about using the /i and /c parameters, see article Q187941, "An Explanation of CHKDSK and the New /C and /I Switches." To find this article, see the Microsoft Knowledge Base link on the Web Resource page at http://www.microsoft.com/windows/reskits/webresources.

Running Chkdsk on Mission-Critical Computers

If you use the Chkntfs or Fsutil command-line tool and discover that a volume in a mission-critical computer is flagged as dirty, you must choose among the following three choices:

Do nothing.   For a mission-critical computer that is expected to be online 24 hours a day, doing nothing might be a necessary choice. The drawback to this option is that relatively minor corruption can become major corruption if you do not repair the volume as soon as possible after you detect the corruption. Therefore, consider this option only if keeping a system online is more important than the integrity of the data stored on the corrupted volume. You must consider all data on the corrupted volume at risk until you run Chkdsk.

Run a full Chkdsk.   This option repairs all file system data, restoring all user data that can be recovered by means of an automated process. The drawback is that a full Chkdsk might require several hours of downtime for a mission-critical computer at an inopportune time.

Run an abbreviated Chkdsk by using a combination of the /c and /i parameters.
This option repairs minor corruption that can become major corruption in much less time than a full Chkdsk requires, but might not repair all corruption. A full Chkdsk is required to guarantee that all the data that can be recovered has been recovered.

Determining How Long Chkdsk Will Run

The best way to predict how long Chkdsk will take to run on a given volume is to perform a trial run in read-only mode during a period of low system usage. However, you must use caution when using read-only mode to estimate run time because of the following reasons:

Chkdsk might fail in read-only mode or might report false errors.   The read-only Chkdsk process involves three phases. If Chkdsk encounters errors in the early phases, Chkdsk might abort before it completes all three phases. In addition, Chkdsk is prone to falsely reporting errors when in read-only mode and might report that a volume is corrupted even when no corruption is present. For example, Chkdsk might report corruption if NTFS modifies an area of the disk on behalf of a program at the same time Chkdsk is examining the same area. To verify a volume correctly, the volume must be in a static state, and the only way to guarantee that state is to lock the volume. Chkdsk locks the volume only when you specify the **/f**, **/r**, or **/x** parameters. Thus, you might need to run Chkdsk more than once for Chkdsk to complete all stages in read-only mode.

System load can influence the time required to run Chkdsk.   Chkdsk is both CPU intensive and disk intensive. If heavy disk I/O or high CPU usage is occurring when you run Chkdsk in read-only mode, the time required to complete the process increases.

Chkdsk and Autochk do not take the same time to complete.   Chkdsk runs while Windows XP Professional is running, and Autochk runs before Windows XP Professional loads. Although running Autochk at startup gives exclusive use of CPU and disk I/O resources to Chkdsk, it also deprives Autochk of the benefit of virtual memory. Thus, while Autochk usually runs faster than Chkdsk, systems with relatively low amounts of RAM might see longer times for Autochk than for Chkdsk.

Repairing corruption lengthens the Chkdsk process.   The read-only Chkdsk process can complete only if no significant corruption is found. If a disk suffers only minor corruption, the time to fix the problems is only slightly longer than the time required for read-only Chkdsk. However, if the volume has major corruption, the time required to run Chkdsk can increase in proportion to the number of files damaged.

Recovering Lost Clusters on FAT Volumes

Because some repairs on FAT volumes, such as correcting lost clusters (also known as allocation units) or cross-linked files, change the volume's file allocation table and can cause data loss, Chkdsk first prompts you with a confirmation message similar to the following:

```
10 lost allocation units found in 3 chains.
Convert lost chains to files? (Y/N)
```

If you press the **N** key, Windows XP Professional fixes the errors on the volume but does not save the contents of the lost clusters.

If you press the **Y** key, Windows XP Professional attempts to identify the folder to which they belong. If the folder is identified, the lost cluster chains are saved as files.

If Windows XP Professional cannot identify the folder or if the folder does not exist, it saves each chain of lost clusters in a folder called Found.*xxx*, where *xxx* is a sequential number starting with 000. If no folder Found.000 exists, one is created at the root. If one or more sequential folders called Found.*xxx* (starting at 000) exist, a folder that uses the next number in the sequence is created.

Windows XP Professional creates Found.xxx folders as hidden system folders. To see a list of Found.xxx folders, at the root folder in the command prompt, type **dir /a**. For information about viewing hidden system folders in My Computer or Windows Explorer, see Windows XP Professional Help.

After the storage folder has been identified or created, one or more files with a name in the format File*nnnn*.chk are saved. (The first saved file is named File0000.chk, the second is named File0001.chk, and so on in sequence.) When Chkdsk finishes, you can examine the contents of these files with a text editor such as Notepad to see whether they contain any needed data (if the converted chains came from corrupted binary files, they are of no value). You can delete the .chk files after you save any useful data.

> **Caution**   Because other programs might create and use files with the .chk extension, you must be careful to delete only the .chk files that are in the Found.xxx folders.

Running Chkdsk from My Computer or Windows Explorer

In addition to using the command-line version of Chkdsk, you can run Chkdsk from My Computer or Windows Explorer. The graphical version of Chkdsk offers the equivalent of read-only mode, the **/f** parameter, and the **/r** parameter.

If Chkdsk cannot lock the volume, you can schedule Autochk to run the next time you restart the computer. You cannot choose to dismount the volume like you can when you use the command-line version of Chkdsk, nor can you use other Chkdsk parameters, such as **/c** or **/i**. To take advantage of all the Chkdsk parameters, use the command-line version of Chkdsk.

To run Chkdsk from My Computer or Windows Explorer

1. In My Computer or Windows Explorer, right-click the volume you want to check, and then click **Properties**.

2. On the **Tools** tab, click **Check Now**.

3. Do one of the following:

- To run Chkdsk in read-only mode, click **Start**.

- To run Chkdsk by using the **/f** parameter, select the **Automatically fix file system errors** check box, and then click **Start**.

- To run Chkdsk by using the **/r** parameter, select the **Scan for and attempt recovery of bad sectors** check box, and then click **Start**.

Disk Defragmenter

Fragmentation causes your disk subsystem to perform more seeks, which slows the transfer rate and results in sluggish disk performance. Defragmenting is occasionally necessary because of the way files are stored on disk. Fragmentation can occur when:

- You create a file, but the volume does not have a group of contiguous, free clusters that is large enough to contain the entire file. Therefore, the file is broken into fragments rather than residing in contiguous clusters on the disk.

- You edit a file so that it outgrows its existing space on the disk. When a file uses all the clusters in a group of contiguous, free clusters, the file is then broken into fragments that are stored in free clusters elsewhere on the disk.

Although FAT and NTFS are designed to make storage faster and more efficient when you save files, these file systems take longer to read and write fragmented files than unfragmented files. When the files on a disk become badly fragmented, performance noticeably suffers because the disk heads must move to different tracks on the disk to locate all the clusters of the file.

Defragmentation tools fix this problem by moving the files into contiguous clusters on the disk. Reducing fragmentation reduces the amount of mechanical movement required to locate all clusters of a file, which improves hard disk performance.

Windows XP Professional provides two methods for defragmenting FAT and NTFS volumes:

- The Disk Defragmenter snap-in (Dfrg.msc).

- The new Disk Defragmenter command-line tool (Defrag.exe).

Both tools rearrange files, folders, programs, and unused space on your computer's hard disk to optimize disk performance. In addition, the defragmentation tools are improved in Windows XP Professional so that you can:

- Defragment volumes that use any cluster size.

- Defragment files that are smaller than 16 clusters.

- Defragment the master file table (MFT).

The amount of time that the defragmentation process takes depends on several factors, including the size of the volume, the number and size of files on the volume, the amount of fragmentation, and how busy the system is during defragmentation.

Before Using the Disk Defragmentation Tools

When you use the disk defragmentation tools, keep the following restrictions in mind:

- You can defragment only local volumes, and you can defragment only one volume at a time.

- You must be logged on as an administrator or as a member of the Administrators group to defragment volumes.

- You cannot use the Disk Defragmenter command-line tool (Defrag.exe) while the Disk Defragmenter snap-in is open.

- You cannot defragment volumes that are marked as dirty by the file system. You must run Chkdsk on the dirty volume before you can defragment it. To determine if a volume is dirty, use the **fsutil dirty query** command. For more information about running Chkdsk, see "Chkdsk" earlier in this chapter.

In addition, to obtain best results when you use the disk defragmentation tools, follow these guidelines:

- Ensure you have at least 15 percent free disk space when you defragment a volume. Windows XP Professional uses the free disk space as a sorting area for file fragments.

    Although the defragmentation tools can partially defragment volumes that have less than 15 percent free space, for best results delete unneeded files or move them to another volume to increase the free space to at least 15 percent. You can also use the Disk Cleanup tool to delete unnecessary files. For more information about Disk Cleanup, see Windows XP Professional Help.

- Do not run Backup (either a manual or a scheduled start) at the same time that you run the defragmentation tools because using Backup causes the defragmentation process to pause.

    The Backup program included with Windows XP Professional uses volume snapshots to allow users or applications to continue working while a backup occurs. The defragmentation process resumes after Backup removes the volume snapshot. For more information about volume snapshots, see "Backup and Restore" in this book.

Running the Disk Defragmenter Snap-in

By using the Disk Defragmenter snap-in, you can analyze the volume before you defragment to see how many fragmented files and folders exist. If 10 percent or more of the files and folders are fragmented, Disk Defragmenter recommends that you defragment the volume. If the volume is less than 10 percent fragmented, you can still defragment the volume or you can simply view the fragmentation report.

To open the Disk Defragmenter snap-in

■ Click **Start**, click **Run**, type **dfrg.msc**, and then click **OK**.

Figure 26-2 shows that the Disk Defragmenter snap-in is divided into two main areas. The upper part lists the volumes on the local computer and allows you to select a volume to analyze and defragment. The lower part displays a graphical representation of how fragmented the volume is. The colors indicate the condition of the volume:

■ Red areas show fragmented files.

■ Blue areas show contiguous (unfragmented) files.

■ White areas show free space on the volume. White areas on an NTFS volume might also represent the MFT zone. For more information about the MFT zone, see "File Systems" in this book.

■ Green areas show files that cannot be moved. The green areas usually represent the paging file, but on NTFS volumes, green areas might also represent space used by the NTFS change journal and the NTFS log file.

Figure 26-2   The Disk Defragmenter snap-in

By comparing the **Estimated disk usage before defragmentation** band to the **Estimated disk usage after defragmentation** band, you can see the improvement in your volume after defragmenting. The defragmentation report provides further details on the fragmentation state of the volume. Analyze volumes regularly and defragment them when Disk Defragmenter recommends it.

Defragmenting Volumes by Using the Defrag Command

The Disk Defragmenter command-line tool and the Disk Defragmenter snap-in both defragment volumes by using the same method. However, the command-line tool differs from the snap-in in the following ways:

- The command does not provide a graphical analysis of a volume's fragmentation status, but it does provide a summary.

- The command does not provide a status indicator.

To see a list of parameters for Defrag.exe, at the command prompt, type:

`defrag /?`

To defragment a volume, specify the drive letter. For example, to defragment the C volume, type:

`defrag c:`

To defragment the C volume and view a detailed report that is similar to the report shown in the Disk Management snap-in, type:

`defrag c -v`

To analyze the C volume and view a detailed analysis report, type:

`defrag c: -a -v`

While the command-line Disk Defragmenter is analyzing and defragmenting a volume, it displays a blinking cursor. When Disk Defragmenter finishes analyzing a volume, it displays the analysis report. When Disk Defragmenter finishes defragmenting a volume, it displays the defragmentation report. After the process completes, Disk Defragmenter exits to the command prompt.

To interrupt the defragmentation process, at the command line, press CTRL+C.

For more information about using Defrag.exe, see Windows XP Professional Help.

Tips for Using the Disk Defragmentation Tools

For best results when defragmenting volumes, follow these tips:

- Before defragmenting a volume, delete any unnecessary files, such as temporary files. You can delete unnecessary files by using Disk Cleanup. For more information about Disk Cleanup, see Windows XP Professional Help.

- Defragment a volume before you add a large number of files to the volume, such as before you install programs. This ensures that the files occupy contiguous space and do not become fragmented after you add them.

- Defragment a volume after you delete a large number of files from the volume.

- Defragment a volume after you install programs on it.

- Defragment the system and boot volumes after installing Windows XP Professional.

- Defragment volumes during periods of low system activity.

Optimizing Startup Times by Using Defragmentation Tools

Windows XP Professional monitors the files that are used when the computer starts and when you start applications. By monitoring these files, Windows XP Professional can prefetch them. Prefetching data is the process whereby data that is expected to be requested is read ahead into the cache. Prefetching boot files and applications decreases the time needed to start Windows XP Professional and start applications.

Prefetching is further improved if the files are located next to each other on the outer edge of the disk. Windows XP Professional optimizes the location of boot files and applications when the computer is idle. The optimization occurs in the background and lasts only a minute or two; you might hear the hard disk being accessed when optimization occurs. After the initial optimization takes place, subsequent optimization occurs, at most, every three days.

When you run the Disk Defragmenter tools that are included with Windows XP Professional, they can perform any optimization updates that are scheduled to take place during the next idle period. The Disk Defragmenter tools do not disturb the existing layout of optimized boot files and applications.

> **Note** Computers running Windows XP Home Edition also prefetch and optimize boot files and applications.

Files That You Cannot Defragment

After you defragment a volume, you can view the defragmentation report to see the results. The report includes a list of files that remain fragmented (having two or more fragments). Some reasons that a file might remain fragmented include:

- The volume lacks adequate contiguous free space to defragment all files. Disk Defragmenter requires at least 15 percent free disk space to completely defragment a volume.

- During defragmentation, a new file is created on the volume in disk space that was previously free space. In this case, if Disk Defragmenter tries to move a file to that space to defragment the file, the move fails and the file remains fragmented.

- The file is the master file table (MFT) on an NTFS volume. Because the first fragment of the MFT cannot be moved, the MFT is typically contained within two fragments when sufficient space is available on the volume. If the MFT is contained within three or more fragments, Disk Defragmenter looks for free space where the MFT might fit. If sufficient free space exists, the MFT is moved as a whole (minus the first fragment). If space is not available, the MFT is not defragmented.

- The file is permanently excluded, in which case it might appear in the defragmentation report as still being fragmented no matter how many times you defragment the volume. The following files are permanently excluded from being defragmented.

    - Bootsect.dos

    - Safeboot.fs

    - Safeboot.csv

    - Safeboot.rsv

    - Hiberfil.sys

    - Memory.dmp

    - Paging file

The paging file is a hidden file on the hard disk that Windows XP Professional uses to hold parts of programs and data files that do not fit in memory. (The paging file and physical memory make up virtual memory.) In Windows 2000, the size of the paging file was conservative and often needed to be increased, which caused the paging file to become fragmented. Because Windows XP Professional creates a larger paging file than the default size used in Windows 2000, it is unlikely that your paging file will become fragmented.

You can determine whether the paging file is fragmented by analyzing the volume that contains the paging file and then viewing the analysis report. The report shows the size of the paging file and the number of fragments. You cannot use Disk Defragmenter to defragment the paging file because Windows XP Professional holds the paging file open for exclusive use. However, you can reduce the degree of fragmentation by deleting and then re-creating the paging file. You must have at least two volumes to perform this procedure.

To defragment the paging file

1. From the **Start** menu, click **Control Panel**, click **Performance and Maintenance**, and then click **System**.

2. On the **Advanced** tab, under **Performance**, click **Settings**.

3. On the **Advanced** tab, click **Change** to open the **Virtual Memory** dialog box.

4. In the list of drives, select a volume to store a temporary paging file.

5. Click **Custom size**, type an initial and maximum size to match the current paging file, and then click **Set**.

6. Select the original paging file in the drive list, reduce the minimum and maximum size of the original paging file to 0 MB, and then click **Set**.

7. Restart your computer to have the system use the new paging file.

8. Run Disk Defragmenter on the original volume to consolidate the free space segments created by moving the paging file.

9. Re-create the paging file on the original volume.

10. Reduce the minimum and maximum size of the temporary paging file to 0 MB.

11. Restart your computer.

Recovery Console

The Recovery Console is a text-mode command-line interpreter that you can use for basic troubleshooting and system maintenance. You can run the Recovery Console directly from the Windows XP operating system CD, or for x86-based systems install it as a startup option. The Recovery Console is separate from the Windows XP Professional command prompt and grants limited local hard disk access for both NTFS and FAT volumes.

Because starting the Windows XP Professional graphical user interface (GUI) is not a prerequisite for using the Recovery Console, it can help you recover a Windows XP Professional-based computer that cannot start in safe mode or normal mode. For example, if the computer does not start because the master boot record (MBR) or boot sector is corrupted, you can use the Recovery Console to repair the MBR or boot sector.

> **Note**   Certain Recovery Console commands are not fully functional on dynamic disks or GPT disks.

For more information about using the Recovery Console to repair MBR and boot sector errors, see "Repairing Damaged MBRs and Boot Sectors in x86-based Computers" later in this chapter.

For more information about installing and using Recovery Console, see "Tools for Troubleshooting" in this book.

Automated System Recovery

If changes to the operating system cause instability or startup problems, you can use the Automated System Recovery (ASR) tool to restore the system state and all files stored on the system volume. The term *system state* refers to all the components that determine the current state of the operating system, including:

- User account information, hard disk configuration, and registry information that includes application, hardware, network, video, and software settings.

- Operating system files that are required to start the system, including those in the systemroot directory and boot files such as Ntldr or IA64ldr.efi.

ASR is a last resort option to use after you have unsuccessfully tried other recovery methods, such as rolling back drivers, restoring from backups, performing parallel installations, and using System Restore. ASR restores system state files and settings, and restores your ability to start your system. For example, hard disk corruption might prevent you from starting Windows XP Professional, and the damage might be serious enough to prevent you from using safe mode, Recovery Console, or the Last Known Good Configuration. ASR automates the process of backing up and restoring system state information and files that are needed on the system volume to start Windows XP Professional.

ASR is accessible through the Windows XP Professional Backup application NTBackup.exe and through other programs created by independent software vendors (ISVs). ASR replaces the Emergency Repair Disk option found in Windows 2000 and Windows NT 4.0. For more information about using ASR and other recovery tools, see "Backup and Restore" in this book.

DiskProbe

DiskProbe is a sector editor tool for Windows XP Professional that allows users who are members of the Administrators group to directly edit, save, and copy data on a physical hard disk. With careful use of DiskProbe, you can replace the master boot record (MBR), repair damaged partition table information, and repair or replace damaged boot sectors or other file system data. You can also use DiskProbe to save MBRs and boot sectors as backup binary files in case the original sectors become damaged by viruses, human error, hardware problems, power outages, or similar events. Unless you are familiar with using DiskProbe, try other troubleshooting tools, such as Recovery Console, before using DiskProbe.

Caution   Be cautious when making any changes to the structures of your hard disk. Because DiskProbe does not validate the proposed changes to records, incorrect values in key data structures can render the hard disk inaccessible or prevent the operating system from starting. If you cannot correct the changes you entered, you must re-create and reformat all volumes on the disk.

DiskProbe can change the values of individual bytes in any sector on a dynamic disk, but it cannot navigate the structure of a dynamic disk. Therefore, it is recommended that you use DiskProbe only on basic disks. You can, however, use DiskProbe to back up and restore the boot sector and MBR of dynamic disks.

DiskProbe is part of Windows Support Tools. For more information about DiskProbe, click **Tools** in Help and Support Center, and then click **Windows Support Tools**.

> **Caution**   Do not use DiskProbe on GPT disks in Itanium-based computers. Structures on GPT disks are self-repairing. Making direct changes to GPT structures could cause the partition table checksums to become invalid, rendering the disk inaccessible. For more information about GPT disks, see "Disk Sectors on GPT Disks" later in this chapter.

Dmdiag

Dmdiag.exe is a command-line tool that displays the location and layout of dynamic disks (MBR and GPT) and dynamic volumes. This information is primarily useful if you are working with Microsoft Product Support Services to troubleshoot problems with dynamic disks and volumes.

Dmdiag.exe is part of Windows Support Tools and can be run from the command line by using the following syntax:

```
dmdiag [-f filename] [-v] [/?]
```

When used without parameters, Dmdiag.exe displays information about the dynamic disks and volumes installed on the computer. Table 26-6 describes the Dmdiag.exe parameters.

Table 26-6   Dmdiag.exe Parameters

Parameter	Description
-f *filename*	Specifies the name of the file that stores the output. If you do not specify an output file, the file is saved as Dmdiag.txt in the same folder where you run Dmdiag.exe. If you do not specify the **-f** parameter, the output is displayed at the command prompt.
-v	Runs Dmdiag in verbose mode, which contains additional information about dynamic disks and volumes. Use this mode to obtain a report that product support can use to help you troubleshoot dynamic disks and volumes.
/?	Displays a Help screen with usage syntax.

For more information about Dmdiag.exe, click **Tools** in Help and Support Center, and then click **Windows Support Tools**.

Disk and Volume Status Descriptions

Members of the Administrators group can use the Disk Management snap-in to view the status of disks and volumes.

To open Disk Management

1. From the **Start** menu, click **Run**.

2. In the **Open** box, type **diskmgmt.msc**, and then click **OK**.

As Figure 26-3 shows, if no errors are present on the disk, Disk Management displays an Online status for disks and a Healthy status for volumes.

Figure 26-3   Online status and Healthy status

You can use the information in this section to diagnose and resolve problems identified by Disk Management, which uses a number of predefined status descriptions to indicate a problem has occurred. In many cases, a problem with the underlying disk also results in a volume error condition. For example, Figure 26-4 shows a disk with the Online (Errors) error condition and a volume with the Healthy (At Risk) error condition.

Figure 26-4   Online (Errors) and Healthy (At Risk) error conditions

You can also use the DiskPart command-line tool to view the status of disks and volumes. DiskPart is a text-mode command interpreter that is separate from the Windows XP Professional command prompt. DiskPart allows you to manage fixed (non-removable) disks and volumes by using scripts or direct input.

To run DiskPart, at the command prompt, type:

```
diskpart
```

To view the status of disks, at the DiskPart command prompt, type:

```
list disk
```

To view the status of volumes, at the DiskPart command prompt, type:

```
list volume
```

To view a list of DiskPart commands, at the DiskPart command prompt, type:

```
commands
```

For more information about using DiskPart, see Windows XP Professional Help.

Disk Status Descriptions

The following status descriptions appear if Disk Management detects a problem with a disk or if Disk Management does not recognize the disk.

Foreign

The **Foreign** status occurs when you install a dynamic disk in the local computer. You must right-click the disk and then click **Import Foreign Disks** before you can access data on the disk. If you do not want to import the disk, you can right-click the disk and click **Convert to Basic Disk**. Disk Management displays a warning message before erasing all data from the disk and converting the disk to basic. For more information about importing foreign disks, see "Disk Management" in this book.

Missing

The **Missing** status occurs when a dynamic disk is corrupted, turned off, or disconnected. After you reconnect or turn on the missing disk, open Disk Management, right-click the missing disk, and then click **Reactivate Disk**.

Not Initialized

The **Not Initialized** status indicates that the disk does not contain a valid disk signature in the master boot record (MBR) or a valid disk GUID in the GUID partition table. After you install a new disk, Windows XP Professional must write the MBR or GUID partition table before you can create partitions on the disk.

When you first start Disk Management after installing a new disk, a wizard appears that provides a list of the new disks that Windows XP Professional detects. If you cancel the wizard before the MBR or GUID partition table is written, the disk status remains **Not Initialized** until you right-click the disk and then click **Initialize Disk**.

Offline

The **Offline** status occurs when a dynamic disk is not accessible. The disk might be corrupted or intermittently unavailable. **Offline** also appears if you attempt to import a foreign (dynamic) disk, but the import fails. An error icon appears on the offline disk. Only dynamic disks display the **Offline** status.

If the disk status is **Offline** and the disk name changes to **Missing**, the disk was recently available on the system but can no longer be located or identified. The missing disk might be damaged, turned off, or disconnected.

To bring a disk that is Offline and Missing back online

1. Repair any disk, controller, or cable problems and make sure that the physical disk is turned on, plugged in, and attached to the computer.

2. In Disk Management, right-click the disk, and then click **Reactivate Disk** to bring the disk back online.

If the disk status remains **Offline** and the disk name remains **Missing**, and you determine that the disk has a problem that cannot be repaired, you can remove the disk from the computer.

After you remove a dynamic disk from a computer, the remaining online dynamic disks retain information about the removed disk and its volumes in the dynamic disk database. You can delete all references to the removed disk by updating the dynamic disk database. To do this, use Disk Management to remove all volumes on the missing disk. After you remove all the volumes, right-click the missing disk and then click **Remove Disk**. The missing disk no longer appears in Disk Management.

> **Caution**   Deleting a volume destroys the data on the volume, so you should remove a disk only if you are absolutely certain that the disk is permanently damaged and unusable.

To bring a disk that is Offline but not Missing back online

1. In Disk Management, use the **Reactivate Disk** command to bring the disk back online.

2. If the disk status remains **Offline**, check the cables and disk controller, and make sure that the physical disk is healthy. Correct any problems and try to reactivate the disk again.

If the disk reactivation succeeds, any volumes on the disk automatically return to the **Healthy** status.

Online (Errors)

The **Online (Errors)** status indicates that I/O errors have been detected on a region of the disk. A warning icon appears on the disk with errors. Only dynamic disks display the **Online (Errors)** status.

If the I/O errors are transient, reactivate the disk by right-clicking the disk and then clicking **Reactivate Disk** to return the disk to the **Online** status.

Unreadable

The **Unreadable** status occurs when the disk is not accessible for the following reasons:

■ The disk is spinning up.

■ The disk might have experienced hardware failure, corruption, or I/O errors.

■ The disk's copy of the dynamic disk database might be corrupted.

An error icon appears on disks that display the **Unreadable** status. Both dynamic and basic disks display the **Unreadable** status.

Disks might display the **Unreadable** status while they are spinning up or when Disk Management is rescanning all the disks on the system. In some cases, an unreadable disk has failed and is not recoverable. For dynamic disks, the **Unreadable** status usually results from corruption or I/O errors on part of the disk, rather than failure of the entire disk. You can rescan the disks (by using the **Rescan Disks** command on the **Action** menu in Disk Management) or restart the computer to see if the disk status changes.

Volume Status Descriptions

The following status descriptions appear if Disk Management detects a problem with dynamic volumes or if Disk Management does not recognize volumes, such as those created by non-Windows-brand operating systems.

Failed

The **Failed** status occurs when the dynamic disk is damaged or the file system is corrupted. Unless you can repair the disk or file system, the **Failed** status might indicate data loss.

To troubleshoot a volume with the **Failed** status, make sure that the underlying physical disk is turned on, plugged in, and attached to the computer. Try returning the disk to the **Online** status by using the **Reactivate Disk** command. If this procedure succeeds, the volume automatically restarts and returns to the **Healthy** status.

If the disk returns to the **Online** status but the volume does not return to the **Healthy** status, you can reactivate the volume manually by using the **Reactivate Volume** command.

In some situations, the **Failed** status does not indicate data loss even though the **Reactivate Disk** and **Reactivate Volume** commands fail. These situations occur when:

- You import a mirrored or RAID-5 volume into a computer running Windows XP Professional or Windows XP 64-Bit Edition. These operating systems do not support mirrored or RAID-5 volumes. You must move the disks back to the original computer to access data on the mirrored or RAID-5 volume.

- You install Windows XP Professional to upgrade a computer that is running Windows NT 4.0 Workstation and that contains multidisk volumes. Because Windows XP Professional cannot access multidisk volumes created by using Windows NT 4.0, you must use Ftonline.exe to return the volumes to Healthy status so that you can access data on them. For more information about managing multidisk volumes during Windows XP Professional Setup, see "Disk Management" in this book. For more information about using Ftonline.exe, click **Tools** in Help and Support Center, and then click **Windows Support Tools**.

Healthy (At Risk)

The **Healthy (At Risk)** status occurs when a dynamic volume is experiencing I/O errors caused by bad sectors on the physical disk. The disk remaps the bad sectors by using sectors reserved exclusively for remapping. If the errors are transient, you can use the **Reactivate Disk** command in Disk Management to return the volume to the **Healthy** status. If the **At Risk** status persists, your disk might be failing. Back up the data and replace the disk as soon as possible.

Healthy (Unknown Partition)

The **Healthy (Unknown Partition)** status occurs when Windows XP Professional or Windows XP 64-Bit Edition does not recognize the System ID of a partition on an MBR disk. Partitions with the **Healthy (Unknown Partition)** status might be unknown original equipment manufacturer (OEM) partitions or partitions created by operating systems other than Windows or third-party utilities. You cannot format, assign drive letters or drive paths to, or access data on partitions with **Healthy (Unknown Partition)** status. You can, however, delete these partitions by using Disk Management or the DiskPart command.

> **Caution** If Windows XP Professional recognizes an OEM partition, Disk Management displays the partition as **Healthy (EISA Configuration)**. You cannot use Disk Management to format, delete, assign drive letters or drive paths to, or access data on **Healthy (EISA Configuration)** partitions. However, you can use DiskPart to delete OEM partitions by using the **delete partition** command and specifying the **override** parameter. Deleting an OEM partition can prevent Windows XP Professional from starting, so it is recommended that you do not delete OEM partitions.

Windows XP 64-Bit Edition recognizes partitions on GPT disks that use known partition type GUIDs. If Windows XP 64-Bit Edition does not recognize the partition type GUID of a partition, then it displays the partition as **Healthy (Unknown Partition)**.

Windows XP 64-Bit Edition recognizes the following partitions on GPT disks and displays them in the Disk Management interface:

- Extensible Firmware Interface (EFI) System partition

- Primary partition on a basic disk

Windows XP 64-Bit Edition also recognizes and displays primary partitions, extended partitions, and logical drives on MBR disks.

Windows XP 64-Bit Edition recognizes the following partitions on GPT disks but does not display them in Disk Management:

- Microsoft Reserved partition (MSR)

- Logical Disk Manager (LDM) Metadata partition on a dynamic disk

- LDM Data partition on a dynamic disk

If an OEM created a primary partition on a GPT disk or if you use an operating system other than Windows XP 64-Bit Edition to create a primary partition on a GPT disk, then Windows XP 64-Bit Edition might not recognize the partition type GUID of the partition. If the partition type GUID is unrecognized, Windows XP 64-Bit Edition displays the partition but does not allow you to assign a drive letter or drive path or to access data on the partition. You can, however, delete these partitions by using Disk Management or the DiskPart command.

For more information about the types of partitions that Windows XP Professional recognizes, see "Master Boot Record on Basic Disks." For more information about the types of partitions that Windows XP 64-Bit Edition recognizes, see "GPT Partition Table Header" later in this chapter. For more information about partitions on GPT disks, see "Disk Management" in this book.

Unknown

The **Unknown** status occurs when the boot sector for the volume is corrupted and you can no longer access data on the volume. The boot sector might be infected by a virus. For more information about cleaning an infected computer, see "Viruses That Affect the MBR and Boot Sectors" later in this chapter. For more information about repairing boot sectors, see "Repairing Damaged MBRs and Boot Sectors in x86-based Computers" later in this chapter.

Viruses That Affect the MBR and Boot Sectors

It is always important to take precautions to protect your computer and the data on it from viruses. Many computer viruses exploit the disk structures that your computer uses to start up by replacing, redirecting, or corrupting the code and data that start the operating system.

For more information about the master boot record (MBR) and boot sector on x86-based computers, see "Disk Sectors on MBR Disks" later in this chapter.

MBR Viruses

MBR viruses exploit the master boot code within the master boot record (MBR) that runs automatically when an x86-based computer starts up. MBR viruses are activated when the BIOS activates the master boot code, before the operating system is loaded.

Many viruses replace the MBR sector with their own code and move the original MBR to another location on the disk. After the virus is activated, it stays in memory and passes the execution to the original MBR so that startup appears to function normally.

Some viruses do not relocate the original MBR, causing all volumes on the disk to become inaccessible. If the listing in the partition table for the active primary partition is destroyed, the computer cannot start. Other viruses relocate the MBR to the last sector of the disk or to an unused sector on the first track of the disk. If the virus does not protect the sector that contains the MBR, normal use of the computer might overwrite the MBR, and the system might not restart.

For more information about the master boot code, see "Disk Sectors on MBR Disks" later in this chapter.

Boot Sector Viruses

As with the master boot code, the boot sector's executable code also runs automatically at startup, creating another vulnerable spot exploited by viruses. Boot sector viruses are activated before the operating system is loaded and run when the master boot code in the MBR identifies the active primary partition and activates the executable boot code for that volume.

Many viruses update the boot sector with their own code and move the original boot sector to another location on the disk. After the virus is activated, it stays in memory and passes the execution to the original boot sector so that startup appears normal.

Some viruses do not relocate the original boot sector, making the volume inaccessible. If the affected volume is the active primary partition, the system cannot start. Other viruses relocate the boot sector to the last sector of the disk or to an unused sector on the first track of the disk. If the virus does not protect the altered boot sector, normal use of the computer might overwrite it, rendering the volume inaccessible or preventing the system from restarting.

How MBR and Boot Sector Viruses Affect Windows XP Professional

Two common ways that a computer can contract an MBR or boot sector virus are: by starting up from an infected floppy disk; or by running an infected program, which causes the virus to drop an altered MBR or boot sector onto the hard disk.

The malicious activity of an MBR or boot sector virus is typically contained after Windows XP Professional starts. If the virus payload (the malicious activity of the virus) does not run during system startup and if the virus does not alter the original MBR or boot sector, Windows XP Professional prevents the virus from self-replicating to other disks.

During normal operation, Windows XP Professional is immune to viruses infecting these disk structures because it accesses physical disks only through protected-mode disk drivers. Viruses typically subvert the BIOS INT 13h disk access routines, which are ignored after Windows XP Professional starts. However, on computers with multiple-boot configurations, such as Windows XP Professional with Microsoft® MS-DOS®, Microsoft® Windows® 95, Microsoft® Windows® 98, or Microsoft® Windows® Millennium Edition (Me), an MBR or boot sector virus might infect the computer when you are running another operating system. If this happens, Windows XP Professional is vulnerable to damage.

Viruses that execute their payload during startup are a threat to computers that are running Windows XP Professional because the virus executes before Windows XP Professional takes control of the computer. After Windows XP Professional activates the protected-mode disk drivers, the virus cannot copy itself to other hard disks or floppy disks because the BIOS mechanism on which the virus depends is not used for disk access.

Guidelines for Avoiding Viruses

Follow these guidelines to avoid infecting computers with viruses:

- Install on your system at least one commercial virus-detection program and use it regularly to check your computers for viruses. Be sure to regularly update the virus signature files. After you install an antivirus program, immediately update the virus signature files from the software manufacturer's Internet site. Check with the software manufacturer's documentation for specific instructions.

> **Warning**   It is extremely important that you regularly update your antivirus program. In most cases, antivirus programs are unable to reliably detect and clean viruses of which they are unaware. Most commercial antivirus software manufacturers offer frequent updates. Take advantage of the latest download to ensure that your system is protected with the latest virus defenses.

- Before you install Windows XP Professional in a multiple-boot configuration, scan the other operating systems for viruses.

- Back up files nightly or as needed so that damage is minimized if a virus attack does occur.

- Before opening a file from a floppy disk or before starting a computer from a floppy disk, scan the floppy disk for viruses.

- Do not open e-mail attachments from unknown senders. Delete the e-mail and attachments immediately.

- When you receive an unexpected e-mail attachment from someone you know, verify that the sender intended to send you the attachment. Simply scanning the attachment for viruses is not sufficient because a new virus can propagate without the sender's knowledge. A virus scanner that does not know about the new virus might not catch the virus.

> If the sender did not intend to send you the attachment, permanently delete the e-mail without opening it.

- Never run a file that has a .vbs or .js file name extension unless you know exactly what it is going to do before you run it.

- Regularly check the Microsoft Windows Update Web site and the Microsoft Office Update Web site for patches that fix vulnerabilities and provide security enhancements. In addition, independent software vendors (ISVs) might also provide security-related patches for other programs installed on the computer. For more information, see the Windows Update and Microsoft Office Update links on the Web Resources Page at http://www.microsoft.com/windows/res-kits/webresources.

- Configure the security settings in Microsoft Internet Explorer to protect against downloading infected files or malicious scripts. For more information about protecting computers from unsafe software, see Internet Explorer Help.

- Do not allow users to log on as members of the Administrators group on their own computers because viruses can do more damage if activated from an account with Administrator permissions. Allow users to log on as members of the Users group so that they have only the permissions that are necessary to perform their tasks.

- Configure Windows Explorer and My Computer to show extensions for known file types, show hidden files and folders, and show protected operating system files. For example, a malicious file with the name Report.doc.vbs appears in Windows Explorer and My Computer as Report.doc unless you deselect the option to hide extensions for known file types. To change these settings, in My Computer, click the **Tools** menu, click **Folder Options**, and then click the **View** tab.

Treating an MBR or Boot Sector Virus Infection

To remove a virus from your computer, use a current, well-known commercial antivirus program that is compatible with Windows XP Professional. In addition to scanning the hard disks on your computer, be sure to scan all floppy disks that have been used in the infected computer, in any other computers, or with other operating systems in an infected multiple-boot configuration. Scan floppy disks even if you believe they are not infected. Many infections recur because one or more copies of the virus were not detected and eliminated.

If the computer is already infected with a boot sector virus and you install Windows XP Professional into a multiple-boot configuration, standard antivirus programs might not completely eliminate the infection because Windows XP Professional copies the original MS-DOS boot sector to a file called Bootsect.dos and replaces it with its own boot sector. The Windows XP Professional installation is not initially infected, but if the user chooses to start MS-DOS, Windows 95, Windows 98, or Windows Me, the infected boot sector is reapplied to the system, reinfecting the computer.

Avoid Using the Fdisk /mbr Command to Treat Viruses

Do not depend on the MS-DOS command **Fdisk /mbr**, which rewrites the MBR on the hard disk, to resolve MBR infections. Many newer viruses have the properties of both file infector and MBR viruses, so restoring the MBR does not solve the problem if the virus immediately reinfects the system. In addition, running **Fdisk /mbr** in MS-DOS on a system infected by an MBR virus that does not preserve or encrypt the original MBR partition table permanently prevents access to the lost partitions. If the disk was configured with a third-party drive overlay program to enable support for large disks, running this command eliminates the drive overlay program and you cannot start up from the disk.

> **Caution**   Before you use the **Fdisk /mbr** command, note the following:
>
> - Running **Fdisk /mbr** is not supported on dynamic disks or GPT disks.
> - Running **Fdisk /mbr** in MS-DOS overwrites only the first 446 bytes of the MBR, the portion known as the master boot code, leaving the existing partition table intact. However, if the signature word (the last two bytes of the MBR) has been deleted, the partition table entries are overwritten with zeros. If an MBR virus overwrites the signature word, access to all partitions and logical volumes is lost.

Avoid Using the Fixmbr Command to Treat Viruses

The Recovery Console, a troubleshooting tool in Windows XP Professional, offers a feature called **Fixmbr**. However, it functions identically to the **Fdisk /mbr** command, replacing only the master boot code and not affecting the partition table. For this reason, it is also unlikely to help resolve an infected MBR.

For more information about the Recovery Console, see "Tools for Troubleshooting" in this book.

Repairing Damaged MBRs and Boot Sectors in x86-based Computers

When you start a computer from the hard disk, the BIOS identifies the startup disk and reads the master boot record (MBR). The master boot code in the MBR searches for the active partition on the hard disk. If the first hard disk on the system does not contain an active partition, or if the master boot code cannot locate the boot sector of the system volume so that it can start the operating system, the MBR displays messages similar to the following:

```
Invalid partition table.
Error loading operating system.
Missing operating system.
```

If the active partition exists and the master boot record locates the boot sector of the system volume, the master boot code loads the boot sector of the active partition and transfers CPU execution to that memory address. On computers that are running Windows XP Professional, the executable boot code in the boot sector finds Ntldr, loads it into memory, and transfers execution to that file. However, if the boot sector cannot find Ntldr, which is the file that loads the operating system files from the boot volume, Windows XP Professional cannot start. Windows XP Professional might be unable to find Ntldr in these circumstances:

- If Ntldr is moved, renamed, or deleted.

- If Ntldr is corrupted.

- If the boot sector is corrupted.

- If you install Windows XP Professional and then later install any of the following on the same computer: MS-DOS, Windows 95, Windows 98, or Windows NT 4.0. For more information about configuring a multiple-boot system, see "Planning Deployments" in this book.

Under the preceding circumstances, the computer might not respond to input or might display one of the following messages:

```
A disk read error occurred.
NTLDR is missing.
NTLDR is compressed.
```

Restoring the MBR

You must repair the MBR if it becomes corrupted and you can no longer access any volumes on that disk. You can use several tools to repair the MBR. Which tool you choose depends on whether the partition table is also damaged and whether you can start Windows XP Professional.

- **Use the Recovery Console.**   You can use the **fixmbr** command in Recovery Console to repair the MBR. You can start Recovery Console by booting from the Windows XP Professional operating system CD; so this troubleshooting method is available even if Windows XP Professional does not start in normal or safe mode. However, you cannot use Recovery Console to repair partition tables that were damaged by viruses or other corruption.

- **Use DiskProbe.**   You can use DiskProbe to restore both the MBR and the partition table, but you must have previously backed up this information by using DiskProbe, and you must be able to start Windows XP Professional.

- **Use a third-party disk editor.**   You can use a third-party MS-DOS-based, low-level disk editor to repair the partition table if Windows XP Professional does not start. This method is for experienced users only and involves manually editing the partition table.

Using the Recovery Console to Replace the MBR

You can use the **fixmbr** command in Recovery Console to rewrite the MBR to resolve a corrupted MBR on a startup disk. However, running **fixmbr** overwrites only the master boot code, leaving the existing partition table intact. If the corruption in the MBR affects the partition table, running **fixmbr** might not resolve the problem.

> **Caution**   Use this command with care because it can damage your partition table if any of the following apply:
>
> - A virus is present and a third-party operating system is installed on the same computer.
> - A nonstandard MBR is installed by a third-party disk utility.
> - A hardware problem exists.
>
>   It is recommended that you run antivirus software before you use the **fixmbr** command.

To start the computer and use the Recovery Console to replace the MBR

1. Insert the Windows XP Professional Setup CD-ROM into the CD-ROM drive.

2. Restart the computer. If prompted to press a key to start the computer from the CD-ROM, press the appropriate key.

3. When the text-based part of Setup begins, follow the prompts. Press the **R** key to repair a Windows XP Professional installation.

4. If you are repairing a system that has more than one operating system installed, from the Recovery Console choose the Windows XP Professional installation that you need to repair.

> **Note**   If you press ENTER without typing a number, the Recovery Console quits and restarts the computer.
>   The Recovery Console might also show valid installations of Windows NT 4.0. However, the results of attempting to access a Windows NT 4.0 installation can be unpredictable.

5. When prompted, type the Administrator password. If you do not have the correct password, or if the security database for the installation of Windows XP Professional you are attempting to access is corrupted, Recovery Console does not allow access to the local disks and you cannot repair the MBR.

6. To replace the MBR, at the Recovery Console command prompt, type:

   `fixmbr`

7. Verify if you want to proceed. Depending upon the location and the cause of the corruption within the damaged MBR, this operation can cause the data on the hard disk to become inaccessible. Press the **Y** key to proceed, or press the **N** key to cancel.

Using DiskProbe to Replace the MBR and Partition Table

If you have backed up the MBR by using DiskProbe, you can use it to restore the MBR on any disk that is not used to start the computer. Restoring the backup MBR rewrites the entire sector, including the partition table. However, DiskProbe only runs under Windows XP Professional, Windows 2000 and Windows NT 4.0. It does not run under MS-DOS, Windows 95, Windows 98, or Windows Me.

If the disk that starts Windows XP Professional has a corrupted MBR, Windows XP Professional does not start. Therefore, you cannot use DiskProbe and must use the Recovery Console to replace the MBR.

For more information about restoring backed up MBRs by using DiskProbe, click **Tools** in Help and Support Center, and then click **Windows Support Tools**.

Using a Third-Party Disk Editor to Replace the Partition Table

Before you can repair the partition table, you must know the exact values to use to recreate the partition table. If you backed up your MBR and partition table by using DiskProbe, and you have the backup available on a floppy disk or on another computer, you can use DiskProbe on a different computer to see the correct values so that you can manually recreate the partition table.

Replacing the Boot Sector

If Ntldr is damaged or missing, or if the boot sector is corrupted, you can resolve either problem by using the Recovery Console.

To start the computer and use the Recovery Console to replace the boot sector

1. Insert the Windows XP Professional Setup CD-ROM into the CD-ROM drive.

2. Restart the computer. If prompted to press a key to start the computer from the CD-ROM, press the appropriate key.

3. When the text-based part of Setup begins, follow the prompts. Press the **R** key to repair a Windows XP Professional installation.

4. If you are repairing a system that has more than one operating system installed, from the Recovery Console choose the Windows XP Professional installation that you need to repair.

> **Note** If you press ENTER without typing a number, the Recovery Console quits and restarts the computer.
>
> The Recovery Console might also show valid installations of Windows NT 4.0. However, the results of attempting to access a Windows NT 4.0 installation can be unpredictable.

5. When prompted, type the Administrator password. If you do not have the correct password, or if the security database for the installation of Windows XP Professional that you are attempting to access is corrupted, Recovery Console does not allow access to the local disks and you cannot replace the boot sector.

6. To replace the boot sector, at the Recovery Console command prompt, type:

```
fixboot [drive:]
```

If you do not specify a drive letter, the Recovery Console replaces the boot sector of the system volume. If you need to replace the boot sector of a volume that is not the system volume, then you must specify the appropriate drive letter.

Using a Disk Editor to Replace the Boot Sector

If the boot sector is not from the boot volume on the hard disk, you can use several methods to replace it. If you backed up the boot sector by using DiskProbe, then restoring it by using DiskProbe is the fastest method.

If you want to replace the boot sector on an NTFS volume, you have another alternative. When you create or reformat an existing volume as an NTFS volume, NTFS writes a duplicate of the boot sector in the following location:

- **At the end of the volume.** On volumes formatted with Windows XP Professional, Windows 2000, and Windows NT 4.0.

- **At the logical center of the volume.** On disks formatted with Windows NT 3.51 and earlier.

You can use DiskProbe to locate and copy a duplicate boot sector to the beginning of the volume. There are also third-party MS-DOS-based disk tools that you can use to locate and copy this backup boot sector to the primary boot sector on the volume.

For specifically replacing corrupted boot sectors from boot volumes, DiskProbe is not always an option. Unless you created a Windows XP Professional startup floppy disk, you cannot start Windows XP Professional, which is required by

DiskProbe. You can use a third-party MS-DOS-based, low-level disk editor to restore the backup boot sector.

For more information about creating a startup floppy disk, see article Q119467, "How to Create a Bootable Disk for an NTFS or FAT Partition." To find this article, see the Microsoft Knowledge Base link on the Web Resources page at http://www.microsoft.com/windows/reskits/webresources.

Stop Messages for Disks and File Systems

When Windows XP Professional detects an error from which it cannot recover, it reports error information in full screen, non-windowed, text mode. These Stop messages, which are also referred to as stop errors or blue screens, provide information that is specific to the problem detected by the Windows XP Professional kernel.

File system errors, viruses, hard disk corruption, or controller problems can cause the following Stop messages.

Stop 0x00000024 or NTFS_FILE_SYSTEM

This Stop message, also known as Stop 0x24, indicates that a problem occurred within Ntfs.sys, which is the driver file that allows the system to read and write to NTFS volumes.

Stop 0x00000050 or PAGE_FAULT_IN_NONPAGED_AREA

This Stop message, also known as Stop 0x50, occurs when requested data is not found in memory. The system generates a fault, which indicates that invalid system memory has been referenced. This fault can occur due to a variety of error conditions, such as bugs in antivirus software, a corrupted NTFS volume, or faulty hardware (typically related to defective RAM, be it main memory, L2 RAM cache, or video RAM).

Stop 0x00000077 or KERNEL_STACK_INPAGE_ERROR

This Stop message, also known as Stop 0x77, indicates that the requested page of kernel data from the paging file could not be read into memory. Stop 0x77 can be caused by a number of problems, such as:

- Bad sectors on the hard disk.

- Defective or loose cabling, improper SCSI termination, or the controller not seeing the hard disk.

- Another device is causing a resource conflict with the storage controller.

- Failing RAM.

Stop 0x0000007A or KERNEL_DATA_INPAGE_ERROR

This Stop message, also known as Stop 0x7A, indicates that the requested page of kernel data from the paging file could not be read into memory.

One of the following conditions usually causes a Stop 0x7A: a bad sector in a paging file, a virus, a disk controller error, defective hardware, or failing RAM. In rare cases, a Stop 0x7A occurs when nonpaged pool resources run out.

Stop 0x0000007B or INACCESSIBLE_BOOT_DEVICE

This Stop message, also known as Stop 0x7B, indicates that Windows XP Professional lost access to the system volume or boot volume during the startup process. This error always occurs while the system is starting and is often caused by one of the following:

■ Hardware problems

■ Corrupted or incompatible storage drivers

■ File system problems

■ Boot sector viruses

■ Outdated firmware

During I/O system initialization, this error can occur when:

■ The controller or driver for the startup device (typically the hard disk) failed to initialize the necessary hardware.

■ File system initialization failed because the system did not recognize the data on the boot device.

For more information about these and other Stop messages, see "Common Stop Messages for Troubleshooting" in this book.

Other Disk Problems

Disk problems can occur that do not involve the MBR, partition table, or boot sector. Typically, you cannot use the Windows XP Professional disk tools to troubleshoot these disk problems.

CMOS Problems

The CMOS setup utility is accessible during startup. CMOS typically stores configuration information about the basic elements of the computer, including RAM, video, and storage devices. If CMOS is damaged or incapable of retaining its configuration data, the computer might be unable to start.

Each manufacturer and BIOS vendor can decide what a user can configure in the CMOS utility, and what the standard configuration is. You can access the CMOS utility by using the keyboard sequence that is displayed during startup or by using a software tool, depending on the manufacturer's specifications. It is recommended that you record or print all CMOS information.

The computer uses the CMOS checksum to determine if any CMOS values have been changed other than by using the CMOS setup program. If the checksum is not correct, the computer cannot start.

After the CMOS is correctly configured, any CMOS problem is usually caused by one of the following situations:

- A weak battery, which can happen when the computer has been turned off for a long time.

- A loose or faulty connection between the CMOS and the battery.

- A damaged CMOS caused by static electric discharge.

Cables and Connectors

Another source of disk problems can be cabling and connectors. Cables can become defective, but if the cable works initially, it is likely to work for a long time. When new disks are added to the computer, check for cabling problems. New problems might stem from a previously unused connector on an existing cable or from a faulty, longer cable used to connect all the disks that might have replaced the working original. Also check the connections to the disk themselves. If the cables are tightly stretched, one or more connectors might work themselves loose over time, resulting in intermittent problems with the disks.

If your system has *small computer system interface* (SCSI) adapters, contact the manufacturer for updated Windows XP Professional drivers. Try disabling **sync negotiation** in the SCSI BIOS, checking the SCSI identifiers of each device, and confirming proper termination. For *AT Attachment* devices, define the onboard IDE port as **Primary only**. Also, check each ATA device for the proper master, slave, or stand-alone setting. Try removing all ATA devices except for hard disks. For universal serial bus and IEEE 1394 disks, verify that the cables are correctly connected and that the adapter card, if used, is securely seated.

To make sure that any new disks and disk controllers are supported, see the Microsoft Windows XP Professional Hardware Compatibility List (HCL) link on the Web Resources page at http://www.microsoft.com/windows/reskits/webresources.

Disk Sectors Critical to Startup

A sector is a unit of storage on a hard disk and is typically 512 bytes. Computers access certain sectors on a hard disk during startup to determine which operating system to start and where the partitions are located. The data stored on these sectors varies depending on the computer platform.

Computers that are x86-based begin the startup process from disks that contain a master boot record and are referred to as MBR disks. Itanium-based computers start up from disks that contain a GUID partition table and are referred to as GPT disks. MBR and GPT disks each have disk sectors critical to startup, but the differences in the sectors are not visible in the graphical user interface. Instead, you must use a disk-editing tool, such as DiskProbe, to see how the data on these sectors is structured. For more information about using DiskProbe, see "DiskProbe" earlier in this chapter.

> **Caution**   The ability to edit and repair these sectors on a byte-by-byte basis after corruption has occurred is invaluable, but using a disk-editing tool requires a thorough understanding of how data is organized on the sectors. If you make a mistake, you can damage or permanently overwrite critical on-disk data structures that might make all data on a disk or volume permanently inaccessible. Therefore, it is a good idea to use the information in this chapter to learn about the sectors used for startup, and then to examine the sectors on your own disks to further your learning.

Disk Sectors on MBR Disks

The two sectors critical to starting x86-based computers are the following:

- The master boot record (MBR), which is always located at sector 1 of cylinder 0, head 0, the first sector of a hard disk.

- The boot sector, which resides at sector 1 of each volume.

These sectors contain both executable code and the data required to run the code.

Master Boot Record on Basic Disks

The MBR, the most important data structure on the disk, is created when the disk is partitioned. The MBR contains a small amount of executable code called the master boot code, the disk signature, and the partition table for the disk. At the end of the MBR is a 2-byte structure called a signature word or end of sector marker, which is always set to 0x55AA. A signature word also marks the end of an *extended boot record* (EBR) and the boot sector.

The disk signature, a unique number at offset 0x01B8, identifies the disk to the operating system. Windows XP Professional uses the disk signature as an index to store and retrieve disk information, such as drive letters, in the registry.

Master Boot Code   The *master boot code* performs the following activities:

1. Scans the partition table for the active partition.

2. Finds the starting sector of the active partition.

3. Loads a copy of the boot sector from the active partition into memory.

4. Transfers control to the executable code in the boot sector.

If the master boot code cannot complete these functions, the system displays a message similar to one of the following:

```
Invalid partition table.
Error loading operating system.
Missing operating system.
```

> **Note** Floppy disks and removable disks, such as Iomega Zip disks, do not contain an MBR. The first sector on these disks is the boot sector. Although every hard disk contains an MBR, the master boot code is used only if the disk contains the active primary partition.

For more information about troubleshooting MBR problems, see "Repairing Damaged MBRs and Boot Sectors in x86-based Computers" earlier in this chapter.

Partition Table on Basic Disks The partition table, which is a 64-byte data structure that is used to identify the type and location of partitions on a hard disk, conforms to a standard layout independent of the operating system. Each partition table entry is 16 bytes long, with a maximum of four entries. Each entry starts at a predetermined offset from the beginning of the sector, as follows:

- Partition 1   0x01BE   (446)

- Partition 2   0x01CE   (462)

- Partition 3   0x01DE   (478)

- Partition 4   0x01EE   (494)

The following example shows a partial printout of an MBR revealing the partition table from a computer with three partitions. When there are fewer than four partitions on a disk, the remaining partition table fields are set to the value 0.

```
000001B0:                                  80 01            ..
000001C0: 01 00 07 FE BF 09 3F 00  - 00 00 4B F5 7F 00 00 00   ......?...K.....
000001D0: 81 0A 07 FE FF FF 8A F5  - 7F 00 3D 26 9C 00 00 00   ..........=&....
000001E0: C1 FF 05 FE FF FF C7 1B  - 1C 01 D6 96 92 00 00 00   ...............
000001F0: 00 00 00 00 00 00 00 00  - 00 00 00 00 00 00         ..............
```

Figure 26-5 provides an example of how to interpret the sector printout of the partition table by using Table 26-7. The Boot indicator, System ID, Relative sectors, and Total sectors values correspond to Table 26-7.

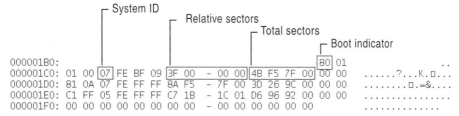

Figure 26-5   Interpreting data in the partition table

Table 26-7 describes the fields in each entry in the partition table. The sample values correspond to the first partition table entry shown in this example. The Byte Offset values correspond to the addresses of the first partition table entry. There are three additional entries whose values can be calculated by adding 10h to the byte offset value specific for each additional partition table entry (for example, add 20h for partition table entry 3 and 30h for partition table entry 4).

The subsections that follow Table 26-7 provide additional detail about these fields.

Table 26-7   Partition Table Fields

Byte Offset	Field Length	Sample Value[*]	Field Name and Definition
0x01BE	1 byte	0x80	**Boot Indicator.** Indicates whether the volume is the active partition. Legal values include: ■ 00. Do not use for booting. ■ 80. Active partition.
0x01BF	1 byte	0x01	**Starting Head.**
0x01C0	6 bits	0x01[†]	**Starting Sector.** Only bits 0–5 are used. The upper two bits, 6 and 7, are used by the Starting Cylinder field.
0x01C1	10 bits	0x00[†]	**Starting Cylinder.** Uses 1 byte in addition to the upper 2 bits from the Starting Sector field to make up the cylinder value. The Starting Cylinder is a 10-bit number that has a maximum value of 1023.
0x01C2	1 byte	0x07	**System ID.** Defines the volume type. See Table 26-8 for sample values.
0x01C3	1 byte	0xFE	**Ending Head.**
0x01C4	6 bits	0xBF[†]	**Ending Sector.** Only bits 0–5 are used. The upper two bits, 6 and 7, are used by the Ending Cylinder field.
0x01C5	10 bits	0x09[†]	**Ending Cylinder.** Uses 1 byte in addition to the upper 2 bits from the Ending Sector field to make up the cylinder value. The Ending Cylinder is a 10-bit number, with a maximum value of 1023.

Table 26-7 Partition Table Fields

Byte Offset	Field Length	Sample Value[*]	Field Name and Definition
0x01C6	4 bytes	0x3F000000	**Relative Sectors.** The offset from the beginning of the disk to the beginning of the volume, counting by sectors.
0x01CA	4 bytes	0x4BF57F00	**Total Sectors.** The total number of sectors in the volume.

[*] Numbers larger than one byte are stored in little endian format, or reverse-byte ordering. Little endian format is a method of storing a number so that the least significant byte appears first in the hexadecimal number notation. For example, the sample value for the Relative Sectors field in the previous table, 0x3F000000, is a little endian representation of 0x0000003F. The decimal equivalent of this little endian number is 63.

[†] This value does not accurately represent the value of the fields, because the fields are either 6 bits or 10 bits and the data is recorded in bytes.

Boot Indicator Field   The first element of the partition table, the **Boot Indicator** field, indicates whether the volume is the active partition. Only one primary partition on the disk can have this field set. See Table 26-7 for the legal values.

It is possible to have different operating systems and different file systems on different volumes. By using disk configuration tools, such as the Windows XP Professional-based Disk Management and DiskPart, or the MS-DOS-based Fdisk to designate a primary partition as active, the **Boot Indicator** field for that partition is set in the partition table.

System ID Field   Another element of the partition table is the **System ID** field. It defines which file system, such as FAT16, FAT32, or NTFS, was used to format the volume. The **System ID** field also identifies an extended partition, if one is defined. Windows XP Professional uses the **System ID** field to determine which file system device drivers to load during startup. Table 26-8 identifies the values for the **System ID** field.

Table 26-8 System ID Values

Partition Type	ID Value
0x01	FAT12 primary partition or logical drive (fewer than 32,680 sectors in the volume)
0x04	FAT16 partition or logical drive (32,680–65,535 sectors or 16 MB–33 MB)
0x05	Extended partition
0x06	BIGDOS FAT16 partition or logical drive (33 MB–4 GB)
0x07	Installable File System (NTFS partition or logical drive)
0x0B	FAT32 partition or logical drive
0x0C	FAT32 partition or logical drive using BIOS INT 13h extensions

Table 26-8 System ID Values

Partition Type	ID Value
0x0E	BIGDOS FAT16 partition or logical drive using BIOS INT 13h extensions
0x0F	Extended partition using BIOS INT 13h extensions
0x12	EISA partition or OEM partition
0x42	Dynamic volume
0x84	Power management hibernation partition
0x86	Multidisk FAT16 volume created by using Windows NT 4.0
0x87	Multidisk NTFS volume created by using Windows NT 4.0
0xA0	Laptop hibernation partition
0xDE	Dell OEM partition
0xFE	IBM OEM partition
0xEE	GPT partition
0xEF	EFI System partition on an MBR disk

Windows XP Professional does not support multidisk volumes that are created by using Windows NT 4.0 and earlier, and that use System ID values 0x86, 0x87, 0x8B, or 0x8C.

If you are upgrading from Windows NT Workstation 4.0 to Windows XP Professional, you must first back up and then delete all multidisk volumes before you upgrade. After you complete the upgrade, create dynamic volumes and restore the data . If you do not delete the multidisk volumes before beginning Setup, you must use the Ftonline tool, which is part of Windows Support Tools, to access the volume after Setup completes. For more information about using Ftonline.exe, click **Tools** in Help and Support Center, and then click **Windows Support Tools**.

If you are upgrading from Windows 2000 to Windows XP Professional, you must convert the multidisk volumes to dynamic before you begin Setup, or Setup does not continue. For more information about multidisk volumes and Setup, see "Disk Management" in this book.

MS-DOS can only access volumes that have a System ID value of 0x01, 0x04, 0x05, or 0x06. However, you can delete volumes that have the other values listed in Table 26-8 by using Disk Management, DiskPart, or the MS-DOS tool Fdisk.

Starting and Ending Cylinder, Head, and Sector Fields The **Starting** and **Ending Cylinder**, **Head**, and **Sector** fields (collectively known as the **CHS** fields) are additional elements of the partition table. These fields are essential for starting the computer. The master boot code uses these fields to find and load the boot sector of the active partition. The **Starting CHS** fields for non-active partitions point to the boot sectors of the remaining primary partitions and the extended boot record (EBR) of the first logical drive in the extended partition, as shown in Figure 26-6.

Knowing the starting sector of an extended partition is very important for low-level disk troubleshooting. If your disk fails, you need to work with the partition starting point (among other factors) to retrieve stored data.

The **Ending Cylinder** field in the partition table is 10 bits long, which limits the number of cylinders that can be described in the partition table to a range of 0 through 1,023. The **Starting Head** and **Ending Head** fields are each one byte long, which limits the field range from 0 through 255. The **Starting Sector** and **Ending Sector** fields are each six bits long, which limits the range of these fields from 0 through 63. However, the enumeration of sectors starts at 1 (not 0, as for other fields), so the maximum number of sectors per track is 63.

Because all hard disks are low-level formatted with a standard 512-byte sector, the maximum disk capacity described by the partition table is calculated as follows:

Maximum capacity = sector size x cylinders (10 bits) x heads (8 bits) x sectors per track (6 bits)

Using the maximum possible values yields:

512 x 1024 x 256 x 63 (or 512 x 2^{24}) = 8,455,716,864 bytes or 7.8 GB

Windows XP Professional and other Windows-based operating systems that support BIOS INT 13h extensions can access partitions that exceed the first 7.8 GB of the disk by ignoring the **Starting** and **Ending CHS** fields in favor of the **Relative Sectors** and **Total Sectors** fields.

Windows 2000 and Windows XP Professional ignore the **Starting** and **Ending CHS** fields regardless of whether the partition exceeds the first 7.8 GB of the disk. However, Windows XP Professional must place the appropriate values in the **Starting** and **Ending CHS** fields because Windows 95, Windows 98, and Windows Me (which all support BIOS INT 13h extensions) use the **Starting** and **Ending CHS** fields if the partition does not exceed the first 7.8 GB of the disk. These fields are also required to maintain compatibility with the BIOS INT 13h for startup.

MS-DOS and other Windows operating systems that do not support BIOS INT 13h extensions ignore partitions that exceed the 7.8 GB boundary because these partitions use a System ID that is recognized only by operating systems that support BIOS INT 13h extensions.

Both the operating system and the computer must support BIOS INT 13h extensions if you want to create partitions that exceed the first 7.8 GB of the disk.

Relative Sectors and Total Sectors Fields   The **Relative Sectors** field represents the offset from the beginning of the disk to the beginning of the volume, counting by sectors, for the volume described by the partition table entry. The **Total Sectors** field represents the total number of sectors in the volume.

Using the **Relative Sectors** and **Total Sectors** fields (resulting in a 32-bit number) provides eight more bits than the CHS scheme to represent the total number of sectors. This allows you to create partitions that contain up to 232 sectors. With a standard sector size of 512 bytes, the 32 bits used to represent the **Relative Sectors** and **Total Sectors** fields translates into a maximum partition size of 2 terabytes (or 2,199,023,255,552 bytes).

Figure 26-6 shows the MBR, partition table, and boot sectors on a basic disk with four partitions. The definitions of the fields in the partition table and the extended partition tables are the same.

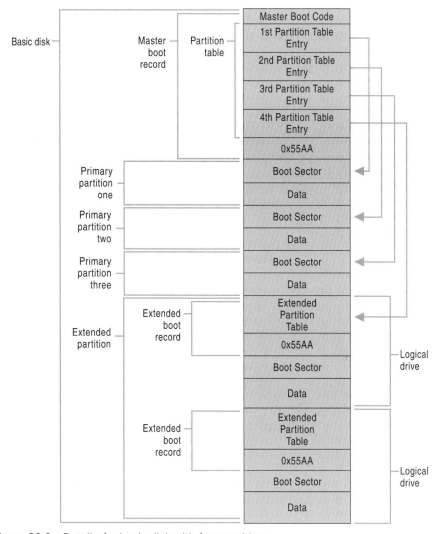

Figure 26-6   Detail of a basic disk with four partitions

Note   For more information about the maximum partition size that each file system supports, see "File Systems" in this book.

Extended Boot Record on Basic Disks   An EBR, which consists of an extended partition table and the signature word for the sector, exists for each logical drive in the extended partition. It contains the only information on the first side of the first cylinder of each logical drive in the extended partition. The boot sector in a logical drive is usually located at either Relative Sector 32 or 63. However, if there is no extended partition on a disk, there are no EBRs and no logical drives.

The first entry in an extended partition table for the first logical drive points to its own boot sector. The second entry points to the EBR of the next logical drive. If no further logical drives exist, the second entry is not used and is recorded as a series of zeros. If there are additional logical drives, the first entry of the extended partition table for the second logical drive points to its own boot sector. The second entry of the extended partition table for the second logical drive points to the EBR of the next logical drive. The third and fourth entries of an extended partition table are never used.

As shown in Figure 27-7, the EBRs of the logical drives in the extended partition are a linked list. The figure shows three logical drives on an extended partition, illustrating the difference in extended partition tables between preceding logical drives and the last logical drive.

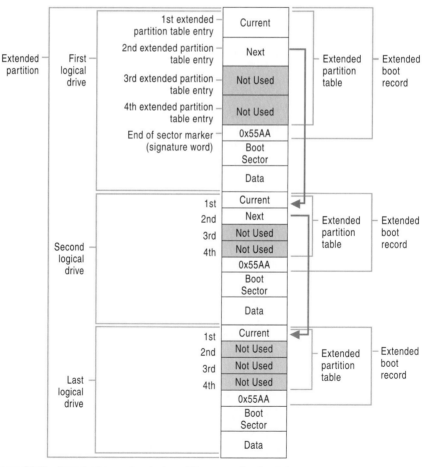

Figure 26-7 Detail of an extended partition on a basic disk

With the exception of the last logical drive on the extended partition, the format of the extended partition table, which is described in Table 26-9, is repeated for each logical drive: the first entry identifies the logical drive's own boot sector and the second entry identifies the next logical drive's EBR. The extended partition table for the last logical drive has only its own partition entry listed. The second through fourth entries of the last extended partition table are not used.

Table 26-9   Contents of Extended Partition Table Entries

Entry	Entry Contents
First	Information about the current logical drive in the extended partition, including the starting address for data.
Second	Information about the next logical drive in the extended partition, including the address of the sector that contains the EBR for the next logical drive. If no additional logical drives exist, this field is not used.
Third	Not used.
Fourth	Not used.

The fields in each entry of the extended partition table are identical to the MBR partition table entries. See Table 26-7 for more information about partition table fields.

The **Relative Sectors** field in an extended partition table entry shows the number of bytes that are offset from the beginning of the extended partition to the first sector in the logical drive. The number in the **Total Sectors** field refers to the number of sectors that make up the logical drive. The value of the **Total Sectors** field equals the number of sectors from the boot sector defined by the extended partition table entry to the end of the logical drive.

Because of the importance of the MBR and EBR sectors, it is recommended that you run disk-scanning tools regularly and that you regularly back up all your data files to protect against losing access to a volume or an entire disk.

Master Boot Record on Dynamic Disks

Like basic disks, dynamic disks contain an MBR that includes the master boot code, the disk signature, and the partition table for the disk. However, the partition table on a dynamic disk does not contain an entry for each volume on the disk because volume information is stored in the dynamic disk database. Instead, the partition table contains entries for the system volume, boot volume (if it is not the same as the system volume), and one or more additional partitions that cover all the remaining unallocated space on the disk. All these partitions use System ID 0x42, which indicates that these partitions are on a dynamic disk. Placing these partitions in the partition table prevents MBR-based disk utilities from interpreting the space as available for new partitions.

> **Note**   In Windows 2000, the partition entries for existing basic volumes were preserved in the partition table when the disk was converted to dynamic. These entries prevented the converted dynamic volumes from being extended. This limitation has been removed from Windows XP Professional for all converted volumes except the boot and system volumes. Partition entries for all other converted volumes are removed from the partition table, and therefore these volumes can be extended.

The following example shows a partial printout of an MBR on a dynamic disk that contains four simple volumes: the system volume, the boot volume, and two data volumes. The first entry is the system volume, which is marked as active. The second entry is the boot volume, and the third entry is the container volume for all other simple volumes on the disk. All entries are type 0x42, which specifies dynamic volumes.

```
000001B0:                                   80 01   ......,Dc!.!.....
000001C0: 01 00 42 FE 7F 04 3F 00 - 00 00 86 FA 3F 00 00 00   ..B...?.....?...
000001D0: 41 05 42 FE FF 02 C5 FA - 3F 00 7E 04 7D 00 00 00   A.B.....?.~.}...
000001E0: C1 03 42 FE FF FF 43 FF - BC 00 58 53 54 00 00 00   ..B...C...XST...
000001F0: 00 00 00 00 00 00 00 00 - 00 00 00 00 00 00 55 AA   ..............U.
```

Boot Sectors on MBR Disks

The boot sector, which is located at sector 1 of each volume, is a critical disk structure for starting your computer. It contains executable code and the data required by the code, including information that the file system uses to access the volume. The boot sector is created when you format a volume. At the end of the boot sector is a 2-byte structure called a signature word or end of sector marker, which is always set to 0x55AA. On computers running Windows XP Professional, the boot sector on the active partition loads into memory and starts Ntldr, which loads the boot menu if multiple versions of Windows are installed or loads the operating system if only one operating system is installed.

A boot sector consists of the following elements:

- An x86-based CPU jump instruction.
- The original equipment manufacturer identification (OEM ID).
- The BIOS parameter block (BPB), a data structure.
- The extended BPB.
- The executable boot code (or bootstrap code) that starts the operating system.

All Windows XP Professional boot sectors contain the preceding elements regardless of the type of disk (basic disk or dynamic disk).

> **Note**   Disk editing tools such as DiskProbe and third-party tools that work with Windows NT 4.0 and NTFS might not support FAT32 boot sectors and volumes.

The BPB describes the physical parameters of the volume: the extended BPB begins immediately after the BPB. Due to differing types of fields and the amount of data they contain, the length of the BPB is different for FAT16, FAT32, and NTFS boot sectors.

Disk device drivers use the information in the BPB and the extended BPB to read and configure volumes. The area following the extended BPB typically contains executable boot code, which performs the actions necessary to continue the startup process.

Boot Sector Startup Processes   Computers use the boot sector to run instructions during startup. The initial startup process is summarized in the following steps:

1. The system BIOS and the CPU initiate the power-on self test (POST).

2. The BIOS finds the boot device, which is typically the first disk the BIOS finds, unless the controller is configured to boot from a different disk.

3. The BIOS loads the first physical sector of the boot device into memory and transfers CPU execution to that memory address.

If the boot device is on a hard disk, the BIOS loads the MBR. The master boot code in the MBR loads the boot sector of the active partition, and transfers CPU execution to that memory address. On computers that are running Windows XP Professional, the executable boot code in the boot sector finds Ntldr, loads it into memory, and transfers execution to that file.

> **Note**   Windows XP Professional cannot start up from a spanned or striped volume on dynamic disks. These disk structures cannot be registered into the MBR partition table; therefore, a system volume that uses these structures cannot start.

If drive A contains a floppy disk, the system BIOS loads the first sector (the boot sector) of the disk into memory. If the disk is a startup disk (formatted by MS-DOS with core operating system files applied), the boot sector loads into memory and uses the executable boot code to transfer CPU execution to Io.sys, a core

MS-DOS operating system file. If the floppy disk is not a startup disk, the executable boot code displays a message such as the following:

```
Non-system disk or disk error.
Replace and press any key when ready.
```

Note These messages do not appear on normally functioning systems that are configured to look for the startup files on drive C first. On many computers, an option in the CMOS setup program allows the user to set the sequence of installed disks that the system searches to find the startup files.

If you get similar errors when trying to start the computer from the hard disk, the boot sector might be corrupted. For more information about troubleshooting boot sector problems, see "Repairing Damaged MBRs and Boot Sectors in x86-based Computers" earlier in this chapter.

Initially, the startup process is independent of disk format and operating system. The unique characteristics of operating and file systems become important when the boot sector's executable boot code starts.

Components of a Boot Sector The MBR transfers CPU execution to the boot sector, so the first three bytes of the boot sector must be valid, executable x86-based CPU instructions. This includes a jump instruction that skips the next several nonexecutable bytes.

Following the jump instruction is the 8-byte OEM ID, a string of characters that identifies the name and version number of the operating system that formatted the volume. To preserve compatibility with MS-DOS, Windows XP Professional records "MSDOS5.0" in this field on FAT16 and FAT32 disks. On NTFS disks, Windows XP Professional records "NTFS."

Note You might also see the OEM ID "MSWIN4.0" on disks formatted by Windows 95 and "MSWIN4.1" on disks formatted by Windows 95 OEM Service Release 2 (OSR2), Windows 98, and Windows Me. Windows XP Professional does not use the OEM ID field in the boot sector except for verifying NTFS volumes.

Following the OEM ID is the BPB, which provides information that enables the executable boot code to locate Ntldr. The BPB always starts at the same offset, so standard parameters are in a known location. Disk size and geometry variables are encapsulated in the BPB. Because the first part of the boot sector is an x86 jump instruction, the BPB can be extended in the future by appending new information at the end. The jump instruction needs only a minor adjustment to accommodate this change. The BPB is stored in a packed (unaligned) format.

FAT16 Boot Sector   Table 26-10 describes the boot sector of a volume formatted with the FAT16 file system.

Table 26-10   Boot Sector Sections on a FAT16 Volume

Byte Offset	Field Length	Field Name
0x00	3 bytes	Jump instruction
0x03	8 bytes	OEM ID
0x0B	25 bytes	BPB
0x24	26 bytes	Extended BPB
0x3E	448 bytes	Bootstrap code
0x01FE	2 bytes	End of sector marker

The following example illustrates a hexadecimal printout of the boot sector on a FAT16 volume. The printout is formatted in three sections:

- Bytes 0x00–0x0A are the jump instruction and the OEM ID (shown in bold print).

- Bytes 0x0B–0x3D are the BPB and the extended BPB.

- The remaining section is the bootstrap code and the end of sector marker (shown in bold print).

```
Physical Sector: Cyl 0, Side 1, Sector 1
00000000: EB 3C 90 4D 53 44 4F 53 - 35 2E 30 00 02 40 01 00   .<.MSDOS5.0..@..
00000010: 02 00 02 00 00 F8 FC 00 - 3F 00 40 00 3F 00 00 00   ........?.@.?...
00000020: 01 F0 3E 00 80 00 29 A8 - 8B 36 52 4E 4F 20 4E 41   ..>....)..6RNO NA
00000030: 4D 45 20 20 20 20 46 41 - 54 31 36 20 20 20 33 C0   ME    FAT16   3.
00000040: 8E D0 BC 00 7C 68 C0 07 - 1F A0 10 00 F7 26 16 00   ....|h......&..
00000050: 03 06 0E 00 50 91 B8 20 - 00 F7 26 11 00 8B 1E 0B   ....P.. ..&.....
00000060: 00 03 C3 48 F7 F3 03 C8 - 89 0E 08 02 68 00 10 07   ...H........h...
00000070: 33 DB 8F 06 13 02 89 1E - 15 02 0E E8 90 00 72 57   3.............rW
00000080: 33 DB 8B 0E 11 00 8B FB - 51 B9 0B 00 BE DC 01 F3   3.......Q.......
00000090: A6 59 74 05 83 C3 20 E2 - ED E3 37 26 8B 57 1A 52   .Yt... ...7&.W.R
000000A0: B8 01 00 68 00 20 07 33 - DB 0E E8 48 00 72 28 5B   ...h. .3...H.r([
000000B0: 8D 36 0B 00 8D 3E 0B 02 - 1E 8F 45 02 C7 05 F5 00   .6...>....E.....
000000C0: 1E 8F 45 06 C7 45 04 0E - 01 8A 16 24 00 EA 03 00   ..E..E.....$....
000000D0: 00 20 BE 86 01 EB 03 BE - A2 01 E8 09 00 BE C1 01   . ..............
000000E0: E8 03 00 FB EB FE AC 0A - C0 74 09 B4 0E BB 07 00   .........t......
000000F0: CD 10 EB F2 C3 50 4A 4A - A0 0D 00 32 E4 F7 E2 03   .....PJJ...2....
00000100: 06 08 02 83 D2 00 A3 13 - 02 89 16 15 02 58 A2 07   .............X..
00000110: 02 A1 13 02 8B 16 15 02 - 03 06 1C 00 13 16 1E 00   ................
00000120: F7 36 18 00 FE C2 88 16 - 06 02 33 D2 F7 36 1A 00   .6........3..6..
00000130: 88 16 25 00 A3 04 02 A1 - 18 00 2A 06 06 02 40 3A   ..%.......*...@:
00000140: 06 07 02 76 05 A0 07 02 - 32 E4 50 B4 02 8B 0E 04   ...v....2.P.....
```

```
00000150: 02 C0 E5 06 0A 2E 06 02  - 86 E9 8B 16 24 00 CD 13   ............$...
00000160: 0F 83 05 00 83 C4 02 F9  - CB 58 28 06 07 02 76 11   .........X(...v.
00000170: 01 06 13 02 83 16 15 02  - 00 F7 26 0B 00 03 D8 EB   ..........&.....
00000180: 90 A2 07 02 F8 CB 42 4F  - 4F 54 3A 20 43 6F 75 6C   ......BOOT: Coul
00000190: 64 6E 27 74 20 66 69 6E  - 64 20 4E 54 4C 44 52 0D   dn't find NTLDR.
000001A0: 0A 00 42 4F 4F 54 3A 20  - 49 2F 4F 20 65 72 72 6F   ..BOOT: I/O erro
000001B0: 72 20 72 65 61 64 69 6E  - 67 20 64 69 73 6B 0D 0A   r reading disk..
000001C0: 00 50 6C 65 61 73 65 20  - 69 6E 73 65 72 74 20 61   .Please insert a
000001D0: 6E 6F 74 68 65 72 20 64  - 69 73 6B 00 4E 54 4C 44   nother disk.NTLD
000001E0: 52 20 20 20 20 20 20 00  - 00 00 00 00 00 00 00 00   R   ........
000001F0: 00 00 00 00 00 00 00 00  - 00 00 00 00 00 00 55 AA   ..............U.
```

Tables 26-11 and 26-12 illustrate the layout of the BPB and the extended BPB for FAT16 volumes. The sample values correspond to the data in this example.

Table 26-11 BPB Fields for FAT16 Volumes

Byte Offset	Field Length	Sample Value	Field Name and Definition
0x0B	2 bytes	0x0002	**Bytes Per Sector.** The size of a hardware sector. Valid decimal values for this field are 512, 1024, 2048, and 4096. For most disks used in the United States, the value of this field is 512.
0x0D	1 byte	0x40	**Sectors Per Cluster.** The number of sectors in a cluster. Because FAT16 can track only a limited number of clusters (up to 65,524), FAT16 supports large volumes by increasing the number of sectors per cluster. The default cluster size for a volume depends on the volume size. Valid decimal values for this field are 1, 2, 4, 8, 16, 32, 64, and 128.
0x0E	2 bytes	0x0100	**Reserved Sectors.** The number of sectors that precede the start of the first FAT, including the boot sector. The value of this field is typically 1.
0x10	1 byte	0x02	**Number of FATs.** The number of copies of the FAT on the volume. The value of this field is typically 2.
0x11	2 bytes	0x0002	**Root Entries.** The total number of 32-byte file and folder name entries that can be stored in the root folder of the volume. On a typical hard disk, the value of this field is 512. One entry can be used as a volume label, and files and folders with long names use multiple entries per file. The largest number of file and folder entries is typically 511; however, if long file names are used, entries usually run out before you reach that number.
0x13	2 bytes	0x0000	**Small Sectors.** The number of sectors on the volume represented in 16 bits (< 65,536). For volumes larger than 65,536 sectors, this field has a value of zero and the **Large Sectors** field is used instead.

Table 26-11   BPB Fields for FAT16 Volumes

Byte Offset	Field Length	Sample Value	Field Name and Definition
0x15	1 byte	0xF8	**Media Descriptor.** Provides information about the media being used. A value of 0xF8 indicates a hard disk and 0xF0 indicates a high-density 3.5-inch floppy disk. Media descriptor entries are a legacy of MS-DOS FAT16 and FAT12 disks and are not used in Windows XP Professional.
0x16	2 bytes	0xFC00	**Sectors Per FAT.** The number of sectors occupied by each FAT on the volume. The computer uses this number and the number of FATs and reserved sectors to determine where the root directory begins. The computer can also determine where the user data area of the volume begins based on the number of entries in the root directory (512).
0x18	2 bytes	0x3F00	**Sectors Per Track.** Part of the apparent disk geometry used on a low-level formatted disk.
0x1A	2 bytes	0x4000	**Number of Heads.** Part of the apparent disk geometry used on a low-level formatted disk.
0x1C	4 bytes	0x3F000000	**Hidden Sectors.** The number of sectors on the volume before the boot sector. This value is used during the boot sequence to calculate the absolute offset to the root directory and data areas.
0x20	4 bytes	0x01F03E00	**Large Sectors.** If the value of the **Small Sectors** field is zero, this field contains the total number of sectors in the FAT16 volume. If the value of the **Small Sectors** field is not zero, the value of this field is zero.

Table 26-12   Extended BPB Fields for FAT16 Volumes

Byte Offset	Field Length	Sample Value	Field Name and Definition
0x24	1 byte	0x80	**Physical Drive Number.** Related to the BIOS physical drive number. Floppy drives are identified as 0x00 and physical hard disks are identified as 0x80, regardless of the number of physical disk drives. Typically, this value is set prior to issuing an INT 13h BIOS call to specify the device to access. This value is only relevant if the device is a boot device.
0x25	1 byte	0x00	**Reserved.** FAT16 volumes are always set to zero.
0x26	1 byte	0x29	**Extended Boot Signature.** A field that must have the value 0x28 or 0x29 to be recognized by Windows XP Professional.

Table 26-12   Extended BPB Fields for FAT16 Volumes

Byte Offset	Field Length	Sample Value	Field Name and Definition
0x27	4 bytes	0xA88B3652	**Volume Serial Number.** A random serial number that is created when a volume is formatted and that helps to distinguish between disks.
0x2B	11 bytes	NO NAME	**Volume Label.** A field that was once used to store the volume label. The volume label is now stored as a special file in the root directory.
0x36	8 bytes	FAT16	Not used by Windows XP Professional.

FAT32 Boot Sector   The FAT32 boot sector is structurally very similar to the FAT16 boot sector, but the FAT32 BPB contains additional fields. The FAT32 extended BPB uses the same fields as FAT16, but the offset addresses of these fields within the boot sector are different than those found in FAT16 boot sectors. Volumes formatted in FAT32 are not readable by operating systems that are incompatible with FAT32.

Table 26-13 describes the boot sector of a volume formatted with the FAT32 file system.

Table 26-13   Boot Sector Sections on a FAT32 Volume

Byte Offset	Field Length	Field Name
0x00	3 bytes	Jump instruction
0x03	8 bytes	OEM ID
0x0B	53 bytes	BPB
0x40	26 bytes	Extended BPB
0x5A	420 bytes	Bootstrap code
0x01FE	2 bytes	End of sector marker

The following example illustrates a hexadecimal printout of the boot sector on a FAT32 volume. The printout is formatted in three sections:

- Bytes 0x00–0x0A are the jump instruction and the OEM ID (shown in bold print).

- Bytes 0x0B–0x59 are the BPB and the extended BPB.

- The remaining section is the bootstrap code and the end of sector marker (shown in bold print).

```
Physical Sector: Cyl 878, Side 0, Sector 1
00000000: EB 58 90 4D 53 44 4F 53 - 35 2E 30 00 02 10 24 00   .X.MSDOS5.0...$.
00000010: 02 00 00 00 00 F8 00 00 - 3F 00 FF 00 3F 00 00 00   ........?...?...
00000020: 1D 91 11 01 2A 22 00 00 - 00 00 00 00 02 00 00 00   ....*"..........
00000030: 01 00 06 00 00 00 00 00 - 00 00 00 00 00 00 00 00   ................
00000040: 80 00 29 F1 9E 5E 5E 4E - 4F 20 4E 41 4D 45 20 20   ..)..^^NO NAME
```

```
00000050: 20 20 46 41 54 33 32 20 - 20 20 33 C9 8E D1 BC F4    FAT32   3.....
00000060: 7B 8E C1 8E D9 BD 00 7C - 88 4E 02 8A 56 40 B4 08    {......|.N..V@..
00000070: CD 13 73 05 B9 FF FF 8A - F1 66 0F B6 C6 40 66 0F    ..s......f...@f.
00000080: B6 D1 80 E2 3F F7 E2 86 - CD C0 ED 06 41 66 0F B7    ....?.......Af..
00000090: C9 66 F7 E1 66 89 46 F8 - 83 7E 16 00 75 38 83 7E    .f..f.F..~..u8.~
000000A0: 2A 00 77 32 66 8B 46 1C - 66 83 C0 0C BB 00 80 B9    *.w2f.F.f.......
000000B0: 01 00 E8 2B 00 E9 48 03 - A0 FA 7D B4 7D 8B F0 AC    ...+..H...}.}...
000000C0: 84 C0 74 17 3C FF 74 09 - B4 0E BB 07 00 CD 10 EB    ..t.<.t.........
000000D0: EE A0 FB 7D EB E5 A0 F9 - 7D EB E0 98 CD 16 CD 19    ...}....}.......
000000E0: 66 60 66 3B 46 F8 0F 82 - 4A 00 66 6A 00 66 50 06    f`f;F...J.fj.fP.
000000F0: 53 66 68 10 00 01 00 80 - 7E 02 00 0F 85 20 00 B4    Sfh.....~.... ..
00000100: 41 BB AA 55 8A 56 40 CD - 13 0F 82 1C 00 81 FB 55    A..U.V@........U
00000110: AA 0F 85 14 00 F6 C1 01 - 0F 84 0D 00 FE 46 02 B4    .............F..
00000120: 42 8A 56 40 8B F4 CD 13 - B0 F9 66 58 66 58 66 58    B.V@......fXfXfX
00000130: 66 58 EB 2A 66 33 D2 66 - 0F B7 4E 18 66 F7 F1 FE    fX.*f3.f..N.f...
00000140: C2 8A CA 66 8B D0 66 C1 - EA 10 F7 76 1A 86 D6 8A    ...f..f....v....
00000150: 56 40 8A E8 C0 E4 06 0A - CC B8 01 02 CD 13 66 61    V@............fa
00000160: 0F 82 54 FF 81 C3 00 02 - 66 40 49 0F 85 71 FF C3    ..T.....f@I..q..
00000170: 4E 54 4C 44 52 20 20 20 - 20 20 20 00 00 00 00 00    NTLDR      .....
00000180: 00 00 00 00 00 00 00 00 - 00 00 00 00 00 00 00 00    ................
00000190: 00 00 00 00 00 00 00 00 - 00 00 00 00 00 00 00 00    ................
000001A0: 00 00 00 00 00 00 00 00 - 00 00 00 00 0D 0A 43 61    ..............Ca
000001B0: 6E 6E 6F 74 20 73 74 61 - 72 74 2E 20 20 52 65 6D    nnot start.  Rem
000001C0: 6F 76 65 20 6D 65 64 69 - 61 2E FF 0D 0A 44 69 73    ove media....Dis
000001D0: 6B 20 65 72 72 6F 72 FF - 0D 0A 50 72 65 73 73 20    k error...Press
000001E0: 61 6E 79 20 6B 65 79 20 - 74 6F 20 72 65 73 74 61    any key to resta
000001F0: 72 74 0D 0A 00 00 00 00 - 00 AC CB D8 00 00 55 AA    rt...........U.
```

Tables 26-14 and 26-15 illustrate the layout of the BPB and the extended BPB for FAT32 volumes. The sample values correspond to the data in this example.

Table 26-14   BPB Fields for FAT32 Volumes

Byte Offset	Field Length	Sample Value	Field Name and Definition
0x0B	2 bytes	0x0002	**Bytes Per Sector.** The size of a hardware sector. Valid decimal values for this field are 512, 1024, 2048, and 4096. For most disks used in the United States, the value of this field is 512.
0x0D	1 byte	0x10	**Sectors Per Cluster.** The number of sectors in a cluster. The default cluster size for a volume depends on the volume size. Valid decimal values for this field are 1, 2, 4, 8, 16, 32, 64, and 128. The Windows XP Professional implementation of FAT32 allows for creation of volumes up to a maximum of 32 GB. However, larger volumes created by other operating systems (Windows 95 OSR2 and later) are accessible in Windows XP Professional.
0x0E	2 bytes	0x2400	**Reserved Sectors.** The number of sectors that precede the start of the first FAT, including the boot sector.

Table 26-14   BPB Fields for FAT32 Volumes

Byte Offset	Field Length	Sample Value	Field Name and Definition
0x10	1 byte	0x02	**Number of FATs.** The number of copies of the FAT on the volume. The value of this field is always 2.
0x11	2 bytes	0x0000	**Root Entries (FAT12/FAT16 only).** For FAT32 volumes, this field must be set to zero.
0x13	2 bytes	0x0000	**Small Sectors (FAT12/FAT16 only).** For FAT32 volumes, this field must be set to zero.
0x15	1 byte	0xF8	**Media Descriptor.** Provides information about the media being used. A value of 0xF8 indicates a hard disk and 0xF0 indicates a high-density 3.5-inch floppy disk. Media descriptor entries are a legacy of MS-DOS FAT16 disks and are not used in Windows XP Professional.
0x16	2 bytes	0x0000	**Sectors Per FAT (FAT12/FAT16 only).** For FAT32 volumes, this field must be set to zero.
0x18	2 bytes	0x3F00	**Sectors Per Track.** Contains the "sectors per track" geometry value for disks that use INT 13h. The volume is broken down into tracks by multiple heads and cylinders.
0x1A	2 bytes	0xFF00	**Number of Heads.** Contains the "count of heads" geometry value for disks that use INT 13h. For example, on a 1.44-MB, 3.5-inch floppy disk this value is 2.
0x1C	4 bytes	0x3F000000	**Hidden Sectors.** The number of sectors on the volume before the boot sector. This value is used during the boot sequence to calculate the absolute offset to the root directory and data areas. This field is generally only relevant for media that are visible on interrupt 13h. It must always be zero on media that are not partitioned.
0x20	4 bytes	0x1D911101	**Large Sectors.** Contains the total number of sectors in the FAT32 volume.
0x24	4 bytes	0x2A220000	**Sectors Per FAT (FAT32 only).** The number of sectors occupied by each FAT on the volume. The computer uses this number and the number of FATs and reserved sectors (described in this table) to determine where the root directory begins. The computer can also determine where the user data area of the volume begins based on the number of entries in the root directory.
0x28	2 bytes	0x0000	Not used by Windows XP Professional.

Table 26-14   BPB Fields for FAT32 Volumes

Byte Offset	Field Length	Sample Value	Field Name and Definition
0x2A	2 bytes	0x0000	**File System Version (FAT32 only).** The high byte is the major revision number; the low byte is the minor revision number. This field supports the ability to extend the FAT32 media type in the future with concern for old FAT32 drivers mounting the volume. Both bytes are zero in Windows XP Professional, Windows 2000, and Windows Me and earlier.
0x2C	4 bytes	0x02000000	**Root Cluster Number (FAT32 only).** The cluster number of the first cluster of the root directory. This value is typically, but not always, 2.
0x30	2 bytes	0x0100	**File System Information Sector Number (FAT32 only).** The sector number of the File System Information (FSINFO) structure in the reserved area of the FAT32 volume. The value is typically 1. A copy of the FSINFO structure is kept in the Backup Boot Sector, but it is not kept up-to-date.
0x32	2 bytes	0x0600	**Backup Boot Sector (FAT32 only).** A value other than zero specifies the sector number in the reserved area of the volume where a copy of the boot sector is stored. The value of this field is typically 6. No other value is recommended.
0x34	12 bytes	0x00000000000 0000000000000	**Reserved (FAT32 only).** Reserved space for future expansion. The value of this field must always be zero.

Table 26-15   Extended BPB Fields for FAT32 Volumes

Byte Offset	Field Length	Sample Value	Field Name and Definition
0x40	1 byte	0x80	**Physical Drive Number.** Related to the BIOS physical drive number. Floppy drives are identified as 0x00 and physical hard disks are identified as 0x80, regardless of the number of physical disk drives. Typically, this value is set prior to issuing an INT 13h BIOS call to specify the device to access. This value is only relevant if the device is a boot device.
0x41	1 byte	0x00	**Reserved.** FAT32 volumes are always set to zero.
0x42	1 byte	0x29	**Extended Boot Signature.** A field that must have the value 0x28 or 0x29 to be recognized by Windows XP Professional.

Table 26-15 Extended BPB Fields for FAT32 Volumes

Byte Offset	Field Length	Sample Value	Field Name and Definition
0x43	4 bytes	0xF19E5E5E	**Volume Serial Number.** A random serial number that is created when a volume is formatted and that helps to distinguish between disks.
0x47	11 bytes	NO NAME	**Volume Label.** A field that was once used to store the volume label. The volume label is now stored as a special file in the root directory.
0x52	8 bytes	FAT32	**System ID.** A text field with a value of FAT32.

NTFS Boot Sector Table 26-16 describes the boot sector of a volume that is formatted with NTFS. When you format an NTFS volume, the format program allocates the first 16 sectors for the boot sector and the bootstrap code.

Table 26-16 Boot Sector Sections on an NTFS Volume

Byte Offset	Field Length	Field Name
0x00	3 bytes	Jump instruction
0x03	8 bytes	OEM ID
0x0B	25 bytes	BPB
0x24	48 bytes	Extended BPB
0x54	426 bytes	Bootstrap code
0x01FE	2 bytes	End of sector marker

On NTFS volumes, the data fields that follow the BPB form an extended BPB. The data in these fields enables Ntldr to find the master file table (MFT) during startup. On NTFS volumes, the MFT is not located in a predefined sector, as on FAT16 and FAT32 volumes. For this reason, NTFS can move the MFT if there is a bad sector in the current location of the MFT. However, if the data is corrupted, the MFT cannot be located, and Windows XP Professional assumes that the volume has not been formatted.

The following example illustrates the boot sector of an NTFS volume that is formatted by using Windows XP Professional. The printout is formatted in three sections:

- Bytes 0x00–0x0A are the jump instruction and the OEM ID (shown in bold print).

- Bytes 0x0B–0x53 are the BPB and the extended BPB.

- The remaining code is the bootstrap code and the end of sector marker (shown in bold print).

```
Physical Sector: Cyl 0, Side 1, Sector 1
00000000: EB 52 90 4E 54 46 53 20 - 20 20 20 00 02 08 00 00   .R.NTFS    .....
00000010: 00 00 00 00 00 F8 00 00 - 3F 00 FF 00 3F 00 00 00   ........?...?...
00000020: 00 00 00 00 80 00 80 00 - 1C 91 11 01 00 00 00 00   ...............
00000030: 00 00 04 00 00 00 00 00 - 11 19 11 00 00 00 00 00   ...............
00000040: F6 00 00 00 01 00 00 00 - 3A B2 7B 82 CD 7B 82 14   ........:.{..{..
00000050: 00 00 00 00 FA 33 C0 8E - D0 BC 00 7C FB B8 C0 07   .....3.....|....
00000060: 8E D8 E8 16 00 B8 00 0D - 8E C0 33 DB C6 06 0E 00   ..........3.....
00000070: 10 E8 53 00 68 00 0D 68 - 6A 02 CB 8A 16 24 00 B4   ..S.h..hj....$..
00000080: 08 CD 13 73 05 B9 FF FF - 8A F1 66 0F B6 C6 40 66   ...s......f...@f
00000090: 0F B6 D1 80 E2 3F F7 E2 - 86 CD C0 ED 06 41 66 0F   .....?.......Af.
000000A0: B7 C9 66 F7 E1 66 A3 20 - 00 C3 B4 41 BB AA 55 8A   ..f..f. ...A..U.
000000B0: 16 24 00 CD 13 72 0F 81 - FB 55 AA 75 09 F6 C1 01   .$...r...U.u....
000000C0: 74 04 FE 06 14 00 C3 66 - 60 1E 06 66 A1 10 00 66   t......f`..f...f
000000D0: 03 06 1C 00 66 3B 06 20 - 00 0F 82 3A 00 1E 66 6A   ....f;. ...:..fj
000000E0: 00 66 50 06 53 66 68 10 - 00 01 00 80 3E 14 00 00   .fP.Sfh.....>...
000000F0: 0F 85 0C 00 E8 B3 FF 80 - 3E 14 00 00 0F 84 61 00   ........>.....a.
00000100: B4 42 8A 16 24 00 16 1F - 8B F4 CD 13 66 58 5B 07   .B..$......fX[.
00000110: 66 58 66 58 1F EB 2D 66 - 33 D2 66 0F B7 0E 18 00   fXfX.-f3.f.....
00000120: 66 F7 F1 FE C2 8A CA 66 - 8B D0 66 C1 EA 10 F7 36   f......f..f....6
00000130: 1A 00 86 D6 8A 16 24 00 - 8A E8 C0 E4 06 0A CC B8   ......$.........
00000140: 01 02 CD 13 0F 82 19 00 - 8C C0 05 20 00 8E C0 66   ........... ...f
00000150: FF 06 10 00 FF 0E 0E 00 - 0F 85 6F FF 07 1F 66 61   ..........o..fa
00000160: C3 A0 F8 01 E8 09 00 A0 - FB 01 E8 03 00 FB EB FE   ................
00000170: B4 01 8B F0 AC 3C 00 74 - 09 B4 0E BB 07 00 CD 10   .....<.t........
00000180: EB F2 C3 0D 0A 41 20 64 - 69 73 6B 20 72 65 61 64   .....A disk read
00000190: 20 65 72 72 6F 72 20 6F - 63 63 75 72 72 65 64 00    error occurred.
000001A0: 0D 0A 4E 54 4C 44 52 20 - 69 73 20 6D 69 73 73 69   ..NTLDR is missi
000001B0: 6E 67 00 0D 0A 4E 54 4C - 44 52 20 69 73 20 63 6F   ng...NTLDR is co
000001C0: 6D 70 72 65 73 73 65 64 - 00 0D 0A 50 72 65 73 73   mpressed...Press
000001D0: 20 43 74 72 6C 2B 41 6C - 74 2B 44 65 6C 20 74 6F   Ctrl+Alt+Del to
000001E0: 20 72 65 73 74 61 72 74 - 0D 0A 00 00 00 00 00 00    restart........
000001F0: 00 00 00 00 00 00 00 00 - 83 A0 B3 C9 00 00 55 AA   ..............U.
```

Table 26-17 describes the fields in the BPB and the extended BPB on NTFS volumes. The fields starting at 0x0B, 0x0D, 0x15, 0x18, 0x1A, and 0x1C match those on FAT16 and FAT32 volumes. The sample values correspond to the data in this example.

Table 26-17   BPB and Extended BPB Fields on NTFS Volumes

Byte Offset	Field Length	Sample Value	Field Name and Definition
0x0B	2 bytes	0x0002	**Bytes Per Sector.** The size of a hardware sector. For most disks used in the United States, the value of this field is 512.
0x0D	1 byte	0x08	**Sectors Per Cluster.** The number of sectors in a cluster.
0x0E	2 bytes	0x0000	**Reserved Sectors.** Always 0 because NTFS places the boot sector at the beginning of the partition. If the value is not 0, NTFS fails to mount the volume.

Table 26-17 BPB and Extended BPB Fields on NTFS Volumes

Byte Offset	Field Length	Sample Value	Field Name and Definition
0x10	3 bytes	0x000000	Value must be 0 or NTFS fails to mount the volume.
0x13	2 bytes	0x0000	Value must be 0 or NTFS fails to mount the volume.
0x15	1 byte	0xF8	**Media Descriptor.** Provides information about the media being used. A value of 0xF8 indicates a hard disk and 0xF0 indicates a high-density 3.5-inch floppy disk. Media descriptor entries are a legacy of MS-DOS FAT16 disks and are not used in Windows XP Professional.
0x16	2 bytes	0x0000	Value must be 0 or NTFS fails to mount the volume.
0x18	2 bytes	0x3F00	Not used or checked by NTFS.
0x1A	2 bytes	0xFF00	Not used or checked by NTFS.
0x1C	4 bytes	0x3F000000	Not used or checked by NTFS.
0x20	4 bytes	0x00000000	The value must be 0 or NTFS fails to mount the volume.
0x24	4 bytes	0x80008000	Not used or checked by NTFS.
0x28	8 bytes	0x1C9111010 0000000	**Total Sectors.** The total number of sectors on the hard disk.
0x30	8 bytes	0x0000040000 000000	**Logical Cluster Number for the File $MFT.** Identifies the location of the MFT by using its logical cluster number.
0x38	8 bytes	0x1119110000 000000	**Logical Cluster Number for the File $MFT-Mirr.** Identifies the location of the mirrored copy of the MFT by using its logical cluster number.
0x40	1 byte	0xF6	**Clusters Per MFT Record.** The size of each record. NTFS creates a file record for each file and a folder record for each folder that is created on an NTFS volume. Files and folders smaller than this size are contained within the MFT. If this number is positive (up to 0x7F), then it represents clusters per MFT record. If the number is negative (0x80 to 0xFF), then the size of the file record is 2 raised to the absolute value of this number.
0x41	3 bytes	0x000000	Not used by NTFS.

Table 26-17 BPB and Extended BPB Fields on NTFS Volumes

Byte Offset	Field Length	Sample Value	Field Name and Definition
0x44	1 byte	0x01	**Clusters Per Index Buffer.** The size of each index buffer, which is used to allocate space for directories. If this number is positive (up to 0x7F), then it represents clusters per MFT record. If the number is negative (0x80 to 0xFF), then the size of the file record is 2 raised to the absolute value of this number.
0x45	3 bytes	0x000000	Not used by NTFS.
0x48	8 bytes	0x3AB27B82C D7B8214	**Volume Serial Number.** The volume's serial number.
0x50	4 bytes	0x00000000	Not used by NTFS.

Protecting the Boot Sector Because a functioning system relies on the boot sector to access a volume, it is highly recommended that you run Chkdsk when needed and back up all your data files regularly to protect against data loss if you lose access to a volume. For more information about Chkdsk, see "Chkdsk" earlier in this chapter. For more information about repairing boot sectors, see "Replacing the Boot Sector" earlier in this chapter.

Disk Sectors on GPT Disks

GPT uses primary and backup partition structures to provide redundancy. These structures are located at the beginning and the end of the disk. GPT identifies these structures by their logical block address (LBA) rather than by their relative sectors. Using this scheme, sectors on a disk are numbered from 0 to n-1, where n is the number of sectors on the disk.

As shown in Figure 26-8, the first structure on a GPT disk is the Protective MBR in LBA 0, followed by the primary GUID partition table (GPT) header in LBA 1. The GPT header is followed by the primary GUID partition entry array, which includes a partition entry for each partition on the disk.

Partitions on the disk are located between the primary and backup GUID partition entry arrays. The partitions must be placed within the first usable and last usable LBAs, as specified in the GPT partition header.

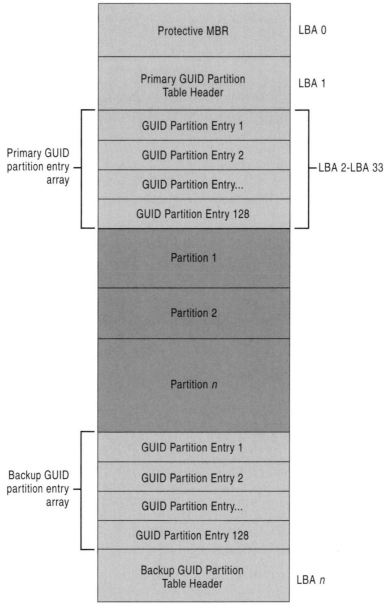

Figure 26-8   Partition structures on a GPT disk

Protective MBR

The Extensible Firmware Interface (EFI) specification requires that LBA 0 be reserved for compatibility code and a Protective MBR. The Protective MBR has the same format as an existing MBR, and it contains one partition entry with a System ID value of 0xEE. This entry reserves the entire space of the disk, including the space used by the GPT header, as a single partition. The Protective MBR is included to prevent disk utilities that were designed for MBR disks from interpreting the disk as having available space and overwriting GPT partitions. The Protective MBR is ignored by EFI; no MBR code is executed.

The following example shows a partial printout of a Protective MBR.

```
000001B0: 00 00 00 00 00 00 00 00 - 04 06 04 06 00 00 00 00   ...............
000001C0: 02 00 EE FF FF FF 01 00 - 00 00 FF FF FF FF 00 00   ...............
000001D0: 00 00 00 00 00 00 00 00 - 00 00 00 00 00 00 00 00   ...............
000001E0: 00 00 00 00 00 00 00 00 - 00 00 00 00 00 00 00 00   ...............
000001F0: 00 00 00 00 00 00 00 00 - 00 00 00 00 00 00 55 AA   ..............U.
```

Table 26-18 describes the fields in each entry in the Protective MBR.

Table 26-18   Protective MBR in GPT Disks

Byte Offset	Field Length	Sample Value*	Field Name and Definition
0x01BE	1 byte	0x00	**Boot Indicator.** Must be set to 0x00 to indicate that this partition cannot be booted.
0x01BF	1 byte	0x00	**Starting Head.** Matches the Starting LBA of the single partition.
0x01C0	1 byte	0x02	**Starting Sector.** Matches the Starting LBA of the single partition.
0x01C1	1 byte	0x00	**Starting Cylinder.** Matches the Starting LBA of the GPT partition.
0x01C2	1 byte	0xEE	**System ID.** Must be 0xEE to specify that the single partition is a GPT partition. If you move a GPT disk to a computer running Windows 2000 with Service Pack 1 or greater or Windows XP Professional, the partition is displayed as a **GPT Protective Partition** and cannot be deleted.
0x01C3	1 byte	0xFF	**Ending Head.** Matches the Ending LBA of the single partition. If the Ending LBA is too large to be represented here, this field is set to 0xFF.
0x01C4	1 byte	0xFF	**Ending Sector.** Matches the Ending LBA of the single partition. If the Ending LBA is too large to be represented here, this field is set to 0xFF.
0x01C5	1 byte	0xFF	**Ending Cylinder.** Matches the Ending LBA of the single partition. If the Ending LBA is too large to be represented here, this field is set to 0xFF.
0x01C6	4 bytes	0x01000000	**Starting LBA.** Always set to 1. The Starting LBA begins at the GPT partition table header, which is located at LBA 1.
0x01CA	4 bytes	0xFFFFFFFF	**Size in LBA.** The size of the single partition. Must be set to 0xFFFFFFFF if this value is too large to be represented here.

* Numbers larger than one byte are stored in little endian format, or reverse-byte ordering. Little endian format is a method of storing a number so that the least significant byte appears first in the hexadecimal number notation.

GPT Partition Table Header

The GPT header defines the range of logical block addresses that are usable by partition entries. The GPT header also defines its location on the disk, its GUID, and a 32-bit cyclic redundancy check (CRC32) checksum that is used to verify the integrity of the GPT header.

GPT disks use a primary and a backup GUID partition table (GPT) header:

■ The primary GPT header is located at LBA 1, directly after the Protective MBR.

■ The backup GPT header is located in the last sector of the disk. No data follows the backup GPT header.

EFI verifies the integrity of the GPT headers by using a CRC32 checksum, which is a calculated value that is used to test data for the presence of errors. If the primary GPT header is corrupted, the system checks the backup GPT header checksum. If the backup checksum is valid, then the backup GPT header is used to restore the primary GPT header. This restoration process works in reverse if the primary GPT header is valid but the backup GPT header is corrupted. If both the primary and backup GPT headers are corrupted, then Windows XP 64-Bit Edition cannot access the disk.

Caution Do not use disk editing tools such as DiskProbe to make changes to GPT disks because any change that you make renders the checksums invalid, which might cause the disk to become inaccessible. To make changes to GPT disks, do either of the following:

■ Use Diskpart.efi in the firmware environment.

■ Use Diskpart.exe or Disk Management in Windows XP 64-Bit Edition.

The following example shows a partial printout of a GPT header.

```
00000000: 45 46 49 20 50 41 52 54 - 00 00 01 00 5C 00 00 00   EFI PART....\...
00000010: 27 6D 9F C9 00 00 00 00 - 01 00 00 00 00 00 00 00   'm..............
00000020: 37 C8 11 01 00 00 00 00 - 22 00 00 00 00 00 00 00   7.......".......
00000030: 17 C8 11 01 00 00 00 00 - 00 A2 DA 98 9F 79 C0 01   .............y..
00000040: A1 F4 04 62 2F D5 EC 6D - 02 00 00 00 00 00 00 00   ...b/..m........
00000050: 80 00 00 00 80 00 00 00 - 27 C3 F3 85 00 00 00 00   ........'.......
00000060: 00 00 00 00 00 00 00 00 - 00 00 00 00 00 00 00 00   ................
```

Table 26-19 describes the fields in the GPT header.

Table 26-19 GUID Partition Table Header

Byte Offset	Field Length	Sample Value	Field Name and Definition
0x00	8 bytes	0x4546492050415254	**Signature.** Used to identify all EFI-compatible GPT headers. The value must always be 0x4546492050415254.
0x08	4 bytes	0x00000100	**Revision.** The revision number of the EFI specification to which the GPT header complies. For version 1.0, the value is 0x00000100.
0x0C	4 bytes	0x5C000000	**Header Size.** The size, in bytes, of the GPT header. The size is always 0x5C000000 or 92 bytes. The remaining bytes in LBA 1 are reserved.
0x10	4 bytes	0x276D9FC9	**CRC32 Checksum.** Used to verify the integrity of the GPT header. The 32-bit cyclic redundancy check (CRC) algorithm is used to perform this calculation.
0x14	4 bytes	0x00000000	**Reserved.** Must be 0.
0x18	8 bytes	0x0100000000000000	**Primary LBA.** The LBA that contains the primary GPT header. The value is always equal to LBA 1.
0x20	8 bytes	0x37C8110100000000	**Backup LBA.** The LBA address of the backup GPT header. This value is always equal to the last LBA on the disk.
0x28	8 bytes	0x2200000000000000	**First Usable LBA.** The first usable LBA that can be contained in a GUID partition entry. In other words, the first partition begins at this LBA. In Windows XP 64-Bit Edition, this number is always LBA 34.
0x30	8 bytes	0x17C8110100000000	**Last Usable LBA.** The last usable LBA that can be contained in a GUID partition entry.
0x38	16 bytes	0x00A2DA989F79C001 A1F404622FD5EC6D	**Disk GUID.** A unique number that identifies the partition table header and the disk itself.
0x48	8 bytes	0x0200000000000000	**Partition Entry LBA.** The starting LBA of the GUID partition entry array. This number is always LBA 2.
0x50	4 bytes	0x80000000	**Number of Partition Entries.** The maximum number of partition entries that can be contained in the GUID partition entry array. In Windows XP 64-Bit Edition, this number is equal to 128.

Table 26-19   GUID Partition Table Header

Byte Offset	Field Length	Sample Value	Field Name and Definition
0x54	4 bytes	0x80000000	**Size of Partition Entry.** The size, in bytes, of each partition entry in the GUID partition entry array. Each partition entry is 128 bytes.
0x58	4 bytes	0x27C3F385	**Partition Entry Array CRC32.** Used to verify the integrity of the GUID partition entry array. The 32-bit CRC algorithm is used to perform this calculation.
0x5C	420 bytes		**Reserved.** Must be 0.

GUID Partition Entry Array

Similar to the partition table on MBR disks, the GUID partition entry array contains partition entries that represent each partition on the disk. Windows XP 64-Bit Edition creates an array that is 16,384 bytes, so the first usable block must start at an LBA greater than or equal to 34. (LBA 0 contains the protective MBR; LBA 1 contains the GPT header; and LBAs 2 through 33 are used by the GUID partition entry array.)

Each GPT disk contains two GUID partition entry arrays:

- The primary GUID partition entry array is located after the GUID partition table header and ends before the first usable LBA.

- The backup GUID partition entry array is located after the last usable LBA and ends before the backup GUID partition table header.

A CRC32 checksum of the GUID partition entry array is stored in the GPT header. When a new partition is added, this checksum is updated in the primary and backup GUID partition entries, and then the GPT header size checksum is updated.

GUID Partition Entry   A GUID partition entry defines a single partition and is 128 bytes long. Because Windows XP 64-Bit Edition creates a GUID partition entry array that has 16,384 bytes, you can have a maximum of 128 partitions on a basic GPT disk.

Each GUID partition entry begins with a partition type GUID. The 16-byte partition type GUID, which is similar to a System ID in the partition table of an MBR disk, identifies the type of data that the partition contains and identifies how the partition is used. Windows XP 64-Bit Edition recognizes only the partition type GUIDs described in Table 26-20 and does not mount any other type of partition. However, original equipment manufacturers (OEMs) and independent software vendors (ISVs), as well as other operating systems might define additional partition type GUIDs.

For more information about the required partitions on GPT disks, see "Disk Management" in this book.

Table 26-20   Partition Type GUIDs

Partition Type	GUID Value
Unused entry	0x00000000000000000000000000000000
EFI System partition	0x28732AC11FF8D211BA4B00A0C93EC93B
Microsoft Reserved partition	0x16E3C9E35C0BB84D817DF92DF00215AE
Primary partition on a basic disk	0xA2A0D0EBE5B9334487C068B6B72699C7
LDM Metadata partition on a dynamic disk	0xAAC808588F7EE04285D2E1E90434CFB3
LDM Data partition on a dynamic disk	0xA0609BAF3114624FBC683311714A69AD

The following example illustrates a partial hexadecimal printout of the GUID partition entry array on a basic GPT disk. This printout shows three partition entries: an EFI System partition, a Microsoft Reserved partition, and a primary partition. The partition type GUIDs are bold and match the entries in Table 26-20.

```
00000000: 28 73 2A C1 1F F8 D2 11 - BA 4B 00 A0 C9 3E C9 3B   (s*......K...>.;
00000010: C0 94 77 FC 43 86 C0 01 - 92 E0 3C 77 2E 43 AC 40   ..w.C.....<w.C.@
00000020: 3F 00 00 00 00 00 00 00 - CC 2F 03 00 00 00 00 00   ?......../......
00000030: 00 00 00 00 00 00 00 00 - 45 00 46 00 49 00 20 00   ........E.F.I. .
00000040: 73 00 79 00 73 00 74 00 - 65 00 6D 00 20 00 70 00   s.y.s.t.e.m. .p.
00000050: 61 00 72 00 74 00 69 00 - 74 00 69 00 6F 00 6E 00   a.r.t.i.t.i.o.n.
00000060: 00 00 00 00 00 00 00 00 - 00 00 00 00 00 00 00 00   ................
00000070: 00 00 00 00 00 00 00 00 - 00 00 00 00 00 00 00 00   ................
00000080: 16 E3 C9 E3 5C 0B B8 4D - 81 7D F9 2D F0 02 15 AE   ....\..M.}.-....
00000090: 80 BC 80 FC 43 86 C0 01 - 50 7B 9E 5F 80 78 F5 31   ....C...P{._.x.1
000000A0: CD 2F 03 00 00 00 00 00 - D0 2A 04 00 00 00 00 00   ./........*......
000000B0: 00 00 00 00 00 00 00 00 - 4D 00 69 00 63 00 72 00   ........M.i.c.r.
000000C0: 6F 00 73 00 6F 00 66 00 - 74 00 20 00 72 00 65 00   o.s.o.f.t. .r.e.
000000D0: 73 00 65 00 72 00 76 00 - 65 00 64 00 20 00 70 00   s.e.r.v.e.d. .p.
000000E0: 61 00 72 00 74 00 69 00 - 74 00 69 00 6F 00 6E 00   a.r.t.i.t.i.o.n.
000000F0: 00 00 00 00 00 00 00 00 - 00 00 00 00 00 00 00 00   ................
00000100: A2 A0 D0 EB E5 B9 33 44 - 87 C0 68 B6 B7 26 99 C7   ......3D..h..&..
00000110: C0 1B 0B 00 44 86 C0 01 - F1 B3 12 71 4F 75 88 21   ....D......qOu.!
00000120: D1 2A 04 00 00 00 00 00 - 4E 2F 81 00 00 00 00 00   .*......N/......
00000130: 00 00 00 00 00 00 00 00 - 42 00 61 00 73 00 69 00   ........B.a.s.i.
00000140: 63 00 20 00 64 00 61 00 - 74 00 61 00 20 00 70 00   c. .d.a.t.a. .p.
00000150: 61 00 72 00 74 00 69 00 - 74 00 69 00 6F 00 6E 00   a.r.t.i.t.i.o.n.
00000160: 00 00 00 00 00 00 00 00 - 00 00 00 00 00 00 00 00   ................
00000170: 00 00 00 00 00 00 00 00 - 00 00 00 00 00 00 00 00   ................
```

Table 26-21 illustrates the layout of a GUID partition entry. The sample values correspond to the EFI System partition entry in the preceding example.

Table 26-21 GUID Partition Entry

Byte Offset	Field Length	Sample Value	Field Name and Definition
0x00	16 bytes	0x28732AC11FF8D211 BA4B00A0C93EC93B	**Partition Type GUID.** Identifies the type of partition. The partition type GUID in this example identifies Microsoft Reserved partitions. See Table 26-20 for a description of the partition type GUIDs.
0x 10	16 bytes	0xC09477FC4386C0019 2E03C772E43AC40	**Unique Partition GUID.** A unique ID created for each partition entry.
0x 20	8 bytes	0x3F00000000000000	**Starting LBA.** The starting LBA of the partition that is defined by this partition entry.
0x 28	8 bytes	0xCC2F030000000000	**Ending LBA.** The ending LBA of the partition that is defined by this partition entry.
0x 30	8 bytes	0x0000000000000000	**Attribute Bits.** Describe how the partition is used. See Table 26-22 for a description of the attribute used by Windows XP 64-Bit Edition.
0x 38	72 bytes	EFI system partition	**Partition Name.** A 36-character Unicode string that can be used to name the partition.

The following example illustrates a partial hexadecimal printout of a GUID partition entry array on a dynamic GPT disk. Notice the differences between this example and the previous example of the basic GPT disk. The GUID partition entry array shows the Microsoft Reserved partition plus additional entries that appear only on dynamic GPT disks:

- The LDM Metadata partition is a 1-MB hidden partition that stores the dynamic disk database, which contains information about all dynamic disks and volumes installed on the computer.

- The LDM Data partition acts as a container for dynamic volumes. Individual dynamic volumes do not contain entries in the GUID partition entry array.

The partition type GUIDs are bold and match the entries in Table 26-20. For more information about partitions on GPT disks, see "Disk Management" in this book.

```
00000000: 16 E3 C9 E3 5C 0B B8 4D - 81 7D F9 2D F0 02 15 AE    ....\..M.}.-....
00000010: 31 C3 97 A6 A4 9F 1D 44 - 85 61 15 49 4A E9 7C 24    1......D.a.IJ.|$
00000020: 22 08 00 00 00 00 00 00 - 21 00 01 00 00 00 00 00    ".......!.......
00000030: 00 00 00 00 00 00 00 00 - 4D 00 69 00 63 00 72 00    ........M.i.c.r.
00000040: 6F 00 73 00 6F 00 66 00 - 74 00 20 00 72 00 65 00    o.s.o.f.t. .r.e.
00000050: 73 00 65 00 72 00 76 00 - 65 00 64 00 20 00 70 00    s.e.r.v.e.d. .p.
00000060: 61 00 72 00 74 00 69 00 - 74 00 69 00 6F 00 6E 00    a.r.t.i.t.i.o.n.
00000070: 00 00 00 00 00 00 00 00 - 00 00 00 00 00 00 00 00    ................
00000080: AA C8 08 58 8F 7E E0 42 - 85 D2 E1 E9 04 34 CF B3    ...X.~.B.....4..
00000090: 66 F2 3F 3A 09 D9 EA 49 - B1 32 75 D5 98 04 3C 34    f.?:...I.2u...<4
```

```
000000A0: 22 00 00 00 00 00 00 00 - 21 08 00 00 00 00 00 00    ".......!.......
000000B0: 00 00 00 00 00 00 00 00 - 4C 00 44 00 4D 00 20 00    ........L.D.M. .
000000C0: 6D 00 65 00 74 00 61 00 - 64 00 61 00 74 00 61 00    m.e.t.a.d.a.t.a.
000000D0: 20 00 70 00 61 00 72 00 - 74 00 69 00 74 00 69 00     .p.a.r.t.i.t.i.
000000E0: 6F 00 6E 00 00 00 00 00 - 00 00 00 00 00 00 00 00    o.n............
000000F0: 00 00 00 00 00 00 00 00 - 00 00 00 00 00 00 00 00    ...............
00000100: A0 60 9B AF 31 14 62 4F - BC 68 33 11 71 4A 69 AD    .`..1.bO.h3.qJi.
00000110: E2 33 A2 82 3A 5E D5 4C - AE 8E 4B EC 6B 76 4D ED    .3..:^.L..K.kvM.
00000120: 22 00 01 00 00 00 00 00 - 09 77 11 01 00 00 00 00    ".......w......
00000130: 00 00 00 00 00 00 00 00 - 4C 00 44 00 4D 00 20 00    ........L.D.M. .
00000140: 64 00 61 00 74 00 61 00 - 20 00 70 00 61 00 72 00    d.a.t.a. .p.a.r.
00000150: 74 00 69 00 74 00 69 00 - 6F 00 6E 00 00 00 00 00    t.i.t.i.o.n.....
00000160: 00 00 00 00 00 00 00 00 - 00 00 00 00 00 00 00 00    ...............
00000170: 00 00 00 00 00 00 00 00 - 00 00 00 00 00 00 00 00    ...............
```

GUID Partition Entry Attributes   GUID partition entry attributes are descriptors for how a partition is used. The attributes are specified within a 64-bit value, so EFI supports up to 64 different attributes. Windows XP 64-Bit Edition uses two attributes as described in Table 26-22.

Table 26-22   GUID Partition Entry Attributes Used by Windows XP 64-Bit Edition

Bits	Description
Bit 0	Specifies that this partition is required for the platform to function.
Bits 48 to 63	Reserved by Microsoft for the following partition types: EFI System partitions, Microsoft Reserved partitions, primary partitions, LDM Metadata partitions, and LDM Data partitions. These partitions use the partition type GUIDs described in Table 26-20.

Boot Sectors on GPT Disks

Boot sectors on GPT disks are similar to boot sectors on MBR disks, except that EFI ignores all x86 code in the boot sector. Instead, EFI uses its own file system driver to read the BPB and then mount the volume.

Additional Resources

- "File Systems" in this book.
- "Disk Management" in this book.
- "Tools for Troubleshooting" in this book.
- "Troubleshooting Concepts and Strategies" in this book.
- *Inside Windows 2000 Server* by William Boswell, 2000, Indianapolis: New Riders Publishing.
- *Inside Microsoft Windows 2000, Third Edition* by David A. Solomon and Mark E. Russinovich, 2000, Redmond: Microsoft Press.
- The Extensible Firmware Interface link on the Web Resources page at http://www.microsoft.com/windows/reskits/webresources.

Chapter 27

Troubleshooting Startup

Diagnosing and correcting hardware and software problems that affect the startup process is an important troubleshooting skill. Resolving startup issues requires a clear understanding of the startup process and core operating system components.

Related Information

- For more information about troubleshooting concepts, see "Troubleshooting Concepts and Strategies" in this book.

- For more information about enabling, disabling, and managing devices, see "Managing Devices" in this book.

- For more information about troubleshooting disk or file system problems, see "Troubleshooting Disks and File Systems" and "Disk Management" in this book.

- For more information about Microsoft® Windows® XP Professional troubleshooting tools, see "Tools for Troubleshooting" in this book.

Understanding the Startup Process

To diagnose and correct a startup problem, you need to understand what occurs during startup. The first step in isolating startup problems is for you to determine whether the problem occurs before, during, or after Microsoft® Windows® XP Professional starts up.

The root cause of startup failure, including contributing factors, can stem from a variety of problems, such as user error, application faults, hardware failures, or virus activity. If the condition is serious enough, you might need to reinstall Windows XP Professional or restore files from backup media.

In *x*86-based systems, startup failures that occur before the operating system loader (Ntldr) starts could indicate missing or deleted files, or damage to the hard disk master boot record (MBR), partition table, or boot sector. If a problem occurs during startup, the system might have incompatible software or drivers, incompatible or improperly configured hardware, or corrupted system files.

The startup process for Itanium-based computers is similar to that of *x*86-based computers. For more information, see "Startup Phases for Itanium-based Systems" later in this chapter.

Startup Phases for x86-based Systems

The Windows XP Professional startup process closely resembles that of Microsoft® Windows NT® version 4.0 and Microsoft® Windows® 2000, but significantly differs from Microsoft® MS-DOS®, Microsoft® Windows® 95, Microsoft® Windows® 98, and Microsoft® Windows® Millennium Edition (Windows Me).

All computers running Windows XP Professional share the same startup sequence:

- Power-on self test (POST) phase

- Initial startup phase

- Boot loader phase

- Detect and configure hardware phase

- Kernel loading phase

- Logon phase

The preceding startup sequence applies to systems started or restarted after a normal shutdown, and does not apply when you bring your computer out of hibernation or standby. See "Resolving Power Management Problems on x86-based Systems" later in this chapter for more information about problems that might occur when you bring your computer out of standby or hibernation.

For Windows XP Professional to start, the system and boot partitions must contain the files listed in Table 27-1.

Table 27-1   Windows XP Professional x86-based Startup Files

File Name	Disk Location	Description
Ntldr	Root of the system partition	The operating system loader.
Boot.ini	Root of the system partition	A file that specifies the paths to Windows XP Professional installations. For multiple-boot systems, Boot.ini contains the operating system choices that display on the startup menu.
Bootsect.dos (multiple-boot systems only)	Root of the system partition	A hidden system file that Ntldr loads for a Windows XP Professional multiple-boot configuration that includes MS-DOS, Windows 95, Windows 98, or Windows Me. Bootsect.dos contains the boot sector for these operating systems.
Ntdetect.com	Root of the system partition	The file that passes information about the hardware configuration to Ntldr.
Ntbootdd.sys	Root of the system partition (required for SCSI or Advanced Technology Attachment (ATA) controllers with firmware disabled or that do not support extended INT-13 calls).	The device driver used to access devices attached to a SCSI or ATA hard disk whose adapter is not using BIOS. The contents of this file depend on the startup controller used.
Ntoskrnl.exe	*systemroot*\System32	The core (also called the kernel) of the Windows XP Professional operating system. Code that runs as part of the kernel does so in privileged processor mode and has direct access to system data and hardware. During installation on single processor systems, Windows XP Professional Setup copies Ntoskrnl.exe from the operating system CD. During installation on multi-processor systems, Windows XP Professional Setup copies Ntoskrnlmp.exe and renames it Ntoskrnl.exe.

Table 27-1   Windows XP Professional x86-based Startup Files

File Name	Disk Location	Description
Hal.dll	*systemroot*\System32	The *Hardware abstraction layer (HAL) dynamic-link library file.* The HAL abstracts low-level hardware details from the operating system and provides a common programming interface to devices of the same type (such as video adapters).
		The Microsoft® Windows® XP Professional operating system CD contains several Hal files. Setup copies to your computer the file that fits your hardware configuration and then renames the file as Hal.dll.
System registry file	*systemroot*\System32\Config\System	The registry file that contains the data used to create the registry key HKEY_LOCAL_MACHINE\SYSTEM. This key contains information that the operating system requires to start devices and system services.
Device drivers	*systemroot*\System32\Drivers	Driver files for hardware devices, such as keyboard, mouse, and video.

Note   Windows NT 4.0, Windows 2000, and Windows XP Professional define the "system" and "boot" partitions differently from other operating systems. The system volume contains files that are needed to start Windows XP Professional, such as the Windows loader (Ntldr). The boot volume contains Windows XP Professional operating system files and folders such as *systemroot* and *systemroot*\System32. In x86-based computers, the boot volume can be, but does not have to be, the same volume as the system volume.

In Table 27-1, the term *systemroot* is one of many *environment variables* used to associate string values, such as folder or file paths, to variables that Windows XP Professional applications and services use. For example, by using environment variables, scripts can run without modification on computers that have different configurations. To obtain a list of environment variables that you can use for troubleshooting, type **set** at the command line.

For more information about environment variables, see "To add or change the values of environment variables" in Windows XP Professional Help and Support Center. For more information about system files, see "System Files Reference" in this book.

Power-on Self Test

As soon as you turn on a computer, its central processing unit (CPU) begins to carry out the programming instructions contained in the basic input/output system (BIOS). The BIOS, which is a type of firmware, contains the processor dependent code that starts the computer regardless of the operating system installed. The first set of startup instructions is the power-on self test (POST). The POST is responsible for the following system and diagnostic functions:

- Performs initial hardware checks, such as determining the amount of memory present.

- Verifies that the devices needed to start an operating system, such as a hard disk, are present.

- Retrieves system configuration settings from non-volatile complementary metal-oxide semiconductor (CMOS) memory, which is located on the motherboard.

    The contents of CMOS memory remain even after you shut down the computer. Examples of hardware settings stored in CMOS memory include boot order and Plug and Play information.

After the motherboard POST completes, add-on adapters that have their own firmware (for example, video and hard drive controllers) carry out internal diagnostic tests.

To access and change system and peripheral firmware settings, consult the system documentation provided by the manufacturer.

Initial Startup Phase

After the POST, the settings that are stored in CMOS memory, such as boot order, determine the devices that the computer can use to start an operating system. For example, if the boot order specifies the floppy disk as the first startup device and the hard disk as second (some firmware displays this order as "A, C"), the following scenarios might occur at startup:

The floppy disk drive contains a floppy disk   The BIOS searches the floppy disk drive for a bootable floppy disk. If one is present, the first sector (the floppy disk boot sector) loads into memory. If the floppy disk is not bootable, an error message similar to the following appears:

```
Non-system disk or disk error
Replace and press any key when ready
```

The computer displays the preceding message until you insert a bootable floppy disk or until you remove the floppy disk and restart the computer.

The floppy disk drive does not contain a floppy disk   If you restart the computer without a floppy disk, the computer reads the boot code instructions located on the master boot record (MBR). The MBR is the first sector of data on the startup hard disk and contains instructions (called *boot code*) and a table (called a *partition table*) that identify primary and extended partitions. The BIOS reads the MBR into memory and transfers control to the code in the MBR.

The computer then searches the partition table for the active partition. The first sector of the active partition contains boot code that enables the computer to do the following:

- Determine the file system used.

- Locate and start the operating system loader file, Ntldr.

If an active partition does not exist or if boot sector information is missing or corrupt, a message similar to any of the following might appear:

```
Invalid partition table
Error loading operating system
Missing operating system
BOOT: Couldn't find NTLDR
NTLDR is missing
```

If an active partition is successfully located, the code in the boot sector locates and starts Ntldr and the BIOS releases control to it.

For more information about disks and file systems, including information about the MBR, partitions, and boot sectors, see "File Systems" and "Troubleshooting Disks and File Systems" in this book.

The boot order specifies another startup device   In addition to floppy disks or hard disks attached to SCSI and ATA controllers, some computer firmware can start an operating system from other devices, such as:

- CD-ROMs

- Network adapters

- Removable disks, such as LS-120 disks or Iomega Zip disks

- Secondary storage devices installed in docking stations for portable computers

It is possible to specify a custom boot order, such as "CDROM, A, C". When you specify "CDROM, A, C" as a boot order, the following events occur at startup:

1. **The computer searches the CD-ROM for bootable media.** If a bootable CD is present, the computer uses the CD-ROM as the startup device. Otherwise, the computer searches the next device in the boot order.

2. **The computer searches the floppy disk for bootable media.** If a bootable floppy is present, the computer uses the floppy disk as the startup device. Otherwise, the computer searches the next device in the boot order or displays an error message.

3. **The computer uses the hard disk as the startup device.** The computer typically uses the hard disk as the startup device only when the CD-ROM drive and the floppy disk drive are empty.

There are exceptions where code on bootable media transfers control to the hard disk. For example, when you start your system by using the bootable Windows XP Professional operating system CD, Setup checks the hard disk for Windows XP Professional installations. If one is found, you have the option of bypassing CD-ROM startup by not responding to the **Press any key to boot from CD** prompt that appears.

You cannot use a nonbootable CD to start your system. The presence of a nonbootable CD in the CD-ROM drive can add to the time the system requires to start. If you do not intend to start the system from CD, remove all CDs from the CD-ROM drive before restarting.

For more information about boot order options, consult your system documentation.

Boot Loader Phase

Ntldr loads startup files from the boot partition and then does the following:

Sets an x86-based processor to run in 32-bit flat memory mode   An $x86$-based computer first starts in real mode. In real mode, the processor disables certain features in order to allow compatibility with software designed to run on 8-bit and 16-bit processors. Ntldr then switches the processor to 32-bit mode, which allows access to large amounts of memory and enables Windows XP Professional to start.

Starts the file system   Ntldr contains the program code that Windows XP Professional needs to read and write to disks formatted by using the NTFS or file allocation table (FAT16 or FAT32) file systems.

Reads the Boot.ini file   Ntldr parses the Boot.ini file to determine the location of the operating system boot partition. For systems that use a single-boot configuration, Ntldr initiates the hardware detection phase by starting Ntdetect.com. For multiple-boot configurations that include Windows XP Professional, Windows 2000, Windows NT 4.0, Windows 95, Windows 98, Windows Me, or MS-DOS, you receive a menu of operating system choices at startup.

Note   Computers running Windows NT 4.0 require Service Pack 4 or later to access NTFS volumes previously mounted by Windows 2000 or Windows XP Professional. For more information about NTFS interoperability, see "File Systems" in this book.

If you choose Windows XP Professional, Windows 2000, or Windows NT 4.0, Ntldr proceeds with the hardware detection phase. If you do not select Windows XP Professional, Windows 2000, or Windows NT 4.0, control is passed to the boot sector for the other operating system. For example, if you select Windows 95, Windows 98, Windows Me, or MS-DOS, Ntldr passes control to Bootsect.dos by reading MBR code that Bootsect.dos contains. This action causes the MBR code in Bootsect.dos to execute as if the instructions were read from the disk. For more information about Boot.ini, see "Reviewing and Correcting Boot.ini Settings on x86-based Systems" later in this chapter.

Detects hardware and hardware profiles   For *x*86-based systems, Ntldr starts Ntdetect.com, a program that performs basic device detection. Ntldr then passes Boot.ini information, as well as hardware and software data in the registry, to Ntoskrnl.exe. Ntdetect.com detects hardware profile information (for example, docked and undocked configurations for portable computers) and also checks for information stored in Advanced Configuration and Power Interface (ACPI) tables. ACPI compliant firmware enables Windows XP Professional to detect device power management features and determine device resource requirements.

For more information about ACPI, see the ACPI link on the Web Resources page at http://www.microsoft.com/windows/reskits/webresources.

Detect and Configure Hardware Phase

After processing the Boot.ini file, Ntldr starts Ntdetect.com. For *x*86-based systems, Ntdetect.com collects information about installed hardware by using calls to system firmware routines. Ntdetect.com then passes this information back to Ntldr. Ntldr gathers the data received from Ntdetect.com and organizes the information into internal data structures. Ntldr then starts Ntoskrnl.exe and provides it with information obtained from Ntdetect.com.

Ntdetect.com collects the following type of hardware and device information:

- System firmware information, such as time and date
- Bus and adapter types
- Video adapters
- Keyboard
- Communication ports
- Disks
- Floppy disks
- Input devices (such as mouse devices)
- Parallel ports
- Devices installed on the Industry Standard Architecture (ISA) bus

Ntdetect.com plays a greater role for device enumeration in computers that are not ACPI compliant because in those computers, the firmware, not the operating system, determines the resources assigned to devices. For computers with ACPI firmware, Windows XP Professional assigns the hardware resources to use.

During this phase, Ntdetect.com searches for *hardware profile* information. Windows XP Professional creates a single default profile for desktop computers and creates two default profiles for portable computers. For portable computers, the operating system selects the appropriate profile based on the hardware state of the computer:

- **Desktop computer**. Profile 1

- **Portable computer**.

  - Docked Profile

  - Undocked Profile

Hardware profiles are especially useful for portable computers because the hardware state of these computers is not static. Drivers for devices not listed in a particular hardware profile are not loaded during startup.

For more information about creating and using hardware profiles, see Windows XP Professional Help and Support Center. Also see article Q225810, "How to Create Hardware Profiles on Windows 2000–Based Mobile Computers," in the Microsoft Knowledge Base. To find this article, see the Microsoft Knowledge Base link on the Web Resources page at http://www.microsoft.com/windows/reskits/webresources. Also, see "Managing Devices" and "Supporting Mobile Users" in this book.

Kernel Loading Phase

Ntldr is responsible for loading the Windows kernel (Ntoskrnl.exe) and the hardware abstraction layer (HAL) into memory. The Hal.dll file that your computer uses can vary. During installation, Windows XP Professional Setup copies one of several HAL files (see Table 27-2 for a list of these files) and renames the file Hal.dll.

To view the computer description in Device Manager

1. In the **Run** dialog box, type **devmgmt.msc**, and then click **OK**.

2. In Device Manager, expand **Computer** to view the description of your computer.

   By comparing the description that Device Manager uses to the descriptions listed in Table 27-2, you can determine the HAL file that is copied to your computer from the Windows XP Professional operating system CD.

Table 27-2   Description of Different Hal.dll Files

Computer Description in Device Manager	HAL File Copied
ACPI Multiprocessor PC	Halmacpi.dll
ACPI Uniprocessor PC	Halaacpi.dll
Advanced Configuration and Power Interface (ACPI) PC	Halacpi.dll
MPS Multiprocessor PC	Halmps.dll
MPS Uniprocessor PC	Halapic.dll
Standard PC	Hal.dll
Compaq SystemPro Multiprocessor or 100% Compatible	Halsp.dll

Together, the kernel and the HAL initialize a group of software components that are called the Windows executive. The Windows executive processes the configuration information stored in registry control sets, and starts services and drivers.

For more information about Windows executive services, see "Common Stop Messages for Troubleshooting" in this book.

Control Sets   Ntldr reads control set information from the HKEY_LOCAL_MACHINE\SYSTEM registry key, which is created from information in the *systemroot*\System32\Config\System file, so that Ntldr can determine which device drivers need to be loaded during startup. Typically, several control sets exist, with the actual number depending on how often system configuration settings change.

> **Caution**   Do not edit the registry unless you have no alternative. The registry editor bypasses standard safeguards, allowing settings that can damage your system, or even require you to reinstall Windows. If you must edit the registry, back it up first and see the Registry Reference in the Microsoft' Windows' 2000 Server Resource Kit at http://www.microsoft.com/windows/reskits/webresources.

Typical registry control set subkeys are:

- \CurrentControlSet, a pointer to a ControlSet*xxx* subkey (*xxx* represents a control set number, such as 001) designated in the \Select**Current** entry.

- \Clone, a copy of \CurrentControlSet, created each time you start your computer.

- \Select, which contains the following entries:

  - **Default**, which points to the control set number (for example, 001=ControlSet001) that the system has specified for use at the next startup. If no error or manual invocation of the **LastKnownGood** startup option occurs, this control set number is designated as the value of the **Default**, **Current**, and **LastKnownGood** entries (assuming that a user is able to log on successfully).

  - **Current**, which points to the last control set that was used to start the system.

  - **Failed**, which points to a control set that did not start Windows XP Professional successfully. This value is updated when the **LastKnownGood** option is used to start the system.

  - **LastKnownGood**, which points to the control set that was used during the last user session. When a user logs on, the **LastKnownGood** control set is updated with configuration information from the previous user session.

Ntldr uses the control set identified by the **Default** value unless you choose the **Last Known Good Configuration** from the **Windows Advanced Options** menu.

The kernel uses the internal data structures provided by Ntldr to create the HKEY_LOCAL_MACHINE\HARDWARE key, which contains the hardware data collected at system startup. The data includes information about various hardware components and system resources allocated to each device. You can monitor the kernel load process by viewing the **Starting up** progress indicator that appears during startup. For more information about Last Known Good Configuration, see "Tools for Troubleshooting" in this book.

Windows XP Professional supports an extensive set of devices. New or updated drivers that are not on the Windows XP Professional operating system CD are provided by hardware manufacturers. *Drivers* are kernel-mode components required by devices to function within an operating system. *Services* are components that support operating system functions and applications. Services can run in a different context than user applications and typically do not offer many user-configurable options. Services, such as the Print Spooler, do not require a user to be logged on to run and act independently of the user who is logged on to the system. Windows XP Professional driver and service files are typically stored in the *systemroot*\System32 and *systemroot*\System32\Drivers folders and use .exe, .sys, or .dll file name extensions.

Drivers are also services. Therefore, during kernel initialization, Ntldr and Ntoskrnl.exe use the information stored in the HKEY_LOCAL_MACHINE\SYSTEM\CurrentControlSet\Services*servicename* registry subkeys to determine both the drivers and services to load. For example, Ntldr searches the Services subkey for drivers with a **Start** value of 0, such as hard disk controllers. After Ntldr starts Ntoskrnl.exe, an Ntoskrnl.exe component searches for and starts drivers, such as network protocols, that have a **Start** value of 1.

Table 27-3 lists the values (in decimal) for the **Start** entry. Boot drivers (those with a **Start** value of 0) and file system drivers are always loaded regardless of their **Start** value because they are required to start Windows XP Professional.

Table 27-3   Values for a <*servicename*> Start Entry

Value	Start Type	Value Descriptions for Start Entries
0	Boot	Specifies a driver that is loaded (but not started) by firmware calls made by the x86-based Ntldr or Itanium-based IA64ldr boot loader. If no errors occur, the kernel starts the driver.
1	System	Specifies a driver that loads at kernel initialization during the startup sequence by calling Windows XP Professional boot drivers.
2	Auto load	Specifies a driver or service that is initialized at system startup by Session Manager (Smss.exe) or Service Controller (Services.exe).
3	Load on demand	Specifies a driver or service that is manually started by a user, a process, or another service.
4	Disabled	Specifies a disabled (not started) driver or service.

Table 27-4 lists some of the values (in decimal) for the **Type** entry.

Table 27-4   Values for a <*servicename*> Type Entry

Value	Value Descriptions for Type Entries
1	Specifies a kernel device driver.
2	Specifies a file system driver (also a kernel device driver).
4	Specifies parameters passed to the device driver.
16	Specifies a service that obeys the service control protocol, can run in a process by itself, and can be started by the Services Controller.
32	Specifies a service that can share a process with other services.

Some drivers and services require that certain dependencies be met before they start. You can find dependencies listed under the **DependOnGroup** and **DependOnService** entries in the HKEY_LOCAL_MACHINE\SYSTEM\CurrentControlSet\ Services*servicename* subkey for each service or driver. For more information about using dependencies to prevent or delay a driver or service from starting, see "Temporarily Disabling Services" later in this chapter. The Services subkey also contains information that affects how drivers and services are loaded, a few of which are listed in Table 27-5.

Table 27-5   Other Registry <*servicename*> Entries

Entry	Description
DependOn-Group	At least one item from this group must start before this service is loaded. The subkey SYSTEM\CurrentControlSet\Control\ServiceGroupOrder contains the service group load order.
DependOn-Service	Lists the specific services that must load before this service loads.
Description	Describes the component.
DisplayName	Specifies the display name of the component.
ErrorControl	Controls whether a driver error requires the system to use the **Last-KnownGood** control set or to display a Stop message.
	■ If the value is 0x0 (Ignore, no error is reported), do not display a warning and proceed with startup.
	■ If the value is 0x1 (Normal, error reported), record the event to the System Event Log and display a warning message, but proceed with startup.
	■ If the value is 0x2 (Severe), record the event to the System Event Log, use the **LastKnownGood** settings, restart the system, and proceed with startup.
	■ If the value is 0x3 (Critical), record the event to the System Event Log, use the **LastKnownGood** settings, and restart the system. If the **LastKnownGood** settings are already in use, display a Stop message.
Group	Designates the group that the driver or service belongs to. This allows related drivers or services to start together (for example, file system drivers). The registry entry **List** in the subkey HKEY_LOCAL_MACHINE\SYSTEM\CurrentControlSet\Control\ServiceGroupOrder specifies the group startup order.
ImagePath	Identifies the path and file name of the driver or service if the **ImagePath** entry is present. You can use Windows Explorer to verify the path and file name.
ObjectName	Specifies an object name. If the **Type** entry specifies a Windows XP Professional service, it represents the account name that the service uses to log on when it runs.
Tag	Designates the order in which a driver starts within a driver group.

Session Manager

After all entries that have Boot and Startup data types are processed, the kernel starts Session Manager. Session Manager (Smss.exe) performs important initialization functions, such as:

■ Creating system environment variables.

■ Starting the kernel-mode portion of the Windows subsystem (implemented by *systemroot*\System32\Win32k.sys), which causes Windows XP Professional to switch from text mode to graphics mode. Windows-based applications run in the Windows subsystem. This environment allows applications to access operating system functions, such as displaying information to the screen.

■ Starting the user-mode portion of the Windows subsystem (implemented by *systemroot*\System32\Csrss.exe).

■ Starting the Logon Manager *(systemroot*\System32\Winlogon.exe).

■ Creating additional virtual memory paging files.

■ Performing delayed rename operations for files listed in the registry entry HKEY_LOCAL_MACHINE\SYSTEM\CurrentControlSet\Control\Session Manager**PendingFileRenameOperations**. For example, you might be prompted to restart the computer after installing a new driver or application so that Windows XP Professional can replace the file in use.

The Windows subsystem and the applications that run within it are user mode processes; they do not have direct access to hardware or device drivers. User-mode processes run at a lower priority than kernel-mode processes. When the operating system needs more memory, it can page to disk the memory that is used by user-mode processes. For more information about user-mode and kernel-mode components, see "Common Stop Messages for Troubleshooting" in this book.

Session Manager searches the registry for service information that is contained in the following subkeys:

■ HKEY_LOCAL_MACHINE\SYSTEM\CurrentControlSet\Control\Session Manager contains a list of commands to run before loading services. The Autochk.exe tool is specified by the value of the **BootExecute** entry and virtual memory (paging file) settings stored in the Memory Management subkey. Autochk, which is a version of the Chkdsk tool, runs at startup if the operating system detects a file system problem that requires repair before completing the startup process. For more information about Autochk and Chkdsk, see "Troubleshooting Disks and File Systems" in this book.

■ HKEY_LOCAL_MACHINE\SYSTEM\CurrentControlSet\Control\Session Manager\Subsystems contains a list of available subsystems. For example, Csrss.exe contains the user-mode portion of the Windows subsystem.

■ HKEY_LOCAL_MACHINE\SYSTEM\CurrentControlSet\Services*servicename*. The Service Control Manager initializes services that the **Start** entry designates as Auto-load.

Logon Phase

The Windows subsystem starts Winlogon.exe, a system service that enables logging on and off. Winlogon.exe then does the following:

■ Starts the Services subsystem (Services.exe), also known as the Service Control Manager (SCM).

- Starts the Local Security Authority (LSA) process (Lsass.exe).

- Parses the CTRL+ALT+DEL key combination at the **Begin Logon** prompt.

The Graphical Identification and Authentication (GINA) component collects the user name and password, and passes this information securely to the LSA for authentication. If the user supplied valid credentials, access is granted by using either the Kerberos V 5 authentication protocol or NTLM. For more information about security components, such as LSA, Kerberos V5 protocol, or NTLM, see the *Distributed Systems Guide* of the *Microsoft® Windows® 2000 Server Resource Kit*.

Winlogon initializes security and authentication components while the Service Control Manager initializes Auto-load services and drivers. After the user logs on, the following events occur:

- **Control sets are updated**. The control set referenced by the **LastKnown-Good** registry entry is updated with the contents in the **Clone** entry. **Clone**, which is a copy of the **CurrentControlSet** entry, is created each time you start your computer. When a user logs on, the **LastKnownGood** control set is updated with configuration information from the previous user session.

- **Group Policy settings take effect**. Group Policy settings that apply to the user and computer take effect. For more information about Group Policy, see "Planning Deployments," "Managing Desktops," and "Authorization and Access Control" in this book, and see "Group Policy" in the Distributed Systems Guide of the *Microsoft Windows 2000 Server Resource Kit*. Also, see the *Change and Configuration Management Deployment Guide* link on the Web Resources page at http://www.microsoft.com/windows/reskits/webresources.

- **Startup programs run**. Windows XP Professional starts logon scripts, startup programs, and services referenced in these registry subkeys and folder locations:

  - HKEY_LOCAL_MACHINE\SOFTWARE\Microsoft\Windows\CurrentVersion\Runonce

  - HKEY_LOCAL_MACHINE\SOFTWARE\Microsoft\Windows\CurrentVersion\policies\Explorer\Run

  - HKEY_LOCAL_MACHINE\SOFTWARE\Microsoft\Windows\CurrentVersion\Run

  - HKEY_CURRENT_USER\Software\Microsoft\Windows NT\CurrentVersion\Windows\Run

  - HKEY_CURRENT_USER\Software\Microsoft\Windows\CurrentVersion\Run

  - HKEY_CURRENT_USER\Software\Microsoft\Windows\CurrentVersion\RunOnce

  - *systemdrive*\Documents and Settings\All Users\Start Menu\Programs\Startup

- *systemdrive*\Documents and Settings*username*\Start Menu\Programs\\
Startup

- *windir*\Profiles\All Users\Start Menu\Programs\Startup

- *windir*\Profiles*username*\Start Menu\Programs\Startup

The *windir*\Profiles folders exist only on systems that are upgraded from Windows NT 4.0.

Windows XP Professional startup is not complete until a user successfully logs on to the computer.

Plug and Play Device Detection

Plug and Play detection runs asynchronously with the logon process and relies on system firmware, hardware, device driver, and operating system features to detect and enumerate new devices. Windows XP Professional optimizes Plug and Play support for computers equipped with ACPI firmware and enables enhanced features, such as hardware resource sharing.

When Plug and Play components are well coordinated, Windows XP Professional can detect new devices, allocate system resources, and install or request drivers with minimal user intervention. ACPI features are especially useful for mobile users who use portable computers that support standby, hibernation, hot and warm docking, or undocking features.

For more information about Plug and Play device detection and system resources, see "Managing Devices" and "Supporting Mobile Users" in this book.

Startup Phases for Itanium-based Systems

Windows XP Professional also runs on Itanium-based systems. The startup process for Itanium-based computers is similar to that of *x*86-based systems. Itanium-based systems proceed through the following startup stages:

- Power-on self test (POST) phase

- Initial startup and boot manager phase

- Kernel loading phase

- Device driver and service initialization phase

- Logon phase

- Plug and Play device detection phase

Power-on Self Test for Itanium-based Systems

The POST process for Itanium-based systems is similar to *x*86-based systems. The Extensible Firmware Interface (EFI) performs rudimentary hardware checks, similar to those performed by BIOS, and verifies that devices needed to start the system are present.

> **Note**   The EFI specification, currently implemented for Itanium-based systems only, defines a new model for the interface between operating systems and platform firmware. For more information about EFI, see the Extensible Firmware Interface link on the Web Resources page at http://www.microsoft.com/windows/reskits/webresources.

Initial Startup and Boot Manager Phase for Itanium-based Systems

After the POST finishes and before Windows XP Professional loads, the boot manager (a part of the EFI) determines the EFI drivers to use, the EFI tool set that is available to the user, and the EFI startup options to display.

The specific set of boot manager features that are available on your computer can vary from one Itanium-based system to another. Check your system documentation for information about additional tools, which might include Nvrboot.efi, Format.efi, Fdisk.efi, Diskpart.efi, and an EFI shell. These tools are either included with the EFI image or can be run from a floppy disk or other removable disks.

You might be able to use these additional tools to perform system tasks, such as restoring the boot manager startup menu, mapping disks, performing file maintenance, updating system firmware, and doing recovery operations.

To start Windows XP Professional, the boot manager performs the following tasks:

- Reads EFI configuration settings, such as the boot order sequence, from non-volatile memory (NVRAM). As with the CMOS settings for $x86$-based systems, the contents of NVRAM are preserved even when you turn off the computer. For more information about boot order options in firmware, see "Startup Phases for x86-based Systems" and "Initial Startup Phase" earlier in this chapter.

- Initializes essential devices needed to start Windows XP Professional. Configuration information for storage and possibly other devices are also kept in non-volatile memory. Before Windows XP Professional starts, only basic functionality (the minimum required to start an operating system) is available for these devices. Devices detected at this stage include the following if they are present:
  - Network adapters
  - Video adapters
  - Keyboard
  - Drive controllers (SCSI or ATA)
  - Storage devices

- Determines which device holds the EFI System partition image. The EFI System partition can range in size from a minimum of 100 megabytes (MB) up to one percent of the available hard disk space or a maximum of 1000 MB. The EFI System partition contains the files required to start Windows XP Professional. The remaining system files in the *systemroot* folder must reside on another partition.

  For more information about Windows XP Professional disk partitions, including a discussion about the structure of the new Itanium globally unique identifier (GUID) partition table, see Windows XP Professional Help and Support Center. Also, see in "File Systems," "Disk Management," and "Troubleshooting Disks and File Systems" this book.

- Locates the operating system partition and locates directories containing Windows XP Professional files.

- Locates and starts the loader file called IA64ldr.efi. IA64ldr.efi starts the 64-bit Windows kernel.

Table 27-6 lists the names and locations of the startup files for Itanium-based systems. The EFI System partition is the first partition of the startup drive.

Table 27-6   Startup Files for Itanium-based Systems

File and Folder Names	Disk Location	Description
Boot*NNNN*	EFI\Microsoft\WINNT50.*x* folder on the EFI System partition	A file that contains a saved copy of the EFI boot manager NVRAM settings.
		A WINNT50.*x* folder exists for each Windows XP Professional installation on your system. The value of *x* indicates the order in which you installed the instance of Windows XP Professional.
		A corresponding Boot*NNNN* file exists for each Windows XP Professional installation. Setup generates a Boot*NNNN* file during installation. The value of *NNNN* corresponds to the installation's NVRAM boot ID entry. For more information about Boot*NNNN* files, see "Reviewing and Correcting NVRAM Startup Settings on Itanium-based Systems" later in this chapter.
FPSWA.efi	EFI\Microsoft\WINNT50.*x* folder on the EFI System partition	A file that supports EFI floating point operations.
MSUtil (folder)	Resides on the root of the EFI System partition	A folder that contains EFI tools.

Table 27-6   Startup Files for Itanium-based Systems

File and Folder Names	Disk Location	Description
Nvrboot.efi	MSUtil folder on the EFI System partition	A tool that enables you to restore boot manager startup options saved to Boot*NNNN* files. It also allows you to back up NVRAM boot entries and edit startup parameters.
		Whenever possible, use Bootcfg.exe to make changes. For more information about Bootcfg.exe, see Windows XP Professional Help and Support Center. For more information about Nvrboot.efi, see "Reviewing and Correcting NVRAM Startup Settings on Itanium-based Systems" later in this chapter.
IA64ldr.efi	EFI\Microsoft\WINNT50.*x* folder on the EFI System partition	The operating system loader.
Ntoskrnl.exe	*systemroot*\System32	The core (also called the kernel) of the Windows XP Professional operating system. Operating system code that runs as part of the kernel does so in a special privileged processor mode, with direct access to system data and hardware.
		During installation, Windows XP Professional Setup copies Ntoskrnl.exe from the operating system CD for single processor systems, or for multi-processor systems, copies Ntoskrnlmp.exe and renames it to Ntoskrnl.exe.
Hal.dll	*systemroot*\System32	The hardware abstraction layer (HAL) dynamic-link library file. The HAL abstracts low-level hardware details from the operating system and provides a common programming interface to devices of the same type (such as video adapters).
System registry file	*systemroot*\System32\Config\System file	The registry file that contains the data used to create the registry key HKEY_LOCAL_MACHINE\SYSTEM. This key contains information that the operating system requires to start devices and system services.
Device drivers	*systemroot*\System32\Drivers folder	Driver files for hardware devices.

Due to the differences between Itanium-based and *x*86-based systems, certain files required for the *x*86-based startup process are not required for Itanium-based computers. Table 27-7 lists *x*86-based files not required by Itanium-based systems.

Table 27-7   x86-based Files Not Used on Itanium-based Systems

File not used	Description
Boot.ini	The Boot.ini file is not required for Itanium-based systems because information previously contained in the file, such as startup options and descriptive menu text, is stored in NVRAM.
Ntdetect.com	Windows XP Professional detects hardware according to the ACPI specification rather than by using Ntdetect.com.
Ntldr	The *x*86-based loader. The loader for Itanium-based versions is IA64ldr.efi.

For more information about system files, see "System Files Reference" in this book.

Kernel Loading for Itanium-based Systems

IA64ldr.efi performs a function similar to that of Ntldr for *x*86-based systems. IA64ldr.efi is responsible for loading the kernel (Ntoskrnl.exe) and the hardware abstraction layer (Hal.dll) into memory.

IA64ldr.efi loads control set information and uses it to initialize hardware and software components. For more information about the kernel loading phase, see "Startup Phases for x86-Based Systems" and "Kernel Loading Phase" earlier in this chapter.

Device Drivers and Services Phase for Itanium-based Systems

The processes that occur for Itanium-based systems during this phase closely resemble the processes for *x*86-based computers. For more information about the device drivers and services phase, see "Startup Phases for x86-based Systems" and "Kernel Loading Phase" earlier in this chapter.

Logon Phase for Itanium-based Systems

During this phase, the processes that occur for Itanium-based systems closely resemble the processes for *x*86-based computers. For more information about the operating system logon phase, see "Startup Phases for x86-based Systems" and "Logon Phase" earlier in this chapter.

Plug and Play Device Detection for Itanium-based Systems

The processes that occur for Itanium-based systems during this phase closely resemble the processes for *x*86-based computers. For more information, see "Startup Phases for x86-based Systems" and "Plug and Play Device Detection" earlier in this chapter.

Summary of the Startup Process

Table 27-8 lists the startup phases and provides a descriptive summary of each one.

Table 27-8   Summary of the Startup Process

Startup Stage	x86-based Systems	Itanium-based Systems
Power-on self test (POST)	CPU initiates motherboard POST routines. Individual adapter POST routines start after the motherboard POST is complete.	CPU initiates motherboard POST routines. Individual adapter POST routines start after the motherboard POST is complete.
Initial startup (before the-operating system loads)	The system searches for a boot device according to the boot order setting stored in CMOS. If the boot device is a hard disk, Ntldr starts.	The EFI starts and the boot manager searches for a boot device according to the boot order settings stored in NVRAM.
Ntldr starts	Ntldr switches the CPU to protected mode, starts the file system, and then reads the contents of the Boot.ini file. This information determines the startup options and initial boot menu selections.	Global system variables and settings are read from NVRAM and boot manager information is used to determine the startup options.
Hardware detection occurs	Ntdetect.com gathers basic hardware configuration data and passes this information to Ntldr. If more than one hardware profile exists, Windows XP Professional attempts to use the one that is correct for the current configuration. If the firmware complies with ACPI specifications, Windows XP Professional uses ACPI functionality to enumerate and initialize devices.	The boot manager searches for and starts IA64ldr.efi. The operating system starts devices by using ACPI functionality.
Kernel loads	Ntldr passes the information collected by Ntdetect.com to Ntoskrnl.exe. Ntoskrnl then loads the kernel, HAL, and registry information. A progress indicator appears near the bottom of the screen.	IA64ldr.efi loads the kernel, the HAL, and registry information. A progress indicator appears near the bottom of the screen.
Drivers load and the user logs on	Networking-related components, such as TCP/IP, load asynchronously with other services and the **Begin Logon** prompt appears on screen. After a user logs on successfully, Windows XP Professional updates the Last Known Good Configuration information to reflect the current state.	
Plug and Play detects and configures new devices	If Windows XP Professional detects new devices, they are assigned system resources. Windows XP Professional extracts the needed driver files from the Driver.cab file or if the driver files are not found, prompts the user to provide them. Device detection occurs asynchronously with the operating system logon process.	

Table 27-9 lists the files that are processed by *x*86-based and Itanium-based systems during the startup process. This information is useful if your organization uses Windows XP Professional on *x*86-based and Itanium-based computers. For example, when diagnosing a problem on an Itanium-based system, you can immediately eliminate Boot.ini and Ntdetect.com from your list of potential causes.

Table 27-9   Files Processed During Startup

File Name	x86-based Systems	Itanium-based Systems
Boot.ini	X	
Bootsect.dos (multiple-boot systems only)	X	
FPSWA.efi		X
Hal.dll	X	X
IA64ldr.efi		X
Ntbootdd.sys	X	
Ntdetect.com	X	
Ntldr	X	
Ntoskrnl.exe	X	X
Files in the *systemroot*\System32\Config folder	X	X
Files in the*systemroot*\System32\Drivers folder	X	X

Following a Process for Startup and Recovery

If you cannot start Windows XP Professional, the operating system provides several options that you can use to identify the cause and resolve the problem.

If the startup problem occurs immediately after updating or installing a specific device driver or application   You can restore previous system settings by using the following features:

1. Use the Last Known Good Configuration.

2. If you are in normal or safe mode, undo a device driver update by rolling back a driver.

3. In normal or safe mode, use System Restore to restore a previous system configuration.

The preceding options are not limited to troubleshooting startup problems, but also apply to any problem affecting the operating system.

If you are still unable to start your system in normal mode   You can restart your computer in safe mode and disable services and software that might be interfering with the startup process. Try disabling the following:

1. Temporarily disable applications and processes.

2. Temporarily disable services.

3. Uninstall software.

If the problem prevents you from starting in safe mode   You can try the following:

1. Use Recovery Console to replace corrupted files or to perform other manual recovery operations.

2. Examine and correct the following:

   ■ Boot.ini settings on *x*86-based systems.

   ■ NVRAM startup settings on Itanium-based systems.

3. Perform a parallel Windows XP Professional installation and use Backup to restore operating system files from backup media.

4. Use Automated System Recovery (ASR) in Windows XP Professional Backup to reformat the system partition and restore operating system files from backup media.

Restoring to the Last Known Good Configuration

Use Last Known Good Configuration to correct instability or startup problems by reversing the most recent system and driver changes within a hardware profile. When you use this feature, you lose all configuration changes that were made since you last successfully started your system.

Using the Last Known Good Configuration restores previous drivers and also restores registry settings for the subkey HKEY_LOCAL_MACHINE\SYSTEM\CurrentControlSet. Windows XP Professional does not update the LastKnownGood control set until you successfully start the operating system in normal mode and log on.

When you are troubleshooting, it is recommended that you use Last Known Good Configuration before you try other options, such as safe mode. However, if you decide to use safe mode first, logging on to the computer in safe mode does not update the LastKnownGood control set. Therefore, Last Known Good Configuration remains an option if you cannot resolve your problem by using safe mode.

To access the Last Known Good Configuration startup option

1. Remove all floppy disks and CDs from your computer, and restart your computer.

2. Press F8 when prompted.

    If Windows XP Professional starts without displaying a menu similar to that shown in Figure 27-4, restart your computer. Press F8 after the firmware POST process completes but before Windows XP Professional displays graphical output.

3. On the **Windows Advanced Options** menu, select **Last Known Good Configuration**.

When Windows XP Professional starts, it reads status information from the file *systemroot*\Bootstat.dat. If Windows XP detects that the last startup attempt was unsuccessful, it automatically displays the message and startup options that are shown in Figure 27-1.

```
We apologize for the inconvenience, but Windows did not start successfully.
A recent hardware or software change might have caused this.

If your computer stopped responding, restarted unexpectedly, or was
automatically shut down to protect your files and folders, choose Last Known
Good Configuration to revert to the most recent settings that worked.

If a previous startup attempt was interrupted due to a power failure or because
the Power or Reset button was pressed, or if you aren't sure what caused the
problem, choose Start Windows Normally.

    Safe Mode
    Safe Mode with Networking
    Safe Mode with Command Prompt

    Last Known Good Configuration (your most recent settings that worked)

    Start Windows Normally

Use the up and down arrow keys to move the highlight to your choice.
Seconds until Windows starts: 29
```

Figure 27-1   Startup options when your system cannot start

Caution   If you suspect that changes made since you last successfully restarted the computer are causing problems, do not log on because logging on causes the Last Known Good Configuration control set to be overwritten. Instead, restart the computer and use the Last Known Good Configuration. For more information about control sets, see "Kernel Loading Phase" earlier in this chapter.

For more information about the Last Known Good Configuration, see Windows XP Professional Help and Support Center, and also see "Tools for Troubleshooting" in this book.

Starting in Safe Mode

Safe mode is a diagnostic startup environment that runs only a subset of the drivers and services that are in your system memory. Safe mode is useful when you install software or a device driver that causes instability or problems with starting in normal mode. In most cases, safe mode allows you to start Windows XP Professional and then troubleshoot problems that prevent startup.

Logging on to the computer in safe mode does not update the LastKnown-Good control set. Therefore, if you log on to your computer in safe mode and then decide you want to try Last Known Good Configuration, the LastKnownGood control set is still available.

In safe mode, Windows XP Professional uses the minimum set required to start the graphical user interface (GUI). The following registry subkeys list the drivers and services that start in safe mode:

- **Safe mode**

    HKEY_LOCAL_MACHINE\SYSTEM\CurrentControlSet\Control\Safe-Boot\Minimal

- **Safe mode with networking**

    HKEY_LOCAL_MACHINE\SYSTEM\CurrentControlSet\Control\Safe-Boot\Network

To access safe mode

1. Remove all floppy disks and CDs from your computer, and restart your computer.

2. Press F8 when prompted.

    If Windows XP Professional starts without displaying the menu shown in Figure 27-4, restart your computer. Press F8 after the firmware POST process completes but before Windows XP Professional displays graphical output.

3. On the **Windows Advanced Options** menu, select **Safe Mode**, **Safe Mode with Networking**, or **Safe Mode with Command Prompt**.

You can also select a safe mode option from the startup recovery menu that appears when Windows XP Professional detects that the startup attempt was unsuccessful. For more information about the startup recovery menu, see "Restoring to the Last Known Good Configuration" earlier in this chapter.

For more information about safe mode, see Windows XP Professional Help and Support Center and "Tools for Troubleshooting" in this book. Also see article Q202485, "Description of Safe Boot Mode in Windows 2000," in the Microsoft Knowledge Base. To find this article, see the Microsoft Knowledge Base link on the Web Resources page at http://www.microsoft.com/windows/reskits/webresources.

Rolling Back Drivers

When you update a device driver, your computer might have problems that it did not have with the previous version. For example, installing an unsigned device driver might cause the device to malfunction or cause resource conflicts with other installed hardware. Installing faulty drivers might cause Stop errors that prevent the operating system from starting in normal mode. Typically, Stop message text displays the file name of the driver that causes the error.

Windows XP Professional provides a feature called Device Driver Roll Back, which can help you restore system stability by rolling back a driver update.

> **Note**   You can use System Information to determine if a driver on your system is signed and to obtain other information about the driver, such as version, date, time, and manufacturer. This data, combined with information from the manufacturer's Web site, can help you decide whether to roll back or update a device driver.

To roll back a driver

1. In **Control Panel**, open **System**.

2. Click the **Hardware** tab, and then click **Device Manager**.

3. Expand a category (**Standard floppy disk controller**, for example), and then double-click a device.

4. Click the **Driver** tab, and then click **Roll Back Driver**.

   You are prompted to confirm that you want to overwrite the current driver. Click **Yes** to roll back the driver. The roll back process proceeds, or you are notified that an older driver is not available.

> **Tip**   You can also open the System Properties box from the Start menu by clicking **Run** and typing **sysdm.cpl** in the **Run** dialog box. Some Control Panel tools are stored in the *systemroot*\System32 folder and use a .cpl file name extension. You can start frequently used Control Panel tools from the Run dialog box or by creating shortcuts.
>
> Other frequently used files include Appwiz.cpl (Add or Remove Programs), Hdwwiz.cpl (Add Hardware Wizard), Mmsys.cpl (Sounds and Audio Devices Properties), Nusrmgr.cpl (User Accounts), and Powercfg.cpl (Power Options Properties).

For more information about Device Driver Roll Back and about using System Information to check for unsigned drivers, see Windows XP Professional Help and Support Center. Also see "Tools for Troubleshooting" in this book.

Using System Restore to Undo Changes

Using System Restore, you can restore your system to an earlier state, a state prior to when you began having problems. System Restore monitors changes to certain system and application files. It functions like an "undo" feature, allowing you to recover from system problems, such as those caused by incorrect system settings, faulty drivers, and incompatible applications. System Restore restores your system state without risk to personal files, such as documents or e-mail.

When you need to restore to an earlier system setting, you can select a restore point that was created when the system functioned correctly. *Restore points* are registry "snapshots" that System Restore creates, stores, and manages. System Restore copies monitored files to data stores on hard disk before Windows XP Professional overwrites, deletes, or changes the files.

When Windows XP Professional is running in normal mode, System Restore creates restore points in the background without user intervention. You can also manually create restore points, for example, before installing new hardware or software. In safe mode, you can use restore points but you cannot create them.

To start the System Restore wizard

- From the **Start** menu, click **Help and Support**, click **Tools**, and then click **System Restore**.

For more information about System Restore, see Windows XP Professional Help and Support Center, and see also "Tools for Troubleshooting" in this book.

Temporarily Disabling Applications and Processes

If a problem occurs after installing new software, you can temporarily disable or uninstall the application to verify that the application is the source of the problem.

Problems with applications that run at startup can cause logon delays or even prevent you from completing Windows XP Professional startup in normal mode. The following subsections provide techniques for temporarily disabling startup programs:

- Disabling Startup Programs by Using the System Configuration Utility
- Disabling Startup Programs by Using the SHIFT Key
- Disabling Startup Programs by Using the Group Policy Snap-in
- Disabling Startup Programs for Computers on a Network
- Manually Disabling Startup Programs

Disabling Startup Programs by Using the System Configuration Utility

System Configuration Utility allows you to disable startup programs individually or several at a time. You can also disable certain startup programs that do not use the registry to store configuration information but that instead use the Win.ini file. For example, on *x*86-based computers, you can use this tool to disable 16-bit startup programs.

To disable a startup program by using the System Configuration Utility

1.   In the **Run** dialog box, type **msconfig**, and then click **OK**.

2.   To disable startup programs, select the **General** tab, click **Selective Startup**, and then click to clear the **Process WIN.INI File** and **Load Startup Items** check boxes.

     –or–

     To disable specific startup items, select the **Startup** or **WIN.INI** tab, and then click to clear the check boxes that correspond to the items you want to disable. You can also click **Disable All** on the **Startup** and **WIN.INI** tabs to disable all items on each tab.

If you change any startup setting by using the System Configuration Utility, Windows XP Professional displays the following message when you log on:

```
You have used the System Configuration Utility to make temporary changes to some of
your system settings. To return to normal operations, choose the Normal option on th
e General tab.
```

The preceding message and the System Configuration Utility continue to appear each time you log on until you restore the original startup settings by clicking **Normal Startup** under **Startup Selection** on the **General** tab. To permanently change a startup setting, you must move or delete startup shortcuts, change a Group Policy setting, or uninstall the application that added the startup application.

For more information about the System Configuration Utility, see Windows XP Professional Help and Support Center, and also see "Tools for Troubleshooting" in this book.

Disabling Startup Programs by Using the SHIFT Key

One way you can simplify your configuration is to disable startup programs. By holding down the SHIFT key during the logon process, you can prevent the operating system from running startup programs or shortcuts in the following folders:

■   *systemdrive*\Documents and Settings*Username*\Start Menu\Programs\Startup

■   *systemdrive*\Documents and Settings\All Users\Start Menu\Programs\Startup

■   *windir*\Profiles*Username*\Start Menu\Programs\Startup

■   *windir*\Profiles\All Users\Start Menu\Programs\Startup

The *windir* folders exist only on computers that are upgraded from Windows NT 4.0.

To disable the programs or shortcuts in the preceding folders, you must hold down the SHIFT key until the desktop icons appear. Holding down the SHIFT key is a better alternative than temporarily deleting or moving programs and shortcuts because this procedure only affects the current user session.

To use the SHIFT key to disable programs and shortcuts in startup folders

1. Log off the computer.

2. In the **Welcome to Windows** dialog box, press CTRL+ALT+DEL.

3. In the **Log On to Windows** dialog box, type your user name and password, and then click **OK**.

4. Immediately hold down the SHIFT key. The mouse cursor changes shape from a plain pointer, to a pointer with an hourglass (it might do this several times).

5. Continue to hold down the SHIFT key until the Windows XP Professional desktop icons appear and the mouse cursor stops changing shape.

Disabling Startup Programs by Using the Group Policy Snap-in

You can use the Group Policy MMC snap-in to disable programs that run at startup. Before you use this snap-in, you must be familiar with Group Policy concepts, and you must understand how to view registry entries and change local Group Policy settings.

For information about Group Policy and about using the Group Policy snap-in, see "Planning Deployments," "Managing Desktops," and "Authorization and Access Control" in this book, and see "Group Policy" in the Distributed Systems Guide of the *Microsoft Windows 2000 Server Resource Kit*. Also see "Using Group Policy" in Windows XP Professional Help and Support Center, and see the *Change and Configuration Management Deployment Guide* link on the Web Resources page at http://www.microsoft.com/windows/reskits/webresources.

If you are uncertain which startup programs to disable, you can view the registry startup information that appears in certain registry subkeys. For information about viewing registry entries, see "To open Registry Editor" in Windows XP Professional Help and Support Center, and also see Table 27-10, Table 27-11, and Table 27-12.

Caution Do not edit the registry unless you have no alternative. The registry editor bypasses standard safeguards, allowing settings that can damage your system, or even require you to reinstall Windows. If you must edit the registry, back it up first and see the Registry Reference in the Microsoft Windows 2000 Server Resource Kit at http://www.microsoft.com/reskit.

To disable startup programs by using the Group Policy snap-in

1. In the **Run** dialog box, type **gpedit.msc**, and then click **OK**.

2. Under **Local Computer**, click the plus sign (+) to expand either of the following:

   - **Computer Configuration**
   - **User Configuration**

3. Expand **Administrative Templates**, expand **System,** and then click **Logon**.

4. Double-click the Group Policy setting **Run these programs at user logon**.

5. For the programs that appear in either registry subkey that shows in Table 27-10, do one of the following:

   - To disable all the programs that are listed in the following subkeys, click **Disabled**.

     Disabling this Group Policy deletes the computer or user Run subkey described in Table 27-10.

   - To selectively disable individual programs that are listed in the computer or user Run subkey, click **Enabled,** and then click **Show**. In the **Show Contents** dialog box, select a program to disable, and then click **Remove**.

     If you enable the preceding Group Policy settings, the programs listed in the corresponding registry subkeys no longer start automatically when a user logs on to the system.

Table 27-10   Registry Subkeys That List the Programs That Run at User Logon

Group Policy Setting	Run List Controlled by the Group Policy setting "Run these programs at user logon"
Computer	HKEY_LOCAL_MACHINE\SOFTWARE\Microsoft\Windows\CurrentVersion\Policies\Explorer\Run
User	HKEY_CURRENT_USER\Software\Microsoft\Windows\CurrentVersion\Policies\Explorer\Run

You can change additional Group Policy settings that might help you simplify your computer configuration when you are troubleshooting startup problems. Table 27-11 lists the registry subkeys that are controlled by the Group Policy setting **Do not process the run once list**. If you enable this Group Policy setting, the system ignores the programs listed in the following RunOnce registry subkeys the next time a user logs on to the system.

Table 27-11   Registry Subkeys That List the Programs That Run Once

Group Policy Setting	RunOnce List Managed by the Group Policy setting "Do not process the run once list"
Computer	HKEY_LOCAL_MACHINE\SOFTWARE\Microsoft\Windows\CurrentVersion\RunOnce
User	HKEY_CURRENT_USER\Software\Microsoft\Windows\CurrentVersion\RunOnce

Table 27-12 lists the computer registry subkey that is controlled by the Group Policy setting **Do not process the legacy run list**. The programs listed in this registry subkey are a customized list of programs that were configured by using the system policy editor for Windows NT 4.0 or earlier. If you enable this Group Policy setting, the system ignores the programs listed in the corresponding registry subkey when you start your computer. If you disable or do not configure this Group Policy setting, the system processes the customized run list that is contained in this registry subkey when you start the computer.

Table 27-12   Registry Subkey That Lists Customized Legacy Programs

Group Policy Setting	Customized Run List Controlled by the Group Policy setting "Do not process the legacy run list"
Computer	HKEY_LOCAL_MACHINE\SOFTWARE\Microsoft\Windows\CurrentVersion\Run

Group Policy changes do not always take effect immediately. You can use the Gpupdate (Gpupdate.exe) tool to refresh local Group Policy changes to computer and user policies. (Gpupdate replaces the **secedit /refreshpolicy** command used in Windows 2000 to refresh Group Policy settings.) After you refresh the policy, you can use the Group Policy Result (Gpresult.exe) tool to verify that the updated settings are in effect. For more information about using Gpupdate, see Windows XP Professional Help and Support Center.

Disabling Startup Programs for Computers on a Network

If your computer is on a network, additional steps might be required to disable startup programs that are started by Group Policy settings, roaming user profiles, logon scripts, or scheduled system management tasks. You can also contact your network administrator and request network test accounts that exclude items, such as logon scripts, that you know are not causing problems on other computers.

To check Group Policy settings, you can use the Resultant Set of Policy (RSoP) MMC snap-in (Rsop.msc) or the Group Policy Result (Gpresult.exe) tool to view the policies currently in effect for your user and computer accounts. The information provided by these tools can assist you with troubleshooting or help you determine the policy settings that might affect your results.

You can also prevent Group Policy, logon scripts, roaming user profiles, scheduled tasks, and network-related issues from affecting your troubleshooting by temporarily disabling the network adapter and then logging on by using a local computer account.

To disable a network adapter

1. Do one of the following:

    ■ In **Control Panel**, open **Network Connections**.

    ■ In the **Run** dialog box, type **ncpa.cpl**, and then click **OK**.

2. Right-click the **Local Area Connection** icon, and then click **Disable**.

If you use roaming user profiles and do not want to disable the network adapter, you can temporarily switch to locally cached user profiles. Making this change preserves local diagnostic changes in case you need to log off and log on, or restart the computer. This change also prevents the roaming user profile from overwriting your diagnostic changes each time you log on to the computer.

To switch from roaming user profiles to locally cached user profiles

1. In **Control Panel**, open **System**, and then click the **Advanced** tab.

2. Under **User Profiles**, click **Settings**, and then click the name of your user profile.

3. Click **Change Type**, and then click **Local profile**.

For more information about roaming user profiles, see Windows XP Professional Help and Support Center, and also see "Managing Desktops" in this book.

Manually Disabling Startup Programs

You can use the registry editor Regedit.exe to disable the registry entries for startup programs. For a list of registry subkeys that contain entries for service and startup programs, see "Logon Phase" earlier in this chapter. Changes made by using the registry editor might not take effect until you restart the computer.

You can also prevent startup programs from running by using Windows Explorer or Recovery Console to temporarily move shortcuts in the following folders to another location on the hard disk:

■ *systemdrive*\Documents and Settings*username*\Start Menu\Programs\Startup

■ *systemdrive*\Documents and Settings\All Users\Start Menu\Programs\Startup

■ *windir*\Profiles*username*\Start Menu\Programs\Startup

■ *windir*\Profiles\All Users\Start Menu\Programs\Startup

The *windir* folders exist only on computers that are upgraded from Windows NT 4.0.

For the startup program changes to take effect, you must log off or restart the computer and log on again.

For more information about disabling startup programs, see article Q270035, "How to Modify the List of Programs that Run at When You Startup Windows," in the Microsoft Knowledge Base. To find this article, see the Microsoft Knowledge Base link on the Web Resources page at http://www.microsoft.com/windows/reskits /webresources.

Ending Processes and Applications That Are Not Responding   A startup program or a process that stops responding can cause delays or prevent you from logging on to Windows XP Professional. A *process* is an instance of an application, including the set of system resources that run an application. By using Task Manager, you can view and selectively end applications and processes, allowing the startup process to continue.

When you are in normal or safe mode, you can also use Task Manager to gather system information, such as CPU and memory statistics.

To start Task Manager

- Press CTRL+ALT+DEL, and then click **Task Manager**.

As Figure 27-2 shows, you can select the **Applications**, **Processes**, **Performance**, and **Networking** tabs. The **Applications** and **Processes** tabs provide a list of active applications and processes, some of which run in the background and might not show activity. You can use the **End Process** button to end most of the items listed. Save all data before ending any process because this action can cause the system to stop responding.

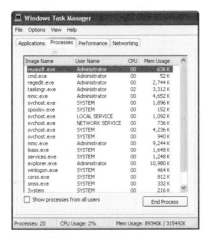

Figure 27-2   Task Manager

You can also customize Task Manager to display more information on the Processes tab.

To display more information on the Processes tab

1. Open Task Manager, and then click the **Processes** tab.

2. On the **View** menu, click **Select Columns**.

3. Select or clear the check box for each item you want to change.

To obtain more information about Task Manager, open Task Manager, and on the **Help** menu, click **Task Manager Help Topics**.

In addition to using Task Manager, you can also end processes by using two command-line tools:

- Task List (Tasklist.exe)

- Task Kill (Taskkill.exe)

Task List displays information similar to that displayed by the Task Manager **Processes** tab. For each process, Task List displays useful information, such as the name of the process, the process identification number (PID), and the amount of memory used.

To end a process, run Task Kill by using the process ID or any part of the process name, such as the title of the application window, as a command-line parameter. For more information about Task List and Task Kill, see Windows XP Professional Help and Support Center.

Preserving the Core System Processes   When you are deciding which processes to temporarily disable, avoid ending the processes that are listed in Table 27-13. This table lists the core processes that are common to all systems running Windows XP Professional. Knowing the core processes is useful because the source of an application or service-related problem is most likely due to non-core processes.

Table 27-13   Core System Processes

Core Process	Process Description
Csrss.exe*	An essential subsystem that is active at all times. Csrss.exe is the user-mode portion of the Windows subsystem and it maintains console windows and creates or deletes threads. *Csrss* stands for client/server runtime subsystem.
Explorer.exe	An interactive graphical user interface shell. It provides the familiar Windows taskbar and desktop environment.
Internat.exe	When enabled, a process that displays the **EN** (English) and other language icons in the system notification area, allowing the user to switch between locales.

Table 27-13   Core System Processes

Core Process	Process Description
Lsass.exe1	The local security authentication (LSA) subsystem server component generates the process that authenticates users for the Winlogon service. The LSA also responds to authentication information received from the Graphical Identification and Authentication (GINA) Msgina.dll component. If authentication is successful, Lsass.exe generates the user's access token, which starts the initial shell. Other processes that the user initiates inherit this token.
Mstask.exe1	The task scheduler service. It runs tasks at a time determined by the user.
Smss.exe1	The Session Manager subsystem, which starts the user session. This process is initiated by the system thread and is responsible for various activities, including starting the Winlogon.exe and Csrss.exe services and setting system variables.
Spoolsv.exe1	The spooler service. It manages spooled print and fax jobs.
Svchost.exe1	A generic process that acts as a host for other processes running from dynamic-link libraries (DLLs). Multiple entries for this process might be present in the Task Manager list. For more information about Svchost.exe, see article Q250320, "Description Of Svchost.exe," in the Microsoft Knowledge Base. To find this article, see the Microsoft Knowledge Base link on the Web Resources page at http://www.microsoft.com/windows/reskits/webresources.
Services.exe1	The Service Control Manager can start, stop, and pause system services.
System1	The system process, which is the process in which most kernel-mode threads run.
System Idle1	A separate instance of this process runs for each processor present, and has the single purpose of accounting for unused processor time.
Taskmgr.exe	The process that runs Task Manager.
Winlogon.exe1	The process that manages user logon and logoff. Winlogon runs when a user presses CTRL+ALT+DEL to open the logon dialog box.
Winmgmt.exe1	A core component of client management. This process starts when the first client application connects, or when management applications request its services.

*   You cannot use Task Manager to end this process.

For more information about threads, processes, and services, see Windows XP Professional Help and Support Center.

Temporarily Disabling Services

Many services automatically run at startup, but others are started only by users or by another process. The operating system, the drivers, and the applications that are loaded on a computer determine the services that run. For example, two

Windows XP Professional systems with identical hardware installed can be running different services if they have a different set of applications installed.

When you troubleshoot startup issues that are related to system services, a useful technique is to simplify your computer configuration so that you can reduce system complexity and isolate operating system services. To decrease the number of variables, temporarily close all applications or services and start them one at a time until you reproduce the problem. Always close applications first, before attempting to disable system services.

This section helps you do the following:

- Use service tools to diagnose and resolve startup issues.

- Determine service dependencies.

- Determine the services and processes to temporarily disable.

Using Service Tools to Diagnose and Resolve Startup Issues

Windows XP Professional provides tools that can help you troubleshoot services:

- System Configuration Utility

- Services snap-in (Services.msc)

- SC (Sc.exe)

Disabling Services with the System Configuration Utility

The System Configuration Utility allows you to disable system services individually or several at a time. You can also disable certain services that do not use the registry to store configuration information, but that instead use the System.ini file. For example, on *x*86-based computers, you can use this tool to disable 16-bit services.

To disable a service by using the System Configuration Utility

1. In the **Run** dialog box, type **msconfig**, and then click **OK**.

2. Do one of the following:

   - To disable services, on the **General** tab, click **Selective Startup**, and then click to clear the **Process SYSTEM.INI File** and **Load System Services** check boxes.

   - To disable specific services, on the **Services** or **SYSTEM.INI** tab, click to clear the check boxes that correspond to the items you want to disable. You can also click **Disable All** on the **Services** and **SYSTEM.INI** tabs to disable all items on each tab.

If you change any startup setting by using the System Configuration Utility, Windows XP Professional prompts you to return to normal operations the next time you log on. A prompt and the System Configuration Utility appear each time you log on until you restore the original startup settings by clicking **Normal Startup** under **Startup Selection** on the **General** tab. To permanently change a startup setting, use Control Panel, change a Group Policy setting, or uninstall the application that added the service.

For more information about the System Configuration Utility, see Windows XP Professional Help and Support Center, and also see "Tools for Troubleshooting" in this book.

Disabling Services by Using the Services Snap-in

When diagnosing startup problems, you can use the Services snap-in (Services.msc) in safe and normal modes to view service information or to temporarily disable a service that is causing problems (for example, a driver mentioned in a Stop message). You must have administrator permissions to disable or change the service startup type. Certain startup changes are not in effect until you restart the computer.

To disable a service by using the Services snap-in

1. In the **Run** dialog box, type **services.msc**, and then click **OK**.

   As Figure 27-3 shows, the Services snap-in displays the name, description, status, and startup type for each service.

2. Double-click a service name and then click the **General** tab. Record the setting for **Startup type** so that you can later restore the original value if you find that the change was not helpful.

3. Change the **Startup type** to **Disabled**.

After disabling the service, try to start your computer in normal mode. If your system starts in normal mode, you can research a permanent solution for the problem by checking technical information resources.

Startup type settings remain in effect even after you restart the system. You must use the Services snap-in to restore the original Startup type setting. On the General tab of the Services snap-in, you can specify the following startup types for services:

- **Automatic**. The operating system automatically starts the service.

- **Manual**. A user or another service starts the service.

- **Disabled**. The service does not start.

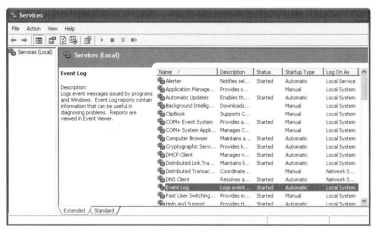

Figure 27-3 Services snap-in

Managing Services by Using Sc.exe

As an alternative to using the Services snap-in, you can use Sc.exe, a command-line tool that communicates with the Service Control Manager and displays information about services running on your computer. Sc.exe enables you to gather the same type of information obtainable from the Services snap-in and to perform many functions including:

- Display service information, such as start type and whether you can pause or end a service.

- Change the Startup type of a service.

- Start, pause, or resume a service.

- Disable a service by using the **sc config** command.

For troubleshooting startup, the **sc query** and **sc config** commands are the most helpful. The report that follows is an example of the information you can obtain by typing **sc query** at the command prompt:

```
SERVICE_NAME: winmgmt
DISPLAY_NAME: Windows Management Instrumentation
        TYPE            : 20  WIN32_SHARE_PROCESS
        STATE           : 4   RUNNING
                              (STOPPABLE,PAUSABLE,ACCEPTS_SHUTDOWN)
        WIN32_EXIT_CODE  : 0  (0x0)
        SERVICE_EXIT_CODE : 0  (0x0)
        CHECKPOINT       : 0x0
        WAIT_HINT        : 0x0
```

For more information about Sc.exe, see Windows XP Professional Help and Support Center.

Determining Service Dependencies

Some services and drivers that rely on other components are initialized before starting. If a service or driver does not start, the cause might be a dependency requirement that is not met. You can obtain a list of dependencies by using any of the following methods:

- Navigate to the registry subkey HKEY_LOCAL_MACHINE\SYSTEM\CurrentControlSet\Services*servicename* and examine the information contained in the **DependOnGroup** and **DependOnService** entries.

- Start the Services tool, double-click the service you want information about, and then click the **Dependencies** tab.

- Use the Dependency Walker (Depends.exe) Support Tool. For more information about Dependency Walker, see "Tools for Troubleshooting" in this book.

You can also check the Event Viewer System log to obtain information about services that do not start due to dependency issues.

For more information about the Services snap-in, see Windows XP Professional Help and Support Center. For more information about adding or changing service dependencies for troubleshooting purposes, see article Q193888, "How to Delay Loading of Specific Services," in the Microsoft Knowledge Base. To find this article, see the Microsoft Knowledge Base link on the Web Resources page at http://www.microsoft.com/windows/reskits/webresources.

Determining Which Services and Processes to Temporarily Disable

When you are troubleshooting, the method for determining which services and processes to temporarily disable varies from one computer to the next. The most reliable way to determine what you can disable is to gather more information about the services and processes enabled on your computer.

These Windows XP Professional tools and features generate a variety of logs that can provide you with valuable troubleshooting information:

- Error Reporting service
- Dr. Watson
- Boot logging
- System Information
- Event Viewer

Error Reporting Service   Windows XP Professional provides a Windows error reporting service that monitors your system for problems that affect services and applications. When a problem occurs, you can send a problem report to Microsoft and receive an automated response with more information, such as news about an update for an application, service, or device driver.

For more information about the Error Reporting service, see Windows XP Professional Help and Support Center, and also see "Tools for Troubleshooting" in this book.

Dr. Watson   If an application error (also known as a program exception) occurs, the Dr. Watson application debugging tool (DrWtsn32.exe) records information about the problem to a log, DrWtsn32.log, located in the *systemdrive*\Documents and Settings\All Users\Application Data\Microsoft\DrWatson folder. This log contains the following information:

- The file name of the program that caused the error.

- Information about the computer and user under which the error occurred.

- A list of the programs and services that were active when the error occurred.

- A list of components, such as dynamic-link libraries (DLLs), that were in memory when the error occurred.

- Additional information that might be useful if you need to contact technical support about an application that is causing errors.

The task and component lists are useful for duplicating the conditions under which an application error occurred. Using the lists as a reference, you can add or remove programs and services until you reproduce the problem. For more information about the Dr. Watson tool, including an overview of the log file and an explanation of the debugging files, see "Setting up Dr. Watson" and "Using the Dr. Watson log file" in Windows XP Professional Help and Support Center.

Boot Logging   Boot logging lists the files that successfully and unsuccessfully processed during startup. Boot logging enables you to log the Windows XP Professional components that are processed when you start your computer in safe mode and also in normal mode. By comparing the differences between the two logs, you can determine which components are not required to start.

You can enable boot logging by using either of these methods:

- Edit the Boot.ini file as described in "Reviewing and Correcting Boot.ini Settings on x86-based Systems" later in this chapter. Add the **/bootlog** parameter, save the revised Boot.ini, and restart the computer. For more information about the **/bootlog** parameter, see Table 27-18 later in this chapter.

- Restart the computer and press **F8** when prompted. On the **Windows Advanced Options** menu, select **Enable Boot Logging**.

Windows XP Professional records in a log, *windir*\Ntbtlog.txt, the name and path of each file that runs during startup. The log marks each file as successful (Loaded driver) or unsuccessful (Did not load driver). Boot logging appends entries to Ntbtlog.txt when you start your system in safe mode. Comparing normal mode and safe mode entries enables you to determine which services run in normal mode only. The following lines are sample Ntbtlog.txt entries:

```
Loaded driver \SystemRoot\System32\DRIVERS\flpydisk.sys
Did not load driver \SystemRoot\System32\DRIVERS\flpydisk.SYS
```

If you cannot start your computer in normal mode, start it in safe mode. For the services that run only in normal mode, disable those services one at a time, trying to restart your computer in normal mode after you disable each service. Continue to individually disable services until your computer starts in normal mode.

For more information about boot logging, see Windows XP Professional Help and Support Center.

System Information If a startup problem occurs inconsistently and if you can start Windows XP Professional in safe or normal mode, you can use System Information to view driver and service name, status, and startup information.

System Information enables you to create lists of drivers that were processed during safe and normal mode startup. By comparing the differences between the two lists, you can determine which components are not required to start Windows XP Professional. For diagnostic purposes, you can use this list of differences to help you determine which services to disable. In safe mode, disable a service and then try to restart the operating system in normal mode. Repeat this process for each service until you are able to start in normal mode.

To view service or driver information

1. In the **Run** dialog box, type **msinfo32**, and then click **OK**.

2. Do any of the following:

   - To view service information, click **Software Environment**, and then click **Services**.

   - To view the state of a driver, click **Software Environment**, and then click **System Drivers**. Information for each driver is in the **State** column.

   - To view driver information arranged by category, click **Components**, and then double-click a category, such as **Storage**.

A related tool, Systeminfo.exe, enables you to view system information, such as processor type, firmware version, and network information, from the command prompt. For more information about System Information and Systeminfo.exe, see Windows XP Professional Help and Support Center.

Event Viewer (Eventvwr.msc)   You can use Event Viewer (Eventvwr.msc) to view logs that can help you to identify system problems. When you are troubleshooting, use these logs to isolate problems by application, driver, or service, and to identify frequently occurring issues. You can save these logs to a file and specify filtering criteria.

Event Viewer provides three logs for computers running Windows XP Professional:

- **Application logs**. The application log contains events logged by applications or programs. For example, a database program might record read or write errors here.

- **Security logs**. The security log holds security event records, such as logon attempts and actions related to creating, opening, or deleting files. An administrator can specify what events to record in the security log.

- **System logs**. The system log contains information about system components. Event Viewer logs an entry when a driver or other system component does not load during startup. Therefore, you can use Event Viewer to search for information about drivers or services that did not load.

To use Event Viewer to obtain driver and service error information from the System log

1. In the **Run** dialog box, type **eventvwr.msc**, and then click **OK**.

2. Click **System**, and on the **View** menu, click **Filter** to open the **System Properties** dialog box.

3. Under **Event types**, click to clear the **Information** and **Warning** check boxes.

4. In the **Event source** list, click **Service Control Manager**, and then click **OK**.

5. Double-click an event entry to view details.

A related command-line tool, Event Query (Eventquery.vbs), enables you to search the event logs by using specified criteria. For troubleshooting, using Event Query enables you to view the Event logs for entries related to specified event properties, including date and time, event ID, and user name.

For more information about using Event Viewer, click the **Action** menu in Event Viewer, and then click **Help**. For more information about Event Query, click **Tools** in Help and Support Center.

Uninstalling Software

You can simplify your system configuration by uninstalling software, which reduces the number of variables to track and helps you to identify problems more quickly.

If you find that recently installed software causes system instability or if error messages consistently point to a specific application, you can use Add or Remove Programs in Control Panel to uninstall the software. If you suspect that an application is causing conflicts, uninstalling software can verify your suspicions. You can then reinstall applications after locating Windows XP Professional updates or other solutions.

For more information about adding or removing programs, see "Add or Remove Programs overview" in Windows XP Professional Help and Support Center, and also see "Tools for Troubleshooting" in this book.

Using Recovery Console

If you cannot start your computer in safe mode or by using the Last Known Good Configuration startup option, you can use Recovery Console. With the appropriate permissions, you can use this command-line interface to start recovery tools, start and stop services, access files on hard disks, and perform advanced tasks, such as manually replacing corrupted system files. You can run Recovery Console from the Windows XP Professional operating system CD, or you can install it as a startup option.

Infrequently, startup files and critical areas on the hard disk become corrupted. If the corruption is extensive, it might prevent you from starting Windows XP Professional in normal or safe modes, or from using the installed Recovery Console or using the Last Known Good Configuration startup option. In these situations, you can run Recovery Console from the Windows XP Professional operating system CD.

To start Recovery Console from the Windows XP Professional operating system CD

1. Insert the Windows XP Professional operating system CD into the CD-ROM drive, and restart the computer. When prompted, press a key to start Setup.

2. At the **Setup Notification** screen, press ENTER.

3. After the **Welcome to Setup** screen appears, select **To repair a Windows XP installation using Recovery Console** by pressing **R**.

   A menu that lists one or more Windows XP Professional installations appears.

4. Type the number corresponding to the installation that you want to use, and then press ENTER.

5. At the prompt, enter the password for the local Administrator account to access the contents of the local hard disk. Recovery Console accepts only the local Administrator account password.

From Recovery Console, you can attempt to replace corrupted files with undamaged copies stored on removable disks, such as a floppy disk or the Windows XP Professional operating system CD.

To use the CD-based Recovery Console, you must set the CD-ROM as the primary boot device (the first item listed in the boot order). If the CD-ROM is not listed as a boot-order option in the computer firmware, you cannot start your system by using the Windows XP Professional operating system CD. You must use startup floppy disks to start Windows XP Professional Setup. For more information about startup floppy disks, see the *Getting Started Guide,* which comes with Microsoft® Windows® XP Professional.

> **Note**   When you start your system by using the bootable Windows XP Professional operating system CD, Setup checks the hard disk for Windows XP Professional or another Windows operating system, such as Windows 2000 or Windows Me. If another operating system is found, you have the option of bypassing CD-ROM startup by not responding to the **Press any key to boot from CD** prompt that appears. If you do not press a key within three seconds, Setup does not run and the computer passes control from the CD-ROM to the hard disk.

To install Recovery Console as a startup option for x86-based systems

1. With Windows XP Professional running, insert the Windows XP Professional operating system CD into your CD-ROM drive.

2. Click **No** when prompted to upgrade to Windows XP Professional.

3. In the **Run** dialog box, type **cmd**, and then click **OK**.

4. At the command prompt, type:
   *drive***:\i386\Winnt32.exe /cmdcons**
   In the preceding command, *drive* represents the letter of the CD-ROM or network drive that holds the Windows XP Professional installation files.

5. Restart your computer. Recovery Console appears as an item on the operating system menu.

> **Note**   Installing Recovery Console on the hard disk is an option only for *x86*-based computers.

Using Recovery Console to Disable Services

If you are unable to start Windows XP Professional in normal or safe mode, the cause might be an incorrectly configured driver or service that has caused a Stop message. Stop messages might provide information about the service or driver name, such as a file name. By using Recovery Console, you might be able to disable the problem component and allow the Windows XP Professional startup process to continue in normal or safe mode.

To enable or disable services by using Recovery Console

1. At the Recovery Console prompt, type **listsvc**.

    The computer displays the service or driver name, startup type, and possibly a friendly driver or service name. Record the name of the driver or service that you want to enable or disable.

2. To disable a driver, type:
    disable *drivername*

3. To enable a driver, type:
    enable *drivername start_type*
    Possible values for *start_type* are:

    ■ SERVICE_BOOT_START

    ■ SERVICE_SYSTEM_START

    ■ SERVICE_AUTO_START

    ■ SERVICE_DEMAND_START

For more information about Stop messages, see "Common Stop Messages for Troubleshooting" in this book.

Using Recovery Console to Restore the Registry Keys HKEY_LOCAL_MACHINE\SYSTEM and HKEY_LOCAL_MACHINE\SOFTWARE

If the previously discussed recovery methods do not enable you to start Windows XP Professional, you can try replacing the System and Software files, which are in the *systemroot*\System32\Config folder, with a backup copy from the *systemroot*\Repair folder. The System and Software files are used by Windows XP Professional to create the registry keys HKEY_LOCAL_MACHINE\SYSTEM and HKEY_LOCAL_MACHINE\SOFTWARE. A corrupted copy of the System or Software file could prevent you from starting Windows XP Professional.

Try other recovery methods before using the manual procedure that follows. The manual procedure enables you to start the operating system, allowing you to perform further repairs by using Windows XP Professional tools.

When using the following procedure, do not replace both the System and Software files as part of a single attempt to start the computer. First, replace one file, and then test whether this action resolves the startup problem. If the problem persists, copy the other file. Which file you decide to replace first (the System or Software file), depends on the information that the Stop error displays (hardware or software related).

Using Recovery Console to replace the System file

1. At the Recovery Console prompt, locate the config folder by typing:
   cd system32\config

2. Create backups of the System or Software files by typing:
   copy system *<drive:\path\filename>*
   -or-
   copy software *<drive:\path\filename>*
   If they exist, save backups of other files that use file names that start with "system" or "software," such as System.sav or Software.sav.

3. Replace the current System or Software file by typing:
   copy ..\..\repair\system
   -or-
   copy ..\..\repair\software

4. Answer the **Overwrite system? (Yes/No/All):** prompt by pressing **Y**.

5. Restart the computer.

If you are still unable to start your computer, consider performing a parallel operating system installation or an ASR restore operation. For more information about these two recovery options, see "Performing a Parallel Windows XP Professional Installation" and "Saving System Files and Settings by Using Automated System Recovery" later in this chapter. For more information about Stop messages, see "Common Stop Messages for Troubleshooting" in this book.

Consider these points when you replace the System or Software file with a backup copy from the *systemroot*\Repair folder:

- The System and Software files in the repair folder might not be current. If the files are not current, you might need to update drivers, reinstall applications and service packs, and perform other configuration to bring your computer up-to-date.

- The Emergency Repair Disk (ERD) that was available in Windows NT 4.0 and Windows 2000 does not exist in Windows XP Professional. The option to create an ERD for updating the *systemroot*\Repair directory is not available.

To update the *systemroot*\Repair directory, use the option to save system state in Backup (Ntbackup.exe). Whenever you perform a backup operation with the **System State** option enabled, Backup updates the repair folder.

For more information about Backup and saving system state, see "Backup and Restore" in this book. Also see "Tools for Troubleshooting" in this book.

For more information about Recovery Console, see Windows XP Professional Help and Support Center, and also see "Tools for Troubleshooting" in this book.

Recovery Console Alternatives

For *x*86-based systems, you have another option in addition to Recovery Console for accessing FAT16 and FAT32 partitions. If the FAT16 and FAT32 partitions were formatted by using an MS-DOS startup floppy disk (FAT16), or an emergency boot disk created in Microsoft® Windows® 95 OSR2, Windows 98, or Windows Me, you can start your computer by using these startup floppy disks. Using the floppy disk method starts the system in a command-line environment that enables read and write access to the disk without using Recovery Console. You can pre-configure startup disks to include commonly used tools and additional drivers that provide CD-ROM or network access.

For information about creating and using a FAT16 or FAT32 emergency boot disk, see Windows 95 OSR2, Windows 98, or Windows Me Help. You cannot use an MS-DOS boot disk or an emergency boot disk to view the contents of NTFS volumes.

Reviewing and Correcting Boot.ini Settings on x86-based Systems

The Boot.ini file, which is created during setup in the system root partition, contains information that Ntldr uses to display the startup menu. The Boot.ini file includes the path to the boot partition, descriptive text to display, and optional parameters. The Boot.ini file supports multiple installations of Windows XP Professional on the same computer and also supports multiple-boot configurations with other Microsoft operating systems installed in separate partitions. The following is an example of a Boot.ini file:

```
[boot loader]
timeout=30
default=multi(0)disk(0)rdisk(0)partition(1)\WINDOWS
[operating systems]
multi(0)disk(0)rdisk(0)partition(1)\Windows="Microsoft Windows XP Professional" /
fastdetect
```

Each Boot.ini file contains two sections:

[boot loader]   Contains settings that apply to all the Windows XP Professional installations on a computer.

[operating systems]   Contains settings that apply to a specific Windows XP Professional installation on the computer.

The default= line in the [boot loader] section points to the default operating system.

For multiple-boot systems that have Windows XP Professional and another Microsoft operating system, such as Windows 2000 Professional, additional entries might appear in the [operating systems] section as shown:

```
[boot loader]
timeout=30
default=multi(0)disk(0)rdisk(0)partition(1)\WINDOWS
```

```
[operating systems]
multi(0)disk(0)rdisk(0)partition(1)\WINDOWS="Microsoft Windows XP Professional" /
fastdetect
multi(0)disk(0)rdisk(0)partition(2)\WINDOWS="Microsoft Windows 2000 Professional" /
fastdetect
```

When more than one operating system is installed on a computer, a startup menu appears that is similar to the one shown in Figure 27-4.

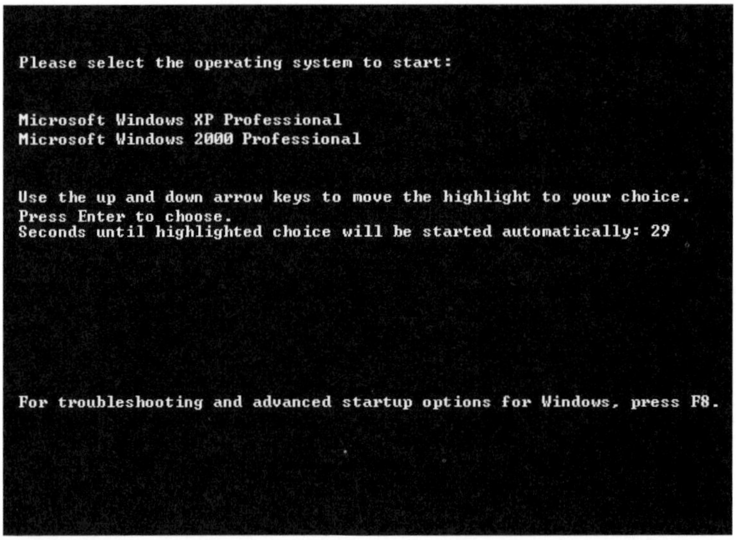

```
Please select the operating system to start:

Microsoft Windows XP Professional
Microsoft Windows 2000 Professional

Use the up and down arrow keys to move the highlight to your choice.
Press Enter to choose.
Seconds until highlighted choice will be started automatically: 29

For troubleshooting and advanced startup options for Windows, press F8.
```

Figure 27-4 Example of a startup menu for multiple-boot systems

Note If only one operating system is installed, Ntldr does not display a startup menu. Instead, the system starts immediately.

The Boot.ini file uses the Advanced RISC Computing (ARC) naming convention to define the path to a Windows XP Professional installation. If the contents of the Boot.ini are incorrectly changed or the file becomes corrupt, you might not be able to start Windows XP Professional. To detect and correct Boot.ini problems you need to understand ARC paths.

ARC paths use the following formats:

```
multi(W)disk(X)rdisk(Y)partition(Z)\systemroot="Description"
scsi(W)disk(X)rdisk(Y)partition(Z)\systemroot="Description"
signature(V)disk(X)rdisk(Y)partition(Z)\systemroot="Description"
```

Windows XP Professional can use any of the preceding formats to locate the *systemroot* directory.

Multi() Syntax   The multi() syntax instructs Windows XP Professional to rely on system BIOS calls to load system files. To achieve this, Ntldr uses interrupt 13 (also called INT-13) firmware instructions to locate Ntoskrnl.exe and other *systemroot* files needed to start Windows XP Professional. The multi() Boot.ini syntax is used for all controllers that provide INT-13 support for ATA and SCSI disks. Table 27-14 describes the multi() parameters, which follow this syntax:

```
multi(W)disk(X)rdisk(Y)partition(Z)
```

Table 27-14 describes the multi() parameters.

Table 27-14   Multi( ) Parameters

Parameter	Multi() Parameter Descriptions
W	Specifies the drive controller number (also known as the ordinal number), typically 0. The first valid number is 0.
X	This value is always 0 when the multi() syntax is used.
Y	Specifies a physical hard disk attached to drive controller *W*. For ATA controllers, this number is typically between 0 and 3. For SCSI controllers, this number is typically between 0 and 7, or 0 and 15, depending on the adapter type. The first valid number is 0.
Z	Specifies the partition number on the physical disk specified by parameter *Y*, attached to the controller specified by parameter *W*. All partitions in use are assigned a number. The first valid number is 1.

SCSI() Syntax   The scsi() syntax informs Windows XP Professional that the startup SCSI controller does not support INT-13 calls and that a device driver, Ntbootdd.sys, is needed to access files on the boot partition.

The scsi() parameters follow this format:

```
scsi(W)disk(X)rdisk(Y)partition(Z)
```

Table 27-15 describes the SCSI() parameters.

Table 27-15   SCSI( ) Parameters

Parameter	SCSI() Parameter Descriptions
W	Specifies the drive controller number (also known as the ordinal number), typically 0. The first valid number is 0.
X	Specifies a physical hard disk attached to drive controller *W*. For SCSI controllers, this number is typically between 0 and 7, or 0 and 15, depending on the adapter type. The first valid number is 0.
Y	Specifies the SCSI logical unit number (LUN) of the disk that contains the boot partition. This value is typically 0 when the scsi() syntax is used.
Z	Specifies the partition number on the physical disk specified by parameter *Y*, attached to the controller specified by parameter *W*. All partitions in use are assigned a number. The first valid number is 1.

Signature() Syntax The signature() syntax shares similarities with the scsi() syntax and was implemented to support Plug and Play scenarios where you install additional drive controllers to your system. Windows XP Professional Setup determines whether to use the signature() syntax during installation. The signature() syntax is valid for systems equipped with either ATA or SCSI hard disks. The signature() parameters follow this syntax:

```
signature(V)disk(X)rdisk(Y)partition(Z)
```

The signature() syntax instructs Ntldr to locate the disk with the signature that matches the first value in parentheses, regardless of the controller number associated with the disk. A disk signature is a globally unique identifier (GUID) that is extracted from information in the MBR and written to the disk during the text-mode portion of Windows XP Professional Setup or during previous Windows 2000 and Windows XP Professional installations. This 128-bit hexadecimal number uniquely identifies the disk.

If you see the signature() syntax used in the Boot.ini file, it means that Ntbootdd.sys is required to access the boot partition and one or both of the following conditions exist:

- You installed Windows XP Professional to a hard disk partition larger than 7.8 gigabytes (GB) in size, the ending cylinder number is higher than 1024 for that partition, and the system firmware or startup controller BIOS cannot gain access by using extended INT-13 calls.

- The hard disk controller BIOS does not support extended INT-13 calls or you have set this option to **disabled** by using the adapter's built-in setup utility. When Windows XP Professional is unable to use INT-13 BIOS calls during the startup process, the file Ntbootdd.sys is required to access the boot partition.

Whenever possible, configure your storage controller to use INT-13 BIOS calls. Consult the documentation for the storage adapter to determine the correct hardware settings.

Table 27-16 describes the signature() parameters.

Table 27-16 Signature() Parameters

Parameter	Signature() Parameter Descriptions
V	A 32-bit hexadecimal number extracted from the MBR that identifies the disk.
X	Specifies a physical hard disk with signature *V*, attached to *any* drive controller that uses Ntbootdd.sys. For SCSI controllers, this number is typically between 0 and 7, or 0 and 15, depending on the adapter type. The first valid number is 0.
Y	This value is always 0 when the signature() syntax is used.
Z	The partition number on the physical disk with a signature matching *V*. The first valid number is 1.

> **Note**   The signature() syntax might increase the time required to start Windows XP Professional, depending on the number of controllers and disks present.

NTBootdd.sys File   Ntbootdd.sys is a copy of a storage controller device driver that resides on the root of the startup partition. Ntbootdd.sys is used when the Boot.ini specifies the scsi() syntax or when the signature() syntax is used for disk controllers with disabled firmware.

The Ntbootdd.sys file can be used for ATA disks, depending upon the type of controller used. Follow the manufacturer's instructions for hardware and driver installation when using add-in Peripheral Component Interconnect (PCI) ATA controllers with Windows XP Professional.

Boot.ini Parameters and Options   The Boot.ini file consists of two sections, [boot loader] and [operating systems]. You can customize the startup process by editing these sections. Table 27-17 lists parameters for the [boot loader] section.

Table 27-17   Boot.ini [Boot Loader] Parameters

Parameter	Boot.ini [Boot Loader] Parameter Descriptions
Timeout= *seconds*	Specifies the number of seconds that the startup menu is displayed before the operating system specified in the **default=** line is loaded. ■ If you set this value to 0, Ntldr immediately starts the default operating system without displaying the bootstrap loader screen. ■ If you set this value to –1, Ntldr displays the menu indefinitely unless you make a choice.
default=	Specifies the ARC path to the default operating system.

Table 27-18 lists optional parameters that you can append to the ARC paths contained in the [operating systems] section of the Boot.ini file. For example, the following optional parameters limit memory usage to 64 MB:

```
multi(0)disk(0)rdisk(0)partition(1)\Windows="Windows XP Professional" /fastdetect /
MAXMEM=64
```

Table 27-18 Boot.ini [Operating System] Parameters

Parameter	Description
/3GB	Specifies for x86-based systems that the operating system allocate 3 GB of virtual address space to applications and 1 GB to kernel and executive components. An application must be designed to take advantage of the additional memory address space.
/basevideo	Directs the operating system to use standard VGA mode for the installed video driver (640 x 480 resolution with 16 available colors). If you install a new video driver, and it fails to work properly, you can use this parameter to start the operating system. You can then remove, update, or roll back the problem video driver.
/baudrate=	Specifies the baud rate used for kernel debugging. The default baud rate is 9600 kilobits per second (Kbps) for modems up to 115,200 Kbps for a null-modem cable. Including this parameter in the Boot.ini file implies the **/debug** parameter.
/bootlog	Enables boot logging to a file called *systemroot*\Ntbtlog.txt. For more information about boot logging, see Windows XP Professional Help and Support Center and "Tools for Troubleshooting" in this book.
/burnmemory=*number*	Specifies an amount of memory, in megabytes, that Windows XP Professional cannot use. Use this parameter to confirm performance or other problems related to RAM depletion. For example, **/burnmemory=**128 would reduce the physical memory available to Windows XP Professional by 128 MB.
/crashdebug	Loads the kernel debugger when you start Windows XP Professional but it remains inactive until a Stop message error occurs. This parameter is useful if you experience random kernel errors. For more information about Stop messages and debugging, see "Common Stop Messages for Troubleshooting" in this book.
/debug	Loads the Windows kernel debugger when you start Windows XP Professional.
/debugport={com1|com2|1 394}	Specifies the communication port for kernel debugging, typically com1, com2, or 1394. Using this parameter in the Boot.ini file implies the **/debug** parameter.
/fastdetect ={com1|com2|comx, *y,z...*}	Turns off serial and bus mouse detection in Ntdetect.com. Use if you have a component other than a mouse attached to a serial port during the startup process. If you use **/fastdetect** without specifying a communication port, serial mouse detection is disabled on all communication ports.

Table 27-18   Boot.ini [Operating System] Parameters

Parameter	Description
/maxmem=_number_	Specifies the maximum amount of RAM that Windows XP Professional can use. Use this parameter to confirm whether a memory chip is faulty. For example, if you have a 128-MB system that is equipped with two 64-MB RAM modules and you are experiencing memory-related Stop messages, you can specify **/maxmem=**_64_. If the computer starts Windows XP Professional and operates without problems, replace the first module to see if this resolves the problem.
/noguiboot	Disables the bitmap that displays the progress bar for Windows XP Professional startup (the progress bar appears just prior to the logon prompt).
/nodebug	Disables kernel debugging.
/numproc=_number_	Allows you to force a multi-CPU system to use only the quantity of processors specified.
/pcilock	For x86-based systems, stops the operating system from dynamically assigning hardware input and output, and interrupt request resources to PCI devices. Allows the BIOS to configure the devices.
/safeboot:_parameter_	Forces a start in safe mode by using the specified parameters. The available parameters are: ■ minimal ■ network ■ safeboot:minimal(alternateshell) You can combine other Boot.ini parameters with the /safeboot: parameter. The following examples illustrate the parameters that are in effect when you select a safe mode option from the startup recovery menu. ■ **Safe Mode with Networking** /safeboot:minimal /sos /bootlog /noguiboot ■ **Safe Mode with Networking** ■ /safeboot:network /sos /bootlog /noguiboot ■ **Safe Mode with Command Prompt** /safeboot:minimal(alternateshell) /sos /bootlog /noguiboot For more information about safe mode, see "Tools for Troubleshooting" in this book.
/sos	Displays the name of each device driver as it loads. Use when startup fails (while loading drivers) to determine which driver is failing to load.

Editing and repairing the Boot.ini file   When you install Windows XP Professional, the hidden file attribute for Boot.ini is set by default. To edit the Boot.ini file, you can use the following tools:

- Bootcfg.exe
- System Configuration Utility (Msconfig.exe)
- Control Panel
- A text editor (such as Notepad.exe)

> **Caution**   Always make a backup copy of the Boot.ini file before editing it.

Bootcfg.exe is a new command-line tool for Windows XP Professional.

To use Bootcfg.exe to view or edit the Boot.ini file

- To view the contents of the Boot.ini file, at the command prompt type **bootcfg /query**.
- To edit the Boot.ini file, use the **bootcfg /Addsw** or **bootcfg /Rmsw** command to change Boot.ini options. For a list of parameters, at the command prompt type **bootcfg /?**.

For more information about Bootcfg.exe, see Windows XP Professional Help and Support Center.

To use the System Configuration Utility to edit the Boot.ini file

1. In the **Run** dialog box, type **msconfig**, and then click **OK**.
2. Click the **BOOT.INI** tab.
   You can move individual Boot.ini lines up or down, or you can add **Boot Options** settings to each ARC path by selecting the check box associated with each parameter.

For more information about the System Configuration Utility, see Windows XP Professional Help and Support Center, also see and "Tools for Troubleshooting" in this book.

To use Control Panel to edit the Boot.ini file

1. In **Control Panel**, open **System**.
2. Click the **Advanced** tab, and in the **Startup and Recovery** box, click **Settings**.

3. In the **System Startup** area, click **Edit** or select from the options listed in **Default operating system**.

   Clicking **Edit** causes Notepad to read the contents of Boot.ini for editing. For multiple-boot systems, the option that you select in **Default operating system** updates the Boot.ini default= ARC path entry in [boot loader].

When you install Windows XP Professional, the **hidden** and **read only** file attributes for the *systemdrive*\Boot.ini file are set by default. Before using the following procedure, you need to clear these attributes by typing **attrib %systemdrive%:\boot.ini -h -r** at the command prompt.

To use Notepad or another text editor to edit the Boot.ini file

1. In the **Run** dialog box, type **cmd**, and then click **OK**.

2. Type **notepad** (or another text-editing program that you prefer to use) at the command prompt.

3. On the **File** menu, click **Open**, and then specify *systemdrive*\Boot.ini. The environment variable *systemdrive* represents the drive letter assigned to the system partition.

Replacing a Damaged Boot.ini   If your system fails to start due to a damaged Boot.ini file, you can use the following methods to replace the file or to correct errors.

   The **bootcfg** command is a new addition to the Windows XP Professional Recovery Console.

To use the Recovery Console bootcfg command to rebuild a Boot.ini file (Automatic Method)

1. Start Recovery Console.

2. At the Recovery Console prompt, type **bootcfg /rebuild**.

   Windows XP Professional scans the hard disks on your system and checks for Windows installations. You can then rebuild the Boot.ini file.

> **Note**   The Recovery Console **bootcfg** command is not the same as the Windows XP Professional Bootcfg.exe command-line tool. Bootcfg.exe resides in the *systemroot*\System32 folder and is a stand-alone command-line tool that you cannot use in Recovery Console.

To use Recovery Console to create a new Boot.ini file (Manual Method)

1. Start Recovery Console.

   For more information about installing and using Recovery Console, see "Using Recovery Console" earlier in this chapter and "Tools for Troubleshooting" in this book.

2. From the Recovery Console prompt, type:

   map

   A list appears containing hard disk and partition information for Windows XP Professional and other operating systems, such as Windows 2000 and Windows NT 4.0. Record and use this information to correct errors to an existing Boot.ini file, or to create a new Boot.ini file by using a text editor, such as Notepad, on another computer. (You must use another computer because Recovery Console does not provide text-editing tools.)

   When you are trying to copy an existing Boot.ini file to a floppy disk to edit on another computer, be aware that floppy disk write access is disabled by default. For information about using Recovery Console to enable write access to floppy disks, see "Tools for Troubleshooting" in this book, and also see article Q235364, "Description of the SET Command in Recovery Console," in the Microsoft Knowledge Base. To find this article, see the Microsoft Knowledge Base link on the Web Resources page at http://www.microsoft.com/windows/reskits/webresources.

Reviewing and Correcting NVRAM Startup Settings on Itanium-based Systems

Unlike *x*86-based systems, Itanium-based systems do not require a Boot.ini file to track ARC paths to Windows XP Professional installations and startup options. Instead, Windows XP Professional writes this information to NVRAM during installation, and the EFI boot manager displays a menu with these options when you start your computer. You can manage NVRAM settings by using the following tools:

- Bootcfg.exe
- Nvrboot.efi

Bootcfg.exe

Bootcfg.exe is a new command-line tool that allows you to add or change Windows XP Professional startup parameters stored in NVRAM. Always use Bootcfg.exe to avoid typing errors that can occur when manually editing settings. For more information about Bootcfg.exe, see Windows XP Professional Help and Support Center.

Nvrboot.efi

To safeguard against corrupted NVRAM data, Setup writes the boot manager entry that corresponds to a specific installation to a file named Boot*NNNN*. Table 27-19 describes a possible scenario where Boot*NNNN* files are written to disk after you install Windows XP Professional three times on the same system (as part of a multiple-boot configuration). In addition, separate WINNT50.*x* folders exist for each Windows XP Professional installation.

Table 27-19   WINNT50.*x* Folder and Boot*NNNN* File Details and Locations

Attribute	File Details and Locations		
Installation	First	Second	Third
Boot*NNNN*	Boot0004	Boot0005	Boot0006
Disk location	EFI\Microsoft\WINNT 50	EFI\Microsoft\WINNT 50.0	EFI\Microsoft\WINNT 50.1

In the preceding table, the value of *x* can vary. For example, if you have also installed two non-Windows-brand operating systems on the computer, the values for *x* in Table 27-19 could be 3, 4, and 5, representing three successive Windows XP Professional installations. Setup determines the value of *NNNN* based on the NVRAM boot id entry used during installation, and the value of *NNNN* depends on the number of boot entries present. Therefore, it is possible for identically named Boot*NNNN* files to exist in two different EFI\Microsoft\WINNT50.x directories.

You can recover from problems caused by corrupted or deleted NVRAM settings by using Nvrboot.efi, which is a menu-driven tool. The Nvrboot.efi tool enables you to restore boot manager startup options saved to Boot*NNNN* files. If the boot manager option that allows you to select one or more Windows XP Professional installations is missing, Nvrboot.efi enables you to restore any or all entries by doing the following:

- Importing individual Boot*NNNN* files that are stored in WINNT50.*x* folders.

- Exporting some or all EFI boot manager entries to a user-specified location. You can then use the backups generated by Nvrboot.efi to restore missing NVRAM entries.

The steps that you must follow to run Nvrboot.efi vary by computer manufacturer. For more information about starting and using Nvrboot.efi, review your system documentation. Methods that the EFI boot manager might provide to start Nvrboot.efi include startup menu items similar to the following:

- **EFI Console**. Selecting this option enables you to navigate to the MSUtil folder on the EFI System partition. From the EFI command-line, type:
  nvrboot

■ **Other Options**. Choosing this option might display a submenu from which you can select the option to start the EFI console. You can then navigate to the MSUtil folder on the EFI System partition and start Nvrboot.efi.

Nvrboot.efi also provides other options, such as appending startup parameters listed in Table 27-18.

> **Note** Windows XP Professional does not update Boot*NNNN* files in EFI\Microsoft\WINNT50.*x* folders when you convert from basic to dynamic disks. You must manually export the boot menu entry corresponding to a Windows XP Professional installation and overwrite the previous versions originally created by Setup. You also need to update NVRAM backup files saved to other folders.

For more information about using Nvrboot.efi, see article Q298872, "How to Modify NVRAM with Nvrboot.efi," in the Microsoft Knowledge Base. To find these articles, see the Microsoft Knowledge Base link on the Web Resources page at http://www.microsoft.com/windows/reskits/webresources.

Performing a Parallel Windows XP Professional Installation

Infrequently, startup files and critical areas on the hard disk become corrupted. If you are mainly concerned with salvaging readable data files and using the Backup tool to copy them to backup media or a network location, you can perform a parallel Windows XP Professional installation.

To perform a parallel installation of Windows XP Professional

1. Restart the computer by using the Windows XP Professional operating system CD. If prompted, press any key to start the system from the CD-ROM.

    If more than one usable disk partition exists, Setup displays a list from which you can select. Setup also allows you to create new partitions or delete existing ones. If installing to the same partition as the existing Windows XP Professional installation, Setup prompts you for a file name (for example, Windows.tmp).

2. Accept default options and proceed through the installation process. When prompted with formatting options, select **Leave the current file system intact (no changes)** if you are performing a parallel installation of Windows XP Professional to a partition that contains data. Do not select the **Format** option because this deletes all data on the partition.

Complete the parallel installation and start the second Windows XP Professional installation. You can now access files on other volumes and copy them to a safe location.

> **Tip**   If your computer supports Remote Installation Services (RIS), you can start a Windows XP Professional parallel installation by using the network. For more information about RIS, see "Applying Change and Configuration Management" and "Automating Client Installation and Upgrade" in the *Deployment Planning Guide* of the *Microsoft Windows 2000 Server Resource Kit*. For more information about deploying Windows XP installations from a Windows 2000 RIS Server, see "Automating and Customizing Installations" in this book.

Saving System Files and Settings by Using Automated System Recovery

The Backup tool adds a new feature called Automated System Recovery (ASR) that enables you to recover from situations where you cannot easily repair system partition damage. ASR works by writing operating system files onto backup media, and hard disk configuration information to floppy disk.

If you have a recent ASR backup set to use, you can begin an ASR restore by using the Windows XP Professional operating system CD to start your system. During the text-mode setup phase, wait for the **Press F5 to run Automated System Recovery (ASR)** prompt to appear. Respond to the prompt by pressing F5, and follow the instructions on the screen.

For more information about ASR or about using Backup to save system state information, see Windows XP Professional Help and Support Center. Also see "Backup and Restore" in this book.

Recovering from Hardware-related Problems

Hardware-related problems typically appear early in the startup process and symptoms include warning messages, startup failures, and Stop messages. The causes are typically due to improper device configuration, incorrect driver settings, or hardware malfunction and failure. You can also use the suggestions provided in this chapter for troubleshooting hardware issues that are not directly related to startup.

Checking Your Hardware

Always remember to check basic issues first before attempting to remove and replace parts:

Review your system documentation   Refer to your motherboard and device manuals before installing new peripherals for helpful information including safety precautions, firmware configuration, and expansion-slot or memory-slot locations. Some peripheral manufacturers recommend that you use a busmastering PCI slot and advise that installing their adapter in a secondary slot might cause it to function improperly. For more information about system resources, see "Managing Devices" in this book.

Confirm that the power cords for all devices are firmly plugged in and that the computer power supply meets hardware specifications   Computer power supplies are available in different sizes and are typically rated at 200, 250, 300, and 400 watts or larger. Some computers are equipped with even smaller power supplies (less than 100 watts) and installing too many devices into a system with an inadequate amount of power can cause reliability problems or even damage the power supply. See the manufacturer's power specifications when installing new devices and verify that your system can handle the increased electrical load.

Verify that you correctly installed and firmly seated all internal adapters
Typically, peripherals such as keyboards and video cards must be installed and functioning to complete the startup process without generating error messages. A faulty video card can cause the POST process to fail on some systems.

Verify that you correctly attached cables   Check that you have firmly seated all cable connectors. Search for damaged or worn cables and replace them as required.

Verify that you correctly configured any jumpers or dual in-line package switches   Jumpers and dual in-line package switches are used to close or open electric contacts on circuit boards. For hard disks, jumper settings are especially important because they can adversely affect the startup process if not correctly set. For example, configuring two master ATA disks that are installed on the same channel or assigning duplicate SCSI ID numbers to devices in the same SCSI chain might cause a Stop error or error messages about hard disk failure.

Verify that system firmware and peripheral firmware are up-to-date   You can sometimes trace instability and compatibility problems to outdated ACPI firmware. If your computer has firmware that is known to cause problems and an update is not yet available, technical support might advise you to disable ACPI and reinstall the operating system for stable operation. Although the option to disable ACPI is an option found on some *x*86-based firmware, it is recommended that you leave this setting at the default value (typically enabled).

To correctly disable or re-enable ACPI, you must first change firmware settings and then re-install Windows XP Professional to avoid a Stop 0x000000A5 or ACPI_BIOS_ERROR message, or a Stop 0x00000079 or MISMATCHED HAL message. Because of the numerous registry and system file changes required, you must rerun Setup (an upgrade installation does not work). For more information about checking firmware versions, see "Troubleshooting Concepts and Strategies" in this book.

If Setup does not respond when you are installing the operating system, the cause might be the firmware for your CD-ROM drives. Try upgrading the CD-ROM firmware to the latest version.

Test your hardware by running diagnostic tools   If the problem occurs after the POST routine finishes but before Windows XP Professional fully loads, run any diagnostic software that the manufacturer of the hardware adapter provides. This software typically includes self-test programs that allow you to quickly verify proper operation of a device and might enable you to obtain additional information about the device, such as model number, hardware, and device firmware version.

Determine if new hard disks were recently installed   Adding new hard disks to the system can cause startup problems. For example, in a two-disk system with Windows XP Professional installed on the first partition of the second hard disk, the Boot.ini file might be referencing a path to the operating system. The path might use a multi() format similar to the following:

```
multi(0)disk(0)rdisk(1)partition(1)
```

For the newly installed disk, you might need to update Boot.ini references so that they point to the correct location. For example, to restore the ability to start Windows XP Professional, you might need to change the multi path so it is similar to the following:

```
multi(0)disk(0)rdisk(2)partition(1)
```

Adding new disks might also affect how logical drive letters are assigned to partitions. For more information about diagnosing and resolving issues due to changed logical drive letters, see Microsoft Knowledge Base articles Q234048, "How Windows 2000 Assigns, Reserves, and Stores Drive Letters," Q249321, "Unable to Log on if the Boot Partition Drive Letter Has Changed," and Q225025, "Setup Changes Drive Letters After a Partition Is Deleted and Reinstalled." To find these articles, see the Microsoft Knowledge Base link on the Web Resources page at http://www.microsoft.com/windows/reskits/webresources.

Configure ISA devices in Plug and Play mode   If ISA devices are present, always configure them in Plug and Play mode if possible. Plug and Play is the default mode for ISA devices that comply with Plug and Play. If necessary, you can switch from Plug and Play to manual mode by using jumpers or software provided by the manufacturer. Use care when configuring ISA devices in manual mode because the operating system depends on the user to select the correct hardware and Device Manager resources. Manually selecting resources is more likely to cause an error because Windows XP Professional cannot resolve resource conflicts for you.

Manually assign interrupt request (IRQ) line numbers for each hardware device Some *x*86-based motherboards force IRQ sharing across two or more expansion slots (or integrated devices) regardless of the adapters installed. In some cases, IRQ sharing can cause conflicts after you install new hardware. If you have a non-ACPI computer equipped with firmware that supports changing IRQ assignments, as a troubleshooting method, try manually changing the IRQ assigned to a problem device.

Because systems that use the ACPI HAL ignore IRQ assignments stored in firmware, you are only able to manually change IRQ settings for non-ACPI (Standard PC HAL) systems. Some *x*86-based systems enable you to toggle ACPI functionality. To disable or re-enable ACPI, you must first change firmware settings and then re-install Windows XP Professional to avoid a Stop 0xA5 message or a Stop 0x79 message. Because of the numerous registry and system file changes required, you must rerun Setup (an upgrade installation does not work).

For more information about system resources, see "Managing Devices" in this book. For more information about Stop messages, see "Common Stop Messages for Troubleshooting" in this book.

Verify SCSI configuration If your computer uses or starts from SCSI devices and if you suspect that these devices are causing startup problems, you need to check the items listed in Table 27-20.

Table 27-20 Checklist for Troubleshooting SCSI Devices

Checklist	Description for Each Item
All devices are correctly terminated	Verify that each SCSI device is correctly terminated. There are specific rules for termination that you must follow to avoid problems with the computer not recognizing a SCSI device. Although these rules can vary slightly from one type of adapter to another, the basic principle is that you must terminate a SCSI chain at both ends.
All devices use unique SCSI ID numbers	Verify that each device located on a particular SCSI chain has a unique identification number. Duplicate identification numbers can cause intermittent failures or even data corruption. For newer devices, you can use the SCSI Configured AutoMatically (SCAM) standard. The host adapter and all devices must support the SCAM standard. Otherwise, ID numbers must be set manually.

Table 27-20   Checklist for Troubleshooting SCSI Devices

Checklist	Description for Each Item
The BIOS on the startup SCSI controller is enabled	Verify that the SCSI BIOS is enabled for the primary SCSI controller and that the BIOS on secondary controllers is disabled. SCSI firmware contains programming instructions that allow the computer to communicate with SCSI disks before Windows XP Professional starts. Disabling this feature for all host adapters causes a startup failure. For information about disabling or enabling the BIOS, refer to the documentation provided with your SCSI controller.
You are using the correct cables	Verify that the connecting cables are the correct type and length, and are compliant with SCSI requirements. Different SCSI standards exist, each with specific cabling requirements. Consult the product documentation for more information.
The firmware settings for the host SCSI adapter match device capabilities	Verify that host adapter BIOS settings for each SCSI device are set correctly. (The BIOS for the SCSI adapter is separate from the system motherboard firmware.) For each SCSI device, you can specify settings, such as **Sync Negotiation**, **Maximum Transfer Rate**, and **Send Start Command**, that can affect performance and compatibility. Certain SCSI devices might not function correctly if settings are set beyond the capabilities of the hardware. Consult the documentation for your SCSI adapter and device before changing default settings.
SCSI adapters are installed in a master PCI slot	Verify that you installed the host adapter in the correct motherboard slot. The documentation for some PCI SCSI adapters recommends using busmaster PCI slots to avoid problems on x86-based systems. Refer to the manufacturer's documentation for your motherboard or computer to locate these busmaster PCI slots. If your SCSI adapter is installed in a non-busmaster PCI slot, move it to a master slot to see if the change improves operation and stability.

> **Note** As a precaution, always shut down the computer before troubleshooting hardware. Never attempt to install or remove internal devices if you are unfamiliar with hardware. Check your system documentation for more information.

For more information about the SCSI standard, see the SCSI link on the Web Resources page at http://www.microsoft.com/windows/reskits/webresources. For more information about SCSI termination, see articles Q92765, "Terminating a SCSI Device," and Q154690, "How to Troubleshoot Event 9 and Event 11 Error Messages," in the Microsoft Knowledge Base. To find these articles, see the Microsoft Knowledge Base link on the Web Resources page at http://www.microsoft.com/windows/reskits/webresources.

Simplifying Your Hardware Configuration

Hardware problems can occur when you have new and older devices installed on your system. If you cannot resolve problems by using safe mode and other options, such as rolling back drivers, temporarily disable or remove ISA devices that do not support Plug and Play. If you can start Windows XP Professional with these older devices removed, this is an indication that they are causing resource conflicts and you need to manually reconfigure the resources assigned to them. For more information about rolling back drivers, see Windows XP Professional Help and Support Center, and also see "Tools for Troubleshooting" in this book.

When you are diagnosing startup problems related to hardware, it is recommended that you simplify your configuration. Avoid troubleshooting when you have several adapters and external peripherals installed. Starting with external and ISA devices, disable or remove hardware devices one at time until you are able to start your system. Reinstall devices by following the manufacturer's instructions, verifying that each is functioning properly before checking the next device. For example, installing a PCI network adapter and a SCSI adapter at the same time can complicate troubleshooting because either adapter might cause a problem. Simplifying your system configuration might enable you to start Windows XP Professional. You can then gradually increase hardware complexity until you reproduce the problem, which allows you to diagnose and resolve the problem.

ISA devices can cause problems because the PCI bus does not have a reliable method for determining ISA resource settings. Device conflicts might occur due to miscommunication between the two bus types. To avoid ISA and PCI conflicts, try temporarily removing ISA devices. After you install a new PCI device, you can use Device Manager to determine which system resources are available to ISA devices. Then reconfigure the ISA devices that do not support Plug and Play so that you eliminate any conflicts. If the problems continue after you reinstall ISA devices and you cannot resolve them with assistance from technical support, consider upgrading to newer hardware.

Simplifying your system configuration also helps when problems prevent you from installing Windows XP Professional. For more information about simplifying your hardware configuration to resolve setup problems, see article Q224826, "Troubleshooting Text-Mode Setup Problems on ACPI Computers," in the Microsoft Knowledge Base. To find this article, see the Microsoft Knowledge Base link on the Web Resources page at http://www.microsoft.com/windows/reskits/webresources. Also, see "Troubleshooting Concepts and Strategies" in this book.

Checking the Operating System Configuration

Installing new hardware or updating drivers can create conflicts, causing devices to become inaccessible. You can isolate and troubleshoot these problems by using System Information and Device Manager.

To use the System Information tool to view problem devices

1. In the **Run** dialog box, type **msinfo32**, and then click **OK**.

2. Click **Components**, and then click **Problem Devices**.

To use the System Information tool to view shared and conflicting resources

1. In the **Run** dialog box, type **msinfo32**, and then click **OK**.

2. Click **Hardware Resources**, and then click **Conflicts/Sharing**.

> **Note**   The Windows NT 4.0 tool Windows Diagnostics (Wlnmsd.exe) is not available in Windows XP Professional. Instead, you can obtain similar information by using System Information. To start System Information at the command prompt, type **winmsd** or **msinfo32**.

To use Device Manager (Devmgmt.msc) to view system resource usage information

■ In the **Run** dialog box, type **devmgmt.msc**, and then click **OK**.

For more information about using Device Manager and resolving hardware conflicts, see Windows XP Professional Help and Support Center, and also see "Managing Devices" in this book.

Diagnosing Disk-related Problems

Disk-related problems typically occur before Windows XP Professional starts or shortly afterwards. Table 27-21 provides a list of symptoms, possible causes, and sources of information that you can refer to.

Table 27-21   Diagnosing Disk-related Startup Problems

Symptom, Message, or Problem	Possible Cause	Where to Find More Information

The POST routine displays messages similar to the following:
 	
`Hard disk error.`
`Hard disk absent/failed.`
	The system self-test routines halt due to improperly installed devices.	See "Recovering from Hardware-related Problems" earlier in this chapter.

Table 27-21   Diagnosing Disk-related Startup Problems

Symptom, Message, or Problem	Possible Cause	Where to Find More Information

The system displays MBR-related or boot sector–related messages similar to the following:
 	
`Missing operating system.`
`Insert a system diskette and`
`restart the system.`
	The MBR or partition boot sector is corrupt due to problems with hardware or viruses.	For more information about recovering from MBR or boot sector problems, see
		
		"Troubleshooting Disks and File Systems" in this book.

The system displays messages about the partition table similar to the following:
 	
`Invalid partition table.`
`A disk-read error occurred.`
	The partition table is invalid due to incorrect configuration of newly added disks.	See "Troubleshooting Disks and File Systems" in this book.

You cannot access Windows XP Professional after installing another operating system.	The Windows XP Professional boot sector is overwritten by the other operating system's setup program.	See "Troubleshooting Disks and File Systems" and "Tools for Troubleshooting" in this book.
In an x86-based system, one of the following files is missing or damaged: ■ Boot.ini ■ Ntoskrnl.exe ■ Ntdetect.com	Required startup files are missing or damaged, or entries in the Boot.ini are pointing to the wrong partition.	See "Troubleshooting Disks and File Systems" and "Tools for Troubleshooting" in this book.

The Windows loader or EFI boot manager displays messages similar to the following:
 	
`Couldn't find loader.`
`Please insert another disk.`
	Ntldr or IA64ldr.efi is missing or corrupted.	See "Troubleshooting Disks and File Systems" in this book.

CMOS or NVRAM disk configuration settings are not retained.	The CMOS memory or NVRAM is faulty, data is corrupted, or the battery that retains these settings needs replacing.	Follow the manufacturer's instructions for replacing or recharging the system battery. For Itanium-based systems, refer to system documentation for how to start the Nvrboot.efi tool. For more information about Nvrboot.efi, see Table 27-6 and "Startup Phases for Itanium-based Systems" Earlier in this chapter.

Infrequently, disk-related issues, such as corrupted files, file system problems, or insufficient free space might cause Stop messages to appear. For more information about maintaining disks and troubleshooting disk-related problems, see "Disk Management" and "Troubleshooting Disks and File Systems" in this book. Also, see "Common Stop Messages for Troubleshooting" in this book.

Resolving Shutdown Problems

At first glance, shutdown and startup problems might appear to be unrelated, but they can stem from the same causes. Components that cause startup problems might also interfere with the shutdown process.

System shutdown is an orderly process and involves the following:

- Winlogon sends specific messages to devices, system services, and applications, notifying them that you are shutting down the computer.

- Winlogon waits for applications to close open files and allows them a certain amount of time to complete clean-up tasks, such as writing unsaved data to disk. Typically, every enabled device, system service, and application replies to the shutdown message request, indicating to Winlogon that shutdown can safely occur.

Shutdown problems can be caused by:

- Device drivers or applications that do not respond to shutdown messages.

- System services that do not respond to shutdown messages or that send busy replies to the system. Busy replies might be due to a *deadlock* condition where two or more processes attempt to access the same resource. Because each process has a request for the other's resource, neither process can finish.

- Faulty or incompatible drivers, services, or applications.

- Hardware changes that cause device conflicts.

- Firmware incompatibility or incorrect changes to firmware settings.

To resolve problems that prevent shutdown, use Task Manager to close the unresponsive application or service.

To end an unresponsive application or service

1. Start Task Manager by pressing CTRL+SHIFT+ESC.

2. Click the **Applications** tab.

   The Applications tab provides status information and displays each task as either **Running** or **Not Responding**.

3. Click the item labeled **Not Responding**, and then click **End Task**.

Resolving Power Management Problems on x86-based Systems

Putting your computer on standby or in hibernation requires firmware that uses Advanced Power Management (APM), or preferably, that is ACPI compliant. To avoid problems, review your system documentation or the manufacturer's support Web page for information about determining whether your firmware is current. Using updated firmware is especially important when you use ACPI functionality.

To determine whether your system is using ACPI features

1. In the **Run** dialog box, type **devmgmt.msc**, and then click **OK**.

2. In the console tree, expand the **Computer** folder.

3. If the computer description includes ACPI, as Figure 27-5 shows, Windows XP Professional is using ACPI functionality.

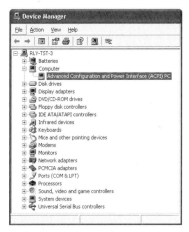

Figure 27-5   Using Device Manager to determine ACPI functionality

For information about using Device Manager, see "Managing Devices" in this book.

To determine if your computer supports hibernate and standby features

1. In the **Run** dialog box, type **powercfg.cpl**, and then click **OK**.

2. In the **Power Options Properties** dialog box, verify that a **Hibernate** tab exists. If present, select the **Hibernate** tab, check the **Enable hibernation** box, and click **Apply**.

3. In the **Power Options Properties** dialog box, verify that an **Advanced** tab exists. If present, verify that **Standby** and **Hibernate** are selectable options in the **Power buttons** drop down lists.

If the **Standby** and **Hibernate** options are not present, then your computer does not support these features.

Symptoms of Power Management Problems and Their Causes

When a computer is entering or leaving hibernation or standby, the following might occur:

- It displays an error message such as "Unable to enter Standby mode," or the option to configure the standby or hibernation feature is not available in Control Panel.

- It cannot leave standby or hibernation.

- It runs differently after leaving hibernation or standby, and you notice audio, mouse control, or video distortion problems.

- It displays Stop messages, such as 0x0000009F: DRIVER_POWER_STATE_FAILURE, when the system is leaving or entering standby or hibernation.

  Typical causes include:

- **Your hardware does not properly support standby and hibernation.** Verify with your computer or peripheral manufacturer that your hardware supports standby or hibernation. Older hardware might not be ACPI-compliant or might predate recent revisions in the Advanced Power Management standard.

- **Your system firmware is out-of-date.** Upgrading to the latest system firmware can resolve problems, especially for ACPI systems. For x86-based systems that are equipped with an APM-based (non-ACPI) BIOS, disabling APM might eliminate startup problems, such as instability or Stop errors, until you can obtain an update. For more information, see article Q237673, "How to Troubleshoot STOP Error Messages After Enabling Advanced Power Management," in the Microsoft Knowledge Base. To find this article, see the Microsoft Knowledge Base link on the Web Resources page at http://www.microsoft.com/windows /reskits/webresources.

- **Your peripheral firmware is out-of-date.** Peripherals are typically packaged with diagnostic software that allows you to check the firmware version installed. You can then visit the manufacturer's Web site to determine whether an upgrade is necessary. Firmware updates for various devices, including SCSI adapters, modems, CD and DVD-ROM drives, and video cards, might be available. If you find updates for several devices, install them one at a time to better observe the effect of each update.

- **You are using outdated driver files that do not support power management.** Using out-of-date drivers might cause incompatibility problems, preventing the system from entering or resuming from standby and hibernation. Be sure to check for the latest Windows XP Professional updates to all your devices (especially audio and video). If you find updates for several devices, observe the rule of simplicity and install them one at a time to better observe the effect of each update.

■ **You are using incompatible software that installs components that either interfere with or do not support power management.** Are incompatible versions of software present on your system? For example, CD-ROM mastering software meant for other versions of Windows might appear to function properly in Windows XP Professional. However, the software might be the source of a message similar to the following:

```
System Standby Failed. The device driver for the 'XXXX CD-
RW' device is preventing the computer from entering standby. Please close all
applications and try again.
```

The preceding message might be misleading because the problem might not be caused by the CD rewriter driver. You query the Microsoft Knowledge Base or review messages on the msnews.microsoft.com newsgroups and find recommendations to update your CD authoring software. Following this advice, you install a Windows XP compatible update, which restores the ability to put the computer on standby and in hibernation.

Recovering from a Failed Standby

When a computer is on standby, the CPU enters a low-power state until an event, such as user or network activity, causes the computer to come out of standby. Using standby conserves power and is typically much faster than shutting down and restarting the computer.

If your computer cannot return to normal mode after being on standby, try the following:

■ Disconnect any devices that you attached after putting the computer on standby. Avoid plugging in devices while the computer is on standby. For best results, bring the computer out of standby first, and then attach peripherals, such as universal serial bus (USB) devices.

■ Avoid major changes to the computer's state after putting the computer on standby. For example, if you place an undocked portable computer on standby, avoid resuming the computer while it is docked. Computers that are not ACPI-compliant might be more sensitive to this type of state change.

■ Reset your computer. If your computer does not restart when you press the reset switch, turn the computer off by pressing the power switch. Some computers require that you press down the power switch for at least four seconds. If your computer does not respond to the power switch, consult your owner's manual to determine how to completely turn off the computer.

Improper shutdowns might cause unsaved data to be lost. Windows XP Professional can detect whether an improper shutdown occurred and might start Autochk to correct file system problems during the startup process. For more information about Autochk and Chkdsk, see "Troubleshooting Disks and File Systems" in this book.

Recovering from a Failed Hibernation

When you put a computer in hibernation, Windows XP Professional writes all memory content to the *systemdrive*\Hiberfil.sys file before shutting down the system. When you turn the computer back on, Ntldr uses firmware calls to locate the startup disk. If Ntldr finds a Hiberfil.sys file on the *systemdrive* root, the information is read back into memory and the computer resumes exactly where it left off without going through a full startup sequence. If the Windows loader cannot locate the Hiberfil.sys file, it processes the Boot.ini file and proceeds with normal startup.

The Hiberfil.sys file can exist in one of the following forms:

- A complete memory image several megabytes in size (equal to the amount of physical memory).

- A text file named Hiberfil.sys that uses a slightly modified ARC format pointing to the boot partition of the last hibernated operating system. That boot partition contains the actual Hiberfil.sys file, which is a full memory image of the hibernating operating system.

In either case, Ntldr locates and reads the Hiberfil.sys memory image and continues without displaying the Boot.ini startup menu.

The modified ARC path specified in the Hiberfil.sys file conforms to one of the following formats:

- linkmulti(W)disk(X)rdisk(Y)partition(Z)

- linkscsi(W)disk(X)rdisk(Y)partition(Z)

- linksignature(V)disk(X)rdisk(Y)partition(Z)

Ntldr checks the integrity of the Hiberfil.sys file and if the file is damaged, displays a prompt similar to the following:

```
Delete restoration data and proceed to system boot menu
```

If you confirm the prompt by pressing ENTER, Windows XP Professional deletes the Hiberfil.sys file and proceeds with normal startup.

To minimize problems, avoid major changes to the computer's state after putting the computer in hibernation. For example, if you hibernate an undocked portable computer, avoid starting the computer in a docked state. Computers that are not ACPI-compliant might be more sensitive to this type of state change.

For more information about using the standby and hibernate features, see Windows XP Professional Help and Support Center. For more information about power management, see "Managing Devices" and "Supporting Mobile Users" in this book. For more information about troubleshooting standby or hibernation issues, see article Q266169, "Troubleshoot Problems with Standby Mode, Hibernate Mode, and Shutting Down Your Computer in Windows 2000," in the Microsoft Knowledge Base. To find this article, see the Microsoft Knowledge Base link on the Web Resources page at http://www.microsoft.com/windows/reskits/webresources.

Additional Resources

These resources contain additional information related to this chapter.

- "Troubleshooting Concepts and Strategies" in this book.

- "File Systems" in this book.

- "Disk Management" in this book.

- "Troubleshooting Disks and File Systems" in this book.

- "Managing Devices" in this book.

- "Tools for Troubleshooting" in this book.

- "Common Stop Messages for Troubleshooting" in this book.

- "Backup and Restore" in this book.

- "System Files Reference" in this book

- "Supporting Mobile Users" in this book.

- For detailed information about the registry and its components, see Windows XP Professional Help and Support Center.

- The Registry Reference at http://www.microsoft.com/reskit.

- The Hardware Compatibility List link on the Web Resources page at http://www.microsoft.com/windows/reskits/webresources.

- The ACPI link on the Web Resources page at http://www.microsoft.com/windows/reskits/webresources.

- The Extensible Firmware Interface link on the Web Resources page at http://www.microsoft.com/windows/reskits/webresources.

- The Debugging Tools link on the Web Resources page at http://www.microsoft.com/windows/reskits/webresources.

- The Driver Development Kits link on the Web Resources page at http://www.microsoft.com/windows/reskits/webresources.

- The Microsoft Product Support Services link on the Web Resources page at http://www.microsoft.com/windows/reskits/webresources.

- The SCSI link on the Web Resources page at http://www.microsoft.com/windows/reskits/webresources.

- For information about the registry and its structure, see "Registry Structure" in Windows XP Professional Help and Support Center.

Part VI

Appendixes

The following appendices provide reference and supplemental information to help you support computers running Microsoft Windows XP Professional in your organization.

APPENDIX A

System Files Reference

When you install the Microsoft® Windows® XP Professional operating system, the Setup program creates folders on your system drive into which it places files that the system requires. Knowing the names and locations of essential system files can help you understand and troubleshoot your Windows XP Professional installation.

Related Information

- For information about troubleshooting Startup and running Recovery Console, see "Troubleshooting Startup" in this book.

- For information about general troubleshooting concepts and strategies, see "Troubleshooting Concepts and Strategies" in this book.

System Files

The following files are core components of the Windows XP Professional operating system. If you install Windows XP Professional as an upgrade from Microsoft® Windows® 2000 or earlier, the files listed in Table A-1 are located in the Windows\System32 folder or in Winnt\System32.

Table A-1   Essential System Files

File Name	Description
Ntoskrnl.exe	Executive and kernel.
Ntkrnlpa.exe	Executive and kernel with support for Physical Address Extension (PAE), which allows addressing of more than 4 gigabytes (GB) of physical memory.
Hal.dll	Hardware abstraction layer.
Win32k.sys	Kernel-mode part of the Win32 subsystem.
Ntdll.dll	Internal support functions and system service dispatch stubs to executive functions.
Kernel32.dll	Core Win32 subsystem DLLs.
Advapi32.dll	
User32.dll	
Gdi32.dll	

Startup Files

The following files are essential to the startup process. All files listed in Table A-2 are located in the boot or root directory (for example, C:\) of your Windows XP Professional installation.

Table A-2   Essential Startup Files

File Name	Description
Ntldr	Reads the Boot.ini file, presents the boot menu, and loads Ntoskrnl.exe, Bootvid.dll, Hal.dll, and boot-start device drivers.
Boot.ini	Contains options for starting the version of Windows that Setup installs and any preexisting Windows installations.

Table A-2   Essential Startup Files

File Name	Description
Ntdetect.com	After the boot selection is made, Ntldr loads and executes this 16-bit real-mode program to query the computer for basic device and configuration information. This information includes the following: ■ The time and date information stored in the system's CMOS (nonvolatile memory). ■ The types of buses (for example, ISA, PCI, EISA, Micro Channel Architecture [MCA]) on the system and identifiers for devices attached to the buses. ■ The number, size, and type of disk drives on the system. ■ The types of mouse input devices connected to the system. ■ The number and type of parallel ports configured on the system.
Pagefile.sys	Contains memory data that Windows is unable to fit into physical RAM. During Startup, the virtual memory manager moves data in and out of the paging file to optimize the amount of physical memory available to the operating system and applications.
Ntbootdd.sys	If either the boot or system drives are SCSI-based, Ntldr loads this file and uses it instead of the boot-code functions for disk access.

Folders on the Local Disk

Setup creates the following folders (shown in Table A-3) on your local disk by default when installing Windows XP Professional.

> **Note**   When Windows XP Professional is installed as an upgrade from Windows 2000 or earlier, Setup installs the operating system into the existing Winnt folder. A Windows folder is not created.

Table A-3   Default Local Disk Folders

Folder Name	Contents
Documents and Settings	Account information for each user who is granted access on the computer. Each user account is represented by a subfolder assigned the user name. Folders under each user account folder include My Documents, Desktop, and Start Menu.
Program Files	Installed applications, such as Microsoft® Internet Explorer or Microsoft® Office.
WINDOWS or WINNT	Entire operating system.

Windows Folder

The Windows folder and its subfolders contain the operating system files for your Windows XP Professional installation (as shown in Table A-4).

Table A-4   Windows Folder and Subfolders

Folder Name	Contents
WINDOWS or WINNT	Miscellaneous operating system and application files (for example, Control.ini, Desktop.ini, Notepad.exe, and System.ini files)
Addins	ActiveX controls (.ocx) files
AppPatch	Application compatibility files
Config	Musical Instrument Digital Interface (MIDI) instrument definition files
Connection Wizard	Internet connection files that are used when a computer starts Windows for the first time
CSC	Offline files that are used during client-side caching
Cursors	Cursor and icon files
Debug	Log files
Downloaded Program Files	Downloaded program files
Driver Cache	Uninstalled driver files
Fonts	All font files
Help	Help files
Ime	Language files
ime (x86)	Language files for x86-based systems
Java	Java files
Media	Sound and music files (for example: *.wav and *.midi)
MS	Installation folder for Microsoft® Systems Management Server (SMS) client
Msagent	Microsoft Agent files (Microsoft Agent is a set of programmable software services that support the presentation of interactive animated characters within the Microsoft® Windows® interface)
Msapps	Files that support backward compatibility in applications
Mui	Multi-user interface files
Offline Web Pages	Downloaded Web pages for offline reading
PCHEALTH	Help and Support Center files
Prefetch	Data files related to enhancing the speed at which applications start

Table A-4   Windows Folder and Subfolders

Folder Name	Contents
Registration	COM+ files. COM+ files are enhancements to the Microsoft Component Object Model (COM)
Repair	Registry backup files (these files are updated if you use NTBackup and choose to back up system state files)
Resources	User interface files
SchCache	Schema cache folder
Security	Log files, templates for snap-ins, and security database files
Setupupd	Dynamic Update storage location
Srchasst	Search assistant files
System	Backward compatibility files related to the System folder (for example, applications that look for a System folder)
system32	Core operating system files (for more information, see "System32 Folder" later in this appendix)
Tasks	Scheduled Task files
Temp	Temporary files
twain_32	Imaging files (for scanners)
Web	Printer and wallpaper files
WinSxS	Side by Side (shared components)

System32 Folder

The System32 folder and its subfolders contain the core operating system files for your Windows XP Professional installation. Table A-5 describes the System32 files.

Table A-5   System32 Folder and Subfolders

Folder Name	Contents
system32	Essential system files (for example, Hal.dll and Ntoskrnl.exe files)
1025, 1028, 1031, 1033, 1037, 1041, 1053, 2052, 3076	Localization (language) files for a specific language, corresponding to the number assigned to this folder. This folder remains empty unless Windows XP Professional is localized for this particular language.
CatRoot	Catalog files and signature files
CatRoot2	Catalog files and signature files
Com	Component Object Model (COM) objects
Config	Registry files and event logs
Dhcp	DHCP database files

Table A-5   System32 Folder and Subfolders

Folder Name	Contents
DirectX	DirectX files
Dllcache	Windows File Protection backup files
Drivers	Installed drivers
Export	Encryption Pack installation files
Ias	Internet Authentication Service files
Icsxml	Universal Plug and Play files
Ime	Language files
Inetsrv	Internet Information Services files
Macromed	Macromedia files
Microsoft	Cryptography files
MsDtc	Microsoft Distributed Transaction Coordinator files
Mui	Multi-user interface files
Npp	Network Monitor and trace files
Oobe	Windows Welcome files
Ras	Remote access server encryption files
Restore	Data files or System Restore related files
Rpcproxy	RPC Proxy files (RPCProxy.dll)
Setup	Optional component manager files
ShellExt	Shell extension components
Smsmsgs	SMS Site Component Manager files
Spool	Print spooling files
Usmt	User State Migration tool
Wbem	Web-based Enterprise Management data files. Windows Management Instrumentation (WMI) is the Microsoft implementation of WBEM.
Wins	WINS database files

Extracting Files from the Operating System CD

It is usually recommended that you use Add or Remove Programs in Control Panel to install and uninstall components, applications, and support software from the Windows XP Professional operating system CD. If system files are missing or damaged, you can run Windows XP Professional Setup from the operating system CD and choose the option to repair your existing installation. In some cases, however, you might need to extract a system or startup file directly from the operating system CD.

> **Warning**   If you install incorrect versions of system or startup files or if you install files to incorrect locations, your system might not operate as expected or might not start. Use the method described in this section only if your product support representative indicates that it is necessary to manually retrieve a compressed file from your operating system CD.

The /i386 folder on your Windows XP Professional operating system CD contains system and startup files in compressed form. If you need to replace a file in your Windows XP Professional installation, you can use the **copy** or **expand** command in Recovery Console to extract the needed file from the operating system CD. Use the **copy** command unless you are extracting a file from a .cab file, such as Driver.cab. When extracting a file from a .cab file, use the **expand** command.

When you use Recovery Console to extract a compressed file from the operating system CD, you must use exact file names for the compressed and uncompressed files. Table A-6 illustrates compressed and uncompressed file names.

Table A-6   Compressed and Uncompressed File Names

Compressed File Name	Uncompressed File Name
Ntoskrnl.ex_	Ntoskrnl.exe
Hal.dl_	Hal.dll

Using the Copy Command in Recovery Console

If a file is not within a .cab file, you can use the **copy** command in Recovery Console to extract the file from the operating system CD and place it on your local disk in a Windows XP Professional installation. When you use the **copy** command to extract a file to a destination on your local disk, the file is automatically uncompressed. For more information about running Recovery Console, including how to add it to your startup options, see "Troubleshooting Startup" in this book.

Use the **copy** command with the following syntax:

```
copy source [destination]
```

Table A-7 describes the parameters that you can use with the **copy** command.

Table A-7   Parameters for the Copy Command

Parameter	Description
Source	Specifies the file to be copied.
Destination	Specifies the directory and/or file name for the new file.

Source can be removable media, any directory within the System32 directory of the current Windows installation, the root of any drive, the local installation sources, or the Cmdcons folder. (The C:\Cmdcons folder is the Recovery Console installation folder.)

Destination can be any directory within the System32 directories of the current Windows installation, the root of any drive, the local installation sources, or the Cmdcons folder. If you do not specify a destination, the command defaults to the current directory. The **copy** command prompts you if the destination file already exists. The destination cannot be removable media.

The **copy** command does not support replaceable parameters (wildcards).

Using the Expand Command in Recovery Console

To extract a file from a .cab file on the operating system CD and place it on your local disk in a Windows XP Professional installation, start Recovery Console and use the **expand** command. When you use the **expand** command to extract a file to a destination on your local disk, the file is automatically uncompressed. For more information about running Recovery Console, including how to add it to your startup options, see "Troubleshooting Startup" in this book.

Use the **expand** command with the following syntax:

```
expand source [/f:filespec] [destination] [/y] [/d]
```

Tables A-8 describes the parameters that you can use with the **expand** command.

Table A-8 Parameters for the Expand Command

Parameter	Description
source	Specifies the file that you want to expand. Cannot include wildcards.
destination	Specifies the directory for the new file; the default is the current directory.
/y	Suppresses the overwrite prompt when you expand or extract files.
/f:*filespec*	If the source contains more than one file, this parameter is required to identify the specific file or files that you want to expand. Can include wildcards.
/d	Lists the files contained in the cabinet file without expanding it or extracting from it.

- The destination can be any folder within the System32 folder of the current Windows installation, the root of any drive, the local installation sources, or the Cmdcons folder.

- The destination cannot be removable media.

- The destination file cannot be read-only. Use the **Attrib** command to remove the read-only attribute.

- If the destination file already exists, the **expand** command prompts you for confirmation to overwrite the file unless you include the **/y** parameter.

Additional Resources

These resources contain additional information related to this appendix.

Related Information

- "Troubleshooting Concepts and Strategies" in this book.

- "Tools for Troubleshooting" in this book.

- "Troubleshooting Disks and File Systems" in this book.

- "Troubleshooting Startup" in this book

- Windows XP Professional Help and Support Center for more information about running and troubleshooting Windows XP Professional. Search using the keywords *troubleshooting* and *recovery console*.

APPENDIX B

User Rights

User rights fall into two general categories: logon rights and privileges. Logon rights control who is authorized to log on to a computer and how they can log on. Privileges control access to system-wide resources on a computer and can override the permissions that are set on particular objects.

Logon Rights

Logon rights control how security principals are allowed access to the computer—whether from the keyboard or through a network connection, or whether as a service or as a batch job. For each logon method, there exists a pair of logon rights—one to allow logging on to the computer and another to deny logging on to the computer. Use a deny logon right as you would use a deny permission—to exclude a subset of a group that has been assigned an allow logon right. For example, suppose that Alice wants all users except the members of the domain Marketing group to be able to log on locally at her computer's keyboard. With this in mind, Alice creates a local group, which she names "LocalLogonDenied." Then she configures her computer as follows:

1. She assigns the log on locally user right to the Users group.

2. She assigns the deny local logon user right to the LocalLogonDenied group.

3. She makes the Marketing group a member of the LocalLogonDenied group.

Deny rights take precedence over allow rights, so members of the Marketing group are denied the right to log on locally even though they are also members of the Users group, which is allowed to log on locally.

> **Warning**   The rule to keep in mind is: "Allow a set, and then deny a subset." Reversing the order can be disastrous. For example, Alice might want to allow no one but herself to log on locally. If she allowed herself the right to log on locally and denied the Users group the right to log on locally, she would be unpleasantly surprised to find that she had locked herself out of the computer. Alice, after all, is a member of the Users group, so the deny right she assigned to the Users group would take precedence over the allow right she assigned to herself.

Logon rights are described in Table B-1. The display names for logon rights are followed by the string constant (in parentheses). Many command-line tools refer to rights by string constant rather than by display name. The default settings are taken from the Windows XP Professional Local Computer policy.

Table B-1   Logon Rights

Right	Description
Access this computer from the network (SeNetworkLogonRight)	Allows a user to connect to the computer from the network.
	Default setting: Administrators, Power Users, Users, Everyone, and Backup Operators.
Allow logon through Terminal Services (SeRemoteInteractiveLogonRight)	Allows a user to log on to the computer by using a Remote Desktop connection.
	Default setting: Administrators and Remote Desktop Users.
Log on as a batch job (SeBatchLogonRight)	Allows a user to log on by using a batch-queue facility such as the Task Scheduler service.
	Default setting: Administrator, System, and Support_xxxxxxxx.
	When an administrator uses the Add Scheduled Task wizard to schedule a task to run under a particular user name and password, that user is automatically assigned the "Log on as a batch job" right. When the scheduled time arrives, the Task Scheduler service logs the user on as a batch job rather than as an interactive user, and the task runs in the user's security context. The Support_xxxxxxxx account is the logon account for Remote Assistance.
Log on locally (SeInteractiveLogonRight)	Allows a user to start an interactive session on the computer.
	Default setting: Administrators, Power Users, Users, Guest, and Backup Operators.
	Users who do not have this right can start a remote interactive session on the computer if they have the "Allow logon through Terminal Services" right.
Log on as a service (SeServiceLogonRight)	Allows a security principal to log on as a service. Services can be configured to run under the Local System, Local Service, or Network Service accounts, which have a built-in right to log on as a service. Any service that runs under a separate user account must be assigned the right.
	Default setting: Network Service.

Table B-1   Logon Rights

Right	Description
Deny access to this computer from the network (SeDenyNetworkLogonRight)	Prohibits a user from connecting to the computer from the network. **Default setting**: The Support_xxxxxxxx account used by Remote Assistance is denied this right.
Deny logon locally (SeDenyInteractiveLogonRight)	Prohibits a user from logging on directly at the keyboard. **Default setting**: Guest.
Deny logon as a batch job (SeDenyBatchLogonRight)	Prohibits a user from logging on by using a batch-queue facility. **Default setting**: Not assigned.
Deny logon as a service (SeDenyServiceLogonRight)	Prohibits a user from logging on as a service. **Default setting**: Not assigned.
Deny logon through Terminal Services (SeDenyRemoteInteractiveLogonRight)	Prohibits a user from logging on to the computer using a Remote Desktop connection. **Default setting**: Not assigned.

Privileges

To ease the task of security administration, it is recommended that you assign privileges primarily to groups rather than to individual user accounts. When you assign privileges to a group, the privileges are assigned automatically to each user who is added to the group. This is easier than assigning privileges to individual user accounts as each account is created.

The privileges that can be assigned are listed and described in Table B-2. The display name for each privilege is followed by the corresponding string constant (in parentheses). Many command-line tools refer to privileges by string constant rather than by display name. The default settings are taken from the Windows XP Professional Local Computer policy.

Table B-2   Privileges

Privilege	Description
Act as part of the operating system (SeTcbPrivilege)	Allows a process to assume the identity of any user and thus gain access to the resources that the user is authorized to access. Typically, only low-level authentication services require this privilege. **Default setting**: Not assigned. Note that potential access is not limited to what is associated with the user by default; the calling process might request that arbitrary additional privileges be added to the access token. The calling process might also build an access token that does not provide a primary identity for tracking events in the audit log. When a service requires this privilege, configure the service to log on using the Local System account, which has the privilege inherently. Do not create a separate account and assign the privilege to it.
Add workstations to domain (SeMachineAccountPrivilege)	Allows the user to add a computer to a specific domain. For the privilege to take effect, it must be assigned to the user as part of the Default Domain Controllers Policy for the domain. A user who has this privilege can add up to 10 workstations to the domain. **Default setting:** Not assigned. Users can also join a computer to a domain if they have Create Computer Objects permission for an organizational unit or for the Computers container in Active Directory. Users who have this permission can add an unlimited number of computers to the domain regardless of whether they have been assigned the "Add workstations to a domain" privilege.
Adjust memory quotas for a process (SeIncreaseQuotaPrivilege)	Allows a process that has access to a second process to increase the processor quota assigned to the second process. This privilege is useful for system tuning, but it can be abused. In the wrong hands, it could be used to launch a denial-of-service attack. **Default setting**: Administrators, Local Service, and Network Service.

Table B-2   Privileges

Privilege	Description
Back up files and directories (SeBackupPrivilege)	Allows the user to circumvent file and directory permissions to back up the system. The privilege is selected only when an application attempts access by using the NTFS backup application programming interface (API). Otherwise, normal file and directory permissions apply. **Default setting**: Administrators and Backup Operators. See also "Restore files and directories" in this table.
Bypass traverse checking (SeChangeNotifyPrivilege)	Allows the user to pass through folders to which the user otherwise has no access while navigating an object path in the NTFS file system or in the registry. This privilege does not allow the user to list the contents of a folder; it allows the user only to traverse its directories. **Default setting**: Administrators, Backup Operators, Power Users, Users, and Everyone.
Change the system time (SeSystemTimePrivilege)	Allows the user to adjust the time on the computer's internal clock. This privilege is not required to change the time zone or other display characteristics of the system time. **Default setting**: Administrators and Power Users.
Create a token object (SeCreateTokenPrivilege)	Allows a process to create an access token by calling NtCreateToken () or other token-creating APIs. **Default setting**: Not assigned. When a process requires this privilege, use the Local System (or System) account, which has the privilege inherently. Do not create a separate user account and assign the privilege to it.
Create a pagefile (SeCreatePagefilePrivilege)	Allows the user to create and change the size of a pagefile. This is done by specifying a paging file size for a particular drive in the **Performance Options** box on the **Advanced** tab of **System Properties**. **Default setting**: Administrators.
Debug programs (SeDebugPrivilege)	Allows the user to attach a debugger to any process. This privilege provides access to sensitive and critical operating system components. **Default setting**: Administrators.

Table B-2   Privileges

Privilege	Description
Enable computer and user accounts to be trusted for delegation (SeEnableDelegationPrivilege)	Allows the user to change the **Trusted for Delegation** setting on a user or computer object in Active Directory. The user or computer that is granted this privilege must also have write access to the account control flags on the object. **Default setting**: Not assigned to anyone on member servers and workstations because it has no meaning in those contexts. Delegation of authentication is a capability that is used by multi-tier client/server applications. It allows a front-end service to use the credentials of a client in authenticating to a back-end service. For this to be possible, both client and server must be running under accounts that are trusted for delegation. Misuse of this privilege or the **Trusted for Delegation** settings can make the network vulnerable to sophisticated attacks that use Trojan horse programs, which impersonate incoming clients and use their credentials to gain access to network resources.
Force shutdown from a remote system (SeRemoteShutdownPrivilege)	Allows a user to shut down a computer from a remote location on the network. **Default setting**: Administrators. See also "Shut down the system" in this table.
Generate security audits (SeAuditPrivilege)	Allows a process to generate audit records in the security log. The security log can be used to trace unauthorized system access. **Default setting**: Local Service and Network Service. Local System (or System) has the privilege inherently. See also "Manage auditing and security log" in this table.
Increase scheduling priority (SeIncreaseBasePriorityPrivilege)	Allows a user to increase the base priority class of a process. (Increasing relative priority within a priority class is not a privileged operation.) This privilege is not required by administrative tools supplied with the operating system but might be required by software development tools. **Default setting**: Administrators.

Table B-2   Privileges

Privilege	Description
Load and unload device drivers (SeLoadDriverPrivilege)	Allows a user to install and remove drivers for Plug and Play devices. This privilege is not required if a signed driver for the new hardware already exists in the Driver.cab file on the computer.
	Default setting: Administrators.
	Do not assign this privilege to any user or group other than Administrators. Device drivers run as trusted (highly privileged) code. A user who has "Load and unload device drivers" privilege could unintentionally install malicious code masquerading as a device driver. It is assumed that administrators will exercise greater care and install only drivers with verified digital signatures.
	Note: You must have this privilege and also be a member of either Administrators or Power Users in order to install a new driver for a local printer or manage a local printer by setting defaults for options such as duplex printing. The requirement to have both the privilege and membership in Administrators or Power Users is new to Windows XP Professional.
Lock pages in memory (SeLockMemoryPrivilege)	Allows a process to keep data in physical memory, which prevents the system from paging the data to virtual memory on disk. Assigning this privilege can result in significant degradation of system performance.
	Default setting: Not assigned. Local System (or System) has the privilege inherently.
Manage auditing and security log (SeSecurityPrivilege)	Allows a user to specify object access auditing options for individual resources such as files, Active Directory objects, and registry keys. Object access auditing is not performed unless you enable it by using **Audit Policy** (under **Security Settings**, **Local Policies**). A user who has this privilege can also view and clear the security log from Event Viewer.
	Default setting: Administrators.
Modify firmware environment values (SeSystemEnvironmentPrivilege)	Allows modification of system environment variables either by a process through an API or by a user through **System Properties**.
	Default setting: Administrators.

Table B-2   Privileges

Privilege	Description
Perform volume maintenance tasks (SeManageVolumePrivilege)	Allows a non-administrative or remote user to manage volumes or disks. The operating system checks for the privilege in a user's access token when a process running in the user's security context calls SetFileValidData(). **Default setting**: Administrators.
Profile single process (SeProfileSingleProcessPrivilege)	Allows a user to sample the performance of an application process. **Default setting**: Administrators and Power Users. Ordinarily, you do not need this privilege to use the Performance snap-in. However, you do need the privilege if System Monitor is configured to collect data by using Windows Management Instrumentation (WMI).
Profile system performance (SeSystemProfilePrivilege)	Allows a user to sample the performance of system processes. This privilege is required by the Performance snap-in only if it is configured to collect data by using Windows Management Instrumentation (WMI). **Default setting**: Administrators. Ordinarily, you do not need this privilege to use the Performance snap-in. However, you do need the privilege if System Monitor is configured to collect data by using Windows Management Instrumentation (WMI).
Remove computer from docking station (SeUndockPrivilege)	Allows the user of a portable computer to undock the computer by clicking **Eject PC** on the **Start** menu. **Default setting**: Administrators, Power Users, and Users.
Replace a process-level token (SeAssignPrimaryTokenPrivilege)	Allows a parent process to replace the access token that is associated with a child process. **Default setting**: Local Service and Network Service. Local System has the privilege inherently.
Restore files and directories (SeRestorePrivilege)	Allows a user to circumvent file and directory permissions when restoring backed-up files and directories and to set any valid security principal as the owner of an object. **Default setting**: Administrators and Backup Operators. See also "Back up files and directories" in this table.

Table B-2   Privileges

Privilege	Description
Shut down the system (SeShutdownPrivilege)	Allows a user to shut down the local computer. **Default setting**: Administrators, Backup Operators, Power Users, and Users. See also "Force shutdown from a remote system" in this table.
Synchronize directory service data (SeSynchAgentPrivilege)	Allows a process to read all objects and properties in the directory, regardless of the protection on the objects and properties. This privilege is required in order to use Lightweight Directory Access Protocol (LDAP) directory synchronization (Dirsync) services. **Default setting**: Not assigned. The privilege is relevant only on domain controllers.
Take ownership of files or other objects (SeTakeOwnershipPrivilege)	Allows a user to take ownership of any securable object in the system, including Active Directory objects, NTFS files and folders, printers, registry keys, services, processes, and threads. **Default setting**: Administrators.

Appendix C

Common Stop Messages for Troubleshooting

When Microsoft® Windows® XP Professional detects a problem from which it cannot recover, it displays a Stop message, which is a text-mode error message that reports information about the condition. Stop messages, sometimes referred to as blue screens, contain specific information that can help you diagnose and possibly resolve the problem detected by the Windows kernel. This appendix describes these Stop messages and helps you understand and interpret them.

Related Information

- For more information about troubleshooting concepts, see "Troubleshooting Concepts and Strategies" in this book.

- For more information about troubleshooting startup problems, see "Troubleshooting Startup" in this book.

- For more information about enabling, disabling, and managing devices, see "Managing Devices" in this book.

Stop Message Overview

Stop messages described in this appendix report information that covers a wide variety of issues. Diagnosing a problem that caused a Stop message to appear, known as a *Stop error*, requires advanced knowledge of Windows XP Professional. Consider the following options when attempting to diagnose or troubleshoot Stop errors or interpreting information in a Stop message:

- See the description and troubleshooting information for your Stop message in this appendix.

- See the Microsoft Knowledge Base for related information. Before searching technical information sources, record as much information about the problem as possible. For guidelines about information to record when diagnosing or troubleshooting problems, see "Troubleshooting Concepts and Strategies" in this book. For information about the Microsoft Knowledge Base, see the Microsoft Knowledge Base link on the Web Resources page at http://www.microsoft.com/windows/reskits/webresources.

- Obtain and install the Debugging Tools Help file that is available from the Microsoft Debugging Tools Web site for a list of Stop messages not covered in this appendix. The Debugging Tools Help file is part of the Microsoft Debugging Tools installation.

To install Debugging Tools, Debugging Tools Help, and view more information about Stop messages

1. Click the Debugging Tools link on the Web Resources page at http://www.microsoft.com/windows/reskits/webresources. This link takes you to the Microsoft Debugging Tools Web site.

2. Click **Debugging Tools for Windows**.
   Follow the steps listed on the **Installing Debugging Tools for Windows** page to install debugging tools.

3. Follow the on-screen setup instructions and when prompted, type a destination folder name.
   The Setup program copies files and creates a **Start** menu folder named **Microsoft Debugging Tools**.

4. From the **Start** menu, point to **All Programs**, point to **Microsoft Debugging Tools**, and then click **Debugging Help** to view the **Using Microsoft Debuggers** Help file.

5. Expand **Using Microsoft Debuggers** and then expand **Reference**. Expand **Bugcheck Codes** to see a list of dozens of Stop messages, also known as bugcheck codes.

You can also download and install Microsoft Debugging Tools by following the instructions in "Using Symbol Files and Debuggers" later in this appendix.

> **Note**   The **Using Microsoft Debuggers** Help file contains extensive information about debugging techniques. It includes debugging examples that show you how to use debuggers to obtain more information about a Stop message. The Help file also documents Stop messages not covered in this appendix.

- Obtain assistance from trained Microsoft support personnel. You might need to furnish specific information and perform certain procedures to provide technical support with the information needed to investigate your problem. For more information about Microsoft Product Support Services, see the Microsoft Product Support Services link on the Web Resources page at http://www.microsoft.com /windows/reskits/webresources. For more information about Microsoft technical support options, see the Support link on the Microsoft Web page at http://www.microsoft.com.

A basic understanding of Stop messages and the underlying causes improves your ability to locate and understand technical information or perform diagnostic procedures requested of you by technical support.

Defining Terms

Throughout this appendix, several important terms are used and it is necessary to define these terms to understand the content in this appendix.

Call Stack.   A stack is fundamental data structure that holds volatile data. The call stack is a type of stack used to track function calls and the parameters passed to these function calls. In debugging terminology, the call stack is sometimes referred to simply as the *stack*.

Exception.   An error condition caused by an illegal instruction. Exceptions can be hardware-related or software-related errors.

Hardware abstraction layer (HAL).   A kernel-mode component that contains hardware-specific code that handles low-level hardware operations such as input/output (I/O) interfaces, interrupt controllers, and multiprocessor communication mechanisms. The HAL abstracts, or hides, hardware-dependent details from the rest of the operating system.

Input/output (I/O) request packet.   A data structure used to represent an input/output request and control its process. The I/O request packet structure consists of a header and one or more stack locations.

Interrupt.   A condition that disrupts normal command implementation and transfers control to an interrupt handler. I/O devices (such as disks and network devices) requiring service from the processor typically initiate interrupts.

Interrupt request level (IRQL).   An internal priority level table used by the kernel to manage interrupt sources, such as hardware or software. Software interrupts are assigned the lowest priorities with hardware interrupt levels assigned higher priorities by the hardware abstraction table (HAL). Only kernel mode threads can change IRQLs.

Interrupt service routine (ISR).   Code that the kernel executes when an interrupt occurs. For example, device drivers provide ISRs for interrupting devices.

Kernel.   The kernel provides low-level operating system functions for managing processor activities such as thread scheduling and dispatching, interrupt and exception handling, and multiprocessor synchronization.

Kernel mode.   The processor access mode in which operating system components and drivers run. Kernel-mode processes can directly access system data and hardware, and are not restricted like user-mode processes. Performance-sensitive drivers and services run in kernel mode to interact with hardware more efficiently. All kernel-mode components are fully protected from applications running in user mode.

Nonpaged pool.   The portion of shared system memory that cannot be paged to the disk paging file. Nonpaged pool memory can be accessed at any time without causing a page fault.

Page fault.   A page fault occurs when a thread accesses a page that is not in memory. For more information about paging and other memory management topics, see "Evaluating Memory and Cache Usage" in the *Operations Guide* of the *Microsoft® Windows® 2000 Server Resource Kit*.

Page table.   A process-specific table that maps paging file virtual memory addresses to physical memory addresses.

Page table entry (PTE).   An item in the page table.

Paged pool.   The portion of shared system memory that can be paged to the disk paging file, *systemdrive*\Pagefile.sys. This includes memory already paged to the disk and memory that the operating system might page, but has not actually done so.

Paging.   A virtual memory operation in which the memory manager transfers pages from memory to the disk *systemdrive*\pagefile.sys file when physical memory becomes full. A page fault occurs when a thread accesses a page that is not in memory. For more information about paging and other memory management topics, see "Evaluating Memory and Cache Usage" in the *Operations Guide* of the *Microsoft® Windows® 2000 Server Resource Kit*.

Process.   A process is an instance of an application, together with the set of resources allocated to run the application.

Stack.   A data structure consisting of a series of memory locations and a pointer to the initial location (also referred to as *top of the stack*). All processors provide instructions for placing and retrieving values to and from the stack. The stack used most often in debugging is the *call stack*.

Thread.   A thread is an object within a process that contains central processing unit (CPU) state information, user, and kernel-mode stacks. Threads are allocated processor time by the operating system to run code. Threads, not processes, run program code. Every process must have at least one thread and a thread can belong to only one process. A thread allows a process to maintain parallel lines of operation.

User mode.   The processor access mode in which applications run. Applications and subsystems run on the computer in user mode. Processes that run in user mode do so within their own virtual address spaces. They are restricted from gaining direct access to many parts of the system, including system hardware, memory not allocated for user mode, and other portions of the system that might compromise system integrity. Processes that run in user mode are effectively isolated from kernel-mode processes and other user-mode processes.

Stop Message Screen Sections

Stop messages use a full-screen character mode format, as shown in Figure C-1. Each message is uniquely associated with alphanumeric characters followed by the error's symbolic name. The Stop error number is the first parameter listed, followed by up to four hexadecimal numbers (shown in parentheses), which identify related error parameters.

Figure C-1   Stop message

As shown in Figure C-1, a Stop message screen has four major sections, which display the following information:

- Bugcheck information

- Recommended user action

- Driver information

- Debug port and dump status information

Bugcheck Information

This **Bugcheck information** section includes the Stop error number, also known as the bugcheck code, followed by up to four developer-defined parameters (enclosed in parentheses) and the symbolic name of the error. Stop error codes contain a "0x" prefix, which indicates hexadecimal numerical format. For example, in Figure C-1, the Stop error hexadecimal code is 0x000000D1 and its symbolic name is DRIVER_IRQL_NOT_LESS_OR_EQUAL.

As shown in Figure C-1, the **Bugcheck information** section frequently includes a line that lists the specific hexadecimal memory address of the Stop error's source, along with the name of the driver or device.

Note   Under certain conditions, the kernel cannot fully display all of the Stop message content; only the first line is visible. This occurs if the problem has caused video display services to stop functioning.

Recommended User Action

The **Recommended user action** section provides a list of suggestions for recovery. In some cases, restarting the computer might be sufficient because the problem is not likely to recur. But if the Stop error persists even after you restart the system, you must determine the root cause to return the system to an operable state. This might involve undoing recent changes, replacing hardware, or updating drivers to eliminate the cause of the problem.

Driver Information

The **Driver information** section identifies the driver associated with the Stop error. If a file is specified by name, you can use Recovery Console or safe mode to verify that the driver is signed or has a date stamp that coincides with other drivers. If necessary, you can replace the file manually, or use Driver Rollback. For more information about Recovery Console and Driver Rollback, see "Tools for Troubleshooting" in this book.

Debug Port and Status Information

The **Debug port and status information** section lists COM port parameters that a kernel debugger uses if enabled. If you have enabled memory dump file saves, this section also indicates whether one was successfully written.

Enabling kernel debugging requires that you:

- Set the Boot.ini file parameters **/crashdebug** and **/debug** (you can also set the optional **/debugport** parameter).

- Restart the computer. When prompted at startup, press F8 to activate the **Advanced Options Menu**, and then select **Debugging Mode**.

For more information about debugging related Boot.ini parameters, see Debugging Tools Help.

Types of Stop Messages

A hardware or software problem can cause a Stop error, which causes a Stop message to appear. Stop messages typically fit into one of the following categories:

- Stop messages caused by faulty software

   This problem occurs as an unplanned event when the central processing unit (CPU) encounters invalid instructions specified by a faulty device driver or other software.

- Installation Stop messages that occur during Windows XP Professional setup

   For new installations, installation Stop messages typically occur because of incompatible hardware, defective hardware, or outdated firmware. During an operating system upgrade, Stop errors can occur when incompatible applications and drivers exist on the system.

- Stop messages caused by hardware issues

    This problem occurs as unplanned event due to defective, malfunctioning, or incorrectly configured hardware.

- Executive initialization Stop messages

    Executive initialization Stop messages appear only during the relatively short Windows executive initialization sequence, before the Logon to Windows dialog box appears.

To find out more information about a Stop message, follow the instructions provided in "Stop Message Overview" earlier in this appendix.

Stop Messages Caused by Faulty Software

A Stop error can occur when a driver, service, application, or system component introduces an exception. For example, an application or driver attempts to perform an operation above its assigned IRQL or tries to write to an invalid memory address. A Stop message might seem to appear randomly, but through careful observations, you might be able to associate the problem with a specific activity. Verify that all installed software in question is fully Windows XP Professional compatible and if not, locate and install the latest updates.

Windows XP Professional compatibility is especially important for applications that might install *file system filter drivers*, such as antivirus, Internet firewall, multimedia, CD mastering, and backup software. File system filter drivers can perform value-added processing to enhance and extend file system functionality, but installing an incompatible file system filter driver might cause Stop errors.

Installation Stop Messages

For a new (non-upgrade) operating system installation, using outdated firmware might cause a Stop message. Update the computer's firmware to the version recommended by the computer manufacturer before installing Windows XP Professional. Consult your system documentation for information about checking and upgrading your computer's firmware.

> **Note** Types of firmware include BIOS for x86-based computers and Extensible Firmware Interface (EFI) for Itanium-based systems. Verify that your system firmware is updated before installing Windows XP Professional, especially for computers using Advanced Configuration and Power Interface (ACPI) firmware. For more information about checking and updating firmware, see "Troubleshooting Concepts and Strategies" in this book.

If you are upgrading to Windows XP Professional from a previous version of Windows, such as Microsoft® Windows® 2000 Professional, Microsoft®

Windows NT 4.0 Workstation, Microsoft® Windows 95, Microsoft® Windows 98, or Microsoft® Windows Millennium Edition, you can identify applications and drivers that might cause Stop errors.

To check system compatibility with Windows XP Professional

Do one of the following:

■ Insert the Windows XP Professional operating system CD into the computer and wait for the **Welcome to Microsoft Windows XP** screen to appear. Click **Check system compatibility**.

-or-

■ Type *drive:***i386\winnt32 /checkupgradeonly** from the command prompt (where *drive:* represents the network or CD-ROM path to the Windows XP Professional installation files).

You can then uninstall the applications and drivers identified, complete the Windows XP Professional setup, and search for updates after you have completed the operating system upgrade.

For more information about upgrading to, or deploying Windows XP Professional, see "Planning Deployments" in this book.

Stop Messages Caused by Hardware Issues

Incorrectly configured or failing hardware can cause a Stop message to appear. For example, a video adapter with defective memory might cause the operating system to display a Stop message when writing to, or reading from, video RAM. A Stop message might also appear after adding a new device, if the device causes resource conflicts with existing hardware.

If the Stop message mentions a specific device, try replacing the device. If more than one device is a possible cause, you can try to isolate the problem hardware by temporarily simplifying your system configuration, removing hardware not required to start the computer or to complete installation. Leave the following essential devices installed:

■ Hard disks and disk controllers

■ Video adapters

■ Pointing devices

Temporarily remove, disconnect, or disable these devices:

■ Audio devices

■ Universal Serial Bus (USB) devices

■ Institute of Electrical and Electronics Engineers (IEEE) 1394 devices (also known as "Firewire")

- Modems and printers

- External small computer system interface (SCSI) devices not used to start the system

For most motherboards, you can disable integrated components by adjusting firmware or onboard jumper settings. Refer to your computer documentation for details about disabling built-in devices.

Completing Installation and Resolving Startup Problems   Continue to remove devices until you can successfully install or start Windows XP Professional. Re-enable or install devices one at a time, according to the manufacturer's instructions. For more information about resolving startup problems, see "Stop Message Checklist" later in this appendix and "Troubleshooting Startup" in this book.

Checking the Hardware Compatibility List   If you still cannot resolve your problem, verify that your computer system and hardware are compatible with Windows XP Professional by checking the latest revision of the Windows XP Professional Hardware Compatibility List (HCL) before contacting technical support. Microsoft includes computers and peripheral hardware on the HCL after performing rigorous component and compatibility testing that verifies that they work well with Windows XP Professional. If your computer or device is not in the HCL, contact the hardware manufacturer for more information. The manufacturer might be in the process of certifying the hardware or testing new drivers.

For more information about the HCL, see the Hardware Compatibility List link on the Web Resources page at http://www.microsoft.com/windows/reskits/webresources.

Executive Initialization Stop Messages

Executive initialization Stop errors occur only during initialization of the Windows executive, a group of components that provides basic operating system services. Windows executive services comprise the low-level kernel mode portion of Windows XP Professional and are contained in the Ntoskrnl.exe file.

After the Windows loader (Ntldr) calls the kernel (Ntoskrnl.exe), executive initialization occurs in two phases:

- **Phase 0**. During Phase 0, interrupts are disabled and only a few executive components, such as the hardware abstraction layer (HAL), are initialized.

- **Phase 1**. During Phase 1, interrupts are enabled and the remaining Windows executive components, including device drivers, are initialized. In addition, the remaining CPUs in multiprocessor systems are initialized.

Phase 0 Initialization Stop Messages   A Stop message during Phase 0 initialization might indicate a problem with outdated firmware or faulty hardware. If you receive one of the Phase 0 initialization Stop messages listed in Table C-1, run the hardware diagnostics program included with your devices or replace them with new parts. Also, verify that your motherboard and peripheral firmware revisions are current and try the suggestions provided in "Stop Message Checklist" later in this appendix. For more information about the startup process and recovering from hardware problems, see "Troubleshooting Startup" and "Managing Devices" in this book. For more information about checking firmware, see "Troubleshooting Concepts and Strategies" in this book.

If you cannot isolate any hardware problems, try running the Windows XP Professional setup again. If the same error message appears, contact a Microsoft support technician.

Table C-1   Phase 0 Initialization Stop Messages

Message ID	Symbolic Name
0x31	PHASE0_INITIALIZATION_FAILED
0x5C	HAL_INITIALIZATION_FAILED
0x5D	HEAP_INITIALIZATION_FAILED
0x5E	OBJECT_INITIALIZATION_FAILED
0x5F	SECURITY_INITIALIZATION_FAILED
0x60	PROCESS_INITIALIZATION_FAILED

Phase 1 Initialization Stop Messages   A Stop message during Phase 1 initialization might indicate a problem with outdated firmware, corrupted system files, or an incompatible HAL type. If you receive any of the Phase 1 initialization Stop messages listed in the Table C-2, reinstall Windows XP Professional and try to initialize it again. Verify that your motherboard and peripheral firmware revisions are current and try the suggestions provided in "Stop Message Checklist" later in this appendix. For more information about the startup process and recovering from hardware problems, see "Troubleshooting Startup" and "Managing Devices" in this book. For more information about checking firmware, see "Troubleshooting Concepts and Strategies" in this book. If you get the same message, contact a Microsoft support technician.

Table C-2   Phase 1 Initialization Stop Messages

Message ID	Symbolic Name
0x32	PHASE1_INITIALIZATION_FAILED
0x61	HAL1_INITIALIZATION_FAILED
0x62	OBJECT1_INITIALIZATION_FAILED
0x63	SECURITY1_INITIALIZATION_FAILED
0x64	SYMBOLIC_INITIALIZATION_FAILED
0x65	MEMORY1_INITIALIZATION_FAILED

Table C-2 Phase 1 Initialization Stop Messages

Message ID	Symbolic Name
0x66	CACHE_INITIALIZATION_FAILED
0x67	CONFIG_INITIALIZATION_FAILED
0x68	FILE_INITIALIZATION_FAILED
0x69	IO1_INITIALIZATION_FAILED
0x6A	LPC_INITIALIZATION_FAILED
0x6B	PROCESS1_INITIALIZATION_FAILED
0x6C	REFMON_INITIALIZATION_FAILED
0x6D	SESSION1_INITIALIZATION_FAILED
0x6E	SESSION2_INITIALIZATION_FAILED
0x6F	SESSION3_INITIALIZATION_FAILED
0x70	SESSION4_INITIALIZATION_FAILED
0x71	SESSION5_INITIALIZATION_FAILED

Memory Dump Files

When a Stop error occurs, Windows XP Professional writes information to the paging file (Pagefile.sys) on the *systemdrive* root by default. When you restart the computer in normal or safe mode after a Stop error occurs, Windows XP Professional uses paging file information to create a memory dump file in the *systemroot* folder. Analyzing the dump file can help provide more information about the root cause of a problem and enables offline analysis by using tools run on another computer. You can configure your system to generate one of three different types of dump files.

Small memory dump   Small memory dump files contain the least information, but consume the least disk space, 64 kilobytes (KB). Small memory dump files are sometimes referred to as "mini" dump files. Unlike kernel and complete memory dump files; Windows XP Professional stores small memory dump files in the *systemroot*\Minidump folder, instead of using the *systemroot*\Memory.dmp file name.

Windows XP Professional always create a small memory dump file when a Stop error occurs, even when you choose the kernel or complete memory dump file options. One of the services that use small memory dump files is the Error Reporting service. The Error Reporting service reads the contents of a small memory dump file to help diagnose problems that cause Stop errors. For more information about the Error Reporting service, see "Using Memory Dump Files to Analyze Stop Errors" later in this appendix.

Kernel memory dump   This is an intermediate size dump file that records only kernel-level memory and can occupy several megabytes (MB) of disk space. When a Stop error occurs, Windows XP Professional saves a kernel memory dump file to a file named *systemroot*\Memory.dmp and create a small memory dump file in the *systemroot*\Minidump folder. You cannot exactly predict the size of a kernel memory dump file because this depends on the amount of kernel-mode memory allocated by the operating system and drivers present on the machine when the Stop error occurred.

Complete memory dump   A complete memory dump file contains the entire contents of physical memory when the Stop error occurred. The file size is equal to the amount of physical memory installed plus 1 MB. When a Stop error occurs, the operating system saves a complete memory dump file to a file named *systemroot*\Memory.dmp and creates a small memory dump file in the *systemroot*\Minidump folder.

To help ensure that your system can save memory dump files:

- Verify that adequate free space exists on *systemdrive* to accommodate the maximum paging file size for the selected dump file. For example, for complete memory dump files, the available space must be at least equal to the amount of physical memory present plus 1 MB.

To view the maximum paging file size for each disk volume

1. In **Control Panel**, click **Performance and Maintenance**, and then click **System**.

2. Select the **Advanced** tab, and then in the **Performance** box, click **Settings**.

3. In the **Performance Options** dialog box, select the **Advanced** tab.

4. In **Virtual memory**, click **Change** to view the **Virtual Memory** dialog box that contains paging file information.

    In **Total paging file size for all drives**, the **Currently allocated** value indicates the paging file disk space used. If you choose to enable the **Custom size** option, you can specify different paging file sizes by entering values for **Initial size (MB)** and **Maximum size (MB)**. Verify that adequate disk space is available on *systemdrive* to accommodate the maximum paging file specified.

    - Verify that the memory dump file path (by default, *systemroot*\ Memory.dmp) contains sufficient free space to store the memory dump file. For more information about specifying the disk dump file location, see the discussions on small, kernel, and complete memory dump files that follow.

    - Verify that the *systemdrive* or the volume containing the memory dump file is not corrupted. To test hard disk or volume integrity, follow the instructions provided in "Stop 0x00000024 or NTFS_FILE_SYSTEM" later in this appendix.

Infrequently, device driver problems might cause failure to save memory dump files. To minimize the potential for problems, use storage devices and controllers listed in the HCL and device drivers digitally signed by Microsoft.

Small Memory Dump File

A small memory dump file records the smallest set of useful information that might identify the cause of the system stopping unexpectedly. A small memory dump file includes the following:

- **Stop error information**. Includes the error number and additional parameters that describe the Stop error.

- **A list of drivers running on the system**. Identifies the modules in memory when the Stop error occurred. Device driver information sent includes the file name, date, version, size, and manufacturer.

- **Processor context information for the process that stopped**. Includes the processor and hardware state, performance counters, multiprocessor packet information, deferred procedure call information, and interrupts.

- **Kernel context information for the process that stopped**. Includes offset of the directory table and the page frame number database (which describes the state of every physical page in memory).

- **Kernel context information for the thread that stopped**. Identifies registers and interrupt request levels, and includes pointers to operating system data structures.

- **Kernel-mode call stack information for the thread that stopped**. Consists of a series of memory locations and includes a pointer to the initial location. If this information is greater than 16 KB, only the top most 16 KB is included.

A small memory dump file requires a paging file of at least 2 MB on the boot volume and specifies that the operating system save each dump file using a unique file name every time a Stop error occurs. Each minidump file has a unique file name, which includes the date encoded in the file name. For example, Mini062701-01.dmp is the first small memory dump generated on June 27, 2001.

Small memory dump files are useful when space is limited or when you are using a slow connection to send information to technical support. Because of the limited amount of information that can be included, errors not directly caused by the thread that was running when the problem occurred are not included.

To configure Windows XP Professional to generate a small memory dump file

1. In **Control Panel**, click **Performance and Maintenance**, and then click **System**.

2. Select the **Advanced** tab, and in **Startup and Recovery**, click **Settings**.

3. In the **Write Debugging Information** list, select **Small Memory Dump (64 KB)**.

4. Click **OK** to close the **Startup and Recovery** dialog box.

5. Click **OK** to close the **System Properties** dialog box, and then restart if prompted.

By default, Windows XP Professional saves small memory dump files to the *systemroot*\Minidump folder. You can change the folder location by typing a new path in the **Dump File** box of the **Write Debugging Information** list.

Kernel Memory Dump File

A kernel memory dump file records only kernel memory information, which expedites the dump file creation process. Although you cannot exactly predict the size of a kernel memory dump file, a good rule of thumb is that roughly 50 MB to 800 MB, or one-third the size of physical memory, must be available on the boot volume for the paging file.

The kernel memory dump file does not include unallocated memory or any memory allocated to user-mode programs. It includes only memory allocated to the kernel and HAL, as well as memory allocated to kernel-mode drivers and other kernel-mode programs. For most purposes, a kernel memory dump file is the most useful kind of file for troubleshooting Stop messages. It contains more information than the small memory dump file and is significantly smaller than the complete memory dump file. It omits only those portions of memory that are unlikely to have been involved in the problem.

To configure Windows XP Professional to generate a kernel memory dump file

1. In **Control Panel**, click **Performance and Maintenance**, and then click **System**.

2. Select the **Advanced** tab, and then in **Startup and Recovery**, click **Settings**.

3. In the **Write Debugging Information** list, select **Kernel Memory Dump**.

4. Click **OK** to close **the Startup and Recovery** dialog box.

5. Click **OK** to close the **System Properties** dialog box, and then restart if prompted.

By default, Windows XP Professional saves a kernel memory dump file to *systemroot*\Memory.dmp. You can change the default output location by typing a new path in the **Dump File** box of the **Write Debugging Information** list.

> **Note**   By default, a new kernel memory dump file overwrites an existing one. To change this, you need to clear the **Overwrite any existing file** check box. You can also choose to archive or move a dump file prior to trouble-shooting.

Complete Memory Dump File

A complete memory dump records the contents of physical memory. If you choose to use complete memory dump files, you must have available space on the *system-drive* partition large enough to hold the contents of physical RAM, plus 1 MB. By default, Windows XP Professional systems create complete memory dump files. A Microsoft technical support engineer might ask you to change this setting to facilitate data uploads over slow connections. Depending upon the speed of your Internet connection, uploading the data might not be practical and you might be requested to provide the memory dump file on higher capacity removable media.

To configure Windows XP Professional to generate a complete memory dump file

1. In Control Panel, click **Performance and Maintenance**, and then click **System**.

2. Select the **Advanced** tab, and then in **Startup and Recovery**, click **Settings**.

3. In the **Write Debugging Information** list, select **Complete Memory Dump**.

4. Click **OK** to close **the Startup and Recovery** dialog box. Click **OK** to close the **System Properties** dialog box, and then restart if prompted.

By default, Windows XP Professional saves a complete memory dump file to *systemroot*\Memory.dmp. You can change the default location by typing in a new path in the **Dump File** box of the **Write Debugging Information** list.

> **Note**   By default, new complete memory dump files overwrite existing files. To change this, you need to clear the **Overwrite any existing file** check box. You can also choose to archive or move a dump file prior to troubleshooting.

For more information about memory dump files, see Windows XP Professional Help and Support Center. Also see Microsoft Knowledge Base articles Q254649, "Windows 2000 Memory Dump Options Overview," Q254723, "Reading Small Memory Dump Files Created by Windows 2000," and Q228524, "New Crash Dump Options in Windows 2000 Reduce Memory.dmp Size." To find these articles, see the Microsoft Knowledge Base link on the Web Resources page at http://www.microsoft.com /windows/reskits/webresources.

Using Memory Dump Files to Analyze Stop Errors

Memory dump files record detailed information about the state of your system when the Stop error occurred. You can analyze memory dump files manually by using debugging tools or by using automated processes provided by Microsoft. The information obtained can help you understand more about the root cause of the problem.

You can use the following resources to upload your memory dump file information to Microsoft:

- Error Reporting service
- Online Crash Analysis Web site

You can also use the following debugging tools to manually analyze your memory dump files.

- Microsoft Kernel Debugger (Kd.exe)
- Microsoft WinDbg Debugger (Windbg.exe)

Using Error Reporting

When enabled, the Error Reporting service monitors your system for kernel and user mode faults related to operating system components and applications. Using kernel-mode reporting enables you to obtain more information about the problem or condition that caused the Stop error.

Kernel Mode Reporting

When a Stop error occurs, Windows XP Professional displays a Stop message and writes diagnostic information to the memory dump file type specified in the Control Panel **Advanced** tab (as described in "Memory Dump Files" earlier in this appendix). For reporting purposes, the operating system also saves a small memory dump file. When you restart your system by using normal mode or safe mode (with networking) and logon to Windows XP Professional, the Error Reporting service gathers information about the problem and provides you with the option to send a report.

Displays an alert   A dialog box appears stating that Windows XP Professional detected a problem. You can click **Send Error Report** or **Don't Send**; or **click here** to view technical information about the problem before sending a report to Microsoft.

Provides the option to sends a problem report to Microsoft   If you click **Send Error Report**, the Error Reporting service anonymously sends the report, which includes the small memory dump file that was just generated, to Microsoft by using a Secure Socket Layer (SSL) encryption secured Internet connection. You might be prompted to provide additional information to complete your error report.

The Error Reporting service displays a dialog box when it has finished sending the report. A **More Information** button in the dialog box directs you to more information about the problem. When you click the **Close** button, you are directed to the Online Crash Analysis Web site, which provides options for tracking your report. For more information about this Web site, see "Using the Online Crash Analysis Web Site" later in this appendix.

To verify that Error Reporting is enabled for Stop messages

1. In **Control Panel**, click **Performance and Maintenance**, and then click **System**.

2. Select the **Advanced** tab, and then click **Error Reporting** to display the dialog box shown in Figure C-2.

3. Select **Enable error reporting**.

4. If not checked, click to select the **Windows Operating System** check box.

Figure C-2   Error reporting options

The operating system always writes a supplemental small memory dump file when a Stop error occurs. Therefore, the Error Reporting service can send a problem report with small memory dump file information, even if you have configured your system to generate kernel or complete memory dump files.

For more information about additional reporting options provided by the Error Reporting service, such as using the **Programs** check box to add or exclude individual applications for monitoring, see Windows XP Professional Help and Support Center and "Tools for Troubleshooting" in this book.

Using the Online Crash Analysis Web Site

The Online Crash Analysis (OCA) Web site enables you to send error reports to Microsoft and track the status by using your Microsoft Passport information. You can access the Online Crash Analysis Web site by using the Error Reporting service or by using your Web browser. For more information about the Error Reporting service, see "Using Error Reporting" earlier in this appendix.

To visit the Online Crash Analysis Web site

1. Click the Online Crash Analysis Web site link on the Web Resources page at http://www.microsoft.com/windows/reskits/webresources. If using Error Reporting, the Error Reporting service client automatically directs you to the OCA Web site when you log on to Windows XP Professional in normal mode or safe mode with networking.

2. Click **Submit an event report** and follow the on-screen instructions for logging on and sending a report. At the **Contact Information** page, you have two options.

    Send an acknowledged upload You have the option of providing your name, e-mail, and telephone number. You are informed of status and future developments about your problem by e-mail. Information sent to you might include news about updated drivers, patches, or Microsoft Knowledge Base articles with troubleshooting and support information. You can also choose to visit the OCA Web site again to check status and view information about your report.

    Send information to Microsoft anonymously If you choose not to provide your e-mail address, you do not receive e-mail updates from Microsoft. Your information is still processed and added to the error report database. To view status and information about your problem, you need to log on to the OCA Web site by using your Microsoft Passport information.

3. At the **Event Reports** screen, specify the path and file name to your small memory dump file by clicking **Browse**.

    You can leave a name, e-mail, and telephone number on the **Contact Information** page to submit an acknowledged upload or you can choose not to provide this information and submit your report anonymously.

    If you choose to send an acknowledged or anonymous report, information is sent to Microsoft over the Internet by using Secure Sockets Layer (SSL) encryption.

Note Microsoft® Windows® 2000 Premier support customers are directed to a page that provides the option to submit a Windows 2000 or Windows XP Professional problem report.

Information sent to Microsoft includes the following:

- **System information**. Includes the operating system version and language.

- **Hardware data**. Includes the number of processors installed and the amount of random access memory (RAM) available.

- **Date and time information**. Indicates when the Stop error event occurred.

- **Stop error information**. Includes the error number and additional parameters that describe the Stop error.

- **A list of drivers running on the system**. Identifies the modules in memory when the Stop error occurred. Device driver information sent includes the file name, date, version, size, and manufacturer.

- **Processor context information for the process that stopped**. Includes the processor and hardware state, performance counters, multiprocessor packet information, deferred procedure call information, and interrupts.

- **Kernel context information for the process that stopped**. Includes offset of the directory table and the page frame number database (which describes the state of every physical page in memory).

- **Kernel context information for the thread that stopped**. Identifies registers and interrupt request levels, and includes pointers to operating system data structures.

- **Kernel-mode call stack information for the thread that stopped**. Consists of a series of memory locations and includes a pointer to the initial location.

Access to the OCA Web site is free of charge to all Windows XP Professional and Windows 2000 Premier support customers.

If you need an immediate response and analysis of your dump file is not yet complete, you can search the Microsoft Knowledge Base or submit a request to the Microsoft Product Support Services Web site. For more information about Microsoft Product Support Services, see the Microsoft Product Support Services link on the Web Resources page at http://www.microsoft.com/windows/reskits/webresources.

Using Symbol Files and Debuggers

You can also analyze memory dump files by using a kernel debugger. Before using a debugger however, install symbol files to reduce debugging complexity. Symbol files enable you to view memory addresses as module and function names.

You can download symbol files directly from Microsoft.

To obtain symbol files from the Windows Downloads Web site

1. Click the **Windows Downloads** link on the Web Resources page at http://www.microsoft.com/windows/reskits/webresources.

2. Click **Tools and Utilities** and then **Windows Customer Support Diagnostics**.

3. Follow the on-screen instructions to install debugging tools, symbol files, or both.

For more information about symbol files, see Debugging Tools Help.

For information about other debugging options, see article Q121652, "List of Debuggers Supported with Windows NT," in the Microsoft Knowledge Base and Debugging Tools Help. To find this article, see the Microsoft Knowledge Base link on the Web Resources page at http://www.microsoft.com/windows/reskits/webresources.

Note   Because of the limited information contained in small memory and kernel memory dump files; you might need to perform other operations, such as setting kernel environment variables, in addition to installing symbol files. For more information about verifying small and kernel memory dump files, see Debugging Tools Help. Also, see article Q254723, "Reading Small Memory Dump Files Created by Windows 2000," in the Microsoft Knowledge Base. To find this article, see the Microsoft Knowledge Base link on the Web Resources page at http://www.microsoft.com/windows/reskits/webresources.

Using Kernel Debugger (Kd.exe)   The Microsoft Kernel Debugger (Kd.exe) is a command-line debugging tool that you can use to analyze memory dump files, debug kernel-mode programs and drivers, or monitor the behavior of the operating system itself. Kd.exe also supports multiprocessor debugging. For more information about using the Microsoft Kernel Debugger, see Debugging Tools Help.

Using WinDbg Debugger (Windbg.exe)   The WinDbg Debugger (Windbg.exe) is a graphical user interface (GUI) mode debugging tool that you can use to analyze the contents of a memory dump file and debug kernel-mode and user-mode programs and drivers. For more information about using the WinDbg debugger, see Debugging Tools Help.

Kernel Debugger and WinDbg Debugger are just a few of the many tools provided. For more information about other kernel debugging tools, such as CDB and NTSD, see Debugging Tools Help.

Stop Message System Event Log Reporting

As an additional troubleshooting option, you can configure your system to write an entry in the system Event Log when a Stop message occurs.

To enable Stop message Event Log reporting

1. In **Control Panel**, click **Performance and Maintenance**, and then click **System**.

2. Click the **Advanced** tab, and then in the **Startup and Recovery** box, click **Settings**.

3. In **System Failure**, verify that the **Write an event to the system log** check box is selected.

For details about interpreting the contents of the resulting log, see the Microsoft Knowledge Base article Q192463, "Gathering Blue Screen Information After Memory Dump." To find this article, see the Microsoft Knowledge Base link on the Web Resources page at http://www.microsoft.com/windows/reskits/webresources.

Preventing System Restarts After a Stop Error

When a Stop error occurs, Windows XP Professional displays a Stop message related to the problem, followed by one of these events:

-   Windows XP Professional becomes unresponsive.

-   Windows XP Professional restarts your system.

If Windows XP Professional restarts your system immediately after a Stop message occurs, you might not be able to record Stop message information quickly enough. Disabling this default behavior is useful when you want to record Stop message details before using other recovery options such as Driver Rollback, System Restore, or Recovery Console. This information could help you analyze the root cause after you have addressed the symptoms of a problem.

To disable restarts when the system stops unexpectedly

1. In **Control Panel**, click **Performance and Maintenance**, and then click **System**.

2. Select the **Advanced** tab. In the **Startup and Recovery** box, click **Settings**.

3. Clear the **Automatically reboot** check box.

If you cannot start your system in normal mode, you can also perform the preceding steps in safe mode.

Common Stop Messages

The following Stop message descriptions can help you to troubleshoot problems that cause Stop messages. Also, the "Stop Message Checklist" at the end of this appendix, provides suggestions useful for resolving all types of Stop errors. If errors persist after you have followed the recommendations given, request assistance from a Microsoft support engineer.

Stop 0x0000000A or IRQL_NOT_LESS_OR_EQUAL

The Stop 0xA message indicates that a kernel-mode process or driver attempted to access a memory location to which it did not have permission, or at a kernel interrupt request level (IRQL) that was too high. A kernel-mode process can access only other processes that have an IRQL lower than, or equal to, its own. This Stop message is typically due to faulty or incompatible hardware or software.

Interpreting the Message

This Stop message has four parameters:

1. Memory address that was improperly referenced.

2. IRQL that was required to access the memory.

3. Type of access (0x00000000 = read operation, 0x00000001 = write operation).

4. Address of the instruction that attempted to reference memory specified in parameter 1.

If the last parameter is within the address range of a device driver used on your system, you can determine which device driver was running when the memory access occurred. You can typically determine the driver name by reading the line that begins with:

```
**Address 0xZZZZZZZZ has base at <address>- <driver name>
```

If the third parameter is the same as the first parameter, a special condition exists in which a system worker routine, carried out by a worker thread to handle background tasks known as work items, returned at a higher IRQL. In that case, some of the four parameters take on new meanings:

1. Address of the worker routine.

2. Kernel interrupt request level (IRQL).

3. Address of the worker routine.

4. Address of the work item.

Resolving the Problem

The following suggestions are specific to Stop 0xA errors. For additional trouble-shooting suggestions that apply to all Stop errors, see "Stop Message Checklist" later in this appendix.

■ A Stop 0xA message might occur after installing a faulty device driver, system service, or firmware. If a Stop message lists a driver by name, disable, remove, or roll back the driver to correct the problem. If disabling or removing drivers resolves the issues, contact the manufacturer about a possible update. Using updated software is especially important for multimedia applications, antivirus scanners, and CD mastering tools.

■ A Stop 0xA message might also be due to failing or defective hardware. If a Stop message points to a category of devices (video or disk adapters, for example), try removing or replacing the hardware to determine if it is causing the problem.

■ If you encounter a Stop 0xA message while upgrading to Windows XP Professional, the problem might be due to an incompatible driver, system service, virus scanner, or backup. To avoid problems while upgrading, simplify your hardware configuration and remove all third-party device drivers and system services (including virus scanners) prior to running setup. After you have successfully installed Windows XP Professional, contact the hardware manufacturer to obtain compatible updates. For more information about simplifying your system for troubleshooting purposes, see " Troubleshooting Concepts and Strategies" and "Troubleshooting Startup" in this book.

For more information about Stop 0xA messages, see the Microsoft Knowledge Base link on the Web Resources page at http://www.microsoft.com/windows /reskits/webresources. Search using keywords *winnt*, *0x0000000A*, and *0xA*.

Stop 0x0000001E or KMODE_EXCEPTION_NOT_HANDLED

The Stop 0x1E message indicates that the Windows XP Professional kernel detected an illegal or unknown processor instruction. The problems that cause Stop 0x1E messages share similarities with those that generate Stop 0xA errors in that they can be due to invalid memory and access violations. This default Windows XP Professional error handler typically intercepts these problems if error-handling routines are not present in the code itself.

Interpreting the Message

This Stop message has four parameters:

1. Exception code that was not handled.

2. Address at which the exception occurred.

3. Parameter 0 of the exception.

4. Parameter 1 of the exception.

The first parameter identifies the exception generated. Common exception codes include:

■ 0x80000002: STATUS_DATATYPE_MISALIGNMENT

An unaligned data reference was encountered. The trap frame supplies additional information.

■ 0x80000003: STATUS_BREAKPOINT

A breakpoint or ASSERT was encountered when no kernel debugger was attached to the system.

■ 0xC0000005: STATUS_ACCESS_VIOLATION

A memory access violation occurred. Parameter 4 of the Stop error (which is Parameter 1 of the exception) is the address that the driver attempted to access.

■ 0xC0000044: STATUS_QUOTA_EXCEEDED

The text `Insufficient quota exists to complete the operation` indicates a pool memory leak. A quota allocation attempt necessary for the system to continue operating normally was unsuccessful due to a program or driver memory leak.

For a complete list of exception codes, see the Ntstatus.h file located in the Inc directory of the Windows XP Professional Driver Development Kit (DDK). For more information about the DDK, see the Driver Development Kits link on the Web Resources page at http://www.microsoft.com/windows/reskits/webresources.

The second parameter identifies the address of the module in which the error occurred. Frequently, the address points to an individual driver or faulty hardware named on the third parameter of the Stop message. Make a note of this address and the link date of the driver or image that contains it.

The last two Stop message parameters vary, depending upon the exception that has occurred. You can typically find a description of the parameters that are included with the name of error code in Ntstatus.h. If the error code has no parameters, the last two parameters of the Stop message are listed as 0x00000000.

Resolving the Problem

The following suggestions are specific to Stop 0x1E errors. For additional troubleshooting suggestions that apply to all Stop errors, see "Stop Message Checklist" later in this appendix.

■ Stop 0x1E messages typically occur after installing faulty drivers or system services, or they can indicate hardware problems, such as memory and IRQ conflicts. If a Stop message lists a driver by name, disable, remove, or roll it back to correct the problem. If disabling or removing applications and drivers resolves the issue, contact the hardware manufacturer about a possible update. Using updated software is especially important for multimedia applications, antivirus scanners, and CD mastering tools.

- If the Stop message mentions the file Win32k.sys, the source of the error might be a third-party "remote control" program. If such software is installed, you might be able to disable it by starting the system in safe mode. If not, use Recovery Console to manually delete the system service file that is causing the problem. For more information about safe mode and Recovery Console, see "Tools for Troubleshooting" in this book.

- Problems can result from system firmware incompatibilities. Many Advanced Configuration and Power Interface (ACPI) issues can be resolved by updating to the latest firmware.

- Other possible causes include insufficient disk space while installing applications or performing certain functions that require more memory. You can free up space by deleting unneeded files. Use Disk Cleanup to increase available disk space. From Recovery Console, remove temporary files (those with .tmp file extensions), Internet cache files, application backup files, and .tmp files generated by Chkdsk.exe or Autochk.exe. You can also choose to install additional applications to another hard disk with more free space or move data files, paging files, and so on. For more information about Autochk.exe and Chkdsk.exe, see "Troubleshooting Disks and File Systems" in this book.

- The problem might be due to a memory leak caused by an application or service that is not releasing memory correctly. Poolmon (Poolmon.exe) helps you to isolate the components that are causing kernel memory leaks. For more information about troubleshooting memory leaks, see Microsoft Knowledgebase articles Q177415, "How to Use Poolmon to Troubleshoot Kernel Mode Memory Leaks," and Q298102, "Finding Pool Tags Used by Third Party Files Without Using the Debugger." To find these articles, see the Microsoft Knowledge Base link on the Web Resources page at http://www.microsoft.com /windows/reskits/webresources.

    To find additional articles, search using keywords *winnt, poolmon, pool tag, pooltag,* and *memory leak.*

For more information about Stop 0x1E messages, see the Microsoft Knowledge Base link on the Web Resources page at http://www.microsoft.com/windows /reskits/webresources. Search using keywords *winnt, 0x0000001E,* and *0x1E.*

Stop 0x00000024 or NTFS_FILE_SYSTEM

The Stop 0x24 message indicates that a problem occurred within Ntfs.sys, the driver file that allows the system to read and write to NTFS file system drives. A similar Stop message, 0x23, exists for the file allocation table (FAT16 or FAT32) file systems.

Interpreting the Message

This Stop message has four parameters:

1. Source file and line number.

2. A non-zero value that contains the address of the exception record (optional).

3. A non-zero value that contains the address of the context record (optional).

4. A non-zero value that contains the address where the original exception occurred (optional).

Parameters for this Stop message are useful only to Microsoft technical support with access to Windows XP Professional source code. Stop messages due to file system issues have the source file and the line number within the source file that generated the error encoded in their first parameter. The first four hexadecimal digits (also known as the high 16 bits) after the "0x" identify the source file number, and the last four hexadecimal digits (the low 16 bits) identify the source line in the file where the stop occurred.

Resolving the Problem

The following suggestions are specific to Stop 0x24 errors. For additional troubleshooting suggestions that apply to all Stop errors, see "Stop Message Checklist" later in this appendix.

- Malfunctioning SCSI and Advanced Technology Attachment (ATA) hardware or drivers can also adversely affect the system's ability to read and write to disk, causing errors. If using SCSI hard disks, check for cabling and termination problems between the SCSI controller and the disks. Periodically check Event Viewer for error messages related to SCSI or FASTFAT in the **System** log or Autochk in the **Application** log. For more information about troubleshooting SCSI adapters and disks, see "Troubleshooting Startup," "Troubleshooting Disks and File Systems," and "Disk Management" in this book.

- Verify that the tools you use to continually monitor your system, such as virus scanners, backup programs, or disk defragmenters are compatible with Windows XP Professional. Some disks and adapters come packaged with diagnostic software that you can use to run hardware tests. For more information, see the owner's manual for your computer, hard disk, or controller. For more information about Autochk, see "Troubleshooting Disks and File Systems" in this book.

To test hard disk or volume integrity
Method 1:

1. In the **Run** dialog box, in the **Open** box type:
   Cmd

2. Start the Chkdsk tool, which detects and attempts to resolve file system structural corruption. At the command prompt type:
   `chkdsk drive: /f`

Method 2:

1. Double-click **My Computer**, and then select the hard disk you want to check.

2. On the **File** menu, click **Properties**.

3. Click the **Tools** tab.

4. In the **Error-checking** box, click **Check Now**.

5. In **Check disk options**, select the **Scan for and attempt recovery of bad sectors** check box. You can also select the **Automatically fix file system errors** check box.

   If the volume you are checking is in use, a message asks whether you want to delay disk error checking until the next time you restart your computer. After you restart, disk error checking runs and the volume chosen is not available to run other tasks during this process. If you cannot restart the computer due to the error, use safe mode or Recovery Console.

   If you are not using the NTFS file system, and the system partition is formatted with the file allocation table (FAT16 or FAT32) file system, long file name (LFN) information can be lost if hard disk tools are started from an MS-DOS command prompt. A command prompt appears when using a startup floppy disk or when using the command prompt startup option on multiple boot systems that use FAT16 or FAT32 partitions with Microsoft® Windows® 95 OEM Service Release 2 (OSR2), Microsoft® Windows® 98, or Microsoft® Windows® Millennium Edition (Me) installed. Do not use tools meant for other operating systems on Windows XP Professional partitions.

   For more information about disks and file systems, see "Disk Management," "File Systems," and "Troubleshooting Disks and File Systems" in this book.

■ Nonpaged pool memory might be depleted, which can cause the system to stop. You can resolve this situation by adding more RAM, which increases the quantity of nonpaged pool memory available to the kernel. You can also reduce the number of files on the Services for Macintosh volume, if applicable.

For more information about Stop 0x24 messages, see the Microsoft Knowledge Base link on the Web Resources page at http://www.microsoft.com/windows /reskits/webresources. Search using keywords *winnt*, *0x00000024*, and *0x24*.

Stop 0x0000002E or DATA_BUS_ERROR

The Stop 0x2E message indicates a system memory parity error. The cause is typically failed or defective RAM (including motherboard, Level 2 cache, or video memory), incompatible or mismatched memory hardware, or when a device driver attempts to access an address in the 0x8*xxxxxxx* range that does not exist (does not map to a physical address). A Stop 0x2E message can also indicate hard disk damage caused by viruses or other problems.

Interpreting the Message

This Stop message has four parameters:

1. Virtual address that caused the fault.

2. Physical address that caused the fault.

3. Processor status register

4. Faulting instruction register

Resolving the Problem

The following suggestions are specific to Stop 0x2E errors. For additional troubleshooting suggestions that apply to all Stop errors, see "Stop Message Checklist" later in this appendix.

■ Stop 0x2E is typically due to defective, malfunctioning, or failed memory hardware, such as memory modules, Level 2 (L2) SRAM cache, or video adapter RAM. If you added new hardware recently, remove and replace it to determine if it is causing or contributing to the problem. Run diagnostics software supplied by the system manufacturer to determine if the component has failed.

■ Stop 0x2E messages can also occur after installing faulty drivers or system services. If a file name is given, you need to disable, remove, or roll back that driver. Disable the service or application and confirm that this resolves the error. If so, contact the hardware manufacturer about a possible update. Using updated software is especially important for backup programs, multimedia applications, antivirus scanners, and CD mastering tools.

■ Hard disk corruption can also cause this Stop message. For more information about checking hard disk integrity, see the instructions provided in "Stop 0x00000024 or NTFS_FILE_SYSTEM" earlier in this appendix. Also see "Troubleshooting Disks and File Systems" in this book.

- The problem might also be due to cracks, scratched traces, or defective components on the motherboard. If all else fails, take the system motherboard to a repair facility for diagnostic testing.

For more information about Stop 0x2E messages, see the Microsoft Knowledge Base link on the Web Resources page at http://www.microsoft.com/windows /reskits/webresources. Search using keywords *winnt, 0x0000002E,* and *0x2E.*

Stop 0x0000003F or NO_MORE_SYSTEM_PTES

The Stop 0x3F message indicates one or more of the following problems:

- The system Page Table Entries (PTEs) are depleted or fragmented due to the system performing a large number of input/output (I/O) actions.

- A faulty device driver is not managing memory properly.

- An application, such as a backup program, is improperly allocating large amounts of kernel memory.

Interpreting the Message

Depending on the configuration of your system, the value of the first parameter might vary. Possible values for the first parameter and the information returned are as follows:

- 0x0000000A - Page Table Entry (PTE) type: 0x00000000 = system expansion, 0x00000001 = nonpaged pool expansion

- 0x0000000B - Requested size

- 0x0000000C - Total free system PTEs

- 0x0000000D - Total system PTEs

Resolving the Problem

The following suggestions are specific to Stop 3F errors. For additional troubleshooting suggestions that apply to all Stop errors, see "Stop Message Checklist" later in this appendix.

- Stop 0x3F messages can occur after installing faulty drivers or system services. If a file name is given, you need to disable, remove, or roll back that driver. Disable the service or application and confirm that this resolves the error. If so, contact the hardware manufacturer about a possible update. Using updated software is especially important for backup programs, multimedia applications, antivirus scanners, and CD mastering tools.

- The system might not actually be out of PTEs, but a contiguous memory block of sufficient size is not available to satisfy a driver or application request. Check for the availability of updated driver or application files and consult the hardware or program documentation for minimum system requirements.

- Another cause is excessive demands for system PTE by applications. This situation is more common in server environments. Windows XP Professional provides a registry entry, **SystemPages**, that you can use to increase the number of PTEs allocated.

> **Caution**   Do not edit the registry unless you have no alternative. The registry editor bypasses standard safeguards, allowing settings that can damage your system, or even require you to reinstall Windows. If you must edit the registry, back it up first and see the Registry Reference in the Microsoft, Windows, 2000 Server Resource Kit at http://www.microsoft.com/reskit.

To increase the number of PTEs allocated in the registry

1. In the **Run** dialog box, and in the **Open** box, type: **regedit**

2. In the registry editor, navigate to the subkey HKEY_LOCAL_MACHINE\SYSTEM\CurrentControlSet\Control\Session Manager\Memory Management.

3. Double-click on **PagedPoolSize** and **SystemPages** to view the value for each entry.

4. If **PagedPoolSize** is not zero, assign a value of **0**.

5. If **SystemPages** is not zero, assign a value of **40000** for systems with 128 MB (or less) of memory, or **110000** for systems with 128 MB to 256 MB of memory. For systems with more memory, do not increase the SystemPages value above 110000 without contacting Microsoft technical support.

6. Click **OK,** and then close the registry editor.

7. Restart your computer.

A related Stop message, 0x000000D8: DRIVER_USED_EXCESSIVE_PTES, is described later in this appendix.

For more information about Stop 0x3F messages, see the Microsoft Knowledge Base link on the Web Resources page at http://www.microsoft.com/windows/reskits/webresources. Search using keywords *winnt, 0x0000003F,* and *0x3F.*

Stop 0x00000050 or PAGE_FAULT_IN_NONPAGED_AREA

The Stop 0x50 message indicates that requested data was not in memory. The system generates an exception error when using a reference to an invalid system memory address. Defective memory (including main memory, L2 RAM cache, video RAM) or incompatible software (including remote control and antivirus software) might cause Stop 0x50 messages.

Interpreting the Message

This Stop message has four parameters:

1. Memory address that caused the fault.

2. Type of access (0x00000000 = read operation, 0x00000001 = write operation).

3. If not zero, the instruction address that referenced the address in parameter 0x00000001.

4. This parameter is reserved (set aside for future use).

Resolving the Problem

The following suggestions are specific to Stop 0x50 errors. For additional troubleshooting suggestions that apply to all Stop errors, see "Stop Message Checklist" later in this appendix.

- If you added new hardware recently, remove and replace the hardware to determine if it is causing or contributing to the problem. Run diagnostics software supplied by the hardware manufacturer to determine if the component has failed.

- Stop 0x50 messages can also occur after installing faulty drivers or system services. If the file name is listed, you need to disable, remove, or roll back that driver. If not, disable the recently installed service or application to determine if this resolves the error. If this does not resolve the problem, contact the hardware manufacturer for updates. Using updated drivers and software is especially important for network interface cards, video adapters, backup programs, multimedia applications, antivirus scanners, and CD mastering tools. If an updated driver is not available, attempt to use a driver from a similar device in the same family. For example, if printing to a Model 1100C printer causes Stop 0x50 errors, using a printer driver meant for a Model 1100A or Model 1000 might temporarily resolve the problem.

For more information about Stop 0x50 messages, see the Microsoft Knowledge Base link on the Web Resources page at http://www.microsoft.com/windows /reskits/webresources. Search using keywords *winnt*, *0x00000050*, and *0x50*.

Stop 0x00000077 or KERNEL_STACK_INPAGE_ERROR

The Stop 0x77 message indicates that a page of kernel data requested from the paging (virtual memory) file could not be found or read into memory. This Stop message can also indicate disk hardware failure, disk data corruption, or possible virus infection.

Interpreting the Message

This Stop message has four parameters. The following set of definitions applies only if the first and third parameters are both zero:

1. This value is 0x00000000 (zero).

2. Value found in the stack.

3. This value is 0x00000000 (zero).

4. Address of signature on kernel stack.

    Otherwise, the following definitions apply:

1. Status code.

2. I/O status code.

3. Page file number.

4. Offset into page file.

    Frequently, the cause of this error can be determined from the second parameter, the I/O status code. Some common status codes are:

- 0xC000009A, or STATUS_INSUFFICIENT_RESOURCES, indicates a lack of nonpaged pool resources.

- 0xC000009C, or STATUS_DEVICE_DATA_ERROR, generally indicates bad blocks (sectors) on the hard disk.

- 0xC000009D, or STATUS_DEVICE_NOT_CONNECTED, indicates defective or loose data or power cables, a problem with SCSI termination, or improper controller or hard disk configuration.

- 0xC000016A, or STATUS_DISK_OPERATION_FAILED, also indicates bad blocks (sectors) on the hard disk.

- 0xC0000185, or STATUS_IO_DEVICE_ERROR, indicates improper termination, defective storage controller hardware, defective disk cabling, or two devices attempting to use the same system resources.

For information about other possible status codes that can be returned, see the file Ntstatus.h of the Windows XP Professional Driver Development Kit (DDK). For more information about the DDK, see the Driver Development Kits link on the Web Resources page at http://www.microsoft.com/windows/reskits/webresources.

Resolving the Problem

The following suggestions are specific to Stop 0x70 errors. For additional troubleshooting suggestions that apply to all Stop errors, see "Stop Message Checklist" later in this appendix.

- Stop 0x77 messages can be caused by bad sectors in the virtual memory paging file or a disk controller error. In extremely rare cases, depleted nonpaged pool resources can cause this error. If the first and third parameters are zero, the stack signature in the kernel stack is missing, which is an error typically caused by defective hardware. If the I/O status is 0xC0000185 and the paging file is on a SCSI disk, check for cabling and termination issues. An I/O status code of 0xC000009C or 0xC000016A indicates that the requested data could not be found. You can try to correct this by restarting the computer. If a problem with disk integrity exists, Autochk, a program that attempts to mark bad disk sectors as defective so that they are not used in the future, starts automatically. If Autochk fails to run, you can manually perform the integrity check yourself by following the instructions to run Chkdsk provided in "Stop 0x00000024 or NTFS_FILE_SYSTEM" earlier in this appendix. For more information about Autochk and Chkdsk, see "Troubleshooting Disks and File Systems" in this book.

- Another cause of Stop 0x77 messages is defective, malfunctioning, or failed memory hardware, such as memory modules, Level 2 (L2) SRAM cache, or video adapter RAM. If you added new hardware recently, remove and replace it to determine if it is causing or contributing to the problem. Run diagnostics software supplied by the system manufacturer to determine if the component has failed.

- The problem might also be due to cracks, scratched traces, or defective components on the motherboard. If all else fails, take the system motherboard to a repair facility for diagnostic testing.

- Problems that cause Stop 0x77 messages can also cause Stop 0x7A messages. For more information about Stop 0x7A messages, see "Stop 0x0000007A or KERNEL_DATA_INPAGE_ERROR" later in this appendix.

For more information about Stop 0x77 messages, see the Microsoft Knowledge Base link on the Web Resources page at http://www.microsoft.com/windows/reskits/webresources. Search using keywords *winnt*, *0x00000077*, and *0x77*.

Stop 0x00000079 or MISMATCHED_HAL

The Stop 0x79 message indicates that the hardware abstraction layer (HAL) and the kernel type for the computer do not match. This error most often occurs when ACPI firmware settings are changed. For example, you might install Windows XP Professional on an x86-based computer with the firmware **ACPI enable** option enabled and later decide to disable it. This error can also result when mismatched single and multi-processor configuration files are copied to the system.

Interpreting the Message

The content of the information provided by a 0x79 Stop message varies according to the value of the first parameter. Three different values for Parameter 1 are possible. The information in the next two parameters depends upon the value of Parameter 1 as shown in Table C-3.

Table C-3   Parameter Listing for Stop Message 0x79

Parameter 1	Parameter 2	Parameter 3	Description
0x00000001	Release level of Ntoskrnl.exe	Release level of Hal.dll	PRCB release level mismatch
0x00000002	Build type of Ntoskrnl.exe	Build type of Hal.dll	Build type mismatch

When the value of Parameter 1 is set to 0x00000002, the following build type codes become effective:

- **0x00000000**: Multiprocessor-enabled free build

- **0x00000001**: Multiprocessor-enabled checked build

- **0x00000002**: Single-processor free build

Resolving the Problem

The following suggestions are specific to Stop 0x79 errors. For additional troubleshooting suggestions that apply to all Stop errors, see "Stop Message Checklist" later in this appendix.

- A Stop 0x79 message occurs when the system is using out-of-date Ntoskrnl.exe or Hal.dll files. This can occur after manual repairs that involve copying incorrect files to the system. This error also occurs when using mismatched files, such as copying a multiprocessor HAL on to a system using a single-processor kernel (or vice versa). The kernel and HAL files for single-processor and multiprocessor systems are stored on the Windows XP Professional operating system CD using two different file names. For example, the single and multiprocessor versions of the kernel, named Ntoskrnl.exe and Ntkrnlmp.exe respectively. Setup copies either Ntoskrnl.exe or Ntkrnlmp.exe to your system as Ntoskrnl.exe. In Recovery Console, you can use the **Copy** command to copy the correct HAL or kernel files from the CD to the appropriate folder on the hard disk. For more information about Recovery Console, see Windows XP Professional Help and Support Center, "Tools for Troubleshooting" and " Troubleshooting Concepts and Strategies" in this book.

■ If you experience Stop 0x79 messages after changing firmware settings, restore the original settings used during Windows XP Professional Setup.

Because systems that use the ACPI HAL ignore IRQ assignments stored in firmware, you can only manually change IRQ settings for non-ACPI (Standard PC HAL) systems. Some *x*86-based provide the option to toggle ACPI functionality. To disable or re-enable ACPI, you must change firmware settings and reinstall Windows XP Professional. Because of the numerous registry and system file changes required, you must run Setup again (an upgrade installation does not work).

For more information about Stop 0x79 messages, see the Microsoft Knowledge Base link on the Web Resources page at http://www.microsoft.com/windows/reskits/webresources. Search using keywords *winnt*, *0x00000079*, and *0x79*.

Stop 0x0000007A or KERNEL_DATA_INPAGE_ERROR

The Stop 0x7A message indicates that a page of kernel data was not found in the paging (virtual memory) file and could not be read into memory. This might be due to incompatible disk or controller drivers, firmware, or hardware.

Interpreting the Message

This Stop message has four parameters:

1. Lock type value (0x00000001, 0x00000002, 0x00000003, or page table entry (PTE) address).

2. I/O status code.

3. If the lock type is 0x00000001, this parameter represents the current process. If the lock type is 0x00000003, this parameter represents the virtual address.

4. The virtual address that could not be read into memory.

Frequently, the cause of this error can be determined from the second parameter, the I/O status code. Some common status codes are:

■ 0xC000009A, or STATUS_INSUFFICIENT_RESOURCES, indicates a lack of nonpaged pool resources.

■ 0xC000009C, or STATUS_DEVICE_DATA_ERROR, indicates bad blocks (sectors) on the hard disk.

- 0xC000009D, or STATUS_DEVICE_NOT_CONNECTED, indicates defective or loose data or power cables, a problem with SCSI termination, or improper controller or disk configuration.

- 0xC000016A, or STATUS_DISK_OPERATION_FAILED, indicates bad blocks (sectors) on the hard disk.

- 0xC0000185, or STATUS_IO_DEVICE_ERROR, indicates improper termination, defective storage controller hardware, or defective disk cabling, or two devices attempting to use the same resources.

For information about other possible status codes that might be returned, see the file Ntstatus.h of the Windows XP Professional Driver Development Kit (DDK). For more information about the DDK, see the Driver Development Kits link on the Web Resources page at http://www.microsoft.com/windows/reskits/webresources.

Resolving the Problem

The following suggestions are specific to Stop 0x7A errors. For additional troubleshooting suggestions that apply to all Stop errors, see "Stop Message Checklist" later in this appendix.

- Stop 0x7A can be caused by bad sectors in the virtual memory paging file, disk controller error, virus infection, or memory hardware problems. In extremely rare cases, depleted nonpaged pool resources can cause this error. If the first and third parameters are zero, the stack signature in the kernel stack is missing, an error typically caused by defective hardware. If the I/O status is 0xC0000185 and the paging file is on a SCSI disk, check for cabling and termination issues. An I/O status code of 0xC000009C or 0xC000016A indicates that the requested data could not be found. You can try to correct this by restarting the computer. If a problem with disk integrity exists, Autochk, a program that attempts to mark bad disk sectors as defective so that they are not used in the future, starts automatically. If Autochk fails to run, you can manually perform the integrity check yourself by following the instructions to run Chkdsk provided in "Stop 0x00000024 or NTFS_FILE_SYSTEM" earlier in this appendix. For more information about Autochk and Chkdsk, see "Troubleshooting Disks and File Systems" in this book.

- Another cause of Stop 0x7A messages is defective, malfunctioning, or failed memory hardware, such as memory modules, Level 2 (L2) SRAM cache, or video adapter RAM. If you added new hardware recently, remove and replace it to determine if it is causing or contributing to the problem. Run diagnostics software supplied by the system manufacturer to determine if the component has failed.

- Check the hardware manufacturer's Web site for updates to disk adapter firmware or drivers that improve compatibility. Verify that your disks and controller support the same set of advanced features, such as higher transfer rates. If necessary, select a slower transfer rate if an update is not yet available. Consult your hardware or device documentation for more information.

> **Warning**   You can install disk controller drivers not present on the Windows XP Professional operating system CD by responding to the following prompt shortly after starting Setup:
> **Press F6 if you need to install a third party SCSI or RAID driver.**
> Press F6, and when prompted, provide the appropriate storage controller driver (ATA or SCSI) supplied by the manufacturer.

- The problem might also be due to cracks, scratched traces, or defective components on the motherboard. If all else fails, take the system motherboard to a repair facility for diagnostic testing.

- Problems that cause Stop 0x7A messages can also cause Stop 0x77 messages. For more information about Stop 0x77 messages, see "Stop 0x00000077 or KERNEL_STACK_INPAGE_ERROR" earlier in this appendix.

For more information about Stop 0x7A messages, see the Microsoft Knowledge Base link on the Web Resources page at http://www.microsoft.com/windows /reskits/webresources. Search using keywords *winnt*, *0x0000007A*, and *0x7A*.

Stop 0x0000007B or INACCESSIBLE_BOOT_DEVICE

The Stop 0x7B message indicates that Windows XP Professional has lost access to the system partition or boot volume during the startup process. Installing incorrect device drivers when installing or upgrading storage adapter hardware typically causes stop 0x7B errors. Stop 0x7B errors could also indicate possible virus infection.

Interpreting the Message

This Stop message has four parameters:

1. The address of a Unicode string data structure representing the Advanced Reduced Instruction Set Computing (RISC) Computing (ARC) specification name of the device at which you attempted startup.

2. Pointer to ARC name string in memory.

3. This value is 0x00000000 (zero).

4. This value is 0x00000000 (zero).

The first parameter typically contains two separate pieces of data. For example, if the parameter is 0x00800020, 0x0020 is the actual length of the Unicode string and 0x0080 is the maximum ARC name string length. The next parameter contains the address of the buffer. This address is in system space, so the high-order bit is set.

If the file system is unable to mount the boot device or simply does not recognize the data on the boot device as a file system structure, the following parameter definition applies:

1. The address of the device object that could not be mounted.

2. Error code value or 0x00000000 (zero).

3. This value is 0x00000000 (zero).

4. This value is 0x00000000 (zero).

The value of the first parameter determines whether the parameter is a pointer to an ARC name string (ARC names are a generic method of identifying devices within the ARC environment) or a device object, because a Unicode string never has an odd number of bytes, and a device object always has a Type code of 0003.

The second parameter is very important because it can indicate whether the 0x7B Stop message was caused by file system issues or problems with storage hardware and drivers. Values of 0xC000034 or 0xC000000E typically indicate:

- Disks or storage controllers that are failing, defective, or improperly configured.

- Storage-related drivers or programs (tape management software, for example) that are not fully compatible with Windows XP Professional.

Resolving the Problem

The following suggestions are specific to Stop 0x7B errors. For additional troubleshooting suggestions that apply to all Stop errors, see "Stop Message Checklist" later in this appendix.

- During I/O system initialization, the controller or driver for the startup device (typically the hard disk) might have failed to initialize the necessary hardware. File system initialization might have failed because of disk or controller failure, or because the file system did not recognize the data on the boot device.

- Repartitioning disks, adding new disks, or upgrading to a new disk controller might cause the information in the Boot.ini file, or Boot Manager, to become outdated. If this Stop message occurs after installing new disks to your system, edit the Boot.ini file or adjust the Boot Manager parameters to allow the system to start. If the error occurs after upgrading the disk controller, verify that the new hardware is functioning and correctly configured. For more information about the Boot.ini file, see "Troubleshooting Startup" in this book.

- Verify that the system firmware and disk controller BIOS settings are correct and that the storage device was properly installed. If you are unsure, consult your computer's documentation about restoring default firmware settings or configuring your system to auto-detect settings. If the error occurs during Windows XP Professional setup, the problem might be due to unsupported disk controller hardware. In some cases, drivers for new hardware are not in the Windows XP Professional Driver.cab library, and you need to provide additional drivers to complete the Windows XP Professional setup successfully. If this is the case, follow the hardware manufacturer's instructions when installing drivers. Periodically check for driver and firmware updates.

■ Hard disk corruption can also cause this Stop message. For more information about checking hard disk integrity, see the instructions provided in "Stop 0x00000024 or NTFS_FILE_SYSTEM" earlier in this appendix.

■ Problems that cause 0x7B errors might also cause Stop 0xED errors. For more information about 0xED Stop messages, see "Stop 0x0000007B or INACCESSIBLE_BOOT_DEVICE" later in this appendix.

For more information about Stop 0x7B messages, see the Microsoft Knowledge Base link on the Web Resources page at http://www.microsoft.com/windows/reskits /webresources. Search using keywords *winnt*, *0x0000007B*, *0x7B*, and *Txtsetup.oem*.

Stop 0x0000007F or UNEXPECTED_KERNEL_MODE_TRAP

The Stop 0x7F message indicates that one of three types of problems occurred in kernel-mode:

■ A condition that the kernel is not allowed to have or intercept (also known as a bound trap).

■ Software problems.

■ Hardware failures.

Interpreting the Message

This Stop message has four parameters:

1. Processor exception code.

2. This value is 0x00000000 (zero).

3. This value is 0x00000000 (zero).

4. This value is 0x00000000 (zero).

The first parameter is the most important and can have several different values, indicating different causes of this error. You can find all conditions that cause a Stop 0x7F in any *x*86 microprocessor reference manual because they are specific to the *x*86 platform. Here are some of the most common exception codes:

■ 0x00000000, or a divide by zero error, occurs when a divide (DIV) instruction is run and the divisor is 0. Memory corruption, other hardware failures, or software problems can cause this message.

- 0x00000004, or Overflow, occurs when the processor carries out a call to an interrupt handler when the overflow (OF) flag is set.

- 0x00000005, or Bounds Check Fault, indicates that the processor, while carrying out a BOUND instruction, found that the operand exceeded the specified limits. BOUND instructions are used to ensure that a signed array index is within a certain range.

- 0x00000006, or Invalid Opcode, is generated when the processor attempts to run an invalid instruction. This typically occurs when the instruction pointer is corrupted due to a hardware memory problem and is pointing to a wrong location.

- 0x00000008, or Double Fault, indicates an exception while trying to call the handler for a prior exception. Normally, two exceptions can be handled serially, but there are certain exceptions (almost always caused by hardware problems) that cause the processor to signal a double fault.

Less common codes include:

- **0x00000001**: A system-debugger call.

- **0x00000003**: A debugger breakpoint.

- **0x0000000A**: A corrupted Task State Segment.

- **0x0000000B**: An access to a memory segment that was not present.

- **0x0000000C**: An access to memory beyond the limits of a stack.

- **0x0000000D**: An exception not covered by some other exception; a protection fault that pertains to access violations for applications.

Resolving the Problem

The following suggestions are specific to Stop 0x7F errors. For additional troubleshooting suggestions that apply to all Stop errors, see "Stop Message Checklist" later in this appendix.

- Stop 0x7F messages are typically due to defective, malfunctioning, or failed memory hardware. If you added new hardware recently, remove and replace it to determine if it is causing or contributing to the problem. Run diagnostics software supplied by the system manufacturer to determine if the component has failed.

- Running the CPU beyond the rated specification, known as "overclocking," can cause Stop 0x7F or other error messages due to heat buildup. When diagnosing problems on overclocked systems, first restore all clock and bus speed settings to the manufacturer recommended values to determine if this resolves the issues.

- The problem might also be due to cracks, scratched traces, or defective components on the motherboard. If all else fails, take the system motherboard to a repair facility for diagnostic testing.

- Stop 0x7F messages can occur after installing incompatible applications, drivers, or system services. Contact the software manufacturer about possible Windows XP Professional-specific updates. Using updated software is especially important for backup programs, multimedia applications, antivirus scanners, and CD mastering tools.

For more information about Stop 0x7F messages, see the Microsoft Knowledge Base link on the Web Resources page at http://www.microsoft.com/windows /reskits/webresources. Search using keywords *winnt*, *0x0000007F*, and *0x7F*.

Stop 0x0000009F or DRIVER_POWER_STATE_FAILURE

The Stop 0x9F message indicates that a driver is in an inconsistent or invalid power state.

Interpreting the Message

Table C-4 describes the information provided by Stop 0x9F messages. The value of the first parameter indicates the type of violation (see the Description column) and determines the meaning of the next three parameters.

Table C-4   Parameter Listing for Stop Message 0x9F

Parameter 1	Parameter 2	Parameter 3	Parameter 4	Description
0x00000001	Pointer to the device object	Reserved	Reserved	The device object being freed still has an incomplete power request pending.
0x00000002	Pointer to the target device object	Pointer to the device object	Reserved	The device object completed the I/O request packet for the system power state request, but failed to call **PoStartNextPowerIrp**.
0x00000003	Pointer to the target device object	Pointer to the device object	The I/O request packet	The device driver did not properly set the I/O request packet as "pending" or complete the I/O request packet.
0x00000100	Pointer to the nonpaged device object	Pointer to the target device object	Pointer to the device object to notify	The device objects in the dev node were inconsistent in their use of DO_POWER_PAGABLE.

Table C-4   Parameter Listing for Stop Message 0x9F

Parameter 1	Parameter 2	Parameter 3	Parameter 4	Description
0x00000101	Child device object	Child device object	Parent device object	A parent device object has detected that a child device has not set the DO_POWER_PAGABLE bit.

This Stop message typically occurs during events that involve power state transitions, such as:

- Shutting down.

- Suspending or resuming from standby mode.

- Suspending or resuming from hibernate mode.

Resolving the Problem

The following suggestions are specific to Stop 0x9F errors. For additional troubleshooting suggestions that apply to all Stop errors, see "Stop Message Checklist" later in this appendix.

- Stop 0x9F messages can occur after installing faulty applications or drivers or system services. If a file is listed by name and you can associate it with an application, uninstall the application. For drivers, disable, remove, or roll back that driver to determine if this resolves the error. If it does, contact the hardware manufacturer for a possible update. Using updated software is especially important for backup programs, multimedia applications, antivirus scanners, and CD mastering tools.

- For information about troubleshooting standby and hibernate mode issues, see "Troubleshooting Startup" in this book. Also see article Q266169, "How to Troubleshoot Problems with Standby Mode, Hibernate Mode, and Shutting Down Your Computer in Windows 2000." To find this article, see the Microsoft Knowledge Base link on the Web Resources page at http://www.microsoft.com /windows/reskits/webresources.

For more information about Stop 0x9F messages, see the Microsoft Knowledge Base link on the Web Resources page at http://www.microsoft.com/windows /reskits/webresources. Search using keywords *winnt*, *0x0000009F*, and *0x9F*.

Stop 0xBE or ATTEMPTED_WRITE_TO_READONLY_MEMORY

The Stop 0xBE message indicates that a driver attempted to write to read-only memory.

Interpreting the Message

This Stop message has four parameters:

1. Virtual address of attempted write.

2. PTE contents.

3. Reserved.

4. Reserved.

Resolving the Problem

The following suggestion is specific to Stop 0xBE errors. For additional troubleshooting suggestions that apply to all Stop errors, see "Stop Message Checklist" later in this appendix.

- A Stop 0xBE message might occur after installing a faulty device driver, system service, or firmware. If a Stop message lists a driver by name, disable, remove, or roll back the driver to correct the problem. If disabling or removing drivers resolves the issues, contact the manufacturer about a possible update. Using updated software is especially important for multimedia applications, antivirus scanners, DVD playback, and CD mastering tools.

For more information about Stop 0xBE messages, see the Microsoft Knowledge Base link on the Web Resources page at http://www.microsoft.com/windows/reskits /webresources. Search using keywords *winnt*, *0x000000BE*, and *0xBE*.

Stop 0xC2 or BAD_POOL_CALLER

The Stop 0xC2 message indicates that a kernel-mode process or driver incorrectly attempted to perform memory operations in the following ways:

- By allocating a memory pool size of zero bytes.

- By allocating a memory pool that does not exist.

- By attempting to free a memory pool that is already free.

- By allocating or freeing a memory pool at an IRQL that was too high.

  This Stop message is typically due to a faulty driver or software.

Interpreting the Message

Table C-5 describes the information provided by Stop 0xC2 messages. The value of the first parameter indicates the type of violation (see the Description column) and determines the meaning of the next three parameters.

Table C-5   Parameter Listing for Stop Message 0xC2

Parameter 1	Parameter 2	Parameter 3	Parameter 4	Description
0x00000000	This value is always 0	The pool type being allocated	The pool tag being used	The caller is requesting a zero byte pool allocation
0x00000001, 0x00000002, or 0x00000004	Pointer to pool header	First part of pool header contents	This value is always zero	Pool header has been corrupted
0x00000006	Reserved	Pointer to pool header	Pool header contents	Attempt to free a memory pool that was already freed
0x00000007	Reserved	Pointer to pool header	This value is always zero	Attempt to free a memory pool that was already freed
0x00000008	Current IRQL	Pool type	Size of allocation	Attempt to allocate pool at invalid IRQL
0x00000009	Current IRQL	Pool type	Address of pool	Attempt to free pool at invalid IRQL
0x00000040	Starting address	Start of system address space	This value is always zero	Attempt to free usermode address to kernel pool
0x00000041	Starting address	Physical page frame	Highest physical page frame	Attempt to free a non-allocated nonpaged pool address
0x00000042 or 0x00000043	Address being freed	This value is always zero	This value is always zero	Attempt to free a virtual address that was never in any pool
0x00000050	Starting address	Start offset in pages from beginning of paged pool	Size in bytes of paged pool	Attempt to free a non-allocated paged pool address
0x00000099	Address being freed	This value is always zero	This value is always zero	Attempt to free pool with invalid address or corruption in pool header
0x0000009A	Pool type	Size of allocation in bytes	Allocation's pool tag	Attempt to allocate must-succeed

Resolving the Problem

The following suggestions are specific to Stop 0xC2 errors. For additional trouble-shooting suggestions that apply to all Stop errors, see "Stop Message Checklist" later in this appendix.

- A Stop 0xC2 message might occur after installing a faulty device driver, system service, or firmware. If a Stop message lists a driver by name, disable, remove, or roll back the driver to correct the problem. If disabling or removing drivers resolves the issues, contact the manufacturer about a possible update. Using updated software is especially important for multimedia applications, antivirus scanners, DVD playback, and CD mastering tools.

- A Stop 0xC2 message might also be due to failing or defective hardware. If a Stop message points to a category of devices (such as disk controllers, for example), try removing or replacing the hardware to determine if it is causing the problem.

- If you encounter a Stop 0xC2 message while upgrading to Windows XP Professional, the problem might be due to an incompatible driver, system service, virus scanner, or backup. To avoid problems while upgrading, simplify your hardware configuration and remove all third-party device drivers and system services (including virus scanners) prior to running setup. After you have successfully installed Windows XP Professional, contact the hardware manufacturer to obtain compatible updates. For more information about simplifying your system for troubleshooting purposes, see " Troubleshooting Concepts and Strategies" and "Troubleshooting Startup" in this book.

For more information about Stop 0xC2 messages, see the Microsoft Knowledge Base link on the Web Resources page at http://www.microsoft.com/windows/reskits /webresources. Search using keywords *winnt*, *0x000000C2*, and *0xC2*.

Stop 0x000000CE or DRIVER_UNLOADED_WITHOUT_CANCELLING_PENDING_OPERATIONS

This Stop message indicates that a driver failed to cancel pending operations before exiting.

Interpreting the Message

This Stop message has four parameters:

1. Memory address referenced.
2. Type of access (0x00000000 = read operation, 0x00000001 = write operation).
3. If non-zero, the address of the instruction that referenced the incorrect memory location.
4. Reserved.

Resolving the Problem

For additional troubleshooting suggestions that apply to all Stop errors, see "Stop Message Checklist" later in this appendix.

■ Stop 0xCE messages can occur after installing faulty drivers or system services. If a driver is listed by name, disable, remove, or roll back that driver to confirm that this resolves the error. If so, contact the manufacturer about a possible update. Using updated software is especially important for backup programs, multimedia applications, antivirus scanners, DVD playback, and CD mastering tools.

For more information about Stop 0xCE messages, see the Microsoft Knowledge Base link on the Web Resources page at http://www.microsoft.com/windows /reskits/webresources. Search using keywords *winnt*, *0x000000CE*, and *0xCE*.

Stop 0x000000D1 or DRIVER_IRQL_NOT_LESS_OR_EQUAL

The Stop 0xD1 message indicates that the system attempted to access pageable memory using a kernel process IRQL that was too high. Drivers that have used improper addresses typically cause this error.

Interpreting the Message

This Stop message has four parameters:

1. Memory referenced.

2. IRQL at time of reference.

3. Type of access (0x00000000 = read operation, 0x00000001 = write operation).

4. Address that referenced memory.

Resolving the Problem

For additional troubleshooting suggestions that apply to all Stop errors, see "Stop Message Checklist" later in this appendix.

■ Stop 0xD1 messages can occur after installing faulty drivers or system services. If a driver is listed by name, disable, remove, or roll back that driver to confirm that this resolves the error. If so, contact the manufacturer about a possible update. Using updated software is especially important for backup programs, multimedia applications, antivirus scanners, DVD playback, and CD mastering tools.

For more information about Stop 0xD1 messages, see the Microsoft Knowledge Base link on the Web Resources page at http://www.microsoft.com/windows /reskits/webresources. Search using keywords *winnt*, *0x000000D1*, and *0xD1*.

Stop 0x000000D8 or DRIVER_USED_EXCESSIVE_PTES

The Stop 0xD8 message typically occurs if your computer runs out of page table entries (PTEs) due to a driver that requests large amounts of kernel memory.

Interpreting the Message

Depending upon the configuration of your system, the number of parameters returned might vary. The four possible values are:

1. If this parameter has a non-null value, it contains the name of the driver that caused the Stop error.

2. If the first parameter has a non-null value, this parameter contains the number of PTEs used by the driver that is causing the error.

3. This parameter represents the total free system PTEs.

4. This parameter represents the total system PTEs.

Resolving the Problem

For additional troubleshooting suggestions that apply to all Stop errors, see "Stop Message Checklist" later in this appendix.

■ For suggestions about resolving problems related to inadequate PTEs, see "0x0000003F or NO_MORE_SYSTEM_PTES" earlier in this appendix.

For more information about Stop 0xD8 messages, see the Microsoft Knowledge Base link on the Web Resources page at http://www.microsoft.com/windows /reskits/webresources. Search using keywords *winnt*, *0x000000D8*, and *0xD8*.

Stop 0x000000EA or THREAD_STUCK_IN_DEVICE_DRIVER

A device driver problem is causing the system to pause indefinitely. Typically, this problem is caused by a display driver waiting for the video hardware to enter an idle state. This might indicate a hardware problem with the video adapter or a faulty video driver.

Interpreting the Message

This Stop message has four parameters:

1. Pointer to the thread object that is caught in an infinite loop.

2. Pointer to a DEFERRED_WATCHDOG object, useful when using a kernel debugger to find out more information about this problem.

3. Pointer to graphics device interface (GDI) supplied context.

4. Additional debugging information.

Resolving the Problem

The following suggestion is specific to Stop 0xEA errors. For additional trouble-shooting suggestions that apply to all Stop errors, see "Stop Message Checklist" later in this appendix.

- Stop 0xD1 messages can occur after installing faulty drivers (especially video drivers) or system services. If a driver is listed by name, disable, remove, or roll back that driver to confirm that this resolves the error. If so, contact the manufacturer about a possible update. Using updated software is especially important for backup programs, multimedia applications, antivirus scanners, DVD playback, and CD mastering tools.

For more information about Stop 0xEA messages, see the Microsoft Knowledge Base link on the Web Resources page at http://www.microsoft.com/windows/reskits/webresources. Search using keywords *winnt*, *0x000000EA*, and *0xEA*.

Stop 0x000000ED or UNMOUNTABLE_BOOT_VOLUME

The kernel mode I/O subsystem attempted to mount the boot volume and it failed. This error might also occur during an upgrade to Windows XP Professional on systems that use higher throughput ATA disks or controllers with incorrect cabling. In some cases, your system might appear to work normally after you restart.

Interpreting the Message

This Stop message has two parameters:

1. Device object of the boot volume

2. Status code from the file system on why it failed to mount the volume

Resolving the Problem

The following suggestions are specific to Stop 0xED errors. For additional trouble-shooting suggestions that apply to all Stop errors, see "Stop Message Checklist" later in this appendix.

- If using higher throughput ATA disks and controllers, those capable of data transfer rates above 33.3 megabytes per second, replace the standard 40-pin cable with an 80-pin cable. Using an 80-pin cable is optional for transfer rates up to and including 33.3 megabytes per second, but is mandatory for higher transfer rates. The additional grounded pins are required to avoid data loss.

- Some firmware enables you to force higher transfer rates even when you are using the incorrect cable type. Your firmware might issue a warning but allow the startup process to proceed. Restore the default firmware setting for ATA cable detection.

- Problems that cause 0xED errors might also cause Stop 0x7B errors. For more information about 0x7B Stop messages, see "Stop 0x0000007B or INACCESSIBLE_BOOT_DEVICE" earlier in this appendix.

For more information about Stop 0xED messages, see the Microsoft Knowledge Base link on the Web Resources page at http://www.microsoft.com/windows /reskits/webresources. Search using keywords *winnt*, *0x000000ED*, and *0xED*.

Stop 0x000000F2 or HARDWARE_INTERRUPT_STORM

The Stop 0xF2 message occurs if the kernel detects an *interrupt storm*. An interrupt storm occurs when a level-interrupt-triggered device fails to release an interrupt request (IRQ). This can result from the following causes:

- A device fails to respond to an interrupt release signal sent from a driver.

- An incorrectly written device driver fails to send an interrupt release request to a device. The driver fails to determine that the interrupt was hardware initiated.

- An incorrectly written device driver claims an interrupt request meant for a different device. This occurs only for multiple devices sharing an IRQ.

- The edge level control register is set incorrectly by system firmware.

- Edge level and level-interrupt-triggered devices are incorrectly assigned the same IRQ (for example, a serial port and a Peripheral Component Interconnect (PCI) SCSI controller).

Interpreting the Message

This Stop message has four parameters:

1. Address of the first or only interrupt service routine (ISR) involved in initiating the interrupt storm.

2. ISR context value.

3. Address of the interrupt object that initiated the storm.

4. 0x00000001 if the ISR is not chained (not part of an interrupt sequence).
   0x00000002 if the ISR is chained (part of an interrupt sequence).

If the fourth parameter is 0x1, the driver module to which parameters 1 and 3 point probably indicates a driver problem or malfunctioning hardware.

If the fourth parameter is 0x2, the driver module to which parameter 1 point is the first ISR in the sequence, and might not be the source of the problem.

When a Stop 0xF2 message occurs, it indicates the driver involved in the ISR on the storming IRQ. In addition to four Stop message parameters, a message similar to the following appears:

```
*** STOP: 0x000000F2 (0xFCA7C55C, 0x817B9B28, 0x817D2AA0, 0x00000002)
An interrupt storm has caused the system to hang.
*** Address FCA7C55C base at FCA72000, Datestamp 3A72BDEF - ACPI.sys
```

Resolving the Problem

The following suggestions are specific to Stop 0xF2 errors. For additional trouble-shooting suggestions that apply to all Stop errors, see "Stop Message Checklist" later in this appendix.

To resolve this problem, simplify your system's hardware configuration by following these procedures:

- Try to identify the device linked to the driver module indicated in the Stop message. Remove the conflicting hardware to determine if this resolves the issue. If the problem persists, identify other devices using the same IRQ by using Device Manager or System Information. Then remove all devices using the same IRQ and reinstall them one at time until you can reproduce the problem. Check for updated drivers for the problem device on the manufacturer's Web site. For more information about Device Manager, see "Managing Devices" in this book. For more information about System Information, see "Tools for Troubleshooting" in this book.

- If you cannot associate the device to the driver module indicated in the Stop message, create a list of devices that are sharing IRQs by using Device Manager or System Information. Remove all devices sharing IRQs and reinstall them one at a time until you can reproduce the problem. For example, you find that devices are sharing IRQs 9 and 11 on your computer. To determine the IRQ affected, remove all devices on IRQs 9 and 11. Reinstall devices assigned to IRQ 9 one at a time. If you cannot reproduce the problem, proceed with reinstalling devices assigned to IRQ 11. Check for updated drivers for the problem device on the manufacturer's Web site.

- Check the computer or motherboard manufacturer's Web site for updated system firmware. For more information about updating firmware, see "Troubleshooting Concepts and Strategies" in this book.

- Verify that all of your internal and external peripherals appear on the HCL as devices that meet Windows Logo Requirements, and use only drivers digitally signed by Microsoft. For more information about the HCL, Windows Logo Requirements, and compatible device designations, see the Hardware Compatibility List link on the Web Resources page at http://www.microsoft.com/windows/reskits/webresources. Also, see "Troubleshooting Concepts and Strategies" in this book.

Note   Although a device might be attached to a bus, a Stop 0xD8 error might occur only when you are actively using a device. For example, you might not experience problems with IEEE 1394, SCSI, or USB host controllers until you attempt to use devices attached to them.

■ For more information about simplifying your system configuration as part of diagnosing and troubleshooting problems, see "Troubleshooting Startup" in this book.

For more information about PCI devices and IRQ sharing, see Microsoft Knowledge Base articles Q170922, "How PCI Devices Are Detected and Why They May Fail," and Q252420, "General Description of IRQ Sharing in Windows 2000," in the Microsoft Knowledge Base. To find these articles, see the Microsoft Knowledge Base link on the Web Resources page at http://www.microsoft.com/windows /reskits/webresources.

For more information about Stop 0xF2 messages, see the Microsoft Knowledge Base link on the Web Resources page at http://www.microsoft.com/windows /reskits/webresources. Search using keywords *winnt*, *0x000000F2*, and *0xF2*.

Stop 0xC000021A or STATUS_SYSTEM_PROCESS_TERMINATED

The Stop 0xC000021A message occurs when Windows XP Professional switches into kernel mode and a user-mode subsystem, such as Winlogon or the Client Server Runtime Subsystem (CSRSS), is compromised and security can no longer be guaranteed. Because Windows XP Professional cannot run without Winlogon or CSRSS, this is one of the few situations where the failure of a user-mode service can cause the system to stop responding. You cannot use the kernel debugger in this situation because the error occurred in a user-mode process.

A Stop 0xC000021A message can also occur when the computer is restarted after a system administrator has modified permissions in such a way that the SYSTEM account no longer has adequate permissions to access system files and folders.

Interpreting the Message

This Stop message has three parameters:

1. Status code.

2. This value is 0x00000000 (zero).

3. This value is 0x00000000 (zero).

For information about all possible status codes that might be returned, see the Ntstatus.h file of the Windows XP Professional Driver Development Kit (DDK). For more information about the DDK, see the Driver Development Kits link on the Web Resources page at http://www.microsoft.com/windows/reskits/webresources.

Resolving the Problem

The following suggestions are specific to Stop 0x21A errors. For additional trouble-shooting suggestions that apply to all Stop errors, see "Stop Message Checklist" later in this appendix.

- Stop 0xC000021A messages occur in a user-mode process and the most common causes are third-party applications. If the error occurred after installing a new or updated device driver, system service, or third-party application, you need to remove, disable, or roll back the driver, or uninstall the new software. Contact the software manufacturer about a possible update.

- System file mismatch caused by partially restoring the system from backup media might cause this error (some backup programs do not restore files that they determine are in use). Always use backup software that is Windows XP Professional compatible.

- If SYSTEM account permissions were altered, follow the procedures below to regain access to the boot partition:

  1. Perform a parallel Windows XP Professional installation onto a separate partition or drive. Do not use the original drive and folder names because the new Windows XP Professional installation overwrites previous settings. Complete the second installation.

  2. In the **Run** dialog box, in the **Open** box, type: **c:**

  3. Right-click the original Windows XP Professional *systemroot* folder, and then click **Properties**.

  4. Click the **Security** tab, and then grant the local **SECURITY** account full control of the *systemroot* folder and its subfolders.

  5. Restart the system, and then select the original Windows XP Professional installation from the startup menu.

For more information about Stop 0xC000021A messages, see the Microsoft Knowledge Base link on the Web Resources page at http://www.microsoft.com /windows/reskits/webresources. Search using keywords *winnt* and *0xC000021A*.

Stop 0xC0000221 or STATUS_IMAGE_CHECKSUM_MISMATCH

This Stop message indicates driver, system file, or disk corruption problems (such as a damaged paging file). Faulty memory hardware can also cause this Stop message to appear.

Interpreting the Message

- This Stop message typically displays the name of the damaged file as follows:

```
STOP: 0xC0000221 STATUS_IMAGE_CHECKSUM_MISMATCH <path>\<file name>
- or -
Unable to load device driver <driver_name>
```

Resolving the Problem

The following suggestions are specific to Stop 0x221 errors. For additional trouble-shooting suggestions that apply to all Stop errors, see "Stop Message Checklist" later in this appendix.

- You can use Driver Rollback or System Restore from safe mode, to restore a previous driver. You can also use Windows XP Professional recovery features such as the Last Known Good Configuration startup option, Backup, or Automated System Recovery to restore a previous working configuration. After restoring from backup media, you might need to reapply service packs or hot-fixes, depending on when the backups were made. For more information about the preceding tools, see "Tools for Troubleshooting" in this book.

- If the Stop message names the specific file, try replacing it manually with a fresh copy from the Windows XP Professional operating system CD using safe mode or Recovery Console. For systems using the FAT16 or FAT32 file system, you have the option of using a Windows 98 or Windows Millennium Edition Emergency Boot Disk to access the hard disk.

    If the original file from the operating system CD has a file name that ends with an underscore (_) character, you cannot use the file until it is uncompressed. The Recovery Console's **Copy** command is ideal for copying compressed files because it detects and expands them. If you do not specify a destination file name, you must rename the expanded file with the correct extension before using it. From safe mode or Recovery Console, you can use the **Expand** command to uncompress and copy a file to a destination location. In Recovery Console, the expanded file is given the correct name after being copied to the destination location. For more information about the Copy or Expand commands, see Windows XP Professional Help and Support Center and "Tools for Troubleshooting" in this book.

- Stop message 0xC000026C, caused by similar conditions, provides the name of the system file. You can also use the preceding suggestions to resolve this error.

For more information about Stop 0xC0000221 messages, see the Microsoft Knowledge Base link on the Web Resources page at http://www.microsoft.com /windows/reskits/webresources. Search using keywords *winnt* and *0xC0000221*.

Hardware Malfunction Messages

Stop messages also take the form of hardware malfunction messages and, like all Stop messages, they are displayed in non-windowed text mode. These Stop messages occur after the processor detects a hardware malfunction, with the first one or two lines of the message containing a description. Depending on the HAL, the error text displayed can vary from one computer to another, even when similar components are involved. However, the error description typically points to a hardware problem, as shown in this example:

```
Hardware malfunction.
Call your hardware vendor for support.
```

The installed HAL determines the format and content of the message. Prior to proceeding with the recommendation provided by the message, it is best to contact the manufacturer for technical support. Record the information displayed after the first two lines of the message, as this might prove useful to the support technician.

Under certain circumstances, driver problems can generate Stop messages that appear to be related to a hardware malfunction. For example, if a driver writes to the wrong I/O port, the device at the destination port might respond by generating a hardware malfunction message. Errors of this kind, which are typically detected and debugged in advance of public release, underscore the need to periodically check for updated drivers.

Stop Message Checklist

Stop messages provide diagnostic information, such as Stop codes and driver names, that you can use to resolve the problem. However, this information disappears when you restart your computer. Therefore, it is important to record the information displayed for future reference. When a Stop message appears, you should do the following before restarting the system:

1. Record data in the **Bugcheck information** and **Driver information** sections for later reference.

2. Record and evaluate suggestions in the **Recommended user action** section. Stop messages typically provide troubleshooting tips relevant to the error.

3. Check the Stop message **Debug port and dump status** section (as shown in Figure C-1) to verify that Windows XP Professional successfully dumped memory contents to the paging file and proceed with your troubleshooting efforts.

    After you resolve the problem or at least able to start the computer, you can copy the memory dump file to another location, such as removable media, for further evaluation. Analyzing memory dump files can assist you with identifying root causes by providing you with detailed information about the system state when the Stop message occurred. For more information about creating and analyzing memory dump files, see "Memory Dump Files" earlier in this appendix.

The preceding steps enable you to save important information that you can refer to when using the resources listed in "Stop Message Overview" earlier in this appendix.

Stop messages do not always point to the root of the problem, but they do provide important clues that you or a trained support technician can use to identify and troubleshoot a problem. For more information about troubleshooting concepts, troubleshooting strategies, and the types of information to record when diagnosing problems, see "Troubleshooting Concepts and Strategies" in this book.

Check Your Software

The following are useful software-related techniques that you can use to recover from problems that cause Stop messages.

Check software disk space requirements   Verify that adequate free space exists on your disk volumes for virtual memory paging files and application data files. Insufficient free space might cause Stop messages and other symptoms, including disk corruption. Always check the minimum system requirements recommended by the software publisher before installing an application. To determine the amount allocated to paging files, see "Memory Dump Files" earlier in this appendix.

You can move, delete, or compress unused files manually, or by using Disk Cleanup (Cleanmgr.exe) to increase free space on disk volumes.

To run Disk Cleanup

1. In the **Run** dialog box, in the **Open** box, type:
   cleanmgr

2. In the **Select Drive** dialog box, select a disk volume to clean.

3. Click the **Disk Cleanup** or the **More Options** tab to specify files to compress or delete.

For more information about Disk Cleanup, see Windows XP Professional Help and Support Center. For more information about checking hard disk integrity, see the instructions provided in "Stop 0x00000024 or NTFS_FILE_SYSTEM" earlier in this appendix. Also, see "Troubleshooting Disks and File Systems" in this book.

Use the Last Known Good Configuration   If a Stop message occurs immediately after installing new software or drivers, use the **Last Known Good Configuration** startup option to undo the registry and driver changes. To use this option, restart your computer, and then press F8 when prompted to activate the **Windows Advanced Options** menu. **Last Known Good Configuration** is one of the available options. For more information about Windows XP Professional startup and recovery options, see "Troubleshooting Startup" and "Tools for Troubleshooting" in this book.

Use disaster recovery features   Disaster recovery features such as System Restore and Driver Rollback can undo recent changes. For more information about recovery options, see "Tools for Troubleshooting" and "Troubleshooting Startup" in this book. Also, see Windows XP Professional Help and Support Center.

Restart the system in safe mode   Safe mode is a diagnostic environment that loads a minimum set of drivers and system services, increasing the chances of starting the operating system. After Windows XP Professional has started, you can enable or disable drivers and make the necessary changes to restore stability. To enter safe mode, restart your computer, and then press F8 when prompted to activate the **Windows Advanced Options** menu. **Safe Mode** is one of the available options. For more information about startup and recovery options, see "Troubleshooting Startup" and "Tools for Troubleshooting" in this book.

Use Recovery Console   You can use Recovery Console to perform advanced operations, such as replacing corrupted files. You can also disable a driver or service causing a Stop error by using the Recovery Console listsvc and disable commands. You can also disable a service by renaming the file specified in a Stop message. For more information about using Recovery Console to recover from startup problems, see "Troubleshooting Startup" and "Tools for Troubleshooting" in this book.

Check Event Viewer logs   Check the Event Viewer **System** and **Application** logs for warnings or error message patterns that point to an application or service. Record this information and refer to it when searching for more information or when contacting technical support. For more information about Event Viewer, see Windows XP Professional Help and Support Center and "Tools for Troubleshooting" in this book.

Check application and driver compatibility   Categories of software that are known to cause Stop messages if they are not fully compatible with Windows XP Professional (such as those meant for previous versions of Windows) include backup, remote control, multimedia, CD mastering, Internet firewall, and antivirus tools. If temporarily disabling a driver or uninstalling software resolves the problem, contact the manufacturer for information about an update or workaround. You need to disable a service that is causing Stop errors or other problems rather than stop or pause it. A stopped or paused service runs after you restart the computer. For more information about disabling services for diagnostic or troubleshooting purposes, see "Troubleshooting Startup" in this book.

Install compatible antivirus tools   Virus infection can cause problems such as Stop errors (for example, Stop 0x7B) and data loss. Before running antivirus software, verify that you are using updated virus signature files. Signature files provide information that enables the antivirus scanning software to identify viruses. Using current signature files increases the chances of detecting the most recent viruses.

Verify that your virus scanner product checks the master boot record (MBR) and the boot sector. For more information about MBR and boot sector viruses, see "Troubleshooting Disks and File Systems" in this book.

Check for and install service pack updates Microsoft periodically releases service packs, which contain updated system files, security enhancements, and other improvements that can resolve problems. You can use Windows Update to check for, and install, the latest versions as they become available. To check the service pack revision installed on your system, in the **Run** dialog box, in the **Open** box, type **winver**. The **About Windows** dialog box displays operating system and service pack revision information. For more information about Windows Update, see "Tools for Troubleshooting" in this book.

Report your errors You can find out more information about the conditions that caused the Stop message by using the Windows Error Reporting service or by using the Online Crash Analysis Web site. For more information about options for analyzing memory dump files, see "Using Memory Dump Files to Analyze Stop Errors" earlier in this appendix.

Check for interim updates Occasionally, interim solutions or workarounds, also known as hotfixes, are available between service pack releases. Do not install these interim updates unless directed to do so by technical support, a Microsoft Knowledge Base article, or a Windows Error Reporting advisory that specifically applies to your problem.

Check information sources You might find information about a workaround or solution to the problem. Information sources include the Microsoft Knowledge Base and manufacturer's technical support Web pages. For more information about the Microsoft Knowledge Base, see the Microsoft Knowledge Base link on the Web Resources page at http://www.microsoft.com/windows/reskits/webresources. For more information about checking information sources, see "Troubleshooting Concepts and Strategies" in this book.

Install and use a kernel debugger You can use a kernel debugger to gather more information about the problem. The Debugging Tools Help file contains instructions and examples that can help you find additional information about the Stop message affecting you. For more information about installing and using debugging tools, see "Stop Message Overview" and "Using Memory Dump Files to Analyze Stop Errors" earlier in this appendix.

Check Your Hardware

The following are useful hardware-related techniques that can enable you to recover from problems that cause Stop messages.

Restore a previous configuration   If a Stop message appears immediately after adding new hardware, see if removing or replacing the part and restoring a previous configuration resolves the problem. You can use recovery features such as Last Known Good Configuration, Driver Rollback, System Restore, or Automated System Recovery, to restore the system to the previous configuration or to remove a specific driver. For more information about startup and recovery options, see "Troubleshooting Startup" and "Tools for Troubleshooting" in this book.

Check for non-default firmware settings   Some *x*86-based and Itanium-based systems have firmware that enables you to change hardware settings such as power management parameters, video configuration, memory timing, and memory shadowing. Do not alter these settings unless there is a specific requirement to do so. If you are experiencing hardware problems, verify that firmware values are set to default values. To restore default firmware values, follow the instructions provided by the computer or motherboard manufacturer.

Check for non-default hardware clock speeds   Verify that hardware is running at the correct speed. Do not set clock speeds for components such as the processor, video adapter, or memory above the rated specification, a practice known as "overclocking," because this can cause random errors that are difficult to diagnose. If you are experiencing problems with overclocked hardware, restore default clock speed and CPU voltage settings according to the instructions provided by the hardware manufacturer.

Check the Hardware Compatibility List   Verify that your hardware appears in the latest revision of the Hardware Compatibility List (HCL) for Windows XP Professional. If your device is not in the HCL, contact the hardware manufacturer for more information. The manufacturer might be in the process of certifying the hardware, testing new drivers, or updating firmware to improve compatibility. For more information about the HCL, see the Hardware Compatibility List link on the Web Resources page at http://www.microsoft.com/windows/reskits/webresources. Also see "Troubleshooting Concepts and Strategies" in this book.

Check for hardware-related updates   Check the manufacturer's Web site to see if updated firmware is available for your system or individual peripherals. For more information about updating firmware, see "Troubleshooting Concepts and Strategies" in this book.

Check by running hardware diagnostic tools Run hardware diagnostic software to verify that your hardware is not defective. These tools are typically built into, or bundled with your hardware.

Check ATA disk and controller settings If your system uses Advanced Technology Attachment (ATA) storage devices such as hard disks, determine if a firmware setting, **Primary IDE only**, is available. If the setting is available, enable it if the second ATA channel is unused. Verify that primary and secondary device jumper settings are set correctly. Storage devices (including CD and DVD-ROM drives) use their own firmware, so check the manufacturer's Web site periodically for updates. Verify that you are using a cable that is compatible with your device because certain ATA standards require you to use a different cable type.

Check for SCSI disk and controller settings If your system uses an SCSI adapter, check for updates to device drivers and adapter firmware. Try disabling advanced SCSI firmware options, such as **sync negotiation** for low-bandwidth devices (tape drives and CD-ROM drives). Verify that you are using cables that meet the SCSI adapter's requirements for termination and maximum cable length. Check SCSI ID settings and termination to ensure that they are correct for all devices. For more information about troubleshooting SCSI devices, see "Troubleshooting Startup" in this book. For more information about the SCSI standard, see the SCSI link on the Web Resources page at http://www.microsoft.com/windows/reskits/webresources.

Check for proper hardware installation and connections Verify that internal expansion boards and external devices are firmly seated and properly installed, and that connecting cables are properly fastened. If necessary, clean adapter card electrical contacts using supplies available at electronics stores. For more information about troubleshooting hardware, see "Troubleshooting Concepts and Strategies" and "Managing Devices" in this book.

Check memory compatibility If a Stop message appears immediately after adding new memory, verify that the new part is compatible with your system. Do not rely solely on physical characteristics (such as chip count or module dimensions) when purchasing new or replacement memory. Always adhere to the manufacturer's specifications when purchasing memory modules. For example, you can fit a memory module rated for 66-megahertz (MHz) or 100-MHz operation (PC66 or PC100 RAM, respectively) into a system using a 133-Mhz memory bus speed, and it might initially appear to work. However, using the slower memory results in system instability.

Check by temporarily remove devices Installing a new device can sometimes cause resource conflicts with existing devices. You might recover from this problem by temporarily removing devices not needed to start the operating system. For example, temporarily removing a CD-ROM or audio adapter might enable you start

Windows XP Professional. You can then examine the device and operating system settings separately to determine what changes you need to make. For more information about simplifying your hardware configuration for troubleshooting purposes, see "Troubleshooting Startup" in this book.

Check by replacing a device   If you are unable to obtain diagnostic software for the problem device, install a replacement to verify that this action resolves the problem. If the problem disappears, then the original hardware might be defective or incorrectly configured.

Check hardware resource settings   Firmware on *x*86-based systems might provide the option to assign specific hardware interrupt requests (IRQs) to specific Peripheral Component Interconnect (PCI) expansion slots for troubleshooting and diagnostic purposes. If you are experiencing problems installing Windows XP Professional on *x*86-based systems and are familiar with hardware, try to minimize the number of devices sharing IRQs.

Other *x*86-based firmware forces IRQ sharing across multiple PCI slots regardless of the devices installed. If you are experiencing problems installing Windows XP Professional on *x*86-based systems and are familiar with the hardware, try moving a device to another PCI slot.

Documentation for certain PCI adapters (for example, network and SCSI adapters) strongly advises that you install them in "master" or busmaster PCI slots on *x*86-based systems. For more information, see your PCI adapter and computer documentation.

For more information about PCI devices and IRQ sharing see Microsoft Knowledge Base articles Q170922, "How PCI Devices Are Detected and Why They May Fail," and Q252420, "General Description of IRQ Sharing in Windows 2000," in the Microsoft Knowledge Base. To find these articles, see the Microsoft Knowledge Base link on the Web Resources page at http://www.microsoft.com/windows/reskits/webresources.

Check information sources   You might be able to find information about a workaround or solution to the problem. Information sources include the Microsoft Knowledge Base and manufacturer's technical support Web pages. For more information about the Microsoft Knowledge Base, see the Microsoft Knowledge Base link on the Web Resources page at http://www.microsoft.com/windows/reskits/webresources. For more information about checking information sources, see "Troubleshooting Concepts and Strategies" in this book.

Contact technical support   As a last resort, Microsoft technical support can assist you with troubleshooting your system. For more information about Microsoft technical support options, see the Support link on the Microsoft Web page at http://www.microsoft.com.

Additional Resources

These resources contain additional information related to this appendix.

- "Troubleshooting Concepts and Strategies" in this book.

- "Troubleshooting Startup" in this book.

- "Managing Devices" in this book.

- "Disk Management" in this book.

- "File Systems" in this book.

- "Troubleshooting Disks and File Systems" in this book.

- "Tools for Troubleshooting" in this book.

- "Backup and Restore" in this book.

- "Evaluating Cache Memory and Cache Usage" in the *Operations Guide* of the *Microsoft® Windows® 2000 Server Resource Kit*.

- The Debugging Tools link on the Web Resources page at http://www.microsoft.com/windows/reskits/webresources.

- The Hardware Compatibility List link on the Web Resources page at http://www.microsoft.com/windows/reskits/webresources.

- The Driver Development Kits link on the Web Resources page at http://www.microsoft.com/windows/reskits/webresources.

- The Microsoft Product Support Services link on the Web Resources page at http://www.microsoft.com/windows/reskits/webresources.

- The ACPI link on the Web Resources page at http://www.microsoft.com/windows/reskits/webresources.

- The Extensible Firmware Interface link on the Web Resources page at http://www.microsoft.com/windows/reskits/webresources.

- Windows XP Professional Help and Support for detailed information about the registry and its components.

Appendix D

Tools for Troubleshooting

Microsoft® Windows® XP Professional provides a number of tools that can help you diagnose and resolve hardware and software problems. The subset of tools discussed here is especially useful for troubleshooting many common problems.

Related Information

- For more information about troubleshooting concepts and strategies, see "Troubleshooting Concepts and Strategies" in this book.

- For more information about troubleshooting startup problems, see "Troubleshooting Startup" in this book.

- For more information about enabling, disabling, and managing devices, see "Managing Devices" in this book.

- For more information about troubleshooting disk problems, see "Troubleshooting Disks and File Systems" and "Disk Management" in this book.

Using This Appendix

This appendix describes the troubleshooting and maintenance tools available in Windows XP Professional. To help you locate the tools needed to solve a problem, Table D-1 describes how this appendix presents related tools.

Table D-1   Using This Appendix

To Find Information About...	See This Section
Identifying the types of tools that Windows XP Professional provides, including: ■ How to install and run the tools. ■ How to get Help about the tools.	Installing and Running Troubleshooting Tools
Troubleshooting instability and startup problems and restoring system and data files.	Disaster Recovery Tools
Troubleshooting problems related to startup, applications, and services.	Application and Service Tools
Troubleshooting a computer that is in a remote location.	Remote Management Tools for Troubleshooting
Maintaining disks and volumes to prevent problems before they occur.	Disk and Maintenance Tools
Troubleshooting problems caused by incompatible, missing, or corrupted driver and system files.	System File Tools
Monitoring and troubleshooting network performance problems.	Networking Tools for Troubleshooting
Locating other chapters related to troubleshooting in *Microsoft*® *Windows*® *XP Professional Resource Kit, Second Edition*.	Additional Resources

Installing and Running Troubleshooting Tools

Tools are small applications that implement a limited set of functions and help you perform management or problem-solving tasks. The subset of tools discussed in this appendix is presented in categories based on tool uses, such as recovery, diagnosis, and system file maintenance. Tools are also described according to where to find them and how to use them. For example, you can download a debugging tool or install Windows Support Tools from the Support folder on the Microsoft® Windows® XP Professional operating system CD.

Installing Tools

When you use the operating system CD to install Windows XP Professional, Setup installs several tools with the operating system. You can install additional tools from the CD or by downloading them as needed. Troubleshooting tools can be described in three categories.

Built-in tools   Setup installs built-in tools as part of the default setup. For each built-in tool, Windows XP Professional Help and Support Center provides an overview, and usage and syntax examples (if applicable).

Support Tools   Windows Support Tools are optional tools that you might find useful for troubleshooting. Setup does not install these tools; instead, use the Support Tools setup program.

To install Support Tools

1. While Windows XP Professional is running, insert the Windows XP Professional operating system CD into your computer.

2. Click **No** if you are prompted to reinstall Microsoft® Windows®.

3. When the **Welcome** screen appears, click **Perform Additional Tasks**, and then click **Browse this CD**.

4. Navigate to the *drive*:\Support\Tools folder on the Windows XP Professional CD and double-click **Setup.exe**.
   The variable *drive* represents the drive letter assigned to the CD-ROM.

5. Follow the instructions that appear on the screen.
   If Support Tools Setup detects an older version of Support Tools, you are prompted to uninstall them. It is recommended that you remove all previous versions of Support Tools before proceeding with the installation.

If you do not have a Windows XP Professional operating system CD available, or for network-based installations, you can install Support Tools by running *server**share*\i386\Support\Tools\Setup.exe on the network distribution share. The Support Tools setup program adds Windows Support Tools to the Start menu, allowing you to view Support Tools Help for more information. For more information about Support Tools setup options, including command-line and unattended setup parameters, see the Readme.htm file in the \Support\Tools folder.

Downloadable debugging tools   Microsoft® Debugging Tools for Windows enables advanced users to diagnose and troubleshoot complex problems that might not be solved by other means. For example, you can use a kernel debugger to determine the cause of a Stop error, such as a Stop 0x0000000A, IRQL_NOT_LESS_OR_EQUAL. The Windows XP Professional operating system CD does not provide debugging tools; you must download them from Microsoft.

To install the debugging tools

1. Click the **Debugging Tools** link on the Web Resources page at http://www.microsoft.com/windows/reskits/webresources.

2. Click **Debugging Tools for Windows**, and follow the instructions under **Installing Debugging Tools for Windows**.

3. At the prompt, specify the destination folder.

Setup copies files and creates a Start menu Microsoft Debugging Tools folder. For more information about Stop messages and debugging tools, see "Common Stop Messages for Troubleshooting" in this book.

Tool Interface Types

Windows XP Professional tools typically implement a command-line interface or a graphical user interface (GUI). The interface type determines how you interact with the tool.

Command-line These tools use a character mode user interface and typically accept only keyboard input. Compared to GUI tools, command-line tools typically require less disk space and fewer system resources to run. In many cases, you can use additional features or change the default behavior of a command-line tool by specifying optional parameters when starting the tool. File name extensions of command-line tools include .vbs, .exe, and .com. For inexperienced users, command-line tools might be more difficult to use than GUI tools.

Graphical user interface GUI tools accept mouse input and have graphical controls such as windows, dialog boxes, and menus. Typically, GUI-based tools require more disk space and system resources than command-line tools. Most GUI tools also accept optional parameters that change default behavior. File name extensions of GUI tools include .exe and .msc. For many users, GUI tools are easier to use than command-line tools.

Starting GUI Tools

You can start GUI tools from the Start menu, by using shortcuts provided by the operating system and software installation programs, or, if you want to specify optional parameters, by using either of the following methods:

■ **From the Run dialog box.** In the **Run** dialog box, start the tool by using the following syntax:

toolname [*/switch1*] [*/switch2*]

The */switch* parameters are optional, and the number of available parameters varies by tool. Typing the file name extension is normally optional. For example, to start Task Manager (Taskman.exe), you can type **taskman** or

taskman.exe. The exception is when two tools have file names that differ only by file name extension (for example, mytool.com and mytool.exe).

– or –

■ **From the command prompt.** At the command prompt, type the file name of the tool and any parameters.

Starting GUI Snap-in Tools

Snap-ins are GUI administrative tools that differ from standard GUI programs in that you can run them individually, or group them together to create a custom set of tools. You can modify, create, and save snap-in consoles by using the Microsoft Management Console (MMC), a framework that hosts administrative tools. You then access a snap-in or a snap-in group by using the console, which displays the tools in a console tree, and the administrative properties, services, and events that are acted on by the items in the tree. An example of a pre-defined Windows XP Professional console is the Computer Management snap-in Compmgmt.msc. You can run a snap-in or snap-in group from the Start menu, by using shortcut icons provided by the operating system and software installation programs, or by using any of the following methods:

■ **From the Run dialog box.** In the **Run** dialog box, start the tool using the following syntax:

toolname.**msc** [*/switch1*] [*/switch2*]

The */switch* parameters are optional and the number of available parameters varies by tool. When starting a snap-in from the **Run** dialog box, you must type the complete file name, including the .msc extension. For example, to start the Services snap-in, you must type: **services.msc**. Starting a snap-in or snap-in group by using this method automatically invokes MMC, which displays the contents of the console.

– or –

■ **From the command prompt.** At the command prompt, type the entire file name of the snap-in, including the .msc extension and any optional parameters.

– or –

■ **From MMC.** In the **Run** dialog box, type **mmc**. To add one or more snap-ins, click **Add/Remove Snap-in** on the **File** menu. You can run a snap-in by clicking the snap-in name from the MMC interface.

For more information about MMC and snap-ins, see Windows XP Professional Help and Support Center.

Starting Command-Line Tools and Logging Output

You can start a command-line tool from the command prompt by typing the tool file name (the .exe extension is optional), including any optional parameters. Use the following syntax:

```
toolname [/switch1] [/switch2]
```

The */switch* parameters are optional and the number of available parameters varies by tool. Typing the file name extension is optional. For example, to start IP Configuration (IPConfig.exe), type **ipconfig** or **ipconfig.exe**.

The exception to this is when two tools have file names that differ only by file name extension. For example, Mytool.com and Mytool.exe.

For more information about the command prompt, see Windows XP Professional Help and Support Center.

How to Obtain a Log of Command-Line Tool Output

Although most command-line tools display useful information, many do not provide a way to permanently record data to a log. If you do not record the information displayed, you must rerun the tool. However, *redirection*, a command-line feature, allows you to direct command-line tool output to disk by using the following command-line syntax:

```
toolname [/switch1] [/switch2] [...] > [drive:]\[path]\filename.txt
```

By using the greater-than (>) sign, called the *redirection symbol*, you can specify the drive, path, and file name to save output to. The */switch* parameters are optional, and the number of available parameters varies by tool. The *drive* and *path* parameters are also optional. If you do not specify a drive or path, output is saved to the current drive and path.

Ways to View Command-Line Help

A common use of redirection is to save or view the help information for a command-line tool. For most command-line tools, you can view a list of parameters by using the back-slash-question-mark (**/?**) parameter. A large amount of help text might cause the page to scroll too quickly for you to read. To read Help for command-line tools, you can use the following syntax to pause the display or to save the information to a file.

To view Help information one screen at a time

■ To display information and pause between each screen of output until the user presses a key, use the following syntax:

```
toolname /? | More
```

For example, to pause help output for the **dir** command, type **dir /? | More**.

To save Help information to a file

- To cause the tool or command to save help information to a file, use the following syntax:

```
toolname /? > [drive:][path]filename.txt
```

For example, to save help information for the **dir** directory list command, type:

```
dir /? > D:\dir_help.txt
```

You can then use a text editor (such as Notepad.exe) to view the help information that you saved to disk.

Help and Support Center

Windows XP Professional Help and Support Center provides a central location to access Help, tool usage and installation information, configuration wizards, search engines, and links to information that covers a wide range of Windows XP Professional topics including:

- Hardware devices such as modems and network adapters

- Internet and networking

- Multimedia applications and devices

- E-mail, printing, and faxing issues

- Working remotely

- Remote assistance and troubleshooting

- System information and diagnostics

- Troubleshooting tools and diagnostic programs provided by Windows XP Professional

To open Help and Support Center

1. Click **Start**, and then click **Help and Support**.

2. For more information about tools, under **Pick a task**, click **Use Tools to view your computer information and diagnose problems**.

You can also use Windows XP Professional Help and Support Center to submit a form describing your problem to Microsoft. A Microsoft Support Professional then evaluates the information and contacts you by using the chosen contact option, such as Remote Assistance, which allows the Microsoft Support Professional to assist you by sharing control of your computer. For more information about Remote Assistance, see "Remote Assistance" later in this appendix.

Disaster Recovery Tools

Software and hardware issues can affect the way that your system functions. Severe problems might prevent you from starting Windows XP Professional normally.

Software problems   Installing incompatible software, incorrectly changing system configuration settings, or installing faulty device drivers can cause system instability or a Stop error.

Hardware problems   Hardware that is defective, malfunctioning, incorrectly installed, or incorrectly configured can also cause instability or a Stop error.

Other problems   Deleted or corrupted system files caused by problems such as user error or virus activity can cause data loss or prevent you from starting the operating system.

Any of the preceding types of problems can prevent you from starting Windows XP Professional in normal mode, causing certain applications or data to become inaccessible. Windows XP Professional provides several tools that enable you to troubleshoot startup and stability problems, and restore system and data files.

Table D-2 lists these tools according to the preferred order of use, from tools that present little or no risk to data, to those that might cause data loss. With the exception of the Automated System Recovery (ASR) restore phase, Last Known Good Configuration, and Recovery Console, the features in the table are available in safe and normal startup modes. If the following tools and features do not resolve the problem, and you upgraded your system from an earlier version of Windows, you might have the option to uninstall Windows XP Professional. For more information, see "Uninstall Windows XP Professional" in this appendix.

Table D-2   Comparison of Windows XP Professional Recovery Tools and Features

Recovery Feature	Function	Tool Type, Interface
Last Known Good Configuration	A startup option to use when the system cannot start in normal or safe mode following a driver or application installation that causes a problem. By using the Last Known Good Configuration, you can recover by reversing the most recent driver and registry changes made since you last started Windows XP Professional.	Built-in, startup option
Device Driver Roll Back	A Device Manager feature that allows you to replace an individual device driver with the previously installed version if the driver was updated after you installed Windows XP Professional. Device Driver Roll Back is available in normal or safe mode.	Built-in, GUI

Table D-2   Comparison of Windows XP Professional Recovery Tools and Features

Recovery Feature	Function	Tool Type, Interface
System Restore	A service for *x*86-based computers that actively monitors your system and records changes to the registry, to system files, and to certain application files. System Restore allows you to undo recent registry and file changes by using information previously saved in restore points. Use to restore the system to a previous state. System Restore is available in normal or safe mode.	Built-in, GUI
Add or Remove Programs in Control Panel	A Control Panel feature you can use to uninstall programs. Use to temporarily uninstall software that you suspect is causing a problem. You can uninstall an application in normal or safe mode.	Built-in, GUI
Recovery Console	A command-line environment that you can use to perform advanced troubleshooting operations. In addition to Last Known Good Configuration and safe mode, advanced users can use Recovery Console to attempt manual recovery operations.	Built-in, command-line environment
Backup	A tool for saving data, such as the system state, before you troubleshoot problems, attempt workarounds, or apply updates. Backup (Ntbackup.exe) enables you to restore system settings and data if your troubleshooting attempts worsen the problem. Use in conjunction with a parallel installation to restore a system that cannot start in normal or safe modes. Backup is available in safe or normal mode. For more information about parallel installations, see "Troubleshooting Startup" in this book.	Built-in, GUI
Automated System Recovery (ASR)	A Backup (Ntbackup.exe) option to use when boot and system files become corrupt, preventing your system from starting in normal or safe modes, or using Recovery Console. This option is more desirable than formatting disks and reinstalling Windows because ASR restores system settings and critical files on the system and boot partitions. The user interface to ASR backup is the ASR wizard in Backup, which steps you through the process of creating an ASR backup set and an ASR floppy. Windows XP Professional Setup provides the user interface to ASR restore. Because the ASR process formats disks, consider this a last resort when using Last Known Good Configuration, Device Driver Roll Back, System Restore, or Recovery Console does not solve the problem. ASR is available in safe or normal mode.	Built-in, GUI (ASR Backup), and text-mode Setup option (ASR Restore)

Last Known Good Configuration

The Last Known Good Configuration startup option allows you to recover from a problem by reversing driver and registry changes made since you last started Windows XP Professional. Windows XP Professional does not update Last Known Good Configuration information in the registry until the operating system successfully restarts in normal mode and a user logs on and is authenticated.

Using Last Known Good Configuration restores information for the registry subkey HKEY_LOCAL_MACHINE\SYSTEM\CurrentControlSet. Additionally, if you updated any device drivers, choosing Last Known Good Configuration restores the previous drivers.

Using Last Known Good Configuration might enable you to resolve startup or stability problems. For example, if a Stop error occurs immediately after installing a new application or device driver, you can restart the computer and use Last Known Good Configuration to recover from the problem.

When you are troubleshooting, it is recommended that you use Last Known Good Configuration before you try other options, such as safe mode. However, even if you decide to use safe mode first, logging on to the computer in safe mode does not update the Last Known Good Configuration. Therefore, using Last Known Good Configuration remains an option if you cannot resolve your problem by using safe mode.

To use Last Known Good Configuration from the Windows Advanced Options Menu

1. Remove any floppy disks or CDs from your computer and restart your computer.

2. When prompted, press F8. If Windows XP Professional starts without displaying the **Please select the operating system to start** menu, restart your computer. Press F8 after the firmware POST process completes, but before Windows XP Professional displays graphical output.

3. On the **Windows Advanced Options Menu**, select **Last Known Good Configuration**

    For more information about other options available on the Windows Advanced Options Menu, see "Using Safe Mode" later in this appendix.

You can also use Last Known Good Configuration by selecting it from the startup recovery menu. Windows XP Professional detects when the last startup attempt was not successful and displays a message that includes a menu of startup options, as shown in Figure D-1.

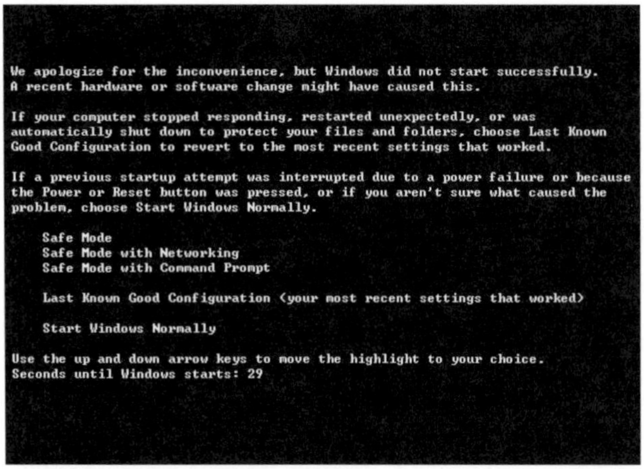

```
We apologize for the inconvenience, but Windows did not start successfully.
A recent hardware or software change might have caused this.

If your computer stopped responding, restarted unexpectedly, or was
automatically shut down to protect your files and folders, choose Last Known
Good Configuration to revert to the most recent settings that worked.

If a previous startup attempt was interrupted due to a power failure or because
the Power or Reset button was pressed, or if you aren't sure what caused the
problem, choose Start Windows Normally.

    Safe Mode
    Safe Mode with Networking
    Safe Mode with Command Prompt

    Last Known Good Configuration (your most recent settings that worked)

    Start Windows Normally

Use the up and down arrow keys to move the highlight to your choice.
Seconds until Windows starts: 29
```

Figure D-1 Startup recovery menu

The startup recovery menu is separate from the Windows Advanced Options Menu. A user manually invokes the Windows Advanced Options Menu by pressing F8, while the operating system automatically displays the startup recovery menu after an unsuccessful startup.

To Use Last Known Good Configuration from the startup recovery menu after an unsuccessful startup

1. Restart your computer. The startup recovery menu appears shortly after Windows XP Professional starts.

2. On the startup recovery menu, select **Last Known Good Configuration (your most recent settings that worked)**.

In some cases, other troubleshooting options might be preferable to choosing Last Known Good Configuration. If you know the specific driver causing the problem, you have the option of using Device Driver Roll Back in safe mode. This might be preferable because Device Driver Roll Back changes are limited to a single device. Also, consider using System Restore because it enables you to revert system registry settings by date. For more information about Device Driver Roll Back and System Restore, see "Device Driver Roll Back" and "System Restore" later in this appendix.

Using Safe Mode

If you are unable to start your system by using Last Known Good Configuration, Windows XP Professional provides *safe mode*, a startup option that disables startup programs and nonessential services to create an environment useful for troubleshooting and diagnosing problems. In safe mode, Windows XP Professional starts a minimal set of drivers that the operating system needs to function. Support for devices such as audio devices, most USB devices, and IEEE 1394 devices is disabled to reduce the variables that you need to account for when diagnosing the cause of startup problems, Stop messages, or system instability.

Logging on to the computer in safe mode does not update Last Known Good Configuration information. Therefore, if you log on to your computer in safe mode and then decide you want to try Last Known Good Configuration, the option to do so is still available.

Safe Mode Enables Only Essential Drivers and Services

Essential drivers and system services enabled in safe mode include the following:

- Drivers for serial or PS/2 mouse devices, standard keyboards, hard disks, CD-ROM drives, and standard VGA devices. Your system firmware must support universal serial bus (USB) mouse and USB keyboard devices in order for you to use these input devices in safe mode.

- System services for the Event Log, Plug and Play, remote procedure calls (RPCs), and Logical Disk Manager.

The following registry keys list the driver and service groups enabled in safe mode.

Safe mode   HKEY_LOCAL_MACHINE\SYSTEM\CurrentControlSet\Control\Safe-Boot\Minimal

Safe mode with networking   HKEY_LOCAL_MACHINE\SYSTEM\CurrentCon-trolSet\Control\SafeBoot\Network

Enabling only components needed for basic functionality allows the operating system to start in the following situations.

The computer consistently stops responding   You can restart the operating system in safe mode and use the tools described in this appendix to diagnose and resolve problems.

The computer starts with a blank or distorted video display   You can start your computer in safe mode and then use Control Panel to select video adapter settings that are compatible with your monitor. New settings take effect when you restart the computer.

The computer does not start normally after you install new hardware or software   If recently installed hardware or software prevents you from starting Windows XP Professional in normal mode, you can use safe mode to uninstall software, or to remove or roll back device drivers.

If you can start the computer in safe mode but not in normal mode, the problem is caused by a driver or service that runs in normal mode.

Safe Mode Bypasses Startup Programs

Bypassing startup programs reduces system complexity and enables you to see whether a startup program is the source of the problem. Safe mode bypasses startup programs in the following locations or of the following types.

Current User, All Users, and Administrator profiles   In safe mode, the operating system does not run startup programs called by shortcuts stored in the Start Menu\Programs\Startup folder in the following directories:

- *USERPROFILE*

- *ALLUSERSPROFILE*

- *SystemDrive*\Documents and Settings\Administrator

Run and RunOnce registry subkeys   In safe mode, Windows XP Professional does not run startup programs specified in registry Run and RunOnce subkeys. For more information about startup programs specified in the registry, see "Troubleshooting Startup" in this book.

Advertised applications and network logon scripts   In safe mode, the operating system does not run network-based startup programs. To enable network logon scripts in safe mode, select **Safe Mode with Networking** on the **Windows Advanced Options Menu**.

For more information about startup programs, startup program registry subkeys, and disabling startup programs for diagnostic purposes, see "Troubleshooting Startup" in this book.

> **Note**   Your computer might take longer to start and shut down when it is running in safe mode because Windows XP Professional disables disk caching in safe mode.

To start your computer in safe mode

1. Remove all floppy disks and CDs from your computer, and then restart your computer.

2. When prompted, press F8. If Windows XP Professional starts without displaying the **Please select the operating system to start** menu, restart your computer. Press F8 after the firmware POST process completes, but before Windows XP Professional displays graphical output.

3. From the **Windows Advanced Options Menu**, select a safe mode option listed in Table D-3. Table D-3 also lists other options available on the Windows Advanced Options Menu.

Table D-3   Options on the Windows Advanced Options Menu

Startup Option	Description
Safe Mode	Loads the minimum set of device drivers and system services required to start Windows XP Professional. User specific startup programs do not run.
Safe Mode with Networking	Includes the services and drivers needed for network connectivity. Safe mode with networking enables logging on to the network, logon scripts, security, and Group Policy settings. Nonessential services and startup programs not related to networking do not run.
Safe Mode with Command Prompt	Starts the computer in safe mode, but displays the command prompt rather than the Windows GUI interface.
Enable Boot Logging	Creates a log file (Ntbtlog.txt) in the *systemroot* folder, which contains the file names and status of all drivers loaded into memory. *Systemroot* is an environment variable that can vary from one system running Windows XP Professional to another. For more information about environment variables, see "Troubleshooting Startup" in this book.
Enable VGA Mode	Starts the computer in standard VGA mode by using the current video driver. This option helps you recover from distorted video displays caused by using incorrect settings for the display adapter or monitor.
Last Known Good Configuration	Restores the registry and driver configuration in use the last time the computer started successfully.
Debugging Mode	Starts Windows XP Professional in kernel debugging mode, which allows you to use a kernel debugger for troubleshooting and system analysis.
Start Windows Normally	Starts Windows XP Professional in normal mode.
Reboot	Restart the computer.

You can also select a safe mode option to use from the startup recovery menu that appears when Windows XP Professional detects that the most recent startup attempt was unsuccessful. For more information about the startup recovery menu, see "Last Known Good Configuration" earlier in this appendix.

For more information about safe mode, see Windows XP Professional Help and Support Center.

Device Driver Roll Back

Updating one or more device drivers might cause problems, such as resource conflicts that prevent devices from functioning, Stop errors, and startup problems. To prevent problems after upgrading a device driver, avoid using beta or unsigned drivers, because these drivers might not be fully tested for Windows XP Professional compatibility.

If a problem does occur immediately after you update a driver, you can revert to the previous version by using a Device Manager feature called Device Driver Roll Back. If the problem prevents you from starting Windows XP Professional in normal mode, you can roll back device drivers in safe mode. You must be logged on as an administrator or a member of the Administrators group to roll back a driver.

To roll back a driver

1. In the **Run** dialog box, type **devmgmt.msc**.

2. Expand a category, such as **Standard floppy disk controller**, and then double-click a device name.

3. On the **Driver** tab, click **Roll Back Driver**.

4. At the prompt, click **Yes** to confirm that you want to roll back to the previous driver.

    The driver roll back process checks for a previous driver, and if one is not found, the following message appears:

    ```
    No driver files have been backed up for this device.
    If you are having problems with this device you should view the Troubleshooter
    information. Would you like to launch the Troubleshooter?
    ```

If rolling back drivers does not resolve the problem, you have the option of using the Last Known Good Configuration or System Restore. For more information about System Restore and Last Known Good Configuration, see "Last Known Good Configuration" and "System Restore" in this appendix.

Driver roll back limitations   When using Device Driver Roll Back, be aware of the following limitations:

- You cannot roll back beyond one driver version. For example, you cannot revert to the second to the last version of a driver.

- You cannot roll back printer drivers.

- You cannot roll back drivers for all functions of a multifunction device simultaneously. You must roll back each driver separately. For example, if you have a multifunction device that provides audio and modem functionality, you must roll back the modem driver and the audio driver separately.

- You cannot uninstall a driver by using Device Driver Roll Back (you must use the Uninstall feature in Device Manager to do this).

For more information about Device Manager and rolling back drivers, see Windows XP Professional Help and Support Center or "Managing Devices" in this book.

System Restore

Using System Restore, you can restore your *x*86-based system to a state prior to the occurrence of a problem. System Restore monitors changes to certain system and application files. System Restore functions like an "undo" feature for Windows XP Professional configuration changes, allowing you to recover from problems caused by such things as incorrect system settings, faulty drivers, incompatible applications and so on, without risk to personal files, such as documents or e-mail.

System Restore enables you to restore your system by automatically creating restore points based on a preset schedule or in response to system events (such as installing a new application or driver). You can also manually create restore points as needed. You must be logged on as an administrator or a member of the Administrators group to use System Restore.

System Restore consists of two parts, file monitoring and restore point management.

File Monitoring

System Restore monitors file operations for a core set of system and application files specified in *systemroot*\System32\Restore\Filelist.xml. System Restore records changes to the original file and sometimes copies it to a hidden archive before Windows XP Professional overwrites, deletes, or changes, the monitored file. System Restore does not monitor the following files and folders:

- The virtual memory paging file.

- Personal user data, such as files in My Documents, Favorites, Recycle Bin, Temporary Internet Files, History, and Temp folders.

- Image and graphics files, such as those with .bmp, .jpg, and .eps extensions.

- Application data files with extensions not listed in *systemroot*\System32\Restore\Filelist.xml such as .doc, .xls, .mdb, and .pst.

Restore Points and Restore Point Management

Restore points contain the following two types of information:

- A snapshot of the registry.

- Certain dynamic system files.

System Restore creates restore points according to the following system events, user actions, or time intervals.

Installing an unsigned device driver   Installing an unsigned driver causes System Restore to create a restore point.

Installing System Restore compliant applications   Installing an application that uses Windows Installer, or Install Shield Pro version 7.0 or later, causes System Restore to create a restore point.

Installing an update by using Automatic Updates   Installing an update by using Automatic Updates or installing an update directly by using Windows Update causes System Restore to create a restore point. For more information about the Automatic Updates feature in Windows XP Professional, see "Windows Update" later in this appendix.

Performing a System Restore operation   System Restore creates a new restore point when you revert your system to a previous state by using a restore point. System Restore implements this safeguard in the event that you use the wrong restore point. You can undo the last restore, rerun System Restore, and select another restore point.

Restoring data from backup media   When you use the Backup tool to restore files, System Restore creates a restore point to use before restoring from backup media. If problems occur with the Backup application, and your system is left in an undetermined state, you can restore your system. System Restore does not revert personal data files copied to the computer by using the Backup tool.

Creating a restore point manually   Creating a restore point manually is an action that you initiate by using the System Restore wizard. For example, before you add new hardware or software, manually create a restore point to record the current system state. If a problem occurs after installation, you can undo the changes.

Creating daily restore points   System Restore creates a restore point every 24 hours if the computer is turned on, or if it has been 24 hours since the last restore point was created. Scheduled restore-point creation occurs when the computer is idle, when there is no mouse, keyboard, or disk activity.

Creating restore points at preset intervals   Restore-point creation at specified intervals is disabled by default but can be enabled by using the registry editor, Regedit.exe. See Table D-4 later in this appendix for a description of the System Restore registry entries **RPSessionInterval** and **RPGlobalInterval**.

For systems using the NTFS file system, System Restore compresses archive information during idle time when there is no mouse, keyboard, or disk activity.

Archiving and Purging of Restore Points

System Restore archives expand to include multiple restore points, each representing unique system states. *System state* refers to the components that define the current state of the operating system and includes the following:

- User account information stored in the registry.

- Application, hardware, and software settings stored in the registry.

- Files that Windows XP Professional requires for startup, including those in the *systemroot* directory and boot files on the system partition, such as Ntldr or IA64ldr.efi.

Archived restore point information is saved to a hidden *systemdrive* folder or an archive on the volume where a monitored file is located. The archive collects multiple restore points, each representing individual system states. The files, registry snapshots, and logs associated with older restore points are purged on a first in, first out (FIFO) basis, optimizing System Restore disk space and making room for new restore points. System Restore uses the following algorithms and conditions to determine whether it is time to purge restore point data.

When System Restore consumes at least 90 percent of allotted space   System Restore purges restore points to reduce the amount of allotted space used from 90 percent to 75 percent. System Restore is limited to 12 percent of available disk space, which is not pre-allocated. Windows XP Professional and applications can use the free portion of this space.

When you reduce the amount of disk space allotted to System Restore   By using Control Panel or Disk Cleanup to reduce the amount of System Restore space you can cause System Restore to purge all but the most recent restore points. For more information about Disk Cleanup, see "Disk Cleanup" in this appendix.

When you disable System Restore   Disabling System Restore deletes all restore points.

When a specified period of time has elapsed   You can configure System Restore to purge restore points by elapsed time. For example, you can specify deletion of restore points older than two months. See Table D-4 for a description of the System Restore registry entry **RPLifeInterval**. By default, System Restore purges restore points older than 90 days.

Using System Restore

Before changing system settings during troubleshooting, create a restore point. If a problem occurs, you can undo the negative effects of diagnostic and troubleshooting changes by reverting to a previous state. The following illustrate situations where System Restore can help you recover from problems that might occur.

Uninstalling incompatible software does not resolve the problem   If the problem persists after uninstalling an application, you can use System Restore to return the system to a state before you installed the new software.

Updating a device driver causes system instability   During the week, you decide to update drivers for five devices. At the end of the week, you find that your system is unstable. If you are not sure which driver is causing conflicts, you can revert your system configuration by using a restore point created the previous week.

Downloading content causes a problem   You visit a Web site and download a program or control that causes problems. By using System Restore, you can undo the negative effects of downloaded software.

Identifying a problem is not possible   If you are unable to diagnose a problem, but know approximately when the problem started, you can use System Restore to restore your system to a state when it was performing normally.

Undoing a System Restore operation that does not solve the problem   You can undo the effects of the last restore point used, by selecting **Undo my last restore** at the **System Restore** screen that appears after a restore operation. You can optionally rerun System Restore and select another restore point.

To restore the system by using a restore point

1. Click **Help and Support Center**, and under **Pick a task**, click **Undo changes to your computer with System Restore**.

2. On the **Welcome to System Restore** screen, click **Restore my computer to an earlier time**, and then click **Next**.

3. Select a restore point on the **Select a Restore Point** screen, and then click **Next**.

4. At the **Confirm Restore Point screen**, click **Next**.

When you choose a specific restore point, System Restore examines the System Restore change logs. These logs contain information that enables System Restore to create a restore map, which outlines how to revert the system to the selected system state. System Restore processes the restore map, reverses file and registry changes (by using information stored in the restore point), and then restarts the computer. If you are not satisfied with the results, you can rerun System Restore and select another restore point, or you can select the **Undo my last restoration** option available on the **Welcome to System Restore** screen.

> **Note**   If you know the specific driver causing the problem, rolling back drivers might be a preferred troubleshooting option because it limits changes to reverting a driver for one device. For more information about rolling back drivers, see "Device Driver Roll Back" earlier in this appendix.

To create a restore point manually

1. Start System Restore.

2. Click **Create a restore point**, and then click **Next**.

3. At the **Create a Restore Point** screen, type a description for the restore point in the **Restore point description** line.

4. Click the **Create** button.

Using Control Panel to Configure System Restore

To configure System Restore settings by using Control Panel

1. In **Control Panel**, open **System**.

2. In the **System Properties** dialog box, click the **System Restore** tab.

3. System Restore is enabled by default. If you have disabled System Restore, you can enable it by clearing the **Turn off System Restore** check box.

   You can also specify the amount of hard disk space that System Restore uses for data archives by adjusting the **Disk space to use** slider for each volume.

Be aware of the following before using System Restore:

- System Restore requires a minimum of 200 MB of disk space when you install Windows XP Professional. If your computer does not have enough disk space available after you install Windows XP Professional, you must first free sufficient disk space and then enable System Restore by using the preceding steps.

- System Restore can consume up to 12 percent of available disk space for systems with hard drives over 4 gigabytes (GB), and up to 400 megabytes (MB) for hard drives under 4 GB. If you require more disk space for applications and data, you can reduce the amount of space dedicated to System Restore archives.

- By default, System Restore monitors all volumes, but you can exclude hard disks (with the exception of the system hard disk) from monitoring. If you exclude a volume, System Restore clears all restore points on the volume. System Restore does not revert changes on excluded volumes. For more information about excluding volumes from System Restore monitoring, see Windows XP Professional Help and Support Center.

- After System Restore is enabled, System Restore can function below the 200 MB disk free space installation requirement. System Restore can continue to monitor and copy files on a volume until the amount of free disk space falls to approximately 50MB.

Using the Group Policy Snap-in to Configure System Restore

You can use the Group Policy snap-in, Gpedit.msc, to modify System Restore Group Policy settings. The following settings affect how System Restore functions.

Turn off System Restore   Enabling this setting disables System Restore. In addition, a user is unable to access the System Restore Wizard and cannot configure System Restore by using the System Restore tab in the System Properties dialog box in Control Panel.

Disabling this setting enables System Restore and blocks a user from disabling System Restore by selecting the **Turn off System Restore** check box on the System Restore tab in the System Properties dialog box in Control Panel. A user might still be able to configure System Restore settings, depending on the value of the **Turn off Configuration** Group Policy setting.

Turn off Configuration   Enabling this setting removes the System Restore configuration tab in the System Properties dialog box in Control Panel.

If this setting is not configured, the System Restore configuration tab remains, and the user retains the ability to configure System Restore.

To configure System Restore settings by using the Group Policy snap-in

1. In the **Run** dialog box, type **gpedit.msc**.

2. In the console tree, expand **Local Computer Policy**, and then expand **Computer Configuration**, **Administrative Templates**, and then **System**.

3. Click **System Restore,** and then double-click **Turn off System Restore** or **Turn off Configuration**.

4. On the **Setting** tab, click **Not Configured**, **Enabled**, or **Disabled**, and then click **OK**.

For more information about Group Policy, see "Authorization and Access Control," "Planning Deployments," and "Managing Desktops" in this book. Also, see the *Distributed Systems Guide* of the *Microsoft Windows 2000 Server Resource Kit* and the Change and Configuration Management Deployment Guide link on the Web Resources page at http://www.microsoft.com/windows/reskits/webresources.

> **Tip**   You can also open System Properties from the Start menu by clicking **Run** and typing **sysdm.cpl** in the **Run** dialog box. Many such Control Panel tools are stored in the *systemroot*\System32 folder and use a .cpl extension. You can start frequently used Control Panel tools from the Run dialog box or by creating shortcuts.
>
> Other frequently used tools include Appwiz.cpl (Add or Remove Programs), Hdwwiz.cpl (Add Hardware Wizard), Mmsys.cpl (Sounds and Audio Devices Properties), Nusrmgr.cpl (User Accounts), and Powercfg.cpl (Power Options Properties).

Using the Registry Editor to Configure System Restore

You can use the registry editor, Regedit.exe, to change entries in the HKEY_LOCAL_MACHINE\SOFTWARE\Microsoft\WindowsNT\CurrentVersion\System-Restore subkey that are not configurable by using Control Panel. Table D-4 lists some of these settings.

Table D-4   Selected System Restore Registry Settings

Registry Value	Description
RPSessionInterval	Specifies the intervals, in seconds, between scheduled restore-point creation during an active user session. The default value is 0 seconds (disabled).
RPGlobalInterval	Specifies the time interval, in seconds, at which scheduled restore points are created (regardless of whether or not there is an active user session). The default value is 86,400 seconds (24 hours).
RPLifeInterval	Specifies the time interval, in seconds, for which restore points are kept. System Restore deletes restore points older than the specified value. The default value is 7,776,000 seconds (90 days).
DiskPercent	Specifies the maximum amount of disk space on each drive that System Restore can use. This value is specified as a percentage of the total drive space. The default value is 12 percent.

Caution   Do not edit the registry unless you have no alternative. The registry editor bypasses standard safeguards, allowing settings that can damage your system, or even require you to reinstall Windows. If you must edit the registry, back it up first and see the Registry Reference in the *Microsoft Windows 2000 Server Resource* Kit at http://www.microsoft.com/reskit.

Using Custom Scripts to Configure System Restore

By using custom scripts that use Windows Management Instrumentation (WMI), you can change System Restore parameters by declaring the WMI class RegSR and changing specific object properties. By using WMI classes that are documented in the Software Development Kit (SDK), you can create custom scripts to perform the following tasks:

- Create restore points
- Enumerate restore points
- Restore the system
- Enable System Restore

- Disable System Restore

- Retrieve status about the last System Restore operation

For more information about WMI, see the Driver Development Kits link on the Web Resources page at http://www.microsoft.com/windows/reskits/webresources. On the Microsoft® Windows® Driver Development Kits Web page, expand **Technology Areas**, and then click **WMI (Windows Management Instrumentation)**. For more information about System Restore scripting, see the Software Development Kit (SDK) information in the MSDN Library link and the Windows Script Technologies link on the Web Resources page at http://www.microsoft.com/windows/reskits/webresources.

How System Restore Works with Other Windows XP Professional Features

Windows XP Professional features, options, and troubleshooting tools can affect the behavior of System Restore. Table D-5 describes how System Restore works with these features.

Table D-5   How System Restore Works with Windows XP Tools and Features

Tool or Feature	Interaction with System Restore
Add or Remove Programs	System Restore does not uninstall applications. To properly remove all files installed by an application's setup program, run the uninstall program provided with the application.
Automated System Recovery (ASR)	A successful ASR restore operation resets restore points. All restore points created prior to the ASR restore operation are lost, with the restored data serving as the basis for subsequent monitoring and restore point management.
Backup	System Restore creates a restore point before you perform a restore operation by using Backup (Ntbackup.exe). If the Backup restore operation fails, or if the user cancels, System Restore reverts the operating system state but does not restore personal data files. If the Backup restore operation succeeds, you cannot use restore points created before the successful Backup restore operation.
Device Driver Roll Back	System Restore reverts drivers and the Device Driver Roll Back state to match the information in the restore point. Use Device Driver Roll Back instead of System Restore if you are certain that a specific driver (for example a video card driver) is the source of a problem. If you already performed a System Restore and want to roll back a specific driver without affecting other system changes, you can undo the last System Restore restore operation and then roll back the problem driver.
Folder Redirection	System Restore does not restore files in redirected folders.

Table D-5   How System Restore Works with Windows XP Tools and Features

Tool or Feature	Interaction with System Restore
Last Known Good Configuration	System Restore applies settings stored in the selected restore point. System Restore reverts the Last Known Good Configuration to match the information in the selected restore point. This guarantees that the restored registry and Last Known Good state are consistent.
Operating System Upgrades	Upgrading from Windows Millennium Edition to Windows XP Professional or upgrading from one Windows XP Professional version to another causes all System Restore restore points to be reset. All restore points created prior to the operating system upgrade are lost.
Plug and Play	System Restore does not alter Plug and Play routines. For example, if you use a restore point created before a device was installed, that device is redetected and Windows XP Professional attempts to initialize new hardware and install drivers after System Restore completes.
Recovery Console	System Restore does not monitor changes made within Recovery Console. You cannot apply restore points in Recovery Console.
Roaming User Profiles	System Restore does not restore roaming user profile information.
Safe mode	You cannot create restore points in safe mode. You can use System Restore to apply restore points in safe mode.
Windows File Protection	System Restore synchronizes Windows File Protection (WFP) data to agree with restored information. For more information about Windows File Protection, see "Windows File Protection" later in this appendix.
Windows Update	Using a restore point might revert recent updates such as a new video card driver or updates downloaded by using Windows Update. By using Automatic Updates, you can help ensure that your system is up-to-date. For example, after you apply a restore point, Automatic Updates can download updates to your system and you can then decide whether to reinstall them. For more information about Automatic Updates, see "Windows Update" in this appendix.

Warning   System Restore is not a backup feature and does not replace Backup. System Restore saves registry information and incremental changes to monitored files. System Restore does not save personal data. In addition, System Restore requires that you be able to start Windows XP Professional in safe or normal mode. You must use Backup or ASR to recover from data loss due to hard disk-related damage that prevents you from starting the operating system in safe mode, normal mode, or Recovery Console.

Add or Remove Programs

If problems occur soon after you install an application, you can use **Add or Remove Programs** in Control Panel to remove the application. You can then focus your efforts on searching for an update or workaround that might permanently resolve the problem.

Software conflicts can cause problems with other software or cause hardware to behave unpredictably or stop responding. For example, after installing an incompatible CD-ROM mastering application, you cannot shut down your system properly. You observe that the problem is consistent, and you decide to uninstall the application. After removing the CD-mastering software, you can successfully shut down the computer. You search for a Windows XP Professional–specific update on the manufacturer's Web site and find that reinstalling the application and applying the update resolves the problem.

To uninstall an application

1. Do one of the following:

   ■ In **Control Panel**, click **Add or Remove Programs**.

   ■ In the **Run** dialog box, type **appwiz.cpl**, and then click **OK**.

2. Under **Currently installed programs**, click an application to uninstall.

3. Click **Change/Remove** and confirm or cancel the uninstall process.

Uninstalling software might not always resolve the problem. However, it does eliminate a possible cause, and it reduces the number of variables to consider while troubleshooting. For more information about adding or removing programs, see Windows XP Professional Help and Support Center.

Recovery Console

Recovery Console is a character-mode environment that you can run directly from the Windows XP Professional operating system CD or, for *x*86-based systems, install as a startup option. Unlike normal or safe mode, the Windows graphical user interface (GUI) is not available within Recovery Console. Recovery Console provides a set of commands for advanced users who are comfortable working outside the Windows GUI environment.

If you cannot start Windows XP Professional in safe mode or normal mode, Recovery Console allows you to perform many troubleshooting and maintenance tasks, such as disabling problem drivers and services that you suspect are causing startup problems. Recovery Console is separate from the command-line Cmd.exe shell and grants limited access to local NTFS and file allocation table (FAT) formatted volumes.

For more information about using Recovery Console to troubleshoot startup and disk problems, see "Troubleshooting Startup" and "Troubleshooting Disks and File Systems" in this book.

Installing and Using Recovery Console

Before you install Recovery Console, you need to be aware of the following disk and file system limitations.

Recovery Console is sensitive to file-system changes   If you install Recovery Console to a hard disk that uses the FAT file system, converting to NTFS causes Recovery Console to stop functioning. You must reinstall Recovery Console after converting to NTFS.

Recovery Console limitations on dynamic disks   Certain Recovery Console limitations exist for dynamic disks. For more information, see article Q227364, "Dynamic Volumes Are Not Displayed Accurately in Text-Mode Setup or Recovery Console," in the Microsoft Knowledge Base. To find this article, see the Microsoft Knowledge Base link on the Web Resources page at http://www.microsoft.com /windows/reskits/webresources.

Installing Recovery Console   You can start Recovery Console directly from the Windows XP Professional operating system CD or, for *x*86-based systems, install it on the hard disk as a startup option.

> **Warning**   To enable your system to start from the Windows XP Professional operating system CD you might need to change the device boot order settings stored in firmware. For more information about changing boot order settings, see "Troubleshooting Startup" in this book.

To start Recovery Console from the Windows XP Professional operating system CD

1. Restart the computer by using the Windows XP Professional operating system CD.

2. Wait for the Windows XP Professional Setup program to display the **Welcome to Setup** screen (this might take a few moments). Choose **To repair a Windows XP Professional installation** by pressing R.

3. Type the number corresponding to the Windows XP Professional installation that you want to use, and then press ENTER. You must type a number when prompted, even if only a single Windows XP Professional installation exists. If you press ENTER without typing a number, Windows XP Professional restarts the computer.

4. At the prompt, enter the password for the local Administrator account so that you can access the contents of the local hard disk. Recovery Console accepts only the password for the local Administrator account. If you do not enter the correct password within three attempts, Windows XP Professional denies access and restarts the computer.

For more information about the password requirements for Recovery Console, see article Q258585, "Recovery Console Prompts for Administrator Password Even If Administrator Account Has Been Renamed," in the Microsoft Knowledge Base. To find this article, see the Microsoft Knowledge Base link on the Web Resources page at http://www.microsoft.com/windows/reskits/webresources.

To install Recovery Console as a hard disk startup option for x86-based systems

1. With Windows running, insert the Windows XP Professional operating system CD into your CD-ROM drive.

2. Click **No** when prompted to upgrade to Windows XP Professional.

3. At the command prompt, type a command using the following syntax:

   `drive :\i386\winnt32.exe /cmdcons`

   In the preceding syntax, *drive* represents the letter of the CD-ROM. For network-based installations, or if you do not have access to a Windows XP Professional operating system CD, you can install Recovery Console from a network distribution share by typing:

   `\\server\share\i386\winnt32.exe /cmdcons`

After you enter this command and restart your computer, Recovery Console appears as a menu item in the operating system startup menu.

Directory and Folder Access If you successfully log on, you can access the following directories and folders by using Recovery Console:

- The root directory of any volume.

- The *systemroot* folder and subfolders of the selected Windows XP Professional installation.

- The Recovery Console Cmdcons folder and any subfolders (if you installed Recovery Console as a startup option).

- Files and directories on removable disks.

Recovery Console Restrictions   By default, Recovery Console enforces the following four restrictions:

- You cannot access certain folders, such as Program Files, Documents and Settings, and disks or folders containing other Windows XP Professional installations.

- You cannot copy files to removable disks because floppy-disk write access is disabled by default. When you attempt to copy files to removable disks, an error message similar to the following appears: "Access is denied."

- You cannot change the local Administrator account password from Recovery Console.

- You do not have access to a text-editing tool in Recovery Console.

You can customize Recovery Console to bypass the first and second restrictions, by using the SET command to modify *environment variables*. Windows XP Professional uses environment variables to associate string values, such as folder or file paths, to variables that applications and the operating system can use. For example, by using environment variables, scripts can run without modification on computers that have different configurations. For more information about environment variables, see "To add or change the values of environment variables" in Windows XP Professional Help and Support Center.

Customizing Recovery Console

You can use the Recovery Console **set** command to display or modify the following four Recovery Console environment variables.

AllowWildCards   Setting the value of this variable to TRUE allows you to use wildcard characters (* and ?) with some commands. For example, typing dir *.txt lists all files in the current directory with the .txt file name extension to the screen.

AllowAllPaths   Setting the value of this variable to TRUE allows you to expand the scope of the change directory **cd** command to include all folders on all disks.

AllowRemovableMedia   Setting the value of this variable to TRUE allows you to copy files from the hard disk to removable disk media.

NoCopyPrompt   Setting the value of this variable to TRUE allows you to copy files without being prompted to continue when overwriting an existing file.

To change the value of the preceding variables from the default value of FALSE to TRUE, use the following syntax:

```
set variable = [TRUE|FALSE]
```

When you first attempt to use the **set** command to change the value of environment variables from FALSE to TRUE, an error message similar to the following appears:

```
The SET command is currently disabled. The SET command is an optional Recovery Conso
le command that can only be enabled by using the Security Configuration and Analysis
 snap-in.
```

To enable the **set** command, enable the **Allow floppy copy and access to all drives and all folders** Group Policy setting by using the Group Policy snap-in.

To enable use of the set command by using the Group Policy snap-in

1. Restart Windows XP Professional in normal mode.

2. In the **Run** dialog box, type **gpedit.msc**.

3. In the console tree, expand **Local Computer Policy**, and then expand **Computer Configuration**, **Windows Settings**, **Security Settings**, and **Local Policies**.

4. Click **Security Options**.

5. Double-click **Recovery Console: Allow floppy copy and access to all drives and all folders**, click **Enabled**, and then click **OK**.

In a Microsoft® Windows® 2000 Server–based network, to enable **set** command functionality for all computers, set Group Policy on a domain controller. Setting up policy from a central location is more efficient than applying settings for each computer.

You can also use the Group Policy snap-in to enable the policy **Recovery Console: Allow automatic administrative logon**, which allows you to bypass the logon process when Recovery Console starts. Activating this policy eliminates a security barrier intended to protect your computer against unauthorized users. Therefore, it is important that you enable this policy only on systems that have secure consoles, such as those in locked rooms. You can also make Group Policy changes by using the Security Configuration and Analysis snap-in.

For more information about Group Policy, see "Authorization and Access Control," "Planning Deployments," and "Managing Desktops" in this book. Also, see the *Distributed Systems Guide* of the *Microsoft® Windows® 2000 Server Resource Kit* and the Change and Configuration Management Deployment Guide link on the Web Resources page at http://www.microsoft.com/windows/reskits/webresources.

Using Recovery Console to Recover from Startup Problems

Using Recovery Console enables you to recover from the following problems:

- Corrupted or deleted startup files caused by incompatible software, user error, or virus activity.

- Disk problems related to damage to the master boot record (MBR), partition table, or boot sector on *x*86-based systems.

- A partition boot sector overwritten by another operating system's setup program.

If critical system files, such as Ntldr or Ntoskrnl.exe, are missing or corrupted, you can restore them by starting Recovery Console and copying fresh files from the Windows XP Professional operating system CD or other removable disk media. For more information about using Recovery Console to recover from startup problems, see "Troubleshooting Startup" in this book.

Boot sector damage can be caused by incompatible software, hardware problems, virus activity, or when you attempt to configure your computer as a multiple-boot system. For example, setup programs for other operating systems might not be compatible with Windows XP Professional, and might attempt to overwrite the boot sector or startup files.

When configuring a multiple-boot system on *x*86-based systems, you must install other operating systems, such as Microsoft® Windows® 95 and Microsoft® Windows® 98, before installing Windows XP Professional. To avoid boot sector problems, install Windows operating systems on different partitions in the following order:

1. Windows 95, Windows 98, or Microsoft® Windows® Millennium Edition (Windows Me)

2. Microsoft® Windows NT® Workstation version 4.0 with Service Pack 4 or later

3. Microsoft® Windows NT® Server version 4.0 with Service Pack 4 or later

4. Microsoft® Windows® 2000 Professional

5. Windows XP Professional

If you do not follow the preceding order, you might lose the ability to start Windows XP Professional. To restore the ability to start your system, use Recovery Console **fixboot** command as described in "Troubleshooting Disks and File Systems" in this book.

> **Note** For a multiple-boot computer that participates in a Windows 2000 domain, use a different computer name for each operating system installation to avoid security identifier (SID) issues.

Leave partitions with Windows 95, Windows 98, or Windows Me installed as FAT16 or FAT32, because these operating systems are not compatible with NTFS. In addition, be aware of the following limitations when running Windows NT 4.0:

- Computers running Windows NT 4.0 cannot access FAT32 partitions. For a multiple-boot computer running Windows NT 4.0 and Windows 95, Windows 98, or Windows Me, you must use a FAT16 formatted system partition.

- Computers running Windows NT 4.0 require Service Pack 4 or later to access NTFS volumes previously mounted by Windows 2000 or Windows XP Professional.

- Computers running Windows NT 4.0 cannot access files stored by using the Encrypting File System.

For more information about file system interoperability, see "File Systems" in this book. For more information about the Encrypting File System, see "Encrypting File System" in this book.

For *x*86-based systems, Microsoft® Windows® 2000 Setup might overwrite the Windows XP Professional versions of system files, Ntldr and Ntdetect.com, if you install Windows 2000 after Windows XP Professional. You cannot use Windows 2000 versions of Ntldr and Ntdetect.com to start Windows XP Professional. To restore these system files, use the procedure that follows.

To restore Windows XP Professional versions of Ntldr and Ntdetect.com on x86-based systems

1. Start Recovery Console by using the Windows XP Professional operating system CD.

2. Navigate to the system partition root and type the following commands from the Recovery Console prompt:
   copy *drive*:**\i386\ntldr**
   copy *drive*:**\i386\ntdetect.com**
   In the preceding two commands, *drive* represents the letter of the CD-ROM that holds the Windows XP Professional installation files.

3. Answer the **Overwrite system? (Yes/No/All):** prompts by pressing Y.

4. Restart the computer.

Using Recovery Console Commands

Recovery Console provides a list of commands that you can use for troubleshooting. When using Recovery Console, you can view and reuse previous commands by pressing the UP ARROW and DOWN ARROW keys, which move you forward or backward through your command history.

For the list of Recovery Console commands that follow, brackets ([]) enclose optional parameters and a pipe (|) separates mutually exclusive choices. Recovery Console commands and parameters are not case sensitive.

Attrib Use the **attrib** command to change the file attributes for a single file or folder. Use the following syntax:

```
attrib -|+[c][h][r][s] [drive:][path]filename
```

Parameter	Description
+	Sets an attribute.
-	Clears an attribute.
c	Sets or clears a compressed file attribute.
h	Sets or clears a hidden file attribute.
r	Sets or clears a read-only file attribute.
s	Sets or clears a system file attribute.
drive:	Specifies the drive letter to use.
path:	Specifies the directory path to use.

Follow these guidelines for using the **attrib** command:

- You must set or clear at least one attribute.

- You can change attributes for only one file or directory at a time.

- You can view attributes by using the **dir** command.

- Do not separate attribute parameters with spaces.

- You can set multiple attributes simultaneously:

  - To change multiple attributes in the same way, use either the set or clear parameter (+ or -). Include all the attribute options to be changed, and do not separate them with spaces. For example, to set the compressed, hidden, and read-only attributes for a single file, use the following syntax:

```
attrib +chr filename
```

  - To change multiple attributes in different ways, use the set parameter (+) and include all the attribute letters to be set, followed without a space by the clear parameter (-) and all the attribute letters to be cleared. For example, to set the compressed and hidden file attributes and to clear the read-only file attribute, use the following syntax:

```
attrib +ch-r filename
```

Batch Use the **batch** command to run the commands specified in a text file. Use the following syntax:

```
batch inputfile [outputfile]
```

Parameter	Description
inputfile	Specifies the text file (by using [*drive*:][*path*][*filename*] format) that contains the list of commands you want to carry out.
outputfile	If specified, stores the output of the Batch command in the specified file. If you do not specify a value for *outputfile*, the Batch command displays its output on the screen. Specify *outputfile* by using [*drive*:][*path*][*filename*] format.

The **batch** command cannot call itself recursively. Do not include the **batch** command in the file specified by the *inputfile* parameter.

Bootcfg   For *x*86-based systems, use the **bootcfg** command to scan your hard disks and use the information to modify the contents of the Boot.ini file or rebuild a new copy. Use the following syntax:

```
bootcfg [/add] [/default]| [/list] [/rebuild] [/scan]
```

Parameter	Description
/add	Adds a Windows installation to the operating system boot menu list.
/default	Sets the default boot menu.
/list	Lists the entries already in the boot menu list.
/rebuild	Scans hard disks for Windows installations and to select which to add.
/scan	Scans all disks for Windows installations and display the results.

Always back up the Boot.ini file before modifying it. For more information about the Boot.ini file, see "Troubleshooting Startup" in this book.

Cd or Chdir   Use the **cd** or **chdir** command to display the name of the current volume or directory, or to change to the folder specified. Use the following syntax:

```
cd [path]|[..]|[drive:]
```

– or –

```
chdir [path]|[..]|[drive:]
```

Parameter	Description
path	Specifies the directory that you want to change to.
..	Displays the parent folder.
drive:	Specifies the drive that you want to change to.

If you want to display the current volume and folder, use the **cd** or **chdir** command without parameters.

Cd and Chdir treat spaces as delimiters, requiring that a space precede all arguments, including double periods. Use quotation marks to enclose a path or file name that contains a space.

Chkdsk Use the **chkdsk** command to check a volume, and if needed, to repair the volume. Also, use Chkdsk to recover and move readable information before marking bad sectors as unusable. Use the following syntax:

```
chkdsk [drive:] [/p]|[/r]
```

You can use Chkdsk without parameters. When you do not specify a volume, Chkdsk runs on the current volume.

Parameter	Description
drive:	Specifies the volume that you want Chkdsk to check.
/p	Performs an exhaustive volume check. This parameter does not make any changes to the volume.
/r	Locates bad sectors and recovers readable information before marking them as unusable. Implies /p.

Chkdsk requires the file Autochk.exe. If Chkdsk cannot find Autochk in the *systemroot*\System32 directory, it attempts to locate Autochk on the Windows XP Professional installation CD. If you are using a multiple boot configuration, verify that you are issuing this command from the volume containing Windows XP Professional.

Cls Use the **cls** command to clear the screen and redisplay the command prompt. Use the following syntax:

```
cls
```

Copy Use the **copy** command to copy a single file to a specified location. Use the following syntax:

```
copy source destination
```

Parameter	Description
source	Specifies the file (by using [*drive*:][*path*][*filename*] format) that you want copied.
destination	Specifies the destination (by using [*drive*:][*path*][*filename*] format) where you want to copy the *source* file .

The following also applies to the **copy** command:

- You cannot use wildcard characters (* and ?) with the **copy** command.

- If you do not specify a destination directory, the **copy** command uses the current folder by default.

- If you do not specify a destination file name, the **copy** command uses the existing file name by default.

- If the *destination* file name already exists, you are warned before overwriting it.

- Compressed files from the Windows XP Professional operating system CD are automatically expanded as they are copied.

Del or Delete   Use the **del** or **delete** command to delete a file or folder. Use the following syntax:

`del [`*drive:*`][`*path*`]`*filename*

– or –

`delete [`*drive:*`][`*path*`]`*filename*

Parameter	Description
drive:	Specifies the volume of the file you want to delete.
path	Specifies the directory of the file you want to delete.
filename	Specifies the file you want to delete.

You cannot use wildcard characters with this command.

Dir   Use the **dir** command to display a list of the files and folders in a directory. Use the following syntax:

`dir [`*drive:*`][`*path*`][`*filename*`]`

Parameter	Description
drive:	Specifies the volume of the directory for which you want a listing.
path	Specifies the directory for which you want a listing.
filename	Specifies the file for which you want a listing.

In Recovery Console, the **dir** command functions differently, listing all folders and files, including those with hidden and system attributes set. For each file and subdirectory, the **dir** command lists its attributes (if they apply) by using the following abbreviations.

a   Archive

c   Compressed

d   Directory

e   Encrypted

h   Hidden

p   Reparse point

r   Read-only

s   System file
   You cannot use wildcard characters with this command.

Disable   Use the **disable** command to disable a service or driver. Use the following syntax:

```
disable servicename
```

Parameter	Description
servicename	Specifies the service or driver that you want to disable.

   Use the related command **listsvc** to view a list of service and driver names for your system. The **disable** command displays the previous start type of a service before changing it to SERVICE_DISABLED. Record this value so that you can restore the original state of a service after troubleshooting a problem.

Diskpart   Use the **diskpart** command to manage the partitions on your hard disk. For example, to create or delete disk partitions, use the following syntax:

```
diskpart[/add|/delete] [device-name|drive-name|partition-name] [size]
```

Parameter	Description
/add	Creates a new disk partition.
/delete	Deletes an existing partition.
device-name	Specifies the name of the device for which you want to create or delete a partition, for example, \Device\HardDisk0. To obtain the name of a device, view the output of the **map** command.
drive-name	Specifies the drive letter of the partition that you want to delete, for example, D:. Use only with **/delete**.
partition-name	Specifies the partition that you want to delete; can be used in place of the *drive-name* parameter. For example, \Device\HardDisk0. Use only with **/delete**.
size	Specifies the size, in megabytes, of the partition you want to create. Use only with **/add**.

   If you do not use a parameter, a user interface for managing your partitions appears.

> **Caution**   This command can damage your partition table if the disk has been upgraded to dynamic disk. Do not modify the structure of dynamic disks unless you are using the Disk Management snap-in.

Enable   Use the **enable** command to enable or change the startup type of a service or driver. Use the following syntax:

```
enable servicename [start_type]
```

Parameter	Description
servicename	Specifies the service or driver that you want to enable.
start_type	Specifies the startup type for a service or driver. Valid values are:
	■ SERVICE_BOOT_START
	■ SERVICE_SYSTEM_START
	■ SERVICE_AUTO_START
	■ SERVICE_DEMAND_START

Use the related command **listsvc** to view a list of service and driver names for your system. The **enable** command displays the previous start type of the service before changing it. Record this value so that you can restore the original state of the service after troubleshooting a problem.

If you do not specify a new start type, the enable command displays the previous start type.

For more information about enabling or disabling services for troubleshooting, see "Troubleshooting Startup" in this book.

Exit   Use the **exit** command to close Recovery Console and restart your computer. Use the following syntax:

```
exit
```

Expand   Use the **expand** command to expand a compressed file stored on the Windows XP Professional operating system CD or in a cabinet (.cab) file, and copy it to a specified destination. Use the following syntax:

```
expand source [/f:filespec] [target] [/y]
expand source [/f:filespec] /d
```

Parameter	Description
source	Specifies the file you want to expand (by using [*drive*:][*path*][*filename*] format). You cannot use wildcard characters (* and ?).
target	Specifies the destination folder and/or file name for the new file using [*drive*:][*path*][*filename*] format.
/f:*filespec*	Specifies the specific file(s) you want to expand if the source contains more than one file. Wildcards are optional.
/y	Specifies that the confirmation prompt that appears when attempting to overwrite an existing file is not required.
/d	Specifies that files display, but does not expand the files in the cabinet file.

Fixboot Use the **fixboot** command to rewrite the boot sector code to the system volume. This is useful for repairing a corrupted boot sector on *x*86-based systems. If you need to replace the boot sector of a volume that is not the system volume, then you must specify the appropriate drive letter. Use the following syntax:

```
fixboot [drive:]
```

Parameter	Description
drive:	Specifies the volume drive letter on which to rewrite a new boot sector.

If you do not specify a drive, the default is the system boot volume.

Fixmbr Use the **fixmbr** command to rewrite the master boot code of the master boot record (MBR) of the startup hard disk. This command is useful for repairing corrupted MBRs. Use the following syntax:

```
fixboot [device-name]
```

Parameter	Description
device-name	Specifies the name of the device that needs a new MBR, for example, \Device\HardDisk1.

If you do not specify a device, the default is disk 0. If disk 0 is not the device that needs repairing, you can obtain the device name of other disks by using the **map** command.

If the **fixmbr** command detects an invalid or nonstandard partition table signature, it prompts you for permission before rewriting the MBR.

Use this command with care because it can damage your partition table if any one or more of the following applies:

- A virus is present and a third-party operating system is installed on the same computer.

- A nonstandard MBR is installed by a third-party disk utility.

- A hardware problem exists.

Always run antivirus software before using this command.

Running the **fixmbr** command overwrites only the master boot code, leaving the existing partition table intact. If corruption in the MBR affects the partition table, running the **fixmbr** command is unlikely to resolve the problem. For more information, see "Troubleshooting Disks and File Systems" in this book.

Format   Use the **format** command to format the specified volume to the specified file system. Use the following syntax:

`format [`*drive:*`] [`**/q**`] [`**/fs:**`file_system]`

Parameter	Description
drive:	Specifies the drive letter for the volume you want to format.
/q	Specifies a quick format (clears only the table of contents).
/fs:*file-system*	Specifies the file system you want to use. Valid values for *file-system* include FAT, FAT32, and NTFS.

Consider the following points before using the Format command:

- If a file system is not specified, the **format** command defaults to the NTFS file system.

- Choosing FAT formats a volume as FAT16. FAT16 volumes *cannot* be larger than 4 GB. Limit FAT16 partitions to 2 GB to increase storage efficiency, and to maintain compatibility with Microsoft® MS-DOS®, Windows 95, Windows 98, and Windows Me.

- Windows XP Professional can format FAT32 volumes up to 32 GB in size. For larger volumes, use NTFS.

For more information about these file systems, see "File Systems" in this book.

Help   Use the **help** command to view Help information for Recovery Console commands. Use the following syntax:

`help [`*command*`]`

Parameter	Description
command	Specifies the command for which you want to view Help information.

Use the *command* parameter to specify a name of any Recovery Console command.

If you do not specify a parameter, Help lists information about all the supported commands.

Listsvc   Use the **listsvc** command to view details about the services and drivers on your system, including service start types. Use the following syntax:

```
listsvc
```

Use the **listsvc** command together with the **disable** and **enable** commands. The information displayed is extracted from the System registry file that is located in the *systemroot*\System32\Config folder. If the file System is damaged or missing, the information displayed might be inaccurate. For more information about enabling or disabling services for troubleshooting, see "Troubleshooting Startup" in this book.

Logon   Use the **logon** command to detect and log on to Windows installations. Use the following syntax:

```
logon
```

You must correctly enter the local Administrator password within three attempts or the computer restarts.

Map   Use the **map** command to list all drive letters, file system types, volume sizes, and mappings to physical devices that are currently active. Use the following syntax:

```
map [arc]
```

Parameter	Description
arc	Use the **arc** parameter to force the use of the Advanced RISC Computing (ARC) specification format to describe paths instead of using device paths. You can use this information to create or repair the Boot.ini file.

The map command might not work correctly with systems using dynamic disk features.

Md or Mkdir   Use the **md** or **mkdir** command to create a new directory or subdirectory. Use the following syntax:

```
md [drive:]path
mkdir [drive:]path
```

Parameter	Description
drive:	Specifies the volume on which to create a folder.
path	Specifies the name of the folder to create.

You cannot use wildcard characters with this command.

This command might not display all the volumes on a disk or the correct volume sizes on dynamic disks.

More or Type   Use the **more** or **type** command to display the contents of a text file. Use the following syntax:

```
more [path\]filename
type [path\]filename
```

Parameter	Description
filename	Specifies the file name to view.
path	Specifies the folder where the file is located.

If a text file is too large to fit on one screen, use the following page viewing options:

- ENTER to scroll down one line at a time

- SPACEBAR to scroll down one page at a time

- ESC to quit viewing the text file

Rd or Rmdir   Use the **rd** or **rmdir** command to delete a directory or subdirectory. Use the following syntax:

```
rm [drive:]path
rmdir [drive:]path
```

Parameter	Description
drive:	Specifies the volume on which to delete a folder.
path	Specifies the name of the folder to delete.

You cannot use wildcard characters with this command.

Ren or Rename   Use the **ren** or **rename** command to rename a file or directory. Use the following syntax:

```
ren [drive:][path]name1 name2
rename [drive:][path]name1 name2
```

Parameter	Description
drive:	Specifies the volume drive letter on which the file to be renamed resides.
path	Specifies the path to the file or folder to be renamed.
name1	Specific the file or folder to be renamed.
name2	Specifies the new name for the file or folder.

You cannot use wildcard characters with this command.

Set   Use the **set** command to set Recovery Console environment variables. Use the following syntax:

```
set [variable = value]
```

Recovery Console disables the **set** command by default and you must use the Group Policy snap-in to enable the **set** command. For more information about enabling the **set** command, see "Customizing Recovery Console" earlier in this appendix.

Environment Variable	Description
AllowWildCards	Set to TRUE to enable wildcard character (* and ?) support for some commands, such as DEL, that do not otherwise support them.
AllowAllPaths	Set to TRUE to allow access to all files and folders on the computer.
AllowRemovable-Media	Set to TRUE to allow files to be copied to removable media, such as floppy disks.
NoCopyPrompt	Set to TRUE to suppress the confirmation prompt that appears when overwriting a file.

To display the list of current environment variables, use the **set** command without specifying a parameter.

Systemroot   Sets the current directory to the *systemroot* directory of the Windows XP Professional installation with which you are currently working. Use the following syntax:

```
systemroot
```

Backup

Troubleshooting a problem eventually requires that you test one or more possible solutions and observe the results. Therefore, you must be able to restore system settings if the changes you make have negative effects. The Backup tool (Ntbackup.exe) allows you to save system files, application files, and data files that might be at risk. Backups enable you to undo sweeping changes and recover data if troubleshooting does not proceed as expected.

For example, you find and apply several changes suggested in Microsoft Knowledge Base articles. Although the problem disappears, you are unable to identify the change or combination of changes responsible. Using a backup set created before you applied the changes, you can restore the problem configuration and re-test possible solutions individually until you identify the exact steps required to resolve the problem. Identifying the exact steps required avoids applying unnecessary changes that might lead to other problems.

Whether you use Backup or an equivalent backup program with similar functionality, enable the **Verify data** and **Save system state** options if available.

Enabling data verification causes Backup to check that files on disk are identical to those stored on the backup media immediately after a backup or restore operation. Enabling the Save system state option causes Backup to include system state information in the list of items to save to backup media. Always follow the backup media manufacturer's recommendations, especially when reusing tape cartridges.

To save system state information in Backup

1. In the **Run** dialog box, type **ntbackup**.

2. In the Backup Utility wizard, click **Advanced Mode**, click the **Backup** tab, and then select **System State**.

3. In the **Backup destination** box, select **File** or a backup device installed on your computer.

4. In the **Backup media or file name** box, type the destination file name.

5. Click **Start Backup**.

If you want to include other files, such as application or personal data files, select the files to save before clicking **Start Backup**.

There are two points that you need to consider when performing backup and restore operations.

Backups might not contain the latest data   If data on backup media is not current, a restore operation might replace application files, drivers, service packs, or hotfixes by copying older files to your system. Always maintain a record of recent driver or service pack changes in case you need to reapply these changes after restoring files.

Plug and Play redetects hardware and might re-install drivers   Windows XP Professional redetects any hardware that you installed since the last backup and, after restoring the system state from a backup, might request drivers from the Windows XP Professional operating system or from removable disks.

For more information about using Backup to save and restore files, see Windows XP Professional Help and Support Center and "Backup and Restore" in this book.

Automated System Recovery

Automated System Recovery (ASR) is a Backup (Ntbackup.exe) and Windows XP Professional Setup option that enables you to restore the ability to start Windows XP Professional when other recovery methods are ineffective or not available. For example, if a hardware problem or virus activity causes disk corruption problems that prevent you from starting in safe mode, using Recovery Console, or using the Last Known Good Configuration.

The ASR user interface consists of the following two parts:

- The ASR wizard provided by Backup
- The ASR restore option provided by Windows XP Professional Setup

ASR automates the process of saving and restoring system state information. For more information about Automated System Recovery, see Windows XP Professional Help and Support Center and "Backup and Restore" in this book.

Application and Service Tools

Windows XP Professional provides tools and features that you can use to diagnose and troubleshoot startup, applications, and services. Table D-6 is an alphabetical list of tools useful for troubleshooting applications and services. When attempting to identify and resolve problems, follow the guidelines discussed in "Troubleshooting Concepts and Strategies" in this book.

Table D-6   Application and Service Tools for Troubleshooting

Tool	Function	Tool Type, Interface
Bootcfg (Bootcfg.exe)	Viewing or editing startup settings in the x86-based Boot.ini file or Itanium-based Boot Manager entries.	Built-in, GUI
Boot logging	Creating a text-based log (Ntbtlog.txt) of listed drivers that loaded or failed at startup.	Built-in, startup option
Dependency Walker (Depends.exe)	Examining a selected application or software component and determining the modules required for it to start.	Support tool, GUI
Device Manager	Viewing and changing hardware and device driver settings.	Built-in, GUI
DirectX Diagnostic Tool (Dxdiag.exe)	Doing the following: ■ Viewing information about installed components and drivers for the Microsoft® DirectX® application programming interface (API). ■ Testing sound, graphics output, and DirectPlay® service providers. ■ Disabling or enabling DirectX hardware acceleration features.	Built-in, GUI
Dr. Watson (Drwtsn32.exe)	Recording detailed information to a log when application errors occur.	Built-in, GUI configuration

Table D-6   Application and Service Tools for Troubleshooting

Tool	Function	Tool Type, Interface
Error Reporting	Monitoring your system for problems that affect Windows XP Professional components and applications. When a problem occurs, you can send a report to Microsoft. An automated process searches the error-reporting database for matching conditions and responds with any troubleshooting information found.	Built-in, GUI
Event Query (Eventquery.vbs)	Displaying events and properties from the event logs.	Built-in, command-line
Event Triggers (Eventtriggers.exe)	Setting triggers based on event log events.	Built-in, command-line
Event Viewer (Eventvwr.msc)	Viewing the Event log, which contains information about application, security, and system events for your computer.	Built-in, GUI
Global Flag Editor (Gflags.exe)	Enabling or disabling advanced internal system diagnostics and troubleshooting tests.	Support Tool, GUI
Group Policy Snap-in (Gpedit.msc)	Viewing, creating, deleting, or editing user and computer Group Policy object (GPO) settings.	Built-in, GUI
Group Policy Results (Gpresult.exe)	Displaying information about the cumulative effect that Group Policy objects have on computers and users.	Built-in, command-line
Group Policy Update (Gpupdate.exe)	Refreshing GPOs so that changes takes effect immediately. GPUpdate replaces the Windows 2000 tool Secedit.exe, and provides increased control and flexibility.	Built-in, command-line
Kernel Debugger	Analyzing computer memory or a memory dump file written to disk when a Stop message occurs.	Debugging Tool, command-line
Memory Pool Monitor (Poolmon.exe)	Detecting and analyzing memory leaks.	Support Tool, GUI
OpenFiles (Openfiles.exe)	Listing or closing connections to files and folders opened remotely through a shared folder.	Built-in, command-line
Online Crash Analysis	Sending kernel memory dump files to a Web site hosted by Microsoft Corporation for evaluation. An automated process searches a database of known issues for matching conditions. You can optionally receive e-mail updates about your problem.	Web site

Table D-6   Application and Service Tools for Troubleshooting

Tool	Function	Tool Type, Interface
Performance Monitor (Perfmon.msc)	Obtaining data that is useful for detecting and diagnosing bottlenecks and changes in overall system performance.	Built-in, GUI
Process and Thread Status (Pstat.exe)	Viewing the status of threads, processes, and drivers.	Support Tool, command-line
Program Compatibility Wizard	Testing and resolving compatibility problems regarding running programs that worked correctly on an earlier version of Windows.	Built-in, GUI
Registry Editor (Regedit.exe)	Searching, viewing, and editing the contents of the registry.	Built-in, GUI
Resultant Set of Policy (Rsop.msc)	Viewing information about the cumulative effect that Group Policy objects have on computers and users.	Built-in, GUI
Runas.exe	Running tools and programs with different permissions than the user's current logon provides.	Built-in, command-line
Runas (GUI feature)	Running tools and programs with different permissions than the user's current logon provides.	Built-in, GUI
SC (Sc.exe)	Viewing, stopping, starting, pausing, and disabling services, or changing service startup types for diagnostic purposes from the command-line.	Built-in, command line
Services snap-in (Services.msc)	Viewing, stopping, starting, pausing, and disabling services, or changing service startup types for diagnostic purposes.	Built-in, GUI
Shutdown Event Tracker	Recording information to the System log, describing the reason for shutting down or restarting the computer.	Built-in, GUI
System Configuration Utility (Msconfig.exe)	Enabling or disabling various settings for troubleshooting and diagnostic purposes.	Built-in, GUI
System Information in Help (Msinfo32.exe)	Collecting and displaying system configuration information about hardware, system components, and software. You can start System Information as a stand-alone tool or by using Windows XP Professional Help and Support Center.	Built-in, GUI
System Information (Systeminfo.exe)	Viewing computer configuration information. This is the character-mode version of the GUI-mode System Information tool.	Built-in, command-line
Task Killing Utility (TsKill.exe)	Ending one or more active tasks or processes.	Built-in, command-line

Table D-6   Application and Service Tools for Troubleshooting

Tool	Function	Tool Type, Interface
Task Lister (Tasklist.exe)	Listing active tasks and processes.	Built-in, command-line
Task Manager (Taskman.exe)	Viewing and ending active processes running on your system. In addition, you can use Task Manager to view system information, such as CPU and memory usage statistics.	Built-in, GUI
Uninstall Windows XP Professional	Uninstalling Windows XP Professional and reverting to the previous operating system.	Built-in, GUI

In the preceding table, *process* refers to an instance of an application together with the set of system resources allocated to run the application. *Thread* refers to an object within a process that is allocated processor time by the operating system to run code. Threads, not processes, run program code. Every process must have at least one thread, which allows a process to maintain parallel lines of execution. This is especially valuable for multiprocessor systems because Windows XP Professional can assign different threads to different processors.

Bootcfg

Bootcfg (Bootcfg.exe) is a command-line tool that reduces the potential for error when adding or editing startup settings in the *x*86-based Boot.ini file or the Itanium-based EFI Boot Manager. You must be logged on as an administrator or a member of the Administrators group to use Bootcfg.

To use Bootcfg to view Boot.ini file settings

■ To view Boot.ini file or EFI Boot Manager Windows XP Professional startup settings from the command prompt, type **bootcfg /query**.

For more information about using Bootcfg, click **Tools** in Help and Support Center.

Boot Logging

If your computer stops responding during startup, Boot logging allows you to identify initialized drivers. This information is useful if your computer cannot complete the startup process. By examining the boot log, you can identify the file name of the last file processed, which might be causing the problem. You can then focus your troubleshooting efforts on the suspect file and replace the file or search for an update.

To enable boot logging

1. Restart the computer.

2. When prompted, press F8, and then select **Enable Boot Logging** on the **Windows Advanced Options Menu**.

Enabling boot logging and restarting causes the operating system to create a log file in the *systemroot* directory named Ntbtlog.txt. You can view the log by double-clicking it. The log lists files that Windows XP Professional attempted to load during startup. In the log, **Loaded driver** or **Did not load driver** precedes the path to each file.

Loaded driver   A phrase that appears next to each driver or service that Windows XP Professional successfully loaded. The path and file name of the specific driver or service follow.

Did not load driver   A phrase that appears next to a driver or service that Windows XP Professional did not successfully load. The path and file name of the specific driver or service follow.

The following lines are sample Ntbtlog.txt entries:

```
Loaded driver \SystemRoot\System32\DRIVERS\flpydisk.sys
Did not load driver \SystemRoot\System32\DRIVERS\sflpydisk.sys
```

Examine the boot log to help identify missing or corrupted files. If a critical system file is corrupted or missing, Windows XP Professional might generate a Stop message or write an entry to the Event logs. To check if a file listed as **Did not load driver** is corrupted, you can do the following:

- Check for zero byte files or files with date and time stamps that do not match the Windows XP Professional installation date.

- Compare files in *systemroot*\System32 to the same files on the Windows XP Professional operating CD or another computer running the same edition (and service pack) of Windows XP Professional.

- Run the System File Checker (Sfc.exe) command-line tool to inspect system files. For more information about the System File Checker, see "System File Checker" later in this appendix.

Note   In safe mode, new boot log entries are appended to the existing Ntbtlog.txt file.

Dependency Walker

Dependency Walker (Depends.exe) is a support tool that enables you to examine a selected application or component to determine what other components are required for the application to start. The tool lists the dependencies in a tree format.

For every component selected, Dependency Walker lists the programming functions of each primary and secondary module. Typically, the system modules have .exe, .dll, .ocx, and .sys file name extensions.

Dependency Walker can also help you identify problems related to missing or corrupt modules, circular dependency errors, and mismatched module types.

For more information about Dependency Walker, click **Tools** in Help and Support Center, and then click **Windows Support Tools**. For more information about service dependencies, see "Troubleshooting Startup" in this book.

Device Manager

Device Manager (Devmgmt.msc) enables you to manage hardware installed on your computer. Use Device Manager to view device settings, to change hardware resource settings to resolve conflicts, and to update, uninstall, or roll back drivers.

For more information about Device Manager, click **Tools** in Help and Support Center. Or see "Managing Devices" in this book and "Driver Signing and Digital Signatures" later in this appendix.

DirectX Diagnostic Tool

The DirectX Diagnostic Tool (Dxdiag.exe) displays information about DirectX application programming interface (API) components and drivers installed on your system. DirectX is found in Windows 95, Windows 98, Windows Me, Windows 2000, and Windows XP Professional. DirectX allows these operating systems to take advantage of new and current hardware acceleration technologies that new video, audio, and input devices offer.

The DirectX APIs enhance multimedia application performance and enable Windows compatibility with a variety of video, audio, and input hardware. Although multimedia devices, such as audio and video adapters, are physically and functionally similar, they can use different hardware architecture and design philosophies. DirectX technology allows manufacturers to devote more time developing new technologies with less concern about low-level Windows programming details.

The DirectX Diagnostic Tool allows you to view and save information about the following types of hardware:

- Audio (DirectMusic® and DirectSound®)
- Video (DirectDraw® and Direct3D®)
- Controller and input devices (DirectInput®)
- Network hardware (DirectPlay®)

Using the DirectX Diagnostic Tool, you can test multimedia driver compatibility and display driver status and version information. If necessary, you can use the tool to disable or reduce hardware acceleration levels to diagnose problems. You can also use the tool to collect information that might be useful during a technical support call.

To start the DirectX Diagnostic Tool

■ In the **Run** dialog box, type **dxdiag**.

The DirectX Diagnostic Tool dialog box reports information on separate tabs about the various components and drivers. Table D-7 describes each tab in the DirectX Diagnostic Tool dialog box.

Table D-7   Tabs in the DirectX Diagnostic Tool Dialog Box

Tab	Description
System	Provides system information about your computer and specifies the version of DirectX that is installed on your computer.
DirectX Files	Lists the file name, version number, date, and size for each DirectX file that is installed on your computer.
Display	Lists current display settings and allows you to disable hardware acceleration and test DirectDraw and Direct3D compatibility.
Sound	Displays current sound settings and tests audio hardware DirectSound compatibility.
Music	Lists music port information, such as Musical Instrument Digital Interface (MIDI) settings, and allows you to test the DirectMusic component of DirectX.
Input	Lists the input devices and drivers installed on your computer.
Network	Lists the registered DirectPlay service providers that are installed on your computer and allows you to test DirectPlay components.
More Help	Offers additional options if you cannot resolve your DirectX issue by using previous tabs. You can start the System Configuration tool (Msconfig.exe) or override DirectDraw video refresh display settings from this tab. For more information about the System Configuration tool, see "System Configuration Utility" later in this appendix.

Recognizing Common DirectX Issues

You can use the DirectX Diagnostic Tool to determine whether the following issues apply to your system.

Incorrect or outdated DirectX components   In the **Notes** section on the **DirectX Files**, **Display**, **Sound**, **Music**, **Input**, and **Network** tabs, look for warnings or files labeled as **Beta**, **Debug**, **Outdated**, or **Unsigned** drivers. For best performance, install the most recent versions of DirectX and use Microsoft-signed drivers. For more information about obtaining and installing the latest version of DirectX, see the DirectX link on the Web Resources page at http://www.microsoft.com/windows/reskits/webresources.

Unsigned or beta drivers   Check the **DirectX Files** tab for drivers labeled **Unsigned** or **Beta**. Unsigned and beta drivers have not been fully tested by Microsoft Corporation for compatibility with the latest version of DirectX.

No video hardware acceleration   Some graphics-intensive programs run slowly or not at all if DirectDraw or Direct3D hardware acceleration is unavailable or disabled. Hardware acceleration offloads a substantial portion of 2D image and 3D geometry processing from the central processing unit (CPU) to the video adapter, resulting in much faster system performance. If you experience poor video performance, use the DirectX Diagnostic Tool to verify acceleration settings.

To check video hardware acceleration settings

1.   Start the DirectX Diagnostic Tool.

2.   Select the **Display** tab, and then in **DirectX features** verify that at least **DirectDraw Acceleration** and **Direct3D Acceleration** are marked as **Enabled**.

If the option to enable acceleration is not available, your video adapter might not support DirectX acceleration in hardware or you might need to install updated drivers.

> **Note**   Features such as AGP or Direct3D acceleration might not be available with older video hardware. You might need to upgrade your video hardware to use certain features in newer technologies.

Testing DirectX Components

You can test the following DirectX components:

- DirectDraw and Direct3D functionality for video adapters

- DirectSound and DirectMusic for audio devices

- DirectPlay for network devices

On the **Display**, **Sound**, **Music**, and **Network** tabs, click a **Test** button. Record any messages that appears, and then watch or listen to the tests. Each test prompts you to answer **Yes** or **No** to verify successful results. The DirectX Diagnostic Tool tests basic features first and progresses to more advanced functions. If you click **No**, the more advanced tests are cancelled.

If the default DirectX driver settings cause problems, you can reduce or disable acceleration features for video and audio adapters. For more information about disabling or reducing hardware acceleration levels, see "Managing Devices" in this book.

Saving Information

To save information gathered by the DirectX Diagnostic Tool, click the **Save All Information** button in the dialog box. You can save information from all DirectX tabs to a user-specified folder and file name.

For more information about DirectX components, architecture, and multimedia in general, see Windows XP Professional Help and Support Center. Also see "Managing Devices" and "Managing Digital Media" in this book. For more information about obtaining and installing the latest version of DirectX, see the DirectX link on the Web Resources page at http://www.microsoft.com/windows/reskits/webresources.

Dr. Watson

In the event of an application error, also known as a user-mode program exception, the Dr. Watson tool (Drwtsn32.exe) writes information to a text-based log file named **DrWtsn32.log**., in *systemdrive*\Documents and Settings\All Users\Application Data\Microsoft\DrWatson (default folder location). This log contains the following information:

- The file name of the program that caused the error.

- Information about the computer and user under which the error occurred.

- A list of programs and services active when the error occurred.

- A list of modules, such as Dynamic Link Library components (DLLs) that were in memory when the error occurred.

- Additional information that might be needed if you decide to contact technical support.

The task and module lists are useful for duplicating the conditions under which an application error occurred. Using the lists as a reference, you can add or remove programs and services until you can reproduce the problem.

To view and configure Dr. Watson logs

1. In the **Run** dialog box, type **drwtsn32**.

   Problem descriptions appear in **Application Errors**.

2. Select an entry, and then click **View** to display more information about the error.

3. To configure reporting settings, select items in the **Options** area.

To view logs directly from the Start menu

- In the **Run** dialog box, type:
  notepad %systemdrive%\documents and settings\all users\documents\drwatson\drwtsn32.log

For more information about the Dr. Watson tool (including a log file overview), click **Tools** in Help and Support Center.

Error Reporting

Windows XP Professional provides the Error Reporting service, which monitors your system for user-mode and kernel-mode faults that affect the operating system and applications. When an error occurs, the Error Reporting service gathers information about your problem and gives you the option to use an automated system to find more information and possibly a resolution.

User Mode Reporting

When a user mode error occurs, such as an application error, the Error Reporting service takes the following steps:

1. **Displays an alert** stating that Windows XP Professional detected a problem. You can click **Report this Problem** or **Don't Report**; or you can click **click here** for technical information before sending a report to Microsoft.

2. **Sends a problem report to Microsoft**. If you click **Report this Problem**, the Error Reporting service sends the error report anonymously to Microsoft by using a Secure Sockets Layer (SSL) encryption secured Internet connection. You might be prompted to provide additional information to complete your error report. When the process is complete, you can click **More Information**, which directs you to updated drivers, patches, or Microsoft Knowledge Base articles.

To verify that Windows Error Reporting is enabled for programs

1. In **Control Panel**, open **System**.

2. Click the **Advanced** tab, and then click **Error Reporting**.

3. In the **Error Reporting** dialog box, select **Enable error reporting**, and if not checked, click to enable the **Programs** check box.

Kernel Mode Reporting

When a Stop error occurs, Windows XP Professional displays a Stop message and writes diagnostic information to a memory dump file. When you restart your system by using normal mode or safe mode (with networking) and log on to Windows XP Professional, the Error Reporting service gathers information about the problem and displays a dialog box that gives you the option of sending a report to Microsoft.

For more information about Error Reporting, click **Tools** in Help and Support Center. For more information about Stop Messages, memory dump files, and using Error Reporting to get information about kernel-mode errors, see "Common Stop Messages for Troubleshooting" in this book.

Event Query

Event Query (Eventquery.vbs) is a command-line tool that you can use to search the event logs by using specified criteria. For troubleshooting, using Event Query enables you to view the event logs for entries related to specified event properties, including date and time, event ID, and user name.

Event Query also enables you to save output to a file and to specify the file format to use. For example, you can save output to a .csv file and further analyze the data by using Microsoft Excel.

For more information about Event Query and the event logs, click **Tools** in Help and Support Center.

Event Triggers

Event Triggers (Eventtriggers.exe) is a command-line tool that you can use to view, set, or delete trigger events. You can specify an error-log trigger condition to monitor and the task to run, including starting other programs, if thresholds are exceeded. For example, you can create a trigger that starts Disk Cleanup (Cleanmgr.exe) when a "Low Disk Space" message is recorded to the System log.

For more information about Event Triggers and the event logs, click **Tools** in Help and Support Center.

Event Viewer

Event Viewer (Eventvwr.msc) maintains application, security, and system logs for your computer. It also contains useful information for diagnosing hardware and software problems. Event Viewer provides three logs.

Application Log   Contains events logged by applications or programs. For example, a database program might record read or write errors to this log.

Security Log   Holds security event records, such as logon attempts and actions related to creating, opening, or deleting files. An administrator can view information or specify events to record in the security log.

System Log   Contains information about system components. For example, an entry is made when a driver or other system component fails to load during startup. For more information about how to insert custom shutdown information into the System log, see "Shutdown Event Tracker" later in this appendix.

You can save Event Viewer logs and specify filtering criteria for viewing information. Event Viewer logs can provide clues to problems that affect the system. When troubleshooting, use the information to identify problems with applications, drivers, or services, and to identify frequently occurring issues.

To start Event Viewer

- In the **Run** dialog box, type **eventvwr.msc**.

  – or –

- Start Event Viewer from the Computer Management snap-in.

For more information about the Computer Management MMC snap-in, see "Computer Management Tool" later in this appendix. For more information about using Event Viewer, see Help on the **Action** menu in Event Viewer.

Global Flags Editor

Global Flags Editor (Gflags.exe) is a GUI-mode Support Tool that allows members of the Administrators group to enable and disable advanced internal system diagnostics and troubleshooting features on computers running Windows XP Professional. Gflags.exe is designed as a debugging tool for application developers. It is most often used to turn on indicators that other tools track, count, and log.

Use it to edit the global flag settings that the kernel uses when starting. The term *global flag* refers to the **GlobalFlag** registry entries that Windows XP Professional checks to enable or disable advanced internal system diagnostics and troubleshooting tests.

> **Caution**   Incorrect use of Global Flags Editor might cause system startup failure or adversely impact performance. Use this tool only as directed by Microsoft Product Support Services.

For more information about Global Flags Editor, click **Tools** in Help and Support Center, and then click **Windows Support Tools**. For more information about memory leaks, see Debugging Tools Help and "Evaluating Memory and Cache Usage" in the *Operations Guide* of the *Microsoft® Windows® 2000 Server Resource Kit*.

Group Policy Snap-in

The Group Policy snap-in (Gpedit.msc) allows you to view, create, delete, or edit user and computer Group Policy objects (GPOs). The Group Policy snap-in enables you to view which Group Policy settings are in effect and simplify troubleshooting by disabling GPOs that can affect the way your system starts and performs. You must be logged on as an administrator or a member of the Administrators group to use the Group Policy snap-in.

To start the Group Policy snap-in

- In the **Run** dialog box, type **gpedit.msc**.

For an illustration of using the Group Policy snap-in to help diagnose a startup problem, see "Troubleshooting Startup" in this book. Also, see article Q256320, "Startup Scripts May Appear to Hang Windows 2000," in the Microsoft Knowledge Base. To find this article, see the Microsoft Knowledge Base link on the Web Resources page at http://www.microsoft.com/windows/reskits/webresources.

Two related tools, Group Policy Results (Gpresult.exe) and the Resultant Set of Policy snap-in (Rsop.msc) enable you to view Group Policy settings. Another related tool, Group Policy Update (Gpupdate.exe) enables you to immediately refresh changes to GPOs. For more information about using the Group Policy snap-in, see Windows XP Professional Help and Support Center.

For more information about Group Policy, see "Authorization and Access Control," "Planning Deployments," and "Managing Desktops" in this book. Also, see the *Distributed Systems Guide* of the *Microsoft Windows 2000 Server Resource Kit* and the Change and Configuration Management Deployment Guide link on the Web Resources page at http://www.microsoft.com/windows/reskits/webresources.

Group Policy Results

Group Policy Results (Gpresult.exe) is a command-line tool that displays information about the cumulative result that Group Policy objects (GPOs) have on computers and users. Use this tool to view which Group Policy settings are in effect for the local computer, sites, domains, and organizational units (OUs). Group Policy Results provides information that can help you identify and troubleshoot problems due to missing or improperly applied GPOs.

Two related tools, the Group Policy snap-in (Gpedit.msc) and the Resultant Set of Policy snap-in (Rsop.msc) enable you to change and view Group Policy information. For more information about using Gpresult.exe, see Windows XP Professional Help and Support Center.

For more information about Group Policy, see "Authorization and Access Control," "Planning Deployments," and "Managing Desktops" in this book. Also, see the *Distributed Systems Guide* of the *Microsoft Windows 2000 Server Resource Kit* and the *Change and Configuration Management Deployment Guide* link on the Web Resources page at http://www.microsoft.com/windows/reskits/webresources.

Group Policy Update

Group Policy changes do not always take effect immediately. You can use the Group Policy Update (Gpupdate.exe) command-line tool to immediately refresh changes to user and computer GPOs. Group Policy Update replaces the **secedit /refreshpolicy** command used in Windows 2000 to refresh Group Policy settings. You must be logged on as an administrator or a member of the Administrators group to run Gpupdate.exe.

After you run Gpupdate.exe, you can use the Resultant Set of Policy snap-in (Rsop.msc) or the Group Policy Results (Gpresult.exe) tool to verify that the updated settings are in effect. For more information about using Gpupdate.exe, see Windows XP Professional Help and Support Center.

For more information about Group Policy, see "Authorization and Access Control," "Planning Deployments," and "Managing Desktops" in this book. Also, see the *Distributed Systems Guide* of the *Microsoft Windows 2000 Server Resource Kit* and the *Change and Configuration Management Deployment Guide* link on the Web Resources page at http://www.microsoft.com/windows/reskits/webresources.

Kernel Debugger

You can use a kernel debugger for real-time computer debugging, or to analyze a memory-dump file saved to disk when a Stop error occurs. A kernel debugger enables advanced users to view the contents of computer memory, including source code and variables. The following are two debuggers that you can obtain from Microsoft.

Kernel Debugger   Kernel Debugger (Kd.exe) is a command-line debugging tool that you can use to analyze a memory dump file written to disk when a Stop message occurs. Kernel Debugger requires that you install symbol files on your system.

WinDbg Debugger   WinDbg Debugger (Windbg.exe) provides functionality similar to Kernel Debugger, but uses a GUI interface.

Kernel Debugger and WinDbg Debugger are two of many available debugging tools. For more information about kernel debugging tools, Stop messages, memory-dump files, or symbol files, see Debugging Tools Help or "Common Stop Messages for Troubleshooting" in this book.

Memory Pool Monitor

Memory Pool Monitor (Poolmon.exe) is a Support Tool used to detect memory leaks.

For more information about the Pool Monitor and a related tool, Global Flags Editor (Gflags.exe), click **Tools** in Help and Support Center, and then click **Windows Support Tools**. Also, see Debugging Tools Help. For more information about memory leaks, see "Evaluating Memory and Cache Usage" in the *Operations Guide* of the *Microsoft Windows 2000 Server Resource Kit*. Also, see "Global Flags Editor" earlier in this appendix.

Online Crash Analysis Web Site

The Online Crash Analysis Web site enables you to send kernel-mode error reports to Microsoft Corporation and track the status of reports previously sent by using your Microsoft Passport information. You can access the Online Crash Analysis Web site by using the Error Reporting service or by using your Web browser. For more information about using the Online Crash Analysis Web site and the Error Reporting service to diagnose Stop errors, see "Common Stop Messages for Troubleshooting" in this book.

OpenFiles

OpenFiles (Openfiles.exe) is command-line tool that you can use to view or disconnect connections to files and folders opened remotely by using a shared folder.

For more information about using OpenFiles, click **Tools** in Help and Support Center.

Performance Snap-in

The Performance (Perfmon.msc) MMC snap-in enables you to establish performance baselines, diagnose system problems, and anticipate increased system resource demands. This tool can be used to obtain useful data for detecting system bottlenecks and changes in system performance.

The Performance snap-in has two components:

- System Monitor
- Performance Logs and Alerts

These components allow you to collect, save, and view real-time data pertaining to memory, disk, processor, network, and other activities in various formats such as graphs, histograms, and reports. You can configure Performance Logs and Alerts to record performance data and set system alerts when a specified parameter is above or below a defined threshold.

To start the Performance snap-in

- In the **Run** dialog box, type **perfmon.msc**.

For more information about the Performance Tool, see Windows XP Professional Help and Support Center and "Overview of Performance Monitoring" in the *Operations Guide* of the *Microsoft Windows 2000 Server Resource Kit*.

Process and Thread Status

Process and Thread Status (Pstat.exe) is a command-line Support Tool that enables you to view the status of threads, processes, and drivers running on your computer.

For an illustration of how to use Process and Thread Status to identify driver problems, see article Q192463, "Gathering Blue Screen Information After Memory Dump," in the Microsoft Knowledge Base. To find this article, see the Microsoft Knowledge Base link on the Web Resources page at http://www.microsoft.com /windows/reskits/webresources.

For more information about Process and Thread Status, click **Tools** in Help and Support Center, and then click **Windows Support Tools**.

Program Compatibility Wizard

The Program Compatibility Wizard allows you to test and resolve compatibility issues with a program that worked correctly on an earlier version of Windows. By using the Program Compatibility Wizard, you might be able to run an older program by using a specific compatibility mode and display resolution.

You can run a program released for an earlier version of Windows by using the following compatibility modes:

- Windows 95
- Windows 98 and Windows Me
- Windows NT 4.0 (Service Pack 5)
- Windows 2000

You can also use the following display options to resolve video driver compatibility problems:

- Run in 256 colors
- Run in 640 x 480 screen resolution
- Disable visual themes

To set compatibility mode options for a program (Method 1)

1. From the **Start** menu, click **Accessories**, and then click **Program Compatibility Wizard**.

2. Follow the on-screen instructions to select a program, and to specify the compatibility options to use when running the program.

To set compatibility mode options for a program (Method 2)

1. Open Windows Explorer to locate the program.

2. Right-click the program's icon, and then click **Properties**.

3. In the **Properties** dialog box, click the **Compatibility** tab.

4. Select the options you want to use, and then click **OK**.

Warning   It is recommended that you do not run virus detection software, backup programs, CD authoring tools, or other programs that install system drivers and services, while in compatibility mode.

Always consult the software manufacturer's Web site for more information about obtaining Windows XP Professional–specific updates. For more information about program compatibility, see Windows XP Professional Help and Support Center.

Registry Editor

Advanced users can use the registry editor, Regedit.exe, to view or change system settings. The registry is a central database that stores information about users, software, and hardware. The registry editor displays the data by using a GUI that lists subtrees, keys, subkeys, and entries. *Subkeys* are similar to folders and can hold entries and other subkeys. Valid data types for entries include strings, dwords (hexadecimal values), and binary values.

Editing the registry directly is seldom required, and using the registry editor is typically a last-resort option. Use caution when editing the registry, because specifying incorrect values can cause instability. The registry editor is intended for advanced users who are familiar with registry concepts and want to configure settings for which a user interface does not exist. If you must edit the registry, back it up first and see the Registry Reference in the Microsoft Windows 2000 Server Resource Kit at http://www.microsoft.com/reskit.

Before Using the Registry Editor

Before you use the registry editor, be sure that you can restore your system if problems occur. Before changing registry values, use System Restore or the Backup tool. For more information about System Restore, see "System Restore" earlier in this appendix. For more information about using the Backup tool for troubleshooting, see "Backup" earlier in this appendix. Also, see "Backup and Restore" in this book.

If you have not saved the system state and encounter problems, you might be able to recover by restarting the computer and using the Last Known Good Configuration startup option. For more information about using this option, see "Last Known Good Configuration" earlier in this appendix.

Features of the Registry Editor

The registry editor, Regedit.exe, in Windows XP Professional provides many improvements and convenient features that enable you to do the following:

■ Make all your changes by using one registry editor, Regedit.exe. Regedit.exe in Windows XP Professional combines the features of the two registry editors in Windows 2000 (Regedit.exe and Regedt32.exe) into a single program. Regedit.exe in Windows XP Professional supports importing portions of the registry that were backed up by using versions of Regedit32.exe included with Windows NT 4.0 and Windows 2000.

■ Perform searches by using criteria that you specify. Performance improvements enable you to view search results more quickly than previous versions.

■ Save commonly used or hard-to-find subkeys and entries in a list of favorites for faster access in the future.

■ Quickly return to a location in the registry, because the registry editor records and opens the last location that you viewed.

■ Export all or a portion of registry content to a file that can be read by using a text editor such as Notepad. Information contained in these exported files is logically organized and labeled.

■ Use the registry editor from the command line by specifying the **/s** parameter. When you use **/s**, Regedit.exe does not display a GUI or pause for user confirmation. This enables you to use the registry editor in batch files.

Registry Subtrees

The registry consists of five subtrees that group computer information and settings by category or scope. Table D-8 lists and describes the five subtrees that make up the registry.

Table D-8   Registry Subtrees

Subtree	Description
HKEY_CLASSES_ROOT	Stores the information that maintains file associations to ensure that the correct program runs when you open a data file. For example, the information in this subkey associates files using a .doc file name extension with Microsoft® Word if Microsoft® Office is installed.
	This subtree also contains information necessary to support core aspects of the Windows user interface, such as drag-and-drop operations.
HKEY_CURRENT_USER	Contains configuration settings for the user currently logged on. Examples of information stored for each user are Desktop wallpaper and custom color settings. User-specific information in HKEY_CURRENT_USER is taken from the HKEY_USERS subtree during the logon process.

Table D-8   Registry Subtrees

Subtree	Description
HKEY_LOCAL_MACHINE	Contains computer-specific hardware and software settings that apply to the entire computer, regardless of the user logged on. An example of this is hard disk configuration settings.
HKEY_USERS	Contains information that applies to all users of the computer. Settings that apply to all users, as well as user-specific settings, are stored in this subtree. User-specific information is grouped by security identifier (SID) values, a unique number assigned to a user account.
HKEY_CURRENT_CONFIG	Contains information about the current hardware profile used by the local computer. HKEY_CURRENT_CONFIG is an alias for information stored in HKEY_LOCAL_MACHINE.

For more information about using the registry editor, Regedit.exe, click **Tools** in Help and Support Center.

Resultant Set of Policy

The Resultant Set of Policy (RSoP) snap-in (Rsop.msc) enables you to poll and evaluate the cumulative effect that local, site, domain, and organizational unit Group Policy objects (GPOs) have on computers and users. Resultant Set of Policy enables you to check for GPOs that might affect your troubleshooting. For example, a GPO setting can cause startup programs to run after you log on to the computer.

Use this snap-in to evaluate the effects of existing GPOs on your computer. This information is helpful for diagnosing deployment or security problems. Rsop.msc reports individual Group Policy settings specific to one or more users and computers, including advertised and assigned applications.

To start the Resultant Set of Policy snap-in

- In the **Run** dialog box, type **rsop.msc**.

For more information about Group Policy, see "Authorization and Access Control," "Planning Deployments," and "Managing Desktops" in this book. Also, see the *Distributed Systems Guide* of the *Microsoft Windows 2000 Server Resource Kit* and the *Change and Configuration Management Deployment Guide* link on the Web Resources page at http://www.microsoft.com/windows/reskits/webresources.

Two related tools, the Group Policy snap-in (Gpedit.msc) and the Group Policy Results tool (Gpresult.exe) allow you to view Group Policy information. For more information about the preceding tools, see "Group Policy Snap-in" and "Group Policy Results" earlier in this appendix.

RunAs (Command-Line Tool)

RunAs (Runas.exe) is a command-line tool that you can use to run tools and programs with different permissions than the user's current logon provides. For troubleshooting, this enables you to run configuration and diagnostic tools with administrator credentials while logged on as another user (for example, a user account that is a member of the Power Users group). You can then test and observe the results that these changes have on user accounts and groups that do not have administrative privileges.

For more information about using the RunAs command-line tool, see Windows XP Professional Help and Support Center.

RunAs (GUI Feature)

Windows XP Professional enables you to run tools and programs from the Start menu, Windows desktop, and Windows Explorer, with different permissions than the user's current logon provides. For troubleshooting, this enables you to run configuration and diagnostic tools with administrator credentials while logged on as another user (for example, a user account that is a member of the Power Users group). You can then test and observe the results that these changes have on user accounts and groups that do not have administrative privileges.

To start a program as an administrator

1. Locate an executable file, snap-in, or shortcut to run by using the **Start** menu, Windows desktop, or Windows Explorer.

2. Press and hold the SHIFT key, right-click the program icon, and then click **Run as**.

3. In the **Run As** dialog box, specify a user account with administrative permissions, and then click **OK**.

For more information about using RunAs functionality from the Windows GUI, see "Use the runas command to start programs as an administrator" in Windows XP Professional Help and Support Center.

SC

SC (Sc.exe) is a command-line tool that communicates with the Windows XP Professional Services Control Manager (SCM) and displays information about processes running on your computer. SC enables you to perform many functions including:

- Display service information such as startup type and whether you can pause or end a process.

- Start, pause, resume, or end a process.

The following illustrates output obtained by typing **sc query** at the command prompt:

```
SERVICE_NAME: winmgmt
DISPLAY_NAME: Windows Management Instrumentation
        TYPE                : 20 WIN32_SHARE_PROCESS
        STATE               : 4 RUNNING
                              (STOPPABLE,PAUSABLE,ACCEPTS_SHUTDOWN)
        WIN32_EXIT_CODE   : 0 (0x0)
        SERVICE_EXIT_CODE : 0 (0x0)
        CHECKPOINT        : 0x0
        WAIT_HINT         : 0x0
```

SC enables you to create lists of components that are running in safe and normal modes. By comparing the differences between the two lists, you can determine which components are not required to start Windows XP Professional. For diagnostic purposes, you can disable services individually in safe mode and then try to start your computer in normal mode.

For more information about SC, click **Tools** in Help and Support Center. For more information about troubleshooting startup problems, see "Troubleshooting Startup" in this book.

Services Snap-in

The Services (Services.msc) snap-in enables you to view service information or to temporarily stop, pause, or disable services for troubleshooting or diagnostic purposes. You must be logged on as an administrator or a member of the Administrators group to change service properties.

To start the Services snap-in

- In the **Run** dialog box, type **services.msc**.

  – or –

- Start the Services snap-in from the Computer Management tool.

  For more information about the Computer Management tool, click **Tools** in Help and Support Center. Also, see "Computer Management Tool" later in this appendix.

To view properties for a service, double-click the service name. For more information about services and using the Services snap-in to troubleshoot application and startup problems, click **Tools** in Help and Support Center and see "Troubleshooting Startup" in this book.

Shutdown Event Tracker

Shutdown Event Tracker provides a mechanism to record reasons in the System log for scheduled (planned), unscheduled (unplanned), and unexpected computer shutdowns or restarts. This mechanism takes the form of a Shutdown Event Tracker dialog box that appears if any of the following events occur:

- Immediately after a user clicks **Shut Down** from the **Start** menu, and then clicks **Shut Down** or **Restart** from the **Shut Down Windows** dialog box.
- After a user resets the computer and logs on to Windows XP Professional.
- After power is disconnected, when a user starts the computer and logs on to Windows XP Professional.

You can indicate whether the shutdown or restart was "planned" or "unplanned." The reasons and comments that you provide are recorded to the System log. Predefined reasons that Windows XP Professional provides for planned and unplanned shutdowns include the following:

- Hardware: Maintenance (Planned and Unplanned)
- Hardware: Installation (Planned and Unplanned)
- Operating System: Upgrade (Planned and Unplanned)
- Operating System: Configuration Change (Planned and Unplanned)
- Application: Maintenance (Planned and Unplanned)
- Application: Unresponsive (Planned and Unplanned)
- Application: Unstable (Unplanned)

A shutdown that is not initiated by the operating system, an application, a service, or the **Shut Down Windows** dialog box is an *unexpected shutdown*. Causes of unexpected shutdown include a power failure or a disconnected power cable. Predefined reasons for unexpected shutdowns include the following:

- System Failure: Stop error
- Power Failure: Cord Unplugged
- Power Failure: Environment
- Other Failure: System Unresponsive
- Unknown

Caution   Do not edit the registry unless you have no alternative. The registry editor bypasses standard safeguards, allowing settings that can damage your system, or even require you to reinstall Windows. If you must edit the registry, back it up first and see the Registry Reference in the *Microsoft® Windows® 2000 Server Resource Kit* at http://www.microsoft.com/reskit.

By default, Shutdown Event Tracker is disabled for Windows XP Professional. Use the following procedure to enable or disable Shutdown Event Tracker.

To enable or disable Shutdown Event Tracker

1. In the **Run** dialog box, start the registry editor by typing **regedit.exe**, and then clicking **OK**.

2. In the registry editor, navigate to HKEY_LOCAL_MACHINE\SOFTWARE\ Microsoft\Windows\CurrentVersion\Reliability, and then double-click **ShutdownReasonUI**.

3. To enable Shutdown Event Tracker, assign a value of **1**.
   – or –
   To disable Shutdown Event Tracker, assign a value of **0**.

4. Click **OK**, and then close the registry editor.

   Use the following procedure to view Shutdown Event Tracker information.

To view Shutdown Event Tracker information

1. In the **Run** dialog box, type **eventvwr.msc**.

2. In **Event Viewer (local)**, click **System Log**.

3. On the **View** menu, click **Find** to open the **Find in local System** dialog box.

4. In the **Event ID** box, type **1074** (planned and unplanned) or **1076** (unexpected shutdown), and then click **Find Next**.

5. Click the up or down arrows to view each matching entry. Shutdown or restart information appears in the **Description** box.

A related command-line tool, Shutdown (Shutdown.exe) enables you to shut down the computer from the command line. By using the **-d** parameter, Shutdown also enables you to record shutdown reasons to the System log. Another related tool, Event Query (Eventquery.vbs) enables you to search the System log on one or more computers for shutdown information, and save the output to a file for further evaluation. For more information about Shutdown Event Tracker and the Shutdown command-line tool, click **Tools** in Help and Support Center.

System Configuration Utility

System Configuration Utility (Msconfig.exe) allows you to temporarily change the way Windows XP Professional starts by disabling startup programs and services individually or several at a time. For example, on *x*86-based computers, you can use this tool to disable 16-bit startup applications specified in Win.ini and System.ini. Figure D-2 shows the tabs available and the options on the **General** tab. You must be logged on as an administrator or a member of the Administrators group to change or restore settings by using System Configuration Utility.

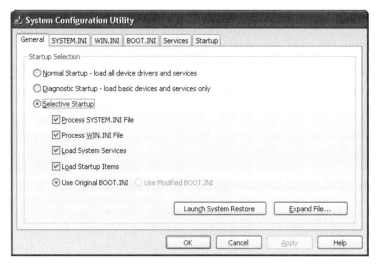

Figure D-2   System Configuration Utility

To change options by using System Configuration Utility

1. In the **Run** dialog box, type **msconfig**.

2. In the **System Configuration Utility** dialog box, click one of the tabs, and then enable or disable the available options by clearing or selecting the check box for a configuration option.

    System Configuration Utility provides several configuration tabs that allow you to enable or disable system services and startup applications.

General

Allows you to start Windows XP Professional in **Normal**, **Diagnostic**, or **Selective Startup** mode.

Diagnostic Startup   Starts Windows XP Professional in safe mode with only basic device drivers and services active. When you select the Diagnostic Startup option, System Configuration Utility disables most services, and you might not be able to run certain Computer Management and Control Panel tools. To use these tools, select the Selective Startup option on the General tab, and then enable the following services listed on the Services tab:

- Cryptographic Services
- Event Log
- Logical Disk Manager

- Help and Support

- Plug and Play

- Remote Procedure Call (RPC)

- System Restore Service

- Windows Management Instrumentation

For more information about the Computer Management tool, see "Computer Management Tool" later in this appendix.

Selective Startup   Allows you to enable or disable programs and services listed in the **SYSTEM.INI**, **WIN.INI**, **BOOT.INI**, **Startup**, and **Services** tabs. Disabling a check box under **Selective Startup** disables all entries in the corresponding tab. You can also enable or disable individual entries on each tab.

WIN.INI and SYSTEM.INI Tabs

On these two tabs, you can enable or disable services and startup programs meant for earlier versions of Windows. Both the *systemroot*\System.ini and *systemroot*\Win.ini files are not required by Windows XP Professional and these files are maintained only for compatibility with older software that does not use the registry to save settings. The System.ini file is used to start and store information for drivers and services; the Win.ini file plays a similar role for applications.

BOOT.INI Tab

On this tab you can customize your Boot.ini file. For more information about the Boot.ini file, see "Troubleshooting Startup" in this book.

Services Tab

On this tab you can enable or disable specific services. Enabling **Hide All Microsoft Services** allows you to isolate and disable third-party services.

Certain applications (such as antivirus programs) run as services. Problems with these applications might prevent you from starting Windows XP Professional in normal mode. You can use System Configuration Utility to disable a service and verify that it is the cause of the problem. For more information about troubleshooting startup problems, see "Troubleshooting Startup" in this book.

Startup Tab

You can enable or disable startup programs on this tab. For more information about disabling startup programs, see "Troubleshooting Startup" in this book.

If you change any startup setting by using System Configuration Utility, the following message appears the next time you log on to the system:

You have used the System Configuration Utility to change the way Windows starts. The System Configuration Utility is currently in Diagnostic or Selective Startup mode, causing this message to be displayed and the utility to run every time Windows starts. Choose the Normal Startup mode on the General tab to start Windows normally and undo the changes you made using the System Configuration Utility.

Simplifying system configuration is an essential part of troubleshooting. For more information about using System Configuration Utility, click **Tools** in Help and Support Center.

Systeminfo

Systeminfo (Systeminfo.exe) is a command-line tool that displays computer configuration information. You can use this tool to gather information useful for troubleshooting, such as the firmware version and any hotfixes applied. This tool is separate from the GUI-based System Information tool (Msinfo32.exe) but provides similar information.

To start Systeminfo, type **systeminfo** at the command prompt.

The following is an illustration of Systeminfo output:

```
Host Name:                RLY-1-TST
BIOS Version:             BIOS v4.51PG
Boot Device:              \Device\HarddiskVolume1
Total Physical Memory:    127.00 M
Available Physical Memory: 8,976.00 K
Virtual Memory: Max Size: 443,176.00 K
Virtual Memory: Available: 190,580.00 K
Virtual Memory: In Use:   252,596.00 K
Domain:                   mydomain.com
Logon Server:             \\LOGON-SRV-1
Hotfix(s):                1 Hotfix(s) Installed.
```

For more information about Systeminfo.exe, click **Tools** in Help and Support Center.

System Information

System Information (Msinfo32.exe) displays configuration information that can help you diagnose and troubleshoot problems.

To start System Information

■ In the **Run** dialog box, type **msinfo32**.

System Information displays and groups information about your computer into categories.

System Summary   **System Summary** displays information about the system, such as processor type, computer name, and the amount of physical memory available. **System Summary** is a good starting point to search for information about the environment in which the problem is occurring.

Hardware Resources   This item displays information such as direct memory access (DMA) channels, free and used interrupt request (IRQ) lines, device conflicts, and resource sharing. **Hardware Resources** contains a **Problem Devices** item, which lists descriptions and error codes for devices that might not be functioning correctly. Expand **Hardware Resources** to obtain information about system hardware resource settings. Table D-9 describes the information displayed.

Table D-9   Hardware Resource Information

Resource	Description
Conflicts/Sharing	Provides information about shared or conflicting devices, including several bus types such as Industry Standard Architecture (ISA), Peripheral Component Interconnect (PCI), Small Computer System Interface (SCSI), and PC Card or Personal Computer Memory Card International Association (PCMCIA).
	Shared resources are not necessarily in conflict. For example, PCI devices can share IRQs.
DMA	Reports the DMA channels in use, the devices that use them, and the channels that are free for use.
Forced Hardware	Lists devices that have manually specified resources, instead of resources that Windows XP Professional assigns. This information is useful for troubleshooting Plug and Play resource conflicts.
I/O	Lists all input and output (I/O) port ranges in use and the devices that use each range.
IRQ	Summarizes IRQ usage by identifying the devices that use each IRQ; also identifies which IRQs are free.
Memory	Lists memory address ranges in use by devices.

For more information about system resources and managing device settings, see "Managing Devices" in this book.

Components   This item displays hardware information for installed devices such as ports, display, and USB. **Components** contains a **Conflicts/Shared** item, which lists descriptions and error codes for devices that might not be functioning correctly. Expand **Components** for information about device component configuration. For information about devices that have assigned error codes from Windows XP Professional, check **Problem Devices** when you are troubleshooting.

For more information about system resources and how to manage device settings, see "Managing Devices" in this book.

Software Environment **Software Environment** displays a list of drivers, environment variables, tasks, and services. You can use this information to verify that a process is running or to determine versions. Expand **Software Environment** for information about software in system memory. Table D-10 describes the information displayed.

Table D-10   Software Environment

Category	Description
System Drivers	Lists and displays status for all enabled drivers.
Signed Drivers	Provides the same type of information as **System Drivers** but limits the scope to signed drivers.
Environment Variables	Lists all system environment variables and their values.
Print Jobs	Lists open print jobs.
Network Connections	Lists all mapped network connections.
Running Tasks	Lists all processes currently running on the system.
Loaded Modules	Lists loaded system-level DLLs and programs, along with their version numbers, size, and file date and path. Useful for debugging software problems, such as application faults.
Services	Lists all available system services, showing current run status and start mode.
Program Groups	Lists all existing program groups for all known users of the system.
Startup Programs	Lists programs started automatically either from the registry, the Startup program group or the Win.ini file.
OLE Registration	Lists OLE file associations controlled by the registry.

Internet Explorer This item displays a list of configuration settings related to Internet Explorer. Expand **Internet Explorer** to obtain information about system configuration. Table D-11 describes the information displayed.

Table D-11   Internet Explorer

Category	Definition
Summary	Lists Internet Explorer information, such as the version and cipher strength.
File Versions	Lists all files associated with Internet Explorer, as well as version numbers, file sizes, file dates, installation paths, and manufacturer.
Connectivity	Lists all the connectivity settings used by Internet Explorer.
Cache	Lists a general summary of cache settings and of cached objects.

Table D-11   Internet Explorer

Category	Definition
Content	Determines if Content Advisor is enabled and lists all installed personal certificates, other people certificates, and publishers.
Security	Lists the settings for Internet security zones.

System Information Menu   The **Tools** menu in System Information provides convenient access to several troubleshooting tools and features including the following:

- Backup
- Disk Cleanup
- Dr. Watson
- DirectX Diagnostic Tool
- File Signature Verification Tool
- Hardware Wizard
- Network Connections
- System Monitor

To save System Information data to a text file

1. Start System Information.
2. On the **File** menu, click **Export**, and then type a file name.
3. To print the information, under the **File** menu, click **Print**.

A full System Information printout is an important record of your computer's baseline configuration that you can use for troubleshooting. For more information about system baselines, see "Troubleshooting Concepts and Strategies" in this book.

Task Kill

Task Kill (Tskill.exe) is a command-line tool used to end one or more processes. You can end processes by using a command-line parameter to Tskill.exe that specifies the process identifier (PID) or any part of the process name, such as the title of the application's main window. You can obtain a list of process names and IDs by using a related tool, Task List (Tasklist.exe).

Use Task Kill for troubleshooting when you suspect that faulty services or applications that stop responding or consume excessive system resources might be adversely affecting the performance of your system. Symptoms typically include sluggish performance, slow screen updates, delayed response to network requests, or slow response to keyboard and mouse input.

You can use Task Kill to specify how to stop processes, such as by:

■ Sending the process a command to halt itself.

■ Forcing the process to end.

Task Kill is useful for terminating tasks when Task Manager is not available or when you are remotely connecting to other computers by using the Telnet protocol.

For more information about Task Kill or the related Task List tool, click **Tools** in Help and Support Center. For more information about using task listing or task ending tools for troubleshooting, see "Troubleshooting Startup"" in this book.

Task List

The Task List command-line tool (Tasklist.exe) allows you to obtain a list of active processes that are running on a local computer. For each process, Task List displays the process name and process identifier (PID). The following is output from Task List:

```
Host Name         Image Name                  PID Session   Mem Usage
================  ==========================  ====== ========  ============
RLY-TST-WXP       System Idle Process            0        0         20 K
RLY-TST-WXP       System                        4        0        216 K
RLY-TST-WXP       smss.exe                    188        0        332 K
RLY-TST-WXP       csrss.exe                   200        0      2,996 K
```

You can terminate a process by specifying the PID number as a command-line parameter to process-ending tools such as Task Kill or Process Viewer. You can disable a process to rule it out as the cause of a problem. For more information about troubleshooting applications and services, see "Troubleshooting Startup" in this book.

For more information about the Task List or the related Task Kill and Process Viewer tools, click **Tools** in Help and Support Center.

Task Manager

Task Manager (Taskmgr.exe) is a GUI tool that enables you to view or end a processes or an unresponsive application. You can also use Task Manager to gather other information, such as CPU statistics.

To start Task Manager

■ At the command prompt, type **taskmgr**.

– or –

■ You can start Task Manager by pressing CTRL+ALT+DEL and then clicking **Task Manager**.

The Task Manager window contains four tabs: **Applications**, **Processes**, **Performance**, and **Networking**. The **Applications** and **Processes** tabs provide a list of applications or processes currently active on your system. These lists are valuable, because active tasks do not always display a user interface, making it difficult to detect activity. Task Manager displays active processes and enables you to end most items by clicking **End Process**. You cannot end some processes immediately, and you might need to use other programs such as the Services snap-in, Task Kill, Process Viewer, or equivalent tools, to end them. You can also customize Task Manager to increase or decrease the level of detail shown on the **Processes** tab.

To display additional information on the Processes tab

1. Start Task Manager, and then click the **Processes** tab.

2. On the **View** menu, click **Select Columns**.

3. Select or clear the columns that you want to add to, or remove from, the **Processes** tab.

For more information about using Task Manager, start the tool, and then on the **Help** menu, click **Task Manager Help Topics**.

Uninstall Windows XP Professional

For systems upgraded to Windows XP Professional from Windows 98 or Windows Me, you might be able to revert to the previous operating system as a method for resolving the following problem.

After upgrading to Windows XP Professional, you might discover that a critical application does not run or a device fails to initialize. Consult the software or hardware manufacturer to determine if a compatibility problem exists. You might also learn that one of the following conditions applies to you:

■ The program does not run correctly, even after running the Program Compatibility Wizard. For more information, see "Program Compatibility Wizard" earlier in this appendix.

■ The manufacturer no longer supports the application or device and an update is not available. Furthermore, device drivers for earlier versions of Windows do not work.

■ The manufacturer supports the device, but a Windows XP Professional update is not yet available. Furthermore, device drivers for earlier versions of Windows do not work.

Reverting to the previous operating system enables you to continue using the application or device while waiting for a compatible update or replacement. You can choose to upgrade to Windows XP Professional at a later date.

To uninstall Windows XP Professional

1. In the **Run** dialog box, type **appwiz.cpl**, and then click **OK**.

2. In the **Currently installed programs** box, click **Windows XP Professional**, and then click **Remove**.

3. Follow the on-screen instructions to uninstall Windows XP Professional.

You can only uninstall Windows XP Professional if your computer meets all of the following requirements:

- The computer was upgraded from Windows 98 or Windows Me.

- The system partition uses the FAT or FAT32 file system. This is the default for computers upgraded from Windows 98 and Windows Me. If you use Convert.exe to convert the file system from FAT to NTFS, you can no longer uninstall Windows XP Professional.

- The computer had sufficient disk space to save uninstall information when you upgraded to Windows XP Professional.

To detect incompatible components before upgrading to Windows XP Professional, run Setup with the **/checkupgradeonly** parameter.

To check system compatibility before installing Windows XP Professional

- Insert the Windows XP Professional operating system CD into the computer, and then wait for the **Welcome to Microsoft Windows XP** screen to appear. Click **Check system compatibility**.

  – or –

- At the command prompt, type **drive:\i386\winnt32.exe /checkupgradeonly** (where *drive*: represents the network or CD-ROM path to the Windows XP Professional installation files).

For more information about uninstalling Windows XP, see Windows XP Professional Help and Support Center. Also see articles Q303661, "How to Uninstall Windows XP and Revert to a Previous Operating System", and Q303678, "How to Uninstall Windows XP if Setup Will Not Continue During Upgrade". To find these articles, see the Microsoft Knowledge Base link on the Web Resources page at http://www.microsoft.com/windows/reskits/webresources.

For more information about upgrading to, or deploying Windows XP Professional, see "Planning Deployments" in this book.

Remote Management Tools

If a computer that you want to troubleshoot is in a remote location, you can use the tools alphabetically listed in Table D-12 to access computers running Windows XP Professional. Table D-12 lists only a few of the Windows XP Professional tools and features that you can use for remote troubleshooting.

Table D-12   Remote Management Tools for Troubleshooting

Tool	Function	Tool Type, Interface
Computer Management Tool (Compmgmt.msc)	Viewing, troubleshooting, and managing local or remote computer settings.	Built-in, GUI
Remote Desktop	Remotely accessing remote computers by using a GUI terminal session. Remote Desktop is a new feature for Windows XP Professional.	Built-in, GUI
Remote Assistance	Remotely sharing input device access to a remote computer by using a GUI terminal session. This option requires two people to function: a remote helper, or expert, and another person seated at the computer experiencing problems. Remote Assistance is a new feature for Windows XP Professional.	Built-in, GUI
Telnet	Establishing remote console sessions and running command-line programs and scripts on remote computers.	Built-in, command-line

For more information about remote troubleshooting tools and features, click **Tools** in Help and Support Center. For more information about configuring remote connections, see "Connecting Remote Offices" and "Configuring Remote Desktop" in this book.

Computer Management Tool

The Computer Management tool (Compmgmt.msc) provides a predefined set of MMC snap-ins for performing common computer management tasks or gathering useful information about local or remote computers for troubleshooting. By using Computer Management, you can view information about the following:

- Event Viewer Logs
- Shared Folders
- Local Users and Groups Accounts
- Performance Logs and Alerts

- Device Manager

- Storage Devices (including Removable Storage, Disk Defragmenter, and Disk Management MMC snap-ins)

- Services and Applications (including the Services snap-in)

To view information or manage a remote computer

1. On the desktop, right-click **My Computer**, and then click **Manage**.

2. Right-click **Computer Management (Local)**, and then click **Connect to another computer**.

3. In the **Select Computer** dialog box, click **Another computer**, and then enter the name of the remote computer to which you want to connect.

4. Select any of the tools listed to view and manage remote computer information.

You can also use Computer Management to view information gathered by applications or custom scripts that implement Windows Management Instrumentation (WMI), a unified architecture for describing and using Windows objects.

For more information about WMI, see the Driver Development Kits link on the Web Resources page at http://www.microsoft.com/windows/reskits/webresources.

Remote Desktop

Although Remote Desktop is not specifically a troubleshooting tool, this feature does enable you to use a local keyboard, mouse, and video display to remotely diagnose and troubleshoot problems that do not require collaboration with someone logged on at the computer. For example, you can use Remote Desktop to verify a problem on a computer within a network domain.

While using Remote Desktop, the remote computer remains locked and any actions that you perform are not visible on the monitor attached to the remote computer. This is intended behavior because Remote Desktop was designed primarily for the following:

- To enable you to work with or troubleshoot a computer (such as your office system) from a remote location by using a direct network, secure virtual private network (VPN), or remote access, connection to your organization's network.

- To enable administrators or other designated users or groups (such as Help Desk) to manage or troubleshoot computers remotely.

- To remotely access a computer without concern about unauthorized users viewing your actions or taking control of the remote system.

Remote Desktop Restrictions

Remote Desktop uses Windows XP Professional security features to grant or deny access based on user permissions. Before using Remote Desktop, be aware of the following restrictions:

- You typically cannot establish connections to external (non-domain) computers that are located outside your organization's firewall. To bypass this limitation use Internet Proxy or Microsoft Internet Security and Acceleration Server client software.

- You typically cannot establish a session from your home computer on the Internet to your office system. To bypass this limitation, you must first establish a secure VPN connection to your office network.

- You cannot establish Remote Desktop connections between two computers connected directly to the Internet.

- Remote Desktop does not allow simultaneous remote and local access to the Windows XP Professional desktop, and one user must log off before another can log on. For members of the Administrators group, Windows XP Professional prompts for confirmation before logging the other user off to avoid loss of unsaved data. Whenever possible, notify the other user before logging the user off.

For more information about planning special Remote Desktop configurations, consult with your network administrator.

Configuring and Using Remote Desktop

Windows 2000 Server–based and Windows XP Professional–based computers can host remote clients. However, Windows XP Professional–based systems can host only one user session at a time.

To configure a computer to host a Remote Desktop session

1. Log on by using a user account that belongs to the local or domain Administrators group.

2. Do one of the following:

   - In **Control Panel**, click **System**.

   - In the **Run** dialog box, type **sysdm.cpl**, and then click **OK**.

3. Click the **Remote** tab, and in **Remote Desktop**, click **Allow users to connect remotely to this computer** check box if not enabled.

4. Click **Select Remote Users**, and then in **Remote Desktop Users**, click **Add** to grant Remote Desktop access to specific users.

When you click **OK**, changes take effect immediately; you do not need to restart your computer. Members of the local or domain Administrators group have Remote Desktop privileges by default.

Unlike members of the Administrators group, nonadministrators granted Remote Desktop access cannot end another user's session. If another user is logged on, a Remote Desktop session requested by a nonadministrator is refused by the remote system.

To connect to a computer by using Remote Desktop

1. In the **Run** dialog box, type **mstsc**.

2. Type the name of the computer to which you want to connect, and then click **Connect**.

A session window opens, and a **Log On to Windows** dialog box prompts you to supply valid user credentials. After you log on to the remote computer, the session window displays the contents of the remote computer's desktop. You can then interact with the remote computer, with your activities limited only by user permission settings.

Other Remote Desktop Features

Remote Desktop also includes these features:

■ **Bandwidth efficiency**. Remote Desktop caches and compresses data to enhance performance.

■ **Terminal Services Compatibility**. Remote Desktop can host sessions with clients running Terminal Services client software. For example, you can use Remote Desktop to establish remote sessions with Windows NT Workstation 4.0–based and Windows 2000 Professional–based computers running Terminal Services client software.

For more information about Remote Desktop, see "Configuring Remote Desktop" in this book and Windows XP Professional Help and Support Center.

Remote Assistance

Remote Assistance for *x*86-based computers allows you to invite a trusted person (a friend or computer expert) to remotely and interactively assist you with a problem. You can also use Remote Assistance to remotely assist a user who trusts you. This feature is useful in situations where detailed or lengthy instructions are required to reproduce or resolve problems.

Problems that are difficult to reproduce   A user requesting assistance reports a problem that is reproducible only under specific circumstances. Instead of having the user describe the problem to you, you can remotely view the problem computer while the user shows you the steps that cause the error to occur.

Problems that require following complicated instructions   A user describes a problem that you know can be fixed by adjusting video display settings. You describe the steps required, but the inexperienced user cannot follow your instructions. You can help by interactively demonstrating the steps required to correct the problem.

Differences Between Remote Assistance and Remote Desktop

In Remote Assistance terminology, the user sending the request for assistance, an *invitation,* is called the *novice,* and the person providing assistance is known as the *expert.* The key distinctions between Remote Assistance and Remote Desktop are:

- Remote Desktop establishes new sessions, while Remote Assistance attaches another user (the expert) to an existing session.

- To use Remote Assistance, both the novice and expert need to be present at their computers and must cooperate with each other. Remote Desktop relies on Windows security features and users with the appropriate privileges do not require permission before establishing new sessions.

- Remote Assistance requires that both computers are running a version of Microsoft® Windows® XP.

Establishing Remote Assistance Connections

You can establish the following types of connections by using Remote Assistance:

- A local area network (LAN) connection between the expert and novice.

- A direct Internet connection between the expert and novice.

- A connection between an expert located behind a firewall and a novice on the Internet.

- A connection between an expert and a novice located behind different firewalls. Establishing Remote Assistance connections through a firewall might require network configuration changes such as opening TCP Port 3389. Consult your network administrator for more information.

To send a Remote Assistance invitation to an expert

1. Notify the expert (by a method such as e-mail, telephone, or instant messaging), that you intend to send a Remote Assistance invitation and provide the password you plan to use (if any). For security purposes, Remote Assistance does not include password information with the invitation, an omission based on the assumption that the expert knows the invitation password.

2. From the **Start** menu, click **Remote Assistance**.

3. Follow the instructions for Remote Assistance and, when prompted, specify options, such as the delivery method, time until expiration, expert's e-mail address, and a message.

4. Click **Send Invitation** to send the invitation to the expert.

   The novice has several options when sending the invitation, including:

- Invitation delivery method (by means of e-mail or instant message notification).

- Time until expiration (in hours, minutes, or days).

- Password protection feature (optional).

   If a problem occurs when you send invitations, verify that Remote Assistance is enabled.

To verify that Remote Assistance is enabled

1. Do one of the following:

   - In **Control Panel**, click **System**.

   - In the **Run** dialog box, type **sysdm.cpl**, and then click **OK**.

2. On the **Remote** tab, in **Remote Assistance**, select the **Allow Remote Assistance invitations to be sent from this computer** check box if it is disabled, and then click **OK**.

To respond to a Remote Assistance invitation sent from a novice

1. Using e-mail or instant messaging software that is installed on the expert computer, wait for the Remote Assistance invitation to arrive from the novice.

2. Open the invitation message and double-click the attachment that is included to start the session. If prompted to do so, provide password information. The following prompt appears on the novice computer:

   ```
   User has accepted your Remote Assistance invitation and is ready to connect to
    your computer.
   Do you want to let this person view your screen and chat with you?
   ```

3. If the information you provided is correct and the novice confirms the preceding prompt, a terminal window appears and displays the novice's desktop. You can now use the Remote Assistance **Chat** window to send or receive text messages.

   Although you can view the remote computer's desktop content, you are initially in read-only mode and are not able to move windows, or manipulate on-screen objects, such as the **Start** menu or desktop icons, until the novice gives you permission to do so.

4. To interact with the novice's desktop, click **Take Control**, and then ask the novice to confirm the **Allow Expert Interaction** button in the **Remote Assistance** window. After the novice clicks this button, you and the novice share access to the novice's desktop, and you can now interact with on-screen objects by using your local mouse and keyboard. At any time, the novice can restrict you to view-only mode by pressing a user-defined hot key (by default, the ESC key).

Invitation Limitations

An expert can reuse a Remote Assistance invitation ticket multiple times as long as both of the following conditions are met:

■ The invitation ticket has not expired.

■ The IP address of the expert computer has not changed since the novice issued the invitation ticket.

The second condition is mainly a concern for experts that use computers that require dial-up connections to Internet service providers (ISPs). Computers that use dial-up connections are typically assigned different IP addresses by Dynamic Host Configuration Protocol (DHCP) servers each time they connect to the Internet. A separate ticket for each IP address is required.

Security Concerns

When using Remote Assistance, consider the following security issues:

■ When the novice clicks the **Allow Expert Interaction** button, a Remote Assistance expert performs all actions under the novice's user security context and has the same level of network access and local computer privileges.

■ To allow experts outside of your organization to establish Remote Assistance connections (for example, outsourced technical support), the preferred connection method is by VPN account. This is the preferred method because it avoids opening TCP Port 3389 to allow traffic through your firewall. Consult your network administrator for more information about your organization's policies towards external technical support providers.

Offer Remote Assistance

An added feature for Windows XP Professional, known as Offer Remote Assistance, enables an expert with Administrators group privileges to initiate a session *without* first receiving an invitation from the novice. This feature allows experts (for example, Domain Administrators) to provide assistance within an organization. Offer Remote Assistance is disabled by default, but you can enable it by modifying a Group Policy setting.

To enable Offer Remote Assistance

1. In the **Run** dialog box, type **gpedit.msc**.

2. Expand **Local Computer Policy**, expand **Computer Configuration**, and then expand **Administrative Templates**.

3. Expand **System**, and then expand **Remote Assistance**.

4. In the details pane, double-click **Offer Remote Assistance**, click **Enabled**, and then click **OK**.

You can also grant Offer Remote Assistance privileges to nonadministrators, by using the following procedure.

To enable Offer Remote Assistance for nonadministrators

1. In the **Run** dialog box, type **gpedit.msc**.

2. Expand **Local Computer Policy**, expand **Computer Configuration**, and then expand **Administrative Templates**.

3. Expand **System**, and then expand **Remote Assistance**.

4. In the details pane, double-click **Offer Remote Assistance** and then click **Enabled**.

5. Click **Show** and then click **Add**. In the **Add Item** dialog box, type the name of the user or group that you want to grant Offer Remote Assistance privileges to by using the following syntax:

   domain\username

   – or –

   domain\groupname

   The computers of the novice and expert users must be members of the same domain, or members of domains that trust each other.

6. Click **OK** and repeat Steps 1-5 for each user or group.

For more information about Group Policy, see "Authorization and Access Control," "Planning Deployments," and "Managing Desktops" in this book. Also, see the *Deployment Planning Guide* of the *Microsoft Windows 2000 Server Resource Kit* and the Change and Configuration Management Deployment Guide link on the Web Resources page at http://www.microsoft.com/windows/reskits/webresources.

To offer remote assistance to a novice

1. You, an expert, inform the novice that you intend to offer Remote Assistance.

2. In **Help and Support Center**, click **Pick a task**, click **Use Tools**, and then click **Offer Remote Assistance**.

3. Follow the instructions and provide the name or IP address for the computer to which the novice is logged on.

The following prompt appears on the novice's computer:

```
The network administrator Domain\User would like to view your screen and chat with
you in real time, and work on your computer.
Would you like to give Domain\User access to your computer?
```

A Remote Assistance session starts after the novice confirms the prompt.

> **Note**   The Offer Remote Assistance feature does not remove the require-ment that the novice be present to accept the session request from the expert. The novice can end the session at any time by clicking **Disconnect** or by pressing the disconnect hot key.

Other Remote Assistance Features

In addition to sharing control of the desktop, Remote Assistance also provides these features useful for troubleshooting problems affecting the novice:

- **File transfers**. This enables the novice and the expert to send or receive files.

- **Voice over IP**. This feature lets the novice and expert to communicate verbally in real-time by using an Internet connection.

- **Chat**. Chat enables the novice and the expert to establish two-way real-time text communication.

- **Desktop scaling**. This feature enables the expert to scale the view of novice's desktop to fit the Remote Assistance view window. This allows the expert to choose between different views, depending on the situation.

- **Bandwidth efficiency**. Remote Assistance automatically senses connection speed and configures settings such as color depth and voice data rate, depend-ing on the available bandwidth.

For more information about Remote Assistance, click **Support** or **Tools** in Help and Support Center.

Telnet

The Microsoft Telnet client (Telnet.exe) and server enable you to establish command console sessions to a remote host. You can then use this session to run command-line programs and scripts on the remote computer. Telnet benefits include low sys-tem resource and bandwidth requirements, as well as interoperability with Telnet clients and servers running on other operating systems, such as UNIX.

The Windows XP Professional Telnet client and server are more robust than their Windows 2000 Professional and Windows NT Workstation 4.0 counterparts and add new features such as auditing.

For more information about Microsoft Telnet, click **Tools** in Help and Support Center.

Disk and Maintenance Tools

Windows XP Professional provides disk and maintenance tools you can use to prevent problems from occurring. Some of the most useful tools are listed alphabetically in Table D-13. The disk-related tools allow you to view disk information and correct a problem before it becomes a serious issue. My Computer Information and Windows Update allow you to periodically check the status of your computer, apply updates that enhance Windows XP Professional, and might also help resolve problems due to causes such as incompatible device drivers.

Table D-13   Disk and Maintenance Tools

Tool	Function	Tool Type, Interface
Chkdsk (Chkdsk.exe)	Verifying and repairing the logical integrity of a file system on a Windows XP Professional–based volume.	Built-in, command-line, GUI
Disk Cleanup (Cleanmgr.exe)	Increasing the amount of disk space that applications and Windows XP Professional can use by deleting unused files.	Built-in, GUI
Disk Defragmenter (Dfrg.msc and Defrag.exe)	Contiguously arranging files, folders, and programs, and grouping unused space on the hard disk to optimize disk performance.	Built-in, GUI, command-line
Disk Management (Diskmgmt.msc) and DiskPart (Diskpart.exe)	Viewing disk information and performing disk related functions such as extending volumes or partitioning disks.	Built-in, GUI, command-line
Fsutil (Fsutil.exe)	Displaying volume and file system information and performing advanced disk-related operations.	Built-in, command-line
My Computer Information in Help and Support	Viewing hardware and software status and obtaining Help and troubleshooting information.	Built-in, GUI
Windows Update (Wupdmgr.exe)	Obtaining updates, service packs, device drivers, and other enhancements.	Built-in, GUI

Chkdsk

Chkdsk (Chkdsk.exe) is a command-line tool that checks volumes for problems and attempts to repair any that it finds. For example, Chkdsk can repair problems related to bad sectors, lost clusters, cross-linked files, and directory errors. For NTFS formatted disks, the Windows XP Professional version of Chkdsk.exe can provide substantial performance improvements (compared to the versions in Windows 2000 Professional and Windows NT Workstation 4.0) when using the new the **/i** and **/c** parameters. These two parameters instruct Chkdsk.exe to skip certain file system checks, which might reduce the time needed to run Chkdsk. You must be logged on as an administrator or a member of the Administrators group to use Chkdsk.

In addition to using the command-line version of Chkdsk, you can run Chkdsk from My Computer or Windows Explorer.

To run Chkdsk from the command prompt

- At the command prompt, type **chkdsk**.

To run Chkdsk from My Computer or Windows Explorer

1. In My Computer or Windows Explorer, right-click the volume you want to check, and then click **Properties**.

2. On the **Tools** tab, click **Check Now**.

3. Do one of the following:

   - To run Chkdsk in read-only mode, click **Start**.

   - To repair errors without scanning the volume for bad sectors, select the **Automatically fix file system errors** check box, and then click **Start**.

   - To repair errors, locate bad sectors, and recover readable information, select the **Scan for and attempt recovery of bad sectors** check box, and then click **Start**.

   Before running Chkdsk, be aware of the following:

- Chkdsk requires exclusive access to a volume while it is running. Chkdsk might display a prompt asking if you want to check the drive the next time you restart your computer.

- Chkdsk might take a long time to run, depending on the number of files and folders, the size of the volume, disk performance, and available system resources (such as processor and memory).

- Chkdsk might not accurately report information in read-only mode.

For more information about using Chkdsk, see "Troubleshooting Disks and File Systems" in this book.

Disk Cleanup

Disk Cleanup (Cleanmgr.exe) enables you to delete unneeded files and periodically compress infrequently accessed files. Insufficient disk free space can cause many problems ranging from Stop messages to file corruption. To increase free space you can do the following:

- Move files to another volume or archive them to backup media.
- Compress files or disks to reduce the space required to store data.
- Delete unneeded files.

To run Disk Cleanup

1. At the command prompt, type `cleanmgr`.
2. Select the drive you want to clean up, and then click **OK**.
3. On the **Disk Cleanup** tab, select an option.
   – or –
   Click the **More Options** tab to remove restore points and uninstall operating system components or applications.

For more information about restore points, see "System Restore" earlier in this appendix.

To compress files by using Disk Cleanup

1. On the **Disk Cleanup** tab, select the **Compress old files** check box.
2. In the **Description** box, click **Options** to specify how many days to wait before compressing a file.

For more information about Disk Cleanup, click **Tools** in Help and Support Center.

Disk Defragmenter

Windows XP Professional provides two methods for defragmenting volumes:

- The Disk Defragmenter snap-in (Dfrg.msc)
- The new Disk Defragmenter command-line tool (Defrag.exe)

Both defragmentation tools rearrange files, folders, and programs so that they occupy contiguous space on the hard disk. The tools also reorder free space, moving it into a contiguous block at the end of each volume. As a result, the operating system can write files to the hard disk sequentially more often, which improves performance. You must be logged on as an administrator or a member of the Administrators group to use the defragmentation tools.

To start the Disk Defragmenter snap-in

■ In the **Run** dialog box, type **dfrg.msc**.

You can also start Disk Defragmenter from the Computer Management tool. For more information about the Computer Management tool, see "Computer Management Tool" earlier in this appendix.

To start the Defrag.exe command-line tool

■ At the command prompt, type `defrag`.

For more information about Disk Defragmenter, see "Troubleshooting Disks and File Systems" in this book.

Disk Management and DiskPart

Windows XP Professional provides two tools that you can use to view the status of disks and volumes:

■ The Disk Management snap-in (Diskmgmt.msc)

■ The command-line tool DiskPart (Diskpart.exe)

Both tools use a number of predefined descriptions to indicate the status of disks and volumes in the computer. For example, if no errors are present on a disk, the tools display an Online status for the disk and a Healthy status for volumes on the disk. By periodically running these tools, you can identify disk or volume problems and repair them before they lead to data loss. You must be logged on as an administrator or a member of the Administrators group to use Disk Management or DiskPart.

To use the Disk Management snap-in

■ In the **Run** dialog box, type **diskmgmt.msc**.

You can also start Disk Defragmenter from the Computer Management tool. For more information about the Computer Management tool, see "Computer Management Tool" earlier in this appendix.

To start DiskPart and view a list of commands

1. At the command prompt, type `diskpart`.

2. At the **DISKPART>** prompt, type `commands`.

DiskPart is a text-mode command interpreter that provides commands for managing disks, volumes, and partitions. The command-line Diskpart.exe tool is separate from the **diskpart** command that you can use in Recovery Console.

For more information about troubleshooting disk-related problems, see "Troubleshooting Disks and File Systems" in this book. For more information about using DiskPart, click **Tools** in Help and Support Center.

Fsutil.exe

Fsutil (Fsutil.exe) is a command-line tool that provides commands for performing file system and volume-related tasks, such as querying or changing file and disk attributes. You must be logged on as an administrator or a member of the Administrators group to use Fsutil.

To obtain a list of Fsutil subcommands

- At the command prompt, type `fsutil`.

To obtain help for an Fsutil subcommand

- At the command prompt, use the following syntax:

    `fsutil` *subcommand* `help`

For more information about Fsutil, click **Tools** in Help and Support Center.

My Computer Information in Help and Support Center

"My Computer Information" in Windows XP Professional Help and Support Center enables you to view your computer's hardware and software status and to gather help and troubleshooting information.

To view My Computer Information in Help and Support Center

1. Under **Pick a task**, click **Use Tools to view your computer information and diagnose problems**.

2. Under **Tools**, click **My Computer Information**, and then follow the instructions displayed on the screen.

Table D-14 lists the type of information available.

Table D-14   Information Available in My Computer Information

Category	Description
General	Displays details about your computer, such as the processor speed and the amount of physical memory and disk space available.
Status	Shows diagnostic information that can help you solve existing problems and read tips that can help you avoid issues.

Table D-14   Information Available in My Computer Information

Category	Description
Hardware	Contains detailed information about internal and external hardware installed on your computer.
Software	Lists system software installed on your computer.
View computer information on another computer	Shows information for a remote computer, if you have administrative permissions on the remote computer.

For more information about My Computer Information, see Windows XP Professional Help and Support Center.

Windows Update

Windows Update is an online extension of Windows XP Professional, and provides a central location to find product enhancements, such as service packs, device drivers, and system security updates.

To obtain a list of the available updates on the Windows Update Web site

1. In the **Run** dialog box, type **wupdmgr**.

2. Click **Pick updates to install** to view the following choices:

   - **Critical Updates**

   - **Windows XP**

   - **Driver Updates**

     At a minimum, download and install all updates listed in **Critical Updates**.

Windows XP Professional provides Automatic Updates, a feature you can enable that eliminates the need to check for new updates posted to the Windows Update Web site. Automatic Updates also conserves network bandwidth by checking for updates during periods of idle network activity.

To enable Automatic Updates

1. In **Control Panel**, open **System**.

2. Click the **Automatic Updates** tab.

3. Under **Notification Settings**, click the option that you want to use:

   - **Download the updates automatically and notify me when they are ready to be installed**.

   - **Notify me before downloading any updates and notify me again before installing them on my computer**.

■ **Turn off automatic updating. I want to update my computer manually**.

When you enable Automatic Updates, an **Install Reminder** appears in the notification area of the taskbar when one or more updates are ready to be downloaded or installed. Double-click the reminder icon to display the list of items.

For more information about Automatic Updates, see Windows XP Professional Help and Support Center.

Restricting Access to Windows Update

You can restrict user access to the Windows Update Web page by using the Group Policy snap-in. You can use Group Policy settings to remove the Windows Update icon from the following locations:

■ Windows Explorer **Start** menu

■ The **Tools** menu in Microsoft® Internet Explorer

■ The **Add or Remove Programs** icon in **Control Panel**. (The **Add programs from Microsoft** option that appears when you click **Add New Programs.**)

To disable access to Windows Update by using the Group Policy snap-in

1. In **Run** dialog box, type **gpedit.msc**.

2. Expand **Local Computer Policy**, expand **User Configuration**, and then expand **Administrative Templates**.

3. Double-click **Start Menu and Taskbar**, and then in the details pane, double-click **Remove links and access to Windows Update**. Click **Enabled**, and then click **OK**.

4. In the **Administrative Templates** node, expand **Windows Components**, double-click **Windows Update**, and in the details pane, double-click **Remove access to use all Windows Update features**. Click **Enabled** and then click **OK**.

5. Under **Administrative Templates**, expand **Control Panel**, double-click **Add or Remove Programs**, and in the details pane, double-click **Hide the "Add programs from Microsoft" option**. Click **Enabled**, and then click **OK**.

System File Tools

Windows XP Professional provides tools to help you troubleshoot problems caused by incompatible, missing, or corrupted driver and system files. Helpful tools for troubleshooting system and driver file issues are listed alphabetically in Table D-15. These tools enable you to detect and correct issues caused by problem files, or prevent their installation.

Table D-15   System File and Driver Tools

Tool	Function	Tool Type, Interface
Driver Query (Driver-query.exe)	Listing information about the drivers on a computer.	Built-in, command-line
Driver Signing and Digital Signatures	Maintaining system stability by verifying that device drivers have passed a series of rigorous tests administered by the Windows Hardware Quality Labs (WHQL).	Built-in, GUI
Windows File Protection	Scanning protected system files and restoring overwritten files with the correct versions provided by Microsoft.	Built-in, GUI

Driver Signing and Digital Signatures

Driver signing is a multistage process in which device drivers are verified. For a driver to earn this certification, it must pass a series of compatibility tests administered by the Windows Hardware Quality Labs (WHQL). Due to stringent WHQL standards, using signed drivers typically result in a more stable system. Microsoft digitally signs drivers that pass the WHQL tests and Windows XP Professional performs signature detection for signed device categories, such as the following:

- Keyboards

- Hard disk controllers

- Modems

- Mouse devices

- Multimedia devices

- Network adapters

- Printers

- SCSI adapters

- Smart card readers

- Video adapters

A Microsoft Corporation digital signature indicates that a driver file is an original, unaltered system file that Microsoft has approved for use with Windows XP Professional.

Windows XP Professional can warn or prevent users from installing unsigned drivers. If a driver is not digitally signed, the user receives a message that requests confirmation to continue.

Microsoft digitally signs all drivers included with the Windows XP Professional operating system CD. When downloading updated drivers from a manufacturer's Web page, always select drivers that are signed by Microsoft.

Windows XP Professional provides the following tools to help you identify digitally signed files:

- File Signature Verification
- Driver Signature Checking
- System Information
- Device Manager
- DirectX Diagnostic Tool
- Hardware Compatibility List

File Signature Verification

The File Signature Verification tool (Sigverif.exe) detects signed files and allows you to do the following:

- View the certificates of signed files to verify that the file has not been tampered with after being digitally signed.
- Search for signed files in a specific location.
- Search for unsigned files in a specific location.

To run File Signature Verification

- In the **Run** dialog box, type **sigverif**.

When you click the **Advanced** button, the **Advanced File Signature Verification Settings** dialog box provides additional configuration options on the **Search** and **Logging** tabs.

Search   You can specify file search options such as whether to search all drivers or limit the scope of your search by using file name and folder criteria.

Logging   You can specify that search results be saved to a file, the log file name to use, and whether to overwrite or append the log file. You can also view the log file by clicking **View Log**.

File Signature Verification writes information to *systemroot*\Sigverif.txt, a log that contains the following information about the scanned files:

- Name
- Modification date
- Version number

- Signed status

- Location (name of catalog file)

Driver Signature Checking

Driver Signature Checking enables you detect unsigned drivers before you install them. Using Control Panel, you can set verification levels for driver signature checking to ensure that Windows XP Professional inspects files for digital signatures whenever you install or update drivers.

To enable Driver Signature Checking

1. In **Control Panel**, open **System**.

2. Click the **Hardware** tab, and then click **Driver Signing**.

Table D-16 describes the three levels of file signature verification that appear in the **Driver Signing Options** box.

Table D-16   Signature Checking Levels

Level	Description
Level 0 (**Ignore**)	Disables digital signature checking. The message that identifies a digitally signed driver does not appear, and all drivers are installed even if they are unsigned.
Level 1 (**Warn**)	Determines whether the driver has passed WHQL testing. A message appears whenever a user tries to install a driver that fails the signature check.
Level 2 (**Block**)	Blocks installation of a driver that fails the signature check. You are notified that Windows XP Professional cannot install the unsigned driver.

System Information

System Information enables you to view a list of signed drivers installed on your system.

To view a list of signed drivers

1. In the **Run** dialog box, type **msinfo32.exe**.

2. Expand **Software Environment**, and then click **Signed Drivers**.

Driver Query

Driver Query (Driverquery.exe) is a command-line tool that displays information about drivers running on your computer.

For more information about using Driver Query to view signing information for drivers, see "Driver Query" later in this appendix.

Device Manager

Device Manager enables you to verify that Microsoft Corporation has provided or digitally signed a driver for a specific device.

To view driver signing information by using Device Manager

1. In the **Run** dialog box, type **devmgmt.msc**.

2. Expand a device category. (For this example, expand **Floppy disk controllers**.)

3. Double-click **Standard floppy disk controller**, and then click the **Driver** tab.

4. Verify that **Driver Provider** is listed as **Microsoft** (for Microsoft-provided drivers) or that **Digital Signer** mentions **Microsoft WHQL** (for manufacturer-provided drivers).

DirectX Diagnostic Tool

The DirectX Diagnostic Tool (Dxdiag.exe) displays file names and properties for multimedia device drivers, such as audio and video. Use this tool to check for beta or unsigned DirectX driver files.

For more information about using the DirectX Diagnostic Tool to view information for multimedia drivers, see "DirectX Diagnostic Tool" earlier in this appendix.

Hardware Compatibility List

The Hardware Compatibility List (HCL) is a Web-based searchable database, which is continuously updated as hardware is tested and approved. The HCL lists devices that have been approved for use with Windows XP Professional. For more information about the HCL, see "Troubleshooting Concepts and Strategies" in this book and the Hardware Compatibility List link on the Web Resources page at http://www.microsoft.com/windows/reskits/webresources.

Driver Query

Driver Query (Driverquery.exe) is a command-line tool that lists information about drivers running on your computer.

> **Tip**   Run the Driver Query tool when your system is working properly and then redirect the information to a file. You can use these results as a comparison later if the system has problems with missing or corrupted drivers.

The information generated by the Driver Query tool can fill several screens, so it is helpful to redirect the video output to a file by using the following syntax:

```
driverquery > drivers_M-D-Y.txt
```

In the preceding syntax, *M* is the numerical month, *D* is the day, and *Y* is the year. Keep this file in a safe location or print it and record the date on the page. Comparing Driver Query output files created on different dates can help you determine which drivers have changed.

Table D-17 describes the output from the Driver Query tool.

Table D-17   Column Names and Descriptions of the Driver Query Tool Output

Column	Description
HostName	The name of the computer queried.
FileName	The driver file name shown without path or file name extension information. To list driver file names with the path and extension, use the **-verbose** parameter.
DisplayName	The friendly name of the driver.
Description	A description of the driver. This can be the same as the DisplayName.
DriverType	The type of driver, for example, kernel or file system.

The following is output from Driver Query:

```
Module Name Display Name            Driver Type   Link Date
============ ====================== ============= ========================
aec         Microsoft Kernel Acous Kernel        07/07/2001 09:50:41 AM
AFD         AFD Networking Support Kernel        07/16/2001 11:47:08 AM
atapi       Standard IDE/ESDI Hard Kernel        07/15/2001 09:02:51 PM
```

When you specify the **/si** parameter, Driver Query displays digital signature information for both signed and unsigned drivers. The following is output obtained by typing **driverquery /si**:

```
DeviceName                        InfName       IsSigned Manufacturer
================================= ============= ======== ====================
Microsoft AC Adapter              battery.inf   TRUE     Microsoft
Microsoft ACPI-Compliant Contr    battery.inf   TRUE     Microsoft
Microsoft ACPI-Compliant Contr    battery.inf   TRUE     Microsoft
```

The information in the IsSigned column is useful for troubleshooting because a value of FALSE indicates that a driver has not been approved by Microsoft for use with Windows.

For more information about Driver Query, click **Tools** in Help and Support Center. For more information about driver signing, see "Driver Signing and Digital Signatures" in this appendix.

Windows File Protection

To maintain operating system stability, Windows XP Professional implements the following mechanisms to ensure that software installation programs do not overwrite critical system files:

■ Windows File Protection (WFP) service

■ System File Checker (Sfc.exe) tool

Windows File Protection Service

The Windows File Protection (WFP) service monitors changes to protected system files. When the WFP service detects that a protected system file has changed, it examines file signature information to determine if the new file is the correct version. If the version is incorrect, the WFP service displays a message similar to the following:

```
A file replacement was attempted on the protected system file filename. To maintain
system stability, the file has been restored to the correct Microsoft version. If
problems occur with your application, please contact the application vendor for
support.
```

The WFP service then records an entry to the System log and replaces the invalid file with a backup copy from the *systemroot*\System32\Dllcache folder. If a backup copy is not found in Dllcache, you are prompted to provide the Windows XP Professional operating system CD or a source file location.

System File Checker

System File Checker (Sfc.exe) is a command-line tool that examines protected system files on your computer and restores the correct versions by using backups stored in the Dllcache folder or files copied from the operating system CD.

Protected files include those with .sys, .dll, .exe, .ttf, .fon and .ocx file name extensions. Due to disk space considerations, storing all protected files in the Dllcache folder might not practical, especially on computers with limited storage space. Therefore, you must be ready to provide the Windows XP Professional operating system CD when prompted to do so.

You can use System File Checker to repopulate the Dllcache folder if the contents become damaged or unusable. To purge and repopulate the contents of the Dllcache folder, in the **Run** dialog box, type:

sfc /purgecache

You can also specify the protected file cache size by using the following syntax:

```
sfc /cachesize=x
```

The value of x represents the number of megabytes (MB) of space to use in hexadecimal notation. For example, to specify 200 MB, type:

sfc /cachesize=C8

> **Note** For network-based installations, the WFP service and the System File Checker tool search the network source file directory if the required backup file is not in the Dllcache folder. You must be a member of the Administrators group to purge or change the space allotted for cached protected files.

For more information about the Windows File Protection service and System File Checker, click **Tools** in Help and Support Center. Also, see article Q222473, "Registry Settings for Windows File Protection," in the Microsoft Knowledge Base. To find this article, see the Microsoft Knowledge Base link on the Web Resources page at http://www.microsoft.com/windows/reskits/webresources.

Networking Tools

Many factors affect network performance and reliability, including remote connections, hardware configuration (network adapters or the physical network connection), and device drivers. Quite often, network difficulties are related to protocol configuration errors. For example, use of incorrect settings in TCP/IP-based networks can affect IP addressing, routing, and IP security.

Windows XP Professional provides a collection of useful troubleshooting tools that allow you to monitor network performance across a variety of connections, including analog and ISDN modems, and broadband connections such as xDSL and cable. Table D-18 is an alphabetical list of tools useful for diagnosing network and protocol configuration issues.

Table D-18 Network Troubleshooting and Diagnostic Tools

Tool	Function	Tool Type, Interface
GetMac (Getmac.exe)	Displaying media access control (MAC) control information for network adapters and protocols installed on a computer.	Built-in, command-line
IP Configuration (Ipconfig.exe)	Displaying the current configuration of the installed IP stack on a networked computer by using TCP/IP.	Built-in, command-line
IP Security Monitor	Confirming that secured communications are successfully established by displaying the active security associations on local or remote computers.	Built-in, GUI

Table D-18   Network Troubleshooting and Diagnostic Tools

Tool	Function	Tool Type, Interface
NetBT Statistics (Nbt-stat.exe)	Displaying protocol statistics and current TCP/IP connections by using NetBIOS over TCP/IP (NetBT), including NetBIOS name resolution to IP addresses.	Built-in, command-line
Netsh(Netsh.exe)	Viewing or modifying TCP/IP network configuration for a computer. Netsh also provides scripting features.	Built-in, command-line
Network Connectivity Tester (NetDiag.exe)	Viewing network-client health by running a wide range of connectivity tests.	Support Tool, Command-line
Netstat	Displaying protocol statistics and current TCP/IP connections.	Built-in, command-line
Network Diagnostics	Viewing network-related information such as network adapter status, and IP addresses for DHCP and Domain Name System (DNS) servers.	Built-in, GUI
Network Monitor Capture Utility (Netcap.exe)	Monitoring network traffic and capturing information to a log file.	Support Tool, command-line
Nslookup.exe	Performing DNS queries and examining content zone files on local and remote servers.	Built-in, command-line
Path Ping (Pathping.exe)	Obtaining network performance statistics. Path Ping displays information for the destination computer and all routers along the way.	Built-in, command-line

For more detailed information about configuring hardware resources for network adapters, see "Managing Devices" in this book.

For more information about preceding tools and configuring and troubleshooting networks, see "Configuring TCP/IP" and "Configuring IP Addressing and Name Resolution" in this book. Also, see the *TCP/IP Core Networking Guide* or the *Internetworking Guide* of the Microsoft® *Microsoft Windows® 2000 Server Resource Kit*.

GetMac

GetMac (Getmac.exe) is a command-line tool that enables you to obtain the media access control (MAC) address for all network adapters and network protocols installed on your computer.

For more information about using GetMac, click **Tools** in Help and Support Center.

IP Config

IP Config (Ipconfig.exe) is a command-line tool that displays the current configuration of the installed IP stack on networked computers that are using the TCP/IP network protocol. You can use Ipconfig.exe to:

- Produce a detailed configuration report for all network interfaces.
- Release or renew IP addresses for specified adapters.
- Remove all entries from, or display the contents of, the Domain Name System (DNS) Resolver Cache.
- Refresh all DHCP leases and reregister DNS names.
- Display or modify the DHCP class IDs that are allowed for specified adapters.

Warning   Incorrect use of IP Config can cause network connectivity issues. Unless you are familiar with IP Config, use this tool without command-line parameters or by using only the **/all** parameter.

For more information about IP Config, see Windows XP Professional Help and Support Center. Also, see "Configuring TCP/IP" and "Configuring IP Addressing and Name Resolution" in this book.

IP Security Monitor

You can use the Internet Protocol Security (IPSec) Monitor snap-in to verify the security IPSec communications. IP Security Monitor displays security information, such as the quantity of packets that you sent by using the Authentication Header (AH) or Encapsulating Security Payload (ESP) security protocols, and the number of security associations and keys generated since the computer was started.

IP Security Monitor monitors the local computer unless you specify a different computer. You can specify a different computer by right-clicking **IP Security Monitor** in the console tree, and then clicking **Add Computer**.

IP Security Monitor shows only active security associations. For a log of successful and unsuccessful security associations, search the Security log for Netlogon events.

For more information about IPSec, see "Configuring TCP/IP" in this book and "Internet Protocol Security" in the *TCP/IP Core Networking Guide* in the *Microsoft Windows 2000 Server Resource Kit*. Also see article Q231587, "Using the IP Security Monitor Tool to View IPSec Communications," in the Microsoft Knowledge Base. To find this article, see the Microsoft Knowledge Base link on the Web Resources page at http://www.microsoft.com/windows/reskits/webresources.

NetBT Statistics

NetBT Statistics (Nbtstat.exe) is a command-line tool for troubleshooting network NetBIOS names over TCP/IP (NetBT) resolution problems. It displays protocol statistics and current TCP/IP connections that are using NetBT.

When a network is functioning, NetBT resolves NetBIOS names to IP addresses. It uses several options for NetBIOS name resolution, including local cache lookup, WINS server query, broadcast, Lmhosts and Hosts file lookup, and DNS server query. The output of the NetBT Statistics tool is in tabular format.

For more information about using NetBT, see "Configuring TCP/IP" and "Configuring IP Addressing and Name Resolution" in this book and **Tools** in Help and Support Center.

Netsh

The Netsh command-line tool (Netsh.exe) enables you to access other tools that you can use to view and modify local network interface TCP/IP configurations. Using the Netsh tool, you can perform a wide variety of tasks, such as:

- Displaying and configuring network interface parameters for local and remote computers.

- Configuring routers including routing protocols and routes.

- Configuring Windows XP Professional remote access routers that are running the Routing and Remote Access service.

- Using the scripting feature to run a series of commands in batch mode against a specified computer or router.

Netsh works by directing your command to an appropriate "helper" network component by using entry points called *contexts*. Helpers are dynamic-link library (DLL) files that extend the functionality of Netsh by enabling access to their network routines. A helper can also extend the capabilities of other helpers.

For more information about Netsh, see "Configuring TCP/IP" in this book and **Tools** in Help and Support Center.

Netstat

Netstat (Netstat.exe) is a command-line tool that displays TCP/IP protocol statistics and active connections to and from your computer. Netstat also provides an option to display the number of bytes sent and received, as well as network packets dropped (if any). You can use this tool to quickly verify that your computer can send and receive information over the network.

For more information about Netstat, click **Tools** in Help and Support Center.

Network Connectivity Tester

Network Connectivity Tester (Netdiag.exe) is a command-line Support Tool that helps to identify network-related problems. Network Connectivity Tester runs several network-related tests to determine client connectivity health. Network Connectivity Tester displays information for each network adapter and marks each connectivity test as **Passed**, **Failed**, or **Skipped**, allowing you to quickly isolate problem areas.

For more information about Network Connectivity Tester, click **Tools** in Help and Support Center, and then click **Windows Support Tools**.

Network Diagnostics

Network Diagnostics enables you to view software and hardware network component information from a central location.

To start Network Diagnostics

1. In **Help and Support Center**, under **Pick a task**, click **Use Tools to view your computer information and diagnose problems**.

2. In **Tools**, click **Network Diagnostics**, and then click **Scan your system**.

The results page includes options to expand or collapse the network data gathered. You can also save the results to a file for later reference. Network Diagnostics organizes information into the categories listed in Table D-19.

Table D-19   Network Diagnostics Information Categories

Name of Log	Overview
Internet Service	Displays information about Internet Explorer Web Proxy and Microsoft® Outlook® Express mail and news configuration.
Computer Information	Displays information such as computer name, hardware state and capabilities, as well as operating system name and version information.
Modems and Network Adapters	Displays network hardware and software information, including domain, media access control (MAC) address, IP address, and subnet information.

For more information about Network Diagnostics, click **Tools** in Help and Support Center.

Network Monitor Capture Utility

Network Monitor Capture Utility (Netcap.exe) is a command-line Support Tool that allows a system administrator to monitor network packets and save the information to a capture (.cap) file. On first use, Network Monitor Capture Utility installs the Network Monitor Driver.

You can use information gathered by using Network Monitor Capture Utility to analyze network use patterns and diagnose specific network problems.

For more information about Network Monitor Capture Utility, click **Tools** in Help and Support Center, and then click **Windows Support Tools**.

NSLookup

This diagnostic tool displays information about Domain Name System (DNS) servers. To use NSLookup, you must first install the TCP/IP network protocol.

For more information about Nslookup and DNS, see Windows XP Professional Help and Support Center. Also, see "Windows 2000 DNS" in the *TCP/IP Core Networking Guide* of the *Microsoft Windows 2000 Server Resource Kit* and "Active Directory Diagnostics, Troubleshooting, and Recovery" in the *Distributed Systems Guide* of the *Microsoft Windows 2000 Server Resource Kit*.

PathPing

You can use PathPing (Pathping.exe) to troubleshoot IP connectivity issues. Path-Ping is a command-line tool that traces network routes. It combines features of Ping (Ping.exe) and Trace Route (Tracert.exe) with features not found in either tool. Path-Ping sends network packets to each router on the way to a final network destination IP address, and then reports information as the packets travel from one router to another. (This point-to-point travel is also referred to as a *hop*). Because PathPing shows the degree of packet loss across router segments or links, you can use it to identify routers or links that might be congested and cause network problems.

PathPing first displays the IP addresses of the destination and each router that it crosses. When the packets reach their destination, PathPing computes and displays a summary of network hop statistics. In the example below, the loss rate is displayed as the percentage value at the far right, preceding the "|" symbol.

The following is a PathPing report.

```
Tracing route to rly-wxp-pro [7.54.1.196]
over a maximum of 30 hops:
 0 rly-srv [172.16.87.35]
 1 tstroute1 [172.16.87.218]
 2 tstroute2 [192.168.52.1]
 3 tstroute3 [192.168.80.1]
 4 tstroute4 [7.54.247.14]
 5 rly-wxp-pro [7.54.1.196]
Computing statistics for 125 seconds...
           Source to Here   This Node/Link
Hop RTT Lost/Sent = Pct Lost/Sent = Pct Address
 0                                       rly-srv [172.16.87.35]
                                0/ 100 = 0% |
 1 41ms       0/ 100 = 0%     0/100 = 0% tstroute1 [172.16.87.218]
                               13/ 100 = 13% |
 2 22ms      16/ 100 = 16%    3/100 = 3% tstroute2 [192.168.52.1]
                                0/ 100 = 0% |
 3 24ms      13/ 100 = 13%    0/100 = 0% tstroute3 [192.168.80.1]
```

```
                                     0/ 100 = 0% |
   4 21ms      14/ 100 = 14%         1/100 = 1% tstroute4 [7.54.247.14]
                                     0/ 100 = 0% |
   5 24ms      13/ 100 = 13%         0/100 = 0% rly-wxp-pro [7.54.1.196]
Trace complete.
```

Analyzing the preceding PathPing report, the link between 172.16.87.218 (hop 1) and 192.168.52.1 (hop 2) has a 13 percent drop-packet rate. Dropped packets represent data that needs to be retransmitted, which adversely affects data throughput. All other links appear to be functioning normally with 0 percent packet-loss rates. Packet loss between the first and second hops could indicate heavy network traffic, congested routers, or slow links.

For information about PathPing (as well as the related Ping and Trace Route tools), see "Configuring TCP/IP" and "Configuring IP Addressing and Name Resolution" in this book, and Windows XP Professional Help and Support Center. Also, see the *TCP/IP Core Networking Guide* of the *Microsoft Windows 2000 Server Resource Kit*.

Additional Resources

These resources contain additional information related to this appendix.

- "Troubleshooting Concepts and Strategies" in this book for more information about troubleshooting methodology.

- "Troubleshooting Disks and File Systems" in this book.

- "Troubleshooting Startup" in this book.

- "File Systems" in this book.

- "Disk Management" in this book.

- "Managing Devices" in this book.

- "Managing Digital Media" in this book.

- "Backup and Restore" in this book.

- "Common Stop Messages for Troubleshooting" in this book.

- "Overview of Performance Monitoring" in the *Operations Guide* of the *Microsoft Windows 2000 Server Resource Kit* for more information about monitoring performance.

- The Debugging Tools link on the Web Resources page at http://www.microsoft.com/windows/reskits/webresources.

- The Driver Development Kits (DDK) link on the Web Resources page at http://www.microsoft.com/windows/reskits/webresources.

Appendix E

Security Event Messages

This appendix contains information that can help you interpret security event messages. When security event auditing is enabled, you can review security-related events by using Event Viewer, a Microsoft Management Console snap-in. For information about enabling security event auditing, see "Logon and Authentication" and "Authorization and Access Control" in this book.

Related Information

- For more information about security events, see "Auditing Microsoft Windows Security Events" in the Microsoft® Windows® Security Resource Kit.

Viewing Security Event Messages

You can review security-related events by using Event Viewer, a Microsoft Management Console snap-in.

To view security event messages

1. Open **Event Viewer**.

2. In the console tree, click **Security**.

3. Sort events based on any column in the details pane, such as **Event ID**, **User**, or **Type**.

4. Filter events based on severity, source, or event ID.

Using the event ID number, you can locate the information you need in this appendix. The security event messages are organized by category and include the following categories of event messages:

- System
- Logon
- Object access
- Privilege use
- Detailed tracking
- Policy change
- User management
- Account logon
- Directory service access

To simplify scanning and finding the information that you need, the event listings are sorted numerically from lowest event ID number to highest. This numerical ordering is also helpful because related security events are generally grouped together.

Note   In several cases, numerical grouping of like events does not apply. These events are cross-referenced in both their numerical and logical locations.

The following information is provided for each event:

- **Event number and title**.

- **Parameters** that describe the types of detailed information that is provided each time this particular event occurs. Parameters are listed in the order in which they appear in the event.

- **Configurable information** that indicates whether the event can be configured to log successes (that is, something happened), failures (something failed to happen), or both failures and successes.

- **Formal name**, which is the formal name for the security event. This information is useful for programmers.

> **Note**   Many of the error event messages in this appendix apply to Active Directory™–based environments and are not seen on Microsoft® Windows® XP Professional.

System Event Messages

The following messages document local system processes such as system startup and shutdown and changes to the system time or audit log.

512 Windows is starting up.
Parameters: None.
> **Configurable Information:** Success
> **Formal name:** SE_AUDITID_SYSTEM_RESTART

513 Windows is shutting down.
Parameters: None.
> **Configurable Information:** Success
> **Formal name:** SE_AUDITID_SYSTEM_SHUTDOWN

514 An authentication package was loaded by the Local Security Authority.
Parameters: Authentication package name.
> **Configurable Information:** Success
> **Formal name:** SE_AUDITID_AUTH_PACKAGE_LOAD

515 A trusted logon process has registered with the Local Security Authority.
Parameters: Logon process name.
> **Configurable Information:** Success
> **Formal name:** SE_AUDITID_SYSTEM_LOGON_PROC_REGISTER

516 Internal resources allocated for the queuing of security event messages have been exhausted, leading to the loss of some security event messages.
Parameters: Number of audit messages discarded.
> **Configurable Information:** Success
> **Formal name:** SE_AUDITID_AUDITS_DISCARDED

517 The audit log was cleared.
Parameters: Primary user name, primary domain, primary logon ID, client user name, client domain, client logon ID
> **Configurable Information:** Success
> **Formal name:** SE_AUDITID_AUDIT_LOG_CLEARED

518 A notification package was loaded by the Security Accounts Manager.
Parameter: Notification package name.
> **Configurable Information:** Success
> **Formal name:** SE_AUDITID_NOTIFY_PACKAGE_LOAD

519 A process is using an invalid local procedure call (LPC) port in an attempt to impersonate a client and reply or read from or write to a client address space.
Parameters: Process ID, type of invalid use (either impersonation or reply), server port name, primary user name, primary domain, primary logon ID, client user name, client domain, client logon ID.
> **Configurable Information:** Success
> **Formal name:** SE_AUDITID_LPC_INVALID_USE

520 The system time was changed.
Parameters: Process ID, process name, primary user name, primary domain, primary logon ID, client user name, client domain, client logon ID, previous time, new time.
> **Configurable Information:** Success
> **Formal name:** SE_AUDITID_SYSTEM_TIME_CHANGE

This audit normally appears twice. This is necessary to deal with time zone changes.

Logon Events

Windows XP Professional and Windows 2000 Server generate logon-related events when a user logs on interactively or remotely. These events are generated on the computer to which the logon attempt was made. For more information about the different types of logons and the logon process, see "Logon and Authentication" in this book.

528 A user successfully logged on to a computer.

Parameters: User name, domain, or workstation involved in the logon attempt, logon ID, logon type, source of the logon attempt, authentication package (NTLM, Kerberos V5, or negotiate) involved in the logon attempt, workstation name.

Configurable Information: Success

Formal names: SE_AUDITID_SUCCESSFUL_LOGON SE_AUDITID_NETWORK_LOGON

This event is identical to event 528.

529 The logon attempt was made with an unknown user name or a known user name with a bad password.

Parameters: User name, domain, or workstation that controls the user account, logon type, source of the logon attempt, authentication package used for the logon attempt, name of the workstation at which the logon attempt was made.

Configurable Information: Failure

Formal name: SE_AUDITID_UNKNOWN_USER_OR_PWD

530 The user account tried to log on outside of the allowed time.

Parameters: User name, domain, or workstation that controls the user account, logon type, source of the logon attempt, authentication package used for the logon attempt, name of the workstation at which the logon attempt was made.

Configurable Information: Failure

Formal name: SE_AUDITID_ACCOUNT_TIME_RESTR

Logon time restrictions can only be configured for domain accounts. However, for non-domain accounts, it is still possible to configure logon time restrictions programmatically.

531 A logon attempt was made by using a disabled account.

Parameters: User name, domain, or workstation that controls the user account, logon type, source of the logon attempt, authentication package used for the logon attempt, name of the workstation at which the logon attempt was made.

Configurable Information: Failure

Formal name: SE_AUDITID_ACCOUNT_DISABLED

532 A logon attempt was made by using an expired account.

Parameters: User name, domain, or workstation that controls the user account, logon type, source of the logon attempt, authentication package used for the logon attempt, name of the workstation at which the logon attempt was made.

Configurable Information: Failure

Formal name: SE_AUDITID_ACCOUNT_EXPIRED

533 The user is not allowed to log on at this computer.

Parameters: User name, domain, or workstation that controls the user account, logon type, source of the logon attempt, authentication package used for the logon attempt, name of the workstation at which the logon attempt was made.

> **Configurable Information:** Failure
>
> **Formal name:** SE_AUDITID_WORKSTATION_RESTR

534 The user attempted to log on with a type (such as network, interactive, batch, service, or remote interactive) that is not allowed.

Parameters: User name, domain, or workstation that controls the user account, logon type, source of the logon attempt, authentication package used for the logon attempt, name of the workstation at which the logon attempt was made.

> **Configurable Information:** Failure
>
> **Formal name:** SE_AUDITID_LOGON_TYPE_RESTR

535 The password for the specified account has expired.

Parameters: User name, domain, or workstation that controls the user account, logon type, source of the logon attempt, authentication package used for the logon attempt, name of the workstation at which the logon attempt was made.

> **Configurable Information:** Failure
>
> **Formal name:** SE_AUDITID_PASSWORD_EXPIRED

536 The Net Logon service is not active.

Parameters: User name, domain, or workstation that controls the user account, logon type, source of the logon attempt, authentication package used for the logon attempt, name of the workstation at which the logon attempt was made.

> **Configurable Information:** Failure
>
> **Formal name:** SE_AUDITID_NETLOGON_NOT_STARTED

The Net Logon service is needed for domain-style logon attempts or logon attempts to an account that does not exist on the workstation at which the logon attempt is occurring.

537 The logon attempt failed for other reasons.

Parameters: User name, domain, or workstation that controls the user account, logon type, source of the logon attempt, authentication package used for the logon attempt, name of the workstation from which the logon attempt was made, one or two status codes indicating why the logon failed.

> **Configurable Information:** Failure
>
> **Formal name:** SE_AUDITID_UNSUCCESSFUL_LOGON

In some cases, the reason for the logon failure might not be known. To find the individual status codes, search for the files Ntstatus.h or Winerror.h, and then open them by using a text editor such as Notepad.

538 A user logged off.

Parameters: User name, domain, or workstation that controls the user account, logon type, source of the logon attempt, authentication package used for the logon attempt, name of the workstation at which the logon attempt was made.

> **Configurable Information:** Success
> **Formal name:** SE_AUDITID_LOGOFF
> The logoff message can be caused by any type of logoff attempt.

539 The account was locked out at the time the logon attempt was made.

Parameters: User name, domain, or workstation that controls the user account, logon type, source of the logon attempt, authentication package used for the logon attempt, name of the workstation from which the logon attempt was made.

> **Configurable Information:** Failure
> **Formal name:** SE_AUDITID_ACCOUNT_LOCKED

540 A user successfully logged on to a computer.

Parameters: User name, domain, or workstation involved in the logon attempt, logon ID, logon type, source of the logon attempt, authentication package (NTLM, Kerberos V5, or negotiate) involved in the logon attempt, workstation name.

> **Configurable Information:** Success
> **Formal names:** SE_AUDITID_SUCCESSFUL_LOGON SE_AUDITID_
NETWORK_LOGON
> This event is identical to event 528.

541 Main mode Internet Key Exchange (IKE) authentication was completed between the local computer and the listed peer identity (establishing a security association), or quick mode has established a data channel.

Parameters: Mode (main or quick), the IP address and name of the other host involved in the authentication, a filter specifying source and destination addresses (address can be either specific IP, IP subnet, or all computers), an encryption algorithm, hashing algorithm, and timeout for the security association.

> **Configurable Information:** Success
> **Formal name:** SE_AUDITID_IPSEC_LOGON_SUCCESS

542 A data channel was terminated.

Parameters: Mode (main or quick), a filter indicating a subnet, a particular host, or all computers, the inbound Service Parameters Index (SPI) or local host, the outbound SPI (the other peer in the connection).

> **Note**   Data transfer mode is the same as quick mode (QM).

Configurable Information: Success
Formal name: SE_AUDITID_IPSEC_LOGOFF_QM

543 Main mode was terminated.

Parameters: A filter indicating a subnet, a particular host, or all computers.
Configurable Information: Success
Formal name: SE_AUDITID_IPSEC_LOGOFF_MM

This might occur as a result of the time limit on the security association expiring (the default is eight hours), policy changes, peer termination, and so on.

544 Main mode authentication failed because the peer did not provide a valid certificate or the signature was not validated.

Parameters: Peer identity (the other host involved in the authentication), a filter indicating a subnet, a particular host, or all computers.
Configurable Information: Failure
Formal name: SE_AUDITID_IPSEC_AUTH_FAIL_CERT_TRUST

545 Main mode authentication failed because of a Kerberos failure or a password that is not valid.

Parameters: Peer identity (the other host involved in the authentication), filter indicating a subnet, a particular host, or all computers.
Configurable Information: Failure
Formal name: SE_AUDITID_IPSEC_AUTH_FAIL

546 IKE security association establishment failed because the peer sent a proposal that is not valid. A packet was received that contained data that is not valid.

Parameters: Mode (main or quick, depending when the error occurred), a filter indicating a subnet, a particular host, or all computers), incorrect attribute, expected value, received value.
Configurable Information: Failure
Formal name: SE_AUDITID_IPSEC_ATTRIB_FAIL

547 A failure occurred during an IKE handshake.

Parameters: Mode (indicates when the failure occurred), a filter indicating a subnet, particular host, or all computers, the point of failure, and the reason for the failure.
Configurable Information: Failure
Formal name: SE_AUDITID_IPSEC_NEGOTIATION_FAIL

548 The security ID (SID) from a trusted domain does not match the home domain SID of the client.

Parameters: User name, domain name, logon type, logon process, authentication package, workstation name, impersonated domain.

> **Configurable Information:** Failure
> **Formal name:** SE_AUDITID_DOMAIN_TRUST_INCONSISTENT

549 All SIDs were filtered out during a cross-forest authentication.

Parameters: User name, domain name, logon type, logon process, authentication package, workstation name.

> **Configurable Information:** Failure
> **Formal name:** SE_AUDITID_ALL_SIDS_FILTERED

During cross-forest authentication, all SIDs corresponding to untrusted namespaces are filtered out. This event is triggered when this filtering action removes all SIDs.

550 Indicates a possible denial-of-service attack.

Parameters: No parameters, other than the above text describing the beginning or ending of a denial-of-service attack.

> **Configurable Information:** Success or Failure
> **Formal name:** SE_AUDITID_IPSEC_IKE_NOTIFICATION

This event message is generated when IKE has a large number of pending requests to establish security associations and is beginning denial-of-service prevention mode. This might be normal if caused by high computer loads or a large number of client connection attempts. It also might be the result of a denial-of-service attack against IKE. If this is a denial-of-service attack, there is usually many audits for failed IKE negotiations to spoofed IP addresses. Otherwise, the computer is only extremely heavily loaded.

682 A user has reconnected to a disconnected terminal server session.

Parameters: User name, domain name, logon ID, session name, client name, client address.

> **Configurable Information:** Success
> **Formal name:** SE_AUDITID_SESSION_RECONNECTED

This event message is generated on a terminal server.

683 A user disconnected a terminal server session without logging off.

Parameters: User name, domain, logon ID, session name, client name, client address.

> **Configurable Information:** Success or Failure.
> **Formal name:** SE_AUDITID_SESSION_DISCONNECTED

This event message is generated when a user is connected to a terminal server session over the network. It appears on the terminal server.

Object Access Events

Object access events must be enabled on a per object basis by configuring the system access control list (SACL) for that object. For information about how to configure SACLs, see "Authorization and Access Control" in this book.

560 Access was granted to an already existing object.

Parameters: Object server, object type, object name, handle ID, operation ID, process ID, image file name, primary user name, primary domain, primary logon ID, client user name, client domain, client logon ID, access privileges, restricted SID count.

> **Configurable Information:** Success
> **Formal name:** SE_AUDITID_OPEN_HANDLE

Objects are accessed with handles. This event means that a handle was opened. It does not mean that the object was actually accessed.

562 A handle to an object was closed.

Parameters: Object server, handle ID, process ID, image file name.

> **Configurable Information:** Failure
> **Formal name:** SE_AUDITID_CLOSE_HANDLE

563 An attempt was made to open an object with the intent to delete it.

Parameters: Object server, object type, object name, handle ID, operation ID, process ID, primary user name, primary domain, primary logon ID, client user name, client domain, client logon ID, accesses, privileges.

> **Configurable Information:** Success or Failure
> **Formal name:** SE_AUDITID_OPEN_OBJECT_FOR_DELETE

This is used by file systems when the FILE_DELETE_ON_CLOSE flag is specified.

564 A protected object was deleted.

Parameters: Object server, handle ID, process ID.

> **Configurable Information:** Success
> **Formal name:** SE_AUDITID_DELETE_OBJECT,

565 Access was granted to an already existing object type.

Parameters: Object server, object type, object name, handle ID, operation ID, process ID, process name, primary user name, primary domain, primary logon ID, client user name, client domain, client logon ID, accesses, privileges, properties.

> **Configurable Information:** Success
> **Formal name:** SE_AUDITID_OPEN_HANDLE_OBJECT_TYPE

566 A generic object operation took place.

Parameters: Operation type, object type, object name, handle ID, primary user name, primary domain, primary logon ID, client user name, client domain, client logon ID, accesses, properties.

Configurable Information: Success

Formal name: SE_AUDITID_OBJECT_OPERATION

This event message is also used to audit directory service access events.

567 A permission associated with a handle was used.

Parameters: Name of the object being accessed, object server, handle ID, object type, process ID, access mask.

Configurable Information: Success

Formal name: SE_AUDITID_OBJECT_ACCESS

A handle is created with certain granted permissions (read, write, and so on). When the handle is used, one audit is generated for each of the permissions that was used.

568 An attempt was made to create a hard link to a file that is being audited.

Parameters: Primary user name, primary domain, primary logon ID, object name, link name.

Configurable Information: Success or Failure

Formal name: SE_AUDITID_HARDLINK_CREATION

Privilege Use Events

Changes to a user's privileges or attempts to use privileges in an unauthorized manner might require investigation. These events help support these queries.

576 Specified privileges were added to a user's token.

Parameters: Special privileges assigned to the new user (SeChangeNotifyPrivilege, SeAuditPrivilege, SeCreateTokenPrivilege, SeAssignPrimaryTokenPrivilege, SeBackupPrivilege, SeRestorePrivilege, SeDebugPrivilege), user name, domain, logon ID, privileges.

Configurable Information: Success

Formal name: SE_AUDITID_ ASSIGN_SPECIAL_PRIV

This event message is generated when the user logs on.

577 A user attempted to perform a privileged system service operation.

Parameters: Privileged service called, server, service, primary user name, primary domain, primary logon ID, client user name, client domain, client logon ID, privileges.

    Configurable Information: Success or Failure

    Formal name: SE_AUDITID_ PRIVILEGED_SERVICE

    Callers of PrivilegedServiceAuditAlarm generate this event.

578 Privileges were used on an already open handle to a protected object.

Parameters: Privileged object operation, object server, object handle, process ID, primary user name, primary domain, primary logon ID, client user name, client domain, client logon ID, privileges.

    Configurable Information: Success

    Formal name: SE_AUDITID_PRIVILEGED_OBJECT

Detailed Tracking Events

In Windows XP Professional and Windows 2000 Server, all processes occur in a security context. At times you might need to investigate the security implications of the processes initiated on a computer. The following messages allow you to see security events that relate to system processes.

592 A new process was created.

Parameters: New process ID, image file name, creator process ID, user name, domain logon ID.

    Configurable Information: Success

    Formal name: SE_AUDITID_PROCESS_CREATED

593 A process exited.

Parameters: Process ID, image file name, user name, domain name, logon ID.

    Configurable Information: Success

    Formal name: SE_AUDITID_PROCESS_EXIT

594 A handle to an object was duplicated.

Parameters: Source handle ID, source process ID, target handle ID, target process ID.

    Configurable Information: Success

    Formal name: SE_AUDITID_DUPLICATE_HANDLE

595 Indirect access to an object was obtained.

Parameters: Object type, object name, process ID, primary user name, primary domain, primary logon ID, client user name, client domain, client logon ID, accesses.

    Configurable Information: Success

    Formal name: SE_AUDITID_INDIRECT_REFERENCE

596 A data protection master key was backed up.

Parameters: Key ID, recovery server (the computer to which the key was backed up), recovery key ID (identifies the key on the domain controller that was used to encrypt the master key), failure reason.

Configurable Information: Success or Failure
Formal name: SE_AUDITID_DPAPI_BACKUP

The master key is used by the CryptProtectData and CryptUnprotectData routines, and Encrypting File System (EFS). The master key is backed up each time a new one is created (the default is 90 days). The key is usually backed up to a domain controller.

597 A data protection master key was recovered from a recovery server.

Parameters: Key ID, recovery server (the computer to which the key was backed up), recovery key ID (identifying the key on the domain controller used to encrypt the master key), failure reason.

Configurable Information: Success or Failure
Formal name: SE_AUDITID_DPAPI_RECOVERY

598 Auditable data was protected.

Parameters: Data description, key ID (the master key GUID), protected data flags (CRYPTPROTECT_AUDIT, which indicates that the audit should be generated or CRYPTPROTECT_SYSTEM, which indicates that this is system information and should not be viewed in the user space), name of the protection algorithm, failure reason.

Configurable Information: Success or Failure
Formal name: SE_AUDITID_DPAPI_PROTECT

599 Auditable data was unprotected.

Parameters: Data description, key ID, protected data flags (including CRYPTPROTECT_AUDIT, which indicates that the audit should be generated, and CRYPTPROTECT_SYSTEM, which indicates that this is system information and should not be viewed in the user space), name of the protection algorithm, failure reason.

Configurable Information: Success or Failure
Formal name: SE_AUDITID_DPAPI_UNPROTECT

600 A process was assigned a primary token.

This often happens when a service starts. The following parameters are tracked for both the assigning process and the new process.

Parameters: Process ID, image file name (the name of the process), user name, domain name, logon ID.

Configurable Information: Success
Formal name: SE_AUDITID_ASSIGN_TOKEN

Policy Change Events

Policy change events include security event messages involving trust relationships, IPSec policy, and user rights assignments.

IPSec policy involves settings that need to be applied to the computer. The IPSec audits include filters (what traffic should be processed by IPSec) and filter actions (such as encryption or authentication).

For more information about the user rights that are being audited, see the appendix "User Rights" in this book.

608 A user right was assigned.
Parameters: User, right, assigned to, assigned by (includes user name, domain name, and logon ID).
> **Configurable Information:** Success
> **Formal name:** SE_AUDITID_USER_RIGHT_ASSIGNED

609 A user right was removed.
Parameters: User, right, assigned to, assigned by (includes user name, domain, and logon ID).
> **Configurable Information:** Success
> **Formal name:** SE_AUDITID_USER_RIGHT_REMOVED

610 A trust relationship with another domain was created.
Parameters: New trusted domain (domain name, domain ID), established by (user name, domain name, logon ID), trust type, trust direction, trust attributes.
> **Configurable Information:** Success
> **Formal name:** SE_AUDITID_TRUSTED_DOMAIN_ADD

This event is recorded on the domain controller on which the trusted domain object (TDO) is created and not on any other domain controller to which the TDO is replicated.

611 A trust relationship with another domain was removed.
Parameters: Trusted domain removed (domain name, domain ID), removed by (user name, domain name, logon ID).
> **Configurable Information:** Success
> **Formal name:** SE_AUDITID_TRUSTED_DOMAIN_REM

This event is only recorded on the domain controller on which the trusted domain object (TDO) is deleted.

612 An audit policy was changed.

Parameters: New policy (includes success, failure, or both for logon/logoff, object access, privilege use, account management, policy change, system, detailed tracking, directory service, access, account logon), changed by (user name, domain name, logon ID).

> **Configurable Information:** Success
> **Formal name:** SE_AUDITID_AUDIT_POLICY_CHANGE
> The new policy is described in the audit body.

613 An IPSec policy agent started.

Parameters: Policy source.

> **Configurable Information:** Success
> **Formal name:** SE_AUDITID_IPSEC_POLICY_START

614 An IPSec policy agent was disabled.

Parameters: Policy source.

> **Configurable Information:** Success
> **Formal name:** SE_AUDITID_IPSEC_POLICY_DISABLED

615 An IPSec policy agent changed.

Parameters: Policy source.

> **Configurable Information:** Success or Failure
> **Formal name:** SE_AUDITID_IPSEC_POLICY_CHANGED

616 An IPSec policy agent encountered a potentially serious failure.

Parameters: Policy source.

> **Configurable Information:** Failure
> **Formal name:** SE_AUDITID_IPSEC_POLICY_FAILURE

617 A Kerberos policy changed.

Parameters: Changed by (user name, domain name, logon ID).

> **Configurable Information:** Success
> **Formal name:** SE_AUDITID_KERBEROS_POLICY_CHANGE

618 Encrypted Data Recovery policy changed.

Parameters: Changed by (user name, domain name, logon ID).

> **Configurable Information:** Success
> **Formal name:** SE_AUDITID_EFS_POLICY_CHANGE

620 A trust relationship with another domain was modified.

Parameters: Trusted domain information modified (domain name, domain ID), modified by (user name, domain name, logon ID), trust type, trust direction, trust attributes.

Configurable Information: Success

Formal name: SE_AUDITID_TRUSTED_DOMAIN_MOD

This event is only recorded on the domain controller on which the trusted domain object (TDO) is modified.

621 System access was granted to an account.

Parameters: Access granted, account modified, assigned by (user name, domain name, and logon ID).

Configurable Information: Success

Formal name: SE_AUDITID_SYSTEM_ACCESS_GRANTED

System access permissions can be interactive, network, batch, service, proxy, deny interactive, deny network, deny batch, deny service, remote interactive, or deny remote interactive.

622 System access was removed from an account.

Parameters: Access removed, account modified, assigned by (user name, domain name, and logon ID).

Configurable Information: Success

Formal name: SE_AUDITID_SYSTEM_ACCESS_REMOVED

System access permissions can be interactive, network, batch, service, proxy, deny interactive, deny network, deny batch, deny service, remote interactive, or deny remote interactive.

768 A collision was detected between a namespace element in one forest and a namespace element in another forest.

Parameters: Target type, target name, forest root, top level name, DNS name, NetBIOS name, SID, new flags.

Configurable Information: Failure

Formal name: SE_AUDITID_NAMESPACE_COLLISION

When a namespace element in one forest overlaps a namespace element in another forest, it can lead to ambiguity in resolving a name belonging to one of the namespace elements. This overlap is also called a collision. Not all parameters are valid for each namespace element. For example, parameters such as DNS name, NetBIOS name, and SID are not valid for a "TopLevelName" namespace element.

769 Trusted forest information was added.

Parameters: Forest root, forest root SID, operation ID, entry type, flags, top level name, DNS name, NetBIOS name, domain SID, added by, client user name, client domain, client logon ID.

> **Configurable Information:** Success or Failure
>
> **Formal name:** SE_AUDITID_TRUSTED_FOREST_INFO_ENTRY_ADD
>
> This event message is generated when forest trust information is updated and one or more entries are added. One event message is generated per added entry. If multiple entries are added, deleted, or modified in a single update of the forest trust information, all the generated event messages have a single unique identifier called an operation ID. This allows you to determine that the multiple generated event messages are the result of a single operation. Not all parameters are valid for each entry type. For example, parameters such as DNS name, NetBIOS name and SID are not valid for an entry of type "TopLevelName".

770 Trusted forest information was deleted.

Parameters: Forest root, forest root SID, operation ID, entry type, flags, top level name, DNS name, NetBIOS name, domain SID, deleted by, client user name, client domain, client logon ID.

> **Configurable Information:** Success or Failure
>
> **Formal name:** SE_AUDITID_TRUSTED_FOREST_INFO_ENTRY_REM
>
> This event message is generated when forest trust information is updated and one or more entries are deleted. One event message is generated per deleted entry. If multiple entries are added, deleted, or modified in a single update of the forest trust information, all the generated event messages have a single unique identifier called an operation ID. This allows you to determine that the multiple generated event messages are the result of a single operation. Not all parameters are valid for each entry type. For example, parameters such as DNS name, NetBIOS name, and SID are not valid for an entry of type "TopLevelName".

771 Trusted forest information was modified.

Parameters: Forest root, forest root SID, operation ID, entry type, flags, top level name, DNS name, NetBIOS name, domain SID, added by, client user name, client domain, client logon ID.

> **Configurable Information:** Success or Failure
>
> **Formal name:** SE_AUDITID_TRUSTED_FOREST_INFO_ENTRY_MOD
>
> This event message is generated when forest trust information is updated and one or more entries are modified. One event message is generated per modified entry. If multiple entries are added, deleted, or modified in a single update of the

forest trust information, all the generated event messages have a single unique identifier called an operation ID. This allows you to determine that the multiple generated event messages are the result of a single operation. Not all parameters are valid for each entry type. For example, parameters such as DNS name, NetBIOS name and SID are not valid for an entry of type "TopLevelName".

User Management Events

The bulk of the user management events are identical, with variation only in the activity (for example, enabled versus disabled) and the security groups (local, global, or universal) to which the audit applies.

In addition, from event 648 to event 685, some events include the phrase SECURITY_DISABLED in their formal names. This means that these groups cannot be used to grant permissions in access checks. If the SID representing a security-disabled group appears in a user's token, it is only used to verify deny access control entries (ACEs) during an access check. A SECURITY_ENABLED group is used to verify all ACEs during an access check.

For more information about access tokens and the roles and use of local, global, or universal groups, see "Authorization and Access Control" in this book.

624 A user account was created.

Parameters: Name of new user account, domain of new user account, SID string of new user account, user name of subject creating the user account, domain name of subject creating the user account, logon ID string of subject creating the user account, privileges used to create the user account.

    Configurable Information: Success
    Formal name: SE_AUDITID_USER_CREATED

627 A user password was changed.

Parameters: Name of target user account, domain of target user account, SID string of target user account, user name of subject changing the user account, domain name of subject changing the user account, logon ID string of subject changing the user account.

    Configurable Information: Success
    Formal name: SE_AUDITID_USER_PWD_CHANGED

628 A user password was set.

Parameters: Name of target user account, domain of target user account, SID string of target user account, user name of subject changing the user account, domain name of subject changing the user account, logon ID string of subject changing the user account.

    Configurable Information: Success
    Formal name: SE_AUDITID_USER_PWD_SET

630 A user account was deleted.

Parameters: Name of target user account, domain of target user account, SID string of target user account, user name of subject deleting the user account, domain name of subject deleting the user account, logon ID string of subject deleting the user account.

    Configurable Information: Success
    Formal name: SE_AUDITID_USER_DELETED

631 A global group was created.

Parameters: Name of new group account, domain of new group account, SID string of new group account, user name of subject creating the account, domain name of subject creating the account, logon ID string of subject creating the account.

    Configurable Information: Success
    Formal name: SE_AUDITID_GLOBAL_GROUP_CREATED

632 A member was added to a global group.

Parameters: SID string of member being added, name of target account, domain of target account, SID string of target account, user name of subject changing the account, domain name of subject changing the account, logon ID string of subject changing the account.

    Configurable Information: Success
    Formal name: SE_AUDITID_GLOBAL_GROUP_ADD

633 A member was removed from a global group.

Parameters: SID string of member being removed, name of target account, domain of target account, SID string of target account, user name of subject changing the account, domain name of subject changing the account, logon ID string of subject changing the account.

    Configurable Information: Success
    Formal name: SE_AUDITID_GLOBAL_GROUP_REM

634 A global group was deleted.

Parameters: Name of the global group account, domain of the global group account, SID string of the global group account, user name of subject deleting the global group, domain name of subject deleting the global group, logon ID string of subject deleting the global group.

    Configurable Information: Success
    Formal name: SE_AUDITID_GLOBAL_GROUP_DELETED

635 A new local group was created.

Parameters: Name of new group account, domain of new group account, SID string of new group account, user name of subject creating the account, domain name of subject creating the account, logon ID string of subject creating the account.

Configurable Information: Success

Formal name: SE_AUDITID_LOCAL_GROUP_CREATED

636 A member was added to a local group.

Parameters: SID string of member being added, name of target account, domain of target account, SID string of target account, user name of subject changing the account, domain name of subject changing the account, logon ID string of subject changing the account.

Configurable Information: Success

Formal name: SE_AUDITID_LOCAL_GROUP_ADD

637 A member was removed from a local group.

Parameters: SID string of member being removed, name of target account, domain of target account, SID string of target account, user name of subject changing the account, domain name of subject changing the account, logon ID string of subject changing the account.

Configurable Information: Success

Formal name: SE_AUDITID_LOCAL_GROUP_REM

638 A local group was deleted.

Parameters: Name of group account being deleted, domain of the group account, SID string of group account, user name of subject deleting the account, domain name of subject deleting the account, logon ID string of subject deleting the account.

Configurable Information: Success

Formal name: SE_AUDITID_LOCAL_GROUP_DELETED

639 A local group account was changed.

Parameters: Name of group account being changed, domain of group account, SID string of group account, user name of subject changing the account, domain name of subject changing the account, logon ID string of subject changing the account.

Configurable Information: Success

Formal name: SE_AUDITID_LOCAL_GROUP_CHANGE

641 A global group account was changed.

Parameters: Name of group account being changed, domain of group account, SID string of target account, user name of subject changing the account, domain name of subject changing the account, logon ID string of subject changing the account.

Configurable Information: Success

Formal name: SE_AUDITID_GLOBAL_GROUP_CHANGE

642 A user account was changed.

Parameters: Name of user account, domain of user account, SID string of user account, user name of subject changing the user account, domain name of subject changing the user account, logon ID string of subject changing the user account.

Configurable Information: Success

Formal name: SE_AUDITID_USER_CHANGE

643 A domain policy was modified.

Parameters: Domain policy that was modified, domain name, domain ID, caller user name, caller domain, caller logon ID, privileges used.

Configurable Information: Success

Formal name: SE_AUDITID_DOMAIN_POLICY_CHANGE

644 A user account was auto locked.

Parameters: Name of target user account, domain of target user account, SID string of target user account, user name of subject changing the user account, domain name of subject changing the user account, logon ID string of subject changing the user account.

Configurable Information: Success

Formal name: SE_AUDITID_ACCOUNT_AUTO_LOCKED

This happens when a user attempts to log on unsuccessfully multiple times (the number of attempts is configured by the administrator).

645 A computer account was created.

Parameters: Name of new computer account, domain of new computer account, SID string of new computer account, user name of subject creating the computer account, domain name of subject creating the computer account, logon ID string of subject creating the computer account, privileges used to create the computer account.

Configurable Information: Success

Formal name: SE_AUDITID_COMPUTER_CREATED

646 A computer account was changed.

Parameters: Name of target computer account, domain of target computer account, SID string of target computer account, user name of subject changing the computer account, domain name of subject changing the computer account, logon ID string of subject changing the computer account, privileges used to change the computer account.

Configurable Information: Success

Formal name: SE_AUDITID_COMPUTER_CHANGE

647 A computer account was deleted.

Parameters: Name of target computer account, domain of target computer account, SID string of target computer account, user name of subject deleting the computer account, domain name of subject deleting the computer account, logon ID string of subject deleting the computer account, privileges used to delete the computer account.

> **Configurable Information:** Success
> **Formal name:** SE_AUDITID_COMPUTER_DELETED

648 A local security group with security disabled was created.

Parameters: Name of new group account, domain of new group account, SID string of new group account, user name of subject creating the account, domain name of subject creating the account, logon ID string of subject creating the account, privileges used to create the account.

> **Configurable Information:** Success
> **Formal name:** SE_AUDITID_SECURITY_DISABLED_LOCAL_GROUP_CREATED

SECURITY_DISABLED in the formal name means that this group cannot be used to grant permissions in access checks. If the SID representing a security-disabled group appears in a user's token, it is only used to verify deny access control entries (ACEs) during an access check. A SECURITY_ENABLED group is used to verify all ACEs during an access check.

For more information about access tokens and the roles and usage of local, global, or universal groups, see "Authorization and Access Control" in this book.

649 A local security group with security disabled was changed.

Parameters: Name of group account, domain of group account, SID string of group account, user name of subject modifying the account, domain name of subject modifying the account, logon ID string of subject modifying the account, privileges used to modify the account.

> **Configurable Information:** Success
> **Formal name:** SE_AUDITID_SECURITY_DISABLED_LOCAL_GROUP_CHANGE

650 A member was added to a security-disabled local security group.

Parameters: SID string of member being added, name of security-disabled local security group account, domain of security group account, SID string of security-disabled local security group account, user name of subject changing the membership of the security-disabled local security group, domain name of subject changing the membership of the security-disabled local security group, logon ID string of subject changing the membership of the security-disabled local security group.

> **Configurable Information:** Success
> **Formal name:** SE_AUDITID_SECURITY_DISABLED_LOCAL_GROUP_ADD

651 A member was removed from a security-disabled local security group.

Parameters: SID string of member being removed, name of security-disabled local security group account, domain of security-disabled security group account, SID string of local security group account, user name of subject changing the membership of the security-disabled local security group, domain name of subject changing the membership of the security-disabled local security group, logon ID string of subject changing the membership of the security-disabled local security group.

> **Configurable Information:** Success
> **Formal name:** SE_AUDITID_SECURITY_DISABLED_LOCAL_GROUP_REM

652 A security-disabled local group was deleted.

Parameters: Name of the security-disabled local group, domain of security-disabled local group, SID string of security-disabled local group, user name of subject deleting the security-disabled local group, domain name of subject deleting the security-disabled local group, logon ID string of subject deleting the security-disabled local group.

> **Configurable Information:** Success
> **Formal name:** SE_AUDITID_SECURITY_DISABLED_LOCAL_GROUP_DELETED

653 A security-disabled global group was created.

Parameters: Name of new security-disabled global group, domain of new security-disabled global group, SID string of new security-disabled global group, user name of subject creating the security-disabled global group, domain name of subject creating the security-disabled global group, logon ID string of subject creating the security-disabled global group.

> **Configurable Information:** Success
> **Formal name:** SE_AUDITID_SECURITY_DISABLED_GLOBAL_GROUP_
CREATED

654 A security-disabled global group was changed.

Parameters: Name of security-disabled global group, domain of security-disabled global group, SID string of security-disabled global group, user name of subject changing the security-disabled global group, domain name of subject changing the security-disabled global group, logon ID string of subject changing the security-disabled global group.

> **Configurable Information:** Success
> **Formal name:** SE_AUDITID_SECURITY_DISABLED_GLOBAL_GROUP_
CHANGE

655 A member was added to a security-disabled global group.

Parameters: SID string of member being added, name of security-disabled global group, domain of security-disabled global group, SID string of security-disabled global group, user name of subject changing the security-disabled global group, domain name of subject changing the security-disabled global group, logon ID string of subject changing the security-disabled global group.

> **Configurable Information:** Success
> **Formal name:** SE_AUDITID_SECURITY_DISABLED_GLOBAL_GROUP_ADD

656 A member was removed from a security-disabled global group.

Parameters: SID string of member being removed, name of security-disabled global group, domain of security-disabled global group, SID string of security-disabled global group, user name of subject changing the security-disabled global group, domain name of subject changing the security-disabled global group, logon ID string of subject changing the security-disabled global group.

> **Configurable Information:** Success
> **Formal name:** SE_AUDITID_SECURITY_DISABLED_GLOBAL_GROUP_REM

657 A security-disabled global group was deleted.

Parameters: Name of security-disabled global group, domain of security-disabled global group, SID string of security-disabled global group, user name of subject deleting the security-disabled global group, domain name of subject deleting the security-disabled global group, logon ID string of subject deleting the security-disabled global group.

> **Configurable Information:** Success
> **Formal name:** SE_AUDITID_SECURITY_DISABLED_GLOBAL_GROUP_
DELETED

658 A security-enabled universal group was created.

Parameters: Name of new group account, domain of new security-enabled universal group, SID string of new security-enabled universal group, user name of subject creating the security-enabled universal group, domain name of subject creating the security-enabled universal group, logon ID string of subject creating the security-enabled universal group.

> **Configurable Information:** Success
> **Formal name:** SE_AUDITID_SECURITY_ENABLED_UNIVERSAL_GROUP_
CREATED

659 A security-enabled universal group was changed.

Parameters: Name of target security-enabled universal group, domain of security-enabled universal group, SID string of security-enabled universal group, user name of subject changing the security-enabled universal group, domain name of subject changing the security-enabled universal group, logon ID string of subject changing the security-enabled universal group.

Configurable Information: Success

Formal name: SE_AUDITID_SECURITY_ENABLED_UNIVERSAL_GROUP_ CHANGE

660 A member was added to a security-enabled universal group.

Parameters: SID string of member being added, name of security-enabled universal group, domain of security-enabled universal group, SID string of security-enabled universal group, user name of subject changing the security-enabled universal group, domain name of subject changing the security-enabled universal group, logon ID string of subject changing the security-enabled universal group.

Configurable Information: Success

Formal name: SE_AUDITID_SECURITY_ENABLED_UNIVERSAL_GROUP_ADD

661 A member was removed from a security-enabled universal group.

Parameters: SID string of member being removed, name of security-enabled universal group, domain of security-enabled universal group, SID string of security-enabled universal group, user name of subject changing the security-enabled universal group, domain name of subject changing the security-enabled universal group, logon ID string of subject changing the security-enabled universal group.

Configurable Information: Success

Formal name: SE_AUDITID_SECURITY_ENABLED_UNIVERSAL_GROUP_REM

662 A security-enabled universal group was deleted.

Parameters: Name of target account, domain of security-enabled universal group, SID string of security-enabled universal group, user name of subject deleting the security-enabled universal group, domain name of subject deleting the security-enabled universal group, logon ID string of subject deleting the security-enabled universal group.

Configurable Information: Success

Formal name: SE_AUDITID_SECURITY_ENABLED_UNIVERSAL_GROUP_ DELETED

663 A security-disabled universal group was created.

Parameters: Name of new security-disabled universal group, domain of new security-disabled universal group, SID string of new security-disabled universal group, user name of subject creating the security-disabled universal group, domain name of subject creating the security-disabled universal group, logon ID string of subject creating the security-disabled universal group.

> **Configurable Information:** Success
> **Formal name:** SE_AUDITID_SECURITY_DISABLED_UNIVERSAL_GROUP_CREATED

664 A security-disabled universal group was changed.

Parameters: Name of security-disabled universal group, domain of security-disabled universal group, SID string of security-disabled universal group, user name of subject changing the security-disabled universal group, domain name of subject changing the security-disabled universal group, logon ID string of subject changing the security-disabled universal group.

> **Configurable Information:** Success
> **Formal name:** SE_AUDITID_SECURITY_DISABLED_UNIVERSAL_GROUP_CHANGE

665 A member was added to a security-disabled universal group.

Parameters: SID string of member being added, name of security-disabled universal group, domain of security-disabled universal group, SID string of security-disabled universal group, user name of subject changing the security-disabled universal group, domain name of subject changing the security-disabled universal group, logon ID string of subject changing the security-disabled universal group.

> **Configurable Information:** Success
> **Formal name:** SE_AUDITID_SECURITY_DISABLED_UNIVERSAL_GROUP_ADD

666 A member was removed from a security-disabled universal group.

Parameters: SID string of member being removed, name of security-disabled universal group, domain of security-disabled universal group, SID string of security-disabled universal group, user name of subject changing the security-disabled universal group, domain name of subject changing the security-disabled universal group, logon ID string of subject changing the security-disabled universal group.

> **Configurable Information:** Success
> **Formal name:** SE_AUDITID_SECURITY_DISABLED_UNIVERSAL_GROUP_REM

667 A security-disabled universal group was deleted.

Parameters: Name of target account, domain of security-disabled universal group, SID string of security-disabled universal group, user name of subject deleting the security-disabled universal group, domain name of subject deleting the security-disabled universal group, logon ID string of subject deleting the security-disabled universal group.

> **Configurable Information:** Success
> **Formal name:** SE_AUDITID_SECURITY_DISABLED_UNIVERSAL_GROUP_DELETED

668 A group type was changed.

Parameters: Nature of group type change, name of group being changed, domain of group being changed, SID string of group being changed, user name of subject changing the group type, domain name of subject changing the group type, logon ID string of subject changing the group type.

> **Configurable Information:** Success
> **Formal name:** SE_AUDITID_GROUP_TYPE_CHANGE

684 Set the security descriptor of members of administrative groups.

Parameters: Domain of target user account, SID string of target user account, user name of subject changing the user account, domain name of subject changing the user account, logon ID string of subject changing the user account.

> **Configurable Information:** Success
> **Formal name:** SE_AUDITID_SECURE_ADMIN_GROUP
>
> Every 60 minutes on a domain controller a background thread searches all members of administrative groups (such as domain, enterprise, and schema administrators) and applies a fixed security descriptor on them. This event is logged.

685 Name of an account was changed.

Parameters: Name of target account, domain of target account, SID string of target account, user name of subject changing the account, domain name of subject changing the account, logon ID string of subject changing the account.

> **Configurable Information:** Success
> **Formal name:** SE_AUDITID_ACCOUNT_NAME_CHANGE

Account Logon Events

Unlike the logon events described earlier in this appendix, the following security event messages track activity specifically in relation to Kerberos logon attempts, which require Active Directory.

672 An authentication service (AS) ticket was successfully issued and validated.

Parameters: User name of client, domain name of client, SID of client, SID of service, ticket options, failure code, ticket encryption type, preauthentication type (such as PK_INIT), client IP address.

Configurable Information: Success

Formal name: SE_AUDITID_AS_TICKET_SUCCESS

This event occurs on the Key Distribution Center (KDC) when a Kerberos logon attempt takes place. One AS ticket is granted per logon session.

673 A ticket granting service (TGS) ticket was granted.

Parameters: User name of client, domain name of client, user name of service, SID of service, ticket options, ticket encryption type, client IP address.

Configurable Information: Success

Formal name: SE_AUDITID_TGS_TICKET_SUCCESS

This event occurs on the KDC and means that a user presented an AS ticket and was given a TGS ticket for some service.

674 A principal renewed an AS ticket or TGS ticket.

Parameters: User name of client, domain name of client, user name of service, SID of service, ticket options, ticket encryption type, client IP address.

Configurable Information: Success

Formal name: SE_AUDITID_TICKET_RENEW_SUCCESS

This event occurs on the KDC and is currently only caused by non-Windows-based clients because Windows-based clients do not renew tickets, but reacquire them instead. This event occurs on the KDC user name of the client.

675 Preauthentication failed.

Parameters: User name of client, SID of client, user name of service, preauthentication type, failure code, client IP address.

Configurable Information: Success or Failure

Formal name: SE_AUDITID_PREAUTH_FAILURE

This event message is generated on the KDC for reasons such as the user typing in a wrong password, a large difference between the clock time on the client and the KDC, or a smart card logon error.

677 A TGS ticket was not granted.

Parameters: User name of client, SID of client, user name of service, SID of service, preauthentication type, failure code, client IP address.

Configurable Information: Failure

Formal name: SE_AUDITID_TGS_TICKET_FAILURE

This audit occurs on the KDC.

678 An account was successfully mapped to a domain account.

Parameters: Source, client name, mapped name.

Configurable Information: Success

Formal name: SE_AUDITID_ACCOUNT_MAPPED

An account mapping is a map of a user authenticated in an MIT Kerberos realm to a domain account.

681 A domain account logon attempt was made.

Parameters: Logon attempt by, logon account, source workstation, error code, if relevant.

Configurable Information: Success or Failure

Formal name: SE_AUDITID_ACCOUNT_LOGON

This audit appears on the domain controller or wherever the account exists. The following error codes are possible:

- Unknown user name or bad password (1326)

- Account logon time restriction violation (1328)

- Account currently disabled (1331)

- The specified user account has expired (1793)

- User not allowed to log on at this computer (1329)

- The user has not been granted the requested logon type at this computer (1327)

- The specified account's password has expired (1330)

- The Net Logon service is not active (1792)

In each of these events, descriptive text gives detailed information about each specific logon attempt. Also, on Windows XP Professional you can enable success and failure auditing of the Account Logon category of events, which enables the following events:

- Authentication ticket granted

- Service ticket granted

- Ticket renewed

- Preauthentication failed

- Authentication ticket request failed

- Service ticket request failed

- Account mapped for logon

- Account could not be mapped for logging on

- Account used for logging on

The following account logon events are included in "Logon Events" earlier in this appendix:

682 A user has reconnected to a disconnected terminal server session.

683 A user disconnected a terminal server session without logging off.

Directory Service Access Events

The only directory service access event is also included in "Object Access Events" earlier in this appendix.

566 A generic object operation took place.

Parameters: Object operation, operation type, object type, object name, handle ID, primary user name, primary domain, primary logon ID, client user name, client domain, client logon ID, accesses, properties.

    Configurable Information: Success or Failure

    Formal name: SE_AUDITID_OBJECT_OPERATION

Appendix F

Device Manager Error Codes

If you experience problems with a device, you can use Device Manager to troubleshoot the problem. Device Manager displays a device tree that includes all devices configured for your system. If there is a problem with a device, it is marked with a yellow exclamation point. If a device is disabled, it is marked with a red "X" Device Manager error codes are provided to aid in troubleshooting problems with devices.

In Device Manager, double-click a device to display its property sheet. Right-click a device to display a menu that allows you to update or uninstall drivers, scan for hardware changes, and display the property sheet of a device. Device Manager also allows you to enable or disable devices, troubleshoot problems with devices, roll back the installed driver to the previously installed driver, and change the resources that are assigned to devices.

The General tab of the device property sheet contains the device status. If there is a problem with the device, an error message and code appear in the device status area. If an error code is shown, you can use Table F-1 to find more information about resolving the error. A troubleshooting wizard is available for some errors. Specific error codes that have troubleshooting wizards are listed in the **Recommended Resolution** column of Table F-1.

In this appendix:

Related Information

- For more information about Device Manager, see "Managing Devices" in this book.

> **Note**   There are gaps in the numbering of these error codes. The missing error codes are not applicable to Microsoft® Windows® XP Professional.

Table F-1   Device Manager Error Codes

Error Code	Display Message	Recommended Resolution
1	This device is not configured correctly. (Code 1)	This device has no drivers installed or is improperly configured. Update the driver(s) by clicking **Update Driver**, which starts the Hardware Update wizard. If updating the driver does not work, see your hardware documentation for more information.
3	The driver for this device might be corrupted, or your system may be running low on memory or other resources. (Code 3)	If the driver is corrupted, uninstall the driver and scan for new hardware to install the driver again. To scan for new hardware, click on the **Action** menu in Device Manager, and then select **Scan for hardware changes**.
		If your computer does not have enough memory to run the device, you can close some applications to make memory available. To check memory and system resources, right-click **My Computer**, click **Properties**, click the **Advanced** tab, and then click **Settings** under **Performance**.
		You may need to install additional random access memory (RAM).
		On the **General Properties** tab of the device, click **Troubleshoot** to start the troubleshooting wizard.
10	This device cannot start. (Code 10)	Device failed to start. Click **Update Driver** to update the drivers for this device.
		On the **General Properties** tab of the device, click **Troubleshoot** to start the troubleshooting wizard.
12	This device cannot find enough free resources that it can use. If you want to use this device, you will need to disable one of the other devices on this system. (Code 12)	Two devices have been assigned the same input/output (I/O) ports, the same interrupt, or the same Direct Memory Access channel (either by the BIOS, the operating system, or a combination of the two). This error message can also appear if the BIOS did not allocate enough resources to the device (for example, if a universal serial bus (USB) controller does not get an interrupt from the BIOS because of a corrupt Multiprocessor System (MPS) table).
		You can use Device Manager to determine where the conflict is and disable the conflicting device.
		On the **General Properties** tab of the device, click **Troubleshoot** to start the troubleshooting wizard.

Table F-1   Device Manager Error Codes

Error Code	Display Message	Recommended Resolution
14	This device cannot work properly until you restart your computer. (Code 14)	Restart your computer.
16	Windows cannot identify all the resources this device uses. (Code 16)	The device is only partially configured. To specify additional resources for this device, click the **Resources** tab in Device Manager. If there is a resource with a question mark next to it in the list of resources assigned to the device, select that resource to assign it to the device. If the resource cannot be changed, click **Change Settings**. If **Change Settings** is unavailable, try clearing the **Use automatic settings** check box to make it available. If this is not a Plug and Play device, check the hardware documentation for more information. On the **General Properties** tab of the device, click **Troubleshoot** to start the troubleshooting wizard.
18	Reinstall the drivers for this device. (Code 18)	The drivers for this device must be reinstalled. Click **Update Driver**, which starts the Hardware Update wizard. Alternately, uninstall the driver, and then click **Scan for hardware changes** to reload the drivers.
19	Windows cannot start this hardware device because its configuration information (in the registry) is incomplete or damaged. To fix this problem you can first try running a troubleshooting wizard. If that does not work, you should uninstall and then reinstall the hardware device. (Code 19)	A registry problem was detected. This can occur when more than one service is defined for a device, if there is a failure opening the service subkey, or if the driver name cannot be obtained from the service subkey. Try these options: On the **General Properties** tab of the device, click **Troubleshoot** to start the troubleshooting wizard. Click **Uninstall**, and then click **Scan for hardware changes** to load a usable driver. Restart the computer in Safe Mode, and then select **Last Known Good Configuration**, which rolls back to the most recent successful registry configuration. As a last resort, you can edit the registry directly. For more information, see the Registry Reference in the Microsoft Windows 2000 Server Resource Kit at http://www.microsoft.com/reskit.
21	Windows is removing this device. (Code 21)	Wait a few seconds, and then refresh the Device Manager view. If the device appears, restart the computer.

Table F-1 Device Manager Error Codes

Error Code	Display Message	Recommended Resolution
22	This device is disabled. (Code 22)	The device is disabled because a user disabled it using Device Manager. Click **Enable Device**, which starts the Enable Device wizard.
24	This device is not present, is not working properly, or does not have all its drivers installed. (Code 24)	The device does not appear to be present. The problem could be bad hardware, or a new driver might be needed. Devices stay in this state if they have been prepared for removal. After you remove the device, this error disappears. On the **General Properties** tab of the device, click **Troubleshoot** to start the troubleshooting wizard.
28	The drivers for this device are not installed. (Code 28)	To install the drivers for this device, click **Update Driver**, which starts the Hardware Update wizard.
29	This device is disabled because the firmware of the device did not give it the required resources. (Code 29)	Enable the device in the BIOS of the device. For information about how to make this change, see the hardware documentation or contact the hardware vendor. On the **General Properties** tab of the device, click **Troubleshoot** to start the troubleshooting wizard.
31	This device is not working properly because Windows cannot load the drivers required for this device. (Code 31)	Windows was unable to load the driver. Try updating the driver for this device. On the **General Properties** tab of the device, click **Troubleshoot** to start the troubleshooting wizard.
32	A driver (service) for this device has been disabled. An alternate driver may be providing this functionality (Code 32)	The start type for this driver is set to disabled in the registry. Uninstall the driver, and then click **Scan for hardware changes** to reinstall or upgrade the driver. On the **General Properties** tab of the device, click **Troubleshoot** to start the troubleshooting wizard. If the driver is required, and if reinstalling or upgrading does not work, change the start type in the registry using the registry editor. For more information, see the Registry Reference in the Microsoft Windows 2000 Server Resource Kit at http://www.microsoft.com/reskit.
33	Windows cannot determine which resources are required for this device. (Code 33)	The translator that determines the types of resources required by the device has failed. Contact the hardware vendor, and configure or replace hardware. On the **General Properties** tab of the device, click **Troubleshoot** to start the troubleshooting wizard.

Table F-1 Device Manager Error Codes

Error Code	Display Message	Recommended Resolution
34	Windows cannot determine the settings for this device. Consult the documentation that came with this device and use the Resource tab to set the configuration. (Code 34)	The device requires manual configuration. Change the hardware settings by setting jumpers or running a vendor-supplied tool, and then use the **Resources** tab in Device Manager to configure the device. On the **General Properties** tab of the device, click **Troubleshoot** to start the troubleshooting wizard.
35	Your computer's system firmware does not include enough information to properly configure and use this device. To use this device, contact your computer manufacturer to obtain a firmware or BIOS update. (Code 35)	The Multiprocessor System (MPS) table, which stores the resource assignments for the BIOS, is missing an entry for your device and needs to be updated. Obtain a new BIOS from the system vendor. On the **General Properties** tab of the device, click **Troubleshoot** to start the troubleshooting wizard.
36	This device is requesting a PCI interrupt but is configured for an ISA interrupt (or vice versa). Please use the computer's system setup program to reconfigure the interrupt for this device. (Code 36)	Interrupt request (IRQ) translation failed. Try using the BIOS setup tool to change settings for IRQ reservations (if such options exist). The BIOS might have options to reserve certain IRQs for peripheral component interconnect (PCI) or ISA devices. For more information about changing BIOS settings, see the hardware documentation. On the **General Properties** tab of the device, click **Troubleshoot** to start the troubleshooting wizard.
37	Windows cannot initialize the device driver for this hardware. (Code 37)	The driver returned failure from its DriverEntry routine. Uninstall the driver, and then click **Scan for hardware changes** to reinstall or upgrade the driver. On the **General Properties** tab of the device, click **Troubleshoot** to start the troubleshooting wizard.
38	Windows cannot load the device driver for this hardware because a previous instance of the device driver is still in memory. (Code 38)	The driver could not be loaded because a previous instance is still loaded. Restart the computer. On the **General Properties** tab of the device, click **Troubleshoot** to start the troubleshooting wizard.

Table F-1   Device Manager Error Codes

Error Code	Display Message	Recommended Resolution
39	Windows cannot load the device driver for this hardware. The driver may be corrupted or missing. (Code 39)	Reasons for this error include a driver that is not present; a binary file that is corrupt; a file I/O problem, or a driver that references an entry point in another binary file that could not be loaded.
		Uninstall the driver, and then click **Scan for hardware changes** to reinstall or upgrade the driver.
		On the **General Properties** tab of the device, click **Troubleshoot** to start the troubleshooting wizard.
40	Windows cannot access this hardware because its service key information in the registry is missing or recorded incorrectly. (Code 40)	Information in the registry's service subkey for the driver is invalid. Uninstall the driver, and then click **Scan for hardware changes** to load the driver again.
		On the **General Properties** tab of the device, click **Troubleshoot** to start the troubleshooting wizard.
41	Windows successfully loaded the device driver for this hardware but cannot find the hardware device. (Code 41)	A driver was loaded but Windows cannot find the device. This happens when Windows does not detect a non-Plug and Play device.
		If the device was removed, uninstall the driver, install the device, and then click **Scan for hardware changes** to reinstall the driver. If the hardware was not removed, obtain a new or updated driver for the device.
		If the device is a non-Plug and Play device, a newer version of the driver might be needed. To install non-Plug and Play devices, use the **Add Hardware** wizard. Click **Performance and Maintenance** on Control Panel, click **System**, and on the **Hardware** tab, click **Add Hardware Wizard**.
		On the **General Properties** tab of the device, click **Troubleshoot** to start the troubleshooting wizard.
42	Windows cannot load the device driver for this hardware because there is a duplicate device already running in the system. (Code 42)	A duplicate device was detected. This error occurs when a bus driver erroneously creates two identically named children (bus driver error), or when a device with a serial number is discovered in a new location before it is removed from the old location.
		Restart the computer.
		On the **General Properties** tab of the device, click **Troubleshoot** to start the troubleshooting wizard.

Table F-1   Device Manager Error Codes

Error Code	Display Message	Recommended Resolution
43	Windows has stopped this device because it has reported problems. (Code 43)	One of the drivers controlling the device notified the operating system that the device failed in some manner. For more information about how to diagnose the problem, see the hardware documentation.
		On the General Properties tab of the device, click Troubleshoot to start the troubleshooting wizard.
44	An application or service has shut down this hardware device. (Code 44)	Restart the computer.
		On the **General Properties** tab of the device, click **Troubleshoot** to start the troubleshooting wizard.
45	Currently, this hardware device is not connected to the computer. (Code 45). To fix this problem, reconnect this hardware device to the computer.	The device is not present or was previously attached to the computer.
		If Device Manager is started with the environment variable DEVMGR_SHOW_NONPRESENT_DEVICES set to 1 (which means show these devices), then any previously attached (NONPRESENT) devices are displayed in the device list and assigned this error code. For more information about using Device Manager to show previously attached devices, see "Managing Devices" in this book.
		No resolution is necessary.
46	Windows cannot gain access to this hardware device because the operating system is in the process of shutting down (Code 46). The hardware device should work correctly next time you start your computer.	The device is not available because the system is shutting down.
		This error code is only set when Driver Verifier is enabled and all applications have already been shut down.
		No resolution is necessary.
47	Windows cannot use this hardware device because it has been prepared for "safe removal", but it has not been removed from the computer (Code 47). To fix this problem, unplug this device from your computer and then plug it in again.	The device has been prepared for ejection.
		This error code occurs only if the user used the Safe Removal application to prepare the device for removal, or pressed a physical eject button. Restarting the computer brings the device online if the user does not want to eject from the dock.
		Unplug the device, and then plug it in again. Alternately, restart the computer to make the device available.
		On the **General Properties** tab of the device, click **Troubleshoot** to start the troubleshooting wizard.

Table F-1   Device Manager Error Codes

Error Code	Display Message	Recommended Resolution
48	The software for this device has been blocked from starting because it is known to have problems with Windows. Contact the hardware vendor for a new driver. (Code 48)	Obtain and install a new or updated driver from the hardware vendor. On the **General Properties** tab of the device, click **Troubleshoot** to start the troubleshooting wizard.
49	Windows cannot start new hardware devices because the system hive is too large (exceeds the Registry Size Limit). (Code 49) To fix this problem, you should first try uninstalling any hardware devices that you are no longer using. If that doesn't solve the problem, then you will have to reinstall Windows.	The system hive has exceeded its maximum size and new devices cannot work until the size is reduced. The system hive is a permanent part of the registry associated with a set of files containing information related to the configuration of the computer on which the operating system is installed. Configured items include applications, user preferences, devices, and so on. The problem might be specific devices that are no longer attached to the computer but are still listed in the system hive. The solution is as stated in the Device Manager error code text. To view devices that are no longer attached to the computer, set the environment variable DEVMGR_SHOW_NONPRESENT_DEVICES to 1. Then run Device Manager to view, uninstall, and reinstall these devices. For more information about using Device Manager to show previously attached (NONPRESENT) devices, see "Managing Devices" in this book.

Additional Resources

These resources contain additional information and tools related to this appendix.

- For more information about troubleshooting, managing, and configuring devices, see "Managing Devices" in this book.

- For more information about troubleshooting, see "Tools for Troubleshooting" in this book.

Appendix G

Differences with Windows XP Home Edition

Microsoft® Windows® XP Home Edition is the new operating system for home users who currently use Microsoft® Windows® 95, Microsoft® Windows® 98, or Microsoft® Windows® Millennium Edition (Me). In addition to features included with Windows XP Home Edition, Windows XP Professional includes advanced and business features that focus on productivity in the workplace.

Related Information

- For more information about installing Windows XP Professional, see "Planning Deployments" in this book.

Windows XP Home Edition Overview

Windows XP provides improvements over Windows 2000 Professional designed to appeal to both business and home users. Enhancements include:

- Improved application and hardware device compatibility

- Simplified security and logging on

- Fast user switching

- A new user interface with simplified WebViews

- Enhanced digital media support for movies, pictures, and music

- A software-based firewall to protect against outside security threats on the Internet

- Support for Direct X version 8.0 technology for gaming

Windows 95, Windows 98, and Windows Me were designed to support both home and business users. Windows XP Home Edition is designed specifically for home users. It provides them with the reliability and security of Windows XP Professional and the efficient simplicity of Windows Me. Windows XP Home Edition offers enhanced support for computer games, storage of digital media (such as the My Movies and My Music folders), and wizards for connecting to the Internet.

The hardware requirements for installing Windows XP Home Edition and Windows XP Professional are similar; however Windows XP Home Edition supports only one CPU.

Users can upgrade to Windows XP Home Edition from Windows 98 or Windows Me—but not from Windows 95, Microsoft® Windows NT® Workstation or Windows 2000 Professional. You can upgrade to Windows XP Professional from any of those operating systems, except Windows 95.

Note   There is no 64-bit version of Windows XP Home Edition.

For more information about hardware requirements and compatibility for installing Windows XP Professional, see "Planning Deployments" in this book.

Comparing Windows XP Home Edition and Windows XP Professional Feature Differences

Because Windows XP Professional is targeted to businesses, it contains several features that are not included with Windows XP Home Edition. These features can be categorized into two groups:

- Functionality that is important for business use but typically not for home use
- Complexity that adds value for business use, but typically not for home use

Although Windows XP Professional is targeted to businesses, home users might also require or gain advantage from using Windows XP Professional features that are not included in Windows XP Home Edition.

Features not included in Windows XP Home Edition are mostly in the following categories:

- Corporate management
- Corporate security
- Networking
- File system
- User Interface
- Advanced and power-user

> **Warning**   Computers running Windows XP Home Edition cannot join corporate domains. For this reason, features that require machine accounts within a domain, such as Group Policy, are not available in Windows XP Home Edition.

Corporate Management

IntelliMirror allows organizations to manage desktop computers by using Active Directory to reduce maintenance and support costs. The features that make up IntelliMirror—including Group Policy, Group Policy Editor (Gpedit.msc), roaming user profiles, and folder redirection—require computers to have accounts in a domain that uses Active Directory. Those features are not included in Windows XP Home Edition. Also, you cannot deploy applications to computers running Windows XP Home Edition by publishing them using Active Directory.

For more information about IntelliMirror features, see "Managing Desktops" in this book.

Because they cannot be joined to a domain, you cannot manage computers running Windows XP Home Edition by using login scripts.

The following corporate management features are not included with Windows XP Home Edition:

- Folder Redirection
- Group Policy settings
- Local Policy settings
- System Policy settings (Poledit.exe)
- Roaming User Profiles
- Offline Files and Folders
- Software Installation and Maintenance
- Remote Installation Services (RIS)

Corporate Security

Features such as Encrypting File System (EFS) and computer domain account support add complexity that is primarily for business use and therefore is not supported in Windows XP Home Edition. Windows XP Home Edition offers security features that are important for home users, especially those using cable modems or other Internet connection methods that do not require dialing into an ISP to browse the Web or read e-mail. Security features such as Personal Firewall are enabled by default in Windows XP Home Edition.

Users of Windows XP Home Edition might need to remotely access resources on corporate local-area networks (LANs). Stored User Names and Passwords allow users to authenticate to remote networks and to access shares on domains. Domain-based credentials cannot be stored on a computer running Windows XP Home Edition. However, when connecting to a domain by using Remote Access or virtual private networking (VPN), the user's remote access credentials are stored during that session to allow user access to domain resources.

In addition, you cannot control access to local shares on a computer running Windows XP Home Edition from the domain's user-level security. For more information about using Stored User Names and Passwords, see "Authorization and Access Control" and "Logon and Authentication" in this book.

Windows XP Home Edition uses a slightly different scheme from Windows XP Professional to identify security groups. Backup Operators, Power Users, and Replicator groups are removed from Windows XP Home Edition. Instead, Restricted Users are added as a group to Windows XP Home Edition, and the Administrators group is replaced by the Owners group. By default, all interactive users are logged on as members of the Owners local group and have rights to install software and modify the system. Network logons are allowed only for the Guest account, which is enabled by default. In addition, in Windows XP Home Edition, users can log on to the Owners account only by using Safe Mode.

The following security features are not included with Windows XP Home Edition:

- Encrypting File System (EFS)

- Computer domain account support

- Access Control List (ACL) Editor

- Administrative shares (available only when joined to a domain)

- **Log on using dial-up connection** option in **Log On to Windows** dialog box

- Security-related Group Policy settings

Because it is not intended for corporate network use, Windows XP Home Edition will not be submitted for Common Criteria for Information Technology Security Evaluation (CCITSE) certification.

For more information about user rights in Windows XP Professional, see "User Rights" in this book. For more information about security groups in Windows XP Home Edition, see Windows XP Home Edition Help and Support Center.

Networking Features

Many networking features are identical in Windows XP Professional and Windows XP Home Edition. The main differences involve connection limits and simplification. While Windows XP Professional allows up to 10 simultaneous file-sharing connections, Windows XP Home Edition allows up to five connections only.

> **Note**   For critical details about the connection limits for each version of Windows XP, see the End User License Agreement (EULA) included with the operating system.

Some advanced network components designed for corporate networks—the user interface for the IPSec manual configuration, for example—are not included in Windows XP Home Edition. Also, Client Service for NetWare is not included.

File System Features

Automated System Recovery (ASR), which is designed for computers such as servers and advanced workstations that have complex disk configurations, is not included with Windows XP Home Edition. Typically, OEMs provide home users with a system recovery CD, and users can use the System Restore feature in Windows XP Home Edition to repair a damaged system. For more information about System Restore, see "Tools for Troubleshooting" in this book.

Dynamic disks are not supported in Windows XP Home Edition, and you cannot convert disks to dynamic disk or import dynamic disks from another computer. Backup is included with Windows XP Home Edition but not installed by default. Users who want to use this feature must install it from the installation CD.

Windows XP Home Edition supports the FAT, FAT32, and NTFS file systems. To take advantage of large disk and file support, performance increases, and file security in Windows XP, use NTFS as your file system. However, Windows XP Home Edition does not support EFS, and it allows only limited control over Access Control Lists (ACLS) to allow simple file sharing. Simplified file sharing in Windows XP allows for three states: Me Only, Local Users, and The World, either the user's network or the Internet, by using the Guest account.

User Interface Features

Most of the user interface differences between Windows XP Professional and Windows XP Home Edition are in the default settings, including those determined by whether the computer is part of a Windows–based domain. For example, because computers running Windows XP Home Edition cannot have computer accounts on Windows domains, the default settings are simple logon and simple user accounts control. There are also some differences in the default settings for the **Quick Launch** toolbar and in **Start** menu options.

Table G-1 compares some of the default settings in Windows XP Professional and Windows XP Home Edition.

Table G-1 Default Settings in Windows XP Professional and Windows XP Home Edition

Feature	Windows XP Professional	Windows XP Home Edition
Guest Logon	Off by default	On by default
Ability to move the taskbar	On by default	Off by default
QuickLaunch bar	On by default	Off by default

Advanced or Power-User Features

Localized versions of Windows XP Home Edition and all versions of Windows XP support character input, display, and printing of over 60 languages. However, the multilanguage user interface that allows you to dynamically change language version user interfaces is only available through licensing intended for corporations and is not included with Windows XP Home Edition. Users who want to remotely administer their computer to manage a simple Web server or to use other advanced features can do so by using Windows XP Professional.

The following advanced features are not included in Windows XP Home Edition:

■ Remote Desktop Service

■ Multiprocessor support

■ Multilanguage user interface

■ **Start** menu option to show administrative tools

■ Internet Information Services (IIS)

> **Note**   Windows XP does not support Personal Web Server (PWS). IIS is included with Windows XP Professional to allow users to manage simple Web servers.

Additional Resources

These resources contain additional information and tools related to this appendix.

■ Windows XP Professional Help and Support Center for more information about configuring and using Windows XP Professional.

■ Windows XP Home Edition Help and Support Center for more information about configuring and using Windows XP Home Edition.

Appendix H

Differences with Windows XP 64-Bit Edition

Microsoft® Windows® XP 64-Bit Edition provides a scalable, high-performance solution for a new generation of Windows®-based applications. While compatible with 32-bit applications and existing deployment and management tools, Windows XP 64-Bit Edition provides more efficient processing of extremely large amounts of data, supporting up to 16 terabytes of virtual memory.

Related Information

- For more information about installing Windows XP 64-Bit Edition, see "Planning Deployments" in this book.

- For more information about managing disks in Windows XP 64-Bit Edition, see "Disk Management" in this book.

- For more information about troubleshooting problems related to disks and file systems in Windows XP 64-Bit Edition, see "Troubleshooting Disks and File Systems" in this book.

Overview of Windows XP 64-Bit Edition

Windows XP 64-Bit Edition supports the latest class of Intel Itanium processors designed for users who need to create and manipulate large amounts of complex data. The high performance of the Intel Itanium processor is targeted toward high-end workstation applications such as large database management, data mining, computer-aided engineering, digital content creation, and scientific and engineering computing. Itanium-based computers running Windows XP 64-Bit Edition can support up to 16 terabytes of virtual memory and up to 16 gigabytes (GB) of physical memory.

Based on the Explicitly Parallel Instruction Set Computing (EPIC) design technology, the Intel Itanium processor can perform up to 20 operations simultaneously by using advanced compiling techniques and large processor resources. In addition, applications can preload substantial amounts of data into virtual memory to enable rapid access by the processor. This reduces the time for loading data into virtual memory and the time for seeking, reading, and writing data to storage devices, thereby allowing applications to run faster and more efficiently.

Using an emulation layer, you can run 32-bit applications on Windows XP 64-Bit Edition. However, such applications run significantly slower on the 64-bit system than on the 32-bit system, because emulation requires additional resources.

Table H-1 describes the architectural differences between Microsoft® Windows® XP Professional and Windows XP 64-Bit Edition.

Table H-1   Architectural Comparison of Windows XP Professional and Windows XP 64-Bit Edition

Architectural Component	Windows XP Professional	Windows XP 64-Bit Edition
Virtual memory	4 gigabytes (GB)	16 terabytes
Paging file size	64 GB	512 terabytes
Paged pool	470 megabytes (MB)	128 GB
Non-paged pool	256 MB	128 GB
System cache	1 GB	1 terabytes
System Page Table Entry (PTE)	1.2GB	128GB

For more information about migrating applications to 64-bit, see the Software Development Kit (SDK) information in the MSDN Library link and the Driver Development Kits link on the Web Resources page at http://www.microsoft.com/windows/reskits/webresources.

Features Not Supported in Windows XP 64-Bit Edition

A number of features in Windows XP Professional are not included with Windows XP 64-Bit Edition. The following is a list of these features.

Digital Media

The following digital media features are not included with Windows XP 64-Bit Edition:

- Digital video disc (DVD) video playback
- CD Recording
- Kodak Imaging Accessory
- Windows Media™ Player
- A subset of Windows Media™ Technologies
    - DirectMusic®
    - Microsoft TV Technologies for Windows®
    - Video mixing renderer (VMR)
- NetMeeting®
- IEEE 1394 audio
- Fax

Subsystems and Protocols

Windows XP 64-Bit Edition does not provide support for a number of older subsystems and transport protocols, including the following:

- Microsoft® MS-DOS® subsystem
- OS/2 subsystems
- 16-bit subsystems
- Portable Operating System Interface for UNIX (POSIX) subsystem
- Legacy transport protocols
    - Internetwork Packet Exchange/Sequenced Packet Exchange (IPX/SPX) LAN and WAN
    - AppleTalk Protocol LAN
    - Services for Macintosh

- Data Link Control (DLC) LAN

- NetBIOS Enhanced User Interface (NetBEUI) LAN

- Service Advertising Protocol (SAP) Agent for Server

- Internetwork Packet Exchange (IPX) router

- Infrared Data Association (IrDA)

- Open Shortest Path First (OSPF)

- Network BIOS (NetBIOS) gateway

Mobile Computing

Windows XP 64-Bit Edition does not provide support for features aimed primarily at users of portable computers. The following features are not included:

- Hot docking/undocking

- PC Card

- IrDA

- Terminal Services client for Handheld PC

- Power Management

System Restore

The System Restore feature is not supported in Windows XP 64-Bit Edition.

Networking and Communications

The following networking and communications features are not included in Windows XP 64-Bit Edition:

- Internet Locator Service (ILS)

- MSN™ Internet Access client

- Message Queuing (MSMQ) Level 8 Listener

- Windows Messenger Service

- SharePoint™ Team Services from Microsoft

Database

The 64-bit versions of these database engines and features are not included in Windows XP 64-Bit Edition; 32-bit versions of Microsoft Database Engine (MSDE) and Jet RED are included.

- Microsoft Database Engine (MSDE) 64-Bit

- Jet RED 64-Bit

- Microsoft Data Access Components (MDAC) Oracle provider

- MDAC Oracle driver

- MDAC Data Access Objects (DAOs)

- MDAC Visual FoxPro® Driver

- Dynamic Data Exchange (DDE) Share

System Administration

These system administration and management features are not supported in Windows XP 64-Bit Edition:

- Winrep (Windows Report Tool)

- Security Dynamics Access Control Entry (ACE) Agent

- Windows Installer

- Fast User Switching

- Remote Assistance

- File and Settings Transfer Wizard

- Windows Product Activation (WPA)

- Installation of Recovery Console on the hard disk; Recovery Console can be run from the operating system CD

- Search Companion

- Speech recognition

Windows XP 64-Bit Edition Requirements

Windows XP Professional and Windows XP 64-Bit Edition differ in performance and capacity. As a result, setup, disk space, and device driver requirements also differ, as do installation of certain software applications and the method for running some applications such as Microsoft Management Console (MMC). These differences are as follows.

System Requirements

Table H-2 shows how system requirements for the two operating systems differ.

Table H-2   Comparison of Setup Requirements Between Windows XP Professional and Windows XP 64-Bit Edition

System Requirements Setup Component	Windows XP Professional	Windows XP 64-Bit Edition
Minimum CPU speed	233 megahertz (MHz)	733 MHz
Recommended CPU speed	300 MHz	N/A
Minimum RAM	64 MB	1 GB
Recommended minimum RAM	128 MB	N/A
Disk space required for Setup	1.5 GB free	1.5 GB free

Multilingual Solutions

Installing certain types of additional language support requires more disk space on a Windows XP 64-Bit Edition–based client. The differences relate to the following two language collections:

- **Complex Script and Right-to-Left Language Collection.** Requires 10 MB of hard drive space on Windows XP Professional, and requires 12 MB of space on Windows XP 64-Bit Edition.

- **East Asian Language Collection.** Requires 230 MB of hard drive space on Windows XP Professional, and requires 280 MB of space on Windows XP 64-Bit Edition.

Device Driver Installation

Windows XP 64-Bit Edition requires the installation of 64-bit drivers only. Some device drivers are modified to allow installation of 64-bit and 32-bit drivers from the same .inf file. These modifications also prevent installation of the wrong driver on the wrong platform. The extension **.ia64** is used in the .inf file of these drivers to identify the installation files and sections in the .inf file that can be installed on the 64-bit platform. Previous versions of Windows do not recognize the .ia64 extension, and ignore any .inf file entries that contain it.

Note   Some device drivers might have packaging that says that the driver works on Microsoft® Windows® XP, but it is designed to work only on Windows XP Professional. In this case, the driver does not work on Windows XP 64-Bit Edition.

Running Microsoft Management Console Snap-Ins

Windows XP 64-Bit Edition includes both 64-bit and 32-bit versions of MMC. The default version of MMC that runs in Windows XP 64-Bit Edition is the 64-bit version. You can, however, manually select which version to run by running MMC from the Run dialog box, and by entering runtime parameters. This might be necessary if certain MMC consoles that you need to use are not available in a 64-bit version.

To manually select the version of the MMC to run

■ To run the 32-bit version of MMC, in the **Run** dialog box, type **mmc -32**.
  – or –
  To run the 64-bit version of MMC, in the **Run** dialog box type **mmc -64**.

If you are running the 64-bit version of MMC, you cannot run 32-bit snap-ins. If the 32-bit version of MMC is running, you cannot run 64-bit snap-ins. However, if you run a particular MMC *console*, or set of administrative tools, without specifying the 64-bit or 32-bit version of MMC as described in the foregoing procedure, the version of MMC that runs is determined by an algorithm that looks at the number of 32-bit and 64-bit snap-ins available for that console. If all 64-bit snap-ins are available for the console, the 64-bit version of MMC runs. If only 32-bit snap-ins are available, then the 32-bit version of MMC runs. Other algorithms determine which version runs if a combination of 32-bit and 64-bit snap-ins is available for a particular MMC console. For more information about running 32-bit and 64-bit MMC snap-ins in Windows XP 64-Bit Edition, see the Microsoft® Platform Software Development Kit (SDK).

Additional Resources

These resources contain additional information and tools related to this appendix.

■ "Planning Deployments" in this book for more information about installing Windows XP Professional.

■ The Windows XP 64-Bit Edition link on the Web Resources page at http: //www.microsoft.com/windows/reskits/webresources for more information about Windows XP 64-Bit Edition.

■ The Microsoft Platform SDK link on the Web Resources page at http: //www.microsoft.com/windows/reskits/webresources for more information about running 32-bit and 64-bit MMC snap-ins in Windows XP 64-Bit Edition.

Appendix I

Accessibility for People with Disabilities

Microsoft is dedicated to making its products and services accessible and usable for everyone. Microsoft® Windows® XP Professional includes accessibility features that benefit all users. These features make it easier to customize the computer and give users with disabilities better access to the applications they need to do their work.

Related Information

- For more information about using accessibility features on the Internet, see "Accessibility Features and Functionality" in the *Microsoft Internet Explorer 5 Resource Kit* of the *Microsoft® Windows® 2000 Server Resource Kit*.

Customizing for Accessibility

Several built-in Windows XP Professional technologies and Windows Explorer options can help administrators and users configure computers with accessibility features. For more information about how users with specific disabilities can use these features, see "Setting Accessibility Options by Type of Disability" later in this appendix.

Windows XP Professional installs built-in accessibility options automatically. Users cannot delete these accessibility options from the operating system after they are installed, including those options available in **Accessibility Wizard** or Control Panel.

> **Note**   Even if all of an individual user's data and applications are stored centrally, some user settings that might include accessibility options are stored on the local computer. When you perform a clean installation, these settings and data must be preserved and reapplied to the system after the installation.

Windows Installer

Windows Installer allows the operating system to install, maintain, and remove software on client computers. The service includes self-repairing applications. If an application is missing or damaged, Windows Installer reinstates the missing files the next time the user tries to open them. The self-repairing feature can alter selected options upon reinstallation. Administrators can configure these options for users.

For more detailed information about Windows Installer, see "Automating and Customizing Installations" in this book.

Group Policy

Group Policy is important to administrators who support users with disabilities because you can use it to ensure that accessibility features and settings are available. You can publish applications for defined groups of users who have assistive needs. And you can verify that the Group Policy settings that are applied to your users or computers allow a flexible user interface (UI) and include compatibility with external software tools.

User Profiles

A user profile is a user-environment setting. Users with disabilities can change their user profiles to suit their accessibility needs. For accessibility purposes, it is important to consider setup options that maintain individual user profiles.

Automatic logon   For many users, pressing CTRL+ALT+DEL before logging on to a computer is difficult or impossible. Some users select the StickyKeys option to allow them to use CTRL+ALT+DEL. The automatic logon feature allows users to bypass this keyboard shortcut and go directly to the logon process, which requires the correct name and password. You can allow a user to log on without using CTRL+ALT+DEL by using the **User Accounts** Control Panel option, on the **Advanced** tab, under **Secure logon**.

Administrative options   You can set Administrative Options for several features by using **Accessibility Wizard** or **Accessibility Options** in Control Panel. Settings you can make in both include automatic time-out, automatic reset, and default accessibility settings.

> **Note**   Automatic reset and automatic time-out do not turn off SerialKeys.

Multiple user profiles   You can use **Accessibility Wizard** to set multiple user profiles. Each user who logs on to the computer can change settings without deleting the previous settings. Each user's settings are restored at the next logon session. Windows XP Professional automatically presets features to default settings for other users. When accessibility features are turned off, users who do not need them do not notice that the features are installed. Multiple users of the same computer can use their logon and password information to set preferences and desktop settings, including any accessibility features that they need.

Roaming user profiles   A user profile is a group of settings and files that defines the environment that the system loads when a user logs on. It includes all the user-specific configuration settings, such as program items, screen colors, network connections, printer connections, mouse settings, and window size and position. Roaming user profiles make it possible for users to use different computers within the corporate network and still retain a consistent desktop, including any accessibility options they need to use.

Fast User Switching   Fast User Switching, a new feature in Windows XP Professional, allows multiple users to log on to a computer without requiring that other users log off. Multiple users can switch back and forth without closing applications or losing settings and data. This feature allows users who need to use accessibility options to more easily share their computers with other users. This feature is only available when a computer is not joined to a domain.

> **Note**   If Fast User Switching is enabled, you cannot use SerialKeys.

Customizing the Desktop

Control over desktop elements such as menus, toolbars, shortcuts, and status indicators is important for users who must customize these features for accessibility in daily operations. In Windows XP Professional, you can customize the desktop to create an arrangement of navigational elements needed for quick access to applications and folders. Users can also assign shortcut keys to allow users to start and use applications and features without using a mouse. You can customize desktop elements in the **Display** Control Panel option by using the **Appearance** tab.

Users can customize toolbars within applications to contain frequently used commands and buttons. The ability to customize toolbars is most useful for people who use the mouse rather than the keyboard. Users who prefer the keyboard usually also prefer to add commands to the **Start** menu. Users can use or create desktop toolbars in the following ways:

- Putting a toolbar in a more convenient place on a desktop or taskbar.
- Using the mouse to drag and drop or pressing SHIFT+F10 on the keyboard to move frequently used files and programs for quick access.
- Adding an address bar to the taskbar or to the desktop to give the user the ability to type an Internet address without first opening the browser.

Start menu options   You can add program shortcuts to the **Start** menu to make the menu more efficient. You can change **Start** menu options by using the **Taskbar and Start Menu** Control Panel option.

System status indicators   From the **Start** menu, you can use the TAB key to move to the status indicators on the notification area of the taskbar. These indicators, or icons, show the user whether MouseKeys, StickyKeys, or FilterKeys are active and the status of certain other programs or hardware.

Windows Explorer   Windows Explorer provides a consistent interface for accessing all files, folders, and applications on the computer and, for some users, can be easier than using the mouse to navigate to objects on the desktop.

Utility Manager

Utility Manager allows faster access to some accessibility tools and also displays the status of the tools or devices that it controls. Administrators can also use Utility Manager to designate features that must start automatically when a user logs on. Utility

Manager includes three built-in accessibility tools: Magnifier, Narrator, and On-Screen Keyboard.

Although only administrators can customize Utility Manager, users can start or stop the individual utilities. Users with administrator rights can also set up additional applications or run programs that install third-party add-on devices.

You can access Utility Manager by pressing the WINDOWS LOGO key+U shortcut key combination or by using the **Start** menu (point to All Programs, Accessories, and then Accessibility). Network policy settings might prevent opening Utility Manager from the **Start** menu if the computer is connected to a network.

To start accessibility features at login

1. Open Utility Manager by pressing WINDOWS LOGO key+U.

2. Select the accessibility feature that must start when a user logs on to the computer.

3. In the **Options** box, select **Start automatically when I log in**.

By setting these options the administrator can provide immediate access for users who must use Narrator, Magnifier, or On-Screen Keyboard to operate the computer. This procedure can also be used to open third-party programs or start devices when Windows starts if the vendor has supplied the installer for them.

Configuring Accessibility Features

Custom interfaces allow users with disabilities to control their computing environments so that they can effectively use the software they need to perform their work. Although accessibility features install automatically with Windows XP Professional, any previously configured options and settings must be reconfigured—and customized options must be configured for individual users.

You can configure most accessibility options in either Control Panel or **Accessibility Wizard**. However, several options are configurable in only one of these tools. In some instances, there are different names for the same, or similar, features. Table I-1 describes such variances.

Table I-1   Variances in Accessibility Wizard and Control Panel Features

Accessibility Wizard	Control Panel
UI elements and schemes organized by category of disability	UI elements and schemes organized by feature
Magnifier	No Magnifier
No SerialKeys	SerialKeys
No customizable keyboard	Dvorak keyboard

Table I-1   Variances in Accessibility Wizard and Control Panel Features

Accessibility Wizard	Control Panel
BounceKeys	FilterKeys
Mouse options in **I have trouble using a keyboard**, on the Mouse menu	Mouse options in **Mouse** properties and the **Mouse** tab in **Accessibility Options**
Personalized menus	No personalized menu options

Configuring options by using Accessibility Wizard Accessibility Wizard makes it easy to set up accessibility preferences to meet a user's particular needs. Available from the **Start** menu, the wizard provides a single entry point for many frequently used features. The wizard controls sound and screen options such as volume and font sizes, keyboard options such as BounceKeys and MouseKeys, and Administrative Options.

Configuring options by using Control Panel Accessibility Options in Control Panel allows users to customize many accessibility features in Windows XP Professional. Users can turn accessibility features on or off and customize keyboard, sound, and mouse operations. **Accessibility Options** gives users access to the following features: StickyKeys, FilterKeys, ToggleKeys, SoundSentry, ShowSounds, MouseKeys, and SerialKeys. Users can also modify settings in Control Panel options such as **Display**, **Keyboard**, **Mouse**, and **Sounds and Audio Devices**.

Setting Accessibility Options by Type of Disability

Accessibility features built into Windows XP Professional make it easier for users to solve a variety of specific problems. Table I-2 summarizes some common difficulties and the solutions that are built into Windows XP Professional. For more detailed descriptions of many of these solutions in the context of specific disabilities, see the sections that follow the table.

Table I-2   Common User Difficulties and Solutions

If the user has difficulty...	Use These Windows XP Professional Features
Customizing settings in a multiple user network.	**Accessibility Wizard**, **Accessibility Options** in Control Panel, Utility Manager.
Remembering what accessibility features are activated.	Status indicators on the notification area of the taskbar.
	In **Accessibility Options**, on the **General** tab, click **Give a warning message when turning a feature on** or **Make a sound when turning a feature on or off**.

Table I-2   Common User Difficulties and Solutions

If the user has difficulty...	Use These Windows XP Professional Features
Finding a needed feature.	Windows XP Professional Help and Support Center and Help in specific applications.
Remembering keyboard navigation shortcuts (underlined access keys).	In **Accessibility Options,** on the **Keyboard** tab, select **Show extra keyboard help in programs**.
Hearing sound prompts, distinguishing sounds, hearing audible cues, or working in a noisy environment.	ShowSounds, SoundSentry, and Notification options.
Using standard keyboard configurations.	Dvorak keyboards, On-Screen Keyboard, MouseKeys.
Using a keyboard due to slow key release or inadvertent repeating of keys.	FilterKeys and StickyKeys in **Accessibility Options**.
Holding down two or more keys at the same time.	StickyKeys.
Using a standard mouse and keyboard.	MouseKeys, On-Screen Keyboard, Utility Manager, third-party assistive technology.
Manipulating a mouse.	MouseKeys in **Accessibility Options**, keyboard shortcuts.
Working with a flashing cursor.	**Cursor Options** in **Accessibility Options**.
Seeing the pointer on the screen.	**Cursor Options** in **Accessibility Options**.
Seeing keyboard status lights.	ToggleKeys in **Accessibility Wizard** and in Control Panel; Narrator, third-party assistive technology.
Seeing screen elements.	Narrator; Magnifier; in **Accessibility Wizard**, select **I am blind or having difficulty seeing things on screen**, third-party assistive technology.
Functioning well with built-in accessibility features.	SerialKeys in Control Panel for third-party assistive technology.
Finding assistive technology and other accessibility information.	See the Microsoft Accessibility link on the Web Resources page at http://windows.microsoft.com/windows/reskits/webresources.

You can use **Accessibility Options** in Control Panel to customize many accessibility features. However, you can also configure many accessibility features by using **Accessibility Wizard**. For example, you can customize display, keyboard, mouse, and sound options for the user's own particular needs by using either method.

Options for Users with Vision Impairments

Features such as text-to-speech tools, keyboard shortcuts, magnifiers, mouse pointers, color and contrast schemes, and other UI elements are useful to people who are blind or have low vision, colorblindness, tunnel vision, or other vision impairments.

Microsoft Narrator

Narrator is a minimally featured text-to-speech utility included with Windows XP Professional that reads objects on the screen, their properties, and their spatial relationships. You can run Narrator from the **Start** menu or by using Utility Manager. Narrator automatically reads certain information when it changes on the screen. Narrator is always available, and the user can later install alternative screen reading devices or features.

Narrator allows users or administrators to customize the way a device reads screen elements. The **Voice** option allows you to adjust the speed, volume, or pitch of the voice. The **Reading** option allows you to select the pressed keys you want Narrator to read aloud, such as DELETE, ENTER, printable characters, or modifiers. The **Move mouse pointer** option causes the mouse pointer to follow the active object on the screen. The **Announce events on screen** option allows you to configure Narrator to announce new windows, menus, or shortcut menus when it displays them.

Many users with low vision need a text-to-speech utility with a higher functionality for daily use. For a list of other text-to-speech tools, see the Microsoft Accessibility link on the Web Resources page at http://www.microsoft.com/windows /reskits/webresources.

> **Note**   Narrator is a temporary aid and is not intended as a replacement for full-featured text-to-speech utilities that are available from other software companies.

Keyboard Audio Cues

People with vision impairments might not be able to see lights on the keyboard that indicate CAPS LOCK, NUM LOCK, and SCROLL LOCK status. ToggleKeys provides audio cues to indicate whether these keys are active or inactive. If ToggleKeys is on, pressing one of these keys to activate it produces a high-pitched beep. Pressing one of these keys to inactivate it produces a beep that is an octave lower. You can activate ToggleKeys in **Accessibility Options** in Control Panel or select **I have trouble using a keyboard or a mouse** in the **Accessibility Wizard**. You can also use a shortcut key to control ToggleKeys.

To turn ToggleKeys on or off by using a shortcut key

■ Press and then hold down the NUM LOCK key for eight seconds. When Tog-gleKeys turns on, a rising series of beeps plays. When it is off, the sound is a descending series of beeps.

ToggleKeys is also useful for people who accidentally press the CAPS LOCK key instead of the TAB key because it provides immediate feedback. For keyboards that do not have indicator lights for the CAPS LOCK, NUM LOCK, and SCROLL LOCK keys, ToggleKeys provides a method for tracking that status of these keys.

FilterKeys and BounceKeys can both be set to provide audio clues when the user presses a key. You can enable the option **Do you want Windows to beep when it accepts a keystroke?** by selecting the check box in either of these features or by using the appropriate shortcut keys.

Magnifier

Magnifier is a screen enlarger that magnifies a portion of the display to make the screen easier to read for some people. Magnifier displays an enlarged portion of the screen in a separate window. While Magnifier can be helpful for occasional use, many users with low vision need a magnification utility with a higher functionality for daily use.

> **Note**   Magnifier is a limited solution and is not intended as a replacement for the full-featured screen-enlargement utilities that are available from other software companies. For more information about screen enlarging tools, see the Microsoft Accessibility link on the Web Resources page at http://www.microsoft.com/windows/reskits/webresources.

Using Magnifier, you can do the following:

■ Magnify an area of the screen up to nine times the standard display size.

■ Choose to have the magnified area follow the mouse pointer, the keyboard focus, the text editing focus, or any combination of these three.

■ Invert colors for contrast.

■ Resize and relocate the Magnifier display area.

When Magnifier is on, the magnified area is a display only, not an active area. The active focus for the cursor, keyboard, and other input devices is in the unmag-nified area.

To start Magnifier press the WINDOWS LOGO key+U to run Utility Manager or from the **Start** menu, point to **All Programs**, **Accessories**, **Accessibility**, and then click **Magnifier**. If Magnifier is already running, select its button on the taskbar to open the dialog box.

You can use the mouse to resize or reposition the magnification window anywhere within the desktop area. Alternatively, you can reposition the window by using the arrow key. You can also dock the magnification window to the top, bottom, or side of the display. Press ALT+F6 to focus on the magnification window, and then type ALT+SPACEBAR to display the System Menu. Type M to invoke the move feature, and then use the arrow keys to move the magnification window.

Customizing Fonts

Users with low vision might benefit from using larger, more legible fonts in applications and in the user interface. You can change text sizes for Windows messages in **Accessibility Wizard** or Control Panel. Set custom options in **Custom Font Size** by choosing **Other** in the **Font Size** list and then either selecting one of the percentage options in the drop-down list or clicking the ruler and dragging the pointer to specify a font size.

You can add or remove fonts and restrict font sizes by removing all TrueType fonts and leaving only raster fonts. TrueType fonts are device-independent fonts that are stored as outlines and that can be scaled to produce characters in varying sizes. Raster fonts are bitmap images that can provide greater visibility at fixed sizes. Removing fonts does not delete them from the hard disk drive. Users can easily reinstall the fonts for later use. To add or remove fonts, in Control Panel, double-click **Fonts**.

Note Limiting fonts also limits the number of fonts available to applications. This operation should be used with caution because it affects the display of documents on the screen and how they are printed.

To limit the system to a single font

1. Create a new folder on the desktop or hard disk.

2. In **Control Panel**, click **Fonts**.

3. Select all the fonts in the **Fonts** folder, move them to the new folder, and then restart the computer.

   The system font is not listed, so it remains even when you delete all other fonts.

   The font size you specify in Control Panel affects all video adapters on your system. To change font settings for individual window objects, double-click **Display** in Control Panel, and then click the **Appearance** tab. To add a new font, in Control Panel, double-click **Fonts**.

Size and Color Schemes

Windows XP Professional includes a new look and feel—the Windows XP theme—although users can choose the Windows Classic theme instead. The Windows XP theme improves the overall user interface, while the Classic theme provides full flexibility for customization. Users who must configure color schemes can change all aspects of the user interface by using the Windows Classic theme. Using the Windows XP theme limits changes to the size of certain elements. You can choose a theme by using the **Display** Control Panel Option and selecting the **Theme** tab.

In the Windows XP Professional **Accessibility Wizard** and in Control Panel, users can adjust the size and color of most screen elements, such as window text, menus, mouse pointer, fonts, and caption bars. This capability can make the system easier to use and can reduce eyestrain. In **Accessibility Wizard**, users can change icon size, mouse pointer size, and text size.

The following are considerations for adjusting the color settings:

- Settings that display a large number of colors require a large amount of computer processor resources.

- A High Color setting (16-bit) includes more than 65,000 colors. A True Color setting (24-bit) includes more than 16 million colors.

- The monitor and display adapter determine the maximum number of colors that can appear on the screen.

- To change settings for another monitor in a multiple-monitor system, in the **Display Properties** dialog box, select the **Extend My Windows Desktop onto this Monitor** check box to change the settings for the other monitor. You can make color settings for each installed monitor.

To change the border width of windows, including command prompt windows, double-click **Display** in Control Panel, and then click the **Appearance** tab to select the preferred scheme. Users can also resize a window by using the keyboard instead of the mouse, or in **Accessibility Wizard** by selecting **I am blind or have difficulty seeing things on screen**. You can adjust the width of the cursor in **Accessibility Options** by moving the slider bar on the **Display** tab.

High-contrast color schemes can be helpful to users with low vision who require a high degree of contrast between foreground and background objects to distinguish the objects. For example, some users cannot easily read black text on a gray background or text drawn over a picture. By selecting a high-contrast display scheme, users can instruct Windows XP Professional and programs to display information with a high degree of contrast. Activating High Contrast mode selects a color scheme that makes it easier for some users to see screen objects. To choose a high-contrast color scheme, in **Accessibility Options**, on the **Display** tab, click **Settings**, and then choose a scheme from the drop-down list.

In addition, while using the **Magnifier** dialog box, users can temporarily invert the colors of the magnification window or display the screen in high contrast. It can take a few seconds for High Contrast Mode to take effect.

Mouse Pointers

Customized through **Accessibility Wizard** or Control Panel, mouse pointers allow the user to select the most visible pointer. Choices include three sizes and a white or black pointer or an inverted pointer that reacts to screen colors and changes to contrast with the background. You can set the following mouse pointer characteristics:

- Pointer size
- Pointer color
- Speed of the pointer
- Visible trails of pointer movement
- Animation of the pointer

Other options for users who have difficulty seeing the mouse pointer include MouseKeys and Snap To. For more information about MouseKeys, see "Options for Users with Mobility Impairments" later in this appendix. For more information about Snap To, see "Options for Users with Cognitive Disabilities" later in this appendix.

Insertion Point Indicator Blink Rate

You can increase the visibility of the insertion point indicator by changing the rate at which it flashes. You can change the insertion point indicator blink rate by using the **Keyboard** Control Panel option.

Sound Schemes

Users with low vision might benefit from reducing distracting movement on screen. You can prevent animations, videos, and sounds from loading. By using Control Panel, you can assign custom sounds to any event. You can also customize sound schemes by turning sound on or off or adjusting the volume up or down.

Options for Users with Mobility Impairments

Some users are unable to perform certain manual tasks, such as using a mouse or typing two keys at the same time. Others tend to hit multiple keys or bounce their fingers off keys. Mobility impairments include paralysis, repetitive stress injuries, cerebral palsy, erratic motion tremors, quadriplegia, or lack of limbs or fingers. Many users need keyboard and mouse functions adapted to their particular needs, or they rely exclusively on an alternative input device. A large number of assistive technology input devices are available to users, including keyboard filters, voice-input utilities for controlling the computer, on-screen keyboards, smaller or larger keyboards, eye-gaze pointing devices, and sip-and-puff systems that the user operates by breath control. For more information about assistive technology and a catalog of third-party assistive technology products, see the Microsoft Accessibility link on the Web Resources page at http://www.microsoft.com/windows/reskits/webresources.

The following options include some of the Windows XP Professional accessibility features that are useful to people with mobility impairments.

Keyboard Options

Impaired dexterity can make it difficult for a person to use a standard keyboard. However, keyboard filters built into Windows XP Professional compensate somewhat by correcting for erratic motion tremors, slow response time, and similar conditions. Other kinds of keyboard filters include typing aids, such as word prediction and abbreviation expansion tools and add-in spelling checkers.

The following sections describe input devices and features that are different from the standard keyboard. These features include alternative keyboard layouts, keyboard shortcuts, and specialized keyboard filters that operate on the standard keyboard but tailor the behavior of keys to specific accessibility needs.

Note   In most cases, it is not possible to apply keyboard-style behavior corrections to pointing devices, such as the mouse. This limitation might affect the use of the mouse by users with impaired dexterity.

On-Screen Keyboard   Some users have difficulty with both the mouse and the keyboard. However, they might be able to use an on-screen keyboard with another input device, such as a pointing device or a joystick that connects to the serial port. They might be able to use the keyboard space bar as a single-switch device. Using the keyboard space bar as a switching device requires additional assistive technology; contact the switch manufacturer for custom cables and any other requirements.

Users can set up and customize the Windows XP Professional On-Screen Keyboard in **Accessibility Options**. The On-Screen Keyboard can also be run through Utility Manager. Many users with physical disabilities need an alternative keyboard with higher functionality for daily use. For a list of other Windows-based on-screen keyboard tools, see the Microsoft Accessibility link on the Web Resources page at http://www.microsoft.com/windows/reskits/webresources.

Note   The On-Screen Keyboard is a limited solution and not a day-to-day alternative keyboard. Third-party on-screen keyboards provide increased functionality.

Dvorak Keyboard Layout for People Who Type with One Hand or Finger   The Dvorak keyboard makes the most frequently typed characters on a keyboard more accessible to people who have difficulty typing on the standard keyboard layout (known as the QWERTY layout). There are three Dvorak layouts: one for people who use two hands to type, one for people who type with their left hand only, and one for people who type with their right hand only. Dvorak layouts reduce the degree of motion required to type common English text. This feature might help avoid some kinds of repetitive strain injuries that are associated with typing. You can add the Dvorak keyboard to a Windows XP Professional installation during setup or add it later. To configure the Dvorak keyboard, double-click the **Keyboard** icon in Control Panel.

Keyboard Shortcuts

Keyboard shortcuts are keyboard-driven commands that allow a user to navigate and enter commands using just the keyboard—and not the mouse. Keyboard shortcuts are important to users with disabilities, and they cover nearly all categories of disabilities. The Microsoft Accessibility Web site includes a searchable database of keyboard shortcuts for many Microsoft products. For more information, see the Accessibility Web site link on the Web Resources Page at http://www.microsoft.com/windows/reskits/webresources.

By using the ALT and CTRL keys in combination with other keys, a user can navigate and enter commands. Even without configuring accessibility features, the user can use the TAB key in dialog boxes to move the focus and then use the arrow keys to select options in a list. In property sheets that have multiple tabs, the user can press CTRL+TAB to select each property sheet in order from left to right. Or the user can press the TAB key until the focus is on the tab for the current property sheet and then press an arrow key to select the next sheet.

Windows indicates keyboard shortcuts by underlining the shortcut letter on menus and buttons. By default, Windows XP Professional does not underline keyboard navigation indicator letters until the ALT key is pressed. You can override this default and always display the underlines.

To reinstate the underlines for keyboard navigation

■   In **Accessibility Options**, on the **Keyboard** tab, select the **Show extra keyboard help in programs** check box.

For a list of keyboard shortcuts, see Windows XP Professional Help and Support Center. For accessibility-specific keyboard shortcuts, see the Microsoft Accessibility link on the Web Resources page at http://www.microsoft.com/windows/reskits/webresources.

Key Sequences for Quick Activation of Accessibility Options   A type of shortcut key sequence, sometimes called "hot keys," provides quick activation of accessibility features for people who cannot use the computer without accessibility features enabled. Key sequences allow the user to turn on a specific feature temporarily. After the feature is enabled, users can use the Accessibility Wizard or **Accessibility Options** to configure the feature to their own needs or to turn on the feature permanently. The same key sequence turns off the feature.

These key sequences ordinarily do not conflict with keys that programs use. If such a conflict does arise, the user can disable the key sequence and still use the feature during the current session or by using the Accessibility Wizard or **Accessibility Options** to turn on the feature permanently. In a typical installation of Windows XP Professional, the accessibility key sequences are inactive by default to prevent them from conflicting with other programs.

You can also assign key sequences to frequently used programs, documents, or folders, and then use a shortcut key to open the object or make it the active window. To turn on the shortcut key for a feature, in **Accessibility Options**, click **Settings** for the feature, and select the **Use Shortcut** check box. You can also create shortcut keys to start programs from the **Start** menu.

As a precaution against accidental use, if the sound features for StickyKeys are turned on, pressing an accessibility shortcut key causes special tones to sound (a rising tone for activation and a falling tone for deactivation). A confirmation dialog box then appears, which briefly explains the feature and how it is turned on. A user who presses the shortcut key unintentionally can cancel the feature's activation at this time. The confirming dialog box also provides a quick path to more detailed help and to Control Panel settings for the shortcut key feature, in case the user wants to turn off the shortcut key permanently.

To assign a shortcut key to start a program

1. Create a shortcut to the object on the desktop or on the **Start** menu.

2. Display the properties for the shortcut by right-clicking the shortcut icon or name and then clicking **Properties** or by using SHIFT+F10.

3. Click the **Shortcut** tab, and then type the key combination that you want to assign to this object in the **Shortcut Key** box.

When a shortcut is placed on the desktop or on the **Start** menu, the user can press the shortcut key for the program at any time, and Windows XP Professional opens that window. Or, if the program is not running, the shortcut key starts it.

Note   Some keyboard shortcuts might not work if the StickyKeys feature is enabled.

Essential Keyboard Shortcuts   Tables I-3 through I-7 list essential keyboard shortcuts for the user who has difficulty using the mouse or other input methods and must rely on the keyboard to navigate through Windows XP Professional. What the shortcut letter designates might vary in some configurations. In such situations, the user must also use directional arrows, the tab key, or repeat the same letter to arrive at the desired icon. The Microsoft Accessibility Web site includes a searchable database of keyboard shortcuts for many Microsoft products. For more information, see the Microsoft Accessibility link on the Web Resources Page at http://www.microsoft.com/windows/reskits/webresources.

Table I-3   Accessibility Shortcut Keys

Accessibility Feature	Keyboard Shortcut
Switch FilterKeys on or off.	RIGHT SHIFT for 8 seconds
Switch High Contrast on and off.	LEFT ALT+LEFT SHIFT+PRINT SCREEN
Switch MouseKeys on and off.	LEFT ALT+LEFT SHIFT+NUM LOCK
Switch StickyKeys on and off.	SHIFT 5 times
Switch ToggleKeys on and off.	NUM LOCK for 5 seconds
Open Utility Manager.	WINDOWS LOGO key+U

Table I-4   Help Shortcuts

Accessibility Topics in Help	Key Sequence
Display Help and Support Center.	WINDOWS LOGO key, H
Select "Accessibility for People with Disabilities."	TAB repeatedly to topic, ENTER
Enter a topic content area.	ENTER
Select a link.	TAB repeatedly, ENTER
Return to Help table of contents (move between panes).	F6
Close Help.	ALT+SPACEBAR, C

Table I-5   Accessibility Wizard Shortcuts

Accessibility Wizard	Key Sequence
Start Accessibility Wizard.	WINDOWS LOGO key, P, A, RIGHT ARROW, ENTER
Select setting.	UP ARROW, SPACEBAR; or DOWN ARROW, SPACEBAR; or TAB, SPACEBAR for setting
Go to next screen or save settings.	ENTER
Close Accessibility Wizard.	ALT+F4

Table I-6   Magnifier and Narrator Shortcuts

Action	Key Sequence
Start Utility Manager.	WINDOWS LOGO key+U
Start Magnifier.	WINDOWS LOGO key+U, ALT+TAB, down-arrow to Magnifier
Start Narrator.	WINDOWS LOGO key+U, ALT+TAB, down-arrow to Narrator

Table I-7   Control Panel Shortcuts

Control Panel Action	Key Sequence
Go to the **Start** menu.	WINDOWS LOGO key or CTRL+ESC
Go to Control Panel.	WINDOWS LOGO key, C (or if another icon in the **Start** menu begins with C, you might need to use the tab key or directional arrows to reach the icon)
Select a Control Panel option.	Select the first letter of the option name, ENTER. If more than one option starts with the same letter, you might need to use the tab key or directional arrows to reach the correct icon.
Move focus to a tab (if present).	CTRL+TAB
Move focus to a dialog box.	TAB
Display predefined schemes (if present).	DOWN ARROW
Respond to the dialog box query **Save the previous scheme?**	"Y" for "Yes," "N" for "No," or ESC to close the dialog box without saving changes
Check/clear check boxes.	SPACEBAR
Move slider bars right or left.	CTRL+RIGHT ARROW or CTRL+LEFT ARROW
Close window	ALT+F4

StickyKeys for One-Finger or Mouthstick Typing   Many software programs require the user to press two or three keys at a time. For people who type using a single finger or a mouthstick, that process is not possible. StickyKeys allows the user to press one key at a time and instructs Windows to respond as if the keys are pressed simultaneously. StickyKeys is especially useful when a user must press CTRL+ALT+DEL to log on to the computer.

To activate the StickyKeys feature

- In **Control Panel**, in **Accessibility Options**, on the **Keyboard** tab, select the **Use StickyKeys** check box.

– or –

To activate StickyKeys from the keyboard, press SHIFT five times. The following are tips for using StickyKeys:

- When StickyKeys is on, pressing any modifier key (SHIFT, CTRL, WINDOWS LOGO, or ALT) latches that key down until the user presses a key that is not a modifier key. If the StickyKeys sound features are on, you hear a short low-pitched beep and then a high-pitched beep. When the next nonmodifier key is pressed, the modifier key(s) are released.

- Pressing a modifier key twice in a row locks the key down until it is tapped a third time. If the StickyKeys sound features are on, you hear a short low-to-high sound after the first tap and a single high-pitched beep after the second tap. After a modifier key is locked, it stays locked until it is pressed a third time.

- Any and all of the modifier keys (SHIFT, CTRL, WINDOWS LOGO, and ALT) can be latched or locked in combination.

- For shared computers, there is an optional feature to keep other users from being confused when StickyKeys is left on. If the option **Turn StickyKeys Off If Two Keys Are Pressed at Once** is activated and two keys are held down simultaneously, StickyKeys automatically turns off.

- Some people do not like to have keyboard sounds, although others find them useful. To turn feedback sounds on or off, in **Accessibility Options**, on the **Keyboard** tab select the **StickyKeys** check box; then either select the **Make Sounds When Modifier Key Is Pressed** check box to activate the feature or click the check box to clear it if the feature is already activated and you do not want it on.

- To turn off the StickyKeys Locked mode, make sure the **Press Modifier Key Twice to Lock** check box is cleared.

- To turn StickyKeys off, press SHIFT five times. This process triggers a high-to-low series of tones.

- To turn StickyKeys on, also press SHIFT five times. This process triggers a low-to-high series of tones.

FilterKeys for Users with Impaired Manual Dexterity   Windows XP Professional includes keyboard filters such as RepeatKeys and SlowKeys that work separately or in combination to make input easier for users who have difficulty with the keyboard because of slow response time, erratic motion tremors, or a tendency to repeat the keys inadvertently. To configure these keys, in Control Panel, in **Accessibility Options**, on the **Keyboard** tab, under **FilterKeys**, click the **Settings** button. Under **Filter options**, click **Settings**.

FilterKeys can perform the following functions:

- RepeatKeys allows the user to adjust the repeat rate or ignore the key repeat function on the keyboard, which compensates for a tendency to hold a key down too long. Most keyboards allow the user to repeat a key just by holding it down. Although this automatic repeat feature can be convenient for some people, it poses a problem for individuals who cannot lift their fingers off the keyboard quickly. This feature can also compensate for a tendency to press the wrong key accidentally.

- SlowKeys also instructs the computer to disregard keystrokes that are repeated quickly. This allows a user to brush against keys without any effect. By placing a finger on the proper key, the user can hold the key down until the character appears on the screen.

In Control Panel, the **Keyboard** option also allows users to alter character repeat rates.

Note   For RepeatKeys, SlowKeys, or BounceKeys (which ignores repeated keystrokes for users who might accidentally press a key too many times), you must define the acceptance delay, which allows you to adjust the amount of time that you must hold a key down before the computer accepts it.

Another useful FilterKeys feature is the option **Beep When a Key Is Pressed**. If this option is on and any FilterKeys functions are active, you hear a beep when you press a key or when a key repeats. For example, if SlowKeys is active, you hear a sound when a key is pressed and also when the computer accepts the key. This feature can be useful when the keyboard is set to respond differently than usual.

To adjust key repeat delay and speed

1. In **Control Panel**, click **Keyboard**, click the **Speed** tab, and then move the slider bar to adjust keyboard behavior.

2. Do the following:

   - To adjust how long you must hold down a key before it begins repeating, move the **Repeat Delay** slider.

   - To adjust how fast a key repeats when you hold it down, move the **Repeat Rate** slider.

ToggleKeys for Users Who Inadvertently Activate the Lock Keys   ToggleKeys instructs Windows to play a high beep or a low beep when the lock keys NUM LOCK, CAPS LOCK, or SCROLL LOCK are on. This sound signals to the user that one of these keys has been turned on.

Mouse Options

To make the mouse pointer automatically move to the default button (such as **OK**, or **Apply**) in dialog boxes and to reverse the buttons so that the right mouse button is the primary (index finger) button, use the **Mouse** option in Control Panel. Users can adjust other mouse settings, such as pointer speed and acceleration, left-right orientation, size, color, shape, time allowed between clicks, or animation. By selecting **I am blind or have difficulty seeing things on screen** and **I have difficulty using the keyboard or mouse**, users can also set several mouse options in **Accessibility Wizard**.

MouseKeys for Keyboard-only Input   Although Windows XP Professional is designed so that users can perform all actions without a mouse, certain programs might require one. MouseKeys in Control Panel is also useful for graphic artists and others who must position the pointer with great accuracy. A user does not need a mouse to use this feature. With MouseKeys, users can control the mouse pointer with one finger or a mouthstick by using the numeric keypad to move the mouse pointer. In this way, users can click, double-click, and move objects as if they were using the mouse. To use shortcut keys to turn the MouseKeys on or off, select the **Use Shortcut** check box in the **Settings for MouseKeys** dialog box or click this check box to clear it.

To turn on MouseKeys from the keyboard

- Press LEFT ALT+ LEFT SHIFT+NUM LOCK.

When MouseKeys is on, it emits a rising tone if sounds are turned on. If a user is using only one finger or a mouthstick to operate the computer, the easiest way to activate MouseKeys is to first activate StickyKeys by tapping the SHIFT key five times. The user can then press the three keys in sequence rather than simultaneously.

> **Note**   If FilterKeys is active, all the MouseKeys control keys respond according to the setting for FilterKeys.

When MouseKeys is on, use the following keys to move the pointer on the screen:

- On the numeric keypad, press any of the numbered keys immediately surrounding the 5 key (also called the "arrow keys") to move the pointer in the direction indicated by the arrows.

- Use the 5 key on the numeric keypad for a single mouse-button click and the PLUS SIGN (+) key for a double-click.

- To drag and release an object, place the pointer on the object and then press the INSERT key to begin dragging. Move the object to its new location, and then press DELETE to release it.

You can use the NUM LOCK key to toggle the MouseKeys control pad back to the numeric keypad and vice versa. This is especially useful with a portable computer that lacks a separate numeric keypad. On these computer keyboards, the numeric keypad is usually overlaid on top of the standard QWERTY keyboard. For example, if you are using the numeric keypad for number entry before starting MouseKeys, when you toggle out of MouseKeys by using the NUM LOCK key, you can enter numbers with the numeric keypad. If you are using the numeric keypad as a cursor keypad before starting MouseKeys, when you toggle out of MouseKeys by using the NUM LOCK key, you have a cursor keypad.

It can be useful to combine MouseKeys and a physical mouse. For example, you can use the standard mouse to move quickly around the screen and then use MouseKeys to move more precisely. Some people cannot use the standard mouse and simultaneously hold down the mouse button. Such users can use MouseKeys to lock down the currently active mouse button, move the mouse pointer by using MouseKeys or the standard mouse, and then release the mouse button by using MouseKeys.

ClickLock   ClickLock allows you to highlight or drag items on the screen without holding down the mouse button. When ClickLock is enabled, press the mouse button briefly to lock your click, and then highlight or drag an item, and then briefly press the mouse button again to release. To enable ClickLock, in Control Panel, click **Mouse**. On the **Buttons** tab, under **ClickLock**, click **Settings**, and then move the **Settings for ClickLock** slider to adjust how long you need to hold down the mouse button to lock the click.

SerialKeys

SerialKeys is a feature designed for users who have difficulty using the keyboard or the mouse. It allows third-party add-on hardware or software, such as single switch or puff and sip devices to interact with the computer. You can enable SerialKeys from **Accessibility Options**. For more information about using SerialKeys with assistive technology, see "Adding Assistive Technology Products" later in this appendix.

Options for Users with Hearing Impairments

Users who have hearing impairments or who work in a noisy environment can adjust the pitch and timbre of sounds, as well as the volume associated with various on-screen events, to make them easier to distinguish. The sounds are customizable either by using **Accessibility Wizard** or by using Control Panel. Windows XP Professional provides sounds that users can associate with many events. These can be events generated either by Windows XP Professional or by programs. If users have difficulty distinguishing identifying a default sound, such as the beep to signal an inoperative keystroke, they can choose a new sound scheme or design their own scheme to make the sounds easier to identify.

If the computer has a sound card, users can adjust the volume for all of the sounds by using the **Volume Control** property sheet under **Sounds and Audio Devices** in Control Panel. They can also adjust the sound volume by using the speaker icon on the taskbar.

Some users require visual feedback instead of sound. Such users are likely to be interested in SoundSentry and closed captioning. The following features are useful to people who are deaf or hard-of-hearing.

ShowSounds

ShowSounds, in **Accessibility Options**, instructs programs that are closed-caption-enabled to display visual feedback in the form of closed captioning. With Show-Sounds enabled, information that is typically conveyed by sounds is provided visually as well, by the use of text captions, informative icons, or other visual cues.

SoundSentry

This feature for users who are deaf or hard of hearing tells Windows XP Professional to send a visual cue, such as a blinking title bar or screen flash, whenever the system generates a sound. Enabling this feature allows users to see when the computer is generating sounds and to be aware of messages that they might not hear. To enable the SoundSentry feature, in **Accessibility Options** click the **Sound** tab, and then select the User SoundSentry check box. To select a visual cue, select an option from the **Choose the visual warning** drop-down list box.

> **Note**   If you choose to flash the active window's title bar, a visual cue might not be visible if the active window has no title bar. Some displays do not have a flashing border, so there is no visual cue when using this option on such display hardware. This is true of some liquid crystal displays typically found on portable computers.

SoundSentry supports only those sounds the computer's internal speaker generates; it cannot detect sounds that are made using multimedia sound cards. If the computer has a multimedia sound card, you might need to disable this hardware to force the computer's built-in speaker to relay the sounds.

To disable the multimedia sound card

1. In the **Control Panel** option **Sounds and Audio Devices**, click the **Hardware** tab.

2. Select the sound card, and then click **Properties**.

3. On the **Properties** tab, expand **Audio Devices**.

4. Select the sound card, and then click **Properties**.

5. Select the **Do not use audio features on this device** check box.

Users with hearing impairments often rely on indicators, such as lights, to replace sound. If the indicator lights for the locking keys NUM LOCK, CAPS LOCK, or SCROLL LOCK are inactive, it can mean that the user selected the ToggleKeys feature in the **Accessibility Options** property sheet under **Keyboard**. To reactivate the indicator lights, click the **ToggleKeys** check box to clear it.

NetMeeting

Microsoft NetMeeting is a package of features designed for Internet-based conferencing. NetMeeting allows users who are deaf or hard-of-hearing to communicate with others in the room or on the Internet though text messages and graphics sharing. It includes a real-time text-based chat feature that allows two or more users to communicate with other users. The bi-directional communication that NetMeeting provides is faster than that available with a TTY device and allows users to save transcripts of discussions. In addition, NetMeeting allows you to share applications, conduct video conferences, and use an electronic whiteboard to create diagrams or display existing ones.

Options for Users with Cognitive Disabilities

Cognitive disabilities include developmental disabilities, such as Down syndrome; learning disabilities; dyslexia; illiteracy; attention deficit disorder; memory loss; and perceptual difficulties, such as slow response time. In addition to third-party assistive technology, such as voice-input utilities, some built-in Windows XP Professional features can be helpful to people with cognitive disabilities. Examples of such built-in features include AutoCorrect and AutoComplete.

For some users, these features facilitate their work considerably. However, it is advantageous for some users with cognitive disabilities to clear, rather than select options such as AutoComplete or certain sound schemes. Such features can cause distractions, especially if the user is working with a text-to-speech utility. There are two types of AutoComplete that affect use of Windows Explorer and the **Run** box and which might be undesirable for users with certain cognitive disabilities. One is an automatic suggestion, with a drop-down list of Web sites with the same letters the user has typed. The other AutoComplete feature, called Inline AutoComplete, automatically completes a line if the user has typed it before. The first feature is turned on by default, but Inline AutoComplete is not. To change these defaults, perform the following steps.

To disable the site-address AutoComplete feature

1. In **Control Panel**, click **Internet Options.**

2. On the **Content** tab. click **AutoComplete**, and then clear the **Web Addresses** check box.

To activate the inline AutoComplete feature

1. In **Control Panel**, click **Internet Options**.

2. On the **Advanced** tab, select the **Use Inline AutoComplete** check box.

Keyboard Filters

The FilterKeys feature allows users to adjust keyboard response time and ignore accidental pressing of keys. In both **Accessibility Wizard** and Control Panel, users can adjust keyboard response time to instruct Windows XP Professional to ignore accidental pressing of keys and slow response time. FilterKeys includes RepeatKeys and SlowKeys. With RepeatKeys, the user can instruct Windows XP Professional to ignore the automatic repeat feature or to slow down the keyboard repeat rate. SlowKeys requires keys to be held down for a specified period of time before the keystroke is accepted. BounceKeys is a FilterKeys option that instructs Windows XP Professional to ignore keystrokes that are faster than a set period of time.

Keyboard Shortcuts

Other options that are useful to people with cognitive disabilities are shortcut keys and other keyboard shortcuts, such as Quick Launch bar, status indicators on the notification area of the taskbar that show which features are on, and sound options. Sound schemes can help draw attention to, or provide additional feedback for, tasks as the user completes them. For a more extensive list of keyboard shortcuts, see "Options for Users with Mobility Impairments" earlier in this appendix.

SerialKeys

SerialKeys allows third-party add-on hardware or software to interact with the computer. For example, you can use SerialKeys with third-party assistive technology that allows the user to press pictures rather than spelling out full words. You can enable SerialKeys from **Accessibility Options** in Control Panel. For more information about using SerialKeys with add-on hardware or software, see "Adding Assistive Technology" later in this appendix.

Snap To

Snap To is helpful for people who have difficulty finding elements on a screen. The feature automatically moves the pointer to the default button in a dialog box. You can enable Snap To from the **Mouse** Control Panel option.

Options for Users Who Experience Seizures

Certain visual elements, such as flashing images, can adversely affect users with seizure disorders. These can be disabled or adjusted. Users who experience seizures, including those with epilepsy, can adjust screen elements, such as timing, color and contrast, and sound by using Accessibility Wizard or **Accessibility Options**. The range of options in many of these features is expanded in Windows XP Professional.

Timing Patterns

Timing patterns can affect users in many adverse ways. Users who have seizures might be sensitive to screen refresh rates and blinking or flashing images. Users or administrators can also adjust the rate at which most objects flash to select a frequency that is less likely to trigger seizures, or they can prevent images from blinking or flashing at all.

Cursor Blink-Rate Options

Users who have seizures might be sensitive to the blink rate of screen images, such as the cursor. You can use the **Keyboard** option in Control Panel to adjust the rate at which the cursor blinks, or you can prevent it from blinking at all. On the **Speed** tab, move the **Cursor blink rate** slider all the way to the left to prevent the cursor from blinking.

Sound Schemes

Users who have seizures can be affected by specific sounds. Settings in Windows XP Professional can prevent the default loading of animations, videos, and sounds. By using Control Panel, users can also assign custom sounds to any event. The ability to customize sound schemes, whether by turning sound on or off or adjusting the volume up or down, is important for people with various kinds of disabilities as well as for other users.

Color and Contrast Settings

In **Accessibility Options** users can adjust color and contrast settings to make objects on the screen easier to distinguish from one another. New to Windows XP Professional is an expanded spectrum of color schemes, customizable to suit a user's individual needs. For more detailed information about color and contrast settings, see "Options for Users with Vision Impairments" earlier in this appendix.

Adding Assistive Technology Products

Although the accessibility features included with Windows XP Professional provide some functionality for users with special needs, many users with disabilities might need assistive technology. With the use of hardware and software available through independent software vendors (ISVs) and independent hardware vendors (IHVs), collectively known as assistive technology vendors (ATVs), people with disabilities can enhance their use of the Windows XP Professional operating system.

Add-on Assistive Technology

Microsoft works with independent manufacturers to produce compatible software and hardware for users with disabilities. Independent vendors that manufacture specialized assistive technology help people with disabilities to make better use of Windows XP Professional. Products available from third-party vendors are many and varied and make it possible for people with disabilities to use computers. Available products include the following:

- Hardware and software that provide alternatives to the mouse and keyboard, such as the following alternative input devices:

    - Tracking devices. These devices enable users who are unable to use standard input devices, such as a mouse or a keyboard, to generate input by moving their eyes or head.

    - Mouthstick. A wooden dowel held in the mouth that allows a user to activate commands by pressing one key at a time.

    - Single-switch. A device that allows a user to scan or select options or text by generating a signal by using a muscle or other controllable movement.

    - Voice-activation device. A type of speech recognition device that allows users with disabilities to control computers with their voices instead of with a mouse or keyboard.

    - Alternative keyboards, such as on-screen keyboards, or variously sized or shaped keyboards that can be activated with one's feet, elbows, and so on.

- Devices that provide synthesized speech or devices that use Braille printers to print out information from the screen for people who are blind or have difficulty reading.

- Word or phrase prediction software that helps users type more quickly and with fewer keystrokes.

- Closed-captioning devices for users with hearing impairments.

- Devices that enlarge or alter the color of information on the screen.

Finding Compatible Hardware and Software

Contact the third-party assistive technology product manufacturer to find products that are compatible with Windows XP Professional. The manufacturer should also be able to provide information about configuring settings to use with Windows XP Professional. Some add-on utilities depend on file formats and programming interfaces to interpret data accurately to the user. Such dependencies can change with each new operating system. Before you add assistive technology, it is important to perform compatibility testing with the operating system and the applications you plan to use.

Using SerialKeys for Add-on Hardware and Software

The SerialKeys feature is designed for people who are unable to use a standard user input method, such as a keyboard or a mouse. SerialKeys allows an augmentative/communication device to emulate the local keyboard and mouse. Users who can point, but not click, can use pointing devices or Morse-code input systems on these devices. The interface device sends coded command strings through the computer's serial port to specify keystrokes and mouse events, which are then treated as typical keyboard or mouse input. Enable SerialKeys from the **General** tab in **Accessibility Options**.

Microsoft provides a catalog of a wide range of assistive technology products that can be used with Windows XP Professional. Additional information is available about support services and documentation for users who are deaf or hard-of-hearing, and users who have difficulties reading or handling printed materials. This information and the catalog are available from the Microsoft Accessibility link on the Web Resources page at http://www.microsoft.com/windows/reskits/webresources, by voice telephone at 1 +(800) 426-9400, or by writing to the Microsoft Sales Information Center, One Microsoft Way, Redmond, Washington 98052-6399.

Additional Resources

These resources contain additional information and tools related to this appendix.

- The Microsoft Accessibility link on the Web Resources page at http://www.microsoft.com/windows/reskits/webresources.

- "Accessibility" in Windows XP Professional Help and Support Center.

Appendix J

Interoperability Solutions

Microsoft® Windows® XP Professional supports a comprehensive set of protocols and solutions to support cross-platform interoperability in a heterogeneous computing environment. Many of the core standards-based protocols that promote interoperability with non-Microsoft operating systems are built into Windows XP Professional. In addition, Microsoft offers specialized products to support comprehensive interoperability with other computing platforms. Because the additional Microsoft interoperability products may be updated as the corresponding non-Microsoft operating systems are released, this appendix provides an overview of the major Microsoft interoperability products and refers to the up-to-date information on the Microsoft Web site.

Related information

- For more detailed information about Windows® Services for UNIX, see http://www.microsoft.com/windows/sfu/

- To support more comprehensive interoperability between the Windows platform and Novell NetWare, see http://www.microsoft.com/windows2000/sfn/.

- For more detailed information about Microsoft® Host Integration Server 2000, see http://www.microsoft.com/hiserver/.

- For more detailed information about Microsoft interoperability solutions for Macintosh computers, see http://www.microsoft.com/mac/.

Overview of Microsoft Interoperability Solutions for Windows XP Professional

The Microsoft Windows XP Professional operating system includes standards-based protocols and services to promote interoperability with non-Microsoft platforms. Microsoft also offers products to support a more comprehensive level of cross-platform interoperability between Windows and UNIX and Linux operating systems, IBM Host Systems, Novell NetWare, and Apple Macintosh computers.

Where applicable, the Microsoft interoperability solutions are designed to provide four layers of cross-platform interoperability:

- **Network interoperability.**   Provides basic network connectivity across heterogeneous platforms. Standards-based network protocols, including terminal access protocols and print service protocols, enable basic network connectivity between Windows XP Professional and non-Microsoft platforms. Network interoperability protocols also provide the basis for more comprehensive data, application, and management interoperability solutions.

- **Data interoperability.**   Allows users and applications to access and query information stored in both structured and unstructured storage engines on multiple platforms. For example, Windows XP Professional users who work in a heterogeneous computing environment might need to access data on NetWare file servers, UNIX Network File System (NFS) hosts, IBM mainframes, or IBM AS/400 systems.

- **Application interoperability.**   Allows Windows-based applications and multi-tier Web applications to interoperate with existing applications and business logic across heterogeneous application platforms. For example, a Windows-based application might need to participate in transactions with systems that use IBM Customer Information Control System (CICS), Advanced Program-to-Program Communications (APPC) protocols, or standards-based Web services.

- **Management interoperability.**   Allows administrators to manage computers, user accounts, security settings, and system events across multiple platforms. For example, an administrator might need to synchronize user accounts and passwords for Windows, UNIX and Linux operating systems, Novell NetWare, and IBM host systems.

Table J-1 summarizes the Microsoft interoperability solutions that support Windows XP Professional interoperability at each interoperability layer for each of the major computing platforms:

Table J-1   Microsoft Interoperability Solutions for Windows XP Professional

Platform	Network	Data	Application	Management
Interoperability with UNIX	Connect to UNIX TCP/IP services through Windows XP TCP/IP protocols	Access UNIX NFS file services through Windows Services for UNIX	Run Telnet terminal sessions, support UNIX application programming interfaces (APIs), port applications with Windows Services for UNIX	Run UNIX shell utilities and synchronize passwords through Windows Services for UNIX
Interoperability with Novell NetWare	Connect to NetWare Servers through Windows XP NWLink protocols	Access NetWare files through Windows XP Client Service for NetWare	Not applicable	Access NetWare bindery-based tools through Windows XP Client Service for NetWare and directory synchronization tools through Microsoft Services for NetWare
Interoperability with IBM host systems	Support secure connections to IBM mainframes and AS/400 systems through standard Web services or through Microsoft Host Integration Server Systems Network Architecture (SNA) network services	Transfer files and access IBM host data through Microsoft Host Integration Server	Support terminal access, integrated transactions and messaging, and Web-to-Host integration through Microsoft Host Integration Server	Map user accounts, synchronize passwords, provide single sign-on, monitor host events and SNA or Advanced Peer-to-Peer Networking (APPN) resources through Microsoft Host Integration Server
Interoperability with Apple Macintosh systems	Provide secure network connectivity and remote access through Windows Server Services for Macintosh	Share files and printers through Windows Server Services for Macintosh	Share application data between Microsoft® Office for Windows and Microsoft® Office for Macintosh.	Administer Services for Macintosh through a remote connection to the Windows Server Microsoft Management Console (MMC).

These Microsoft interoperability solutions are described in more detail in the following sections.

Interoperability with UNIX

Microsoft's primary interoperability solution for UNIX is Microsoft® Windows® Services for UNIX. At the time of this writing, the current version is Microsoft Windows Services for UNIX 3.0.

Microsoft Windows Services for UNIX provides a comprehensive set of services, tools, and applications that allow you to integrate Windows-based computers, including Windows XP Professional-based computers, into your existing UNIX environment. Windows Services for UNIX supports flexible file sharing between Windows-based and UNIX-based computers. Additionally, Windows network administrators can use Windows Services for UNIX to manage Network Information Service (NIS) domains.

Windows Services for UNIX 3.0 includes the following components:

- **Interix.** A comprehensive implementation of a POSIX-compliant environment that includes the C and Korn command shells and over 350 utilities. These utilities enable you to leverage your existing scripts and UNIX knowledge to administer Windows computers and run UNIX applications directly on Windows computers.

> **Note**   Some of the Interix utilities are covered by the GNU General Public License (GPL), and you may choose not to install these GPL utilities. Note, however, that if you do not install these utilities, the overall functionality of Interix will be limited.

- **Interix Software Development Kit.**   Using the tools, libraries, and documentation provided in the Interix Software Development Kit (SDK), you can port your UNIX applications to run on Windows computers through the Interix subsystem. Some of the SDK tools are covered by the GPL; you may choose not to install these tools.

- **User Name Mapping.**   This component provides centralized mapping between Windows user accounts and UNIX accounts for Client for NFS, Server for NFS, Gateway for NFS, and Interix. With User Name Mapping, Windows and UNIX users can access files on each other's computers transparently and without compromising security. User Name Mapping can use UNIX accounts from Personal Computer Network File System (PCNFS) servers or Network Information System (NIS) servers.

- **Client for NFS.**   With Client for NFS, Windows-based computers can map an exported NFS share to a drive letter. This lets users access files on the file system as though they were on a local disk drive. They can also access NFS shares using Universal Naming Convention (UNC) names. Users can receive UNIX authentication credentials through User Name Mapping or from a PCNFS server (either UNIX–based PCNFS daemon (PCNFSD) or Server for PCNFS running on a Microsoft® Windows NT®–based or Microsoft® Windows® 2000–based computer).

- **Server for NFS.** The administrator of a Windows computer can use Server for NFS to share directories as NFS exported file systems, which makes it possible for UNIX-based clients to mount a shared directory just as they would an exported file system located on a UNIX server. User-level security is maintained because, in conjunction with Server for NFS Authentication, User Name Mapping maps the UNIX client's user identifier (UID) and group identifier (GID) to existing Windows user accounts. This ensures that UNIX clients are given appropriate access to files on Windows-based servers.

- **Gateway for NFS.** With Gateway for NFS, Windows users can access exported file systems on NFS without running special client software on their computers. The Windows server running Gateway for NFS mounts exported file systems on UNIX-based NFS servers and then shares those mounted file systems as Windows networking shared folders. Gateway for NFS relies on User Name Mapping to provide the appropriate UID and GID for the Windows user, which allows transparent access to UNIX-based files without requiring users to log on to Windows and UNIX systems separately.

Note   Gateway for NFS runs only on Windows Server servers. It does not run on Windows XP Professional–based computers.

- **Server for PCNFS.** This component is similar to a PCNFS daemon (PCNFSD) running on a UNIX server. Windows users running PCNFS or Windows Services for UNIX Client for NFS version 1.0 software on their computers can access NFS file systems by providing the required UNIX user name and password when they attempt to access an NFS file.

- **Server for NIS.** This component completely integrates UNIX Network Information System (NIS) networks with Windows Active Directory™. Windows Services for UNIX includes a wizard that a Windows domain administrator can use to export NIS domain maps to Active Directory entries. Once this is done, an Active Directory domain controller running Server for NIS becomes the master server for the NIS domain.

Note   Server for NIS runs only on Windows Server servers. It does not run on Windows XP Professional–based computers.

- **Password Synchronization.**   This feature automatically changes a user's password on the UNIX network when the user changes his or her Windows password, or vice versa. This allows users to maintain just one password for both networks.

- **Telnet Client and Telnet Server.**   Windows users are given command-line access to UNIX systems through the popular Telnet terminal protocol. By taking advantage of Windows authentication, users of Telnet Client can log on directly to computers running Telnet Server, eliminating the need to send unencrypted passwords over the network.

Note   Telnet Server runs only on Windows Server servers. It does not run on Windows XP Professional–based computers.

- **The Windows-based Remote Shell service.**   Users of remote computers use the Windows-based Remote Shell service to carry out commands on the server.

- **The Windows-based Cron service.**   Runs commands scheduled using the crontab utility.

- **ActiveState ActivePerl.**   Allows Perl scripts to run on a Windows computer.

For more detailed information about Windows Services for UNIX, see http://www.microsoft.com/windows/sfu/.

Interoperability with Novell NetWare

Windows XP Professional uses the NWLink protocol and Client Service for NetWare to provide connectivity between Windows XP Professional and servers running Novell Directory Services (NDS) or Netware bindery-based servers by using the following components:

- **NWLink Network Protocols.**   If a NetWare network is running Internetwork Packet Exchange/Sequenced Packet Exchange (IPX/SPX) instead of Transmission Control Protocol/Internet Protocol (TCP/IP), Windows XP Professional provides NWLink IPX/SPX/NetBIOS–Compatible Transport Protocol (NWLink). NWLink is the Microsoft implementation of the IPX/SPX protocol.

- **Client Service for NetWare.**   Allows the Windows XP Professional client to access NetWare file, print, and directory services. Both Novell and Microsoft provide a client service for these purposes. Each client service includes a redirector component that enables packet forwarding for the differing file and print service protocols.

> **Note**   To support more comprehensive interoperability between the Windows platform and Novell NetWare, Microsoft provides a separate, standalone Windows Server-based interoperability product, Microsoft Services for NetWare. The utilities available in Windows® Services For NetWare (SFN) version 5.0 include Microsoft Directory Synchronization Services (MSDSS), Microsoft File Migration Utility (MSFMU), and File and Print Services for NetWare (v.5). For more detailed information, see http://www.microsoft.com /windows2000/sfn/.

Interoperability with IBM Host Systems

Windows XP Professional uses TCP/IP as its primary networking protocol suite. IBM host systems, primarily IBM mainframes and AS/400 systems, increasingly use TCP/IP, but many installations still use Systems Network Architecture (SNA). In order for Windows XP Professional–based computers to communicate with IBM host systems, either a gateway device to interpret the two different network protocols or a common network protocol is required.

Microsoft Host Integration Server

To connect to IBM hosts by using a gateway device, you must have a local area network (LAN) protocol on Windows XP Professional, typically TCP/IP, and a gateway that provides the translation between the LAN protocol and the IBM host protocol or data stream. Microsoft® Host Integration Server 2000 is a gateway that provides the translation service to establish network connectivity with IBM host systems.

After SNA-based or TCP/IP-based network connectivity is established, the advanced host integration features of Host Integration Server 2000 allow Windows users to gain secure access to IBM host data, applications, and network services without leaving the familiar Windows desktop or Web browser interface.

The following list describes these host integration services and how they apply to each layer of the Windows 2000 interoperability model.

- **Network integration.**   Provides cross-platform network connectivity and protocols, security integration, and single sign-on between clients, including Windows clients, and IBM host systems. The single sign-on feature allows users to log on once for access to multiple servers, systems, or applications.

- **Data access.** Enables transparent file transfer services, universal data access technologies such as OLE DB and open database connectivity (ODBC), and host data replication.

- **Application interoperability.** Provides terminal access, integrated transaction services, and Web-to-host integration.

- **Network management integration.** Network management integration provides integration between Windows XP network management services and IBM NetView–based management services.

Host Integration Server Client Software Components

When Host Integration Server 2000 is implemented as a gateway to an IBM host, Windows XP Professional uses Host Integration Server 2000 client software to establish connectivity. The Host Integration Server 2000 client software (either Administrator's Client or End-User Client) includes terminal emulation programs. For connecting to an IBM mainframe using the SNA 3270 data stream, the 3270 Client is provided. For connecting to an IBM AS/400 system using the SNA 5250 data stream, the 5250 Client is provided.

Administrators can install Host Integration Server 2000 client software on Windows XP Professional–based computers. Host Integration Server 2000 Administrator Client allows you to use the interface in SNA Manager—or the snacfg command—to read and change the configuration file, start and stop services and connections, or reset SNA Logical Units (LUs). Table J-2 describes the components you can select during the installation of Host Integration Server 2000 client software.

Table J-2 Host Integration Server Client Software Components

Client Component	Description
SNA Manager	Allows you to manage Host Integration Server 2000 from Windows XP Professional. Users who have network administration privileges can use SNA Manager to configure a Host Integration Server 2000 computer, LUs, LU pools, users, Host Print Service, Shared Folders Gateway Service, APPC modes, CPI-C symbolic names, and host security domains.
3270 Client	Allows access to an IBM host on an SNA network.
5250 Client	Allows access to IBM AS/400 systems.
COM Transaction Integrator for CICS and IMS (COMTI)	Provides access to IBM Customer Information Control System (CICS) and Information Management System (IMS) programs that run on Multiple Virtual Storage (MVS) mainframes.
Microsoft OLE DB Provider for AS/400 and VSAM	Allows record-level access to mainframe and AS/400 files.

Table J-2   Host Integration Server Client Software Components

Client Component	Description
APPC File Transfer Protocol (AFTP) Client	Allows client computers to connect to the AFTP service to share files across platforms.
Host Account Manager	Connects users to all servers and domains to which they have access with a single password.
Host Integration Server 2000 Remote Access Service	Enables an administrator to create a virtual LAN connection between Windows Server systems across an existing SNA network without having redundant LAN-to-LAN networks or having to install dial-up connections at each site.
Host Connectivity SDK	Provides access to the Software Development Kit (SDK), making it possible for software developers to create specialized Host Integration Server 2000 applications.
SNA NetView Alerter	Allows the IBM NetView reporting system to send alerts and other messages between a host and the computers that connect to it.

For more detailed information about Host Integration Server 2000, see http://www.microsoft.com/hiserver/.

Interoperability with Apple Macintosh Systems

Microsoft provides a comprehensive set of products and services to support interoperability between Windows operating systems, including Windows XP Professional, and Apple Macintosh computers. These include:

- Microsoft® Windows Server™ 2003 Services for Macintosh
- Microsoft® Office for Apple Macintosh computers
- Microsoft® Internet applications for Apple Macintosh computers

Windows Server 2003 Services for Macintosh

Services for Macintosh provides server-based interoperability services to allow Windows clients, including Windows XP Professional clients, and Apple Macintosh clients to share files and printers. The three primary components of Services for Macintosh are:

- **AppleTalk Phase 2 Protocol Suite.**   A set of network protocols on which AppleTalk network architecture is based.
- **File Services for Macintosh.**   Allows users of Macintosh computers to store, access, and share files on servers running Services for Macintosh. This service

supports AppleTalk Filing Protocol (AFP) over TCP/IP support. This enables earlier Macintosh clients to access shared resources through the faster TCP/IP protocol. With this feature, you can completely remove the AppleTalk protocol from your network and Macintosh clients will still have the ability to access shared volumes.

- **Print Services for Macintosh.**   Enables Macintosh clients to send and spool documents to printers attached to a computer running Windows NT Server; Windows 2000 Server; or an operating system in the Windows Server 2003 family, excluding 64-bit editions.

Microsoft Office for Apple Macintosh Operating Systems

Microsoft provides a full set of Microsoft Office applications for Macintosh computers. At the time of this writing, the most recent release of Microsoft Office for Macintosh is Microsoft® Office v. X for Mac. Because Microsoft Office v. X uses the same file format as Office XP, Office 2000, and Office 97 on the Windows platform, as well as Office 2001 for Mac and Office 98 Macintosh Edition, users can share files and data easily across multiple versions of Windows and Macintosh-based computers.

Microsoft Office v. X for Mac includes the following applications, each of which are also available as separate applications outside of the Microsoft Office v. X for Mac suite:

- **Microsoft® Word X.**   A word processing and Web authoring program designed specifically for Mac OS X.

- **Microsoft® Excel X.**   A spreadsheet program for evaluating, calculating, and analyzing data, as well as creating charts and reports.

- **Microsoft® PowerPoint® X.**   A business tool used to create dynamic presentations.

- **Microsoft® Entourage™ X.**   An e-mail and personal information management program designed specifically for Mac OS X. Entourage X combines e-mail, calendar, address book, and tasks into one program and is tightly integrated with the other Microsoft Office v. X applications.

Microsoft Internet Applications for Apple Macintosh Computers

Microsoft provides the following Macintosh applications to support Web browsing, Internet-based e-mail, and instant messaging:

- **Microsoft® Internet Explore for Mac.**   Web browsing software in two versions; Internet Explorer 5 for Mac OS X and Internet Explorer 5 for Mac OS 8.1 to 9.x.

- **Microsoft® Outlook® and Outlook® Express for Mac.**   Microsoft Outlook 2001 for Mac is an e-mail and collaboration client for Macintosh computers accessing Microsoft Exchange Server–based e-mail services. Microsoft Outlook Express for Mac is a free Internet-based e-mail and newsgroup client and contact management system for Mac OS v. 8.1 and 9.x. Mac OS X computers use Microsoft Entourage X.

- **MSN® Messenger for Mac.**   Free instant messaging software for Mac OS X allows users to exchange instant messaging with Windows-based computers, other Mac users, and mobile devices.

For more detailed information about Microsoft interoperability solutions for Macintosh computers, see http://www.microsoft.com/mac/.

Glossary

Symbols

3270 A class of IBM Systems Network Architecture terminal and related protocol used to communicate with IBM mainframe host systems.

3DES An encrypting algorithm that processes each data block three times, using a unique key each time. 3DES is much more difficult to break than straight DES. It is the most secure of the DES combinations, and is therefore slower in performance. See also Data Encryption Standard (DES).

5250 A class of IBM Systems Network Architecture terminal and related protocol used to communicate with AS/400 host systems.

802.1p A protocol that supports the mapping of Resource Reservation Protocol (RSVP) signals to Layer 2 signals by using 802.1p priority markings to enable the prioritization of traffic across Layer 2 devices, such as switches, on a network segment. IEEE 802 refers to the Layer 2 technology used by LANs including the data-link layer and the media access control layer.

8mm cassette A tape cartridge format used for data backups, similar to that used for some video cameras except that the tape is rated for data storage. The capacity is 5 GB or more of (optionally compressed) data.

A

AC-3 The coding system used by Dolby Digital. A standard for high quality digital audio that is used for the sound portion of video stored in digital format.

Accelerated Graphics Port (AGP) A type of expansion slot that is solely for video cards. Designed by Intel, AGP is a dedicated bus that provides fast, high-quality video and graphics performance.

access control entry (ACE) An entry in an object's discretionary access control list (DACL) that grants permissions to a user or group. An ACE is also an entry in an object's system access control list (SACL) that specifies the security events to be audited for a user or group. See also access control list (ACL); access mask; discretionary access control list (DACL); object; permission; security descriptor; system access control list (SACL).

access control list (ACL) A list of security protections that apply to an entire object, a set of the object's properties, or an individual property of an object. There are two types of access control lists: discretionary and system. See also access control entry (ACE); discretionary access control list (DACL); object; security descriptor; system access control list (SACL).

access mask   A 32-bit value that specifies the rights that are allowed or denied in an access control entry (ACE) of an access control list (ACL). An access mask is also used to request access rights when an object is opened. See also access control entry (ACE).

access token   A data structure that contains the security identifier (SID) for a security principal, SIDs for the groups that the security principal belongs to, and a list of the security principal's privileges (also called *user rights*) on the local computer. See also security ID (SID); security principal.

accessibility   The quality of a system incorporating hardware or software to engage a flexible, customizable user interface, alternative input and output methods, and greater exposure of screen elements to make the computer usable by people with cognitive, hearing, physical, or visual disabilities.

Accessibility Wizard   An interactive tool that makes it easier to set up commonly used accessibility features by specifying options by type of disability, rather than by numeric value changes.

ACPI   See definition for Advanced Configuration and Power Interface (ACPI).

Active Directory   The directory service that stores information about objects on a network and makes this information available to users and network administrators. Active Directory gives network users access to permitted resources anywhere on the network using a single logon process. It provides network administrators with an intuitive, hierarchical view of the network and a single point of administration for all network objects. See also directory; directory service.

active partition   A partition from which an x86-based computer starts up. The active partition must be a primary partition on a basic disk. If you use Windows exclusively, the active partition can be the same as the system volume. See also basic disk; primary partition; system partition; system volume.

active volume   The volume from which the computer starts up. The active volume must be a simple volume on a dynamic disk. You cannot mark an existing dynamic volume as the active volume, but you can upgrade a basic disk containing the active partition to a dynamic disk. After the disk is upgraded to dynamic, the partition becomes a simple volume that is active. See also active partition; basic disk; dynamic disk; dynamic volume; simple volume.

ActiveX   A set of technologies that allows software components to interact with one another in a networked environment, regardless of the language in which the components were created.

Advanced Configuration and Power Interface (ACPI)   An open industry specification that defines power management on a wide range of mobile, desktop, and server computers and peripherals. ACPI is the foundation for the OnNow industry initiative that allows system manufacturers to deliver computers that start at the touch of a keyboard. ACPI design is essential to take full advantage of power management and Plug and Play. See also Plug and Play.

Advanced Power Management (APM)   A software interface (designed by Microsoft and Intel) between hardware-specific power management software (such as that located in a system BIOS) and an operating system power management driver. See also basic input/output system (BIOS).

advertisement   In Systems Management Server, a notification sent by the site server to the client access points (CAPs) specifying that a software distribution program is available for clients to use. In Windows 2000 and Windows XP, the Software Installation snap-in generates an application advertisement script and stores this script in the appropriate locations in Active Directory and the Group Policy object.

allocation unit   The smallest amount of disk space that can be allocated to hold a file. All file systems used by Windows organize hard disks based on allocation units. The smaller the allocation unit size, the more efficiently a disk stores information. If you do not specify an allocation unit size when formatting the disk, Windows picks default sizes based on the size of the volume. These default sizes are selected to reduce the amount of space that is lost and the amount of fragmentation on the volume. An allocation unit is also called a cluster. See also file system; volume.

American Standard Code for Information Interchange (ASCII)   A standard single-byte character encoding scheme used for text-based data. ASCII uses designated 7-bit or 8-bit number combinations to represent either 128 or 256 possible characters. Standard ASCII uses 7 bits to represent all uppercase and lowercase letters, the numbers 0 through 9, punctuation marks, and special control characters used in U.S. English. Most current x86-based systems support the use of extended (or "high") ASCII. Extended ASCII allows the eighth bit of each character to identify an additional 128 special symbol characters, foreign-language letters, and graphic symbols. See also Unicode.

answer file   A text file that you can use to provide automated input for unattended installation of Windows XP and Windows 2000. This input includes parameters to answer the questions included in Setup for specific installations. In some cases, you can use this text file to provide input to wizards, such as the Active Directory Installation Wizard, which is used to add Active Directory to Windows 2000 Server through Setup. The default answer file for Setup is known as Unattend.txt. See also Active Directory.

API   See definition for application programming interface (API).

APM   See definition for Advanced Power Management (APM).

application media pool   A data repository that determines which media can be accessed by which applications and that sets the policies for that media. There can be any number of application media pools in a Removable Storage system. Applications create application media pools. See also Removable Storage.

application programming interface (API)   A set of routines that an application uses to request and carry out lower-level services performed by a computer's operating system. These routines usually carry out maintenance tasks such as managing files and displaying information.

assistive technology   System extensions, programs, devices, and tools added to a computer to make it more accessible to users with disabilities.

asynchronous communication   A form of data transmission in which information is sent and received at irregular intervals, one character at a time. Because data is received at irregular intervals, the receiving modem must be signaled to let it know when the data bits of a character begin and end. This is done by means of start and stop bits.

Asynchronous Transfer Mode (ATM)   A high-speed, connection-oriented protocol used to transport many different types of network traffic. ATM packages data in a 53-byte, fixed-length cell that can be switched quickly between logical connections on a network. See also protocol.

ATM   See definition for Asynchronous Transfer Mode (ATM).

attribute   For files, information that indicates whether a file is read-only, hidden, ready for archiving (backing up), compressed, or encrypted, and whether the file contents should be indexed for fast file searching. See also object; schema.

auditing   The process that tracks the activities of users by recording selected types of events in the security log of a server or a workstation.

authentication   The process for verifying that an entity or object is who or what it claims to be. Examples include confirming the source and integrity of information, such as verifying a digital signature or verifying the identity of a user or computer. See also confidentiality; cryptography; integrity; Kerberos V5 authentication protocol; nonrepudiation; NTLM authentication protocol; smart card; trust relationship.

Authentication Header (AH)   A header that provides authentication, integrity, and anti-replay for the entire packet (the IP header and the data payload carried in the packet).

authoritative   For DNS, describes a DNS server hosting a zone, or a zone containing a name or record. When a DNS server is configured to host a zone, it is said to be authoritative for names that do exist or could exist within that zone. A DNS server is allowed to respond authoritatively to queries for domain names for which it is authoritative. A zone is said to be authoritative for a name if the name exists or could exist within a zone, and it is said to be authoritiative for a record if the owner name of the record exists or could exist within a zone. See also DNS server; domain name; Domain Name System (DNS).

automated installation   An unattended setup using one or more of several methods such as Remote Installation Services, bootable CD, and Sysprep. See also Remote Installation Services (RIS); Sysprep.

automatic caching   A method of automatically storing network files on a user's hard disk drive whenever a file is open so the files can be accessed when the user is not connected to the network.

Automatic Private IP Addressing (APIPA)   A feature of Windows XP TCP/IP that automatically configures a unique IP address from the range 169.254.0.1 through 169.254.255.254 and a subnet mask of 255.255.0.0 when the TCP/IP protocol is configured for dynamic addressing and a Dynamic Host Configuration Protocol (DHCP) is not available. See also Dynamic Host Configuration Protocol (DHCP); IP address; Transmission Control Protocol/Internet Protocol (TCP/IP).

available state   A state in which media can be allocated for use by applications.

B

B-tree   A tree structure for storing database indexes. Each node in the tree contains a sorted list of key values and links that correspond to ranges of key values between the listed values. To find a specific data record given its key value, the program reads the first node, or root, from the disk and compares the desired key with the keys in the node to select a subrange of key values to search. It repeats the process with the node indicated by the corresponding link. At the lowest level, the links indicate the data records. The database system can thus rapidly search through the levels of the tree structure to find the simple index entries that contain the location of the desired records or rows.

backup   A duplicate copy of a program, a disk, or data, made either for archiving purposes or for safeguarding valuable files from loss in case the active copy is damaged or destroyed. Some application programs automatically make backup copies of data files, maintaining both the current version and the preceding version.

backup operator   A type of local or global group that contains the user rights you need to back up and restore files and folders. Members of the Backup Operators group can back up and restore files and folders regardless of ownership, permissions, encryption, or auditing settings. See also auditing; global group; local group; user rights.

backup types   A type that determines which data is backed up and how it is backed up. There are five backup types: copy, daily, differential, incremental, and normal. See also copy backup; daily backup; differential backup; incremental backup; normal backup.

bad block   A disk sector that can no longer be used for data storage, usually due to media damage or imperfections. Also known as bad sector.

bad sector   A disk sector that can no longer be used for data storage, usually due to media damage or imperfections. Also known as bad block.

bandwidth   In analog communications, the difference between the highest and lowest frequencies in a spcific range. For example, an analog telephone line accommodates a bandwidth of 3,000 hertz (Hz), the difference between the lowest (300 Hz) and highest (3,300 Hz) frequencies it can carry. In digital communications, bandwidth is expressed in bits per second (bps).

bar code   A machine-readable label that identifies objects, such as physical media.

base file record   The first file record in the master file table (MFT) for a file that has multiple file records. The base file record is the record to which the file's file reference corresponds. See also master file table (MFT).

baseline   A range of measurements derived from performance monitoring that represents acceptable performance under typical operating conditions.

basic disk   A physical disk that can be accessed by MS-DOS and all Windows-based operating systems. Basic disks can contain up to four primary partitions, or three primary partitions and an extended partition with multiple logical drives. If you want to create partitions that span multiple disks, you must first convert the basic disk to a dynamic disk using Disk Management or the Diskpart.exe command-line utility. See also dynamic disk; extended partition; logical drive; MS-DOS (Microsoft Disk Operating System); primary partition.

basic input/output system (BIOS)   On x86-based computers, the set of essential software routines that test hardware at startup, start the operating system, and support the transfer of data among hardware devices. The BIOS is stored in read-only memory (ROM) so that it can be executed when you turn on the computer. Although critical to performance, the BIOS is usually invisible to computer users. See also Extensible Firmware Interface (EFI); read-only memory (ROM).

basic volume   A primary partition or logical drive that resides on a basic disk. See also basic disk; logical drive; primary partition.

batch program   An ASCII (unformatted text) file that contains one or more operating system commands. A batch program's file name has a .cmd or .bat extension. When you type the file name at the command prompt, or when the batch program is run from another program, its commands are processed sequentially. Batch programs are also called *batch files*. See also American Standard Code for Information Interchange (ASCII); logon script.

bidirectional communication   Communication that occurs in two directions simultaneously. Bidirectional communication is useful in printing where jobs can be sent and printer status can be returned at the same time.

binding   A process by which software components and layers are linked together. When a network component is installed, the binding relationships and dependencies for the components are established. Binding allows components to communicate with each other.

binding order   The sequence in which software components, network protocols, and network adapters are linked together. When a network component is installed, the binding relationships and dependencies for the components are established.

BIOS   See definition for basic input/output system (BIOS).

BIOS parameter block (BPB)   A series of fields containing data on disk size, geometry variables, and the physical parameters of the volume. The BPB is located within the boot sector.

Boot Information Negotiation Layer (BINL) service   A service that runs on the server running Windows 2000 Server that acts on client boot requests.

boot sector   A critical disk structure for starting your computer, located at sector 1 of each volume or floppy disk. It contains executable code and data that is required by the code, including information used by the file system to access the volume. The boot sector is created when you format the volume.

boot volume   The volume that contains the Windows operating system and its support files. The boot volume can be, but does not have to be, the same as the system volume. See also system volume; volume.

bootable CD   An automated installation method that runs Setup from a CD-ROM. This method is useful for computers at remote sites with slow links and no local IT department. See also automated installation.

bootstrap loader   A program that is run automatically when a computer is turned on, or booted. After first performing a few basic hardware tests, the bootstrap loader loads and passes control to a larger loader program, which typically then loads the operating system. The bootstrap loader typically resides in the computer's read-only memory (ROM). See also read-only memory (ROM).

bottleneck   A condition, usually involving a hardware resource, that causes the entire system to perform poorly.

BounceKeys   A keyboard filter that assists users whose fingers bounce on the keys when pressing or releasing them.

bound trap   In programming, a problem in which a set of conditions exceeds a permitted range of values that causes the microprocessor to stop what it is doing and handle the situation in a separate routine.

Bourne shell   A UNIX command processor developed by Steven Bourne.

browsing   The process of creating and maintaining an up-to-date list of computers and resources on a network or part of a network by one or more designated computers running the Computer Browser service.

C

cable modem   A device that enables a broadband connection to the Internet by using cable television infrastructure. Access speeds vary greatly, with a maximum throughput of 10 megabits per second (Mbps).

cache   For DNS and WINS, a local information store of resource records for recently resolved names of remote hosts. Typically, the cache is built dynamically as the computer queries and resolves names. It also helps optimize the time required to resolve queried names. See also cache file; naming service; resource record (RR).

cache file   A file used by the Domain Name System (DNS) server to preload its names cache when the service is started. Also known as the root hints file because DNS uses resource records stored in this file to help locate root servers that provide referral to authoritative servers for remote names. For Windows DNS servers, the cache file is named Cache.dns and is located in the %SystemRoot%\System32\Dns folder. See also authoritative; cache; Domain Name System (DNS); systemroot.

caching   The process of temporarily storing recently used data values in a special pool in memory for quicker subsequent access. For DNS, typically the ability of the DNS server to store information learned about the DNS namespace during the resolution of DNS queries. (For example, the DNS server can cache DNS records received from other DNS servers.) Caching is also available through the DNS Client service as a way for DNS clients to keep a cache of information learned during recent queries. See also caching resolver; DNS server; Domain Name System (DNS).

caching resolver   A client-side DNS name resolution service that performs caching of recently learned DNS domain name information. The caching resolver service provides system-wide access to DNS-aware programs for resource records obtained from DNS servers during processing of name queries. Cached data is used for a limited period of time and aged according to the active Time-to-Live (TTL) value. You can set the TTL individually for each resource record (RR). Otherwise, it defaults to the minimum TTL set in the SOA RR for the zone. See also cache; caching; expire interval; resolver; resource record (RR); Time to Live (TTL).

callback number   The number that a remote access server uses to call back a user. This number can be preset by the administrator or specified by the user at the time of each call, depending on how the administrator configures the user's callback options. The callback number should be the number of the phone line to which the user's modem is connected. See also remote access server.

CardBus   A 32-bit PC Card.

cartridge   A unit of media of a certain type, such as 8mm tape, magnetic disk, optical disk, or CD-ROM, used by Removable Storage. See also Removable Storage.

central processing unit (CPU)   The part of a computer that has the ability to retrieve, interpret, and execute instructions and to transfer information to and from other resources over the computer's main data-transfer path, the bus. By definition, the CPU is the chip that functions as the "brain" of a computer.

certificate   A digital document that is commonly used for authentication and secure exchange of information on open networks, such as the Internet, extranets, and intranets. A certificate securely binds a public key to the entity that holds the corresponding private key. Certificates are digitally signed by the issuing certification authority and can be issued for a user, a computer, or a service. The most widely accepted format for certificates is defined by the ITU-T X.509 version 3 international standard. See also certification authority (CA); International Telecommunication Union - Telecommunication [Standardization Sector] (ITU-T); private key.

Certificate Services   A software service that issues certificates for a particular certification authority (CA). It provides customizable services for issuing and managing certificates for the enterprise. Certificates can be used to provide authentication support, including secure e-mail, Web-based authentication, and smart card authentication. See also authentication; certificate; certification authority (CA).

certificate template   A Windows construct that prespecifies format and content of certificates based on their intended usage. When requesting a certificate from a Windows enterprise certification authority (CA), certificate requestors are, depending on their access rights, able to select from a variety of certificate types that are based on certificate templates, such as *User* and *Code Signing*. See also certificate; certification authority (CA).

certification authority (CA)   An entity responsible for establishing and vouching for the authenticity of public keys belonging to users (end entities) or other certification authorities. Activities of a certification authority can include binding public keys to distinguished names through signed certificates, managing certificate serial numbers, and certificate revocation. See also certificate.

Challenge Handshake Authentication Protocol (CHAP)   A challenge-response authentication protocol for PPP connections documented in RFC 1994 that uses the industry-standard Message Digest 5 (MD5) one-way encryption scheme to hash the response to a challenge issued by the remote access server. See also Point-to-Point Protocol (PPP).

change journal   A feature new to Windows 2000 that tracks changes to NTFS volumes, including additions, deletions, and modifications. The change journal exists on the volume as a sparse file. See also NTFS file system; volume.

changer   The robotic element of an online library unit.

child object   An object that resides in another object. A child object implies relation. For example, a file is a child object that resides in a folder, which is the parent object. See also object; parent object.

ciphertext   Text that has been encrypted using an encryption key. Ciphertext is meaningless to anyone who does not have the decryption key. See also decryption; encryption; encryption key; plaintext.

client   Any computer or program connecting to, or requesting the services of, another computer or program. Client can also refer to the software that enables the computer or program to establish the connection.

For a local area network (LAN) or the Internet, a computer that uses shared network resources provided by another computer (called a server). See also server.

cluster   In data storage, the smallest amount of disk space that can be allocated to hold a file. All file systems used by Windows organize hard disks based on clusters, which consist of one or more contiguous sectors. The smaller the cluster size, the more efficiently a disk stores information. If no cluster size is specified during formatting, Windows picks defaults based on the size of the volume. These defaults are selected to reduce the amount of space that is lost and the amount of fragmentation on the volume. A cluster is also called an allocation unit.

In computer networking, a group of independent computers that work together to provide a common set of services and present a single-system image to clients. The use of a cluster enhances the availability of the services and the scalability and manageability of the operating system that provides the services. See also client; file system; volume.

cluster disk   A disk on a shared bus connected to the cluster nodes, which all the cluster nodes can access (though not at the same time).

cluster remapping   A recovery technique used when NTFS detects a bad sector. NTFS dynamically replaces the cluster containing the bad sector and allocates a new cluster for the data. If the error occurs during a read, NTFS returns a read error to the calling program, and the data is lost. If the error occurs during a write, NTFS writes the data to the new cluster, and no data is lost. See also NTFS file system.

code page   A means of providing support for character sets and keyboard layouts for different countries or regions. A code page is a table that relates the binary character codes used by a program to keys on the keyboard or to characters on the display.

codec   Hardware that can convert audio or video signals between analog and digital forms (coder/decoder); hardware or software that can compress and uncompress audio or video data (compression/decompression); or the combination of coder/decoder and compression/decompression. Generally, a codec compresses uncompressed digital data so that the data uses less memory.

COM   See definition for Component Object Model (COM).

COM port   See definition for communication port.

Common Internet File System (CIFS)   A protocol and a corresponding API used by application programs to request higher level application services. CIFS was formerly known as *Server Message Block (SMB)*.

communication port   A port on a computer that allows asynchronous communication of one byte at a time. A communication port is also called a serial port. See also asynchronous communication.

Compact Disc File System (CDFS)   A 32-bit protected-mode file system that controls access to the contents of CD-ROM drives.

compact disc-recordable (CD-R)   A type of CD-ROM that can be written on a CD recorder and read on a CD-ROM drive.

complementary metal-oxide semiconductor (CMOS)   The battery-packed memory that stores information, such as disk types and amount of memory, used to start the computer.

Component Object Model (COM)   An object-based programming model designed to promote software interoperability; it allows two or more applications or components to easily cooperate with one another, even if they were written by different vendors, at different times, in different programming languages, or if they are running on different computers running different operating systems. Object linking and embedding (OLE) technology and ActiveX are both built on top of COM. See also ActiveX; object linking and embedding (OLE).

confidentiality   A basic security function of cryptography. Confidentiality provides assurance that only authorized users can read or use confidential or secret information. Without confidentiality, anyone with network access can use readily available tools to eavesdrop on network traffic and intercept valuable proprietary information. For example, an Internet Protocol security service that ensures a message is disclosed only to intended recipients by encrypting the data. See also authentication; cryptography; integrity; non-repudiation.

console tree   The left pane in Microsoft Management Console (MMC) that displays the items contained in the console. By default it is the left pane of a console window, but it can be hidden. The items in the console tree and their hierarchical organization determine the capabilities of a console. See also Microsoft Management Console (MMC).

container object   An object that can logically contain other objects. For example, a folder is a container object. See also noncontainer object; object.

copy backup   A backup that copies all selected files but does not mark each file as having been backed up (in other words, the archive attribute is not cleared). Copying is useful if you want to back up files between normal and incremental backups because copying does not affect these other backup operations. See also daily backup; differential backup; incremental backup; normal backup.

CPU   See definition for central processing unit (CPU).

credentials   A set of information that includes identification and proof of identification that is used to gain access to local and network resources. Examples of credentials are user names and passwords, smart cards, and certificates.

CryptoAPI   An application programming interface (API) that is provided as part of Microsoft Windows. CryptoAPI provides a set of functions that allows applications to encrypt or digitally sign data in a flexible manner while providing protection for the user's sensitive private key data. Actual cryptographic operations are performed by independent modules known as cryptographic service providers (CSPs). See also application programming interface (API); cryptographic service provider (CSP); private key.

cryptographic service provider (CSP)   The code that performs authentication, encoding, and encryption services that Windows-based applications access through CryptoAPI. A CSP is responsible for creating keys, destroying them, and using them to perform a variety of cryptographic operations. Each CSP provides a different implementation of the CryptoAPI. Some provide stronger cryptographic algorithms, while others contain hardware components, such as smart cards. See also CryptoAPI; smart card.

cryptography   The processes, art, and science of keeping messages and data secure. Cryptography is used to enable and ensure confidentiality, data integrity, authentication (entity and data origin), and nonrepudiation. See also authentication; confidentiality; integrity; nonrepudiation.

cylinder   The set of tracks that are at the same head position on a hard disk. Cylinder numbers start at 0, with cylinder 0 at the outer edge of the platters. A cylinder is approximately 8 megabytes. See also head; track.

D

daily backup   A backup that copies all selected files that have been modified the day the daily backup is performed. The backed-up files are not marked as having been backed up (in other words, the archive attribute is not cleared). See also copy backup; differential backup; incremental backup; normal backup.

data confidentiality   A service provided by cryptographic technology to ensure that data can be read only by authorized users or programs. In a network, data confidentiality ensures that data cannot be read by intruders. Windows 2000 and Windows XP Professional use access control mechanisms and encryption, such as DES, 3DES, and RSA encryption algorithms, to ensure data confidentiality. See also 3DES; cryptography; Data Encryption Standard (DES); RSA.

Data Encryption Standard (DES)   An encryption algorithm that uses a 56-bit key, and maps a 64-bit input block to a 64-bit output block. The key appears to be a 64-bit key, but one bit in each of the 8 bytes is used for odd parity, resulting in 56 bits of usable key.

data integrity   A service provided by cryptographic technology that ensures data has not been modified. In a network environment, data integrity allows the receiver of a message to verify that data has not been modified in transit. Windows 2000 and Windows XP Professional use access control mechanisms and cryptography, such as RSA public-key signing and shared symmetric key one-way hash algorithms, to ensure data integrity. See also cryptography.

data packet   A unit of information transmitted as a whole from one device to another on a network.

data-link layer   A layer that packages raw bits from the physical layer into frames (logical, structured packets for data). This layer is responsible for transferring frames from one computer to another, without errors. After sending a frame, the data-link layer waits for an acknowledgment from the receiving computer.

deallocate   To return media to the available state after they have been used by an application.

decommissioned state   A state that indicates that media have reached their allocation maximum.

decryption   The process of making encrypted data readable again by converting ciphertext to plaintext. See also ciphertext; encryption; plaintext.

default gateway   A configuration item for the TCP/IP protocol that is the IP address of a directly reachable IP router. Configuring a default gateway creates a default route in the IP routing table.

defragmentation   The process of rewriting parts of a file to contiguous sectors on a hard disk to increase the speed of access and retrieval. See also fragmentation.

denial-of-service attack   An attack in which an attacker exploits a weakness or a design limitation of a network service to overload or halt the service, so that the service is not available for use. This type of attack is typically launched to prevent other users from using a network service such as a Web server or a file server.

desktop   The on-screen work area on which windows, icons, menus, and dialog boxes appear.

destination directory   The directory (or folder) to which files are copied or moved. See also source directory.

device driver   A program that allows a specific device, such as a modem, network adapter, or printer, to communicate with the operating system. Although a device might be installed on your system, Windows cannot use the device until you have installed and configured the appropriate driver.

If a device is listed in the Hardware Compatibility List (HCL), a driver is usually included with Windows. Device drivers load automatically (for all enabled devices) when a computer is started, and thereafter run invisibly. See also Hardware Compatibility List (HCL).

Device Manager   An administrative tool that can be used to manage the devices on your computer. Use Device Manager to view and change device properties, update device drivers, configure device settings, and remove devices.

device tree   A hierarchical tree that contains the devices configured on a computer.

DHCP   See definition for Dynamic Host Configuration Protocol (DHCP).

DHCP service   A service that enables a computer to function as a DHCP server and configure DHCP-enabled clients on a network. DHCP runs on a server, enabling the automatic, centralized management of IP addresses and other TCP/IP configuration settings for network clients.

dial-up connection   The connection to your network if you are using a device that uses the telephone network. This includes modems with a standard phone line, ISDN cards with high-speed ISDN lines, or X.25 networks.

If you are a typical user, you might have one or two dial-up connections, for example, to the Internet and to your corporate network. In a more complex server situation, multiple network modem connections might be used to implement advanced routing.

differential backup   A backup that copies files created or changed since the last normal or incremental backup. It does not mark files as having been backed up (in other words, the archive attribute is not cleared). If you are performing a combination of normal and differential backups, restoring files and folders requires that you have the last normal as well as the last differential backup. See also copy backup; daily backup; incremental backup; normal backup.

differential data   Saved copies of changed data that can be applied to an original volume to generate a volume shadow copy. See also volume; volume shadow copy.

digital audio tape (DAT)   A magnetic medium for recording and storing digital audio data.

digital certificate   An electronic certification issued by certification authorities that shows where a program comes from and proves that the installation package has not been altered. Administrators should sign their code with a digital certificate if planning to distribute an Internet Explorer package over the Internet. See also certification authority (CA).

digital linear tape (DLT)   A magnetic medium for backing up data. DLT can transfer data faster than many other types of tape media.

digital signature   A means for originators of a message, file, or other digitally encoded information to bind their identity to the information. The process of digitally signing information entails transforming the information, as well as some secret information held by the sender, into a tag called a signature. Digital signatures are used in public key environments, and they provide nonrepudiation and integrity services. See also public key cryptography; timestamp.

digital subscriber line (DSL)   A special communication line that uses modulation technology to maximize the amount of data that can be sent over copper wires. DSL is used for connections from telephone switching stations to a subscriber rather than between switching stations.

digital video disc (DVD)   A type of optical disc storage technology. A digital video disc (DVD) looks like a CD-ROM disc, but it can store greater amounts of data. DVDs are often used to store full-length movies and other multimedia content that requires large amounts of storage space. See also DVD decoder; DVD drive.

direct hosting   For Microsoft networking, the sending of messages directly over the IPX protocol without the use of NetBIOS. While direct hosting may be more efficient, a direct hosting client can connect only to a direct hosting server. Windows XP Professional does not support direct hosting. See also Internetwork Packet Exchange (IPX); network basic input/output system (NetBIOS); NWLink.

direct memory access (DMA)   Memory access that does not involve the microprocessor. DMA is frequently used for data transfer directly between memory and a peripheral device such as a disk drive. See also hardware configuration.

directory   An information source that contains information about users, computer files, or other objects. In a file system, a directory stores information about files. In a distributed computing environment (such as a Windows domain), the directory stores information about objects such as printers, fax servers, applications, databases, and other users. See also domain.

directory service   Both the directory information source and the service that makes the information available and usable. A directory service enables the user to find an object when given any one of its attributes. See also Active Directory; directory.

disable   To make a device nonfunctional. For example, if you disable a device in a hardware configuration, you cannot use the device when your computer uses that hardware configuration. Disabling a device frees the resources that were allocated to the device. See also hardware configuration.

discretionary access control list (DACL)   The part of an object's security descriptor that grants or denies specific users and groups permission to access the object. Only the owner of an object can change permissions granted or denied in a DACL; thus, access to the object is at the owner's discretion. See also access control entry (ACE); object; security descriptor; security group; system access control list (SACL).

disk bottleneck   A condition that occurs when disk performance is reduced to the extent that overall system performance is affected.

disk quota   The maximum amount of disk space available to a user.

dismount   To remove a removable tape or disc from a drive. See also library; mount.

Distributed File System (DFS)   A service that allows system administrators to organize distributed network shares into a logical namespace, enabling users to access files without specifying their physical location and providing load sharing across network shares.

distribution folder   The folder created on the Windows 2000-based distribution server to contain the Setup files.

DMA   See definition for direct memory access (DMA).

DNS   See definition for Domain Name System (DNS).

DNS client   A client computer that queries Domain Name System (DNS) servers in an attempt to resolve DNS domain names. DNS clients maintain a temporary cache of resolved DNS domain names. See also DNS server; Domain Name System (DNS).

DNS dynamic update protocol   An updated specification to the DNS standard that permits hosts that store name information in DNS to dynamically register and update their records in zones maintained by DNS servers that can accept and process dynamic update messages. See also DNS; DNS server.

DNS server   A server that maintains information about a portion of the Domain Name System (DNS) database and that responds to and resolves DNS queries. See also DNS client; Domain Name System (DNS).

DNS zone   In a DNS database, a zone is a contiguous portion of the DNS tree that is administered as a single separate entity by a DNS server. The zone contains resource records for all the names within the zone.

domain   In Active Directory, a collection of computers defined by the administrator. These computers share a common directory database, security policies, and security relationships with other domains.

In DNS, any tree or subtree within the DNS namespace. Although the names for DNS domains often correspond to Active Directory domains, DNS domains should not be confused with Active Directory domains. See also Active Directory; Domain Name System (DNS).

domain controller   In an Active Directory forest, a server that contains a writable copy of the Active Directory database, participates in Active Directory replication, and controls access to network resources. Administrators can manage user accounts, network access, shared resources, site topology, and other directory objects from any domain controller in the forest. See also Active Directory; authentication; directory; shared resource.

domain DFS   An implementation of DFS in which DFS topological information is stored in Active Directory. Because this information is made available on multiple domain controllers in the domain, domain DFS provides fault-tolerance for any distributed file system in the domain. See also fault tolerance.

domain local group   A security or distribution group that can contain universal groups, global groups, other domain local groups from its own domain, and accounts from any domain in the forest. Domain local security groups can be granted rights and permissions on resources that reside only in the same domain where the domain local group is located. See also domain tree; forest; global group; security group; universal group.

domain name   The name given by an administrator to a collection of networked computers that share a common directory. Part of the Domain Name System (DNS) naming structure, domain names consist of a sequence of name labels separated by periods. See also domain; Domain Name System (DNS).

Domain Name System (DNS)   A hierarchical, distributed database that contains mappings of DNS domain names to various types of data, such as IP addresses. DNS enables the location of computers and services by user-friendly names, and it also enables the discovery of other information stored in the database. See also domain; IP address; Transmission Control Protocol/Internet Protocol (TCP/IP).

domain tree   In DNS, the inverted hierarchical tree structure that is used to index domain names. Domain trees are similar in purpose and concept to the directory trees used by computer filing systems for disk storage. For example, when numerous files are stored on disk, directories can be used to organize the files into logical collections. When a domain tree has one or more branches, each branch can organize domain names used in the namespace into logical collections.

In Active Directory, a hierarchical structure of one or more domains, connected by transitive, bidirectional trusts, that forms a contiguous namespace. Multiple domain trees can belong to the same forest. See also Active Directory; domain; domain name; Domain Name System (DNS); forest.

dual boot   A computer configuration that can start two different operating systems. See also multiple boot; startup environment.

DVD decoder   A hardware or software component that allows a digital video disc (DVD) drive to display movies on your computer screen. See also digital video disc (DVD); DVD drive; hardware decoder; software decoder.

DVD drive   A disk storage device that uses digital video disc (DVD) technology. A DVD drive reads both CD-ROM and DVDs; however, you must have a DVD decoder to display DVD movies on your computer screen. See also digital video disc (DVD); DVD decoder.

Dvorak keyboard   An alternative keyboard with a layout that makes the most frequently typed characters more accessible to people who have difficulty typing on the standard QWERTY layout.

dynamic disk   A physical disk that can be accessed only by Windows 2000 and Windows XP. Dynamic disks provide features that basic disks do not, such as support for volumes that span multiple disks. Dynamic disks use a hidden database to track information about dynamic volumes on the disk and other dynamic disks in the computer. You convert basic disks to dynamic by using the Disk Management snap-in or the DiskPart command-line tool. When you convert a basic disk to dynamic, all existing basic volumes become dynamic volumes. See also active volume; basic disk; basic volume; dynamic volume; partition; volume.

Dynamic Host Configuration Protocol (DHCP)   A TCP/IP service protocol that offers dynamic leased configuration of host IP addresses and distributes other configuration parameters to eligible network clients. DHCP provides safe, reliable, and simple TCP/IP network configuration, prevents address conflicts, and helps conserve the use of client IP addresses on the network.

DHCP uses a client/server model where the DHCP server maintains centralized management of IP addresses that are used on the network. DHCP-supporting clients can then request and obtain lease of an IP address from a DHCP server as part of their network boot process. See also IP address; Transmission Control Protocol/Internet Protocol (TCP/IP).

dynamic volume   A volume that resides on a dynamic disk. Windows supports five types of dynamic volumes: simple, spanned, striped, mirrored, and RAID-5. A dynamic volume is formatted by using a file system, such as FAT or NTFS, and has a drive letter assigned to it. See also basic disk; basic volume; dynamic disk; mirrored volume; RAID-5 volume; simple volume; spanned volume; striped volume; volume.

dynamic-link library (DLL)   An operating system feature that allows executable routines (generally serving a specific function or set of functions) to be stored separately as files with .dll extensions. These routines are loaded only when needed by the program that calls them.

E

EAP   See definition for Extensible Authentication Protocol (EAP).

EFI system partition   On Itanium-based computers, a portion on a GUID partition table (GPT) disk that is formatted with the FAT file system and contains the files necessary to start the computer. Every Itanium-based computer must have at least one GPT disk with an EFI system partition. The EFI system partition serves the same purpose as the system volume found on *x*86-based computers. See also Extensible Firmware Interface (EFI); GUID partition table (GPT); Microsoft Reserved (MSR) partition.

Encapsulating Security Payload (ESP)   An IPSec protocol that provides confidentiality, in addition to authentication, integrity, and anti-replay. ESP can be used alone, in combination with AH, or nested with the Layer Two Tunneling Protocol (L2TP). ESP does not normally sign the entire packet unless it is being tunneled. Ordinarily, just the data payload is protected, not the IP header. See also authentication; Authentication Header (AH); integrity; Internet Protocol security (IPSec); Layer Two Tunneling Protocol (L2TP).

Encrypting File System (EFS)   A feature in this version of Windows that enables users to encrypt files and folders on an NTFS volume disk to keep them safe from access by intruders. See also NTFS file system.

encryption   The process of disguising a message or data in such a way as to hide its substance. See also public key encryption.

encryption key   A bit string that is used in conjunction with an encryption algorithm to encrypt and decrypt data. See also private key; symmetric key.

environment variable   A string consisting of environment information, such as a drive, path, or file name, associated with a symbolic name that can be used by Windows. You use System in Control Panel or the **set** command from the command prompt to define environment variables. See also variable.

Ethernet   An IEEE 802.3 standard for contention networks. Ethernet uses a bus or star topology and relies on the form of access known as Carrier Sense Multiple Access with Collision Detection (CSMA/DC) to regulate communication line traffic. Network nodes are linked by coaxial cable, fiber-optic cable, or by twisted-pair wiring. Data is transmitted in variable-length frames containing delivery and control information and up to 1,500 bytes of data. The Ethernet standard provides for baseband transmission at 10 megabits (10 million bits) per second.

exabyte   Approximately one quintillion bytes, or one billion billion bytes.

expire interval   For DNS, the number of seconds that DNS servers operating as secondary masters for a zone will use to determine if zone data should be expired when the zone is not refreshed and renewed. See also DNS server; Domain Name System (DNS).

export   In Network File System (NFS), to make a file system available by a server to a client for mounting. See also Network File System (NFS).

Extended Industry Standard Architecture (EISA)   A 32-bit bus standard introduced in 1988 by a consortium of nine computer-industry companies. EISA maintains compatibility with the earlier Industry Standard Architecture (ISA) but provides for additional features. See also Industry Standard Architecture (ISA).

extended partition   A type of partition that you can create only on basic master boot record (MBR) disks. Extended partitions are useful if you want to create more than four volumes on a basic MBR disk. Unlike primary partitions, you do not format an extended partition with a file system and then assign a drive letter to it. Instead, you create one or more logical drives within the extended partition. After you create a logical drive, you format it and assign it a drive letter. An MBR disk can have up to four primary partitions, or three primary partitions, one extended partition, and multiple logical drives. See also basic disk; logical drive; master boot record (MBR); partition; primary partition; unallocated space; volume.

Extensible Authentication Protocol (EAP)   An extension to the Point-to-Point Protocol (PPP) that allows for arbitrary authentication mechanisms to be employed for the validation of a PPP connection. See also Point-to-Point Protocol (PPP).

Extensible Firmware Interface (EFI)   In computers with the Intel Itanium processor, the interface between a computer's firmware, hardware, and the operating system. The Extensible Firmware Interface (EFI) defines a new partition style called GUID partition table (GPT). EFI serves the same purpose for Itanium-based computers as the BIOS found in x86-based computers. However, it has expanded capabilities that provide a consistent way to start any compatible operating system and an easy way to add EFI drivers for new bootable devices without the need to update the computer's firmware. See also basic input/output system (BIOS); GUID partition table (GPT).

Extensible Markup Language (XML)   A meta-markup language that provides a format for describing structured data. This facilitates more precise declarations of content and more meaningful search results across multiple platforms. In addition, XML enables a new generation of Web-based data viewing and manipulation applications.

F

FAT32   A derivative of the file allocation table (FAT) file system. FAT32 supports smaller cluster sizes and larger volumes than FAT, which results in more efficient space allocation on FAT32 volumes. See also file allocation table (FAT).

fault tolerance   The ability of computer hardware or software to ensure data integrity when hardware failures occur. Fault tolerant features appear in many server operating systems and include mirrored volumes, RAID-5 volumes, and server clusters. See also cluster; mirrored volume; RAID-5 volume.

FDDI   See definition for Fiber Distributed Data Interface (FDDI).

Fiber Distributed Data Interface (FDDI)   A type of network media designed for use with fiber-optic cabling.

file allocation table (FAT)   A file system used by MS-DOS and other Windows operating systems to organize and manage files. The file allocation table (FAT) is a data structure that Windows creates when you format a volume by using the FAT or FAT32 file systems. Windows stores information about each file in the FAT so that it can retrieve the file later. See also FAT32; file system; NTFS file system.

file record   The row in the master file table (MFT) that corresponds to a particular disk file. The file record is identified by its file reference.

file system   In an operating system, the overall structure in which files are named, stored, and organized. NTFS, FAT, and FAT32 are types of file systems. See also FAT32; NTFS file system.

file system cache   An area of physical memory that holds frequently used pages. It allows applications and services to locate pages rapidly and reduces disk activity.

File Transfer Protocol (FTP)   A member of the TCP/IP suite of protocols, used to copy files between two computers on the Internet. Both computers must support their respective FTP roles: one must be an FTP client and the other an FTP server. See also Transmission Control Protocol/Internet Protocol (TCP/IP).

filter   For Indexing Service, software that extracts content and property values from a document in order to index them.

For IPSec, a specification of IP traffic that provides the ability to trigger security negotiations for a communication based on the source, destination, and type of IP traffic.

FilterKeys   A keyboard feature that instructs your keyboard to ignore brief or repeated keystrokes. You can also adjust the keyboard repeat rate, which is the rate at which a key repeats when you hold it down. See also ToggleKeys.

firewall   A combination of hardware and software that provides a security system, usually to prevent unauthorized access from outside to an internal network or intranet. A firewall prevents direct communication between network and external computers by routing communication through a proxy server outside of the network. The proxy server determines whether it is safe to let a file pass through to the network. A firewall is also called a *security-edge gateway.*

Firewire   See definition for IEEE 1394.

Folder Redirection   A Group Policy option that allows you to redirect designated folders to the network.

font   A graphic design applied to a collection of numbers, symbols, and characters. A font describes a certain typeface, along with other qualities such as size, spacing, and pitch. See also OpenType fonts; PostScript fonts; screen font; Type 1 fonts.

forest   A collection of one or more Active Directory domain trees that share a common schema, configuration, and global catalog and are linked with two-way transitive trusts. See also domain; domain tree; schema.

fragmentation   The scattering of parts of the same disk file over different areas of the disk. Fragmentation occurs as files on a disk are deleted and new files are added. It slows disk access and degrades the overall performance of disk operations, although usually not severely. See also defragmentation.

free media pool   A logical collection of unused data-storage media that can be used by applications or other media pools. When media are no longer needed by an application, they are returned to a free media pool so that they can be used again. See also media pool; Removable Storage.

free space   Available space that you use to create logical drives within an extended partition. See also extended partition; logical drive; unallocated space.

G

gatekeeper   A server that uses a directory to perform name-to-IP address translation, admission control, and call management services in H.323 conferencing. See also H.323.

gateway   A device connected to multiple physical TCP/IP networks capable of routing or delivering IP packets between them. A gateway translates between different transport protocols or data formats (for example, IPX and IP) and is generally added to a network primarily for its translation ability.

In the context of interoperating with Novell NetWare networks, a gateway acts as a bridge between the server message block (SMB) protocol used by Windows networks and the NetWare Core Protocol (NCP) used by NetWare networks. A gateway is also called an *IP router.*

global group   A security or distribution group that can contain users, groups, and computers from its own domain as members. Global security groups can be granted rights and permissions on resources in any domain in its forest.

Global groups cannot be created or maintained on computers running Windows XP Professional. However, for Windows XP Professional-based computers that participate in a domain, domain global groups can be granted rights and permissions at those workstations and can become members of local groups at those workstations. See also group; local group; permission; user account.

globally unique identifier (GUID)   A 16-byte value generated from the unique identifier on a device, the current date and time, and a sequence number. A GUID is used to identify a particular device or component.

GPT   See definition for GUID partition table (GPT).

GPT disk   A disk that uses the GUID partition table (GPT) partition style. A partition style is the method that Windows XP uses to organize partitions on the disk. The GPT partition style supports volumes up to 18 exabytes and 128 partitions per disk. Only Itanium-based computers can use GPT disks. See also GUID partition table (GPT).

Graphical Identification and Authentication (GINA)   A DLL loaded during the Windows 2000 Winlogon process, which displays the standard logon dialog box and collects and processes user logon data for verification. See also dynamic-link library (DLL).

graphical user interface (GUI)   A display format, like that of Windows, that represents a program's functions with graphic images such as buttons and icons. GUIs allow a user to perform operations and make choices by pointing and clicking with a mouse.

group   A collection of users, computers, contacts, and other groups. Groups can be used as security or as e-mail distribution collections. Distribution groups are used only for e-mail. Security groups are used both to grant access to resources and as e-mail distribution lists. See also domain; global group; local group.

group memberships   The groups to which a user account belongs. Permissions and rights granted to a group are also provided to its members. In most cases, the actions a user can perform in Windows are determined by the group memberships of the user account to which the user is logged on. See also group; user account.

Group Policy   The Microsoft Management Console (MMC) snap-in that is used to edit Group Policy objects.

Group Policy object   A collection of Group Policy settings. Group Policy objects are essentially the documents created by the Group Policy snap-in, a Windows tool. Group Policy objects are stored at the domain level, and they affect users and computers contained in sites, domains, and organizational units. In addition, each Windows computer has exactly one group of settings stored locally, called the local Group Policy object. See also Group Policy; object.

GUI mode   The portion of Setup that uses a graphical user interface (GUI).

GUID partition table (GPT)   A disk-partitioning scheme that is used by the Extensible Firmware Interface (EFI) in Itanium-based computers. GPT offers more advantages than master boot record (MBR) partitioning because it allows up to 128 partitions per disk, provides support for volumes up to 18 exabytes in size, allows primary and backup partition tables for redundancy, and supports unique disk and partition IDs (GUIDs). See also Extensible Firmware Interface (EFI); globally unique identifier (GUID); master boot record (MBR).

H

H.323   The ITU-T standard for multimedia communications over networks that do not provide a guaranteed quality of service (QoS). This standard provides specifications for workstations, devices, and services to carry real-time video, audio, and data or any combination of these elements. See also International Telecommunication Union - Telecommunication [Standardization Sector] (ITU-T); Quality of Service (QoS).

hardware abstraction layer (HAL)   A thin layer of software provided by the hardware manufacturer that hides, or abstracts, hardware differences from higher layers of the operating system. By means of the filter provided by the HAL, different types of hardware look alike to the rest of the operating system. This allows the operating system to be portable from one hardware platform to another. The HAL also provides routines that allow a single device driver to support the same device on all platforms.

Hardware Compatibility List (HCL)   A hardware list that Microsoft compiles for a specific product. The Windows HCL, which is posted on the Web, lists the hardware devices and computer systems that are compatible with specific versions of Windows.

hardware configuration   Resource settings that have been allocated for a specific device. Each device on your computer has a hardware configuration, which can consist of interrupt request (IRQ) lines, DMA, an I/O port, or memory address settings. See also direct memory access (DMA); input/output (I/O) port.

hardware decoder   A type of digital video disc (DVD) decoder that allows a DVD drive to display movies on your computer screen. A hardware decoder uses both software and hardware to display movies. See also DVD decoder; DVD drive; software decoder.

hardware malfunction message   A character-based, full-screen error message displayed on a blue background. It indicates that the microprocessor detected a hardware error condition from which the system cannot recover.

head   The mechanism that reads data from and writes data to a hard disk. Hard disks use one head for each side of each platter. The heads are attached to a common head-movement area, so that all heads move in unison. The heads are always positioned over the same logical track on each side of each platter. See also track.

high byte   The byte containing the most significant bits (bits 8 through 15) in a 2-byte grouping representing a 16-bit (bits 0 through 15) value.

hop   In data communications, one segment of the path between routers on a geographically dispersed network. A hop is comparable to one "leg" of a journey that includes intervening stops between the starting point and the destination. The distance between each of those stops (routers) is a communications hop.

Hosts file   A local text file in the same format as the 4.3 Berkeley Software Distribution (BSD) UNIX /etc/hosts file. This file maps host names to IP addresses, and it is stored in the \%Systemroot%\System32\Drivers\Etc folder. See also systemroot.

HTML   See definition for Hypertext Markup Language (HTML).

HTML+TIME   A feature in Microsoft Internet Explorer 5 that adds timing and media synchronization support to HTML pages. Using a few Extensible Markup Language (XML)-based elements and attributes, you can add images, video, and sounds to an HTML page, and synchronize them with HTML text elements over a specified amount of time. In short, you can use HTML+TIME technology to quickly and easily create multimedia-rich, interactive presentations, with little or no scripting.

HTTP   See definition for Hypertext Transfer Protocol (HTTP).

hubbed mode   A mode in which the ARP/MARS provides ATM addresses to requesting clients in the form of a multicast server (MCS) list value. In this mode, the ARP/MARS acts as a multicast server, providing active forwarding of all multicast and broadcast traffic destined for IP addresses contained within the ranges specified in the list. See also Asynchronous Transfer Mode (ATM); IP address.

Human Interface Device (HID)   A firmware specification that is a new standard for input and output devices such as drawing tablets, keyboards, USB speakers, and other specialized devices designed to improve accessibility. See also universal serial bus (USB).

Hypertext Markup Language (HTML)   A simple markup language used to create hypertext documents that are portable from one platform to another. HTML files are simple ASCII text files with codes embedded (indicated by markup tags) to denote formatting and hypertext links. See also American Standard Code for Information Interchange (ASCII).

Hypertext Transfer Protocol (HTTP)   The protocol used to transfer information on the World Wide Web. An HTTP address (one kind of Uniform Resource Locator [URL]) takes the form: http://www.microsoft.com.

I

I/O request packet (IRP)   Data structures that drivers use to communicate with each other.

ICM   See definition for Image Color Management (ICM).

IDE   See definition for integrated device electronics (IDE).

IEEE 1284.4   An IEEE specification for supporting multifunction peripherals (MFPs). Windows 2000 has a driver that creates different port settings for each function of an MFP, enabling Windows 2000 print servers to simultaneously send data to multiple parts of an MFP.

IEEE 1394   A standard for high-speed serial devices such as digital video and digital audio editing equipment.

IIS   See definition for Internet Information Services (IIS).

ILS   See definition for Internet locator service (ILS).

Image Color Management (ICM)   The process of image output correction. ICM attempts to make the output more closely match the colors that are input or scanned.

import media pool   A logical collection of data-storage media that has not been cataloged by Removable Storage. Media in an import media pool should be cataloged as soon as possible so that they can be used by an application. See also media pool; Removable Storage.

incremental backup   A backup that copies only those files created or changed since the last normal or incremental backup. It marks files as having been backed up (in other words, the archive attribute is cleared). If you use a combination of normal and incremental backups to restore your data, you will need to have the last normal backup and all incremental backup sets. See also copy backup; daily backup; differential backup; normal backup.

independent client   A computer with Message Queuing installed that can host queues and store messages locally. Independent clients do not require synchronous access to a Message Queuing server to send and receive messages, but they can use Message Queuing servers with routing enabled for efficient message routing.

independent software vendors (ISVs)   A third-party software developer; an individual or an organization that independently creates computer software.

Industry Standard Architecture (ISA)   A bus design specification that allows components to be added as cards plugged into standard expansion slots in IBM Personal Computers and IBM-compatible computers.

infrared (IR)   Light that is beyond red in the color spectrum. While the light is not visible to the human eye, infrared transmitters and receivers can send and receive infrared signals. See also Infrared Data Association (IrDA); infrared device; infrared port.

Infrared Data Association (IrDA)   The industry organization of computer, component, and tele-communications vendors who establish the standards for infrared communication between computers and peripheral devices, such as printers. See also infrared (IR).

infrared device   A computer, or a computer peripheral such as a printer, that can communicate by using infrared light. See also infrared (IR).

infrared port   An optical port on a computer that enables communication with other computers or devices by using infrared light, without cables. Infrared ports can be found on some portable computers, printers, and cameras. See also infrared (IR); infrared device.

inheritance   In security, a mechanism that allows a specific access control entry (ACE) to be copied from the container where it was applied to all children of the container. Inheritance can be used to manage access to a whole subtree of objects in a single update operation. See also access control entry (ACE); Active Directory.

initialize   In Disk Management, the process of detecting a disk or volume and assigning it a status (for example, healthy) and a type (for example, dynamic). See also basic disk; basic volume; dynamic disk; dynamic volume.

Input language   A Regional and Language Options setting that specifies the combination of the language being entered and the keyboard layout, Input Method Editor (IME), speech-to-text converter, or other device being used to enter it. Formerly known as *input locale*.

input locale   See definition for Input language.

input/output (I/O) port   A channel through which data is transferred between a device and the microprocessor. The port appears to the microprocessor as one or more memory addresses that it can use to send or receive data.

insert/eject port   A port that offers limited access to the cartridges in a library managed by Removable Storage. Also known as a *mailslot*. See also cartridge; library; Removable Storage.

install   When referring to software, to add program files and folders to your hard disk and related data to your registry so that the software runs properly. Installing contrasts with upgrading, where existing program files, folders, and registry entries are updated to a more recent version.

When referring to hardware, to physically connect the device to your computer, to load device drivers onto your computer, and to configure device properties and settings. See also device driver; registry; uninstall.

Institute of Electrical and Electronics Engineers (IEEE)   An organization of engineering and electronics professionals that are notable for developing standards for hardware and software.

integrated device electronics (IDE)   A type of disk-drive interface in which the controller electronics reside on the drive itself, eliminating the need for a separate adapter card. IDE offers advantages such as look-ahead caching to increase overall performance.

integrity   A basic security function of cryptography. Integrity provides verification that the original contents of information have not been altered or corrupted. Without integrity, someone might alter information or the information might become corrupted, but the alteration can go undetected. For example, an Internet Protocol security property that protects data from unauthorized modification in transit, ensuring that the data received is exactly the same as the data sent. Hash functions sign each packet with a cryptographic checksum, which the receiving computer checks before opening the packet. If the packet—and therefore signature—has changed, the packet is discarded.

IntelliMirror   A set of directory-based change and configuration management features introduced in Windows 2000 and enhanced in Windows XP. When IntelliMirror is used in both the server and client, the users' data, applications, and settings follow them when they move to another computer.

interactive logon   A network logon from a computer keyboard, when the user types information in the **Logon Information** dialog box displayed by the computer's operating system.

International Telecommunication Union - Telecommunication [Standardization Sector] (ITU-T)   The sector of the International Telecommunication Union (ITU) responsible for telecommunication standards. ITU-T replaces the Comite Consultatif International Telegraphique et Telephonique (CCITT). Its responsibilities include standardizing modem design and operations, and standardizing protocols for networks and facsimile transmission. ITU is an international organization within which governments and the private sector coordinate global telecom networks and services.

internet   *internet*. Two or more network segments connected by routers. Another term for *internetwork*.

Internet. A worldwide network of computers. If you have access to the Internet, you can retrieve information from millions of sources, including schools, governments, businesses, and individuals. See also World Wide Web.

Internet Control Message Protocol (ICMP)   A required maintenance protocol in the TCP/IP suite that reports errors and allows simple connectivity. ICMP is used by the Ping tool to perform TCP/IP troubleshooting. See also Internet Protocol (IP); protocol; Transmission Control Protocol/Internet Protocol (TCP/IP).

Internet Information Services (IIS)   Software services that support Web site creation, configuration, and management, along with other Internet functions. Internet Information Services include Network News Transfer Protocol (NNTP), File Transfer Protocol (FTP), and Simple Mail Transfer Protocol (SMTP). See also File Transfer Protocol (FTP); Simple Mail Transfer Protocol (SMTP).

Internet Key Exchange (IKE)   A protocol that establishes the security association and shared keys necessary for two parties to communicate by using Internet Protocol security. See also Internet Protocol security (IPSec).

Internet locator service (ILS)   An optional component of Microsoft Site Server that creates a dynamic directory of videoconferencing users.

Internet Printing Protocol (IPP)   The protocol that uses the Hypertext Transfer Protocol (HTTP) to send print jobs to printers throughout the world. Windows 2000 and Windows XP Professional support Internet Printing Protocol (IPP) version 1.0.

Internet Protocol (IP)   A routable protocol in the TCP/IP protocol suite that is responsible for IP addressing, routing, and the fragmentation and reassembly of IP packets. See also packet; Transmission Control Protocol/Internet Protocol (TCP/IP); voluntary tunnel.

Internet Protocol security (IPSec)   A set of industry-standard, cryptography-based protection services and protocols. IPSec protects all protocols in the TCP/IP protocol suite and Internet communications by using L2TP. See also Layer Two Tunneling Protocol (L2TP); protocol; Transmission Control Protocol/Internet Protocol (TCP/IP).

Internet service provider (ISP)   A company that provides individuals or companies access to the Internet and the World Wide Web. An ISP provides a telephone number, a user name, a password, and other connection information so users can connect their computers to the ISP's computers. An ISP typically charges a monthly or hourly connection fee.

Internetwork Packet Exchange (IPX)   A network protocol native to NetWare that controls addressing and routing of packets within and between LANs. IPX does not guarantee that a message will be complete (no lost packets). See also Internetwork Packet Exchange/Sequenced Packet Exchange (IPX/SPX); local area network (LAN); Routing Information Protocol over IPX (RIPX).

Internetwork Packet Exchange/Sequenced Packet Exchange (IPX/SPX)   Transport protocols used in Novell NetWare networks, which together correspond to the combination of TCP and IP in the TCP/IP protocol suite. Windows implements IPX through NWLink. See also Internetwork Packet Exchange (IPX); NWLink; Transmission Control Protocol/Internet Protocol (TCP/IP).

interrupt   A request for attention from the processor. When the processor receives an interrupt, it suspends its current operations, saves the status of its work, and transfers control to a special routine known as an interrupt handler, which contains the instructions for dealing with the particular situation that caused the interrupt.

interrupt request (IRQ)   A signal sent by a device to get the attention of the processor when the device is ready to accept or send information. Each device sends its interrupt requests over a specific hardware line. Each device must be assigned a unique IRQ number.

intranet   A network within an organization that uses Internet technologies and protocols, but is available only to certain people, such as employees of a company. An intranet is also called a private network.

IP   See definition for Internet Protocol (IP).

IP address   A 32-bit address used to identify a node on an IP internetwork. Each node on the IP internetwork must be assigned a unique IP address, which is made up of the network ID, plus a unique host ID. This address is typically represented with the decimal value of each octet separated by a period (for example, 192.168.7.27). You can configure the IP address statically or dynamically by using DHCP. See also Dynamic Host Configuration Protocol (DHCP).

IP router   A system connected to multiple physical TCP/IP networks that can route or deliver IP packets between the networks.

IPP   See definition for Internet Printing Protocol (IPP).

IPSec   See definition for Internet Protocol security (IPSec).

IPSec driver   A driver that uses the IP Filter List from the active IPSec policy to watch for outbound IP packets that must be secured and inbound IP packets that need to be verified and decrypted. See also IPSec.

IPX   See definition for Internetwork Packet Exchange (IPX).

IPX/SPX   See definition for Internetwork Packet Exchange/Sequenced Packet Exchange (IPX/SPX).

IrDA   See definition for Infrared Data Association (IrDA).

IRP   See definition for I/O request packet (IRP).

IRQ   See definition for interrupt request (IRQ).

IrTran-p   A protocol that transfers images from cameras to computers by using infrared transmissions, making a physical cable connection unnecessary. See also infrared (IR).

isochronous   Time dependent. Refers to processes where data must be delivered within certain time constraints. Multimedia streams require an isochronous transport mechanism to ensure that data is delivered as fast as it is displayed, and to ensure that the audio is synchronized with the video.

J, K

Kerberos V5 authentication protocol   An authentication mechanism used to verify user or host identity. The Kerberos V5 authentication protocol is the default authentication service for Windows 2000. Internet Protocol security (IPSec) and the QoS Admission Control Service use the Kerberos protocol for authentication. See also Internet Protocol security (IPSec); Key Distribution Center (KDC).

kernel   The core of layered architecture that manages the most basic operations of the operating system and the computer's processor. The kernel schedules different blocks of executing code, called threads, for the processor to keep it as busy as possible and coordinates multiple processors to optimize performance. The kernel also synchronizes activities among Executive-level subcomponents, such as I/O Manager and Process Manager, and handles hardware exceptions and other hardware-dependent functions. The kernel works closely with the hardware abstraction layer.

key   In Registry Editor, a folder that appears in the left pane of the Registry Editor window. A key can contain subkeys and value entries. For example, Environment is a key of HKEY_CURRENT_USER.

In IP security (IPSec), a value used in combination with an algorithm to encrypt or decrypt data. Key settings for IP security are configurable to provide greater security.

Key Distribution Center (KDC)   A network service that supplies session tickets and temporary session keys used in the Kerberos V5 authentication protocol. In Windows 2000 and Windows XP, the KDC runs as a privileged process on all domain controllers. See also Kerberos V5 authentication protocol.

keyboard filters   Special timing and other devices that compensate for erratic motion tremors, slow response time, and other mobility impairments.

Korn shell (ksh)   A command shell that provides the following functionality: file input and output redirection; command-line editing by using **vi**; command history; integer arithmetic; pattern matching and variable substitution; command name abbreviation (aliasing); and built-in commands for writing shell programs.

L

L2TP   See definition for Layer Two Tunneling Protocol (L2TP).

LAN   See definition for local area network (LAN).

Language for non-Unicode programs   A Regional and Language Options setting that specifies the default code pages and associated bitmap font files for a specific computer that affects all of that computer's users. The default code pages and fonts enable a non-Unicode application written for one operating system language version to run correctly on another operating system language version. Formerly known as *system locale*.

Last Known Good Configuration   A hardware configuration available by pressing F8 during startup. If the current hardware settings prevent the computer from starting, the last known good configuration can allow you to start the computer and examine the configuration. When the last known good configuration is used, later configuration changes are lost.

Layer 2 forwarding (L2F)   Permits the tunneling of the link layer of higher-level protocols. Using these tunnels, it is possible to separate the location of the initial dial-up server from the physical location at which the dial-up protocol connection is terminated and access to the network is provided. See also tunnel.

Layer Two Tunneling Protocol (L2TP)   An industry-standard Internet tunneling protocol that provides encapsulation for sending Point-to-Point Protocol (PPP) frames across packet-oriented media. For IP networks, L2TP traffic is sent as User Datagram Protocol (UDP) messages. In Microsoft operating systems, L2TP is used in conjunction with Internet Protocol security (IPSec) as a virtual private network (VPN) technology to provide remote access or router-to-router VPN connections. L2TP is described in RFC 2661. See also Internet Protocol security (IPSec); Point-to-Point Protocol (PPP); tunnel.

library   A data-storage system, usually managed by Removable Storage. A library consists of removable media (such as tapes or discs) and a hardware device that can read from or write to the media. There are two major types of libraries: robotic libraries (automated multiple-media, multidrive devices) and stand-alone drive libraries (manually operated, single-drive devices). A robotic library is also called a *jukebox* or *changer*. See also Removable Storage.

library request   A request for an online library or stand-alone drive to perform a task. This request can be issued by an application or by Removable Storage.

Lightweight Directory Access Protocol (LDAP)   The primary access protocol for Active Directory. LDAP version 3 is defined by a set of Proposed Standard documents in Internet Engineering Task Force (IETF) RFC 2251. See also Active Directory; protocol.

Line Printer   A connectivity tool that runs on client systems and is used to print files to a computer running an LPD server.

Line Printer Daemon (LPD)   A service on the print server that receives documents (print jobs) from Line Printer Remote (LPR) tools running on client systems. See also Line Printer Remote (LPR); print job; print server.

Line Printer Port Monitor   A port monitor that is used to send jobs over TCP/IP from the client running Lprmon.dll to a print server running a Line Printer Daemon (LPD) service. Line Printer Port Monitor can be used to enable Internet printing, UNIX print servers, or Windows 2000 print servers over a TCP/IP network. See also Line Printer Daemon (LPD); Transmission Control Protocol/Internet Protocol (TCP/IP).

Line Printer Remote (LPR)   A connectivity tool that runs on client systems and is used to print files to a computer running an LPD server. See also Line Printer Daemon (LPD).

local area network (LAN)   A communications network connecting a group of computers, printers, and other devices located within a relatively limited area (for example, a building). A LAN allows any connected device to interact with any other on the network. See also NetBIOS Extended User Interface (NetBEUI); network basic input/output system (NetBIOS); virtual local area network (VLAN); workgroup.

local group   A security group that can be granted rights and permissions on only resources on the computer on which the group is created. Local groups can have any user accounts that are local to the computer as members, as well as users, groups, and computers from a domain to which the computer belongs. See also global group; user account.

Local Security Authority (LSA)   A protected subsystem that authenticates and logs users on to the local system. In addition, the LSA maintains information about all aspects of local security on a system (collectively known as the *local security policy*), and provides various services for translation between names and identifiers.

local security policy   Security information about all aspects of local security on a system. The local security policy identifies who is assigned privileges and what security auditing is to be performed.

local user profile   A computer-based record about an authorized user that is created automatically on the computer the first time a user logs on to a workstation or server computer.

Localmon.dll   The standard print monitor for use with printers connected directly to your computer. If you add a printer to your computer using a serial or parallel port (such as COM1 or LPT1), this is the monitor that is used.

locator service   In a distributed system, a feature that allows a client to find a shared resource or server without providing an address or full name. Generally associated with Active Directory, which provides a locator service.

logical drive   A volume that you create within an extended partition on a basic master boot record (MBR) disk. Logical drives are similar to primary partitions, except that you are limited to four primary partitions per disk, whereas you can create an unlimited number of logical drives per disk. A logical drive can be formatted and assigned a drive letter. See also basic disk; basic volume; extended partition; master boot record (MBR); primary partition; volume.

logical printer   The software interface between the operating system and the printer in Windows. While a printer is the device that does the actual printing, a logical printer is its software interface on the print server. This software interface determines how a print job is processed and how it is routed to its destination (to a local or network port, to a file, or to a remote print share). When you print a document, it is spooled (or stored) on the logical printer before it is sent to the printer itself. See also printer.

logical volume   A volume created within an extended partition on a basic disk. You can format and assign a drive letter to a logical drive. Only basic disks can contain logical drives. A logical drive cannot span multiple disks. See also basic disk; extended partition; logical drive.

logon script   Files that can be assigned to user accounts. Typically a batch file, a logon script runs automatically every time the user logs on. It can be used to configure a user's working environment at every logon, and it allows an administrator to influence a user's environment without managing all aspects of it. A logon script can be assigned to one or more user accounts. See also user account.

long name   A folder name or file name longer than the 8.3 file name standard (up to eight characters followed by a period and an extension of up to three characters) of the FAT file system. This version of Windows supports long file names up to 255 characters. See also file allocation table (FAT); MS-DOS (Microsoft Disk Operating System).

loopback address   The address of the local computer used for routing outgoing packets back to the source computer. This address is used primarily for testing.

M

MAC   See definition for media access control.

magazine   A collection of storage locations, also known as *slots*, for cartridges in a library managed by Removable Storage. Magazines are usually removable. See also cartridge; library; Removable Storage.

Magnifier   A screen enlarger that magnifies a portion of the screen in a separate window for users with low vision and for those who require occasional screen magnification for such tasks as editing art.

mandatory user profile   A user profile that is not updated when the user logs off. It is downloaded to the user's desktop each time the user logs on, and is created by an administrator and assigned to one or more users to create consistent or job-specific user profiles. Only members of the Administrators group can change profiles. See also roaming user profile.

manual caching   A method of manually designating network files and folders so they are stored on a user's hard disk and accessible when the user is not connected to the network.

master boot record (MBR)   The first sector on a hard disk, which begins the process of starting the computer. The MBR contains the partition table for the disk and a small amount of executable code called the *master boot code*. See also Recovery Console.

master file table (MFT)   An NTFS system file on NTFS-formatted volumes that contains information about each file and folder on the volume. The MFT is the first file on an NTFS volume. See also file allocation table (FAT); NTFS file system; volume.

maximum password age   The period of time a password can be used before the system requires the user to change it.

MBR disk   A disk that uses the master boot record (MBR) partition style. A *partition style* is the method that Windows XP uses to organize partitions on the disk. All x86-based computers use MBR disks. Itanium-based computers can use MBR disks and GPT disks. See also GPT disk; master boot record (MBR).

media   Any fixed or removable objects that store computer data. Examples include hard disks, floppy disks, tapes, and compact discs.

media access control   A sublayer of the IEEE 802 specifications that defines network access methods and framing.

media pool   A logical collection of removable media that have the same management policies. Media pools are used by applications to control access to specific tapes or discs within libraries managed by Removable Storage. There are four media pools: unrecognized, import, free, and application-specific. Each media pool can only hold either media or other media pools. See also free media pool; import media pool; Removable Storage.

memory leak   A condition that occurs when applications allocate memory for use but do not free allocated memory when finished.

metric   A number used to indicate the cost of a route in the IP routing table that enables the selection of the best route among possible multiple routes to the same destination.

Microsoft Challenge Handshake Authentication Protocol version 1 (MS-CHAP v1)   An encrypted authentication mechanism for PPP connections similar to CHAP. The remote access server sends a challenge to the remote access client that consists of a session ID and an arbitrary challenge string. The remote access client must return the user name and a Message Digest 4 (MD4) hash of the challenge string, the session ID, and the MD4-hashed password. See also Challenge Handshake Authentication Protocol (CHAP); Point-to-Point Protocol (PPP).

Microsoft Challenge Handshake Authentication Protocol version 2 (MS-CHAP v2)   An encrypted authentication mechanism for PPP connections that provides stronger security than CHAP and MS-CHAP v1. MS-CHAP v2 provides mutual authentication and asymmetric encryption keys. See also Challenge Handshake Authentication Protocol (CHAP); Point-to-Point Protocol (PPP).

Microsoft Management Console (MMC)   A framework for hosting administrative tools called *snap-ins*. A console might contain tools, folders or other containers, World Wide Web pages, and other administrative items. These items are displayed in the left pane of the console, called a *console tree*. A console has one or more windows that can provide views of the console tree. The main MMC window provides commands and tools for authoring consoles. The authoring features of MMC and the console tree itself might be hidden when a console is in User Mode. See also console tree; snap-in.

Microsoft Reserved (MSR) partition   A required partition on every GUID partition table (GPT) disk. System components can allocate portions of the MSR partition into new partitions for their own use. For example, when you convert a basic GPT disk to dynamic, the system allocates a portion of the MSR partition to be used as the Logical Disk Manager (LDM) metadata partition. The MSR partition varies in size based on the size of the GPT disk. For disks smaller than 16 GB, the MSR partition is 32 MB. For disks larger than 16 GB, the MSR partition is 128 MB. The MSR partition is not visible in Disk Management, and you cannot store data on the MSR partition or delete it. See also GUID partition table (GPT); partition.

Microsoft Tape Format (MTF)   The data format used for tapes supported by the Backup feature of Windows 2000.

Mini-Setup wizard   A wizard that starts the first time a computer boots from a hard disk that has been duplicated. The wizard gathers any information that is needed for the newly duplicated hard disk.

minidriver   A relatively small, simple driver or file that contains additional instructions needed by a specific hardware device to interface with the universal driver for a class of devices.

mirror   One of the two volumes that make up a mirrored volume. Each mirror of a mirrored volume resides on a different disk. If one mirror becomes unavailable (due to a disk failure, for example), Windows can use the remaining mirror to gain access to the volume's data. See also fault tolerance; mirrored volume; volume.

mirror set   A fault-tolerant partition created with Windows NT 4.0 or earlier that duplicates data on two physical disks. You can only repair, resynchronize, break, or delete mirror sets in Windows 2000. To create new volumes that are mirrored, use mirrored volumes on dynamic disks. See also dynamic disk; mirrored volume.

mirrored volume   A fault-tolerant volume that duplicates data on two physical disks. A mirrored volume provides data redundancy by using two identical volumes, which are called *mirrors*, to duplicate the information contained on the volume. A mirror is always located on a different disk. If one of the physical disks fails, the data on the failed disk becomes unavailable, but the system continues to operate in the mirror on the remaining disk. You can create mirrored volumes only on dynamic disks. See also dynamic disk; dynamic volume; fault tolerance; RAID-5 volume; volume.

mixed mode   In a Windows 2000 domain, the default domain mode setting. Mixed mode allows Windows NT-based backup domain controllers to coexist with Windows 2000-based domain controllers. Mixed mode does not support universal groups or the nesting of groups. You can change the domain mode setting to native mode when all Windows NT-based domain controllers are removed from a domain. See also native mode.

MMC   See definition for Microsoft Management Console (MMC).

Mode Pruning   A Windows 2000 feature that can be used to remove display modes that the monitor cannot support.

mount   To place a removable tape or disc into a drive. See also dismount; library.

MP3   Audio compressed in the MPEG1 Layer 3 format.

MPEG-2   A standard of video compression and file format developed by the Moving Pictures Experts Group. MPEG-2 offers video resolutions of 720 x 480 and 128 x 720 at 60 frames per second, with full CD-quality audio.

MS-CHAP v2   See definition for Microsoft Challenge Handshake Authentication Protocol version 2 (MS-CHAP v2).

MS-DOS (Microsoft Disk Operating System)   An operating system used on all personal computers and compatibles. As with other operating systems, such as OS/2, it translates user keyboard input into operations the computer can perform. MS-DOS can be easily accessed by using the command prompt, while MS-DOS-based programs can be accessed through the use of shortcuts on the desktop.

multicasting   The process of sending a message simultaneously to more than one destination on a network.

multihomed computer   A computer that has multiple network adapters or that has been configured with multiple IP addresses for a single network adapter. See also IP address; network adapter; virtual IP address.

multiple boot   A computer configuration that runs two or more operating systems. See also dual boot; startup environment.

N

name devolution   A process by which a DNS resolver appends one or more domain names to an unqualified domain name, making it a fully qualified domain name, and then submits the fully qualified domain name to a DNS server.

naming service   A service, such as that provided by WINS or DNS, that allows friendly names to be resolved to an address, or other specially defined resource data used to locate network resources of various types and purposes. See also Domain Name System (DNS); Windows Internet Name Service (WINS).

Narrator   A synthesized text-to-speech tool for users who have low vision. Narrator reads aloud most of what the screen displays.

native mode   The condition in which all domain controllers in a domain are running Windows 2000 and a domain administrator has switched the domain operation mode from mixed mode to native mode.

NDIS miniport drivers   A type of minidriver that interfaces network class devices to NDIS.

nested groups   A Windows 2000 capability available only in native mode that allows the creation of groups within groups. See also group; native mode.

Net Logon service   A service that runs in the Windows 2000 security subsystem in user mode, and performs the following functions; Replication of Windows NT 3.*x* and Windows NT 4.0 backup domain controllers with the Windows 2000 PDC emulator; NTLM passthrough authentication; Periodic password updates for computer accounts and interdomain trust relationships; Domain controller discovery using NetBIOS naming for nondirectory-aware domain controllers (domain controllers that run Windows NT 3.5 and Windows NT 4.0); Domain controller discovery in closest site using NetBIOS naming or DNS naming for directory-aware domain controllers (domain controllers that run Windows 2000).

NetBEUI   See definition for NetBIOS Extended User Interface (NetBEUI).

NetBIOS Extended User Interface (NetBEUI)   A network protocol native to Microsoft Networking. It is usually used in small, department-size local area networks (LANs) of 1 to 200 clients. It can use Token Ring source routing as its only method of routing. It is the Microsoft implementation of the NetBIOS standard. See also local area network (LAN); network basic input/output system (NetBIOS); protocol.

NetBIOS over TCP/IP (NetBT)   A feature that provides the NetBIOS programming interface over the TCP/IP protocol. It is used for monitoring routed servers that use NetBIOS name resolution.

NetWare   Novell's network operating system.

network adapter   A device that connects your computer to a network. This device is sometimes called an adapter card or network interface card.

network basic input/output system (NetBIOS)   An application programming interface (API) that can be used by programs on a local area network (LAN). NetBIOS provides programs with a uniform set of commands for requesting the lower-level services required to manage names, conduct sessions, and send datagrams between nodes on a network. See also application programming interface (API); basic input/output system (BIOS); local area network (LAN); node.

network card driver   A device driver that works directly with the network card, acting as an intermediary between the card and the protocol driver. See also device driver.

Network Control Protocol (NCP)   A protocol within the PPP protocol suite that negotiates the parameters of an individual LAN protocol such as TCP/IP or IPX. See also Internetwork Packet Exchange (IPX); local area network (LAN); Point-to-Point Protocol (PPP); Transmission Control Protocol/Internet Protocol (TCP/IP).

Network Driver Interface Specification (NDIS)   A Microsoft/3Com specification establishing a common shared interface for Microsoft operating systems to support protocol-independent transport of multiple network transport protocols (such as TCP/IP, NetBEUI, IPX/SPX, and AppleTalk). NDIS allows more than one transport protocol to be bound and to operate simultaneously over a single network adapter. See also Internetwork Packet Exchange (IPX); Internetwork Packet Exchange/Sequenced Packet Exchange (IPX/SPX); NetBIOS Extended User Interface (NetBEUI); Transmission Control Protocol/Internet Protocol (TCP/IP).

Network File System (NFS)   A service for distributed computing systems that provides a distributed file system, eliminating the need for keeping multiple copies of files on separate computers.

network security administrator   A users who manages network and information security. A network security administrator should implement a security plan that addresses network security threats.

node   For tree structures, a location on the tree that can have links to one or more items below it.

For local area networks (LANs), a device that is connected to the network and is capable of communicating with other network devices. See also local area network (LAN).

noncontainer object   An object that cannot logically contain other objects. For example, a file is a noncontainer object. See also container object; object.

nonrepudiation   A basic security function of cryptography that ensures that a party in a communication cannot falsely deny that a part of the communication occurred. Without nonrepudiation, someone can communicate and then later deny the communication or claim that the communication occurred at a different time.

nonresident attribute   A file attribute whose value is contained in one or more runs, or extents, outside the master file table (MFT) record and separate from the MFT. See also master file table (MFT).

nontransitive trust   A type of trust relationship that is bounded by the two domains in the relationship. For example, if domain A trusts domain B and domain B trusts domain C, there is no trust relationship between domain A and domain C.

Nontransitive trusts can be one-way or two-way relationships. This is the only type of trust that can exist between a Windows 2000 domain and a Windows NT domain or between Windows 2000 domains in different forests. See also forest.

normal backup   A backup that copies all selected files and marks each file as having been backed up (in other words, the archive attribute is cleared). With normal backups, you need only the most recent copy of the backup file or tape to restore all of the files. You usually perform a normal backup the first time you create a backup set. See also copy backup; daily backup; differential backup; incremental backup.

notification area   The area on the taskbar to the right of the taskbar buttons. The notification area displays the time and can also contain shortcuts that provide quick access to programs, such as Volume Control and Power Options. Other shortcuts can appear temporarily, providing information about the status of activities. For example, the printer shortcut icon appears after a document has been sent to the printer and disappears when printing is complete.

NT-1 (Network Terminator 1)   A device that terminates an ISDN line at the connection location, commonly through a connection port.

NTFS file system   An advanced file system that provides performance, security, reliability, and advanced features that are not found in any version of FAT. For example, NTFS guarantees volume consistency by using standard transaction logging and recovery techniques. If a system fails, NTFS uses its log file and checkpoint information to restore the consistency of the file system. In Windows 2000 and Windows XP, NTFS also provides advanced features such as file and folder permissions, encryption, disk quotas, and compression. See also FAT32; file allocation table (FAT); file system.

NTLM   A security package that provides authentication between clients and servers.

NTLM authentication protocol   A challenge/response authentication protocol. The NTLM authentication protocol was the default for network authentication in Windows NT version 4.0 and earlier and Windows Millennium Edition and earlier. The protocol continues to be supported in Windows 2000 and Windows XP but no longer is the default.

null modem cable   Special cabling that eliminates the modem's need for asynchronous communications between two computers over short distances. A null modem cable emulates modem communication.

NWLink   An implementation of the Internetwork Packet Exchange (IPX), Sequenced Packet Exchange (SPX), and NetBIOS protocols used in Novell networks. NWLink is a standard network protocol that supports routing and can support NetWare client-server applications, where NetWare-aware Sockets-based applications communicate with IPX/SPX Sockets-based applications. See also Internetwork Packet Exchange/Sequenced Packet Exchange (IPX/SPX); network basic input/output system (NetBIOS); Routing Information Protocol over IPX (RIPX).

O

object   An entity, such as a file, folder, shared folder, printer, or Active Directory object, described by a distinct, named set of attributes. For example, the attributes of a File object include its name, location, and size; the attributes of an Active Directory User object might include the user's first name, last name, and e-mail address.

For OLE and ActiveX, an object can also be any piece of information that can be linked to, or embedded into, another object. See also attribute; child object; parent object.

object linking and embedding (OLE)   A method for sharing information among applications. Linking an object, such as a graphic, from one document to another inserts a reference to the object into the second document. Any changes you make in the object in the first document will also be made in the second document. Embedding an object inserts a copy of an object from one document into another document. Changes you make in the object in the first document will not be updated in the second unless the embedded object is explicitly updated.

offline media   Media that are not connected to the computer and require external assistance to be accessed.

on-media identifier (OMID)   A label that is electronically recorded on each medium in a Removable Storage system. Removable Storage uses on-media identifiers to track media in the Removable Storage database. An application on-media identifier is a subset of the media label.

on-screen keyboard   A tool that displays a virtual keyboard on a computer screen and allows users with mobility impairments to type using a pointing device or joystick.

OnNow   See definition for Advanced Configuration and Power Interface (ACPI).

open database connectivity (ODBC)   An application programming interface (API) that enables database applications to access data from a variety of existing data sources. See also application programming interface (API).

OpenType fonts   Outline fonts that are rendered from line and curve commands, and can be scaled and rotated. OpenType fonts are clear and readable in all sizes and on all output devices supported by Windows. OpenType is an extension of TrueType font technology. See also font; TrueType fonts.

operator request   A request for the operator to perform a task. This request can be issued by an application or by Removable Storage.

organizational unit   An Active Directory container object used within domains. An organizational unit is a logical container into which users, groups, computers, and other organizational units are placed. It can contain objects only from its parent domain. An organizational unit is the smallest scope to which a Group Policy object can be linked, or over which administrative authority can be delegated. See also Active Directory; container object; Group Policy object.

original equipment manufacturer (OEM)   A company that typically purchases computer components from other manufacturers, uses the components to build a personal computer, preinstalls Windows onto that computer, and then sells the computer to the public.

orphan   A member of a mirrored volume or a RAID-5 volume that has failed due to a severe cause, such as a loss of power or a complete hard-disk head failure. When this happens, the fault-tolerant driver determines that it can no longer use the orphaned member and directs all new reads and writes to the remaining members of the fault-tolerant volume. See also fault tolerance; mirrored volume; RAID-5 volume.

OSChooser   The client-side wizard that walks a user through the installation of an operating system or provides access to maintenance and troubleshooting utilities.

out-of-process application   An application that runs in an isolated process and does not share the same memory and CPU resources (process boundaries) as the application or server that calls it.

overclocking   Setting a microprocessor to run at speeds above the rated specification.

P

packet   An Open Systems Interconnection (OSI) network layer transmission unit that consists of binary information representing both data and a header containing an identification number, source and destination addresses, and error-control data.

packet header   In network protocol communications, a specially reserved field of a defined bit length that is attached to the front of a packet for carry and transfer of control information. When the packet arrives at its destination, the field is then detached and discarded as the packet is processed and disassembled in a corresponding reverse order for each protocol layer. See also packet.

page fault   The interrupt that occurs when software attempts to read from or write to a virtual memory location that is marked *not present*.

In Task Manager, page fault is the number of times data has to be retrieved from disk for a process because it was not found in memory. The page fault value accumulates from the time the process started. See also virtual memory.

page-description language (PDL)   A computer language that describes the arrangement of text and graphics on a printed page. See also PostScript; PostScript fonts; Printer Control Language (PCL).

paged pool   The system-allocated virtual memory that has been charged to a process and that can be paged. Paging is the moving of infrequently-used parts of a program's working memory from RAM to another storage medium, usually the hard disk.

In Task Manager, the amount of system-allocated virtual memory, in kilobytes, used by a process. See also registry size limit (RSL); virtual memory.

paging   The process of moving virtual memory back and forth between physical memory and the disk. Paging occurs when physical memory limitations are reached and only occurs for data that is not already "backed" by disk space. For example, file data is not paged out because it already has allocated disk space within a file system.

paging file   A hidden file on the hard disk that Windows uses to hold parts of programs and data files that do not fit in memory. The paging file and physical memory, or RAM, comprise virtual memory. Windows moves data from the paging file to memory as needed and moves data from memory to the paging file to make room for new data. Paging file is also called a swap file. See also registry size limit (RSL); virtual memory.

PAP   See definition for Password Authentication Protocol (PAP).

parallel connection   A connection that simultaneously transmits both data and control bits over wires connected in parallel. In general, a parallel connection can move data between devices faster than a serial connection.

parallel device   A device that uses a parallel connection.

parallel port   The input/output connector for a parallel interface device. Printers are generally plugged into a parallel port.

parent object   An object in which another object resides. For example, a folder is a parent object in which a file, or child object, resides. An object can be both a parent and a child object. For example, a subfolder that contains files is both the child of the parent folder and the parent folder of the files. See also child object; object.

parity   A calculated value that is used to reconstruct data after a failure. RAID-5 volumes stripe data and parity intermittently across a set of disks. When a disk fails, some server operating systems use the parity information together with the data on good disks to recreate the data on the failed disk. See also fault tolerance; RAID-5 volume; striped volume.

parity bit   In asynchronous communications, an extra bit used in checking for errors in groups of data bits transferred within or between computer systems. In modem-to-modem communications, a parity bit is often used to check the accuracy with which each character is transmitted. See also parity.

partition   A portion of a physical disk that functions as though it were a physically separate disk. After you create a partition, you must format it and assign it a drive letter before you can store data on it.

On basic disks, partitions are known as basic volumes, which include primary partitions and logical drives. On dynamic disks, partitions are known as dynamic volumes, which include simple, striped, spanned, mirrored, and RAID-5 volumes. See also basic disk; basic volume; dynamic volume; extended partition; primary partition; system partition.

partition table   On a hard disk, the data structure that stores the offset (location) and size of each primary partition on the disk. On MBR disks, the partition table is located in the master boot record. On GPT disks, the partition table is located in the GUID partition entry array. See also globally unique identifier (GUID); GPT disk; master boot record (MBR); MBR disk; partition.

Password Authentication Protocol (PAP)   A simple, plaintext authentication scheme for authenticating PPP connections. The user name and password are requested by the remote access server and returned by the remote access client in plaintext. See also Point-to-Point Protocol (PPP); remote access.

path   A sequence of directory (or folder) names that specifies the location of a directory, file, or folder within the Windows directory tree. Each directory name and file name within the path must be preceded by a backslash (\). For example, to specify the path of a file named Readme.doc located in the Windows directory on drive C, type C:\Windows\Readme.doc.

PC Card   A removable device, approximately the size of a credit card, that can be plugged into a Personal Computer Memory Card International Association (PCMCIA) slot in a portable computer. PCMCIA devices can include modems, network cards, and hard disk drives.

PCI   See definition for peripheral component interconnect (PCI).

PCMCIA device   A removable device, approximately the size of a credit card, that can be plugged into a PCMCIA slot in a portable computer. PCMCIA devices can include modems, network adapters, and hard disk drives.

Some PCMCIA cards can be connected to and disconnected from your computer without restarting it. Before you remove the PCMCIA card, however, you should use the Add Hardware Wizard to notify Windows that you are doing so. Windows will then notify you when you can remove the device.

PCNFS Daemon (PCNFSD)   A program that receives requests from PCNFS clients for authentication on remote computers.

peer-to-peer network   See definition for workgroup.

performance counter   In System Monitor, a data item that is associated with a performance object. For each counter selected, System Monitor presents a value corresponding to a particular aspect of the performance that is defined for the performance object.

peripheral   A device, such as a disk drive, printer, modem, or joystick, that is connected to a computer and is controlled by the computer's microprocessor.

peripheral component interconnect (PCI)   A specification introduced by Intel Corporation that defines a local bus system that allows up to 10 PCI-compliant expansion cards to be installed in the computer.

permission   A rule associated with an object to regulate which users can gain access to the object and in what manner. Permissions are granted or denied by the object's owner.

physical location   The location designation assigned to media managed by Removable Storage. The two classes of physical locations include libraries and offline media physical locations. The offline media physical location is where Removable Storage lists the cartridges that are not in a library. The physical location of cartridges in an online library is the library in which it resides.

physical media   A storage object that data can be written to, such as a disk or magnetic tape. A physical medium is referenced by its physical media ID (PMID).

physical object   An object, such as an ATM card or smart card used in conjunction with a piece of information, such as a personal identification number (PIN), to authenticate users. In two-factor authentication, physical objects are used in conjunction with another secret piece of identification, such as a password, to authenticate users. In two-factor authentication, the physical object might be an ATM card, which is used in combination with a PIN to authenticate the user.

pinning   To make a network file or folder available for offline use.

PKCS #10   The Certification Request Syntax Standard, developed and maintained by RSA Data Security, Inc. See also certificate; RSA.

PKCS #12   The Personal Information Exchange Syntax Standard, developed and maintained by RSA Data Security, Inc. This syntax standard specifies a portable format for storing or transporting a user's private keys, certificates, and miscellaneous secrets. See also certificate.

PKCS #7   The Cryptographic Message Syntax Standard. It is a general syntax, developed and maintained by RSA Data Security, Inc., for data to which cryptography may be applied, such as digital signatures and encryption. It also provides a syntax for disseminating certificates or certificate revocation lists. See also certificate; encryption.

plaintext   Data that is not encrypted. Sometimes also called *cleartext*.

Plug and Play   A set of specifications developed by Intel Corporation that allows a computer to automatically detect and configure a device and install the appropriate device drivers. See also universal serial bus (USB).

Point and Print   A way of installing network printers on a user's local computer. Point and Print allows users to initiate a connection to a network printer and loads any required drivers onto the client's computer. When users know which network printer they want to use, Point and Print greatly simplifies the installation process.

point of presence (POP)   The local access point for a network provider. Each POP provides a telephone number that allows users to make a local call for access to online services.

Point-to-Point Protocol (PPP)   An industry standard suite of protocols for the use of point-to-point links to transport multiprotocol datagrams. PPP is documented in RFC 1661. See also remote access; Transmission Control Protocol/Internet Protocol (TCP/IP); voluntary tunnel.

Point-to-Point Tunneling Protocol (PPTP)   Networking technology that supports multiprotocol virtual private networks (VPNs), enabling remote users to access corporate networks securely across the Internet or other networks by dialing into an Internet service provider (ISP) or by connecting directly to the Internet. PPTP tunnels, or encapsulates, IP, IPX, or NetBEUI traffic inside of IP packets. This means that users can remotely run applications that are dependent upon particular network protocols. See also Internet Protocol (IP); Internetwork Packet Exchange (IPX); NetBIOS Extended User Interface (NetBEUI); packet; tunnel; virtual private network (VPN).

Portable Operating System Interface for UNIX (POSIX)   An Institute of Electrical and Electronics Engineers (IEEE) standard that defines a set of operating-system services. Programs that adhere to the POSIX standard can be easily ported from one system to another. POSIX was based on UNIX system services, but it was created in a way that allows it to be implemented by other operating systems.

POSIX   See definition for Portable Operating System Interface for UNIX (POSIX).

POST   See definition for power-on self test (POST).

PostScript   A page-description language (PDL), developed by Adobe Systems for printing on laser printers. PostScript offers flexible font capability and high-quality graphics. It is the standard for desktop publishing because it is supported by imagesetters, the high-resolution printers used by printing services for commercial typesetting. See also page-description language (PDL); PostScript fonts; Printer Control Language (PCL); Type 1 fonts.

PostScript fonts   Fonts that are defined in terms of the PostScript page-description language (PDL) rules and are intended to be printed on a PostScript-compatible printer. When a document displayed in a screen font is sent to a PostScript printer, the printer uses the PostScript version if the font exists. If the font doesn't exist but a version is installed on the computer, that font is downloaded to the printer. If there is no PostScript font installed in either the printer or the computer, the bit-mapped (raster) font is translated into PostScript and the printer produces text using the bit-mapped font. PostScript fonts are distinguished from bit-mapped fonts by their smoothness, detail, and faithfulness to standards of quality established in the typographic industry. See also font; page-description language (PDL); PostScript; raster fonts.

power-on self test (POST)   A set of routines stored in read-only memory (ROM) that tests various system components such as RAM, the disk drives, and the keyboard, to see if they are properly connected and operating. If problems are found, these routines alert the user with a series of beeps or a message, often accompanied by a diagnostic numeric value. If the POST is successful, it passes control to the bootstrap loader. See also bootstrap loader.

PPTP   See definition for Point-to-Point Tunneling Protocol (PPTP).

predefined key   A key that represents one of the main divisions of the registry. Each predefined key is displayed in a separate Registry Editor window, with the key's name appearing in the window's title bar. For example, HKEY_CLASSES_ROOT is a predefined key. See also key; registry.

primary partition   A type of partition that you can create on basic disks. A primary partition is a portion of a physical disk that functions as though it were a physically separate disk. On basic master boot record (MBR) disks, you can create up to four primary partitions on a basic disk, or three primary partitions and an extended partition with multiple logical drives. On basic GPT disks, you can create up to 128 primary partitions. Primary partitions are also known as volumes. See also basic disk; extended partition; GPT disk; GUID partition table (GPT); logical drive; master boot record (MBR); partition; volume.

print job   The source code that contains both the data to be printed and the commands for print. Print jobs are classified into data types based on what modifications, if any, the spooler must make to the job for it to print correctly. See also printing pool.

print server   A computer that is dedicated to managing the printers on a network. The print server can be any computer on the network.

printer   A device that puts text or images on paper or other print media. Examples are laser printers or dot-matrix printers. See also logical printer; printing pool.

Printer Control Language (PCL)   The page-description language (PDL) developed by Hewlett-Packard for their laser and inkjet printers. Because of the widespread use of laser printers, this command language has become a standard in many printers. See also page-description language (PDL); PostScript.

printer driver   A program designed to allow other programs to work with a particular printer without concerning themselves with the specifics of the printer's hardware and internal language. By using printer drivers that handle the subtleties of each printer, programs can communicate properly with a variety of printers. See also device driver.

printing pool   Two or more identical printers that are connected to one print server and act as a single printer. In this case, when you print a document, the print job will be sent to the first available printer in the pool. See also print job; printer.

priority inversion   The mechanism that allows low-priority threads to run and complete execution rather than being preempted and locking up a resource such as an I/O device.

private branch exchange (PBX)   An automatic telephone switching system that enables users within an organization to place calls to each other without going through the public telephone network. Users can also place calls to outside numbers.

private key   The secret half of a cryptographic key pair that is used with a public key algorithm. Private keys are typically used to decrypt a symmetric session key, digitally sign data, or decrypt data that has been encrypted with the corresponding public key. See also public key encryption.

privileged mode   Also known as kernel mode, the processing mode that allows code to have direct access to all hardware and memory in the system.

process   An operating system object that consists of an executable program, a set of virtual memory addresses, and one or more threads. When a program runs, a process is created.

process throttling   A method of restricting the amount of processor time a process consumes, for example, using job object functions.

Product Key   A 25-character, alpha-numeric string. Customers must enter this string to activate their installation of Windows. The product key is located on the certificate of authenticity.

protocol   A set of rules and conventions for sending information over a network. These rules govern the content, format, timing, sequencing, and error control of messages exchanged among network devices.

proxy server   A firewall component that manages Internet traffic to and from a local area network (LAN) and can provide other features, such as document caching and access control. A proxy server can improve performance by supplying frequently requested data, such as a popular Web page, and can filter and discard requests that the owner does not consider appropriate, such as requests for unauthorized access to proprietary files. See also firewall.

public key certificate   A digital passport that serves as proof of identity. Public key certificates are issued by a certification authority (CA).

public key cryptography   A method of cryptography in which two different keys are used: a public key for encrypting data and a private key for decrypting data. Public key cryptography is also called asymmetric cryptography. See also cryptography; private key.

public key encryption   A method of encryption that uses two encryption keys that are mathematically related. One key is called the private key and is kept confidential. The other is called the public key and is freely given out to all potential correspondents. In a typical scenario, a sender uses the receiver's public key to encrypt a message. Only the receiver has the related private key to decrypt the message. The complexity of the relationship between the public key and the private key means that, provided the keys are long enough, it is computationally infeasible to determine one from the other. Public key encryption is also called asymmetric encryption. See also encryption; private key.

public key infrastructure (PKI)   The laws, policies, standards, and software that regulate or manipulate certificates and public and private keys. In practice, it is a system of digital certificates, certification authorities, and other registration authorities that verify and authenticate the validity of each party involved in an electronic transaction. Standards for PKI are still evolving, even though they are being widely implemented as a necessary element of electronic commerce. See also certificate; certification authority (CA).

Public Switched Telephone Network (PSTN)   Standard analog telephone lines, available worldwide.

Q

Quality of Service (QoS)   A set of quality assurance standards and mechanisms for data transmission, implemented in this version of Windows.

quantum   Also known as a time slice, the maximum amount of time a thread can run before the system checks for another ready thread of the same priority to run.

quarter-inch cartridge (QIC)   An older storage technology used with tape backup drives and cartridges. A means of backing up data on computer systems, QIC represents a set of standards devised to enable tapes to be used with drives from different manufacturers. The QIC standards specify the length of tape, the number of recording tracks, and the magnetic strength of the tape coating, all of which determine the amount of information that can be written to the tape. Older QIC-80 drives can hold up to 340 MB of compressed data. Newer versions can hold more than 1 GB of information.

R

RAID-5 volume   A fault-tolerant volume with data and parity striped intermittently across three or more physical disks. Parity is a calculated value that is used to reconstruct data after a failure. If a portion of a physical disk fails, Windows recreates the data that was on the failed portion from the remaining data and parity. You can create RAID-5 volumes only on dynamic disks, and you cannot mirror or extend RAID-5 volumes. See also dynamic disk; dynamic volume; fault tolerance; parity; volume.

raster fonts   Fonts that are stored as bitmaps. Raster fonts are designed with a specific size and resolution for a specific printer and cannot be scaled or rotated. If a printer does not support raster fonts, it will not print them. The five raster fonts are Courier, MS Sans Serif, MS Serif, Small, and Symbol. Raster fonts are also called bit-mapped fonts. See also font; printer.

read-only memory (ROM)   A semiconductor circuit that contains information that cannot be modified.

recoverable file system   A file system that ensures that if a power outage or other catastrophic system failure occurs, the file system will not be corrupted and disk modifications will not be left incomplete. The structure of the disk volume is restored to a consistent state when the system restarts.

Recovery Console   A command-line interface that provides a limited set of administrative commands that are useful for repairing a computer. See also NTFS file system.

Redundant Array of Independent Disks (RAID)   A method used to standardize and categorize fault-tolerant disk systems. RAID levels provide various mixes of performance, reliability, and cost. Some servers provide three of the RAID levels: Level 0 (striping), Level 1 (mirroring), and Level 5 (RAID-5).

registry   A database repository for information about a computer's configuration. The registry contains information that Windows continually references during operation, such as: profiles for each user; the programs installed on the computer and the types of documents each can create; property settings for folders and program icons; what hardware exists on the system; and Which ports are being used. The registry is organized hierarchically as a tree and is made up of keys and their subkeys, hives, and entries. See also key; registry size limit (RSL); subkey.

registry size limit (RSL)   A universal maximum for the space that registry files (hives) can consume in the paged pool. This maximum prevents an application from filling the paged pool with registry data. See also paged pool; registry.

relative ID (RID)   The part of a security ID (SID) that uniquely identifies an account or group within a domain. See also domain; forest; group; security ID (SID).

remote access   Part of the integrated Routing and Remote Access service that provides remote networking for telecommuters, mobile workers, and system administrators who monitor and manage servers at multiple branch offices. Users can use Network Connections to dial in to remotely access their networks for services such as file and printer sharing, electronic mail, scheduling, and SQL database access. See also remote access server.

remote access server   A Windows-based computer running the Routing and Remote Access service and configured to provide remote access. See also remote access.

remote installation boot floppy (RBFG.exe)   A tool used to generate a remote installation boot floppy disk. The remote installation boot floppy disk is used to start the process of remote operating system installation for computers which lack a supported Pre-Boot eXecution Environment (PXE)-based remote boot ROM.

Remote Installation Preparation wizard (RIPrep.exe)   A component in Remote Installation Services that is used to create operating system images and to install them on the RIS server.

Remote Installation Services (RIS)   Software services that allow an administrator to set up new client computers remotely, without having to visit each client. The target clients must support remote booting. See also Single Instance Store (SIS).

remote procedure call (RPC)   A message-passing facility that allows a distributed application to call services that are available on various computers on a network. Used during remote administration of computers.

Removable Storage   A service used for managing removable media (such as tapes and discs) and storage devices (libraries). Removable Storage allows applications to access and share the same media resources. See also library.

reparse points   NTFS file system objects that have a definable attribute containing user-controlled data and are used to extend functionality in the input/output (I/O) subsystem.

RepeatKeys   A feature that allows users with mobility impairments to adjust the repeat rate or to disable the key-repeat function on the keyboard.

Request for Comments (RFC)   An official document of the Internet Engineering Task Force (IETF) that specifies the details for networking protocols, such as those included in the TCP/IP family, and other aspects of computer communication. See also protocol; Transmission Control Protocol/Internet Protocol (TCP/IP).

resident attribute   A file attribute whose value is wholly contained in the file's file record in the master file table (MFT).

resolver   DNS client programs used to look up DNS name information. Resolvers can be either a small *stub* (a limited set of programming routines that provide basic query functionality) or larger programs that provide additional lookup DNS client functions, such as caching. See also caching; caching resolver; Domain Name System (DNS).

resource   Generally, any part of a computer system or network, such as a disk drive, printer, or memory, that can be allotted to a running program or a process.

For Device Manager, any of four system components that control how the devices on a computer work. These four system resources are interrupt request (IRQ) lines, direct memory access (DMA) channels, input/output (I/O) ports, and memory addresses. See also direct memory access (DMA); input/output (I/O) port; node.

resource publishing The process of making an object visible and accessible to users in a Windows 2000 domain. For example, a shared printer resource is published by creating a reference to the printer object in Active Directory. See also Active Directory.

resource record (RR) A standard DNS database structure containing information used to process DNS queries. For example, an address (A) resource record contains an IP address corresponding to a host name. Most of the basic resource record types are defined in RFC 1035, but additional RR types have been defined in other RFCs and approved for use with DNS. See also Domain Name System (DNS); Request for Comments (RFC).

response time The amount of time required to do work from start to finish. In a client/server environment, this is typically measured on the client side.

RGB The initials of red, green, and blue. Used to describe a color monitor or color value.

roaming user profile A server-based user profile that is downloaded to the local computer when a user logs on and that is updated both locally and on the server when the user logs off. A roaming user profile is available from the server when logging on to a workstation or server computer. When logging on, the user can use the local user profile if it is more current than the copy on the server. See also local user profile; mandatory user profile.

route table See definition for routing table.

router In a Windows environment, hardware that helps LANs and WANs achieve interoperability and connectivity, and can link LANs that have different network topologies (such as Ethernet and Token Ring). Routers match packet headers to a LAN segment and choose the best path for the packet, optimizing network performance. See also local area network (LAN); packet header; routing; Routing Information Protocol over IPX (RIPX); static routes; wide area network (WAN).

routing The process of forwarding a packet through an internetwork from a source host to a destination host. See also packet.

Routing Information Protocol (RIP) An industry standard, distance vector routing protocol used in small to medium sized IP and IPX internetworks. See also Internet Protocol (IP); Internetwork Packet Exchange (IPX); protocol.

Routing Information Protocol over IPX (RIPX) A protocol used by routers to exchange information between routers on an IPX network and by hosts to determine the best router to use when forwarding IPX traffic to a remote IPX network. See also Internetwork Packet Exchange (IPX); NWLink; protocol; router.

routing table A database of routes containing information on network IDs, forwarding addresses, and metrics for reachable network segments on an internetwork.

RSA A widely used public/private key algorithm. It is the default cryptographic service provider (CSP) for Windows. It was patented by RSA Data Security, Inc. in 1977. See also cryptographic service provider (CSP).

rules An IPSec policy mechanism that governs how and when an IPSec policy protects communication. A rule provides the ability to trigger and control secure communication based on the source, destination, and type of IP traffic. Each rule contains a list of IP filters and a collection of security actions that take place upon a match with that filter list.

S

safe mode A method of starting Windows using basic files and drivers only, without networking. Safe mode is available by pressing the F8 key when prompted during startup. This allows you to start your computer when a problem prevents it from starting normally.

schema The set of definitions for the universe of objects that can be stored in a directory. For each object class, the schema defines which attributes an instance of the class must have, which additional attributes it can have, and which other object classes can be its parent object class. See also attribute; object; parent object.

screen font A typeface designed for display on a computer monitor screen. A screen font often has an accompanying PostScript font for printing to PostScript-compatible printers. See also font; PostScript.

screen-enlargement tool A tool that allows the user to magnify a portion of the screen for greater visibility. Also called a screen magnifier or large-print program.

script A type of program consisting of a set of instructions to an application or tool program. A script usually expresses instructions by using the application's or tool's rules and syntax, combined with simple control structures such as loops and if/then expressions. "Batch program" is often used interchangeably with "script" in the Windows environment.

SCSI connection A standard high-speed parallel interface defined by the X3T9.2 committee of the American National Standards Institute (ANSI). A SCSI interface is used to connect microcomputers to SCSI peripheral devices, such as many hard disks and printers, and to other computers and local area networks.

search filter An argument in an LDAP search that allows certain entries in the subtree and excludes others. Filters allow you to define search criteria and give you better control to achieve more effective and efficient searches.

secondary logon The practice of logging on by using one security context and then, within the initial logon session, authenticating and using a second account is a secondary logon. To facilitate secondary logons, Windows 2000 introduced the RunAs.exe program and the RunAs.exe service.

Secure Sockets Layer (SSL) A proposed open standard for establishing a secure communications channel to prevent the interception of critical information, such as credit card numbers. Primarily, it enables secure electronic financial transactions on the World Wide Web, although it is designed to work on other Internet services as well.

Security Accounts Manager (SAM)   A Windows service used during the logon process. SAM maintains user account information, including groups to which a user belongs. See also group; user account.

security association (SA)   A combination of identifiers, which together define the Internet Protocol Security (IPSec) that protects communication between sender and receiver. An SA is identified by the combination of a Security Parameters Index (SPI), destination IP address, and security protocol (AH or ESP). An SA must be negotiated before secured data can be sent. See also Authentication Header (AH); Encapsulating Security Payload (ESP); Internet Protocol security (IPSec); Security Parameters Index (SPI).

security context   The security attributes or rules that are currently in effect. For example, the rules that govern what a user can do to a protected object are determined by security information in the user's access token and in the object's security descriptor. Together, the access token and the security descriptor form a security context for the user's actions on the object. See also object.

security descriptor   A data structure that contains security information associated with a protected object. Security descriptors include information about who owns the object, who can access it and in what way, and what types of access are audited. See also discretionary access control list (DACL); group; object; permission; system access control list (SACL).

security event types   Categories of events about which Windows can create auditing events. Account logon or object access are examples of security event types.

security group   A group that can be listed in discretionary access control lists (DACLs) used to define permissions on resources and objects. A security group can also be used as an e-mail entity. Sending an e-mail message to the group sends the message to all the members of the group. See also discretionary access control list (DACL).

security ID (SID)   A data structure of variable length that identifies user, group, and computer accounts. Every account on a network is issued a unique SID when the account is first created. Internal processes in Windows refer to an account's SID rather than the account's user or group name. See also user account.

security method   A process that determines the Internet Protocol security (IPSec) services, key settings, and algorithms that will be used to protect the data during the communication. See also Internet Protocol security (IPSec).

Security Parameters Index (SPI)   A unique, identifying value in the security association (SA) used to distinguish among multiple security associations existing at the receiving computer. See also security association (SA).

security principal   An account holder that is automatically assigned a security identifier (SID) for access to resources. A security principal can be a user, group, service, or computer. See also security ID (SID).

security principal name   A name that uniquely identifies a user, group, or computer within a single domain. This name is not guaranteed to be unique across domains. See also domain; group; security principal.

security template   A physical file representation of a security configuration that can be applied to a local computer or imported to a Group Policy object in Active Directory. When you import a security template to a Group Policy object, Group Policy processes the template and makes the corresponding changes to the members of that Group Policy object, which can be users or computers. See also Active Directory; Group Policy object.

Serial Bus Protocol (SBP-2)   A standard for storage devices, printers, and scanners that is a supplement to the IEEE 1394 specification. See also IEEE 1394.

serial connection   A connection that exchanges information between computers or between computers and peripheral devices one bit at a time over a single channel. Serial communications can be synchronous or asynchronous. Both sender and receiver must use the same baud rate, parity, and control information. See also asynchronous communication.

serial device   A device that uses a serial connection. See also serial connection.

SerialKeys   A Windows feature that uses a communications aid interface device to allow keystrokes and mouse controls to be accepted through a computer's serial port.

server   In general, a computer that provides shared resources to network users. See also client; shared resource.

Server Message Block (SMB)   A file-sharing protocol designed to allow networked computers to transparently access files that reside on remote systems over a variety of networks. The SMB protocol defines a series of commands that pass information between computers. SMB uses four message types: session control, file, printer, and message.

service access point   A logical address that allows a system to route data between a remote device and the appropriate communications support.

Service Pack   A software upgrade to an existing software distribution that contains updated files consisting of patches and hot fixes.

Service Profile Identifier (SPID)   An 8-digit to 14-digit number that identifies the services that you order for each B-channel. For example, when you order Primary Rate ISDN, you obtain two phone numbers and two SPIDs from your ISDN provider. Typical ISDN adapters cannot operate without configuring SPIDs.

service provider   In TAPI, a dynamic-link library (DLL) that provides an interface between an application requesting services and the controlling hardware device. TAPI supports two classes of service providers, media service providers and telephony service providers. See also dynamic-link library (DLL); Telephony API (TAPI).

session key   A key used primarily for encryption and decryption. Session keys are typically used with symmetric encryption algorithms where the same key is used for both encryption and decryption. For this reason, session and symmetric keys usually refer to the same type of key. See also symmetric key encryption.

share   To make resources, such as folders and printers, available to others. See also resource.

shared folder permissions   Permissions that restrict a shared resource's availability over the network to only certain users. See also permission.

shared resource   Any device, data, or program that is used by more than one program or one other device. For Windows, *shared resource* refers to any resource that is made available to network users, such as folders, files, printers, and named pipes. A shared resource can also refer to a resource on a server that is available to network users. See also resource; server.

Shiva Password Authentication Protocol (SPAP)   A two-way, reversible encryption mechanism for authenticating PPP connections employed by Shiva remote access servers.

shortcut key navigation indicators   Underlined letters on a menu or control. Also called *access keys* or *quick-access letters*.

ShowSounds   A feature that instructs programs that usually convey information only by sound to also provide all information visually, such as by displaying text captions or informative icons.

Simple Mail Transfer Protocol (SMTP)   A member of the TCP/IP suite of protocols that governs the exchange of electronic mail between message transfer agents. See also protocol; Transmission Control Protocol/Internet Protocol (TCP/IP).

Simple Network Management Protocol (SNMP)   A network protocol used to manage TCP/IP networks. In Windows, the SNMP service is used to provide status information about a host on a TCP/IP network. See also protocol; Transmission Control Protocol/Internet Protocol (TCP/IP).

simple volume   A dynamic volume made up of disk space from a single dynamic disk. A simple volume can consist of a single region on a disk or multiple regions of the same disk that are linked together. You can extend a simple volume within the same disk or onto additional disks. If you extend a simple volume across multiple disks, it becomes a spanned volume. You can create simple volumes only on dynamic disks. Simple volumes are not fault tolerant, but you can mirror them to create mirrored volumes. See also dynamic disk; dynamic volume; fault tolerance; mirrored volume; spanned volume; volume.

Single Instance Store (SIS)   A component that saves disk space on the server by maintaining a single physical copy of all identical files found. If SIS finds a duplicate file on the server, it copies the original file into the SIS store and leaves a link where the original resided. This technology is used only with Remote Installation Services. See also Remote Installation Services (RIS).

Single Sign-On Daemon (SSOD)   A program installed on a UNIX-based system to handle password synchronization requests.

site   One or more well-connected (highly reliable and fast) TCP/IP subnets. A site allows administrators to configure Active Directory access and replication topology to take advantage of the physical network. See also Active Directory; subnet; Transmission Control Protocol/Internet Protocol (TCP/IP).

slot   A storage location for cartridges in a library of removable media managed by Removable Storage. See also library.

SlowKeys   A Windows feature that instructs the computer to disregard keystrokes that are not held down for a minimum period of time, which allows the user to brush against keys without any effect.

small computer system interface (SCSI)   A standard high-speed parallel interface defined by the American National Standards Institute (ANSI). A SCSI interface is used for connecting microcomputers to peripheral devices such as hard disks and printers, and to other computers and local area networks (LANs). See also local area network (LAN).

Small Office/Home Office (SOHO)   An office with a few computers that can be considered a small business or part of a larger network.

smart card   A credit card–sized device that is used with an access code to enable certificate-based authentication and single sign-on to the enterprise. Smart cards securely store certificates, public and private keys, passwords, and other types of personal information. A smart card reader attached to the computer reads the smart card. See also authentication.

SNA Server Client   Software that allows workstations to communicate through SNA Server and support SNA Server advanced host integration features. SNA Server Client software also provides application programming interfaces (APIs) that are used by third-party vendors to gain access to IBM host systems and applications.

snap-in   A type of tool you can add to a console supported by Microsoft Management Console (MMC). A stand-alone snap-in can be added by itself; an extension snap-in can only be added to extend the function of another snap-in. See also Microsoft Management Console (MMC).

SNMP   See definition for Simple Network Management Protocol (SNMP).

software decoder   A type of digital video disc (DVD) decoder that allows a DVD drive to display movies on your computer screen. A software decoder uses only software to display movies. See also DVD decoder; DVD drive; hardware decoder.

SoundSentry   A Windows feature that produces a visual cue, such as a screen flash or a blinking title bar, whenever the computer plays a system sound.

source directory   The folder that contains the file or files to be copied or moved.

spanned volume   A dynamic volume consisting of disk space on more than one physical disk. You can increase the size of a spanned volume by extending it onto additional dynamic disks. You can create spanned volumes only on dynamic disks. Spanned volumes are not fault tolerant and cannot be mirrored. See also dynamic disk; dynamic volume; fault tolerance; mirrored volume; simple volume; volume.

SPAP   See definition for Shiva Password Authentication Protocol (SPAP).

special permissions   On NTFS volumes, a custom set of permissions. You can customize permissions on files and directories by selecting the individual components of the standard sets of permissions. See also NTFS file system; permission; volume.

speech synthesizer   An assistive device that produces spoken words, either by splicing together prerecorded words or by programming the computer to produce the sounds that make up spoken words.

stand-alone drive   An online drive that is not part of a library unit. Removable Storage treats stand-alone drives as online libraries with one drive and a port. See also Removable Storage.

Standards and formats   A Regional and Language Options setting that determines the formats used to display dates, times, currency, numbers, and the sorting order of text. Formerly known as *user locale*.

startup environment   In dual-boot or multiple-boot systems, the configuration settings that specify which system to start and how each system should be started. See also dual boot; multiple boot.

startup key   A random 128-bit symmetric cryptographic key created at system startup and used to encrypt all of the user's symmetric cryptographic keys. See also encryption; symmetric key.

static routes   Routes in the routing table that are permanent. Static routes are manually configured by a network administrator. They change only if the network administrator changes them. If the routing protocol is configured to support auto-static routes (automatically added static routes), then the router can issue a request to a protocol to get an update of routing information on a specific interface. The results of such an update are then converted and kept as static routes. See also protocol; router; routing.

status area   See definition for notification area.

stream   A sequence of bits, bytes, or other small structurally uniform units.

streaming media servers   Software (such as Windows Media Technologies) that provides multimedia support, allowing you to deliver content by using advanced streaming format over an intranet or the Internet.

stripe set   A volume that stores data in stripes on two or more physical disks. A stripe set is created by using Windows NT 4.0 or earlier. Windows XP Professional does not support stripe sets. Instead, you must create a striped volume on dynamic disks. See also dynamic disk; striped volume.

striped volume   A dynamic volume that stores data in stripes on two or more physical disks. Data in a striped volume is allocated alternately and evenly (in stripes) across the disks. Striped volumes offer the best performance of all the volumes that are available in Windows, but they do not provide fault tolerance. If a disk in a striped volume fails, the data in the entire volume is lost. You can create striped volumes only on dynamic disks. Striped volumes cannot be mirrored or extended. See also dynamic disk; dynamic volume; fault tolerance; volume.

subkey   An element of the registry that contains entries or other subkeys. A tier of the registry that is immediately below a key or a subtree (if the subtree has no keys). See also key; registry.

subnet   A subdivision of an IP network. Each subnet has its own unique subnetted network ID.

subnet mask   A 32-bit value that enables the recipient of IP packets to distinguish the network ID and host ID portions of the IP address. Typically, subnet masks use the format 255.*x.x.x*. See also IP address.

subnet prioritization   The ordering of multiple IP address mappings from a DNS server so that the resolver orders local resource records first. This reduces network traffic across subnets by forcing computers to connect to network resources that are closer to them.

subpicture   A data stream contained within a DVD. The subpicture stream delivers the subtitles and any other add-on data, such as system help or director's comments, that can be displayed while playing multimedia.

subtree   Any node within a tree, along with any selection of connected descendant nodes.

The highest level of the registry (for example, HKEY_LOCAL_MACHINE). See also key; node; registry; subkey.

symmetric key   A single key that is used with symmetric encryption algorithms for both encryption and decryption.

symmetric key encryption   An encryption algorithm that requires the same secret key to be used for both encryption and decryption. This is often called *secret key encryption*. Because of its speed, symmetric encryption is typically used rather than public key encryption when a message sender needs to encrypt large amounts of data. See also public key encryption.

Synchronization Manager   A tool used to ensure that a file or directory on a client computer contains the same data as a matching file or directory on a server.

syntax   The order in which a command must be typed and the elements that follow the command.

Sysprep   A tool that prepares the hard disk on a source computer for duplication to target computers and then runs a non-Microsoft disk-imaging process. This automated installation method is used when the hard disk on the master computer is identical to those of the target computers. See also security ID (SID).

system access control list (SACL)   The part of an object's security descriptor that specifies which events are to be audited per user or group. Examples of auditing events are file access, logon attempts, and system shutdowns. See also discretionary access control list (DACL); object; security descriptor.

system files   Files used by Windows to load, configure, and run the operating system. Generally, system files must never be deleted or moved.

system locale   See definition for Language for non-Unicode programs.

system media pool   A pool used to hold cartridges that are not in use. The free pool holds unused cartridges that are available to applications, and the unrecognized and import pools are temporary holding places for cartridges that have been newly placed in a library.

system partition   The partition that contains the hardware-specific files needed to load Windows (for example, Ntldr, Osloader, Boot.ini, Ntdetect.com). The system partition can be, but does not have to be, the same as the boot partition. See also partition.

System Policy Editor   The Poledit.exe tool, used by administrators to set System Policy on Windows NT 4.0–based and Windows 95–based computers.

system volume   The volume that contains the hardware-specific files that are needed to load Windows on x86-based computers with a BIOS. The system volume can be, but does not have to be, the same volume as the boot volume. See also basic input/output system (BIOS); boot volume; volume.

systemroot   The path and folder name where the Windows system files are located. Typically, this is C:\Windows, although you can designate a different drive or folder when you install Windows. You can use the value *%systemroot%* to replace the actual location of the folder that contains the Windows system files.

Systems Management Server (SMS)   A Microsoft product that includes inventory collection, software deployment, and diagnostic tools. SMS automates the task of upgrading software, allows remote problem solving, provides asset management information, and monitors software usage, computers, and networks.

Systems Network Architecture (SNA)   A communications framework developed by IBM to define network functions and establish standards for enabling computers to share and process data.

T

T.120   The ITU-T standard for multipoint data conferencing. T.120 provides the protocols for establishing and managing data flow, connections, and conferences. Support for T.120 enables data transfer from conferencing applications, such as file transfer and application sharing, to operate in conjunction with H.323 connections. See also H.323; International Telecommunication Union - Telecommunication [Standardization Sector] (ITU-T).

taskbar   The bar that contains the **Start** button and appears by default at the bottom of the desktop. You can click the taskbar buttons to switch between programs. You can also hide the taskbar, move it to the sides or top of the desktop, and customize it in other ways. See also desktop; notification area; taskbar button.

taskbar button   A button that appears on the taskbar and corresponds to a running application. See also taskbar.

TCP/IP   See definition for Transmission Control Protocol/Internet Protocol (TCP/IP).

Tcpmon.ini   The file that specifies whether a device supports multiple ports. If the Tcpmon.ini file indicates that a device can support multiple ports, users are prompted to pick which port should be used during device installation.

Telephony API (TAPI)   An application programming interface (API) used by communications programs to work with telephony and network services. Communications programs like HyperTerminal and Phone Dialer use TAPI to dial, answer, and route telephone calls on conventional telephony devices, including PBXs, modems, and fax machines. TAPI 3.0 also provides Internet Protocol (IP) telephony support, which Phone Dialer and other programs use to transmit, route, and control real-time audio and video signals over IP-based networks such as the Internet. See also application programming interface (API); Internet Protocol (IP).

Telnet 3270 (TN3270)   Terminal emulation software, similar to Telnet, that allows a personal computer to log on to an IBM mainframe over a TCP/IP network.

Telnet 5250 (TN5250)   Terminal emulation software, similar to Telnet, that allows a personal computer to log on to an IBM AS/400 host system over a TCP/IP network.

terabyte   Approximately one trillion bytes, or one million million bytes.

Terminal Services   The underlying technology on that enables Remote Desktop, Remote Assistance, and Terminal Server.

third-party accessibility aids   Non-Microsoft add-on, augmentative hardware and software devices, such as accessibility products that assist users with disabilities.

thread   A type of object within a process that runs program instructions. Using multiple threads allows concurrent operations within a process and enables one process to run different parts of its program on different processors simultaneously. A thread has its own set of registers, its own kernel stack, a thread environment block, and a user stack in the address space of its process. See also kernel.

thread state   A numeric value indicating the execution state of the thread. Numbered 0 through 5, the states seen most often are 1 for ready, 2 for running, and 5 for waiting. See also thread.

Throughput   For disks, the transfer capacity of the disk system.

Time to Live (TTL)   A timer value included in packets sent over TCP/IP-based networks that tells the recipients how long to hold or use the packet or any of its included data before expiring and discarding the packet or data. For DNS, TTL values are used in resource records within a zone to determine how long requesting clients should cache and use this information when it appears in a query response answered by a DNS server for the zone. See also DNS server; Domain Name System (DNS); packet; resource record (RR); Transmission Control Protocol/Internet Protocol (TCP/IP).

timer bar   The colored bar that moves across the screen according to the frequency of the data-collection update interval.

timestamp   A certification by a trusted third party specifying that a particular message existed at a specific time and date. In a digital context, trusted third parties generate a trusted timestamp for a particular message by having a timestamping service append a time value to a message and then digitally signing the result. See also digital signature.

ToggleKeys   A feature that sets your keyboard to beep when one of the locking keys (CAPS LOCK, NUM LOCK, or SCROLL LOCK) is turned on or off. See also FilterKeys; SerialKeys.

Token Ring   A type of network media that connects clients in a closed ring and uses token passing to allow clients to use the network.

track   A thin concentric band that stores data on a hard disk. A hard disk contains multiple platters, and each platter contains many tracks. Each track is divided into units of storage called sectors. Track numbers start at 0 and progress in order with track 0 at the outer track of a hard disk. See also cylinder.

Transmission Control Protocol/Internet Protocol (TCP/IP)   A set of networking protocols widely used on the Internet that provides communications across interconnected networks of computers with diverse hardware architectures and various operating systems. TCP/IP includes standards for how computers communicate and conventions for connecting networks and routing traffic. See also Internet Protocol (IP); protocol.

transmitting station ID (TSID) string   A string that specifies the transmitter subscriber ID sent by the fax machine when sending a fax to a receiving machine. This string is usually a combination of the fax or telephone number and the name of the business. It is often the same as the called subscriber ID.

Transport Layer Security (TLS)   A standard protocol that is used to provide secure Web communications on the Internet or intranets. It enables clients to authenticate servers or, optionally, servers to authenticate clients. It also provides a secure channel by encrypting communications. TLS is the latest and a more secure version of the SSL protocol. See also authentication; protocol; Secure Sockets Layer (SSL).

transport protocol   A protocol that defines how data should be presented to the next receiving layer in the Windows NT and Windows 2000 networking model and packages the data accordingly. The transport protocol passes data to the network adapter driver through the Network Driver Interface Specification (NDIS) interface and to the redirector through the Transport Driver Interface (TDI). See also Network Driver Interface Specification (NDIS).

Trivial File Transfer Protocol (TFTP)   A protocol used to download the initial files needed to begin the installation process. See also protocol.

TrueType fonts   Fonts that are scalable and sometimes generated as bitmaps or soft fonts, depending on the capabilities of your printer. TrueType fonts are device-independent fonts that are stored as outlines. They can be sized to any height, and they can be printed exactly as they appear on the screen. See also font.

trust relationship   A logical relationship established between domains to allow pass-through authentication, in which a trusting domain honors the logon authentications of a trusted domain. User accounts and global groups defined in a trusted domain can be given rights and permissions in a trusting domain, even though the user accounts or groups don't exist in the trusting domain's directory. See also authentication; domain; global group; group; permission; user account.

trusted forest   A forest that is connected to another forest by explicit or transitive trust.

TSID   See definition for transmitting station ID (TSID) string.

tunnel   A logical connection over which data is encapsulated. Typically, both encapsulation and encryption are performed and the tunnel is a private, secure link between a remote user or host and a private network. See also encryption; tunnel server; voluntary tunnel.

tunnel server   A server or router that terminates tunnels and forwards traffic to the hosts on the target network. See also router; server; tunnel.

TWAIN   An acronym for Technology Without An Interesting Name. An industry-standard software protocol and API that provides easy integration of image data between input devices, such as scanners and still image digital cameras, and software applications. See also application programming interface (API).

Type 1 fonts   Scalable fonts designed to work with PostScript devices. See also font; PostScript.

U

UART   See definition for Universal Asynchronous Receiver/Transmitter (UART).

unallocated space   Available disk space that is not allocated to any volume. The type of volume that you can create on unallocated space depends on the disk type. On basic disks, you can use unallocated space to create primary or extended partitions. On dynamic disks, you can use unallocated space to create dynamic volumes. See also basic disk; dynamic disk; extended partition; logical drive; object; partition; primary partition; volume.

unattended Setup   An automated, hands-free method of installing Windows. During installation, unattended Setup uses an answer file to supply data to Setup instead of requiring that an administrator interactively provide the answers.

Unicode   A character encoding standard developed by the Unicode Consortium that represents almost all of the written languages of the world. The Unicode character repertoire has multiple representation forms, including UTF-8, UTF-16, and UTF-32. Most Windows interfaces use the UTF-16 form. See also American Standard Code for Information Interchange (ASCII).

UniDriver   The UniDriver (or Universal Print Driver) carries out requests (such as printing text, rendering bitmaps, or advancing a page) on most types of printers. The UniDriver accepts information from a printer-specific minidriver and uses this information to complete tasks.

Uniform Resource Locator (URL)   An address that uniquely identifies a location on the Internet. A URL for a World Wide Web site is preceded by *http://*, as in the fictitious URL *http://www.example.microsoft.com*. A URL can contain more detail, such as the name of a page of hypertext, usually identified by the file name extension .html or .htm.

uninstall   When referring to software, the act of removing program files and folders from your hard disk and removing related data from your registry so the software is no longer available.

When referring to a device, the act of removing the corresponding device drivers from your hard disk and physically removing the device from your computer. See also device driver; install.

uninterruptible power supply (UPS)   A device that connects a computer and a power source to ensure that electrical flow is not interrupted. UPS devices use batteries to keep the computer running for a period of time after a power failure. UPS devices usually provide protection against power surges and brownouts as well.

Universal Asynchronous Receiver/Transmitter (UART)   An integrated circuit (silicon chip) that is commonly used in microcomputers to provide asynchronous communication. The UART provides parallel-to-serial conversion of data to be transmitted and serial-to-parallel conversion of data received. See also asynchronous communication.

Universal Disk Format (UDF)   A file system defined by the Optical Storage Technology Association (OSTA) that is the successor to the CD-ROM file system (CDFS). UDF is used for removable disk media like DVD, CD, and magneto-optic (MO) disks.

universal group   A security or distribution group that can contain users, groups, and computers from any domain in its forest as members.

Universal security groups can be granted rights and permissions on resources in any domain in the forest. Universal security groups are available only in native mode domains. See also domain; forest; Group Policy; security group.

Universal Naming Convention (UNC) A convention for naming files and other resources beginning with two backslashes (\), indicating that the resource exists on a network computer. UNC names conform to the *servername**sharename* syntax, where *servername* is the server's name and *sharename* is the name of the shared resource. The UNC name of a directory or file can also include the directory path after the share name, by using the following syntax: *servername**sharename**directory**filename*.

universal serial bus (USB) An external bus that supports Plug and Play installation. Using USB, you can connect and disconnect devices without shutting down or restarting your computer. You can use a single USB port to connect up to 127 peripheral devices, including speakers, telephones, CD-ROM drives, joysticks, tape drives, keyboards, scanners, and cameras. A USB port is usually located on the back of your computer near the serial port or parallel port. See also Plug and Play.

UNIX A powerful, multiuser, multitasking operating system initially developed at AT&T Bell Laboratories in 1969 for use on minicomputers. UNIX is considered more portable, that is, less computer-specific, than other operating systems because it is written in C language. Newer versions of UNIX have been developed at the University of California at Berkeley and by AT&T.

unrecognized media pool A repository of blank media and media that are not recognized by Removable Storage.

upgrade When referring to software, to update existing program files, folders, and registry entries to a more recent version. Upgrading, unlike performing a new installation, leaves existing settings and files in place. See also registry.

UPS service A service that manages an uninterruptible power supply (UPS) connected to a computer. See also uninterruptible power supply (UPS).

user account A record that consists of all the information that defines a user to Windows. This includes the user name and password required for the user to log on, the groups in which the user account has membership, and the rights and permissions the user has for using the computer and network, and accessing their resources. For Windows XP Professional and member servers, user accounts are managed with Local Users and Groups. For Windows Server domain controllers, user accounts are managed with Microsoft Active Directory Users and Computers. See also group; permission; resource.

user identifier (UID) An identifier for a specific user. UNIX-based systems use the UID to identify the owner of files and processes, and to determine access permissions.

user locale See definition for Standards and formats.

user mode The processing mode in which applications run.

user principal name (UPN) A user account name (sometimes referred to as the user logon name) and a domain name identifying the domain in which the user account is located. This is the standard usage for logging on to a Windows domain. The format is: *user@domain*.com (as for an e-mail address). See also domain; domain name; user account.

user rights   Tasks that a user is permitted to perform on a computer system or domain. There are two types of user rights: privileges and logon rights. An example of a privilege is the right to shut down the system. An example of a logon right is the right to log on to a computer locally. Both types are assigned by administrators to individual users or groups as part of the security settings for the computer. See also domain; group.

user rights policy   Security settings that manage the assignment of rights to groups and user accounts. See also group; user account; user rights.

Utility Manager   A function of Windows 2000 that allows administrators to review the status of applications and tools and to customize features and add tools more easily.

V

V.34   Data transmission standard that provides for up to 33,600 bits per second (bps) communications over telephone lines. It defines a full-duplex (two-way) modulation technique and includes error-correcting and negotiation. See also V.90.

V.90   Data transmission standard that provides for up to 56,000 bits per second (bps) communications over telephone lines. The transmission speed from the client-side modem is 33,600 bps, the same as for V.34. The transmission speed from the host-side modem, such as an Internet service provider (ISP) or corporate network, is up to 56,000 bps, with an average speed of 40,000 to 50,000 bps. When the host-side modem does not support this standard, the alternative is V.34. See also client; Internet service provider (ISP); V.34.

value bar   The area of the System Monitor graph or histogram display that shows last, average, minimum, and maximum statistics for the selected counter.

variable   In programming, a named storage location capable of containing a certain type of data that can be modified during program execution. See also environment variable.

vector font   A font rendered from a mathematical model, in which each character is defined as a set of lines drawn between points. Vector fonts can be cleanly scaled to any size or aspect ratio. See also font.

vertical blanking interval (VBI)   The part of a TV transmission that is blanked, or left clear of viewable content, to allow time for the TV's electron gun to move from the bottom to the top of the screen as it scans images. This blank area is now being used to broadcast closed captioned and HTML-formatted information.

Video for Windows (VfW)   A format developed by Microsoft for storing video and audio information. Files in this format have an .avi extension. AVI files are limited to 320 x 240 resolution at 30 frames per second, neither of which is adequate for full-screen, full-motion video.

Virtual Device Driver (VxD)   Software for Windows that manages a hardware or software system resource. The middle letter in the abbreviation indicates the type of device; **x** is used where the type of device is not under discussion.

virtual IP address   An IP address that is shared among the hosts of a Network Load Balancing cluster. A Network Load Balancing cluster might also use multiple virtual IP addresses, for example, in a cluster of multihomed Web servers. See also IP address; multihomed computer.

virtual local area network (VLAN)   A logical grouping of hosts on one or more LANs that allows communication to occur between hosts as if they were on the same physical LAN. See also local area network (LAN).

virtual memory   Temporary storage used by a computer to run programs that need more memory than it has. For example, programs could have access to 4 gigabytes (GB) of virtual memory on a computer's hard drive, even if the computer has only 32 megabytes (MB) of RAM. The program data that does not currently fit in the computer's memory is saved into paging files. See also paging file; Virtual Memory Size; virtual printer memory.

Virtual Memory Size   In Task Manager, the amount of virtual memory, or address space, committed to a process. See also virtual memory.

virtual printer memory   In a PostScript printer, a part of memory that stores font information. The memory in PostScript printers is divided into two areas: banded memory and virtual memory. The banded memory contains graphics and page-layout information needed to print your documents. The virtual memory contains any font information that is sent to your printer either when you print a document or when you download fonts. See also virtual memory.

virtual private network (VPN)   The extension of a private network that encompasses encapsulated, encrypted, and authenticated links across shared or public networks. VPN connections can provide remote access and routed connections to private networks over the Internet. See also authentication; encryption; remote access; routing; tunnel.

virus   A program that attempts to spread from computer to computer and either cause damage (by erasing or corrupting data) or annoy users (by printing messages or altering what is displayed on the screen).

virus scanner   Software used to scan for and eradicate computer viruses, worms, and Trojan horses.

VoIP (Voice over Internet Protocol)   A method for sending voice over a LAN, a WAN, or the Internet using TCP/IP packets. See also local area network (LAN); Transmission Control Protocol/Internet Protocol (TCP/IP); wide area network (WAN).

volume   An area of storage on a hard disk. A volume is formatted by using a file system, such as FAT or NTFS, and has a drive letter assigned to it. You can view the contents of a volume by clicking its icon in Windows Explorer or in My Computer. A single hard disk can have multiple volumes, and volumes can also span multiple disks. See also file allocation table (FAT); NTFS file system; simple volume; spanned volume.

volume mount points System objects in the version of NTFS included with Windows 2000 and Windows XP Professional that represent storage volumes in a persistent, robust manner. Volume mount points allow the operating system to graft the root of a volume onto a directory. See also NTFS file system; volume.

volume set A volume that consists of disk space on one or more physical disks. A volume set is created by using Windows NT 4.0 or earlier. Windows XP Professional does not support volume sets. Instead, you must create a spanned volume on dynamic disks. See also basic disk; dynamic disk; partition; spanned volume; volume.

volume shadow copy A volume that represents a duplicate of the original volume taken at the time the copy began. See also differential data; volume.

voluntary tunnel A tunnel that is initiated by the client. It tunnels PPP over IP from the client to the tunnel server, then the data is forwarded to the target host by the tunnel server. See also client; Internet Protocol (IP); Point-to-Point Protocol (PPP); tunnel; tunnel server.

W

WDM Streaming class The means by which Windows XP Professional supports digital video and audio. Enables support for such components as DVD decoders, MPEG decoders, video decoders, tuners, and audio codecs.

wide area network (WAN) A communications network connecting geographically separated computers, printers, and other devices. A WAN allows any connected device to interact with any other on the network. See also local area network (LAN).

Windows File Protection (WFP) A feature that runs in the background and protects your system files from being overwritten. When a file in a protected folder is modified, WFP determines whether the new file is the correct Microsoft version or whether the file is digitally signed. If not, the modified file is replaced with a valid version.

Windows Installer An operating system service that allows the operating system to manage the installation process. Windows Installer technologies are divided into two parts that work in combination: a clientside installer service (Msiexec.exe) and a package (.msi) file. Windows Installer uses the information contained within a package file to install the application.

Windows Internet Name Service (WINS) A software service that dynamically maps IP addresses to computer names (NetBIOS names). This allows users to access resources by name instead of requiring them to use IP addresses that are difficult to recognize and remember. WINS servers support clients running Windows NT 4.0 and earlier versions of Microsoft operating systems. See also Domain Name System (DNS); IP address; network basic input/output system (NetBIOS); resource.

Windows Management Instrumentation (WMI)   A management infrastructure in Windows that supports monitoring and controlling system resources through a common set of interfaces and provides a logically organized, consistent model of Windows operation, configuration, and status. See also resource.

Windows MultiLanguage Version   A version of Windows that extends the native language support in Windows by allowing user interface languages to be changed on a per-user basis. This version also minimizes the number of language versions you need to deploy across a network.

Windows Update   A Microsoft-owned Web site from which Windows users can install or update device drivers. By using an ActiveX control, Windows Update compares the available drivers with those on the user's system and offers to install new or updated versions.

WINS   See definition for Windows Internet Name Service (WINS).

Winsock   Windows Sockets. An application programming interface (API) standard for software that provides a TCP/IP interface under Windows. See also application programming interface (API); Transmission Control Protocol/Internet Protocol (TCP/IP).

work queue item   A job request to an existing library, made by an application that supports Removable Storage, which is placed in a queue and processed when the library resource becomes available. See also library; Removable Storage.

workgroup   A simple grouping of computers, intended only to help users find such things as printers and shared folders within that group. Workgroups in Windows do not offer the centralized user accounts and authentication offered by domains. See also authentication; domain; user account.

World Wide Web   A system for exploring the Internet by using hyperlinks. When you use a Web browser, the Web appears as a collection of text, pictures, sounds, and digital movies. See also internet.

Index

Numbers

3DES encryption algorithm, 771, 815–816, 871
8.3 short file names
  converting to long file names, 99
  FAT volumes, 616
  NTFS, 597, 609
  Windows XP Professional, 622–623
56-bit DESX encryption algorithm, 871
64-Bit Edition. *See* Windows XP 64-Bit Edition
802.1x, 328–331, 877
802.11
  architecture, 324–325
  authentication, 326–327
  encryption, 327–328
  open system authentication, 326
  overview, 323
  security, 326–331, 874–878
  shared key authentication, 327
802.11a, 324
802.11b, 324
61883 Protocol, 383

A

AC-3 audio, 433
Accelerated Graphics Port (AGP), 385, 441
access control
  access tokens, 701
  ACE, 724
  ACL. *See* ACL (access control list)
  anonymous logons, managing, 736
  applying to new objects, 725–728
  auditing Account Management, 758
  auditing and analyzing, 754–764
  auditing privilege use, 757–758
  auditing system events, 702
  Cacls.exe, 732
  configuring and analyzing operations, 763–764
  DACL, 725
  default permissions, 728–732
  default user rights for clean-installed
    workstations, 734–735

  default Write access permissions for Users
    group, 734
  deployment strategies, 28–30
  discretionary access to securable objects, 702
  enabling auditing policies, 755–758
  Event Viewer, 758–759
  Guest accounts, 737–739
  inheritance, 701–702, 726
  key concepts, 702–705
  local computer policy databases, 760–763
  Local Security Policy. *See* Local Security Policy
  multi-user access to encrypted files, 797–801
  network, 1059
  network authentication management, 736–739
  overview, 699–700
  ownership permissions, 726–728
  permission inheritance, 702, 726
  permissions overview, 703
  planning, 706–707
  rights, 703
  Secedit.exe, 763–764
  Security Configuration and Analysis snap-in,
    747, 759–763
  security configuration databases, 760–763
  security context, 700
  security descriptors, 701, 705
  security groups. *See* security groups
  security policy overview, 739–740
  security principals, 700
  security settings, 702
  security templates. *See* security templates
  sharing files and folders, 738
  SID, 700
  Software Restriction Policies, 740–742
  system event auditing, 702
  user accounts. *See* user accounts
  user rights, managing using security groups, 733
  user-based authorization, 703–705
  validating requests for access, 704
access control entries (ACE), 724
access control lists. *See* ACL (access control list)
access tokens, 658–659, 701

1643

Get a **Free**
e-mail newsletter, updates,
special offers, links to related books,
and more when you
register online!

Register your Microsoft Press® title on our Web site and you'll get a FREE subscription to our e-mail newsletter, *Microsoft Press Book Connections*. You'll find out about newly released and upcoming books and learning tools, online events, software downloads, special offers and coupons for Microsoft Press customers, and information about major Microsoft® product releases. You can also read useful additional information about all the titles we publish, such as detailed book descriptions, tables of contents and indexes, sample chapters, links to related books and book series, author biographies, and reviews by other customers.

Registration is easy. Just visit this Web page and fill in your information:

http://www.microsoft.com/mspress/register

Microsoft

System Requirements

To use the *Microsoft Windows XP Profession Resource Kit, Second Edition*, companion CD-ROM, you'll need to have a computer equipped with the following configuration:

- Pentium II with 266 MHz or higher processor
- Microsoft Windows 2000, Microsoft Windows XP, or Microsoft Windows Server 2003
- Microsoft Internet Explorer 5.5 or later
- Adobe Acrobat or Acrobat Reader

To install the Windows Resource Kit Tools contained on the companion CD-ROM, you'll need 30 MB of free disk space. See the Windows Resource Kit Tools Help file that is installed with the tools for each tool's system requirements.